CHRYSLE CORPORATION

SERVICE MANUAL

1997 JEEP® WRANGLER

VOLUME 2

To order the special service tools used and illustrated, please refer to the instructions on inside back cover.

CHRYSLER CORPORATION

Chrysler Corporation reserves the right to make changes in design or to make additions to or improvements in its products without imposing any obligations upon itself to install them on its products previously manufactured.

Paper Content
50% Recycled

GROUP TAB LOCATOR

ENGINE

CONTENTS

STANDARD SERVICE INFORMATION

INDEX

GENERAL INFORMATION

FORM-IN-PLACE GASKETS

There are several places where form-in-place gaskets are used on the engine. **DO NOT use form-in-place gasket material unless specified.** Care must be taken when applying form-in-place gaskets. Bead size, continuity and location are of great importance. Too thin a bead can result in leakage while too much can result in spill-over. A continuous bead of the proper width is essential to obtain a leak-free joint.

Two types of form-in-place gasket materials are used in the engine area (Mopar Silicone Rubber Adhesive Sealant and Mopar Gasket Maker). Each have different properties and cannot be used interchangeably.

MOPAR SILICONE RUBBER ADHESIVE SEALANT

Mopar Silicone Rubber Adhesive Sealant, normally black in color, is available in 3 ounce tubes. Moisture in the air causes the sealant material to cure. This material is normally used on flexible metal flanges. It has a shelf life of a year and will not properly cure if over aged. Always inspect the package for the expiration date before use.

MOPAR GASKET MAKER

Mopar Gasket Maker, normally red in color, is available in 6 cc tubes. This anaerobic type gasket material cures in the absence of air when squeezed between smooth machined metallic surfaces. It will not cure if left in the uncovered tube. DO NOT use on flexible metal flanges.

SURFACE PREPARATION

Parts assembled with form-in-place gaskets may be disassembled without unusual effort. In some instances, it may be necessary to lightly tap the part with a mallet or other suitable tool to break the seal between the mating surfaces. A flat gasket scraper may also be lightly tapped into the joint but care must be taken not to damage the mating surfaces.

Scrape or wire brush all gasket surfaces to remove all loose material. Inspect stamped parts to ensure gasket rails are flat. Flatten rails with a hammer on a flat plate, if required. Gasket surfaces must be free of oil and dirt. Make sure the old gasket material is removed from blind attaching holes.

GASKET APPLICATION

Assembling parts using a form-in-place gasket requires care.

Mopar Silicone Rubber Adhesive Sealant should be applied in a continuous bead approximately 3 mm (0.12 inch) in diameter. All mounting holes must be circled. For corner sealing, a 3 or 6 mm (1/8 or 1/4

GENERAL INFORMATION (Continued)

inch) drop is placed in the center of the gasket contact area. Uncured sealant may be removed with a shop towel. Components should be torqued in place while the sealant is still wet to the touch (within 10 minutes). The use of a locating dowel is recommended during assembly to prevent smearing the material off location.

Mopar Gasket Maker should be applied sparingly to one gasket surface. The sealant diameter should be 1.00 mm (0.04 inch) or less. Be certain the material surrounds each mounting hole. Excess material can easily be wiped off. Components should be torqued in place within 15 minutes. The use of a locating dowel is recommended during assembly to prevent smearing the material off location.

ENGINE PERFORMANCE

To provide best vehicle performance and lowest vehicle emissions, it is most important that the tune-up be done accurately. Use the specifications listed on the Vehicle Emission Control Information label found on the engine compartment hood.

(1) Test battery specific gravity. Add water, if necessary. Clean and tighten battery connections.

(2) Test cranking amperage draw (refer to Group 8B, Battery/Starter Service for the proper procedures).

(3) Tighten the intake manifold bolts (refer to Group 11, Exhaust System and Intake Manifold for the proper specifications).

(4) Perform cylinder compression test:

CAUTION: DO NOT overspeed the engine.

(a) Check engine oil level and add oil, if necessary.

(b) Drive the vehicle until engine reaches normal operating temperature.

(c) Select a route free from traffic and other forms of congestion, observe all traffic laws and briskly accelerate through the gears several times. The higher engine speed may help clean out valve seat deposits which can prevent accurate compression readings.

(d) Remove all spark plugs from engine. As spark plugs are being removed, check electrodes for abnormal firing indicators—fouled, hot, oily, etc. Record cylinder number of spark plug for future reference.

(e) Disconnect coil wire from distributor and secure to good ground to prevent a spark from starting a fire.

(f) Be sure throttle blades are fully open during the compression check.

(g) Insert compression gage adaptor into the No.1 spark plug hole. Crank engine until maximum pressure is reached on gauge. Record this pressure as No.1 cylinder pressure.

(h) Repeat Step 4g for all remaining cylinders.

(i) Compression should not be less than 689 kPa (100 psi) and not vary more than 172 kPa (25 psi) from cylinder to cylinder.

(j) If cylinder(s) have abnormally low compression pressures, repeat procedure.

(k) If the same cylinder(s) repeat an abnormally low reading, it could indicate the existence of a problem in the cylinder.

NOTE: The recommended compression pressures are to be used only as a guide to diagnosing engine problems. An engine should NOT be disassembled to determine the cause of low compression unless some malfunction is present.

(5) Clean or replace spark plugs as necessary. Adjust gap (refer to Group 8D, Ignition System for gap adjustment and torque).

(6) Test resistance of spark plug cables (refer to Group 8D, Ignition System).

(7) Inspect the primary wire. Test coil output voltage, primary and secondary resistance. Replace parts as necessary (refer to Group 8D, Ignition System and make necessary adjustment).

(8) Perform a combustion analysis.

(9) Test fuel pump for pressure (refer to Group 14, Fuel System for the proper specifications).

(10) Inspect air filter element (refer to Group 0, Lubrication and Maintenance for the proper procedure).

(11) Inspect crankcase ventilation system (refer to Group 0, Lubrication and Maintenance for the proper procedure).

(12) For emission controls refer to Group 25, Emission Controls System for service procedures.

(13) Inspect and adjust accessory belt drives (refer to Group 7, Cooling System for the proper adjustments).

(14) Road test vehicle as a final test.

HONING CYLINDER BORES

Before honing, stuff plenty of clean shop towels under the bores and over the crankshaft to keep abrasive materials from entering the crankshaft area.

(1) Used carefully, the Cylinder Bore Sizing Hone C-823 equipped with 220 grit stones, is the best tool for this job. In addition to deglazing, it will reduce taper and out-of-round as well as removing light scuffing, scoring or scratches. Usually a few strokes will clean up a bore and maintain the required limits.

CAUTION: DO NOT use rigid type hones to remove cylinder wall glaze.

(2) Deglazing of the cylinder walls may be done if the cylinder bore is straight and round. Use a cylin-

GENERAL INFORMATION (Continued)

der surfacing hone, Honing Tool C-3501, equipped with 280 grit stones (C-3501-3810). 20-60 strokes, depending on the bore condition, will be sufficient to provide a satisfactory surface. Using honing oil C-3501-3880 or a light honing oil available from major oil distributors.

CAUTION: DO NOT use engine or transmission oil, mineral spirits or kerosene.

(3) Honing should be done by moving the hone up and down fast enough to get a crosshatch pattern. The hone marks should INTERSECT at 50° to 60° for proper seating of rings (Fig. 1).

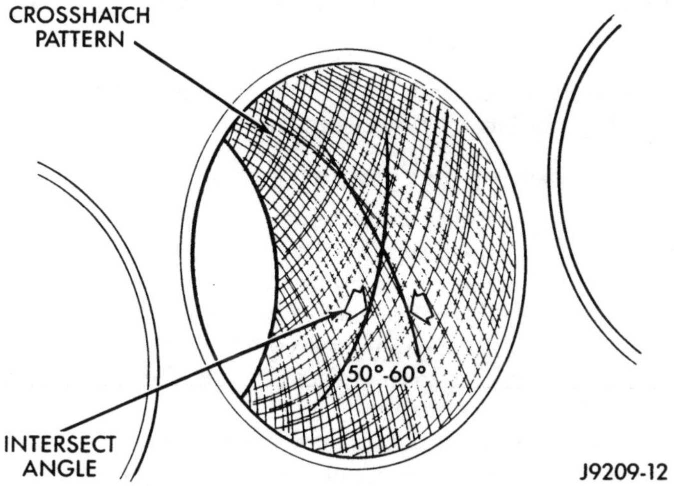

Fig. 1 Cylinder Bore Crosshatch Pattern

(4) A controlled hone motor speed between 200 and 300 RPM is necessary to obtain the proper crosshatch angle. The number of up and down strokes per minute can be regulated to get the desired 50° to 60° angle. Faster up and down strokes increase the crosshatch angle.

(5) After honing, it is necessary that the block be cleaned to remove all traces of abrasive. Use a brush to wash parts with a solution of hot water and detergent. Dry parts thoroughly. Use a clean, white, lint-free cloth to check that the bore is clean. Oil the bores after cleaning to prevent rusting.

MEASURING WITH PLASTIGAGE

CRANKSHAFT MAIN BEARING CLEARANCE

Engine crankshaft bearing clearances can be determined by use of Plastigage, or equivalent. The following is the recommended procedures for the use of Plastigage:

(1) Remove oil film from surface to be checked. Plastigage is soluble in oil.

(2) The total clearance of the main bearings can only be determined by removing the weight of the crankshaft. This can be accomplished by either of two methods:

METHOD - 1 (PREFERRED)

Shim the bearings adjacent to the bearing to be checked. This will remove the clearance between upper bearing shell and the crankshaft. Place a minimum of 0.254 mm (0.010 inch) shim between the bearing shell and the adjacent bearing cap. Tighten the bolts to 18 N·m (13 ft. lbs.) torque.

- **ALL ENGINES**—When checking No.1 main bearing; shim No.2 main bearing.
- **ALL ENGINES**—When checking No.2 main bearing; shim No.1 and No.3 main bearing.
- **ALL ENGINES**—When checking No.3 main bearing; shim No.2 and No.4 main bearing.
- **ALL ENGINES**—When checking No.4 main bearing; shim No.3 and No.5 main bearing.
- **2.5L ENGINE**—When checking No.5 main bearing; shim No.4 main bearing.
- **4.0L ENGINE**—When checking No.5 main bearing; shim No.4 and No.6 main bearing.
- **4.0L ENGINE**—When checking No.6 main bearing; shim No.5 and No.7 main bearing.
- **4.0L ENGINE**—When checking No.7 main bearing; shim No.6 main bearing.

NOTE: Remove all shims before assembling engine.

METHOD - 2 (ALTERNATIVE)

The weight of the crankshaft is supported by a jack under the counterweight adjacent to the bearing being checked.

(1) Place a piece of Plastigage across the entire width of the bearing cap shell (Fig. 2). Position the Plastigage approximately 6.35 mm (1/4 inch) off center and away from the oil holes. In addition, suspect areas can be checked by placing the Plastigage in that area. Tighten the bearing cap bolts of the bearing being checked to 108 N·m (80 ft. lbs.) torque. **DO NOT rotate the crankshaft or the Plastigage may be smeared, giving inaccurate results.**

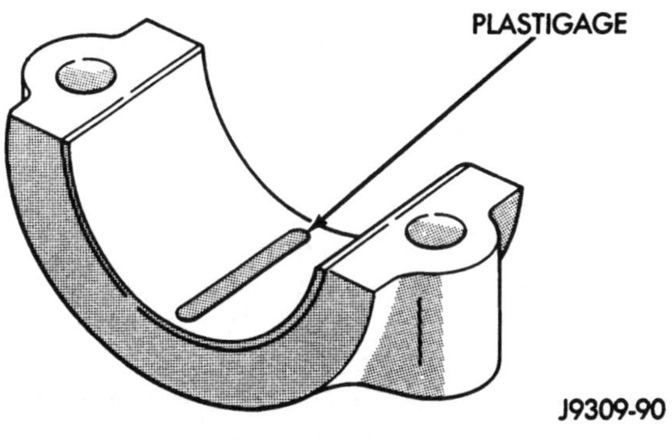

Fig. 2 Placement of Plastigage in Bearing Shell

GENERAL INFORMATION (Continued)

(2) Remove the bearing cap and compare the width of the flattened Plastigage with the scale provided on the package (Fig. 3). Plastigage generally comes in 2 scales (one scale is in inches and the other is a metric scale). Locate the band closest to the same width. This band shows the amount of clearance. Differences in readings between the ends indicate the amount of taper present. Record all readings taken (refer to Engine Specifications).

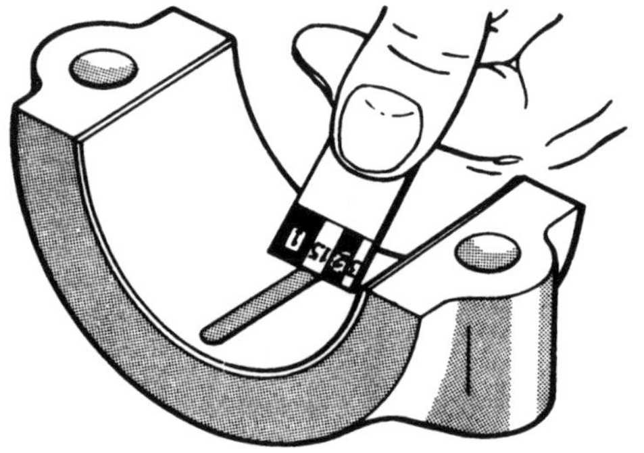

Fig. 3 Clearance Measurement

(3) Plastigage is available in a variety of clearance ranges. The 0.025-0.076 mm (0.001-0.003 inch) range is usually the most appropriate for checking engine bearing clearances.

CONNECTING ROD BEARING CLEARANCE

Engine connecting rod bearing clearances can be determined by use of Plastigage, or equivalent. The following is the recommended procedures for the use of Plastigage:

(1) Remove oil film from surface to be checked. Plastigage is soluble in oil.

(2) Place a piece of Plastigage across the entire width of the bearing cap shell (Fig. 2). Position the Plastigage approximately 6.35 mm (1/4 inch) off center and away from the oil holes. In addition, suspect areas can be checked by placing the Plastigage in the suspect area.

(3) The crankshaft must be turned until the connecting rod to be checked starts moving toward the top of the engine. Only then should the rod cap with Plastigage in place be assembled. Tighten the rod cap nut to 45 N·m (33 ft. lbs.) torque. **DO NOT rotate the crankshaft or the Plastigage may be smeared, giving inaccurate results.**

(4) Remove the bearing cap and compare the width of the flattened Plastigage with the scale provided on the package (Fig. 3). Plastigage generally comes in 2 scales (one scale is in inches and the other is a metric scale). Locate the band closest to the same width. This band shows the amount of clearance. Differences in readings between the ends indicate the amount of taper present. Record all readings taken (refer to Engine Specifications).

(5) Plastigage is available in a variety of clearance ranges. The 0.025-0.076 mm (0.001-0.003 inch) range is usually the most appropriate for checking engine bearing clearances.

REPAIR DAMAGED OR WORN THREADS

Damaged or worn threads can be repaired. Essentially, this repair consists of:

- Drilling out worn or damaged threads.
- Tapping the hole with a special Heli-Coil Tap, or equivalent.
- Installing an insert into the tapped hole to bring the hole back to its original thread size.

CAUTION: Be sure that the tapped holes maintain the original center line.

Heli-Coil tools and inserts are readily available from automotive parts jobbers.

SERVICE ENGINE ASSEMBLY (SHORT BLOCK)

A service replacement engine assembly (short block) may be installed whenever the original cylinder block is defective or damaged beyond repair. It consists of the cylinder block, crankshaft, piston and rod assemblies. If needed, the camshaft must be procured separately and installed before the engine is installed in the vehicle.

A short block is identified with the letter “S” stamped on the same machined surface where the build date code is stamped for complete engine assemblies.

Installation includes the transfer of components from the defective or damaged original engine. Follow the appropriate procedures for cleaning, inspection and torque tightening.

HYDROSTATIC LOCK

When an engine is suspected of hydrostatic lock (regardless of what caused the problem), follow the steps below.

(1) Perform the Fuel Pressure Release Procedure (refer to Group 14, Fuel System).

(2) Disconnect the negative cable from the battery.

(3) Inspect air cleaner, induction system and intake manifold to ensure system is dry and clear of foreign material.

(4) Place a shop towel around the spark plugs to catch any fluid that may possibly be under pressure in the cylinder head. Remove the plugs from the engine.

CAUTION: DO NOT use the starter motor to rotate the crankshaft. Severe damage could occur.

(5) With all spark plugs removed, rotate the crankshaft using a breaker bar and socket.

GENERAL INFORMATION (Continued)

(6) Identify the fluid in the cylinders (i.e. coolant, fuel, oil, etc.).
(7) Make sure all fluid has been removed from the cylinders.
(8) Repair engine or components as necessary to prevent this problem from occurring again.
(9) Squirt engine oil into the cylinders to lubricate the walls. This will prevent damage on restart.
(10) Install new spark plugs. Tighten the spark plugs to 37 N·m (27 ft. lbs.) torque.
(11) Drain engine oil. Remove and discard the oil filter.
(12) Install the drain plug. Tighten the plug to 34 N·m (25 ft. lbs.) torque.
(13) Install a new oil filter.
(14) Fill engine crankcase with the specified amount and grade of oil (refer to Group 0, Lubrication and Maintenance).
(15) Connect the negative cable to the battery.
(16) Start the engine and check for any leaks.

ENGINE OIL

WARNING: NEW OR USED ENGINE OIL CAN BE IRRITATING TO THE SKIN. AVOID PROLONGED OR REPEATED SKIN CONTACT WITH ENGINE OIL. CONTAMINANTS IN USED ENGINE OIL, CAUSED BY INTERNAL COMBUSTION, CAN BE HAZARDOUS TO YOUR HEALTH. THOROUGHLY WASH EXPOSED SKIN WITH SOAP AND WATER. DO NOT WASH SKIN WITH GASOLINE, DIESEL FUEL, THINNER, OR SOLVENTS, HEALTH PROBLEMS CAN RESULT. DO NOT POLLUTE, DISPOSE OF USED ENGINE OIL PROPERLY.

ENGINE OIL SPECIFICATION

CAUTION: Do not use non-detergent or straight mineral oil when adding or changing crankcase lubricant. Engine failure can result.

API SERVICE GRADE CERTIFIED

Use an engine oil that is API Service Grade Certified or an oil that conforms to the API Service Grade SH or SH/CD. MOPAR provides engine oils that conform to all of these service grades.

SAE VISCOSITY

An SAE viscosity grade is used to specify the viscosity of engine oil. SAE 30 specifies a single viscosity engine oil. Engine oils also have multiple viscosities. These are specified with a dual SAE viscosity grade which indicates the cold-to-hot temperature viscosity range. Select an engine oil that is best suited to your particular temperature range and variation (Fig. 4).

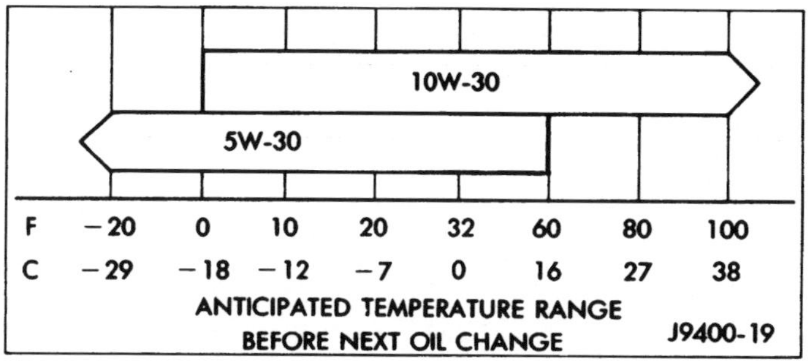

Fig. 4 Temperature/Engine Oil Viscosity

ENERGY CONSERVING OIL

An Energy Conserving type oil is recommended for gasoline engines. They are designated as either ENERGY CONSERVING or ENERGY CONSERVING II.

CONTAINER IDENTIFICATION

Standard engine oil identification notations have been adopted to aid in the proper selection of engine oil. The identifying notations are located on the label of engine oil plastic bottles and the top of engine oil cans (Fig. 5).

9400-9

Fig. 5 Engine Oil Container Standard Notations

ENGINE OIL ADDITIVES

In some instances, such as infrequent operation, short trip driving, and during break-in after a major overhaul, addition of special materials containing anti-rust and anti-scuff additives are beneficial. A suitable product for this purpose is MOPAR Engine Oil Supplement.

OIL LEVEL INDICATOR (DIPSTICK)

The engine oil level indicator (Dipstick) is located at the right rear of both 2.5L engines and 4.0L engines (Fig. 6).

CRANKCASE OIL LEVEL INSPECTION

CAUTION: Do not overfill crankcase with engine oil, oil foaming and oil pressure loss can result.

Inspect engine oil level approximately every 800 kilometers (500 miles). Unless the engine has exhib-

GENERAL INFORMATION (Continued)

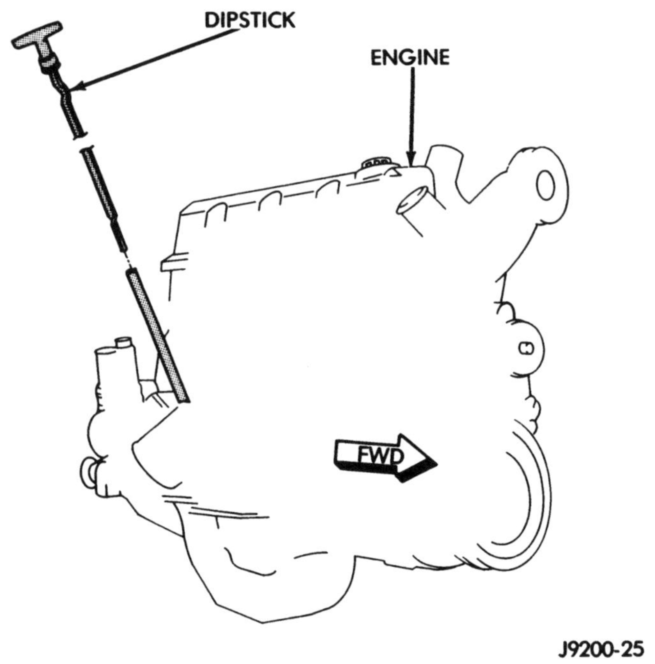

Fig. 6 Engine Oil Dipstick Location—Typical

ited loss of oil pressure, run the engine for about five minutes before checking oil level. Checking engine oil level on a cold engine is not accurate.

To ensure proper lubrication of an engine, the engine oil must be maintained at an acceptable level. The acceptable levels are indicated between the ADD and SAFE marks on the engine oil dipstick (Fig. 7) (Fig. 8).

(1) Position vehicle on level surface.

(2) With engine OFF, allow approximately ten minutes for oil to settle to bottom of crankcase, remove engine oil dipstick.

(3) Wipe dipstick clean.

(4) Install dipstick and verify it is seated in the tube.

(5) Remove dipstick, with handle held above the tip, take oil level reading (Fig. 7) (Fig. 8).

(6) Add oil only if level is below the ADD mark on dipstick.

ENGINE OIL CHANGE

Change engine oil at mileage and time intervals described in Maintenance Schedules.

Run engine until achieving normal operating temperature.

(1) Position the vehicle on a level surface and turn engine off.

(2) Hoist and support vehicle on safety stands.

(3) Remove oil fill cap.

(4) Place a suitable drain pan under crankcase drain.

(5) Remove drain plug from crankcase and allow oil to drain into pan. Inspect drain plug threads for

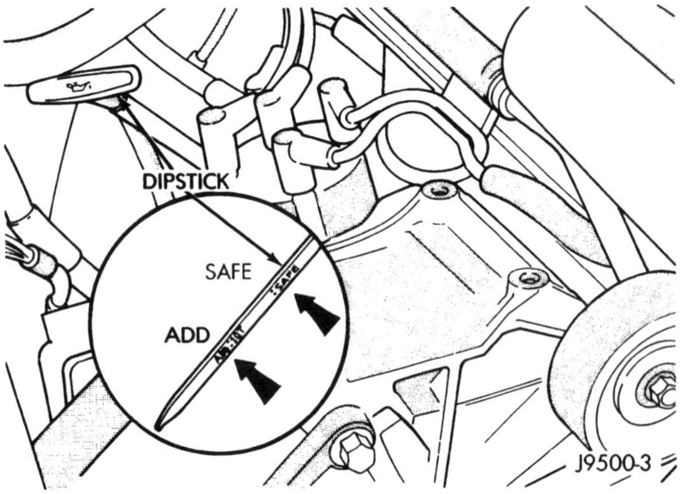

Fig. 7 Engine Oil Dipstick—2.5L Engine

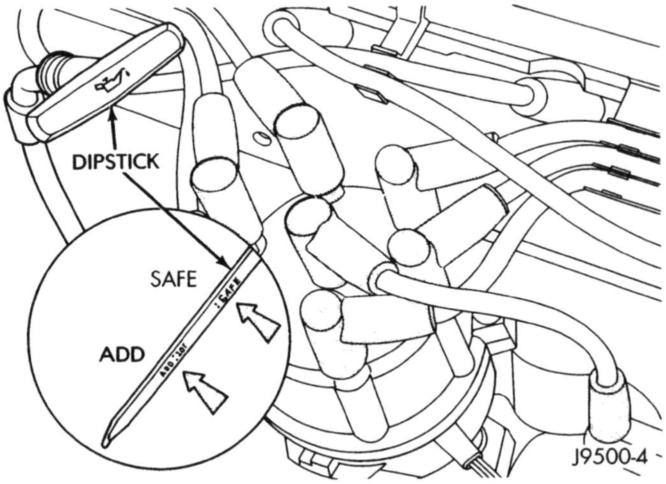

Fig. 8 Engine Oil Dipstick—4.0L Engine

stretching or other damage. Replace drain plug if damaged.

(6) Install drain plug in crankcase.

(7) Lower vehicle and fill crankcase with specified type and amount of engine oil described in this section.

(8) Install oil fill cap.

(9) Start engine and inspect for leaks.

(10) Stop engine and inspect oil level.

ENGINE OIL FILTER CHANGE

FILTER SPECIFICATION

CAUTION: Do not use oil filter with metric threads. The proper oil filter has SAE type 3/4 X 16 threads. An oil filter with metric threads can result in oil leaks and engine failure.

All Jeep engines are equipped with a high quality full-flow, throw-away type oil filter. Chrysler Corpo-

GENERAL INFORMATION (Continued)

ration recommends a Mopar or equivalent oil filter be used.

OIL FILTER REMOVAL

(1) Position a drain pan under the oil filter.

(2) Using a suitable oil filter wrench loosen filter.

(3) Rotate the oil filter counterclockwise to remove it from the cylinder block oil filter boss (Fig. 9).

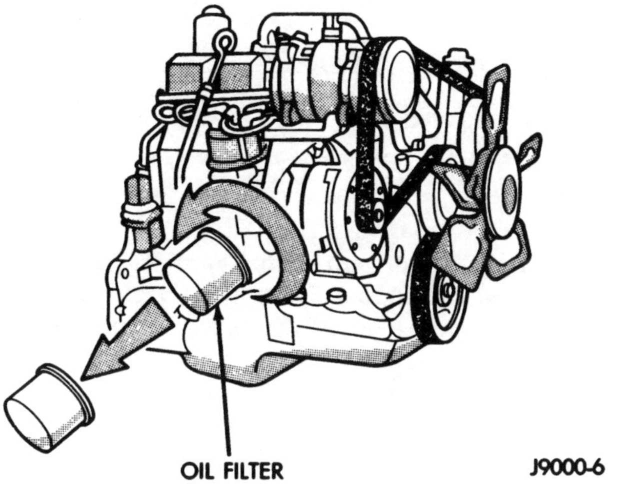

Fig. 9 Oil Filter—2.5L Engine

(4) When filter separates from adapter nipple, tip gasket end upward to minimize oil spill. Remove filter from vehicle.

(5) With a wiping cloth, clean the gasket sealing surface (Fig. 10) of oil and grime.

OIL FILTER INSTALLATION

(1) Lightly lubricate oil filter gasket with engine oil or chassis grease.

(2) Thread filter onto adapter nipple. When gasket makes contact with sealing surface, (Fig. 10) hand tighten filter one full turn, do not over tighten.

(3) Add oil, verify crankcase oil level and start engine. Inspect for oil leaks.

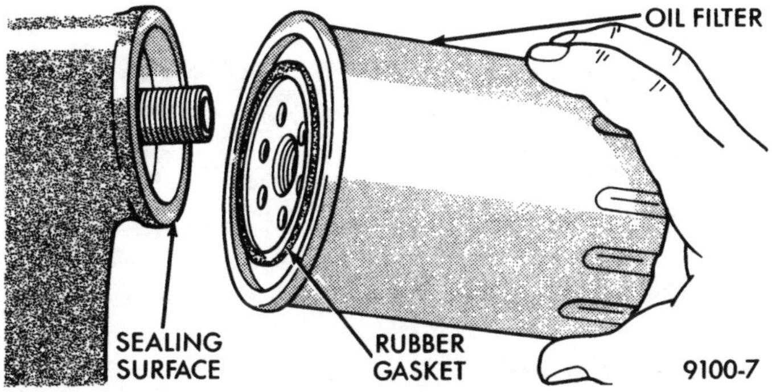

Fig. 10 Oil Filter Sealing Surface—Typical

USED ENGINE OIL DISPOSAL

Care should be exercised when disposing used engine oil after it has been drained from a vehicle engine. Refer to the WARNING at beginning of this section.

ENGINE DIAGNOSIS

INDEX

DIAGNOSIS AND TESTING

GENERAL INFORMATION

Engine diagnosis is helpful in determining the causes of malfunctions not detected and remedied by routine tune-ups.

These malfunctions may be classified as either performance (e.g., engine idles rough and stalls) or mechanical (e.g., a strange noise).

Refer to the Service Diagnosis—Performance chart and the Service Diagnosis—Mechanical chart for possible causes and corrections of malfunctions. Refer to Group 14, Fuel System for the fuel system diagnosis.

Additional tests and diagnostic procedures may be necessary for specific engine malfunctions that can not be isolated with the Service Diagnosis charts. Information concerning additional tests and diagnosis is provided within the following diagnosis:

- Cylinder Compression Pressure Test.
- Cylinder Combustion Pressure Leakage Test.
- Engine Cylinder Head Gasket Failure Diagnosis.
- Intake Manifold Leakage Diagnosis.

HYDRAULIC TAPPETS

LEAK-DOWN TEST

After cleaning and inspection, test each tappet for specified leak-down rate tolerance to ensure zero-lash operation (Fig. 1).

Swing the weighted arm of the hydraulic valve tappet tester away from the ram of the Leak-Down Tester.

(1) Place a 7.925-7.950 mm (0.312-0.313 inch) diameter ball bearing on the plunger cap of the tappet.

(2) Lift the ram and position the tappet (with the ball bearing) inside the tester cup.

(3) Lower the ram, then adjust the nose of the ram until it contacts the ball bearing. DO NOT tighten the hex nut on the ram.

(4) Fill the tester cup with hydraulic valve tappet test oil until the tappet is completely submerged.

(5) Swing the weighted arm onto the push rod and pump the tappet plunger up and down to remove air. When the air bubbles cease, swing the weighted arm away and allow the plunger to rise to the normal position.

(6) Adjust the nose of the ram to align the pointer with the SET mark on the scale of the tester and tighten the hex nut.

(7) Slowly swing the weighted arm onto the push rod.

(8) Rotate the cup by turning the handle at the base of the tester clockwise one revolution every 2 seconds.

(9) Observe the leak-down time interval from the instant the pointer aligns with the START mark on the scale until the pointer aligns with the 0.125 mark. A normally functioning tappet will require 20-110 seconds to leak-down. Discard tappets with leak-down time interval not within this specification.

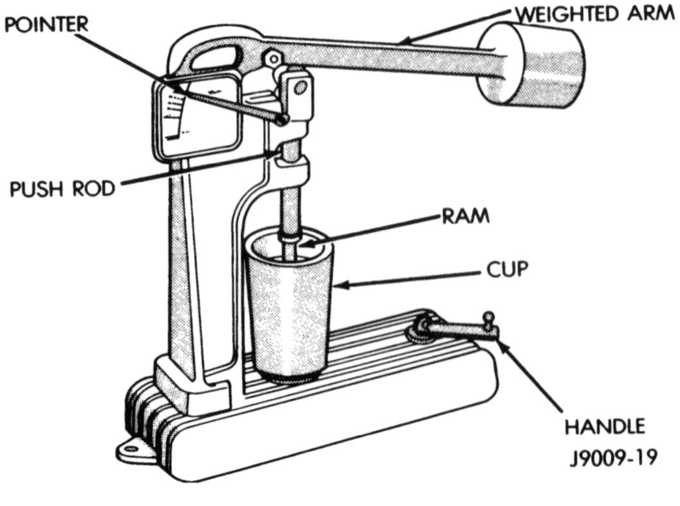

Fig. 1 Leak-Down Tester

DIAGNOSIS AND TESTING (Continued)

INTAKE MANIFOLD LEAKAGE DIAGNOSIS

An intake manifold air leak is characterized by lower than normal manifold vacuum. Also, one or more cylinders may not be functioning.

WARNING: USE EXTREME CAUTION WHEN THE ENGINE IS OPERATING. DO NOT STAND IN A DIRECT LINE WITH THE FAN. DO NOT PUT YOUR HANDS NEAR THE PULLEYS, BELTS OR THE FAN. DO NOT WEAR LOOSE CLOTHING.

(1) Start the engine.
(2) Spray a small stream of water at the suspected leak area.
(3) If a change in RPM is observed the area of the suspected leak has been found.
(4) Repair as required.

CYLINDER COMPRESSION PRESSURE TEST

The results of a cylinder compression pressure test can be utilized to diagnose several engine malfunctions.

Ensure the battery is completely charged and the engine starter motor is in good operating condition. Otherwise the indicated compression pressures may not be valid for diagnosis purposes.

(1) Clean the spark plug recesses with compressed air.
(2) Remove the spark plugs.
(3) Secure the throttle in the wide-open position.
(4) Disconnect the ignition coil.
(5) Insert a compression pressure gauge and rotate the engine with the engine starter motor for three revolutions.
(6) Record the compression pressure on the 3rd revolution. Continue the test for the remaining cylinders.

Refer to Engine Specifications for the correct engine compression pressures.

ENGINE CYLINDER HEAD GASKET FAILURE DIAGNOSIS

A leaking engine cylinder head gasket usually results in loss of power, loss of coolant and engine misfiring.

An engine cylinder head gasket leak can be located between adjacent cylinders or between a cylinder and the adjacent water jacket.

- An engine cylinder head gasket leaking between adjacent cylinders is indicated by a loss of power and/or engine misfire.
- An engine cylinder head gasket leaking between a cylinder and an adjacent water jacket is indicated by coolant foaming or overheating and loss of coolant.

CYLINDER-TO-CYLINDER LEAKAGE TEST

To determine if an engine cylinder head gasket is leaking between adjacent cylinders; follow the procedures outlined in Cylinder Compression Pressure Test. An engine cylinder head gasket leaking between adjacent cylinders will result in approximately a 50-70% reduction in compression pressure.

CYLINDER-TO-WATER JACKET LEAKAGE TEST

WARNING: USE EXTREME CAUTION WHEN THE ENGINE IS OPERATING. DO NOT STAND IN A DIRECT LINE WITH THE FAN. DO NOT PUT YOUR HANDS NEAR THE PULLEYS, BELTS OR THE FAN. DO NOT WEAR LOOSE CLOTHING.

Remove the radiator cap.

Start the engine and allow it to warm up until the engine thermostat opens.

If a large combustion/compression pressure leak exists, bubbles will be visible in the coolant.

If bubbles are not visible, install a radiator pressure tester and pressurize the coolant system.

If a cylinder is leaking combustion pressure into the water jacket, the tester pointer will pulsate with every combustion stroke of the cylinder.

CYLINDER COMBUSTION PRESSURE LEAKAGE TEST

The combustion pressure leakage test provides an accurate means for determining engine condition.

Combustion pressure leakage testing will detect:

- Exhaust and intake valve leaks (improper seating).
- Leaks between adjacent cylinders or into water jacket.
- Any causes for combustion/compression pressure loss.

(1) Check the coolant level and fill as required. DO NOT install the radiator cap.
(2) Start and operate the engine until it attains normal operating temperature, then turn the engine OFF.
(3) Remove the spark plugs.
(4) Remove the oil filler cap.
(5) Remove the air cleaner.
(6) Calibrate the tester according to the manufacturer's instructions. The shop air source for testing should maintain 483 kPa (70 psi) minimum, 1 379 kPa (200 psi) maximum and 552 kPa (80 psi) recommended.
(7) Perform the test procedures on each cylinder according to the tester manufacturer's instructions. While testing, listen for pressurized air escaping through the throttle body, tailpipe and oil filler cap opening. Check for bubbles in the radiator coolant.

DIAGNOSIS AND TESTING (Continued)

CONDITION	POSSIBLE CAUSE	CORRECTION
AIR ESCAPES THROUGH CARBURETOR/THROTTLE BODY	Intake valve not seated properly.	Inspect valve. Reface or replace, if necessary.
AIR ESCAPES THROUGH TAILPIPE	Exhaust valve not seated properly.	Inspect valve.Reface or replace, if necessary.
AIR ESCAPES THROUGH RADIATOR	Head gasket leaks or crack in cylinder block.	Remove cylinder head and inspect. Replace, if necessary.
MORE THAN 50% LEAKAGE FROM ADJACENT CYLINDERS	Head gasket leaks or crack in cylinder block or head between adjacent cylinders.	Remove cylinder head and inspect. Replace gasket or head, if necessary.
MORE THAN 25% LEAKAGE AND AIR ESCAPES THROUGH OIL FILLER CAP OPENING ONLY	Stuck or broken piston ring(s); cracked piston; worn rings and/or cylinder wall.	Inspect for broken ring(s) or piston. Measure ring gap and cylinder diameter, taper, and out-of-round. Replace affected part, if necessary.

J8909-78

All gauge pressure indications should be equal, with no more than 25% leakage.

FOR EXAMPLE: At 552 kPa (80 psi) input pressure, a minimum of 414 kPa (60 psi) should be maintained in the cylinder.

Refer to the Cylinder Combustion Pressure Leakage Test Diagnosis chart.

INSPECTION (ENGINE OIL LEAKS IN GENERAL)

Begin with a through visual inspection of the engine, particularly at the area of the suspected leak. If an oil leak source is not readily identifiable, the following steps should be followed:

(1) Do not clean or degrease the engine at this time because some solvents may cause rubber to swell, temporarily stopping the leak.

(2) Add an oil soluble dye (use as recommended by manufacturer). Start the engine and let idle for approximately 15 minutes. Check the oil dipstick to make sure the dye is thoroughly mixed as indicated with a bright yellow color under a black light.

(3) Using a black light, inspect the entire engine for fluorescent dye, particularly at the suspected area of oil leak. If the oil leak is found and identified, repair per service manual instructions.

(4) If dye is not observed, drive the vehicle at various speeds for approximately 24km (15 miles), and repeat inspection.

(5) **If the oil leak source is not positively identified at this time**, proceed with the air leak detection test method.

Air Leak Detection Test Method

(1) Disconnect the breather cap to air cleaner hose at the breather cap end. Cap or plug breather cap nipple.

(2) Remove the PCV valve from the cylinder head cover. Cap or plug the PCV valve grommet.

(3) Attach an air hose with pressure gauge and regulator to the dipstick tube.

CAUTION: Do not subject the engine assembly to more than 20.6 kpa (3 PSI) of test pressure.

(4) Gradually apply air pressure from 1 psi to 2.5 psi maximum while applying soapy water at the suspected source. Adjust the regulator to the suitable test pressure that provide the best bubbles which will pinpoint the leak source. If the oil leak is detected and identified, repair per service manual procedures.

(5) If the leakage occurs at the rear oil seal area, refer to the section, Inspection for Rear Seal Area Leak.

(6) If no leaks are detected, turn off the air supply and remove the air hose and all plugs and caps. Install the PCV valve and breather cap hose.

(7) Clean the oil off the suspect oil leak area using a suitable solvent. Drive the vehicle at various speeds approximately 24 km (15 miles). Inspect the engine for signs of an oil leak by using a black light.

INSPECTION FOR REAR SEAL AREA LEAKS

Since it is sometimes difficult to determine the source of an oil leak in the rear seal area of the engine, a more involved inspection is necessary. The

DIAGNOSIS AND TESTING (Continued)

following steps should be followed to help pinpoint the source of the leak.

If the leakage occurs at the crankshaft rear oil seal area:

(1) Disconnect the battery.

(2) Raise the vehicle.

(3) Remove torque converter or clutch housing cover and inspect rear of block for evidence of oil. Use a black light to check for the oil leak:

(a) Circular spray pattern generally indicates seal leakage or crankshaft damage.

(b) Where leakage tends to run straight down, possible causes are a porous block, distributor seal, camshaft bore cup plugs oil galley pipe plugs, oil filter runoff, and main bearing cap to cylinder block mating surfaces.

(4) If no leaks are detected, pressurize the crankcase as outlined in the, Inspection (Engine oil Leaks in general)

CAUTION: Do not exceed 20.6 kPa (3 psi).

(5) If the leak is not detected, very slowly turn the crankshaft and watch for leakage. If a leak is detected between the crankshaft and seal while slowly turning the crankshaft, it is possible the crankshaft seal surface is damaged. The seal area on the crankshaft could have minor nicks or scratches that can be polished out with emery cloth.

CAUTION: Use extreme caution when crankshaft polishing is necessary to remove minor nicks and scratches. The crankshaft seal flange is especially machined to complement the function of the rear oil seal.

(6) For bubbles that remain steady with shaft rotation, no further inspection can be done until disassembled.

ENGINE OIL PRESSURE

(1) Remove oil pressure sending unit.

(2) Install Oil Pressure Line and Gauge Tool C-3292. Start engine and record pressure. Refer to Oil Pressure in Engine Specifications for the proper pressures.

DIAGNOSIS AND TESTING (Continued)

SERVICE DIAGNOSIS—PERFORMANCE

CONDITION	POSSIBLE CAUSES	CORRECTION
ENGINE WILL NOT START	1. Weak battery. 2. Corroded or loose battery connections. 3. Faulty starter. 4. Moisture on ignition wires and distributor cap. 5. Faulty ignition cables. 6. Faulty coil or control unit. 7. Incorrect spark plug gap. 8. Incorrect ignition timing. 9. Dirt or water in fuel system. 10. Faulty fuel pump. 11. Faulty connectors for crankshaft or camshaft position sensors.	1. Test battery specific gravity. Charge or replace as necessary. 2. Clean and tighten battery connections. Apply a coat of light mineral grease to the terminals. 3. Refer to Group 8A, Battery/Starter/Charging System Diagnostics. 4. Wipe wires and cap clean and dry. 5. Replace any cracked or shorted cables. 6. Test and replace, if necessary (refer to Group 8D, Ignition System). 7. Set gap (refer to Group 8D, Ignition System). 8. Refer to Group 8D, Ignition System. 9. Clean system and replace fuel filter. 10. Install new fuel pump (refer to Group 14, Fuel System). 11. Rebuild or replace the connectors.
ENGINE STALLS OR ROUGH IDLE	1. Idle speed set too low. 2. Idle mixture too lean or too rich. 3. Leak in intake manifold. 4. Worn or burned distributor rotor. 5. Incorrect ignition wiring. 6. Faulty coil. 7. EGR valve leaking.	1. Refer to Group 14, Fuel System. 2. Refer to Group 14, Fuel System. 3. Inspect intake manifold gasket and vacuum hoses. Replace, if necessary (refer to Group 11, Exhaust System & Intake Manifold). 4. Install new distributor rotor. 5. Install correct wiring. 6. Test and replace, if necessary (refer to Group 8D, Ignition System). 7. Test and replace, if necessary (refer to Group 25, Emissions Control System).

J9409-91

DIAGNOSIS AND TESTING (Continued)

CONDITION	POSSIBLE CAUSES	CORRECTION
ENGINE LOSS OF POWER	1. Incorrect ignition timing. 2. Worn or burned distributor rotor. 3. Worn distributor shaft. 4. Dirty or incorrectly gapped spark plugs. 5. Dirt or water in fuel system. 6. Faulty fuel pump. 7. Incorrect valve timing. 8. Blown cylinder head gasket. 9. Low compression. 10. Burned, warped or pitted valves. 11. Plugged or restricted exhaust system. 12. Faulty ignition cables. 13. Faulty coil. 14. Faulty crankshaft or camshaft sensor.	1. Refer to Group 8D, Ignition System. 2. Install new distributor rotor. 3. Remove and repair distributor (refer to Group 8D, Ignition System). 4. Clean plugs and set gap (refer to Group 8D, Ignition System). 5. Clean system and replace fuel filter. 6. Install new fuel pump. 7. Correct valve timing. 8. Install new cylinder head gasket. 9. Test compression of each cylinder. 10. Install new valves. 11. Install new parts, as necessary. 12. Replace any cracked or shorted cables. 13. Test and replace, as necessary (refer to Group 8D, Ignition System). 14. Replace sensor.
ENGINE MISSES ON ACCELERATION	1. Dirty or gap set too wide in spark plug. 2. Incorrect ignition timing. 3. Dirt in fuel system. 4. Burned, warped or pitted valves. 5. Faulty coil.	1. Clean spark plugs and set gap (refer to Group 8D, Ignition System). 2. Refer to Group 8D, Ignition System. 3. Clean fuel system. 4. Install new valves. 5. Test and replace, if necessary, (refer to Group 8D, Ignition System).
ENGINE MISSES AT HIGH SPEED	1. Dirty or gap set too wide in spark plug. 2. Worn distributor shaft. 3. Worn or burned distributor rotor. 4. Faulty coil. 5. Incorrect ignition timing. 6. Dirty injector in throttle body. 7. Dirt or water in fuel system.	1. Clean spark plugs and set gap (refer to Group 8D, Ignition System). 2. Remove and repair distributor (refer to Group 8D, Ignition System). 3. Install new distributor rotor. 4. Test and replace, as necessary (refer to Group 8D, Ignition System). 5. Refer to Group 8D, Ignition System. 6. Clean injector. 7. Clean system and replace fuel filter.

J9409-92

SERVICE DIAGNOSIS—PERFORMANCE—CONT.

DIAGNOSIS AND TESTING (Continued)

SERVICE DIAGNOSIS—MECHANICAL

CONDITION	POSSIBLE CAUSES	CORRECTION
NOISY VALVES	1. High or low oil level in crankcase.	1. Check for correct oil level (refer to Group 0, Lubrication and Maintenance.
	2. Thin or diluted oil.	2. Change oil (refer to Group 0, Lubrication and Maintenance).
	3. Low oil pressure.	3. Check engine oil level.
	4. Dirt in tappets/lash adjusters.	4. Clean hydraulic tappets/hydraulic lash adjusters.
	5. Bent push rods.	5. Install new push rods.
	6. Worn rocker arms.	6. Inspect oil supply to rocker arms.
	7. Worn tappets/lash adjusters.	7. Install new hydraulic tappets/ hydraulic lash adjusters.
	8. Worn valve guides.	8. Ream and install new valves with oversize stems.
	9. Excessive runout of valve seats on valve faces.	9. Grind valve seats and valves.
CONNECTING ROD NOISE	1. Insufficient oil supply.	1. Check engine oil level (refer to Group 0, Lubrication and Maintenance).
	2. Low oil pressure.	2. Check engine oil level. Inspect oil pump relief valve and spring.
	3. Thin or diluted oil.	3. Change oil to correct viscosity.
	4. Excessive bearing clearance.	4. Measure bearings for correct clearance. Repair as necessary.
	5. Connecting rod journal out-of-round.	5. Replace crankshaft or grind journals.
	6. Misaligned connecting rods.	6. Replace bent connecting rods.
MAIN BEARING NOISE	1. Insufficient oil supply.	1. Check engine oil level (refer to Group 0, Lubrication and Maintenance).
	2. Low oil pressure.	2. Check engine oil level. Inspect oil pump relief valve and spring.
	3. Thin or diluted oil.	3. Change oil to correct viscosity.
	4. Excessive bearing clearance.	4. Measure bearings for correct clearance. Repair as necessary.
	5. Excessive end play.	5. Check No. 3 main bearing for wear on flanges.
	6. Crankshaft journal out-of-round, worn.	6. Grind journals or replace crankshaft.
	7. Loose flywheel or torque converter.	7. Tighten to correct torque.

J9509-62

DIAGNOSIS AND TESTING (Continued)

SERVICE DIAGNOSIS—LUBRICATION

CONDITION	POSSIBLE CAUSES	CORRECTION
OIL LEAKS	1. Gaskets and O-Rings. (a) Misaligned, deteriorated or torn. (b) Loose fastener, broken or porous metal part. 2. Crankshaft Rear Seal (a) Misinstalled, inverted or torn lip (b) Torn, cut or shaved seal back bead. 3. Crankshaft Seal Flange. Scratched, nicked or grooved. 4. Cylinder block to Cap Mating Surface. (a) Inadequate Loctite sealant. (b) Oil hole burr. 5. Oil Pan to Rear Main Cap Sealant (Slots 3.9 - 5.2 only). (a) Inadequate or mislocated sealant. (b) Torn, cut or misinstalled oil pan. (c) Cracked or damaged oil pan flange. 6. Chain Case Cover Seal. (a) Misinstalled, cocked or misaligned. (b) Torn, cut or damaged seal lips. (c) Scratched or damaged seal casing or cover bore. (d) Scratched or damaged vibration damper hub.	1. (a) Replace the part. (b) Tighten, repair or replace the part. 2. (a) Replace the seal. (b) Replace the seal. 3. Replace or polish if necessary. 4. (a) Apply sealant per sealant per service manual. (b) Carefully stone or chamfer hole. 5. (a) Apply sealant per service manual procedures. (b) Replace the gasket. (c) Replace the oil pan. 6. (a) Replace per service manual procedures. (b) Replace the seal. (c) Replace the seal. (d) Minor damage can be polished out; otherwise replace the part.
OIL PRESSURE DROP	1. Low oil level. 2. Faulty oil pressure sending unit. 3. Low oil pressure. 4. Clogged oil filter. 5. Worn parts in oil pump. 6. Thin or diluted oil. 7. Excessive bearing clearance. 8. Oil pump relief valve stuck. 9. Oil pump suction tube loose, bent or cracked. 10. Oil pump cover warped or cracked.	1. Check engine oil level. 2. Install new sending unit. 3. Check sending unit and check main bearing oil clearance. 4. Install new oil filter. 5. Replace worn parts or pump. 6. Change oil to correct viscosity. 7. Measure bearings for correct clearance. 8. Remove valve and inspect, clean and install. 9. Remove oil pan and install new tube, if necessary. 10. Install new oil pump.
OIL PUMPING AT RINGS; SPARK PLUGS FOULING	1. Worn, scuffed or broken rings. 2. Carbon in oil ring slot. 3. Rings fitted too tightly in grooves. 4. Worn valve guides. 5. Leaking intake gasket (3.9L & 5.2L engines). 6. Leaking valve guide seals (3.9L & 5.2L engines). 7. Dislodged valve guide seals (3.9L & 5.2L engines).	1. Hone cylinder bores and install new rings. 2. Install new rings. 3. Remove the rings. Check grooves. If grooves are not proper width, replace piston. 4. Ream guides and replace valves with oversize valves and seals. 5. Replace gasket and tighten intake manifold to proper torque. 6. Replace seals. 7. Seat valve guide seals or replace, as needed.

J9509-61

1997 Wrangler
Publication No. 81-370-7148
TSB 26-10-96 Oct. 1996

2.5L ENGINE

INDEX

DESCRIPTION AND OPERATION

ENGINE DESCRIPTION

The 2.5 liter (150 CID) four-cylinder engine is an In-line, lightweight, overhead valve engine.

Engine Type . . . . . In-line 4 Cylinder
Bore and Stroke . . . . 98.4 x 81.0 mm (3.88 x 3.19 in.)
Displacement . . . . . 2.5 (150 cu. in.)
Compression Ratio 9.2:1
Torque . . . . . 190 N·m (140 ft. lbs.) @ 3500 rpm
Firing Order 1–3–4–2
Lubrication . . . . . Pressure Feed–Full Flow Filtration
**Engine Oil Capacity . . . . . 3.8L (4 Quarts) **
Cooling System . . . Liquid Cooled–Forced Circulation
Cooling System Capacity . . . . . 8.5L (9 Quarts)
Cylinder Block . . . . . Cast Iron
Crankshaft . . . . . Cast Nodular Iron
Cylinder Head . . . . . Cast Nodular Iron
Camshaft . . . . . Cast Nodular Iron
Pistons . . . . . Aluminum Alloy (with Struts)
Pistons Combustion Cavity . . . . . Double Quench
Connecting Rods . . . . . Cast Nodular Iron

This engine is designed for unleaded fuel.

The engine cylinder head has dual quench-type combustion chambers that create turbulence and fast burning of the air/fuel mixture. This results in good fuel economy.

The cylinders are numbered 1 through 4 from front to rear. The firing order is 1-3-4-2 (Fig. 1).

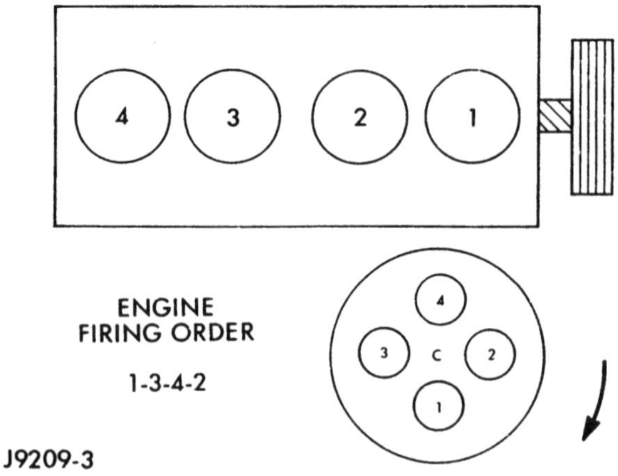

Fig. 1 Engine Firing Order

DESCRIPTION AND OPERATION (Continued)

The crankshaft rotation is clockwise, when viewed from the front of the engine. The crankshaft rotates within five main bearings and the camshaft rotates within four bearings.

BUILD DATE CODE

The engine Build Date Code is located on a machined surface on the right side of the cylinder block between the No.3 and No.4 cylinders (Fig. 2).

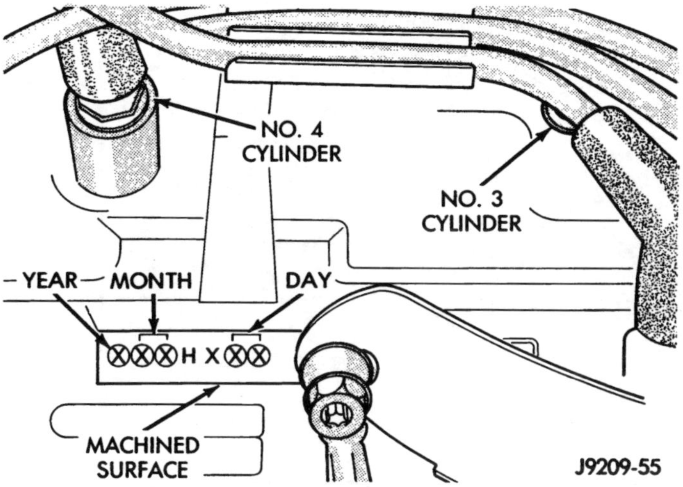

Fig. 2 Build Date Code Location

The digits of the code identify:

- 1st Digit—The year (6 = 1996).
- 2nd & 3rd Digits—The month (01 - 12).
- 4th & 5th Digits—The engine type/fuel system/compression ratio (HX = A 2.5 liter (150 CID) 9.2:1 compression ratio engine with a multi-point fuel injection system).
- 6th & 7th Digits—The day of engine build (01 - 31).

FOR EXAMPLE: Code * 601HX23 * identifies a 2.5 liter (150 CID) engine with a multi-point fuel injection system, 9.2:1 compression ratio and built on January 23, 1996.

LUBRICATION SYSTEM

A gear—type positive displacement pump is mounted at the underside of the block opposite the No. 4 main bearing. The pump draws oil through the screen and inlet tube from the sump at the rear of the oil pan. The oil is driven between the drive and idler gears and pump body, then forced through the outlet to the block. An oil gallery in the block channels the oil to the inlet side of the full flow oil filter. After passing through the filter element, the oil passes from the center outlet of the filter through an oil gallery that channels the oil up to the main gallery which extends the entire length of the block.

Galleries extend downward from the main oil gallery to the upper shell of each main bearing. The crankshaft is drilled internally to pass oil from the main bearing journals (except number 4 main bearing journal) to the connecting rod journals. Each connecting rod bearing cap has a small squirt hole, oil passes through the squirt hole and is thrown off as the rod rotates. This oil throwoff lubricates the camshaft lobes, distributor drive gear, cylinder walls, and piston pins.

The hydraulic valve tappets receive oil directly from the main oil gallery. Oil is provided to the camshaft bearing through galleries. The front camshaft bearing journal passes oil through the camshaft sprocket to the timing chain. Oil drains back to the oil pan under the number one main bearing cap.

The oil supply for the rocker arms and bridged pivot assemblies is provided by the hydraulic valve tappets which pass oil through hollow push rods to a hole in the corresponding rocker arm. Oil from the rocker arm lubricates the valve train components, then passes down through the push rod guide holes in the cylinder head past the valve tappet area, and returns to the oil pan.

DESCRIPTION AND OPERATION (Continued)

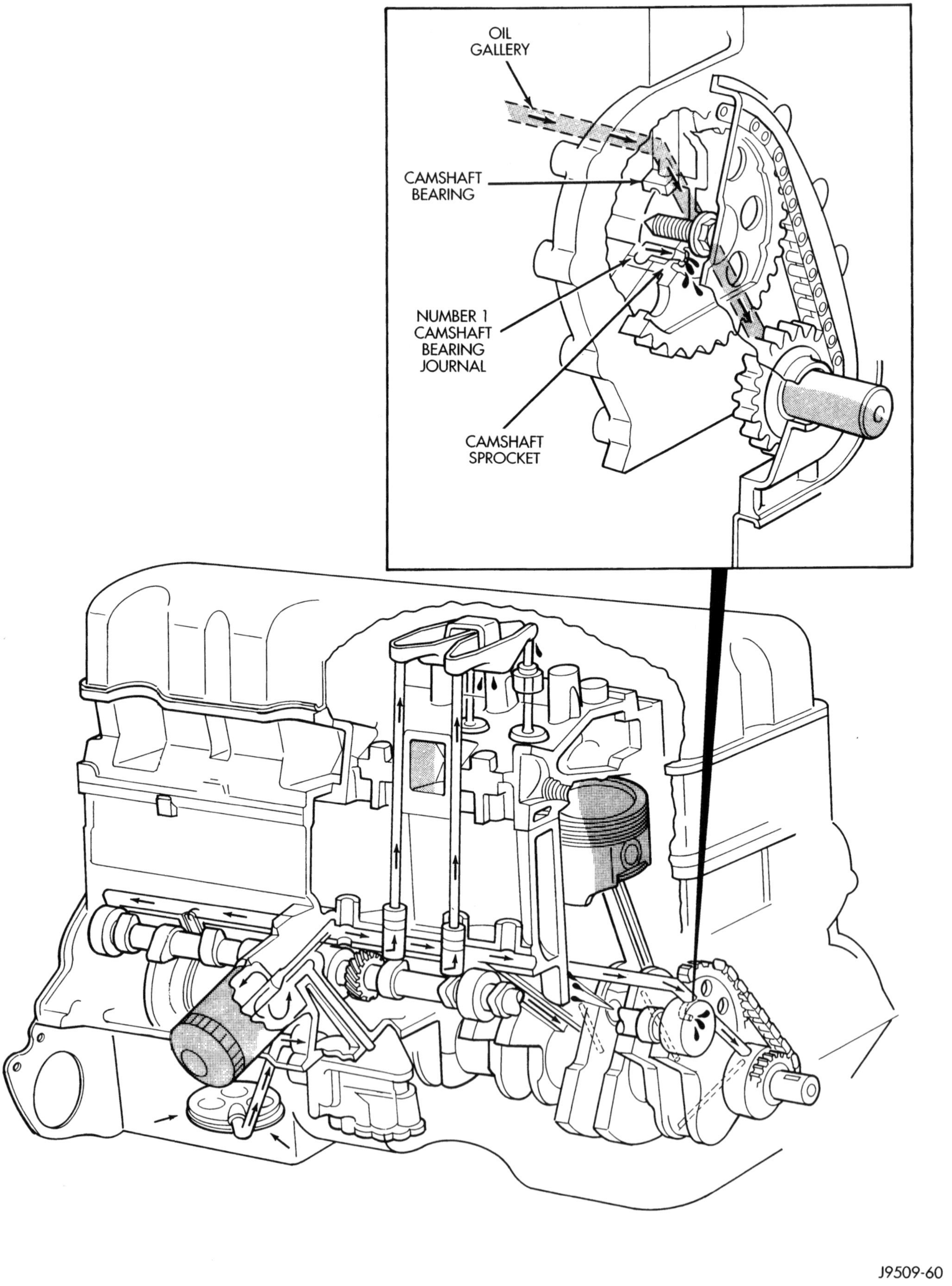

Oil Lubrication System

DESCRIPTION AND OPERATION (Continued)

OIL PUMP PRESSURE

The MINIMUM oil pump pressure is 89.6 kPa (13 psi) at 600 rpm. The MAXIMUM oil pump pressure is 255-517 kPa (37-75 psi) at 1600 rpm or more.

OVERSIZE AND UNDERSIZE COMPONENT CODES

Some engines may be built with oversize or undersize components such as:

- Oversize cylinder bores.
- Oversize camshaft bearing bores.
- Undersize crankshaft main bearing journals.
- Undersize connecting rod journals.

These engines are identified by a letter code (Fig. 3) stamped on the oil filter boss near the distributor (Fig. 4).

CODE	COMPONENT	UNDERSIZE
P	One or more connecting rod bearing journals	0.254 mm (0.010 in)
M	All crankshaft main bearing journals	0.254 mm (0.010 in)
PM	All crankshaft main bearing journals and one or more connecting rod journals	0.254 mm (0.010 in)
CODE	**COMPONENT**	**OVERSIZE**
B	All cylinder bores	0.254 mm (0.010 in)
C	All camshaft bearing bores	0.254 mm (0.010 in)

J8909-54

Fig. 3 Oversize and Undersize Component Codes

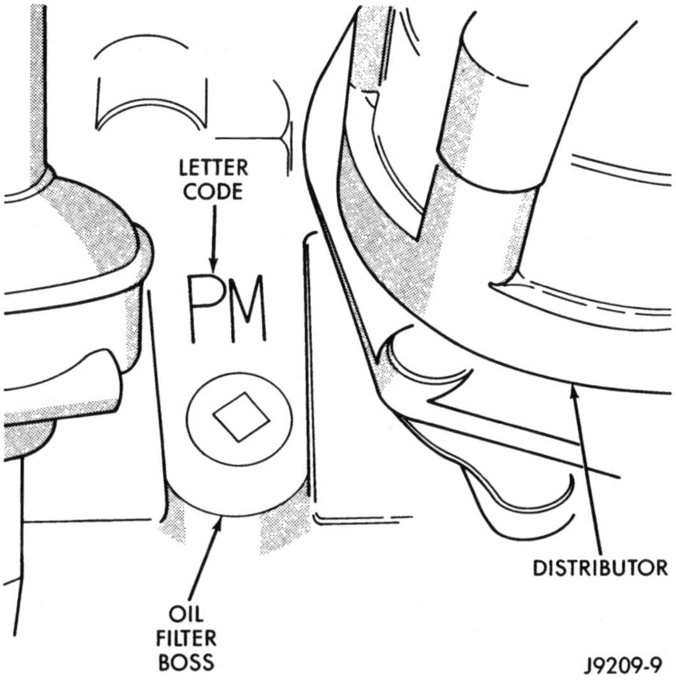

Fig. 4 Oversize and Undersize Component Code Location

SERVICE PROCEDURES

VALVE TIMING

Disconnect the spark plug wires and remove the spark plugs.

Remove the engine cylinder head cover.

Remove the capscrews, bridge and pivot assembly, and rocker arms from above the No.1 cylinder.

Alternately loosen each capscrew, one turn at a time, to avoid damaging the bridge.

Rotate the crankshaft until the No.4 piston is at top dead center (TDC) on the compression stroke.

Rotate the crankshaft counterclockwise (viewed from the front of the engine) 90°.

Install a dial indicator on the end of the No.1 cylinder intake valve push rod. Use rubber tubing to secure the indicator stem on the push rod.

Set the dial indicator pointer at zero.

Rotate the crankshaft clockwise (viewed from the front of the engine) until the dial indicator pointer indicates 0.305 mm (0.012 inch) travel distance (lift).

The timing notch index on the vibration damper should be aligned with the TDC mark on the timing degree scale.

If the timing notch is more than 13 mm (1/2 inch) away from the TDC mark in either direction, the valve timing is incorrect.

If the valve timing is incorrect, the cause may be a broken camshaft pin. It is not necessary to replace the camshaft because of pin failure. A spring pin is available for service replacement.

PISTON FITTING

BORE GAGE METHOD

(1) To correctly select the proper size piston, a cylinder bore gauge, capable of reading in 0.003 mm (.0001 in.) INCREMENTS is required. If a bore gauge is not available, do not use an inside micrometer.

(2) Measure the inside diameter of the cylinder bore at a point 49.5 mm (1-15/16 inches) below top of bore. Start perpendicular (across or at 90 degrees) to the axis of the crankshaft at point A and then take

SERVICE PROCEDURES (Continued)

an additional bore reading 90 degrees to that at point B (Fig. 5).

(3) The coated pistons will be serviced with the piston pin and connecting rod pre-assembled. **The coated piston connecting rod assembly can be used to service previous built engines and MUST be replaced as complete sets.** Tin coated pistons should not be used as replacements for coated pistons.

(4) The coating material is applied to the piston after the final piston machining process. Measuring the outside diameter of a coated piston will not provide accurate results. Therefore measuring the inside diameter of the cylinder bore with a dial Bore Gauge is **MANDATORY.**. To correctly select the proper size piston, a cylinder bore gauge capable of reading in 0.001 mm (.0001 in.) increments is required.

(5) Piston installation into the cylinder bore requires slightly more pressure than that required for non-coated pistons. The bonded coating on the piston will give the appearance of a line-to-line fit with the cylinder bore.

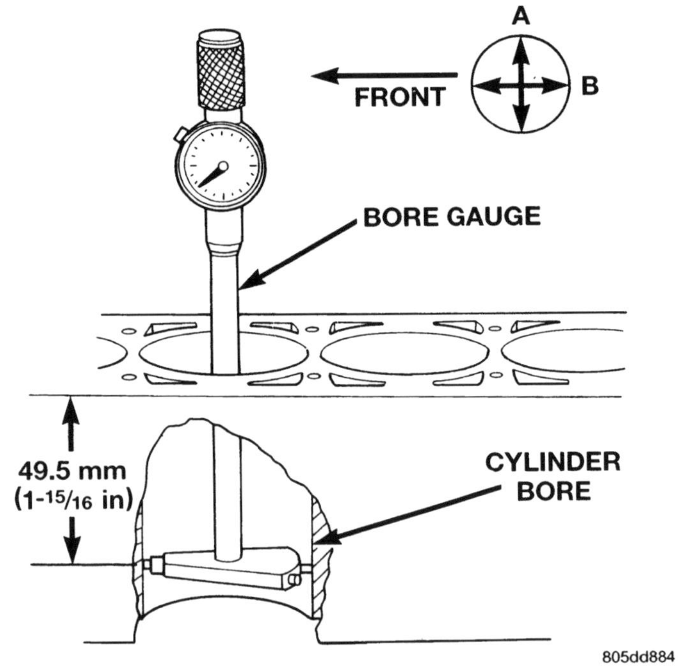

Fig. 5 Bore Gauge

PISTON SIZE CHART

CYLINDER BORE SIZE	PISTON LETTER SIZE
98.438 to 98.448 mm (3.8755 to 3.8759 in.)	A
98.448 to 98.458 mm (3.8759 to 3.8763 in.)	B
98.458 to 98.468 mm (3.8763 to 3.8767 in.)	C
98.468 to 98.478 mm (3.8767 to 3.8771 in.)	D
98.478 to 98.488 mm (3.8771 to 3.8775 in.)	E
98.488 to 98.498 mm (3.8775 to 3.8779 in.)	F

PISTON RING FITTING

(1) Carefully clean the carbon from all ring grooves. Oil drain openings in the oil ring groove and pin boss must be clear. DO NOT remove metal from the grooves or lands. This will change ring-to-groove clearances and will damage the ring-to-land seating.

(2) Be sure the piston ring grooves are free of nicks and burrs.

(3) Measure the ring side clearance with a feeler gauge fitted snugly between the ring land and ring (Fig. 6) (Fig. 7). Rotate the ring in the groove. It must move freely around circumference of the groove.

Ring Side Clearance Measurement

Top Compression Ring	0.042to 0.084 mm (0.0017 to 0.0033 in.)
Second Compression Ring	0.042to 0.084 mm (0.0017 to 0.0033 in.)
Oil Control Ring	0.06 to 0.21 mm (0.0024 to 0.0083 in.)

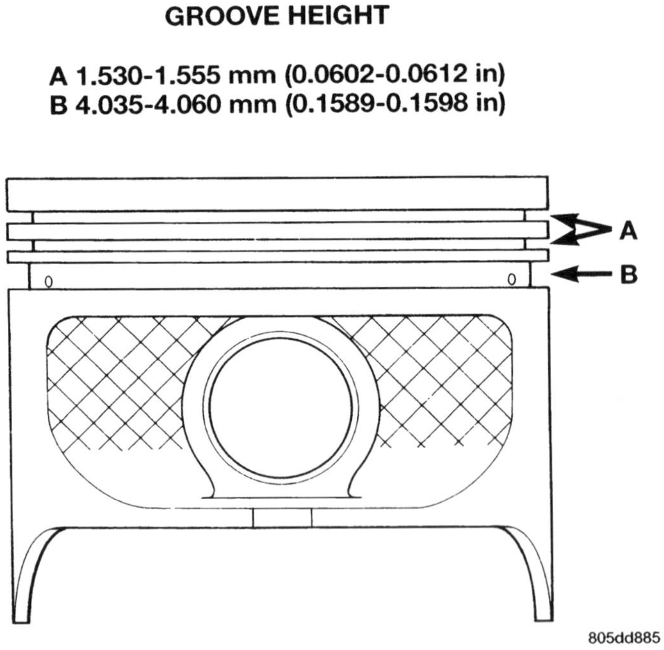

Fig. 6 Piston Dimensions

(4) Place ring in the cylinder bore and push down with inverted piston to position near lower end of the ring travel. Measure ring gap with a feeler gauge fitting snugly between ring ends (Fig. 8).

SERVICE PROCEDURES (Continued)

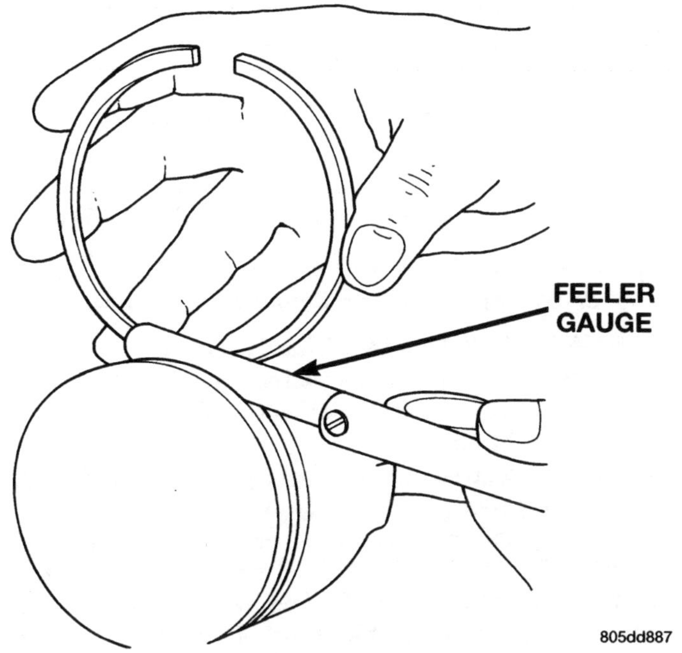

Fig. 7 Ring Side Clearance Measurement

Ring Gap Measurement

Top Compression Ring	0.229 to 0.610 mm (0.0090 to 0.0240 inch)
Second Compresion Ring	0.483 to 0.965 mm (0.0190 to 0.0380 inch)
Oil Control Ring	0.254 to 1.500 mm (0.010 to 0.060 inch)

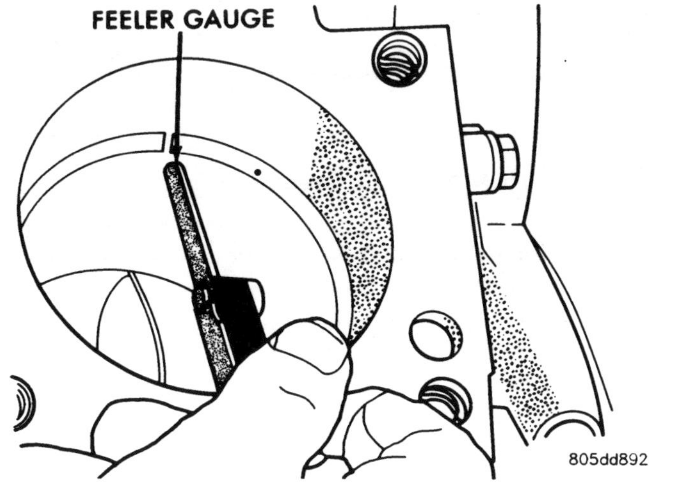

Fig. 8 Gap Measurement

(5) The oil control rings are symmetrical, no top or bottom, install anyside up. It is not necessary to use a tool to install the upper and lower rails. Insert oil rail spacer first, then side rails.

(6) The two compression rings are different and cannot be interchanged. The TOP compression ring can be identified by the shiny coating on the outer sealing surface. This ring is symmetrical, no top or bottom, install anyside up.

(7) The second compression ring has a dot or drill mark denoting the topside of ring. There is also a slight chamfer on the inside bottom edge, therefore dot mark up chamfer face down for installationon.

(8) Using a ring installer, install the second compression ring. (Fig. 9).

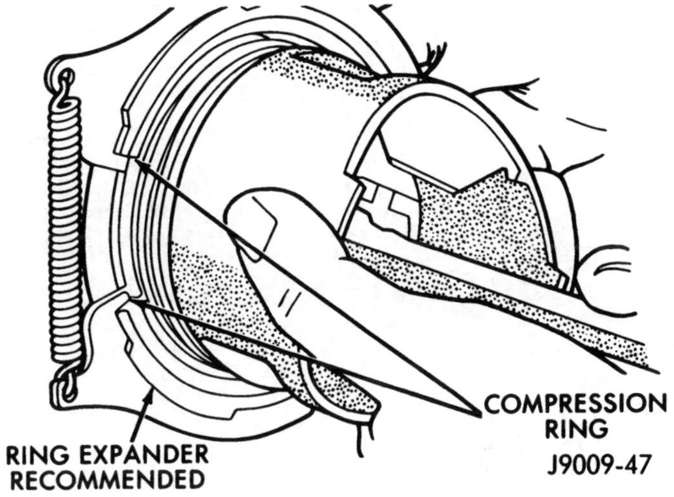

Fig. 9 Compression Ring Installation

(9) The top compression ring has a shiny coating on the outer sealing surface.

(10) Using a ring installer, install the top ring. (Fig. 9).

(11) Position top and second ring 180° apart. Split the oil rings 60° to 90° apart and away from the second ring gap. (Fig. 10) Example: Top oil ring at 12:00, expander at 3:00 or 9:00, bottom oil ring at 6:00.

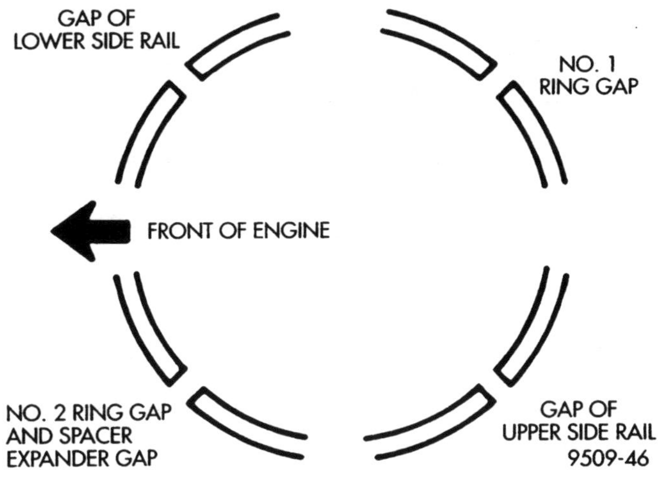

Fig. 10 Piston Ring End Gap Position

SERVICE PROCEDURES (Continued)

FITTING CONNECTING ROD BEARINGS

INSPECTION

BEARINGS

Inspect the connecting rod bearings for scoring and bent alignment tabs (Fig. 11) (Fig. 12). Check the bearings for normal wear patterns, scoring, grooving, fatigue and pitting (Fig. 13). Replace any bearing that shows abnormal wear.

Inspect the connecting rod journals for signs of scoring, nicks and burrs.

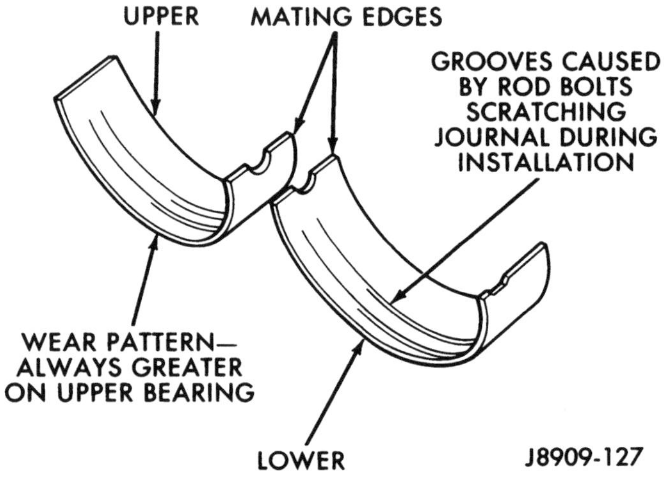

Fig. 11 Connecting Rod Bearing Inspection

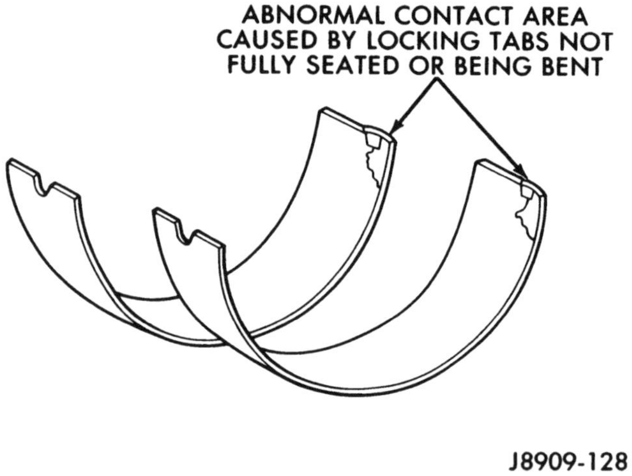

Fig. 12 Locking Tab Inspection

CONNECTING RODS

Misaligned or bent connecting rods can cause abnormal wear on pistons, piston rings, cylinder walls, connecting rod bearings and crankshaft connecting rod journals. If wear patterns or damage to any of these components indicate the probability of a misaligned connecting rod, inspect it for correct rod alignment. Replace misaligned, bent or twisted connecting rods.

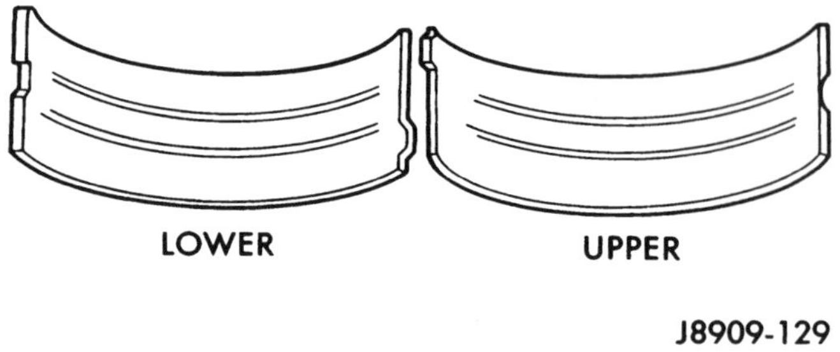

Fig. 13 Scoring Caused by Insufficient Lubrication or by Damaged Crankshaft Pin Journal

BEARING-TO-JOURNAL CLEARANCE

(1) Wipe the oil from the connecting rod journal.

(2) Use short rubber hose sections over rod bolts during installation.

(3) Lubricate the upper bearing insert and install in connecting rod.

(4) Use piston ring compressor to install the rod and piston assemblies. The oil squirt holes in the rods must face the camshaft. The arrow on the piston crown should point to the front of the engine (Fig. 14). Verify that the oil squirt holes in the rods face the camshaft and that the arrows on the pistons face the front of the engine.

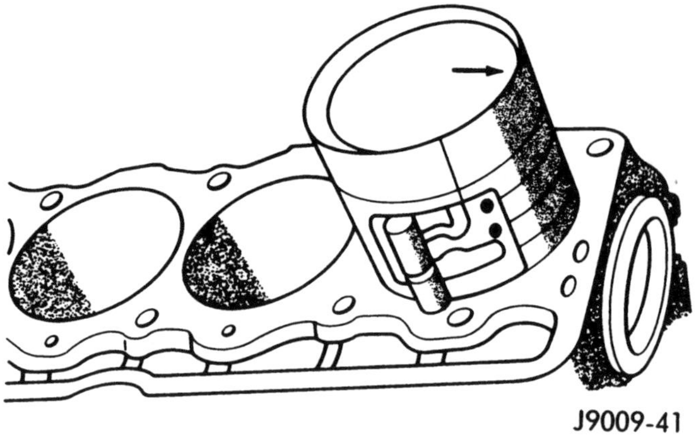

Fig. 14 Rod and Piston Assembly Installation

(5) Install the lower bearing insert in the bearing cap. The lower insert must be dry. Place strip of Plastigage across full width of the lower insert at the center of bearing cap. Plastigage must not crumble in use. If brittle, obtain fresh stock.

(6) Install bearing cap and connecting rod on the journal and tighten nuts to 45 N·m (33 ft. lbs.) torque. DO NOT rotate crankshaft. Plastigage will smear, resulting in inaccurate indication.

(7) Remove the bearing cap and determine amount of bearing-to- journal clearance by measuring the width of compressed Plastigage (Fig. 15). Refer to Engine Specifications for the proper clearance. **Plastigage should indicate the same clearance across the entire width of the insert. If the clearance varies, it may be caused by either a**

SERVICE PROCEDURES (Continued)

tapered journal, bent connecting rod or foreign material trapped between the insert and cap or rod.

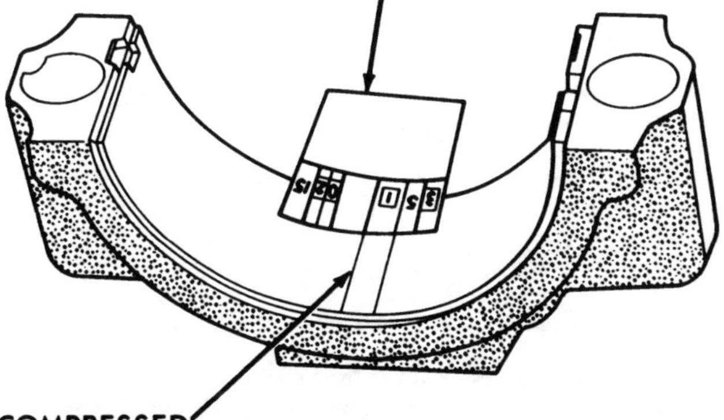

Fig. 15 Measuring Bearing Clearance with Plastigage

(8) If the correct clearance is indicated, replacement of the bearing inserts is not necessary. Remove the Plastigage from crankshaft journal and bearing insert. Proceed with installation.

(9) If bearing-to-journal clearance exceeds the specification, install a pair of 0.0254 mm (0.001 inch) undersize bearing inserts. All the odd size inserts must be on the bottom. The sizes of the service replacement bearing inserts are stamped on the backs of the inserts. Measure the clearance as described in the previous steps.

(10) The clearance is measured with a pair of 0.0254 mm (0.001 inch) undersize bearing inserts installed. This will determine if two 0.0254 mm (0.001 inch) undersize inserts or another combination is needed to provide the correct clearance (refer to Connecting Rod Bearing Fitting Chart).

(11) **FOR EXAMPLE:** If the initial clearance was 0.0762 mm (0.003 inch), 0.025 mm (0.001 inch) undersize inserts would reduce the clearance by 0.025 mm (0.001 inch). The clearance would be 0.002 inch and within specification. A 0.051 mm (0.002 inch) undersize insert would reduce the initial clearance an additional 0.013 mm (0.0005 inch). The clearance would then be 0.038 mm (0.0015 inch).

(12) Repeat the Plastigage measurement to verify your bearing selection prior to final assembly.

(13) Once you have selected the proper insert, install the insert and cap. Tighten the connecting rod bolts to 45 N·m (33 ft. lbs.) torque.

SIDE CLEARANCE MEASUREMENT

Slide snug-fitting feeler gauge between the connecting rod and crankshaft journal flange. Refer to Engine Specifications for the proper clearance. Replace the connecting rod if the side clearance is not within specification.

Crankshaft Journal		Corresponding Connecting Rod Bearing Insert	
Color Code	Diameter	Upper Insert Size	Lower Insert Size
Yellow	53.2257-53.2079 mm (2.0955-2.0948 in.)	Yellow - Standard	Yellow - Standard
Orange	53.2079-53.1901 mm (2.0948-2.0941 in.) 0.0178 mm (0.0007 in.) Undersize	Yellow - Standard	Blue - Undersize 0.025 mm (0.001 in.)
Blue	53.1901-53.1724 mm (2.0941-2.0934 in.) 0.0356 mm (0.0014 in.) Undersize	Blue - Undersize 0.025 mm (0.001 in.)	Blue - Undersize 0.025 mm (0.001 in.)
Red	52.9717-52.9539 mm (2.0855-2.0848 in.) 0.254 mm (0.010 in.) Undersize	Red - Undersize 0.254 mm (0.010 in.)	Red - Undersize 0.254 mm (0.010 in.)

J9409-24

CONNECTING ROD BEARING FITTING CHART

SERVICE PROCEDURES (Continued)

FITTING CRANKSHAFT MAIN BEARINGS

INSPECTION

Wipe the inserts clean and inspect for abnormal wear patterns and for metal or other foreign material imbedded in the lining. Normal main bearing insert wear patterns are illustrated (Fig. 16).

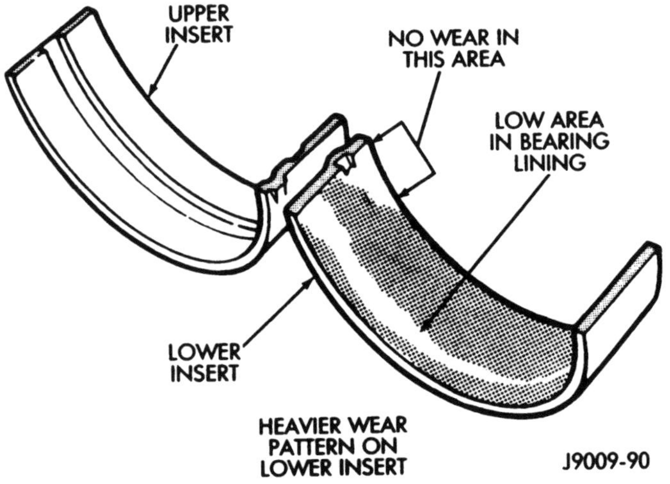

Fig. 16 Main Bearing Wear Patterns

NOTE: If any of the crankshaft journals are scored, remove the engine for crankshaft repair.

Inspect the back of the inserts for fractures, scrapings or irregular wear patterns.

Inspect the upper insert locking tabs for damage.

Replace all damaged or worn bearing inserts.

FITTING BEARINGS (CRANKSHAFT INSTALLED)

The main bearing caps, numbered (front to rear) from 1 through 5 have an arrow to indicate the forward position. The upper main bearing inserts are grooved to provide oil channels while the lower inserts are smooth.

Each bearing insert pair is selectively fitted to its respective journal to obtain the specified operating clearance. In production, the select fit is obtained by using various-sized color-coded bearing insert pairs as listed in the Main Bearing Fitting Chart. The bearing color code appears on the edge of the insert. **The size is not stamped on bearing inserts used for engine production.**

The main bearing journal size (diameter) is identified by a color-coded paint mark on the adjacent cheek. The rear main journal, is identified by a color-coded paint mark on the crankshaft rear flange.

When required, upper and lower bearing inserts of different sizes may be used as a pair. A standard size insert is sometimes used in combination with a 0.025 mm (0.001 inch) undersize insert to reduce the clearance by 0.013 mm (0.0005 inch). **Never use a pair of bearing inserts with greater than a 0.025 mm (0.001 inch) difference in size (Fig. 17).**

Insert	Correct	Incorrect
Upper	Standard	Standard
Lower	0.025 mm (0.001 in.) Undersize	0.051 mm (0.002 in.) Undersize

J9109-179

Fig. 17 Bearing Insert Pairs

NOTE: When replacing inserts, the odd size inserts must be either all on the top (in cylinder block) or all on the bottom (in main bearing cap).

Once the bearings have been properly fitted, proceed to Crankshaft Main Bearing—Installation.

BEARING-TO-JOURNAL CLEARANCE (CRANKSHAFT INSTALLED)

When using Plastigage, check only one bearing clearance at a time.

Install the grooved main bearings into the cylinder block and the non-grooved bearings into the bearing caps.

Install the crankshaft into the upper bearings dry.

Place a strip of Plastigage across full width of the crankshaft journal to be checked.

Install the bearing cap and tighten the bolts to 108 N·m (80 ft. lbs.) torque.

NOTE: DO NOT rotate the crankshaft. This will cause the Plastigage to shift, resulting in an inaccurate reading. Plastigage must not be permitted to crumble. If brittle, obtain fresh stock.

Remove the bearing cap. Determine the amount of clearance by measuring the width of the compressed Plastigage with the scale on the Plastigage envelope (Fig. 18). Refer to Engine Specifications for the proper clearance.

Plastigage should indicate the same clearance across the entire width of the insert. If clearance varies, it may indicate a tapered journal or foreign material trapped behind the insert.

If the specified clearance is indicated and there are no abnormal wear patterns, replacement of the bearing inserts is not necessary. Remove the Plastigage from the crankshaft journal and bearing insert. Proceed to Crankshaft Main Bearing—Installation.

If the clearance exceeds specification, install a pair of 0.025 mm (0.001 inch) undersize bearing inserts

SERVICE PROCEDURES (Continued)

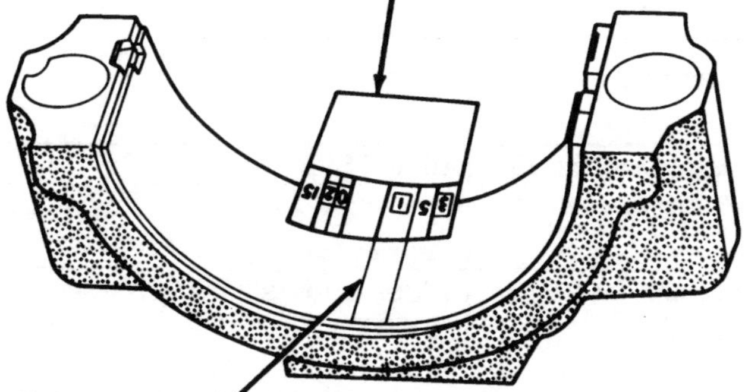

Fig. 18 Measuring Bearing Clearance with Plastigage

and measure the clearance as described in the previous steps.

The clearance indicated with the 0.025 mm (0.001 inch) undersize insert pair installed will determine if this insert size or some other combination will provide the specified clearance. **FOR EXAMPLE:** If the clearance was 0.0762 mm (0.003 inch) originally, a pair of 0.0254 mm (0.001 inch) undersize inserts would reduce the clearance by 0.0254 mm (0.001 inch). The clearance would then be 0.0508 mm (0.002 inch) and within the specification. A 0.051 mm (0.002 inch) undersize bearing insert and a 0.0254 mm (0.001 inch) undersize insert would reduce the original clearance an additional 0.0127 mm (0.0005 inch). The clearance would then be 0.0381 mm (0.0015 inch).

CAUTION: Never use a pair of inserts that differ more than one bearing size as a pair.

FOR EXAMPLE: DO NOT use a standard size upper insert and a 0.051 mm (0.002 inch) undersize lower insert.

If the clearance exceeds specification using a pair of 0.051 mm (0.002 inch) undersize bearing inserts, measure crankshaft journal diameter with a micrometer. If the journal diameter is correct, the crankshaft bore in the cylinder block may be misaligned, which requires cylinder block replacement or machining to true bore.

If journals 1 through 5 diameters are less than 63.4517 mm (2.4981 inches), replace crankshaft or grind crankshaft down to accept the appropriate undersize bearing inserts.

Once the proper clearances have been obtained, proceed to Crankshaft Main Bearing—Installation.

MAIN BEARING JOURNAL DIAMETER (CRANKSHAFT REMOVED)

Remove the crankshaft from the cylinder block (refer to Cylinder Block - Disassemble).

Clean the oil off the main bearing journal.

Determine the maximum diameter of the journal with a micrometer. Measure at two locations 90° apart at each end of the journal.

The maximum allowable taper and out of round is 0.013 mm (0.0005 inch). Compare the measured diameter with the journal diameter specification (Main Bearing Fitting Chart). Select inserts required to obtain the specified bearing-to-journal clearance.

Once the proper clearances have been obtained, proceed to Crankshaft Main Bearing—Installation.

SERVICE PROCEDURES (Continued)

MAIN BEARING FITTING CHART

CRANKSHAFT JOURNALS #1 - #4		CORRESPONDING CRANKSHAFT BEARING INSERT	
Color Code	Diameter	Upper Insert Size	Lower Insert Size
Yellow	63.5025 - 63.4898 mm (2.5001 - 2.4996 in.)	Yellow - Standard	Yellow - Standard
Orange	63.4898 - 63.4771mm (2.4996 - 2.4991 in.) 0.0127 mm (0.0005 in.) Undersize	Yellow - Undersize 0.025 mm (0.001 in.)	Blue - Standard
Blue	63.4771 - 63.4644 mm (2.4991 - 2.4986 in.) 0.0254 mm (0.001 in.) Undersize	Blue- Undersize 0.025 mm (0.001 in.)	Blue- Undersize 0.025 mm (0.001 in.)
Green	63.4644 - 63.4517 mm (2.4986 - 2.4981 in.) 0.0381 mm (0.0015 in.) Undersize	Blue - Undersize 0.025 mm (0.001 in.)	Green - Undersize 0.051 mm (0.002 in.)
Red	63.2485 - 63.2358 mm (2.4901 - 2.4896 in.) 0.254 mm (0.010 in.) Undersize	Red - Undersize 0.254 mm (0.010 in.)	Red - Undersize 0.254 mm (0.010 in.)
CRANKSHAFT JOURNAL #5 ONLY		**CORRESPONDING CRANKSHAFT BEARING INSERT**	
Color Code	Diameter	Upper Insert Size	Lower Insert Size
Yellow	63.4873 - 63.4746 mm (2.4995 - 2.4990 in.)	Yellow - Standard	Yellow - Standard
Orange	63.4746 - 63.4619 mm (2.4990 - 2.4985 in.) 0.0127 mm (0.0005 in. Undersize	Yellow - Undersize 0.025 mm (0.001 in.)	Blue - Standard
Blue	63.4619 - 63.4492 mm (2.4985 - 2.4980 in.) 0.0254 mm (0.001 in.) Undersize	Blue- Undersize 0.025 mm (0.001 in.)	Blue- Undersize 0.025 mm (0.001 in.)
Green	63.4492 - 63.4365 mm (2.4980- 2.4975 in.) 0.0381 mm (0.0015 in.) Undersize	Blue - Undersize 0.025 mm (0.001 in.)	Green - Undersize 0.051 mm (0.002 in.)
Red	63.2333 - 63.2206 mm (2.4895 - 2.4890 in.) 0.254 mm (0.010 in.) Undersize	Red - Undersize 0.254 mm (0.010 in.)	Red - Undersize 0.254 mm (0.010 in.)

REMOVAL AND INSTALLATION

ENGINE MOUNTS—FRONT

The front mounts support the engine at each side. These supports are made of resilient rubber.

REMOVAL

(1) Disconnect negative cable from battery.
(2) Raise the vehicle.
(3) Support the engine.

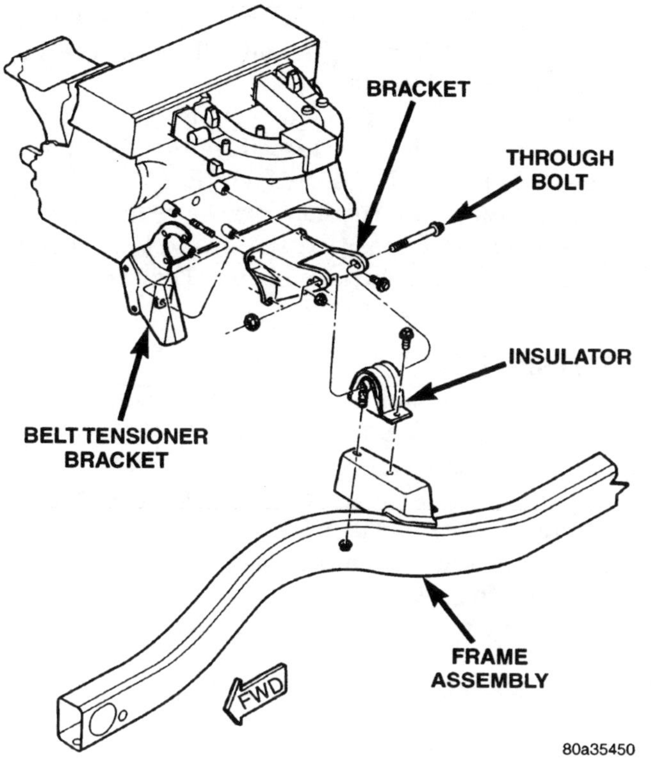

Fig. 19 Left Front Mount—2.5L Engine

(4) Remove through bolt nut (Fig. 19) (Fig. 20). DO NOT remove the through bolt.
(5) Remove the retaining bolts and nuts from the support cushions.
(6) Remove the through bolt.
(7) Remove the engine mount insulator.

INSTALLATION

(1) If the engine support bracket was removed, position the bracket onto the block and install the attaching bolts. Tighten the bolts to 62 N·m (46 ft. lbs.) torque.
(2) Place the insulator on the support bracket. Install the insulator retaining bolts and nuts. Tighten the bolts and nuts to 52 N·m (38 ft. lbs.) torque.
(3) Install the through bolt and the retaining nut. Tighten the through bolt nut to 69 N·m (51 ft. lbs.) torque.
(4) Remove the engine support.

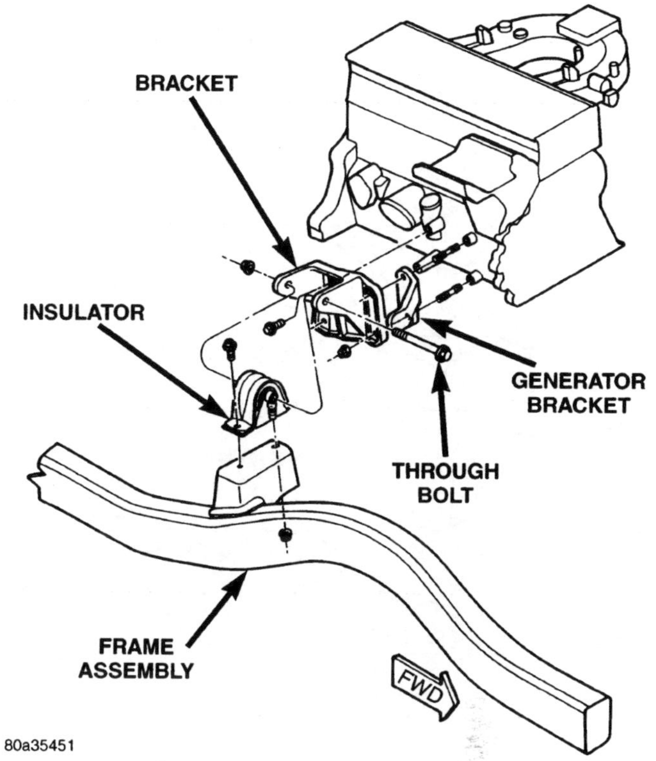

Fig. 20 Right Front Mount—2.5L Engine

(5) Lower the vehicle.
(6) Connect negative cable to battery.

ENGINE MOUNT—REAR

A resilient rubber cushion supports the transmission at the rear between the transmission extension housing and the rear support crossmember or skid plate.

REMOVAL

ALL TRANSMISSIONS

(1) Disconnect negative cable from battery.
(2) Raise the vehicle and support the transmission.
(3) Remove the nuts holding the support cushion to the skid plate (Fig. 21) (Fig. 22).
(4) Remove the skid plate bolts and the skid plate.

MANUAL TRANSMISSIONS

(1) Remove nuts holding support cushion to transmission support bracket.
(2) Remove the support cushion.
(3) Remove bolts holding transmission support bracket to transmission.
(4) Remove the transmission support bracket.

AUTOMATIC TRANSMISSIONS

(1) Remove nuts holding support cushion to transmission support bracket (Fig. 22). Remove the support cushion.

REMOVAL AND INSTALLATION (Continued)

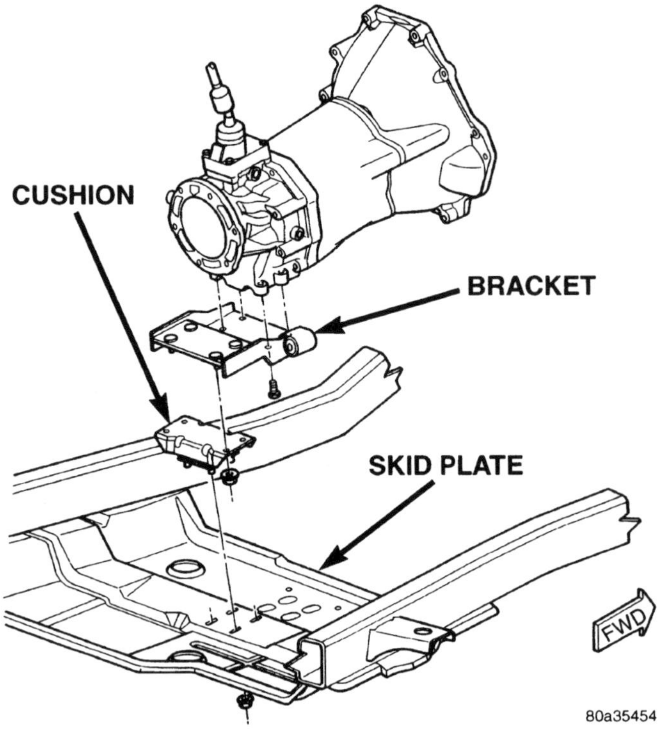

Fig. 21 Rear Mount (Manual Transmission)

(2) Remove the bolts holding the transmission support bracket to transmission.

(3) Remove the transmission support bracket.

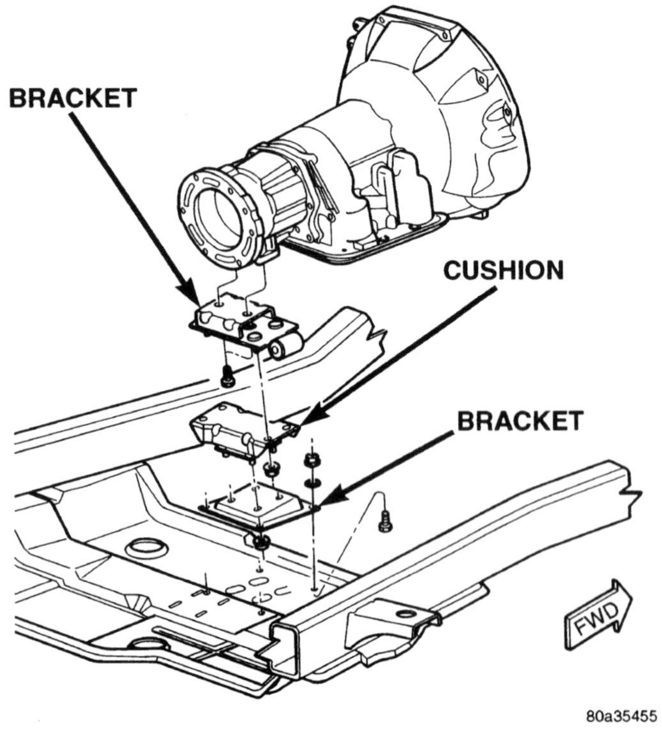

Fig. 22 Rear Mount (AutomaticTransmission)

INSTALLATION

MANUAL TRANSMISSION:

(1) Position the transmission mount bracket to the transmission and install the bolts (Fig. 21).

(2) Tighten the bolts to 54 N·m (40 ft. lbs.) torque.

(3) Position the support cushion to the transmission mount bracket and install nuts (Fig. 21).

(4) Tighten the nuts to 41 N·m (30 ft. lbs.) torque.

AUTOMATIC TRANSMISSION:

(1) Position the transmission mount bracket to the transmission and install the bolts. Tighten the bolts to 54 N·m (40 ft. lbs.) torque.

(2) Position the support cushion to the transmission mount bracket and install nuts. Tighten the nuts to 41 N·m (30 ft. lbs.) torque (Fig. 22).

(3) If the support cushion bracket was removed from the skid plate, position the bracket on the skid plate and install the nuts and bolts. Tighten the nuts to 28 N·m (21 ft. lbs.) torque.

ALL TRANSMISSIONS

(1) Position the skid plate to the studs of the support cushion and install the nuts (Fig. 21) (Fig. 22). Tighten the nuts to 28 N·m (21 ft. lbs.) torque.

(2) Install the skid plate bolts to the sill and tighten to 75 N·m (55 ft. lbs.) torque.

(3) Remove the transmission support.

(4) Lower the vehicle.

(5) Connect negative cable to battery.

ENGINE ASSEMBLY

REMOVAL

(1) Place a protective cloth over the windshield frame. Raise the hood and rest it on the windshield frame.

(2) Disconnect the battery cable clamps and remove the battery.

WARNING: THE COOLANT IN A RECENTLY OPERATED ENGINE IS HOT AND PRESSURIZED. USE CARE TO PREVENT SCALDING BY HOT COOLANT. CAREFULLY RELEASE THE PRESSURE BEFORE REMOVING THE RADIATOR DRAIN COCK AND CAP.

(3) Remove the radiator drain cock and radiator cap to drain the coolant. DO NOT waste usable coolant. If the solution is clean, drain the coolant into a clean container for reuse.

(4) Disconnect the wire connectors from the generator.

(5) Disconnect the ignition coil and distributor wire connectors.

(6) Disconnect the oil pressure sender wire connector.

REMOVAL AND INSTALLATION (Continued)

(7) Disconnect the wires at the starter motor solenoid and injection wire harness connector.

(8) Disconnect the quick-connect fuel lines at the fuel rail and return line by squeezing the two retaining tabs against the fuel tube (Fig. 23). Pull the fuel tube and retainer from the quick-connect fitting (refer to Group 14, Fuel System for the proper procedure).

(9) Remove the fuel line bracket from the intake manifold.

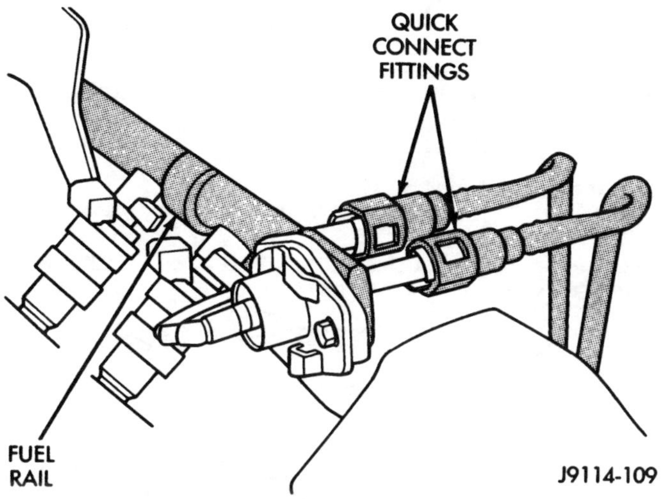

Fig. 23 Fuel Line Quick-Connect Couplings

(10) Disconnect the engine ground strap.

(11) Remove the air cleaner assembly.

(12) Disconnect the vacuum purge hose at the fuel vapor canister tee.

(13) Disconnect the idle speed actuator wire connector.

(14) Disconnect the throttle cable and remove it from the bracket.

(15) Disconnect the throttle rod at the bellcrank.

(16) Disconnect the speed control cable, if equipped.

(17) Disconnect the oxygen sensor wire connector.

(18) Disconnect the upper and lower radiator hoses at the radiator.

(19) Disconnect the coolant hoses from the rear of the intake manifold and thermostat housing.

(20) Disconnect the heater hoses.

(21) Remove the fan shroud screws.

(22) Remove the radiator attaching bolts.

(23) Remove the radiator and fan shroud.

(24) Remove the fan and spacer or Tempatrol fan assembly.

(25) Install a 5/16 X 1/2-inch SAE capscrew through fan pulley into water pump flange. This will maintain the pulley and water pump in alignment when crankshaft is rotated.

(26) Remove the power brake vacuum check valve from the booster, if equipped.

(27) If equipped with power steering:

(a) Disconnect the hoses from the fittings at the steering gear.

(b) Drain the pump reservoir.

(c) Cap the fittings on the hoses and steering gear to prevent foreign objects from entering the system.

(28) Lift the vehicle and support it with support stands.

(29) Remove the oil filter.

(30) Remove the starter motor.

(31) Remove the flywheel housing access cover.

(32) Remove the engine support cushion-to-bracket through bolts.

(33) Disconnect the exhaust pipe from the manifold.

(34) Remove the upper flywheel housing bolts and loosen the bottom bolts.

(35) Remove the engine shock damper bracket from the sill.

(36) Lower the vehicle.

(37) Attach a lifting device to the engine.

(38) Raise the engine off the front supports.

(39) Place a support stand under the flywheel housing.

(40) Remove the remaining flywheel housing bolts.

(41) Lift the engine out of the engine compartment and install on an engine stand.

(42) Install the oil filter to keep foreign material out of the engine.

INSTALLATION

(1) Remove the oil filter.

(2) Lift the engine off the stand and lower it into the engine compartment. For easier installation, it may be useful to remove the engine support cushions from the engine support brackets as an aide for alignment of the engine-to-transmission.

(3) Insert the transmission shaft into the clutch spline.

(4) Align the flywheel housing with the engine.

(5) Install and finger tighten the flywheel housing lower bolts.

(6) Install the engine support cushions (if removed).

(7) Remove the support stand from beneath the flywheel housing.

(8) Lower the engine and engine support cushions onto the engine compartment brackets. Ensure that the bolt holes are aligned. Install the bolts and tighten.

(9) Remove the engine lifting device.

(10) Raise the vehicle.

(11) Attach the engine shock damper bracket to the sill.

REMOVAL AND INSTALLATION (Continued)

(12) Attach the exhaust pipe to the manifold. Install and tighten the nuts to 31 N·m (23 ft. lbs.) torque.

(13) Install the flywheel housing access cover.

(14) Install the remaining flywheel housing bolts. Tighten the bolts to 38 N·m (28 ft. lbs.) torque.

(15) Install the starter motor and connect the cable. Tighten the bolts to 45 N·m (33 ft. lbs.) torque.

(16) Install the oil filter.

(17) Lower the vehicle.

(18) Connect the coolant hoses and tighten the clamps.

(19) If equipped with power steering:

(a) Remove the protective caps

(b) Connect the hoses to the fittings at the steering gear. Tighten the nut to 52 N·m (38 ft. lbs.) torque.

(c) Fill the pump reservoir with fluid.

(20) Remove the pulley-to-water pump flange alignment capscrew and install the fan and spacer or Tempatrol fan assembly.

(21) Tighten the serpentine drive belt according to the specifications listed in Group 7, Cooling System.

(22) Install the fan shroud and radiator.

(23) Connect the radiator hoses.

(24) Connect the heater hoses.

(25) Connect the throttle valve rod and retainer.

(26) Connect the throttle cable and install the rod.

(27) Install the throttle valve rod spring.

(28) Connect the speed control cable, if equipped.

(29) Connect the oxygen sensor wire connector.

(30) Install the vacuum hose and check valve on the brake booster.

(31) Connect the coolant temperature sensor wire connector.

(32) Connect the idle speed actuator wire connector.

(33) Connect the fuel inlet and return hoses at the fuel rail. Verify that the quick-connect fitting assembly fits securely over the fuel lines by giving the fuel lines a firm tug.

(34) Install the fuel line bracket to the intake manifold.

(35) Connect all fuel injection wire connections.

(36) Install the engine ground strap.

(37) Connect the ignition coil wire connector.

(38) Remove the coolant temperature sending unit to permit air to escape from the block. Fill the cooling system with coolant. Install the coolant temperature sending unit when the system is filled.

(39) Install the battery and connect the battery cables.

(40) Install the air cleaner bonnet to the throttle body.

(41) Install the air cleaner.

(42) Lower the hood and secure in place.

(43) Start the engine and inspect for leaks.

(44) Stop the engine and check the fluid levels. Add fluid, as required.

CYLINDER HEAD COVER

A cured gasket is part of the engine cylinder head cover.

REMOVAL

(1) Disconnect negative cable from battery.

(2) Disconnect the Crankcase Ventilation (CCV) vacuum hose from engine cylinder head cover (Fig. 24).

(3) Disconnect the fresh air inlet hose from the engine cylinder head cover (Fig. 24).

(4) Remove the engine cylinder head cover mounting bolts.

(5) Remove the engine cylinder head cover.

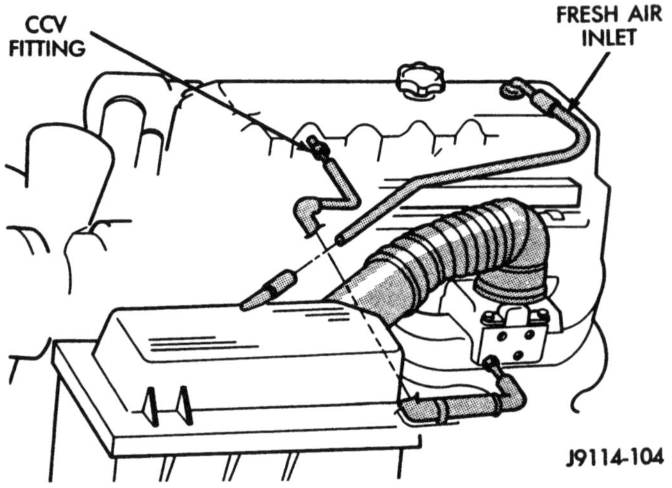

Fig. 24 Engine Cylinder Head Cover

(6) Remove any original sealer from the cover sealing surface of the engine cylinder head and clean the surface using a fabric cleaner.

(7) Remove all residue from the sealing surface using a clean, dry cloth.

INSTALLATION

(1) Inspect the engine cylinder head cover for cracks. Replace the cover, if cracked.

NOTE: The original dark grey gasket material should NOT be removed. If sections of the gasket material are missing or are compressed, replace the engine cylinder head cover. However, sections with minor damage such as small cracks, cuts or chips may be repaired with a hand held applicator. The new material must be smoothed over to maintain gasket height. Allow the gasket material to cure prior to engine cylinder head cover installation.

REMOVAL AND INSTALLATION (Continued)

(2) If a replacement cover is installed, transfer the CCV valve grommet the oil filler cap from the original cover to the replacement cover.

(3) Install engine cylinder head cover. Tighten the mounting bolts to 14 N·m (115 in. lbs.) torque.

(4) Connect the CCV hoses (Fig. 24).

(5) Connect negative cable to battery.

ROCKER ARMS AND PUSH RODS

This procedure can be done with the engine in or out of the vehicle.

REMOVAL

(1) Remove the engine cylinder head cover.

(2) Remove the capscrews at each bridge and pivot assembly (Fig. 25). Alternately loosen the capscrews one turn at a time to avoid damaging the bridges.

(3) Check for rocker arm bridges which are causing misalignment of the rocker arm to valve tip area.

(4) Remove the bridges, pivots and corresponding pairs of rocker arms (Fig. 25). Place them on a bench in the same order as removed.

(5) Remove the push rods and place them on a bench in the same order as removed.

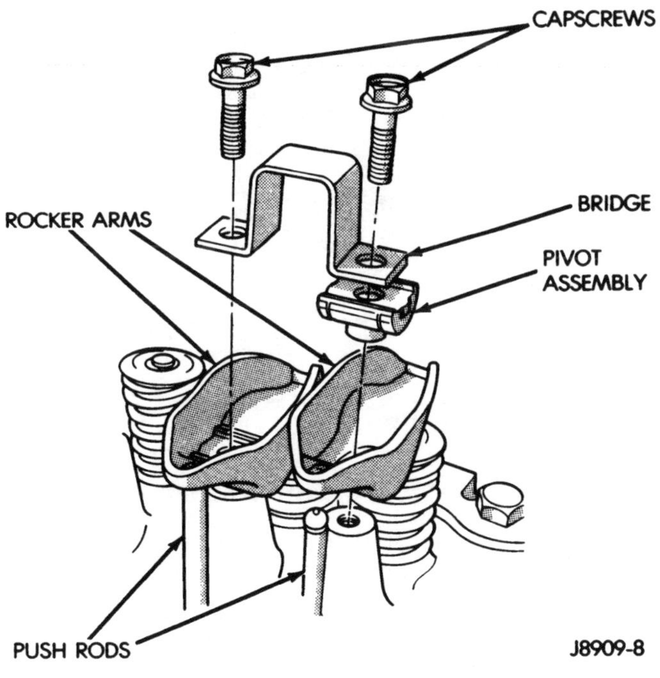

Fig. 25 Rocker Arm Assembly

(6) Clean all the components with cleaning solvent.

(7) Use compressed air to blow out the oil passages in the rocker arms and push rods.

INSTALLATION

(1) Lubricate the ball ends of the push rods with Mopar Engine Oil Supplement, or equivalent and install push rods in their original locations. Ensure that the bottom end of each push rod is centered in the tappet plunger cap seat.

(2) Using Mopar Engine Oil Supplement, or equivalent, lubricate the area of the rocker arm that the pivot contacts. Install rocker arms, pivots and bridge above each cylinder in their original position.

(3) Loosely install the capscrews through each bridge.

(4) At each bridge, tighten the capscrews alternately, one turn at a time, to avoid damaging the bridge. Tighten the capscrews to 28 N·m (21 ft. lbs.) torque.

(5) Install the engine cylinder head cover.

VALVE SPRINGS AND OIL SEALS

This procedure can be done with the engine cylinder head installed on the block.

REMOVAL

Each valve spring is held in place by a retainer and a set of conical valve locks. The locks can be removed only by compressing the valve spring.

(1) Remove the engine cylinder head cover.

(2) Remove capscrews, bridge and pivot assemblies and rocker arms for access to each valve spring to be removed.

(3) Remove push rods. Retain the push rods, bridges, pivots and rocker arms in the same order and position as removed.

(4) Inspect the springs and retainer for cracks and possible signs of weakening.

(5) Remove the spark plug(s) adjacent to the cylinder(s) below the valve springs to be removed.

(6) Install a 14 mm (1/2 inch) (thread size) air hose adaptor in the spark plug hole.

(7) Connect an air hose to the adapter and apply air pressure slowly. Maintain at least 621 kPa (90 psi) of air pressure in the cylinder to hold the valves against their seats. For vehicles equipped with an air conditioner, use a flexible air adaptor when servicing the No.1 cylinder.

(8) Tap the retainer or tip with a rawhide hammer to loosen the lock from the retainer. Use Valve Spring Compressor Tool MD-998772A to compress the spring and remove the locks (Fig. 26).

(9) Remove valve spring and retainer (Fig. 26).

(10) Remove valve stem oil seals (Fig. 26). Note the valve seals are different for intake and exhaust valves. The top of each seal is marked either INT (Intake) or EXH (Exhaust). DO NOT mix the seals.

INSTALLATION

Inspect the valve stems, especially the grooves. An Arkansas smooth stone should be used to remove nicks and high spots.

REMOVAL AND INSTALLATION (Continued)

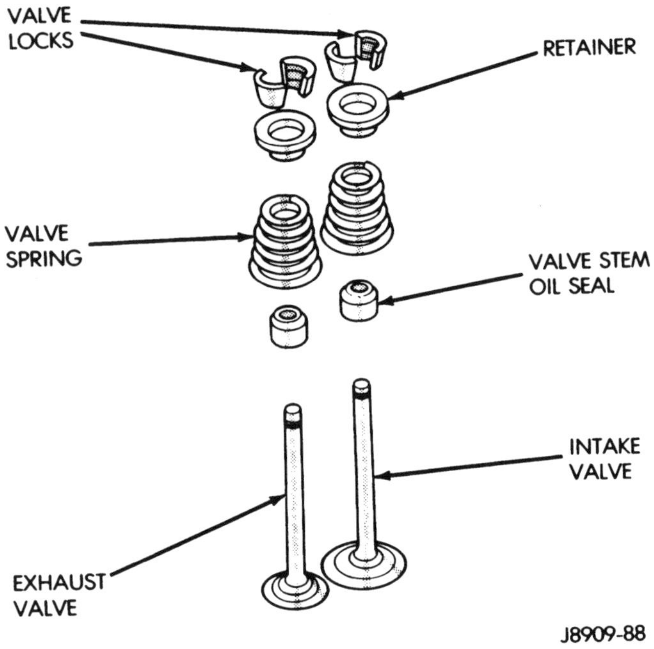

Fig. 26 Valve and Valve Components

CAUTION: Install oil seals carefully to prevent damage from the sharp edges of the valve spring lock grove.

(1) Lightly push the valve seal over the valve stem and valve guide boss. Be sure the seal is completely seated on the valve guide boss.

(2) Install valve spring and retainer.

(3) Compress the valve spring with Valve Spring Compressor Tool MD-998772A and insert the valve locks. Release the spring tension and remove the tool. Tap the spring from side-to-side to ensure that the spring is seated properly on the engine cylinder head.

(4) Disconnect the air hose. Remove the adaptor from the spark plug hole and install the spark plug.

(5) Repeat the procedures for each remaining valve spring to be removed.

(6) Install the push rods. Ensure the bottom end of each rod is centered in the plunger cap seat of the hydraulic valve tappet.

(7) Install the rocker arms, pivots and bridge at their original location.

(8) Tighten the bridge capscrews alternately, one at a time, to avoid damaging the bridge. Tighten the capscrews to 28 N·m (21 ft. lbs.) torque.

(9) Install the engine cylinder head cover.

ENGINE CYLINDER HEAD

This procedure can be done with the engine in or out of the vehicle.

REMOVAL

(1) Disconnect negative cable from battery.

WARNING: DO NOT REMOVE THE CYLINDER BLOCK DRAIN PLUGS OR LOOSEN THE RADIATOR DRAIN COCK WITH THE SYSTEM HOT AND PRESSURIZED BECAUSE SERIOUS BURNS FROM THE COOLANT CAN OCCUR.

(2) Drain the coolant and disconnect the hoses at the engine thermostat housing. DO NOT waste reusable coolant. If the solution is clean and is being drained only to service the engine or cooling system, drain the coolant into a clean container for reuse.

(3) Remove the air cleaner assembly.

(4) Remove the engine cylinder head cover.

(5) Remove the capscrews, bridge and pivot assemblies and rocker arms (Fig. 27).

(6) Remove the push rods (Fig. 27). **Retain the push rods, bridges, pivots and rocker arms in the same order as removed.**

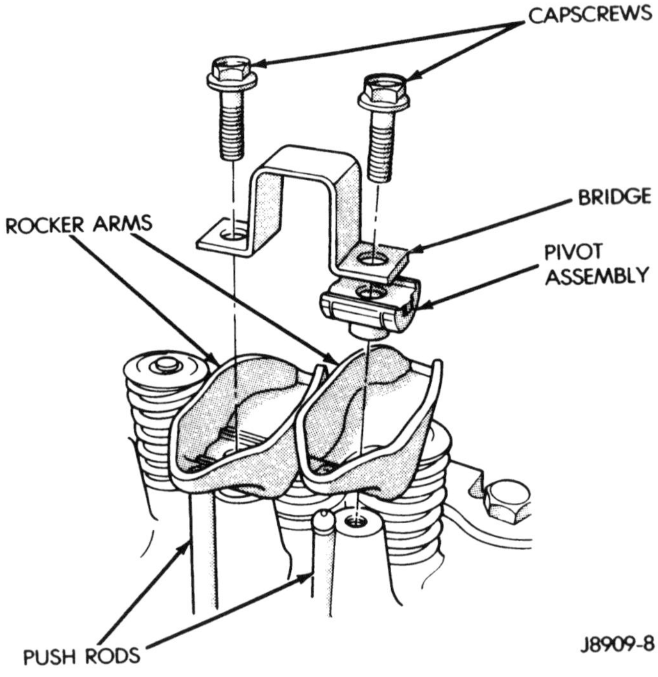

Fig. 27 Rocker Arm Assembly

(7) Loosen the serpentine drive belt at the power steering pump, if equipped or at the idler pulley (refer to Group 7, Cooling System for the proper procedure).

(8) If equipped with air conditioning, perform the following:

(a) Remove the bolts from the A/C compressor mounting bracket and set the compressor aside.

(b) Remove the air conditioner compressor bracket bolts from the engine cylinder head.

(c) Loosen the through bolt at the bottom of the bracket.

(9) If equipped, disconnect the power steering pump bracket. Set the pump and bracket aside. DO NOT disconnect the hoses.

REMOVAL AND INSTALLATION (Continued)

(10) Remove the fuel lines and vacuum advance hose.

(11) Remove the intake and engine exhaust manifolds from the engine cylinder head (refer to Group 11, Exhaust System and Intake Manifold for the proper procedures).

(12) Disconnect the ignition wires and remove the spark plugs.

(13) Disconnect the temperature sending unit wire connector.

(14) Remove the ignition coil and bracket assembly.

(15) Remove the engine cylinder head bolts.

(16) Remove the engine cylinder head and gasket (Fig. 28).

(17) If this was the first time the bolts were removed, put a paint dab on the top of the bolt. If the bolts have a paint dab on the top of the bolt or it isn't known if they were used before, discard the bolts.

(18) Stuff clean lint free shop towels into the cylinder bores.

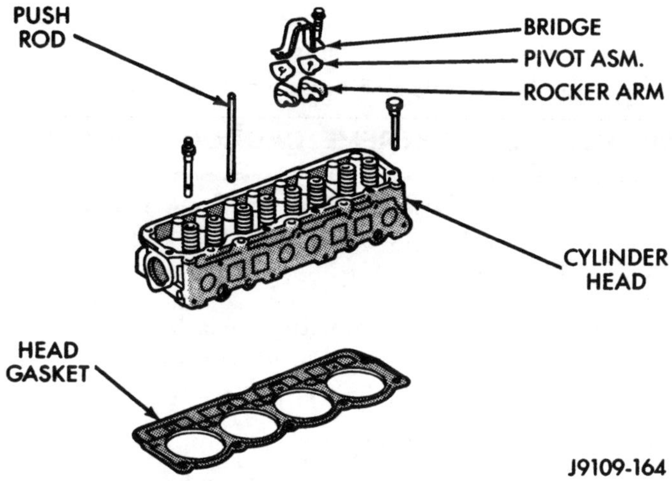

Fig. 28 Engine Cylinder Head Assembly

INSTALLATION

The engine cylinder head gasket is a composition gasket. The gasket is to be installed DRY. **DO NOT use a gasket sealing compound on the gasket.**

If the engine cylinder head is to be replaced and the original valves used, measure the valve stem diameter. Only standard size valves can be used with a service replacement engine cylinder head unless the replacement head valve stem guide bores are reamed to accommodate oversize valve stems. Remove all carbon buildup and reface the valves.

(1) Fabricate two engine cylinder head alignment dowels from used head bolts (Fig. 29). Use the longest head bolt. Cut the head of the bolt off below the hex head. Then cut a slot in the top of the dowel to allow easier removal with a screwdriver.

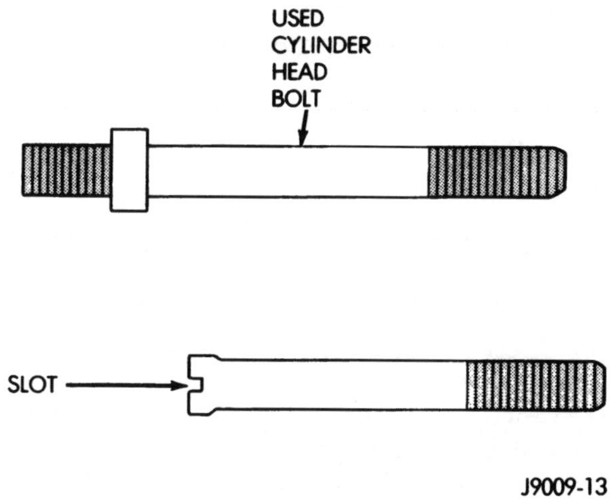

Fig. 29 Fabricate Alignment Dowels

(2) Install one dowel in bolt hole No.10 and the other dowel in bolt hole No.8 (Fig. 30).

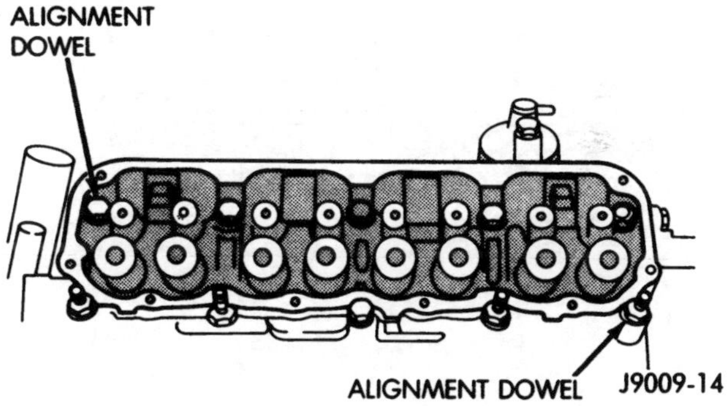

Fig. 30 Alignment Dowel Locations

(3) Remove the shop towels from the cylinder bores. Coat the bores with clean engine oil.

(4) Place the engine cylinder head gasket (with the numbers facing up) over the dowels.

(5) Place the engine cylinder head over the dowels.

CAUTION: Engine cylinder head bolts should be reused only once. Replace the head bolts if they were used before or if they have a paint dab on the top of the bolt.

(6) Coat the threads of bolt No.7, only, with Loctite PST sealant or equivalent.

(7) Install all head bolts, except No.8 and No.10.

(8) Remove the dowels.

(9) Install No.8 and No.10 head bolts.

CAUTION: During the final tightening sequence, bolt No.7 will be tightened to a lower torque than the rest of the bolts. DO NOT overtighten bolt No.7.

(10) Tighten the engine cylinder head bolts in sequence according to the following procedure (Fig. 31):

(a) Tighten all bolts in sequence (1 through 10) to 30 N·m (22 ft. lbs.) torque.

REMOVAL AND INSTALLATION (Continued)

(b) Tighten all bolts in sequence (1 through 10) to 61 N·m (45 ft. lbs.) torque.

(c) Check all bolts to verify they are set to 61 N·m (45 ft. lbs.) torque.

(d) Tighten bolts (in sequence):

- Bolts 1 through 6 to 149 N·m (110 ft. lbs.) torque.
- Bolt 7 to 136 N·m (100 ft. lbs.) torque.
- Bolts 8 through 10 to 149 N·m (110 ft. lbs.) torque.

(e) Check all bolts in sequence to verify the correct torque.

(f) If not already done, clean and mark each bolt with a dab of paint after tightening. Should you encounter bolts which were painted in an earlier service operation, replace them.

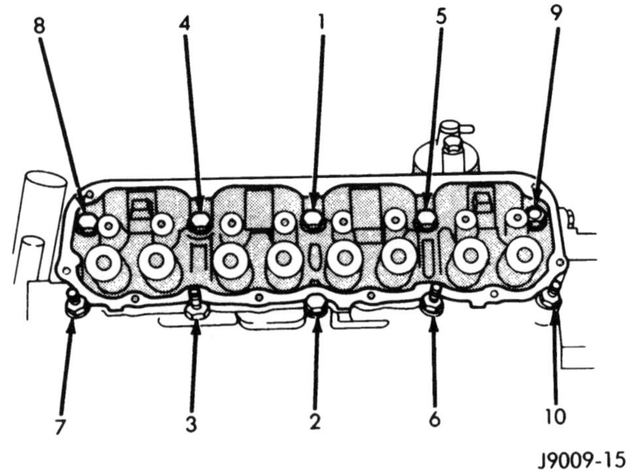

Fig. 31 Engine cylinder head Bolt Tightening Sequence

(11) Install the ignition coil and bracket assembly.

(12) Connect the temperature sending unit wire connector.

(13) Install the spark plugs and tighten to 37 N·m (27 ft. lbs.) torque. Connect the ignition wires.

(14) Install the intake and exhaust manifolds (refer to Group 11, Exhaust System and Intake Manifold for the proper procedures).

(15) Install the fuel lines and the vacuum advance hose.

(16) If equipped, attach the power steering pump and bracket.

(17) Install the push rods, rocker arms, pivots and bridges in the order they were removed.

(18) Install the engine cylinder head cover.

(19) Attach the air conditioning compressor mounting bracket to the engine cylinder head and block. Tighten the bolts to 40 N·m (30 ft. lbs.) torque.

(20) Attach the air conditioning compressor to the bracket. Tighten the bolts to 27 N·m (20 ft. lbs.) torque.

CAUTION: The serpentine drive belt must be routed correctly. Incorrect routing can cause the water pump to turn in the opposite direction causing the engine to overheat.

(21) Install the serpentine drive belt and correctly tension the belt (refer to Group 7, Cooling System for the proper procedure).

(22) Install the air cleaner and ducting.

(23) Install the engine cylinder head cover.

(24) Connect the hoses to the thermostat housing and fill the cooling system to the specified level (refer to Group 7, Cooling Systems for the proper procedure).

(25) The automatic transmission throttle linkage and cable must be adjusted after completing the engine cylinder head installation (refer to Group 21, Transmissions for the proper procedures).

(26) Install the temperature sending unit and connect the wire connector.

(27) Connect the fuel pipe and vacuum advance hose.

(28) Connect negative cable to battery.

(29) Connect the upper radiator hose and heater hose at the thermostat housing.

(30) Fill the cooling system. Check for leaks.

WARNING: USE EXTREME CAUTION WHEN THE ENGINE IS OPERATING. DO NOT STAND IN DIRECT LINE WITH THE FAN. DO NOT PUT HANDS NEAR THE PULLEYS, BELTS OR FAN. DO NOT WEAR LOOSE CLOTHING.

(31) Operate the engine with the radiator cap off. Inspect for leaks and continue operating the engine until the thermostat opens. Add coolant, if required.

VALVES AND VALVE SPRINGS

This procedure is done with the engine cylinder head removed from the block.

REMOVAL

(1) Remove the engine cylinder head from the cylinder block.

(2) Use Valve Spring Compressor Tool MD-998772A and compress each valve spring.

(3) Remove the valve locks, retainers, springs and valve stem oil seals. Discard the oil seals.

(4) Use an Arkansas smooth stone or a jewelers file to remove any burrs on the top of the valve stem, especially around the groove for the locks.

(5) Remove the valves, and place them in a rack in the same order as removed.

INSTALLATION

(1) Thoroughly clean the valve stems and the valve guide bores.

REMOVAL AND INSTALLATION (Continued)

(2) Lightly lubricate the stem.

(3) Install the valve in the original valve guide bore.

(4) Install the replacement valve stem oil seals on the valve stems. If the 0.381 mm (0.015 inch) oversize valve stems are used, oversize oil seals are required.

(5) Position the valve spring and retainer on the engine cylinder head and compress the valve spring with Valve Spring Compressor Tool MD-998772A.

(6) Install the valve locks and release the tool.

(7) Tap the valve spring from side to side with a hammer to ensure that the spring is properly seated at the engine cylinder head. Also tap the top of the retainer to seat the valve locks.

(8) Install the engine cylinder head.

HYDRAULIC TAPPETS

REMOVAL

Retain all the components in the same order as removed.

(1) Remove the engine cylinder head cover.

(2) Remove the bridge and pivot assemblies and rocker arms by removing the capscrews at each bridge. Alternately loosen each capscrew, one turn at a time, to avoid damaging the bridges.

(3) Remove the push rods.

(4) Remove the tappets through the push rod openings in the cylinder head with a Hydraulic Valve Tappet Removal/Installation Tool (Fig. 32).

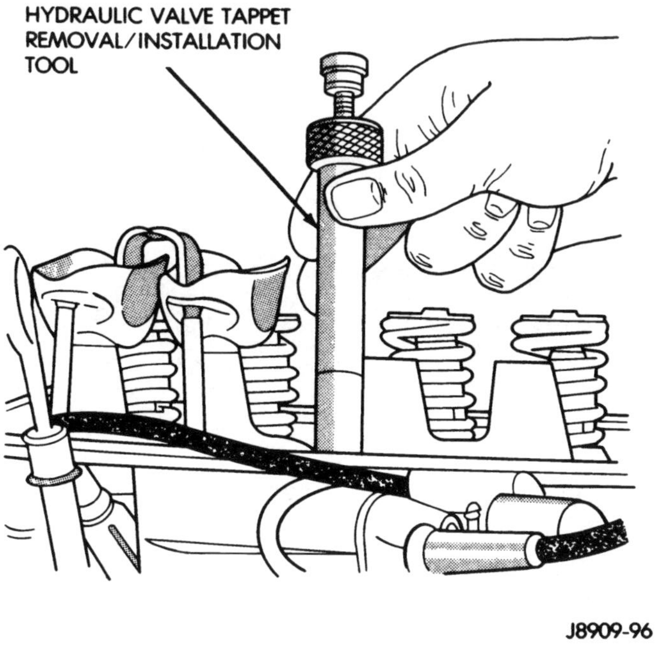

Fig. 32 Hydraulic Valve Tappet Removal/Installation Tool

INSTALLATION

It is not necessary to charge the tappets with engine oil. They will charge themselves within a very short period of engine operation.

(1) Dip each tappet in Mopar Engine Oil Supplement, or equivalent.

(2) Use Hydraulic Valve Tappet Removal/Installation Tool to install each tappet in the same bore from where it was originally removed.

(3) Install the push rods in their original locations.

(4) Install the rocker arms and bridge and pivot assemblies at their original locations. Loosely install the capscrews at each bridge.

(5) Tighten the capscrews alternately, one turn at a time, to avoid damaging the bridges. Tighten the capscrews to 28 N·m (21 ft. lbs.) torque.

(6) Pour the remaining Mopar Engine Oil Supplement, or equivalent over the entire valve actuating assembly. The Mopar Engine Oil Supplement, or equivalent must remain with the engine oil for at least 1 600 km (1,000 miles). The oil supplement need not be drained until the next scheduled oil change.

(7) Install the engine cylinder head cover.

VIBRATION DAMPER

REMOVAL

(1) Disconnect negative cable from battery.

(2) Remove the serpentine drive belt and fan shroud.

(3) Remove the vibration damper retaining bolt and washer.

(4) Use Vibration Damper Removal Tool 7697 to remove the damper from the crankshaft (Fig. 33).

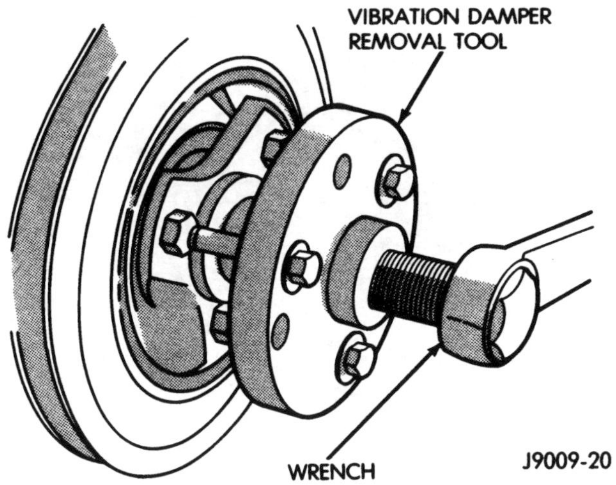

Fig. 33 Vibration Damper Removal Tool 7697

INSTALLATION

(1) Apply Mopar Silicone Rubber Adhesive Sealant to the keyway in the crankshaft and insert the key. With the key in position, align the keyway on the

REMOVAL AND INSTALLATION (Continued)

vibration damper hub with the crankshaft key and tap the damper onto the crankshaft.

(2) Install the vibration damper retaining bolt and washer.

(3) Tighten the damper retaining bolt to 108 N·m (80 ft. lbs.) torque.

(4) Install the serpentine drive belt and tighten to the specified tension (refer to Group 7, Cooling Systems for the proper specifications and procedures).

(5) Connect negative cable to battery.

TIMING CASE COVER OIL SEAL

REMOVAL

This procedure is done with the timing case cover installed.

(1) Disconnect negative cable from battery.

(2) Remove the serpentine drive belt.

(3) Remove the vibration damper.

(4) Remove the radiator shroud.

(5) Carefully remove the oil seal. Make sure seal bore is clean.

INSTALLATION

(1) Position the replacement oil seal on Timing Case Cover Alignment and Seal Installation Tool 6139 with seal open end facing inward. Apply a light film of Perfect Seal, or equivalent, on the outside diameter of the seal. Lightly coat the crankshaft with engine oil.

(2) Position the tool and seal over the end of the crankshaft and insert a draw screw tool into Seal Installation Tool 6139 (Fig. 34). Tighten the nut against the tool until it contacts the cover.

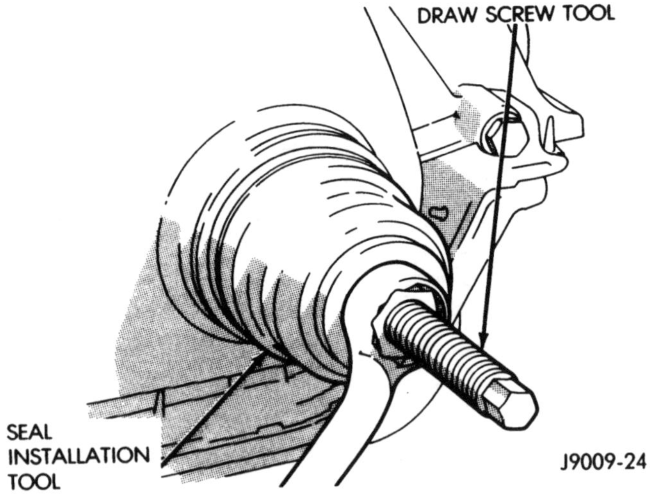

Fig. 34 Timing Case Cover Oil Seal Installation

(3) Remove the tools. Apply a light film of engine oil on the vibration damper hub contact surface of the seal.

(4) Apply Mopar Silicone Rubber Adhesive Sealant to the keyway in the crankshaft and insert the key. With the key inserted in the keyway in the crankshaft, install the vibration damper, washer and bolt. Lubricate and tighten the bolt to 108 N·m (80 ft. lbs.) torque.

(5) Install the serpentine belt and tighten to the specified tension (refer to Group 7, Cooling Systems for the proper specifications and procedures).

(6) Install the radiator shroud.

(7) Connect negative cable to battery.

TIMING CASE COVER

REMOVAL

(1) Disconnect negative cable from battery.

(2) Remove the vibration damper (Fig. 35).

(3) Remove the fan and hub assembly and remove the fan shroud.

(4) Remove the accessory drive brackets that are attached to the timing case cover.

(5) Remove the A/C compressor (if equipped) and generator bracket assembly from the engine cylinder head and move to one side.

(6) Remove the oil pan-to-timing case cover bolts and timing case cover-to-cylinder block bolts.

(7) Remove the timing case cover and gasket from the engine.

(8) Pry the crankshaft oil seal from the front of the timing case cover (Fig. 35).

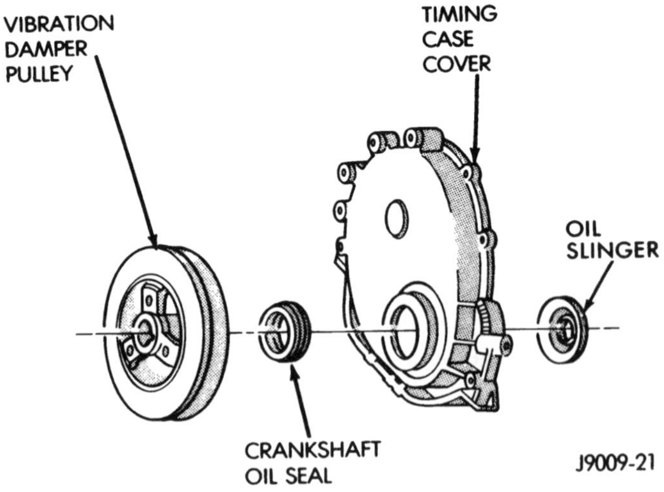

Fig. 35 Timing Case Cover Components

INSTALLATION

(1) Clean the timing case cover, oil pan and cylinder block gasket surfaces.

(2) Install a new crankshaft oil seal in the timing case cover. The open end of the seal should be toward the inside of the cover. Support the cover at the seal area while installing the seal. Force it into position with Seal Installation Tool 6139.

(3) Position the gasket on the cylinder block.

REMOVAL AND INSTALLATION (Continued)

(4) Position the timing case cover on the oil pan gasket and the cylinder block.

(5) Insert Timing Case Cover Alignment and Seal Installation Tool 6139 in the crankshaft opening in the cover (Fig. 36).

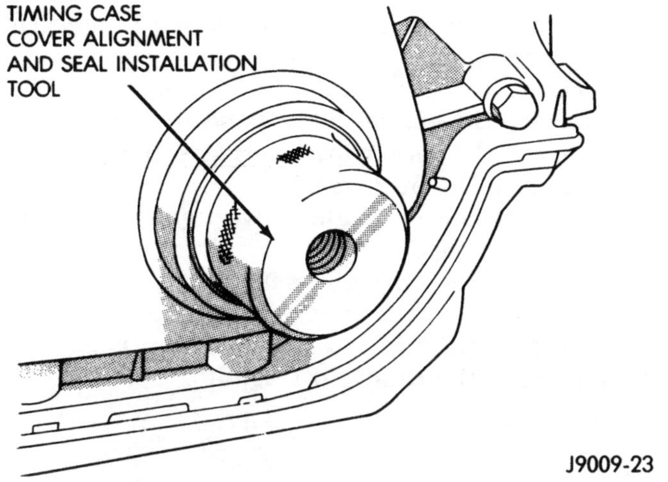

Fig. 36 Timing Case Cover Alignment and Seal Installation Tool 6139

(6) Install the timing case cover-to-cylinder block and the oil pan-to-timing case cover bolts.

(7) Tighten the 1/4 inch cover-to-block bolts to 7 N·m (60 in. lbs.) torque. Tighten the 5/16 inch front cover-to-block bolts to 22 N·m (192 in. lbs.) torque. Tighten the oil pan-to-cover 1/4 inch bolts to 14 N·m (120 in. lbs.) torque. Tighten the oil pan-to-cover 5/16 inch bolts to 9.5 N·m (84 in. lbs.) torque.

(8) Remove the cover alignment tool.

(9) Apply a light film of engine oil on the vibration damper hub contact surface of the seal.

(10) Apply Mopar Silicone Rubber Adhesive Sealant to the keyway in the crankshaft and insert the key. With the key inserted in the keyway in the crankshaft, install the vibration damper, washer and bolt. Lubricate and tighten the bolt to 108 N·m (80 ft. lbs.) torque.

(11) Install the A/C compressor (if equipped) and generator bracket assembly.

(12) Install the engine fan and hub assembly and shroud.

(13) Install the serpentine drive belt and tighten to obtain the specified tension.

(14) Connect negative cable to battery.

TIMING CHAIN AND SPROCKETS

The timing chain tensioner reduces noise and prolongs timing chain life. In addition, it compensates for slack in a worn or stretched chain and maintains the correct valve timing.

REMOVAL

(1) Disconnect negative cable from battery.

(2) Remove the fan and shroud.

(3) Remove the serpentine drive belt.

(4) Remove the crankshaft vibration damper.

(5) Remove the timing case cover.

(6) Rotate crankshaft until the "0" timing mark is closest to and on the center line with camshaft sprocket timing mark (Fig. 37).

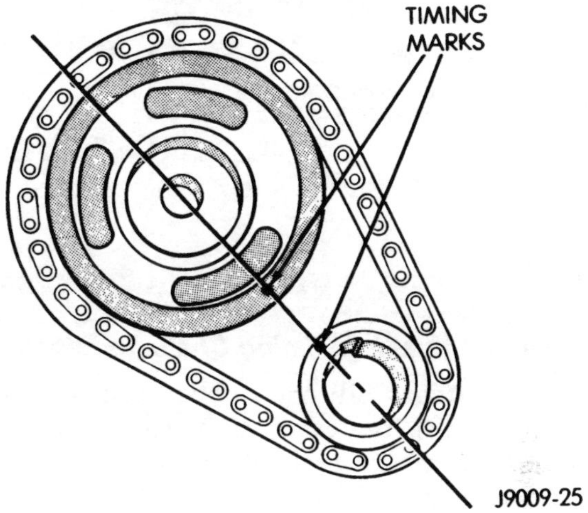

Fig. 37 Crankshaft—Camshaft Alignment

(7) Remove the oil slinger from the crankshaft.

(8) Remove the camshaft retaining bolt and remove the sprockets and chain as an assembly (Fig. 38).

(9) To replace the timing chain tensioner, the oil pan must be removed.

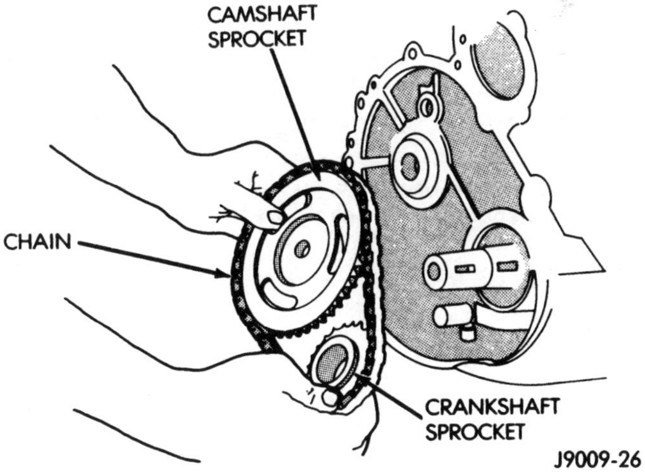

Fig. 38 Camshaft and Crankshaft Sprockets and Chain

INSTALLATION

(1) Turn the tensioner lever to the unlocked (down) position (Fig. 39).

REMOVAL AND INSTALLATION (Continued)

(2) Pull the tensioner block toward the tensioner lever to compress the spring. Hold the block and turn the tensioner lever to the lock position (Fig. 39).

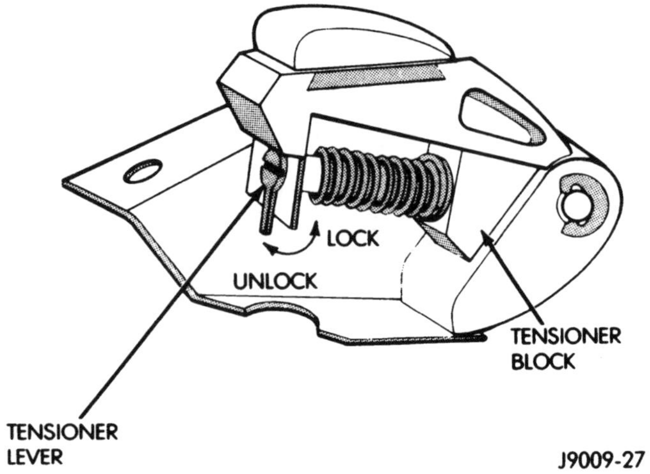

Fig. 39 Loading Timing Chain Tensioner

(3) Apply Mopar Silicone Rubber Adhesive Sealant to the keyway in the crankshaft and insert the key. With the key in the crankshaft keyway, install the crankshaft, camshaft sprockets and timing chain. Ensure the timing marks on the sprockets are properly aligned (Fig. 37).

(4) Install the camshaft sprocket retaining bolt and washer. Tighten the bolt to 108 N·m (80 ft. lbs.) torque.

(5) Turn the chain tensioner lever to the unlocked (down) position (Fig. 39).

(6) Install the oil slinger.

(7) Replace the oil seal in the timing case cover.

(8) Install the timing case cover and gasket.

(9) With the key inserted in the keyway in the crankshaft, install the vibration damper, washer and bolt. Lubricate and tighten the bolt to 108 N·m (80 ft. lbs.) torque.

(10) Install the fan and shroud.

(11) Connect negative cable to battery.

CAMSHAFT

REMOVAL

WARNING: THE COOLANT IN A RECENTLY OPERATED ENGINE IS HOT AND PRESSURIZED. RELEASE THE PRESSURE BEFORE REMOVING THE DRAIN COCK, CAP AND DRAIN PLUGS.

(1) Disconnect negative cable from battery.

(2) Drain the cooling system. DO NOT waste reusable coolant. If the solution is clean, drain it into a clean container for reuse.

(3) Remove the radiator or radiator and condenser, if equipped with A/C.

(4) Scribe a mark on the distributor housing in line with the lip of the rotor.

(5) Scribe a mark on the distributor housing near the clamp and continue the scribe mark on the cylinder block in line with the distributor mark.

(6) For ease of installation, note the position of the rotor and distributor housing in relation to adjacent engine components.

(7) Remove the distributor and ignition wires.

(8) Remove the engine cylinder head cover.

(9) Remove the rocker arms, bridges and pivots.

(10) Remove the push rods.

(11) Remove the hydraulic valve tappets from the engine cylinder head.

(12) Remove the vibration damper.

(13) Remove the timing case cover.

(14) Remove the timing chain and sprockets.

(15) Remove the camshaft (Fig. 40).

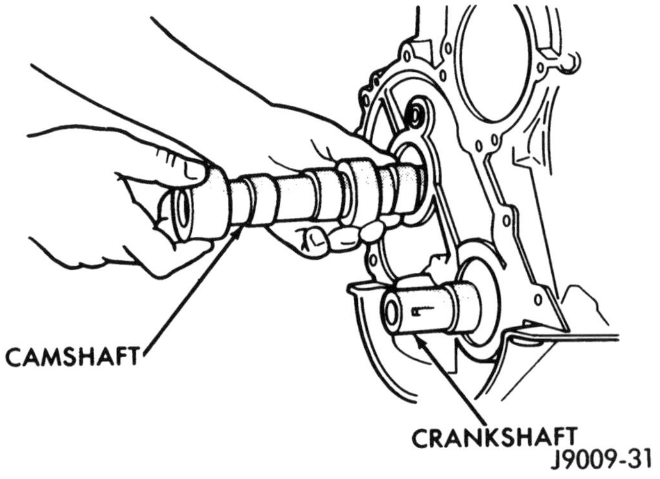

Fig. 40 Camshaft

INSTALLATION

(1) Inspect the cam lobes for wear.

(2) Inspect the bearing journals for uneven wear pattern or finish.

(3) Inspect the bearings for wear.

(4) Inspect the distributor drive gear for wear.

(5) If the camshaft appears to have been rubbing against the timing case cover, examine the oil pressure relief holes in the rear cam journal. The oil pressure relief holes must be free of debris.

(6) Lubricate the camshaft with Mopar Engine Oil Supplement, or equivalent.

(7) Carefully install the camshaft to prevent damage to the camshaft bearings (Fig. 40).

(8) Turn the tensioner lever to the unlocked (down) position (Fig. 41).

NOTE: Pull the tensioner block toward the tensioner lever to compress the spring. Hold the block and turn the tensioner lever to the lock position (Fig. 41).

REMOVAL AND INSTALLATION (Continued)

(9) Install the timing chain, crankshaft sprocket and camshaft sprocket with the timing marks aligned.

(10) Install the camshaft sprocket retaining bolt and washer. Tighten the bolt to 108 N·m (80 ft. lbs.) torque.

(11) Install the timing case cover with a replacement oil seal (Fig. 42). Refer to Timing Case Cover Installation.

(12) Install the vibration damper.

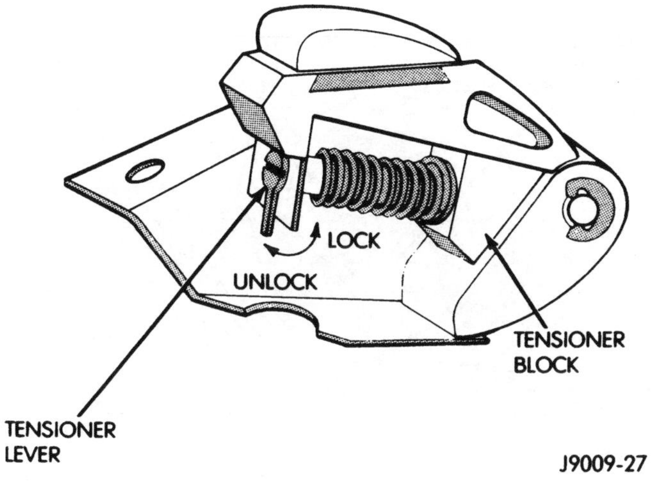

Fig. 41 Loading Timing Chain Tensioner

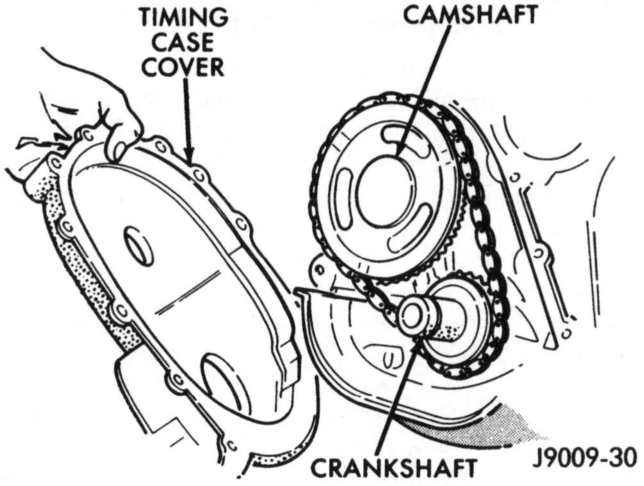

Fig. 42 Timing Case Cover

(13) Install the hydraulic valve tappets.

(14) Install the push rods.

(15) Install the rocker arms, bridges and pivots.

(16) Install the engine cylinder head cover.

(17) Position the oil pump gear. Refer to Distributor in the Component Removal/Installation section of Group 8D, Ignition Systems.

(18) Install the distributor and ignition wires. Refer to Distributor in the Component Removal/Installation section of Group 8D, Ignition Systems.

(19) Install the radiator or radiator and condenser, if equipped with A/C.

(20) Fill the cooling system.

(21) Connect negative cable to battery.

CAMSHAFT PIN REPLACEMENT

REMOVAL

WARNING: DO NOT LOOSEN THE RADIATOR DRAIN COCK WITH THE SYSTEM HOT AND PRESSURIZED BECAUSE SERIOUS BURNS FROM COOLANT CAN OCCUR.

(1) Disconnect negative cable from battery.

(2) Drain the radiator. DO NOT waste reusable coolant. Drain the coolant into a clean container.

(3) Remove the fan and shroud.

(4) Disconnect the radiator overflow tube, radiator hoses, automatic transmission fluid cooler pipes (if equipped).

(5) Remove the radiator.

(6) If equipped with air conditioning:

CAUTION: DO NOT loosen or disconnect any air conditioner system fittings. Move the condenser and receiver/drier aside as a complete assembly.

(a) Remove the A/C compressor serpentine drive belt idler pulley.

(b) Disconnect and remove the generator.

(c) Remove the A/C condenser attaching bolts and move the condenser and receiver/drier assembly up and out of the way.

(7) Remove the serpentine drive belt.

(8) Remove the crankshaft vibration damper.

(9) Remove the timing case cover. Clean the gasket material from the cover.

(10) Rotate crankshaft until the crankshaft sprocket timing mark is closest to and on the center line with the camshaft sprocket timing mark (Fig. 43).

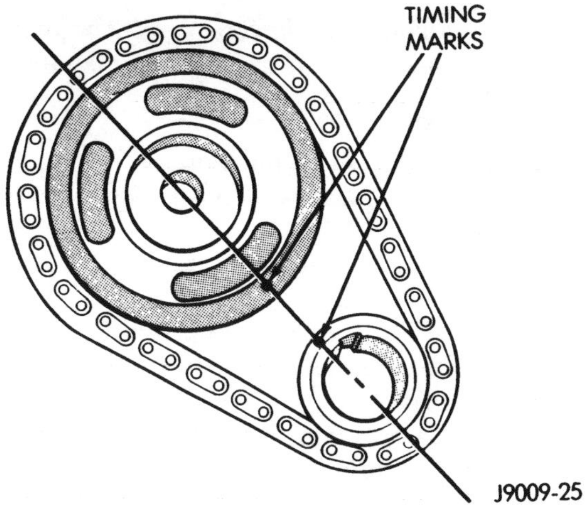

Fig. 43 Timing Chain Alignment

REMOVAL AND INSTALLATION (Continued)

(11) Remove camshaft sprocket retaining bolt.
(12) Remove the crankshaft oil slinger.
(13) Remove the sprockets and chain as an assembly (Fig. 44).

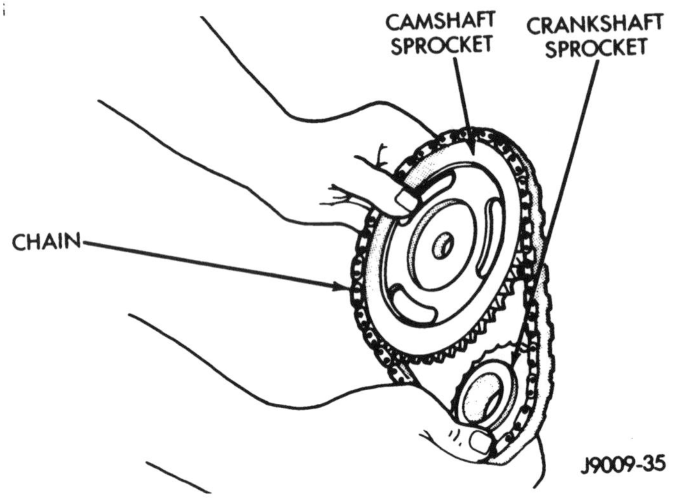

Fig. 44 Camshaft and Crankshaft Sprocket and Chain

CAUTION: The following procedural step must be accomplished to prevent the camshaft from damaging the rear camshaft plug during pin installation.

(14) Inspect the damaged camshaft pin.
(15) If the pin is a spring-type pin, remove the broken pin by inserting a self-tapping screw into the pin and carefully pulling the pin from the camshaft.
(16) If the pin is a dowel-type pin, center-punch it. Ensure the exact center is located when center-punching the pin.

CAUTION: Cover the opened oil pan area to prevent metal chips from entering the pan.

(17) Drill into the pin center with a 4 mm (5/32 inch) drill bit.
(18) Insert a self-tapping screw into the drilled pin and carefully pull the pin from the camshaft.

INSTALLATION

(1) Clean the camshaft pin hole.
(2) Compress the center of the replacement spring pin with vise grips.
(3) Carefully drive the pin into the camshaft pin hole until it is seated.
(4) Install the camshaft sprocket, crankshaft sprocket and timing chain with the timing marks aligned (Fig. 43).
(5) Install the crankshaft oil slinger.
(6) Tighten the camshaft sprocket bolt to 108 N·m (80 ft. lbs.) torque.
(7) Check the valve timing.
(8) Coat both sides of the replacement timing case cover gasket with gasket sealer. Apply a 3 mm (1/8 inch) bead of Mopar Silicone Rubber Adhesive Sealant, or equivalent to the joint formed at the timing case cover and cylinder block.
(9) Position the timing case cover on the oil pan gasket and the cylinder block.
(10) Place Timing Case Cover Alignment and Seal Installation Tool 6139 in the crankshaft opening of the cover (Fig. 45).

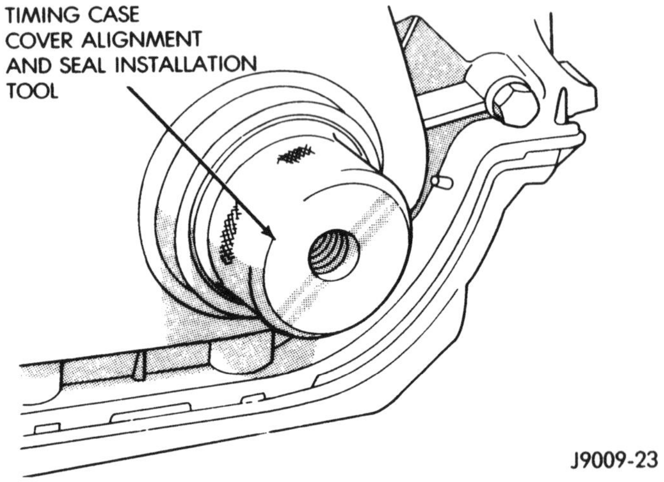

Fig. 45 Timing Case Cover Alignment and Seal Installation Tool 6139

(11) Install the timing case cover-to-cylinder block bolts. Install the oil pan-to-timing case cover bolts.
(12) Tighten the 1/4 inch cover-to-block bolts to 7 N·m (60 in. lbs.) torque. Tighten the 5/16 inch front cover-to-block bolts to 22 N·m (192 in. lbs.) torque. Tighten the oil pan-to-cover 1/4 inch bolts to 14 N·m (120 in. lbs.) torque. Tighten the oil pan-to-cover 5/16 inch bolts to 18 N·m (156 in. lbs.) torque.
(13) Remove the cover alignment tool and install a replacement oil seal into the cover.
(14) Install the vibration damper on the crankshaft.
(15) Lubricate and tighten the damper bolt to 108 N·m (80 ft. lbs.) torque.
(16) If equipped with air conditioning:
(a) Install the A/C compressor serpentine drive belt idler pulley.
(b) Install the generator.
(c) Install the A/C condenser and receiver/drier assembly.
(17) Install the serpentine drive belt on the pulleys and tighten (refer to Group 7, Cooling System for the specifications and procedures).
(18) Install the radiator. Connect the radiator hoses and automatic transmission fluid cooler pipes, if equipped. Fill the cooling system.
(19) Install the fan and shroud.
(20) Connect negative cable to battery.

REMOVAL AND INSTALLATION (Continued)

CAMSHAFT BEARINGS

The camshaft rotates within four steel-shelled, babbitt-lined bearings that are pressed into the cylinder block and then line reamed. The camshaft bearing bores and bearing diameters are not the same size. They are stepped down in 0.254 mm (0.010 inch) increments from the front bearing (largest) to the rear bearing (smallest). This permits easier removal and installation of the camshaft. The camshaft bearings are pressure lubricated.

NOTE: It is not advisable to attempt to replace camshaft bearings unless special removal and installation tools are available.

Camshaft end play is maintained by the load placed on the camshaft by the oil pump and distributor drive gear. The helical cut of the gear holds the camshaft sprocket thrust face against the cylinder block face.

CRANKSHAFT MAIN BEARINGS

REMOVAL

(1) Disconnect negative cable from battery.

(2) Remove the spark plugs.

(3) Raise the vehicle.

(4) Remove the oil pan and oil pump.

(5) Remove only one main bearing cap and lower insert at a time (Fig. 46).

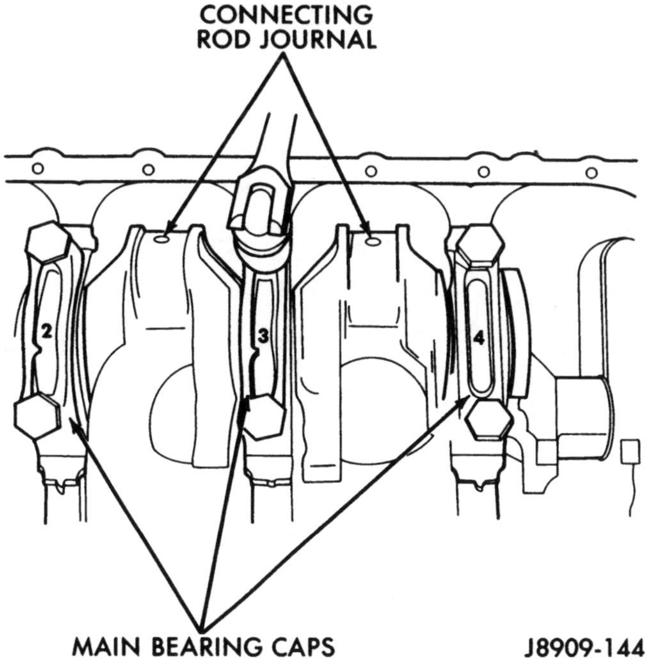

Fig. 46 Removing Main Bearing Caps and Lower Inserts

(6) Remove the lower insert from the bearing cap.

(7) Remove the upper insert by LOOSENING (DO NOT REMOVE) all of the other bearing caps. Now insert a small cotter pin tool in the crankshaft journal oil hole. Bend the cotter pin as illustrated to fabricate the tool (Fig. 47). With the cotter pin tool in place, rotate the crankshaft so that the upper bearing insert will rotate in the direction of its locking tab. Because there is no hole in the No.3 main journal, use a tongue depressor or similar soft-faced tool to remove the bearing insert (Fig. 47). After moving the insert approximately 25 mm (1 inch), it can be removed by applying pressure under the tab.

(8) Using the same procedure described above, remove the remaining bearing inserts one at a time for inspection.

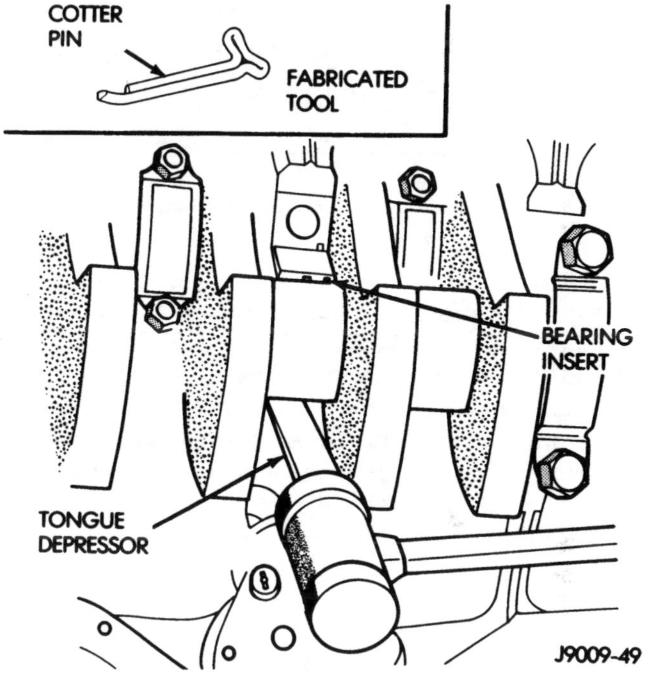

Fig. 47 Removing Upper Inserts

INSTALLATION

(1) Lubricate the bearing surface of each insert with engine oil.

(2) Loosen all the main bearing caps. Install the main bearing upper inserts.

(3) Install the lower bearing inserts into the main bearing caps.

(4) Install the main bearing cap(s) and lower insert(s).

(5) Clean the rear main bearing cap (No.5) mating surfaces.

(6) Apply Loctite 518, or equivalent on the rear bearing cap (Fig. 48). The bead should be 3 mm (0.125 in) thick. DO NOT apply Loctite 518, or equivalent to the lip of the seal.

(7) Install the rear main bearing cap. DO NOT strike the cap more than twice for proper engagement.

REMOVAL AND INSTALLATION (Continued)

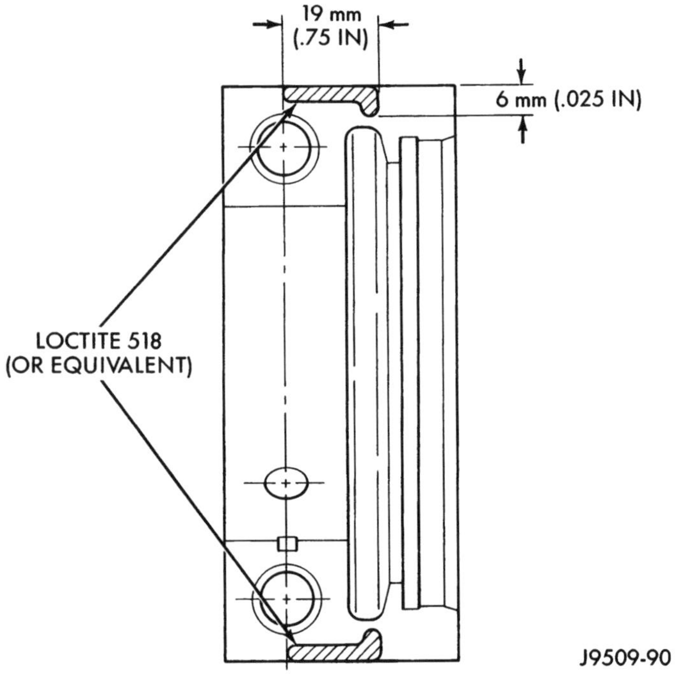

Fig. 48 Location of Loctite 518 (or equivalent)

(8) Tighten the bolts of caps 1, 3, 4 and 5 to 54 N·m (40 ft. lbs.) torque. Now tighten these bolts to 95 N·m (70 ft. lbs.) torque. Finally, tighten these bolts to 108 N·m (80 ft. lbs.) torque.

(9) Push the crankshaft forward and backward. Load the crankshaft front or rear and tighten cap bolt No.2 to 54 N·m (40 ft. lbs.) torque. Then tighten to 95 N·m (70 ft. lbs.) torque and finally tighten to 108 N·m (80 ft. lbs.) torque.

(10) Rotate the crankshaft after tightening each main bearing cap to ensure the crankshaft rotates freely.

(11) Check crankshaft end play. Crankshaft end play is controlled by the thrust bearing which is flange and installed at the No.2 main bearing position.

(a) Attach a magnetic base dial indicator to the cylinder block at either the front or rear of the engine.

(b) Position the dial indicator rod so that it is parallel to the center line of the crankshaft.

(c) Pry the crankshaft forward, position the dial indicator to zero.

(d) Pry the crankshaft forward and backward. Note the dial indicator readings. End play is the difference between the high and low measurements (Fig. 49). Correct end play is 0.038-0.165 mm (0.0015-0.0065 inch). The desired specifications are 0.051-0.064 mm (0.002-0.0025 inch).

(e) If end play is not within specification, inspect crankshaft thrust faces for wear. If no wear is apparent, replace the thrust bearing and measure end play. If end play is still not within specification, replace the crankshaft.

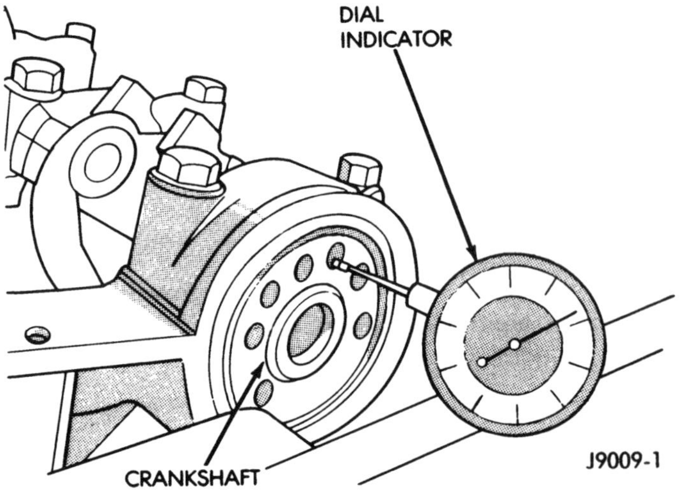

Fig. 49 Crankshaft End Play Measurement

(12) If the crankshaft was removed, install the crankshaft into the cylinder block (refer to Cylinder Block - Assemble).

(13) Install the oil pan.

(14) Install the drain plug. Tighten the plug to 34 N·m (25 ft. lbs.) torque.

(15) Lower the vehicle.

(16) Install the spark plugs. Tighten the plugs to 37 N·m (27 ft. lbs.) torque.

(17) Fill the oil pan with engine oil to the full mark on the dipstick level.

(18) Connect negative cable to battery.

OIL PAN

REMOVAL

(1) Disconnect negative cable from battery.

(2) Raise the vehicle.

(3) Remove the oil pan drain plug and drain the engine oil.

(4) Remove the engine starter motor.

(5) Remove the flywheel/torque converter housing access cover.

(6) Position a jack stand directly under the engine vibration damper.

(7) Place a piece of wood (2 x 2) between the jack stand and the engine vibration damper.

(8) Remove the engine mount through bolts.

(9) Using the jack stand, raise the engine until adequate clearance is obtained to remove the oil pan.

(10) Remove the oil pan bolts. Carefully remove the oil pan and gasket.

INSTALLATION

(1) Clean the block and pan gasket surfaces.

(2) Fabricate 4 alignment dowels from 1/4 x 1 1/2 inch bolts. Cut the head off the bolts and cut a slot

REMOVAL AND INSTALLATION (Continued)

into the top of the dowel. This will allow easier installation and removal with a screwdriver (Fig. 50).

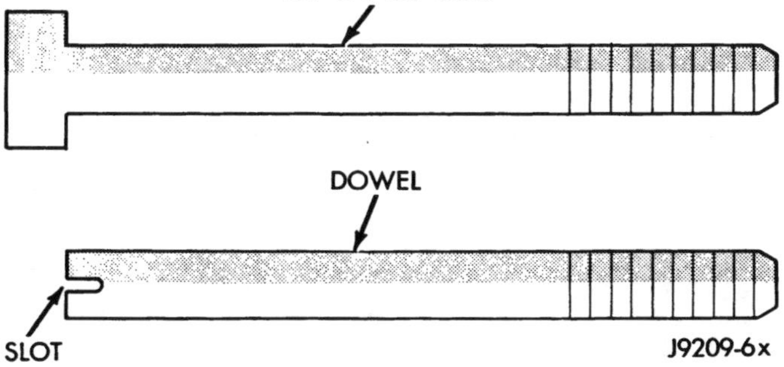

Fig. 50 Fabrication of Alignment Dowels

(3) Install two dowels in the timing case cover. Install the other two dowels in the cylinder block (Fig. 51).

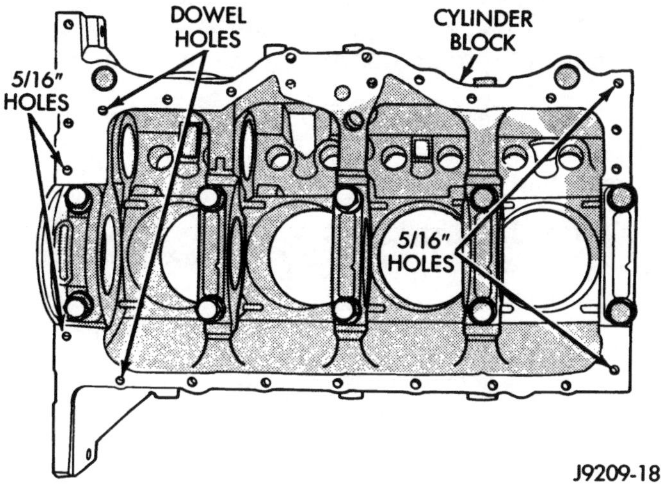

Fig. 51 Position of Dowels in Cylinder Block

(4) Slide the one-piece gasket over the dowels and onto the block and timing case cover.

(5) Position the oil pan over the dowels and onto the gasket.

(6) Install the 1/4 inch oil pan bolts. Tighten these bolts to 9.5 N·m (84 in. lbs.) torque. Install the 5/16 inch oil pan bolts (Fig. 52). Tighten these bolts to 15 N·m (132 in. lbs.) torque.

(7) Remove the dowels. Install the remaining 1/4 inch oil pan bolts. Tighten these bolts to 9.5 N·m (84 in. lbs.) torque.

(8) Lower the engine until it is properly located on the engine mounts.

(9) Install the through bolts and tighten the nuts.

(10) Lower the jack stand and remove the piece of wood.

(11) Install the flywheel and torque converter housing access cover.

(12) Install the engine starter motor.

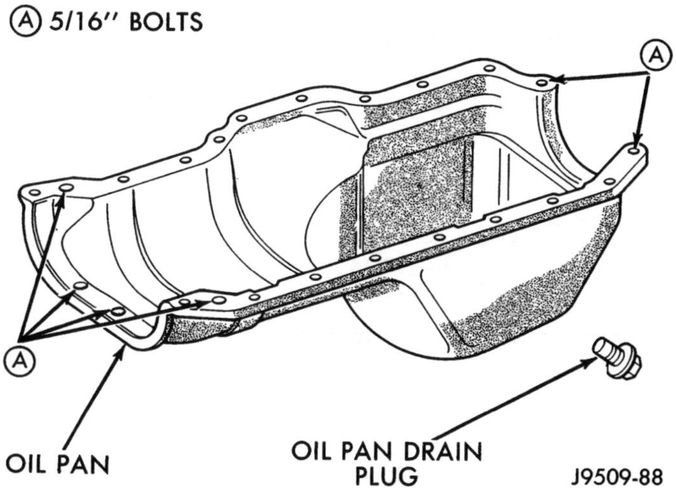

Fig. 52 Position of 5/16 inch Oil Pan Bolts

(13) Connect the exhaust pipe to the hanger and to the engine exhaust manifold.

(14) Install the oil pan drain plug (Fig. 52). Tighten the plug to 34 N·m (25 ft. lbs.) torque.

(15) Lower the vehicle.

(16) Connect negative cable to battery.

(17) Fill the oil pan with engine oil to the specified level.

WARNING: USE EXTREME CAUTION WHEN THE ENGINE IS OPERATING. DO NOT STAND IN A DIRECT LINE WITH THE FAN. DO NOT PUT YOUR HANDS NEAR THE PULLEYS, BELTS OR FAN. DO NOT WEAR LOOSE CLOTHING.

(18) Start the engine and inspect for leaks.

OIL PUMP

The positive-displacement gear-type oil pump is driven by the distributor shaft, which is driven by a gear on the camshaft. Oil is siphoned into the pump through an inlet tube and strainer assembly that is pressed into the pump body.

The pump incorporates a nonadjustable pressure relief valve to limit maximum pressure to 517 kPa (75 psi). In the relief position, the valve permits oil to bypass through a passage in the pump body to the inlet side of the pump.

Oil pump removal or replacement will not affect the distributor timing because the distributor drive gear remains in mesh with the camshaft gear.

REMOVAL

(1) Drain the engine oil.

(2) Remove the oil pan.

(3) Remove the pump-to-cylinder block attaching bolts. Remove the pump assembly with gasket (Fig. 53).

REMOVAL AND INSTALLATION (Continued)

CAUTION: If the oil pump is not to be serviced, DO NOT disturb position of oil inlet tube and strainer assembly in pump body. If the tube is moved within the pump body, a replacement tube and strainer assembly must be installed to assure an airtight seal.

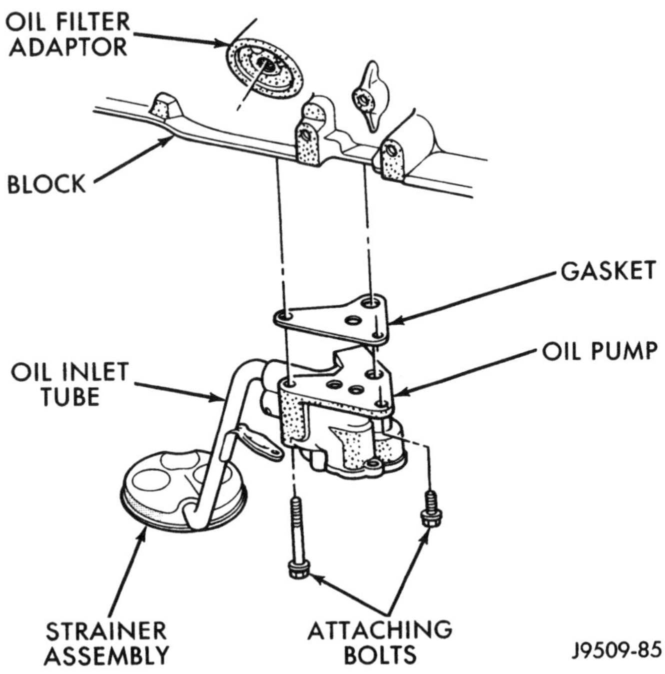

Fig. 53 Oil Pump Assembly

INSTALLATION

(1) Install the oil pump on the cylinder block using a replacement gasket. Tighten the bolts to 23 N·m (17 ft. lbs.) torque.

(2) Install the oil pan and gasket.

(3) Fill the oil pan with oil to the specified level.

PISTONS AND CONNECTING RODS

REMOVAL

(1) Remove the engine cylinder head cover.

(2) Remove the rocker arms, bridges and pivots.

(3) Remove the push rods.

(4) Remove the engine cylinder head.

(5) Position the pistons one at a time near the bottom of the stroke. Use a ridge reamer to remove the ridge from the top end of the cylinder walls. Use a protective cloth to collect the cuttings.

(6) Raise the vehicle.

(7) Drain the engine oil.

(8) Remove the oil pan and gasket.

(9) Remove the connecting rod bearing caps and inserts. Mark the caps and rods with the cylinder bore location. The connecting rods and caps are stamped with a two letter combination (Fig. 54).

(10) Lower the vehicle until it is about 2 feet from the floor.

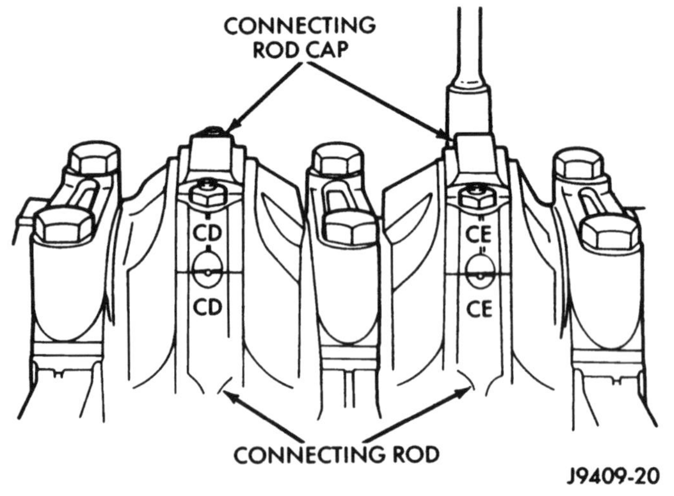

Fig. 54 Stamped Connecting Rods and Caps

CAUTION: Ensure that the connecting rod bolts DO NOT scratch the crankshaft journals or cylinder walls. Short pieces of rubber hose, slipped over the rod bolts will provide protection during removal.

(11) Have an assistant push the piston and connecting rod assemblies up and through the top of the cylinder bores (Fig. 55).

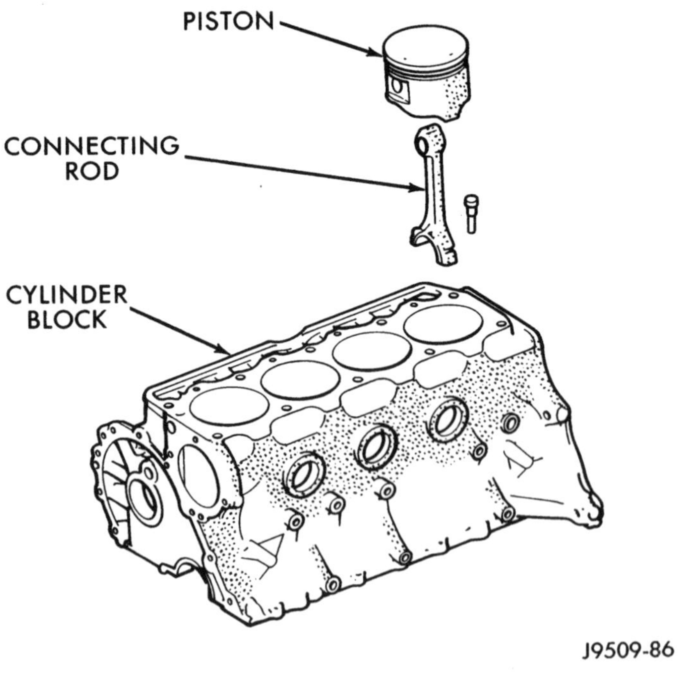

Fig. 55 Removal of Connecting Rod and Piston Assembly

INSTALLATION

(1) Clean the cylinder bores thoroughly. Apply a light film of clean engine oil to the bores with a clean lint-free cloth.

(2) Install the piston rings on the pistons if removed.

REMOVAL AND INSTALLATION (Continued)

(3) Lubricate the piston and rings with clean engine oil.

CAUTION: Ensure that connecting rod bolts do not scratch the crankshaft journals or cylinder walls. Short pieces of rubber hose slipped over the connecting rod bolts will provide protection during installation.

(4) Use a piston ring compressor to install the connecting rod and piston assemblies through the top of the cylinder bores (Fig. 56).
(5) Ensure the arrow on the piston top points to the front of the engine (Fig. 56).

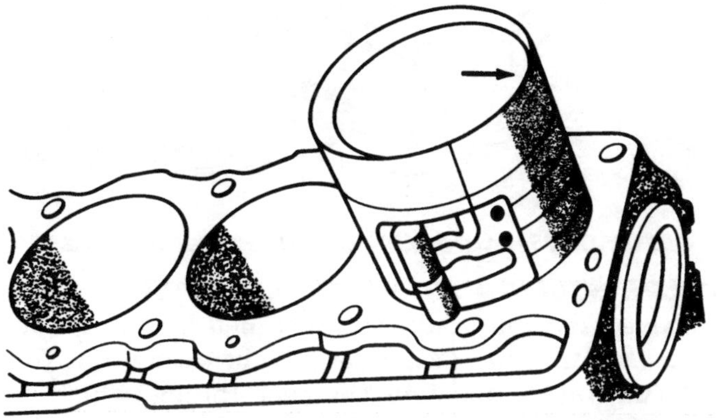

Fig. 56 Rod and Piston Assembly Installation

(6) Raise the vehicle.
(7) Each bearing insert is fitted to its respective journal to obtain the specified clearance between the bearing and the journal. In production, the select fit is obtained by using various-sized, color-coded bearing inserts as listed in the Connecting Rod Bearing Fitting Chart. The color code appears on the edge of the bearing insert. The size is not stamped on inserts used for production of engines.
(8) The rod journal is identified during the engine production by a color-coded paint mark on the adjacent cheek or counterweight toward the flange (rear) end of the crankshaft. The color codes used to indicate journal sizes are listed in the Connecting Rod Bearing Fitting Chart.
(9) When required, upper and lower bearing inserts of different sizes may be used as a pair (refer to Connecting Rod Bearing Fitting Chart). A standard size insert is sometimes used in combination with a 0.025 mm (0.001 inch) undersize insert to reduce clearance 0.013 mm (0.0005 inch).

CAUTION: DO NOT intermix bearing caps. Each connecting rod and bearing cap are stamped with the cylinder number. The stamp is located on a machined surface adjacent to the oil squirt hole that faces the camshaft side of the cylinder block.

(10) Install the connecting rod bearing caps and inserts in the same positions as removed.

CAUTION: Verify that the oil squirt holes in the rods face the camshaft and that the arrows on the pistons face the front of the engine.

(11) Install the oil pan and gaskets as outlined in the installation procedure.
(12) Lower the vehicle.
(13) Install the engine cylinder head, push rods, rocker arms, bridges, pivots and engine cylinder head cover.
(14) Fill the crankcase with engine oil.

REAR MAIN OIL SEALS

REMOVAL

(1) Remove the flywheel or converter drive plate. Discard the old bolts.
(2) Pry out the seal from around the crankshaft flange (Fig. 57).

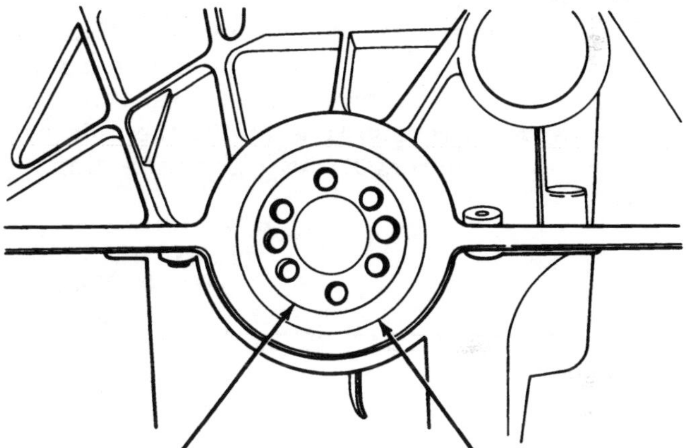

Fig. 57 Replacement of Rear Crankshaft Oil Seal

INSTALLATION

(1) Coat the outer lip of the replacement rear main bearing seal with engine oil.
(2) Carefully position the seal into place. Use rear main Seal Installer Tool 6271A to install the seal flush with the cylinder block.

CAUTION: The felt lip must be located inside the flywheel mounting surface. If the lip is not positioned correctly the flywheel could tear the seal.

(3) Install the flywheel or converter drive plate. New bolts MUST be used when installing the flywheel or converter plate. Tighten the new bolts to 68

REMOVAL AND INSTALLATION (Continued)

N·m (50 ft. lbs.) torque. Turn the bolts an additional 60°.

DISASSEMBLY AND ASSEMBLY

VALVE SERVICE

Clean all carbon deposits from the combustion chambers, valve ports, valve stems, valve stem guides and head.

Clean all grime and gasket material from the engine cylinder head machined gasket surface.

Inspect for cracks in the combustion chambers and valve ports.

Inspect for cracks on the exhaust seat.

Inspect for cracks in the gasket surface at each coolant passage.

Inspect valves for burned, cracked or warped heads.

Inspect for scuffed or bent valve stems.

Replace valves displaying any damage.

VALVE REFACING

(1) Use a valve refacing machine to reface the intake and exhaust valves to the specified angle.

(2) After refacing, a margin of at least 0.787 mm (0.031 inch) must remain (Fig. 58). If the margin is less than 0.787 mm (0.031 inch), the valve must be replaced.

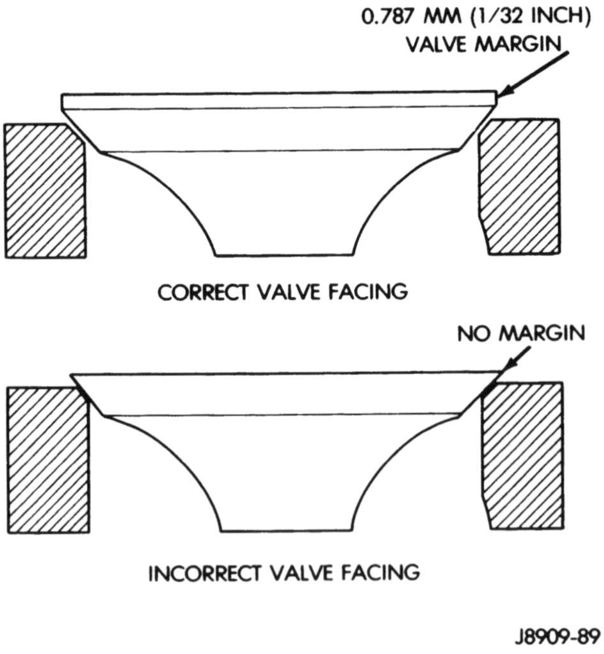

Fig. 58 Valve Facing Margin

VALVE SEAT REFACING

(1) Install a pilot of the correct size in the valve guide bore. Reface the valve seat to the specified angle with a good dressing stone. Remove only enough metal to provide a smooth finish.

(2) Use tapered stones to obtain the specified seat width when required.

(3) Control valve seat runout to a maximum of 0.0635 mm (0.0025 in.)— (Fig. 59).

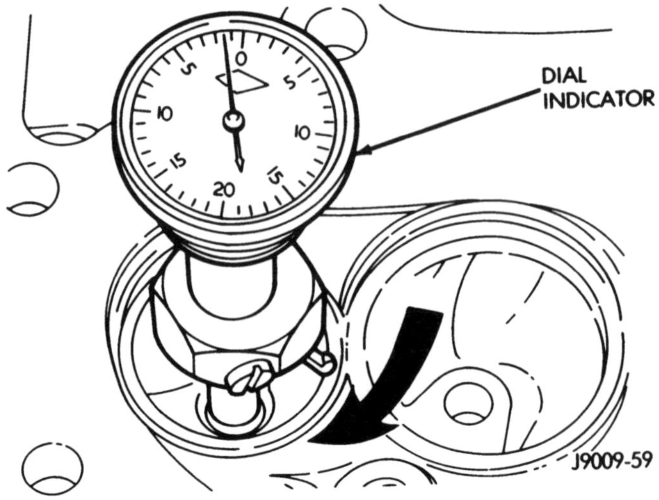

Fig. 59 Measurement of Valve Seat Runout

VALVE STEM OIL SEAL REPLACEMENT

Valve stem oil seals are installed on each valve stem to prevent rocker arm lubricating oil from entering the combustion chamber through the valve guide bores. One seal is marked INT (intake valve) and the other is marked EXH (exhaust valve).

Replace the oil seals whenever valve service is performed or if the seals have deteriorated.

VALVE GUIDES

The valve guides are an integral part of the engine cylinder head and are not replaceable.

When the valve stem guide clearance is excessive, the valve guide bores must be reamed oversize. Service valves with oversize stems are available in 0.076 mm (0.003 inch) and 0.381 mm (0.015 inch) increments.

Corresponding oversize valve stem seals are also available and must be used with valves having 0.381 mm (0.015 inch) oversize stems, 0.076mm (.003in.) oversize stems do not require oversize seals.

NOTE: If the valve guides are reamed oversize, the valve seats must be ground to ensure that the valve seat is concentric to the valve guide.

VALVE STEM-TO-GUIDE CLEARANCE MEASUREMENT

Valve stem-to-guide clearance may be measured by either of the following two methods.

PREFERRED METHOD:

(1) Remove the valve from the head.

DISASSEMBLY AND ASSEMBLY (Continued)

(2) Clean the valve stem guide bore with solvent and a bristle brush.

(3) Insert a telescoping gauge into the valve stem guide bore approximately 9.525 mm (.375 inch) from the valve spring side of the head (Fig. 60).

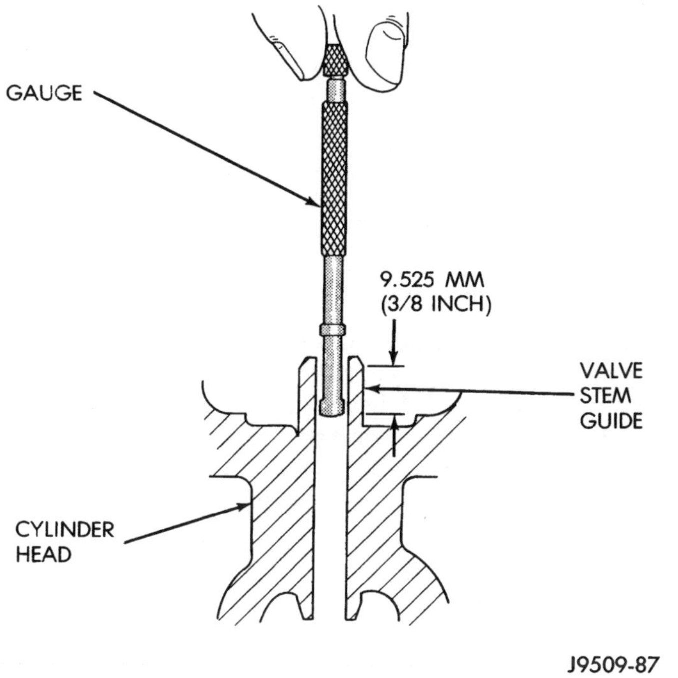

Fig. 60 Measurement of Valve Guide Bore Diameter

(4) Remove and measure telescoping gauge with a micrometer.

(5) Repeat the measurement with contacts lengthwise to engine cylinder head.

(6) Compare the crosswise to lengthwise measurements to determine out-of-roundness. If the measurements differ by more than 0.0635 mm (0.0025 in.), ream the guide bore to accommodate an oversize valve stem.

(7) Compare the measured valve guide bore diameter with specifications (7.95-7.97 mm or 0.313-0.314 inch). If the measurement differs from specification by more than 0.076 mm (0.003 inch), ream the guide bore to accommodate an oversize valve stem.

ALTERNATIVE METHOD:

(1) Use a dial indicator to measure the lateral movement of the valve stem (stem-to-guide clearance). This must be done with the valve installed in its guide and just off the valve seat (Fig. 61).

(2) Correct clearance is 0.025-0.0762 mm (0.001-0.003 inch). If indicated movement exceeds the specification ream the valve guide to accommodate an oversize valve stem.

NOTE: Valve seats must be ground after reaming the valve guides to ensure that the valve seat is concentric to the valve guide.

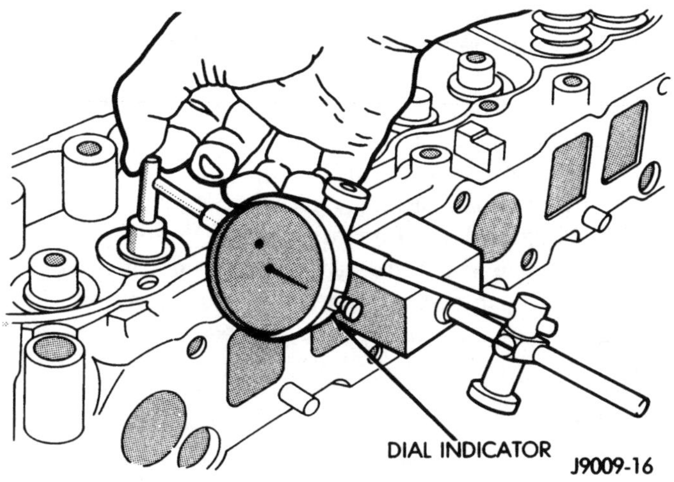

Fig. 61 Measurement of Lateral Movement Of Valve Stem

VALVE SPRING TENSION TEST

Use a Universal Valve Spring Tester and a torque wrench to test each valve spring for the specified tension value (Fig. 62).

Replace valve springs that are not within specifications.

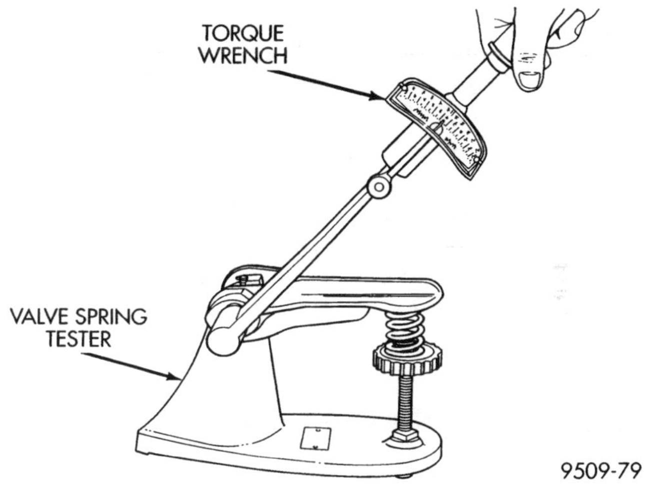

Fig. 62 Valve Spring Tester

CYLINDER BLOCK

Remove the Engine Assembly from the vehicle.

DISASSEMBLY

(1) Drain the engine oil. Remove and discard the oil filter.

(2) Remove the water pump from the cylinder block.

(3) Remove the distributor from the cylinder block.

(4) Remove the vibration damper.

(5) Remove the timing case cover and lay the cover upside down.

(6) Position a drift punch into the slot in the back of the cover and tap the old seal out.

DISASSEMBLY AND ASSEMBLY (Continued)

(7) Remove the timing chain bumper.
(8) Remove the oil slinger from crankshaft.
(9) Remove the camshaft retaining bolt and remove the sprockets and chain as an assembly.
(10) Remove the camshaft.
(11) Remove the oil pan and gasket.
(12) Remove the timing chain tensioner.
(13) Remove the front and rear oil galley plugs.
(14) Remove the connecting rods and the pistons. Remove the connecting rod and piston assemblies through the top of the cylinder bores.
(15) Remove the crankshaft.

ASSEMBLY

(1) Install the crankshaft.
(2) Install the connecting rods and the pistons through the top of the cylinder bores.
(3) Install the front and rear oil galley plugs.
(4) Install the timing chain tensioner.
(5) Install the camshaft.
(6) Install the sprockets and chain as an assembly.
(7) Install the oil slinger to the crankshaft.
(8) Install the timing chain bumper.
(9) Install the timing case cover seal.
(10) Install the timing case cover.
(11) Install the oil pan gasket and oil pan.
(12) Install the vibration damper.
(13) Install the water pump. Tighten the mounting bolts to 31 N·m (270 in. lbs.) torque.
(14) Remove the distributor from the cylinder block.
(15) Lubricate the oil filter seal with clean engine oil. Tighten oil filter to 18 N·m (13 ft. lbs.) torque.
(16) Install the engine into the vehicle.
(17) Fill the engine with clean lubrication oil.
(18) Fill the cooling system.

CLEANING AND INSPECTION

ROCKER ARMS AND PUSH RODS

CLEANING

Clean all the components with cleaning solvent.

Use compressed air to blow out the oil passages in the rocker arms and push rods.

INSPECTION

Inspect the pivot surface area of each rocker arm. Replace any that are scuffed, pitted, cracked or excessively worn.

Inspect the valve stem tip contact surface of each rocker arm and replace any rocker arm that is deeply pitted.

Inspect each push rod end for excessive wear and replace as required. If any push rod is excessively worn because of lack of oil, replace it and inspect the corresponding hydraulic tappet for excessive wear.

Inspect the push rods for straightness by rolling them on a flat surface or by shining a light between the push rod and the flat surface.

A wear pattern along the length of the push rod is not normal. Inspect the engine cylinder head for obstruction if this condition exists.

HYDRAULIC TAPPETS

CLEANING

Clean each tappet assembly in cleaning solvent to remove all varnish, gum and sludge deposits.

INSPECTION

Inspect for indications of scuffing on the side and base of each tappet body.

Inspect each tappet base for concave wear with a straightedge positioned across the base. If the base is concave, the corresponding lobe on the camshaft is also worn. Replace the camshaft and defective tappets.

ENGINE CYLINDER HEAD

CLEANING

Thoroughly clean the engine cylinder head and cylinder block mating surfaces. Clean the intake and exhaust manifold and engine cylinder head mating surfaces. Remove all gasket material and carbon.

Check to ensure that no coolant or foreign material has fallen into the tappet bore area.

Remove the carbon deposits from the combustion chambers and top of the pistons.

INSPECTION

Use a straightedge and feeler gauge to check the flatness of the engine cylinder head and block mating surfaces.

CYLINDER BLOCK

CLEANING

Thoroughly clean the oil pan and engine block gasket surfaces.

Use compressed air to clean out:

• The galley at the oil filter adaptor hole, the filter bypass hole (Fig. 63).

• The front and rear oil galley holes (Fig. 64) (Fig. 65).

• The feed holes for the crankshaft main bearings.

Once the block has been completely cleaned, apply Loctite PST pipe sealant with Teflon 592 to the threads of the front and rear oil galley plugs. Tighten the plugs to 41 N·m (30 ft. lbs.) torque.

CLEANING AND INSPECTION (Continued)

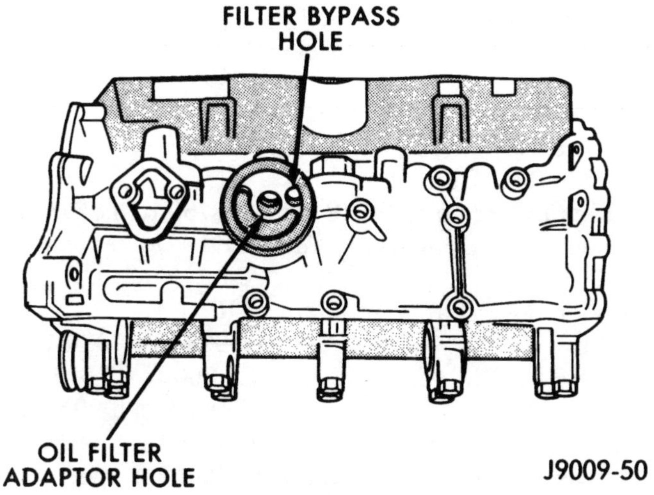

Fig. 63 Oil Filter Adaptor Hole

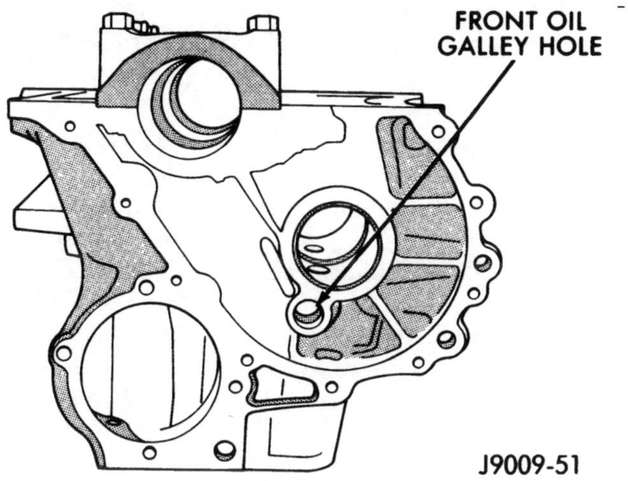

Fig. 64 Front Oil Galley Hole

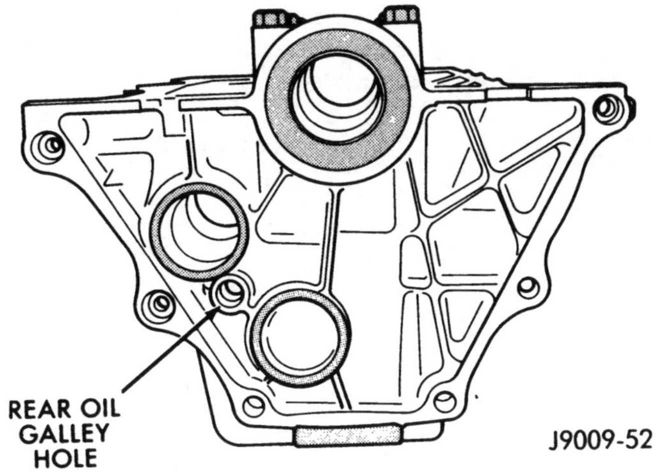

Fig. 65 Rear Oil Galley Hole

INSPECTION—CYLINDER BORE

(1) It is mandatory to use a dial bore gauge to measure each cylinder bore diameter (Fig. 66). To correctly select the proper size piston, a cylinder bore gauge, capable of reading in 0.003 mm (.0001in.) INCREMENTS is required. If a bore gauge is not available, do not use an inside micrometer.

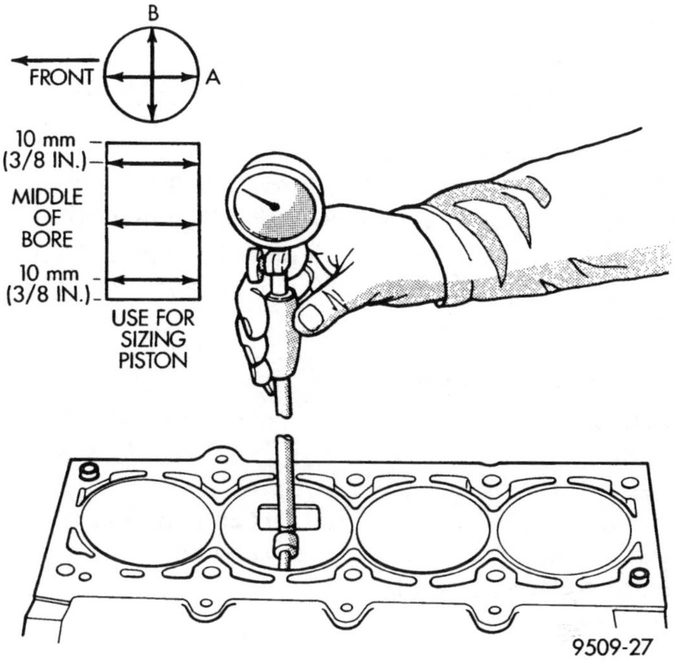

Fig. 66 Cylinder Bore Measurement

(2) Measure the inside diameter of the cylinder bore at three levels below top of bore. Start perpendicular (across or at 90 degrees) to the axis of the crankshaft and then take two additional reading.

(3) Measure the cylinder bore diameter crosswise to the cylinder block near the top of the bore. Repeat the measurement near the middle of the bore, then repeat the measurement near the bottom of the bore.

(4) Determine taper by subtracting the smaller diameter from the larger diameter.

(5) Rotate measuring device 90° and repeat steps above.

(6) Determine out-of-roundness by comparing the difference between each measurement.

(7) If cylinder bore taper does not exceed 0.025 mm (0.001 inch) and out-of-roundness does not exceed 0.025 mm (0.001 inch), the cylinder bore can be honed. If the cylinder bore taper or out- of-round condition exceeds these maximum limits, the cylinder must be bored and then honed to accept an oversize piston. A slight amount of taper always exists in the cylinder bore after the engine has been in use for a period of time.

HONING—CYLINDER BORE

The honing operation should be closely coordinated with the fitting of pistons and rings. This will ensure specified clearances are maintained.

SPECIFICATIONS

2.5L ENGINE SPECIFICATIONS

Camshaft

Hydraulic Tappet Clearance . . . . .Zero Lash
Bearing Clearance. . . . . .0.025 to 0.076 mm (0.001 to 0.003 in.)

Bearing Journal Diameter

No. 1. . . . . . . .51.54 to 51.56 mm (2.029 to 2.030 in.)
No. 2. . . . . . . .51.28 to 51.31 mm (2.019 to 2.020 in.)
No. 3. . . . . . . .51.03 to 51.05 mm (2.009 to 2.010 in.)
No. 4. . . . . . . .50.78 to 50.80 mm (1.999 to 2.000 in.)
Base Circle Runout . . . . .0.03 mm - max. (0.001 in. - max.)

Camshaft Lobe Lift

Exhaust . . . . .6.579 mm (0.259 in.)
Intake . . . . .6.477 mm (0.255 in.)

Valve Lift

Exhaust . . . . .10.528 mm (0.4145 in.)
Intake. . . . . .10.350 mm (0.4075 in.)

Intake Valve Timing

Opens . . . . .15.4° BTDC
Closes. . . . . .58° ABDC

Exhaust Valve Timing

Opens . . . . .52.8 BBDC
Closes. . . . . .26.2° ATDC
Valve Overlap. . . . . .41.6°
Intake Duration . . . . .253.3°
Exhaust Duration. . . . . .259.°

Crankshaft

End Play . . .0.038 to 0.165 mm (0.0015 to 0.0065 in.)
Main Bearing Journal Diameter . . . . .63.489 to 63.502 mm (2.4996 to 2.5001 in.)
Main Bearing Journal Width No. 1. . . . . .27.58 to 27.89 mm (1.086 to 1.098 in.)
Main Bearing Journal Width No. 2. . . . . .32.28 to 32.33 mm (1.271 to 1.273 in.)
Main Bearing Journal Width No. 3-4-5 . . .30.02 to 30.18 mm (1.182 to 1.188 in.)
Main Bearing Clearance . . . . .0.03 to 0.06 mm (0.001 to 0.0025 in.)
Main Bearing Clearance (Preferred). . . . . .0.051 mm (0.002 in.)
Connecting Rod Journal Diameter. . . . . .53.17 to 53.23 mm (2.0934 to 2.0955 in.)
Connecting Rod Journal Width . . .27.18 to 27.33 mm (1.070 to 1.076 in.)
Out-of-Round (Max. All Journals). . . . . . . .0.013 mm (0.0005 in.)
Taper (Max. – All Journals) . . .0.013 mm (0.0005 in.)

Cylinder Block

Deck Height. . . . . .236.73 mm (9.320 in.)
Deck Clearance . . . . .0.000 mm (0.000 in.)
Cylinder Bore Diameter— Standard .98.45 to 98.48 mm (3.8759 to 3.8775 in.)
Cylinder Bore Diameter— Taper (Max.) . . . . .0.025 mm (0.001 in.)
Cylinder Bore Diameter— Out-of-Round (Max.) . . . . .0.025 mm (0.001 in.)
Tappet Bore Diameter . . . . .23.000 to 23.025 mm (0.9055 to 0.9065 in.)
Flatness. . . .0.03 mm per 25 mm (0.001 in. per 1 in.)
Flatness. . .0.05 mm per 152 mm (0.002 in. per 6 in.)
Flatness Max. . . . . .0.20 mm for total length (0.008 in. for total length)
Main Bearing Bore Diameter . . . . .68.3514 to 68.3768 mm (2.691 to 2.692 in.)

Connecting Rods

Total Weight (Less Bearing) . . . . . .657 to 665 grams (23.17 to 23.45 oz.)
Length (Center-to-Center) . . . . .155.52 to 155.62 mm (6.123 to 6.127 in.)
Piston Pin Bore Diameter . . . . . . .23.59 to 23.62 mm (0.9288 to 0.9298 in.)
Bore (Less Bearings). . . . . .56.08 to 56.09 mm (2.2080 to 2.2085 in.)
Bearing Clearance. . . . . .0.025 to 0.076 mm (0.001 to 0.003 in.)
Bearing Clearance (Preferred). . . .0.044 to 0.050 mm (0.0015 to 0.0020 in.)
Side Clearance . .0.25 to 0.48 mm (0.010 to 0.019 in.)
Twist (Max.) . .0.001 mm per mm (0.001 in. per inch)
Bend Max.) . .0.001 mm per mm (0.001 in. per inch.)

Cylinder Compression Pressure

Ratio. 9.1:1
Pressure Range. . . .827 to 1,034 kPa (120 to 150 psi)
Max. Variation Between Cylinders . .206 kPa (30 psi)

Cylinder Head

Combustion Chamber . . . . .49.9 to 52.9 cc (3.04 to 3.23 cu. in.)
Valve Guide I.D. (Integral) . . . . .7.95 to 7.97 mm (0.313 to 0.314 in.)
Valve Stem-to-Guide Clearance. . .0.025 to 0.076 mm (0.001 to 0.003 in.)
Intake Valve Seat Angle. . . . . .44.5°
Exhaust Valve Seat Angle . . . . .44.5°
Valve Seat Width . . . . .1.01 to 1.52 mm (0.040 to 0.060 in.)
Valve Seat Runout . . . . .0.064 mm (0.0025 in.)
Flatness . . . . .0.03 mm per 25 mm (0.001 in. per 1 in.)
Flatness. . .0.05 mm per 152 mm (0.002 in. per 6 in.)

SPECIFICATIONS (Continued)

Flatness Max. . . . . .0.20 mm for total length (0.008 in. for total length)

Rocker Arms, Push Rods & Tappets

Rocker Arm Ratio 1.6:1
Push Rod Length . . . . .241.300 to 241.808 mm (9.500 to 9.520in.)
Push Rod Diameter. . . . . .7.92 to 8.00 mm (0.312 to 0.315 in.)
Hydraulic Tappet Diameter . . . .22.962 to 22.974 mm (0.904 to 0.9045 in.)
Tappet-to-Bore Clearance . . . . . . .0.025 to 0.063 mm (0.001 to 0.0025 in.)

Valves

Length (Tip-to-Gauge Dimension Line) Intake . . . . .124.435 to 125.070 mm (4.899 to 4.924 in.)
Length (Tip-to-Gauge Dimension Line) Exhaust . . . . .125.120 to 125.755 mm (4.927 to 4.952 in.)
Valve Stem Diameter . . . . .7.899 to 7.925 mm (0.311 to 0.312 in.)
Stem-to-Guide Clearance. . . . . . . .0.025 to 0.076 mm (0.001 to 0.003 in.)
Valve Head Diameter— Intake . . .48.387 to 48.641 mm (1.905 to 1.915 in.)
Valve Head Diameter— Exhaust. . . . . .37.973 to 38.227 mm (1.495 to 1.505 in.)
Valve Face Angle—Intake . . . . .45°
Valve Face Angle—Exhaust. . . . . .45°
Tip Refinishing (Max. Allowable) . . . . .0.25 mm (0.010 in.)

Valve Springs

Free Length (Approx.) . . . . .47.65 mm (1.876 in.)
Spring Tension—Valve Closed . . . . .271 to 307 N @ 41.656 mm (61 to 69 lbf. @ 1.64 in.)
Spring Tension—Valve Open. . . . . .818.5 to 871.9 N @ 30.89 mm (184 to 196 lbf @ 1.216 in.)
Inside Diameter . . . . .21.0 mm to 21.51 mm (0.827 to 0.847 in.)

Pistons

Weight (Less Pin) . . . . .563 to 567 grams (19.86 to 20.00 oz.)
Piston Pin Bore (Centerline to Piston Top). . . . . . .40.61 to 40.72 mm (1.599 to 1.603 in.)
Piston-to-Bore Clearance. . . . . . . .0.033 to 0.053 mm (0.0013 to 0.0021 in.)
Piston-to-Bore Clearance (Preferred). . . . . .0.033 to 0.038 mm (0.0013 to 0.0015 in.)
Ring Gap Clearance—Top Compression Ring . . . .0.229 to 0.610 mm (0.0090 to 0.0240 in.)
Ring Gap Clearance—2nd Compression Ring . . . .0.483 to 0.965 mm (0.0190 to 0.0380 in.)
Ring Gap Clearance—Oil Control Steel Rails . . . . . .0.254 to 1.500 mm (0.010 to 0.060 in.)
Ring Side Clearance—Compression Rings. . . .0.042 to 0.084 mm (0.0017 to 0.0033 in.)
Ring Side Clearance—Oil Control Ring . . . . . .0.06 to 0.21 mm (0.0024 to 0.0083 in.)
Piston Ring Groove Height—Compression Rings . . . .1.530 to 1.555mm (0.0602 to 0.0612 in.)
Piston Ring Groove Height—Oil Control Ring . . . .4.035 to 4.060 mm (0.1589 to 0.1598 in.)
Piston Ring Groove Diameter—Compression Rings. . . . . .87.78 to 87.90 mm (3.456 to 3.461 in.)
Piston Ring Groove Diameter—Oil Control Ring . . . . . .87.50 to 87.75 mm (3.445 to 3.455 in.)
Piston Pin Bore Diameter . . . . .23.647 to 23.655 mm (0.9310 to 0.9313 in.)
Piston Pin Diameter . . . . .23.637 to 23.640 mm (0.9306 to 0.9307 in.)
Piston-to-Pin Clearance . . . . . . .0.0076 to 0.0178 mm (0.0003 to 0.0007 in.)
Piston-to-Pin Clearance (Preferred) . . . . .0.015 mm—Loose (0.0006 in.—Loose)
Piston-to-Pin Connecting Rod (Press Fit). . . . . .8.9 kN (2000 lbf.)

Oil Pump

Gear-to-Body Clearance (Radial). . . .0.051 to 0.102 mm (0.002 to 0.004 in.)
Gear-to-Body Clearance (Radial) (Preferred) . . . . .0.051 mm (0.002 in.)
Gear End Clearance— Plastigage . .0.051 to 0.152 mm (0.002 to 0.006 in.)
Gear End Clearance—Plastigage (Preferred) . . . . .0.051 mm (0.002 in.)
Gear End Clearance—Feeler Gauge . . .0.1016 to 0.2032 mm (0.004 to 0.008 in.)
Gear End Clearance—Feeler Gauge (Preferred) . . . . .0.1778 mm (0.007 in.)

Oil Pressure

Min. Pressure (600 rpm) . . . . .89.6 kPa (13 psi)
At Idle Speed (800 rpm) . . . . .172 to 241 kPa (25 to 35 psi)
At 1600 rpm & Higher . . . . .255 to 517 kPa (37 to 75 psi)
Oil Pressure Relief . . . . .517 kPa (75 psi)

SPECIFICATIONS (Continued)

TORQUE SPECIFICATIONS

DESCRIPTION	TORQUE
A/C Compressor Bracket-to-Engine	
Bolts	34 N·m (25 ft. lbs.)
A/C Compressor	
Mounting Bolts	27 N·m (20 ft. lbs.)
A/C Low Pressure Service Valve	
Nut	38 N·m (28 ft. lbs.)
Block Heater	
Nut	1.8 N·m (16 in. lbs.)
Camshaft Sprocket	
Bolt	108 N·m (80 ft. lbs.)
Connecting Rod	
Nuts	45 N·m (33 ft. lbs.)
Converter Plate	
Bolts	68 N·m +60° (50 ft. lbs. +60°)
Cylinder Block	
Drain Plugs	41 N·m (30 ft. lbs.)
Cylinder Head	
Bolts #1–10 & #12–14	149 N·m (110 ft. lbs.)
Bolt #11	135 N·m (100 ft. lbs.)
Cylinder Head Cover	
Bolts	13 N·m (115 in. lbs.)
Drive Plate-to-Torque Converter	
Bolts	54 N·m (40 ft. lbs.)
Engine Shock Damper	
Stud Nuts	23 N·m (17 ft. lbs.)
Engine Mounts—Front	
Cushion to Block Bracket Nuts	69 N·m (51 ft. lbs.)
Cushion to Frame Bolts	61 N·m (38 ft. lbs.)
Bracket to Engine Block Screw	61 N·m (45 ft. lbs.)
Bracket to Engine Block Nut	61 N·m (45 ft. lbs.)
Bracket to Engine Block Stud	61 N·m (45 ft. lbs.)
Engine Mounts—Rear	
Trans. Cushion to Crossmember Nut	28 N·m (21 ft. lbs.)
Trans. Bracket to Skid Plate Nut	28 N·m (21 ft. lbs.)
Trans. Mount to Trans. Bracket Nut	41 N·m (30 ft. lbs.)
Trans. Bracket to Trans.	54 N·m (40 ft. lbs.)
Exhaust Manifold/Pipe	
Nuts	27 N·m (20 ft. lbs.)
Flywheel/Converter Housing	
Bolts	38 N·m (28 ft. lbs.)
Flywheel/Crankshaft	
Bolts	143 N·m (105 ft. lbs.)
Front Cover-to-Block	
Bolts 1/4–20	7N·m (60 in. lbs.)
Bolts 5/16–18	22N·m (192 in. lbs.)
Fuel Pump	
Bolts	22 N·m (16 ft. lbs.)
Generator	
Adjusting Bolt	24 N·m (18 ft. lbs.)
Pivot Bolt/Nut	38 N·m (28 ft. lbs.)
Mounting Bracket-to–Engine Bolts	38 N·m (28 ft. lbs.)
Mounting/Head Bolts	45 N·m (33 ft. lbs.)
Main Bearing	
Bolts	108 N·m (80 ft. lbs.)
Oil Filter	
Filter	18 N·m (13 ft. lbs.)
Oil Filter	
Connector	54 N·m (40 ft. lbs.)
Oil Galley	
Plug	41 N·m (30 ft. lbs.)
Oil Pan	
1/4–20 Bolts	9.5 N·m (84 in. lbs.)
5/16–18 Bolts	15 N·m (132 in. lbs.)
Drain Plug	34 N·m (25 ft. lbs.)
Oil Pump	
Short Attaching Bolts	23 N·m (17 ft. lbs.)
Long Attaching Bolts	23 N·m (17 ft. lbs.)
Cover Bolts	8 N·m (70 in. lbs.)
Power Steering Pump Pressure Hose	
Nut	52 N·m (38 ft. lbs.)
Rocker Arm Assembly-to-Cylinder Head	
Capscrews	28 N·m (21ft. lbs.)
Spark Plugs	
Plugs	37 N·m (27 ft. lbs.)
Starting Motor	
Mounting Bolts	45 N·m (33 ft. lbs.)
Thermostat Housing	
Bolts	18 N·m (13 ft. lbs.)
Vibration Damper	
Bolts	108 N·m (80 ft. lbs.)
Water Pump/Block	
Bolts	31 N·m (270 in. lbs.)

1997 Wrangler
Publication No. 81-370-7148
TSB 26-10-96 Oct. 1996

4.0L ENGINE

INDEX

DESCRIPTION AND OPERATION

ENGINE DESCRIPTION

The 4.0 Liter (242 CID) six-cylinder engine is an In-line, lightweight, overhead valve engine.

Engine Type . . . . In-line 6 Cylinder
Bore and Stroke . . 98.4 x 86.69 mm (3.88 x 3.413 in.)
Displacement . . . . 4.0 (242 cu. in.)
Compression Ratio 8.8:1
Torque . . . . 301 N·m (222 ft. lbs.) @ 2800 rpm
Firing Order 1–5–3–6–2–4
Lubrication . . . . . Pressure Feed–Full Flow Filtration
**Engine Oil Capacity . . . . 5.7L (6 Quarts) **
Cooling System . . . Liquid Cooled–Forced Circulation
Cooling System Capacity . . . . 9.9L (10.5 Quarts)
Cylinder Block . . . . Cast Iron
Crankshaft . . . . Cast Nodular Iron
Cylinder Head . . . . Cast Iron
Camshaft . . . . Cast Iron
Pistons . . . . Aluminum Alloy (with Struts)
Pistons Combustion Cavity . . . . Double Quench
Connecting Rods . . . . Cast Iron

This engine is designed for unleaded fuel.

The engine cylinder head has dual quench-type combustion chambers that create turbulence and fast burning of the air/fuel mixture. This results in good fuel economy.

The cylinders are numbered 1 through 6 from front to rear. The firing order is 1-5-3-6-2-4 (Fig. 1).

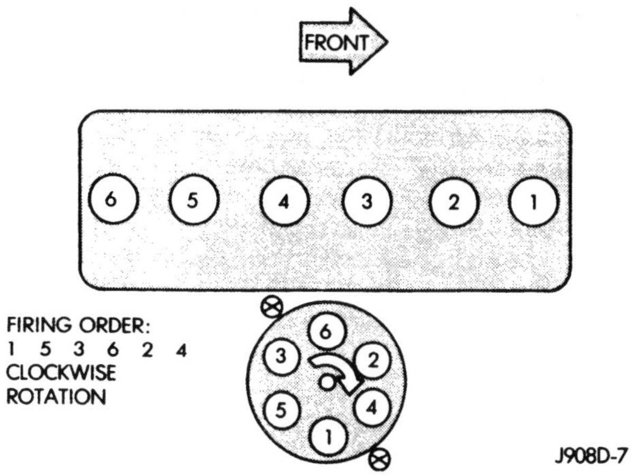

Fig. 1 Engine Firing Order

DESCRIPTION AND OPERATION (Continued)

The crankshaft rotation is clockwise, when viewed from the front of the engine. The crankshaft rotates within seven main bearings. The camshaft rotates within four bearings.

BUILD DATE CODE

The engine Build Date Code is located on a machined surface on the right side of the cylinder block between the No.2 and No.3 cylinders (Fig. 2).

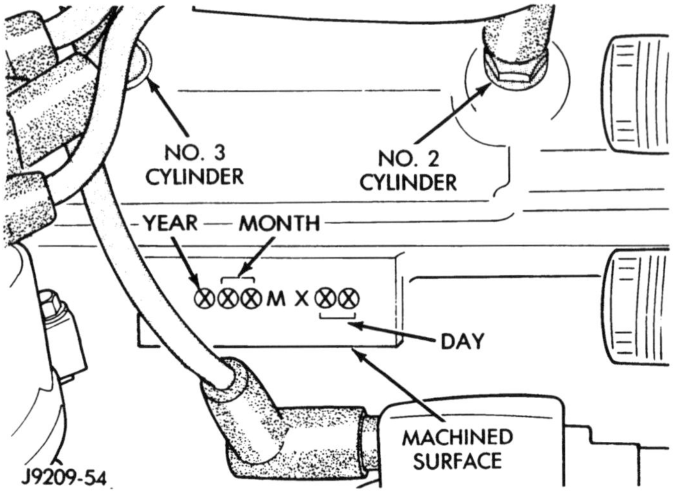

Fig. 2 Build Date Code Location

The digits of the code identify:

- 1st Digit—The year (6 = 1996).
- 2nd & 3rd Digits—The month (01 - 12).
- 4th & 5th Digits—The engine type/fuel system/ compression ratio (MX = A 4.0 Liter (242 CID) 8.8:1 compression ratio engine with a multi-point fuel injection system).
- 6th & 7th Digits—The day of engine build (01 - 31).

(1) **FOR EXAMPLE:** Code * 601MX12 * identifies a 4.0 Liter (242 CID) engine with a multi-point fuel injection system, 8.8:1 compression ratio and built on January 12, 1996.

LUBRICATION SYSTEM

A gear—type positive displacement pump is mounted at the underside of the block opposite the No. 4 main bearing. The pump draws oil through the screen and inlet tube from the sump at the rear of the oil pan. The oil is driven between the drive and idler gears and pump body, then forced through the outlet to the block. An oil gallery in the block channels the oil to the inlet side of the full flow oil filter. After passing through the filter element, the oil passes from the center outlet of the filter through an oil gallery that channels the oil up to the main gallery which extends the entire length of the block.

Galleries extend downward from the main oil gallery to the upper shell of each main bearing. The crankshaft is drilled internally to pass oil from the main bearing journals (except number 4 main bearing journal) to the connecting rod journals. Each connecting rod bearing cap has a small squirt hole, oil passes through the squirt hole and is thrown off as the rod rotates. This oil throwoff lubricates the camshaft lobes, distributor drive gear, cylinder walls, and piston pins.

The hydraulic valve tappets receive oil directly from the main oil gallery. Oil is provided to the camshaft bearing through galleries. The front camshaft bearing journal passes oil through the camshaft sprocket to the timing chain. Oil drains back to the oil pan under the number one main bearing cap.

The oil supply for the rocker arms and bridged pivot assemblies is provided by the hydraulic valve tappets which pass oil through hollow push rods to a hole in the corresponding rocker arm. Oil from the rocker arm lubricates the valve train components, then passes down through the push rod guide holes in the cylinder head past the valve tappet area, and returns to the oil pan.

OIL PUMP PRESSURE

The MINIMUM oil pump pressure is 89.6 kPa (13 psi) at 600 rpm. The MAXIMUM oil pump pressure is 255-517 kPa (37-75 psi) at 1600 rpm or more.

OVERSIZE AND UNDERSIZE COMPONENT CODES

Some engines may be built with oversize or undersize components such as:

- Oversize cylinder bores.
- Oversize camshaft bearing bores.
- Undersize crankshaft main bearing journals.
- Undersize connecting rod journals.

These engines are identified by a letter code (Fig. 3) stamped on a boss between the ignition coil and the distributor (Fig. 4).

SERVICE PROCEDURES

VALVE TIMING

Disconnect the spark plug wires and remove the spark plugs.

Remove the engine cylinder head cover.

Remove the capscrews, bridge and pivot assembly, and rocker arms from above the No.1 cylinder.

Alternately loosen each capscrew, one turn at a time, to avoid damaging the bridge.

Rotate the crankshaft until the No.6 piston is at top dead center (TDC) on the compression stroke.

Rotate the crankshaft counterclockwise (viewed from the front of the engine) 90°.

Install a dial indicator on the end of the No.1 cylinder intake valve push rod. Use rubber tubing to secure the indicator stem on the push rod.

Set the dial indicator pointer at zero.

SERVICE PROCEDURES (Continued)

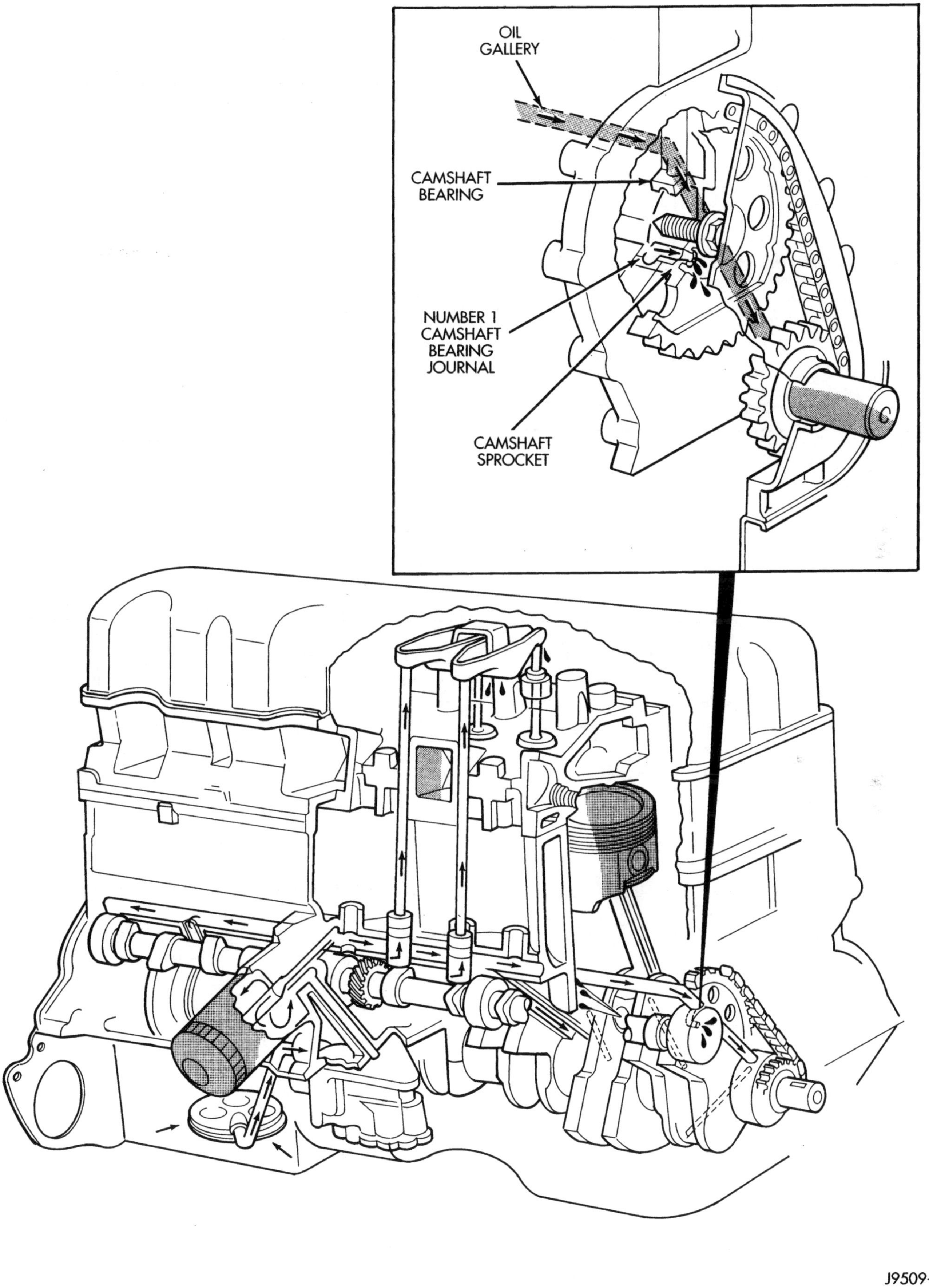

Oil Lubrication System

SERVICE PROCEDURES (Continued)

CODE	COMPONENT	UNDERSIZE
P	One or more connecting rod bearing journals	0.254 mm (0.010 in)
M	All crankshaft main bearing journals	0.254 mm (0.010 in)
PM	All crankshaft main bearing journals and one or more connecting rod journals	0.254 mm (0.010 in)
CODE	**COMPONENT**	**OVERSIZE**
B	All cylinder bores	0.254 mm (0.010 in)
C	All camshaft bearing bores	0.254 mm (0.010 in)

J8909-54

Fig. 3 Oversize and Undersize Component Codes

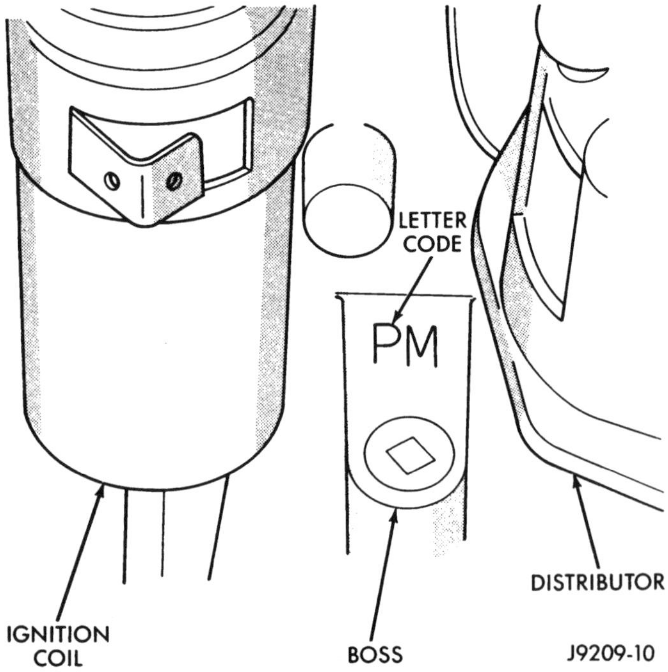

Fig. 4 Oversize and Undersize Component Code Location

Rotate the crankshaft clockwise (viewed from the front of the engine) until the dial indicator pointer indicates 0.305 mm (0.012 inch) travel distance (lift).

The timing notch index on the vibration damper should be aligned with the TDC mark on the timing degree scale.

If the timing notch is more than 13 mm (1/2 inch) away from the TDC mark in either direction, the valve timing is incorrect.

If the valve timing is incorrect, the cause may be a broken camshaft pin. It is not necessary to replace the camshaft because of pin failure. A spring pin is available for service replacement.

PISTON FITTING

BORE GAGE METHOD

(1) To correctly select the proper size piston, a cylinder bore gauge, capable of reading in 0.003 mm (.0001 in.) INCREMENTS is required. If a bore gauge is not available, do not use an inside micrometer.

(2) Measure the inside diameter of the cylinder bore at a point 49.5 mm (1-15/16 inches) below top of bore. Start perpendicular (across or at 90 degrees) to the axis of the crankshaft at point A and then take an additional bore reading 90 degrees to that at point B (Fig. 5).

(3) The coated pistons will be serviced with the piston pin and connecting rod pre-assembled. **The coated piston connecting rod assembly can be used to service previous built engines and MUST be replaced as complete sets.** Tin coated pistons should not be used as replacements for coated pistons.

(4) The coating material is applied to the piston after the final piston machining process. Measuring the outside diameter of a coated piston will not provide accurate results. Therefore measuring the inside diameter of the cylinder bore with a dial Bore Gauge is **MANDATORY.**. To correctly select the proper size piston, a cylinder bore gauge capable of reading in 0.003 mm (.0001 in.) increments is required.

(5) Piston installation into the cylinder bore requires slightly more pressure than that required for non-coated pistons. The bonded coating on the piston will give the appearance of a line-to-line fit with the cylinder bore.

PISTON SIZE CHART

CYLINDER BORE SIZE	PISTON LETTER SIZE
98.438 to 98.448 mm (3.8755 to 3.8759 in.)	A
98.448 to 98.458 mm (3.8759 to 3.8763 in.)	B
98.458 to 98.468 mm (3.8763 to 3.8767 in.)	C
98.468 to 98.478 mm (3.8767 to 3.8771 in.)	D
98.478 to 98.488 mm (3.8771 to 3.8775 in.)	E
98.488 to 98.498 mm (3.8775 to 3.8779 in.)	F

SERVICE PROCEDURES (Continued)

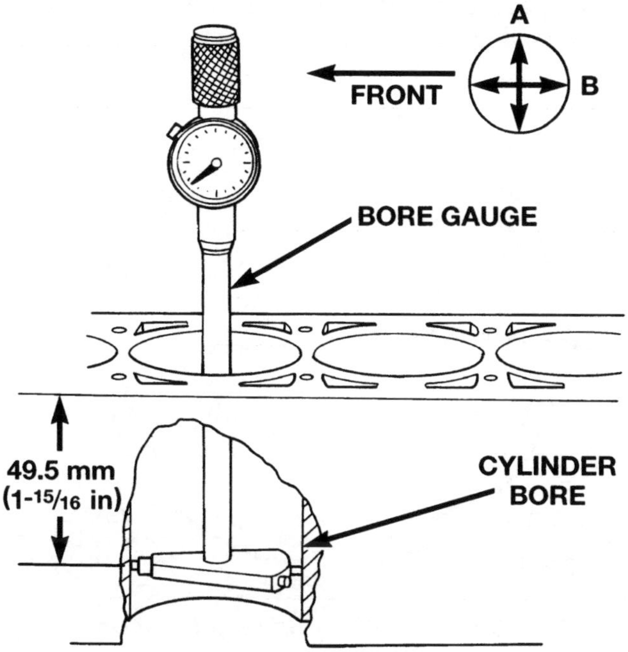

Fig. 5 Bore Gauge

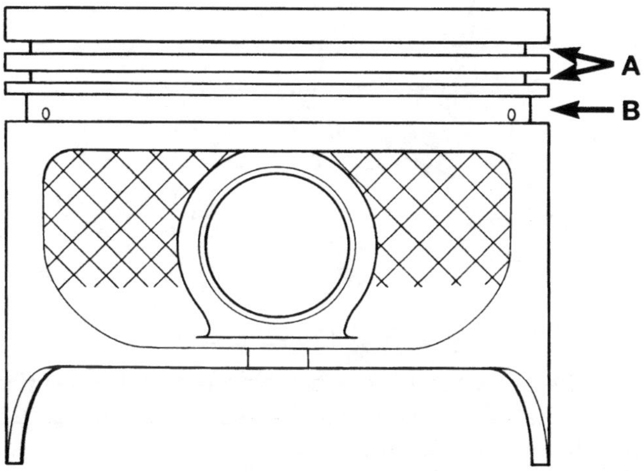

Fig. 6 Piston Dimensions

PISTON RING FITTING

(1) Carefully clean the carbon from all ring grooves. Oil drain openings in the oil ring groove and pin boss must be clear. DO NOT remove metal from the grooves or lands. This will change ring-to-groove clearances and will damage the ring-to-land seating.

(2) Be sure the piston ring grooves are free of nicks and burrs.

(3) Measure the ring side clearance with a feeler gauge fitted snugly between the ring land and ring (Fig. 6) (Fig. 7). Rotate the ring in the groove. It must move freely around circumference of the groove.

Ring Side Clearance Measurement

Top Compression Ring . . . . .0.042to 0.084 mm (0.0017 to 0.0033 in.)
Second Compression Ring. . . . . . . .0.042to 0.084 mm (0.0017 to 0.0033 in.)
Oil Control Ring . . . . .0.06 to 0.21 mm (0.0024 to 0.0083 in.)

(4) Place ring in the cylinder bore and push down with inverted piston to position near lower end of the ring travel. Measure ring gap with a feeler gauge fitting snugly between ring ends (Fig. 8).

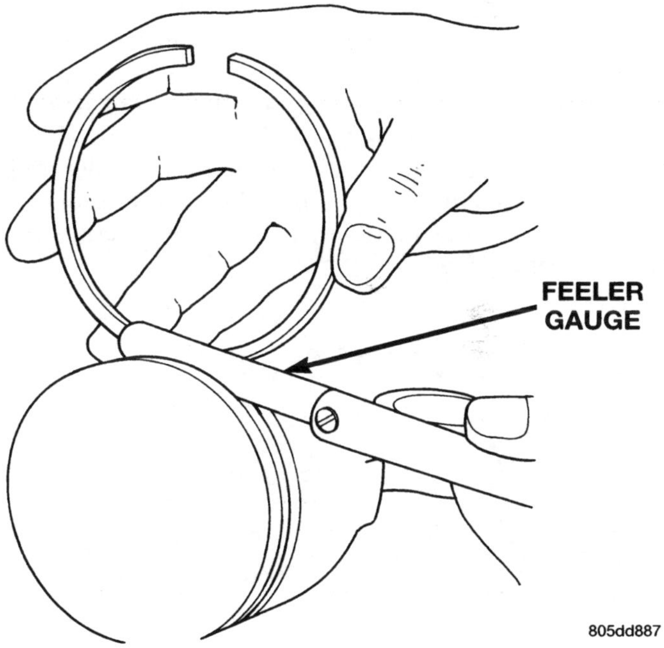

Fig. 7 Ring Side Clearance Measurement

Ring Gap Measurement

Top Compression Ring . . . . 0.229 to 0.610 mm (0.0090 to 0.0240 inch)
Second Compresion Ring. . . . . . . .0.483 to 0.965 mm (0.0190 to 0.0380 inch)
Oil Control Ring . . . . .0.254 to 1.500 mm (0.010 to 0.060 inch)

SERVICE PROCEDURES (Continued)

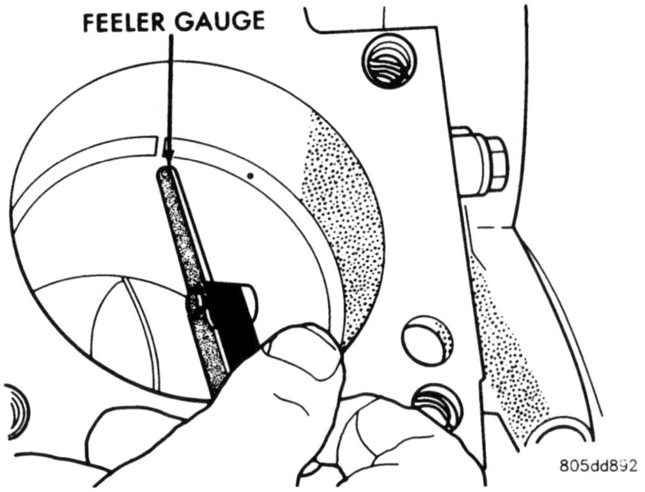

Fig. 8 Gap Measurement

(5) The oil control rings are symmetrical, no top or bottom, install anyside up. It is not necessary to use a tool to install the upper and lower rails. Insert oil rail spacer first, then side rails.

(6) The two compression rings are different and cannot be interchanged. The TOP compression ring can be identified by the shiny coating on the outer sealing surface. This ring is symmetrical, no top or bottom, install anyside up.

(7) The second compression ring has a dot or drill mark denoting the topside of ring. There is also a slight chamfer on the inside bottom edge, therefore dot mark up chamfer face down, for installationon.

(8) Using a ring installer, install the second compression ring. (Fig. 9).

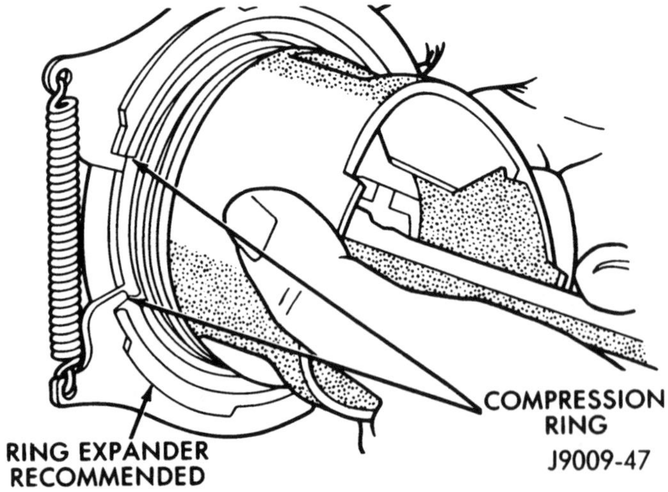

Fig. 9 Compression Ring Installation

(9) The top compression ring has a shiny coating on the outer sealing surface.

(10) Using a ring installer, install the top ring. (Fig. 9).

(11) Position top and second ring 180° apart. Split the oil rings 60° to 90° apart and away from the second ring gap. (Fig. 10) Example: Top oil ring at 12:00, expander at 3:00 or 9:00, bottom oil ring at 6:00.

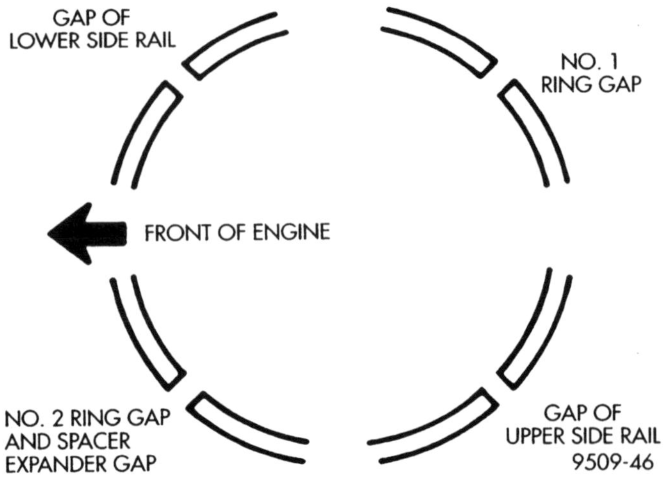

Fig. 10 Piston Ring End Gap Position

FITTING CONNECTING ROD BEARINGS

INSPECTION

BEARINGS

Inspect the connecting rod bearings for scoring and bent alignment tabs (Fig. 11) (Fig. 12). Check the bearings for normal wear patterns, scoring, grooving, fatigue and pitting (Fig. 13). Replace any bearing that shows abnormal wear.

Inspect the connecting rod journals for signs of scoring, nicks and burrs.

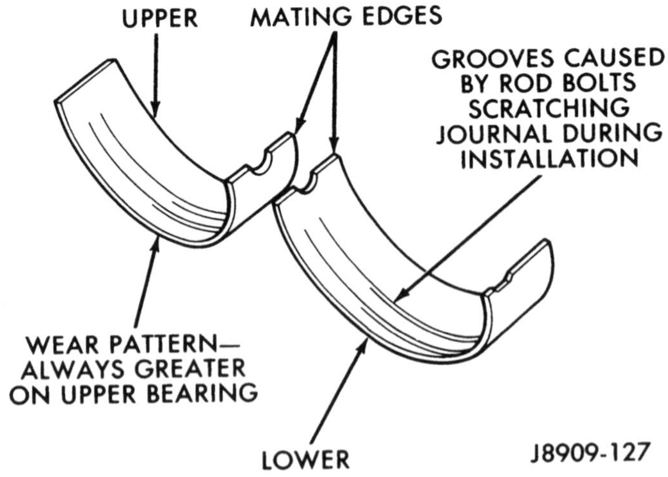

Fig. 11 Connecting Rod Bearing Inspection

CONNECTING RODS

Misaligned or bent connecting rods can cause abnormal wear on pistons, piston rings, cylinder walls, connecting rod bearings and crankshaft connecting rod journals. If wear patterns or damage to any of these components indicate the probability of a

SERVICE PROCEDURES (Continued)

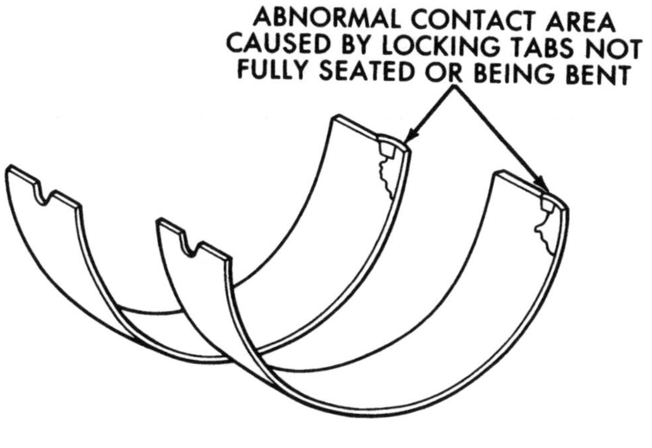

Fig. 12 Locking Tab Inspection

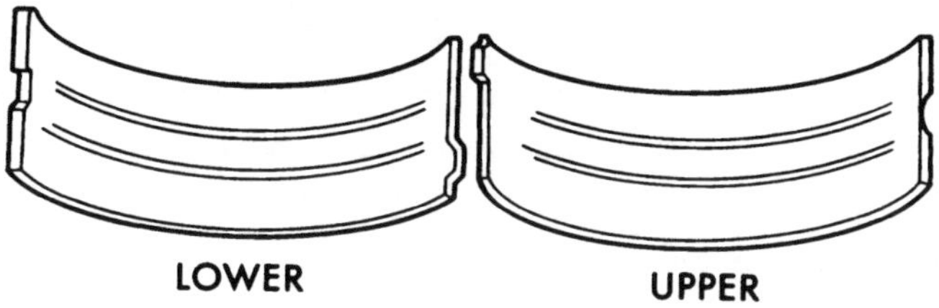

Fig. 13 Scoring Caused by Insufficient Lubrication or by Damaged Crankshaft Pin Journal

misaligned connecting rod, inspect it for correct rod alignment. Replace misaligned, bent or twisted connecting rods.

BEARING-TO-JOURNAL CLEARANCE

(1) Wipe the oil from the connecting rod journal.

(2) Use short rubber hose sections over rod bolts during installation.

(3) Lubricate the upper bearing insert and install in connecting rod.

(4) Use piston ring compressor to install the rod and piston assemblies. The oil squirt holes in the rods must face the camshaft. The arrow on the piston crown should point to the front of the engine (Fig. 14). Verify that the oil squirt holes in the rods face the camshaft and that the arrows on the pistons face the front of the engine.

(5) Install the lower bearing insert in the bearing cap. The lower insert must be dry. Place strip of Plastigage across full width of the lower insert at the center of bearing cap. Plastigage must not crumble in use. If brittle, obtain fresh stock.

(6) Install bearing cap and connecting rod on the journal and tighten nuts to 45 N·m (33 ft. lbs.) torque. DO NOT rotate crankshaft. Plastigage will smear, resulting in inaccurate indication.

(7) Remove the bearing cap and determine amount of bearing-to- journal clearance by measuring the width of

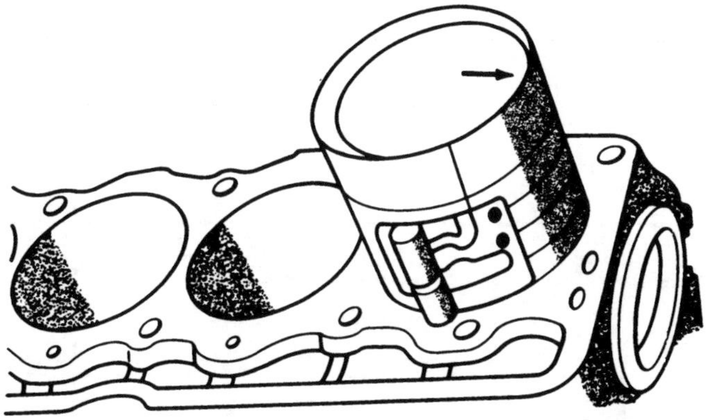

Fig. 14 Rod and Piston Assembly Installation

compressed Plastigage (Fig. 15). Refer to Engine Specifications for the proper clearance. **Plastigage should indicate the same clearance across the entire width of the insert. If the clearance varies, it may be caused by either a tapered journal, bent connecting rod or foreign material trapped between the insert and cap or rod.**

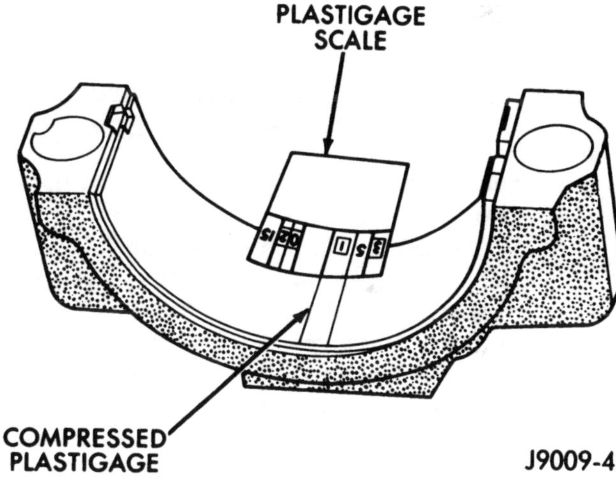

Fig. 15 Measuring Bearing Clearance with Plastigage

(8) If the correct clearance is indicated, replacement of the bearing inserts is not necessary. Remove the Plastigage from crankshaft journal and bearing insert. Proceed with installation.

(9) If bearing-to-journal clearance exceeds the specification, install a pair of 0.0254 mm (0.001 inch) undersize bearing inserts. All the odd size inserts must be on the bottom. The sizes of the service replacement bearing inserts are stamped on the backs of the inserts. Measure the clearance as described in the previous steps.

(10) The clearance is measured with a pair of 0.0254 mm (0.001 inch) undersize bearing inserts installed. This will determine if two 0.0254 mm (0.001 inch) undersize inserts or another combination

SERVICE PROCEDURES (Continued)

Crankshaft Journal		Corresponding Connecting Rod Bearing Insert	
Color Code	Diameter	Upper Insert Size	Lower Insert Size
Yellow	53.2257-53.2079 mm (2.0955-2.0948 in.)	Yellow - Standard	Yellow - Standard
Orange	53.2079-53.1901 mm (2.0948-2.0941 in.) 0.0178 mm (0.0007 in.) Undersize	Yellow - Standard	Blue - Undersize 0.025 mm (0.001 in.)
Blue	53.1901-53.1724 mm (2.0941-2.0934 in.) 0.0356 mm (0.0014 in.) Undersize	Blue - Undersize 0.025 mm (0.001 in.)	Blue - Undersize 0.025 mm (0.001 in.)
Red	52.9717-52.9539 mm (2.0855-2.0848 in.) 0.254 mm (0.010 in.) Undersize	Red - Undersize 0.254 mm (0.010 in.)	Red - Undersize 0.254 mm (0.010 in.)

J9409-24

CONNECTING ROD BEARING FITTING CHART

is needed to provide the correct clearance (refer to Connecting Rod Bearing Fitting Chart).

(11) **FOR EXAMPLE:** If the initial clearance was 0.0762 mm (0.003 inch), 0.025 mm (0.001 inch) undersize inserts would reduce the clearance by 0.025 mm (0.001 inch). The clearance would be 0.002 inch and within specification. A 0.051 mm (0.002 inch) undersize insert would reduce the initial clearance an additional 0.013 mm (0.0005 inch). The clearance would then be 0.038 mm (0.0015 inch).

(12) Repeat the Plastigage measurement to verify your bearing selection prior to final assembly.

(13) Once you have selected the proper insert, install the insert and cap. Tighten the connecting rod bolts to 45 N·m (33 ft. lbs.) torque.

SIDE CLEARANCE MEASUREMENT

Slide snug-fitting feeler gauge between the connecting rod and crankshaft journal flange. Refer to Engine Specifications for the proper clearance. Replace the connecting rod if the side clearance is not within specification.

FITTING CRANKSHAFT MAIN BEARINGS

INSPECTION

Wipe the inserts clean and inspect for abnormal wear patterns and for metal or other foreign material imbedded in the lining. Normal main bearing insert wear patterns are illustrated (Fig. 16).

NOTE: If any of the crankshaft journals are scored, remove the engine for crankshaft repair.

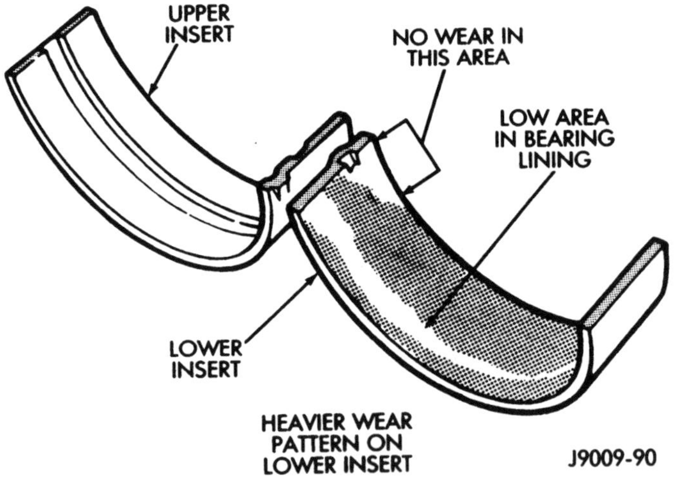

Fig. 16 Main Bearing Wear Patterns

Inspect the back of the inserts for fractures, scrapings or irregular wear patterns.

Inspect the upper insert locking tabs for damage.

Replace all damaged or worn bearing inserts.

FITTING BEARINGS (CRANKSHAFT INSTALLED)

The main bearing caps, numbered (front to rear) from 1 through 7 have an arrow to indicate the forward position. The upper main bearing inserts are grooved to provide oil channels while the lower inserts are smooth.

Each bearing insert pair is selectively fitted to its respective journal to obtain the specified operating clearance. In production, the select fit is obtained by

SERVICE PROCEDURES (Continued)

using various-sized color-coded bearing insert pairs as listed in the Main Bearing Fitting Chart. The bearing color code appears on the edge of the insert. **The size is not stamped on bearing inserts used for engine production.**

The main bearing journal size (diameter) is identified by a color-coded paint mark on the adjacent cheek. The rear main journal, is identified by a color-coded paint mark on the crankshaft rear flange.

When required, upper and lower bearing inserts of different sizes may be used as a pair. A standard size insert is sometimes used in combination with a 0.025 mm (0.001 inch) undersize insert to reduce the clearance by 0.013 mm (0.0005 inch). **Never use a pair of bearing inserts with greater than a 0.025 mm (0.001 inch) difference in size (Fig. 17).**

Insert	Correct	Incorrect
Upper	Standard	Standard
Lower	0.025 mm (0.001 in.) Undersize	0.051 mm (0.002 in.) Undersize

J9109-179

Fig. 17 Bearing Insert Pairs

NOTE: When replacing inserts, the odd size inserts must be either all on the top (in cylinder block) or all on the bottom (in main bearing cap).

Once the bearings have been properly fitted, proceed to Crankshaft Main Bearing—Installation.

BEARING-TO-JOURNAL CLEARANCE (CRANKSHAFT INSTALLED)

When using Plastigage, check only one bearing clearance at a time.

Install the grooved main bearings into the cylinder block and the non-grooved bearings into the bearing caps.

Install the crankshaft into the upper bearings dry.

Place a strip of Plastigage across full width of the crankshaft journal to be checked.

Install the bearing cap and tighten the bolts to 108 N·m (80 ft. lbs.) torque.

NOTE: DO NOT rotate the crankshaft. This will cause the Plastigage to shift, resulting in an inaccurate reading. Plastigage must not be permitted to crumble. If brittle, obtain fresh stock.

Remove the bearing cap. Determine the amount of clearance by measuring the width of the compressed Plastigage with the scale on the Plastigage envelope (Fig. 18). Refer to Engine Specifications for the proper clearance.

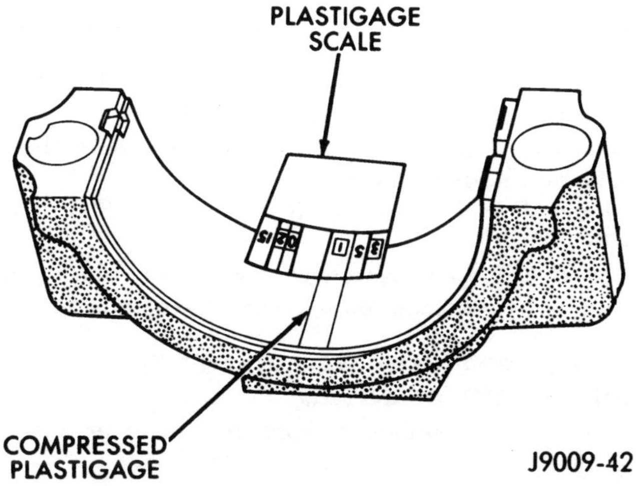

Fig. 18 Measuring Bearing Clearance with Plastigage

Plastigage should indicate the same clearance across the entire width of the insert. If clearance varies, it may indicate a tapered journal or foreign material trapped behind the insert.

If the specified clearance is indicated and there are no abnormal wear patterns, replacement of the bearing inserts is not necessary. Remove the Plastigage from the crankshaft journal and bearing insert. Proceed to Crankshaft Main Bearing—Installation.

If the clearance exceeds specification, install a pair of 0.025 mm (0.001 inch) undersize bearing inserts and measure the clearance as described in the previous steps.

The clearance indicate with the 0.025 mm (0.001 inch) undersize insert pair installed will determine if this insert size or some other combination will provide the specified clearance. **FOR EXAMPLE:** If the clearance was 0q762 mm (0.003 inch) originally, a pair of 0.0254 mm (0.001 inch) undersize inserts would reduce the clearance by 0.0254 mm (0.001 inch). The clearance would then be 0.0508 mm (0.002 inch) and within the specification. A 0.051 mm (0.002 inch) undersize bearing insert and a 0.0254 mm (0.001 inch) undersize insert would reduce the original clearance an additional 0.0127 mm (0.0005 inch). The clearance would then be 0.0381 mm (0.0015 inch).

CAUTION: Never use a pair of inserts that differ more than one bearing size as a pair.

FOR EXAMPLE: DO NOT use a standard size upper insert and a 0.051 mm (0.002 inch) undersize lower insert.

If the clearance exceeds specification using a pair of 0.051 mm (0.002 inch) undersize bearing inserts,

SERVICE PROCEDURES (Continued)

measure crankshaft journal diameter with a micrometer. If the journal diameter is correct, the crankshaft bore in the cylinder block may be misaligned, which requires cylinder block replacement or machining to true bore.

Replace the crankshaft or grind to accept the appropriate undersize bearing inserts if:

- Journal diameters 1 through 6 are less than 63.4517 mm (2.4981 inches)
- Journal 7 diameter is less than 63.4365 mm (2.4975 inches).

Once the proper clearances have been obtained, proceed to Crankshaft Main Bearing—Installation.

MAIN BEARING JOURNAL DIAMETER (CRANKSHAFT REMOVED)

Remove the crankshaft from the cylinder block (refer to Cylinder Block - Disassemble).

Clean the oil off the main bearing journal.

Determine the maximum diameter of the journal with a micrometer. Measure at two locations 90° apart at each end of the journal.

The maximum allowable taper and out of round is 0.013 mm (0.0005 inch). Compare the measured diameter with the journal diameter specification (Main Bearing Fitting Chart). Select inserts required to obtain the specified bearing-to-journal clearance.

Install the crankshaft into the cylinder block (refer to Cylinder Block - Assemble and Crankshaft Main Bearings - Installation).

MAIN BEARING FITTING CHART

CRANKSHAFT JOURNALS #1 - #6		CORRESPONDING CRANKSHAFT BEARING INSERT	
Color Code	Diameter	Upper Insert Size	Lower Insert Size
Yellow	63.5025 - 63.4898 mm (2.5001 - 2.4996 in.)	Yellow - Standard	Yellow - Standard
Orange	63.4898 - 63.4771mm (2.4996 - 2.4991 in.) 0.0127 mm (0.0005 in.) Undersize	Yellow - Undersize 0.025 mm (0.001 in.)	Blue - Standard
Blue	63.4771 - 63.4644 mm (2.4991 - 2.4986 in.) 0.0254 mm (0.001 in.) Undersize	Blue- Undersize 0.025 mm (0.001 in.)	Blue- Undersize 0.025 mm (0.001 in.)
Green	63.4644 - 63.4517 mm (2.4986 - 2.4981 in.) 0.0381 mm (0.0015 in.) Undersize	Blue - Undersize 0.025 mm (0.001 in.)	Green - Undersize 0.051 mm (0.002 in.)
Red	63.2485 - 63.2358 mm (2.4901 - 2.4896 in.) 0.254 mm (0.010 in.) Undersize	Red - Undersize 0.254 mm (0.010 in.)	Red - Undersize 0.254 mm (0.010 in.)
CRANKSHAFT JOURNAL #7 ONLY		**CORRESPONDING CRANKSHAFT BEARING INSERT**	
Color Code	Diameter	Upper Insert Size	Lower Insert Size
Yellow	63.4873 - 63.4746 mm (2.4995 - 2.4990 in.)	Yellow - Standard	Yellow - Standard
Orange	63.4746 - 63.4619 mm (2.4990 - 2.4985 in.) 0.0127 mm (0.0005 in. Undersize	Yellow - Undersize 0.025 mm (0.001 in.)	Blue - Standard
Blue	63.4619 - 63.4492 mm (2.4985 - 2.4980 in.) 0.0254 mm (0.001 in.) Undersize	Blue- Undersize 0.025 mm (0.001 in.)	Blue- Undersize 0.025 mm (0.001 in.)
Green	63.4492 - 63.4365 mm (2.4980- 2.4975 in.) 0.0381 mm (0.0015 in.) Undersize	Blue - Undersize 0.025 mm (0.001 in.)	Green - Undersize 0.051 mm (0.002 in.)
Red	63.2333 - 63.2206 mm (2.4895 - 2.4890 in.) 0.254 mm (0.010 in.) Undersize	Red - Undersize 0.254 mm (0.010 in.)	Red - Undersize 0.254 mm (0.010 in.)

REMOVAL AND INSTALLATION

ENGINE MOUNTS—FRONT

The front mounts support the engine at each side. These supports are made of resilient rubber.

REMOVAL

(1) Disconnect negative cable from battery.
(2) Raise the vehicle.
(3) Support the engine.
(4) Remove the nut from the through bolt (Fig. 19) (Fig. 20). DO NOT remove the through bolt.

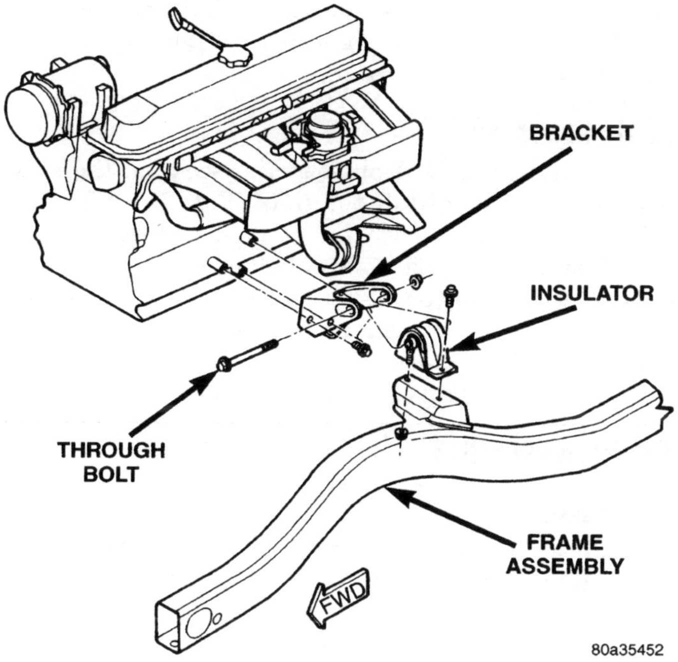

Fig. 19 Left Front Engine Mount

(5) Remove the retaining bolts and nuts from the insulator.
(6) Remove the through bolt.
(7) Remove the insulator.

INSTALLATION

(1) If the engine support bracket was removed, position the bracket onto the block and install the attaching bolts (Fig. 19) (Fig. 20). Tighten the bolts to 62 N·m (46 ft. lbs.) torque.
(2) Place the insulator on the support bracket. Install the insulator retaining bolts and nuts. Tighten the bolts and nuts to 52 N·m (38 ft. lbs) torque.
(3) Install the through bolt and the retaining nut. Tighten the through bolt nut to 69 N·m (51 ft. lbs.) torque.
(4) Remove the engine support.
(5) Lower the vehicle.
(6) Connect negative cable to battery.

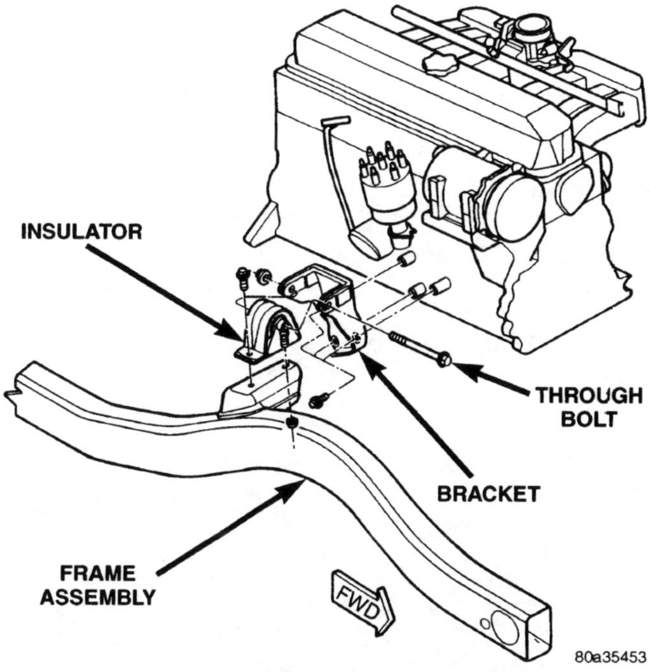

Fig. 20 Right Front Engine Mount

ENGINE MOUNT—REAR

A resilient rubber cushion supports the transmission at the rear between the transmission extension housing and the rear support crossmember or skid plate.

REMOVAL

ALL TRANSMISSIONS

(1) Disconnect negative cable from battery.
(2) Raise the vehicle and support the transmission.
(3) Remove the nuts holding the support cushion to the skid plate (Fig. 21) (Fig. 21).
(4) Remove the skid plate bolts and the skid plate.

MANUAL TRANSMISSIONS

(1) Remove nuts holding support cushion to transmission support bracket.
(2) Remove the support cushion.
(3) Remove bolts holding transmission support bracket to transmission.
(4) Remove the transmission support bracket.

AUTOMATIC TRANSMISSIONS

(1) Remove nuts holding support cushion to transmission support bracket (Fig. 21). Remove the support cushion.
(2) Remove the bolts holding the transmission support bracket to transmission.
(3) Remove the transmission support bracket.

REMOVAL AND INSTALLATION (Continued)

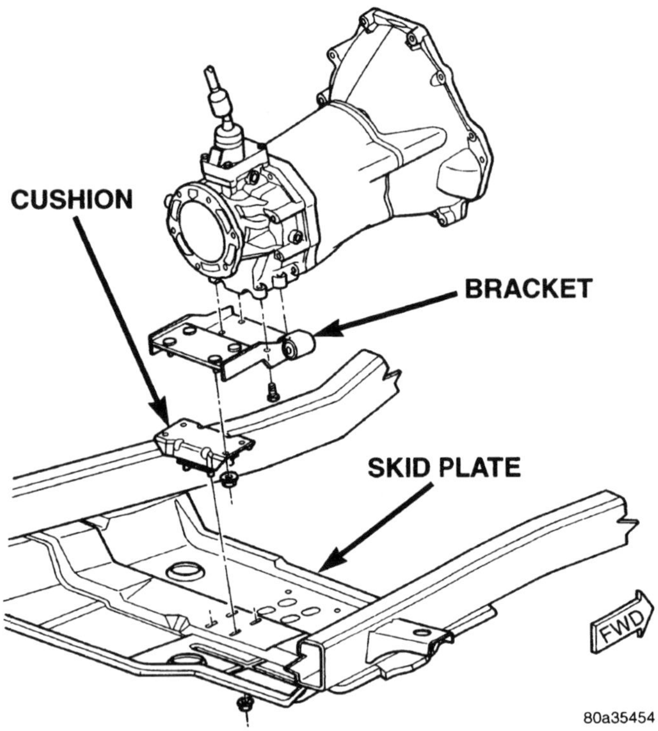

Fig. 21 Rear Mount (Manual Transmission)

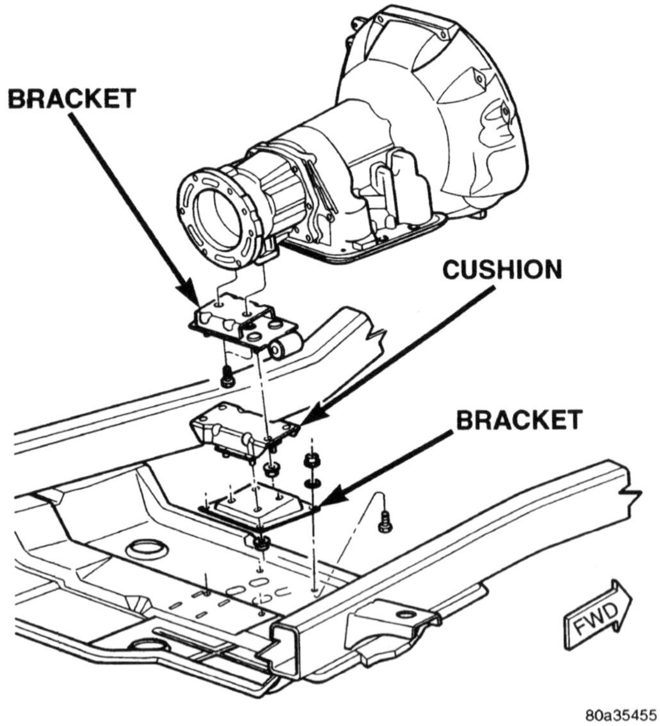

Fig. 22 Rear Mount (AutomaticTransmission)

INSTALLATION

MANUAL TRANSMISSION:

(1) Position the transmission mount bracket to the transmission and install the bolts (Fig. 21).

(2) Tighten the bolts to 54 N·m (40 ft. lbs.) torque.

(3) Position the support cushion to the transmission mount bracket and install nuts (Fig. 21).

(4) Tighten the nuts to 41 N·m (30 ft. lbs.) torque.

AUTOMATIC TRANSMISSION:

(1) Position the transmission mount bracket to the transmission and install the bolts. Tighten the bolts to 54 N·m (40 ft. lbs.) torque.

(2) Position the support cushion to the transmission mount bracket and install nuts. Tighten the nuts to 41 N·m (30 ft. lbs.) torque (Fig. 21).

(3) If the support cushion bracket was removed from the skid plate, position the bracket on the skid plate and install the nuts and bolts. Tighten the nuts to 28 N·m (21 ft. lbs.) torque.

ALL TRANSMISSIONS

(1) Position the skid plate to the studs of the support cushion and install the nuts (Fig. 21) (Fig. 21). Tighten the nuts to 28 N·m (21 ft. lbs.) torque.

(2) Install the skid plate bolts to the sill and tighten to 75 N·m (55 ft. lbs.) torque.

(3) Remove the transmission support.

(4) Lower the vehicle.

(5) Connect negative cable to battery.

ENGINE ASSEMBLY

REMOVAL

(1) Place a protective cloth over the windshield frame. Raise the hood and rest it on the windshield frame.

(2) Disconnect the battery cables. Remove the battery.

WARNING: THE COOLANT IN A RECENTLY OPERATED ENGINE IS HOT AND PRESSURIZED. USE CARE TO PREVENT SCALDING BY HOT COOLANT. CAREFULLY RELEASE THE PRESSURE BEFORE REMOVING THE RADIATOR DRAIN COCK AND CAP.

(3) Remove the radiator drain cock and radiator cap to drain the coolant. DO NOT waste reusable coolant. If the solution is clean, drain the coolant into a clean container for reuse.

(4) Disconnect the wire connectors from the generator.

(5) If equipped with air conditioning, remove the air conditioning compressor, (refer to Group 24, Heating and Air Conditioning).

(6) Disconnect the ignition coil and distributor wire connectors.

(7) Disconnect the oil pressure sender wire connector.

(8) Disconnect the wires at the starter motor solenoid and injection wire harness connector.

REMOVAL AND INSTALLATION (Continued)

(9) Perform the Fuel System Pressure Release procedure (refer to Group 14, Fuel System).

(10) Disconnect the quick-connect fuel lines at the fuel rail and return line by squeezing the retaining tabs against the fuel tube. Pull the fuel tube and retainer from the quick- connect fitting (refer to Group 14, Fuel System for the proper procedure).

(11) Remove the fuel line bracket from the intake manifold.

(12) Disconnect the engine ground strap.

(13) Remove the air cleaner.

(14) Disconnect the vacuum purge hose at the fuel vapor canister tee.

(15) Disconnect the idle speed actuator wire connector.

(16) Disconnect the throttle cable and remove it from the bracket.

(17) Disconnect the throttle rod at the bellcrank.

(18) Disconnect the speed control cable, if equipped.

(19) Disconnect the oxygen sensor wire connector.

(20) Remove the upper radiator hose and coolant recovery hose.

(21) Disconnect lower radiator hoses at the radiator.

(22) Disconnect the coolant hoses from the rear of the intake manifold and thermostat housing.

(23) Remove the fan shroud screws.

(24) Remove the radiator attaching bolts.

(25) Remove the radiator and fan shroud. Refer to Group 7, Cooling System for the proper procedure.

(26) Remove the fan and spacer or Tempatrol fan assembly.

(27) Install a 5/16 X 1/2-inch SAE capscrew through fan pulley into water pump flange. This will maintain the pulley and water pump in alignment when crankshaft is rotated.

(28) Remove the power brake vacuum check valve from the booster, if equipped.

(29) If equipped with power steering:

(a) Disconnect the hoses from the fittings at the steering gear.

(b) Drain the pump reservoir.

(c) Cap the fittings on the hoses and steering gear to prevent foreign objects from entering the system.

(30) Lift the vehicle and support it with support stands.

(31) Remove the starter motor.

(32) Remove the flywheel housing access cover.

(33) Remove the engine support cushion-to-bracket through bolts.

(34) Disconnect the exhaust pipe from the manifold.

(35) Remove the upper flywheel housing bolts and loosen the bottom bolts.

(36) Lower the vehicle.

(37) Attach a lifting device to the engine.

(38) Raise the engine off the front supports.

(39) Place a support stand under the flywheel housing.

(40) Remove the remaining flywheel housing bolts.

(41) Lift the engine out of the engine compartment and install on an engine stand.

INSTALLATION

(1) Lift the engine off the stand and lower it into the engine compartment. For easier installation, it may be useful to remove the engine support cushions from the engine support brackets as an aide for alignment of the engine-to-transmission.

(2) Insert the transmission shaft into the clutch spline.

(3) Align the flywheel housing with the engine.

(4) Install and finger tighten the flywheel housing lower bolts.

(5) Install the engine support cushions (if removed).

(6) Remove the support stand from beneath the flywheel housing.

(7) Lower the engine and engine support cushions onto the engine compartment brackets. Ensure that the bolt holes are aligned. Install the bolts and tighten the nuts.

(8) Remove the engine lifting device.

(9) Raise the vehicle.

(10) Attach the exhaust pipe to the manifold. Install and tighten the nuts to 31 N·m (23 ft. lbs.) torque.

(11) Install the flywheel housing access cover.

(12) Install the remaining flywheel housing bolts. Tighten the bolts to 38 N·m (28 ft. lbs.) torque.

(13) Install the starter motor and connect the cable. Tighten the bolts to 45 N·m (33 ft. lbs.) torque.

(14) Lower the vehicle.

(15) Connect the coolant hoses and tighten the clamps.

(16) Remove the pulley-to-water pump flange alignment capscrew and install the fan and spacer or Tempatrol fan assembly.

(17) Tighten the serpentine drive belt according to the specifications listed in Group 7, Cooling System.

(18) Install the fan shroud and radiator (refer to Group 7, Cooling System for the proper procedure).

(19) Connect the radiator hoses.

(20) Connect the throttle valve rod and retainer.

(21) Connect the throttle cable and install the rod.

(22) Install the throttle valve rod spring.

(23) Connect the speed control cable, if equipped.

(24) Connect the oxygen sensor wire connector.

(25) Install the vacuum hose and check valve on the brake booster.

REMOVAL AND INSTALLATION (Continued)

(26) Connect the coolant temperature sensor wire connector.

(27) Connect the idle speed actuator wire connector.

(28) Connect the fuel inlet and return hoses at the fuel rail. Verify that the quick-connect fitting assembly fits securely over the fuel lines by giving the fuel lines a firm tug.

(29) Install the fuel line bracket to the intake manifold.

(30) Connect all fuel injection wire connections.

(31) Install the engine ground strap.

(32) Connect the ignition coil wire connector.

(33) Remove the coolant temperature sending unit to permit air to escape from the block. Fill the cooling system with coolant. Install the coolant temperature sending unit when the system is filled.

(34) If equipped with power steering:

(a) Remove the protective caps

(b) Connect the hoses to the fittings at the steering gear. Tighten the nut to 52 N·m (38 ft. lbs.) torque.

(c) Fill the pump reservoir with fluid.

(35) If equipped with air conditioning, install air compressor and charge A/C system (refer to Group 24 Heating and Air Conditioning).

(36) Install the battery and connect the battery cables.

(37) Install the air cleaner bonnet to the throttle body.

(38) Install the air cleaner.

(39) Lower the hood and secure in place.

(40) Start the engine and inspect for leaks.

(41) Stop the engine and check the fluid levels. Add fluid, as required.

ENGINE CYLINDER HEAD COVER

The cylinder head cover is isolated from the cylinder head via grommets and a molded rubber gasket. The grommet and limiter are retained in the cylinder head cover.

REMOVAL

(1) Disconnect negative cable from battery.

(2) Disconnect the Crankcase Ventilation (CCV) vacuum hose from engine cylinder head cover (Fig. 23).

(3) Disconnect the fresh air inlet hose from the engine cylinder head cover (Fig. 23).

(4) Remove the engine cylinder head cover mounting bolts.

(5) Remove the engine cylinder head cover.

INSTALLATION

(1) If a replacement cover is installed, transfer the CCV valve grommet and oil filler cap from the original cover to the replacement cover.

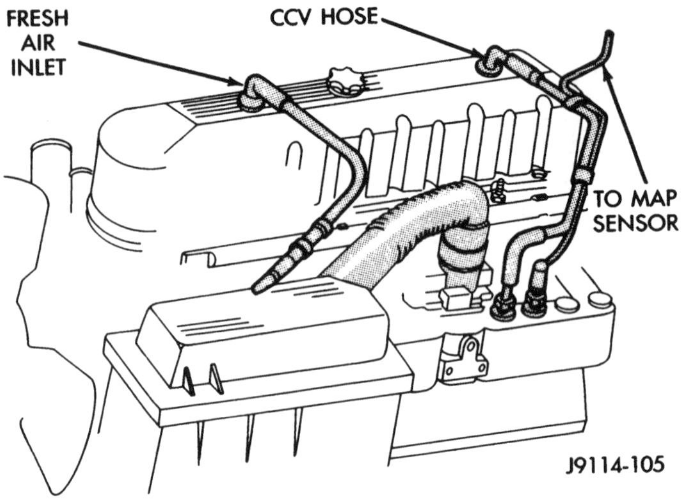

Fig. 23 Engine Cylinder Head Cover

(2) Install engine cylinder head cover. Tighten the mounting bolts to 9.6 N·m (85 in. lbs.) torque.

(3) Connect the CCV hoses (Fig. 23).

(4) Connect negative cable to battery.

ROCKER ARMS AND PUSH RODS

This procedure can be done with the engine in or out of the vehicle.

REMOVAL

(1) Remove the engine cylinder head cover.

(2) Remove the capscrews at each bridge and pivot assembly (Fig. 24). Alternately loosen the capscrews one turn at a time to avoid damaging the bridges.

(3) Check for rocker arm bridges which are causing misalignment of the rocker arm to valve tip area.

(4) Remove the bridges, pivots and corresponding pairs of rocker arms (Fig. 24). Place them on a bench in the same order as removed.

(5) Remove the push rods and place them on a bench in the same order as removed.

INSTALLATION

(1) Lubricate the ball ends of the push rods with Mopar Engine Oil Supplement, or equivalent and install push rods in their original locations. Ensure that the bottom end of each push rod is centered in the tappet plunger cap seat.

(2) Using Mopar Engine Oil Supplement, or equivalent, lubricate the area of the rocker arm that the pivot contacts. Install rocker arms, pivots and bridge above each cylinder in their originally position.

(3) Loosely install the capscrews through each bridge.

(4) At each bridge, tighten the capscrews alternately, one turn at a time, to avoid damaging the bridge. Tighten the capscrews to 28 N·m (21 ft. lbs.) torque.

(5) Install the engine cylinder head cover.

REMOVAL AND INSTALLATION (Continued)

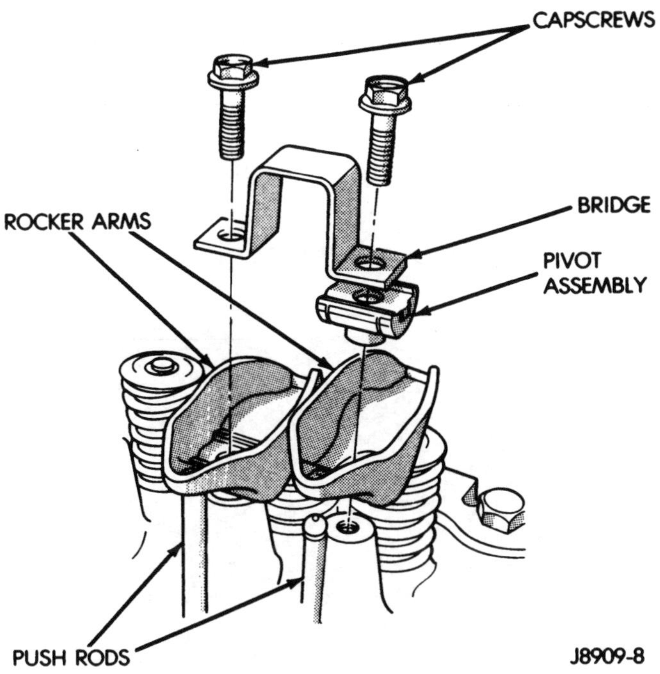

Fig. 24 Rocker Arm Assembly

VALVE STEM SEAL AND SPRING

This procedure can be done with the engine cylinder head installed on the block.

REMOVAL

Inspect the valve stems, especially the grooves. An Arkansas smooth stone should be used to remove nicks and high spots.

Each valve spring is held in place by a retainer and a set of conical valve locks. The locks can be removed only by compressing the valve spring.

(1) Remove the engine cylinder head cover.

(2) Remove capscrews, bridge and pivot assemblies and rocker arms for access to each valve spring to be removed.

(3) Remove push rods. Retain the push rods, bridges, pivots and rocker arms in the same order and position as removed.

(4) Inspect the springs and retainer for cracks and possible signs of weakening.

(5) Remove the spark plug(s) adjacent to the cylinder(s) below the valve springs to be removed.

(6) Connect an air hose to the adapter and apply air pressure slowly. Maintain at least 621 kPa (90 psi) of air pressure in the cylinder to hold the valves against their seats. For vehicles equipped with an air conditioner, use a flexible air adaptor when servicing the No.1 cylinder.

(7) Tap the retainer or tip with a rawhide hammer to loosen the lock from the retainer. Use Valve Spring Compressor Tool MD-998772A to compress the spring and remove the locks (Fig. 25).

(8) Remove valve spring and retainer (Fig. 25).

(9) Remove valve stem oil seals (Fig. 25). Note the valve seals are different for intake and exhaust valves. The top of each seal is marked either INT (Intake) or EXH (Exhaust). DO NOT mix the seals.

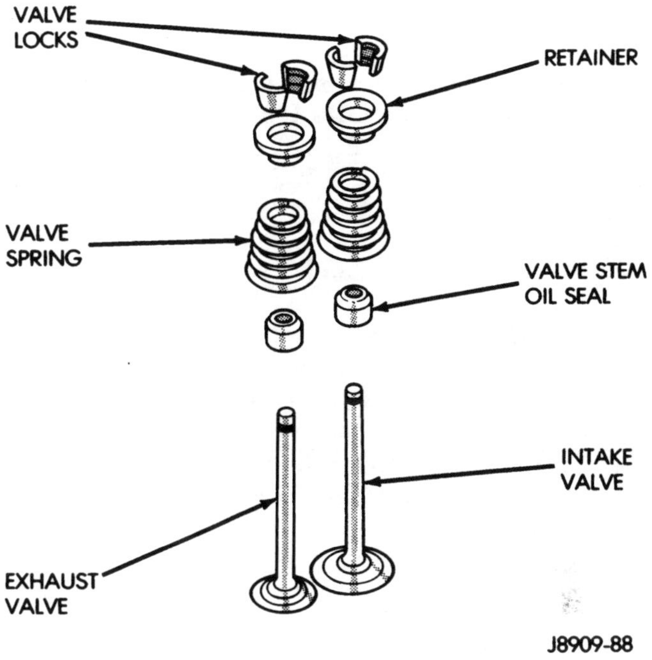

Fig. 25 Valve and Valve Components

INSTALLATION

CAUTION: Install oil seals carefully to prevent damage from the sharp edges of the valve spring lock grove.

(1) Lightly push the valve seal over the valve stem and valve guide boss. Be sure the seal is completely seated on the valve guide boss.

(2) Install valve spring and retainer.

(3) Compress the valve spring with Valve Spring Compressor Tool MD-998772A and insert the valve locks. Release the spring tension and remove the tool. Tap the spring from side-to-side to ensure that the spring is seated properly on the engine cylinder head.

(4) Disconnect the air hose. Remove the adaptor from the spark plug hole and install the spark plug.

(5) Repeat the procedures for each remaining valve spring to be removed.

(6) Install the push rods. Ensure the bottom end of each rod is centered in the plunger cap seat of the hydraulic valve tappet.

(7) Install the rocker arms, pivots and bridge at their original location.

(8) Tighten the bridge capscrews alternately, one at a time, to avoid damaging the bridge. Tighten the capscrews to 28 N·m (21 ft. lbs.) torque.

(9) Install the engine cylinder head cover.

REMOVAL AND INSTALLATION (Continued)

ENGINE CYLINDER HEAD

This procedure can be done with the engine in or out of the vehicle.

REMOVAL

(1) Disconnect negative cable from battery.

WARNING: DO NOT REMOVE THE CYLINDER BLOCK DRAIN PLUGS OR LOOSEN THE RADIATOR DRAIN COCK WITH THE SYSTEM HOT AND PRESSURIZED BECAUSE SERIOUS BURNS FROM THE COOLANT CAN OCCUR.

(2) Drain the coolant and disconnect the hoses at the engine thermostat housing. DO NOT waste reusable coolant. If the solution is clean and is being drained only to service the engine or cooling system, drain the coolant into a clean container for reuse.

(3) Remove the air cleaner assembly.

(4) Remove the engine cylinder head cover.

(5) Remove the capscrews, bridge and pivot assemblies and rocker arms.

(6) Remove the push rods. **Retain the push rods, bridges, pivots and rocker arms in the same order as removed.**

(7) Loosen the serpentine drive belt at the power steering pump, if equipped or at the idler pulley (refer to Group 7, Cooling System for the proper procedure).

(8) If equipped with air conditioning, remove the air conditioning compressor, (refer to Group 24, Heating and Air Conditioning).

(9) If equipped, disconnect the power steering pump bracket. Set the pump and bracket aside. DO NOT disconnect the hoses.

(10) Perform the Fuel System Pressure Release procedure (refer to Group 14, Fuel System).

(11) Remove the fuel lines and vacuum advance hose.

(12) Remove the intake and engine exhaust manifolds from the engine cylinder head (refer to Group 11, Exhaust System and Intake Manifold for the proper procedures).

(13) Disconnect the ignition wires and remove the spark plugs.

(14) Disconnect the temperature sending unit wire connector.

(15) Remove the ignition coil and bracket assembly.

(16) Remove the engine cylinder head bolts. Bolt No.14 cannot be removed until the head is moved forward (Fig. 26). Pull bolt No.14 out as far as it will go and then suspend the bolt in this position (tape around the bolt).

(17) Remove the engine cylinder head and gasket (Fig. 26).

(18) If this was the first time the bolts were removed, put a paint dab on the top of the bolt. If the bolts have a paint dab on the top of the bolt or it isn't known if they were used before, discard the bolts.

(19) Stuff clean lint free shop towels into the cylinder bores.

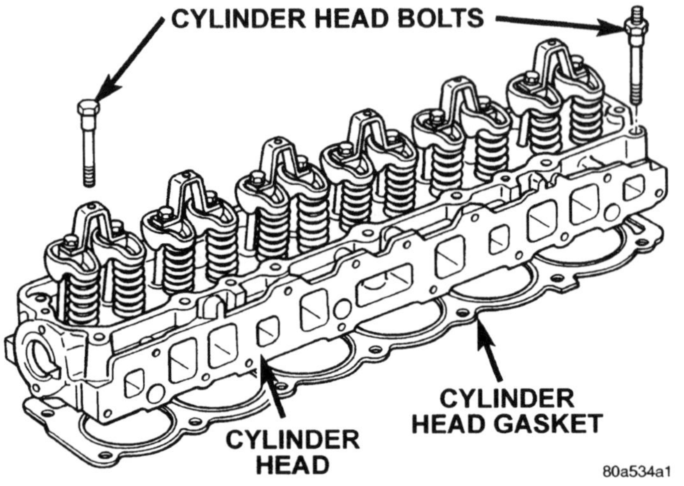

Fig. 26 Engine Cylinder Head Assembly

INSTALLATION

The engine cylinder head gasket is a composition gasket. The gasket is to be installed DRY. **DO NOT use a gasket sealing compound on the gasket.**

If the engine cylinder head is to be replaced and the original valves used, measure the valve stem diameter. Only standard size valves can be used with a service replacement engine cylinder head unless the replacement head valve stem guide bores are reamed to accommodate oversize valve stems. Remove all carbon buildup and reface the valves.

(1) Remove the shop towels from the cylinder bores. Coat the bores with clean engine oil.

(2) Position the engine cylinder head gasket (with the numbers facing up) using the alignment dowels in the cylinder block, to position the gasket.

CAUTION: Engine cylinder head bolts should be reused only once. Replace the head bolts if they were used before or if they have a paint dab on the top of the bolt.

(3) With bolt No.14 held in place (tape around bolt), install the engine cylinder head over the same dowels used to locate the gasket. Remove the tape from bolt No.14.

(4) Coat the threads of stud bolt No.11 with Loctite 592 sealant, or equivalent.

(5) Tighten the engine cylinder head bolts in sequence according to the following procedure (Fig. 27).

REMOVAL AND INSTALLATION (Continued)

CAUTION: During the final tightening sequence, bolt No.11 will be tightened to a lower torque than the rest of the bolts. DO NOT overtighten bolt No.11.

(a) Tighten all bolts in sequence (1 through 14) to 30 N·m (22 ft. lbs.) torque.

(b) Tighten all bolts in sequence (1 through 14) to 61 N·m (45 ft. lbs.) torque.

(c) Check all bolts to verify they are set to 61 N·m (45 ft. lbs.) torque.

(d) Tighten bolts in sequence:

- Bolts 1 through 10 to 149 N·m (110 ft. lbs.) torque.
- Bolt 11 to 13 N·m (100 ft. lbs.) torque.
- Bolts 12 through 14 to 149 N·m (110 ft. lbs.) torque.

CYLINDER HEAD BOLTS

POSITION	DESCRIPTION
1,4,5,12,13	1/2 in.-13 BOLT
8,9	1/2 in.-13 BOLT WITH DOWEL POINT
2,3,6,7,10,11,14	1/2 in.-13 WITH 7/16 in.-14 STUD END
All bolts are 12 point drives for rocker cover clearance	

(e) Check all bolts in sequence to verify the correct torque.

(f) If not already done, clean and mark each bolt with a dab of paint after tightening. Should you encounter bolts which were painted in an earlier service operation, replace them.

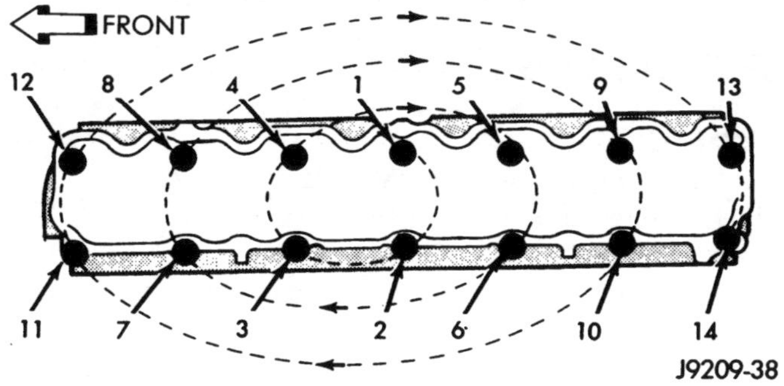

Fig. 27 Engine Cylinder Head Bolt Tightening Sequence

(6) Install the ignition coil and bracket assembly.

(7) Connect the temperature sending unit wire connector.

(8) Install the spark plugs and tighten to 37 N·m (27 ft. lbs.) torque. Connect the ignition wires.

(9) Install the intake and engine exhaust manifolds (refer to Group 11, Exhaust System and Intake Manifold for the proper procedures).

(10) Install the fuel lines and the vacuum advance hose.

(11) If equipped, attach the power steering pump and bracket.

(12) Install the push rods, rocker arms, pivots and bridges in the order they were removed (refer to Rocker Arms and Push Rods in this section).

(13) Install the engine cylinder head cover.

(14) Attach the air conditioner compressor mounting bracket to the engine cylinder head and block. Tighten the bolts to 40 N·m (30 ft. lbs.) torque.

(15) Attach the air conditioning compressor to the bracket. Tighten the bolts to 27 N·m (20 ft. lbs.) torque.

CAUTION: The serpentine drive belt must be routed correctly. Incorrect routing can cause the water pump to turn in the opposite direction causing the engine to overheat.

(16) Install the serpentine drive belt and correctly tension the belt (refer to Group 7, Cooling System for the proper procedure).

(17) Install the air cleaner and ducting.

(18) Install the engine cylinder head cover.

(19) Connect the hoses to the engine thermostat housing and fill the cooling system to the specified level (refer to Group 7, Cooling Systems for the proper procedure).

(20) The automatic transmission throttle linkage and cable must be adjusted after completing the engine cylinder head installation (refer to Group 21, Transmissions for the proper procedures).

(21) Install the temperature sending unit and connect the wire connector.

(22) Connect the fuel line.

(23) If equipped with air conditioning, install air compressor and charge A/C system (refer to Group 24 Heating and Air Conditioning).

(24) Connect negative cable to battery.

(25) Connect the upper radiator hose and heater hose at the engine thermostat housing.

(26) Fill the cooling system. Check for leaks.

WARNING: USE EXTREME CAUTION WHEN THE ENGINE IS OPERATING. DO NOT STAND IN DIRECT LINE WITH THE FAN. DO NOT PUT HANDS NEAR THE PULLEYS, BELTS OR FAN. DO NOT WEAR LOOSE CLOTHING.

(27) Operate the engine with the radiator cap off. Inspect for leaks and continue operating the engine until the engine thermostat opens. Add coolant, if required.

REMOVAL AND INSTALLATION (Continued)

VALVES AND VALVE SPRINGS

This procedure is done with the engine cylinder head removed from the block.

REMOVAL

(1) Remove the engine cylinder head from the cylinder block.

(2) Use Valve Spring Compressor Tool MD-998772A and compress each valve spring.

(3) Remove the valve locks, retainers, springs and valve stem oil seals. Discard the oil seals.

(4) Use a smooth stone or a jewelers file to remove any burrs on the top of the valve stem, especially around the groove for the locks.

(5) Remove the valves, and place them in a rack in the same order as removed.

INSTALLATION

(1) Thoroughly clean the valve stems and the valve guide bores.

(2) Lightly lubricate the stem.

(3) Install the valve in the original valve guide bore.

(4) Install the replacement valve stem oil seals on the valve stems. If the 0.381 mm (0.015 inch) oversize valve stems are used, oversize oil seals are required.

(5) Position the valve spring and retainer on the engine cylinder head and compress the valve spring with Valve Spring Compressor Tool MD-998772A.

(6) Install the valve locks and release the tool.

(7) Tap the valve spring from side to side with a hammer to ensure that the spring is properly seated at the engine cylinder head. Also tap the top of the retainer to seat the valve locks.

(8) Install the engine cylinder head.

HYDRAULIC TAPPETS

Retain all the components in the same order as removed.

REMOVAL

(1) Remove the engine cylinder head cover.

(2) Remove the bridge and pivot assemblies and rocker arms by removing the capscrews at each bridge. Alternately loosen each capscrew, one turn at a time, to avoid damaging the bridges.

(3) Remove the push rods.

(4) Remove cylinder head and gasket.

(5) Remove the tappets through the push rod openings in the cylinder block with a Hydraulic Valve Tappet Removal/Installation Tool (Fig. 28).

INSTALLATION

It is not necessary to charge the tappets with engine oil. They will charge themselves within a very short period of engine operation.

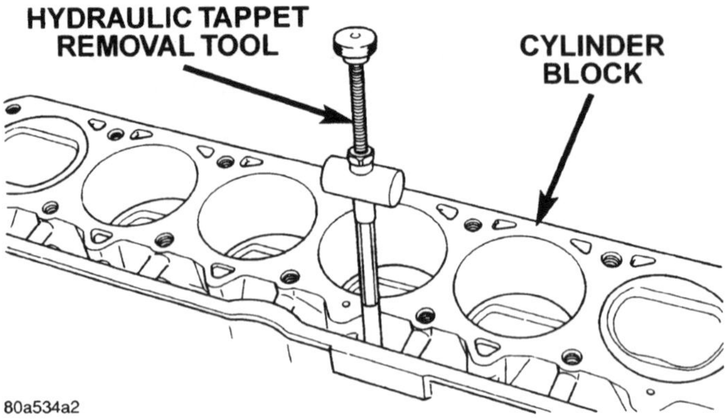

Fig. 28 Hydraulic Valve Tappet Removal—Installation Tool

(1) Dip each tappet in Mopar Engine Oil Supplement, or equivalent.

(2) Use Hydraulic Valve Tappet Removal/Installation Tool to install each tappet in the same bore from where it was originally removed.

(3) Install cylinder head and gasket.

(4) Install the push rods in their original locations.

(5) Install the rocker arms and bridge and pivot assemblies at their original locations. Loosely install the capscrews at each bridge.

(6) Tighten the capscrews alternately, one turn at a time, to avoid damaging the bridges. Tighten the capscrews to 28 N·m (21 ft. lbs.) torque.

(7) Pour the remaining Mopar Engine Oil Supplement, or equivalent over the entire valve actuating assembly. The Mopar Engine Oil Supplement, or equivalent must remain with the engine oil for at least 1 609 km (1,000 miles). The oil supplement need not be drained until the next scheduled oil change.

(8) Install the engine cylinder head cover.

VIBRATION DAMPER

REMOVAL

(1) Disconnect negative cable from battery.

(2) Remove the serpentine drive belt and fan shroud.

(3) Remove the vibration damper retaining bolt and washer.

(4) Use Vibration Damper Removal Tool 7697 to remove the damper from the crankshaft (Fig. 29).

INSTALLATION

(1) Apply Mopar Silicone Rubber Adhesive Sealant to the keyway in the crankshaft and insert the key. With the key in position, align the keyway on the vibration damper hub with the crankshaft key and tap the damper onto the crankshaft.

(2) Install the vibration damper retaining bolt and washer.

REMOVAL AND INSTALLATION (Continued)

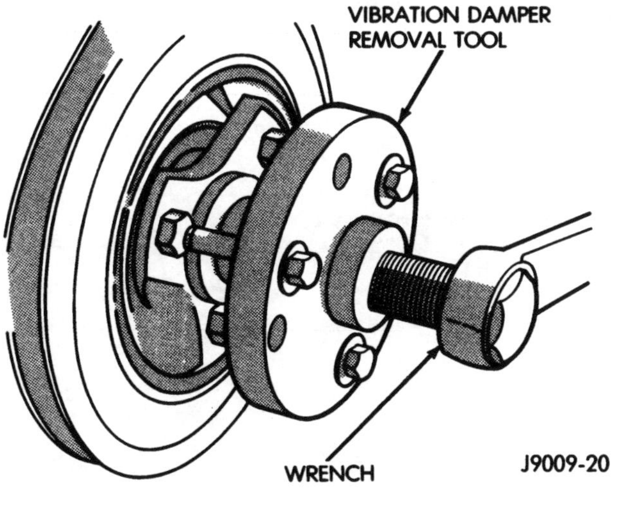

Fig. 29 Vibration Damper Removal Tool 7697

(3) Tighten the damper retaining bolt to 108 N·m (80 ft. lbs.) torque.

(4) Install the serpentine drive belt and tighten to the specified tension (refer to Group 7, Cooling Systems for the proper specifications and procedures).

(5) Connect negative cable to battery.

TIMING CASE COVER

REMOVAL

(1) Disconnect negative cable from battery.

(2) Remove the vibration damper.

(3) Remove the fan and hub assembly and remove the fan shroud.

(4) Remove the accessory drive brackets that are attached to the timing case cover.

(5) Remove the A/C compressor (if equipped) and generator bracket assembly from the engine cylinder head and move to one side.

(6) Remove the oil pan-to-timing case cover bolts and timing case cover-to-cylinder block bolts.

(7) Remove the timing case cover and gasket from the engine. Make sure the tension spring and thrust pin do not fall out of the preload bolt.

(8) Pry the crankshaft oil seal from the front of the timing case cover (Fig. 30).

INSTALLATION

Clean the timing case cover, oil pan and cylinder block gasket surfaces.

(1) Install a new crankshaft oil seal in the timing case cover. The open end of the seal should be toward the inside of the cover. Support the cover at the seal area while installing the seal. Force it into position with Seal Installation Tool 6139.

(2) Position the gasket on the cylinder block.

(3) Position the timing case cover on the oil pan gasket and the cylinder block. Make sure the tension spring and thrust pin are in place in the camshaft preload bolt.

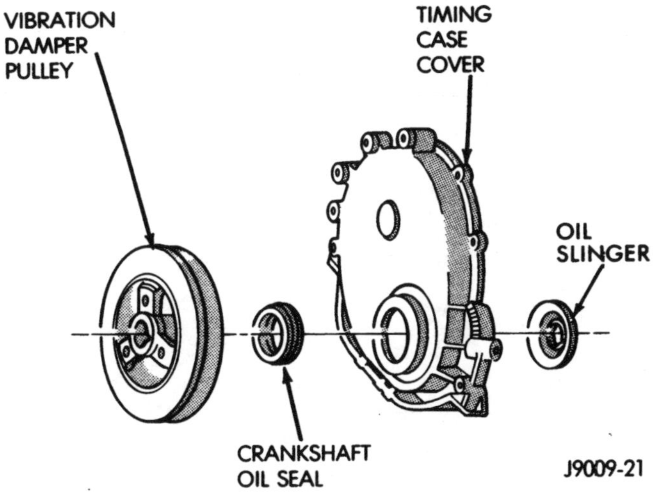

Fig. 30 Timing Case Cover Components

(4) Insert Timing Case Cover Alignment and Seal Installation Tool 6139 in the crankshaft opening in the cover (Fig. 31).

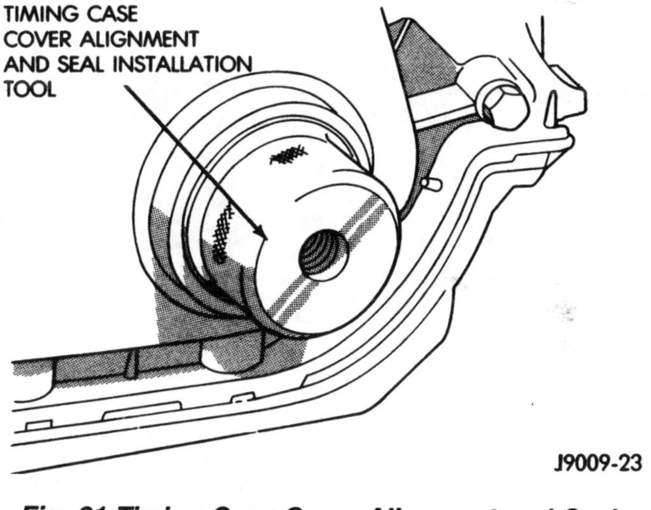

Fig. 31 Timing Case Cover Alignment and Seal Installation Tool 6139

(5) Install the timing case cover-to-cylinder block and the oil pan-to-timing case cover bolts.

(6) Tighten the 1/4 inch cover-to-block bolts to 7 N·m (60 in. lbs.) torque. Tighten the 5/16 inch front cover-to-block bolts to 22 N·m (192 in. lbs.) torque. Tighten the oil pan-to-cover 1/4 inch bolts to 9.5 N·m (84 in. lbs.) torque. Tighten the oil pan-to-cover 5/16 inch bolts to 15 N·m (132 in. lbs.) torque.

(7) Remove the cover alignment tool.

(8) Apply a light film of engine oil on the vibration damper hub contact surface of the seal.

(9) Apply Mopar Silicone Rubber Adhesive Sealant to the keyway in the crankshaft and insert the key. With the key inserted in the keyway in the crankshaft, install the vibration damper, washer and bolt.

REMOVAL AND INSTALLATION (Continued)

Lubricate and tighten the bolt to 108 N·m (80 ft. lbs.) torque.

(10) Install the A/C compressor (if equipped) and generator bracket assembly.

(11) Install the engine fan and hub assembly and shroud.

(12) Install the serpentine drive belt and tighten to obtain the specified tension.

(13) Connect negative cable to battery.

TIMING CHAIN AND SPROCKETS

REMOVAL

(1) Disconnect negative cable from battery.

(2) Remove the fan and shroud.

(3) Remove the serpentine drive belt.

(4) Remove the crankshaft vibration damper.

(5) Remove the timing case cover.

(6) Rotate crankshaft until the "0" timing mark is closest to and on the center line with camshaft sprocket timing mark (Fig. 32).

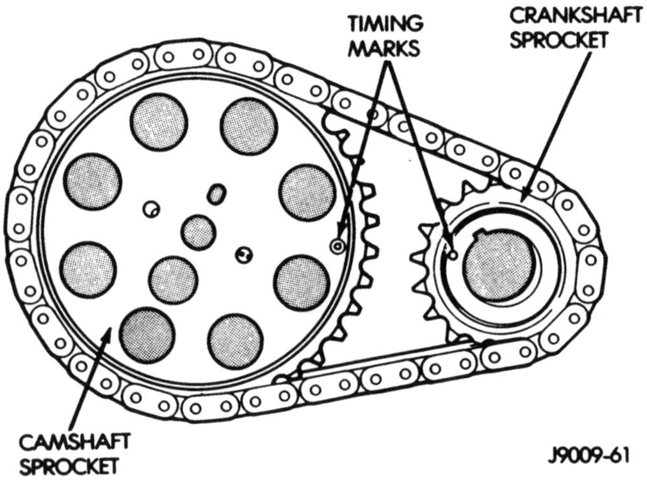

Fig. 32 Crankshaft—Camshaft Alignment—Typical

(7) Remove the oil slinger from the crankshaft.

(8) Remove the tension spring and thrust pin from the preload bolt (Fig. 33). Remove the camshaft sprocket retaining preload bolt and washer.

(9) Remove the crankshaft sprocket, camshaft sprocket and timing chain as an assembly.

(10) Installation of the timing chain with the timing marks on the crankshaft and camshaft sprockets properly aligned ensures correct valve timing. A worn or stretched timing chain will adversely affect valve timing. If the timing chain deflects more than 12.7 mm (1/2 inch) replace it. The correct timing chain has 48 pins. A chain with more than 48 pins will cause excessive slack.

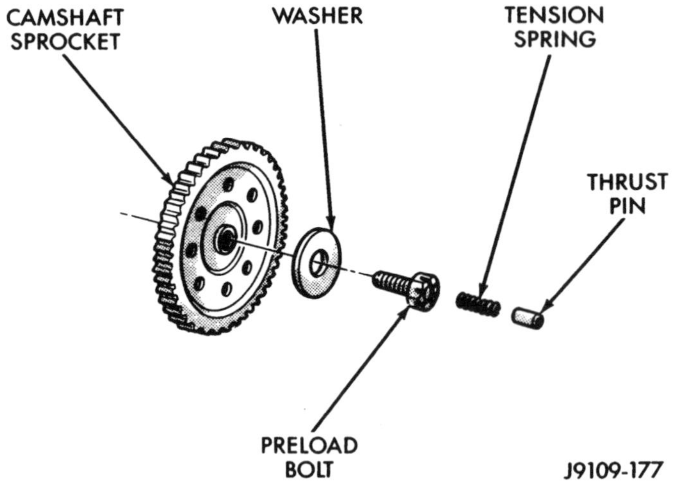

Fig. 33 Camshaft Sprocket Preload Bolt

INSTALLATION

Assemble the timing chain, crankshaft sprocket and camshaft sprocket with the timing marks aligned (Fig. 32).

(1) Apply Mopar Silicone Rubber Adhesive Sealant to the keyway in the crankshaft and insert the key. With the key in the keyway on the crankshaft, install the assembly on the crankshaft and camshaft.

(2) Install the camshaft sprocket retaining preload bolt and washer (Fig. 33). Tighten the preload bolt to 108 N·m (80 ft. lbs.) torque.

(3) Install the crankshaft oil slinger.

(4) Replace the oil seal in the timing case cover.

(5) Lubricate the tension spring, thrust pin and pin bore in the preload bolt with Mopar Engine Oil Supplement, or equivalent. Install the spring and thrust pin in the preload bolt head (Fig. 33).

(6) Install the timing case cover and gasket.

(7) With the key installed in the crankshaft keyway, install the vibration damper, washer and bolt. Lubricate and tighten the bolt to 108 N·m (80 ft. lbs.) torque.

(8) Install the serpentine drive belt and tighten to the specified tension (refer to Group 7, Cooling System for the proper procedure).

(9) Install the fan and hub assembly. Install the shroud.

(10) Connect negative cable to battery.

CAMSHAFT

REMOVAL

WARNING: THE COOLANT IN A RECENTLY OPERATED ENGINE IS HOT AND PRESSURIZED. RELEASE THE PRESSURE BEFORE REMOVING THE DRAIN COCK, CAP AND DRAIN PLUGS.

(1) Disconnect negative cable from battery.

REMOVAL AND INSTALLATION (Continued)

(2) Drain the cooling system. DO NOT waste reusable coolant. If the solution is clean, drain it into a clean container for reuse.

(3) Remove the radiator or radiator and condenser, if equipped with A/C (refer to Group 7, Cooling System for the proper procedure).

(4) Remove the air conditioner condenser and receiver/drier assembly as a charged unit, if equipped (refer to Group 24, Heating and Air Conditioning).

(5) Remove the distributor cap and mark the position of the rotor.

(6) Remove the distributor and ignition wires.

(7) Remove the engine cylinder head cover.

(8) Remove the rocker arms, bridges and pivots.

(9) Remove the push rods.

(10) Remove the engine cylinder head and gasket.

(11) Remove the hydraulic valve tappets from the engine cylinder head.

(12) Remove the vibration damper.

(13) Remove the timing case cover.

(14) Remove the timing chain and sprockets.

(15) Remove the front bumper and/or grille, as required.

(16) Remove the camshaft (Fig. 34).

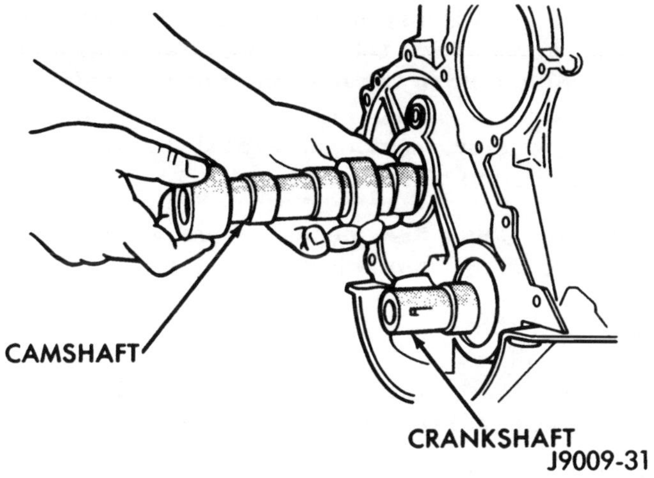

Fig. 34 Camshaft

INSTALLATION

(1) Inspect the cam lobes for wear.

(2) Inspect the bearing journals for uneven wear pattern or finish.

(3) Inspect the bearings for wear.

(4) Inspect the distributor drive gear for wear.

(5) If the camshaft appears to have been rubbing against the timing case cover, examine the oil pressure relief holes in the rear cam journal. The oil pressure relief holes must be free of debris.

(6) Lubricate the camshaft with Mopar Engine Oil Supplement, or equivalent.

(7) Carefully install the camshaft to prevent damage to the camshaft bearings (Fig. 34).

(8) Install the timing chain, crankshaft sprocket and camshaft sprocket with the timing marks aligned.

(9) Install the camshaft sprocket retaining preload bolt. Tighten the bolt to 108 N·m (80 ft. lbs.) torque.

(10) Lubricate the tension spring, the thrust pin and the pin bore in the preload bolt with Mopar Engine Oil Supplement, or equivalent. Install the spring and thrust pin in the preload bolt head.

(11) Install the timing case cover with a replacement oil seal (Fig. 35). Refer to Timing Case Cover Installation.

(12) Install the vibration damper (Fig. 35).

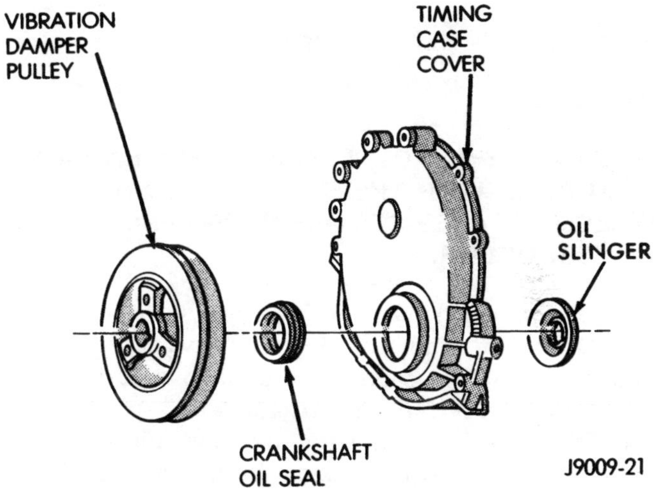

Fig. 35 Timing Case Cover Components

(13) Install the hydraulic valve tappets.

(14) Install the engine cylinder head.

(15) Install the push rods.

(16) Install the rocker arms and pivot and bridge assemblies. Tighten each of the capscrews for each bridge alternately, one turn at a time, to avoid damaging the bridge.

(17) Install the engine cylinder head cover.

(18) Position the oil pump gear. Refer to Distributor in the Component Removal/Installation section of Group 8D, Ignition Systems.

(19) Install the distributor and ignition wires. Refer to Distributor in the Component Removal/Installation section of Group 8D, Ignition Systems.

(20) Install the serpentine drive belt and tighten to the specified tension (refer to Group 7, Cooling System for the proper procedure).

NOTE: During installation, lubricate the hydraulic valve tappets and all valve components with Mopar Engine Oil Supplement, or equivalent. The Mopar Engine Oil Supplement, or equivalent must remain with the engine oil for at least 1 609 km (1,000 miles). The oil supplement need not be drained until the next scheduled oil change.

REMOVAL AND INSTALLATION (Continued)

(21) Install the A/C condenser and receiver/drier assembly, if equipped (refer to Group 24, Heating and Air Conditioning).

CAUTION: Both service valves must be opened before the air conditioning system is operated.

(22) Install the radiator, connect the hoses and fill the cooling system to the specified level (refer to Group 7, Cooling System for the proper procedure).

(23) Check the ignition timing and adjust as necessary.

(24) Install the grille and bumper, if removed.

(25) Connect negative cable to battery.

CAMSHAFT PIN REPLACEMENT

REMOVAL

WARNING: DO NOT LOOSEN THE RADIATOR DRAIN COCK WITH THE SYSTEM HOT AND PRESSURIZED BECAUSE SERIOUS BURNS FROM COOLANT CAN OCCUR.

(1) Disconnect negative cable from battery.

(2) Drain the radiator. DO NOT waste reusable coolant. Drain the coolant into a clean container.

(3) Remove the fan and shroud.

(4) Disconnect the radiator overflow tube, radiator hoses, automatic transmission fluid cooler pipes (if equipped).

(5) Remove the radiator.

(6) If equipped with air conditioning:

CAUTION: DO NOT loosen or disconnect any air conditioner system fittings. Move the condenser and receiver/drier aside as a complete assembly.

(a) Remove the A/C compressor serpentine drive belt idler pulley.

(b) Disconnect and remove the generator.

(c) Remove the A/C condenser attaching bolts and move the condenser and receiver/drier assembly up and out of the way.

(7) Remove the serpentine drive belt.

(8) Remove the crankshaft vibration damper.

(9) Remove the timing case cover. Clean the gasket material from the cover.

(10) Remove the thrust pin and tension spring from the preload bolt head.

(11) Rotate crankshaft until the crankshaft sprocket timing mark is closest to and on the center line with the camshaft sprocket timing mark (Fig. 36).

(12) Remove the camshaft sprocket preload retaining bolt and washer.

(13) Remove the crankshaft oil slinger.

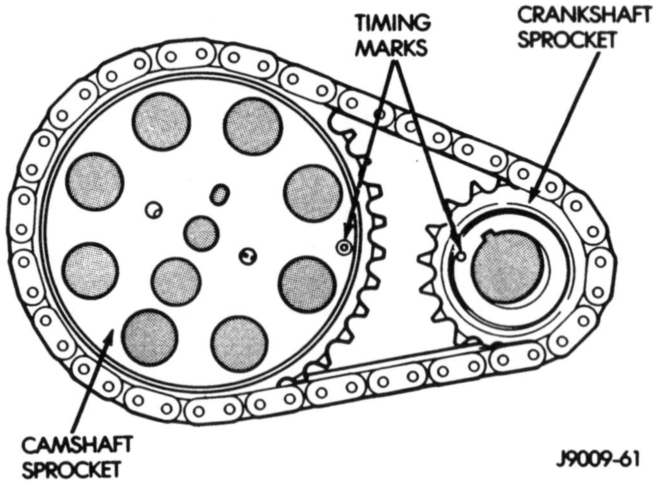

Fig. 36 Timing Chain Alignment—Typical

(14) Remove the sprockets and chain as an assembly.

CAUTION: The following procedural step must be accomplished to prevent the camshaft from damaging the rear camshaft plug during pin installation.

(15) Inspect the damaged camshaft pin.

(16) If the pin is a spring-type pin, remove the broken pin by inserting a self-tapping screw into the pin and carefully pulling the pin from the camshaft.

(17) If the pin is a dowel-type pin, center-punch it. Ensure the exact center is located when center-punching the pin.

CAUTION: Cover the opened oil pan area to prevent metal chips from entering the pan.

(18) Drill into the pin center with a 4 mm (5/32 inch) drill bit.

(19) Insert a self-tapping screw into the drilled pin and carefully pull the pin from the camshaft.

CAMSHAFT BEARINGS

The camshaft rotates within four steel-shelled, babbitt-lined bearings that are pressed into the cylinder block and then line reamed. The camshaft bearing bores and bearing diameters are not the same size. They are stepped down in 0.254 mm (0.010 inch) increments from the front bearing (largest) to the rear bearing (smallest). This permits easier removal and installation of the camshaft. The camshaft bearings are pressure lubricated.

NOTE: It is not advisable to attempt to replace camshaft bearings unless special removal and installation tools are available.

REMOVAL AND INSTALLATION (Continued)

Camshaft end play is maintained by the load placed on the camshaft by the sprocket preload bolt tension spring and thrust pin.

INSTALLATION

(1) Clean the camshaft pin hole.

(2) Compress the center of the replacement spring pin with vise grips.

(3) Carefully drive the pin into the camshaft pin hole until it is seated.

(4) Install the camshaft sprocket, crankshaft sprocket and timing chain with the timing marks aligned (Fig. 36).

(5) Install the crankshaft oil slinger.

(6) Tighten the camshaft sprocket preload bolt to 108 N·m (80 ft. lbs.) torque.

(7) Check the valve timing.

(8) Lubricate the tension spring, the thrust pin and the pin bore in the preload bolt with Mopar Engine Oil Supplement, or equivalent. Install the spring and thrust pin in the preload bolt head.

(9) Coat both sides of the replacement timing case cover gasket with gasket sealer. Apply a 3 mm (1/8 inch) bead of Mopar Silicone Rubber Adhesive Sealant, or equivalent to the joint formed at the oil pan and cylinder block.

(10) Position the timing case cover on the oil pan gasket and the cylinder block.

(11) Place Timing Case Cover Alignment and Seal Installation Tool 6139 in the crankshaft opening in the cover (Fig. 37).

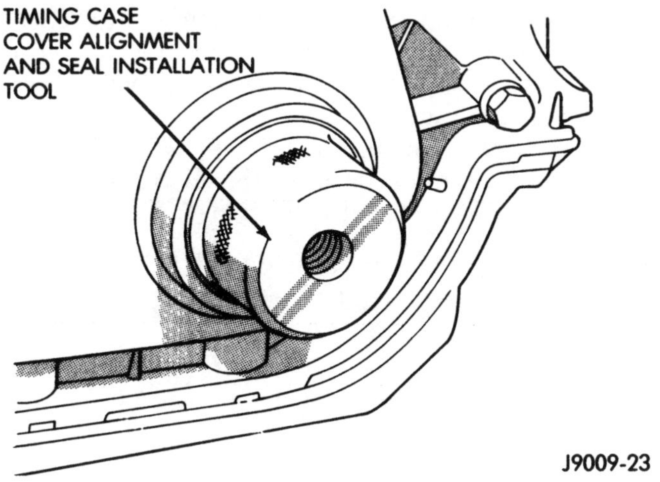

Fig. 37 Timing Case Cover Alignment and Seal Installation Tool 6139

(12) Install the timing case cover-to-cylinder block bolts. Install the oil pan-to-timing case cover bolts.

(13) Tighten the 1/4 inch cover-to-block bolts to 7 N·m (60 in. lbs.) torque. Tighten the 5/16 inch front cover-to-block bolts to 22 N·m (192 in. lbs.) torque. Tighten the oil pan-to-cover 1/4 inch bolts to 14 N·m (120 in. lbs.) torque. Tighten the oil pan-to-cover 5/16 inch bolts to 18 N·m (156 in. lbs.) torque.

(14) Remove the cover alignment tool and install a replacement oil seal into the cover.

(15) Install the vibration damper on the crankshaft.

(16) Lubricate and tighten the damper bolt to 108 N·m (80 ft. lbs.) torque.

(17) If equipped with air conditioning:

(a) Install the A/C compressor serpentine drive belt idler pulley.

(b) Install the generator.

(c) Install the A/C condenser and receiver/drier assembly.

(18) Install the serpentine drive belt on the pulleys and tighten (refer to Group 7, Cooling System for the specifications and procedures).

(19) Install the radiator. Connect the radiator hoses and automatic transmission fluid cooler pipes, if equipped. Fill the cooling system.

(20) Install the fan and shroud.

(21) Connect negative cable to battery.

OIL PAN

REMOVAL

(1) Disconnect negative cable from battery.

(2) Raise the vehicle.

(3) Remove the oil pan drain plug and drain the engine oil.

(4) Disconnect the exhaust pipe at the exhaust manifold.

(5) Disconnect the exhaust hanger at the catalytic converter and lower the pipe.

(6) Remove the starter motor.

(7) Remove the engine flywheel and transmission torque converter housing access cover.

(8) If equipped with an oil level sensor, disconnect the sensor.

(9) Position a jack stand directly under the engine vibration damper.

(10) Place a piece of wood (2 x 2) between the jack stand and the engine vibration damper.

(11) Remove the engine mount through bolts.

(12) Using the jack stand, raise the engine until adequate clearance is obtained to remove the oil pan.

(13) Remove the oil pan bolts. Carefully slide the oil pan and gasket to the rear. If equipped with an oil level sensor, take care not to damage the sensor.

INSTALLATION

(1) Clean the block and pan gasket surfaces.

(2) Fabricate 4 alignment dowels from 1 1/2 x 1/4 inch bolts. Cut the head off the bolts and cut a slot into the top of the dowel. This will allow easier installation and removal with a screwdriver (Fig. 38).

REMOVAL AND INSTALLATION (Continued)

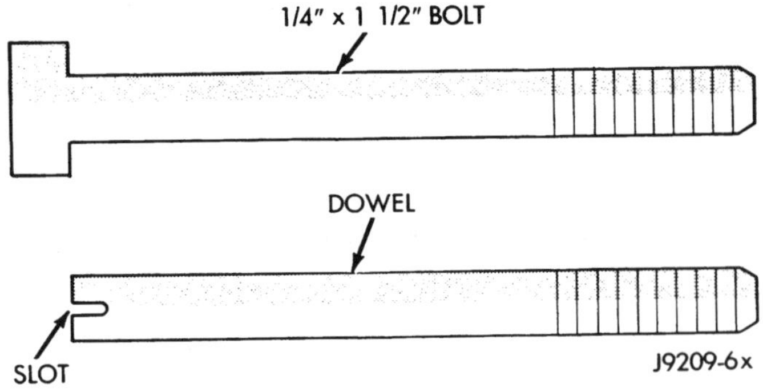

Fig. 38 Fabrication of Alignment Dowels

(3) Install two dowels in the timing case cover. Install the other two dowels in the cylinder block (Fig. 39).

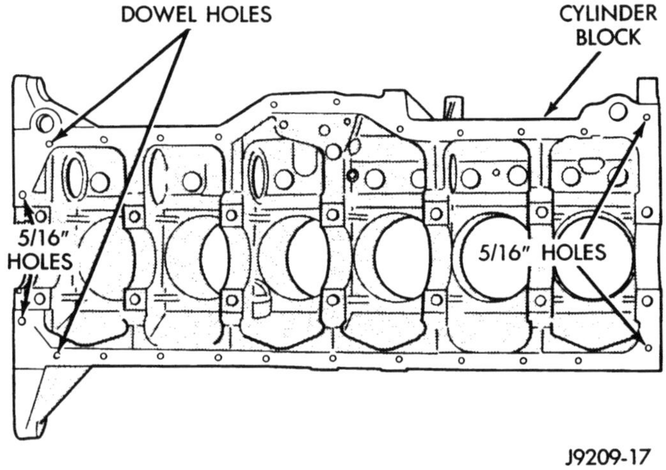

Fig. 39 Position of Dowels in Cylinder Block

(4) Slide the one-piece gasket over the dowels and onto the block and timing case cover.

(5) Position the oil pan over the dowels and onto the gasket. If equipped with an oil level sensor, take care not to damage the sensor.

(6) Install the 1/4 inch oil pan bolts. Tighten these bolts to 9.5 N·m (84 in. lbs.) torque. Install the 5/16 inch oil pan bolts (Fig. 40). Tighten these bolts to 15 N·m (132 in. lbs.) torque.

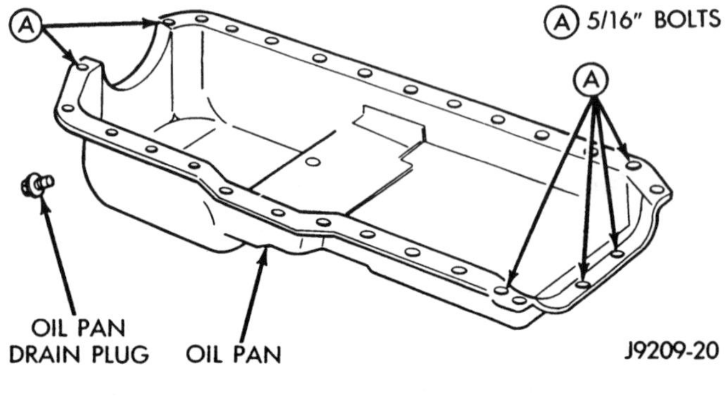

Fig. 40 Position of 5/16 inch Oil Pan Bolts

(7) Remove the dowels. Install the remaining 1/4 inch oil pan bolts. Tighten these bolts to 9.5 N·m (84 in. lbs.) torque.

(8) Lower the engine until it is properly located on the engine mounts.

(9) Install the through bolts and tighten the nuts.

(10) Lower the jack stand and remove the piece of wood.

(11) Install the engine flywheel and transmission torque converter housing access cover.

(12) Install the engine starter motor.

(13) Connect the exhaust pipe to the hanger and to the engine exhaust manifold.

(14) Install the oil pan drain plug (Fig. 40). Tighten the plug to 34 N·m (25 ft. lbs.) torque.

(15) Lower the vehicle.

(16) Connect negative cable to battery.

(17) Fill the oil pan with engine oil to the specified level.

WARNING: USE EXTREME CAUTION WHEN THE ENGINE IS OPERATING. DO NOT STAND IN A DIRECT LINE WITH THE FAN. DO NOT PUT YOUR HANDS NEAR THE PULLEYS, BELTS OR FAN. DO NOT WEAR LOOSE CLOTHING.

(18) Start the engine and inspect for leaks.

OIL PUMP

A gear-type oil pump is mounted at the underside of the cylinder block opposite the No.4 main bearing.

The pump incorporates a nonadjustable pressure relief valve to limit maximum pressure to 517 kPa (75 psi). In the relief position, the valve permits oil to bypass through a passage in the pump body to the inlet side of the pump.

Oil pump removal or replacement will not affect the distributor timing because the distributor drive gear remains in mesh with the camshaft gear.

REMOVAL

(1) Drain the engine oil.

(2) Remove the oil pan.

(3) Remove the pump-to-cylinder block attaching bolts. Remove the pump assembly with gasket (Fig. 41).

CAUTION: If the oil pump is not to be serviced, DO NOT disturb position of oil inlet tube and strainer assembly in pump body. If the tube is moved within the pump body, a replacement tube and strainer assembly must be installed to assure an airtight seal.

REMOVAL AND INSTALLATION (Continued)

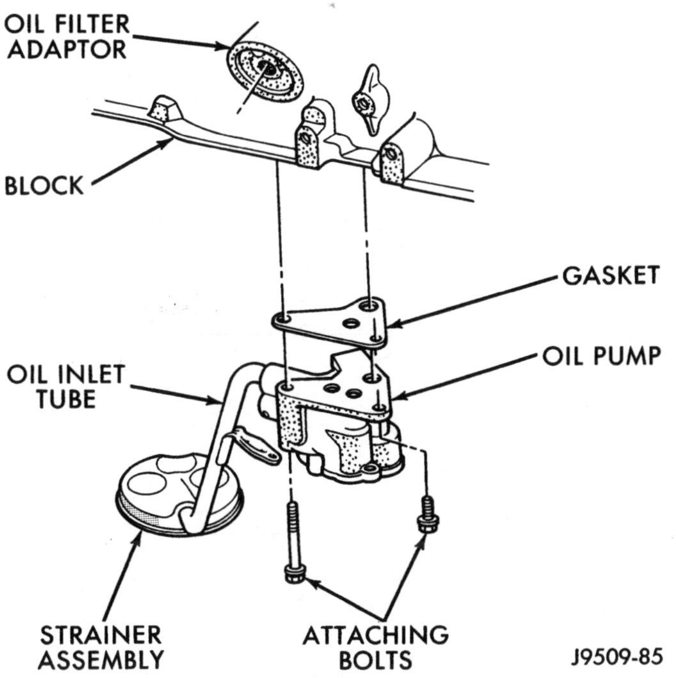

Fig. 41 Oil Pump Assembly

INSTALLATION

(1) Install the oil pump on the cylinder block using a replacement gasket. Tighten the bolts to 23 N·m (17 ft. lbs.) torque.

(2) Install the oil pan.

(3) Fill the oil pan with oil to the specified level.

CRANKSHAFT MAIN BEARINGS

REMOVAL

(1) Disconnect negative cable from battery.

(2) Remove the spark plugs.

(3) Raise the vehicle.

(4) Remove the oil pan and oil pump.

(5) Remove main bearing cap brace (Fig. 42).

(6) Remove only one main bearing cap and lower insert at a time (Fig. 43).

(7) Remove the lower insert from the bearing cap.

(8) Remove the upper insert by LOOSENING (DO NOT REMOVE) all of the other bearing caps. Now insert a small cotter pin tool in the crankshaft journal oil hole. Bend the cotter pin as illustrated to fabricate the tool (Fig. 44). With the cotter pin tool in place, rotate the crankshaft so that the upper bearing insert will rotate in the direction of its locking tab. Because there is no hole in the No.3 main journal, use a tongue depressor or similar soft-faced tool to remove the bearing insert (Fig. 44). After moving the insert approximately 25 mm (1 inch), it can be removed by applying pressure under the tab.

(9) Using the same procedure described above, remove the remaining bearing inserts one at a time for inspection.

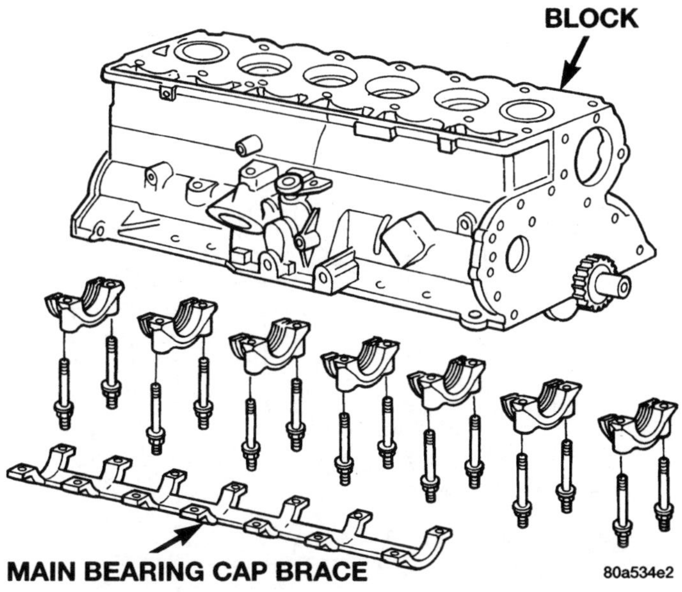

Fig. 42 Main Bearing Caps and Brace.

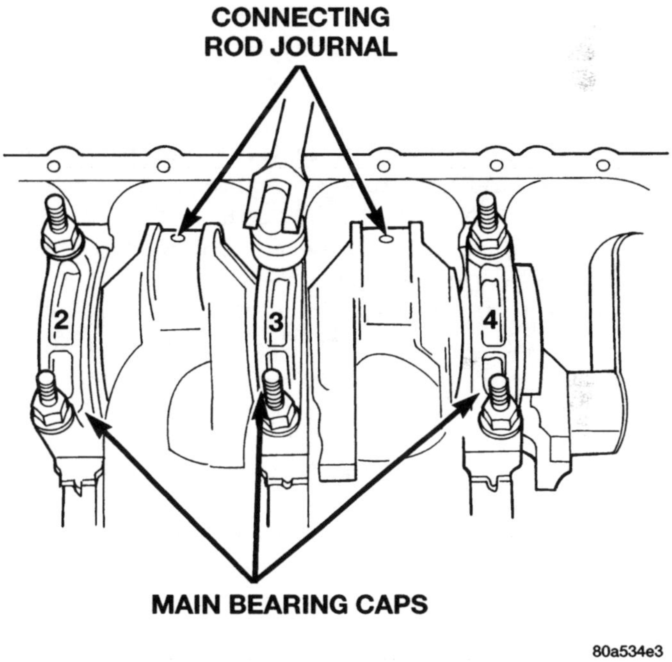

Fig. 43 Removing Main Bearing Caps and Lower Inserts

INSTALLATION

(1) Lubricate the bearing surface of each insert with engine oil.

(2) Loosen all the main bearing caps. Install the main bearing upper inserts.

(3) Install the lower bearing inserts into the main bearing caps.

(4) Install the main bearing cap(s) and lower insert(s).

(5) Tighten the bolts of caps 1, 2, 4, 5, 6, and 7 to 54 N·m (40 ft. lbs.) torque. Now tighten these bolts to

REMOVAL AND INSTALLATION (Continued)

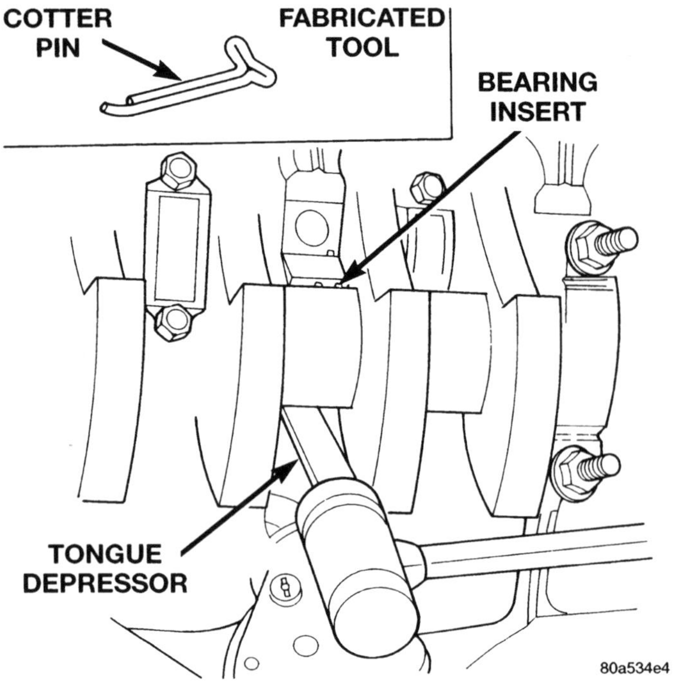

Fig. 44 Removing Upper Inserts

95 N·m (70 ft. lbs.) torque. Finally, tighten these bolts to 108 N·m (80 ft. lbs.) torque.

(6) Push the crankshaft forward and backward. Load the crankshaft front or rear and tighten cap bolt No.3 to 54 N·m (40 ft. lbs.) torque. Then tighten to 95 N·m (70 ft. lbs.) torque and finally tighten to 108 N·m (80 ft. lbs.) torque.

(7) Rotate the crankshaft after tightening each main bearing cap to ensure the crankshaft rotates freely.

(8) Check crankshaft end play. Crankshaft end play is controlled by the thrust bearing which is flange and installed at the No.2 main bearing position.

(a) Attach a magnetic base dial indicator to the cylinder block at either the front or rear of the engine.

(b) Position the dial indicator rod so that it is parallel to the center line of the crankshaft.

(c) Pry the crankshaft forward, position the dial indicator to zero.

(d) Pry the crankshaft forward and backward. Note the dial indicator readings. End play is the difference between the high and low measurements (Fig. 45). Correct end play is 0.038-0.165 mm (0.0015-0.0065 inch). The desired specifications are 0.051-0.064 mm (0.002-0.0025 inch).

(e) If end play is not within specification, inspect crankshaft thrust faces for wear. If no wear is apparent, replace the thrust bearing and measure end play. If end play is still not within specification, replace the crankshaft.

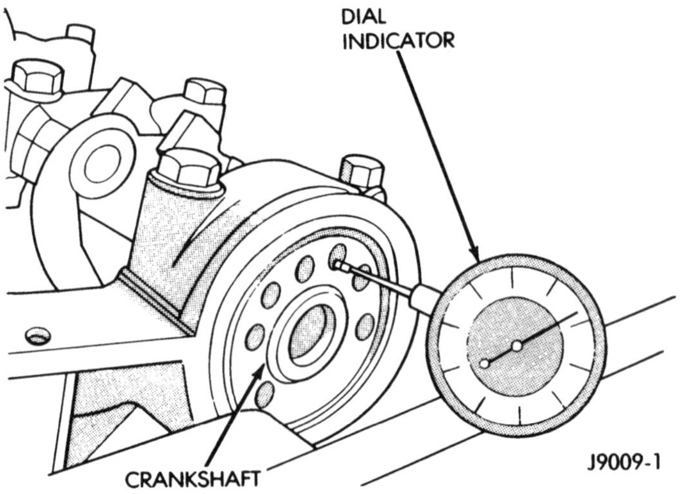

Fig. 45 Crankshaft End Play Measurement

(9) If the crankshaft was removed, install the crankshaft into the cylinder block (refer to Cylinder Block - Assemble).

(10) Install main bearing cap brace tighten nuts to 47 N·m (35 ft. lbs.) torque.

(11) Install the oil pan.

(12) Install the drain plug. Tighten the plug to 34 N·m (25 ft. lbs.) torque.

(13) Lower the vehicle.

(14) Install the spark plugs. Tighten the plugs to 37 N·m (27 ft. lbs.) torque.

(15) Fill the oil pan with engine oil to the full mark on the dipstick level.

(16) Connect negative cable to battery.

PISTONS AND CONNECTING RODS

REMOVAL

(1) Remove the engine cylinder head cover.

(2) Remove the rocker arms, bridges and pivots.

(3) Remove the push rods.

(4) Remove the engine cylinder head.

(5) Position the pistons one at a time near the bottom of the stroke. Use a ridge reamer to remove the ridge from the top end of the cylinder walls. Use a protective cloth to collect the cuttings.

(6) Raise the vehicle.

(7) Drain the engine oil.

(8) Remove the oil pan and gasket.

(9) Remove main bearing cap brace (Fig. 46).

(10) Remove the connecting rod bearing caps and inserts. Mark the caps and rods with the cylinder bore location. The connecting rods and caps are stamped with a two letter combination (Fig. 47).

(11) Lower the vehicle until it is about 2 feet from the floor.

REMOVAL AND INSTALLATION (Continued)

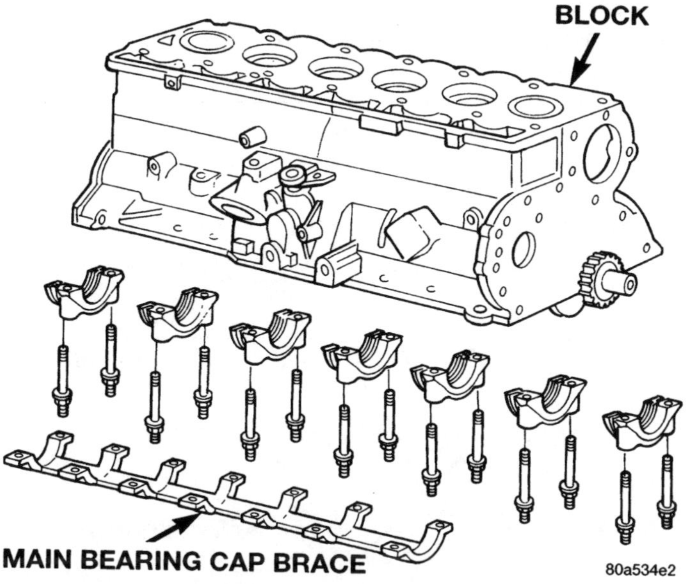

Fig. 46 Main Bearing Caps and Brace.

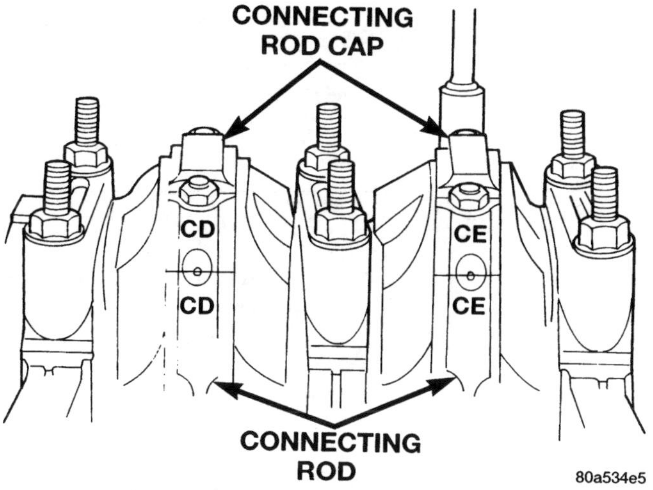

Fig. 47 Stamped Connecting Rods and Caps

CAUTION: Ensure that the connecting rod bolts DO NOT scratch the crankshaft journals or cylinder walls. Short pieces of rubber hose, slipped over the rod bolts will provide protection during removal.

(12) Have an assistant push the piston and connecting rod assemblies up and through the top of the cylinder bores (Fig. 48).

INSTALLATION

(1) Clean the cylinder bores thoroughly. Apply a light film of clean engine oil to the bores with a clean lint-free cloth.

(2) Install the piston rings on the pistons if removed.

(3) Lubricate the piston and rings with clean engine oil.

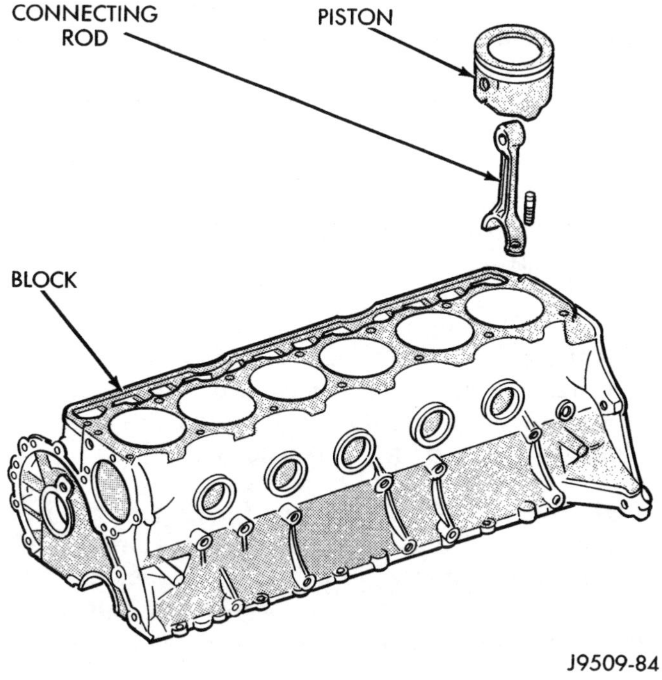

Fig. 48 Removal of Connecting Rod and Piston Assembly

CAUTION: Ensure that connecting rod bolts DO NOT scratch the crankshaft journals or cylinder walls. Short pieces of rubber hose slipped over the connecting rod bolts will provide protection during installation.

(4) Use a piston ring compressor to install the connecting rod and piston assemblies through the top of the cylinder bores (Fig. 49).

(5) Ensure the arrow on the piston top points to the front of the engine (Fig. 49).

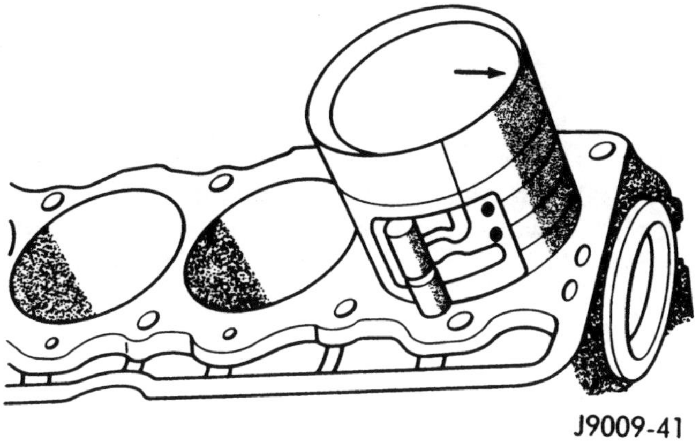

Fig. 49 Rod and Piston Assembly Installation

(6) Raise the vehicle.

(7) Each bearing insert is fitted to its respective journal to obtain the specified clearance between the bearing and the journal. In production, the select fit is obtained by using various-sized, color-coded bearing inserts as listed in the Connecting Rod Bearing

REMOVAL AND INSTALLATION (Continued)

Fitting Chart. The color code appears on the edge of the bearing insert. The size is not stamped on inserts used for production of engines.

(8) The rod journal is identified during the engine production by a color-coded paint mark on the adjacent cheek or counterweight toward the flange (rear) end of the crankshaft. The color codes used to indicate journal sizes are listed in the Connecting Rod Bearing Fitting Chart.

(9) When required, upper and lower bearing inserts of different sizes may be used as a pair (refer to Connecting Rod Bearing Fitting Chart). A standard size insert is sometimes used in combination with a 0.025 mm (0.001 inch) undersize insert to reduce clearance 0.013 mm (0.0005 inch).

CAUTION: DO NOT intermix bearing caps. Each connecting rod and bearing cap are stamped with the cylinder number. The stamp is located on a machined surface adjacent to the oil squirt hole that faces the camshaft side of the cylinder block.

(10) Install the connecting rod bearing caps and inserts in the same positions as removed.

CAUTION: Verify that the oil squirt holes in the rods face the camshaft and that the arrows on the pistons face the front of the engine.

(11) Install main bearing cap brace tighten nuts to 47 N·m (35 ft. lbs.) torque.

(12) Install the oil pan and gaskets as outlined in the installation procedure.

(13) Lower the vehicle.

(14) Install the engine cylinder head, push rods, rocker arms, bridges, pivots and engine cylinder head cover.

(15) Fill the crankcase with engine oil.

REAR MAIN OIL SEALS

The crankshaft rear main bearing oil seal consists of two half pieces of viton with a single lip that effectively seals the rear of the crankshaft. Replace the upper and lower seal halves as a unit to ensure leak-free operation.

REMOVAL

(1) Remove the transmission inspection cover.

(2) Remove the oil pan.

(3) Remove the rear main bearing cap (No.7).

(4) Push the upper seal out of the groove. Ensure that the crankshaft and seal groove are not damaged.

(5) Remove the lower half of the seal from the bearing cap.

INSTALLATION

(1) Wipe the seal surface area of the crankshaft until it is clean.

(2) Apply a thin coat of engine oil.

(3) Coat the lip of the seal with engine oil.

(4) Carefully position the upper seal into the groove in the cylinder block. The lip of the seal faces toward the front of the engine.

(5) Place the lower half of the seal into bearing cap No.7 (Fig. 50).

(6) Coat the outer curved surface of the lower seal with soap and the lip of the seal with engine oil (Fig. 50).

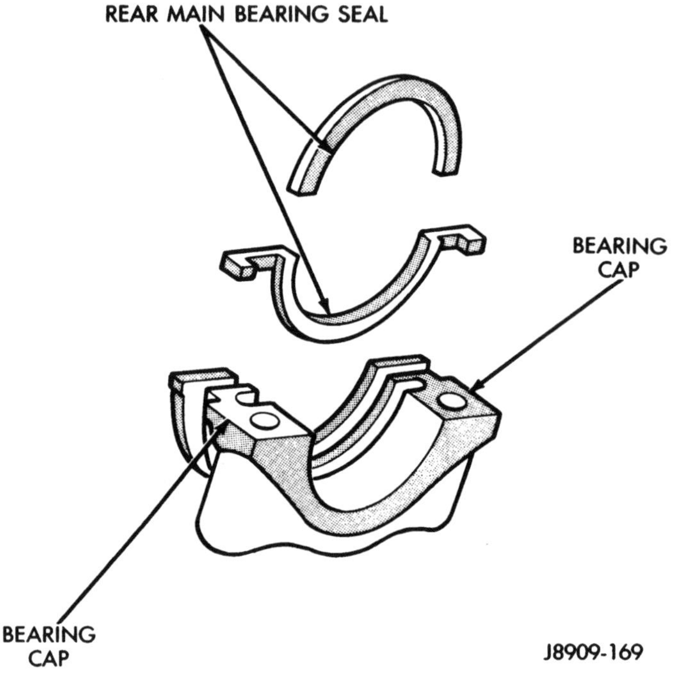

Fig. 50 Rear Main Bearing Oil Seal

(7) Position the lower seal into the bearing cap recess and seat it firmly. Be sure the seal is flush with the cylinder block pan rail.

(8) Apply Loctite 518, or equivalent on the rear bearing cap (Fig. 51). The bead should be 3 mm (0.125 in) thick. DO NOT apply Loctite 518, or equivalent to the lip of the seal.

(9) Install the rear main bearing cap. DO NOT strike the cap more than twice for proper engagement.

(10) Tighten all main bearing bolts to 108 N·m (80 ft. lbs.) torque.

(11) Install the oil pan gasket and oil pan.

(12) Install the engine flywheel or converter drive plate.

TIMING CASE COVER OIL SEAL

This procedure is done with the timing case cover installed.

REMOVAL AND INSTALLATION (Continued)

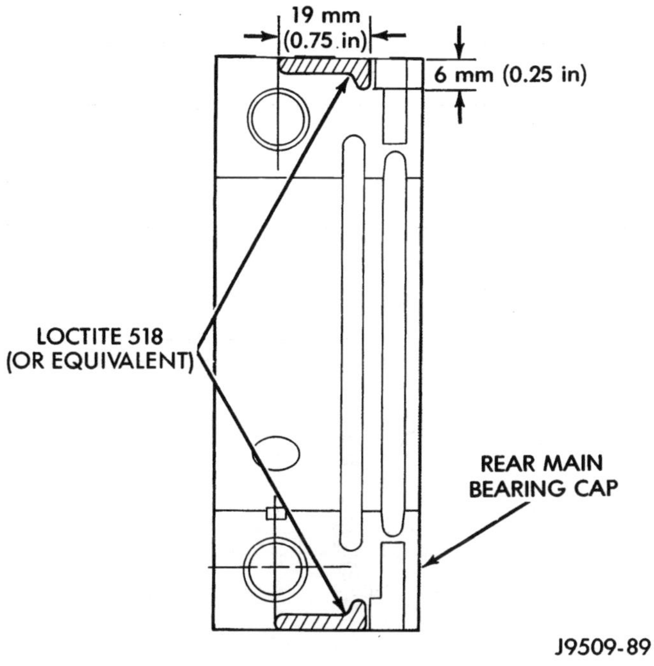

Fig. 51 Location of Loctite 518 (or equivalent)

REMOVAL

(1) Disconnect negative cable from battery.
(2) Remove the serpentine drive belt.
(3) Remove the vibration damper.
(4) Remove the radiator shroud.
(5) Carefully remove the oil seal. Make sure seal bore is clean.

INSTALLATION

(1) Position the replacement oil seal on Timing Case Cover Alignment and Seal Installation Tool 6139 with seal open end facing inward. Apply a light film of Perfect Seal, or equivalent, on the outside diameter of the seal. Lightly coat the crankshaft with engine oil.

(2) Position the tool and seal over the end of the crankshaft and insert a draw screw tool into Seal Installation Tool 6139 (Fig. 52). Tighten the nut against the tool until it contacts the cover.

(3) Remove the tools. Apply a light film of engine oil on the vibration damper hub contact surface of the seal.

(4) Apply Mopar Silicone Rubber Adhesive Sealant to the keyway in the crankshaft and insert the key. With the key inserted in the keyway in the crankshaft, install the vibration damper, washer and bolt. Lubricate and tighten the bolt to 108 N·m (80 ft. lbs.) torque.

(5) Install the serpentine belt and tighten to the specified tension (refer to Group 7, Cooling Systems for the proper specifications and procedures).

(6) Install the radiator shroud.
(7) Connect negative cable to battery.

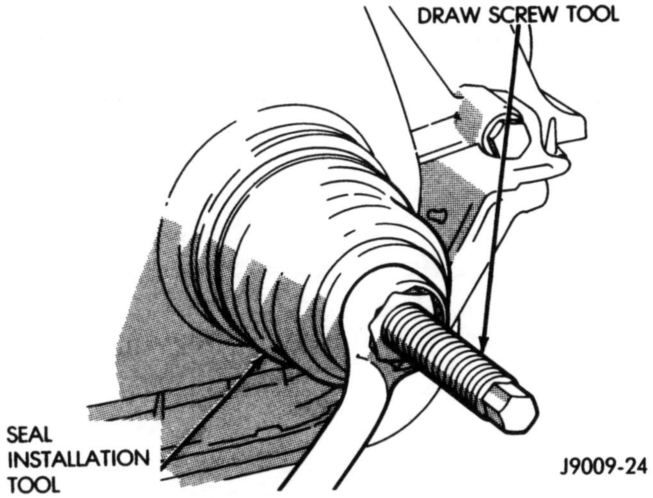

Fig. 52 Timing Case Cover Oil Seal Installation

DISASSEMBLY AND ASSEMBLY

VALVE SERVICE

Clean all carbon deposits from the combustion chambers, valve ports, valve stems, valve stem guides and head.

Clean all grime and gasket material from the engine cylinder head machined gasket surface.

Inspect for cracks in the combustion chambers and valve ports.

Inspect for cracks on the exhaust seat.

Inspect for cracks in the gasket surface at each coolant passage.

Inspect valves for burned, cracked or warped heads.

Inspect for scuffed or bent valve stems.

Replace valves displaying any damage.

VALVE REFACING

(1) Use a valve refacing machine to reface the intake and exhaust valves to the specified angle.

(2) After refacing, a margin of at least 0.787 mm (0.031 inch) must remain (Fig. 53). If the margin is less than 0.787 mm (0.031 inch), the valve must be replaced.

VALVE SEAT REFACING

(1) Install a pilot of the correct size in the valve guide bore. Reface the valve seat to the specified angle with a good dressing stone. Remove only enough metal to provide a smooth finish.

(2) Use tapered stones to obtain the specified seat width when required.

(3) Control valve seat runout to a maximum of 0.0635 mm (0.0025 in.) (Fig. 54).

VALVE STEM OIL SEAL REPLACEMENT

Valve stem oil seals are installed on each valve stem to prevent rocker arm lubricating oil from

DISASSEMBLY AND ASSEMBLY (Continued)

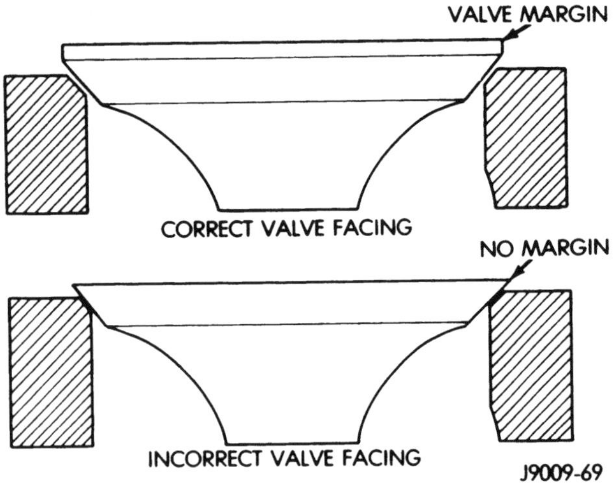

Fig. 53 Valve Facing Margin

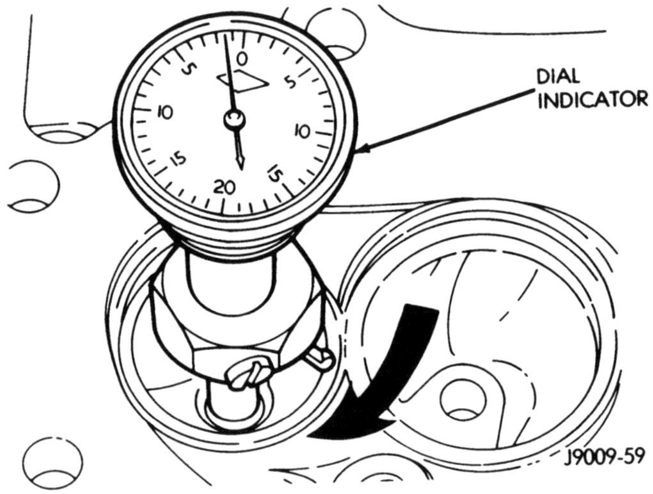

Fig. 54 Measurement of Valve Seat Runout

entering the combustion chamber through the valve guide bores. One seal is marked INT (intake valve) and the other is marked EXH (exhaust valve).

Replace the oil seals whenever valve service is performed or if the seals have deteriorated.

VALVE GUIDES

The valve guides are an integral part of the engine cylinder head and are not replaceable.

When the valve stem guide clearance is excessive, the valve guide bores must be reamed oversize. Service valves with oversize stems are available in 0.076 mm (0.003 inch) and 0.381 mm (0.015 inch) increments.

Corresponding oversize valve stem seals are also available and must be used with valves having 0.381 mm (0.015 inch) oversize stems.

NOTE: If the valve guides are reamed oversize, the valve seats must be ground to ensure that the valve seat is concentric to the valve guide.

VALVE STEM-TO-GUIDE CLEARANCE MEASUREMENT

Valve stem-to-guide clearance may be measured by either of the following two methods.

PREFERRED METHOD

(1) Remove the valve from the head.

(2) Clean the valve stem guide bore with solvent and a bristle brush.

(3) Insert a telescoping gauge into the valve stem guide bore approximately 9.525 mm (.375 inch) from the valve spring side of the head (Fig. 55).

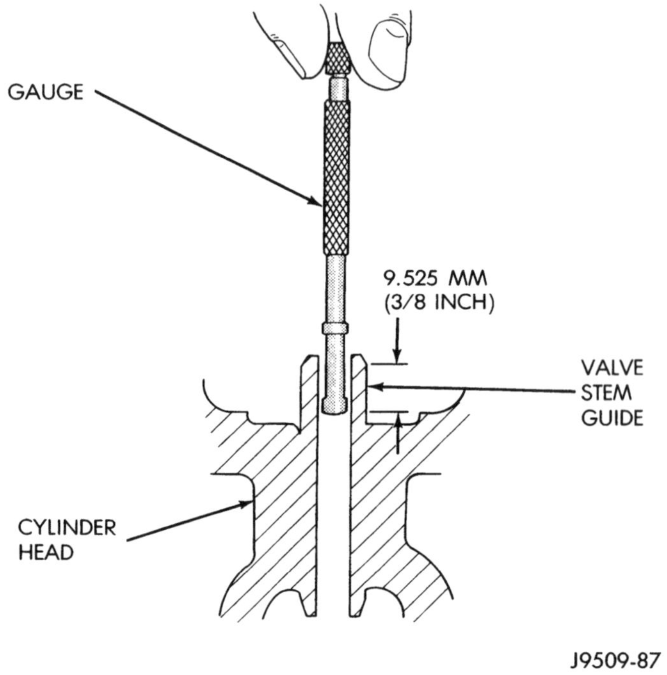

Fig. 55 Measurement of Valve Guide Bore Diameter

(4) Remove and measure telescoping gauge with a micrometer.

(5) Repeat the measurement with contacts lengthwise to engine cylinder head.

(6) Compare the crosswise to lengthwise measurements to determine out-of-roundness. If the measurements differ by more than 0.0635 mm (0.0025 in.), ream the guide bore to accommodate an oversize valve stem.

(7) Compare the measured valve guide bore diameter with specifications (7.95-7.97 mm or 0.313-0.314 inch). If the measurement differs from specification by more than 0.076 mm (0.003 inch), ream the guide bore to accommodate an oversize valve stem.

ALTERNATIVE METHOD

(1) Use a dial indicator to measure the lateral movement of the valve stem (stem-to-guide clearance). This must be done with the valve installed in its guide and just off the valve seat (Fig. 56).

DISASSEMBLY AND ASSEMBLY (Continued)

(2) Correct clearance is 0.025-0.0762 mm (0.001-0.003 inch). If indicated movement exceeds the specification ream the valve guide to accommodate an oversize valve stem.

NOTE: Valve seats must be ground after reaming the valve guides to ensure that the valve seat is concentric to the valve guide.

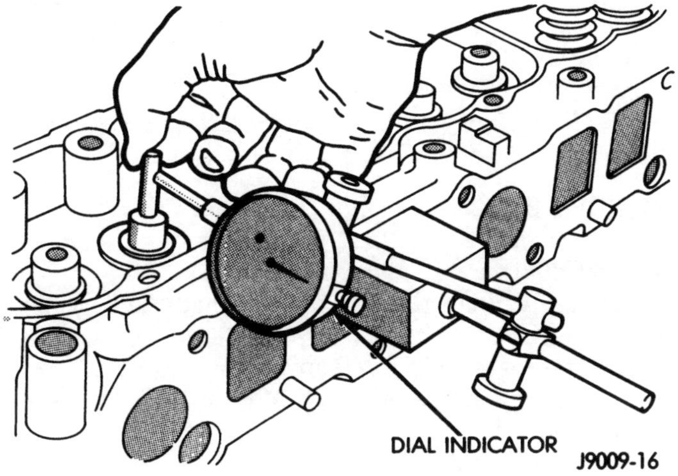

Fig. 56 Measurement of Lateral Movement of Valve Stem

VALVE SPRING TENSION TEST

Use a universal Valve Spring Tester and a torque wrench to test each valve spring for the specified tension value (Fig. 57).

Replace valve springs that are not within specifications.

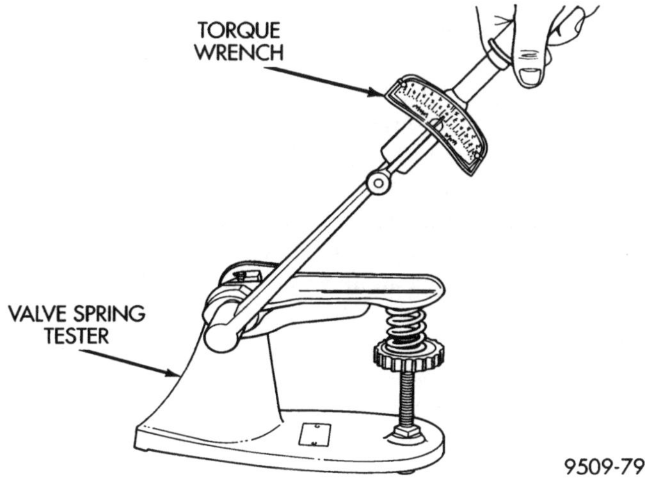

Fig. 57 Valve Spring Tester

CYLINDER BLOCK

DISASSEMBLY

Refer to the applicable sections for detailed instructions.

(1) Drain the engine oil. Remove and discard the oil filter.

(2) Remove the water pump from the cylinder block.

(3) Remove the vibration damper.

(4) Remove the timing case cover and lay the cover upside down.

(5) Position a drift punch into the slot in the back of the cover and tap the old seal out.

(6) Remove the oil slinger from crankshaft.

(7) Remove the camshaft retaining bolt and remove the sprockets and chain as an assembly.

(8) Remove the camshaft.

(9) Remove the oil pan and gasket.

(10) Remove the front and rear oil galley plugs.

(11) Remove the oil pump.

(12) Remove the connecting rods and the pistons. Remove the connecting rod and piston assemblies through the top of the cylinder bores.

(13) Remove the crankshaft.

ASSEMBLY

Refer to the applicable sections for detailed instructions.

(1) Install the crankshaft.

(2) Install the connecting rods and the pistons through the top of the cylinder bores.

(3) Install the oil pump.

(4) Install the oil pan and gasket.

(5) Install the camshaft.

(6) Install the sprockets and chain as an assembly.

(7) Install the oil slinger from the crankshaft.

(8) Install the timing case cover seal.

(9) Install the timing case cover.

(10) Install the vibration damper.

(11) Install the water pump. Tighten the mounting bolts to 31 N·m (270 in. lbs.) torque.

(12) Lubricate the oil filter seal with clean engine oil. Tighten oil filter to 18 N·m (13 ft. lbs.) torque.

(13) Install the engine into the vehicle.

(14) Fill the engine with clean lubrication oil (refer to Group 0, Lubrication and Maintenance).

(15) Fill the cooling system.

CLEANING AND INSPECTION

ENGINE CYLINDER HEAD

CLEANING

Thoroughly clean the engine cylinder head and cylinder block mating surfaces. Clean the intake and engine exhaust manifold and engine cylinder head mating surfaces. Remove all gasket material and carbon.

Check to ensure that no coolant or foreign material has fallen into the tappet bore area.

CLEANING AND INSPECTION (Continued)

Remove the carbon deposits from the combustion chambers and top of the pistons.

INSPECTION

Use a straightedge and feeler gauge to check the flatness of the engine cylinder head and block mating surfaces.

ENGINE CYLINDER HEAD COVER

CLEANING

Remove any original sealer from the cover sealing surface of the engine cylinder head and clean the surface using a fabric cleaner.

Remove all residue from the sealing surface using a clean, dry cloth.

INSPECTION

Inspect the engine cylinder head cover for cracks. Replace the cover, if cracked.

The original dark grey gasket material should NOT be removed. If sections of the gasket material are missing or are compressed, replace the engine cylinder head cover. However, sections with minor damage such as small cracks, cuts or chips may be repaired with a hand held applicator. The new material must be smoothed over to maintain gasket height. Allow the gasket material to cure prior to engine cylinder head cover installation.

ROCKER ARMS AND PUSH RODS

CLEANING

Clean all the components with cleaning solvent.

Use compressed air to blow out the oil passages in the rocker arms and push rods.

INSPECTION

Inspect the pivot surface area of each rocker arm. Replace any that are scuffed, pitted, cracked or excessively worn.

Inspect the valve stem tip contact surface of each rocker arm and replace any rocker arm that is deeply pitted.

Inspect each push rod end for excessive wear and replace as required. If any push rod is excessively worn because of lack of oil, replace it and inspect the corresponding hydraulic tappet for excessive wear.

Inspect the push rods for straightness by rolling them on a flat surface or by shining a light between the push rod and the flat surface.

A wear pattern along the length of the push rod is not normal. Inspect the engine cylinder head for obstruction if this condition exists.

HYDRAULIC TAPPETS

CLEANING

Clean each tappet assembly in cleaning solvent to remove all varnish, gum and sludge deposits.

INSPECTION

Inspect for indications of scuffing on the side and base of each tappet body.

Inspect each tappet base for concave wear with a straightedge positioned across the base. If the base is concave, the corresponding lobe on the camshaft is also worn. Replace the camshaft and defective tappets.

CYLINDER BLOCK

CLEANING

Thoroughly clean the oil pan and engine block gasket surfaces.

Use compressed air to clean out:

- The galley at the oil filter adaptor hole, the filter bypass hole.
- The front and rear oil galley holes.
- The feed holes for the crankshaft main bearings.

Once the block has been completely cleaned, apply Loctite PST pipe sealant with Teflon 592 to the threads of the front and rear oil galley plugs. Tighten the plugs to 41 N·m (30 ft. lbs.) torque.

INSPECTION—CYLINDER BORE

(1) It is mandatory to use a dial bore gauge to measure each cylinder bore diameter (Fig. 58). To correctly select the proper size piston, a cylinder bore gauge, capable of reading in 0.003 mm (.0001 in.) INCREMENTS is required. If a bore gauge is not available, do not use an inside micrometer.

(2) Measure the inside diameter of the cylinder bore at three levels below top of bore. Start perpendicular (across or at 90 degrees) to the axis of the crankshaft and then take two additional reading.

(3) Measure the cylinder bore diameter crosswise to the cylinder block near the top of the bore. Repeat the measurement near the middle of the bore, then repeat the measurement near the bottom of the bore.

(4) Determine taper by subtracting the smaller diameter from the larger diameter.

(5) Rotate measuring device 90° and repeat steps above.

(6) Determine out-of-roundness by comparing the difference between each measurement.

(7) If cylinder bore taper does not exceed 0.025 mm (0.001 inch) and out-of-roundness does not exceed 0.025 mm (0.001 inch), the cylinder bore can be honed. If the cylinder bore taper or out- of-round condition exceeds these maximum limits, the cylinder must be bored and then honed to accept an oversize

CLEANING AND INSPECTION (Continued)

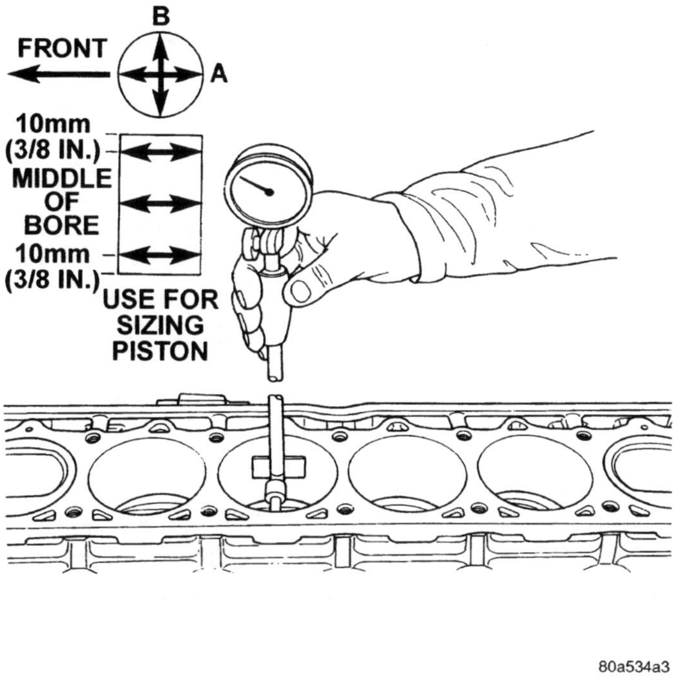

Fig. 58 Cylinder Bore Measurement

piston. A slight amount of taper always exists in the cylinder bore after the engine has been in use for a period of time.

HONING—CYLINDER BORE

The honing operation should be closely coordinated with the fitting of pistons and rings. This will ensure specified clearances are maintained.

Refer to Standard Service Procedures in the beginning of this Group for the proper honing of cylinder bores.

SPECIFICATIONS

4.0L ENGINE SPECIFICATIONS

Camshaft
Hydraulic Tappet Clearance . . . . .Zero Lash
Bearing Clearance. . . . . .0.025 to 0.076 mm (0.001 to 0.003 in.)
Bearing Journal Diameter
No. 1 . . . . .51.54 to 51.56 mm (2.029 to 2.030 in.)
No. 2 . . . . .51.28 to 51.31 mm (2.019 to 2.020 in.)
No. 3 . . . . .51.03 to 51.05 mm (2.009 to 2.010 in.)
No. 4 . . . . .50.78 to 50.80 mm (1.999 to 2.000 in.)
Base Circle Runout . . . . .0.03 mm - max. (0.001 in. - max.)
Valve Lift . . . . .10.29 mm (0.405 in.)
Intake Valve Timing
Opens . . . . .12.4° BTDC
Closes . . . . .60.9° ABDC
Exhaust Valve Timing
Opens . . . . .49.8 BBDC
Closes. . . . . .29.2° ATDC
Valve Overlap. . . . . .42.6°
Intake Duration . . . . .253.3°
Exhaust Duration. . . . . .259.°
Crankshaft
End Play . . .0.038 to 0.165 mm (0.0015 to 0.0065 in.)
Main Bearing Journal Diameter
No. 1-6.63.489 to 63.502 mm (2.4996 to 2.5001 in.)
Main Bearing Journal Diameter
No. 7 . .63.449 to 63.487 mm (2.4980 to 2.4995 in.)
Main Bearing Journal Width
No. 1 . . . . . .27.58 to 27.89 mm (1.086 to 1.098 in.)
Main Bearing Journal Width
No. 3 . . . . . .32.28 to 32.33 mm (1.271 to 1.273 in.)
Main Bearing Journal Width
No. 2-4-5-6-7 . . . . .30.02 to 30.18 mm (1.182 to 1.188 in.)
Main Bearing Clearance . . . . .0.03 to 0.06 mm (0.001 to 0.0025 in.)
Main Bearing Clearance (Preferred) . . . . . .0.051 mm (0.002 in.)
Connecting Rod Journal Diameter . . . . .53.17 to 53.23 mm (2.0934 to 2.0955 in.)
Connecting Rod Journal Width . . .27.18 to 27.33 mm (1.070 to 1.076 in.)
Out-of-Round (Max. All Journals) . . . . .0.013 mm (0.0005 in.)
Taper (Max. – All Journals) . . .0.013 mm (0.0005 in.)
Cylinder Block
Deck Height. . . . . .240.03 to 240.18 mm (9.450 to 9.456 in.)
Deck Clearance (Below Block) . . . . .0.546 mm (0.0215 in.)

SPECIFICATIONS (Continued)

Cylinder Bore Diameter—
Standard . . . . .98.45 to 98.48 mm (3.8759 to 3.8775 in.)
Cylinder Bore Diameter— Taper (Max.) . . .0.025 mm (0.001 in.)
Cylinder Bore Diameter—
Out-of-Round . . . . .0.025 mm (0.001 in.)
Tappet Bore Diameter . . . . .23.000 to 23.025 mm (0.9055 to 0.9065 in.)
Flatness. . . .0.03 mm per 25 mm (0.001 in. per 1 in.)
Flatness. . .0.05 mm per 152 mm (0.002 in. per 6 in.)
Flatness Max. . . . . . . .0.20 mm max. for total length (0.008 in. max. for total length)
Main Bearing Bore
Diameter . . . . .68.3514 to 68.3768 mm (2.691 to 2.692 in.)

Connecting Rods

Total Weight (Less Bearing) . . . . . .657 to 665 grams (23.17 to 23.45 oz.)
Length (Center-to-Center) . . . . .155.52 to 155.62 mm (6.123 to 6.127 in.)
Piston Pin Bore Diameter . . . . . . .23.59 to 23.62 mm (0.9288 to 0.9298 in.)
Bore (Less Bearings) . . . . .56.08 to 56.09 mm (2.2080 to 2.2085 in.)
Bearing Clearance. . . . . .0.025 to 0.076 mm (0.001 to 0.003 in.)
Bearing Clearance (Preferred). . . .0.044 to 0.050 mm (0.0015 to 0.0020 in.)
Side Clearance . .0.25 to 0.48 mm (0.010 to 0.019 in.)
Twist (Max.) . .0.001 mm per mm (0.001 in. per inch)
Bend Max.) . .0.001 mm per mm (0.001 in. per inch.)

Cylinder Compression Pressure

Ratio. 8.7:1
Pressure Range. . . .827 to 1,034 kPa (120 to 150 psi)
Max. Variation Between Cylinders . .206 kPa (30 psi)

Cylinder Head

Combustion Chamber. . . . . .52.22 to 58.22 cc (3.37 to 3.55 cu. in.)
Valve Guide I.D. (Integral). . . . . . .7.9 mm (0.312 in.)
Valve Stem-to-Guide Clearance . . .0.025 to 0.076 mm (0.001 to 0.003 in.)
Intake Valve Seat Angle . . . . .44.5°
Exhaust Valve Seat Angle . . . . .44.5°
Valve Seat Width . . . . .1.02 to 1.52 mm (0.040 to 0.060 in.)
Valve Seat Runout . . . . .0.064 mm (0.0025 in.)
Flatness. . . .0.03 mm per 25 mm (0.001 in. per 1 in.)
Flatness. . .0.05 mm per 152 mm (0.002 in. per 6 in.)
Flatness Max. . . . . . .0.20 mm - max. for total length (0.008 in. max. for total length)

Rocker Arms, Push Rods & Tappets

Rocker Arm Ratio 1.6:1
Push Rod Length . . . . .244.856 to 245.364 mm (9.640 to 9.660 in.)
Push Rod Diameter. . . . . .7.92 to 8.00 mm (0.312 to 0.315 in.)
Hydraulic Tappet Diameter . . . .22.962 to 22.974 mm (0.904 to 0.9045 in.)
Tappet-to-Bore Clearance . . . . . . .0.025 to 0.063 mm (0.001 to 0.0025 in.)

Valves

Length (Tip-to-Gauge Dimension Line)
Intake . . . . .122.479 to 122.860 mm (4.822 to 4.837 in.)
Length (Tip-to-Gauge Dimension Line)
Exhaust . . . . .122.860 to 123.241 mm (4.837 to 4.852 in.)
Valve Stem Diameter . . . . .7.899 to 7.925 mm (0.311 to 0.312 in.)
Stem-to-Guide Clearance. . . . . . . .0.025 to 0.076 mm (0.001 to 0.003 in.)
Valve Head Diameter—Intake. .48.387 to 48.641 mm (1.905 to 1.915 in.)
Valve Head Diameter—
Exhaust. .37.973 to 38.227 mm (1.495 to 1.505 in.)
Valve Face Angle—Intake . . . . .45°
Valve Face Angle—Exhaust. . . . . .45°
Tip Refinishing (Max. Allowable) .0.25 mm (0.010 in.)

Valve Springs

Free Length (Approx.) . . . . .47.65 mm (1.876 in.)
Spring Tension—Valve
Closed . . . . .271 to 307 N @ 41.656 mm (61 to 69 lbf. @ 1.64 in.)
Spring Tension—Valve
Open. . . . . .818.5 to 871.9 N @ 30.89 mm (184 to 196 lbf @ 1.216 in.)
Inside Diameter . . . . .21.0 mm to 21.51 mm (0.827 to 0.847 in.)

Pistons

Weight (Less Pin) . . . . .563 to 567 grams (19.86 to 20.00 oz.)
Piston Pin Bore (Centerline to Piston
Top). . . . . . .40.61 to 40.72 mm (1.599 to 1.603 in.)
Piston-to-Bore Clearance. . . . . . . .0.033 to 0.053 mm (0.0013 to 0.0021 in.)
Piston-to-Bore Clearance
(Preferred). . . . . .0.033 to 0.038 mm (0.0013 to 0.0015 in.)
Ring Gap Clearance— Top Compression
Ring . . . . .0.229 to 0.610mm (0.0090 to 0.0240 in.)
Ring Gap Clearance— 2nd Compression
Ring . . . .0.483 to 0.965 mm (0.0190 to 0.0380 in.)
Ring Gap Clearance—Oil Control Steel
Rails . . . . . .0.254 to 1.500 mm (0.010 to 0.060 in.)
Ring Side Clearance—Compression
Rings. . . .0.042 to 0.084 mm (0.0017 to 0.0033 in.)
Ring Side Clearance—Oil Control
Rings. . . . . .0.06 to 0.21 mm (0.0024 to 0.0083 in.)

SPECIFICATIONS (Continued)

Piston Ring Groove Height—Compression Rings. . . .1.530 to 1.555 mm (0.0602 to 0.0612 in.)
Piston Ring Groove Height—Oil Control Ring . . . .4.035 to 4.060 mm (0.1589 to 0.1598 in.)
Piston Ring Groove Diameter—Compression Rings . . . . . .88.3 to 88.55 mm (3.476 to 3.486 in.)
Piston Ring Groove Diameter—Oil Control Ring . . . . . .90.35 to 90.60 mm (3.557 to 3.566 in.)
Piston Pin Bore Diameter . . . . .23.647 to 23.655 mm (0.9310 to 0.9313 in.)
Piston Pin Diameter . . . . .23.637 to 23.640 mm (0.9306 to 0.9307 in.)
Piston-to-Pin Clearance . . . . .0.0076 to 0.0178 mm—Loose (0.0003 to 0.0007 in. Loose)
Piston-to-Pin Clearance (Preferred) . . . . .0.013 mm (0.0005 in.)
Piston-to-Pin Connecting Rod (Press Fit). . . . .8.9 kN (2000 lbf.)

Oil Pump
Gear-to-Body Clearance (Radial). .0.051 to 0.102 mm (0.002 to 0.004 in.)
Gear-to-Body Clearance (Radial) (Preferred) . . . . .0.051 mm (0.002 in.)
Gear End Clearance—Plastigage . .0.051 to 0.152 mm (0.002 to 0.006 in.)
Gear End Clearance—Plastigage (Preferred) . . . . .0.051 mm (0.002 in.)
Gear End Clearance—Feeler Gauge . . .0.1016 to 0.2032 mm (0.004 to 0.008 in.)
Gear End Clearance—Feeler Gauge (Preferred) . . . . .0.1778 mm (0.007 in.)

Oil Pressure
At Idle Speed (600 rpm). . . . . .89.6 kPa (13 psi)
At 1600 rpm & Higher .255 to 517 kPa (37 to 75 psi)
Oil Pressure Relief . . . . .517 kPa (75 psi)

TORQUE SPECIFICATIONS

DESCRIPTION	TORQUE
A/C Compressor Bracket-to-Engine	
Bolts	34 N·m (25 ft. lbs.)
A/C Compressor	
Mounting Bolts	27 N·m (20 ft. lbs.)
A/C Low Pressure Service Valve	
Nut	38 N·m (28 ft. lbs.)
Block Heater	
Nut	1.8 N·m (16 in. lbs.)
Camshaft Sprocket	
Bolt	108 N·m (80 ft. lbs.)
Connecting Rod	
Nuts	45 N·m (33 ft. lbs.)
Cylinder Block	
Drain Plugs	41 N·m (30 ft. lbs.)
Cylinder Head	
Bolts #1–10 & #12–14	149 N·m (110 ft. lbs.)
Bolt #11	135 N·m (100 ft. lbs.)
Cylinder Head Cover	
Bolts	13 N·m (115 in. lbs.)
Engine Mounts—Front	
Support Bracket Bolts	61 N·m (45 ft. lbs.)
Support Cushion Bolts/Nuts	41 N·m (30 ft. lbs.)
Support Cushion Bracket Bolts	54 N·m (40 ft. lbs.)
Support Cushion Bracket Stud Nuts	41 N·m (30 ft. lbs.)
Support Cushion Thru-Bolt	65 N·m (48 ft. lbs.)
Engine Mounts—Rear	
Crossmember-to-Sill Bolts (Automatic)	41 N·m (30 ft. lbs.)
Insulator Stud Assembly Nut	41 N·m (30 ft. lbs.)
Support Cushion/Crossmember Nuts	22 N·m (192 in. lbs.)
Support Cushion/Bracket Nuts (Manual)	75 N·m (55 ft. lbs.)
Transmission Support Bracket Bolt (Manual)	46 N·m (34 ft. lbs.)
Transmission Support Bracket/Cushion Bolt (4WD Auto)	75N·m (55 ft. lbs.)
Transmission Support Adaptor Bracket Bolts (2WD Auto)	75N·m (55 ft. lbs.)
Exhaust Manifold/Pipe	
Nuts	27 N·m (20 ft. lbs.)
Flywheel/Converter Housing	
Bolts	38 N·m (28 ft. lbs.)
Flywheel/Crankshaft	
Bolts	143 N·m (105 ft. lbs.)
Front Cover-to-Block	
Bolts 1/4–20	7N·m (60 in. lbs.)
Bolts 5/16–18	22N·m (192 in. lbs.)
Fuel Pump	
Bolts	22 N·m (16 ft. lbs.)
Generator	
Adjusting Bolt	24 N·m (18 ft. lbs.)
Pivot Bolt/Nut	38 N·m (28 ft. lbs.)
Main Bearing	
Bolts	108 N·m (80 ft. lbs.)
Oil Filter	
Filter	18 N·m (13 ft. lbs.)
Oil Galley	
Plug	41 N·m (30 ft. lbs.)

SPECIFICATIONS (Continued)

DESCRIPTION	TORQUE
Oil Pan	
1/4–20 Bolts	9.5 N·m (84 in. lbs.)
5/16–18 Bolts	15 N·m (132 in. lbs.)
Drain Plug	34 N·m (25 ft. lbs.)
Oil Pump	
Short Attaching Bolts	23 N·m (17 ft. lbs.)
Long Attaching Bolts	23 N·m (17 ft. lbs.)
Cover Bolts	8 N·m (70 in. lbs.)
Power Steering Pump Pressure Hose	
Nut	52 N·m (38 ft. lbs.)
Rocker Arm Assembly-to-Cylinder Head	
Capscrews	28 N·m (21ft. lbs.)
Spark Plugs	
Plugs	37 N·m (27 ft. lbs.)
Starting Motor	
Mounting Bolts	45 N·m (33 ft. lbs.)
Thermostat Housing	
Bolts	18 N·m (13 ft. lbs.)
Vibration Damper	
Bolts	108 N·m (80 ft. lbs.)
Water Pump/Block	
Bolts	31 N·m (270 in. lbs.)

SPECIAL TOOLS

2.5L/4.0L ENGINE

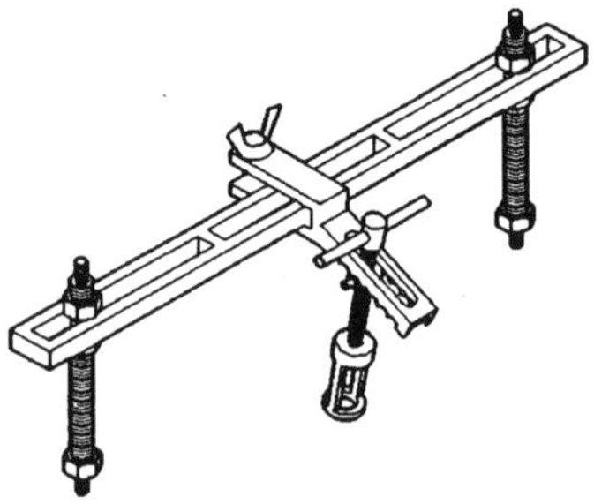

Valve Spring Compressor Tool MD-998772A

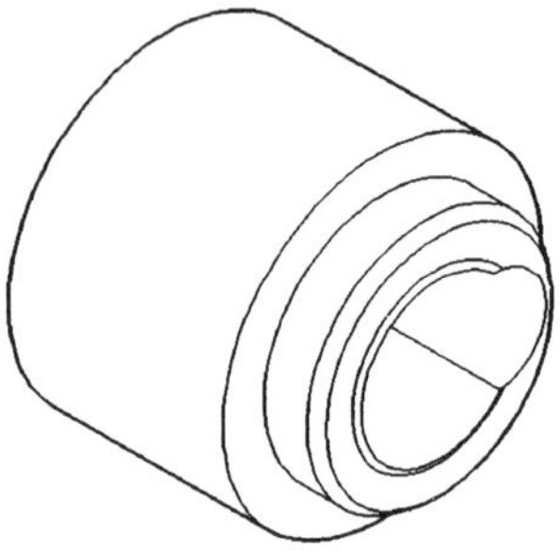

Timing Case Cover Alignment and Seal installation Tool 6139

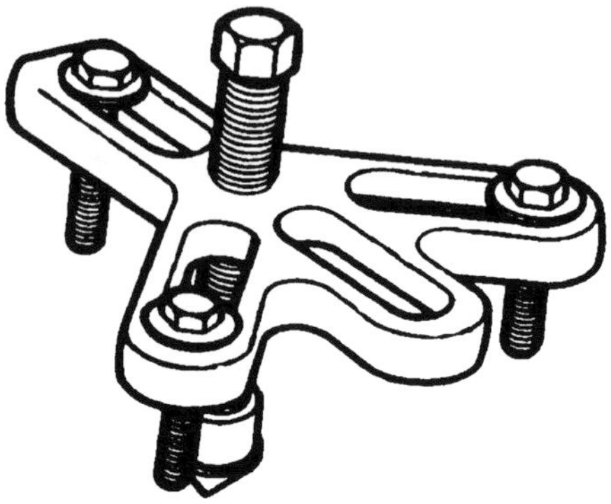

Vibration Damper Removal Tool 7697

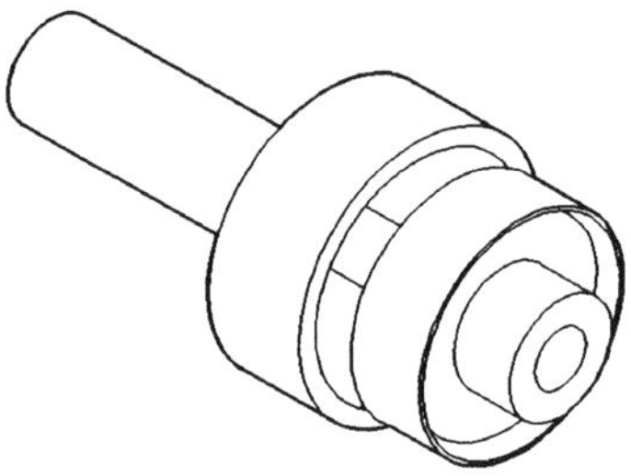

Rear Main Seal Installer Tool 6271A

EXHAUST SYSTEM AND INTAKE MANIFOLD

CONTENTS

GENERAL INFORMATION

EXHAUST SYSTEM

The basic exhaust system consists of an engine exhaust manifold, exhaust pipe with oxygen sensor, catalytic converter with oxygen sensor, exhaust heat shield(s), muffler and exhaust tailpipe (Fig. 1) (Fig. 2).

The exhaust system uses a single muffler with a catalytic converter consisting of dual ceramic monoliths.

The 4.0L engines use a seal between the engine exhaust manifold and exhaust pipe to assure a tight seal and strain free connections (Fig. 2).

The exhaust system must be properly aligned to prevent stress, leakage and body contact. If the system contacts any body panel, it may amplify objectionable noises originating from the engine or body.

When inspecting an exhaust system, critically inspect for cracked or loose joints, stripped screw or bolt threads, corrosion damage and worn, cracked or broken hangers. Replace all components that are badly corroded or damaged. DO NOT attempt to repair.

When replacement is required, use original equipment parts (or their equivalent). This will assure proper alignment and provide acceptable exhaust noise levels.

CAUTION: Avoid application of rust prevention compounds or undercoating materials to exhaust system floor pan exhaust heat shields. Light overspray near the edges is permitted. Application of coating will result in excessive floor pan temperatures and objectionable fumes.

CATALYTIC CONVERTER

The stainless steel catalytic converter body is designed to last the life of the vehicle. Excessive heat can result in bulging or other distortion, but excessive heat will not be the fault of the converter. If unburned fuel enters the converter, overheating may occur. If a converter is heat-damaged, correct the cause of the damage at the same time the converter is replaced. Also, inspect all other components of the exhaust system for heat damage.

Unleaded gasoline must be used to avoid contaminating the catalyst core.

EXHAUST HEAT SHIELDS

Exhaust heat shields are needed to protect both the vehicle and the environment from the high temperatures developed by the catalytic converter. The catalytic converter releases additional heat into the exhaust system. Under severe operating conditions, the temperature increases in the area of the converter. Such conditions can exist when the engine misfires or otherwise does not operate at peak efficiency.

DO NOT remove spark plug wires from plugs or by any other means short out cylinders. Failure of the catalytic converter can occur due to a temperature increase caused by unburned fuel passing through the converter.

DO NOT allow the engine to operate at fast idle for extended periods (over 5 minutes). This condition may result in excessive temperatures in the exhaust system and on the floor pan.

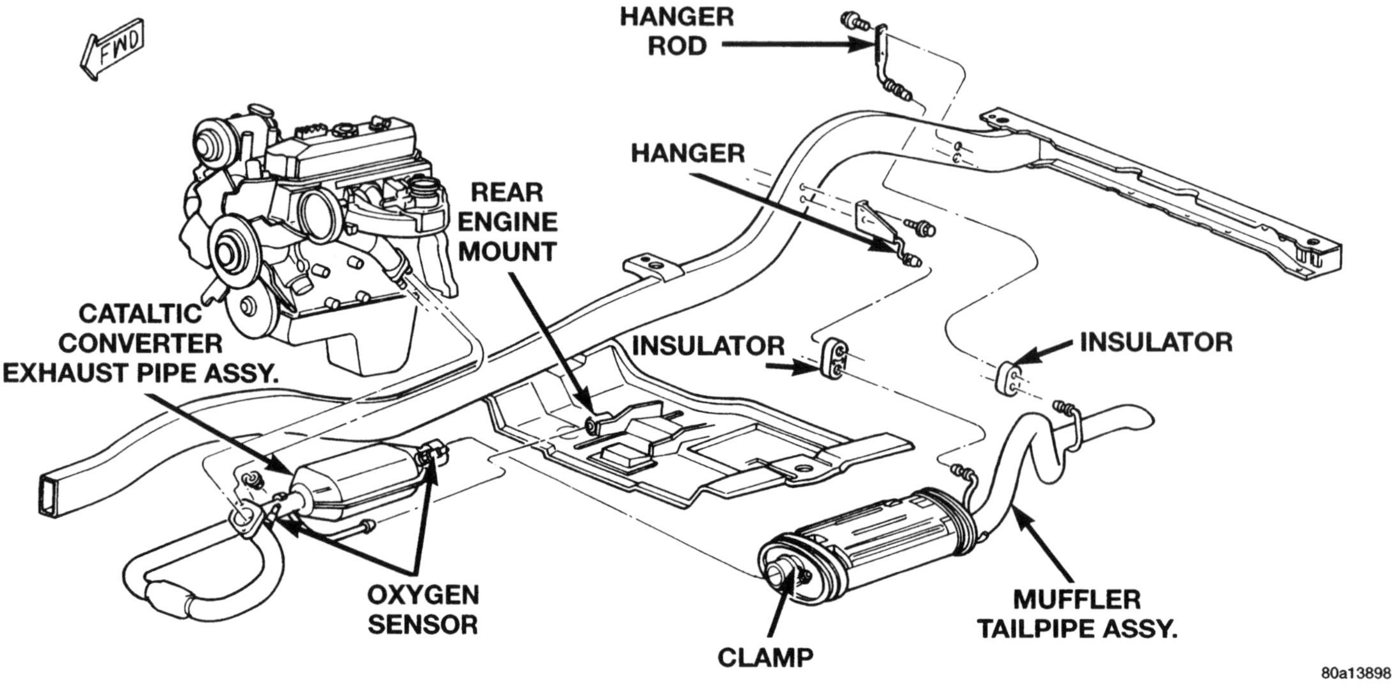

Fig. 1 Exhaust System 2.5 liter Engine

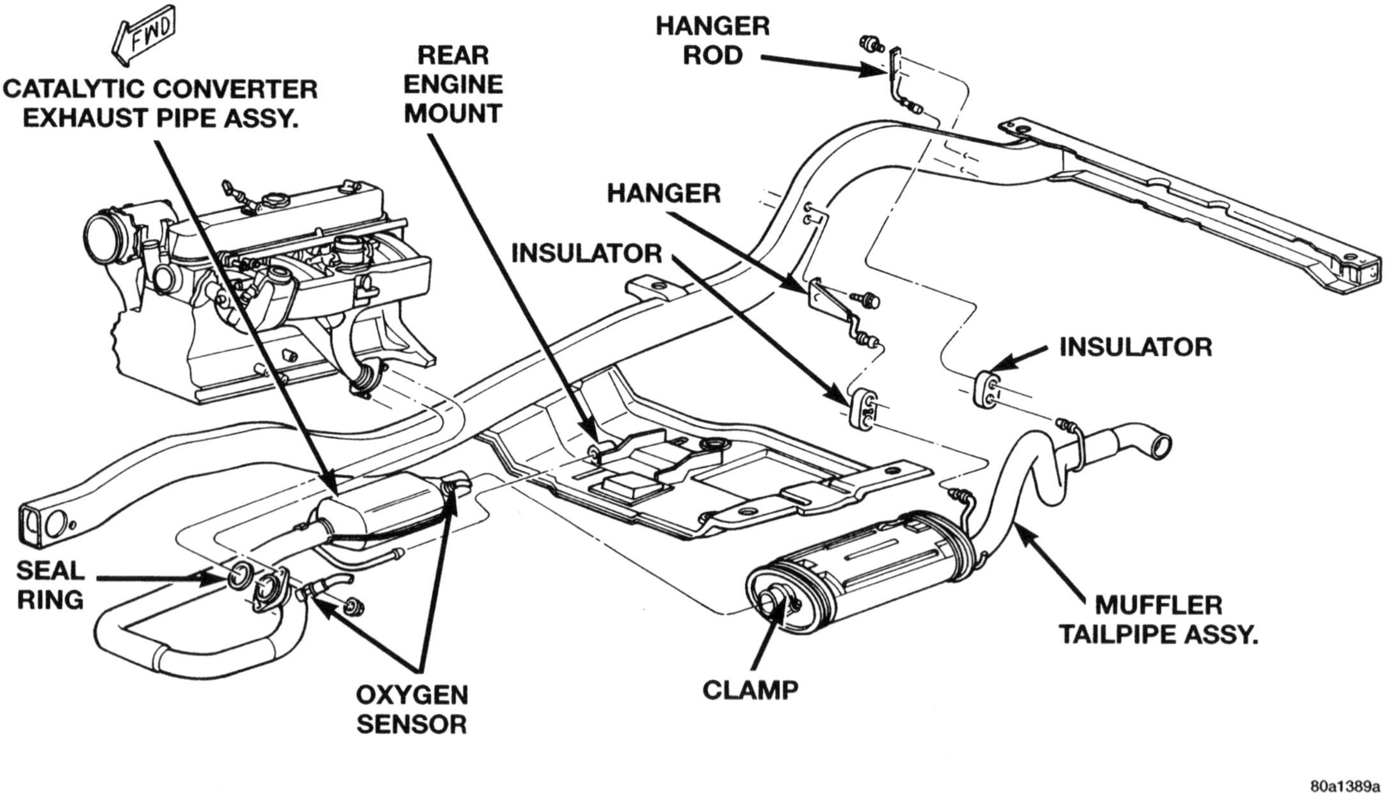

Fig. 2 Exhaust System 4.0 liter Engine

DIAGNOSIS AND TESTING

EXHAUST SYSTEM DIAGNOSIS

CONDITION	POSSIBLE CAUSE	CORRECTION
EXCESSIVE EXHAUST NOISE	1. Leaks at pipe joints.	1. Tighten clamps at leaking joints.
	2. Burned or blown-out muffler.	2. Replace muffler assembly. Check exhaust system.
	3. Burned or rusted-out exhaust pipe.	3. Replace exhaust pipe.
	4. Exhaust pipe leaking at manifold flange.	4. Tighten connection attaching nuts.
	5. Exhaust manifold cracked or broken.	5. Replace exhaust manifold.
	6. Leak between exhaust manifold and cylinder head.	6. Tighten exhaust manifold to cylinder head stud nuts or bolts.
	7. Restriction in muffler or tail pipe.	7. Remove restriction, if possible. Replace muffler or tail pipe, as necessary.
LEAKING EXHAUST GASES	1. Leaks at pipe joints.	1. Tighten clamps at leaking joints.
	2. Damaged or improperly installed gaskets.	2. Replace gaskets, as necessary.
ENGINE HARD TO WARM UP OR WILL NOT RETURN TO NORMAL IDLE	1. Blocked crossover passage in intake manifold.	1. Remove restriction or replace intake manifold.
	2. Thermostat broken.	2. Replace thermostat.

J9311-13

Exhaust System Diagnosis

REMOVAL AND INSTALLATION

EXHAUST PIPE

WARNING: IF TORCHES ARE USED WHEN WORKING ON THE EXHAUST SYSTEM, DO NOT ALLOW THE FLAME NEAR THE FUEL LINES.

REMOVAL

(1) Raise and support the vehicle.
(2) Saturate the studs and nuts with heat valve lubricant. Allow 5 minutes for penetration (Fig. 3) (Fig. 4).
(3) Remove the oxygen sensors from the exhaust pipe and the catalytic converter (Fig. 3) (Fig. 4).
(4) Disconnect the exhaust pipe from the engine exhaust manifold. Discard the seal (4.0L engine, only) (Fig. 4).
(5) Support the transmission and remove the rear crossmember.
(6) Remove the clamp from the catalytic converter and muffler connection.
(7) Heat the catalytic converter and muffler connection with an oxyacetylene torch until the metal becomes cherry red.
(8) While the metal is still cherry red, twist the muffler assembly back and forth to seperate it from the catalytic converter.

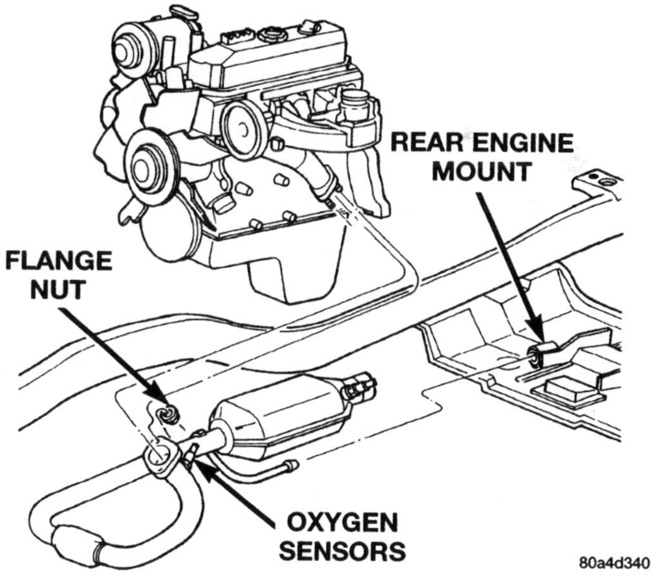

Fig. 3 Exhaust Pipe with Catalytic Converter 2.5 L Engine

INSTALLATION

(1) Assemble catalytic converter and muffler loosely to permit proper alignment of all parts.
(2) Use a new clamp and tighten the nut to 71 N·m (52 ft. lbs.) torque.
(3) Connect the exhaust pipe to the engine exhaust manifold. Install a new seal between the exhaust

REMOVAL AND INSTALLATION (Continued)

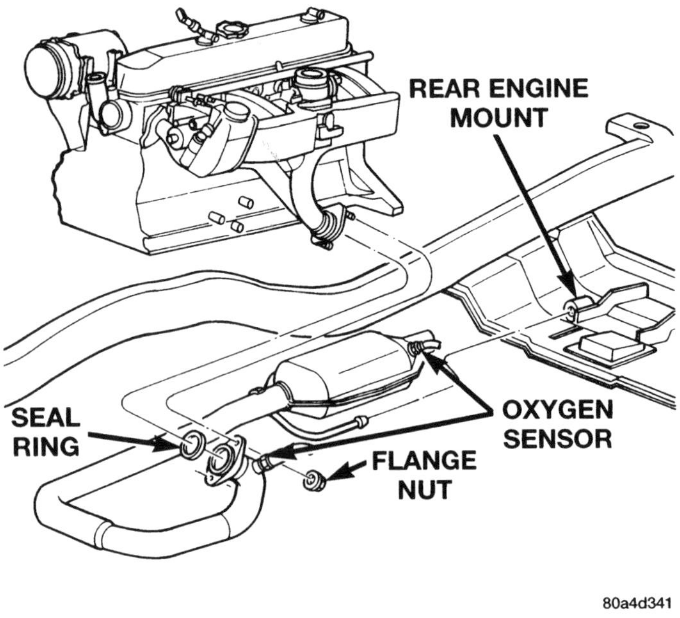

Fig. 4 Exhaust Pipe with Catalytic Converter 4.0 L Engine

manifold and the exhaust pipe (4.0L engine, only). Tighten the nuts to 31 N·m (23 ft. lbs.) torque.

(4) Install the rear crossmember. Tighten the crossmember-to-sill bolts to 41 N·m (30 ft. lbs.) torque. Remove the support from the transmission.

(5) Coat the oxygen sensors with anti-seize compound. Install the sensors and tighten the nut to 48 N·m (35 ft. lbs.) torque.

(6) Lower the vehicle.

(7) Start the engine and inspect for exhaust leaks and exhaust system contact with the body panels. Adjust the alignment, if needed.

MUFFLER TAILPIPE ASSEMBLY

All original equipment exhaust systems are manufactured with the exhaust tailpipe welded to the muffler. Service replacement mufflers and exhaust tailpipes are either clamped together or welded together.

WARNING: IF TORCHES ARE USED WHEN WORKING ON THE EXHAUST SYSTEM, DO NOT ALLOW THE FLAME NEAR THE FUEL LINES.

REMOVAL

(1) Raise the vehicle and support the rear of the vehicle by the side rails and allow the axle to hang free.

(2) Remove the clamp from the catalytic converter and muffler connection (Fig. 5).

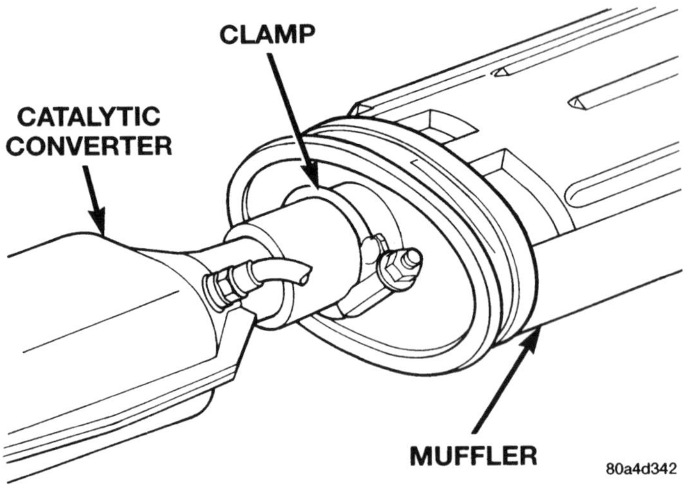

Fig. 5 Catalytic Converter to Muffler Connection

(3) Remove the tailpipe hangers from the insulators (Fig. 6).

(4) Heat the catalytic converter-to-muffler connection with an oxyacetylene torch until the metal becomes cherry red.

(5) While the metal is still cherry red, twist the exhaust tailpipe/muffler assembly back and forth to seperate it from the catalytic converter.

- To separate an original equipment exhaust tailpipe/muffler combination, cut the exhaust tailpipe close to the muffler. Collapse the part remaining in the muffler and remove.
- To remove a service exhaust tailpipe/muffler combination, apply heat until the metal becomes cherry red. Remove the exhaust tailpipe/muffler clamp and twist the exhaust tailpipe out of the muffler.

INSTALLATION

(1) Assemble catalytic converter and muffler loosely to permit proper alignment of all parts.

(2) Install the exhaust tailpipe into the rear of the muffler.

(3) Install the exhaust tailpipe/muffler assembly on the rear exhaust tailpipe hanger. Make sure that the exhaust tailpipe has sufficient clearance from the floor pan.

(4) Tighten the nut on the muffler-to-catalytic converter clamp to 48 N·m (35 ft. lbs.) torque.

(5) Insert rods into isolators.

(6) Lower the vehicle.

(7) Start the engine and inspect for exhaust leaks and exhaust system contact with the body panels. Adjust the alignment, if needed.

INTAKE MANIFOLD—2.5L ENGINE

REMOVAL

(1) Disconnect the battery negative cable.

REMOVAL AND INSTALLATION (Continued)

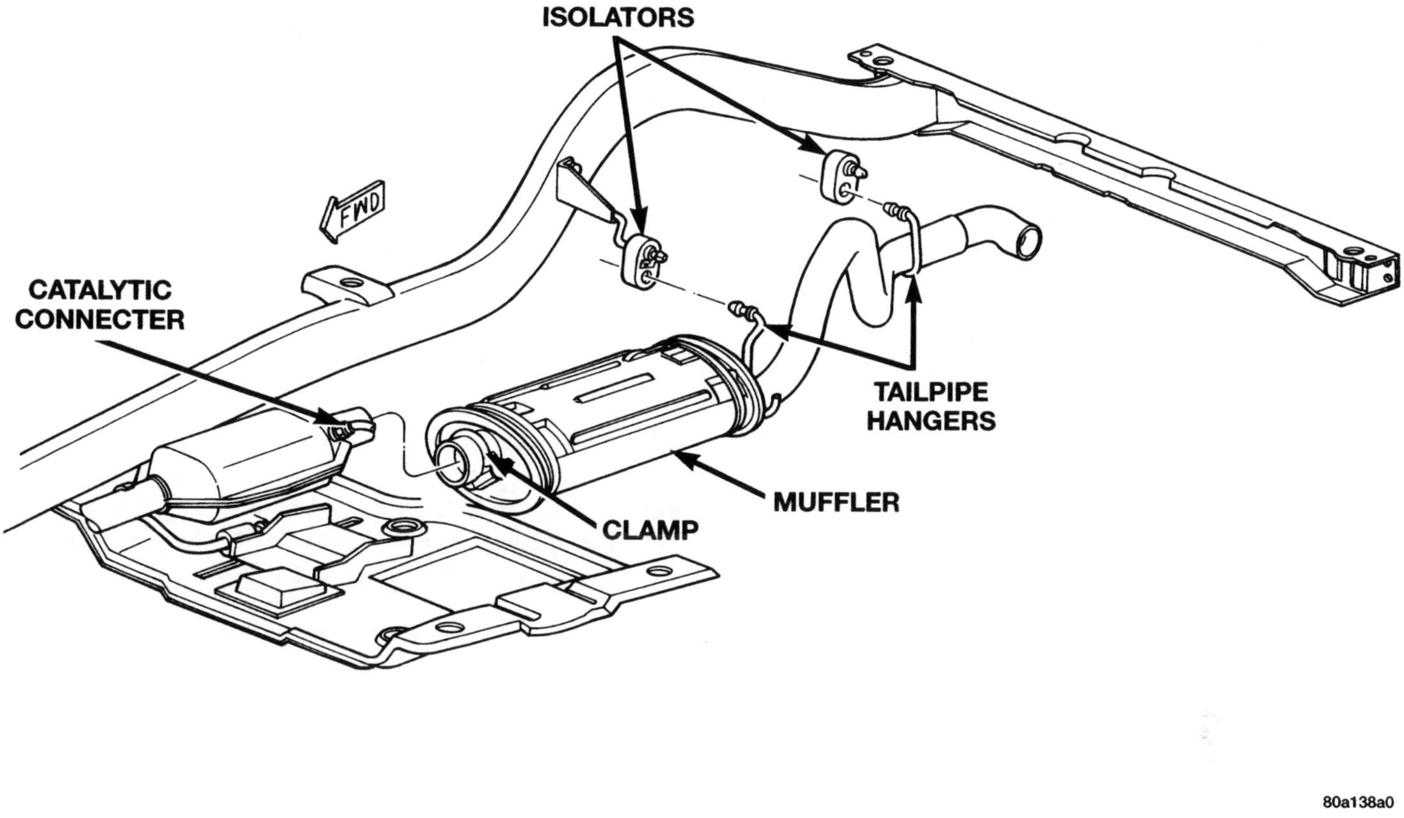

Fig. 6 Muffler Tailpipe Assembly

(2) Remove the air inlet hose from the throttle body and air cleaner.

(3) Loosen the accessory drive belt tension and remove the belt from the power steering pump.

(4) Remove the power steering pump and brackets from the water pump and intake manifold. Support power steering pump and bracket with mechanics wire attached to the radiator upper crossmember.

(5) Remove the fuel tank filler cap to relieve the fuel tank pressure.

(6) Install the fuel tank filler cap.

(7) Disconnect fuel supply and return tube from the fuel rail (refer to Group 14, Fuel System - Quick Connect Fittings).

(8) Disconnect the accelerator cable from the throttle body and the holddown bracket.

CAUTION: When disconnecting the cruise control connector at the throttle body, DO NOT pry the connector off with pliers or screwdriver. Use finger pressure only. Prying the connector off could break it.

(9) Disconnect the electrical connectors. Pull the harnesses away from the manifold.

- The throttle position sensor.
- The idle speed control motor.
- The coolant temperature sensor at the thermostat.
- The manifold air temperature sensor at the intake manifold.
- The fuel injectors.
- The oxygen sensor.

(10) Disconnect the crankcase ventilation (CCV) vacuum hose and manifold absolute pressure (MAP) sensor vacuum hose connector at the intake manifold.

(11) Disconnect vacuum hose from vacuum port on the intake manifold.

(12) Disconnect CCV hose at the cylinder head cover (Fig. 7).

(13) Remove the molded vacuum harness.

(14) Disconnect the vacuum brake booster hose at the intake manifold.

(15) Remove bolts 2 through 5 securing the intake manifold to the cylinder head (Fig. 8). Slightly loosen bolt No.1 and nuts 6 and 7.

(16) Remove the intake manifold and gaskets. Drain the coolant from the manifold.

INSTALLATION

(1) Clean the intake manifold and cylinder head mating surfaces. **DO NOT allow foreign material to enter either the intake manifold or the ports in the cylinder head.**

(2) Install the new intake manifold gasket over the locating dowels.

REMOVAL AND INSTALLATION (Continued)

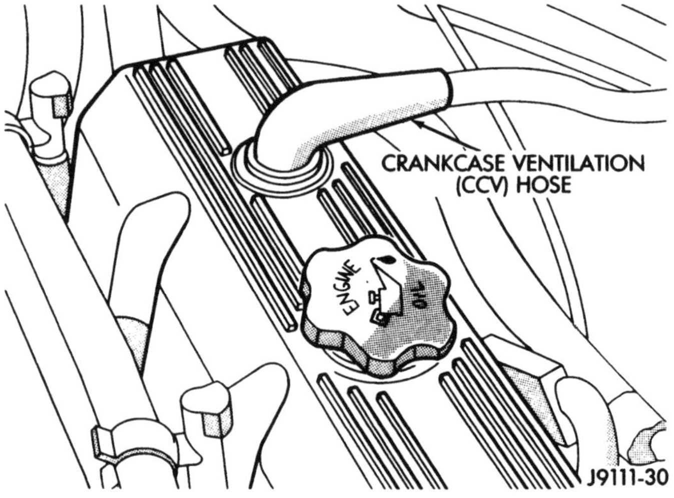

Fig. 7 Crankcase Ventilation (CCV) Hose (2.5L Engine)

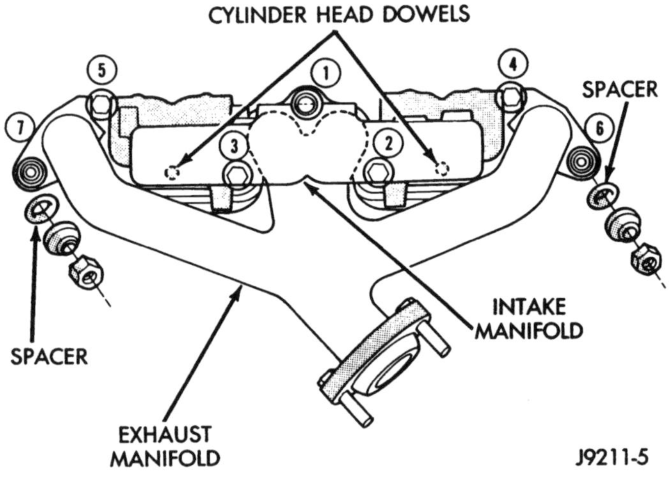

Fig. 8 Intake/Exhaust Manifold 2.5L Engine

(3) Position the manifold in place and finger tighten the mounting bolts.

(4) Tighten the fasteners in sequence and to the specified torque (Fig. 8).

- Fastener No.1—Tighten to 41 N·m (30 ft. lbs.) torque.
- Fasteners Nos.2 through 7—Tighten to 31 N·m (23 ft. lbs.) torque.

(5) Connect the fuel return and supply tube to the connector next to the fuel rail. Push them into the fitting until a click is heard. Verify that the connections are complete.

- First, ensure only the retainer tabs protrude from the connectors.
- Second, pull out on the fuel tubes to ensure they are locked in place.

(6) Connect the molded vacuum hoses to the vacuum port on the intake manifold and the cylinder head cover.

(7) Connect the electrical connectors.

- The throttle position sensor.
- The automatic idle speed control motor.
- The coolant temperature sensor at the thermostat housing.
- The fuel injectors.
- The air manifold temperature sensor.
- The oxygen sensor.

(8) Connect the CCV vacuum hose and MAP sensor vacuum hose connectors to the throttle body.

(9) Install the power steering pump and bracket assembly to the water pump and intake manifold.

(10) Connect the accelerator cable and cruise control cable to the holddown bracket and the throttle arm.

CAUTION: Ensure that the accessory drive belt is routed correctly. Failure to do so can cause the water pump to turn in the opposite direction resulting in engine overheating. Refer to Group 7, Cooling System for the proper procedure.

(11) Tension the accessory drive belt. Refer to Group 7, Cooling System for the proper procedure.

(12) Connect the air inlet hose to the throttle body and the air cleaner.

(13) Connect the battery negative cable.

(14) Start the engine and check for leaks.

INTAKE MANIFOLD—4.0L ENGINE

The intake and engine exhaust manifolds on the 4.0L engine must be removed and installed together. The two manifolds use a common gasket at the cylinder head.

REMOVAL

(1) Disconnect the battery negative cable.

(2) Remove air cleaner inlet hose from throttle plate assembly.

(3) Remove the air cleaner assembly.

(4) Remove the throttle cable, cruise control cable (if equipped) and the transmission line pressure cable.

(5) Disconnect all electrical connectors on the intake manifold.

(6) Disconnect and remove the fuel supply and return lines from the fuel rail assembly (refer to Group 14, Fuel System).

(7) Loosen the accessory drive belt (refer to Group 7, Cooling System). Loosen the tensioner.

(8) Remove the power steering pump and bracket from the intake manifold and set aside.

(9) Remove the fuel rail and injectors (refer to Group 14, Fuel System).

(10) Raise the vehicle.

(11) Disconnect the exhaust pipe from the engine exhaust manifold. Discard the seal.

(12) Lower the vehicle.

REMOVAL AND INSTALLATION (Continued)

(13) Remove the intake manifold and engine exhaust manifold.

INSTALLATION

(1) Clean the mating surfaces of the cylinder head and the manifold if the original manifold is to be installed.

(2) If the manifold is being replaced, ensure all the fitting, etc. are transferred to the replacement manifold.

(3) Install a new exhaust/intake manifold gasket over the alignment dowels on the cylinder head.

(4) Position the engine exhaust manifold to the cylinder head. Install fastener No.3 and finger tighten at this time (Fig. 9).

(5) Install intake manifold on the cylinder head dowels.

(6) Install washers and fasteners Nos.1, 2, 4, 5, 8, 9, 10 and 11 (Fig. 9).

(7) Install washers and fasteners Nos.6 and 7 (Fig. 9).

(8) Tighten the fasteners in sequence and to the specified torque (Fig. 9).

- Fasteners Nos.1 through 5—Tighten to 33 N·m (24 ft. lbs.) torque.
- Fasteners Nos.6 and 7—Tighten to 31 N·m (23 ft. lbs.) torque.
- Fasteners Nos.8 through 11—Tighten to 33 N·m (24 ft. lbs.) torque.

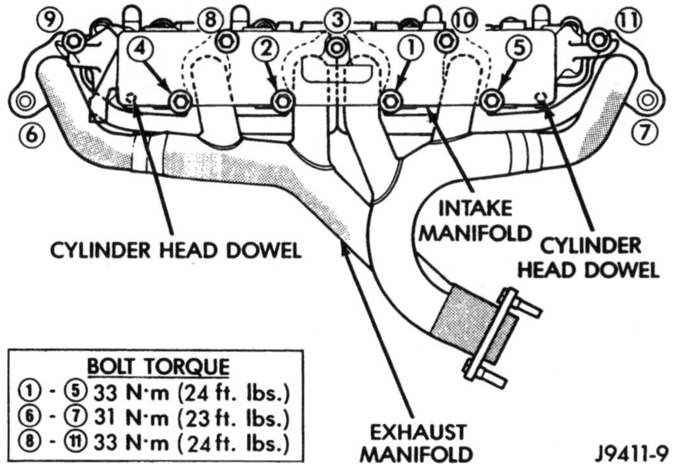

Fig. 9 Intake/Engine Exhaust Manifold Installation 4.0L Engine

(9) Install the fuel rail and injectors.

(10) Install the power steering pump and bracket to the intake manifold. Tighten the belt to specification. Refer to Group 7, Cooling System for the proper procedures.

(11) Install the fuel supply and return lines to the fuel rail assembly. **Before connecting the fuel lines to the fuel rail replace the O-rings in the quick-connect fuel line couplings.** Refer to Group 14, Fuel System for the proper procedure.

(12) Connect all electrical connections on the intake manifold.

(13) Connect the vacuum connector on the intake manifold and install it in the bracket.

(14) Install throttle cable, cruise control cable (if equipped).

(15) Install the transmission line pressure cable (if equipped). Refer to Group 21, Transmission for the adjustment procedures.

(16) Install air cleaner assembly.

(17) Connect air inlet hose to the throttle plate assembly.

(18) Raise the vehicle on a side mounted hoist.

(19) Using a new seal, connect the exhaust pipe to the engine exhaust manifold. Tighten the bolts to 31 N·m (23 ft. lbs.) torque.

(20) Lower the vehicle.

(21) Connect the battery negative cable.

(22) Start the engine and check for leaks.

EXHAUST MANIFOLD—2.5L ENGINE

REMOVAL

(1) Disconnect the battery negative cable.

(2) Remove all components attached to the intake manifold.

(3) Raise the vehicle.

(4) Disconnect the exhaust pipe from the engine exhaust manifold.

(5) Lower the vehicle.

(6) Remove Intake Manifold refer to procedure in this section.

(7) Remove fasteners 2 through 5 and remove the intake manifold (Fig. 10).

(8) Remove fasteners 1, 6 and 7 and remove the engine exhaust manifold (Fig. 10).

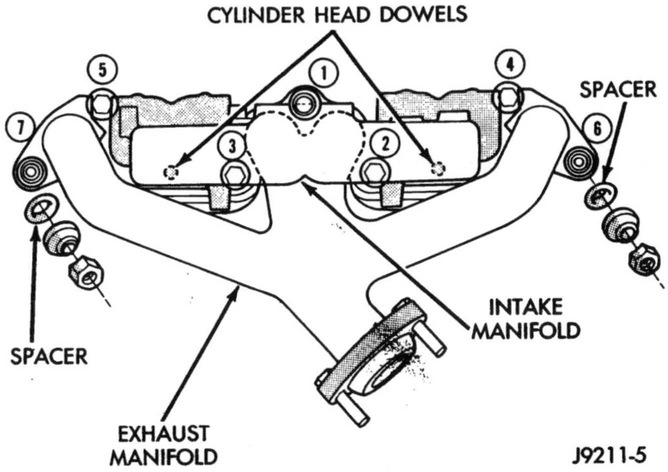

Fig. 10 Intake/Engine Exhaust Manifold Installation 2.5L Engine

REMOVAL AND INSTALLATION (Continued)

INSTALLATION

(1) Clean the intake and engine exhaust manifolds and cylinder head mating surfaces. **DO NOT allow foreign material to enter either the intake manifold or the ports in the cylinder head.**

(2) Install a new intake manifold gasket over the alignment dowels on the cylinder head.

(3) Install the engine exhaust manifold assembly. **Exhaust manifold must be centrally located over the end studs and spacer (Fig. 10).**

(4) Tighten bolt No.1 to 41 N·m (30 ft. lbs.) torque (Fig. 10).

(5) Install the intake manifold on the cylinder head dowels (Fig. 10).

(6) Install bolts 2 through 5 (Fig. 10). Tighten these bolts to 31 N·m (23 ft. lbs.) torque.

(7) Install new engine exhaust manifold spacers over the engine exhaust manifold mounting studs in the cylinder head (Fig. 10).

(8) Tighten nuts 6 and 7 to 31 N·m (23 ft. lbs.) torque (Fig. 10).

(9) Install all components to the intake manifold.

(10) Raise the vehicle.

(11) Connect the exhaust pipe to the engine exhaust manifold. Tighten the bolts to 31 N·m (23 ft. lbs.) torque.

(12) Lower the vehicle.

(13) Connect the battery negative cable.

(14) Start the engine and check for leaks.

EXHAUST MANIFOLD—4.0L ENGINE

The intake and engine exhaust manifolds on the 4.0L engine must be removed and installed together. The manifolds use a common gasket at the cylinder head.

Refer to Intake Manifold—4.0L Engine in this section for the proper removal and installation procedures.

SPECIFICATIONS

TORQUE SPECIFICATIONS

Description	**Torque**
Exhaust Pipe to Manifold Nuts	31 N·m (23 ft. lbs.)
Exhaust Manifold 2.5L Engine Bolt #1	41 N·m (30 ft. lbs.)
Exhaust Manifold 2.5L Engine Bolts #2–5	31 N·m (23 ft. lbs.)
Exhaust Manifold 4.0L Engine Nuts/Bolts #1–5 & #8–11	33 N·m (24 ft. lbs.)
Exhaust Manifold 2.5L Engine Nuts #6&7	31 N·m (23 ft. lbs.)
Exhaust Manifold 4.0L Engine Nuts #6&7	31 N·m (23 ft. lbs.)
Intake Manifold 2.5L Engine Bolt #1	41 N·m (30 ft. lbs.)
Intake Manifold 2.5L Engine Bolt #2–5	31 N·m (23 ft. lbs.)
Mufler to Catalytic Converter Clamp Nut	48 N·m (35 ft. lbs.)
Oxygen Sensors Nut	48 N·m (35 ft. lbs.)

FRAME AND BUMPERS

CONTENTS

BUMPERS

INDEX

REMOVAL AND INSTALLATION

FRONT TOW HOOK

Some Jeep vehicles are equipped with front emergency tow hooks. The tow hooks should be used for **EMERGENCY** purposes only.

REMOVAL

(1) Remove the torx bolts that attach the tow hook to the bumper (Fig. 1).

(2) Separate the tow hook from the bumper.

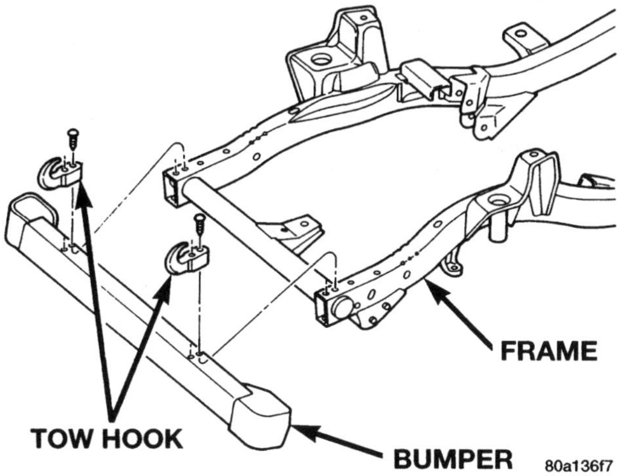

Fig. 1 Front Tow Hook

INSTALLATION

(1) Position the tow hook on the bumper.

(2) Install the torx bolts that attach the tow hook to the bumper. Tighten the bolts to 108 N·m (80 ft. lbs.) torque.

FRONT TOW EYE

REMOVAL

(1) Remove the cap from the tow eye.

(2) Remove the screws that attach the tow eye to the bumper (Fig. 2).

(3) Separate the tow eye from the bumper.

INSTALLATION

(1) Position the tow eye on the bumper.

(2) Install the screws that attach the tow eye to the bumper. Tighten screws to 98 N·m (73 ft. lbs.) torque.

(3) Install the cap on the tow eye.

FRONT BUMPER EXTENSION

REMOVAL

(1) If equipped, remove the extension cover (Fig. 2).

(2) Remove the screws attaching the bumper extension to the bumper (Fig. 3).

(3) Separate the extension from the bumper.

INSTALLATION

(1) Position the extension on the bumper.

(2) Install the screws attaching the bumper extension to the bumper.

(3) If equipped, install the extension cover.

REMOVAL AND INSTALLATION (Continued)

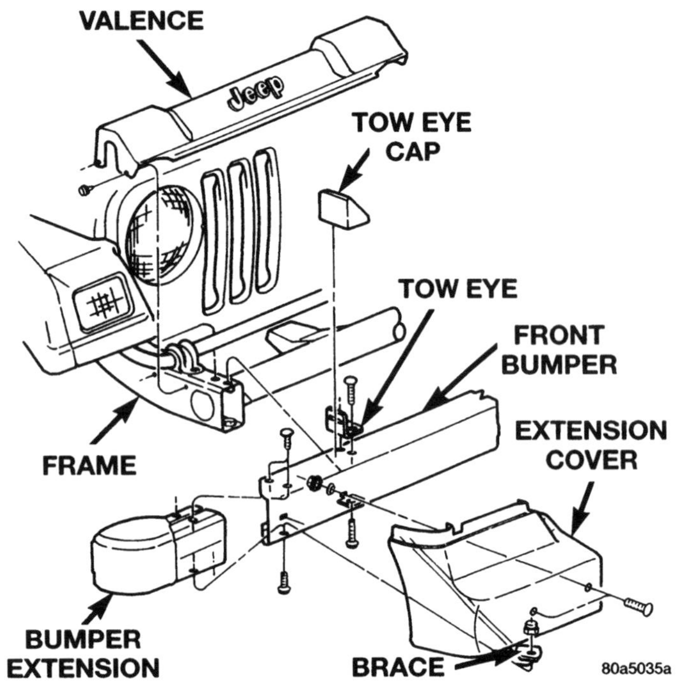

Fig. 2 Front Bumper Components

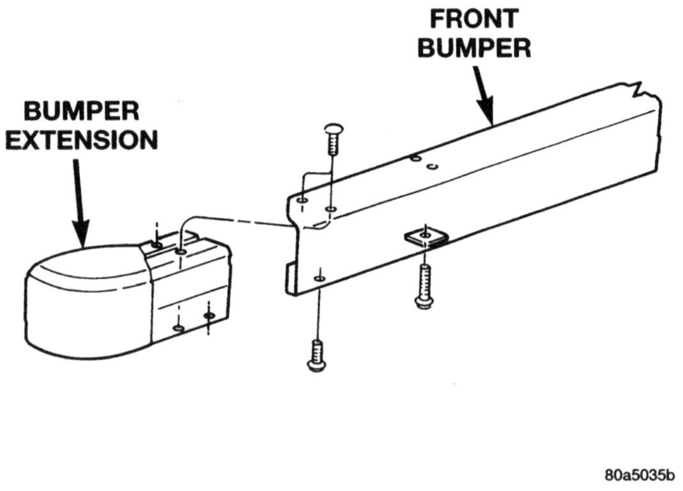

Fig. 3 Bumper Extension

FRONT BUMPER

REMOVAL

(1) If equipped, disconnect the fog lamp harness connector.

(2) Remove the screws that attach the bumper to the frame rail (Fig. 2).

(3) If equipped, separate the tow hook or tow eye from the bumper.

(4) Separate the bumper from the vehicle.

INSTALLATION

(1) Position the bumper on the vehicle.

(2) If equipped, position the tow hook or tow eye on the bumper.

(3) Install the screws that attach the bumper to the frame rail. Tighten the screws to 104 N·m (77 ft. lbs.) torque.

(4) If equipped, Connect the fog lamp harness connector.

REAR TOW EYE

REMOVAL

(1) Remove the screw attaching the tow eye to the frame rail (Fig. 4).

(2) Separate the tow eye from the vehicle.

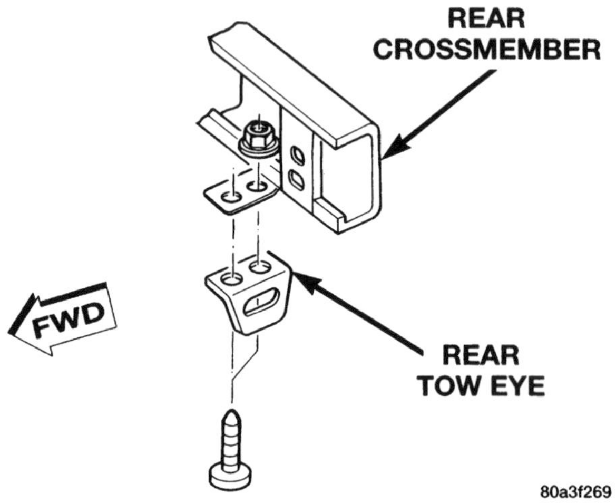

Fig. 4 Rear Tow Eye

INSTALLATION

(1) Position the tow eye on the vehicle.

(2) Install the screw attaching the tow eye to the frame rail. Tighten the screw to 47 N·m (35 ft. lbs.) torque.

REAR BUMPER EXTENSION

REMOVAL

(1) Remove the screws attaching the bumper extension to the bumper (Fig. 5).

(2) Separate the extension from the bumper.

INSTALLATION

(1) Position the extension on the bumper.

(2) Install the screws attaching the bumper extension to the bumper.

REAR BUMPER

REMOVAL

(1) Remove the bolt attaching the bumper to frame rail (Fig. 5).

(2) If equipped, separate the rear tow eye from the bumper.

REMOVAL AND INSTALLATION (Continued)

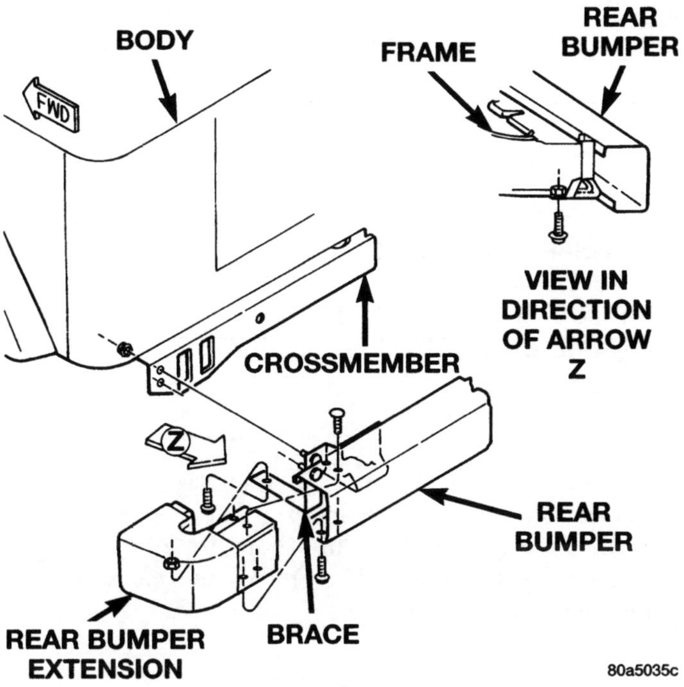

Fig. 5 Bumper Components

(3) Remove the nuts attaching the bumper to the rear frame crossmember.

(4) Separate the bumper from the vehicle.

INSTALLATION

(1) Position the bumper on the vehicle.

(2) Install the nuts attaching the bumper to the rear frame crossmember. Tighten the nuts to 67 N·m (50 ft.lbs.) torque.

(3) If equipped, position the rear tow eye on the bumper.

(4) Install the bolt attaching the bumper to frame rail. Tighten the bolts to 67 N·m (50 ft.lbs.) torque.

FRAME

INDEX

GENERAL INFORMATION

GENERAL INFORMATION

The Jeep TJ frame is the structural center of the vehicle. In addition to supporting the body and payload, the frame provides a station for the engine. The vehicle body is attached to the frame with holddowns (Fig. 1).

The frame is constructed of mild-strength rectangular tubing and crossmembers. The crossmembers join the siderails and retain them in alignment in relation to each other. This provides resistance to frame twists and strains.

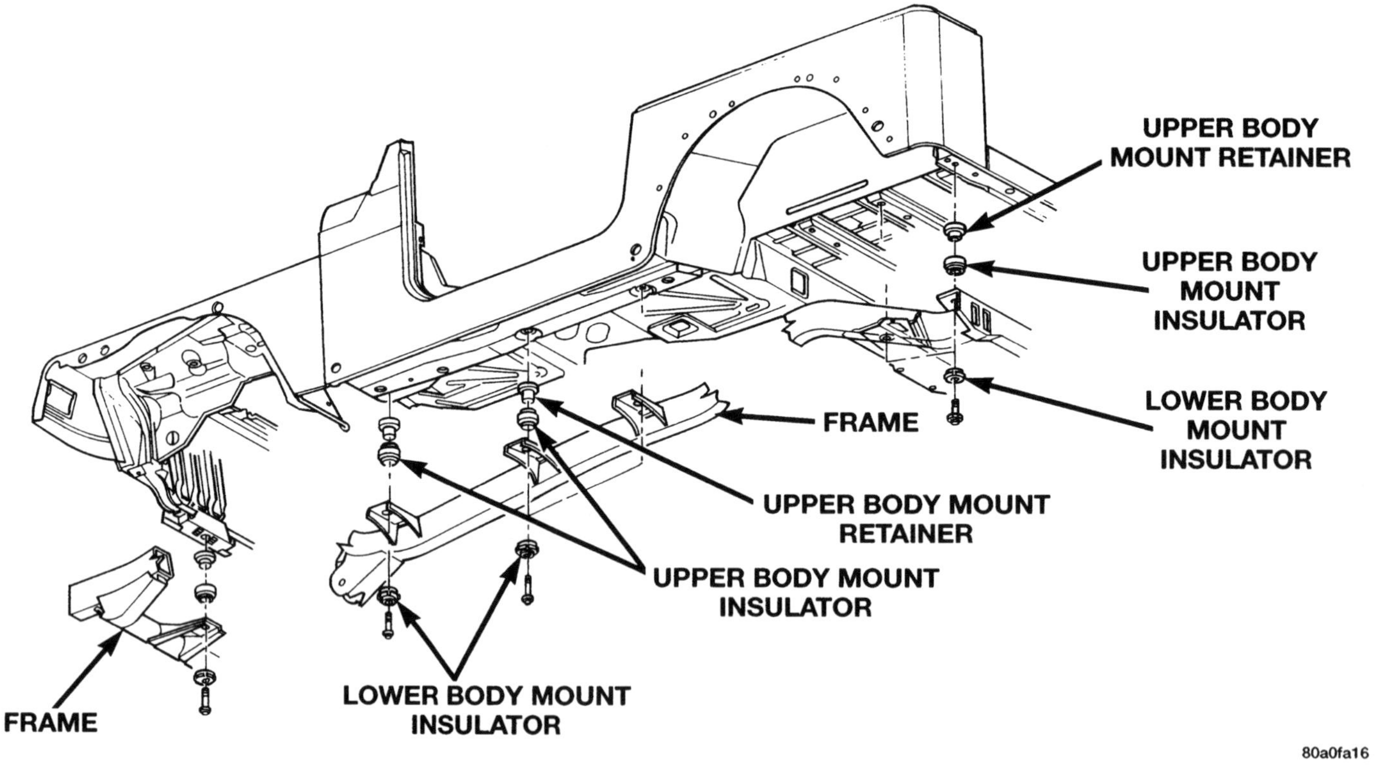

Fig. 1 Body Holddowns

SERVICE PROCEDURES

FRAME SERVICE

SAFETY PRECAUTIONS AND WARNINGS

WARNING: USE EYE PROTECTION WHEN GRINDING OR WELDING METAL, SERIOUS EYE INJURY CAN RESULT. BEFORE PROCEEDING WITH FRAME REPAIR INVOLVING GRINDING OR WELDING, VERIFY THAT VEHICLE FUEL SYSTEM IS NOT LEAKING OR IN CONTACT WITH REPAIR AREA, PERSONAL INJURY CAN RESULT. DO NOT ALLOW OPEN FLAME TO CONTACT PLASTIC BODY PANELS. FIRE OR EXPLOSION CAN RESULT. WHEN WELDED FRAME COMPONENTS ARE REPLACED, 100% PENETRATION WELD MUST BE ACHIEVED DURING INSTALLATION. IF NOT, DANGEROUS OPERATING CONDITIONS CAN RESULT. STAND CLEAR OF CABLES OR CHAINS ON PULLING EQUIPMENT DURING FRAME STRAIGHTENING OPERATIONS, PERSONAL INJURY CAN RESULT. DO NOT VENTURE UNDER A HOISTED VEHICLE THAT IS NOT SUPPORTED ON SAFETY STANDS, PERSONAL INJURY CAN RESULT.

CAUTION: Do not reuse damaged fasteners, quality of repair would be suspect. Do not drill holes in top or bottom frame rail flanges, frame rail failure can result. Do Not use softer than Grade 3 bolts to replace production fasteners, loosening or failure can result. When using heat to straighten frame components do not exceed 566°C (1050°F), metal fatigue can result. Welding the joints around riveted cross members and frame side rails can weaken frame.

FRAME STRAIGHTENING

When necessary, a conventional frame that is bent or twisted can be straightened by application of heat. The temperature must not exceed 566°C (1050°F). The metal will have a dull red glow at the desired temperature. Excessive heat will decrease the strength of the metal and result in a weakened frame.

Welding the joints around riveted cross members and frame side rails is not recommended.

A straightening repair process should be limited to frame members that are not severely damaged. The replacement bolts, nuts and rivets that are used to join the frame members should conform to the same specifications as the original bolts, nuts and rivets.

FRAME REPAIRS

DRILLING HOLES

Do not drill holes in the top and bottom of frame rail, metal fatigue can result causing frame failure. Holes drilled in the side of the frame rail must be at least 38 mm (1.5 in.) from the top and bottom flanges.

Additional drill holes should be located away from existing holes.

WELDING

Use MIG, TIG or arc welding equipment to repair welded frame components.

Frame components that have been damaged should be inspected for cracks before returning the vehicle to use. If cracks are found in accessible frame components perform the following procedures.

(1) Drill a hole at each end of the crack with a 3 mm (0.125 in.) diameter drill bit.

(2) Using a suitable die grinder with 3 inch cut off wheel, V-groove the crack to allow 100% weld penetration.

(3) Weld the crack.

(4) If necessary when a side rail is repaired, grind the weld smooth and install a reinforcement channel (Fig. 2) over the repaired area.

CAUTION: A reinforcement should never be used on the front section of the frame. The frame section forward of the suspension mounts contains energy management holes (Fig. 3). Reinforcing this area may effect energy management.

NOTE: If a reinforcement is required, it should completely cover the repaired area. The reinforcement should also overlap the top and bottom of the frame by more than 50% of its width. Weld as indicated (Fig. 2).

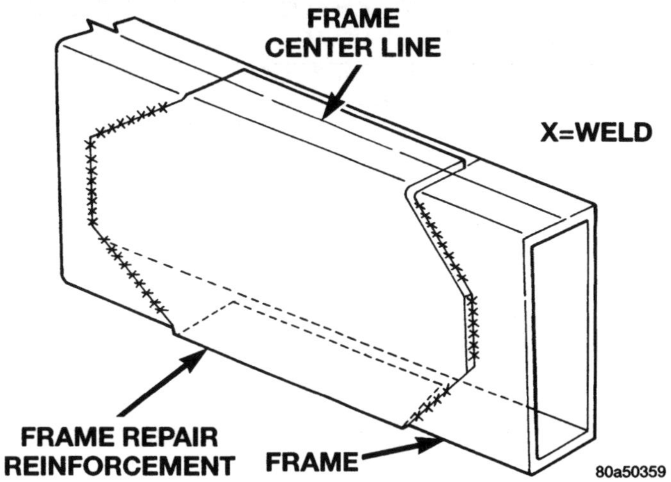

Fig. 2 Frame Reinforcement

SERVICE PROCEDURES (Continued)

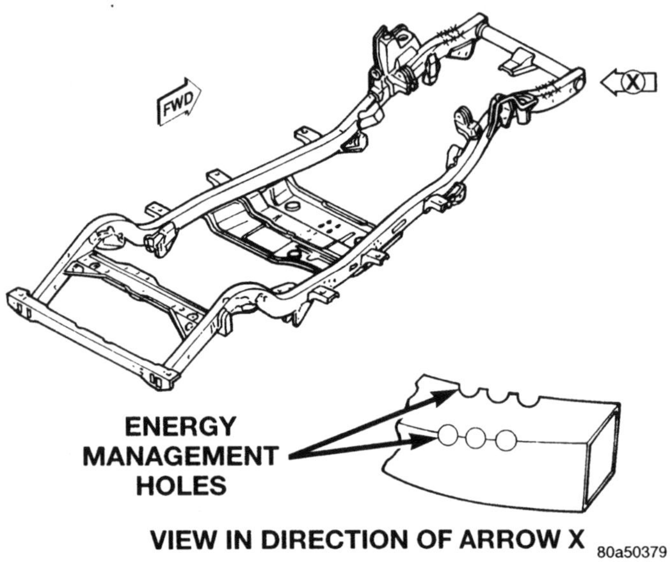

Fig. 3 Energy Management Holes

FRAME FASTENERS

Bolts and nuts and can be used to repair frames or to install a reinforcement section on the frame.

Conical-type washers are preferred over the split-ring type lock washers. Normally, grade-5 bolts are adequate for frame repair. **Grade-3 bolts or softer should not be used.** Tightening bolts/nuts with the correct torque, refer to the Introduction Group at the front of this manual for tightening information.

REMOVAL AND INSTALLATION

TRANSFER CASE SKID PLATE

The transmission and transfer case crossmember is integrated with the transfer case skid plate.

REMOVAL

WARNING: THE TRANSFER CASE AND TRANSMISSION ARE SUPPORTED BY THE TRANSFER CASE SKID PLATE. BEFORE REMOVING THE TRANSFER CASE SKID PLATE, ENSURE THAT THE TRANSMISSION IS PROPERLY SUPPORTED.

(1) Raise and support the vehicle.

(2) Place a support under the transmission.

(3) Remove the nuts attaching the transmission mount to the skid plate (Fig. 4) and (Fig. 5).

(4) Remove the bolts attaching the skid plate to the frame (Fig. 6).

(5) Separate the skid plate from the vehicle.

INSTALLATION

(1) Position the skid plate on the vehicle.

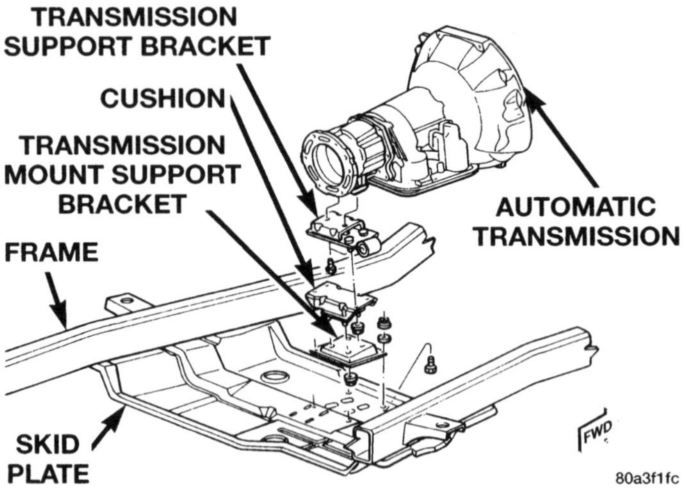

Fig. 4 Transmission Mount—Automatic Transmission

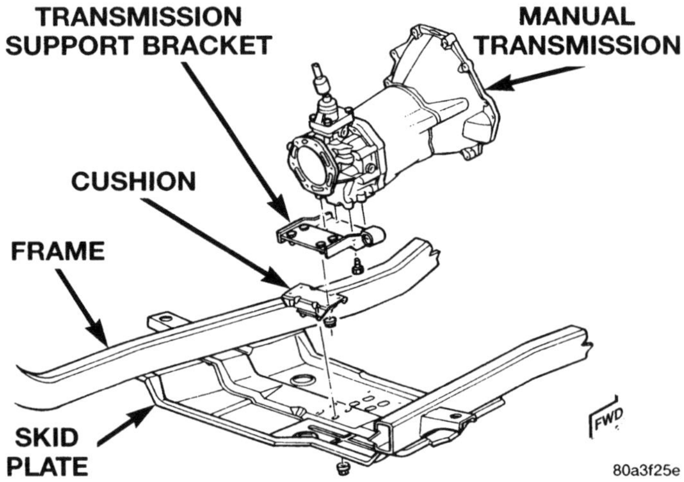

Fig. 5 Transmission Mount—Manual Transmission

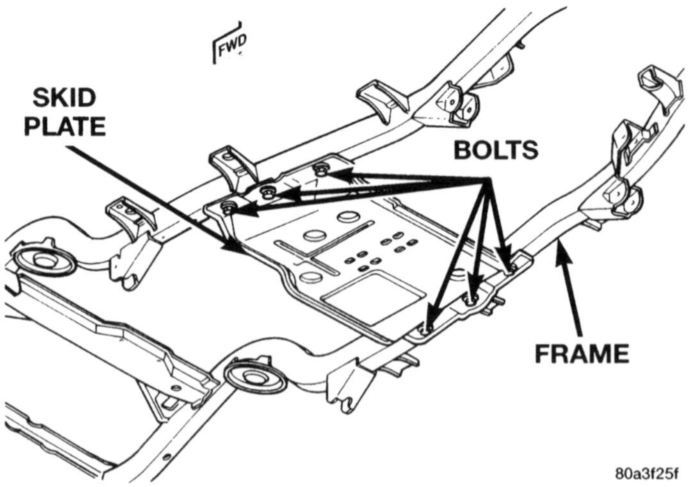

Fig. 6 Transfer Case Skid Plate

(2) Install the bolts attaching the skid plate to the frame. Tighten the bolts to 74 N·m (55 ft. lbs.) torque.

REMOVAL AND INSTALLATION (Continued)

(3) Install the nuts attaching the transmission mount to the skid plate. Tighten the nuts to 28 N·m (21 ft. lbs.) torque.

(4) Remove the support under the transmission.

(5) Remove the support from under the vehicle and lower the vehicle.

FUEL TANK SKID PLATE

REMOVAL

(1) Position a support under the fuel tank skid plate.

(2) Remove the protective caps from the end of the strap studs.

(3) Remove the nuts that attach the skid plate to the straps and to the crossmembers (Fig. 7).

(4) Separate the fuel tank strap from the skid plate.

(5) Support the fuel tank and remove the skid plate from the vehicle.

INSTALLATION

(1) Attach the skid plate to the fuel tank strap.

(2) Position and support the skid plate under the fuel tank.

(3) Install the nuts to attach the skid plate to the straps and to the frame crossmembers. Tighten the fuel tank strap nuts to 5 N·m (40 in. lbs.) torque. Tighten the skid plate-to-crossmember nuts with 16 N·m (138 in. lbs.) torque.

(4) Install the protective caps on the end of the strap studs.

(5) Remove the support from under the skid plate.

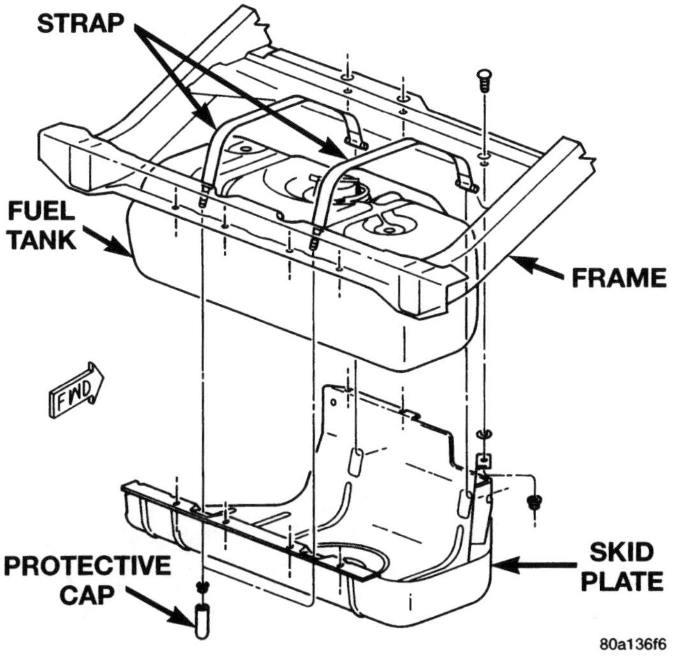

Fig. 7 Fuel Tank Skid Plate

SPECIFICATIONS

VEHICLE DIMENSIONS

WINDSHIELD OPENING

- A & B. Center of radius at bottom to center of radius top.

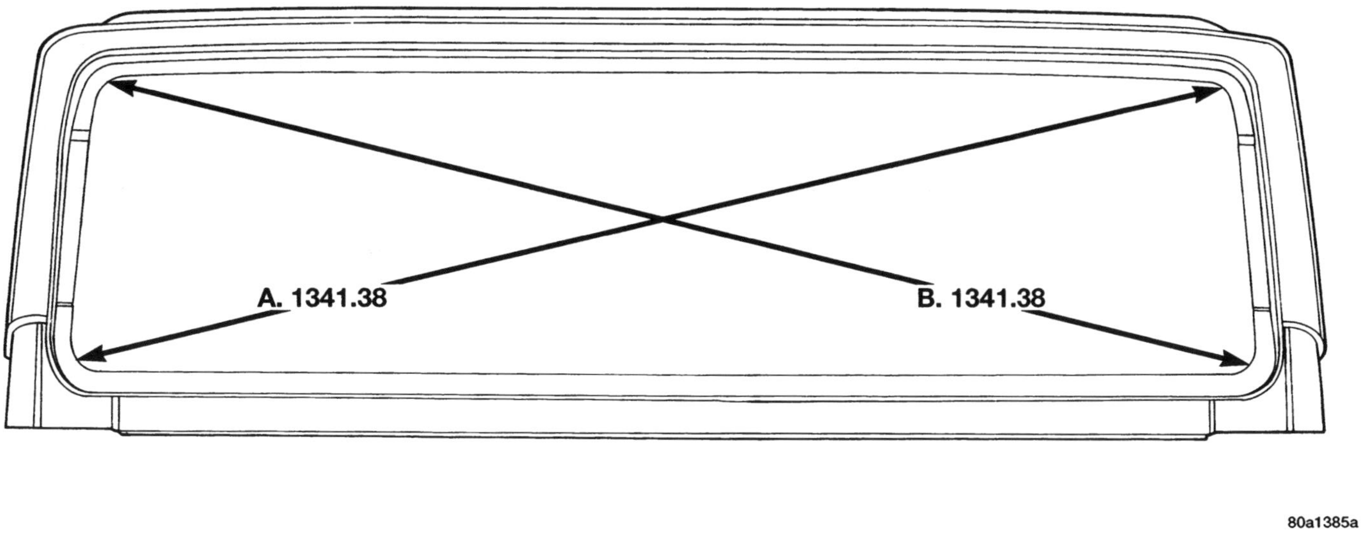

SPECIFICATIONS (Continued)

DOOR OPENING

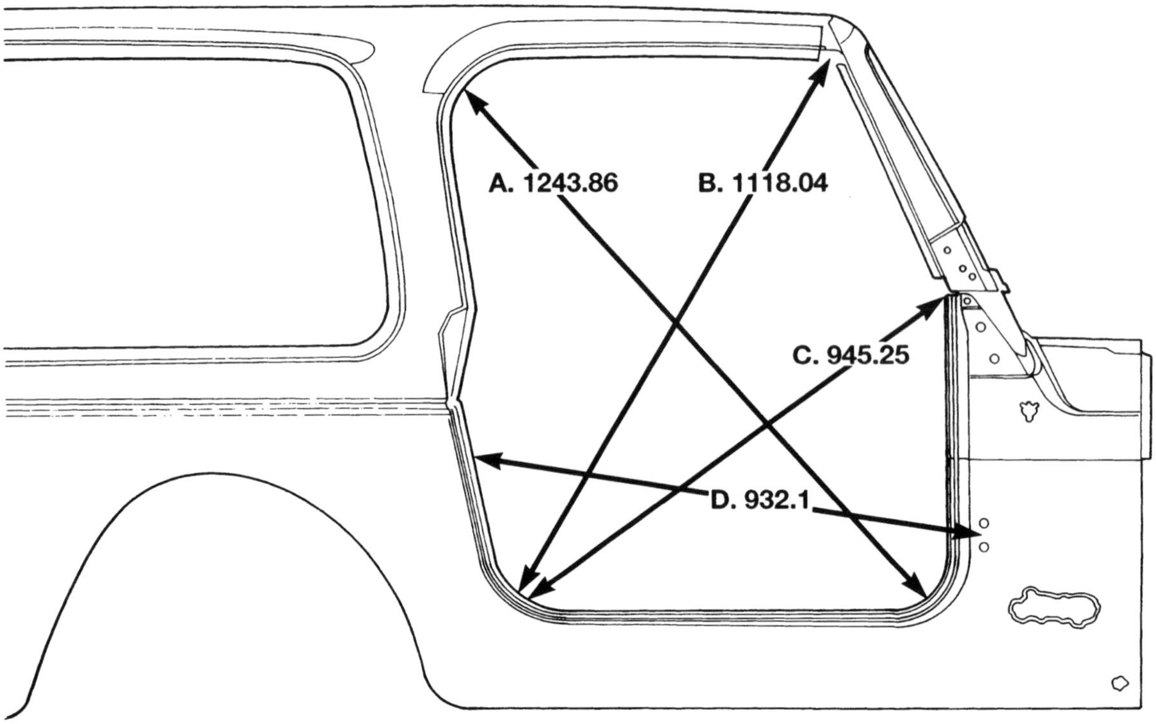

80a1385c

- A. Center of radius at bottom front to center of radius at top rear.
- B. Center of door lower rear corner to center of top of windshield frame.
- C. Center of door lower rear corner to top of cowl.
- D. Center of door hinge mount to center of door striker mount.

SPECIFICATIONS (Continued)

QUARTER WINDOW OPENING

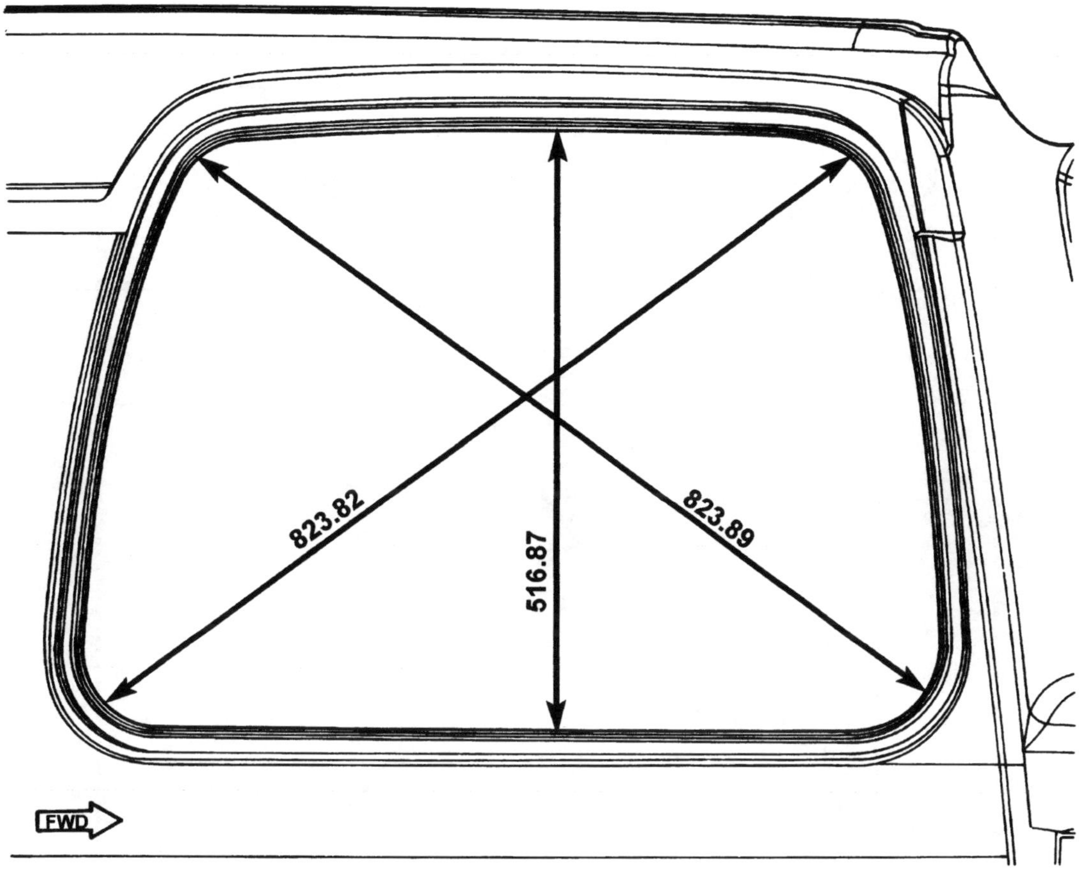

80a1386d

SPECIFICATIONS (Continued)

ENGINE COMPARTMENT

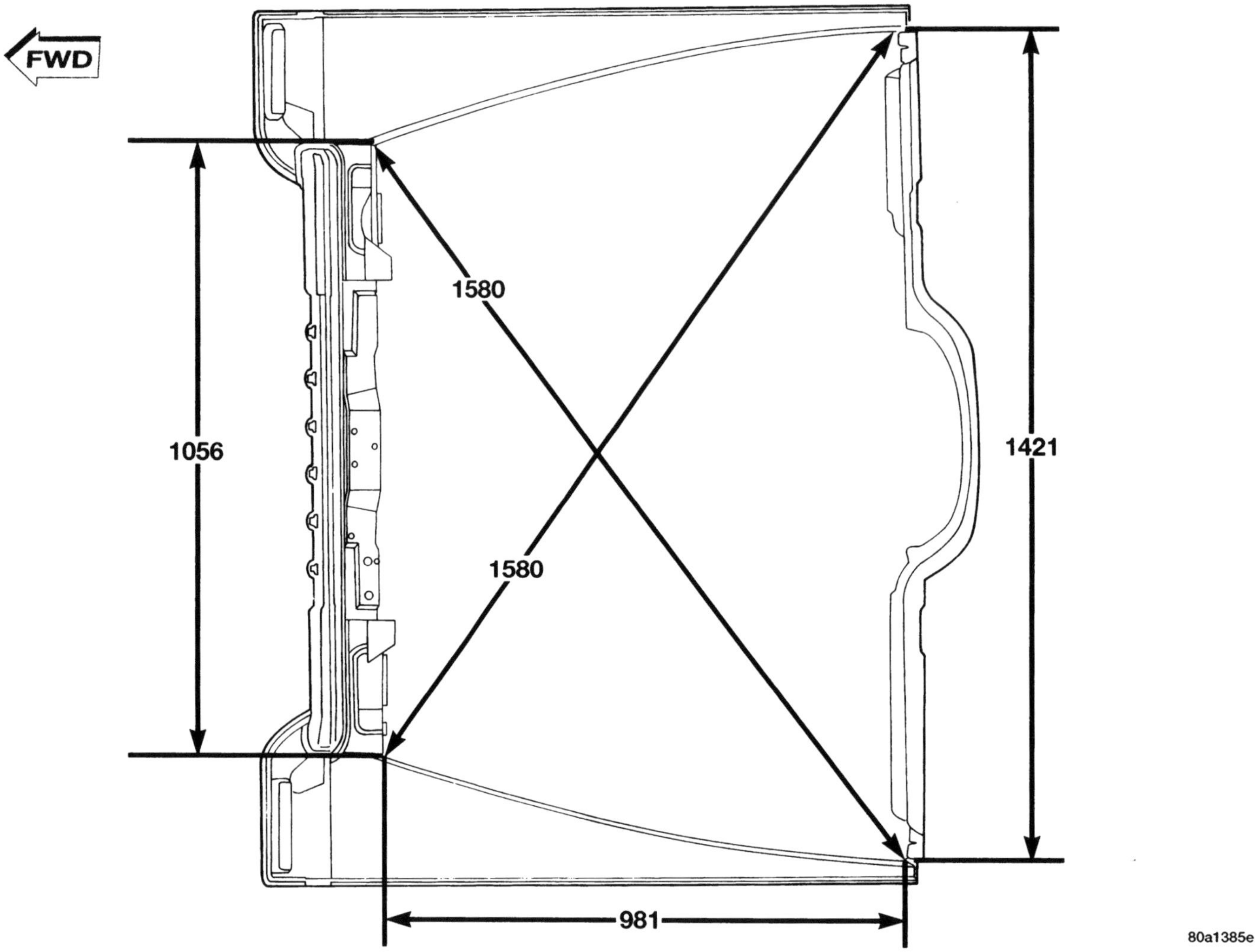

SPECIFICATIONS (Continued)

TAILGATE AND LIFTGATE OPENING

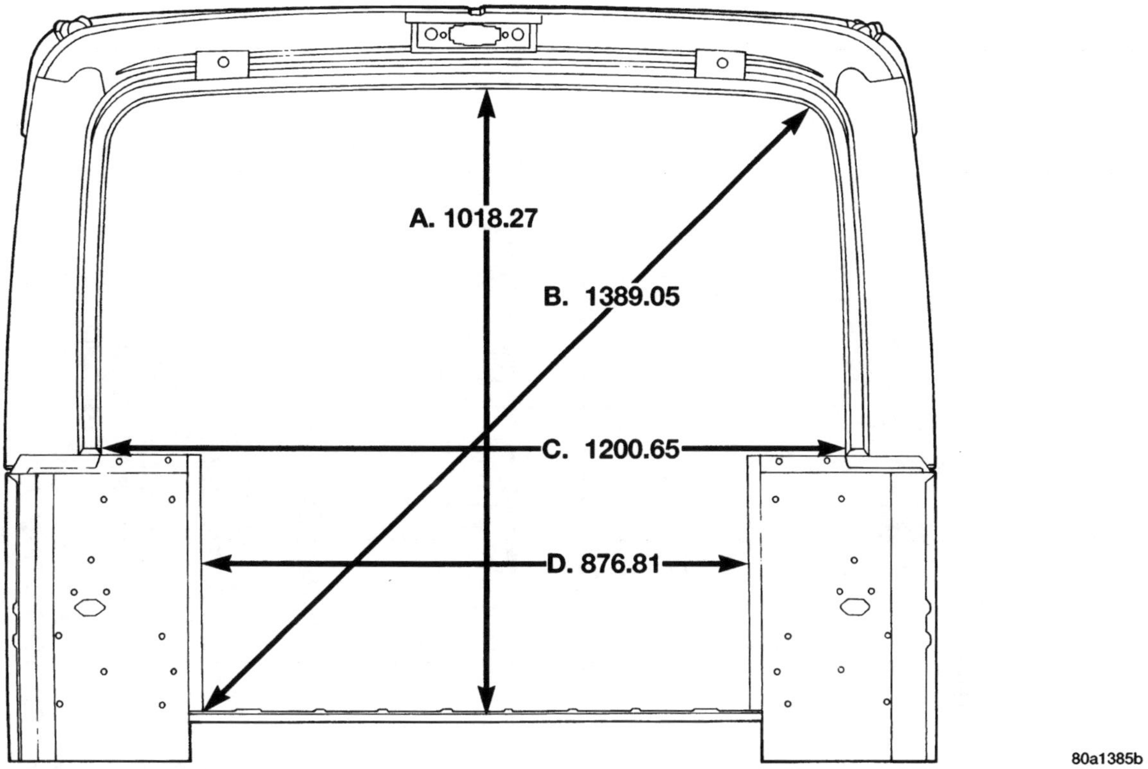

- A. Center of liftgate opening to floor.
- B. Center of radius upper corner to center of body and floor corner.
- C. Liftgate opening distance.
- D. Tailgate opening distance.

SPECIFICATIONS (Continued)

FRAME SIDE VIEW

805fe562

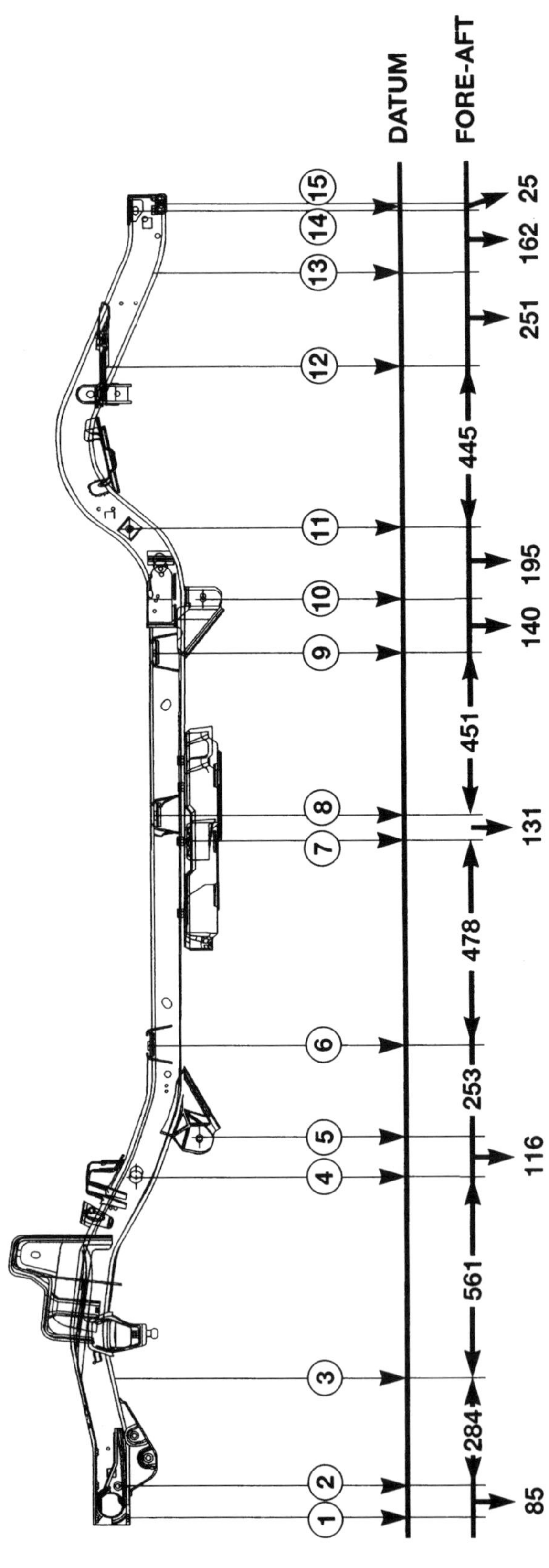

POINT #	DISTANCE TO DATUM (mm)	
1.	500	BOTTOM OF SIDERAIL
2.	534	CENTER OF HOLE
3.	543	BOTTOM OF SIDERAIL, CENTER OF SLOT
4.	494	CENTER OF HOLE, OUTBOARD
5.	317	CENTER OF HOLE, OUTBOARD
6.	460	BOTTOM OF BRACKET
7.	359	BOTTOM OF SIDERAIL

POINT #	DISTANCE TO DATUM (mm)	
8.	445	BOTTOM OF BRACKET
9.	445	BOTTOM OF BRACKET
10.	309	CENTER OF HOLE, OUTBOARD
11.	512	CENTER OF HOLE, INBOARD
12.	577	BOTTOM OF CROSSMEMBER
13.	474	CENTER OF HOLE, OUTBOARD
14.	505	BOTTOM OF BRACKET
15.	406	BOTTOM OF FRAME

SPECIFICATIONS (Continued)

FRAME TOP VIEW

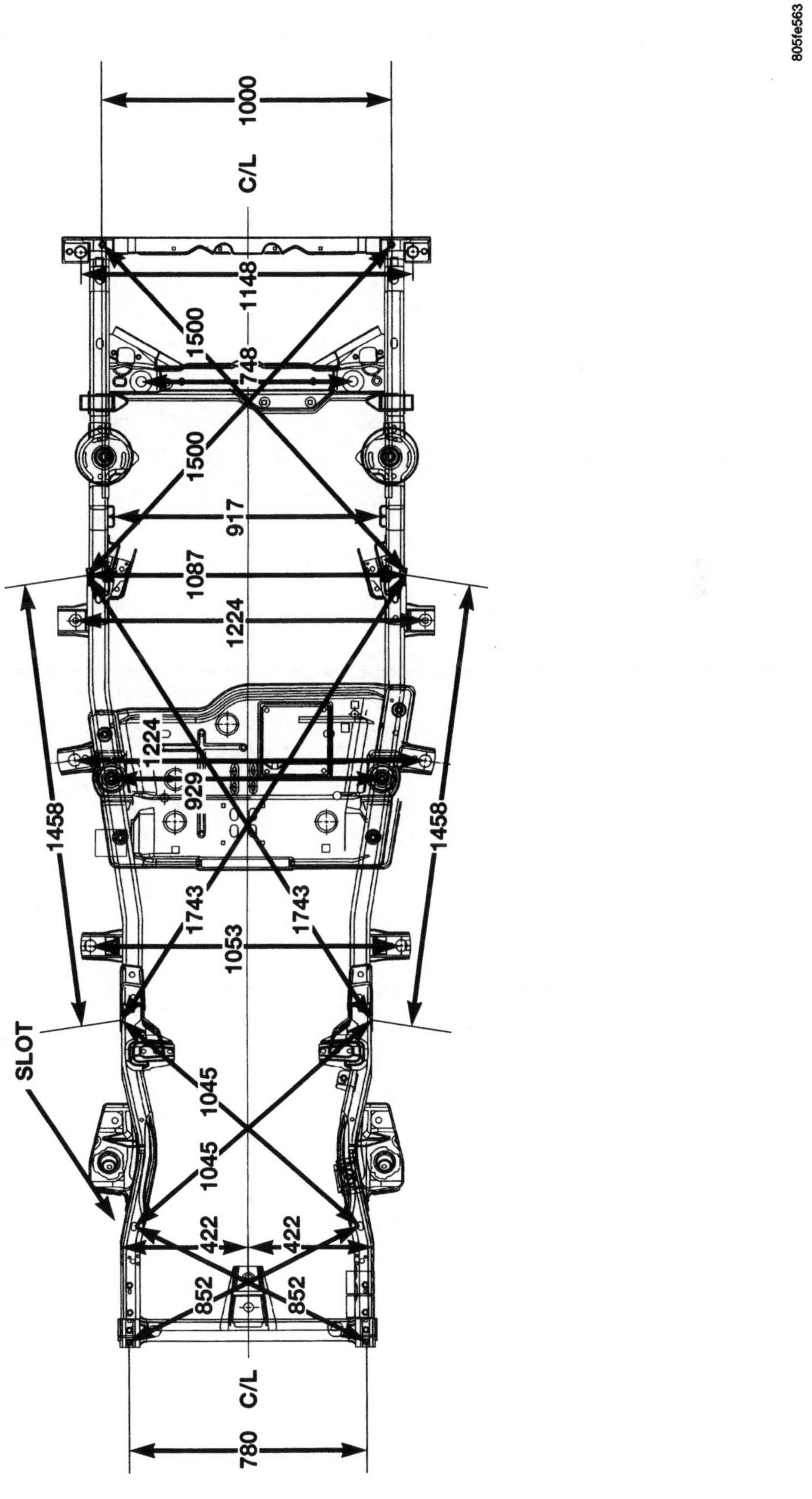

SPECIFICATIONS (Continued)

TORQUE SPECIFICATIONS

DESCRIPTION	TORQUE
Front Bumper Screw	104 N·m (77 ft. lbs.)
Front Tow Hook Screw	108 N·m (80 ft. lbs.)
Front Tow Eye Screw	108 N·m (80 ft. lbs.)
Fuel Tank Skid Plate Nuts	16 N·m (138 in. lbs.)
Fuel Tank Strap Nuts	5 N·m (40 in. lbs.)
Rear Bumper Bolt	67 N·m (50 ft. lbs.)
Rear Bumper Nut	67 N·m (50 ft. lbs.)
Rear Tow Eye Screw	47 N·m (35 ft. lbs.)
Transfer Case Skid Plate Bolts	74 N·m (55 ft. lbs.)
Transmission Mount Nuts	28 N·m (21 ft. lbs.)

FUEL SYSTEM

CONTENTS

GENERAL INFORMATION

INDEX

GENERAL INFORMATION

INTRODUCTION

Throughout this group, references may be made to a particular vehicle by letter or number designation. A chart showing the breakdown of these designations is included in the Introduction Section at the front of this service manual.

The Evaporation Control System, is also considered part of the fuel system. The system reduces the emission of fuel vapor into the atmosphere.

The description and function of the Evaporation Control System is found in Group 25 of this manual.

FUEL REQUIREMENTS

Light spark knock at low engine speeds is not harmful to your engine. However, continued heavy spark knock at high speeds can cause damage and should be reported to your dealer immediately. Engine damage resulting from operating with a heavy spark knock may not be covered by the new vehicle warranty.

In addition to using unleaded gasoline with the proper octane rating, gasolines that contain detergents, corrosion and stability additives are recommended. Using gasolines that have these additives will help improve fuel economy, reduce emissions, and maintain vehicle performance. Generally, premium unleaded gasolines contain more additive than regular unleaded.

Poor quality gasoline can cause problems such as hard starting, stalling, and stumble. If you experience these problems, try another brand of gasoline before considering service for the vehicle.

GASOLINE/OXYGENATE BLENDS

Some fuel suppliers blend gasoline with materials that contain oxygen such as alcohol, MTBE (Methyl Tertiary Butyl Ether) and ETBE (Ethyl Tertiary Butyl Ether). Oxygenates are required in some areas of the country during winter months to reduce carbon monoxide emissions. The type and amount of oxygenate used in the blend is important.

The following are generally used in gasoline blends:

Ethanol - (Ethyl or Grain Alcohol) properly blended, is used as a mixture of 10 percent ethanol and 90 percent gasoline. Gasoline blended with ethanol may be used in your vehicle.

Methanol - (Methyl or Wood Alcohol) is used in a variety of concentrations when blended with unleaded gasoline. You may find fuels containing 3 percent or more methanol along with other alcohols called cosolvents.

Do not use gasolines containing Methanol.

Use of methanol/gasoline blends may result in starting and driveability problems and damage critical fuel system components.

Problems that are the result of using methanol/gasoline blends are not the responsibility of Chrysler Motors and may not be covered by the new vehicle warranty.

MTBE/ETBE - Gasoline and MTBE (Methyl Tertiary Butyl Ether) blends are a mixture of unleaded gasoline blended and up to 15 percent MTBE. Gaso-

GENERAL INFORMATION (Continued)

line and ETBE (Ethyl Tertiary Butly Ether) are blends of gasoline and up to 17 percent ETBE. Gasoline blended with MTBE or ETBE may be used in your vehicle.

Many gasolines are now being blended that contribute to cleaner air, especially in those areas of the country where pollution levels are high. These new blends provide a cleaner burning fuel and some are referred to as reformulated gasoline.

Reformulated Gasoline

Many areas of the country are requiring the use of cleaner-burning fuel referred to as **Reformulated Gasoline**. Reformulated gasolines are specially blended to reduce vehicle emissions and improve air quality.

Chrysler Corporation strongly supports the use of reformulated gasolines whenever available. Although your vehicle was designed to provide optimum performance and lowest emissions operating on high quality unleaded gasoline, it will perform equally well and produce even lower emissions when operating on reformulated gasoline.

Materials Added to Fuel

Indiscriminate use of fuel system cleaning agents should be avoided. Many of these materials intended for gum and varnish removal may contain active solvents of similar ingredients that can be harmful to fuel system gasket and diaphragm materials.

FUEL DELIVERY SYSTEM

INDEX

DESCRIPTION AND OPERATION

FUEL DELIVERY SYSTEM

The fuel delivery system consists of: the electric fuel pump, fuel filter, fuel pressure regulator, fuel pump module, fuel gauge sending unit, fuel tubes/lines/hoses, quick-connect fittings, fuel rail, fuel injectors, fuel tank, accelerator pedal, fuel tank filler cap and throttle cable.

A fuel return system is used on all models (all engines). Fuel is returned through the fuel pump module and back into the fuel tank through the fuel pressure regulator. A separate fuel return line from the engine to the tank is not used with any 2.5L or 4.0L engine.

The fuel tank assembly consists of: the fuel tank, filler tubes/hoses, fuel gauge sending unit/electric fuel pump module, two interconnected pressure relief/rollover valves and a pressure-vacuum filler cap.

Also to be considered part of the fuel system is the evaporation control system. This is designed to reduce the emission of fuel vapors into the atmosphere. Description and function of the Evaporative Control System can be found in Group 25, Emission Control Systems.

FUEL PUMP MODULE

The fuel pump module on all models is installed into the top of the fuel tank (Fig. 1). The fuel pump module contains the following components (Fig. 1) or (Fig. 2):

- A combination fuel filter/fuel pressure regulator
- A separate fuel pick-up filter (strainer)
- An electric fuel pump
- A threaded locknut to retain module to tank
- Fuel gauge sending unit (fuel level sensor)
- Fuel supply tube (line) connection

The fuel gauge sending unit, pick-up filter and fuel filter/fuel pressure regulator may be serviced separately. If the electrical fuel pump requires service, the entire fuel pump module must be replaced.

FUEL PUMP

The fuel pump used in this system has a permanent magnet electric motor. The pump is part of the fuel pump module. The fuel pump module is suspended in fuel in the fuel tank. Fuel is drawn in through a filter and pushed through the electric motor to the outlet. The pump contains a check valve. This valve is located near the pump outlet. It restricts fuel movement in either direction to maintain fuel supply line pressure when the pump is not operational. Voltage to operate the pump is supplied through the fuel pump relay.

DESCRIPTION AND OPERATION (Continued)

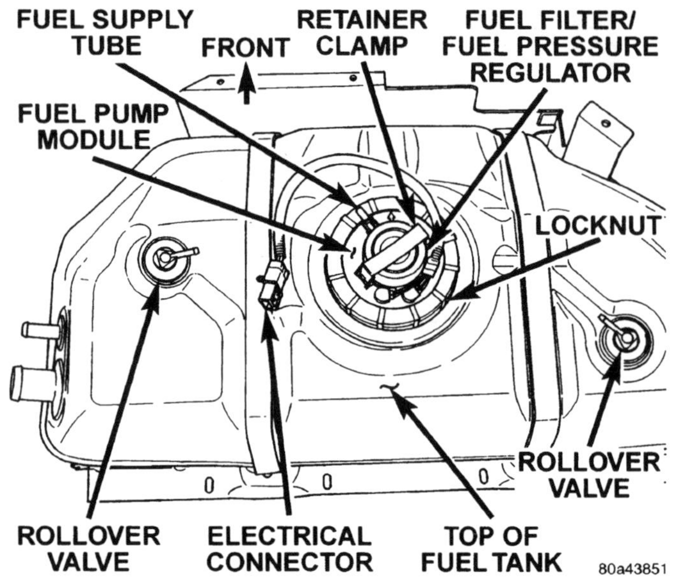

Fig. 1 Fuel Tank/Fuel Pump Module (Top View)

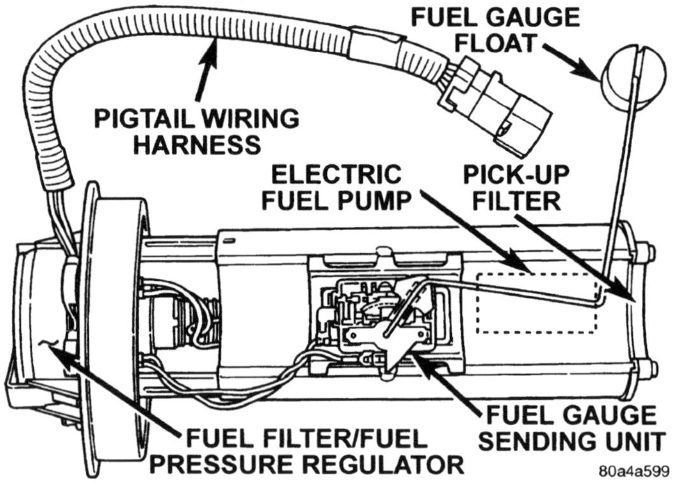

Fig. 2 Fuel Pump Module Components

FUEL GAUGE SENDING UNIT

The fuel gauge sending unit is attached to the side of the fuel pump module (Fig. 2). The sending unit consists of a float, an arm, and a variable resistor (track). The resistor track is used to send electrical signals to the Powertrain Control Module (PCM) for fuel gauge operation and for OBD II emission requirements.

For fuel gauge operation: As fuel level increases, the float and arm move up. This decreases the sending unit resistance, causing the fuel gauge to read full. As fuel level decreases, the float and arm move down. This increases the sending unit resistance causing the fuel gauge to read empty.

After this fuel level signal is sent to the PCM, the PCM will transmit the data across the CCD bus circuits to the instrument panel. Here it is translated into the appropriate fuel gauge level reading.

For OBD II emission requirements: The voltage signal is sent from the resistor track to the PCM to indicate fuel level. The purpose of this feature is to prevent a false setting of misfire and fuel system monitor trouble codes if the fuel level in the tank is less than 15 percent of its rated capacity.

FUEL FILTER/FUEL PRESSURE REGULATOR

A combination fuel filter and fuel pressure regulator is used on all engines. It is located on the top of fuel pump module (Fig. 1). A separate frame mounted fuel filter is not used with any engine.

Fuel Pressure Regulator Operation: The pressure regulator is a mechanical device that is not controlled by engine vacuum or the Powertrain Control Module (PCM).

The regulator is calibrated to maintain fuel system operating pressure of approximately 338 kPa (49 psi) at the fuel injectors. It contains a diaphragm, calibrated springs and a fuel return valve. The internal fuel filter is also part of the assembly.

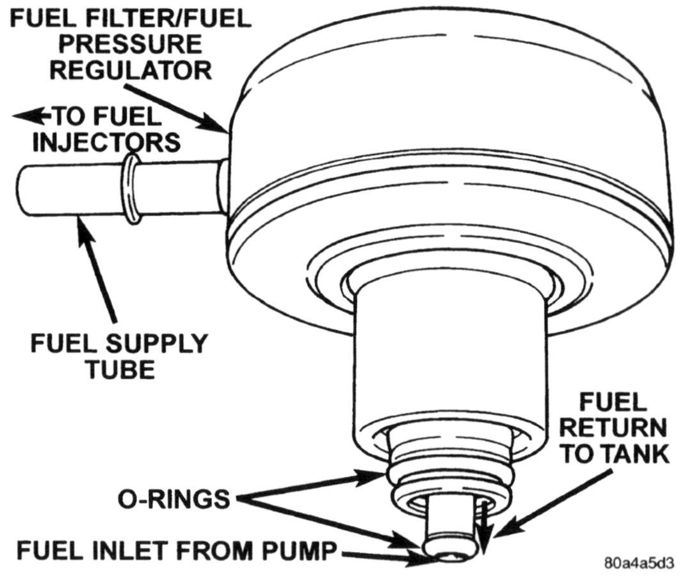

Fig. 3 Fuel Filter/Fuel Pressure Regulator

Fuel is supplied to the filter/regulator by the electric fuel pump through an opening tube at the bottom of filter/regulator (Fig. 3).

The fuel pump module contains a check valve to maintain some fuel pressure when the engine is not operating. This will help to start the engine.

If fuel pressure at the pressure regulator exceeds approximately 49 psi, an internal diaphragm closes and excess fuel pressure is routed back into the tank through the pressure regulator. A separate fuel return line is not used with any engine.

FUEL TANK

All models pass a full 360 degree rollover test without fuel leakage. To accomplish this, fuel and

DESCRIPTION AND OPERATION (Continued)

vapor flow controls are required for all fuel tank connections.

All models are equipped with two rollover valves mounted into the top of the fuel tank (Fig. 1).

An evaporation control system is used to reduce emissions of fuel vapors into atmosphere by evaporation and to reduce unburned hydrocarbons emitted by vehicle engine. When fuel evaporates from fuel tank, vapors pass through vent hoses or tubes to a charcoal canister. The are temporarily held in the canister. When the engine is running, the vapors are drawn into the intake manifold. Refer to Group 25, Emission Control System for additional information.

FUEL INJECTORS

Six individual fuel injectors are used with the 4.0L 6-cylinder engine. Four individual fuel injectors are used with the 2.5L 4-cylinder engine. The injectors are attached to the fuel rail (Fig. 4).

The nozzle ends of the injectors are positioned into openings in the intake manifold just above the intake valve ports of the cylinder head. The engine wiring harness connector for each fuel injector is equipped with an attached numerical tag (INJ 1, INJ 2 etc.). This is used to identify each fuel injector.

The injectors are energized individually in a sequential order by the powertrain control module (PCM). The PCM will adjust injector pulse width by switching the ground path to each individual injector on and off. Injector pulse width is the period of time that the injector is energized. The PCM will adjust injector pulse width based on various inputs it receives.

During start up, battery voltage is supplied to the injectors through the ASD relay. When the engine is operating, voltage is supplied by the charging system. The PCM determines injector pulse width based on various inputs.

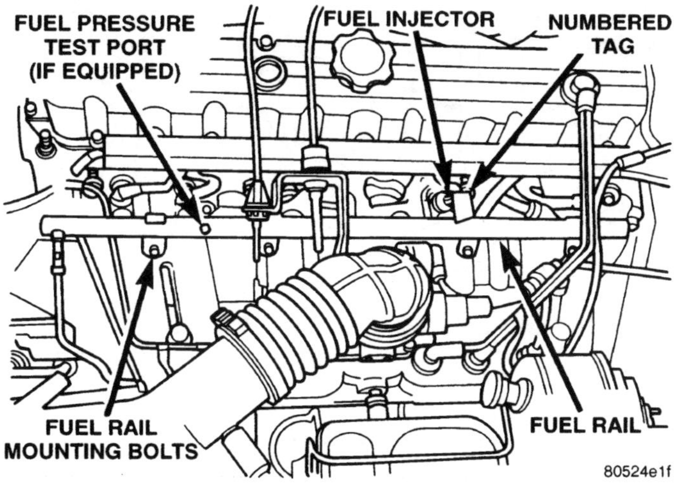

Fig. 4 Fuel Injectors—Typical—4.0L Shown

FUEL RAIL

The fuel rail supplies the necessary fuel to each individual fuel injector and is mounted to the intake manifold (Fig. 4).

Certain engines are equipped with a fuel pressure test port (Fig. 4). **Not all engines are equipped with this test port.**

The fuel rail is not repairable.

FUEL TANK FILLER TUBE CAP

The loss of any fuel or vapor out of filler neck is prevented by the use of a pressure-vacuum fuel tank filler tube cap. Relief valves inside cap will release only under significant pressure of 6.58 to 8.44 kPa (1.95 to 2.5 psi). The vacuum release for all fuel filler tube caps is between .97 and 2.0 kPa (.14 and .29 psi). This cap must be replaced by a similar unit if replacement is necessary. This is in order for the system to remain effective.

CAUTION: Remove fuel tank filler tube cap before servicing any fuel system component. This is done to help relieve tank pressure.

QUICK-CONNECT FITTINGS

Two different types of quick-connect fittings are used to attach various fuel system components. These are: a two-tab type or a plastic retainer ring type. The plastic retainer type will require a special tool for disconnection. Some quick-connect fittings are equipped with safety latch clips. Refer to Quick-Connect Fittings in the Removal/Installation section for more information.

CAUTION: The interior components (o-rings, spacers) of quick-connect fitting are not serviced separately. Do not attempt to repair damaged fittings or fuel lines/tubes. If repair is necessary, replace the complete fuel tube (line) assembly.

DIAGNOSIS AND TESTING

FUEL PUMP PRESSURE TEST—2.5L ENGINE

NOTE: The fuel pressure test port is used on certain engines only. If equipped, the test port will be located on the fuel rail. If not equipped, refer to the following procedure:

All fuel systems are equipped with a fuel tank module mounted, combination fuel filter/fuel pressure regulator. The fuel pressure regulator is not controlled by engine vacuum.

With engine at idle speed, system fuel pressure should be 338 kPa ± 5 kPa (49.0 psi ± 2 psi).

DIAGNOSIS AND TESTING (Continued)

WARNING: THE FUEL SYSTEM IS UNDER CONSTANT FUEL PRESSURE EVEN WITH THE ENGINE OFF. BEFORE DISCONNECTING FUEL LINE AT FUEL RAIL, THIS PRESSURE MUST BE RELEASED. REFER TO THE FUEL SYSTEM PRESSURE RELEASE PROCEDURE.

(1) Release fuel pressure. Refer to the Fuel System Pressure Release Procedure.

(2) Disconnect latch clip and fuel line at fuel rail. Refer to Quick-Connect Fittings for procedures. This can be found in this section of the group.

(3) Connect adapter tool number 6539 or 6631 (Fig. 5) into fuel rail. **Be sure adapter tool is fully seated into fuel rail.**

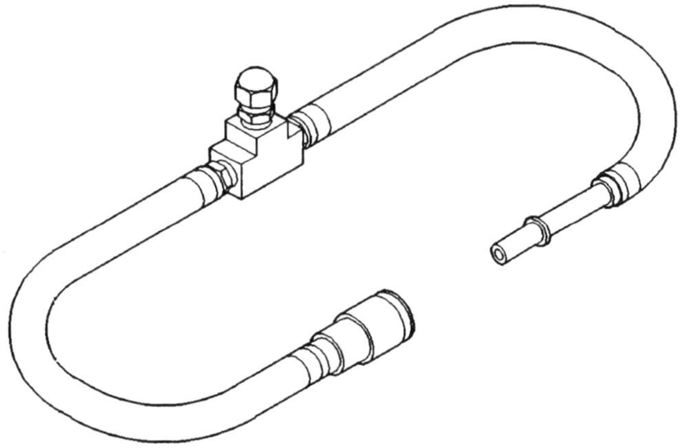

Fig. 5 Adapter Tool 6539 or 6631

(4) Install latch clip to fuel rail. If latch clip can not be fully seated into fuel rail, check for adapter tool not fully seated to fuel rail.

(5) Connect vehicle fuel line into adapter tool. Be sure fuel line is fully seated into adapter tool.

(6) Remove protective cap at test port "T" on adapter tool.

(7) Connect the 0–414 kPa (0-60 psi) fuel pressure gauge (from gauge set 5069) to the test port "T".

(8) Start engine and note pressure gauge reading. Fuel pressure should be 338 kPa ± 5 kPa (49.0 psi ± 2 psi) at idle.

(9) If pressure is at 0 psi, connect DRB scan tool and refer to the appropriate Powertrain Diagnostics Procedures service manual.

(10) If operating pressure is above 51.0 psi, fuel pump is OK but pressure regulator is defective. Replace fuel filter/fuel pressure regulator assembly.

(11) After performing pressure test, install fuel line into fuel rail. Install latch clip into fuel rail. Refer to Quick-Connect Fittings in the Removal/Installation section of this group for procedures.

FUEL PUMP PRESSURE TEST–4.0L ENGINE

NOTE: The fuel pressure test port is used on certain engines only. If equipped, the test port will be located on the fuel rail (Fig. 4). A sealing cap is screwed onto the test port.

All fuel systems are equipped with a fuel tank module mounted, combination fuel filter/fuel pressure regulator. The fuel pressure regulator is not controlled by engine vacuum.

With engine at idle speed, system fuel pressure should be 338 kPa ± 5 kPa (49.0 psi ± 2 psi).

WARNING: DO NOT ALLOW FUEL TO SPILL ONTO THE ENGINE INTAKE OR EXHAUST MANIFOLDS. PLACE SHOP TOWELS UNDER AND AROUND THE PRESSURE PORT TO ABSORB FUEL.

WARNING: WEAR PROPER EYE PROTECTION WHEN TESTING FUEL SYSTEM PRESSURE.

(1) Remove protective cap at fuel rail test port. Connect the 0–414 kPa (0-60 psi) fuel pressure gauge (from gauge set 5069) to test port pressure fitting on fuel rail (Fig. 6).

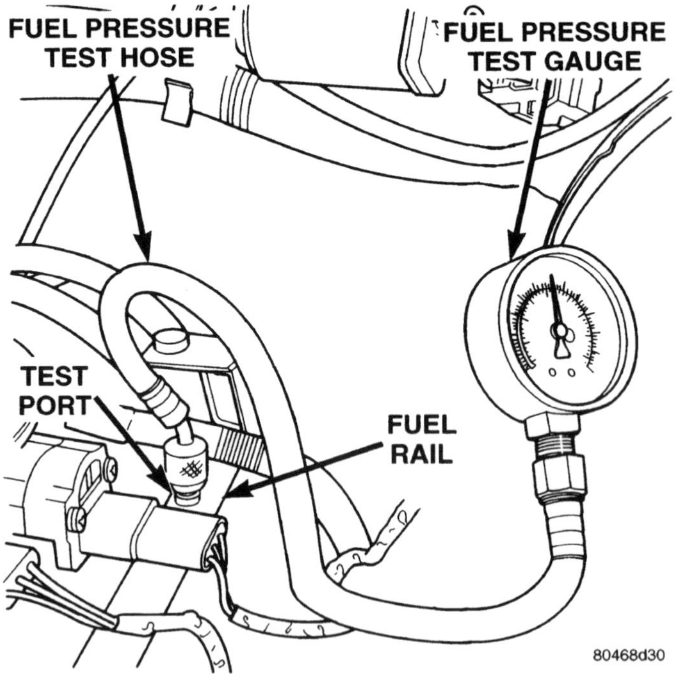

Fig. 6 Fuel Pressure Gauge Installation—Typical Test Port Shown

(2) Start engine and note pressure gauge reading. Fuel pressure should be 338 kPa ± 5 kPa (49.0 psi ± 2 psi) at idle.

DIAGNOSIS AND TESTING (Continued)

(3) If pressure is at O psi, connect DRB scan tool and refer to the appropriate Powertrain Diagnostics Procedures service manual.

(4) If operating pressure is above 51.0 psi, fuel pump is OK but pressure regulator is defective. Replace fuel filter/fuel pressure regulator assembly.

FUEL GAUGE SENDING UNIT

The fuel gauge sending unit contains a variable resistor (track). As the float moves up or down, electrical resistance will change. Refer to Group 8E, Instrument Panel and Gauges for Fuel Gauge testing. To test the gauge sending unit only, it must be removed from vehicle. The unit is part of the fuel pump module. Refer to Fuel Pump Module Removal/ Installation for procedures. Measure the resistance across the sending unit terminals. With float in up position, resistance should be 20 ohms. With float in down position, resistance should be 220 ohms.

FUEL INJECTOR TEST

To perform a complete test of the fuel injectors and their circuitry, refer to DRB scan tool and appropriate Powertrain Diagnostics Procedures manual. To test the injector only, refer to the following:

Disconnect the fuel injector wire harness connector from the injector. Place an ohmmeter across the injector electrical terminals. Resistance reading should be approximately 14.5 ohms ±1.2 ohms at 20°C (68°F).

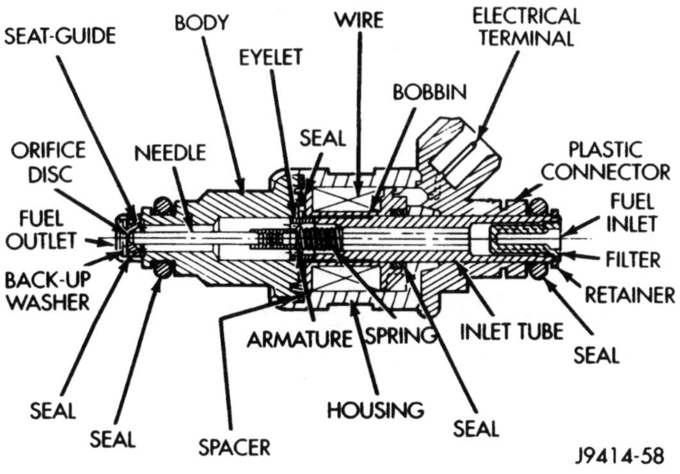

Fig. 7 Fuel Injector Internal Components—Typical

SERVICE PROCEDURES

FUEL SYSTEM PRESSURE RELEASE PROCEDURE—WITHOUT TEST PORT

Use the following procedure if the fuel rail is not equipped with a fuel pressure test port.

(1) Remove fuel pump relay from Power Distribution Center (PDC). For location of relay, refer to label on underside of PDC cover.

(2) Start and run engine it stalls.

(3) Attempt restarting engine until it will no longer run.

(4) Turn ignition key to OFF position.

CAUTION: Steps 1, 2, 3 and 4 must be performed to relieve high pressure fuel from within the fuel rail. Do not attempt to use the following steps to relieve this pressure as excessive fuel will be forced into a cylinder chamber.

(5) Unplug connector from any injector.

(6) Attach one end of a jumper wire with alligator clips (18 gauge or smaller) to either injector terminal.

(7) Connect other end of jumper wire to positive side of battery.

(8) Connect one end of a second jumper wire to remaining injector terminal.

CAUTION: Supplying power to an injector for more than 4 seconds will permanently damage the injector. Do not leave the injector connected to power for more than 4 seconds.

(9) Momentarily touch the other end of this jumper wire to negative terminal of battery for no more than 4 seconds.

(10) Place a rag or towel below fuel line at quick connect to rail.

(11) Disconnect quick connect fitting to rail. Refer to Quick-Connect Fittings in this section.

(12) Return fuel pump relay to PDC.

(13) One or more Diagnostic Trouble Codes (DTC's) may have been stored in the PCM memory due to fuel pump relay removal. The DRB scan tool must be used to erase a DTC. Refer to Group 25, Emission Control System. See On-Board Diagnostics.

FUEL SYSTEM PRESSURE RELEASE PROCEDURE–WITH TEST PORT

NOTE: The fuel pressure test port is used on certain engines only. If equipped, the test port will be located on the fuel rail (Fig. 4). A sealing cap is screwed onto the test port.

The fuel system is under constant fuel pressure (even with the engine off).

WARNING: BECAUSE THE FUEL SYSTEM IS UNDER CONSTANT FUEL PRESSURE, THE PRESSURE MUST BE RELEASED BEFORE SERVICING ANY FUEL SYSTEM COMPONENT. THIS DOES NOT APPLY TO THROTTLE BODY REMOVAL.

SERVICE PROCEDURES (Continued)

(1) Disconnect negative battery cable at battery.
(2) Remove fuel tank filler tube cap to release fuel tank pressure.
(3) Remove protective cap from pressure test port on fuel rail.

WARNING: DO NOT ALLOW FUEL TO SPILL ONTO THE ENGINE INTAKE OR EXHAUST MANIFOLDS. PLACE SHOP TOWELS UNDER AND AROUND THE PRESSURE PORT TO ABSORB FUEL WHEN THE PRESSURE IS RELEASED FROM THE FUEL RAIL.

WARNING: WEAR PROPER EYE PROTECTION WHEN RELEASING FUEL SYSTEM PRESSURE.

(4) Obtain the fuel pressure gauge/hose assembly from fuel pressure gauge tool set 5069. Remove gauge from hose.
(5) Place one end of hose (gauge end) into an approved gasoline container.
(6) Place a shop towel under test port.
(7) To release fuel pressure, screw other end of hose onto fuel pressure test port.
(8) After fuel pressure has been released, remove hose from test port.
(9) Install protective cap to fuel test port.

FUEL TUBES/LINES/HOSES AND CLAMPS

Also refer to the section on Quick-Connect Fittings.

WARNING: THE FUEL SYSTEM IS UNDER A CONSTANT PRESSURE (EVEN WITH THE ENGINE OFF). BEFORE SERVICING ANY FUEL SYSTEM HOSES, FITTINGS OR LINES, THE FUEL SYSTEM PRESSURE MUST BE RELEASED. REFER TO THE FUEL SYSTEM PRESSURE RELEASE PROCEDURE IN THIS GROUP.

Inspect all hose connections such as clamps, couplings and fittings to make sure they are secure and leaks are not present. The component should be replaced immediately if there is any evidence of degradation that could result in failure.

Never attempt to repair a plastic fuel line/tube. Replace as necessary.

Avoid contact of any fuel tubes/hoses with other vehicle components that could cause abrasions or scuffing. Be sure that the plastic fuel lines/tubes are properly routed to prevent pinching and to avoid heat sources.

The lines/tubes/hoses used on fuel injected vehicles are of a special construction. This is due to the higher fuel pressures and the possibility of contaminated fuel in this system. If it is necessary to replace these lines/tubes/hoses, only those marked EFM/EFI may be used.

When Used: The hose clamps used to secure rubber hoses on fuel injected vehicles are of a special rolled edge construction. This construction is used to prevent the edge of the clamp from cutting into the hose. Only these rolled edge type clamps may be used in this system. All other types of clamps may cut into the hoses and cause high-pressure fuel leaks.

When Used: Use new original equipment type hose clamps. Tighten hose clamps to 1 N·m (15 in. lbs.) torque.

QUICK-CONNECT FITTINGS

Also refer to the Fuel Tubes/Lines/Hoses and Clamps section.

Two different types of quick-connect fittings are used to attach various fuel system components. These are: a two-tab type, or a plastic retainer ring type using a latch clip.

TWO-TAB TYPE FITTING

This type of fitting is equipped with tabs located on both sides of the fitting (Fig. 8). These tabs are supplied for disconnecting the quick-connect fitting from component being serviced.

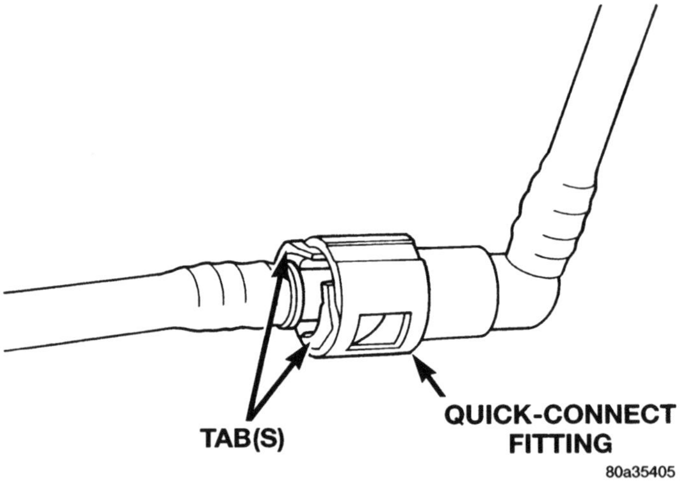

Fig. 8 Typical Two-Tab Type Quick-Connect Fitting

CAUTION: The interior components (o-rings, spacers) of this type of quick-connect fitting are not serviced separately, but new plastic retainers are available. Do not attempt to repair damaged fittings or fuel lines/tubes. If repair is necessary, replace the complete fuel tube assembly.

WARNING: THE FUEL SYSTEM IS UNDER A CONSTANT PRESSURE (EVEN WITH THE ENGINE OFF). BEFORE SERVICING ANY FUEL SYSTEM HOSES, FITTINGS OR LINES, THE FUEL SYSTEM PRESSURE MUST BE RELEASED. REFER TO THE FUEL PRESSURE RELEASE PROCEDURE IN THIS GROUP.

SERVICE PROCEDURES (Continued)

DISCONNECTION/CONNECTION

(1) Disconnect negative battery cable from the battery.

(2) Perform the fuel pressure release procedure. Refer to the Fuel Pressure Release Procedure in this section.

(3) Clean the fitting of any foreign material before disassembly.

(4) To disconnect the quick-connect fitting, squeeze the plastic retainer tabs (Fig. 8) against the sides of the quick-connect fitting with your fingers. Tool use is not required for removal and may damage plastic retainer. Pull the fitting from the fuel system component being serviced. The plastic retainer will remain on the component being serviced after fitting is disconnected. The o-rings and spacer will remain in the quick-connect fitting connector body.

(5) Inspect the quick-connect fitting body and component for damage. Replace as necessary.

CAUTION: When the quick-connect fitting was disconnected, the plastic retainer will remain on the component being serviced. If this retainer must be removed, very carefully release the retainer from the component with two small screwdrivers. After removal, inspect the retainer for cracks or any damage.

(6) Prior to connecting the quick-connect fitting to component being serviced, check condition of fitting and component. Clean the parts with a lint-free cloth. Lubricate them with clean engine oil.

(7) Insert the quick-connect fitting to the component being serviced and into the plastic retainer. When a connection is made, a click will be heard.

(8) Verify a locked condition by firmly pulling on fuel tube and fitting (15-30 lbs.).

(9) Connect negative cable to battery.

(10) Start engine and check for leaks.

FUEL LINE AT FUEL RAIL

A plastic retainer ring type quick-connect fitting is used at the fuel rail. A latch clip is used to secure the fuel line to the fuel rail on certain engines (Fig. 9). A special tool will be necessary to separate the fuel line from the fuel rail after the latch clip is removed.

DISCONNECTION/CONNECTION AT FUEL RAIL

(1) Disconnect the negative battery cable from battery.

(2) Perform the fuel pressure release procedure. Refer to the Fuel Pressure Release Procedure in this section.

(3) Clean the fitting of any foreign material before disassembly.

(4) Pry up on the latch clip with a screwdriver (Fig. 9).

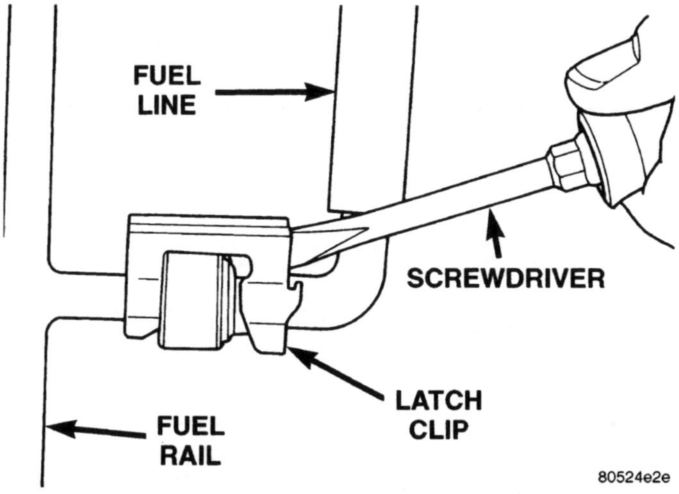

Fig. 9 Latch Clip Removal—Typical

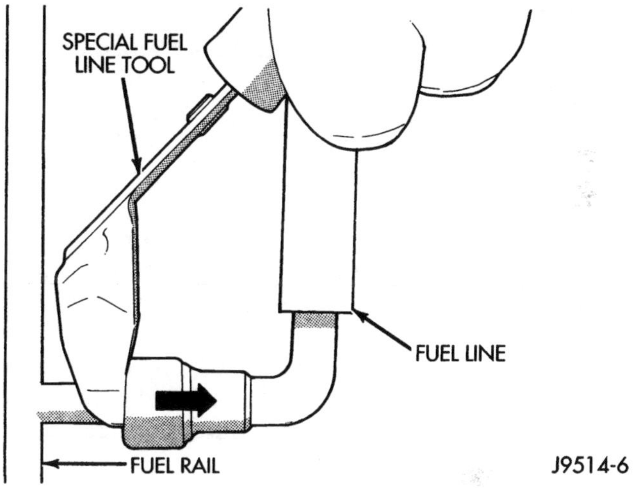

Fig. 10 Fuel Line Disconnection—Typical

(5) Slide the latch clip toward the fuel rail while lifting with the screwdriver.

(6) Insert special fuel line removal tool (Snap-On number FIH 9055-1 or equivalent) into the fuel line (Fig. 10). Use this tool to release the locking fingers in the end of the line.

(7) With the special tool still inserted, pull the fuel line from the fuel rail.

(8) After disconnection, the locking fingers will remain within the quick-connect fitting at the end of the fuel line.

(9) Inspect fuel line fitting, locking fingers and fuel rail fitting for damage. Replace as necessary.

(10) Prior to connecting the fuel line to the fuel rail, check condition of both fittings. Clean the parts with a lint-free cloth. Lubricate them with clean engine oil.

(11) Insert the fuel line onto the fuel rail until a click is felt.

(12) Verify a locked condition by firmly pulling on fuel line and fitting (15-30 lbs.).

SERVICE PROCEDURES (Continued)

(13) Install latch clip (snaps into position). **If the latch clip will not fit, this indicates the fuel line is not properly installed to the fuel rail. Recheck the fuel line connection.**

(14) Connect negative battery cable to battery.

(15) Start engine and check for leaks.

REMOVAL AND INSTALLATION

FUEL FILTER/FUEL PRESSURE REGULATOR

The combination Fuel Filter/Fuel Pressure Regulator is located on the fuel pump module. The fuel pump module is located on top of fuel tank.

The filter/regulator may be removed without removing fuel pump module although fuel tank must be removed.

REMOVAL

(1) Remove fuel tank. Refer to Fuel Tank Removal/Installation.

(2) Clean area around filter/regulator.

(3) Remove retainer clamp from top of filter/regulator (Fig. 11). Clamp snaps to tabs on pump module. Discard old clamp.

(4) Pry filter/regulator from top of pump module with 2 screwdrivers. Unit is snapped into module.

(5) Discard gasket below filter/regulator (Fig. 12).

(6) Discard o-rings on bottom of filter/regulator (Fig. 13). If the smallest of the two o-rings can not be found on bottom of filter/regulator, it may be necessary to remove it from the fuel inlet passage in fuel pump module.

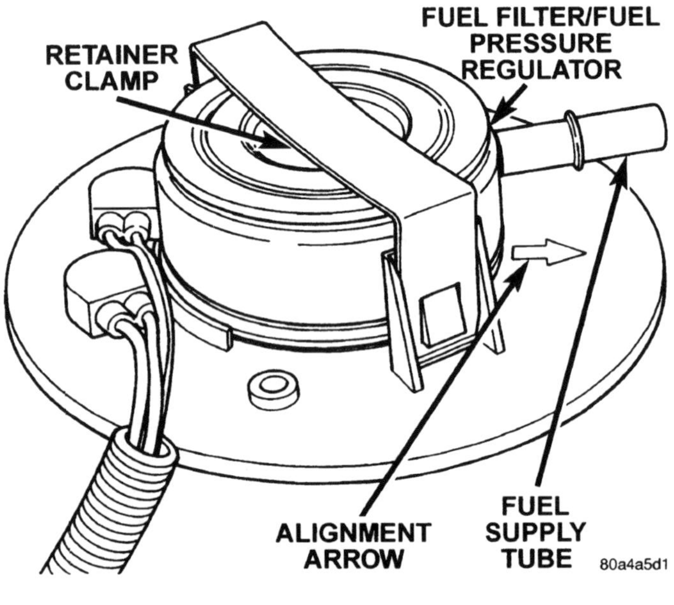

Fig. 11 Fuel Filter/Fuel Pressure Regulator

INSTALLATION

(1) Install new o-rings to grooves on filter/regulator. Apply a small amount of clean engine oil to

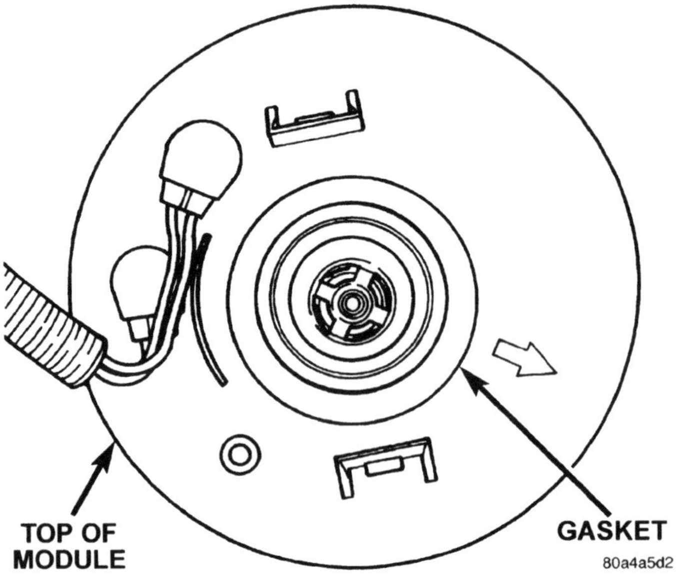

Fig. 12 Fuel Filter/Fuel Pressure Regulator Gasket

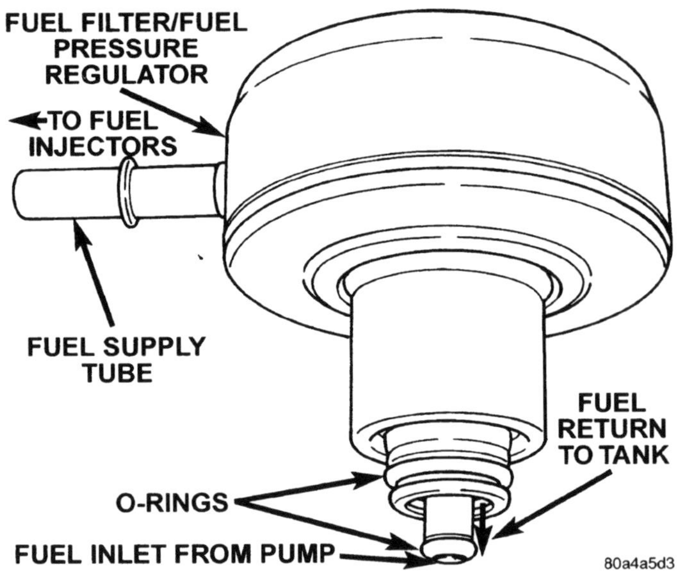

Fig. 13 Fuel Filter/Fuel Pressure Regulator O-Rings

o-rings. **Do not install o-rings separately into fuel pump module. They will be damaged when installing filter/regulator.**

(2) Install new gasket to top of fuel pump module.

(3) Press filter/regulator into top of pump module until it snaps into position (a positive click must be heard or felt).

(4) The arrow (Fig. 11) on top of fuel pump module should be pointed towards front of vehicle (12 o'clock position).

(5) Rotate filter/regulator until fuel supply tube (fitting) is pointed to 10 o'clock position.

(6) Install new retainer clamp (snaps) to top of filter/regulator.

(7) Install fuel tank. Refer to Fuel Tank Removal/Installation.

REMOVAL AND INSTALLATION (Continued)

FUEL PUMP MODULE

Fuel tank removal will be necessary for fuel pump module removal.

REMOVAL

WARNING: THE FUEL SYSTEM IS UNDER A CONSTANT PRESSURE (EVEN WITH THE ENGINE OFF). BEFORE SERVICING THE FUEL PUMP MODULE, THE FUEL SYSTEM PRESSURE MUST BE RELEASED.

(1) Drain fuel tank and remove tank. Refer to the Fuel Tank Removal/Installation section of this group.

(2) The plastic fuel pump module locknut is threaded onto fuel tank (Fig. 14). Install Special Tool 6856 to fuel pump module locknut and remove locknut (Fig. 15). The fuel pump module will spring up when locknut is removed.

(3) Remove module from fuel tank.

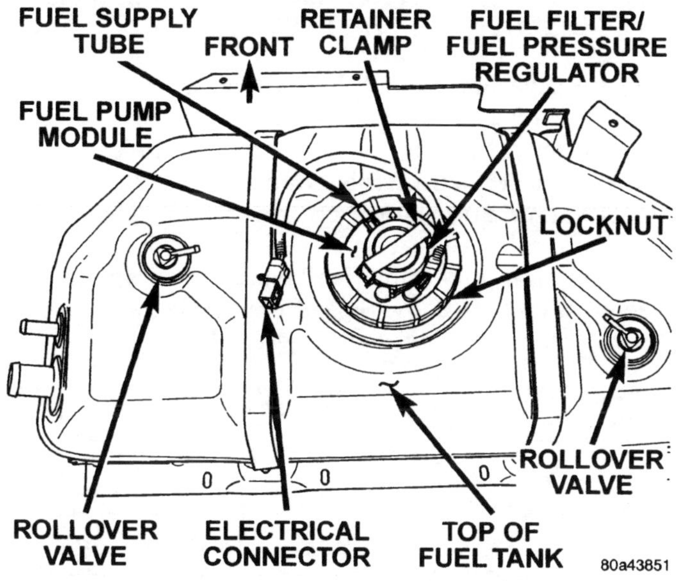

Fig. 14 Top View of Fuel Tank and Fuel Pump Module

INSTALLATION

CAUTION: Whenever the fuel pump module is serviced, the module gasket must be replaced.

(1) Using a new gasket, position fuel pump module into opening in fuel tank.

(2) Position locknut over top of fuel pump module.

(3) Rotate module until arrow (Fig. 11) is pointed toward front of vehicle (12 o'clock position). This step must be done to prevent float/float rod assembly from contacting sides of fuel tank.

(4) Install Special Tool 6856 to locknut.

(5) Tighten locknut to 34 N·m (25 ft. lbs.) torque.

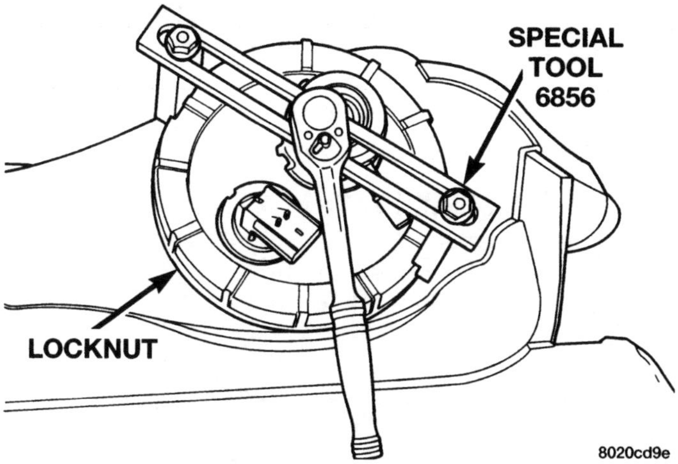

Fig. 15 Locknut Removal/Installation—Typical

(6) Rotate fuel filter/fuel pressure regulator until its fitting is pointed to 10 o'clock position.

(7) Install fuel tank. Refer to Fuel Tank Installation in this section.

FUEL PUMP INLET FILTER

The fuel pump inlet filter (strainer) is located on the bottom of fuel pump module (Fig. 16). The fuel pump module is located on top of fuel tank.

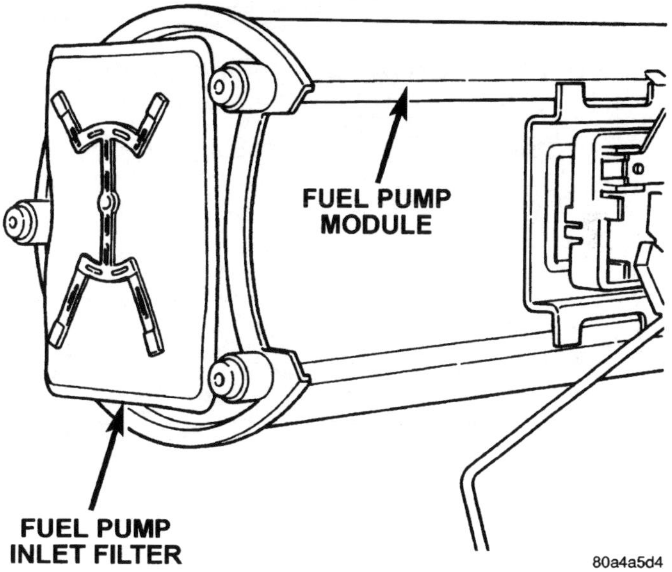

Fig. 16 Fuel Pump Inlet Filter

REMOVAL

(1) Remove fuel tank. Refer to Fuel Tank Removal/Installation.

(2) Remove fuel pump module. Refer to Fuel Pump Module Removal/Installation.

(3) Remove filter by prying from bottom of module with 2 screwdrivers. Filter is snapped to module.

(4) Clean bottom of pump module.

REMOVAL AND INSTALLATION (Continued)

INSTALLATION

(1) Snap new filter to bottom of module.

(2) Install fuel pump module. Refer to Fuel Pump Module Removal/Installation.

(3) Install fuel tank. Refer to Fuel Tank Removal/ Installation.

FUEL GAUGE SENDING UNIT

The fuel gauge sending unit (fuel level sensor) and float assembly is located on the side of fuel pump module (Fig. 17). The fuel pump module is located on top of fuel tank.

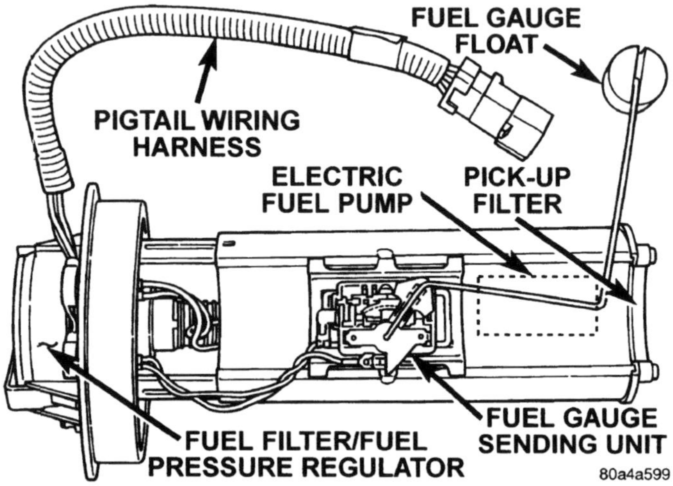

Fig. 17 Fuel Gauge Sending Unit Location

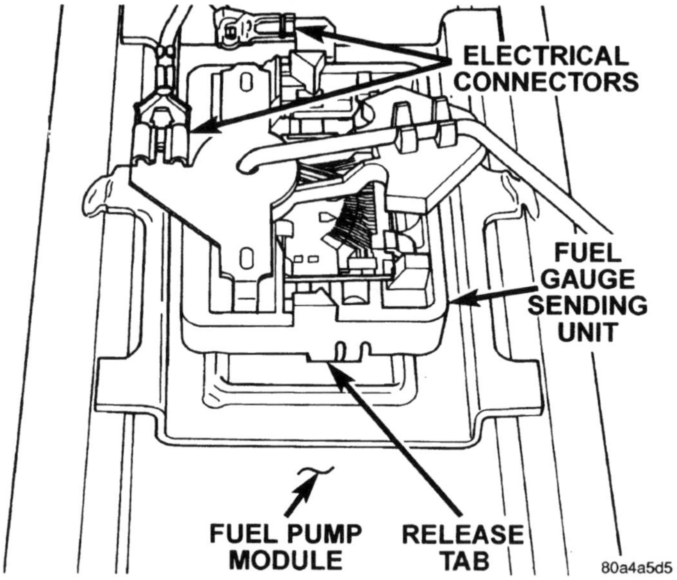

Fig. 18 Fuel Gauge Sending Unit Release Tab

REMOVAL

(1) Remove fuel tank. Refer to Fuel Tank Removal/ Installation.

(2) Remove fuel pump module. Refer to Fuel Pump Module Removal/Installation.

(3) Remove electrical wire connector at sending unit terminals.

(4) Press on release tab (Fig. 18) to remove sending unit from pump module.

INSTALLATION

(1) Position sending unit to pump module and snap into place.

(2) Connect electrical connector to terminals.

(3) Install fuel pump module. Refer to Fuel Pump Module Removal/Installation.

(4) Install fuel tank. Refer to Fuel Tank Removal/ Installation.

FUEL INJECTOR RAIL

REMOVAL

WARNING: THE FUEL SYSTEM IS UNDER CONSTANT FUEL PRESSURE EVEN WITH THE ENGINE OFF. THIS PRESSURE MUST BE RELEASED BEFORE SERVICING THE FUEL RAIL.

(1) Remove fuel tank filler tube cap.

(2) Disconnect negative battery cable from battery.

(3) Perform the Fuel System Pressure Release Procedure as described in this Group.

(4) Remove air cleaner crossover tube above fuel rail.

(5) Remove and numerically attach a tag (if fuel injector is not already tagged), the injector harness connectors. Do this at each injector (Fig. 19).

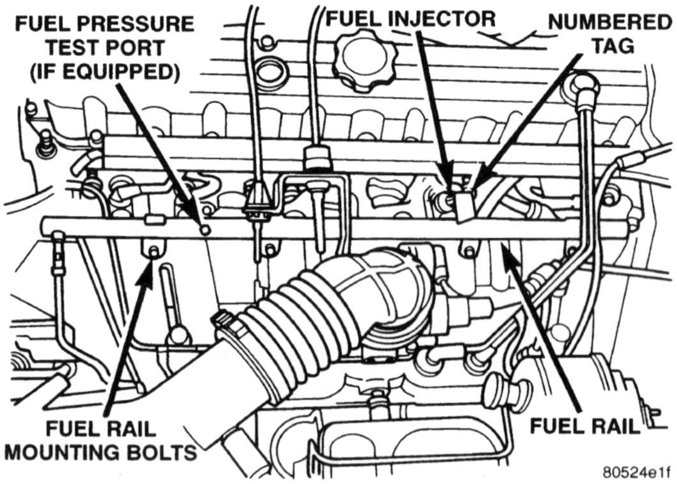

Fig. 19 Fuel Rail Mounting—Typical

(6) Disconnect fuel supply line latch clip and fuel line at fuel rail. Refer to Fuel Tubes/Lines/Hoses and Clamps, and/or Quick-Connect Fittings. These can both be found in the Fuel Delivery section of this group.

(7) Remove fuel rail mounting bolts (Fig. 19).

REMOVAL AND INSTALLATION (Continued)

(8) On models with automatic transmissions, it may be necessary to remove automatic transmission throttle line pressure cable and bracket. This will aid in fuel rail assembly removal.

(9) Remove fuel rail by gently rocking until all fuel injectors are out of intake manifold.

INSTALLATION

(1) Apply a small amount of clean engine oil to each injector o-ring. This will aid in installation.

(2) Position tips of all fuel injectors into corresponding injector bore in intake manifold. Seat injectors into manifold.

(3) Tighten fuel rail mounting bolts and nuts to 11 N·m (100 ft. lbs.) torque.

(4) Connect injector harness connectors to appropriate (tagged) injector.

(5) Connect fuel line and fuel line latch clip to fuel rail. Refer to this group for procedures.

(6) Install protective cap to pressure test port fitting (if equipped).

(7) Install air cleaner crossover tube.

(8) Install fuel tank cap.

(9) Connect negative battery cable to battery.

(10) Start engine and check for fuel leaks.

FUEL INJECTORS

REMOVAL

(1) Remove fuel rail. Refer to Fuel Rail Removal in this section.

(2) Remove clip(s) that retain fuel injector(s) to fuel rail (Fig. 20) or (Fig. 21).

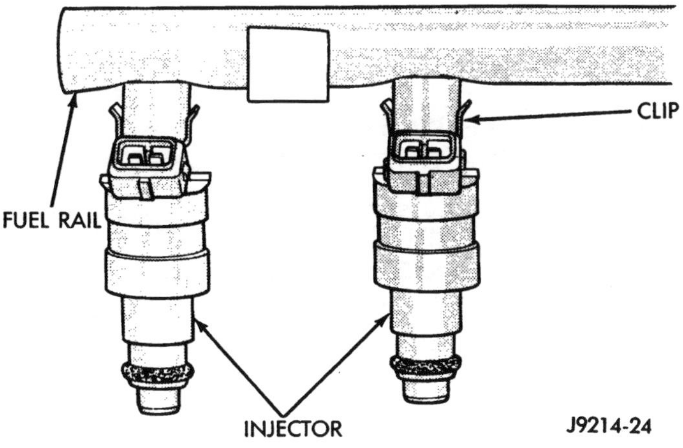

Fig. 20 Injector Mounting

INSTALLATION

(1) Install fuel injector(s) into fuel rail assembly and install retaining clip(s).

(2) If same injector(s) is being reinstalled, install new o-ring(s).

(3) Apply a small amount of clean engine oil to each injector o-ring. This will aid in installation.

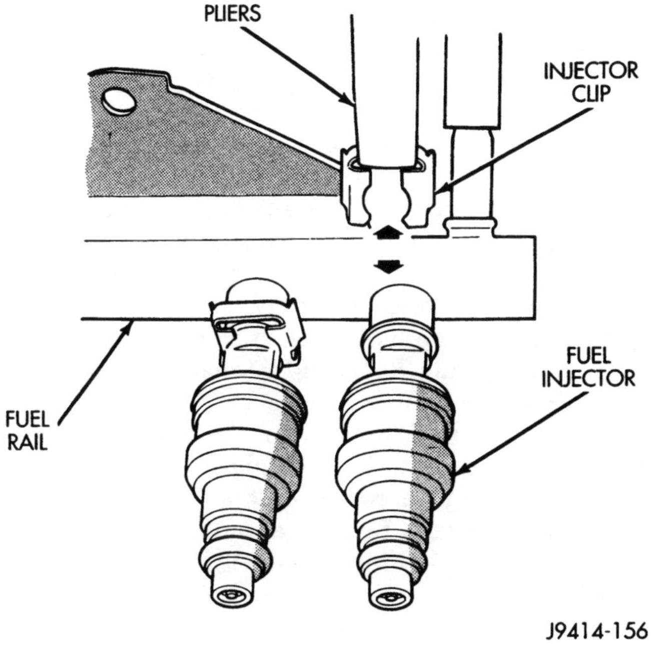

Fig. 21 Injector Retaining Clips—Typical Injector

(4) Install fuel rail. Refer to Fuel Rail Installation in this section.

(5) Start engine and check for fuel leaks.

FUEL TANK

WARNING: THE FUEL SYSTEM IS UNDER CONSTANT FUEL PRESSURE EVEN WITH THE ENGINE OFF. THIS PRESSURE MUST BE RELEASED BEFORE SERVICING FUEL TANK.

REMOVAL

WARNING: KEEP OPEN FLAME AWAY FROM FUEL SYSTEM COMPONENTS.

(1) Disconnect negative battery cable.

(2) Remove fuel filler cap.

(3) Perform the Fuel System Pressure Release Procedure as described elsewhere in this group.

(4) Remove 8 screws retaining plastic fuel filler bezel to body (Fig. 22). Remove fuel filler bezel.

(5) To prevent contaminants from entering tank, temporarily install fuel cap to fill hoses.

(6) Cut plastic tie wrap securing rear axle vent hose to fuel filler hoses.

(7) Disconnect electrical connector at front of fuel tank (Fig. 23).

(8) Disconnect EVAP hose from EVAP line at front of fuel tank (Fig. 23).

(9) Disconnect quick-connect fitting from fuel line at front of fuel tank (Fig. 23). Refer to Quick-Connect Fittings in this group for procedures.

REMOVAL AND INSTALLATION (Continued)

(10) The fuel tank and skid plate are removed as an assembly. Centrally position a transmission jack (or equivalent lifting device) under skid plate/fuel tank assembly. Secure tank assembly to jack.

(11) Remove three skid plate-to-body nuts at front of tank (Fig. 25). Remove one of the nuts through access hole on skid plate (Fig. 25).

(12) Remove four skid plate-to-body nuts at rear of tank (Fig. 24). **Do not loosen tank strap nuts (Fig. 24).**

(13) Lower the tank assembly.

(14) If fuel pump module is to be removed, refer to Fuel Pump Module Removal/Installation.

(15) Disconnect fuel filler hoses at tank. Before disconnecting, mark and note the hose rotational position in relation to tank fittings.

(16) Using an approved portable gasoline siphon/storage tank, drain fuel from tank. To drain fuel, position drain hose into vent fitting (smallest of 2) on side of tank.

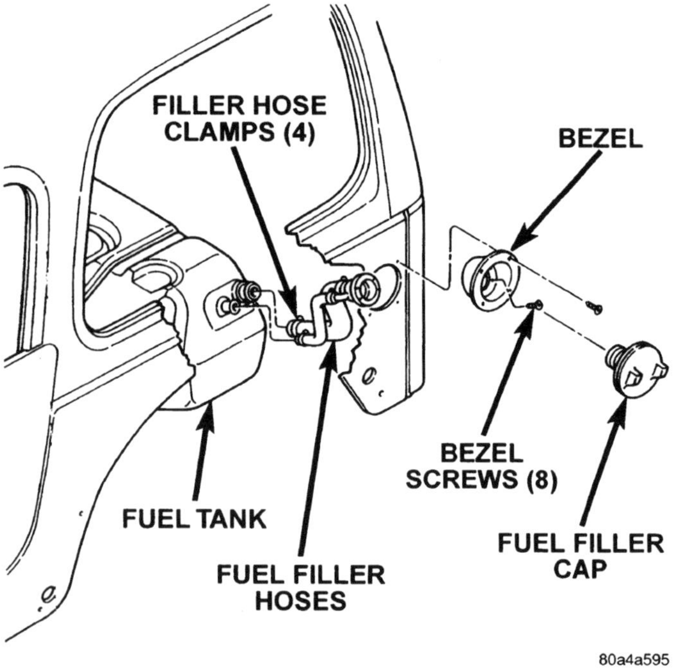

Fig. 22 Fuel Filler Hoses/Fuel Fill Cap

(17) To separate tank from skid plate, remove two protective caps at tank strap studs (Fig. 24) and remove tank strap nuts.

(18) Remove both straps and remove tank from skid plate.

INSTALLATION

(1) Place fuel tank into skid plate. Wrap straps around tank with strap studs inserted through holes in skid plate. Tighten strap nuts to attain 30 mm (±2 mm) between bottom of nut to end of strap stud (Fig. 24). **Do not over tighten nuts.**

(2) Install two protective caps to tank strap studs.

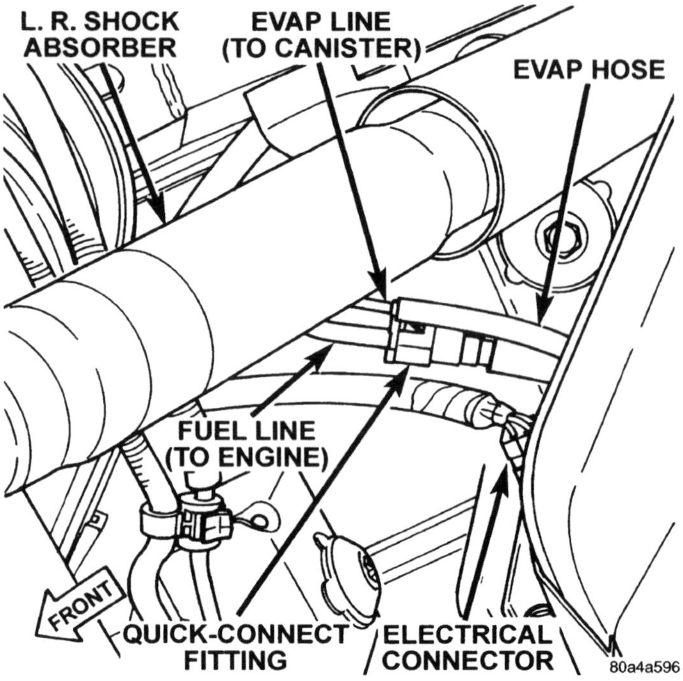

Fig. 23 Fuel Tank Connections

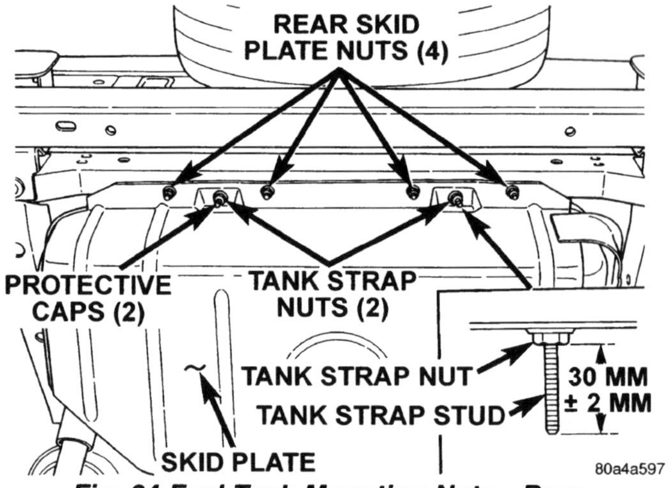

Fig. 24 Fuel Tank Mounting Nuts—Rear

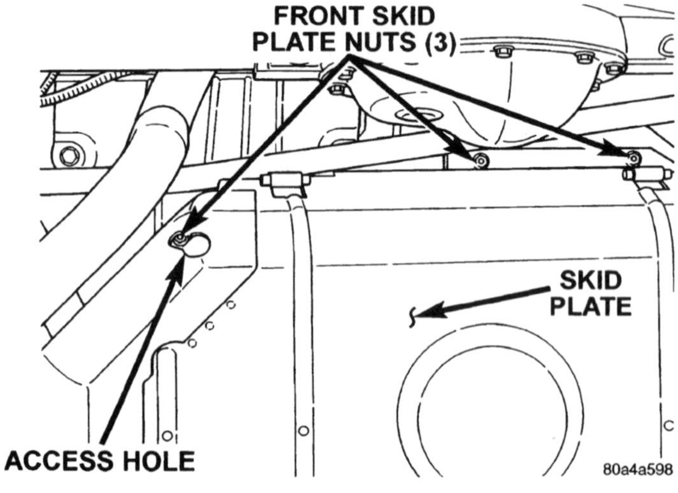

Fig. 25 Fuel Tank Mounting Nuts—Front

REMOVAL AND INSTALLATION (Continued)

(3) Connect fuel filler hoses at tank. Tighten hose clamps.

(4) Raise skid plate/fuel tank assembly into position on body while guiding filler hoses.

(5) Install 7 skid plate mounting nuts. Tighten to 16 N·m (141 in. lbs.) torque.

(6) Remove tank jacking device.

(7) Connect electrical connector at front of fuel tank.

(8) Connect EVAP hose to EVAP line at front of fuel tank.

(9) Connect quick-connect fitting to fuel line at front of fuel tank. Refer to Quick-Connect Fittings in this group for procedures.

(10) Use a new plastic tie wrap to secure rear axle vent hose to fuel filler hoses.

(11) Position fuel filler bezel to body. Install 8 screws and tighten.

(12) Fill fuel tank. Install filler cap.

(13) Connect negative battery cable to battery.

(14) Start vehicle and inspect for leaks.

ACCELERATOR PEDAL

The accelerator pedal is connected to the throttle body linkage by the throttle cable. The cable is protected by a plastic sheathing and is connected to the throttle body linkage by a ball socket. It is connected to the upper part of the accelerator pedal arm by a plastic retainer (clip) (Fig. 26). This retainer (clip) snaps into the top of the accelerator pedal arm. Retainer tabs (built into the cable sheathing) (Fig. 26) fasten the cable to the dash panel.

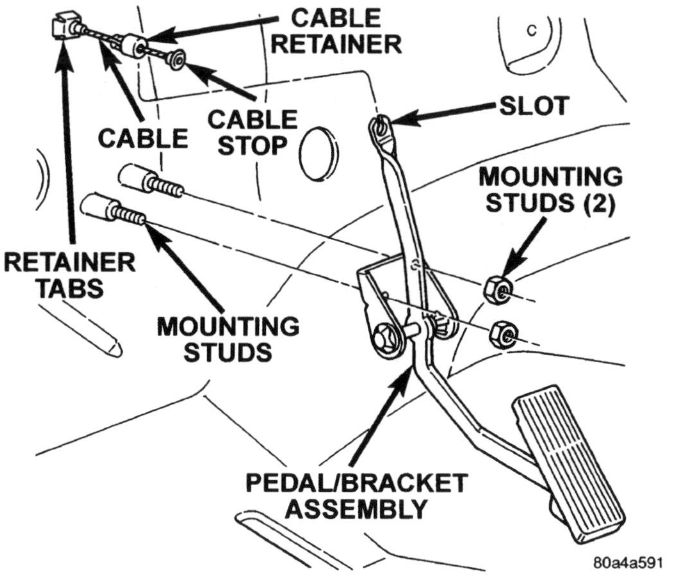

Fig. 26 Accelerator Pedal Mounting

CAUTION: Be careful not to damage or kink the cable core wire (within the cable sheathing) while servicing the accelerator pedal or throttle cable.

REMOVAL

(1) From inside vehicle, hold up accelerator pedal. Remove plastic cable retainer (clip) and throttle cable core wire from upper end of accelerator pedal arm (Fig. 26). Plastic cable retainer (clip) snaps into pedal arm.

(2) Remove accelerator pedal mounting bracket nuts.

(3) Remove accelerator pedal assembly.

INSTALLATION

(1) Place accelerator pedal assembly over mounting studs protruding from floor pan. Tighten mounting nuts to 8.5 N·m (75 in. lbs.) torque.

(2) Slide throttle cable into opening (slot) in top of pedal arm. An index tab is located on pedal arm. Rotate and push plastic cable retainer (clip) into accelerator pedal arm opening until it snaps into place on index tab.

(3) Before starting engine, operate accelerator pedal to check for any binding.

THROTTLE CABLE

REMOVAL

(1) From inside vehicle, hold up accelerator pedal. Remove plastic cable retainer (clip) and throttle cable core wire from upper end of accelerator pedal arm (Fig. 26). Plastic cable retainer (clip) snaps into pedal arm.

(2) Remove cable core wire at pedal arm.

(3) From inside vehicle, pinch both sides of cable housing retainer tabs (Fig. 26) at dash panel. Remove cable housing from dash panel and pull into engine compartment.

(4) Remove cable from clip guides on engine cylinder head (valve) cover (Fig. 27).

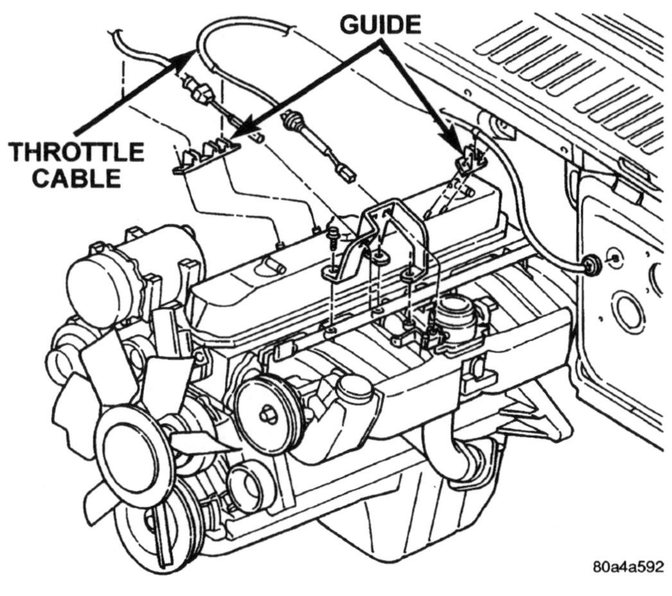

Fig. 27 Throttle Cable Routing

REMOVAL AND INSTALLATION (Continued)

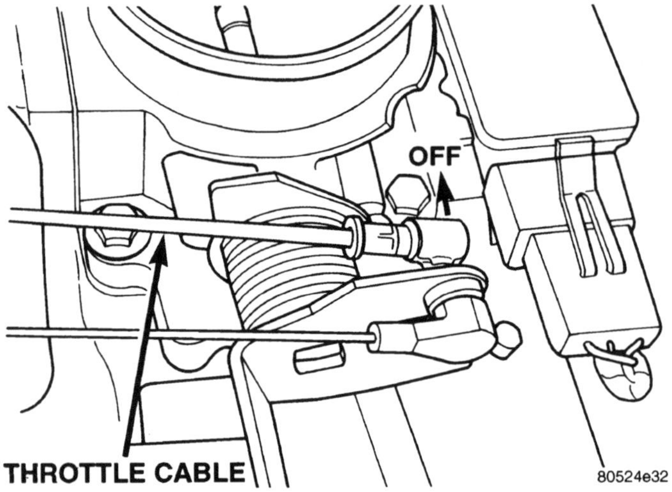

Fig. 28 Throttle Cable at Throttle Body—Typical

(5) Remove throttle cable ball end socket at throttle body linkage (snaps off) (Fig. 28).

(6) Remove throttle cable from throttle body mounting bracket by compressing retainer tabs and pushing cable through hole in bracket.

(7) Remove throttle cable from vehicle.

INSTALLATION

(1) Slide throttle cable through hole in throttle body bracket until retainer tabs lock into bracket. Connect cable ball end to throttle body linkage ball (snaps on).

(2) Snap cable into clip guides on engine cylinder head (valve) cover.

(3) Push other end of cable through opening in dash panel until retaining tabs lock into panel.

(4) From inside drivers compartment, slide throttle cable core wire into opening in top of accelerator pedal arm. An index tab is located on pedal arm. Rotate and push cable retainer (clip) into pedal arm opening until it snaps in place on index tab.

(5) Before starting engine, operate accelerator pedal to check for any binding.

SPECIFICATIONS

VECI LABEL SPECIFICATIONS

If anything differs between the specifications found on the Vehicle Emission Control Information (VECI) label and the following specifications, use specifications on VECI label. The VECI label is located in the engine compartment.

FUEL TANK CAPACITY

Models	Liters	U.S. Gallons
All	57L	15
All	72L	19
Nominal refill capacities are shown. A variation may be observed from vehicle to vehicle due to manufacturing tolerance and refill procedure.		

FUEL SYSTEM PRESSURE

338 kPa ± 5 kPa (49.0 psi ± 2 psi).

TORQUE CHART

DESCRIPTION — **TORQUE**

Accelerator Pedal Bracket Mounting
Nuts . . . . .8.5 N·m (75 in. lbs.)
Fuel Pump Module Locknut . . . . .34 N·m (25 ft. lbs.)
Fuel Rail Mounting Bolts or
Nuts .11 N·m (100 in. lbs.)
Fuel Tank Skidplate Bolts . . . . .16 N·m (141 in. lbs.)
Fuel Tank Mounting Strap
Bolts . . . . .Refer to manual text

FUEL INJECTION SYSTEM

INDEX

GENERAL INFORMATION

INTRODUCTION

All engines are equipped with sequential Multi-Port Fuel Injection (MFI). The MFI system provides precise air/fuel ratios for all driving conditions.

The Powertrain Control Module (PCM) (Fig. 1) operates the fuel system.

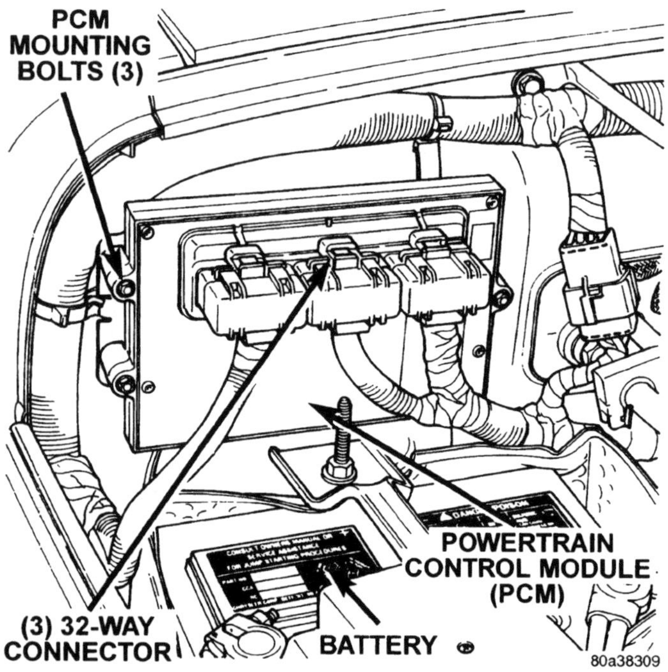

Fig. 1 Powertrain Control Module (PCM) Location

MODES OF OPERATION

As input signals to the Powertrain Control Module (PCM) change, the PCM adjusts its response to the output devices. For example, the PCM must calculate different injector pulse width and ignition timing for idle than it does for Wide Open Throttle (WOT).

There are two different areas of operation: Open Loop and Closed Loop.

During Open Loop modes, the PCM receives input signals and responds only according to preset PCM programming. Input from the oxygen (O2S) sensor is not monitored during Open Loop modes.

During Closed Loop modes, the PCM will monitor the oxygen (O2S) sensor input. This input indicates to the PCM whether or not the calculated injector pulse width results in the ideal air-fuel ratio. This ratio is 14.7 parts air-to-1 part fuel. By monitoring the exhaust oxygen content through the O2S sensor, the PCM can fine tune the injector pulse width. This is done to achieve optimum fuel economy combined with low emission engine performance.

The fuel injection system has the following modes of operation:

- Ignition switch ON
- Engine start-up (crank)
- Engine warm-up
- Idle
- Cruise
- Acceleration
- Deceleration
- Wide Open Throttle (WOT)
- Ignition switch OFF

The ignition switch On, engine start-up (crank), engine warm-up, acceleration, deceleration and wide open throttle modes are Open Loop modes. The idle and cruise modes, (with the engine at operating temperature) are Closed Loop modes.

IGNITION SWITCH (KEY-ON) MODE

This is an Open Loop mode. When the fuel system is activated by the ignition switch, the following actions occur:

- The PCM pre-positions the Idle Air Control (IAC) motor.
- The PCM determines atmospheric air pressure from the MAP sensor input to determine basic fuel strategy.
- The PCM monitors the engine coolant temperature sensor input. The PCM modifies fuel strategy based on this input.
- Intake manifold air temperature sensor input is monitored
- Throttle Position Sensor (TPS) is monitored
- The Auto Shutdown (ASD) relay is energized by the PCM for approximately three seconds.
- The fuel pump is energized through the fuel pump relay by the PCM. The fuel pump will operate for approximately three seconds unless the engine is operating or the starter motor is engaged
- The O2S sensor heater element is energized through the ASD relay. The O2S sensor input is not used by the PCM to calibrate air-fuel ratio during this mode of operation.
- The up-shift indicator lamp is illuminated (manual transmission only).

ENGINE START-UP MODE

This is an Open Loop mode. The following actions occur when the starter motor is engaged.

The PCM receives inputs from:

- Battery voltage
- Engine coolant temperature sensor
- Crankshaft position sensor
- Intake manifold air temperature sensor
- Manifold Absolute Pressure (MAP) sensor
- Throttle Position Sensor (TPS)
- Camshaft position sensor signal

The PCM monitors the crankshaft position sensor. If the PCM does not receive a crankshaft position sensor signal within 3 seconds of cranking the engine, it will shut down the fuel injection system.

GENERAL INFORMATION (Continued)

The fuel pump is activated by the PCM through the fuel pump relay.

Voltage is applied to the fuel injectors with the PCM. The PCM will then control the injection sequence and injector pulse width by turning the ground circuit to each individual injector on and off.

The PCM determines the proper ignition timing according to input received from the crankshaft position sensor.

ENGINE WARM-UP MODE

This is an Open Loop mode. During engine warm-up, the PCM receives inputs from:

- Battery voltage
- Crankshaft position sensor
- Engine coolant temperature sensor
- Intake manifold air temperature sensor
- Manifold Absolute Pressure (MAP) sensor
- Throttle Position Sensor (TPS)
- Camshaft position sensor signal (in the distributor)
- Park/neutral switch (gear indicator signal—auto. trans. only)
- Air conditioning select signal (if equipped)
- Air conditioning request signal (if equipped)

Based on these inputs the following occurs:

- Voltage is applied to the fuel injectors with the PCM. The PCM will then control the injection sequence and injector pulse width by turning the ground circuit to each individual injector on and off.
- The PCM adjusts engine idle speed through the Idle Air Control (IAC) motor and adjusts ignition timing.
- The PCM operates the A/C compressor clutch through the clutch relay. This is done if A/C has been selected by the vehicle operator and requested by the A/C thermostat.
- If the vehicle has a manual transmission, the up-shift lamp is operated by the PCM.
- When engine has reached operating temperature, the PCM will begin monitoring O2S sensor input. The system will then leave the warm-up mode and go into closed loop operation.

IDLE MODE

When the engine is at operating temperature, this is a Closed Loop mode. At idle speed, the PCM receives inputs from:

- Air conditioning select signal (if equipped)
- Air conditioning request signal (if equipped)
- Battery voltage
- Crankshaft position sensor
- Engine coolant temperature sensor
- Intake manifold air temperature sensor
- Manifold Absolute Pressure (MAP) sensor
- Throttle Position Sensor (TPS)
- Camshaft position sensor signal (in the distributor)
- Battery voltage
- Park/neutral switch (gear indicator signal—auto. trans. only)
- Oxygen sensor

Based on these inputs, the following occurs:

- Voltage is applied to the fuel injectors with the PCM. The PCM will then control injection sequence and injector pulse width by turning the ground circuit to each individual injector on and off.
- The PCM monitors the O2S sensor input and adjusts air-fuel ratio by varying injector pulse width. It also adjusts engine idle speed through the Idle Air Control (IAC) motor.
- The PCM adjusts ignition timing by increasing and decreasing spark advance.
- The PCM operates the A/C compressor clutch through the clutch relay. This happens if A/C has been selected by the vehicle operator and requested by the A/C thermostat.

CRUISE MODE

When the engine is at operating temperature, this is a Closed Loop mode. At cruising speed, the PCM receives inputs from:

- Air conditioning select signal (if equipped)
- Air conditioning request signal (if equipped)
- Battery voltage
- Engine coolant temperature sensor
- Crankshaft position sensor
- Intake manifold air temperature sensor
- Manifold Absolute Pressure (MAP) sensor
- Throttle Position Sensor (TPS)
- Camshaft position sensor signal (in the distributor)
- Park/neutral switch (gear indicator signal—auto. trans. only)
- Oxygen (O2S) sensor

Based on these inputs, the following occurs:

- Voltage is applied to the fuel injectors with the PCM. The PCM will then adjust the injector pulse width by turning the ground circuit to each individual injector on and off.
- The PCM monitors the O2S sensor input and adjusts air-fuel ratio. It also adjusts engine idle speed through the Idle Air Control (IAC) motor.
- The PCM adjusts ignition timing by turning the ground path to the coil on and off.
- The PCM operates the A/C compressor clutch through the clutch relay. This happens if A/C has been selected by the vehicle operator and requested by the A/C thermostat.

ACCELERATION MODE

This is an Open Loop mode. The PCM recognizes an abrupt increase in throttle position or MAP pres-

GENERAL INFORMATION (Continued)

sure as a demand for increased engine output and vehicle acceleration. The PCM increases injector pulse width in response to increased throttle opening.

DECELERATION MODE

When the engine is at operating temperature, this is an Open Loop mode. During hard deceleration, the PCM receives the following inputs.

- Air conditioning select signal (if equipped)
- Air conditioning request signal (if equipped)
- Battery voltage
- Engine coolant temperature sensor
- Crankshaft position sensor
- Intake manifold air temperature sensor
- Manifold Absolute Pressure (MAP) sensor
- Throttle Position Sensor (TPS)
- Camshaft position sensor signal (in the distributor)
- Park/neutral switch (gear indicator signal—auto. trans. only)

If the vehicle is under hard deceleration with the proper rpm and closed throttle conditions, the PCM will ignore the oxygen sensor input signal. The PCM will enter a fuel cut-off strategy in which it will not supply ground to the injectors. If a hard deceleration does not exist, the PCM will determine the proper injector pulse width and continue injection.

Based on the above inputs, the PCM will adjust engine idle speed through the Idle Air Control (IAC) motor.

The PCM adjusts ignition timing by turning the ground path to the coil on and off.

The PCM opens the ground circuit to the A/C clutch relay to disengage the A/C compressor clutch. This is done until the vehicle is no longer under deceleration (if the A/C system is operating).

WIDE OPEN THROTTLE MODE

This is an Open Loop mode. During wide open throttle operation, the PCM receives the following inputs.

- Battery voltage
- Crankshaft position sensor
- Engine coolant temperature sensor
- Intake manifold air temperature sensor
- Manifold Absolute Pressure (MAP) sensor
- Throttle Position Sensor (TPS)
- Camshaft position sensor signal (in the distributor)

During wide open throttle conditions, the following occurs:

- Voltage is applied to the fuel injectors with the PCM. The PCM will then control the injection sequence and injector pulse width by turning the ground circuit to each individual injector on and off. The PCM ignores the oxygen sensor input signal and provides a predetermined amount of additional fuel. This is done by adjusting injector pulse width.
- The PCM adjusts ignition timing by turning the ground path to the coil on and off.
- The PCM opens the ground circuit to the A/C clutch relay to disengage the A/C compressor clutch. This will be done for approximately 15 seconds (if the air conditioning system is operating).

If the vehicle has a manual transmission, the upshift lamp is operated by the PCM.

IGNITION SWITCH OFF MODE

When ignition switch is turned to OFF position, the PCM stops operating the injectors, ignition coil, ASD relay and fuel pump relay.

DESCRIPTION AND OPERATION

SYSTEM DIAGNOSIS

The Powertrain Control Module (PCM) can test many of its own input and output circuits. If the PCM senses a fault in a major system, it stores a Diagnostic Trouble Code (DTC) in its memory.

Technicians can display stored DTC's with different methods. One way is using the DRB scan tool. Another way is using the malfunction indicator (check engine) lamp. On certain models the vehicle odometer can be used to display the numeric DTC.

For DTC information, refer to Group 25, Emission Control Systems. See On-Board Diagnostics.

POWERTRAIN CONTROL MODULE (PCM)

The PCM (Fig. 1) operates the fuel system. The PCM was formerly referred to as the SBEC or engine controller. The PCM is a pre-programmed, digital computer. It regulates ignition timing, air-fuel ratio, emission control devices, charging system, speed control (if equipped), air conditioning compressor clutch engagement and idle speed. The PCM can adapt its programming to meet changing operating conditions.

The PCM receives input signals from various switches and sensors. Based on these inputs, the PCM regulates various engine and vehicle operations through different system components. These components are referred to as PCM Outputs. The sensors and switches that provide inputs to the PCM are considered PCM Inputs.

The PCM adjusts ignition timing based upon inputs it receives from sensors that react to: engine rpm, manifold absolute pressure, engine coolant temperature, throttle position, transmission gear selection (automatic transmission), vehicle speed and the brake switch.

The PCM adjusts idle speed based on inputs it receives from sensors that react to: throttle position, vehicle speed, transmission gear selection, engine

DESCRIPTION AND OPERATION (Continued)

coolant temperature and from inputs it receives from the air conditioning clutch switch and brake switch.

Based on inputs that it receives, the PCM adjusts ignition coil dwell. The PCM also adjusts the generator charge rate through control of the generator field and provides speed control operation.

NOTE: Powertrain Control Module (PCM) Inputs:

- A/C request (if equipped with factory A/C)
- A/C select (if equipped with factory A/C)
- Auto shutdown (ASD) sense
- Battery temperature
- Battery voltage
- Brake switch
- Camshaft position sensor signal
- Crankshaft position sensor
- Engine coolant temperature sensor
- Fuel level
- Ignition circuit sense (ignition switch in run position)
- Intake manifold air temperature sensor
- Manifold Absolute Pressure (MAP) sensor
- Oxygen sensors
- Oil pressure
- Park/neutral switch (auto. trans. only)
- Power ground
- SCI receive (DRB scan tool 16–way connection)
- Sensor return
- Signal ground
- Throttle position sensor
- Vehicle speed sensor

NOTE: Powertrain Control Module (PCM) Outputs:

- A/C clutch relay
- Auto Shutdown (ASD) relay
- CCD bus (+) circuits
- CCD bus (-) circuits
- Duty cycle EVAP canister purge solenoid
- Fuel injectors
- Fuel pump relay
- Generator field driver (-)
- Generator field source (+)
- Idle Air Control (IAC) motor
- Ignition coil
- SCI transmit (DRB scan tool 16–way connection)
- Transmission convertor clutch solenoid

The PCM contains a voltage convertor. This converts battery voltage to a regulated 5.0 volts.

AIR CONDITIONING (A/C) CONTROLS—PCM INPUT

The A/C control system information applies to factory installed air conditioning units.

A/C SELECT SIGNAL: When the A/C switch is in the ON position, an input signal is sent to the powertrain control module (PCM). The signal informs the PCM that the A/C has been selected. The PCM adjusts idle speed to a pre-programmed rpm through the idle air control (IAC) motor to compensate for increased engine load.

A/C REQUEST SIGNAL: Once A/C has been selected, the powertrain control module (PCM) receives the A/C request signal from the evaporator switch. The input indicates that the evaporator temperature is in the proper range for A/C application. The PCM uses this input to cycle the A/C compressor clutch (through the A/C relay). It will also determine the correct engine idle speed through the idle air control (IAC) motor position.

If the A/C low-pressure switch opens (indicating a low refrigerant level), the PCM will not receive an A/C receive signal. The PCM will then remove the ground from the A/C relay. This will deactivate the A/C compressor clutch.

If the evaporator switch opens, (indicating that evaporator is not in proper temperature range), the PCM will not receive the A/C request signal. The PCM will then remove the ground from the A/C relay, deactivating the A/C compressor clutch.

AUTOMATIC SHUTDOWN (ASD) RELAY SENSE—PCM INPUT

A 12 volt signal at this input indicates to the powertrain control module (PCM) that the ASD has been activated. The ASD relay is located in the Power Distribution Center (PDC). The PDC is located in the engine compartment (Fig. 2). Refer to label on PDC cover for relay location. The ASD relay is used to connect the oxygen sensor heater elements, ignition coil, and fuel injectors to the 12 volt + power supply. Jeep models of previous years had used the ASD relay to apply the 12 volt + power supply to the generator field source (+) circuit. This generator circuit is now supplied 12 volts + directly from the PCM.

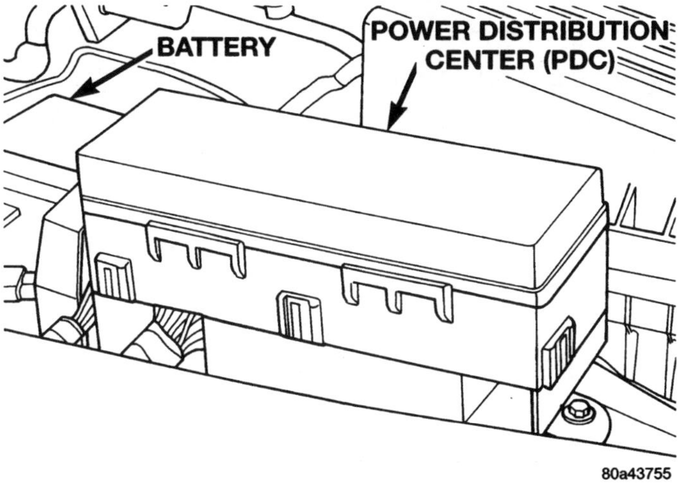

Fig. 2 Power Distribution Center (PDC)

DESCRIPTION AND OPERATION (Continued)

This input is used only to sense that the ASD relay is energized. If the PCM does not see 12 volts at this input when the ASD should be activated, it will set a Diagnostic Trouble Code (DTC).

BATTERY TEMPERATURE SENSOR—PCM INPUT

Provides a signal to the PCM corresponding to the battery temperature. Refer to Group 8C, Charging System for additional information.

BATTERY VOLTAGE—PCM INPUT

The battery voltage input provides power to the Powertrain Control Module (PCM). It also informs the PCM what voltage level is supplied to the ignition coil and fuel injectors.

If battery voltage is low, the PCM will increase injector pulse width (period of time that the injector is energized). This is done to compensate for the reduced flow through injector caused by the lowered voltage.

FIVE VOLT SENSOR SUPPLY—PRIMARY

Supplies the required 5 volt power source to the crankshaft position sensor, camshaft position sensor, MAP sensor and throttle position sensor.

FIVE VOLT SENSOR SUPPLY—SECONDARY

Supplies the required 5 volt source to the vehicle speed sensor.

FUEL LEVEL SENSOR—PCM INPUT

The fuel level sensor (fuel gauge sending unit) sends a variable voltage to the PCM to indicate fuel level. The purpose of this feature is to prevent a false setting of misfire and fuel system monitor trouble codes if the fuel level is less than 15 percent of its rated capacity.

Refer to Fuel Gauge Sending Unit Description and Operation in the Fuel Delivery section of this group for additional information.

BRAKE SWITCH—PCM INPUT

When the brake light switch is activated, the Powertrain Control Module (PCM) receives an input indicating that the brakes are being applied. After receiving this input, the PCM maintains idle speed to a scheduled rpm through control of the Idle Air Control (IAC) motor. The brake switch input is also used to operate the speed control system.

CAMSHAFT POSITION SENSOR—PCM INPUT

A sync' signal is provide by the camshaft position sensor located in the distributor (Fig. 3). The sync signal from this sensor works in conjunction with the crankshaft position sensor to provide the Powertrain Control Module (PCM) with inputs. This is done to establish and maintain correct injector firing order.

Refer to Camshaft Position Sensor in Group 8D, Ignition System for more information.

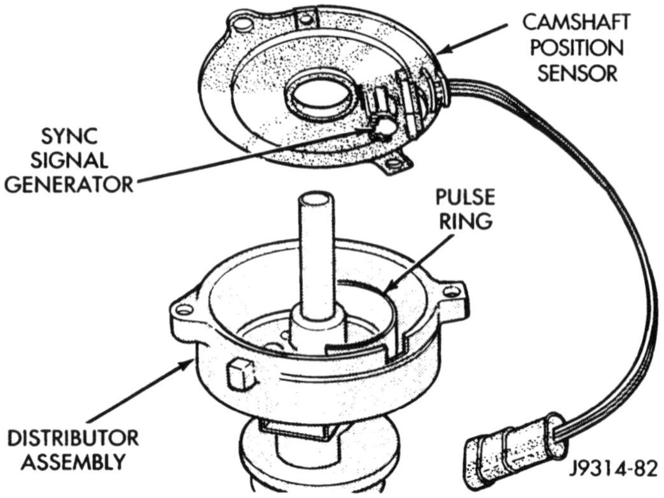

Fig. 3 Camshaft Position Sensor—Typical

CRANKSHAFT POSITION SENSOR—PCM INPUT

This sensor is a hall effect device that detects notches in the flywheel (manual transmission) or flexplate (automatic transmission).

This sensor is used to indicate to the Powertrain Control Module (PCM) that a spark and or fuel injection event is to be required. The output from this sensor, in conjunction with the camshaft position sensor signal, is used to differentiate between fuel injection and spark events. It is also used to synchronize the fuel injectors with their respective cylinders.

The sensor is bolted to the transmission bellhousing.

Refer to Group 8D, Ignition System for more crankshaft position sensor information.

The engine will not operate if the PCM does not receive a crankshaft position sensor input.

ENGINE COOLANT TEMPERATURE SENSOR—PCM INPUT

The engine coolant temperature sensor is installed in the thermostat housing (Fig. 4) and protrudes into the water jacket. The sensor provides an input voltage to the Powertrain Control Module (PCM) relating coolant temperature. The PCM uses this input along with inputs from other sensors to determine injector pulse width and ignition timing. As coolant temperature varies, the coolant temperature sensor's resistance changes. The change in resistance results in a different input voltage to the PCM.

When the engine is cold, the PCM will operate in Open Loop cycle. It will demand slightly richer air-fuel mixtures and higher idle speeds. This is done until normal operating temperatures are reached.

DESCRIPTION AND OPERATION (Continued)

Refer to Open Loop/Closed Loop Modes of Operation in this section of the group for more information.

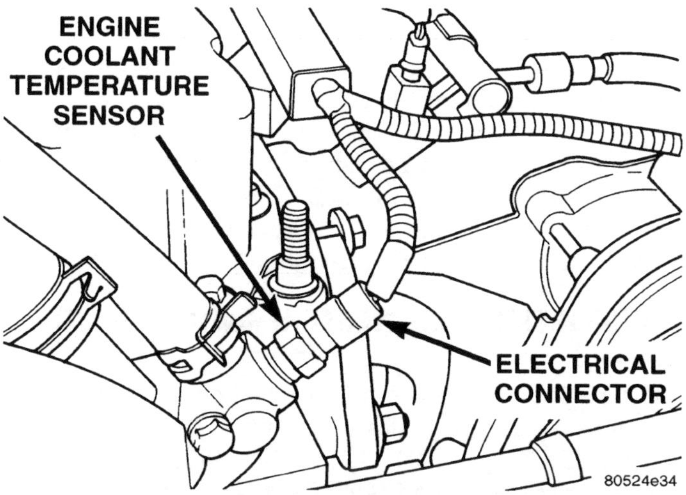

Fig. 4 Engine Coolant Temperature Sensor—Typical

OXYGEN SENSOR (O2S)—PCM INPUT

Two heated O2S sensors are used. When the key is turned ON, and the engine is cold, the sensors will have an initial voltage of 5 volts. The sensors themselves produce voltages from 0 to 1 volt, depending upon the oxygen content of the exhaust gas in the exhaust manifold. When a large amount of oxygen is present (caused by a lean air/fuel mixture), the sensors produces a low voltage. When there is a lesser amount present (rich air/fuel mixture) it produces a higher voltage. By monitoring the oxygen content and converting it to electrical voltage, the sensors act as a rich-lean switch.

Both oxygen sensors are equipped with a heating element that reduces the time required for the sensors to reach operating temperature allowing the system to enter into closed loop operation sooner. Maintaining correct sensor temperature at all times allows the system to remain in closed loop operation during periods of extended idle. The Automatic Shutdown (ASD) relay supplies battery voltage to both the upstream and downstream oxygen sensor heating elements.

In Closed Loop operation, the Powertrain Control Module (PCM) monitors both O2S sensor inputs (along with other inputs) and adjusts the injector pulse width accordingly. During Open Loop operation, the PCM ignores the O2 sensor input. The PCM adjusts injector pulse width based on preprogrammed (fixed) values and inputs from other sensors.

For more O2S information, refer to Monitored Systems in Group 25, Emission Control Systems.

UPSTREAM HEATED OXYGEN SENSOR

The upstream O2S sensor is located in the exhaust downpipe (Fig. 5). It provides an input voltage to the PCM. The input tells the PCM the oxygen content of the exhaust gas. The PCM uses this information to fine tune the air/fuel ratio by adjusting injector pulse width.

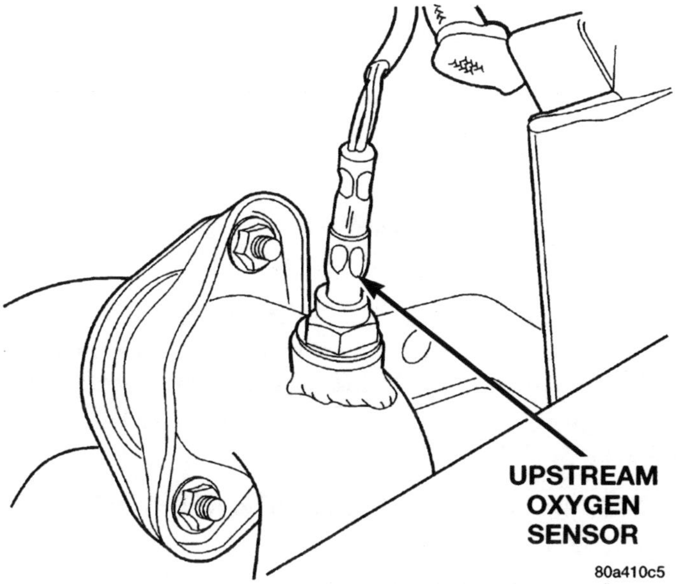

Fig. 5 Upstream Oxygen Sensor

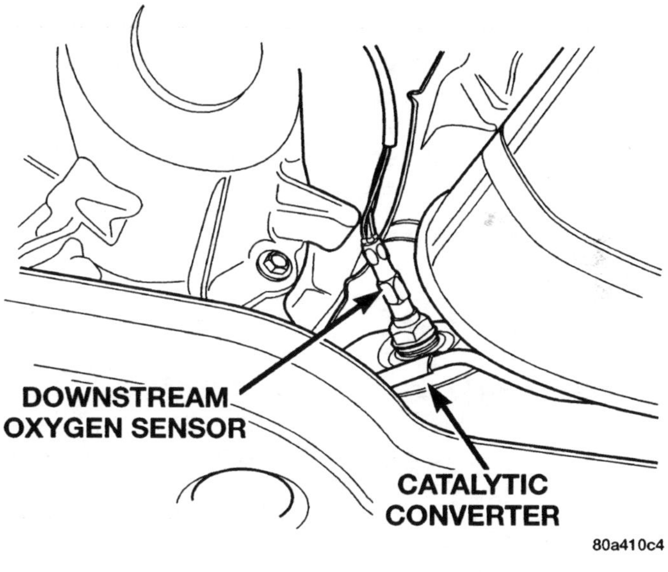

Fig. 6 Downstream Oxygen Sensor

DOWNSTREAM HEATED OXYGEN SENSOR

The downstream heated oxygen sensor is located near the outlet end of the catalytic convertor (Fig. 6). The downstream heated oxygen sensor input is used to detect catalytic convertor deterioration and provide fuel adjustment information.

As the convertor deteriorates, the input from the downstream sensor begins to match the upstream sensor input except for a slight time delay. By comparing the downstream heated oxygen sensor input

DESCRIPTION AND OPERATION (Continued)

to the input from the upstream sensor, the PCM calculates catalytic convertor efficiency.

When the catalytic converter efficiency drops below emission standards, the PCM stores a diagnostic trouble code and illuminates the Malfunction Indicator (MIL) (or Check Engine) lamp. For more information, refer to Group 25, Emission Control Systems.

The downstream sensor input is also used to adjust the upstream O2S goal voltage. This allows a better control of the exhaust gases as the catalytic convertor ages.

The upstream and downstream sensors may look exactly alike, but are not interchangeable.

IGNITION CIRCUIT SENSE—PCM INPUT

The ignition circuit sense input tells the Powertrain Control Module (PCM) the ignition switch has energized the ignition circuit. Refer to the wiring diagrams for circuit information.

INTAKE MANIFOLD AIR TEMPERATURE SENSOR—PCM INPUT

The intake manifold air temperature sensor is installed in the intake manifold with the sensor element extending into the air stream (Fig. 7). The sensor provides an input voltage to the Powertrain Control Module (PCM) indicating intake manifold air temperature. The input is used along with inputs from other sensors to determine injector pulse width. As the temperature of the air-fuel stream in the manifold varies, the sensor resistance changes. This results in a different input voltage to the PCM.

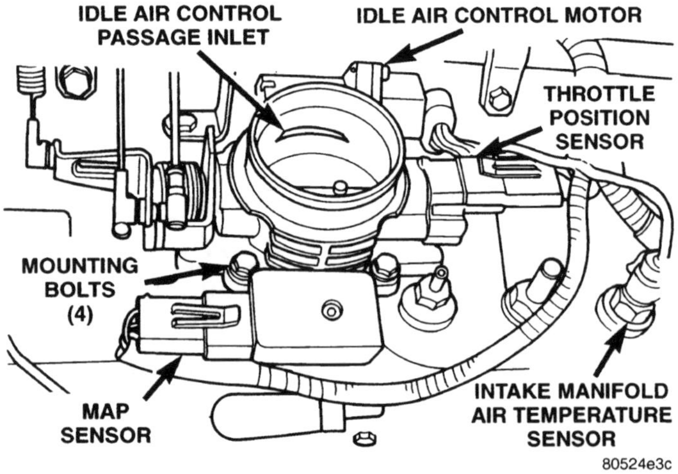

Fig. 7 Intake Air Temp. Sensor Location—Typical

MANIFOLD ABSOLUTE PRESSURE (MAP) SENSOR—PCM INPUT

The MAP sensor reacts to absolute pressure in the intake manifold. It provides an input voltage to the Powertrain Control Module (PCM). As engine load changes, manifold pressure varies. The change in manifold pressure causes MAP sensor voltage to change. The change in MAP sensor voltage results in a different input voltage to the PCM. The input voltage level supplies the PCM with information about ambient barometric pressure during engine start-up (cranking) and engine load while the engine is running. The PCM uses this input along with inputs from other sensors to adjust air-fuel mixture.

The MAP sensor is mounted on the side of the engine throttle body (Fig. 7). The sensor is connected to the throttle body with a rubber L-shaped fitting.

TRANSMISSION PARK/NEUTRAL SWITCH—PCM INPUT

The park/neutral switch is located on the transmission housing and provides an input to the Powertrain Control Module (PCM). This will indicate that the automatic transmission is in Park, Neutral or a drive gear selection. This input is used to determine idle speed (varying with gear selection), fuel injector pulse width and ignition timing advance. Refer to Group 21, Transmissions, for testing, replacement and adjustment information.

THROTTLE POSITION SENSOR (TPS)—PCM INPUT

The TPS is mounted on the throttle body (Fig. 7). The TPS is a variable resistor that provides the Powertrain Control Module (PCM) with an input signal (voltage) that represents throttle blade position. The sensor is connected to the throttle blade shaft. As the position of the throttle blade changes, the resistance of the TPS changes.

The PCM supplies approximately 5 volts to the TPS. The TPS output voltage (input signal to the PCM) represents the throttle blade position. The PCM receives an input signal voltage from the TPS. This will vary in an approximate range of from 1 volt at minimum throttle opening (idle), to 4 volts at wide open throttle. Along with inputs from other sensors, the PCM uses the TPS input to determine current engine operating conditions. In response to engine operating conditions, the PCM will adjust fuel injector pulse width and ignition timing.

VEHICLE SPEED AND DISTANCE SENSOR—PCM INPUT

The vehicle speed sensor is located on the speedometer pinion gear adapter (Fig. 8). The pinion gear adapter is located on the extension housing of the transfer case (drivers side). The sensor input is used by the Powertrain Control Module (PCM) to determine vehicle speed and distance traveled.

The speed sensor generates 8 pulses per sensor revolution. These signals, in conjunction with a closed throttle signal from the throttle position sensor, indicate a closed throttle deceleration to the

DESCRIPTION AND OPERATION (Continued)

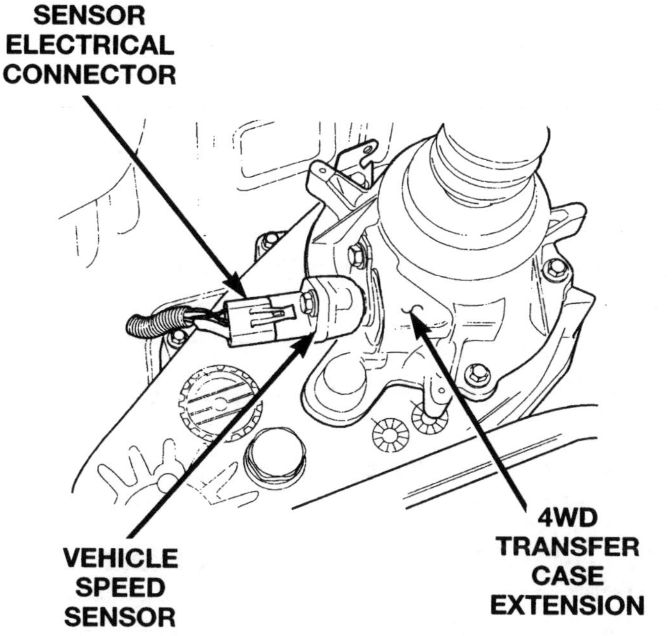

Fig. 8 Vehicle Speed Sensor Location—Typical

PCM. When the vehicle is stopped at idle, a closed throttle signal is received by the PCM (but a speed sensor signal is not received).

Under deceleration conditions, the PCM adjusts the Idle Air Control (IAC) motor to maintain a desired MAP value. Under idle conditions, the PCM adjusts the IAC motor to maintain a desired engine speed.

POWER STEERING PRESSURE SWITCH—PCM INPUT

A pressure sensing switch is included in the power steering system (mounted on the high-pressure line). This switch will be on vehicles equipped with a 2.5L engine and power steering. The switch (Fig. 9) provides an input to the Powertrain Control Module (PCM). This input is provided during periods of high pump load and low engine rpm; such as during parking maneuvers. The PCM will then increase the idle speed through the Idle Air Control (IAC) motor. This is done to prevent the engine from stalling under the increased load.

When steering pump pressure exceeds 1896 kPa ± 345 kPa (275 psi ± 50 psi), the normally closed switch will open and the PCM will increase the engine idle speed. This will prevent the engine from stalling.

When steering pump pressure drops below approximately 70 psi, the switch circuit will close and engine idle speed will return to its previous setting.

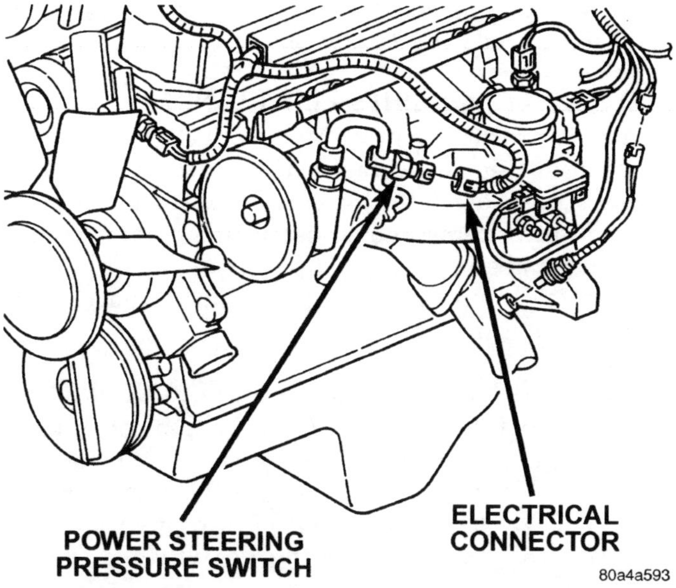

Fig. 9 Power Steering Pump Pressure Switch—2.5L Engine

POWER GROUND

The power ground is used to control ground circuits for the following Powertrain Control Module (PCM) loads:

- Generator field winding
- Fuel injectors
- Ignition coil

AIR CONDITIONING (A/C) CLUTCH RELAY—PCM OUTPUT

The A/C relay is located in the Power Distribution Center (PDC). The PDC is located in the engine compartment (Fig. 2). Refer to label on PDC cover for relay location.

The Powertrain Control Module (PCM) activates the A/C compressor through the A/C clutch relay. The PCM regulates A/C compressor operation by switching the ground circuit for the A/C clutch relay on and off.

When the PCM receives a request for A/C from A/C evaporator switch, it will adjust Idle Air Control (IAC) motor position. This is done to increase idle speed. The PCM will then activate the A/C clutch through the A/C clutch relay. The PCM adjusts IAC stepper motor position to compensate for increased engine load from the A/C compressor.

By switching the ground path for the relay on and off, the PCM is able to cycle the A/C compressor clutch. This is based on changes in engine operating conditions. If, during A/C operation, the PCM senses low idle speeds or a wide open throttle condition, it will de-energize the relay. This prevents A/C clutch engagement. The relay will remain de-energized until the idle speed increases or the wide open throttle condition exceeds 15 seconds or no longer exists. The

DESCRIPTION AND OPERATION (Continued)

PCM will also de-energize the relay if coolant temperature exceeds 125°C (257°F).

CCD BUS (+/-) CIRCUITS-PCM OUTPUTS

The Powertrain Control Module (PCM) sends certain output signals through the CCD bus circuits. These signals are used to control certain instrument panel located items and to determine certain identification numbers.

Refer to Group 8E, Instrument Panel and Gauges for additional information.

GENERATOR FIELD SOURCE (+)—PCM OUTPUT

This output from the Powertrain Control Module (PCM) regulates charging system voltage to the generator field source (+) circuit. The voltage range is 12.9 to 15.0 volts. Jeep models of previous years had used the ASD relay to apply the 12 volt + power supply to the generator field source (+) circuit. Refer to Groups 8A and 8C for charging system information.

GENERATOR FIELD DRIVER (-)—PCM OUTPUT

This output from the Powertrain Control Module (PCM) regulates charging system ground control to the generator field driver (-) circuit. Refer to Groups 8A and 8C for charging system information.

AUTO SHUTDOWN (ASD) RELAY—PCM OUTPUT

The ASD relay is located in the Power Distribution Center (PDC) (Fig. 2).

The ASD relay supplies battery voltage to the fuel pump, fuel injector, ignition coil and both oxygen (O2S) sensor heating elements. The ground circuit for the coil in the ASD relay is controlled by the Powertrain Control Module (PCM). The PCM operates the ASD relay by switching the ground circuit on and off.

FUEL PUMP RELAY-PCM OUTPUT

The PCM energizes the electric fuel pump through the fuel pump relay. Battery voltage is applied to the fuel pump relay when the ignition key is ON. The relay is energized when a ground signal is provided by the PCM.

The fuel pump will operate for approximately one second unless the engine is operating or the starter motor is engaged.

The fuel pump relay is located in the Power Distribution Center (PDC) (Fig. 2).

IDLE AIR CONTROL (IAC) MOTOR—PCM OUTPUT

The IAC motor is mounted on the throttle body (Fig. 7) and is controlled by the Powertrain Control Module (PCM).

The throttle body has an air control passage that provides air for the engine at idle (the throttle plate is closed). The IAC motor pintle protrudes into the air control passage and regulates air flow through it. Based on various sensor inputs, the PCM adjusts engine idle speed by moving the IAC motor pintle in and out of the air control passage. The IAC motor is positioned when the ignition key is turned to the On position.

A (factory adjusted) set screw is used to mechanically limit the position of the throttle body throttle plate. **Never attempt to adjust the engine idle speed using this screw.** All idle speed functions are controlled by the PCM.

DUTY CYCLE EVAP PURGE SOLENOID VALVE-PCM OUTPUT

Refer to Group 25, Emission Control System for information.

DATA LINK CONNECTOR—PCM INPUT AND OUTPUT

The 16–way data link connector (diagnostic scan tool connector) links the Diagnostic Readout Box (DRB) scan tool or the Mopar Diagnostic System (MDS) with the powertrain control module (PCM). The data link connector is located under the instrument panel to the left of the steering column (Fig. 10). For operation of the DRB scan tool, refer to the appropriate Powertrain Diagnostic Procedures service manual.

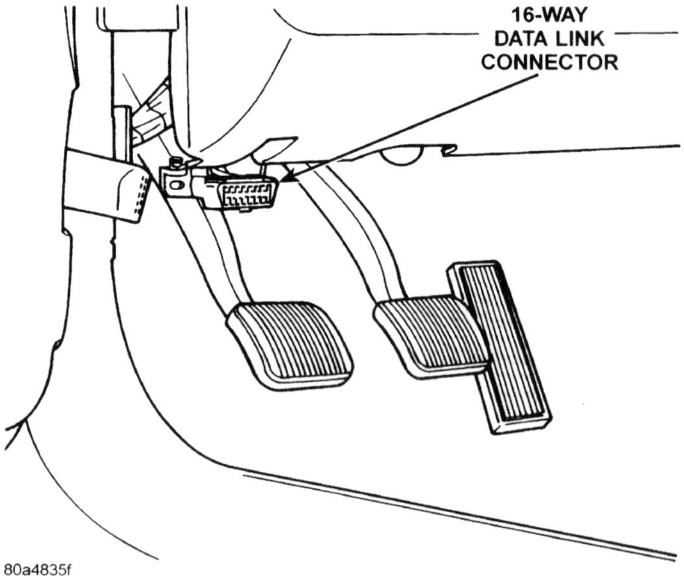

Fig. 10 Data Link Connector Location

FUEL INJECTORS—PCM OUTPUT

Six individual fuel injectors are used with the 4.0L 6-cylinder engine. Four individual fuel injectors are used with the 2.5L 4-cylinder engine. The injectors are attached to the fuel rail (Fig. 11).

The nozzle ends of the injectors are positioned into openings in the intake manifold just above the intake

DESCRIPTION AND OPERATION (Continued)

valve ports of the cylinder head. The engine wiring harness connector for each fuel injector is equipped with an attached numerical tag (INJ 1, INJ 2 etc.). This is used to identify each fuel injector.

The injectors are energized individually in a sequential order by the Powertrain Control Module (PCM). The PCM will adjust injector pulse width by switching the ground path to each individual injector on and off. Injector pulse width is the period of time that the injector is energized. The PCM will adjust injector pulse width based on various inputs it receives.

During start up, battery voltage is supplied to the injectors through the ASD relay. When the engine is operating, voltage is supplied by the charging system. The PCM determines injector pulse width based on various inputs.

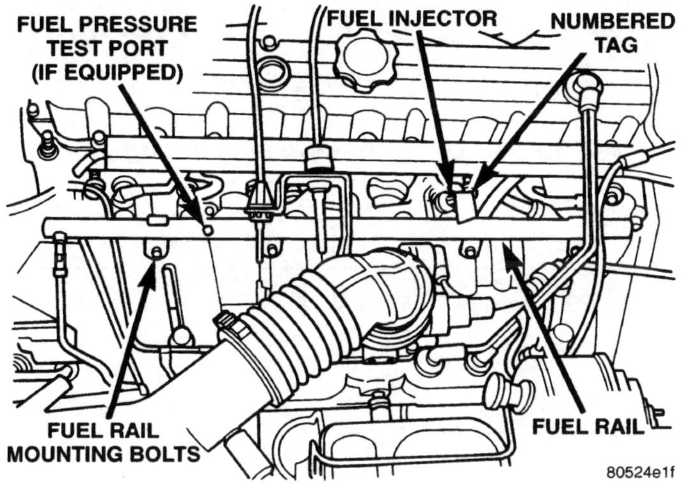

Fig. 11 Fuel Injectors—Typical 4.0L Shown

IGNITION COIL—PCM OUTPUT

System voltage from the Automatic Shutdown (ASD) relay is supplied to the ignition coil positive terminal. The Powertrain Control Module (PCM) operates the ignition coil. **Ignition timing is not adjustable.** The PCM adjusts ignition timing to meet changing engine operating conditions.

Refer to Group 8D, Ignition System for additional information.

MALFUNCTION INDICATOR LAMP—PCM OUTPUT

The malfunction indicator lamp illuminates each time the ignition key is turned on. It will stay on for approximately three seconds as a bulb test. The lamp is displayed on the instrument panel as the CHECK ENGINE lamp (Fig. 12).

The signals needed to activate the lamp are sent from the Powertrain Control Module (PCM) to the instrument panel through the CCD bus circuits.

If the PCM receives an incorrect signal, or no signal from certain sensors or emission related systems,

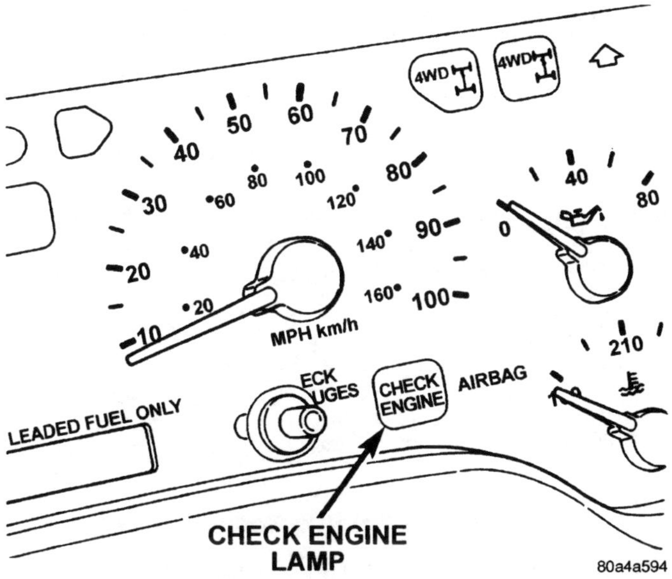

Fig. 12 Check Engine Lamp—Typical

the lamp is turned on. This is a warning that the PCM has recorded a system or sensor malfunction. In some cases, when a problem is declared, the PCM will go into a limp-in mode. This is an attempt to keep the system operating. It signals an immediate need for service.

The lamp can also be used to display a Diagnostic Trouble Code (DTC). Refer to On-Board Diagnostics in Group 25, Emission Control System for additional information.

The lamp is also used to display certain engine misfires. Refer to Group 25, Emission Control System for additional information.

TACHOMETER—PCM OUTPUT

The Powertrain Control Module (PCM) supplies engine rpm values to the instrument cluster tachometer through the PCM's CCD bus circuits. Refer to Group 8E, Instrument Panel and Gauges for tachometer information.

THROTTLE BODY

Filtered air from the air cleaner enters the intake manifold through the throttle body (Fig. 13). Fuel does not enter the intake manifold through the throttle body. Fuel is sprayed into the manifold by the fuel injectors. The throttle body is mounted on the intake manifold. It contains an air control passage (Fig. 13) controlled by an Idle Air Control (IAC) motor. The air control passage is used to supply air for idle conditions. A throttle valve (plate) is used to supply air for above idle conditions.

The Throttle Position Sensor (TPS), IAC motor and Manifold Absolute Pressure sensor (MAP) are attached to the throttle body. The accelerator pedal cable, speed control cable (when equipped) and auto-

DESCRIPTION AND OPERATION (Continued)

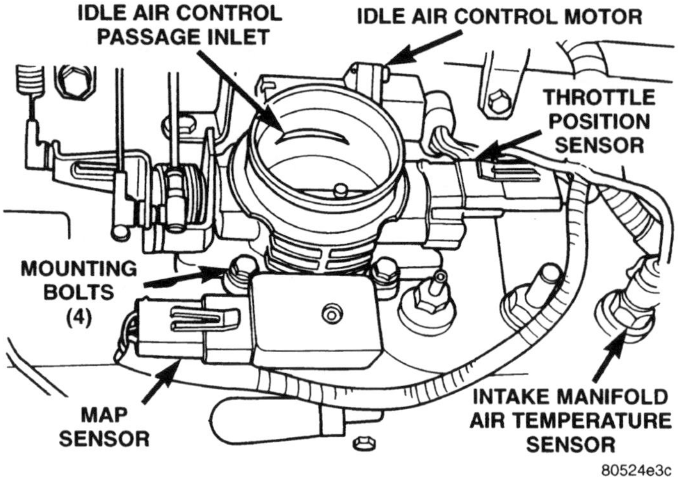

Fig. 13 Throttle Body

matic transmission control cable (when equipped) are connected to the throttle arm.

A (factory adjusted) set screw is used to mechanically limit the position of the throttle body throttle plate. **Never attempt to adjust the engine idle speed using this screw.** All idle speed functions are controlled by the PCM.

DIAGNOSIS AND TESTING

VISUAL INSPECTION

A visual inspection for loose, disconnected or incorrectly routed wires and hoses should be made. This should be done before attempting to diagnose or service the fuel injection system. A visual check will help spot these faults and save unnecessary test and diagnostic time. A thorough visual inspection will include the following checks:

(1) Verify that the three 32–way electrical connectors are fully inserted into connector of Powertrain Control Module (PCM) (Fig. 14).

(2) Inspect battery cable connections. Be sure that they are clean and tight.

(3) Inspect fuel pump relay and ASD relay connections. Inspect starter motor relay connections. Inspect relays for signs of physical damage and corrosion. The relays are located in Power Distribution Center (PDC) (Fig. 15). Refer to label on PDC cover for relay location.

(4) Inspect ignition coil connections. Verify that coil secondary cable is firmly connected to coil (Fig. 16).

(5) Verify that distributor cap is correctly attached to distributor. Be sure that spark plug cables are firmly connected to the distributor cap and spark plugs are in their correct firing order (Fig. 17). Be sure that coil cable is firmly connected to distributor cap and coil. Be sure that camshaft position sensor

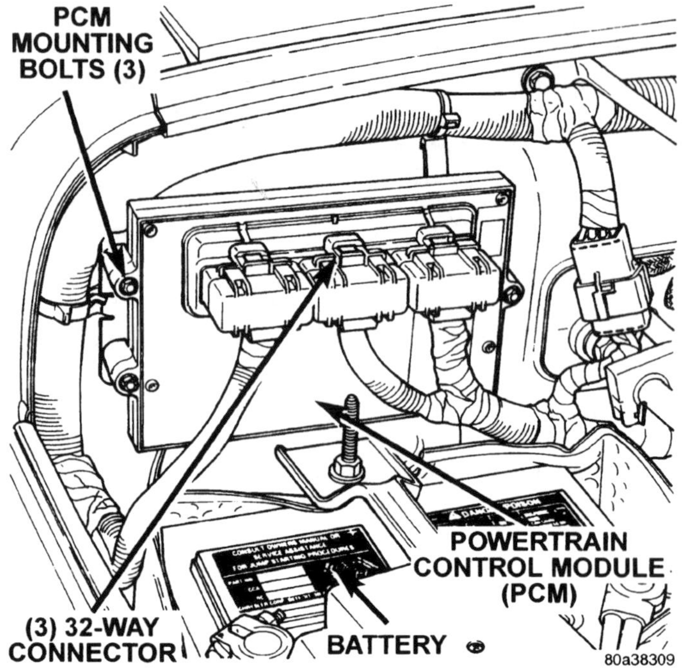

Fig. 14 Powertrain Control Module (PCM)

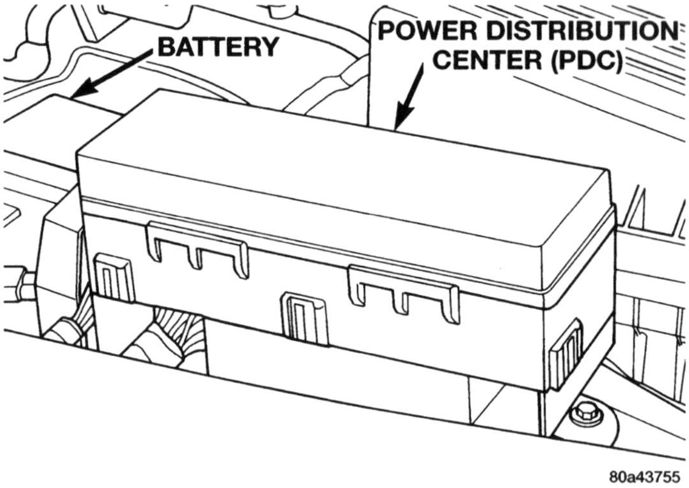

Fig. 15 Power Distribution Center (PDC)

wire connector (at distributor) is firmly connected to harness connector. Inspect spark plug condition. Refer to Group 8D, Ignition. Connect vehicle to an oscilloscope and inspect spark events for fouled or damaged spark plugs or cables.

(6) Verify that generator output wire, generator connector and ground wire are firmly connected to the generator.

(7) Inspect system body grounds for loose or dirty connections. Refer to Group 8, Wiring for ground locations.

(8) Verify Crankcase Ventilation (CCV) operation. Refer to Group 25, Emission Control System for additional information.

(9) Inspect fuel tube quick-connect fitting-to-fuel rail connections.

DIAGNOSIS AND TESTING (Continued)

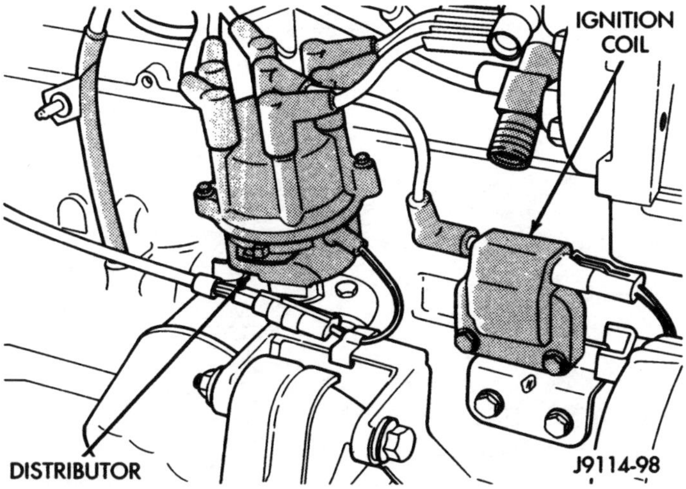

Fig. 16 Ignition Coil—Typical (4.0L Engine Shown)

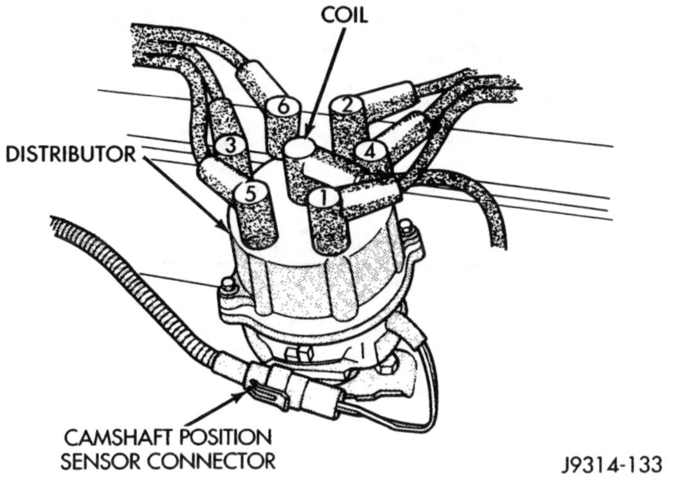

Fig. 17 Distributor and Wiring—Typical (4.0L Engine Shown)

(10) Verify that hose connections to all ports of vacuum fittings on intake manifold are tight and not leaking.

(11) Inspect accelerator cable and transmission throttle cable (if equipped). Check their connections to throttle arm of throttle body for any binding or restrictions.

(12) If equipped with vacuum brake booster, verify that vacuum booster hose is firmly connected to fitting on intake manifold. Also check connection to brake vacuum booster.

(13) Inspect air cleaner inlet and air cleaner element for dirt or restrictions.

(14) Inspect radiator grille area, radiator fins and air conditioning condenser for restrictions.

(15) Verify that intake manifold air temperature sensor wire connector is firmly connected to harness connector (Fig. 18).

(16) Verify that MAP sensor electrical connector is firmly connected to MAP sensor (Fig. 18). Also verify that rubber L-shaped fitting from MAP sensor to throttle body is firmly connected (Fig. 19).

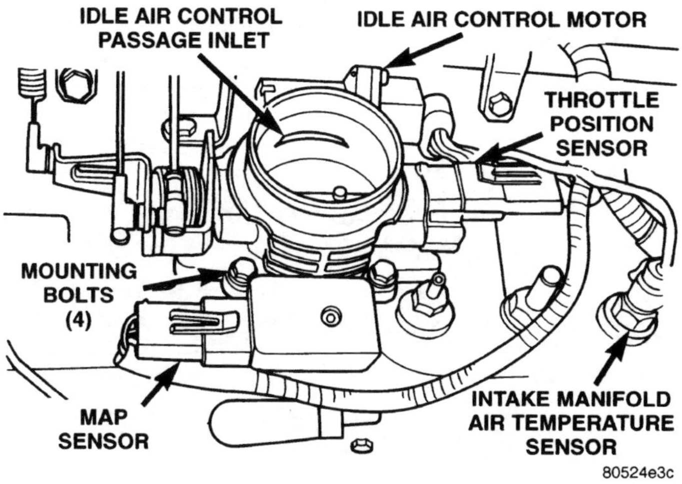

Fig. 18 Sensor Locations—4.0L Engine Shown

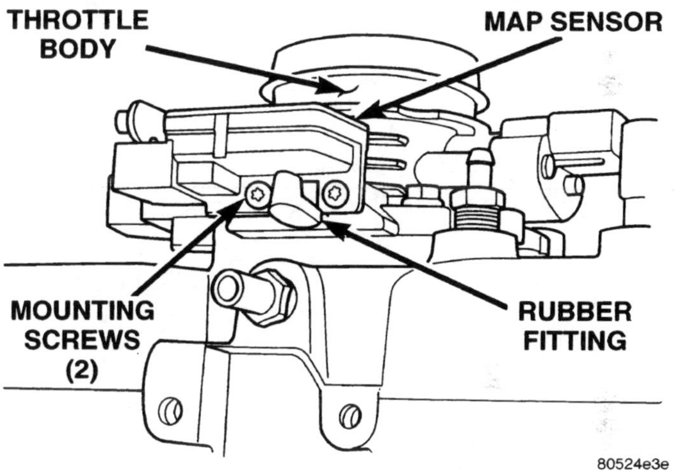

Fig. 19 Rubber L-Shaped Fitting—MAP Sensor-to-Throttle Body

(17) Verify that fuel injector wire harness connectors are firmly connected to injectors in the correct order. Each harness connector is numerically tagged with injector number (INJ 1, INJ 2 etc.) of its corresponding fuel injector and cylinder number.

(18) Verify harness connectors are firmly connected to Idle Air Control (IAC) motor and Throttle Position Sensor (TPS) (Fig. 18).

(19) Verify that wire harness connector is firmly connected to engine coolant temperature sensor (Fig. 20).

(20) Raise and support vehicle.

(21) Verify that both oxygen sensor wire connectors are firmly connected to sensors. Inspect sensors and connectors for damage (Fig. 21) or (Fig. 22).

(22) Inspect for pinched or leaking fuel tubes. Inspect for pinched, cracked or leaking fuel hoses.

DIAGNOSIS AND TESTING (Continued)

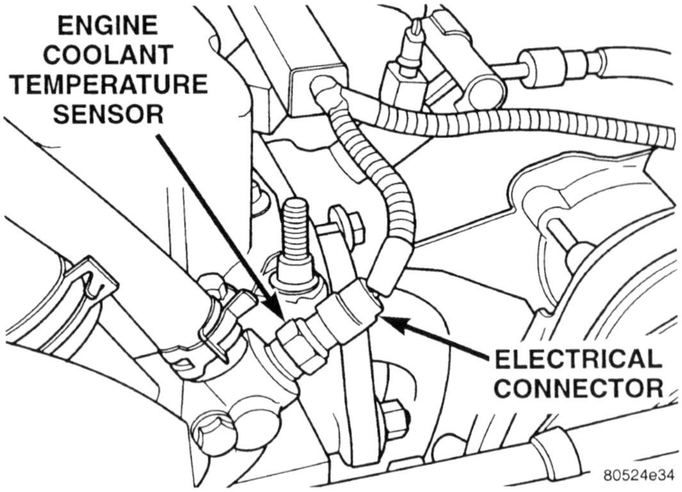

Fig. 20 Engine Coolant Temp. Sensor—4.0L Shown

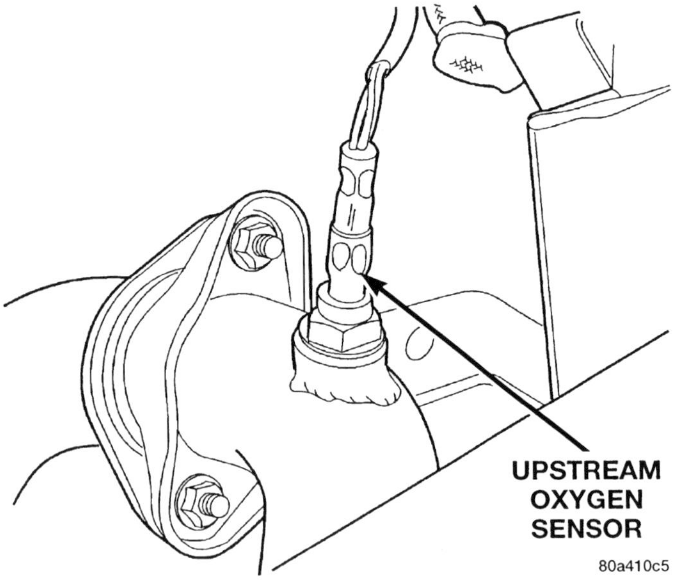

Fig. 21 Upstream Oxygen Sensor

(23) Inspect for exhaust system restrictions such as pinched exhaust pipes, collapsed muffler or plugged catalytic convertor.

(24) If equipped with automatic transmission, verify that electrical harness is firmly connected to park/neutral switch. Refer to Automatic Transmission section of Group 21.

(25) Verify that electrical harness connector is firmly connected to the vehicle speed sensor (Fig. 23).

(26) Verify that fuel pump/gauge sender unit wire connector is firmly connected to harness connector.

(27) Inspect fuel hoses at fuel pump/gauge sender unit for cracks or leaks.

(28) Inspect transmission torque convertor housing (automatic transmission) or clutch housing (manual transmission) for damage to timing ring on drive plate/flywheel.

(29) Verify that battery cable and solenoid feed wire connections to starter solenoid are tight and clean. Inspect for chaffed wires or wires rubbing up against other components.

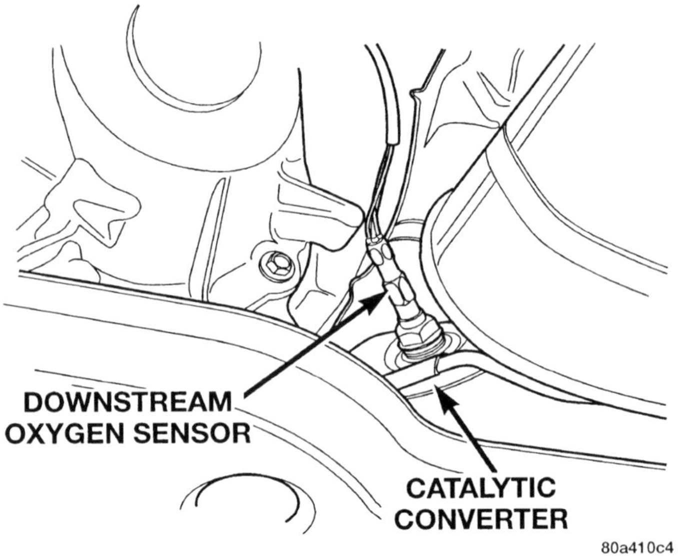

Fig. 22 Downstream Oxygen Sensor

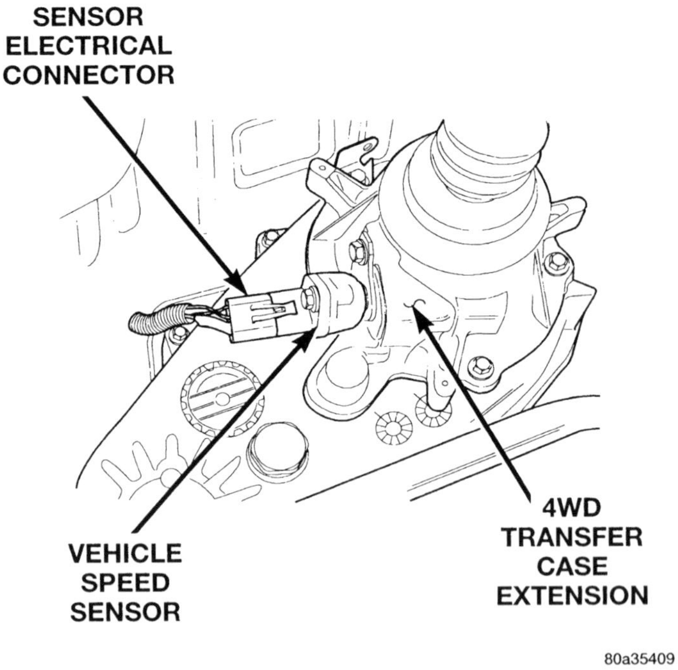

Fig. 23 Vehicle Speed Sensor—Typical

ASD AND FUEL PUMP RELAYS

The following description of operation and tests apply only to the Automatic Shutdown (ASD) and fuel pump relays. The terminals on the bottom of each relay are numbered (Fig. 24).

OPERATION

- Terminal number 30 is connected to battery voltage. For both the ASD and fuel pump relays, terminal 30 is connected to battery voltage at all times.

DIAGNOSIS AND TESTING (Continued)

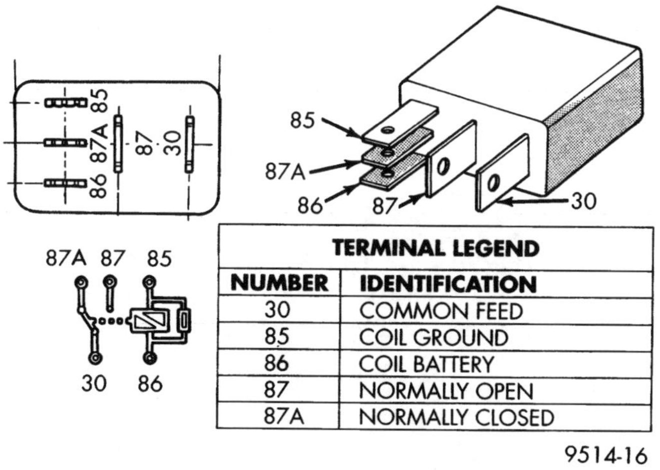

TERMINAL LEGEND	
NUMBER	IDENTIFICATION
30	COMMON FEED
85	COIL GROUND
86	COIL BATTERY
87	NORMALLY OPEN
87A	NORMALLY CLOSED

Fig. 24 ASD and Fuel Pump Relay Terminals

- The PCM grounds the coil side of the relay through terminal number 85.
- Terminal number 86 supplies voltage to the coil side of the relay.
- When the PCM de-energizes the ASD and fuel pump relays, terminal number 87A connects to terminal 30. This is the Off position. In the off position, voltage is not supplied to the rest of the circuit. Terminal 87A is the center terminal on the relay.
- When the PCM energizes the ASD and fuel pump relays, terminal 87 connects to terminal 30. This is the On position. Terminal 87 supplies voltage to the rest of the circuit.

TESTING

The following procedure applies to the ASD and fuel pump relays.

(1) Remove relay from connector before testing.

(2) With the relay removed from the vehicle, use an ohmmeter to check the resistance between terminals 85 and 86. The resistance should be between 75 ±5 ohms.

(3) Connect the ohmmeter between terminals 30 and 87A. The ohmmeter should show continuity between terminals 30 and 87A.

(4) Connect the ohmmeter between terminals 87 and 30. The ohmmeter should not show continuity at this time.

(5) Connect one end of a jumper wire (16 gauge or smaller) to relay terminal 85. Connect the other end of the jumper wire to the ground side of a 12 volt power source.

(6) Connect one end of another jumper wire (16 gauge or smaller) to the power side of the 12 volt power source. **Do not attach the other end of the jumper wire to the relay at this time.**

WARNING: DO NOT ALLOW OHMMETER TO CONTACT TERMINALS 85 OR 86 DURING THIS TEST.

(7) Attach the other end of the jumper wire to relay terminal 86. This activates the relay. The ohmmeter should now show continuity between relay terminals 87 and 30. The ohmmeter should not show continuity between relay terminals 87A and 30.

(8) Disconnect jumper wires.

(9) Replace the relay if it did not pass the continuity and resistance tests. If the relay passed the tests, it operates properly. Check the remainder of the ASD and fuel pump relay circuits. Refer to group 8W, Wiring Diagrams.

MANIFOLD ABSOLUTE PRESSURE (MAP) SENSOR TEST

To perform a complete test of MAP sensor (Fig. 25) and its circuitry, refer to DRB scan tool and appropriate Powertrain Diagnostics Procedures manual. To test the MAP sensor only, refer to the following:

(1) Inspect rubber L-shaped fitting from MAP sensor to throttle body (Fig. 26). Repair as necessary.

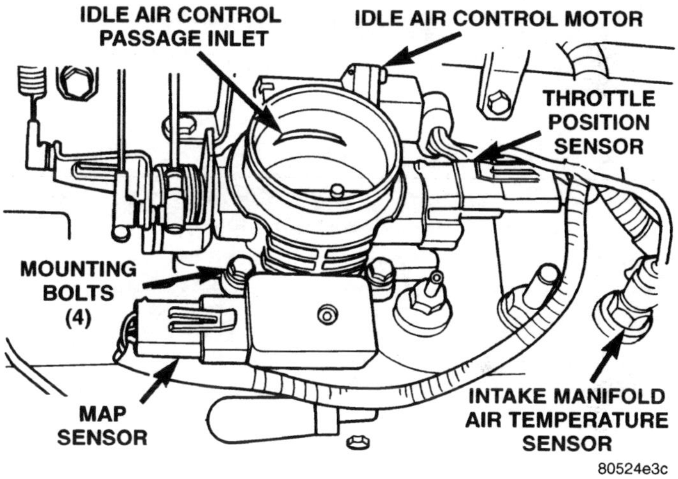

Fig. 25 Sensor Location—4.0L Shown

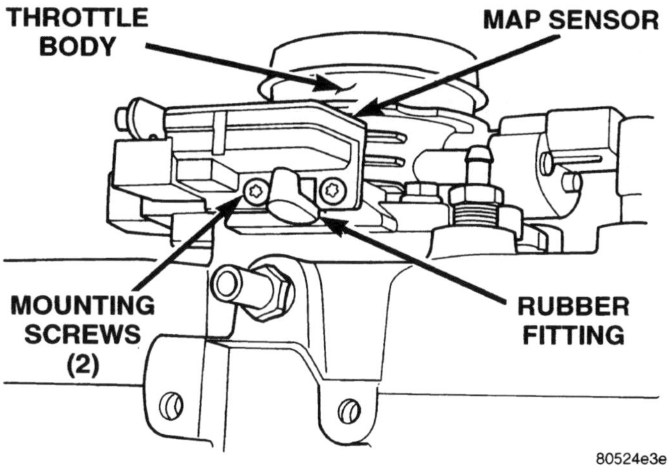

Fig. 26 Rubber L-Shaped Fitting—MAP Sensor-to-Throttle Body

DIAGNOSIS AND TESTING (Continued)

CAUTION: When testing the MAP sensor, be sure that the harness wires are not damaged by the test meter probes.

(2) Test MAP sensor output voltage at MAP sensor connector between terminals A and B (Fig. 27). With ignition switch ON and engine OFF, output voltage should be 4-to-5 volts. The voltage should drop to 1.5-to-2.1 volts with a hot, neutral idle speed condition.

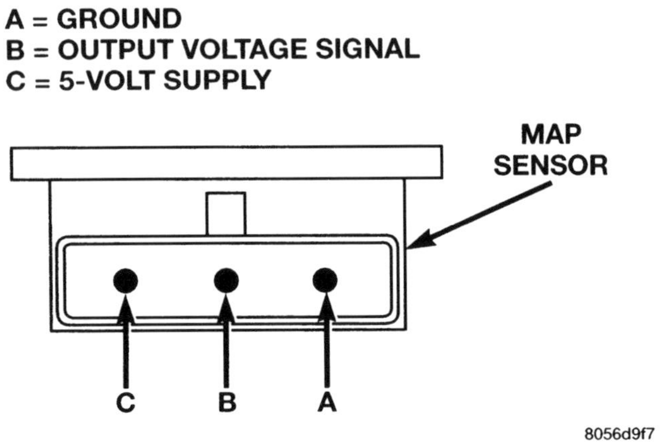

Fig. 27 MAP Sensor Connector Terminals—Typical

(3) Test Powertrain Control Module (PCM) cavity A-27 for same voltage described above to verify wire harness condition. Repair as necessary.

(4) Test MAP sensor supply voltage at sensor connector between terminals A and C (Fig. 27) with ignition ON. The voltage should be approximately 5 volts (±0.5V). Five volts (±0.5V) should also be at cavity A-17 of the PCM wire harness connector. Repair or replace wire harness as necessary.

(5) Test the MAP sensor ground circuit at sensor connector terminal—A (Fig. 27) and PCM connector A-4. Repair wire harness if necessary.

Refer to Group 8W, Wiring Diagrams for cavity locations.

OXYGEN (O2S) SENSORS

To perform a complete test of the O2S sensors and their circuitry, refer to the DRB scan tool and appropriate Powertrain Diagnostics Procedures manual. To test the O2S sensors only, refer to the following:

The upstream O2S sensor is located on the exhaust downpipe (Fig. 28).

The downstream O2S sensor is located near the outlet end of the catalytic converter (Fig. 29).

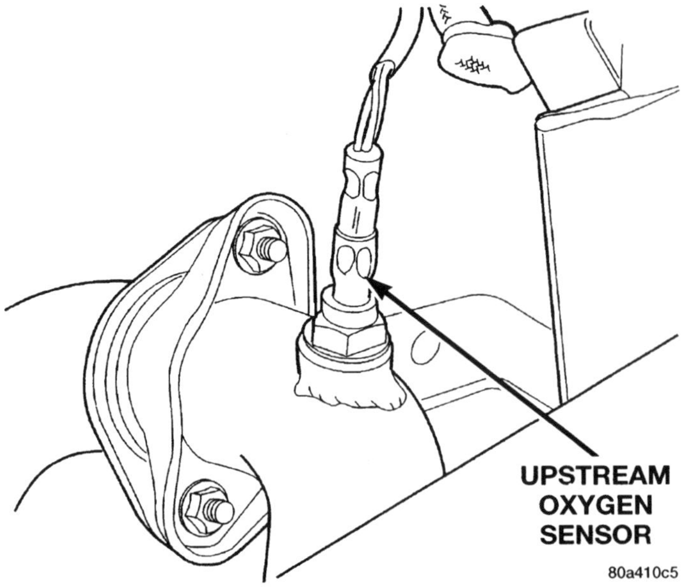

Fig. 28 Upstream Oxygen Sensor Location

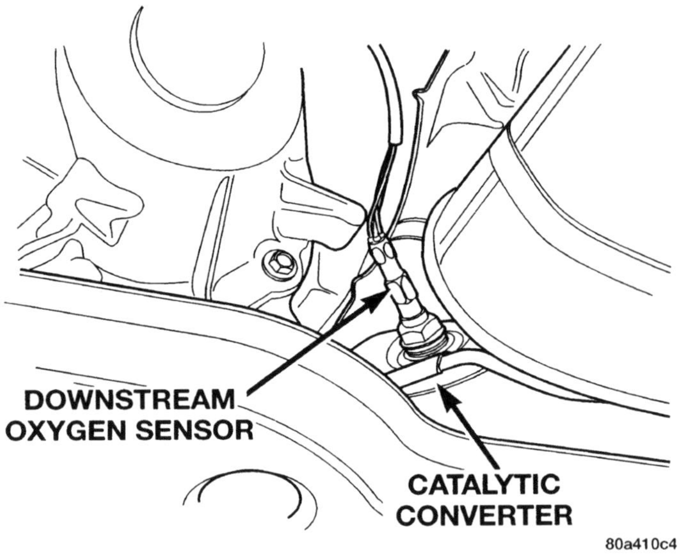

Fig. 29 Downstream Oxygen Sensor Location

Each O2S heating element can be tested with an ohmmeter as follows:

Disconnect the O2S sensor connector. Connect the ohmmeter test leads across the white wire terminals of the sensor connector. Resistance should be between 5 and 7 ohms. Replace the sensor if the ohmmeter displays an infinity (open) reading.

CAMSHAFT AND CRANKSHAFT POSITION SENSORS

Refer to Group 8D, Ignition System for information.

ENGINE COOLANT TEMPERATURE SENSOR

To perform a complete test of the engine coolant temperature sensor and its circuitry, refer to DRB scan tool and appropriate Powertrain Diagnostics Procedures manual. To test the sensor only, refer to the following:

DIAGNOSIS AND TESTING (Continued)

(1) Disconnect wire harness connector from coolant temperature sensor (Fig. 30).

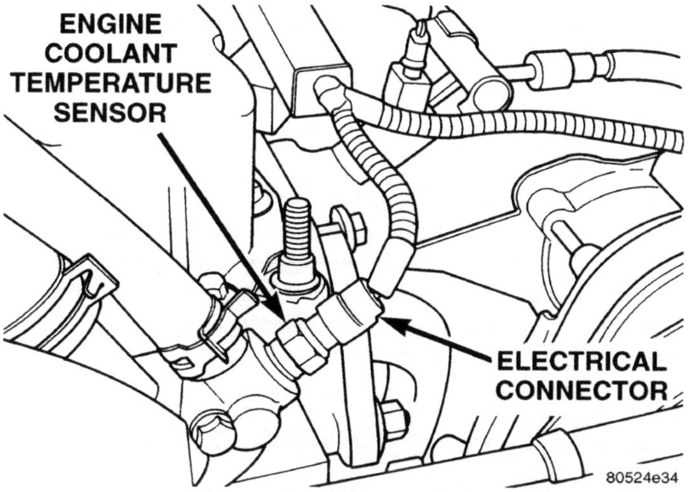

Fig. 30 Engine Coolant Temperature Sensor—Typical

(2) Test the resistance of the sensor with a high input impedance (digital) volt-ohmmeter. The resistance (as measured across the sensor terminals) should be as shown in the Coolant Temperature Sensor/Intake Air Temperature Sensor resistance chart. Replace the sensor if it is not within the range of resistance specified in the chart.

TEMPERATURE		RESISTANCE (OHMS)	
C	F	MIN	MAX
-40	-40	291,490	381,710
-20	-4	85,850	108,390
-10	14	49,250	61,430
0	32	29,330	35,990
10	50	17,990	21,810
20	68	11,370	13,610
25	77	9,120	10,880
30	86	7,370	8,750
40	104	4,900	5,750
50	122	3,330	3,880
60	140	2,310	2,670
70	158	1,630	1,870
80	176	1,170	1,340
90	194	860	970
100	212	640	720
110	230	480	540
120	248	370	410

J928D-4

SENSOR RESISTANCE (OHMS)—COOLANT TEMPERATURE SENSOR/INTAKE AIR TEMPERATURE SENSOR

(3) Test continuity of the wire harness between the PCM wire harness connector and the coolant sensor connector terminals. Refer to Group 8, Wiring for terminal/cavity locations. Repair the wire harness if an open circuit is indicated.

IDLE AIR CONTROL (IAC) MOTOR

To perform a complete test of the IAC motor and its circuitry, refer to DRB scan tool and appropriate Powertrain Diagnostics Procedures manual.

INTAKE MANIFOLD AIR TEMPERATURE SENSOR

To perform a complete test of the intake manifold air temperature sensor and its circuitry, refer to DRB tester and appropriate Powertrain Diagnostics Procedures manual. To test the sensor only, refer to the following:

(1) Disconnect wire harness connector from intake manifold air temperature sensor (Fig. 31).

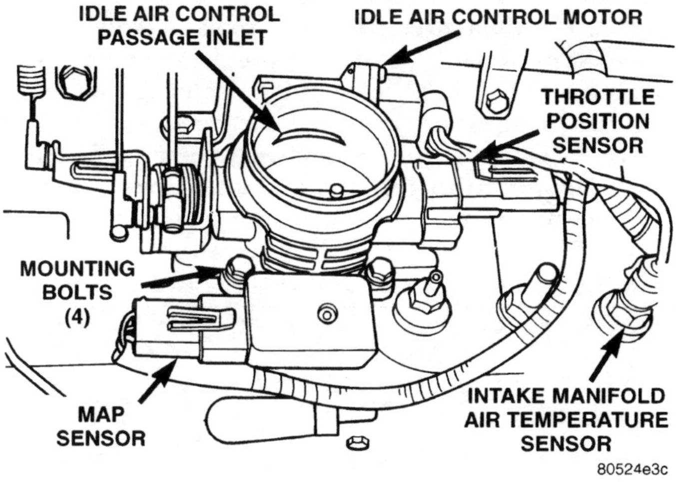

Fig. 31 Intake Manifold Air Temperature Sensor—Typical

(2) Test resistance of sensor with an input impedance (digital) volt-ohmmeter. The resistance (as measured across the sensor terminals) should be as shown in the Coolant Temperature Sensor/Intake Air Temperature Sensor resistance chart. Replace sensor if it is not within range of resistance specified in chart.

(3) Test resistance of wire harness. Do this between PCM wire harness connector A-15 and sensor connector terminal. Also check between PCM connector A-4 to sensor connector terminal. Repair wire harness as necessary if resistance is greater than 1 ohm.

POWER STEERING PRESSURE SWITCH

2.5L 4-Cylinder Engine Only

This switch (Fig. 32) provides an input to the Powertrain Control Module (PCM). The input is provided during periods of high pump load and low engine rpm; such as during parking maneuvers. The PCM will then increase idle speed through the Idle Air

DIAGNOSIS AND TESTING (Continued)

Control (IAC) motor. This is done to prevent the engine from stalling under the increased load.

When steering pump pressure exceeds 1896 kPa ± 345 kPa (275 psi ± 50 psi), the normally closed switch circuit will open and the PCM will increase the engine idle speed.

When power steering pump pressure drops below approximately 70 psi, the switch circuit will close and idle speed will return to normal.

To test switch:

(1) Disconnect electrical connector at switch.

(2) Connect a pair of jumper wires to switch terminals. Route and secure jumper wires away from fan blades and fan belt.

(3) Connect an ohmmeter to jumper wires and observe continuity. Circuit should be closed with engine not running. If continuity is observed, switch is OK. If switch circuit is open, replace switch.

(4) Start engine and observe ohmmeter. With engine at idle speed, continuity should be observed until steering wheel has been turned to left or right position. **Do not hold steering wheel in full left or right position for more than a few seconds. Damage to power steering pump may occur.**

(5) If continuity is still observed after turning wheel (circuit did not open), replace switch.

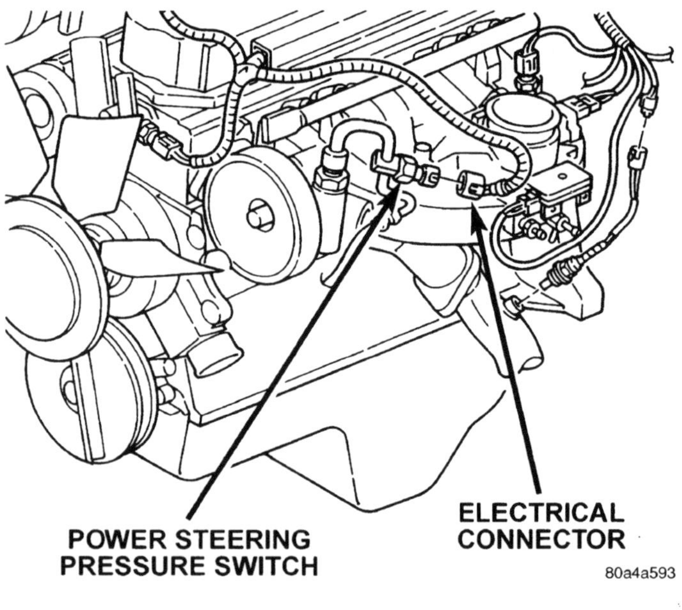

Fig. 32 Power Steering Pump Pressure Switch

VEHICLE SPEED SENSOR

To perform a complete test of the sensor and its circuitry, refer to DRB scan tool and appropriate Powertrain Diagnostics Procedures manual.

THROTTLE POSITION SENSOR (TPS)

To perform a complete test of the TPS (Fig. 31) and its circuitry, refer to the DRB scan tool and appropriate Powertrain Diagnostics Procedures manual. To test the TPS only, refer to the following:

The TPS can be tested with a digital voltmeter. The center terminal of the TPS is the output terminal.

With the ignition key in the ON position, check the TPS output voltage at the center terminal wire of the connector. Check this at idle (throttle plate closed) and at Wide Open Throttle (WOT). At idle, TPS output voltage should must be greater than 200 millivolts. At wide open throttle, TPS output voltage must be less than 4.8 volts. The output voltage should increase gradually as the throttle plate is slowly opened from idle to WOT.

REMOVAL AND INSTALLATION

AUTOMATIC SHUTDOWN (ASD) RELAY

The ASD relay is located in the Power Distribution Center (PDC) (Fig. 33). Refer to label on PDC cover for relay location. Check condition of relay terminals and connector terminals for corrosion and for pin height (pin height should be the same for all terminals within the connector). Repair if necessary before installing relay.

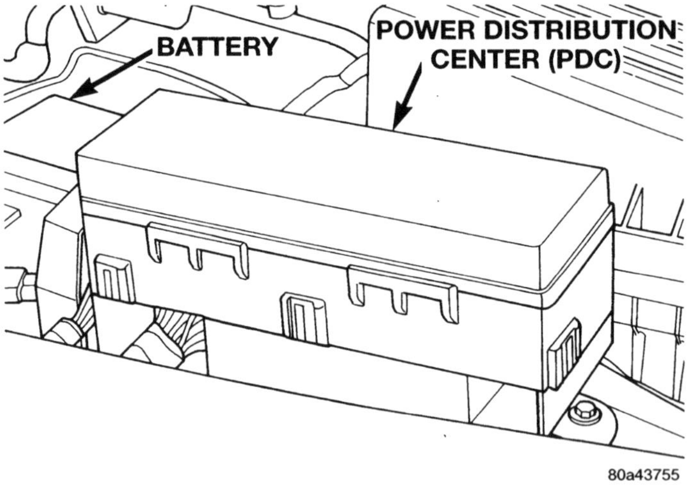

Fig. 33 Power Distribution Center (PDC)

FUEL PUMP RELAY

The fuel pump relay is located in the Power Distribution Center (PDC) (Fig. 33). Refer to label on PDC cover for relay location. Check condition of relay terminals and connector terminals for corrosion and for pin height (pin height should be the same for all terminals within the connector). Repair if necessary before installing relay.

THROTTLE BODY

A (factory adjusted) set screw is used to mechanically limit the position of the throttle body throttle plate. **Never attempt to adjust the engine idle**

REMOVAL AND INSTALLATION (Continued)

speed using this screw. All idle speed functions are controlled by the Powertrain Control Module (PCM).

REMOVAL

(1) Remove air cleaner tube at throttle body.

(2) Disconnect throttle body electrical connectors at MAP sensor, IAC motor and TPS (Fig. 34).

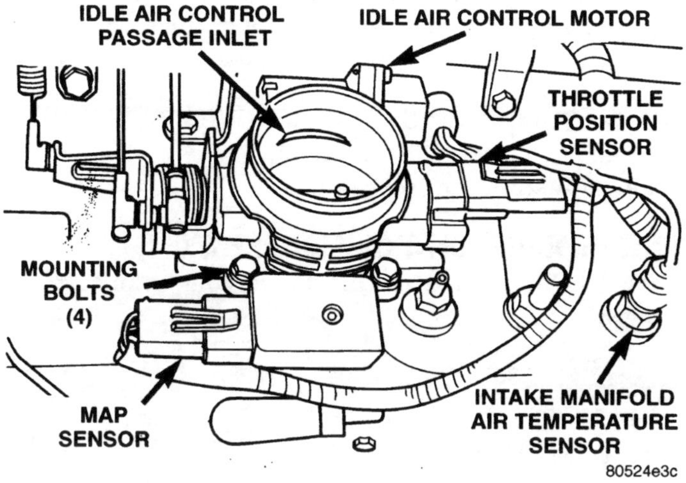

Fig. 34 Throttle Body and Sensor Locations—4.0L Shown

(3) Remove all control cables from throttle body (lever) arm. Refer to the Accelerator Pedal and Throttle Cable section of this group for additional information.

(4) Remove four throttle body mounting bolts.

(5) Remove throttle body from intake manifold.

(6) Discard old throttle body-to-intake manifold gasket.

INSTALLATION

(1) Clean mating surfaces of throttle body and intake manifold.

(2) Install new throttle body-to-intake manifold gasket.

(3) Install throttle body to intake manifold.

(4) Install four mounting bolts. Tighten bolts to 12 N·m (108 in. lbs.) torque.

(5) Install control cables.

(6) Install electrical connectors.

(7) Install air cleaner at throttle body.

THROTTLE POSITION SENSOR (TPS)

The TPS is mounted to the throttle body (Fig. 34).

REMOVAL

(1) Disconnect TPS electrical connector.

(2) Remove TPS mounting screws (Fig. 35).

(3) Remove TPS.

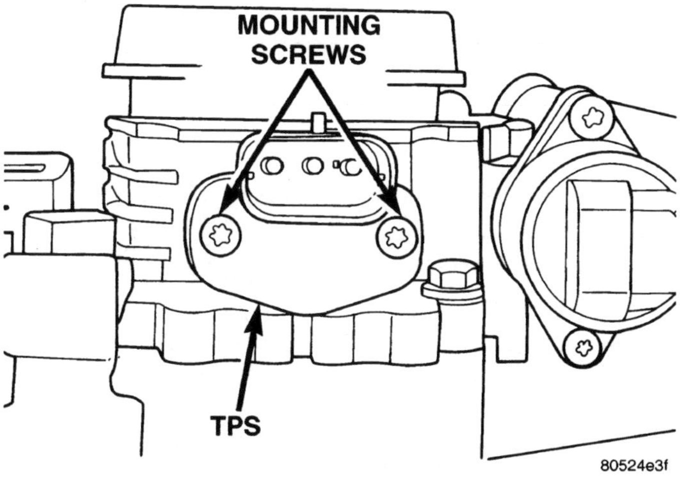

Fig. 35 TPS Mounting Screws

INSTALLATION

The throttle shaft end of the throttle body slides into a socket in the TPS (Fig. 36). The TPS must be installed so that it can be rotated a few degrees. (If the sensor will not rotate, install the sensor with the throttle shaft on the other side of the socket tangs). The TPS will be under slight tension when rotated.

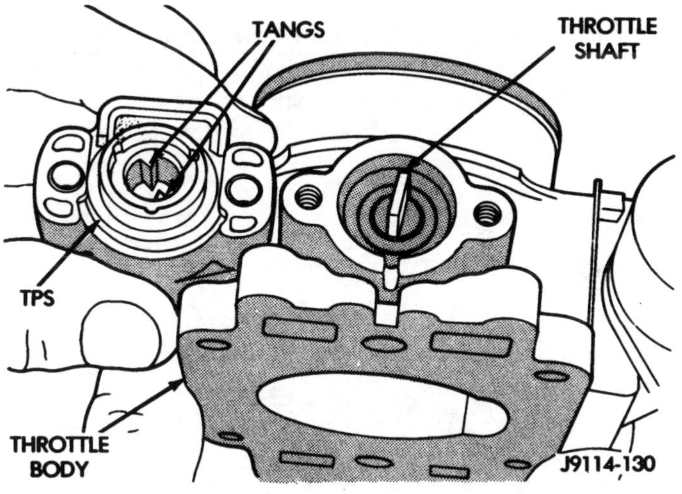

Fig. 36 Throttle Position Sensor—Installation

(1) Install TPS and retaining screws.

(2) Tighten screws to 7 N·m (60 in. lbs.) torque.

(3) Connect TPS electrical connector to TPS.

(4) Manually operate throttle (by hand) to check for any TPS binding before starting engine.

IDLE AIR CONTROL (IAC) MOTOR

The IAC motor is located on the side of the throttle body (Fig. 34).

REMOVAL

(1) Remove air cleaner tube at throttle body.

(2) Disconnect electrical connector from IAC motor.

(3) Remove two mounting bolts (screws) (Fig. 37).

REMOVAL AND INSTALLATION (Continued)

(4) Remove IAC motor from throttle body.

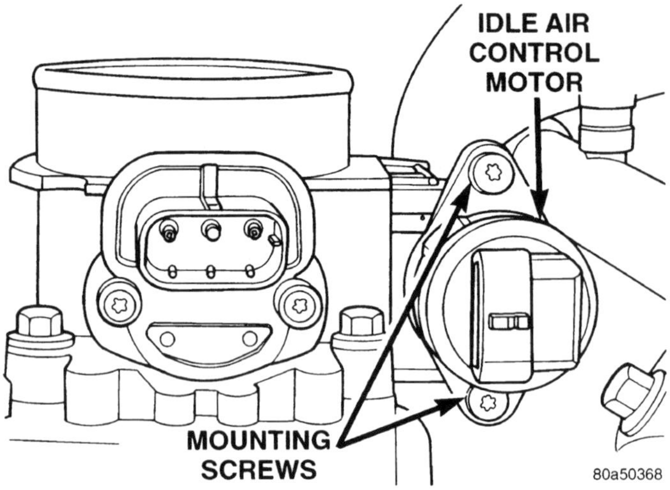

Fig. 37 Mounting Bolts (Screws)—IAC Motor

INSTALLATION

(1) Install IAC motor to throttle body.

(2) Install and tighten two mounting bolts (screws) to 7 N·m (60 in. lbs.) torque.

(3) Install electrical connector.

(4) Install air cleaner tube to throttle body.

MANIFOLD ABSOLUTE PRESSURE (MAP) SENSOR

The MAP sensor is mounted to the side of the throttle body (Fig. 34). An L-shaped rubber fitting is used to connect the MAP sensor to throttle body (Fig. 38).

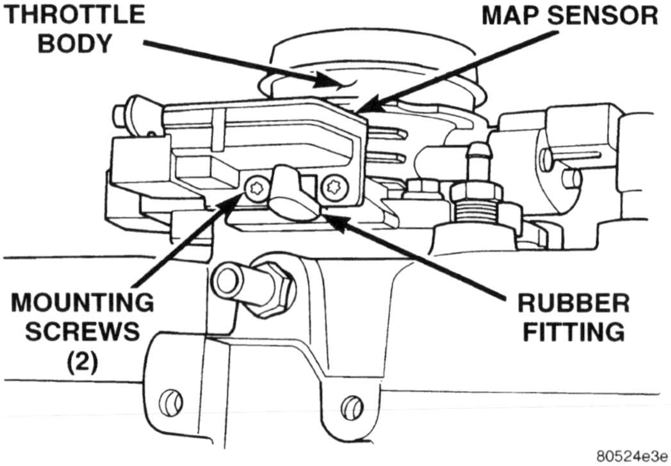

Fig. 38 MAP Sensor Mounting

REMOVAL

(1) Remove air cleaner intake tube at throttle body.

(2) Remove two MAP sensor mounting bolts (screws) (Fig. 38).

(3) While removing MAP sensor, slide the rubber L-shaped fitting (Fig. 38) from throttle body.

(4) Remove rubber L-shaped fitting from MAP sensor.

INSTALLATION

(1) Install rubber L-shaped fitting to MAP sensor.

(2) Position sensor to throttle body while guiding rubber fitting over throttle body vacuum nipple.

(3) Install MAP sensor mounting bolts (screws). Tighten screws to 3 N·m (25 in. lbs.) torque.

(4) Install air cleaner intake tube.

DUTY CYCLE EVAP CANISTER PURGE SOLENOID

Refer to Group 25, Emission Control System for removal/installation procedures.

POWERTRAIN CONTROL MODULE (PCM)

The PCM is located in the engine compartment (Fig. 39).

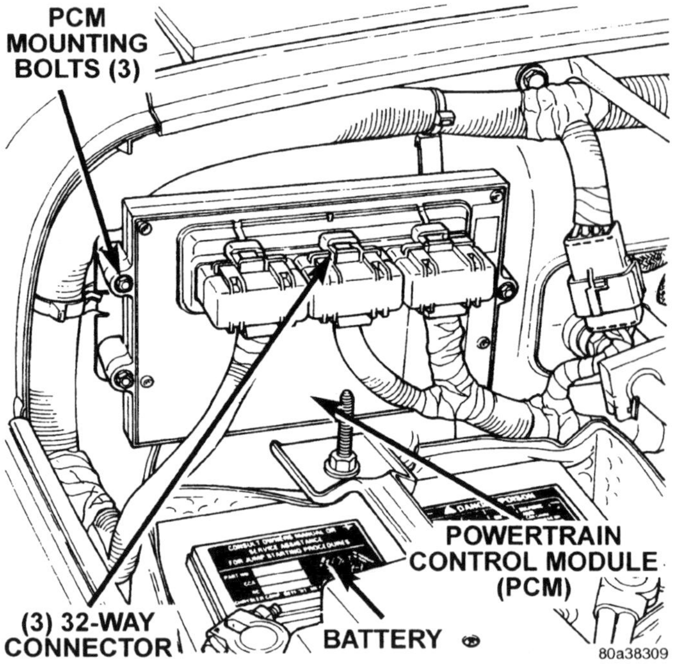

Fig. 39 PCM Location

REMOVAL

(1) Disconnect negative battery cable at battery.

(2) Remove plastic shield from over 32–way connectors. Shield snaps to connectors.

(3) Carefully unplug three 32–way connectors (Fig. 39) from PCM.

(4) Remove three PCM mounting bolts and remove PCM from vehicle.

INSTALLATION

(1) Install PCM and mounting bolts to vehicle.

(2) Tighten bolts to 4 N·m (35 in. lbs.).

(3) Check pin connectors in PCM and three 32–way connectors for corrosion or damage. Also check pin heights in connectors. Pin heights should

REMOVAL AND INSTALLATION (Continued)

all be the same. Repair as necessary before installing 32–way connectors.

(4) Install three 32–way connectors.

(5) Install plastic shield to 32–way connectors. Shield snaps to connectors.

(6) Install battery cable.

POWER STEERING PRESSURE SWITCH—2.5L ENGINE

This switch is not used with 4.0L six-cylinder engines.

The power steering pressure switch is installed in the power steering high-pressure hose (line) (Fig. 40).

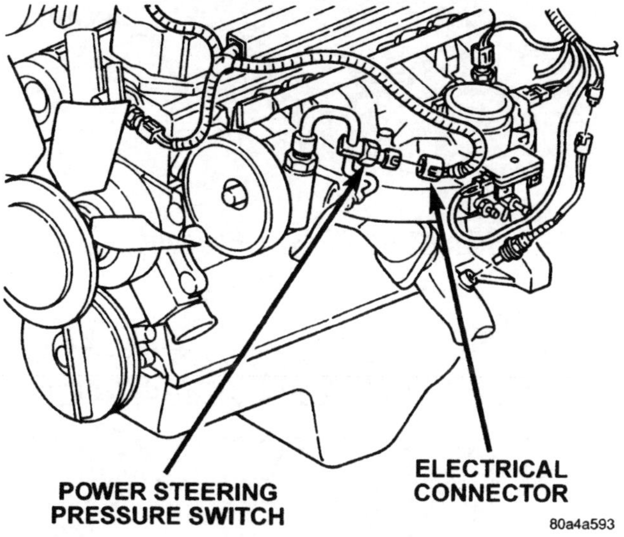

Fig. 40 Power Steering Pressure Switch

REMOVAL

(1) Disconnect electrical connector from power steering pressure switch.

(2) Place a small container or shop towel beneath switch to collect any excess fluid.

(3) Remove switch. Use a back-up wrench on power steering line to prevent bending line.

INSTALLATION

(1) Install power steering switch into power steering line.

(2) Tighten to 14-22 N•m (124-195 in. lbs.) torque.

(3) Connect electrical connector to switch.

(4) Check power steering fluid and add as necessary.

(5) Start engine and again check power steering fluid. Add fluid if necessary.

CRANKSHAFT POSITION SENSOR

Refer to Group 8D, Ignition System for removal/installation procedures.

CAMSHAFT POSITION SENSOR

For removal/installation procedures, refer to Group 8D, Ignition System. See Camshaft Position Sensor.

OXYGEN SENSOR

The upstream O2S sensor is located in the exhaust downpipe (Fig. 41). The downstream sensor is located near outlet end of catalytic converter. Refer to (Fig. 42).

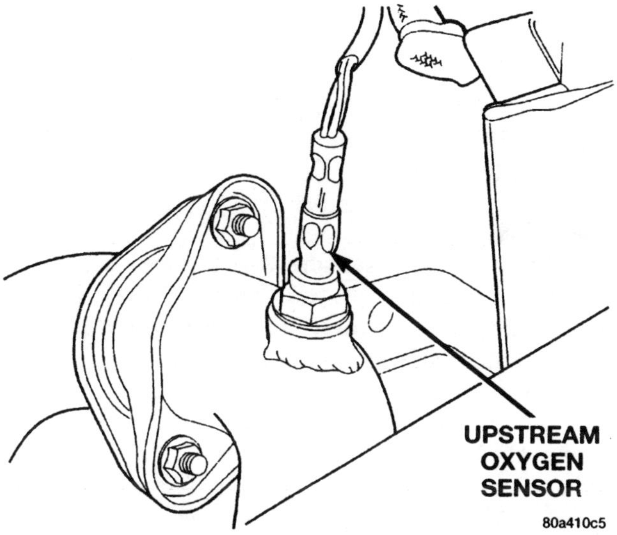

Fig. 41 Upstream Oxygen Sensor Location

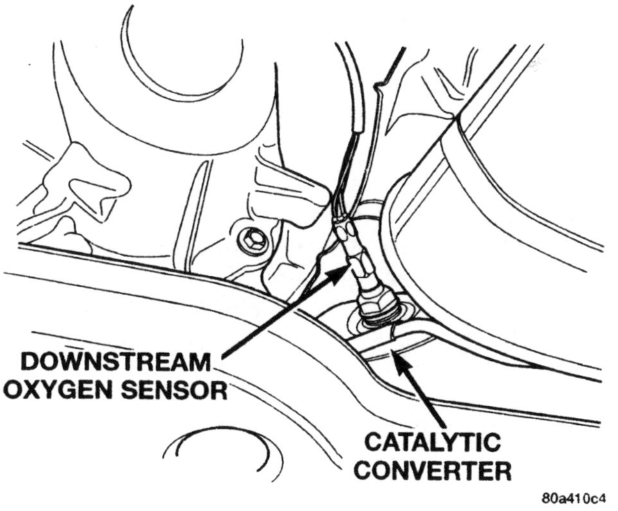

Fig. 42 Downstream Oxygen Sensor Location

1997 Wrangler
Publication No. 81-370-7148
TSB 26-10-96 Oct. 1996

REMOVAL AND INSTALLATION (Continued)

REMOVAL

WARNING: THE EXHAUST MANIFOLD, EXHAUST PIPES AND CATALYTIC CONVERTER BECOME VERY HOT DURING ENGINE OPERATION. ALLOW ENGINE TO COOL BEFORE REMOVING OXYGEN SENSOR.

(1) Raise and support vehicle.
(2) Disconnect wire connector from O2S sensor.

CAUTION: When disconnecting sensor electrical connector, do not pull directly on wire going into sensor.

(3) Remove O2S sensor. Snap-On oxygen sensor wrench number YA 8875 (or equivalent) may be used for removal and installation.

INSTALLATION

Threads of new oxygen sensors are factory coated with anti-seize compound to aid in removal. **DO NOT add any additional anti-seize compound to the threads of a new oxygen sensor.**

(1) Install O2S sensor. Tighten to 30 N·m (22 ft. lbs.) torque.
(2) Connect O2S sensor wire connector.
(3) Lower vehicle.

AIR CLEANER ELEMENT

REMOVAL/INSTALLATION

(1) Loosen air tube clamp at housing cover (Fig. 43).
(2) Disconnect air tube at cover.
(3) Pry back the clips retaining air cleaner cover to air cleaner housing.
(4) Lift cover up to expose air cleaner element.
(5) Remove air cleaner element.
(6) Clean inside of air cleaner housing and its cover before installing new element.
(7) Reverse the preceding operation for installation. Be sure air cleaner cover is properly seated to air cleaner housing.

ENGINE COOLANT TEMPERATURE SENSOR

The coolant temperature sensor is installed in the thermostat housing (Fig. 44).

REMOVAL

(1) Partially drain cooling system until coolant level is below cylinder head. Observe the **WARNINGS** in Group 7, Cooling.
(2) Disconnect coolant temperature sensor wire connector.
(3) Remove sensor from thermostat housing.

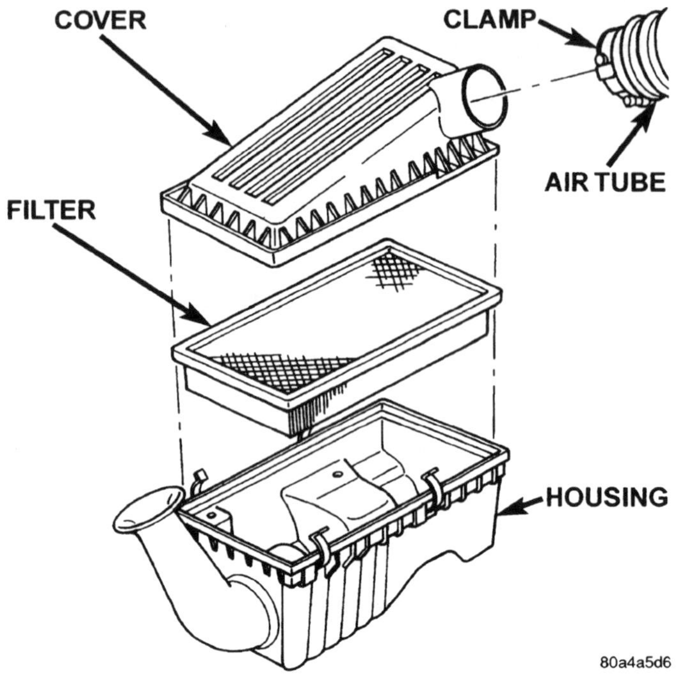

Fig. 43 Air Cleaner Element

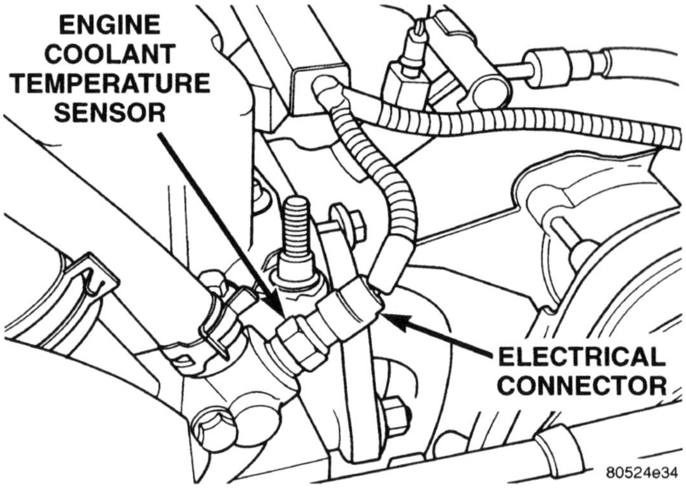

Fig. 44 Engine Coolant Temperature Sensor—Typical

INSTALLATION

(1) Apply sealant to sensor threads (new replacement sensors will have sealant already applied).
(2) Install coolant temperature sensor into thermostat housing. Tighten to 11 N·m (8 ft. lbs.) torque.
(3) Connect wire connector.
(4) Fill cooling system. Refer to Group 7, Cooling System.

INTAKE MANIFOLD AIR TEMPERATURE SENSOR

The intake manifold air temperature sensor is installed into the intake manifold plenum near the throttle body (Fig. 45).

REMOVAL AND INSTALLATION (Continued)

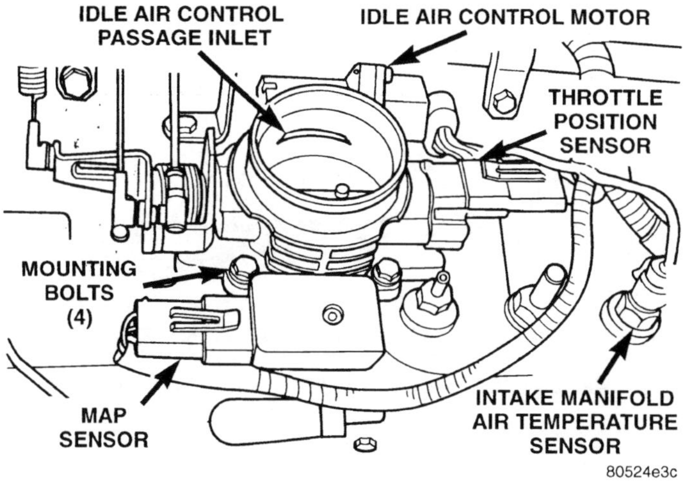

Fig. 45 Intake Air Sensor Location—Typical—4.0L Shown

REMOVAL

(1) Disconnect electrical connector from sensor.
(2) Remove sensor from intake manifold.

INSTALLATION

(1) Install sensor into intake manifold. Tighten sensor to 28 N·m (20 ft. lbs.) torque.
(2) Connect electrical connector to sensor.

VEHICLE SPEED SENSOR

The vehicle speed sensor is located on the speedometer pinion gear adapter. The pinion gear adapter is located on the transfer case extension (drivers side) (Fig. 46).

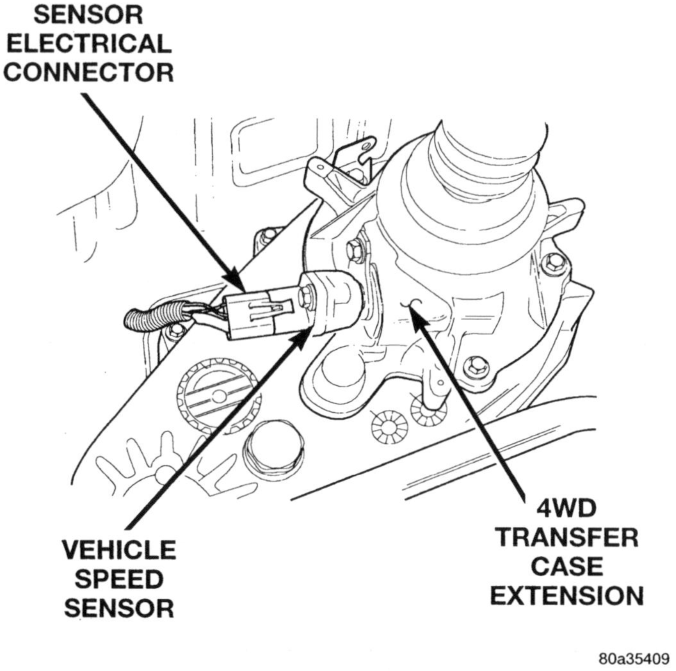

Fig. 46 Vehicle Speed Sensor Location—Typical

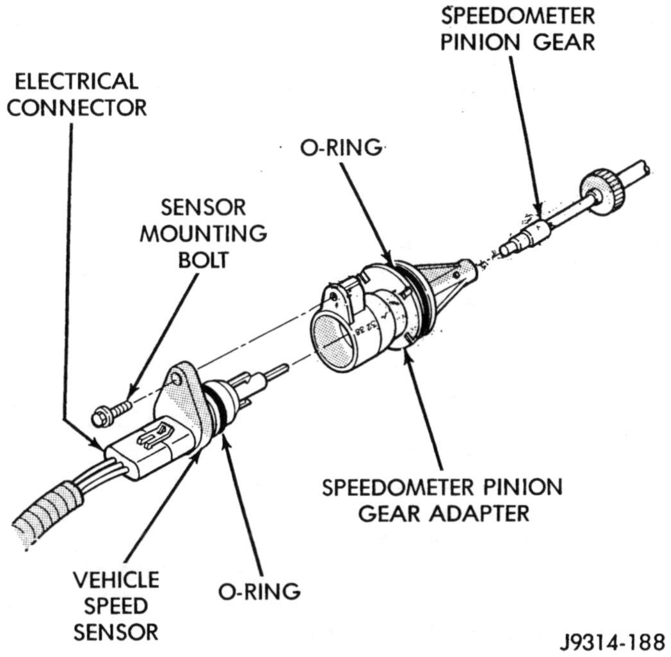

Fig. 47 Sensor Removal/Installation

REMOVAL

(1) Raise and support vehicle.
(2) Disconnect electrical connector from sensor.
(3) Remove sensor mounting bolt (Fig. 47).
(4) Remove sensor (pull straight out) from speedometer pinion gear adapter (Fig. 47). Do not remove gear adapter from transmission.

INSTALLATION

(1) Clean inside of speedometer pinion gear adapter before installing speed sensor.
(2) Install sensor into speedometer gear adapter and install mounting bolt. **Before tightening bolt, verify speed sensor is fully seated (mounted flush) to speedometer pinion gear adapter.**
(3) Tighten sensor mounting bolt to 2.2 N·m (20 in. lbs.) torque.
(4) Connect electrical connector to sensor.

SPECIFICATIONS

VECI LABEL SPECIFICATIONS

If anything differs between the specifications found on the Vehicle Emission Control Information (VECI) label and the following specifications, use specifications on VECI label. The VECI label is located in the engine compartment.

TORQUE CHART

DESCRIPTION	TORQUE
Accelerator Pedal Bracket Mounting Nuts. . .	8.5 N·m (75 in. lbs.)

SPECIFICATIONS (Continued)

DESCRIPTION	TORQUE
Engine Coolant Temperature Sensor	11 N·m (96 in. lbs.)
Fuel Tank Mounting Nuts	Refer to manual text
Fuel Hose Clamps	1 N·m (10 in. lbs.)
IAC Motor-To-Throttle Body Bolts	7 N·m (60 in. lbs.)
Intake Manifold Air Temp. Sensor	28 N·m (20 ft. lbs.)
MAP Sensor Mounting Screws	3 N·m (25 in. lbs.)
Oxygen Sensor	30 N·m (22 ft. lbs.)
PCM Mounting Screws	4 N·m (35 in. lbs.)
** Power Steering Pressure Switch	14-22 N•m (124-195 in. lbs.)**
Throttle Body Mounting Bolts	12 N·m (108 in. lbs.)
Throttle Position Sensor Mounting Screws	7 N·m (60 in. lbs.)
Vehicle Speed Sensor Mounting Bolt	2.2 N·m (20 in. lbs.)

SPECIAL TOOLS

FUEL SYSTEM

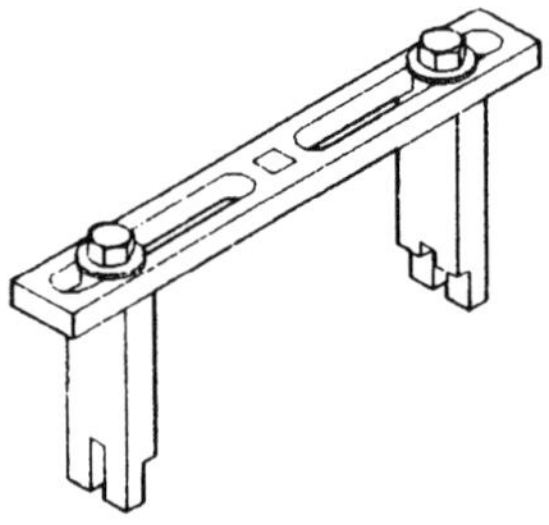

Spanner Wrench—6856

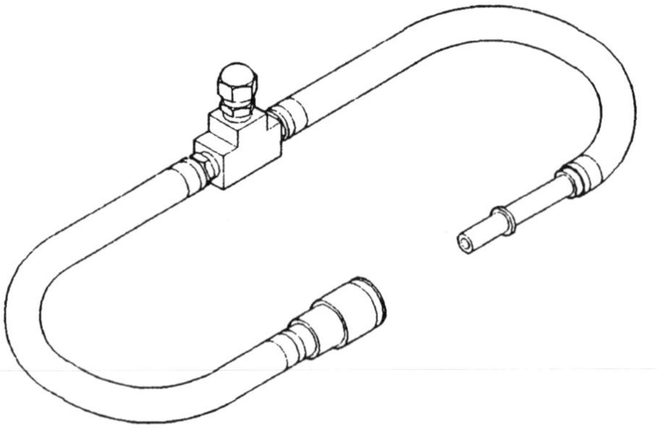

Adapters, Fuel Pressure Test—6541, 6539, 6631 or 6923

O2S (Oxygen Sensor) Remover/Installer—C-4907

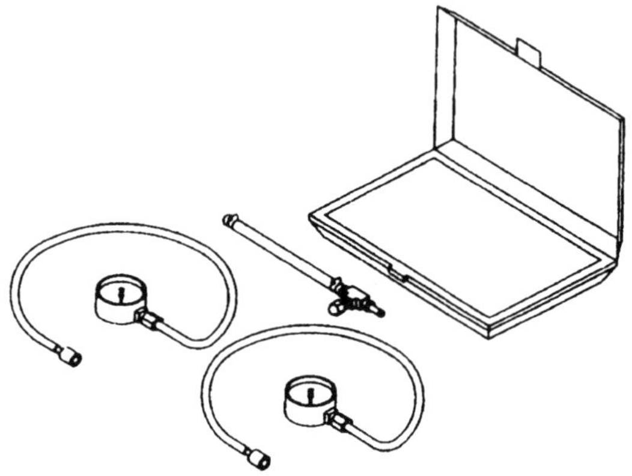

Test Kit, Fuel Pressure—5069

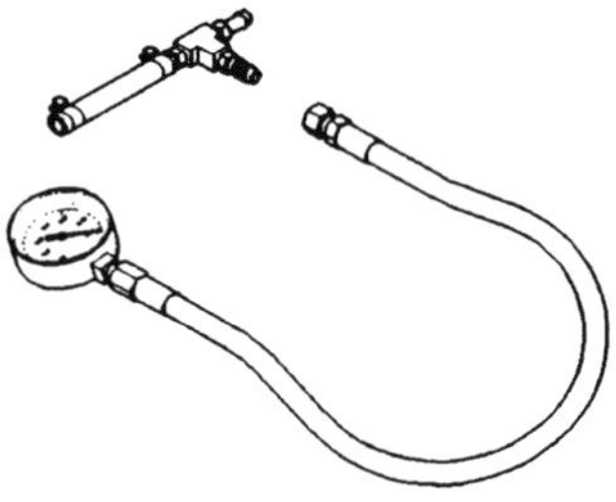

Test Kit, Fuel Pressure—C-4799-B

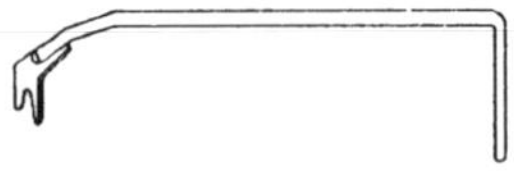

Fuel Line Removal Tool—6782

1997 Wrangler
Publication No. 81-370-7148
TSB 26-10-96 Oct. 1996

STEERING

CONTENTS

POWER STEERING

INDEX

GENERAL INFORMATION

STEERING SYSTEM

The vehicle uses manual steering or optional power steering.

The power steering system has a hydraulic pump. The pump is a constant flow rate and displacement, vane-type pump. The pump on the 4.0L engine has a reservoir mounted to it (Fig. 1). The 2.5L engine has a separate pump reservoir mounted to the fan shroud (Fig. 2).

The steering gear used is a recirculating ball type gear. The gear acts as a rolling thread between the worm shaft and rack piston. The worm shaft is supported by a thrust bearing at the lower end and a bearing assembly at the upper end. When the worm shaft is turned the rack piston moves. The rack piston teeth mesh with the pitman shaft. Turning the worm shaft turns the pitman shaft, which turns the steering linkage. This gear is used on all models.

The power steering system consists of:
- Hydraulic pump
- Recirculating ball steering gear
- Steering column
- Steering linkage

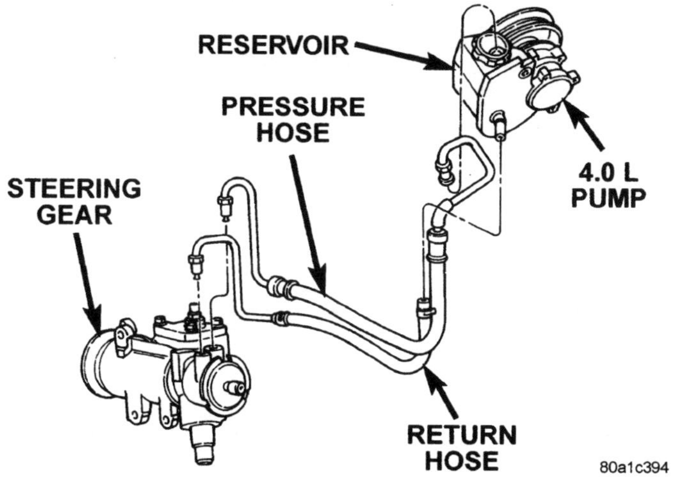

Fig. 1 Power Steering Gear & Pump—4.0L

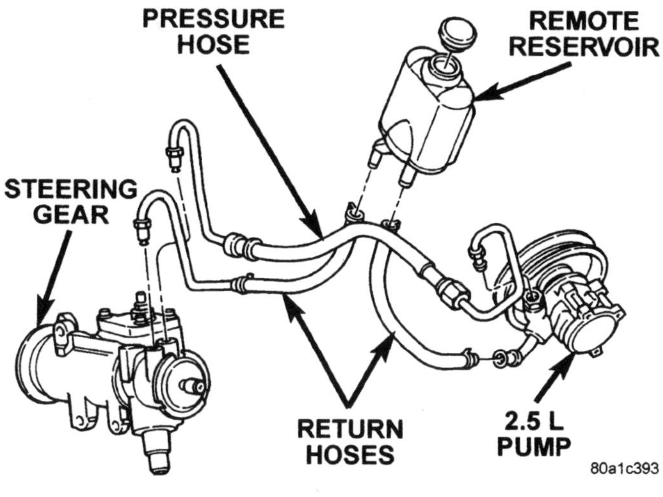

Fig. 2 Power Steering Gear & Pump—2.5L

DIAGNOSIS AND TESTING

POWER STEERING SYSTEM DIAGNOSIS CHARTS

STEERING NOISE

There is some noise in all power steering systems. One of the most common is a hissing sound evident at a standstill parking. Or when the steering wheel is at the end of it's travel. Hiss is a high frequency noise similar to that of a water tap being closed slowly. The noise is present in all valves that have a high velocity fluid passing through an orifice. There is no relationship between this noise and steering performance.

CONDITION	POSSIBLE CAUSES	CORRECTION
OBJECTIONAL HISS OR WHISTLE	1. Steering intermediate shaft to dash panel seal. 2. Noisy valve in power steering gear.	1. Check and repair seal at dash panel. 2. Replace steering gear.
RATTLE OR CLUNK	1. Gear mounting bolts loose. 2. Loose or damaged suspension components. 3. Loose or damaged steering linkage. 4. Internal gear noise. 5. Pressure hose in contact with other components.	1. Tighten bolts to specification. 2. Inspect and repair suspension. 3. Inspect and repair steering linkage. 4. Replace gear. 5. Reposition hose.
CHIRP OR SQUEAL	1. Loose belt.	1. Adjust or replace.
WHINE OR GROWL	1. Low fluid level. 2. Pressure hose in contact with other components. 3. Internal pump noise.	1. Fill to proper level. 2. Reposition hose. 3. Replace pump.
SUCKING AIR SOUND	1. Loose return line clamp. 2. O-ring missing or damaged on hose fitting. 3. Low fluid level. 4. Air leak between pump and reservoir.	1. Replace clamp. 2. Replace o-ring. 3. Fill to proper level. 4. Repair as necessary.
SCRUBBING OR KNOCKING	1. Wrong tire size. 2. Wrong gear.	1. Verify tire size. 2. Verify gear.

BINDING AND STICKING

CONDITION	POSSIBLE CAUSE	CORRECTION
DIFFICULT TO TURN WHEEL STICKS OR BINDS	1. Low fluid level. 2. Tire pressure. 3. Steering components . 4. Loose belt. 5. Low pump pressure. 6. Column shaft coupler binding. 7. Steering gear worn or out of adjustment.	1. Fill to proper level. 2. Adjust tire pressure. 3. Inspect and lube. 4. Adjust or replace. 5. Pressure test and replace if necessary. 6. Replace coupler. 7. Repair or replace gear.

DIAGNOSIS AND TESTING (Continued)

INSUFFICIENT ASSIST OR POOR RETURN TO CENTER

CONDITION	POSSIBLE CAUSE	CORRECTION
HARD TURNING OR MOMENTARY INCREASE IN TURNING EFFORT	1. Tire pressure. 2. Low fluid level. 3. Loose belt. 4. Lack of lubrication. 5. Low pump pressure. 6. Internal gear leak.	1. Adjust tire pressure. 2. Fill to proper level. 3. Adjust or replace. 4. Inspect and lubricate steering and suspension compnents. 5. Pressure test and repair as necessary. 6. Pressure and flow test, and repair as necessary.
STEERING WHEEL DOES NOT WANT TO RETURN TO CENTER POSITION	1. Tire pressure. 2. Wheel alignment. 3. Lack of lubrication. 4. High friction in steering gear.	1. Adjust tire pressure. 2. Align front end. 3. Inspect and lubricate steering and suspension compnents. 4. Test and adjust as necessary.

LOOSE STEERING AND VEHICLE LEAD

CONDITION	POSSIBLE CAUSE	CORRECTION
EXCESSIVE PLAY IN STEERING WHEEL	1. Worn or loose suspension or steering components. 2. Worn or loose wheel bearings. 3. Steering gear mounting. 4. Gear out of adjustment. 5. Worn or loose steering coupler.	1. Inspect and repair as necessary. 2. Inspect and repair or adjust bearings. 3. Tighten gear mounting bolts to specification. 4. Adjust gear to specification. 5. Inspect and replace as necessary.
VEHICLE PULLS OR LEADS TO ONE SIDE.	1. Tire Pressure. 2. Radial tire lead. 3. Brakes dragging. 4. Wheel alignment.	1. Adjust tire pressure. 2. Rotate tires. 3. Repair as necessary. 4. Align front end.

POWER STEERING PUMP

INDEX

DESCRIPTION AND OPERATION

POWER STEERING PUMP

Hydraulic pressure is provided for operation of the power steering gear by a belt driven power steering pump. The power steering pump is a constant flow rate and displacement, vane-type pump. The internal parts in the housing operate submerged in fluid. The flow control orifice is part of the high pressure line fitting. The pressure relief valve inside the flow control valve limits the pump pressure. The reservoir is attached to the pump body with spring clips on the 4.0 L engine. On the 2.5 L engine the reservoir is separate from the pump. It is mounted to the fan shroud.

The power steering pump is connected to the steering gear by the pressure and return hoses. The pump shaft has a pressed-on drive pulley that is belt driven by the crankshaft pulley (Fig. 1).

NOTE: Power steering pumps have different pressure rates and are not interchangeable with other pumps.

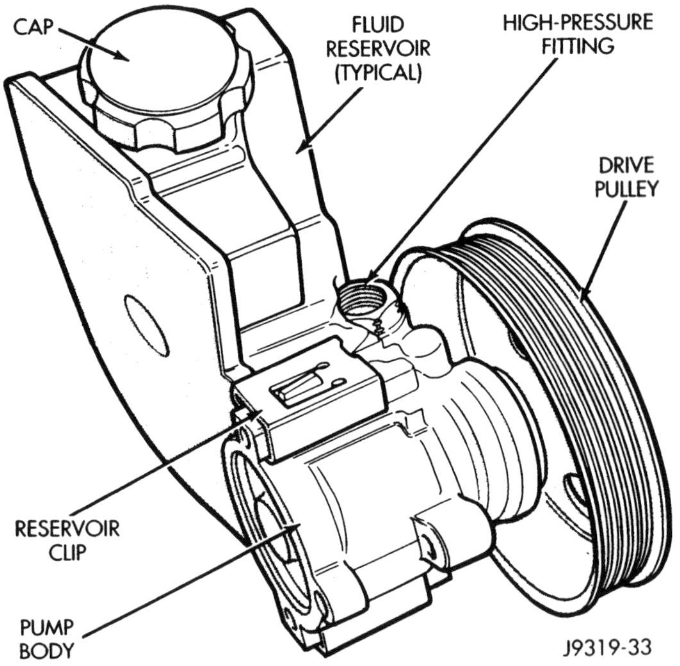

Fig. 1 Typical TC Series Pump With Integral Reservoir

DIAGNOSIS AND TESTING

POWER STEERING PUMP PRESSURE TEST

The following procedure is used to test the operation of the power steering system on the vehicle. This test will provide the flow rate of the power steering pump along with the maximum relief pressure. Perform test any time a power steering system problem is present. This test will determine if the power steering pump or power steering gear is not functioning properly. The following pressure and flow test is performed using Pressure/Flow tester, Special Tool 6815 (Fig. 2).

PUMP PRESSURE TEST

(1) Check belt tension and adjust as necessary.

(2) Disconnect high pressure hose at gear or pump. Use a container for dripping fluid.

(3) Connect Pressure Gauge/Flow Meter Tool 6815 between the pump pressure fitting and pressure hose using adapters from Adapter Kit 6893.

(4) Open the test valve completely.

(5) Start engine and let idle long enough to circulate power steering fluid through flow/pressure test

DIAGNOSIS AND TESTING (Continued)

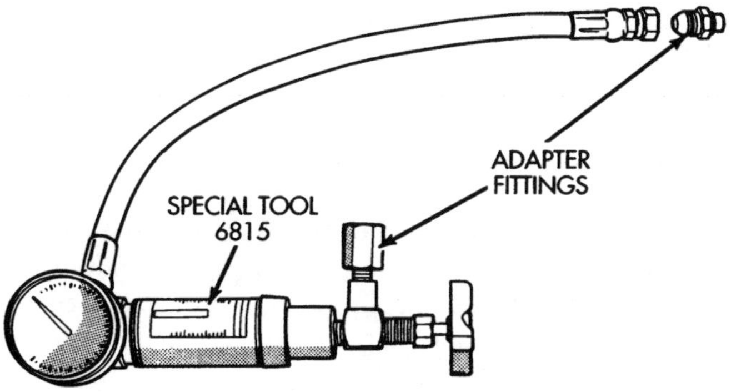

Fig. 2 Pressure Test Gauge

gauge and to get air out of the fluid. Then shut off engine.

(6) Check fluid level, add fluid as necessary. Start engine again and let idle.

(7) Gauge should read below 862 kPa (125 psi), if above, inspect the hoses for restrictions and repair as necessary. The initial pressure reading should be in the range of 345-552 kPa (50-80 psi).

CAUTION: The following test procedure involves testing maximum pump pressure output and flow control valve operation. Do not leave valve closed for more than three seconds as the pump could be damaged.

(8) Close valve fully three times for three seconds and record highest pressure indicated each time. **All three readings must be above specifications and within 345 kPa (50 psi) of each other.**

- Pressures above specifications but not within 345 kPa (50 psi) of each other, replace pump.
- Pressures within 345 kPa (50 psi) of each other but below specifications, replace pump.

NOTE: Refer to pump relief pressure chart.

CAUTION: Do not force the pump to operate against the stops for more than 2 to 4 seconds at a time because, pump damage will result.

(9) Open the test valve, turn steering wheel extreme left and right positions against the stops. Record the highest indicated pressure at each position. Compare readings to specifications. If highest output pressures are not within 50 psi. against either stop, the gear is leaking internally and must be repaired.

ENGINE	RELIEF PRESSURE ± 50
2.5L	9653 kPa (1400 psi)
4.0L	9653 kPa (1400 psi)

PUMP LEAKAGE DIAGNOSIS

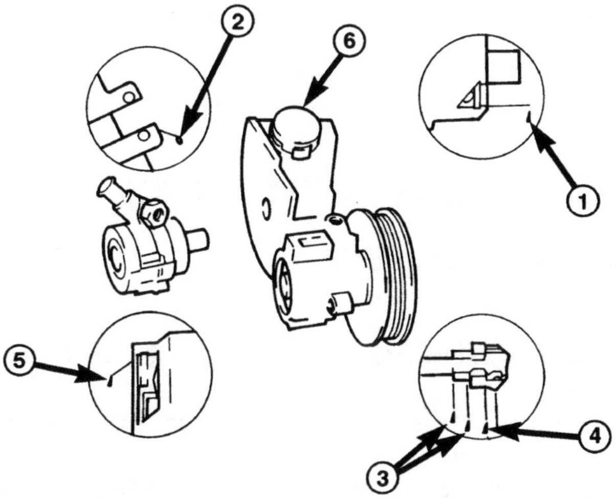

1. BUSHING (BEARING) WORN, SEAL WORN. REPLACE PUMP.
2. REPLACE RESERVOIR O-RING SEAL.
3. TORQUE HOSE FITTING NUT TO SPECIFICATIONS. IF LEAKAGE PERSISTS, REPLACE O-RING SEAL.
4. TORQUE FITTING TO SPECIFICATIONS. IF LEAKAGE PERSISTS, REPLACE O-RING SEAL.
5. REPLACE PUMP.
6. CHECK OIL LEVEL: IF LEAKAGE PERSISTS WITH THE LEVEL CORRECT AND CAP TIGHT, REPLACE THE CAP.

80a1c3c3

SERVICE PROCEDURES

POWER STEERING PUMP—INITIAL OPERATION

WARNING: THE FLUID LEVEL SHOULD BE CHECKED WITH ENGINE OFF TO PREVENT INJURY FROM MOVING COMPONENTS.

CAUTION: Use MOPAR Power Steering Fluid or equivalent. Do not use automatic transmission fluid and do not overfill.

Wipe filler cap clean, then check the fluid level. The dipstick should indicate **COLD** when the fluid is at normal temperature.

(1) Fill the pump fluid reservoir to the proper level and let the fluid settle for at least two (2) minutes.

(2) Start the engine and let run for a few seconds then turn engine off.

(3) Add fluid if necessary. Repeat the above procedure until the fluid level remains constant after running the engine.

(4) Raise the front wheels off the ground.

(5) Slowly turn the steering wheel right and left, lightly contacting the wheel stops at least 20 times.

SERVICE PROCEDURES (Continued)

(6) Check the fluid level add if necessary.

(7) Lower the vehicle, start the engine and turn the steering wheel slowly from lock to lock.

(8) Stop the engine and check the fluid level and refill as required.

(9) If the fluid is extremely foamy or milky looking, allow the vehicle to stand a few minutes and repeat the procedure.

CAUTION: Do not run a vehicle with foamy fluid for an extended period. This may cause pump damage.

REMOVAL AND INSTALLATION

POWER STEERING PUMP

REMOVAL

(1) Remove serpentine drive belt, refer to Group 7 Cooling.

(2) Remove pressure and return hoses from pump, and drain pump.

(3) Remove 3 pump mounting bolts through pulley access holes.

(4) Loosen the 3 pump bracket bolts (Fig. 3).

(5) Tilt pump downward and remove from engine.

(6) Remove pulley from pump.

INSTALLATION

(1) Install pulley on pump.

(2) Install pump on engine.

(3) Tighten pump bracket bolts to 47 N·m (35 ft. lbs.).

(4) Install 3 pump mounting bolts and tighten to 27 N·m (20 ft. lbs.).

(5) Install the pressure and return hoses on pump.

(6) Install drive belt, refer to Group 7 Cooling.

(7) Add power steering fluid. Refer to Power Steering Pump Initial Operation in this section.

PUMP REMOTE RESERVOIR–2.5L

REMOVAL

(1) Remove the pump return hoses from the reservoir and drain the reservoir.

(2) Remove the reservoir mounting bolt (Fig. 4).

(3) Slide the reservoir up out of the fan shroud mount.

INSTALLATION

(1) Slide reservoir down onto the fan shroud mount until it clicks in place.

(2) Install the reservoir mounting bolt.

(3) Install the pump return hoses.

(4) Fill reservoir to proper level. Refer to Power Steering Pump Initial Operation in this section.

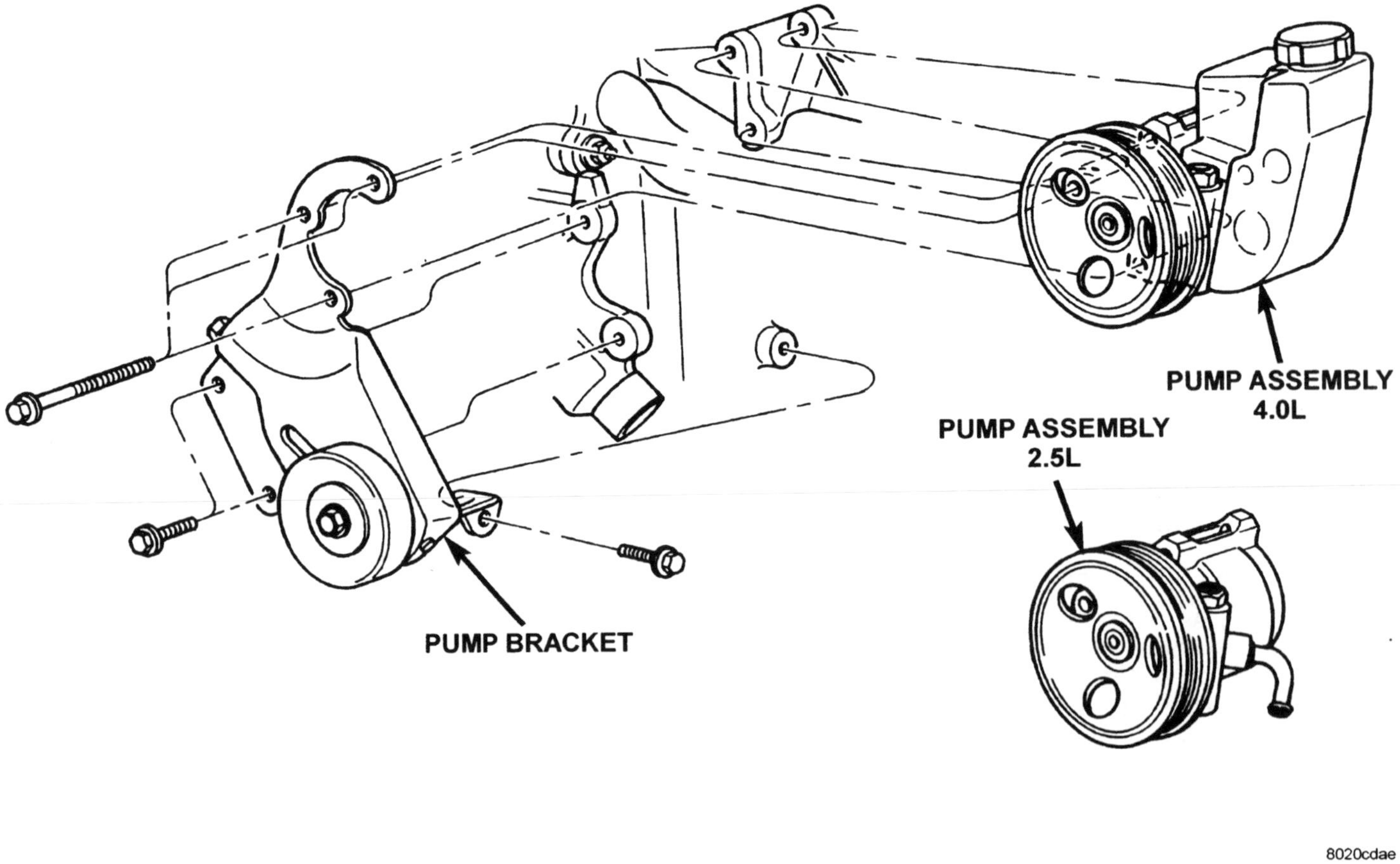

Fig. 3 Pump Mounting

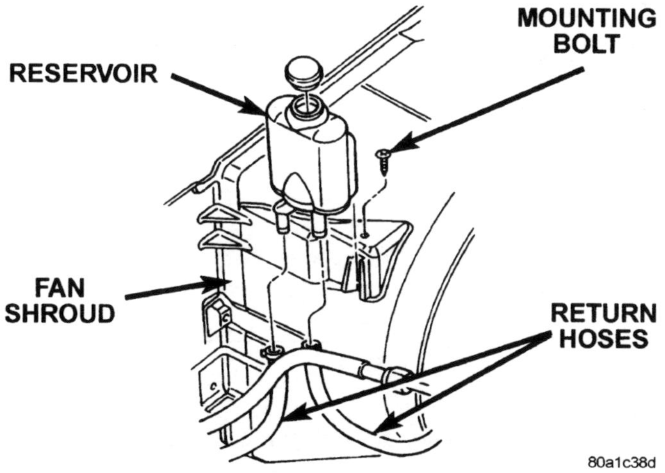

Fig. 4 Pump Reservoir–2.5L

DISASSEMBLY AND ASSEMBLY

TC-SERIES PUMP PULLEY

DISASSEMBLY

(1) Remove pump assembly.

(2) Remove pulley from pump with Puller C-4333 (Fig. 5).

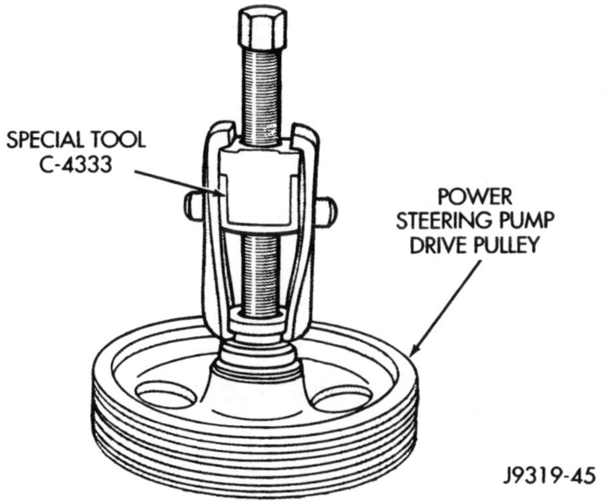

Fig. 5 Pulley Removal

ASSEMBLY

(1) Replace pulley if bent, cracked, or loose.

(2) Install pulley on pump with Installer C-4063-B (Fig. 6) flush with the end of the shaft. Ensure the tool and pulley remain aligned with the pump shaft.

(3) Install pump assembly.

(4) With Serpentine Belts; Run engine until warm (5 min.) and note any belt chirp. If chirp exists, move pulley outward approximately 0.5 mm (0.020 in.). If noise increases, press on 1.0 mm (0.040 in.). **Be careful that pulley does not contact mounting bolts.**

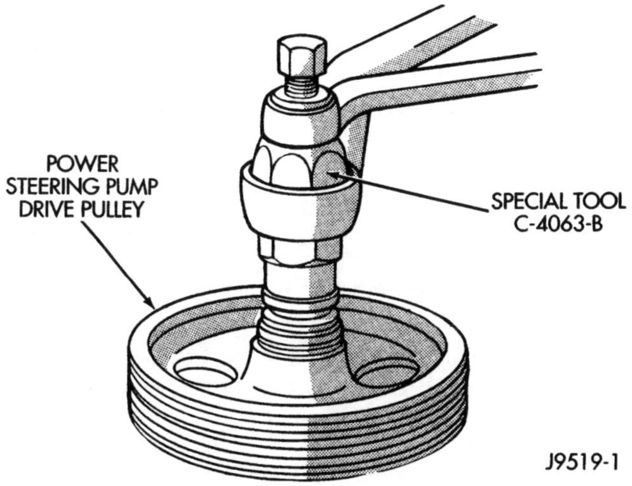

Fig. 6 Pulley Installation

TC-SERIES PUMP RESERVOIR

DISASSEMBLY

(1) Remove power steering pump.

(2) Clean exterior of pump.

(3) Clamp the pump body in a soft jaw vice.

(4) Pry up tab and slide the retaining clips off (Fig. 7).

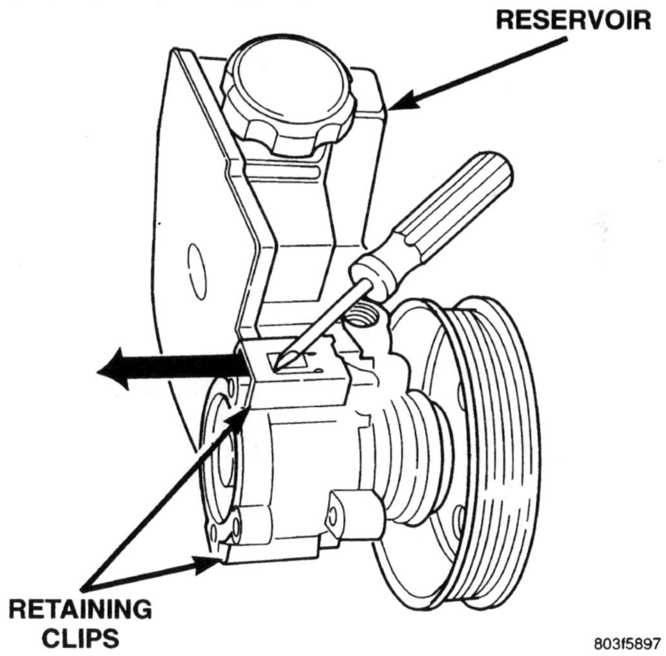

Fig. 7 Pump Reservoir Clips

(5) Remove fluid reservoir from pump body. Remove and discard O-ring seal.

ASSEMBLY

(1) Lubricate new O-ring Seal with Mopar Power Steering Fluid or equivalent.

(2) Install O-ring seal in housing.

DISASSEMBLY AND ASSEMBLY (Continued)

(3) Install reservoir onto housing.

(4) Slide and tap in reservoir retainer clips until tab locks to housing.

(5) Install power steering pump. Refer to Pump Replacement in this section.

FLOW CONTROL VALVE

DISASSEMBLY

(1) Clean area around fitting to prevent dirt from entering pump. Remove pressure hose from pump fitting.

(2) Remove fitting from pump housing (Fig. 8). **Prevent flow control valve and spring from sliding out of housing bore.**

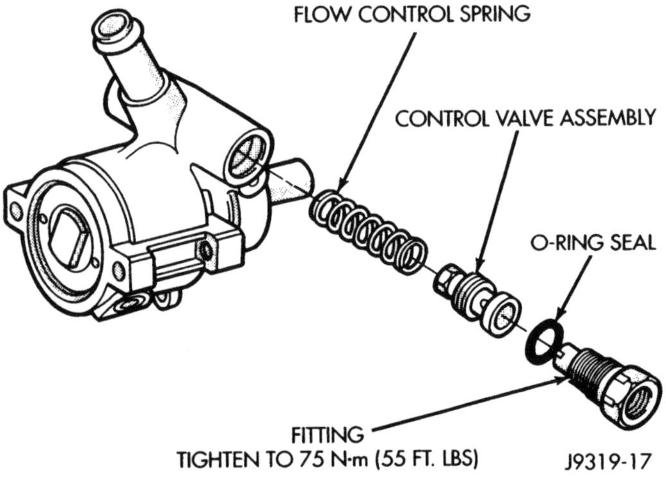

Fig. 8 Flow Control Valve

(3) Remove and discard O-ring seal.

ASSEMBLY

(1) Install spring and flow control valve into pump housing bore. **Be sure the hex nut end of the valve is facing in toward pump.**

(2) Install O-ring seal onto fitting.

(3) Install flow control valve in pump housing and tighten to 75 N·m (55 ft. lbs.).

(4) Install pressure hose to valve.

SPECIFICATIONS

TORQUE CHART

DESCRIPTION	TORQUE
Power Steering Pump	
Bracket to Pump	28 N·m (21 ft. lbs.)
Bracket to Engine	47 N·m (35 ft. lbs.)
Flow Control Valve	75 N·m (55 ft. lbs.)
Pressure Line	28 N·m (21 ft. lbs.)

SPECIAL TOOLS

POWER STEERING PUMP

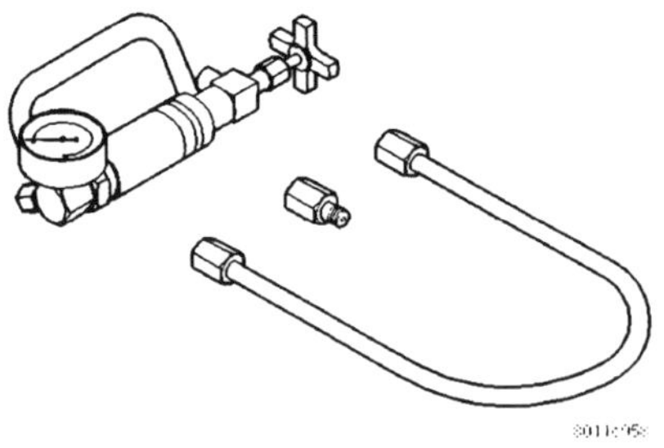

Analyzer Set, Power Steering Flow/Pressure 6815

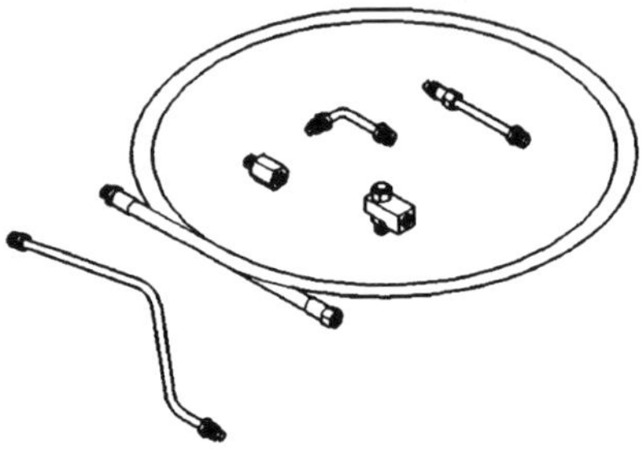

Adapters, Power Steering Flow/Pressure Tester 6893

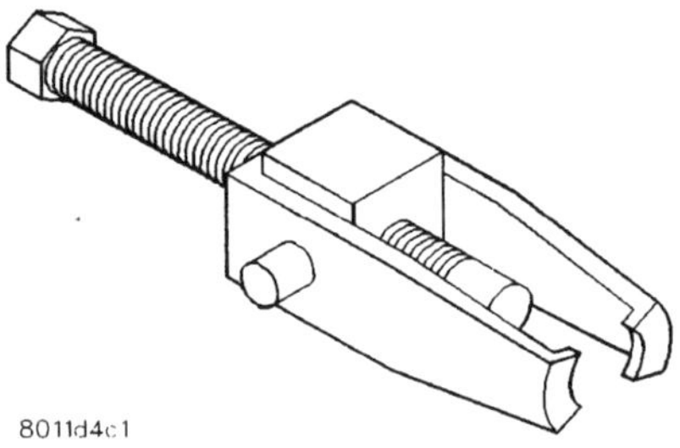

Puller C-4333

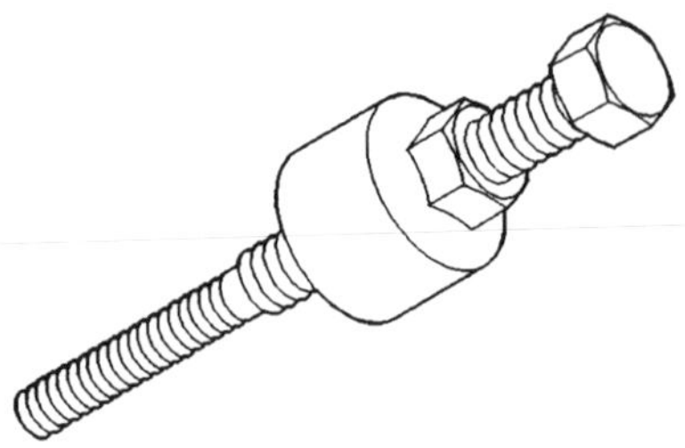

Installer, Power Steering Pulley C-4063–B

POWER STEERING GEAR

INDEX

DESCRIPTION AND OPERATION

POWER STEERING GEAR

The power steering gear is a recirculating ball type gear (Fig. 1). The gear acts as a rolling thread between the worm shaft and rack piston. The worm shaft is supported by a thrust bearing at the lower end and a bearing assembly at the upper end. When the worm shaft is turned the rack piston moves. The rack piston teeth mesh with the pitman shaft. Turning the worm shaft turns the pitman shaft, which turns the steering linkage.

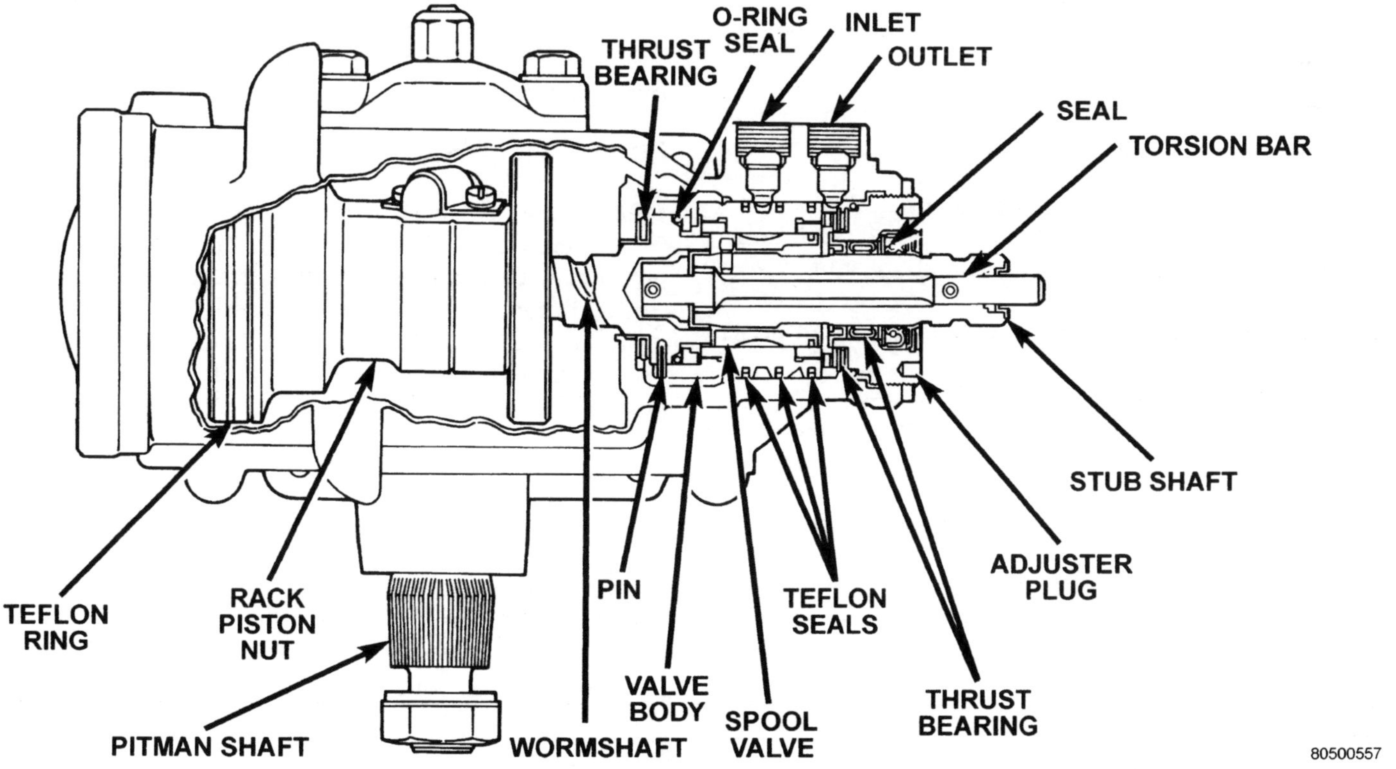

Fig. 1 Power Steering Gear

DIAGNOSIS AND TESTING

POWER STEERING GEAR LEAKAGE DIAGNOSIS

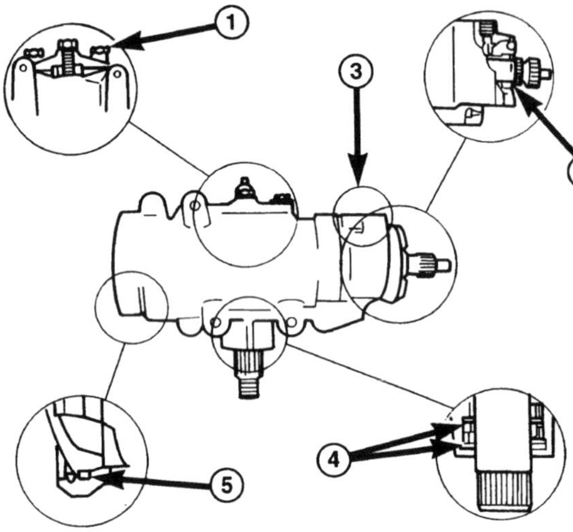

1. SIDE COVER LEAK - TORQUE SIDE COVER BOLTS TO SPECIFICATION. REPLACE THE SIDE COVER SEAL IF THE LEAKAGE PERSISTS.
2. ADJUSTER PLUG SEAL - REPLACE THE ADJUSTER PLUG SEALS.
3. PRESSURE LINE FITTING - TORQUE THE HOSE FITTING NUT TO SPECIFICATIONS. IF LEAKAGE PERSISTS, REPLACE THE SEAL.
4. PITMAN SHAFT SEALS - REPLACE THE SEALS.
5. TOP COVER SEAL - REPLACE THE SEAL.

80a1c3c2

REMOVAL AND INSTALLATION

PITMAN SHAFT SEALS–IN VEHICLE

REMOVAL

CAUTION: Use care not to score the housing bore when prying out seals and washers.

(1) Remove pitman arm from gear.

(2) Clean exposed end of pitman shaft and housing. Use a wire brush to clean the shaft splines.

(3) Remove dust seal.

(4) Remove retaining ring with snap ring pliers (Fig. 2).

(5) Remove backup washer with screwdriver.

(6) Start the engine and turn steering wheel fully to the LEFT. Hydraulic pressure will force the oil seal out.

(7) Turn off engine and remove oil seal with screwdriver.

(8) Inspect the housing for burrs and remove if necessary. Inspect the pitman shaft seal surface for roughness and pitting. If shaft is damaged it will have to be replaced.

INSTALLATION

(1) Coat the seals and washers with grease.

(2) Install oil seal with a suitable size deep socket.

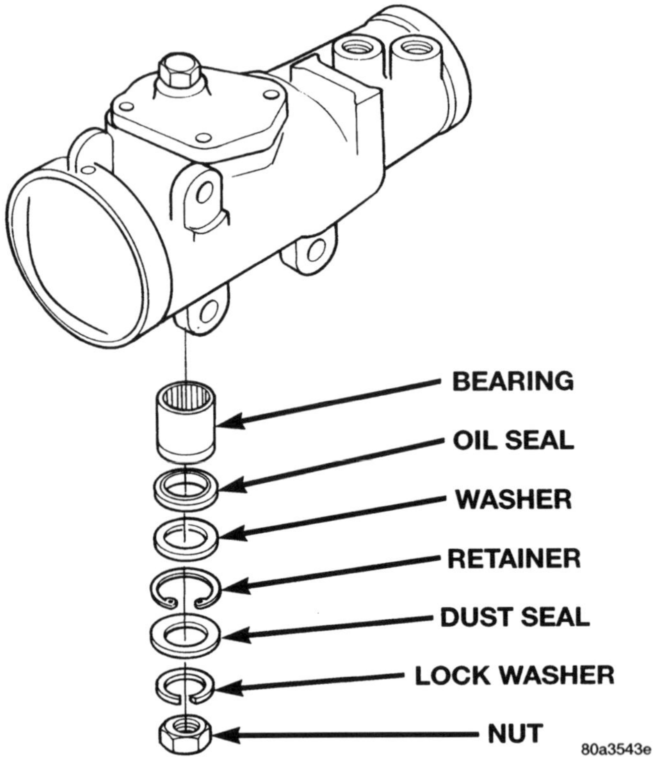

Fig. 2 Pitman Shaft Seal

(3) Install backup washer.

(4) Install the retainer ring with snap ring pliers.

(5) Install dust seal with a suitable size deep socket.

(6) Center the steering gear and install pitman arm.

(7) Add power steering fluid, refer to Power Steering Initial Operation.

POWER STEERING GEAR

REMOVAL

(1) Place the front wheels in the straight ahead position with the steering wheel centered.

(2) Disconnect and cap the fluid hoses/tubes from power steering pump.

(3) Remove the column coupler shaft from the gear.

(4) Remove pitman arm from gear.

(5) Remove the steering gear retaining bolts and remove the gear (Fig. 3).

(6) Remove power steering hoses/tubes from steering gear.

INSTALLATION

(1) Install power steering hoses/tubes to steering gear and tighten to 28 N·m (21 ft. lbs.).

(2) Install steering gear on the frame rail and tighten bolts to 95 N·m (70 ft. lbs.)

REMOVAL AND INSTALLATION (Continued)

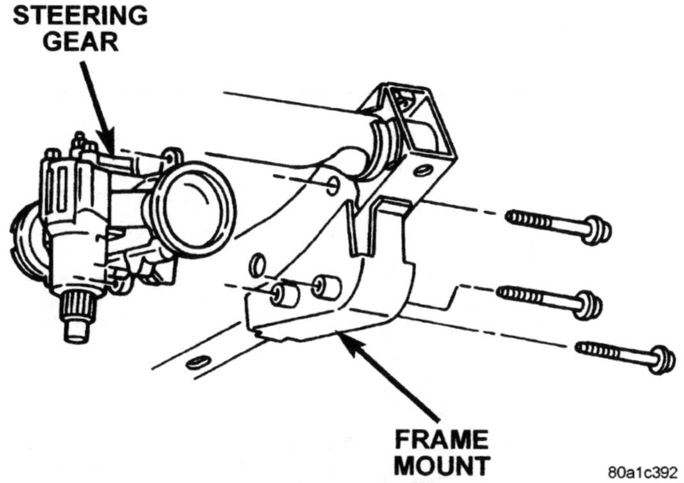

Fig. 3 Steering Gear Mounting

(3) Align the column coupler shaft to steering gear and tighten coupler bolt.

(4) Align and install the pitman arm and tighten nut to 251 N·m (185 ft. lbs.).

(5) Install power steering hoses/tubes to power steering pump.

(6) Fill power steering system to proper level, refer to Steering Pump Initial Operation.

DISASSEMBLY AND ASSEMBLY

PITMAN SHAFT

Steering gear must be removed from the vehicle for this procedure.

DISASSEMBLY

(1) Clean exposed end of pitman shaft and housing with a wire brush.

(2) Remove preload adjuster nut.

(3) Rotate stub shaft with socket to center gear.

(4) Remove side cover bolts and remove side cover, gasket and pitman shaft as an assembly.

(5) Remove pitman shaft from the side cover (Fig. 4).

ASSEMBLY

(1) Install pitman shaft to side cover by screwing shaft in until it fully seats to side cover.

(2) Install preload adjuster nut. **Do not tighten nut until after pitman shaft adjustment has been made.**

(3) Install gasket to side cover and bend tabs around edges of side cover.

(4) Install pitman shaft assembly and side cover to housing.

(5) Install side cover bolts and tighten to 60 N·m (44 ft. lbs.).

(6) Adjust pitman shaft, refer to Over-Center Adjustment.

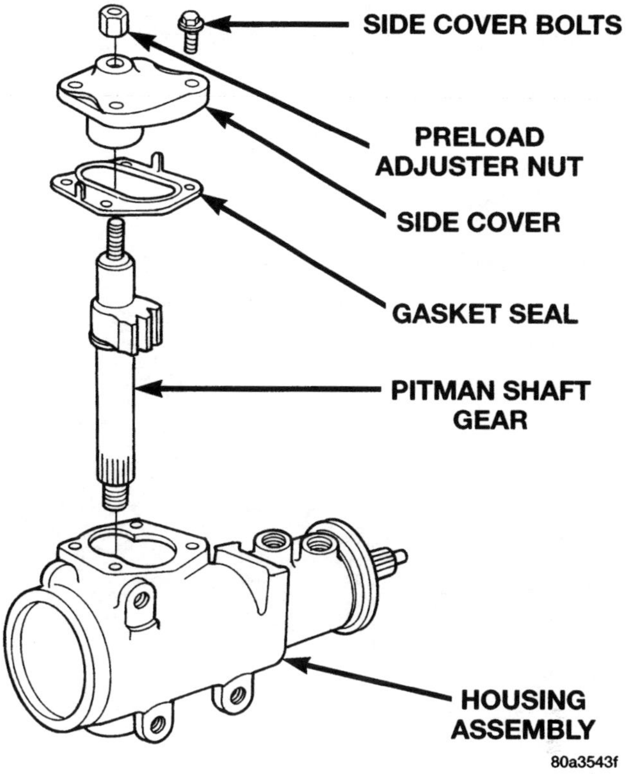

Fig. 4 Side Cover and Pitman Shaft

HOUSING END PLUG

Steering gear must be removed from the vehicle for this procedure.

DISASSEMBLY

(1) Rotate retaining ring until one end is under the hole in the housing. Unseat and force ring from groove (Fig. 5).

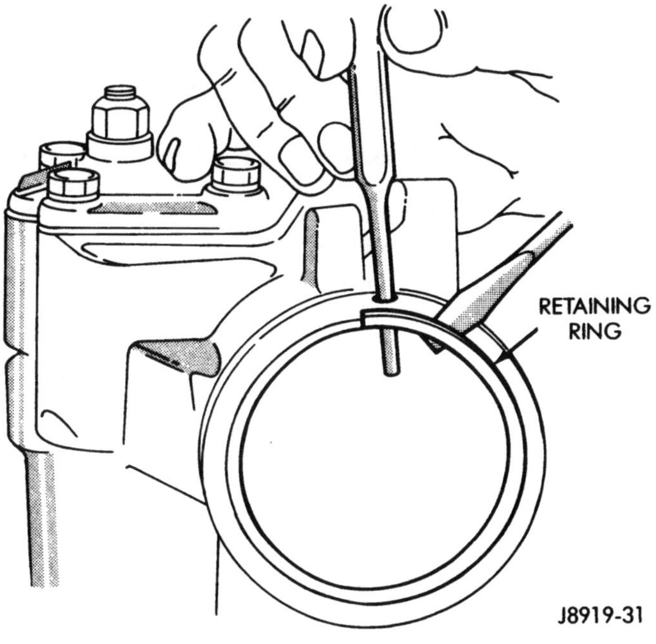

Fig. 5 End Plug Retaining Ring

DISASSEMBLY AND ASSEMBLY (Continued)

(2) Rotate stub shaft slowly COUNTER-CLOCKWISE to remove end plug out from housing.

CAUTION: Do not turn stub shaft any further than necessary. The recirculating balls will drop out of the rack piston circuit and fall inside the rack piston chamber.

(3) Remove O-ring seal (Fig. 6).

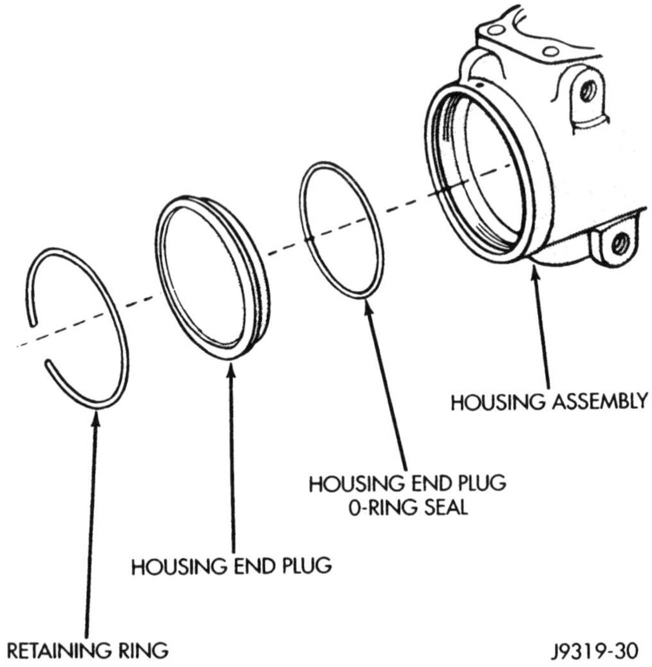

Fig. 6 End Plug Components

ASSEMBLY

(1) Lubricate O-ring seal with power steering fluid.
(2) Install O-ring into housing.
(3) Install plug, tap lightly with a plastic mallet to seat it.
(4) Install retaining ring with open end 25 mm (1 inch) from access hole (Fig. 7).
(5) Adjust pitman arm shaft, refer to Over-Center Adjustment.

ADJUSTER PLUG ASSEMBLY

Steering gear must be removed from the vehicle for this procedure.

DISASSEMBLY

(1) Remove adjuster plug lock nut from housing.
(2) Remove adjuster plug from housing with Spanner Wrench C-4381 (Fig. 8).
(3) Remove thrust washer bearing retainer from adjuster plug with screwdriver (Fig. 9).
(4) Remove bearing spacer, races and thrust bearing (Fig. 10).
(5) Remove O-ring seal and retaining snap ring.

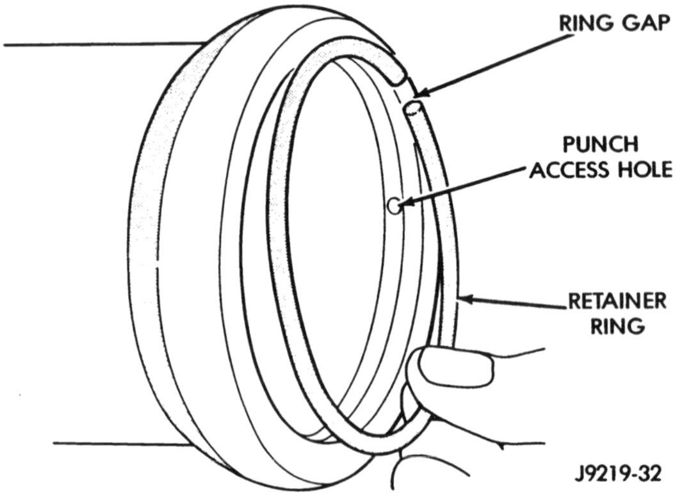

Fig. 7 Installing The Retaining Ring

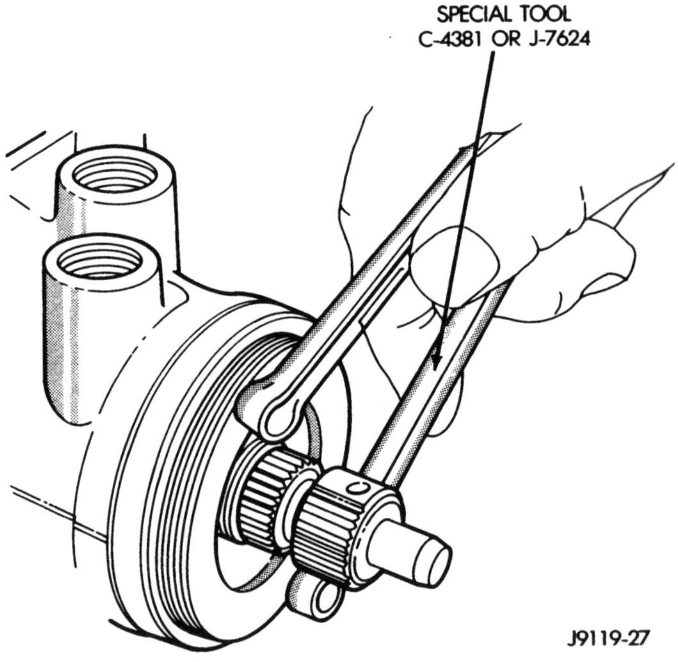

Fig. 8 Adjustment Plug

(6) Remove needle bearing, dust seal and oil seal with remover/installer C-4177 and handle C-4171 (Fig. 11).

ASSEMBLY

CAUTION: Needle bearing must be installed with identification on bearing facing tool to prevent damage to bearing.

(1) Install needle bearing into adjuster plug with remover/install C-4177 and handle C-4171.
(2) Apply white petroleum grease on oil seal. Install oil seal into adjuster plug with remover/installer C-4177 and handle C-4171.

DISASSEMBLY AND ASSEMBLY (Continued)

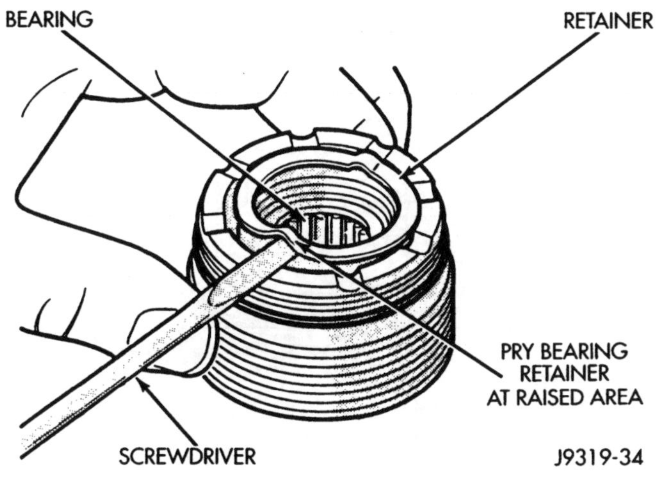

Fig. 9 Bearing Retainer

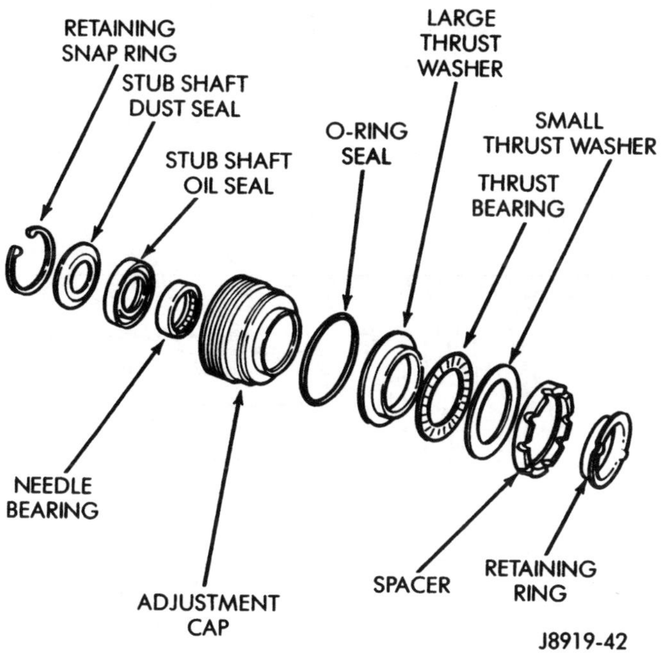

Fig. 10 Adjustment Plug Components

(3) Apply white petroleum grease to dust seal cavity and install dust seal into adjuster plug with remover/installer C-4177 and handle C-4171.

(4) Install retainer snap ring.

(5) Install O-ring seal to adjuster plug.

(6) Install large bearing race, thrust bearing, small bearing race and bearing spacer to adjuster plug.

(7) Install thrust washer bearing retainer to adjuster plug (Fig. 12).

CAUTION: When installing adjuster plug, care should be taken not to cut the seals.

(8) Install adjuster plug into housing with Spanner Wrench C-4381.

(9) Adjust bearing preload, refer to Thrust Bearing Preload Adjustment.

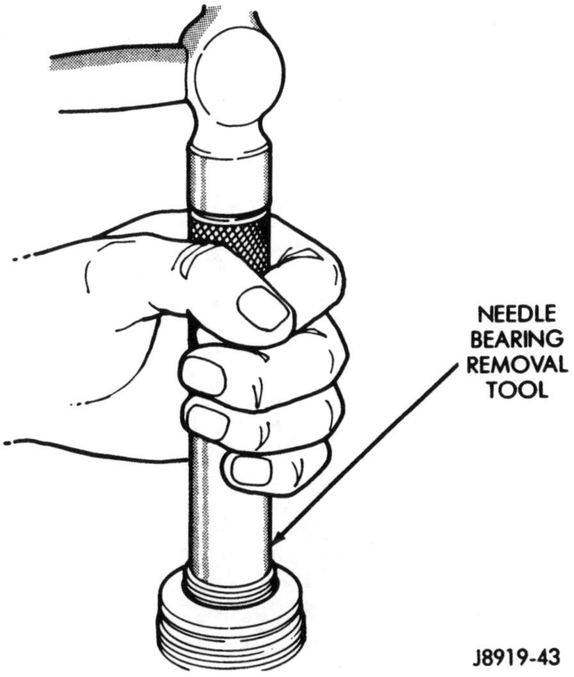

Fig. 11 Needle Bearing Removal

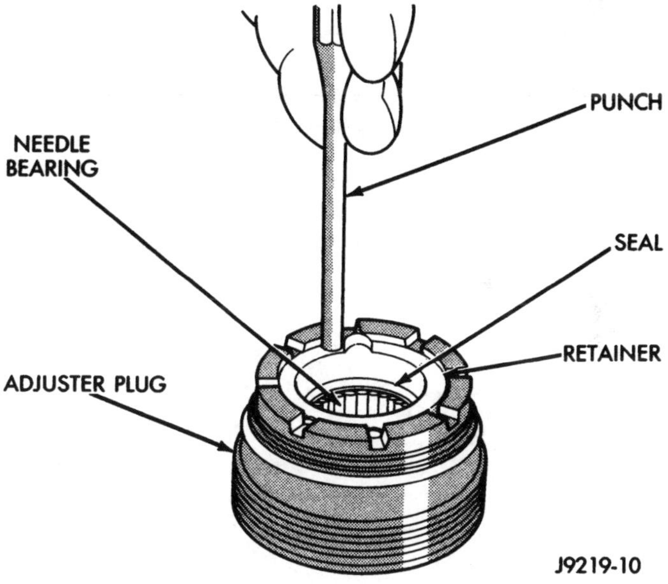

Fig. 12 Install Retainer

(10) Install adjuster plug lock nut, and using a punch (drift) in a notch, tighten securely (Fig. 13). **Hold adjuster plug to maintain alignment of the marks.**

(11) Adjust pitman shaft, refer to Over-Center Adjustment.

SPOOL VALVE

Steering gear must be removed from the vehicle for this procedure.

DISASSEMBLY AND ASSEMBLY (Continued)

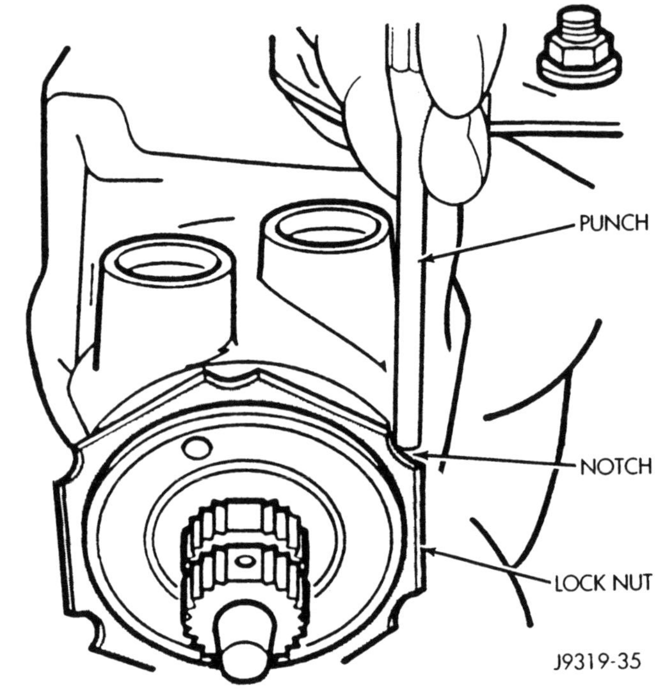

Fig. 13 Tighten Lock Nut

DISASSEMBLY

(1) Remove adjuster plug, refer to Adjuster Plug Assembly Replacement.

(2) Remove stub shaft and valve assembly (Fig. 14).

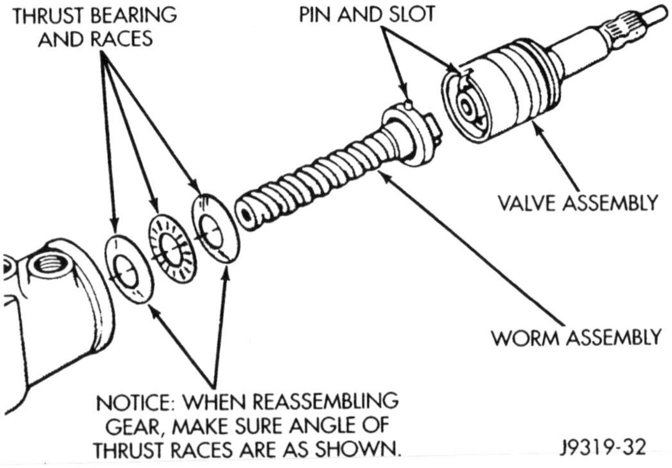

Fig. 14 Bearing, Worm and Valve Assembly

(3) Remove stub shaft from valve assembly by lightly tapping on a block of wood to loosen shaft cap. Then pull cap and valve body and disengage stub shaft pin from hole in valve body (Fig. 15).

(4) Remove valve spool by pulling and rotating from valve body (Fig. 16).

(5) Remove valve spool O-ring seal and valve body teflon rings and O-ring seals (Fig. 17).

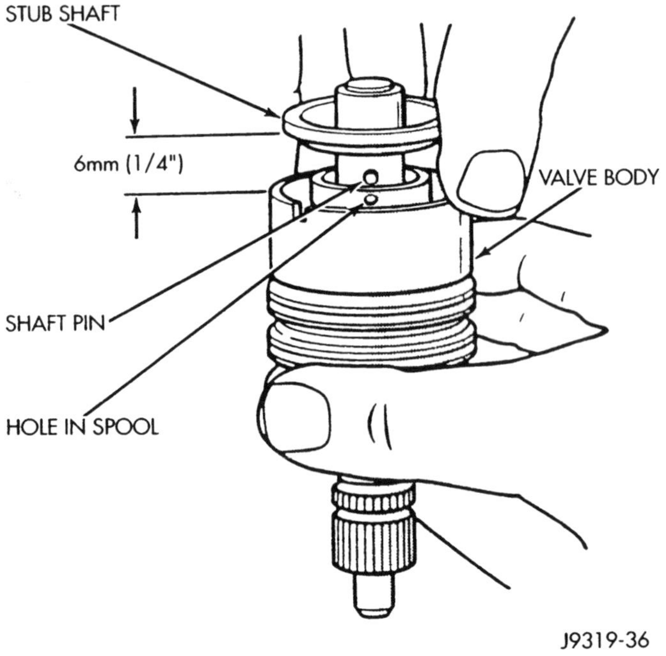

Fig. 15 Stub Shaft

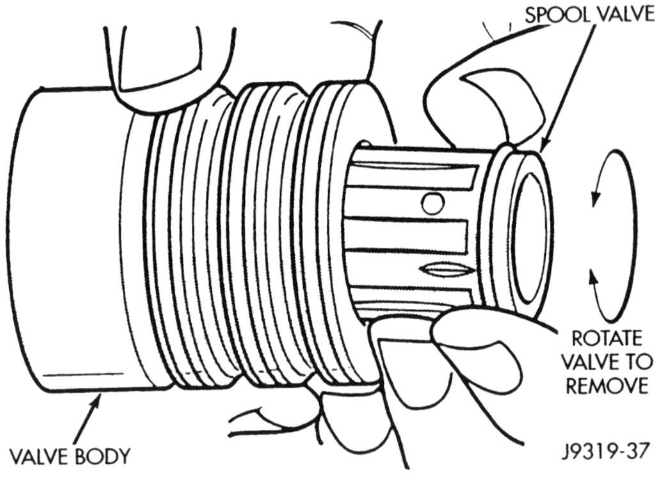

Fig. 16 Spool Valve

ASSEMBLY

(1) Install valve spool O-ring seal to valve spool.

(2) Lubricate valve spool and O-ring seal with power steering fluid.

(3) Install valve spool to valve body by pushing and rotating. Hole in valve spool for stub pin must be accessible from opposite end of valve body.

(4) Assemble stub shaft to valve spool, if necessary and insert pin (Fig. 18).

NOTE: Notch in stub shaft cap must fully engage valve body pin and seat against valve body shoulder.

(5) Install O-ring seals and teflon rings to valve body.

DISASSEMBLY AND ASSEMBLY (Continued)

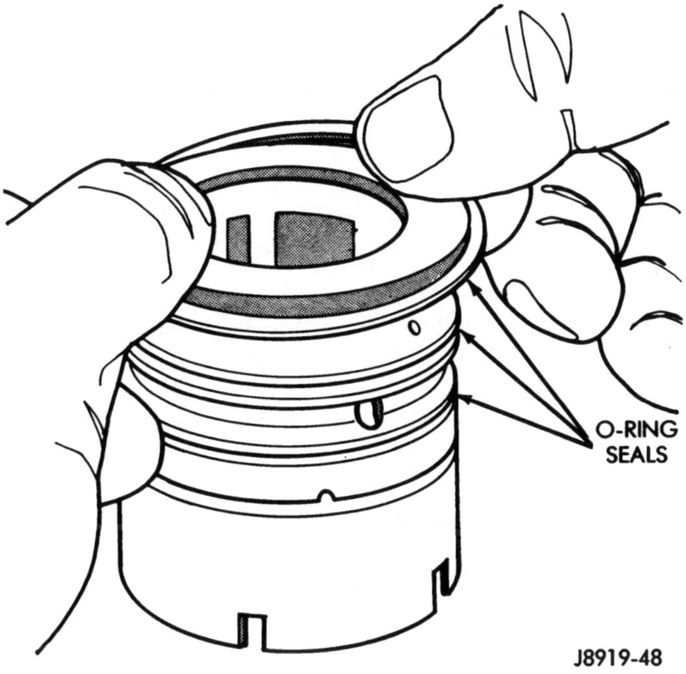

Fig. 17 Valve Seals

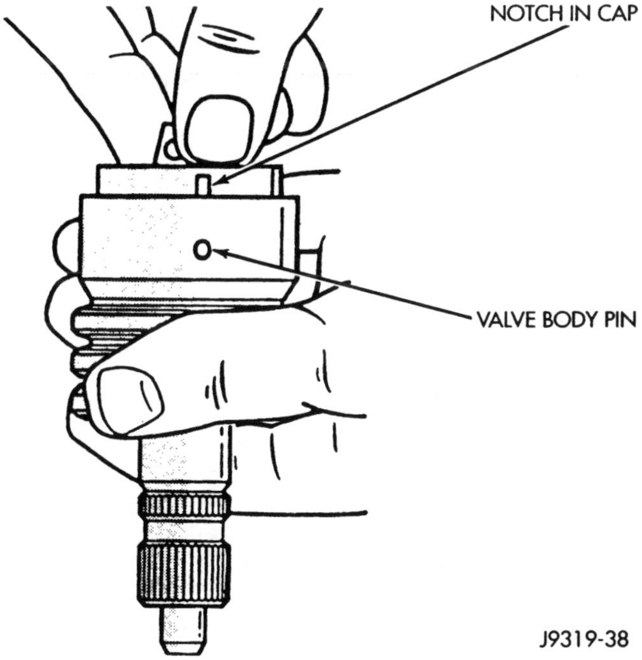

Fig. 18 Stub Shaft Installation

(6) Lubricate O-ring seals and teflon rings with power steering fluid.

(7) Install stub shaft and valve assembly to worm shaft. Line up worm shaft to slot in the valve assembly.

(8) Install adjuster plug.

(9) Adjust Thrust Bearing Preload Adjustment and Over-Center Adjustment.

RACK PISTON AND WORM SHAFT

Steering gear must be removed from the vehicle for this procedure.

DISASSEMBLY

(1) Remove pitman shaft and side cover.

(2) Remove housing end plug.

(3) Turn stub shaft COUNTERCLOCKWISE until the rack piston begins to come out of the housing.

(4) Remove rack piston plug (Fig. 19).

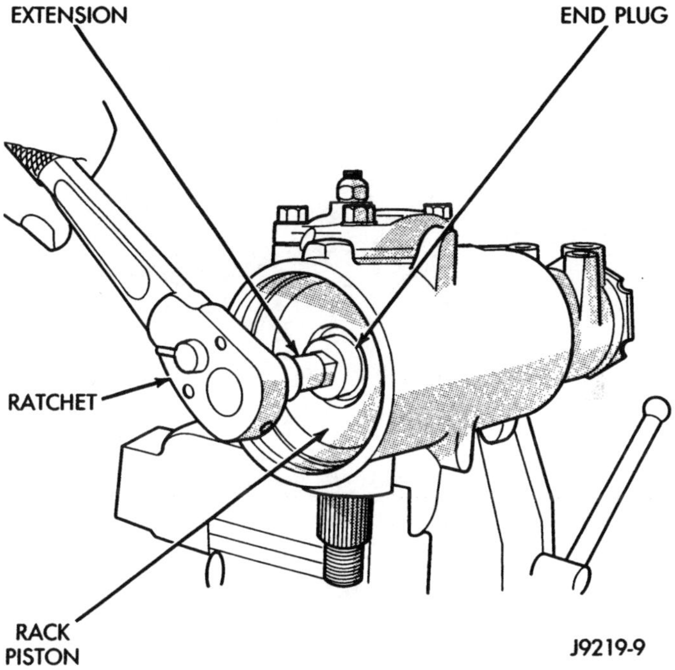

Fig. 19 Rack Piston End Plug

(5) Insert Arbor C-4175 into bore of rack piston (Fig. 20). Hold tool tightly against worm shaft while turning the stub shaft COUNTERCLOCKWISE.

(6) The rack piston will be forced onto the tool and hold the rack piston balls in place.

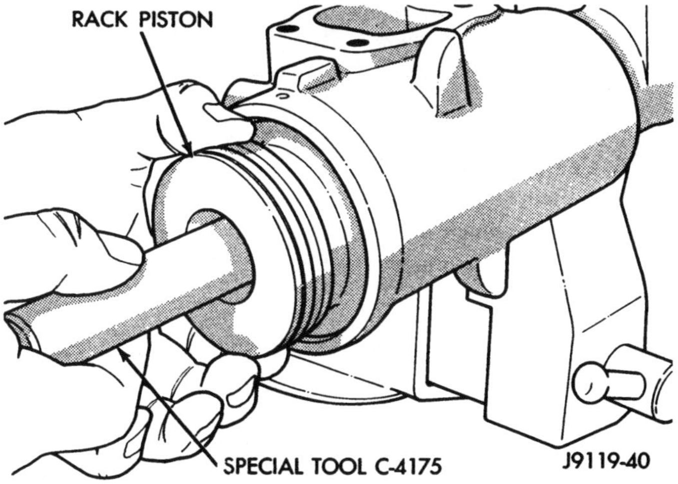

Fig. 20 Rack Piston

DISASSEMBLY AND ASSEMBLY (Continued)

(7) Remove the rack piston, rack balls, and tool together from housing.

(8) Remove valve, worm shaft and thrust bearing and races.

(9) Remove tool from rack piston.

(10) Remove rack piston balls.

(11) Remove screws, clamp and ball guide.

(12) Remove teflon ring and O-ring seal (Fig. 21).

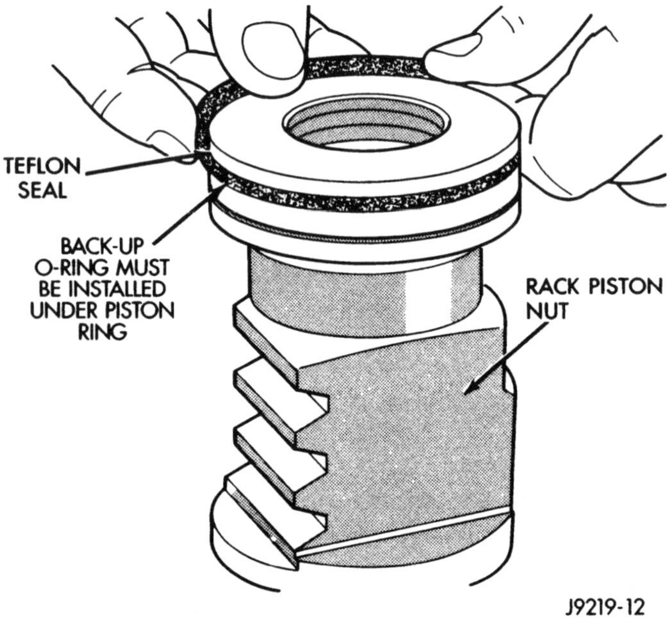

Fig. 21 Rack Piston Teflon Ring and O-Ring

ASSEMBLY

(1) Clean all components in solvent and dry with compressed air.

(2) Check for scores, nicks or burrs on the rack piston finished surface. Slight wear is normal on the worm gear surfaces.

(3) Install O-ring seal and teflon ring and lubricate with power steering fluid.

(4) Install worm shaft to rack piston outside of housing. Fully seat worm shaft to rack piston. Align worm shaft spiral groove with rack piston ball guide hole (Fig. 22).

NOTE: There are 12 black and 12 silver (Chrome) balls in the rack piston circuit. The black balls are smaller than the silver balls. The balls must be installed alternately into the rack piston and ball guide. This procedure will maintain worm shaft pre-load.

(5) Lubricate and install rack piston balls through return guide hole while turning worm shaft COUNTERCLOCKWISE.

WARNING: MAKE SURE ALL RACK PISTON BALLS ARE INSTALLED PROPERLY. IMPROPER INSTALLATION MAY RESULT IN PERSONAL INJURY.

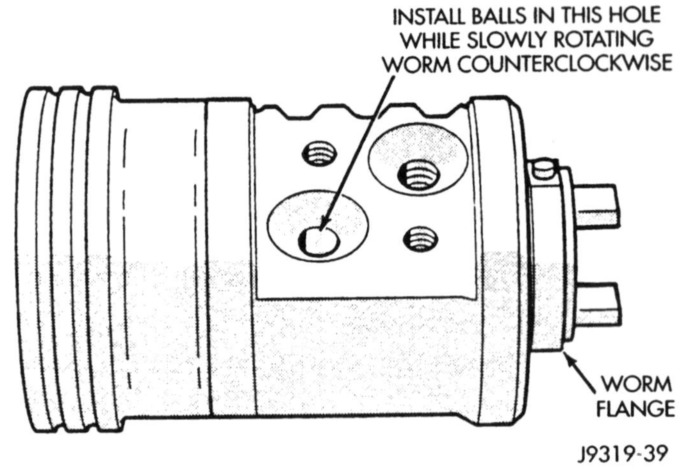

Fig. 22 Installing Balls in Rack Piston

(6) Install remaining balls to guide using grease or petroleum jelly at each end to hold in place (Fig. 23).

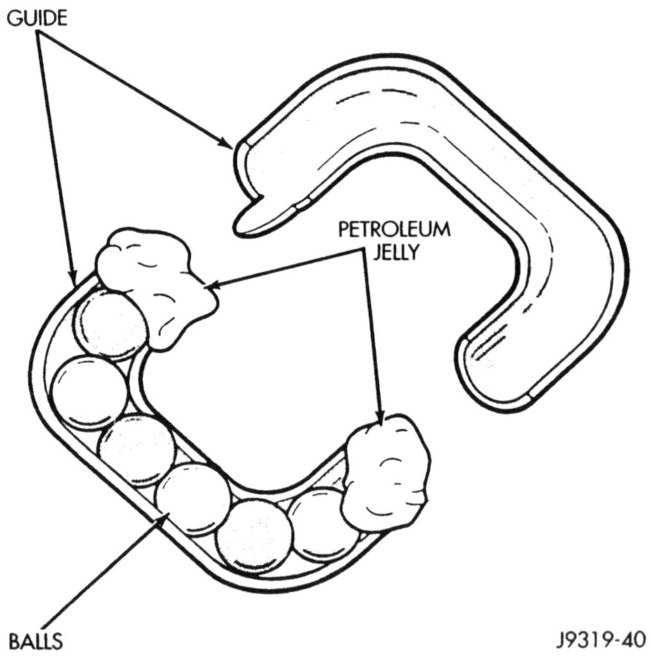

Fig. 23 Balls in the Return Guide

(7) Install guide onto rack piston and return with clamp and screws. Tighten screws to 58 N·m (43 ft. lbs.).

(8) Insert Arbor C-4175 into bore of rack piston. Hold tool tightly against worm shaft while turning the stub shaft COUNTERCLOCKWISE.

(9) The rack piston will be forced onto the tool and hold the rack piston balls in place.

(10) Install the races and thrust bearing to worm shaft (Fig. 24).

(11) Install worm shaft to housing.

(12) Install valve

(13) Install rack piston to worm shaft from tool, compress seals.

DISASSEMBLY AND ASSEMBLY (Continued)

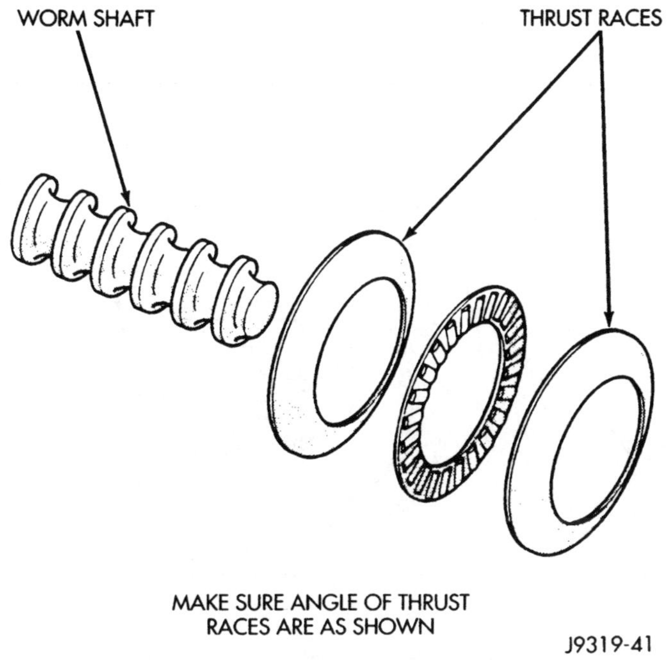

Fig. 24 Worm Shaft and Bearing

(14) Hold Arbor tightly against worm shaft and turn stub shaft CLOCKWISE until rack piston is seated on worm shaft.

(15) Install rack piston plug and tighten to 150 N·m (111 ft. lbs.).

(16) Install housing end plug.

(17) Install pitman shaft and side cover.

(18) Adjust steering gear.

PITMAN SHAFT SEALS AND BEARING

DISASSEMBLY

(1) Remove pitman arm from gear.

(2) Clean exposed end of pitman shaft and housing with a wire brush.

(3) Remove dust seal.

(4) Remove retaining ring with snap ring pliers (Fig. 25).

(5) Remove backup washer with screwdriver.

CAUTION: Use care not to score the housing bore when prying out seals and washers.

(6) Remove oil seal with screwdriver.

(7) Inspect the housing for burrs and remove if necessary.

(8) Remove needle bearing from housing (Fig. 26).

ASSEMBLY

(1) Install needle bearing into housing (Fig. 25).

(2) Coat the oil seal and washers with grease.

(3) Install the oil seal with a suitable size deep socket.

(4) Install backup washer.

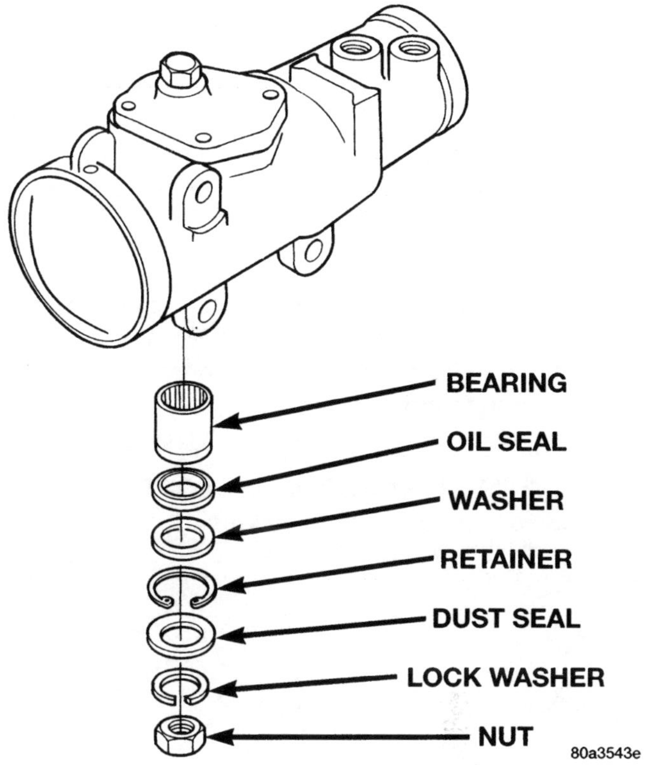

Fig. 25 Pitman Shaft Seals & Bearing

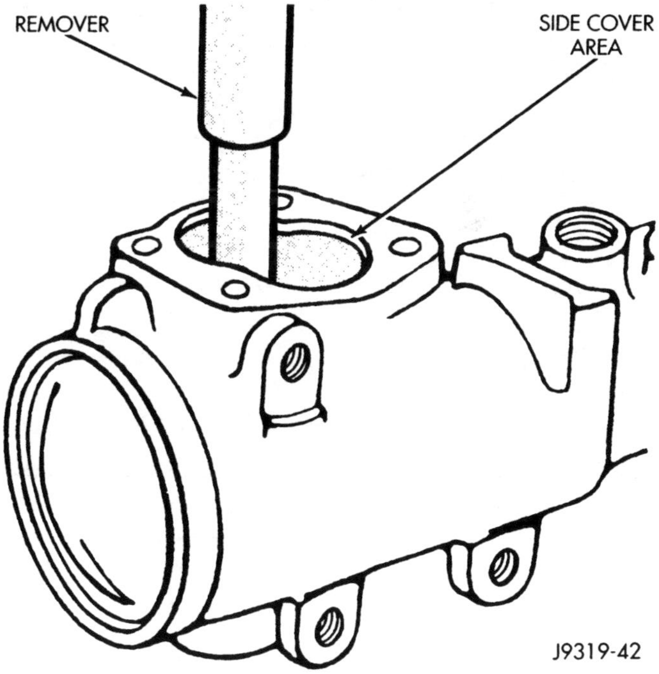

Fig. 26 Needle Bearing Removal

(5) Install the retainer ring with snap ring pliers.

(6) Install dust seal with a suitable size deep socket.

ADJUSTMENTS

STEERING GEAR

CAUTION: Steering gear must be adjusted in the proper order. If adjustments are not performed in order, gear damage and improper steering response may result.

NOTE: Adjusting the steering gear in the vehicle is not recommended. Remove gear from the vehicle and drain the fluid. Then mount gear in a vise to perform adjustments.

WORM THRUST BEARING PRELOAD

(1) Remove adjuster plug locknut (Fig. 27).

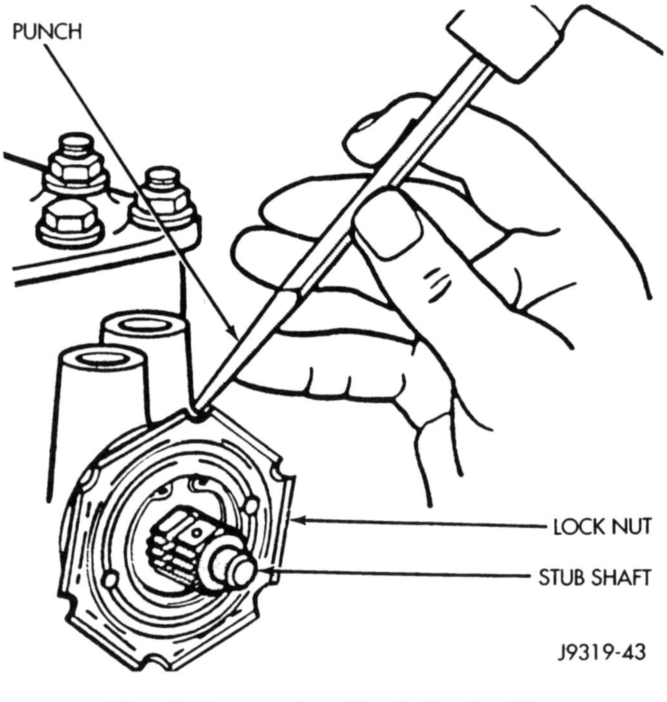

Fig. 27 Loosening the Adjuster Plug

(2) Turn the adjuster in with Spanner Wrench C-4381. Tighten the plug and thrust bearing in the housing until firmly bottomed in housing.

(3) Place an index mark on the housing even with one of the holes in adjuster plug (Fig. 28).

(4) Measure back (counterclockwise) 13 mm (0.50 in) and mark housing (Fig. 29).

(5) Rotate adjustment cap back (counterclockwise) with spanner wrench until hole is aligned with the second mark (Fig. 30).

(6) Install and tighten locknut to 108 N·m (80 ft. lbs.). Be sure adjustment cap does not turn while tightening the locknut.

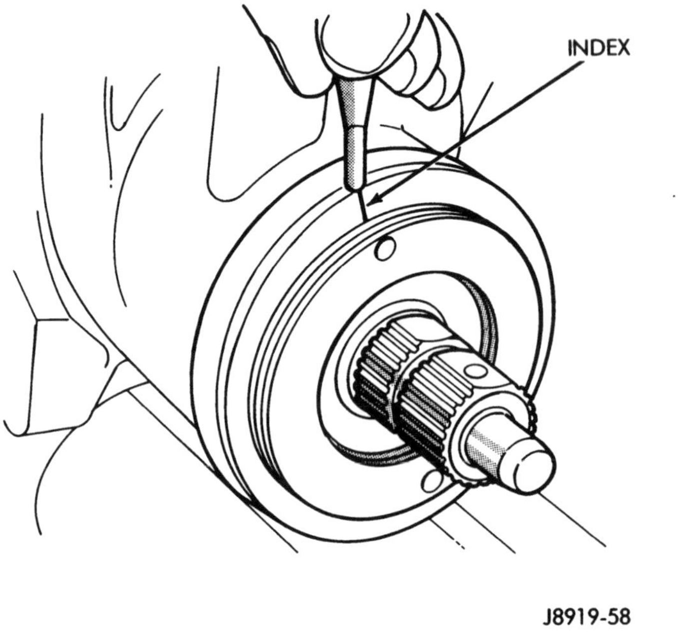

Fig. 28 Alignment Marking On Housing

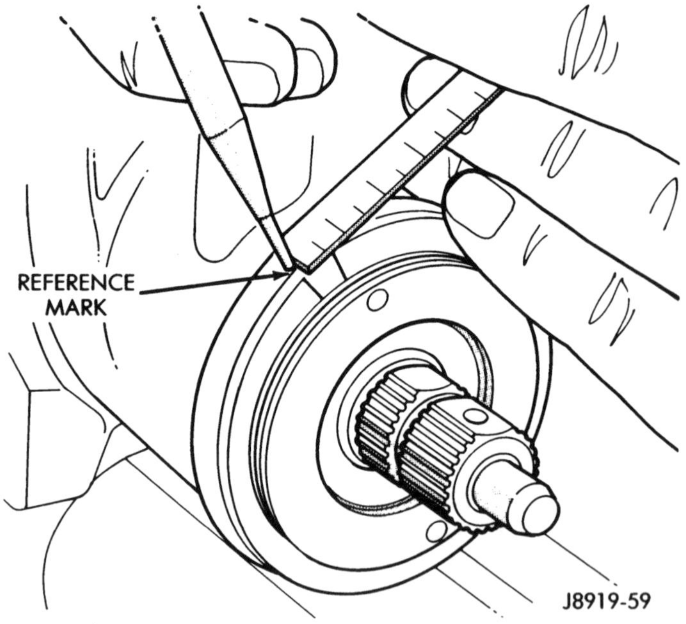

Fig. 29 Remarking The Housing

OVER-CENTER

(1) Rotate the stub shaft from stop to stop and count the number of turns.

(2) Starting at either stop turn the stub shaft back 1/2 the total number of turns. This is the center of the gear travel (Fig. 31).

(3) Turn the pitman shaft adjuster screw back (COUNTERCLOCKWISE) until extended, then turn back in (CLOCKWISE) one full turn.

(4) Place the torque wrench in the vertical position on the stub shaft. Rotate the wrench 45 degrees each

ADJUSTMENTS (Continued)

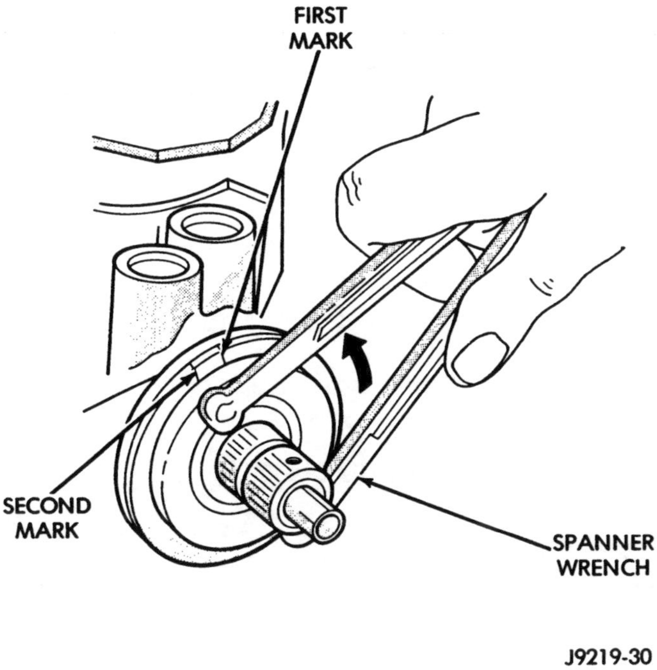

Fig. 30 Aligning To The Second Mark

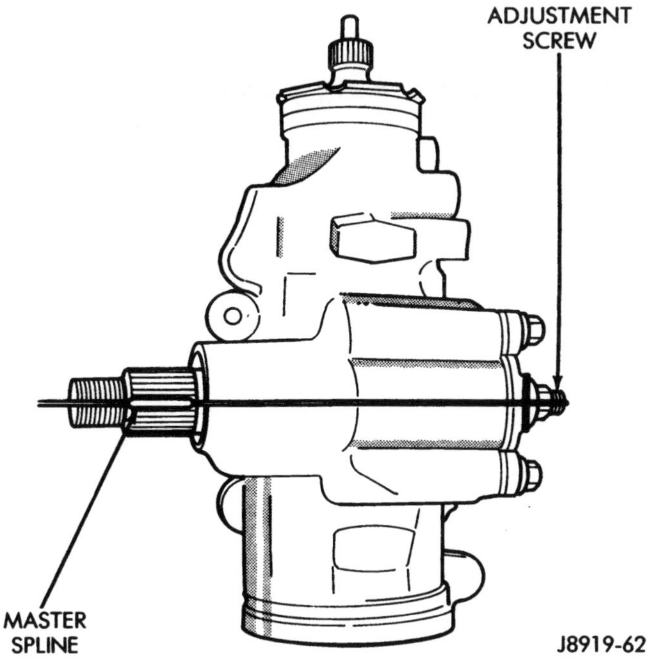

Fig. 31 Steering Gear Centered

side of the center and record the highest rotational torque on center (Fig. 32).

(5) Turn the adjuster in until torque to turn stub shaft is 0.6 to 1.2 N·m (6.0 to 10.0 in. lbs.) more than previous reading recorded.

(6) Prevent the adjuster screw from turning while tightening adjuster lock nut. Tighten the adjuster lock nut to 27 N·m (20 ft. lbs.).

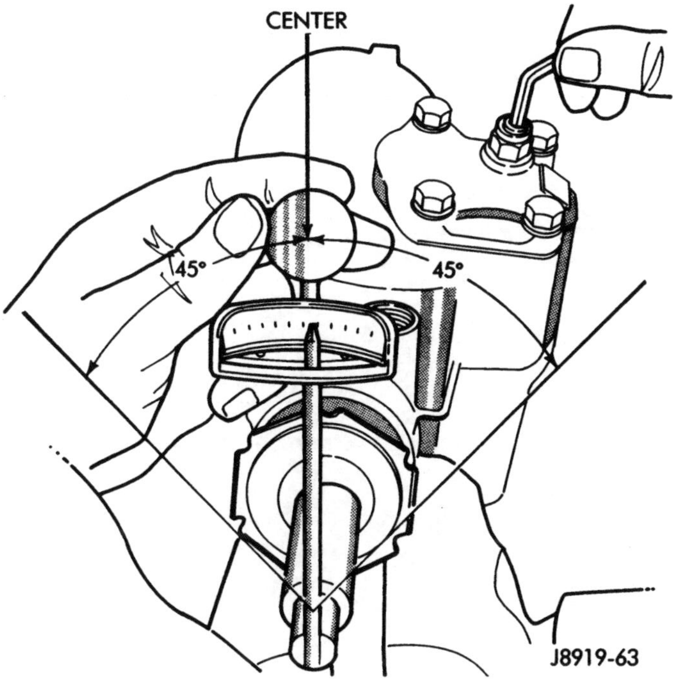

Fig. 32 Checking Over-center Rotation Torque

SPECIFICATIONS

POWER STEERING GEAR

Steering Gear
Type . . . . .Recirculating Ball
Gear Ratio 14:1
Worm Shaft Bearing
Preload. . . . . .0.45–1.13 N·m (4–10 in. lbs.)
Pitman Shaft Over-Center Drag
New Gear (under 400 miles). . .0.45–0.90 N·m (4–8 in. lbs.) + Worm Shaft Preload
Used Gear (over 400 miles). . .0.5–0.6 N·m (4–5 in. lbs.) + Worm Shaft Preload

TORQUE CHART

DESCRIPTION	TORQUE
Power Steering Gear	
Adjustment Cap Locknut	108 N·m (80 ft. lbs.)
Adjustment Screw Locknut	49 N·m (36 ft. lbs.)
Gear to Frame Bolts	95 N·m (70 ft. lbs.)
Pitman Shaft Nut	251 N·m (185 ft. lbs.)
Rack Piston Plug	102 N·m (75 ft. lbs.)
Side Cover Bolts	60 N·m (44 ft. lbs.)
Pressure Line	28 N·m (21 ft. lbs.)
Return Line	28 N·m (21 ft. lbs.)

SPECIAL TOOLS

POWER STEERING GEAR

Remover/Installer, Steering Plug C-4381

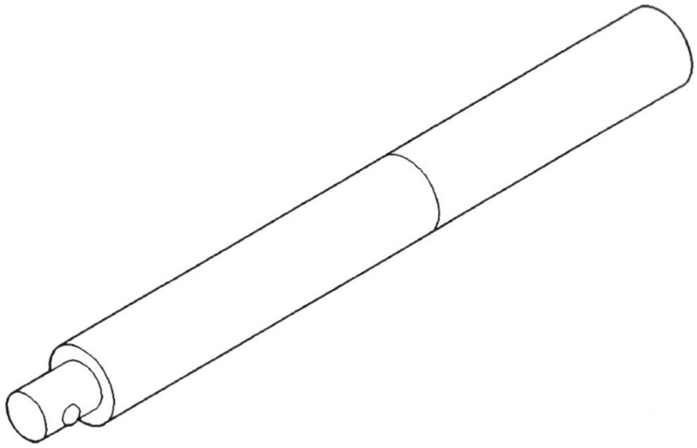

Handle C-4171

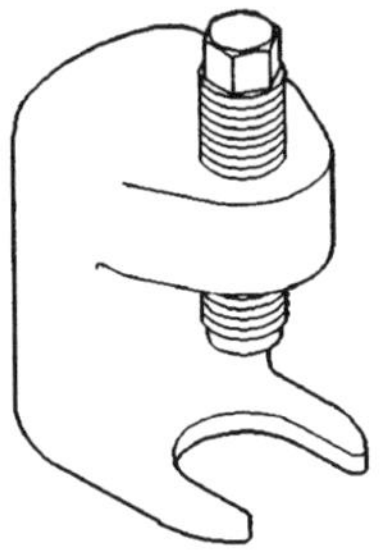

Remover, Pitman Arm C-4150A

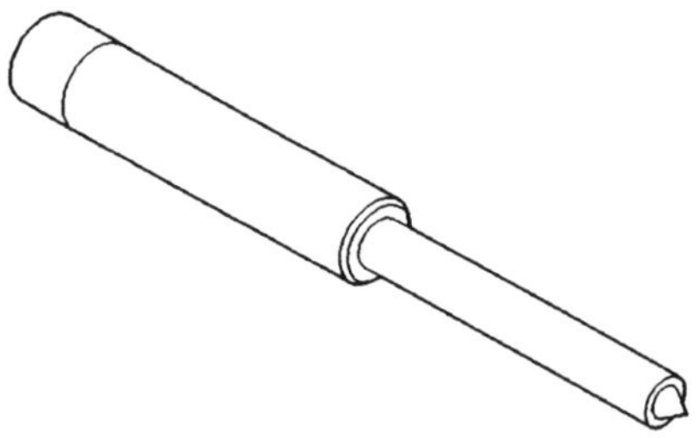

Remover/Installer Steering Rack Piston C-4175

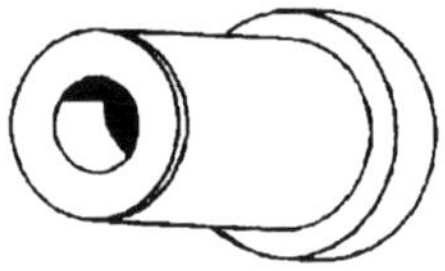

Remover, Pitman Shaft Bearing C-4177

MANUAL STEERING GEAR

INDEX

DESCRIPTION AND OPERATION

MANUAL STEERING GEAR

The manual steering gear is a recirculating-ball, nut and worm type (Fig. 1). The worm is located on the lower end of the worm shaft. The ball nut is mounted on the worm and the balls act as a rolling thread between the worm and nut. Teeth on the ball nut engage teeth on the pitman shaft. The teeth on the ball nut are made to fit tighter between the ball nut and pitman shaft when the front wheels are position straight ahead.

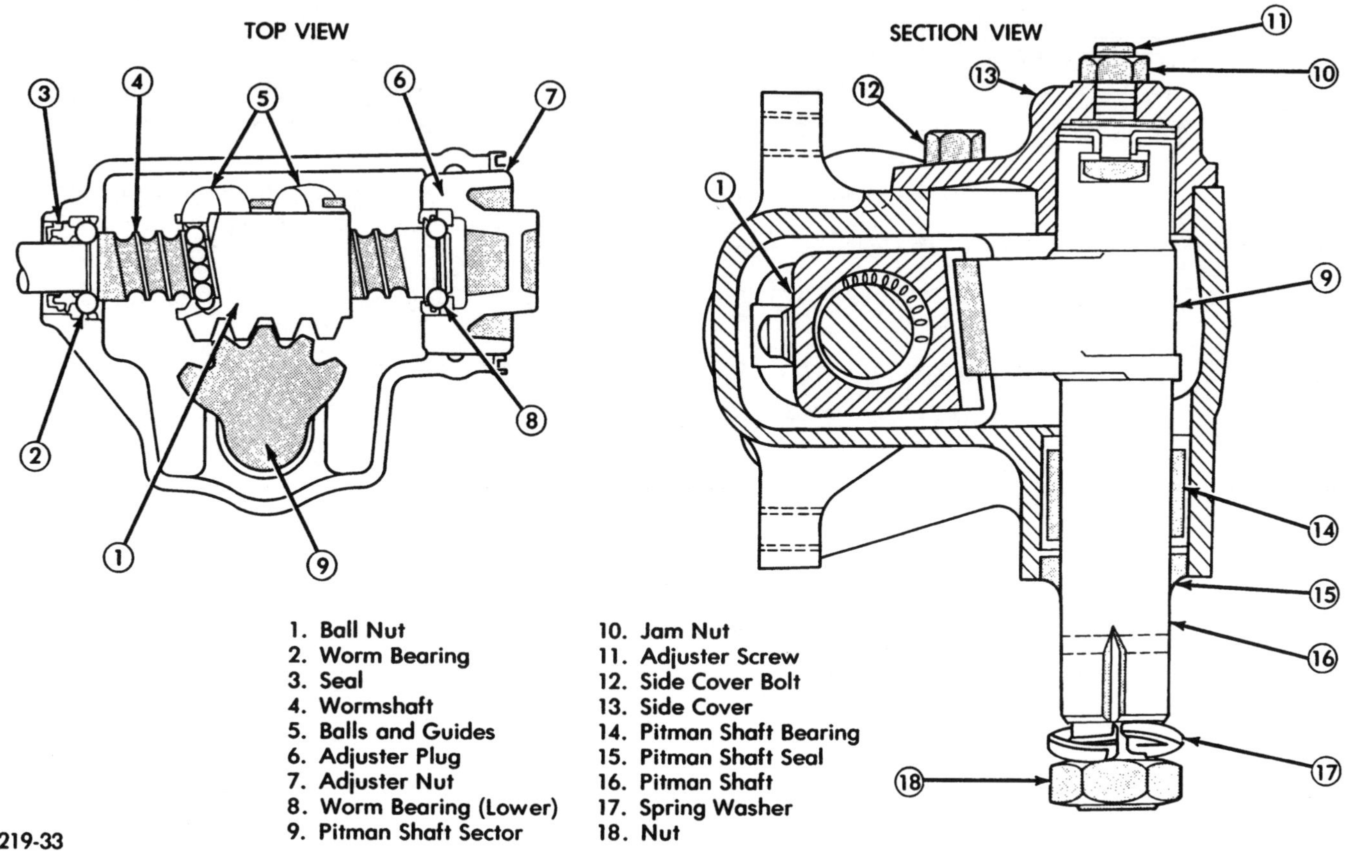

Fig. 1 Manual Steering Gear

DIAGNOSIS AND TESTING

MANUAL STEERING SYSTEM

NOTE: On turns a slight rattle may occur from the steering gear. This is caused by increased gear tooth clearance between the ball nut and pitman shaft as the gear moves off center of the high point position. This is normal and lash must not be reduced to eliminate this slight rattle.

CONDITION	POSSIBLE CAUSES	CORRECTION
RATTLE OR CHUCKLE IN STEERING GEAR.	1. Insufficient lubricant in gear. 2. Loose or damaged suspension components. 3. Pitman arm or steering gear loose. 4. Loose or worn steering shaft bearing. 5. Excessive over-center lash.	1. Add lubricant as required. 2. Inspect and repair as necessary. 3. Tighten to specifications. 4. Replace bearing. 5. Adjust steering to specifications.
POOR STEERING WHEEL RETURN.	1. Insufficient lubricate. 2. Steering gear adjusted too tight. 3. Vehicle out of alignment. 4. Worn or binding steering linkage.	1. Add lubricate as required. 2. Adjust steering gear to specifications. 3. Align vehicle to specifications. 4. Inspect and repair as necessary.
EXCESSIVE STEERING WHEEL PLAY	1.Vehicle out of alignment. 2. Worn or loose wheel bearings. 3. Worn or loose steering components. 4. Improper steering gear adjustment.	1. Align vehicle to specifications. 2. Replace or adjust wheel bearings. 3. Inspect and repair as necessary. 4. Adjust steering gear to specifications.
EXCESSIVE STEERING WHEEL EFFORT.	1. Low or uneven tire pressure. 2. Vehicle out of alignment. 3. Improper steering gear adjustment. 4. Lack of lubricant to steering linkage or suspension components.	1. Inflate tires to specifications. 2. Align vehicle to specifications. 3. Adjust steering gear to specifications. 4. Lubricate steering linkage and suspension components.

REMOVAL AND INSTALLATION

PITMAN SHAFT SEAL

REMOVAL

(1) Raise and support vehicle.
(2) Mark the pitman arm and shaft position for installation reference.
(3) Remove pitman arm retaining nut and remove the pitman arm with Puller C-4150A (Fig. 2).
(4) Remove pitman shaft seal with a seal pick.

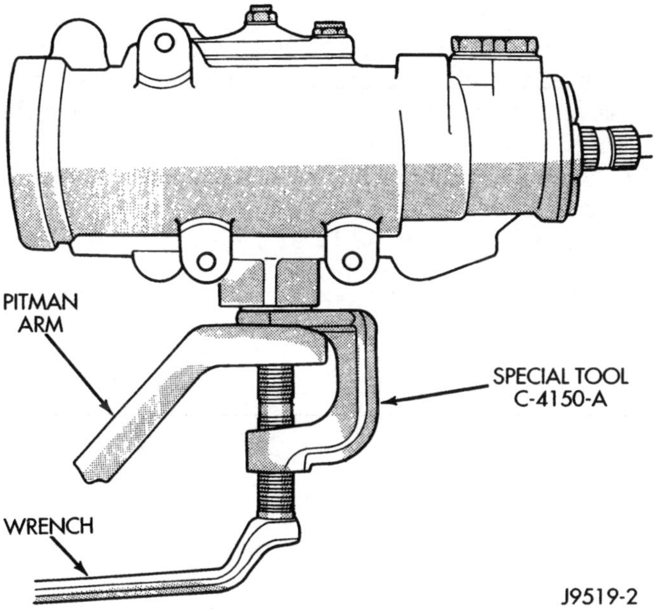

Fig. 2 Pitman Arm Puller

INSTALLATION

NOTE: Tape pitman shaft threads and spline with plastic tape, to protect the seal during installation.

(1) Coat new seal with grease and install seal with suitable size socket.
(2) Remove tape from the pitman arm shaft.
(3) Align pitman arm with the shaft reference mark and install pitman arm.
(4) Install washer and retaining nut and tighten to 251 N·m (185 ft. lbs.).
(5) Remove support and lower vehicle.

MANUAL STEERING GEAR

REMOVAL

(1) Raise and support vehicle.
(2) Remove tie rod from pitman arm with puller (Fig. 3).
(3) Remove pitman arm with Remover C-4150A.
(4) Remove gear mounting bolts and remove gear (Fig. 4).

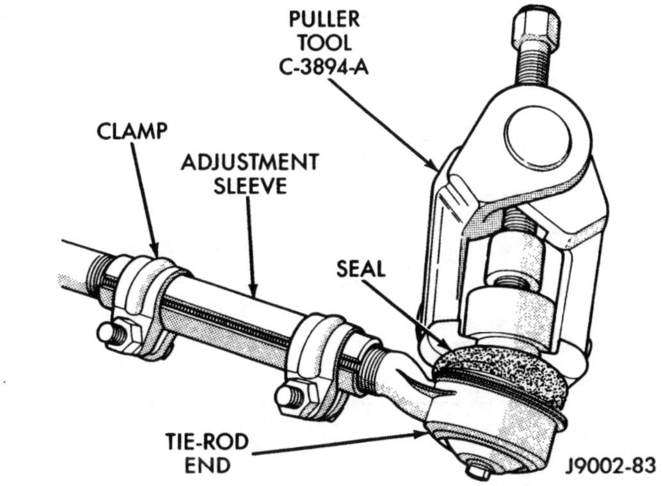

Fig. 3 Tie Rod End

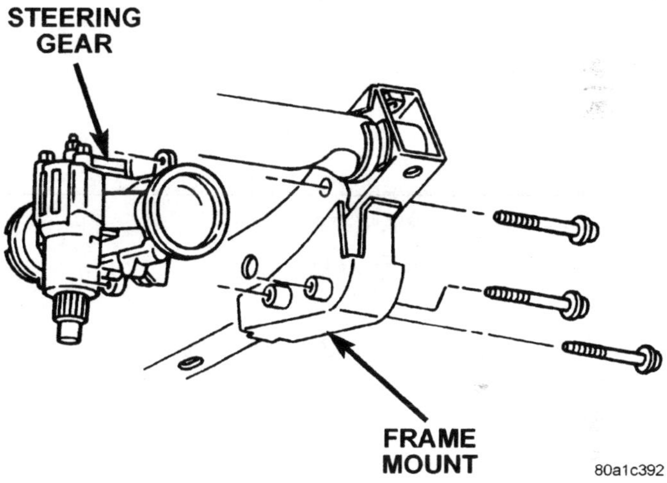

Fig. 4 Steering Gear

INSTALLATION

(1) Install gear on frame rail and install mounting bolts.
(2) Tighten mounting bolts to 95 N·m (70 ft. lbs.).
(3) Install pitman arm and tighten mounting nut to 251 N·m (185 ft. lbs.).
(4) Install tie rod end on pitman arm and tighten nut to 74 N·m (55 ft. lbs.). Install cotter pin.
(5) Remove support and lower vehicle.

DISASSEMBLY AND ASSEMBLY

PITMAN SHAFT AND COVER

DISASSEMBLY

(1) Remove steering gear from the vehicle.
(2) Center the steering gear.
(3) Remove pitman shaft preload adjustment lock-nut (Fig. 5).

DISASSEMBLY AND ASSEMBLY (Continued)

(4) Remove cover bolts and remove cover.

(5) Remove preload adjuster and shim(s) from pitman shaft T-slot (Fig. 5).

(6) Remove pitman shaft from the gear housing.

(7) Pry out pitman shaft seal (Fig. 6).

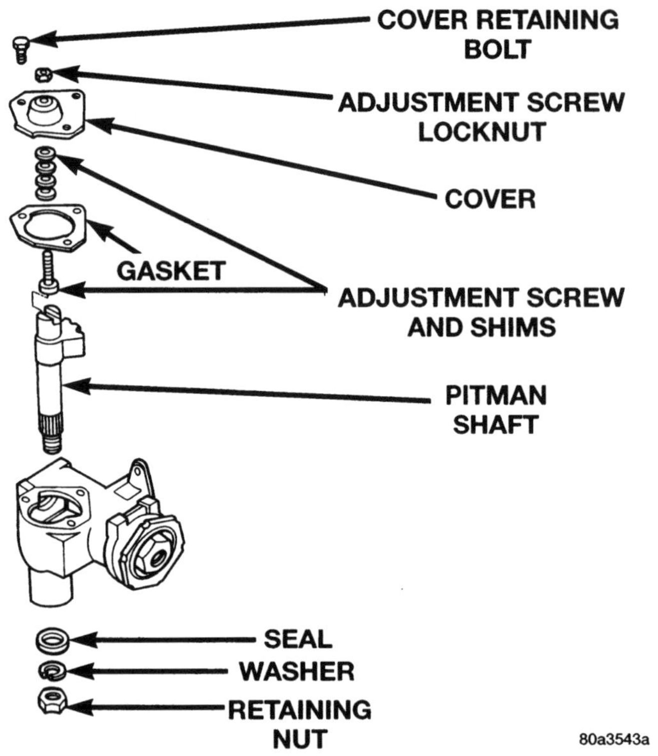

Fig. 5 Manual Steering Gear

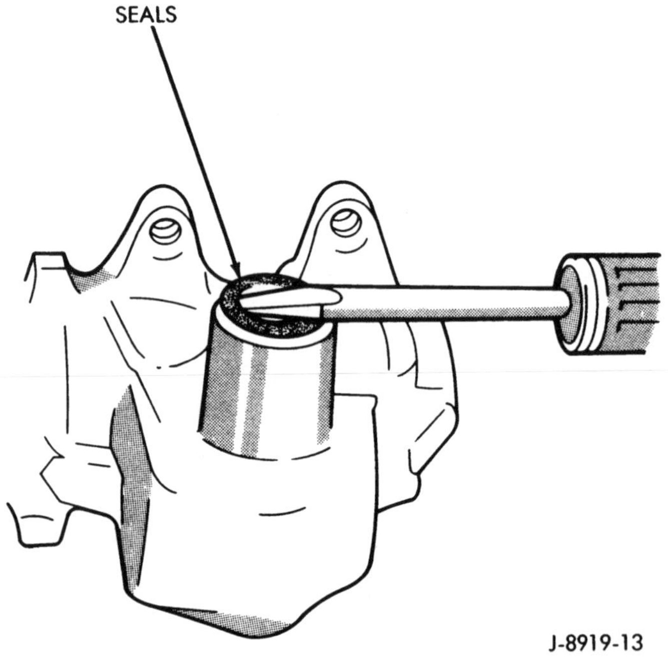

Fig. 6 Pitman Shaft Seal

ASSEMBLY

(1) Install new pitman shaft seal with suitable size socket.

(2) Install preload adjuster in pitman shaft T-slot.

(3) Measure the end-play of preload adjuster with a feeler gauge (Fig. 7). End-play must not exceed .05 mm (.002 in.). If end-play exceeds specifications install replacement shim to obtain correct end-play.

(4) Tape threads and spline of the pitman shaft to protect the seal during shaft installation.

(5) Lubricate the pitman shaft and install the shaft into the gear housing. The pitman shaft center tooth must be engaged with the center groove of the ball nut (Fig. 8).

(6) Install the cover gasket and cover on the housing. Thread preload adjuster counter-clockwise into the cover until the cover makes contact with the housing.

(7) Install cover bolts finger tight, then back off adjuster 1/2 turn.

(8) Tighten cover bolts to 61 N·m (45 ft. lbs.).

(9) Adjust over-center preload.

(10) Install steering gear.

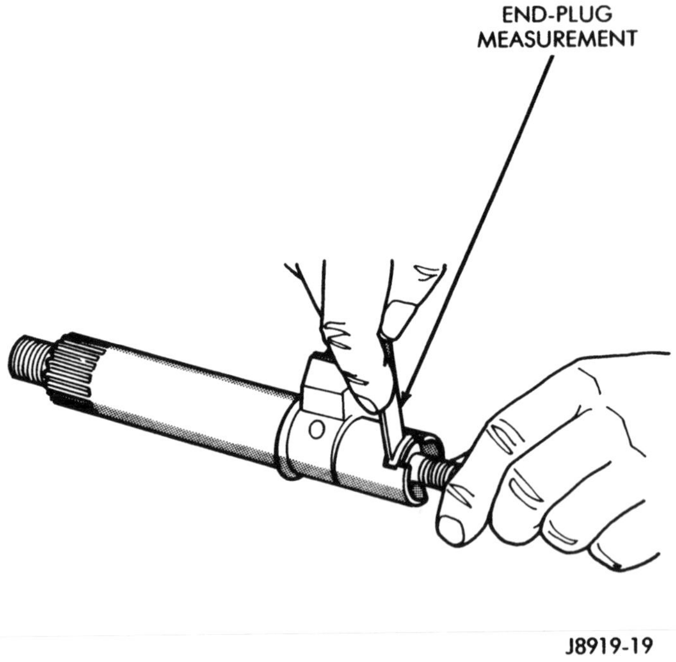

Fig. 7 Preload Adjuster End-Play

WORM SHAFT AND BALL NUT

DISASSEMBLY

(1) Remove the pitman shaft.

(2) Remove the worm bearing adjuster locknut and adjuster (Fig. 9).

(3) Remove worm shaft and ball nut.

DISASSEMBLY AND ASSEMBLY (Continued)

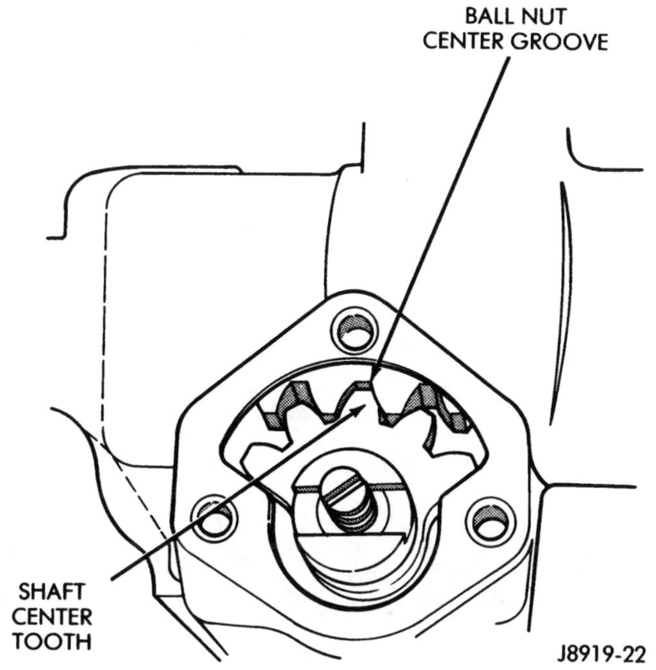

Fig. 8 Pitman Shaft and Ball Nut

CAUTION: Do not allow ball nut to run down to either end of the worm shaft. The ball guides may be damaged if ball nut is stopped by the end of the worm.

(4) Pry worm shaft seal out of the gear housing.

(5) Remove ball guide clamp screws and clamp.

(6) Separate the guides and remove balls from the guides. Remove the remaining balls by rotating the worm shaft back and forth.

NOTE: There are 50 balls, 25 in each circuit of the ball nut.

(7) Remove the ball nut from the worm shaft.

(8) Remove upper worm shaft bearing cup from the gear housing with a brass punch (Fig. 10).

(9) Clean and inspect all components for wear, scoring, and pitting.

ASSEMBLY

(1) Install ball nut onto the worm shaft until an equal amount of threads are showing on either side of the ball nut (Fig. 11).

(2) Install one ball into each ball nut guide hole. Move worm shaft around until the balls roll to the bottom of the worm shaft and support the shaft.

(3) Assemble and install ball guides into ball nut.

(4) Install the remaining balls into the guide holes (Fig. 12). Each guide has a total of 25 balls.

(5) Install the guide clamp and tighten screws to 14 N·m (10 ft. lbs.)

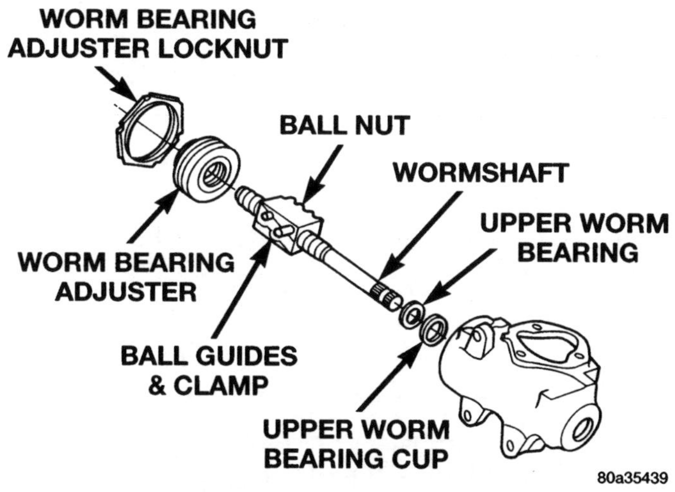

Fig. 9 Worm Shaft and Ball Nut

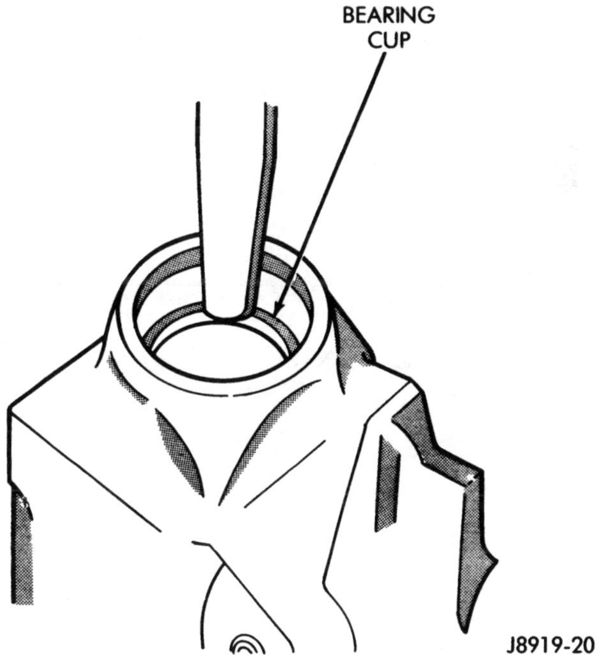

Fig. 10 Upper Bearing Cup

(6) Lubricate worm shaft with chassis lubricate and thread worm shaft in and out of the ball nut to lubricate balls.

(7) Install upper bearing cup into gear housing with a bearing cup driver (Fig. 13).

(8) Install worm shaft seal into gear housing.

(9) Lubricate upper bearing and install on the worm shaft.

(10) Install worm shaft into the steering gear.

NOTE: Wide/deep side of the ball nut teeth face the cover opening.

(11) Install worm shaft adjuster cap and adjust shaft to zero end-play. Install adjuster locknut.

DISASSEMBLY AND ASSEMBLY (Continued)

(12) Install pitman shaft and fill gear with lubricate.

(13) Adjust worm bearing preload and over-center preload.

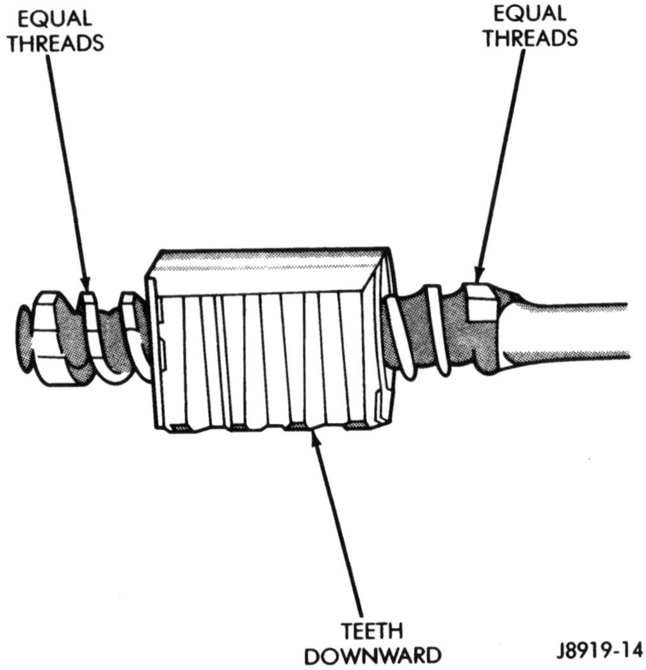

Fig. 11 Worm Shaft and Ball Nut

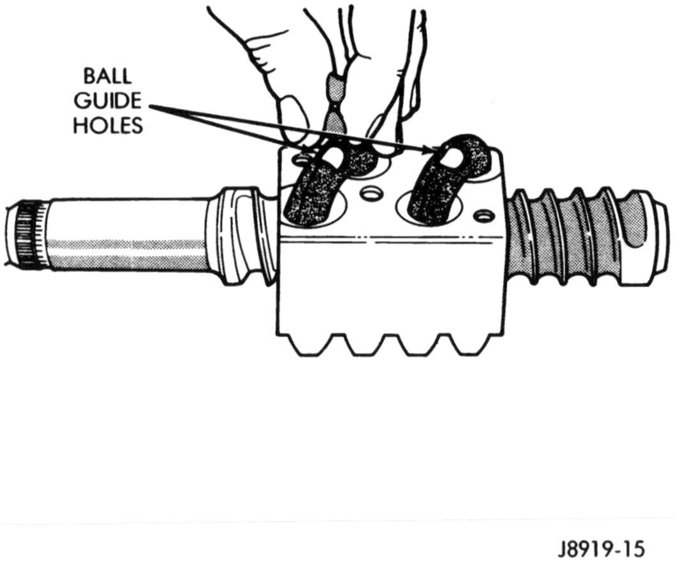

Fig. 12 Ball Nut Guide Holes

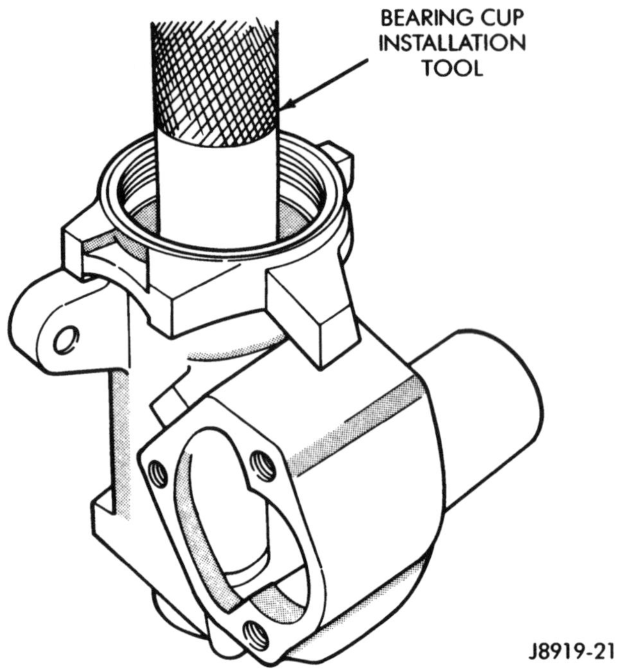

Fig. 13 Upper Bearing Cup Installation

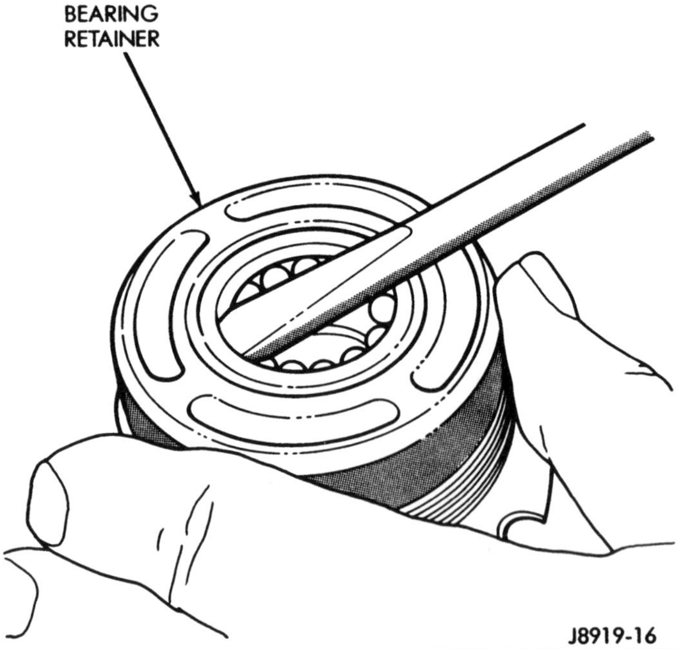

Fig. 14 Lower Bearing Retainer

WORM BEARING ADJUSTER

DISASSEMBLY

(1) Pry out the lower bearing retainer (Fig. 14).

(2) Remove lower bearing (Fig. 15).

(3) Place locknut on the adjuster and place in a vise. Remove lower bearing cup with Puller 7794–A and a slid hammer.

ASSEMBLY

(1) Install lower bearing cup with a bearing cup driver.

(2) Lubricate lower bearing and install into the adjuster.

(3) Install the retainer by tapping it in with a plastic hammer.

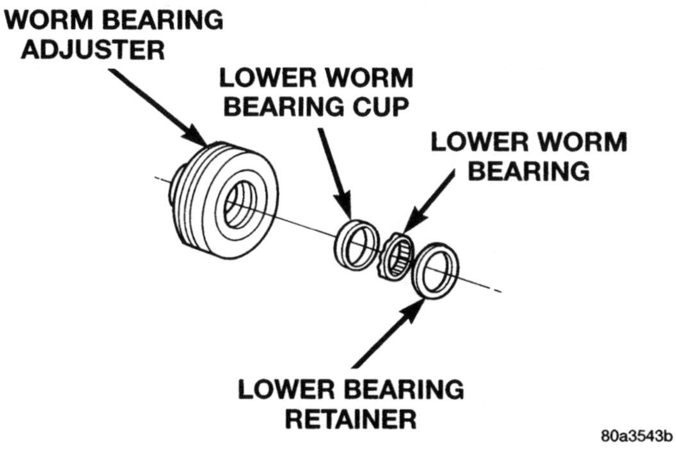

Fig. 15 Lower Bearing Cup

ADJUSTMENTS

WORM BEARING PRELOAD

(1) Tighten the worm bearing adjuster plug until it bottoms, then loosen 1/4 turn.

(2) Carefully turn the worm shaft all the way to the end of travel, then turn back 1/2 turn.

(3) Tighten adjuster plug until torque wrench indicates 0.6 to 1.0 N·m (5 to 8 in. lbs.) torque (Fig. 16).

(4) Tighten the adjuster plug locknut to 68 N·m (50 ft. lbs.).

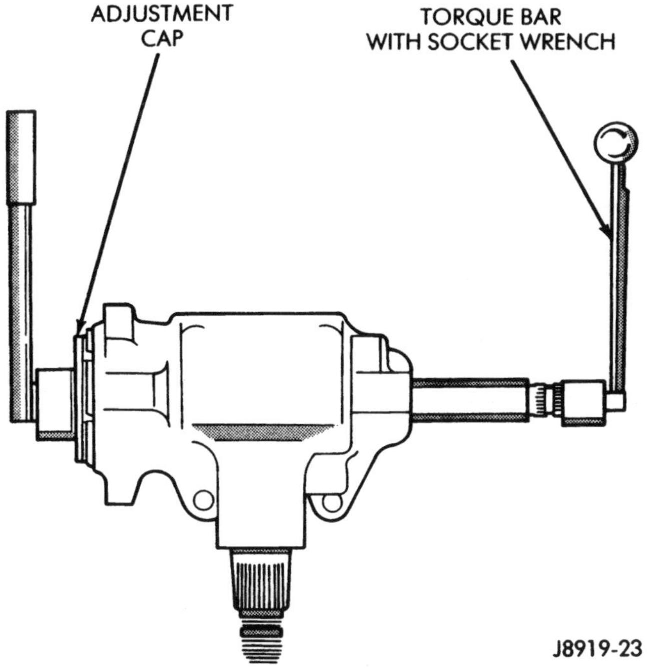

Fig. 16 Worm Bearing Preload

OVER-CENTER PRELOAD

NOTE: Adjust worm bearing preload before adjusting over-center preload if worm shaft was serviced.

(1) Back off preload adjuster until it stops, then turn it in one full turn.

(2) With gear at center of travel, check torque to turn stub shaft and record this reading (Fig. 17).

(3) Turn adjuster in until torque to turn stub shaft is 0.5 to 1 N·m (4 to 10 in. lbs.) more than recorded reading.

(4) Hold pitman shaft adjustment screw and tighten adjuster lock nut to 34 N·m (25 ft. lbs.).

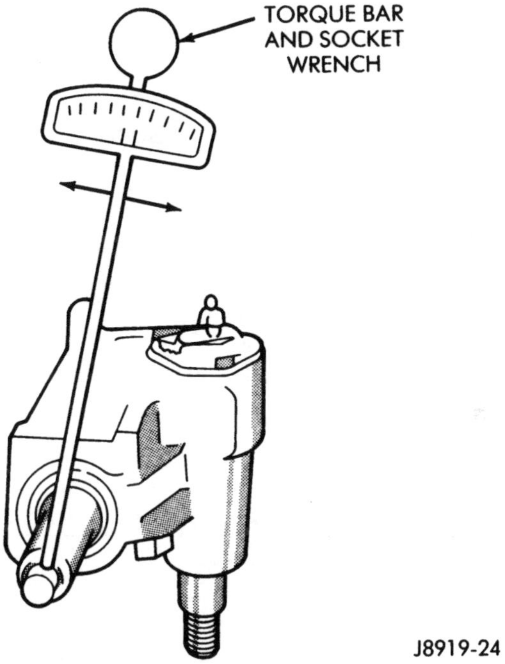

Fig. 17 Over-Center Preload

SPECIFICATIONS

MANUAL STEERING GEAR

Steering Gear
- Type . . . . .Recirculating Ball
- Gear Ratio 24:1

Worm Shaft Bearing
- Preload . . . . .0.6–1.0 N·m (5–8 in. lbs.)

Pitman Shaft Over-Center Drag
- Preload . . . . .0.5–1.0 N·m (4–10 in. lbs.) + Worm Shaft Preload

TORQUE CHART

DESCRIPTION	TORQUE
Manual Steering Gear	
Adjustment Cap Locknut	68 N·m (50 ft. lbs.)
Adjustment Screw Locknut	34 N·m (25 ft. lbs.)
Pitman Shaft Nut	251 N·m (185 ft. lbs.)
Guide Clamp Screws	14 N·m (10 ft. lbs.)
Cover Bolts	61 N·m (45 ft. lbs.)
Gear to Frame Bolts	105 N·m (78 ft. lbs.)

SPECIAL TOOLS

MANUAL STEERING GEAR

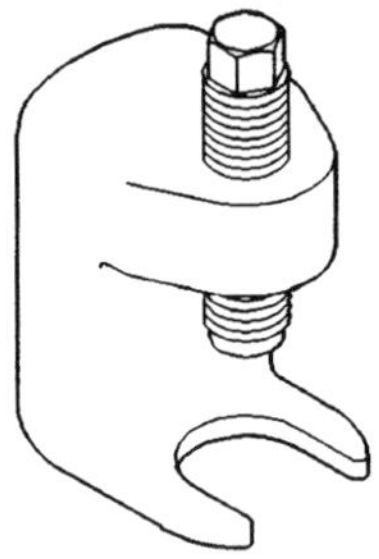

Remover C-41509A

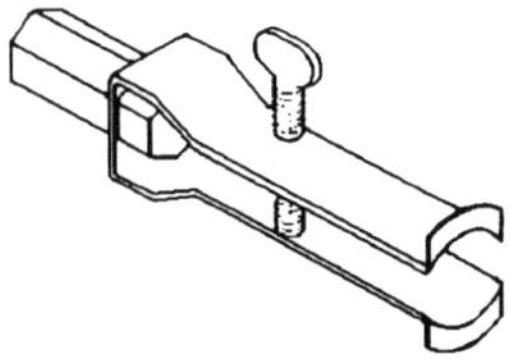

Puller 7794–A

STEERING COLUMN

INDEX

GENERAL INFORMATION

STEERING COLUMN

The standard non-tilt and tilt steering column has been designed to be serviced as an assembly. The key cylinder, switches, clock spring, trim shrouds and steering wheel are serviced separately.

The column is connected to the steering gear with an upper and lower shaft. The lower shaft has a support bearing mounted to a bracket. The bracket mounts to the frame rail with two bolts. These shafts and bearing are serviceable.

REMOVAL AND INSTALLATION

STEERING COLUMN

WARNING: BEFORE SERVICING THE STEERING COLUMN THE AIRBAG SYSTEM MUST BE DISARMED. REFER TO GROUP 8M RESTRAINT SYSTEMS FOR SERVICE PROCEDURES. FAILURE TO DO SO MAY RESULT IN ACCIDENTAL DEPLOYMENT OF THE AIRBAG AND POSSIBLE PERSONAL INJURY.

REMOVAL

(1) Position front wheels **straight ahead.**

(2) Remove negative ground cable from the battery.

(3) Remove the airbag, refer to Group 8M Restraint Systems for service procedures.

(4) Remove the steering wheel with an appropriate puller (Fig. 1).

(5) Turn ignition cylinder to the on position and remove cylinder by pressing release through lower shroud access hole (Fig. 2).

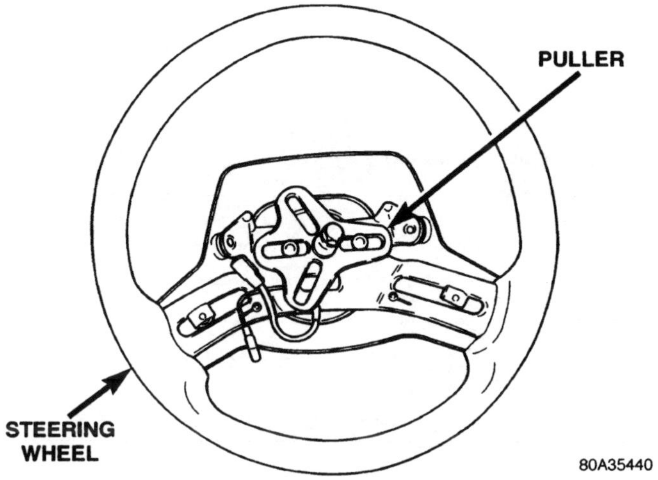

Fig. 1 Steering Wheel

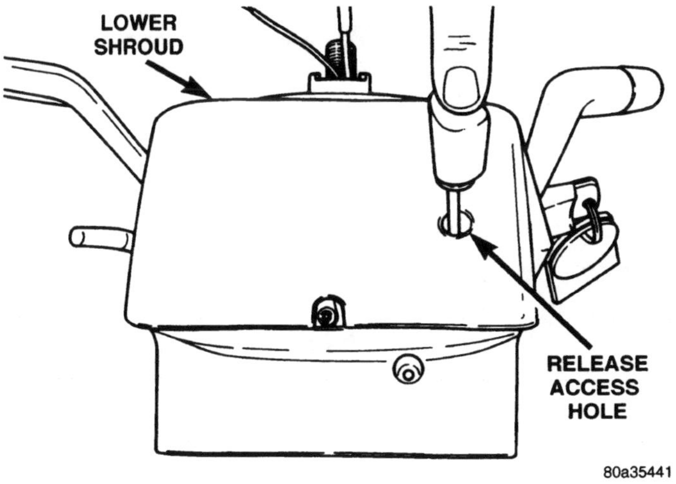

Fig. 2 Key Cylinder Release Access Hole

REMOVAL AND INSTALLATION (Continued)

(6) Remove knee blocker cover and knee blocker.
(7) Remove lower column shroud (Fig. 3).
(8) Remove the steering coupler bolt and column mounting nuts (Fig. 5) and lower column.
(9) Remove upper column shroud (Fig. 3).
(10) Disconnect and remove the wiring harness from the column (Fig. 4).

NOTE: If vehicle is equipped with automatic transmission remove shifter interlock cable. Refer to Group 3 Differential and Driveline for procedure.

(11) Remove column.
(12) Remove switches and clock spring refer to Group 8 Electrical for service procedures.

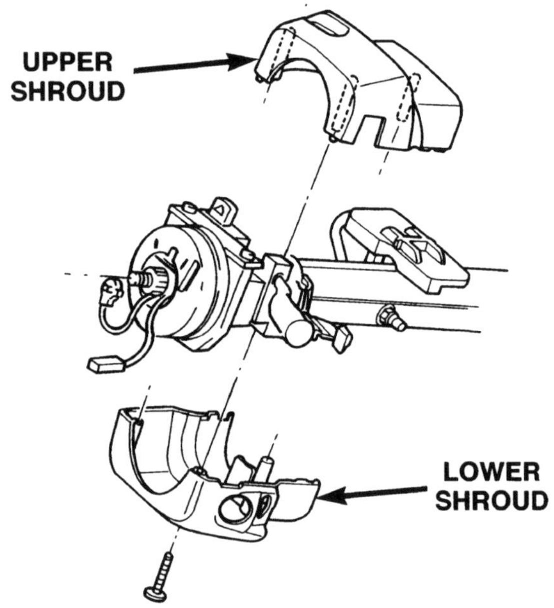

Fig. 3 Column Shrouds

INSTALLATION

(1) Install switches and clock spring refer to Group 8 Electrical for service procedures.
(2) Align and install column into the steering coupler.
(3) Install column harness and connect harness to switches.
(4) If vehicle is equipped with automatic transmission install shifter interlock cable. Refer to Group 3 Differential and Driveline for procedure.
(5) Install upper column shrouds.
(6) Install column onto the mounting studs.
(7) Install mounting nuts and tighten to 23 N·m (17 ft. lbs.).

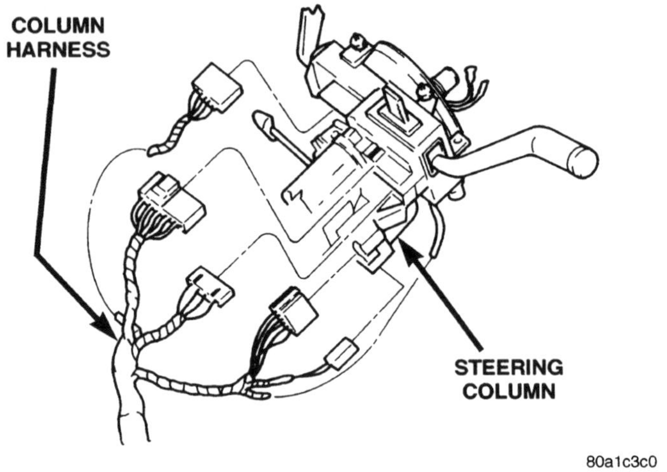

Fig. 4 Steering Column Harness

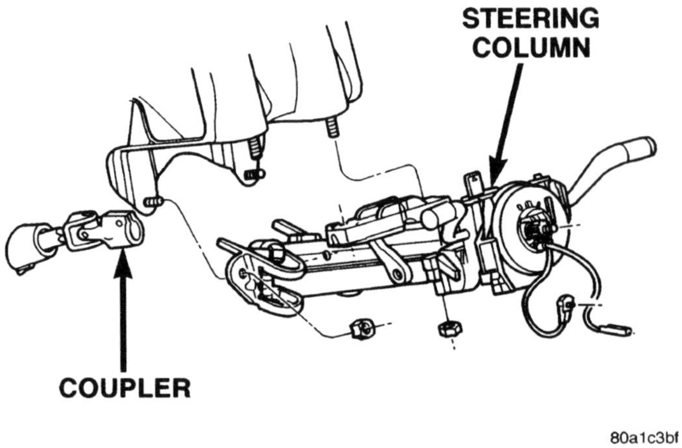

Fig. 5 Steering Column Mounting

(8) Install steering column coupler bolt and tighten to 49 N·m (36 ft. lbs.).
(9) Install lower column shrouds.
(10) Install ignition cylinder.
(11) Install knee blocker and knee blocker cover.
(12) Install steering wheel.
(13) Install airbag, refer to Group 8M Restraint Systems for service procedures.
(14) Install negative battery terminal.

SPECIFICATIONS

TORQUE CHART

DESCRIPTION	TORQUE
Steering Column	
Mounting Nuts	23 N·m (17 ft. lbs.)
Coupler Bolt	49 N·m (36 ft. lbs.)

STEERING LINKAGE

INDEX

GENERAL INFORMATION

STEERING LINKAGE

The steering linkage consists of a pitman arm, drag link, tie rod, and steering dampener (Fig. 1). Adjustment sleeves are used on the tie rod and drag link for toe and steering wheel alignment.

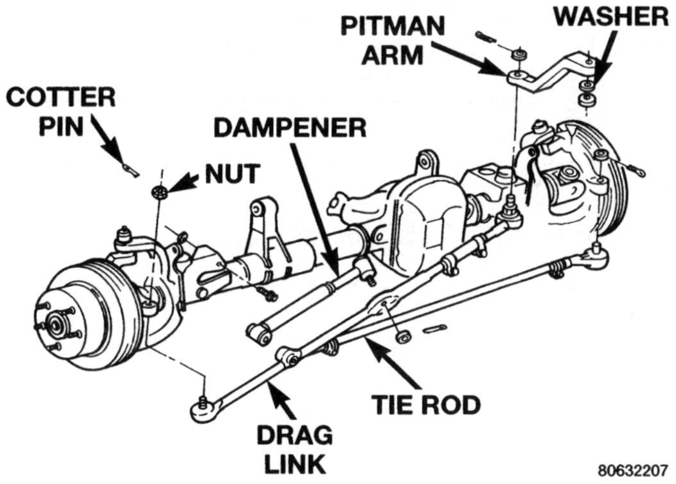

Fig. 1 Steering Linkage

SERVICE PROCEDURES

STEERING LINKAGE

The tie rod end and ball stud seals should be inspected during all oil changes. If a seal is damaged, it should be replaced. Before installing a new seal, inspect ball stud at the throat opening. Check for lubricant loss, contamination, ball stud wear or corrosion. If these conditions exist, replace the tie rod. A replacement seal can be installed if lubricant is in good condition. Otherwise, a complete replacement ball stud end should be installed.

CAUTION: Use a Puller tool C-3894-A for tie rod removal. Failure to use this tool could damage the ball stud and seal (Fig. 2).

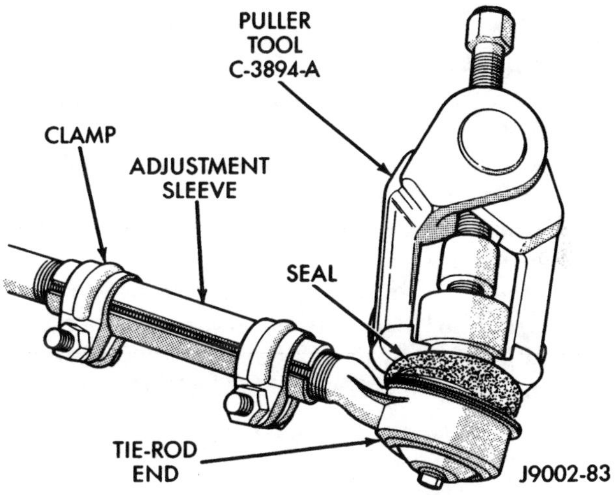

Fig. 2 Ball Stud Removal

REMOVAL AND INSTALLATION

TIE ROD

REMOVAL

(1) Remove the cotter pins and nuts at the steering knuckle and drag link (Fig. 1).

(2) Remove the ball studs with puller tool.

(3) If necessary, loosen the end clamp bolts and remove the tie rod ends from the tube.

INSTALLATION

(1) If necessary, install the tie rod ends in the tube. Position the tie rod clamp (Fig. 3) and tighten to 27 N·m (20 ft. lbs.).

(2) Install the tie rod on the drag link and steering knuckle.

(3) Tighten the ball stud nut on the steering knuckle to 47 N·m (35 ft. lbs.). Tighten the ball stud nut to drag link to 47 N·m (35 ft. lbs.) torque. Install new cotter pins.

REMOVAL AND INSTALLATION (Continued)

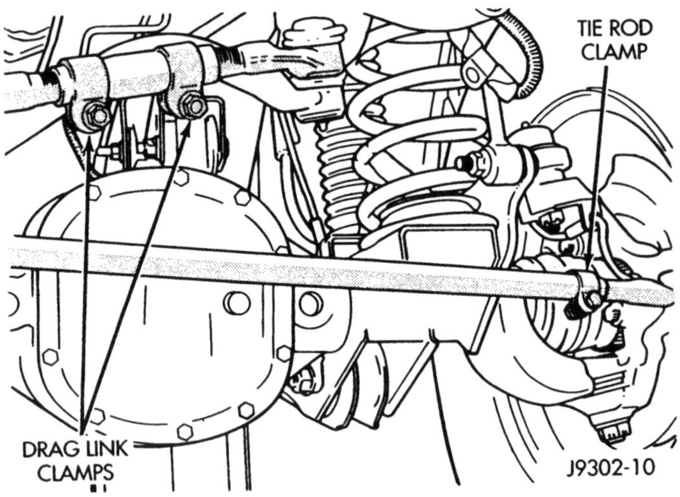

Fig. 3 Tie Rod/Drag Link Clamp Bolt

PITMAN ARM

REMOVAL

(1) Remove the cotter pin and nut from the drag link at the pitman arm.

(2) Remove the drag link ball stud from the pitman arm with a puller.

(3) Remove the nut and washer from the steering gear shaft. Mark the pitman shaft and pitman arm for installation reference. Remove the pitman arm from steering gear with Puller C-4150A (Fig. 4).

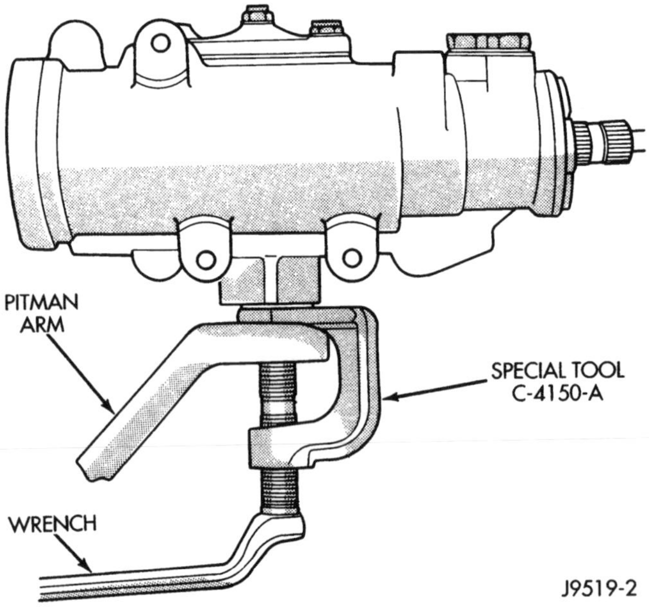

Fig. 4 Pitman Arm Removal

INSTALLATION

(1) Align and install the pitman arm on steering gear shaft.

(2) Install the washer and nut on the shaft and tighten the nut to 251 N·m (185 ft. lbs.).

(3) Install drag link ball stud to pitman arm. Install nut and tighten to 81 N·m (60 ft. lbs.). Install a new cotter pin.

DRAG LINK

REMOVAL

(1) Remove the cotter pins and nuts at the steering knuckle and drag link (Fig. 1).

(2) Remove the steering dampener ball stud from the drag link with a puller tool.

(3) Remove the drag link from the steering knuckle with a puller tool. Remove the same for tie rod and pitman arm.

(4) If necessary, loosen the end clamp bolts and remove the tie rod end from the link.

INSTALLATION

(1) Install the drag link adjustment sleeve and tie rod end. Position clamp bolts (Fig. 3).

(2) Position the drag link at the steering linkage. Install the drag link to the steering knuckle nut. Do the same for the tie rod and pitman arm.

(3) Tighten the nut at the steering knuckle to 47 N·m (35 ft. lbs.). Tighten the pitman nut to 81 N·m (60 ft. lbs.) and tie rod ball stud nut to 47 N·m (35 ft. lbs.). Install new cotter pins and bend end 60°.

(4) Install the steering dampener onto the drag link and tighten the nut to 74 N·m (55 ft. lbs.). Install a new cotter pin and bend end 60°.

STEERING DAMPENER

REMOVAL

(1) Place the front wheels in a straight ahead position.

(2) Remove the steering dampener retaining nut and bolt from the axle bracket (Fig. 1).

(3) Remove the cotter pin and nut from the ball stud at the drag link.

(4) Remove the steering dampener ball stud from the drag link using C-3894-A puller.

INSTALLATION

(1) Install the steering dampener to the axle bracket and drag link.

(2) Install the steering dampener bolt in the axle bracket and tighten nut to 74 N·m (55 ft. lbs.).

(3) Install the ball stud nut at the drag link and tighten nut to 74 N·m (55 ft. lbs.). Install a new cotter pin.

SPECIFICATIONS

TORQUE CHART

DESCRIPTION	TORQUE
Pitman Arm	
Shaft	251 N·m (185 ft. lbs.)
Drag Link	
Ball Studs	74 N·m (55 ft. lbs.)
Clamp	49 N·m (36 ft. lbs.)
Tie Rod Ends	
Ball Studs	74 N·m (55 ft. lbs.)
Clamp	27 N·m (20 ft. lbs.)
Tie Rod	
Ball Stud	88 N·m (65 ft. lbs.)
Steering Damper	
Frame	74 N·m (55 ft. lbs.)
Drag Link	74 N·m (55 ft. lbs.)

SPECIAL TOOLS

STEERING LINKAGE

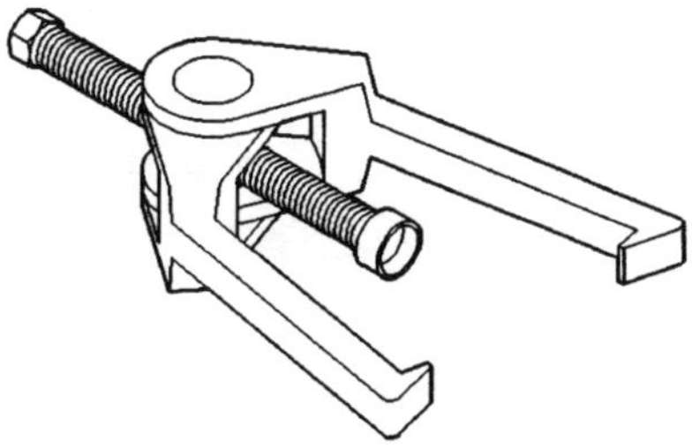

Puller C-3894–A

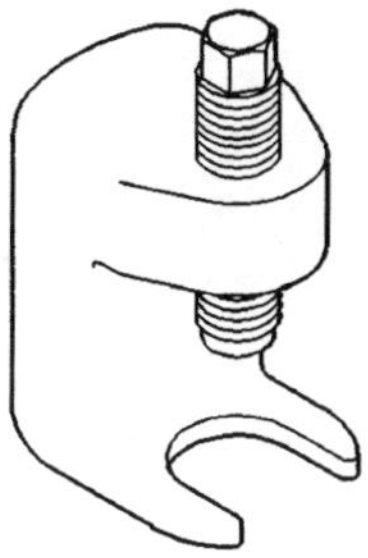

Remover Pitman C-4150A

TRANSMISSION AND TRANSFER CASE

CONTENTS

MANUAL TRANSMISSION—AX5

INDEX

GENERAL INFORMATION

GENERAL INFORMATION

The AX-5 is a five speed manual transmission. Fifth gear in the AX-5 is an overdrive range. The shift mechanism in both models is integral and mounted in the shift tower portion of the adapter housing (Fig. 1). The AX-5 is used for 2.5L engine applications.

TRAMSMISSION IDENTIFICATION

The AX-5 identification code is on the bottom surface of the transmission case near the fill plug (Fig. 2). The first number is year of manufacture. The second and third numbers indicate month of manufacture. The next series of numbers is the transmission serial number.

GEAR RATIOS

Gear ratios are as follows:

- First gear: 3.93:1
- Second gear: 2.33:1
- Third gear: 1.45:1
- Fourth gear: 1.00:1
- Fifth gear: 0.85:1
- Reverse gear: 4.74:1

SHIFT PATTERN

The shift configuration is a modified H-pattern with fifth gear above reverse on the right side of the pattern. The neutral gate runs across the pattern (Fig. 3).

RECOMMENDED LUBRICANT

The recommended lubricant is Mopar 75W–90, API Grade GL–5 gear lubricant, or equivalent.

Correct lubricant level is from the bottom edge, to no more than 6 mm (1/4 in.) below the bottom edge of the fill plug hole.

The fill plug is at the passenger side of the adapter housing (Fig. 4). The drain plug is at the bottom of the case.

Approximate dry fill lubricant capacity is 3.3 liters (3.5 qts.).

GENERAL INFORMATION (Continued)

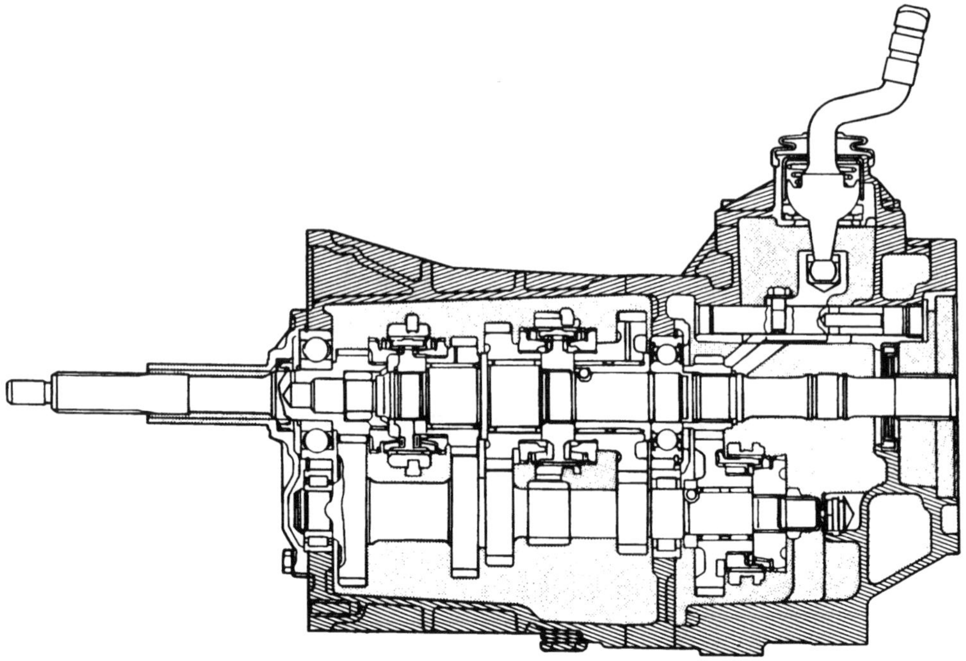

Fig. 1 AX-5 Manual Transmission

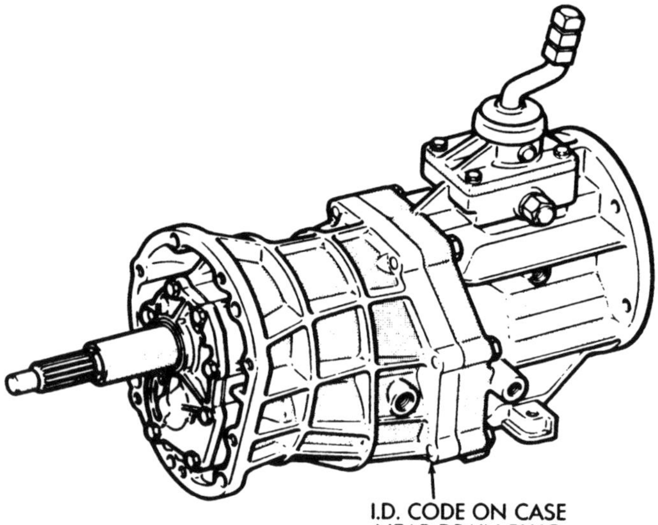

Fig. 2 Transmission Identification

TRANSMISSION ASSEMBLY INFORMATION

Lubricate the transmission components with Mopar 75W–90, GL 5 gear lubricant during assembly. Use petroleum jelly to lubricate seal lips and/or hold parts in place during installation.

Refer to (Fig. 5) during assembly.

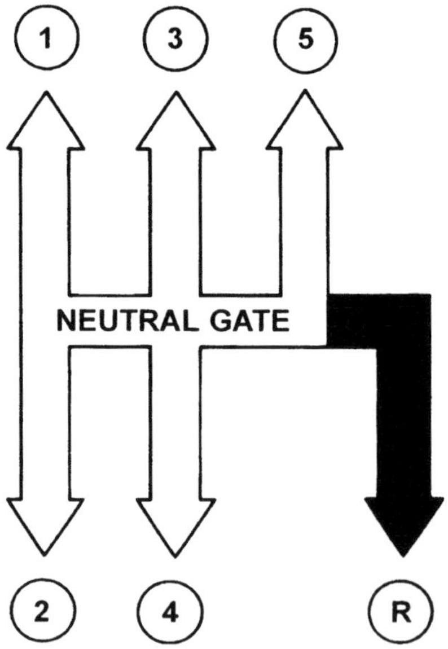

Fig. 3 Shift Pattern

DIAGNOSIS AND TESTING

LOW LUBRICANT LEVEL

A low transmission lubricant level is generally the result of a leak, inadequate lubricant fill, or an incorrect lubricant level check.

Leaks can occur at the mating surfaces of the gear case, intermediate plate and adaptor or extension housing, or from the front/rear seals. A suspected leak could also be the result of an overfill condition.

Leaks at the rear of the extension or adapter housing will be from the housing oil seals. Leaks at com-

DIAGNOSIS AND TESTING (Continued)

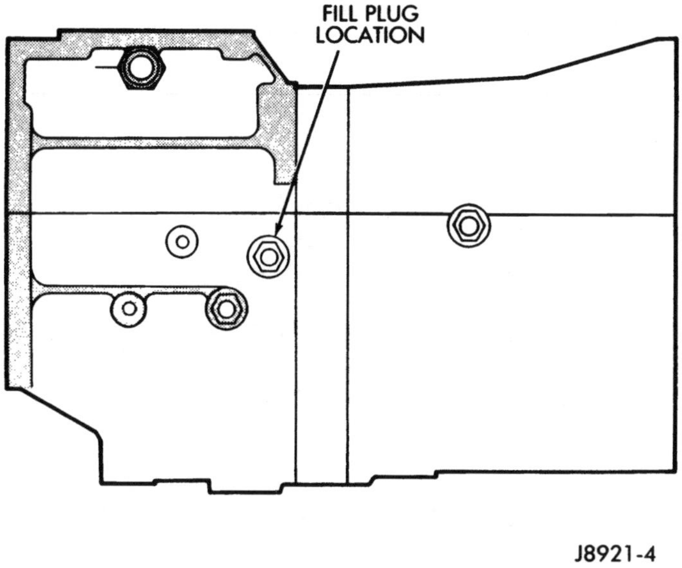

Fig. 4 Fill Plug Location

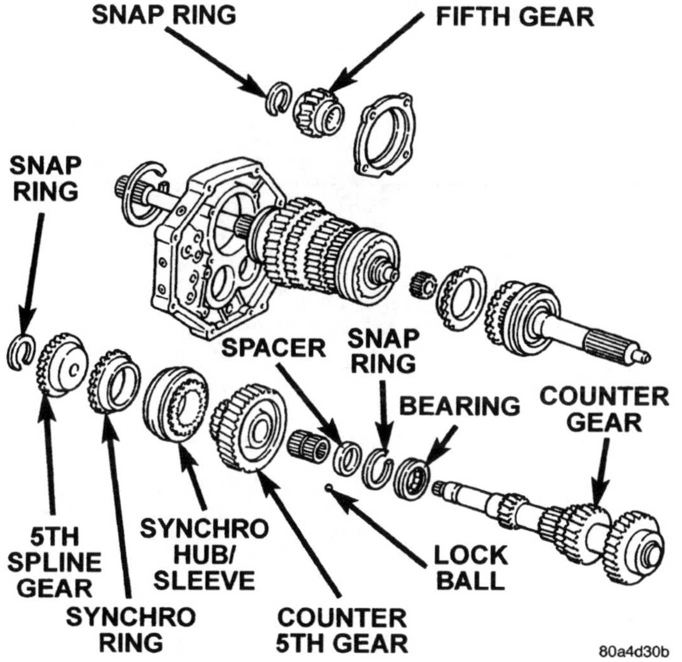

Fig. 5 Counter Gear Components

ponent mating surfaces will probably be the result of inadequate sealer, gaps in the sealer, incorrect bolt tightening, or use of a non–recommended sealer.

A leak at the front of the transmission will be from either the front bearing retainer or retainer seal. Lubricant may be seen dripping from the clutch housing after extended operation. If the leak is severe, it may also contaminate the clutch disc causing slip, grab and chatter.

Transmissions filled from air or electrically powered lubricant containers can be under filled. This generally happens when the container delivery mechanism is improperly calibrated. Always check the lubricant level after filling to avoid an under fill condition.

A correct lubricant level check can only be made when the vehicle is level; use a drive–on hoist to ensure this. Also allow the lubricant to settle for a minute or so before checking. These recommendations will ensure an accurate check and avoid an under– or–overfill condition.

HARD SHIFTING

Hard shifting is usually caused by a low lubricant level, improper or contaminated lubricants, component damage, incorrect clutch adjustment, or by a damaged clutch pressure plate or disc.

Substantial lubricant leaks can result in gear, shift rail, synchro and bearing damage. If a leak goes undetected for an extended period, the first indications of a problem are usually hard shifting and noise.

Incorrect or contaminated lubricants can also contribute to hard shifting. The consequence of using non–recommended lubricants is noise, excessive wear, internal bind and hard shifting.

Improper clutch release is a frequent cause of hard shifting. Incorrect adjustment or a worn, damaged pressure plate or disc can cause incorrect release. If the clutch problem is advanced, gear clash during shifts can result.

Worn or damaged synchro rings can cause gear clash when shifting into any forward gear. In some new or rebuilt transmissions, new synchro rings may tend to stick slightly causing hard or noisy shifts. In most cases, this condition will decline as the rings wear–in.

TRANSMISSION NOISE

Most manual transmissions make some noise during normal operation. Rotating gears generate a mild whine that is audible but only at extreme speeds.

Severe, highly audible transmission noise is generally the result of a lubricant problem. Insufficient, improper, or contaminated lubricant will promote rapid wear of gears, synchros, shift rails, forks and bearings. The overheating caused by a lubricant problem, can also lead to gear breakage.

REMOVAL AND INSTALLATION

TRANSMISSION

REMOVAL

(1) Shift transmission into first or third gear. Then raise vehicle on hoist.

(2) Support engine with adjustable jack stand. Position wood block between jack and oil pan to avoid damaging pan.

REMOVAL AND INSTALLATION (Continued)

(3) Disconnect necessary exhaust system components.

(4) Remove skid plate.

(5) Disconnect rear cushion and bracket from transmission.

(6) Remove rear crossmember.

(7) Disconnect transfer case shift linkage at transfer case.

(8) Disconnect vehicle speed sensor wires and transfer case vent hose.

(9) Remove slave cylinder from clutch housing.

(10) Disconnect transmission shift lever as follows:

(a) Lower transmission–transfer case assembly approximately 7–8 cm (3 in.) for access to shift lever.

(b) Reach up and around transmission case and unseat shift lever dust boot from transmission shift tower (Fig. 6). Move boot upward on shift lever for access to retainer that secures lever in shift tower.

(c) Reach up and around transmission case and press shift lever retainer downward with your fingers. Turn retainer counterclockwise to release it.

(d) Lift lever and retainer out of shift tower (Fig. 6). **Do not remove the shift lever from the floorpan boots. Leave the lever in place for later transmission installation.**

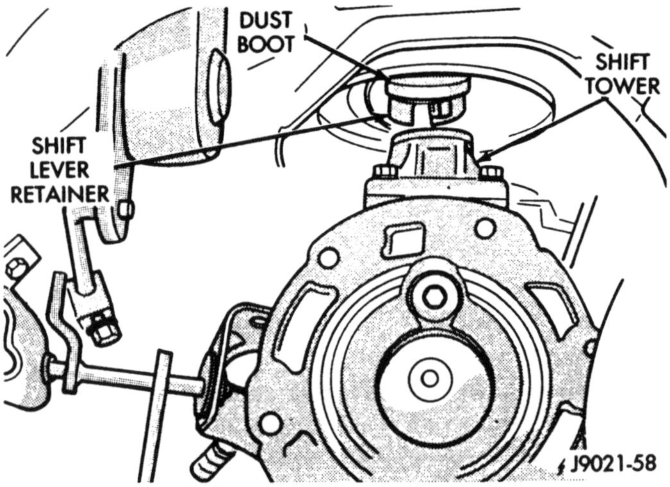

Fig. 6 Removing/Installing Shift Lever

(11) Mark front and rear propeller shafts for installation alignment (Fig. 7). Then remove both shafts.

(12) Remove crankshaft position sensor (Fig. 8).

CAUTION: It is important that the crankshaft position sensor be removed prior to transmission removal. The sensor can easily be damaged if left in place during removal operations.

(13) Unclip wire harnesses from transmission and transfer case.

(14) Remove slave cylinder from clutch housing.

Fig. 7 Marking Propeller Shaft And Axle Yokes

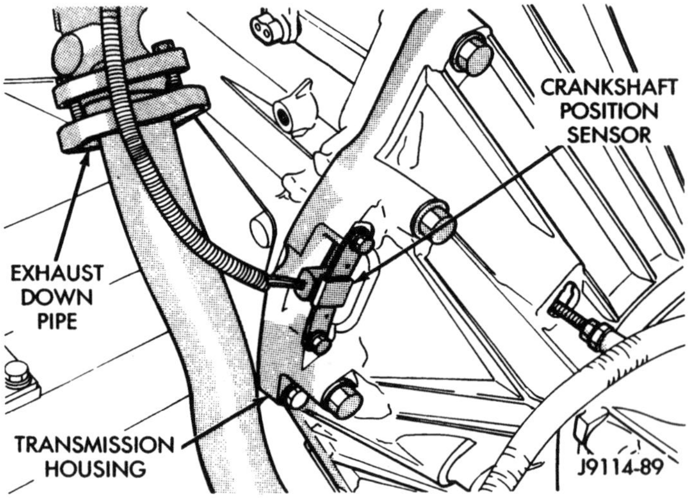

Fig. 8 Crankshaft Position Sensor—2.5L Engine

(15) Support transmission with transmission jack.

(16) Remove nuts attaching transfer case to transmission and remove transfer case.

(17) Secure transmission to jack with safety chains.

(18) Remove clutch housing brace rod.

(19) Remove clutch housing–to–engine bolts.

(20) Pull transmission jack rearward until input shaft clears clutch. Then slide transmission out from under vehicle.

(21) Remove clutch release bearing, release fork and retainer clip.

(22) Remove clutch housing from transmission.

TRANSMISSION INSTALLATION

(1) Install clutch housing on transmission. Tighten housing bolts to 37 N·m (27 ft. lbs.) torque.

(2) Lubricate contact surfaces of release fork pivot ball stud and release fork with high temp grease. Then install release bearing, fork and retainer clip.

(3) Mount transmission on transmission jack.

REMOVAL AND INSTALLATION (Continued)

(4) Lightly lubricate pilot bearing and transmission input shaft splines with Mopar high temp grease.

(5) Align transmission input shaft, release bearing, and clutch disc splines. Then slide transmission into place.

(6) Install and tighten clutch housing–to–engine bolts to 75 N·m (55 ft. lbs.) torque. **Be sure the housing is properly seated on engine block before tightening bolts.**

(7) Lower transmission approximately 7–8 cm (3 in.) for access to shift tower. Be sure transmission is in first or third gear.

(8) Reach up and around transmission and insert shift lever in shift tower. Press lever retainer downward and turn it clockwise to lock it in place. Then install lever dust boot on shift tower.

(9) Install slave cylinder in clutch housing.

(10) Align and install transfer case on and transmission. Tighten transfer case–to–transmission nuts to 35 N·m (26 ft. lbs.) torque.

(11) Connect transfer case vent hose and shift linkage. Check and adjust linkage if necessary.

(12) Connect transfer case vent hose.

(13) Secure wire harnesses in clips/tie straps on transmission and transfer case.

(14) Connect backup light switch wires.

(15) Connect vehicle speed sensor wires.

(16) Install and connect crankshaft position sensor.

(17) Install rear crossmember. Tighten crossmember–to–frame bolts to 41 N·m (31 ft. lbs.) torque. Then tighten transmission–to–rear support bolts/nuts to 45 N·m (33 ft. lbs.) torque.

(18) Remove jack stand.

(19) Align and install front/rear propeller shafts. Tighten shaft U–joint clamp bolts to 19 N·m (170 in. lbs.) torque.

(20) Install skid plate, if equipped. Tighten bolts to 42 N·m (31 ft. lbs.) torque. Tighten stud nuts to 17 N·m (150 in. lbs.) torque.

(21) Top off transmission and transfer case lubricant levels.

(22) Lower vehicle.

DISASSEMBLY AND ASSEMBLY

ADAPTER HOUSING AND FRONT BEARING RETAINER

REMOVAL

(1) Drain transmission lubricant.

(2) Remove release bearing and lever.

(3) Remove clutch housing bolts and remove housing.

(4) Remove adapter housing.

(5) Remove detent spring and ball. Remove detent plug (Fig. 9) and remove detent spring and ball with pencil magnet.

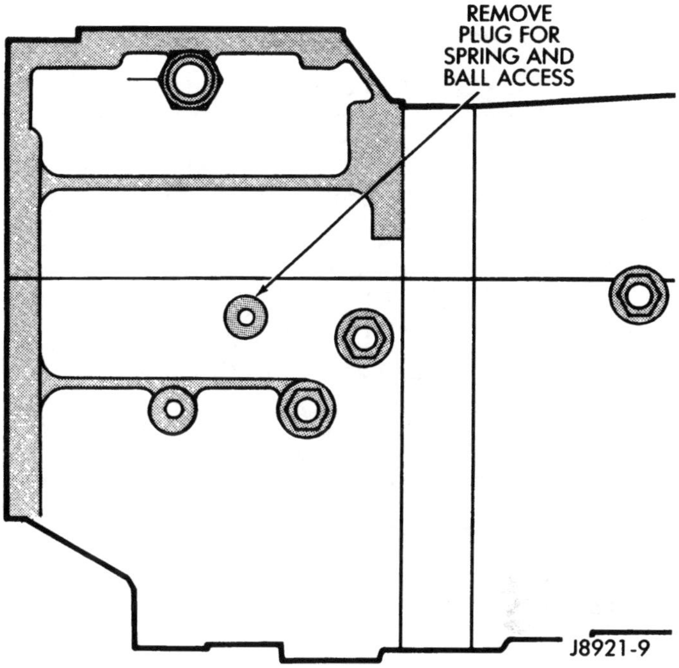

Fig. 9 Detent Ball Plug Location

(6) Remove shift arm set bolt (Fig. 10) and remove bolt and lockplate.

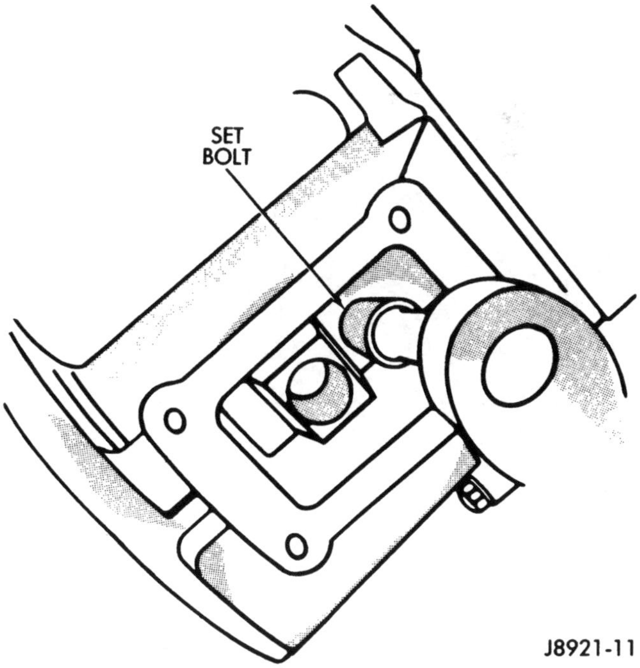

Fig. 10 Set Bolt Removal

DISASSEMBLY AND ASSEMBLY (Continued)

(7) Remove shift lever shaft plug (Fig. 11). Then pull shaft out with large magnet.

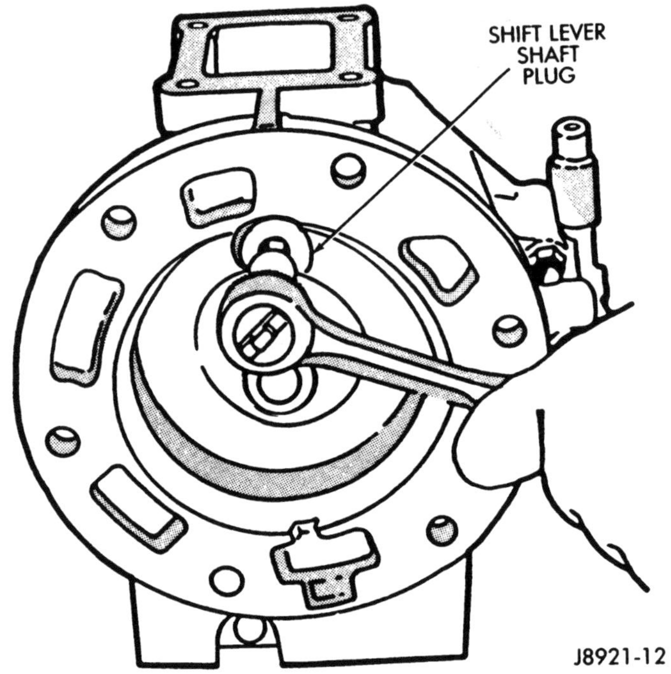

Fig. 11 Removing Shift Lever Shaft Plug

(8) Remove adapter housing bolts.

(9) Remove adapter housing by tapping it loose with plastic mallet.

(10) Remove front bearing snap rings (Fig. 12).

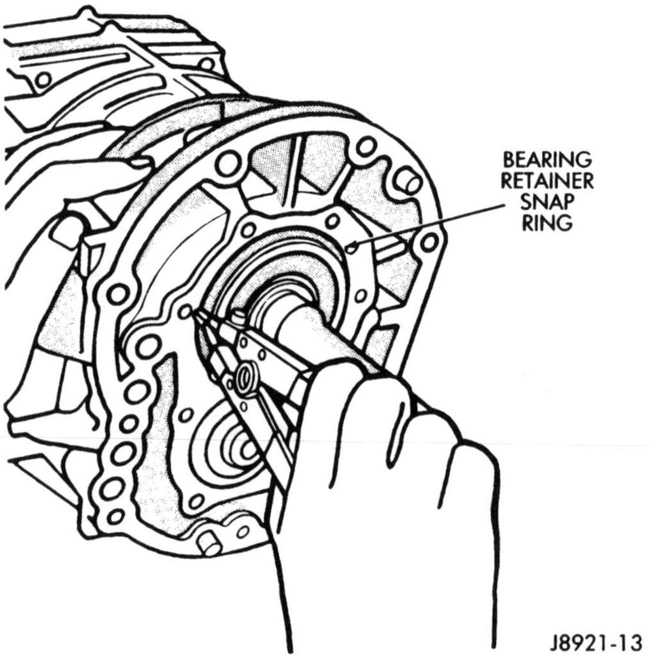

Fig. 12 Removing Bearing Retainer Snap Ring

(11) Remove front bearing retainer and intermediate plate by tapping them loose with plastic mallet (Fig. 13).

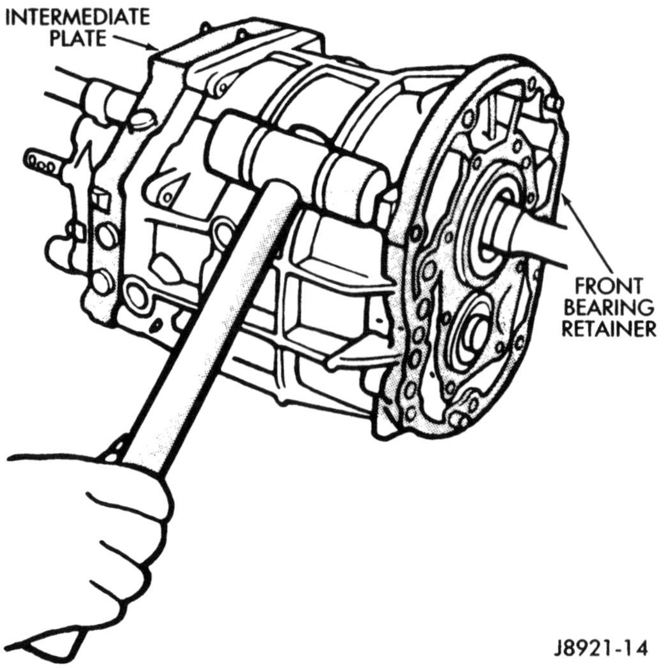

Fig. 13 Front Bearing Retainer And Intermediate Plate Removal

ASSEMBLING GEARTRAIN AND TRANSMISSION CASE

(1) Remove intermediate plate from vise.

(2) Install new gaskets on intermediate plate.

(3) Install transmission case on intermediate plate (Fig. 14).

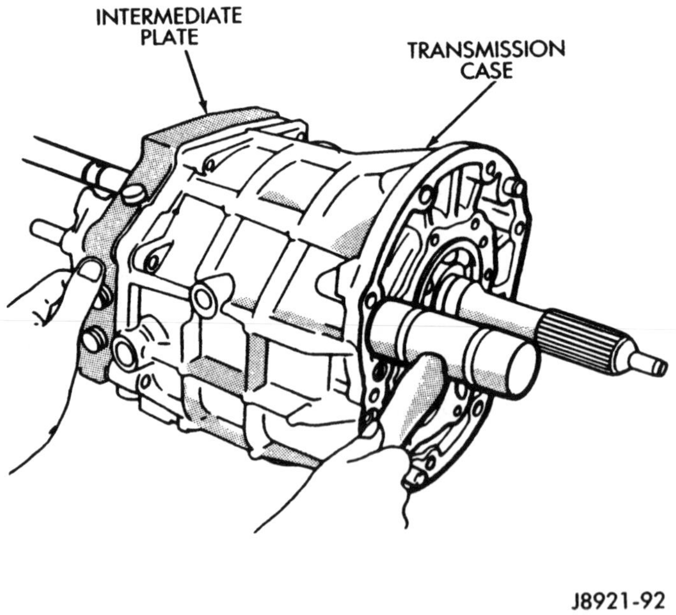

Fig. 14 Installing Transmission Case

DISASSEMBLY AND ASSEMBLY (Continued)

(4) Install new front bearing snap ring (Fig. 15).

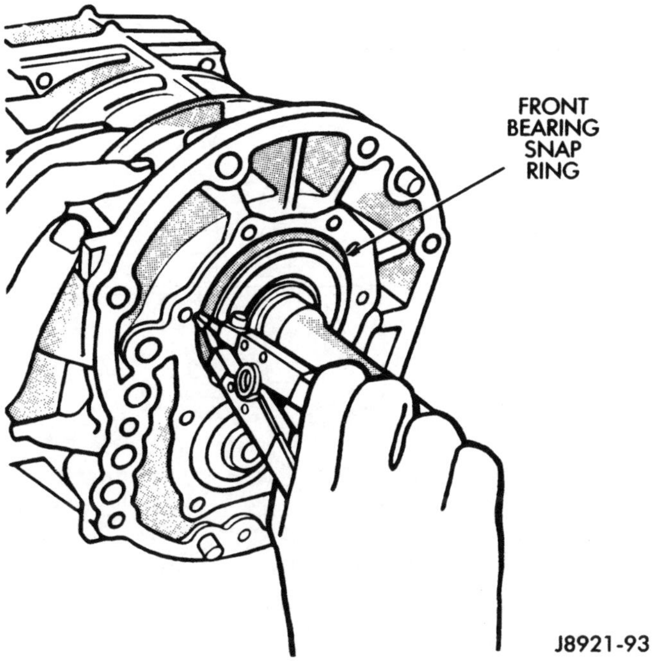

Fig. 15 Installing Front Bearing Snap Ring

(5) Install new gasket on front bearing retainer and install retainer on case (Fig. 16).

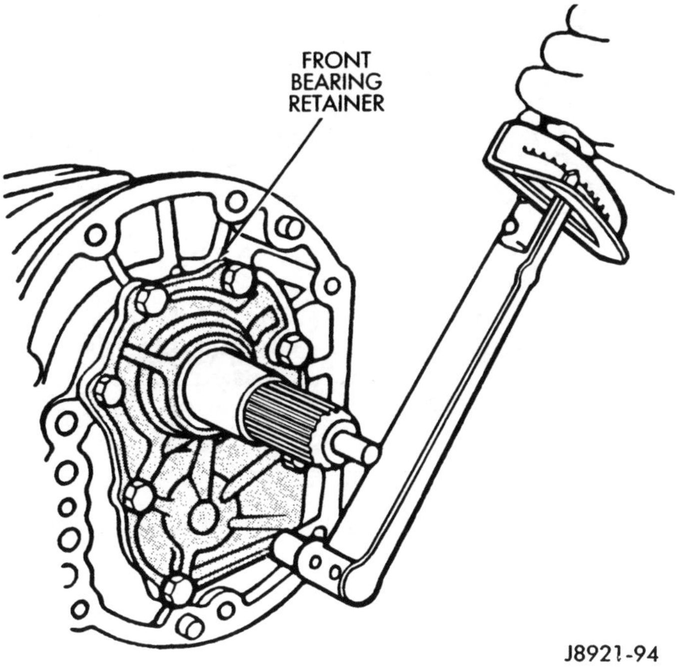

Fig. 16 Installing Front Bearing Retainer

(6) Install adapter or extension housing on intermediate plate (Fig. 17). Tighten housing bolts to 37 N·m (27 ft. lbs.) torque.

(7) Install shift arm (Fig. 17).

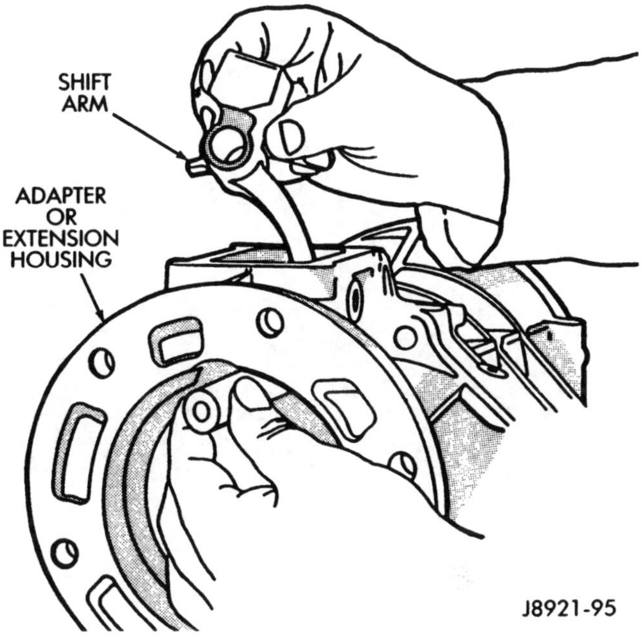

Fig. 17 Installing Adapter Housing And Shift Arm

(8) Install shift arm lock plate with pliers (Fig. 18). Then install and tighten lock plate set bolt to 38 N·m (28 ft. lbs.) torque.

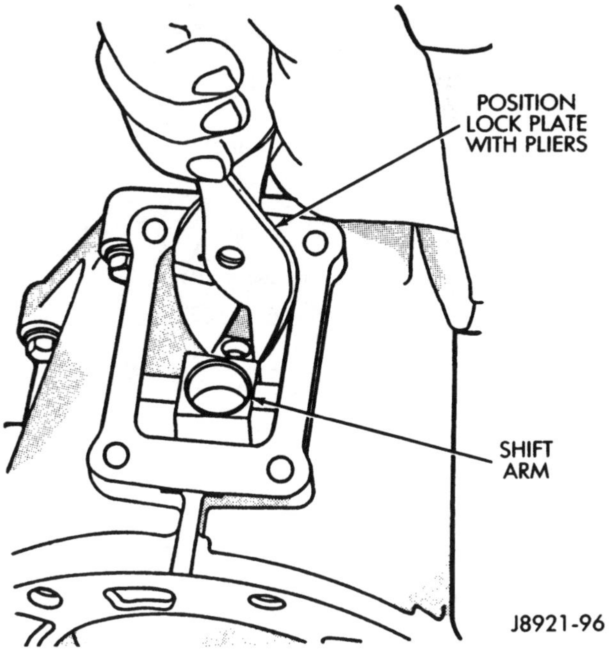

Fig. 18 Shift Arm Lock Plate Installation

DISASSEMBLY AND ASSEMBLY (Continued)

(9) Install and tighten shaft plug to 18 N·m (13 ft. lbs.) torque (Fig. 19).

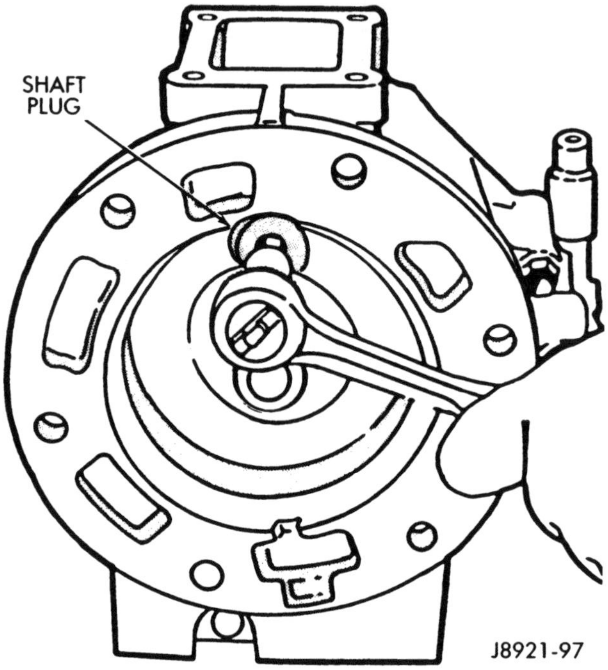

Fig. 19 Shaft Plug Installation

(10) Install lock ball and spring in housing. Then apply sealer to ball plug and install plug (Fig. 20). Tighten plug to 19 N·m (14 ft. lbs.) torque.

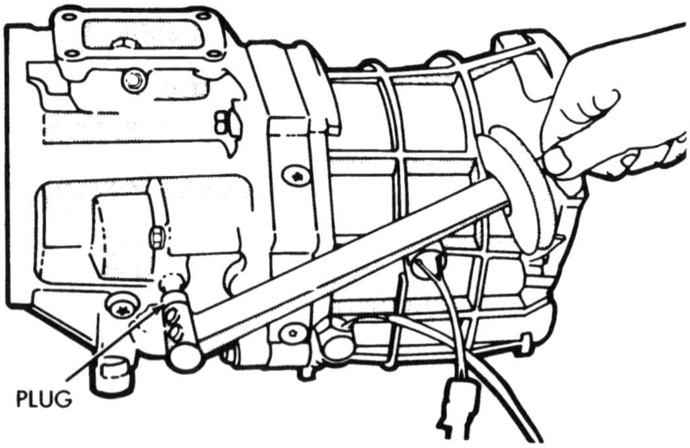

Fig. 20 Installing Ball Plug

(11) Install restrictor pins in housing (Fig. 21). Tighten pins to 27 N·m (20 ft. lbs.) torque.

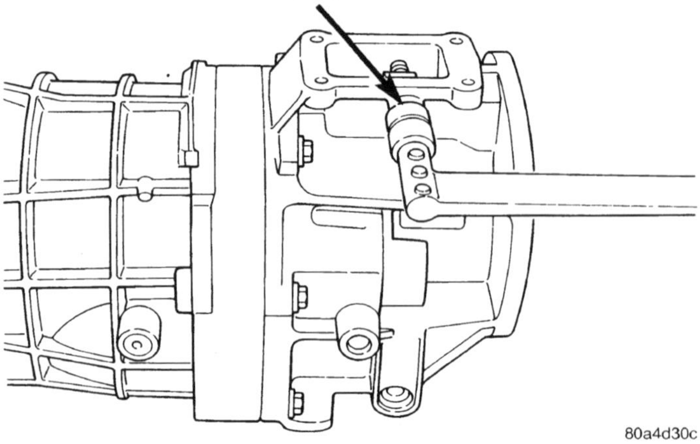

Fig. 21 Install Restrictor Pins

(12) Install shift tower and new gasket/splash plate on housing (Fig. 22). Tighten tower bolts to 18 N·m (13 ft. lbs.) torque.

(13) Install backup lamp switch (Fig. 22). Tighten switch to 37 N·m (27 ft. lbs.) torque.

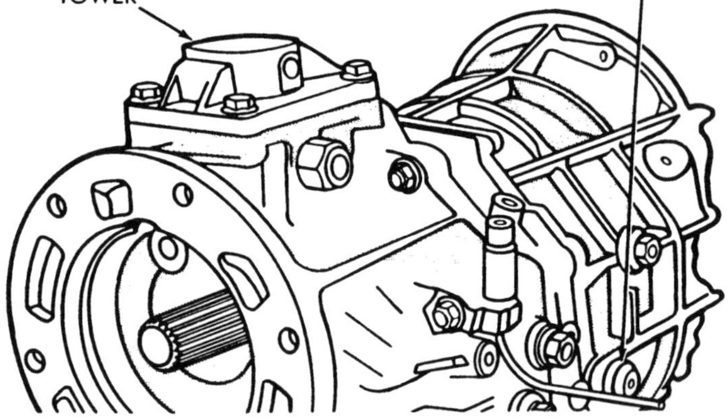

Fig. 22 Installing Shift Tower And Backup Lamp Switch

(14) Install adapter housing on transmission

(15) Install vehicle speed sensor.

(16) Install clutch housing, release bearing, release fork and retainer clip.

DISASSEMBLY AND ASSEMBLY (Continued)

SHIFT MECHANISM

DISASSEMBLE

(1) Install two clutch housing bolts and spare washers in intermediate plate (Fig. 23). Then clamp plate and gear assembly in vise. **Use enough washers to prevent bolts from touching. Also be sure vise jaws are clamped on bolt heads (Fig. 23).**

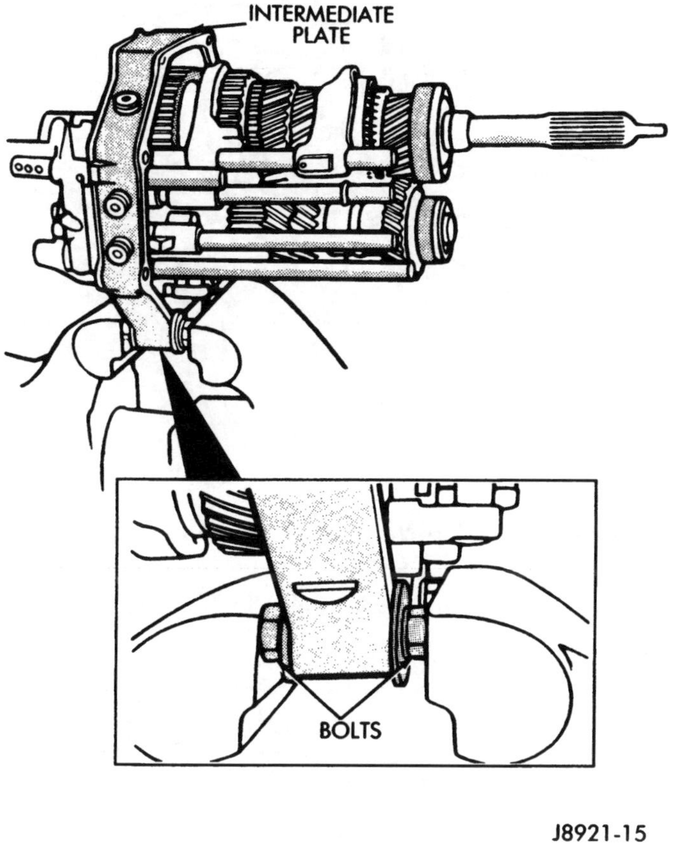

Fig. 23 Positioning Intermediate Plate In Vise

(2) Remove threaded plugs from intermediate plate. Then remove lock ball and spring from plug holes with pencil magnet (Fig. 24).

(3) Remove shift fork bolts (Fig. 25).

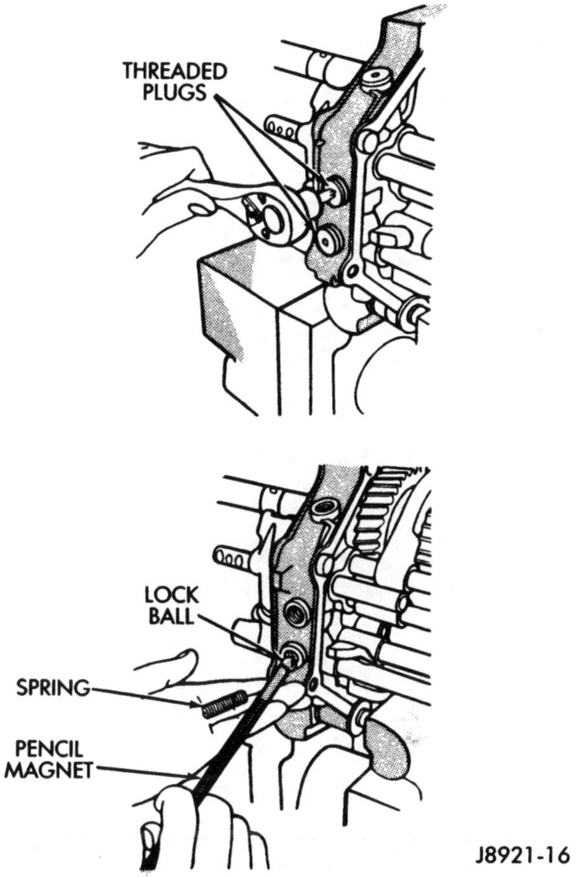

Fig. 24 Lock Ball And Spring Removal

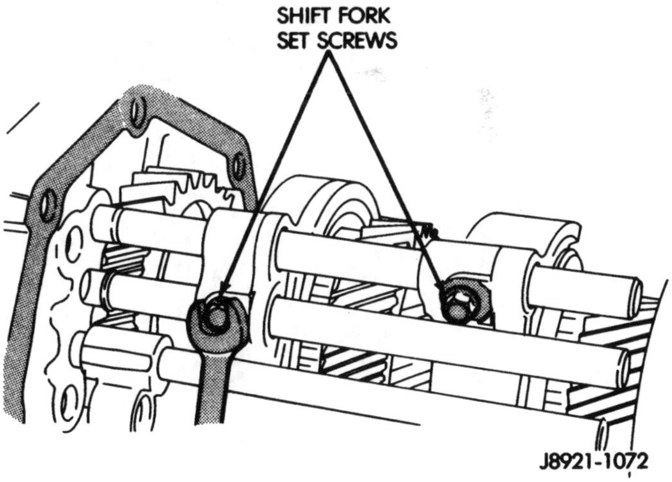

Fig. 25 Removing Shift Fork Pin

DISASSEMBLY AND ASSEMBLY (Continued)

(4) Remove shift rail C–rings (Fig. 26).

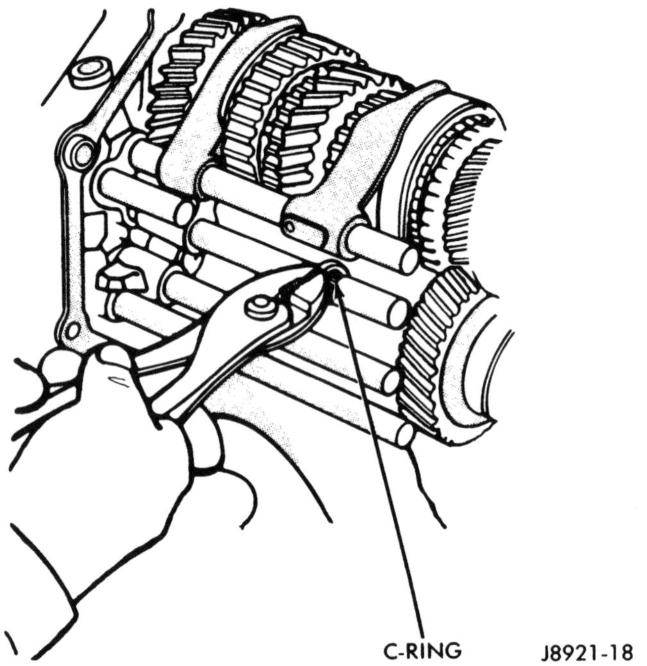

Fig. 26 Shift Rail C–Ring Removal

(5) Pull No. 4 shift rail outward and remove lock balls and pin (Fig. 27).

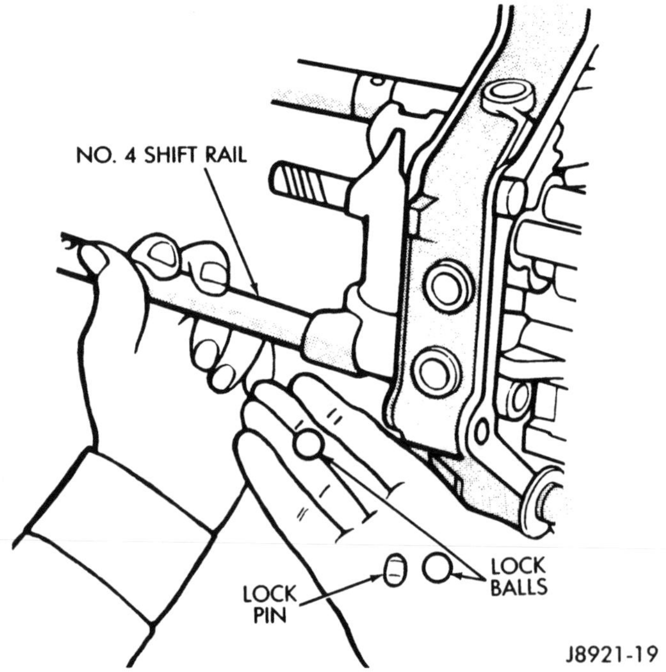

Fig. 27 Removing No. 4 Shift Rail, Lock Balls And Pin

(6) Remove No. 4 shift rail, fifth gear and No. 3 shift fork (Fig. 28).

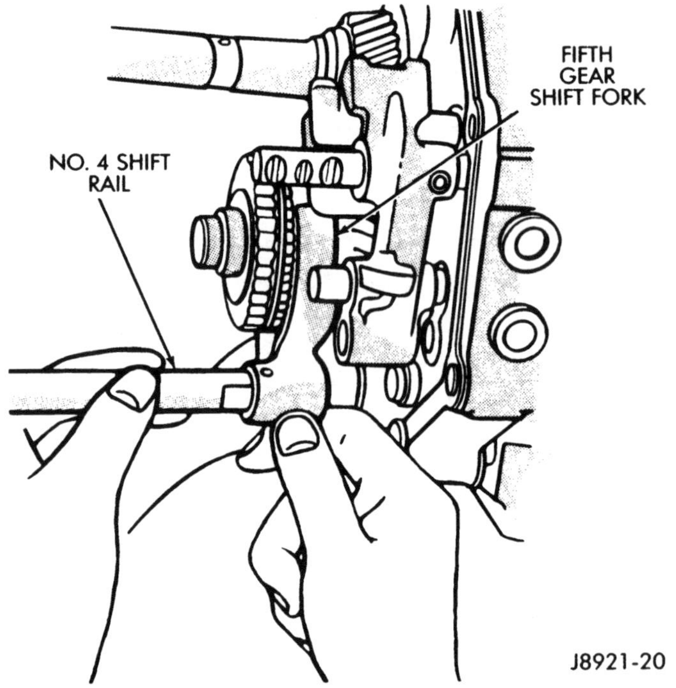

Fig. 28 Removing No. 4 Shift Rail And Fifth Gear Shift Fork

(7) Pull No. 5 shift rail and shift head out of plate (Fig. 29).

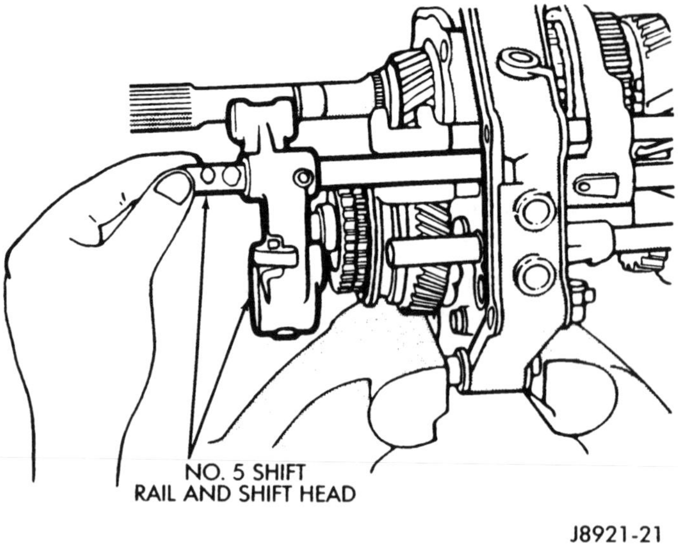

Fig. 29 Removing No. 5 Shift Rail And Shift Head

DISASSEMBLY AND ASSEMBLY (Continued)

(8) Remove shift rail No.3. **Catch interlock pins as rail is removed (Fig. 30).**

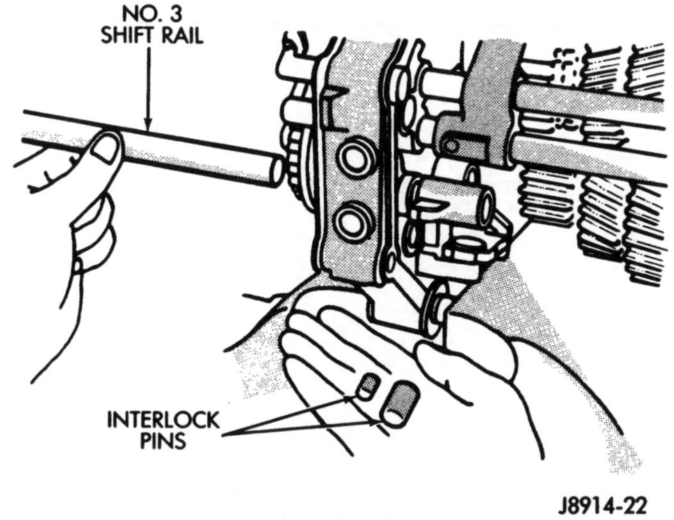

Fig. 30 Removing No. 3 Shift Rail And Interlock Pin

(9) Remove No. 1 shift rail and interlock pin (Fig. 31).

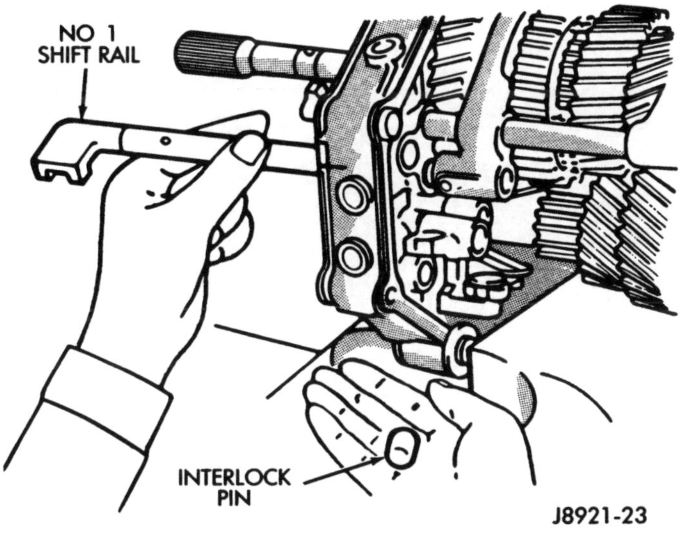

Fig. 31 Removing No. 1 Shift Rail And Interlock Pin

(10) Remove shift rail No. 2 and shift forks 1 and 2 (Fig. 32).

(11) Remove reverse idler gear and shaft (Fig. 33).

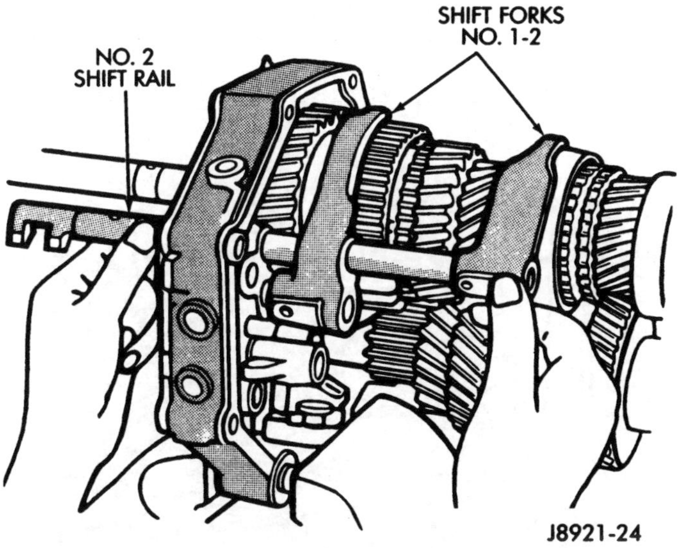

Fig. 32 Removing Shift Forks And No. 2 Shift Rail

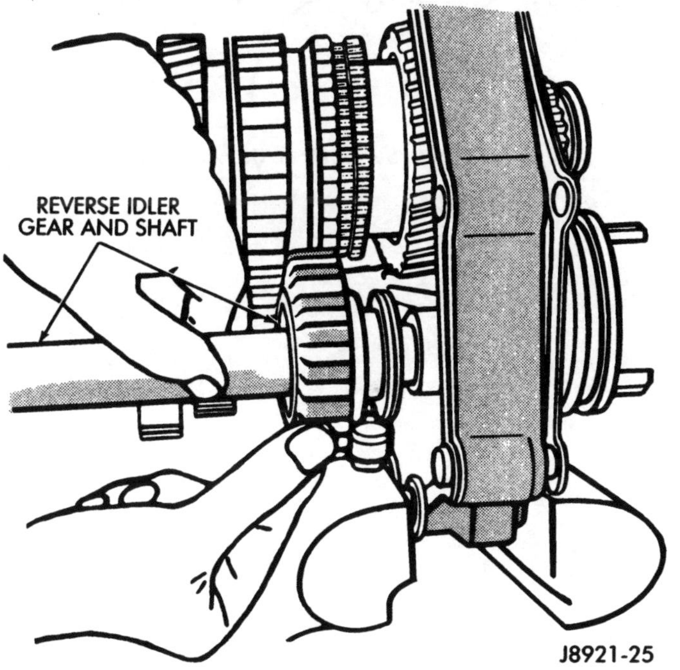

Fig. 33 Removing Reverse Idler Gear And Shaft

DISASSEMBLY AND ASSEMBLY (Continued)

(12) Remove reverse shift arm and fork (Fig. 34).

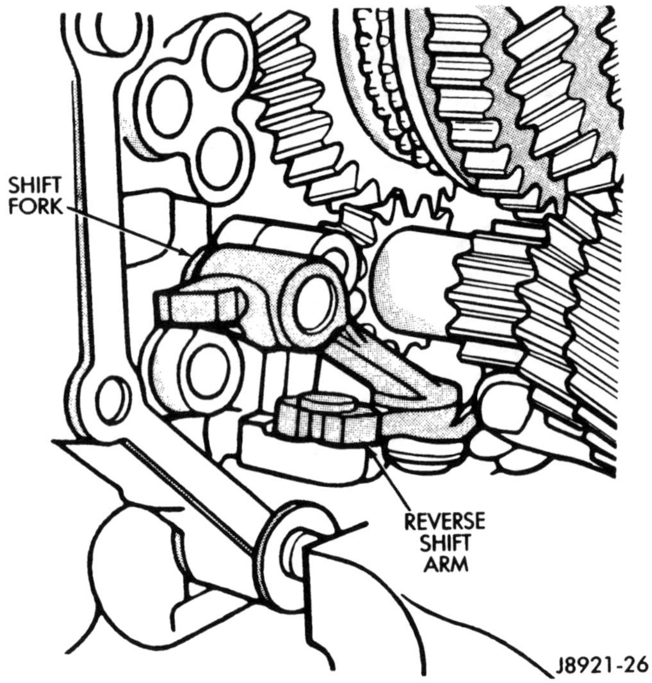

Fig. 34 Reverse Shift Arm Removal

SHIFT MECHANISM ASSEMBLY AND INSTALLATION

When assembling the shift mechanism, refer to (Fig. 35) for component details and location.

DISASSEMBLY AND ASSEMBLY (Continued)

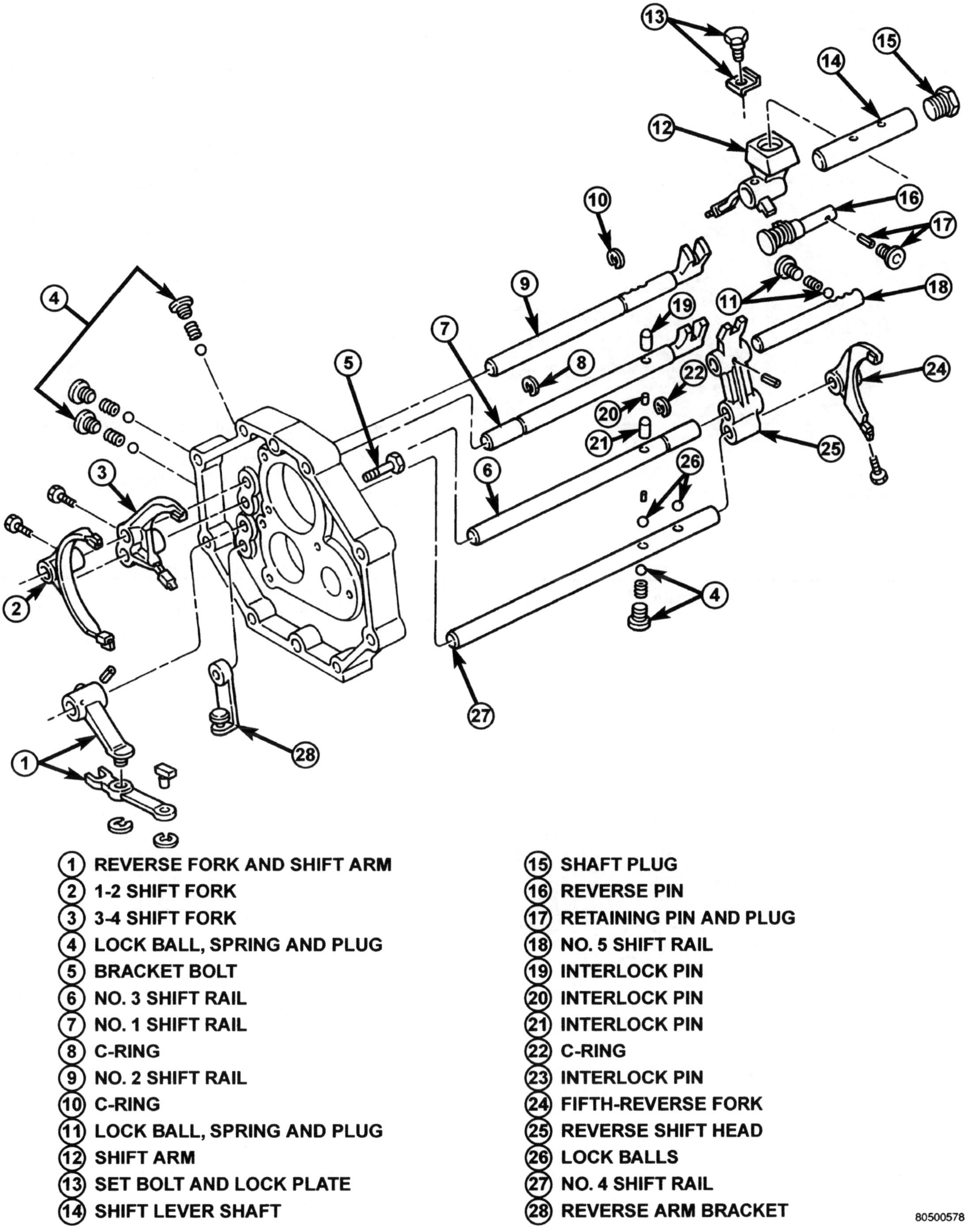

Fig. 35 Shift Components

DISASSEMBLY AND ASSEMBLY (Continued)

(1) Install reverse shift arm. Then seat shift fork in bracket (Fig. 36).

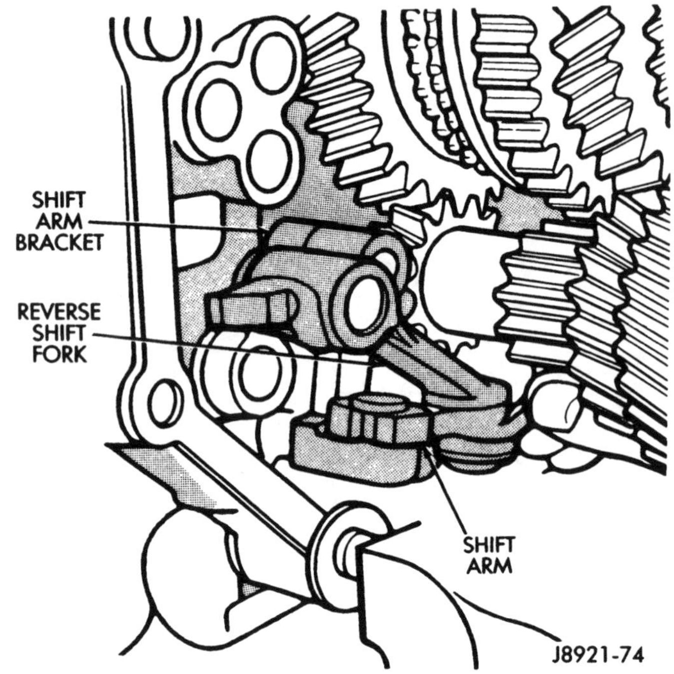

Fig. 36 Installing Reverse Shift Arm

(2) Install reverse idler gear on shaft. Then install shaft and gear in intermediate plate (Fig. 37). Install shaft lock plate and tighten attaching bolt to 18 N·m (13 ft. lbs.) torque.

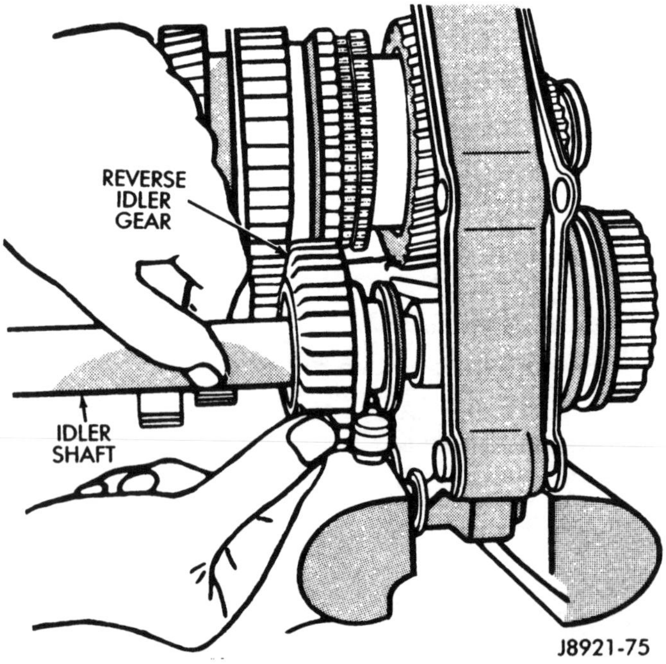

Fig. 37 Installing Reverse Idler Gear And Shaft

(3) Install 1–2 and 3–4 shift forks in synchronizer sleeves. Then slide No. 2 shift rail through intermediate plate and into forks (Fig. 38).

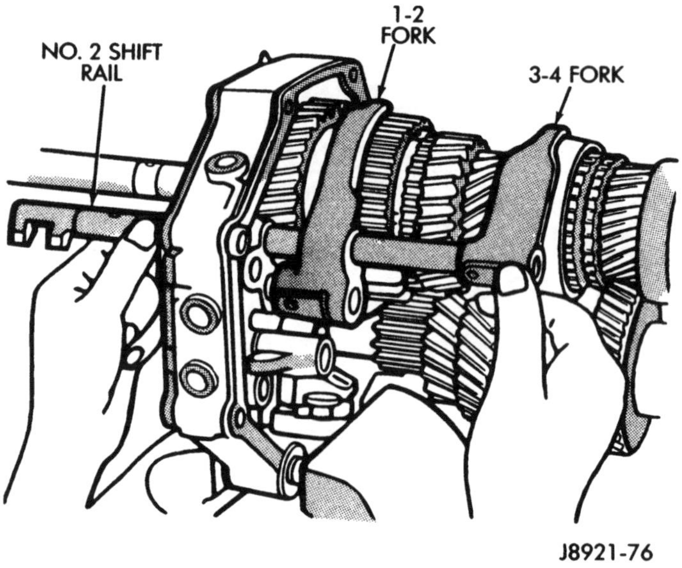

Fig. 38 Installing No. 2 Shift Rail and Shift Forks

(4) Coat shift rail interlock pins and balls with liberal quantity petroleum jelly to hold them in place.

(5) Refer to (Fig. 39) for interlock ball and pin positions during following assembly steps.

(6) Insert first interlock pin in intermediate plate (Fig. 40). Use pencil magnet and screwdriver to install pin.

(7) Install smaller diameter interlock pin in No. 1 rail (Fig. 41).

DISASSEMBLY AND ASSEMBLY (Continued)

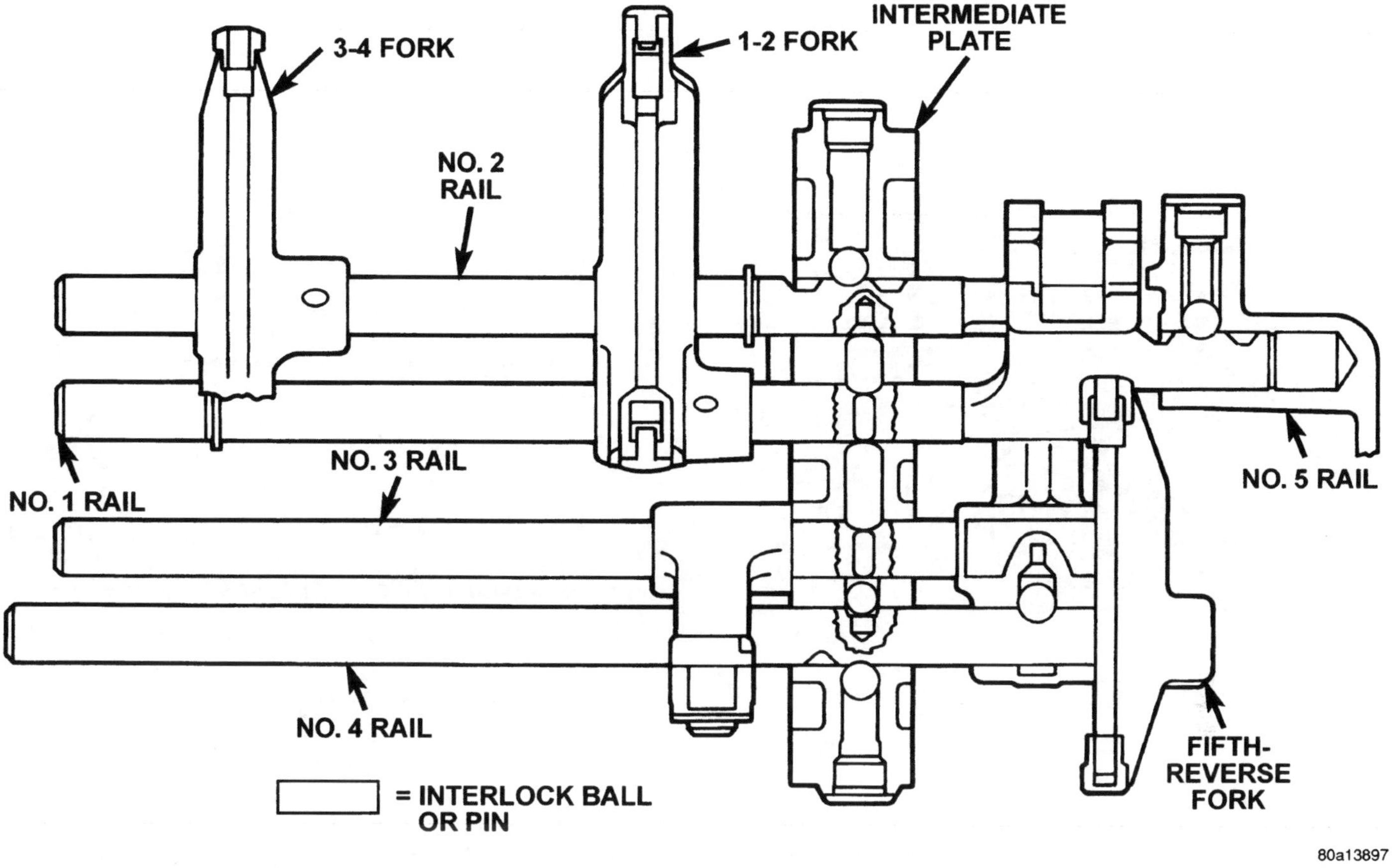

Fig. 39 Interlock Ball And Pin Position

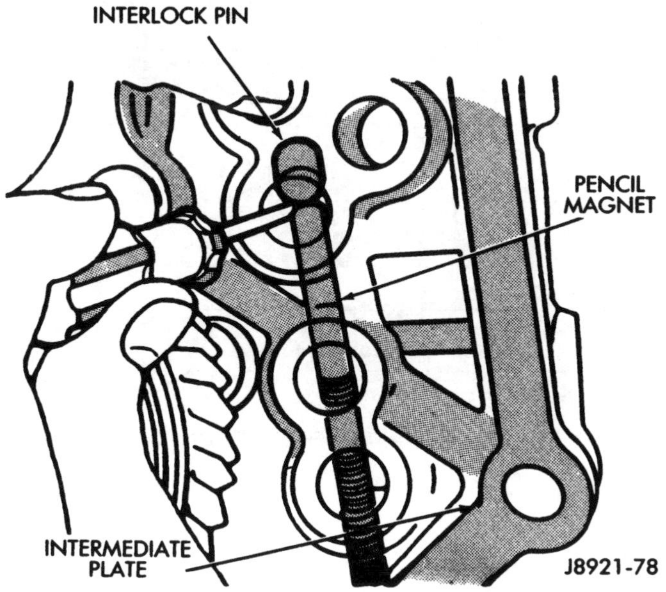

Fig. 40 Installing First Interlock Pin

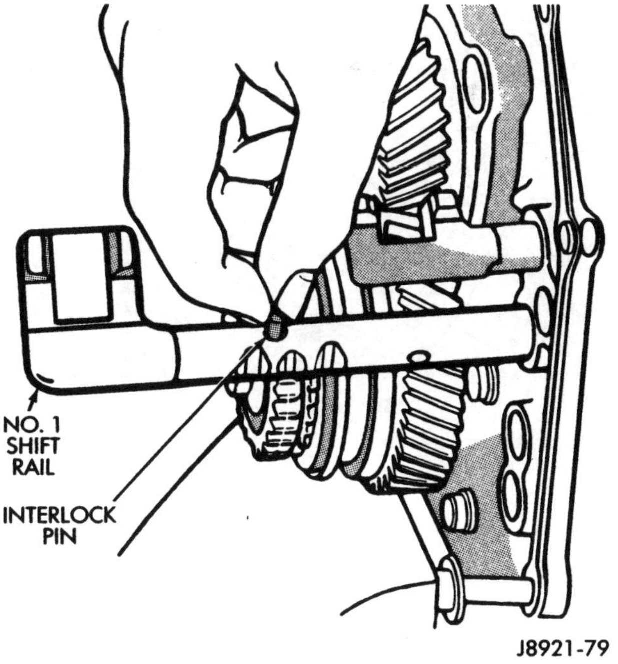

Fig. 41 Installing Interlock Pin In No. 1 Shift Rail

DISASSEMBLY AND ASSEMBLY (Continued)

(8) Slide No. 1 rail through 1–2 shift fork (Fig. 42).

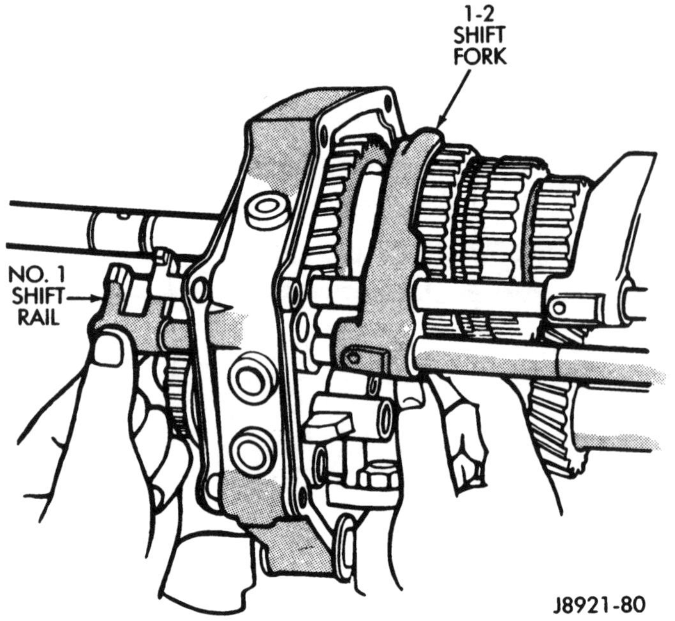

Fig. 42 Installing No. 1 Shift Rail

(9) Install largest interlock pin between Nos. 1 and 3 shift rails (Fig. 43).

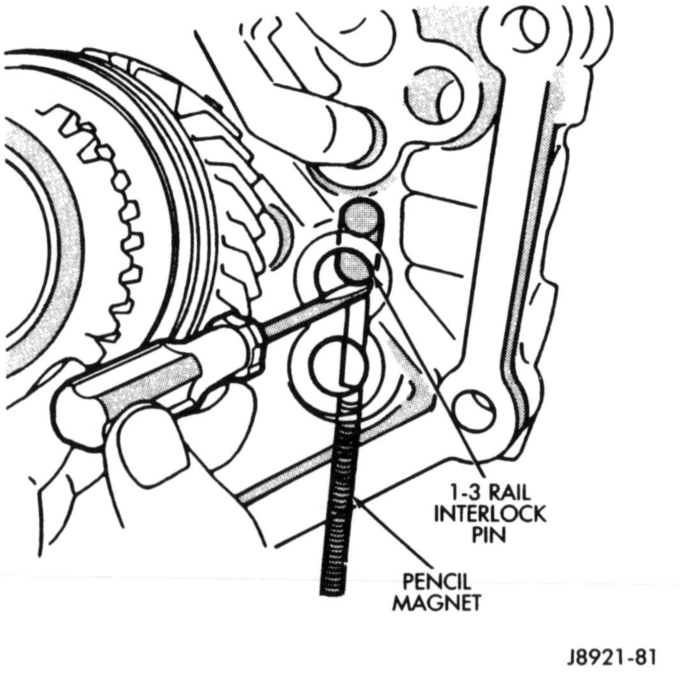

Fig. 43 Installing 1–3 Shift Rail Interlock Pin

(10) Install interlock pin in No. 3 shift rail (Fig. 44).

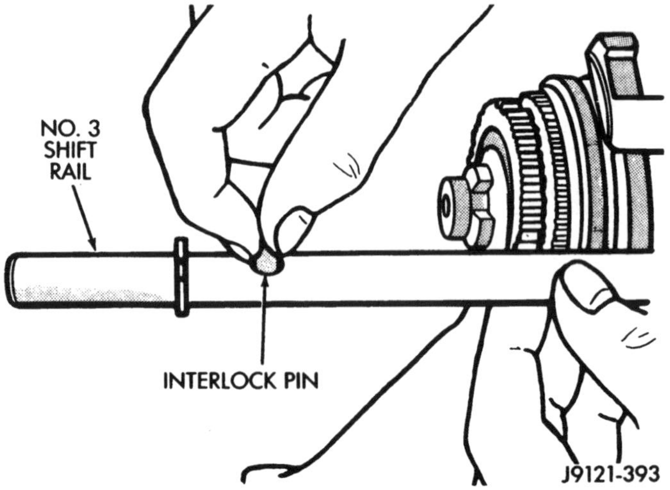

Fig. 44 Installing No. 3 Shift Rail Interlock Pin

(11) Slide No. 3 rail into reverse shift head (Fig. 45).

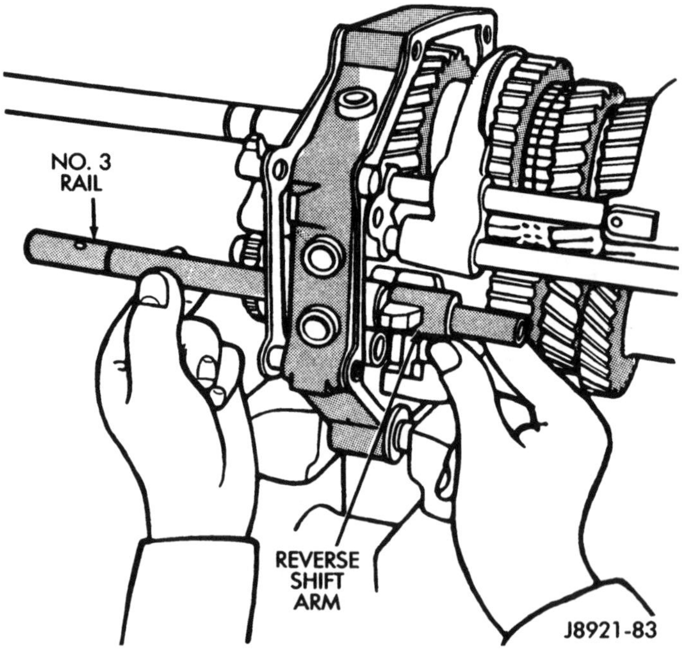

Fig. 45 Installing No. 3 Shift Rail

DISASSEMBLY AND ASSEMBLY (Continued)

(12) Assemble reverse shift head and No. 5 shift rail.

(13) Install No. 5 shift rail in intermediate plate and engage shift head on No. 3 shift rail (Fig. 46).

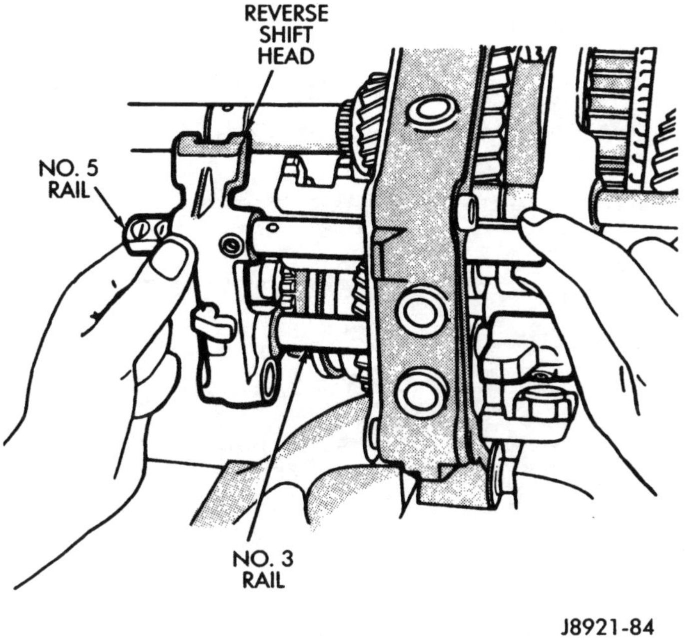

Fig. 46 Installing Reverse Shift Head

(14) Install reverse shift head lock ball with screwdriver and pencil magnet (Fig. 47).

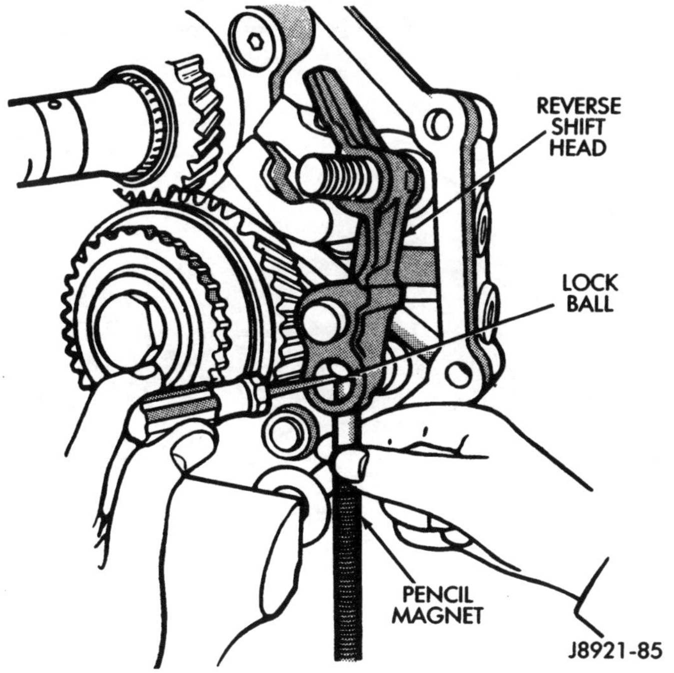

Fig. 47 Installing Reverse Shift Head Lock Ball

(15) Shift fifth gear synchronizer sleeve rearward to lock it (Fig. 48).

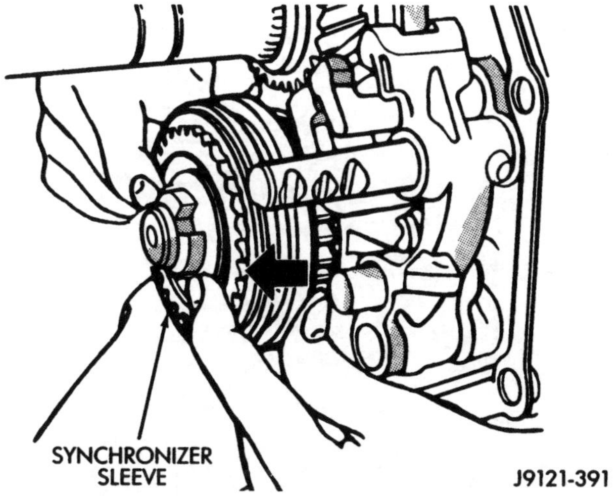

Fig. 48 Locking Fifth Synchronizer

(16) On AX 5, install fifth–reverse shift fork in synchronizer sleeve. Then slide No. 4 shift rail into fork (Fig. 49).

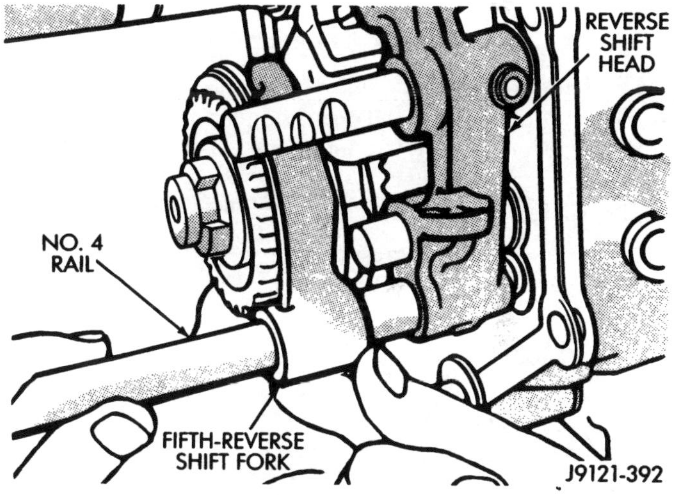

Fig. 49 Fifth–Reverse Shift Fork Installation

DISASSEMBLY AND ASSEMBLY (Continued)

(17) Install shift rail lock ball with pencil magnet and screwdriver (Fig. 50).

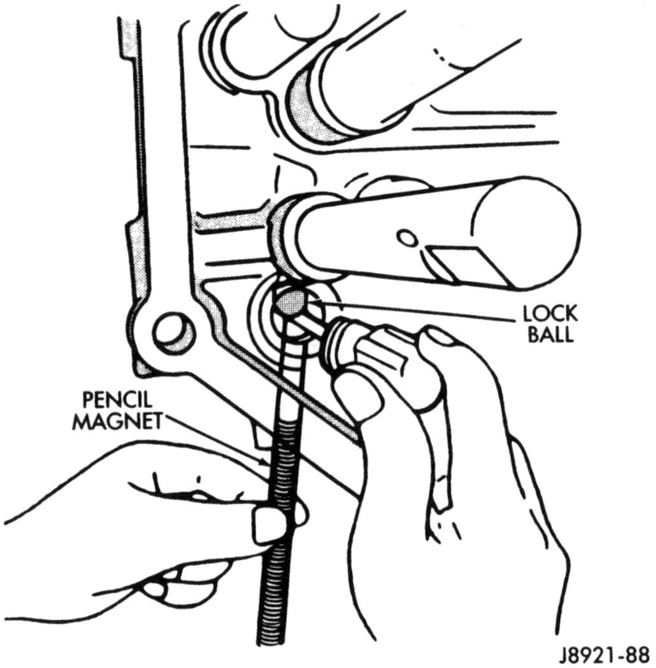

Fig. 50 Lock Ball Installation

(18) Check interlock operation as follows: Move No. 1 shift rail rearward to first gear position. Interlock operation is OK if remaining shift rails did not move.

(19) Install new shift fork pins (Fig. 51).

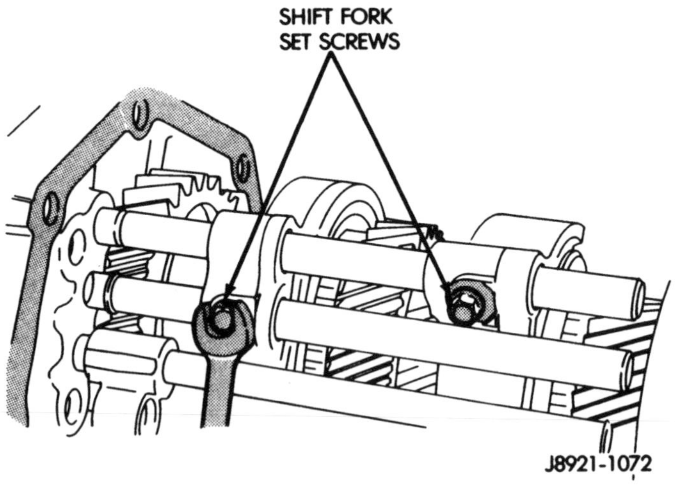

Fig. 51 Installing Shift Fork Pins

(20) Install new shift rail C–rings (Fig. 52).

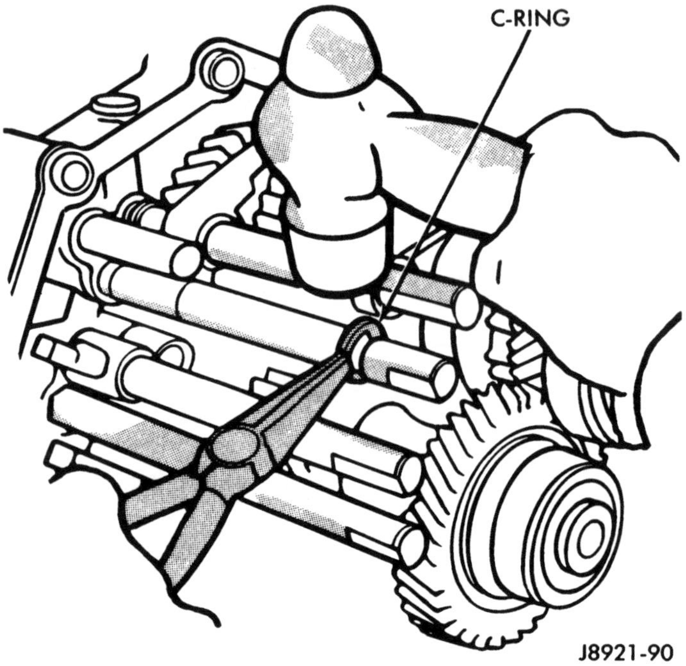

Fig. 52 Installing Shift Rail C–Rings

(21) Apply sealer to threads of lock ball plugs.

(22) Install lock balls and springs in intermediate plate. **Short spring goes in top hole of intermediate plate.**

(23) Install lock ball and spring plugs (Fig. 53). Tighten plugs to 19 N·m (14 ft. lbs.) torque.

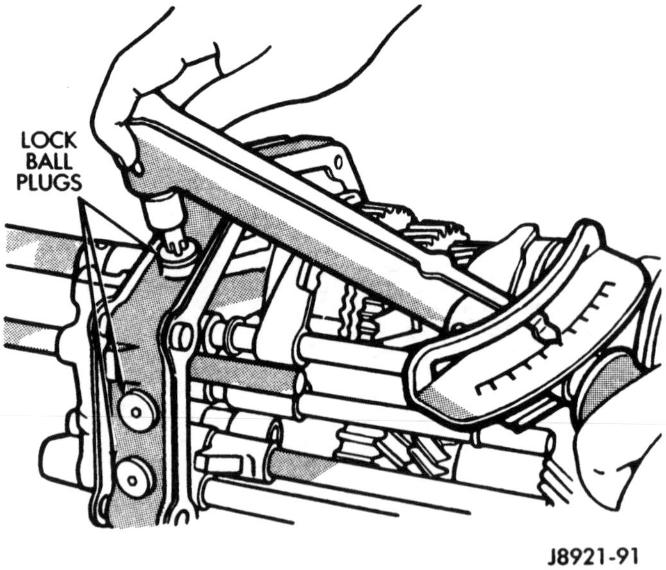

Fig. 53 Installing Lock Ball Plugs

DISASSEMBLY AND ASSEMBLY (Continued)

MAINSHAFT

DISASSEMBLE

(1) Measure fifth counter gear thrust clearance with feeler gauge (Fig. 54). Clearance should be 0.10–0.30 mm (0.004– 0.012 in.).

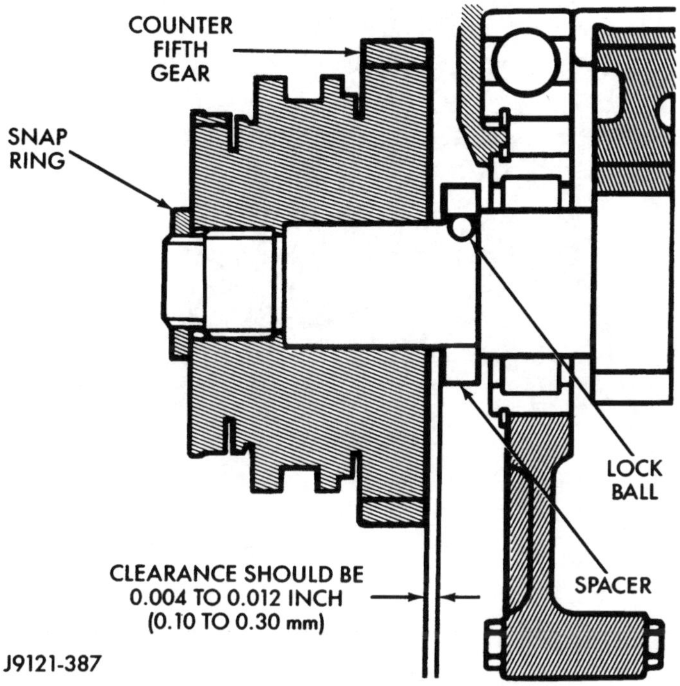

Fig. 54 Measuring Counter Fifth Gear Thrust Clearance

(2) Engage two synchro sleeves to lock mainshaft gears (Fig. 55).

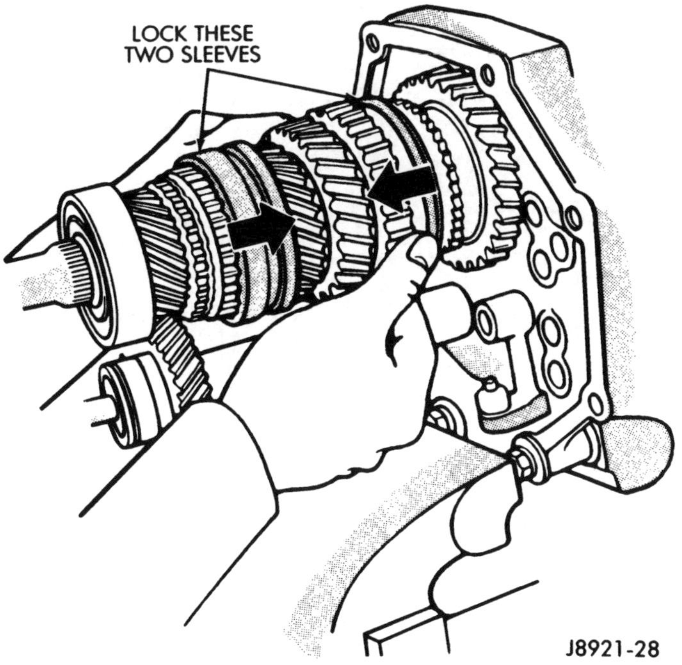

Fig. 55 Locking Mainshaft Gears

(3) Remove select fit snap ring that secures fifth spline gear and counter fifth gear on shaft (Fig. 56).

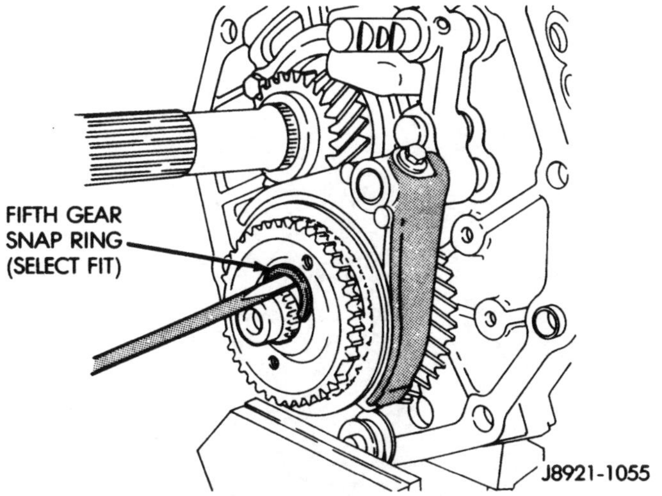

Fig. 56 Removing Fifth Gear Snap Ring

(4) Remove fifth spline gear, synchronizer and counter fifth gear using a suitable puller (Fig. 57).

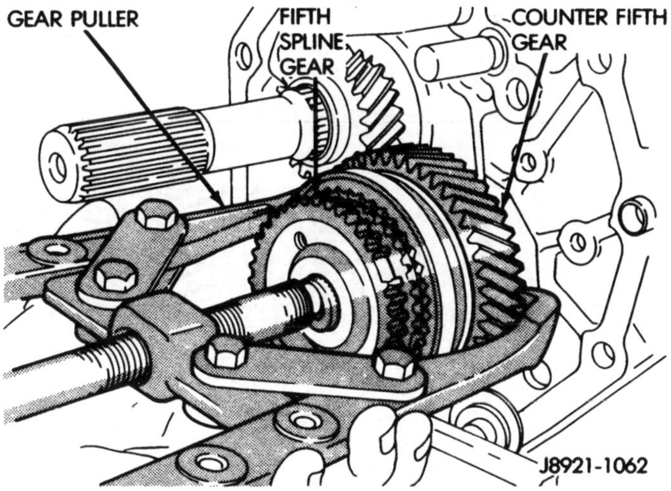

Fig. 57 Removing Fifth Gear Assembly

DISASSEMBLY AND ASSEMBLY (Continued)

(5) Remove spacer and remove lock ball with pencil magnet (Fig. 58).

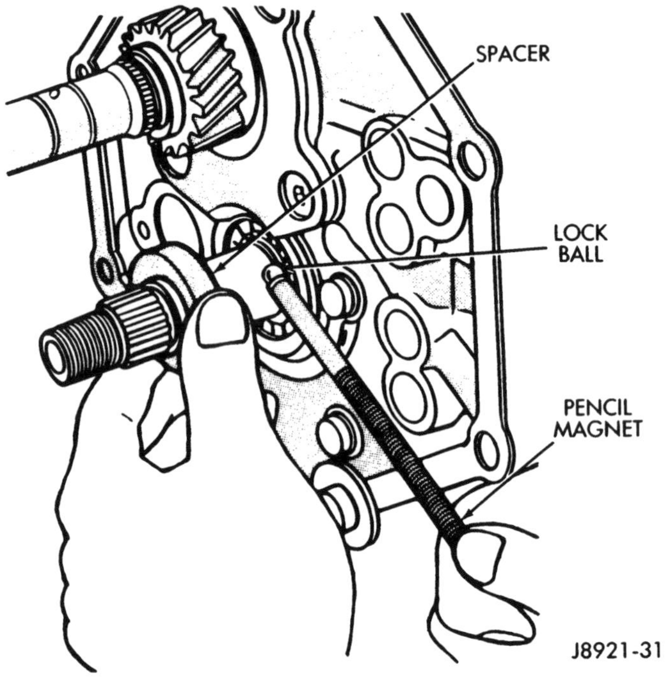

Fig. 58 Spacer and Lock Ball Removal

(6) Remove reverse shift arm bracket (Fig. 59).

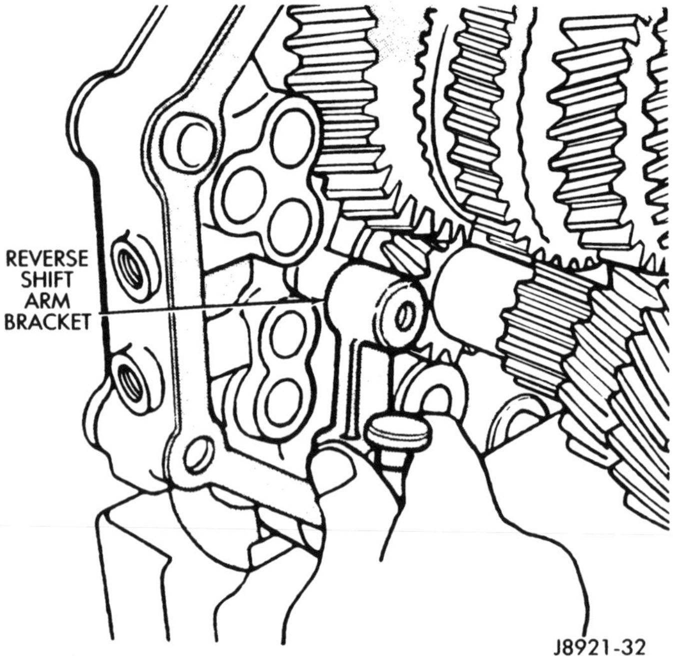

Fig. 59 Removing Reverse Shift Arm Bracket

(7) Remove rear bearing retainer bolts with appropriate size torx bit and remove retainer (Fig. 60).

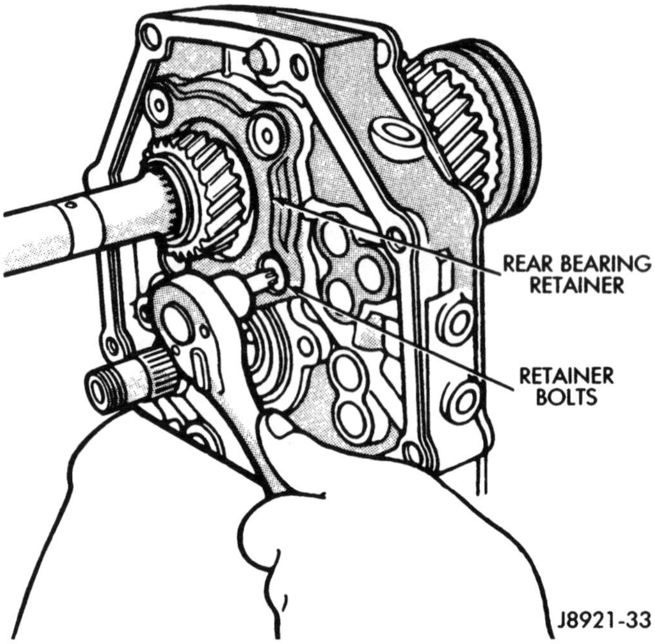

Fig. 60 Removing Rear Bearing Retainer

(8) Remove rear bearing snap ring (Fig. 61).

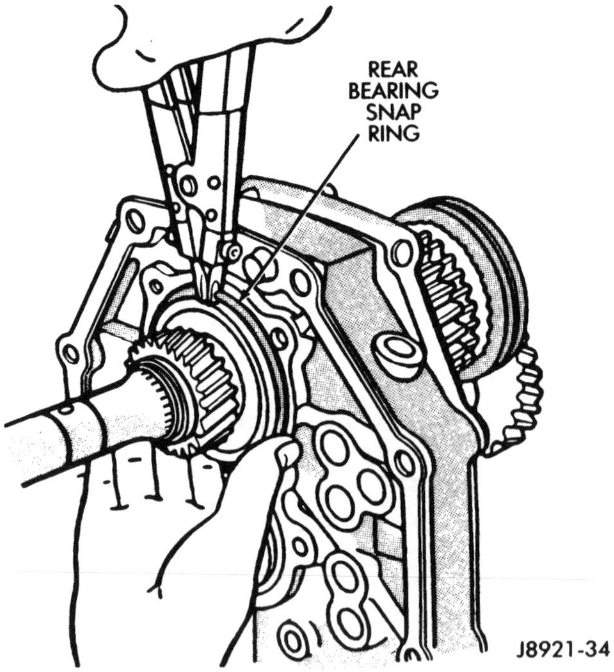

Fig. 61 Removing Rear Bearing Snap Ring

DISASSEMBLY AND ASSEMBLY (Continued)

(9) Tap intermediate plate with plastic mallet and pull output shaft–counter gear assemblies out of plate (Fig. 62).

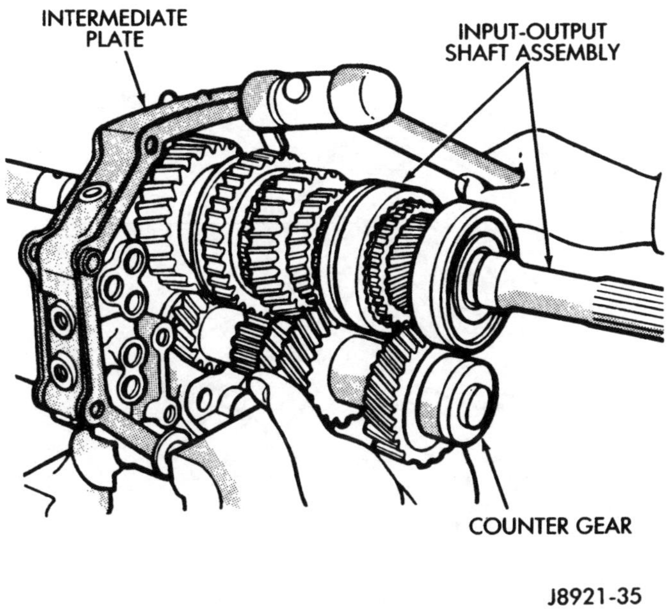

Fig. 62 Removing Counter Gear and Output Shaft

(10) Remove rear bearing from intermediate plate.

(11) Remove input shaft and shaft roller bearings from output shaft.

(12) Measure thrust clearance of output shaft gears (Fig. 63). Clearance should be 0.10 – 0.25 mm (0.004 – 0.010 in.).

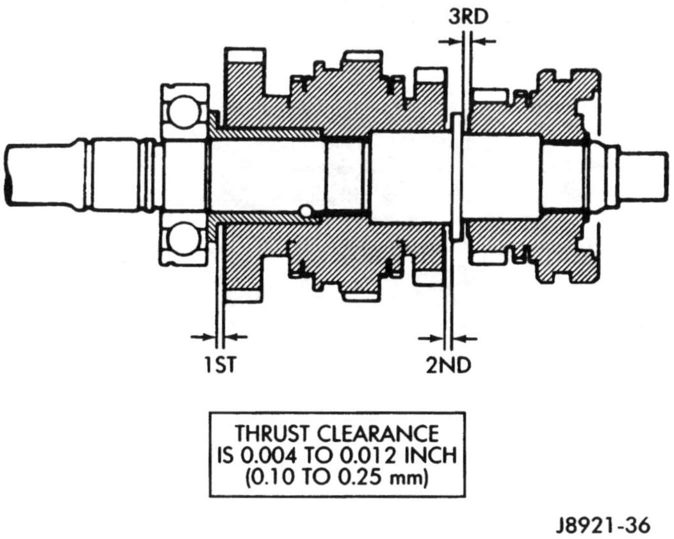

Fig. 63 Checking Output Shaft Gear Thrust Clearance

(13) Remove output shaft fifth gear snap ring with two screwdrivers (Fig. 64).

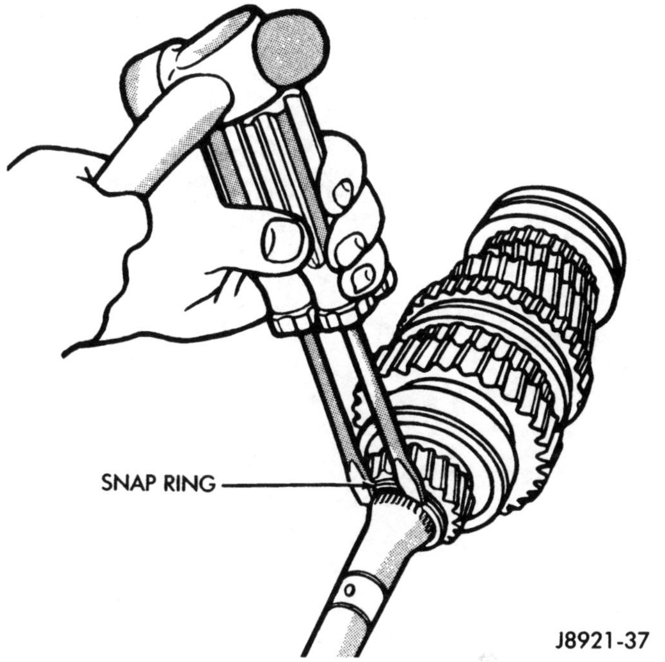

Fig. 64 Removing Fifth Gear Snap Ring

(14) Press fifth gear, rear bearing, first gear and inner race off output shaft (Fig. 65).

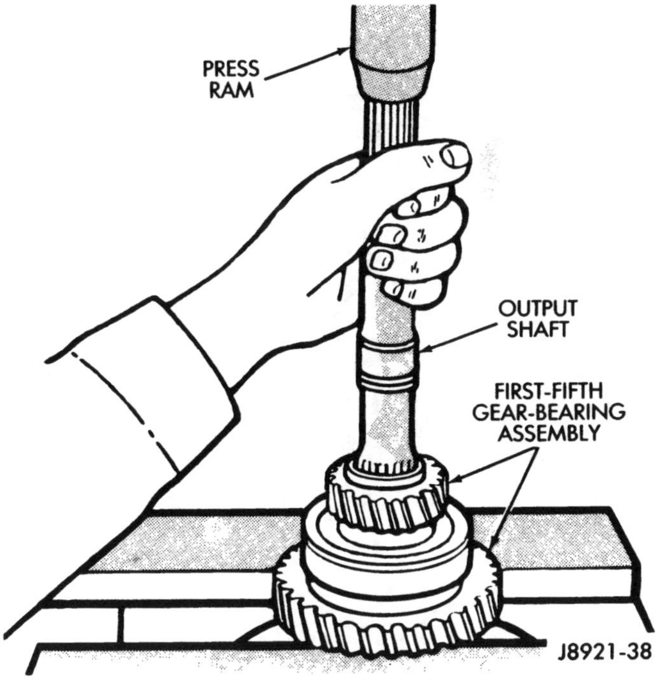

Fig. 65 Removing Fifth Gear and First Gear Bearing and Race

DISASSEMBLY AND ASSEMBLY (Continued)

(15) Remove needle roller bearing.

(16) Remove synchronizer ring.

(17) Remove synchronizer lock ball with pencil magnet (Fig. 66).

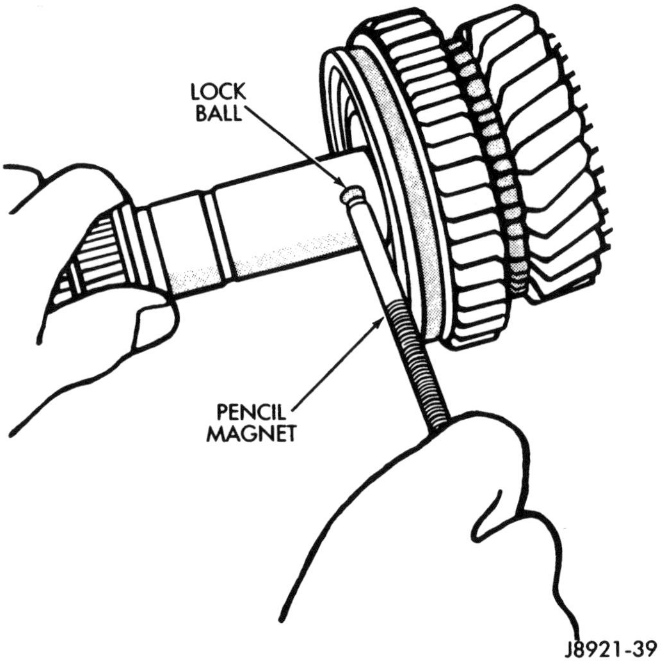

Fig. 66 Synchronizer Lock Ball Removal

(18) Press 1–2 synchronizer and second gear off output shaft (Fig. 67).

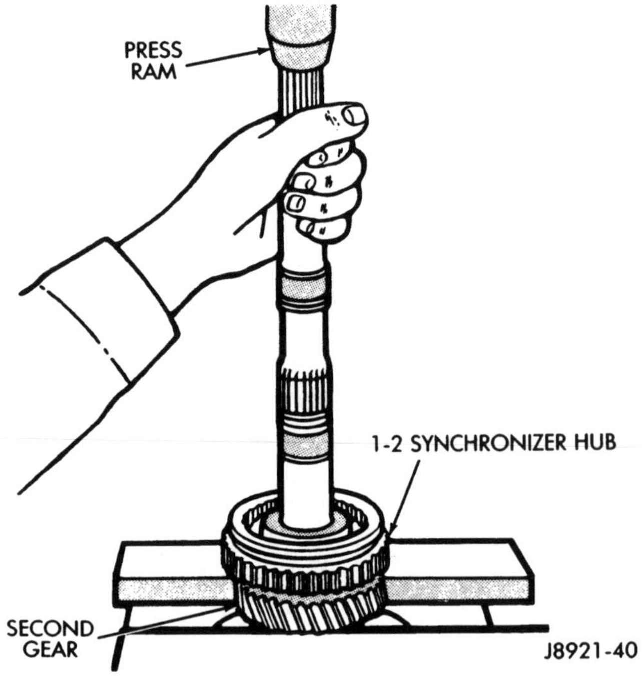

Fig. 67 Second Gear and 1–2 Synchronizer Removal

(19) Remove needle roller bearing from the shaft or second gear.

(20) Remove 3–4 synchronizer snap ring (Fig. 68).

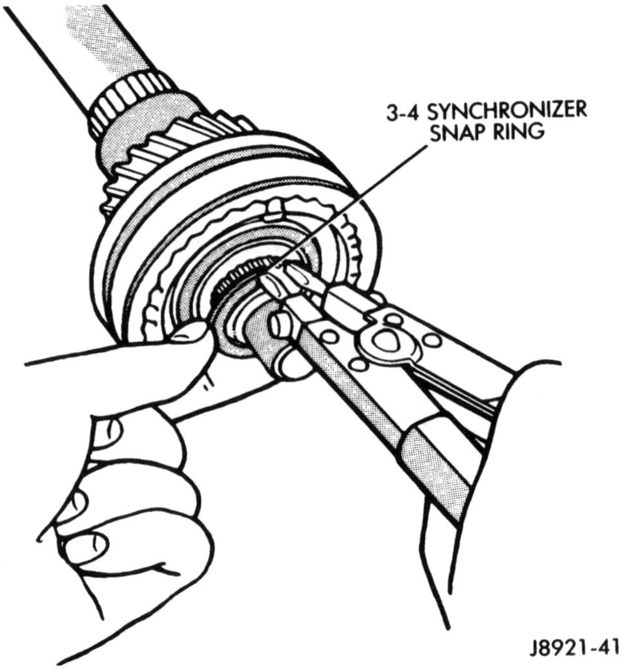

Fig. 68 Removing 3–4 Synchronizer Snap Ring

(21) Press 3–4 synchronizer and third gear off shaft (Fig. 69).

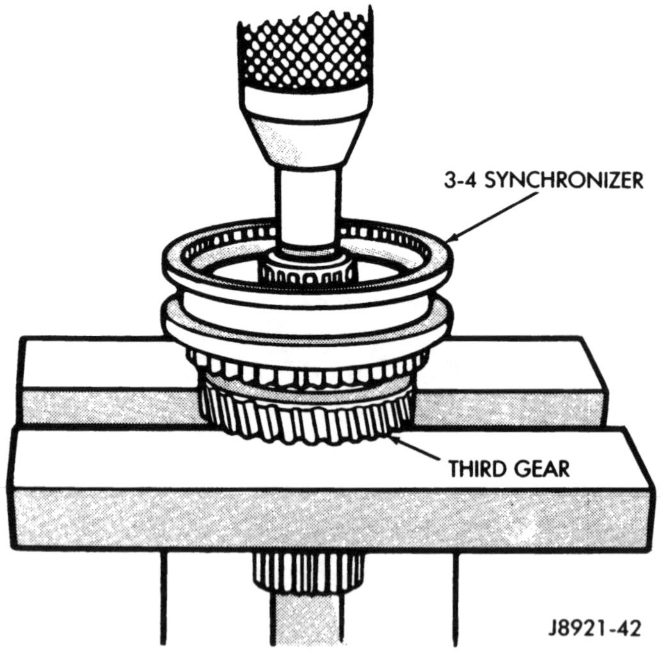

Fig. 69 Removing 3–4 Synchronizer and Third Gear

(22) Remove needle roller bearing from shaft or gear.

ASSEMBLING MAINSHAFT

(1) If front bearing was removed from input shaft, press new bearing on shaft (Fig. 70).

DISASSEMBLY AND ASSEMBLY (Continued)

(2) Secure front bearing with thickest snap ring that will fit in groove (Fig. 70).

(3) Press front bearing on counter gear. Secure bearing with thickest snap ring that will fit in ring groove (Fig. 71).

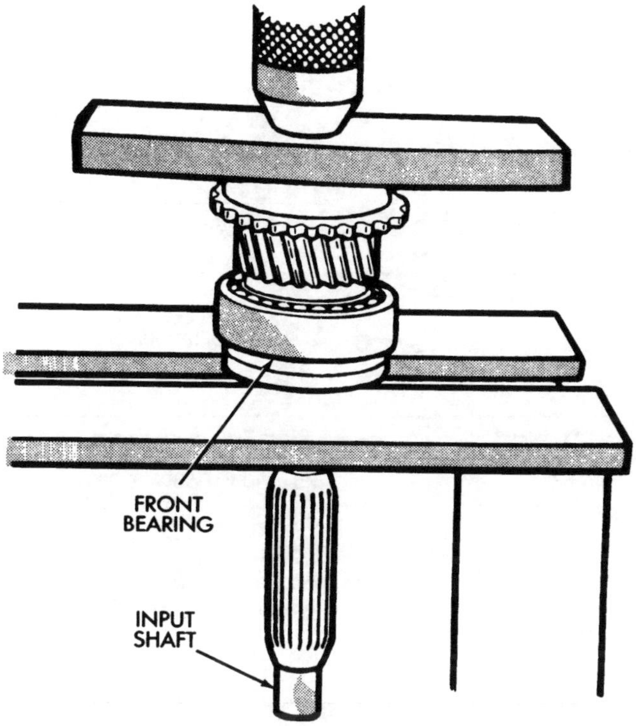

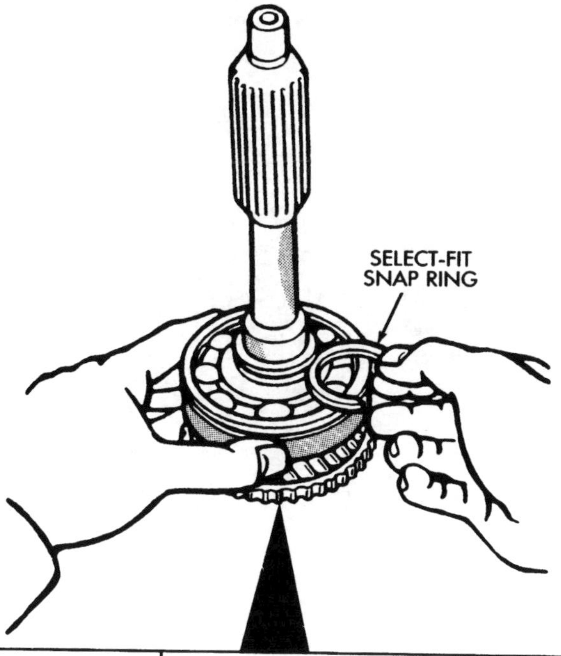

I.D. Mark	Snap Ring Thickness mm (in.)
0	2.05-2.10 (0.0807-0.0827)
1	2.10-2.15 (0.0827-0.0846)
2	2.15-2.20 (0.0846-0.0866)
3	2.20-2.25 (0.0866-0.0886)
4	2.25-2.30 (0.0886-0.0906)
5	2.30-2.35 (0.0906-0.0925)

J8921-50

Fig. 70 Installing Front Bearing and Snap Ring

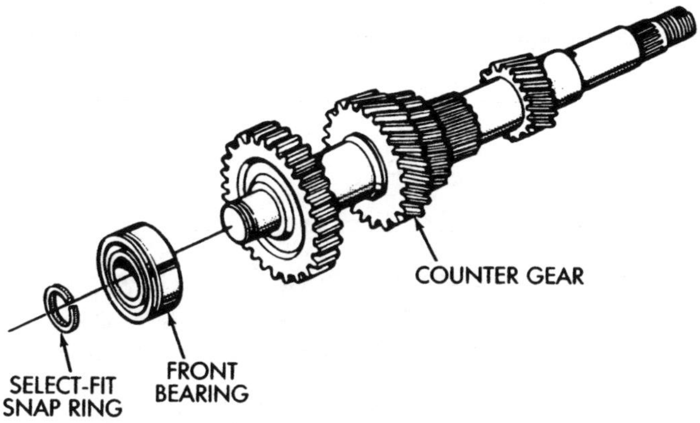

I.D. Mark	Snap Ring Thickness mm (in.)
1	2.05-2.10 (0.0807-0.0827)
2	2.10-2.15 (0.0827-0.0846)
3	2.15-2.20 (0.0846-0.0866)
4	2.20-2.25 (0.0866-0.0886)
5	2.25-2.30 (0.0886-0.0906)
6	2.30-2.35 (0.0906-0.0925)

J8921-51

Fig. 71 Installing Counter Gear Front Bearing and Snap Ring

(4) Install new oil seals in front bearing retainer and adapter (Fig. 72). Bearing retainer seal depth is 11.2 – 12.1 mm (0.441 – 0.480 in.).

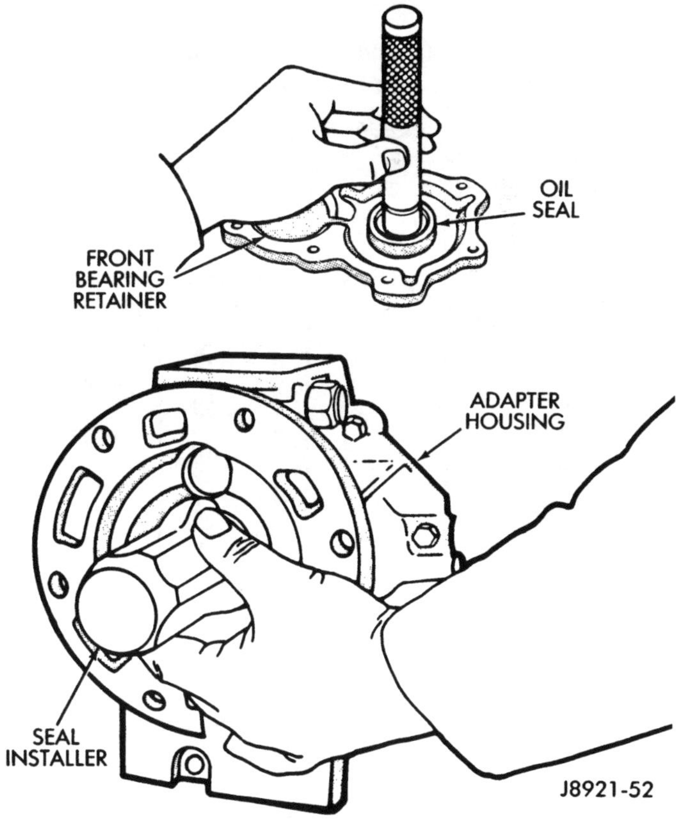

Fig. 72 Oil Seal Installation

DISASSEMBLY AND ASSEMBLY (Continued)

(5) Install reverse shaft and shaft retaining pin in adapter. Then install access hole plug with torx bit (Fig. 73).

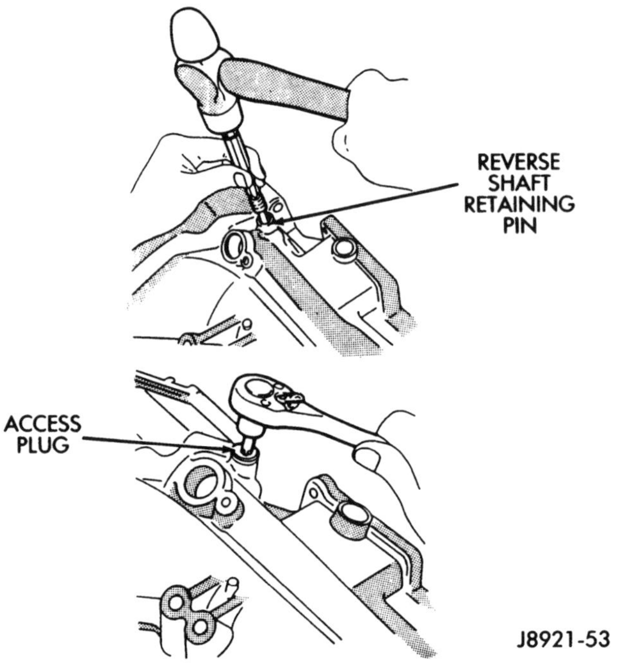

Fig. 73 Installing Reverse Shaft Pin

(6) Lubricate transmission components with specified gear lubricant.

(7) Assemble 1–2 and 3–4 synchronizer hubs, sleeves, springs and key inserts (Fig. 74).

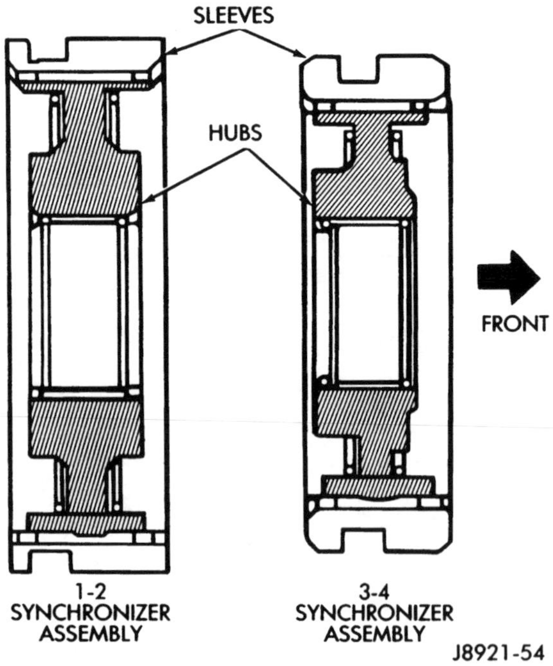

Fig. 74 Synchronizer Identification

(8) Assemble and install third gear, needle bearing, synchronizer ring, 3–4 synchronizer and snap ring on output shaft (Fig. 75). Use thickest snap ring that fits in shaft groove.

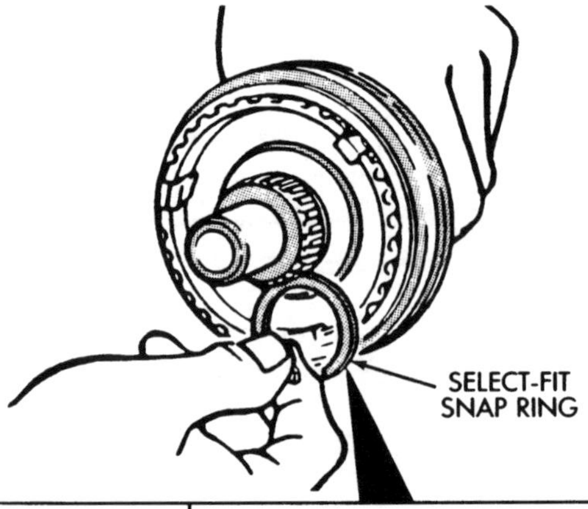

I.D. Mark	Snap Ring Thickness mm (in.)
C-1	1.75-1.80 (0.0689-0.0709)
D	1.80-1.85 (0.0709-0.0728)
D-1	1.85-1.90 (0.0728-0.0748)
E	1.90-1.95 (0.0748-0.0768)
E-1	1.95-2.00 (0.0768-0.0787)
F	2.00-2.05 (0.0788-0.0807)
F-1	2.05-2.10 (0.0807-0.0827)

J8921-55

Fig. 75 Installing Third Gear and 3–4 Synchronizer

(9) Verify third gear thrust clearance with feeler gauge (Fig. 76). Clearance should be 0.10 – 0.25 mm (0.004 – 0.010 in.).

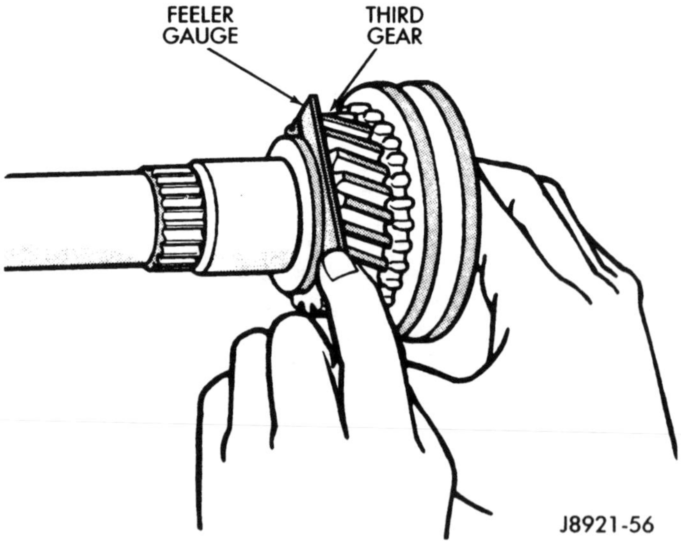

Fig. 76 Checking Third Gear Clearance

DISASSEMBLY AND ASSEMBLY (Continued)

(10) Assemble second gear, gear needle bearing, synchronizer ring and 1–2 synchronizer. Then press assembly on output shaft (Fig. 77).

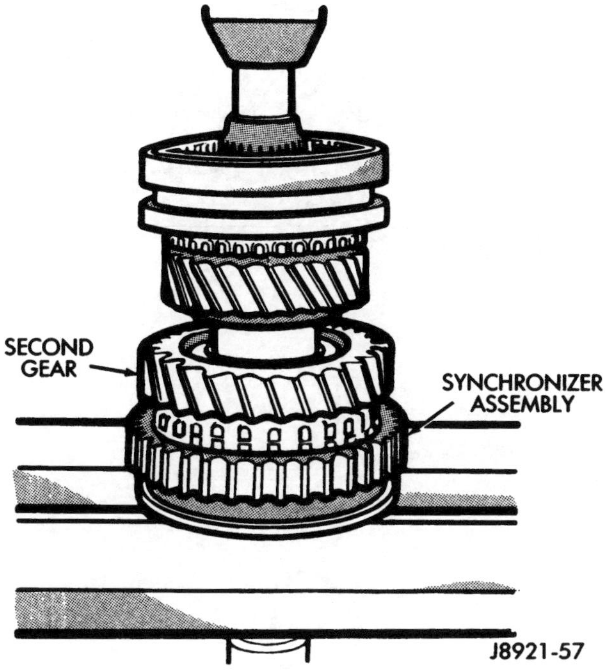

Fig. 77 Installing Second Gear and Synchronizer

(11) Install first gear lock ball in output shaft (Fig. 78).

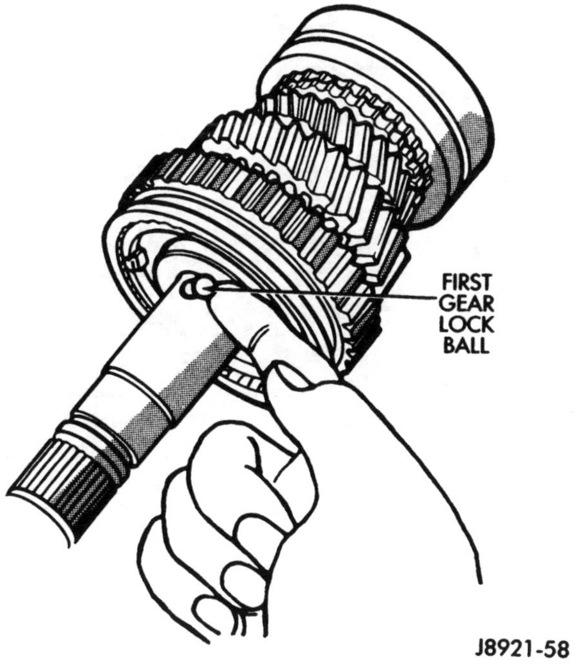

Fig. 78 Installing First Gear and Lock Ball

(12) Assemble first gear, synchronizer ring, gear needle bearing and inner race (Fig. 79). Then install assembly on output shaft. **Rotate inner race until aligned with locking ball.**

(13) Press rear bearing on shaft (Fig. 79). Snap ring groove in bearing goes toward rear. Use screwdriver to hold inner race in position when installing bearing (Fig. 80).

(14) Install snap ring on rear bearing.

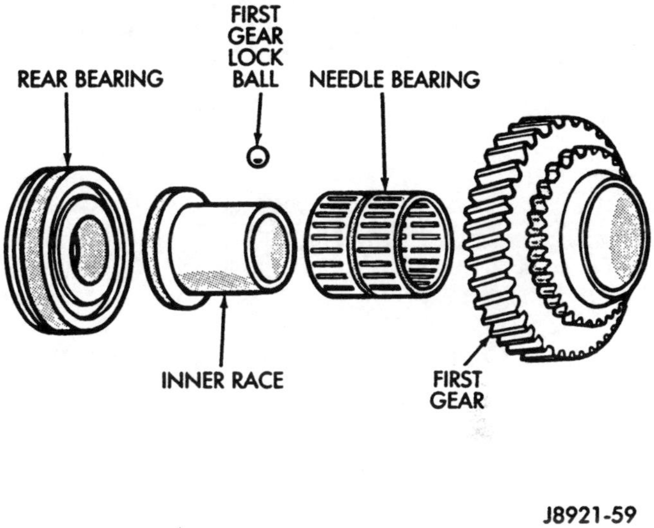

Fig. 79 Assembling First Gear Components

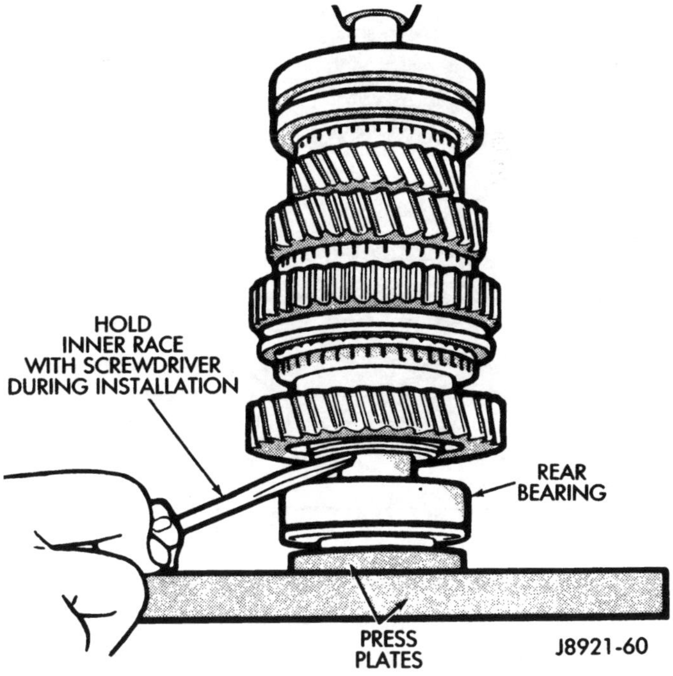

Fig. 80 Installing Output Shaft Rear Bearing

DISASSEMBLY AND ASSEMBLY (Continued)

(15) Check first–second gear thrust clearance (Fig. 81). Standard clearance is 0.10 – 0.25 mm (0.004 – 0.010 in.).

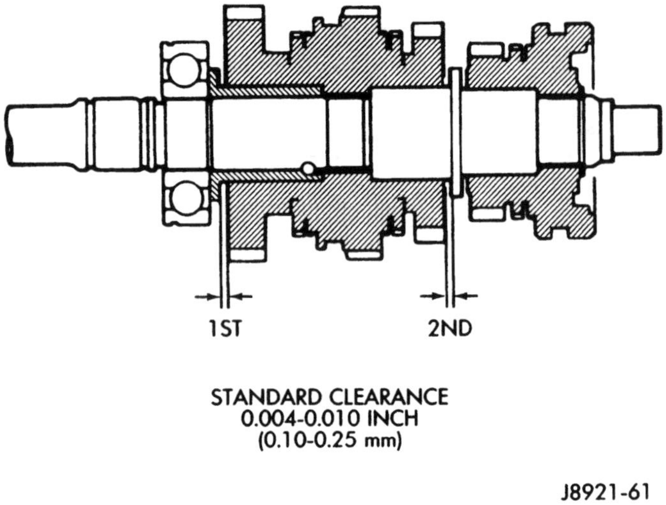

Fig. 81 Checking First–Second Gear Thrust Clearance

(16) Press fifth gear on output shaft (Fig. 82).

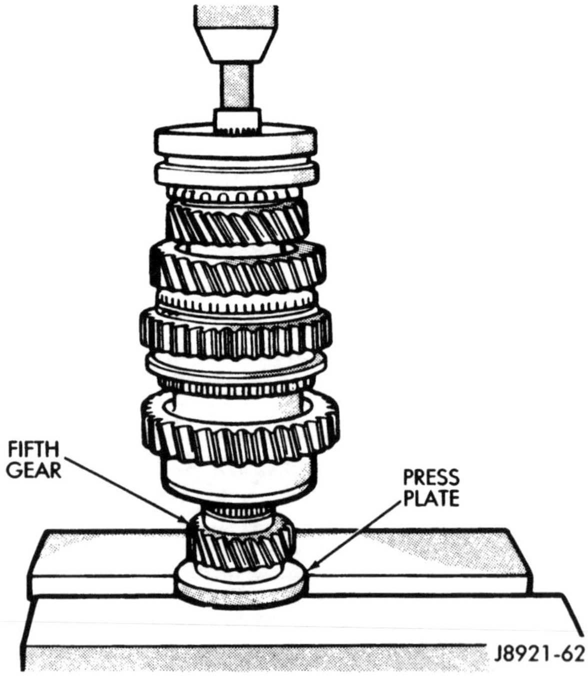

Fig. 82 Installing Output Shaft Fifth Gear

(17) Install fifth gear snap ring (Fig. 83). Use thickest snap ring that will fit in shaft groove.

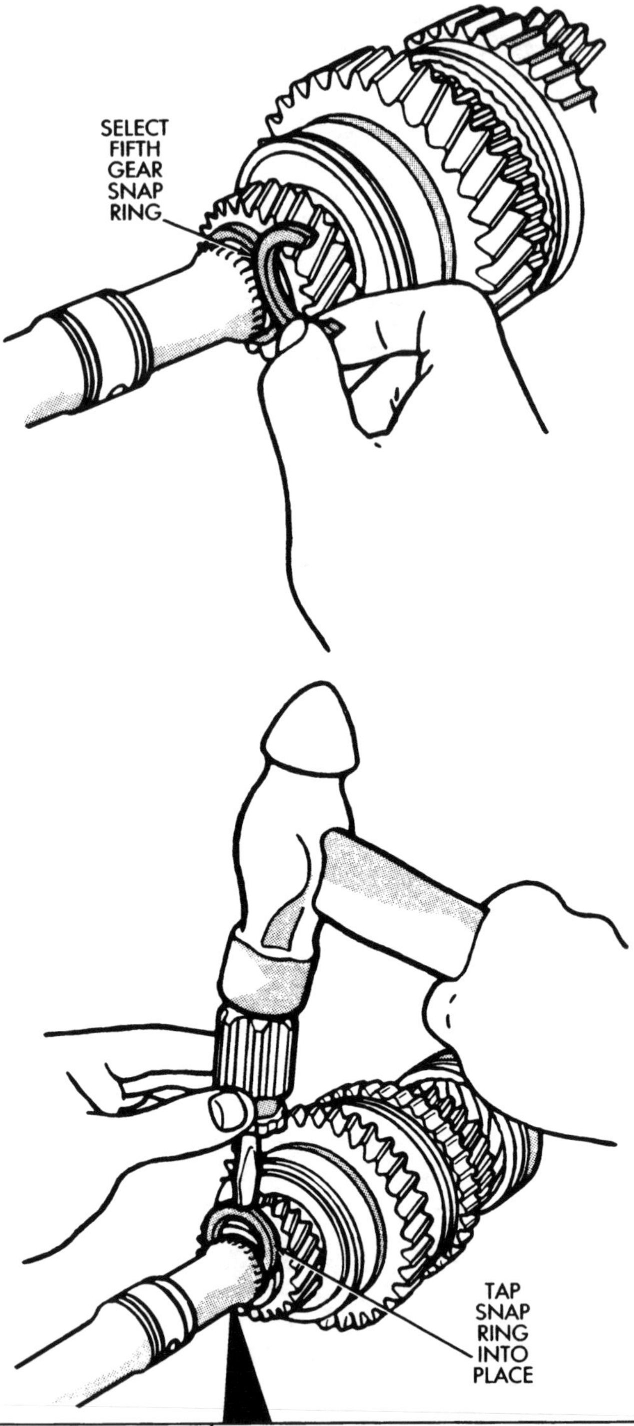

I.D. Mark	Snap Ring Thickness mm (in.)
A	2.67-2.72 (0.1051-0.1071)
B	2.73-2.78 (0.1075-0.1094)
C	2.79-2.84 (0.1098-0.1118)
D	2.85-2.90 (0.1122-0.1142)
E	2.91-2.96 (0.1146-0.1165)
F	2.97-3.02 (0.1169-0.1189)
G	3.03-3.08 (0.1193-0.1213)
H	3.09-3.14 (0.1217-0.1236)
J	3.15-3.20 (0.1240-0.1260)
K	3.21-3.26 (0.1264-0.1283)
L	3.27-3.32 (0.1287-0.1307)

J8921-63

Fig. 83 Selecting/Installing Fifth Gear Snap Ring

DISASSEMBLY AND ASSEMBLY (Continued)

(18) Lubricate input shaft roller bearings with petroleum jelly and install rollers in shaft (Fig. 84).

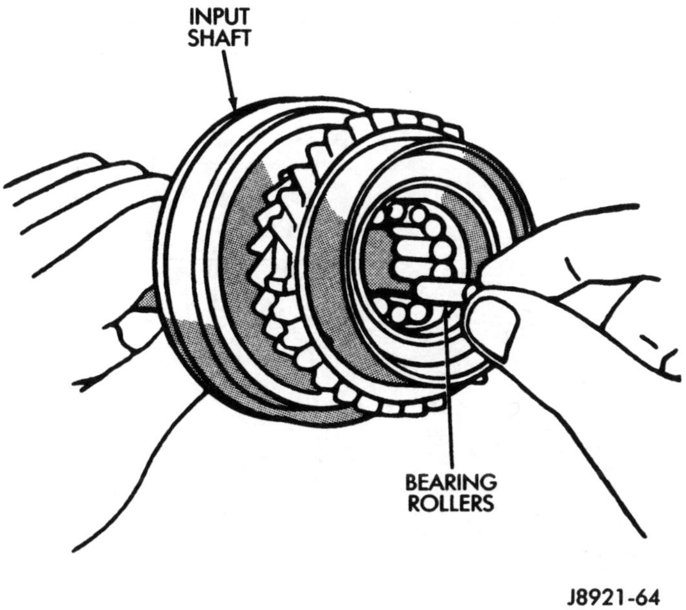

Fig. 84 Installing Input Shaft Bearing Rollers

(19) Install output shaft assembly in intermediate plate (Fig. 85). Tap plate with mallet and pull on shaft to seat assembly.

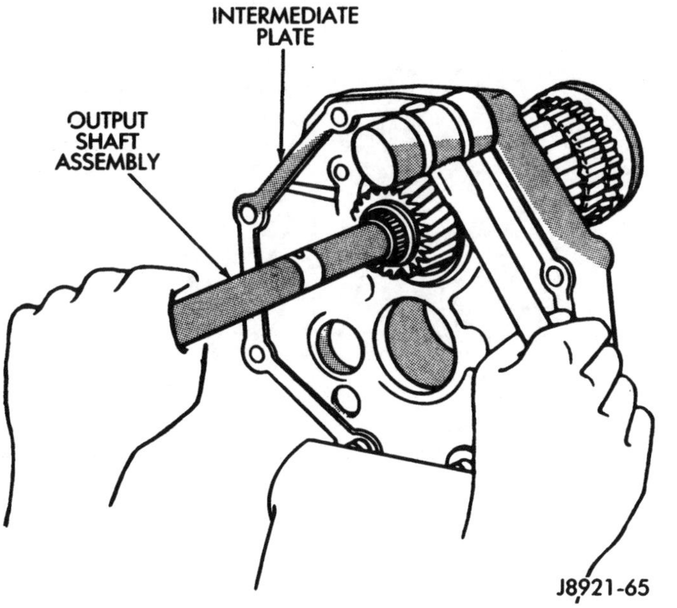

Fig. 85 Installing Output Shaft In Intermediate Plate

(20) Install input shaft on output shaft.

(21) Install counter gear in intermediate plate (Fig. 86).

(22) Install rear bearing snap ring and install bearing retainer (Fig. 87). Tighten retainer screws to 18 N·m (13 ft. lbs.) torque.

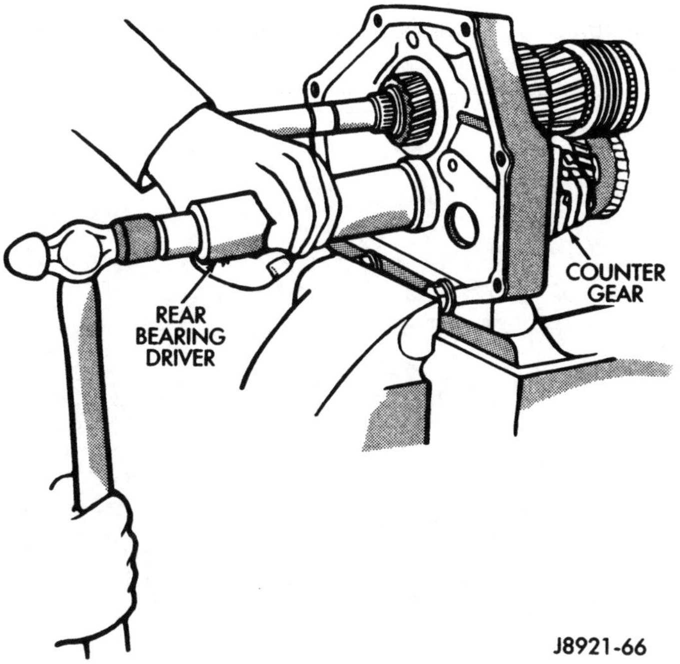

Fig. 86 Counter Gear Installation

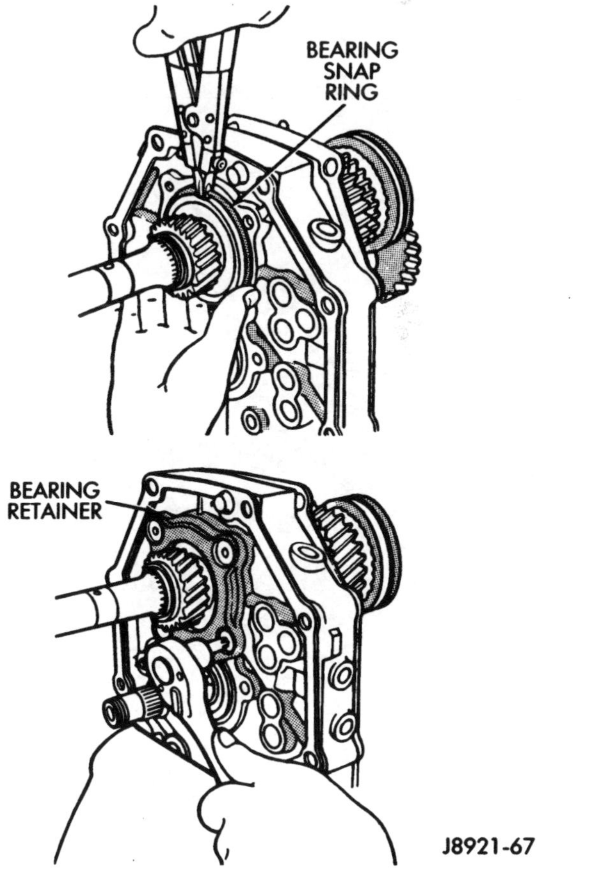

Fig. 87 Installing Bearing Retainer and Snap Ring

DISASSEMBLY AND ASSEMBLY (Continued)

(23) Install reverse shift arm (Fig. 88). Tighten attaching bolt to 18 N·m (13 ft. lbs.) torque.

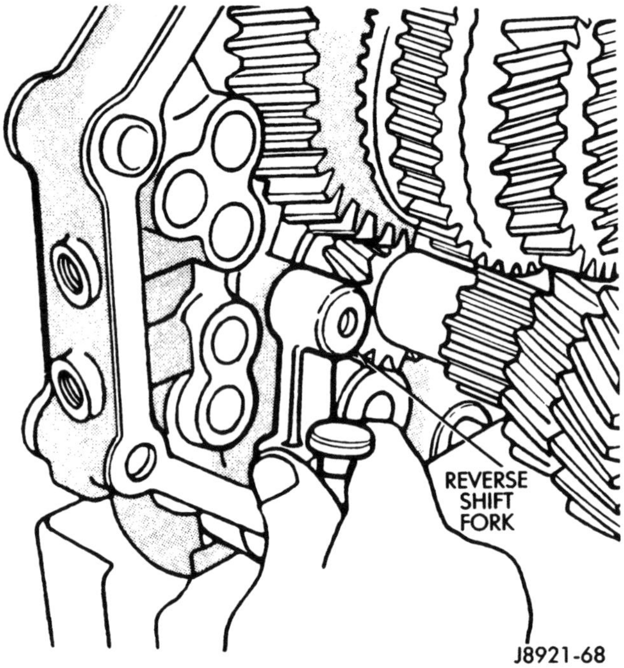

Fig. 88 Installing Reverse Shift Fork

(24) Assemble counter fifth gear and synchro components (Fig. 89).

(25) .

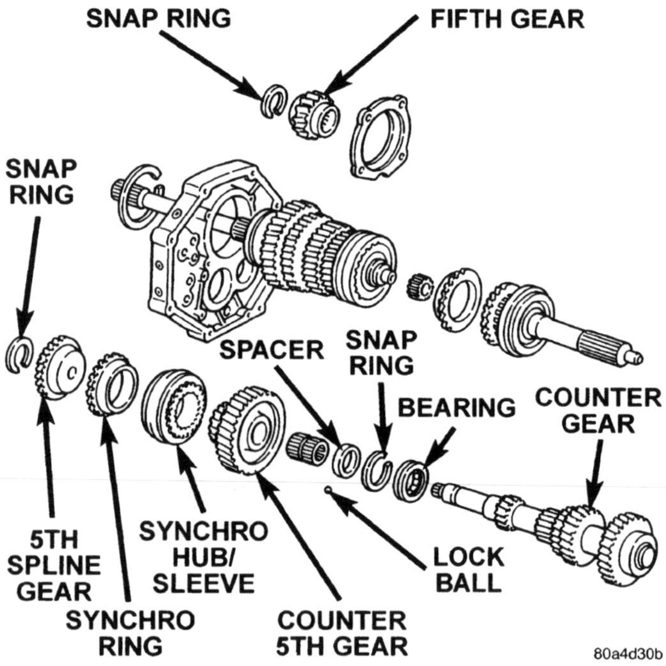

Fig. 89 Counter Gear Components

(26) Install lock ball, spacer and needle bearing (Fig. 90) on counter shaft.

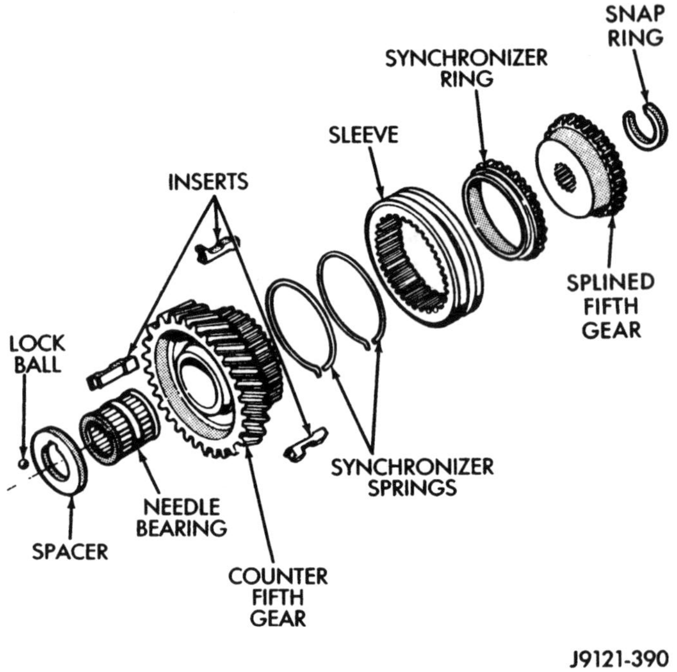

Fig. 90 Counter Fifth Gear and Synchronizer Assembly

(27) Install assembled gear and synchronizer on counter shaft (Fig. 91).

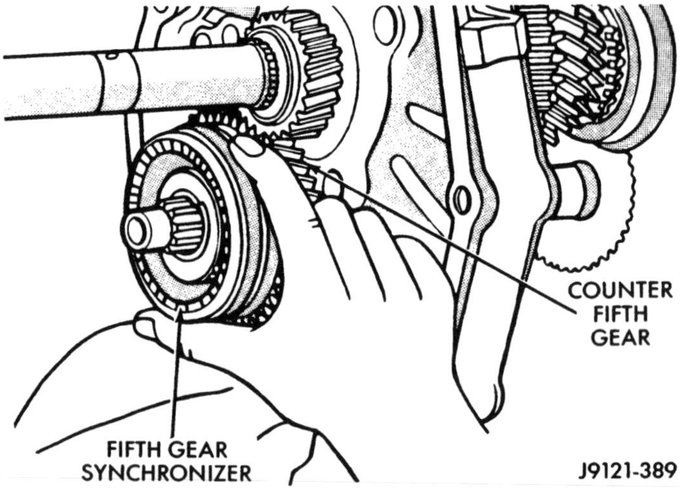

Fig. 91 Fifth Gear and Synchronizer Installation

DISASSEMBLY AND ASSEMBLY (Continued)

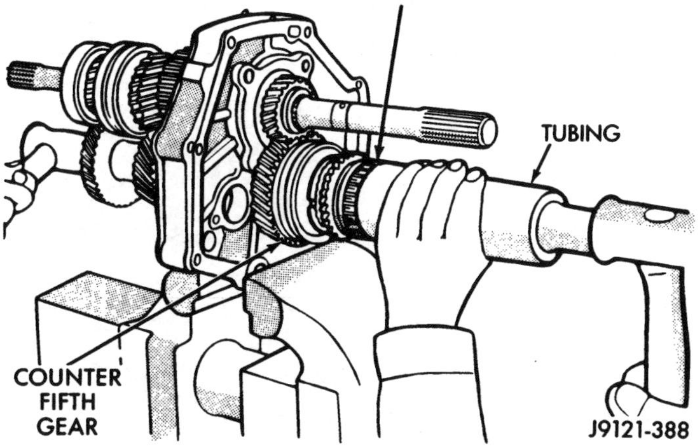

Fig. 92 Installing Fifth Gear

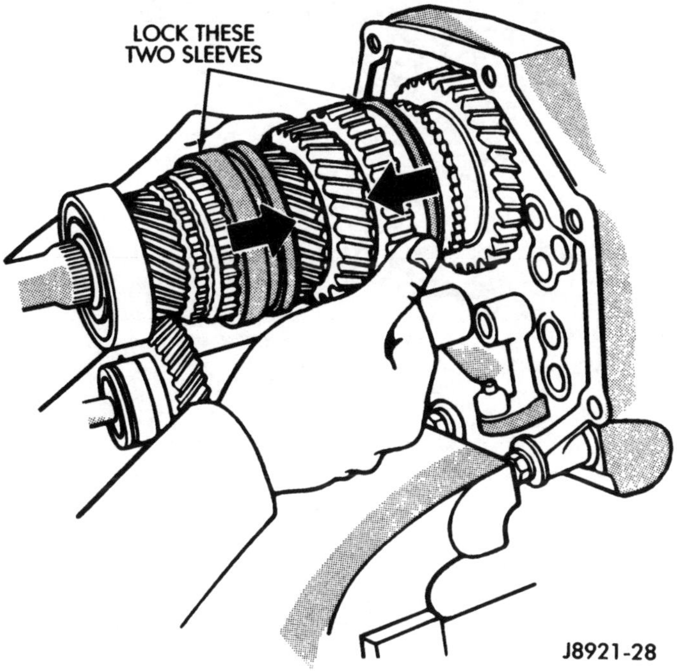

Fig. 93 Locking Mainshaft Gears

(28) Install remaining synchronizer ring and spline fifth gear (Fig. 92). Use length of pipe to tap gear into place.

(29) Shift 1–2 and 3–4 synchronizer sleeves into gear to lock output shaft and counter gear (Fig. 93).

(30) Install fifth gear snap ring (Fig. 94).

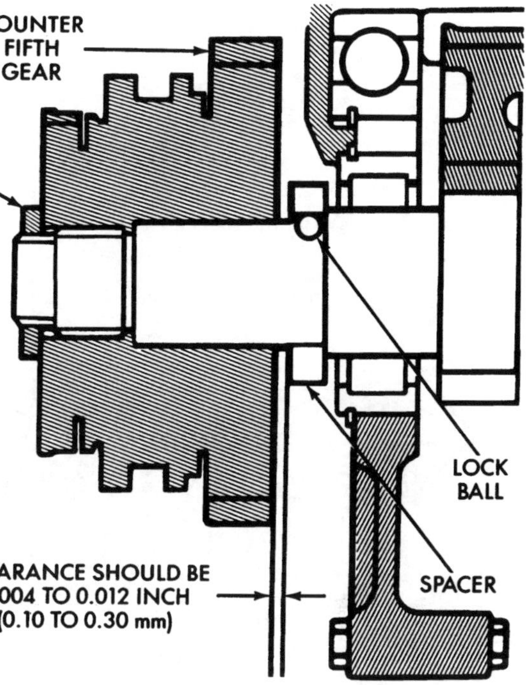

Fig. 94 Checking Fifth Gear Thrust Clearance

(31) Disengage 1–2 and 3–4 synchronizer sleeves.

(32) Check counter fifth gear thrust clearance (Fig. 95). Standard clearance is 0.10 – 0.30 mm (0.004 – 0.010 in.). Adjust clearance with different thickness snap ring if necessary.

DISASSEMBLY AND ASSEMBLY (Continued)

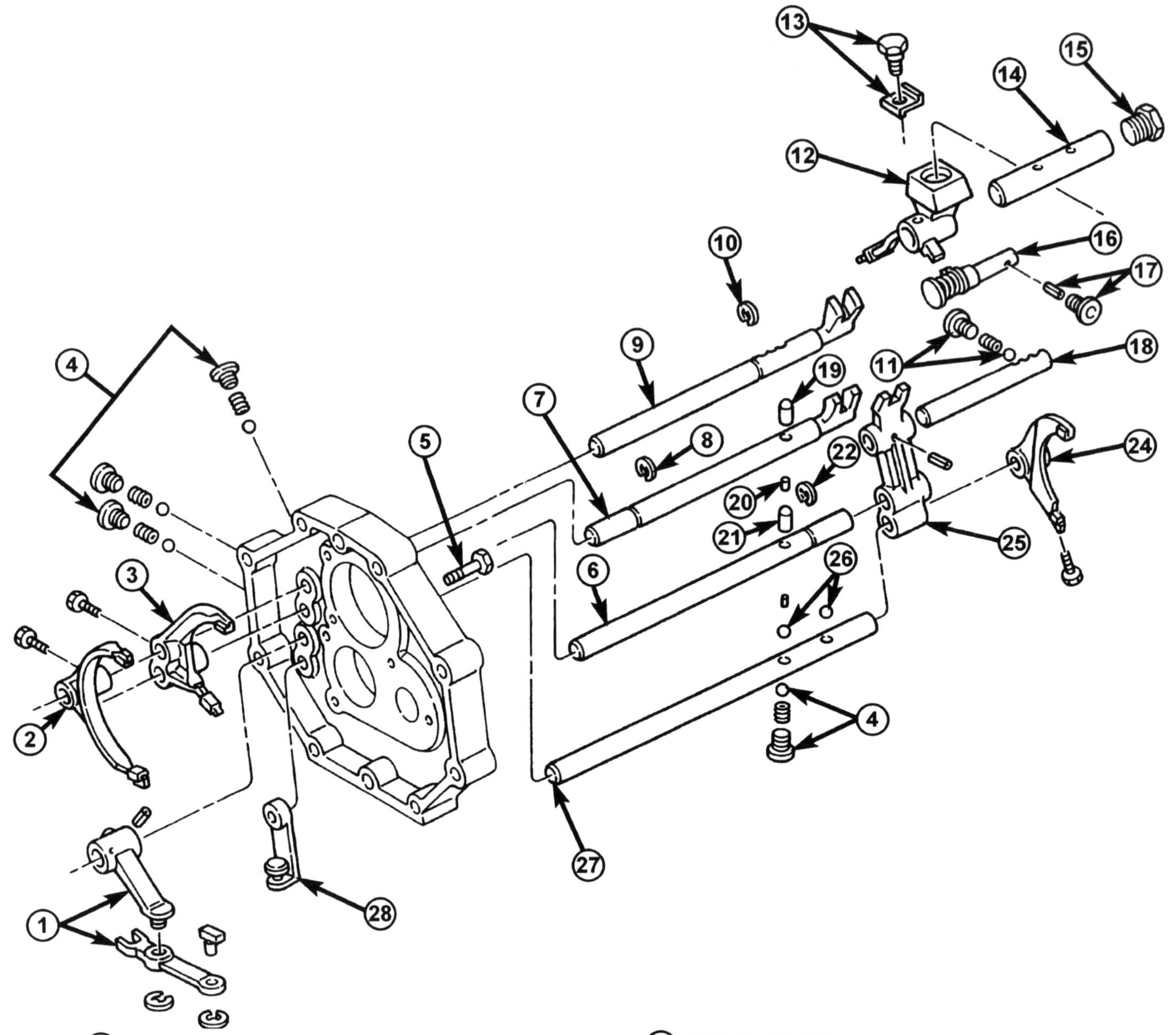

(1) REVERSE FORK AND SHIFT ARM
(2) 1-2 SHIFT FORK
(3) 3-4 SHIFT FORK
(4) LOCK BALL, SPRING AND PLUG
(5) BRACKET BOLT
(6) NO. 3 SHIFT RAIL
(7) NO. 1 SHIFT RAIL
(8) C-RING
(9) NO. 2 SHIFT RAIL
(10) C-RING
(11) LOCK BALL, SPRING AND PLUG
(12) SHIFT ARM
(13) SET BOLT AND LOCK PLATE
(14) SHIFT LEVER SHAFT
(15) SHAFT PLUG
(16) REVERSE PIN
(17) RETAINING PIN AND PLUG
(18) NO. 5 SHIFT RAIL
(19) INTERLOCK PIN
(20) INTERLOCK PIN
(21) INTERLOCK PIN
(22) C-RING
(23) INTERLOCK PIN
(24) FIFTH-REVERSE FORK
(25) REVERSE SHIFT HEAD
(26) LOCK BALLS
(27) NO. 4 SHIFT RAIL
(28) REVERSE ARM BRACKET

80500578

Fig. 95 Shift Components

CLEANING AND INSPECTION

AX-5 MANUAL TRANSMISSION COMPONENTS

Clean the transmission components in solvent. Dry the cases, gears, shift mechanism and shafts with compressed air. **Dry the bearings with clean, dry shop towels only. Never use compressed air on the bearings. This could cause severe damage to the bearing roller and race surfaces.**

Inspect the transmission case. Replace the case if cracked, porous, or if any of the bearing and gear bores are damaged.

Check thickness of the output shaft and inner bearing race flanges with a micrometer or vernier calipers (Fig. 96).

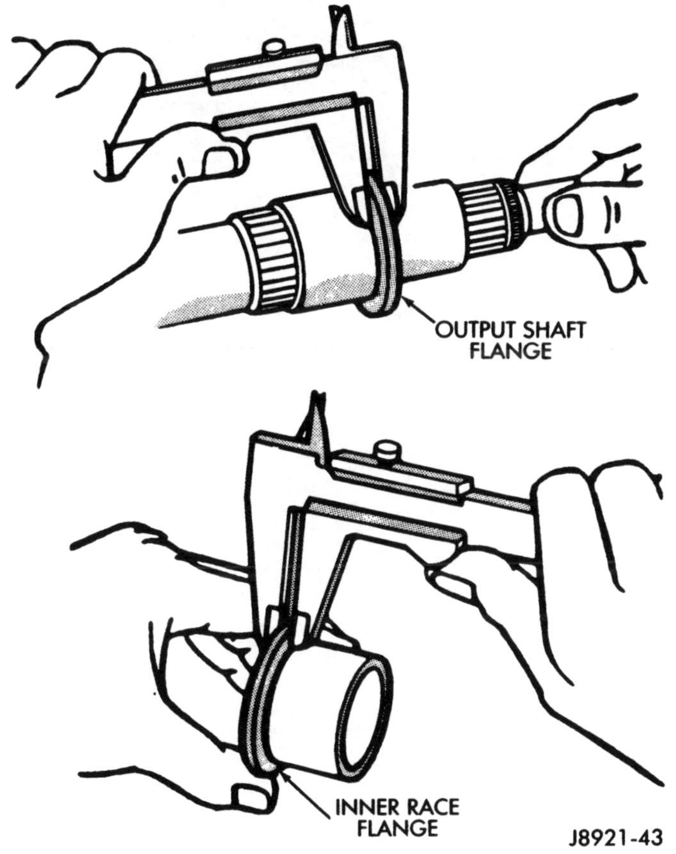

Fig. 96 Checking Shaft and Bearing Race Flange Thickness

- Minimum thickness for shaft flange is 4.8 mm (0.189 in.)
- Minimum thickness for bearing race flange is 3.99 mm (0.157 in.)

Measure diameter of the output shaft journal surfaces with a micrometer. Replace the shaft if either of these surfaces are worn beyond specified limits.

- Second gear surface minimum diameter is 37.96 mm (1.495 in.)
- Third gear surface minimum diameter is 34.98 mm (1.377 in.)

Measure output shaft runout with a dial indicator (Fig. 97). Runout should not exceed 0.05 mm (0.002 in.).

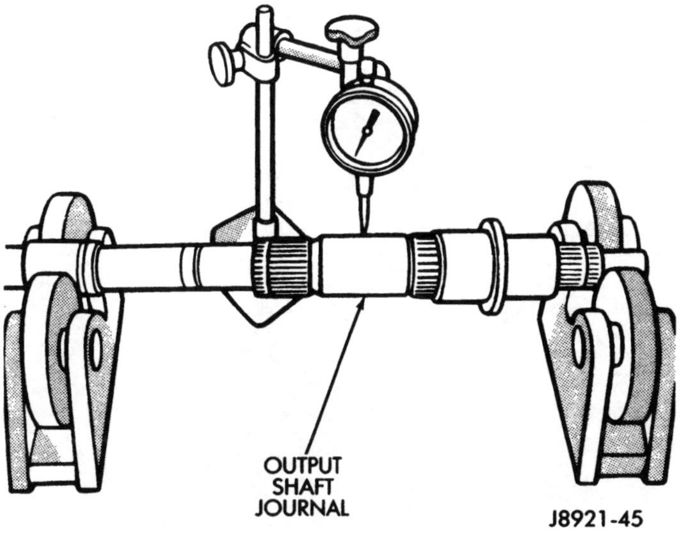

Fig. 97 Checking Output Shaft Runout

Install the needle bearing and inner race in the first gear. Then check oil clearance between the gear and inner race (Fig. 98). Clearance should be 0.009 – 0.032 mm (0.0004 – 0.0013 in.).

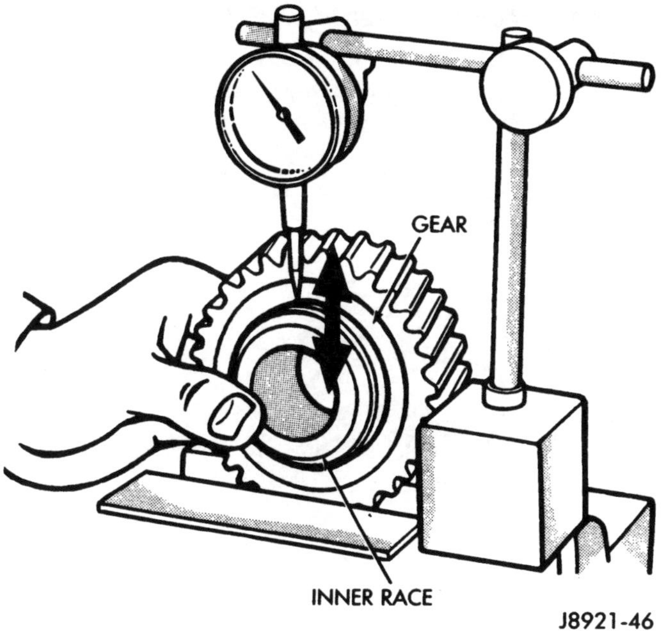

Fig. 98 Checking Gear-to-race Clearance

CLEANING AND INSPECTION (Continued)

Install the needle bearings and the second, third and counter fifth gears on the output shaft. Then check oil clearance between the gears and shaft with a dial indicator (Fig. 99). Oil clearance for all three gears is 0.009 – 0.0013 mm (0.0004 – 0.0013 in.).

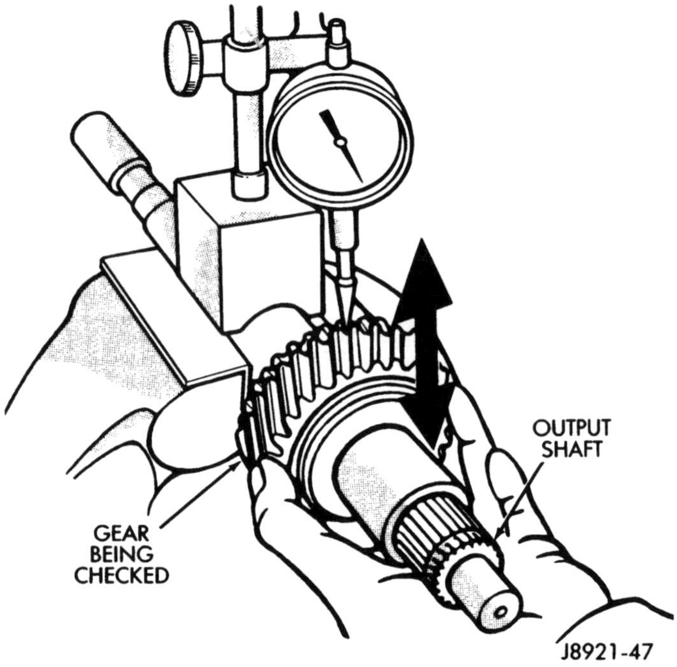

Fig. 99 Checking Gear-to-shaft Oil Clearance

Check synchronizer ring wear (Fig. 100). Insert each ring in matching gear. Measure clearance between each ring and gear with feeler gauge. Replace ring if clearance exceeds 2.0 mm (0.078 in.).

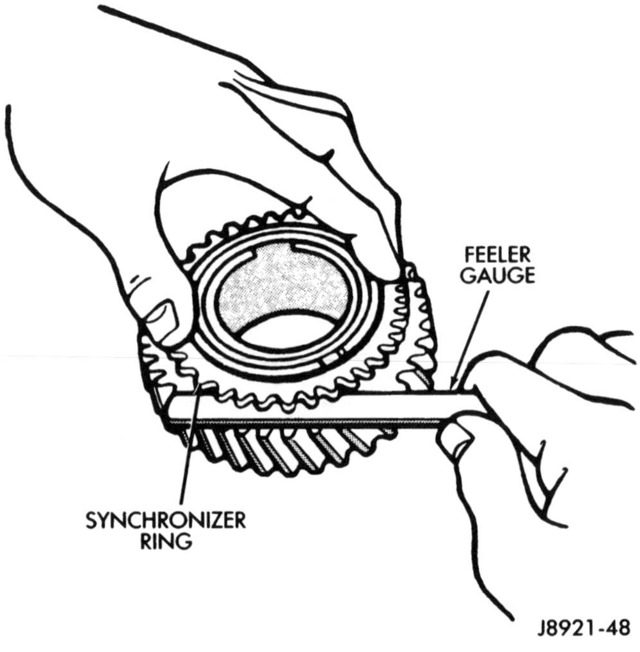

Fig. 100 Checking Synchronizer Ring Wear

Check shift fork–to–synchronizer hub clearance with a feeler gauge (Fig. 101). Replace the fork if clearance exceeds 1.0 mm (0.039 in.).

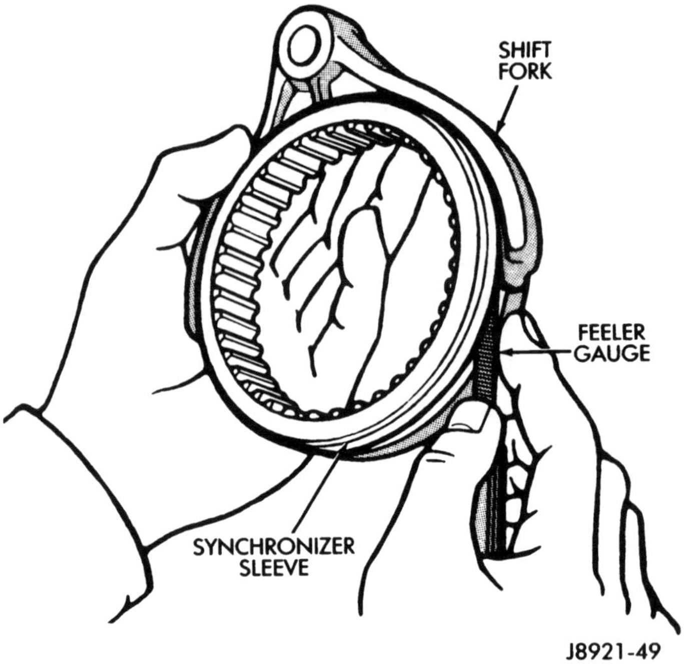

Fig. 101 Checking Fork-to-hub Clearance

SPECIFICATIONS

AX-5 MANUAL TRANSMISSION TORQUE

Description	Torque
Access Plugs	19 N•m (14 ft. lbs.)
Adapter Housing Bolts	37 N•m (27 ft. lbs.)
Backup Light Switch	37 N•m (27 ft. lbs.)
Drain and Fill Plugs	37 N•m (27 ft. lbs.)
Front Bearing Retainer Bolts	17 N•m (12 ft. lbs.)
Interlock and Detent Ball Plugs	19 N•m (14 ft. lbs.)
Propeller Shaft Clamp Screws	16-23 N•m (140-200 in. lbs.)
Rear Mount-To-Transmission Bolts	33-60 N•m (24-44 ft. lbs.)
Rear Mount Clevis Bolt/Nut	54-75 N•m (40-55 ft. lbs.)
Rear Mount-To-Crossmember Nuts	33-49 N•m (24-36 ft. lbs.)
Restrictor Pins	19 N•m (14 ft. lbs.)
Reverse Shift Arm Bracket Bolts	18 N•m (13 ft. lbs.)
Shift Arm Set Screw	38 N•m (28 ft. lbs.)
Shift Fork Set Screws	20 N•m (15 ft. lbs.)
Shift Knob Nut	20-34 N•m (15-25 ft. lbs.)
Shift Lever Floor Cover Screws	2-3 N•m (17-30 in. lbs.)
Shift Tower Bolts	18 N•m (13 ft. lbs.)
Transfer Case Mounting Nuts	30-41 N•m (22-30 ft. lbs.)

J9321-89

SPECIAL TOOLS

AX-5

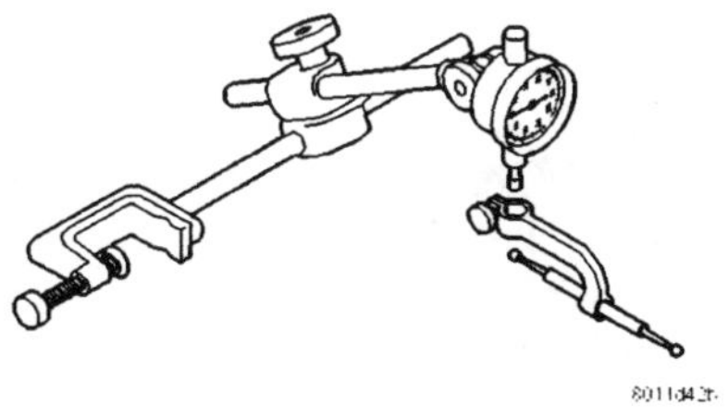

C-3339 Dial Indicator Set

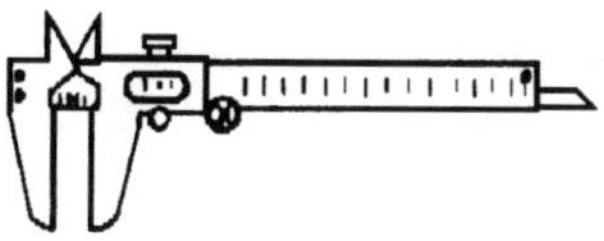

C-4959 Caliper, Metric Vernier

MANUAL TRANSMISSION—AX15

INDEX

GENERAL INFORMATION

AX15 MANUAL TRANSMISSION

The AX 15 is used with a 4.0L engine. The AX 15 is a 5–speed, synchromesh, manual transmission. Fifth gear is an overdrive range with a ratio of 0.79:1. The shift mechanism is integral and mounted in the shift tower portion of the adapter housing (Fig. 1). An adapter housing is used to attach the transmission to the transfer case.

TRANSMISSION IDENTIFICATION

The AX-15 identification code numbers are on the bottom surface of the transmission gear case (Fig. 2). The first number is year of manufacture. The second and third numbers indicate month of manufacture. The next series of numbers is the transmission serial number.

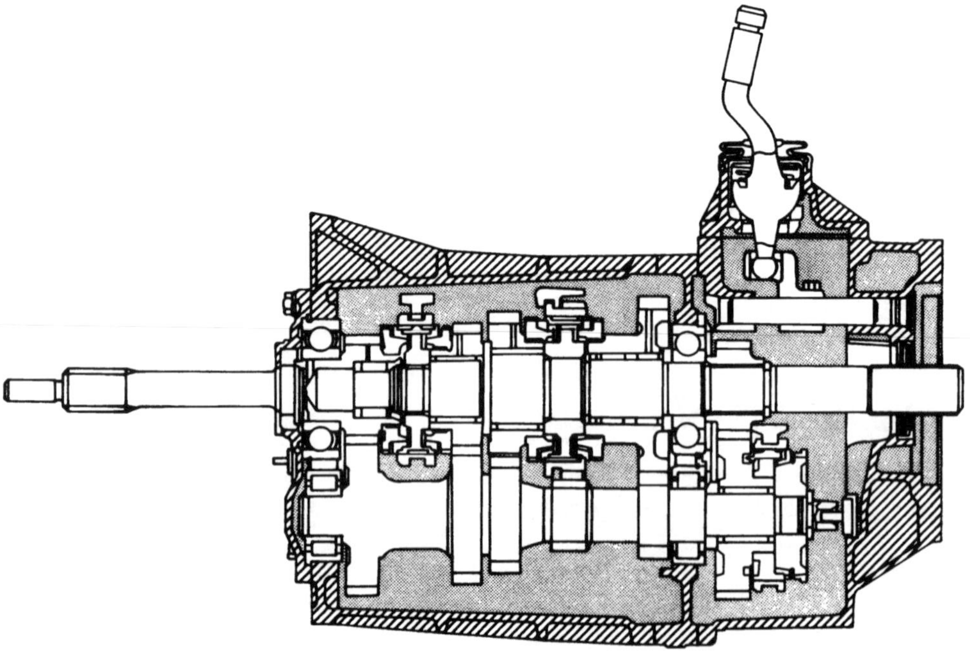

Fig. 1 AX-15 Manual Transmission

GENERAL INFORMATION (Continued)

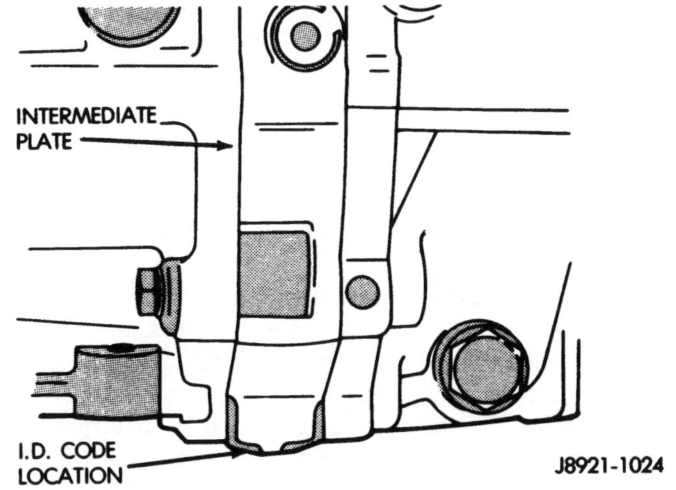

Fig. 2 Identification Code Number Location

TRANSMISSION SHIFT PATTERN

The AX-15 shift pattern is shown in (Fig. 3). First and second and third and fourth gear ranges are in line for improved shifting. Fifth and reverse gear ranges are also in line at the extreme right of the pattern (Fig. 3). The AX-15 is equipped with a reverse lockout mechanism. The shift lever must be moved through the Neutral detent before making a shift to reverse.

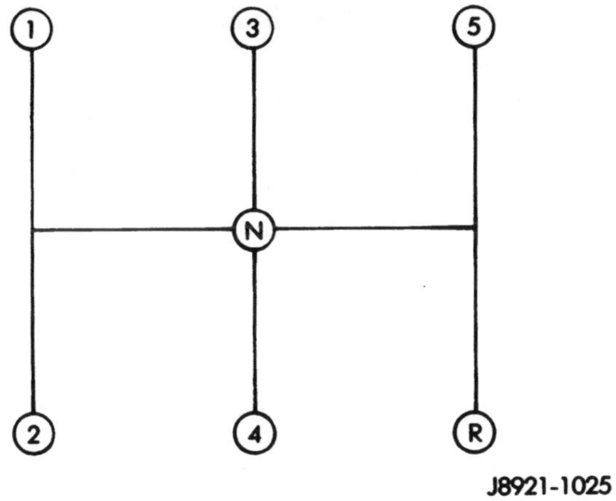

Fig. 3 AX-15 Shift Pattern

TRANSMISSION LUBRICANT

Recommended lubricant for AX-15 transmissions is Mopar 75W–90, API Grade GL–5 gear lubricant, or equivalent.

Correct lubricant level is from the bottom edge, to no more than 6 mm (0.25 in.) below the bottom edge of the fill plug hole.

Approximate dry fill lubricant capacity is 3.10 liters (3.27 qts.).

TRANSMISSION SWITCH AND PLUG LOCATIONS

The fill plug is at the driver side of the gear case (Fig. 4).

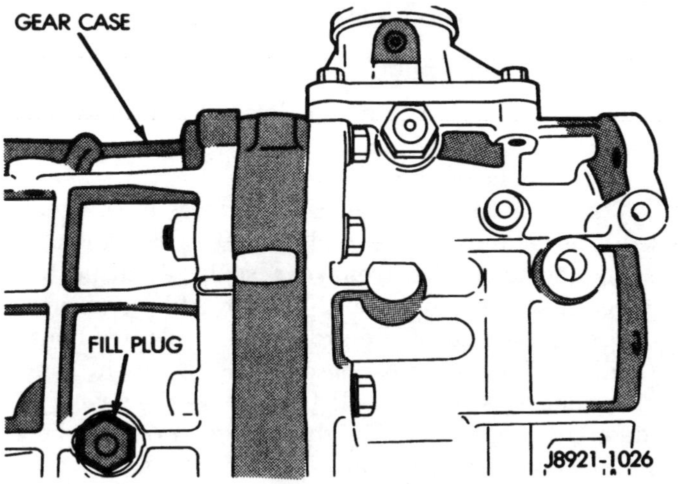

Fig. 4 Fill Plug Location

The drain plug and backup light switch are on the passenger side of the gear case (Fig. 5).

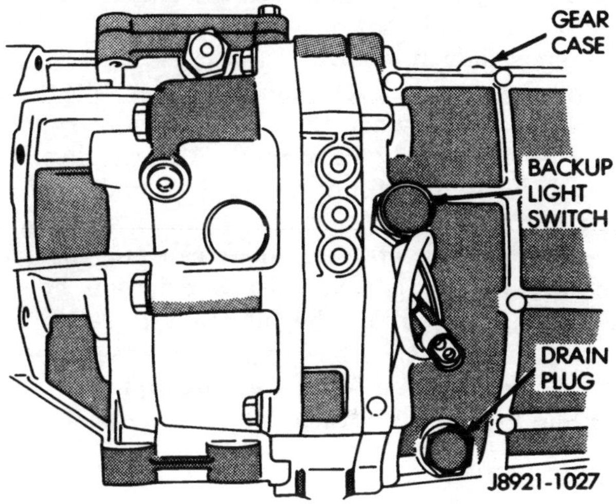

Fig. 5 Drain Plug/Backup Light Switch Location

TRANSMISSION GEAR RATIOS

AX 15 gear ratios are:

First gear	3.83:1
Second gear	2.33:1
Third gear	1.44:1
Fourth gear	1.00:1
Fifth gear	0.79:1
Reverse	4.22:1

TRANSMISSION ASSEMBLY INFORMATION

Lubricate the transmission components with gear lubricant during assembly. Use petroleum jelly to lubricate seal lips and/or hold parts in place during installation.

DIAGNOSIS AND TESTING

LOW LUBRICANT LEVEL

A low transmission lubricant level is generally the result of a leak, inadequate lubricant fill, or an incorrect lubricant level check.

Leaks can occur at the mating surfaces of the gear case, intermediate plate and adapter or extension housing, or from the front/rear seals. A suspected leak could also be the result of an overfill condition.

Leaks at the rear of the extension or adapter housing will be from the housing oil seals. Leaks at component mating surfaces will usually be the result of inadequate sealer, gaps in the sealer, incorrect bolt tightening, or use of a non–recommended sealer.

A leak at the front of the transmission will be from either the front bearing retainer or retainer seal. Lubricant may be seen dripping from the clutch housing after extended operation. If the leak is severe, it may also contaminate the clutch disc causing slip, grab and chatter.

Transmissions filled from air or electrically powered lubricant containers can be under filled. This generally happens when the container delivery mechanism is improperly calibrated. Always check the lubricant level after filling to avoid an under fill condition.

A correct lubricant level check can only be made when the vehicle is level; use a drive–on hoist to ensure this. Also allow the lubricant to settle for a minute or so before checking. These recommendations will ensure an accurate check and avoid an under–or–over fill condition.

HARD SHIFTING

Hard shifting is usually caused by a low lubricant level, improper or contaminated lubricants, component damage, incorrect clutch adjustment, or by a damaged clutch pressure plate or disc.

Substantial lubricant leaks can result in gear, shift rail, synchro and bearing damage. If a leak goes undetected for an extended period, the first indications of a problem are usually hard shifting and noise.

Incorrect or contaminated lubricants can also contribute to hard shifting. The consequence of using non–recommended lubricants is noise, excessive wear, internal bind and hard shifting.

Improper clutch release is a frequent cause of hard shifting. Incorrect adjustment or a worn, damaged pressure plate or disc can cause incorrect release. If the clutch problem is advanced, gear clash during shifts can result.

Worn or damaged synchro rings can cause gear clash when shifting into any forward gear. In some new or rebuilt transmissions, new synchro rings may tend to stick slightly causing hard or noisy shifts. In most cases, this condition will decline as the rings wear–in.

TRANSMISSION NOISE

Most manual transmissions make some noise during normal operation. Rotating gears can generate a mild whine that may only be audible at extreme speeds.

Severe, obviously audible transmission noise is generally the result of a lubricant problem. Insufficient, improper, or contaminated lubricant can promote rapid wear of gears, synchros, shift rails, forks and bearings. The overheating caused by a lubricant problem, can also lead to gear breakage.

REMOVAL AND INSTALLATION

TRANSMISSION

REMOVAL

(1) Shift transmission into first or third gear.

(2) Raise vehicle on a hoist.

(3) Disconnect necessary exhaust system components.

(4) Support transmission with adjustable jack stand.

(5) Disconnect rear cushion and mounting bracket from transmission, or transfer case.

(6) Remove rear crossmember.

(7) Disconnect transmission shift linkage, speedometer cable, transfer case vacuum lines and clutch hydraulic lines.

(8) Lower transmission–transfer case assembly no more than 7.6 cm (3 in.) for access to shift lever.

(9) Reach up and around transmission case and unseat shift lever dust boot from transmission shift tower (Fig. 6). Move boot upward on shift lever for access to lever retainer.

(10) Disengage shift lever as follows:

(a) Reach up and around transmission case and press shift lever retainer downward with your fingers.

(b) Turn retainer counterclockwise to release it.

(c) Lift lever and retainer out of shift tower (Fig. 6). **It is not necessary to remove shift lever from floorpan boot. Simply leave lever in place for later installation.**

(11) Mark front and rear propeller shafts for installation alignment (Fig. 7). Then remove both shafts.

(12) Remove crankshaft position sensor (Fig. 8).

(13) Disconnect transmission and transfer case vent hoses.

(14) Remove slave cylinder from clutch housing.

REMOVAL AND INSTALLATION (Continued)

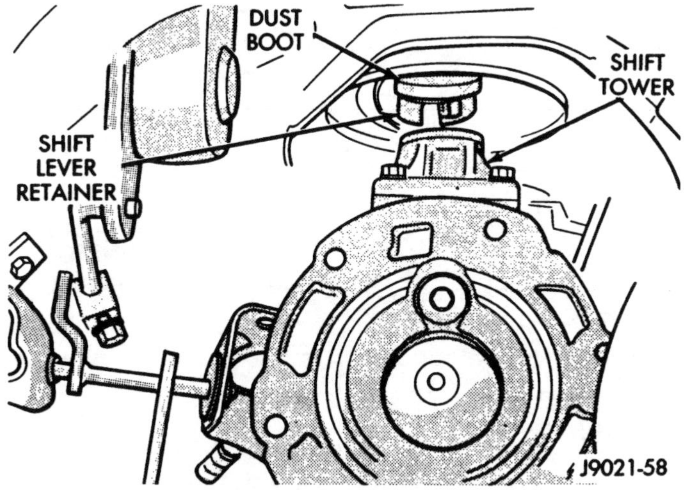

Fig. 6 Removing/Installing Shift Lever

Fig. 7 Marking Propeller Shaft And Axle Yoke

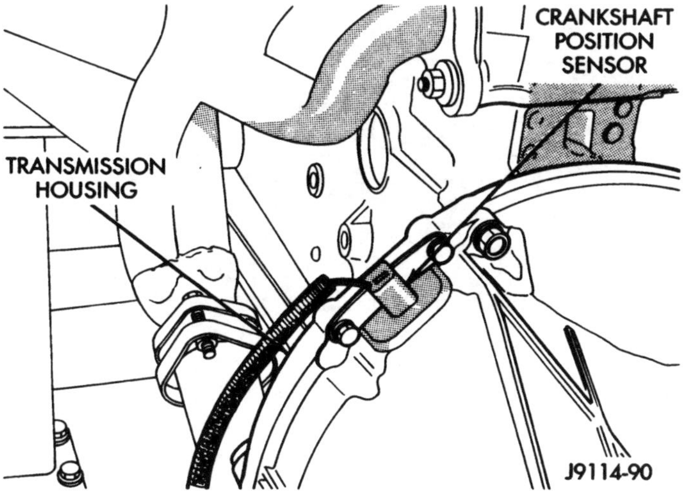

Fig. 8 Crankshaft Position Sensor Location—4.0 L Engine

(15) Remove wire harnesses from clips/tie straps on transmission and transfer case.

(16) Support transmission–transfer case assembly with transmission jack. Secure assembly to jack with safety chains.

(17) Reposition adjustable jack stand under engine. Be sure to place wood block between jack and oil pan.

(18) Remove clutch housing brace rod.

(19) Remove clutch housing–to–engine bolts and remove transmission–transfer case assembly.

(20) Remove bolts attaching transmission to transfer case and separate components.

(21) Remove release bearing, fork and retainer clip.

(22) Remove clutch housing from transmission.

TRANSMISSION INSTALLATION

(1) Install clutch housing on transmission. Tighten 3/8 in. housing bolts to 37 N·m (27 ft. lbs.) and 7/16 in. housing bolts to 58 N·m (43 ft. lbs.) torque.

(2) Lubricate contact surfaces of release fork, lever and pivot ball stud. Then install bearing, fork and clip in clutch housing.

(3) Mount transmission on transmission jack. Secure transmission with safety chains.

(4) Lightly lubricate pilot bearing and transmission input shaft splines with Mopar high temperature grease.

(5) Align transmission input shaft and clutch disc splines and install transmission.

(6) Install and tighten clutch housing–to–engine bolts to 38 N·m (28 ft. lbs.) torque. **Be sure housing is properly seated on engine before tightening bolts.**

(7) Lower transmission no more than 7.6 cm (3 in.) for access to the shift tower.

(8) Reach up and around the transmission and insert shift lever in shift tower. Press lever retainer downward and turn it clockwise to lock it in place. Then install lever dust boot on shift tower.

(9) Install and connect crankshaft position sensor.

(10) Align and install transfer case on transmission. Tighten transfer case attaching nuts to 35 N·m (26 ft. lbs.) torque.

(11) Connect transfer case vacuum and vent hoses.

(12) Install and connect transfer case shift linkage. Check and adjust linkage if necessary.

(13) Secure wire harnesses to clips/tie straps on transmission and transfer case.

(14) Connect backup light switch wires.

(15) Install clutch slave cylinder.

(16) Connect vehicle speed sensor wires.

(17) Install rear crossmember and attach cushion and bracket. Tighten crossmember–to–frame bolts to 41 N·m (30 ft. lbs.) torque. Tighten transmission–to–rear cushion and bracket bolts/nuts to 45 N·m (33 ft. lbs.) torque.

REMOVAL AND INSTALLATION (Continued)

(18) Align and install front/rear propeller shafts. Tighten shaft U–joint clamp bolts to 19 N·m (170 in. lbs.) torque.

(19) Install skid plate if removed. Tighten bolts to 42 N·m (31 ft. lbs.) torque. Tighten stud nuts to 17 N·m (150 in. lbs.) torque.

(20) Top off transmission and transfer lubricant levels.

(21) Remove supports and lower vehicle.

DISASSEMBLY AND ASSEMBLY

ADAPTER HOUSING

REMOVAL

(1) Remove release bearing, release lever and release fork from clutch housing. Then remove clutch housing from transmission.

(2) Remove backup light switch. Then remove drain plug (Fig. 9) and drain transmission lubricant into pan.

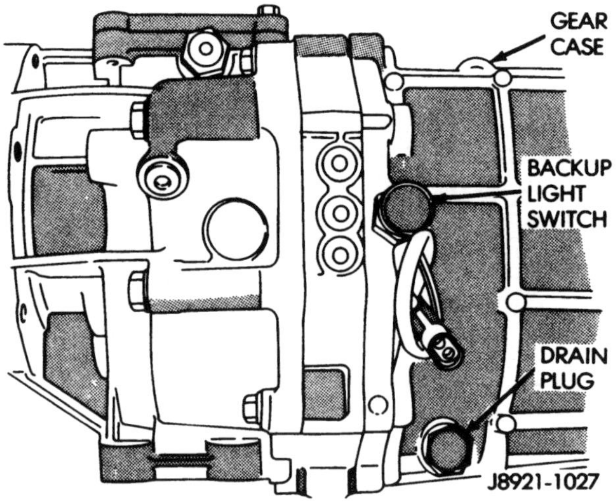

Fig. 9 Drain Plug And Backup Light Switch Location

(3) Remove shift tower bolts and remove tower from adapter housing (Fig. 10).

(4) Remove gasket/slinger from shift tower.

(5) Remove shift arm retainer bolt (Fig. 11).

(6) Loosen and remove restrictor pins (Fig. 12).

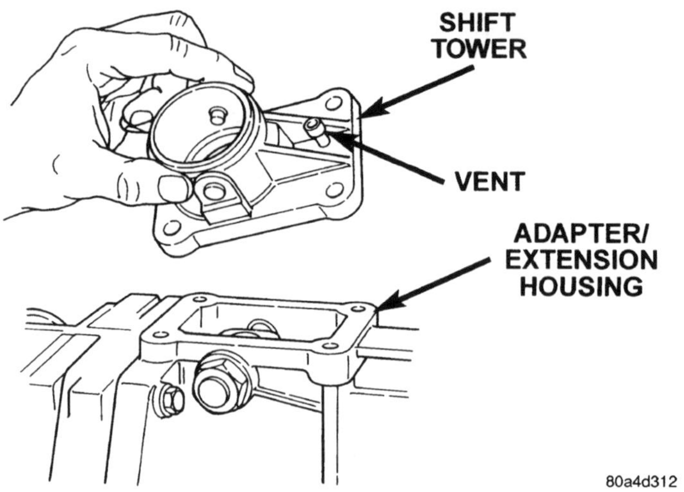

Fig. 10 Shift Tower

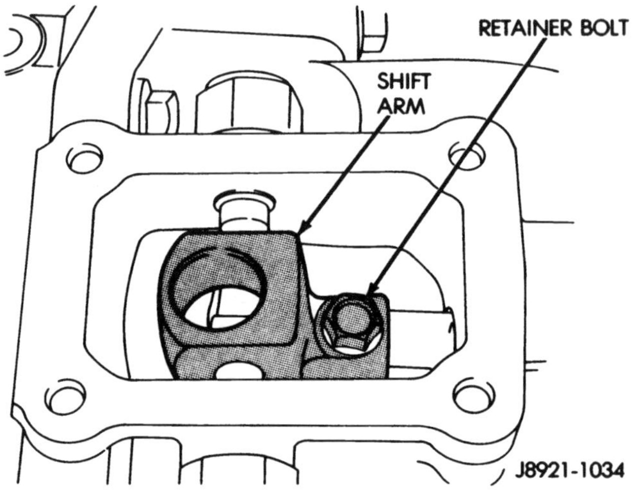

Fig. 11 Shift Arm Retainer Bolt Removal/Installation

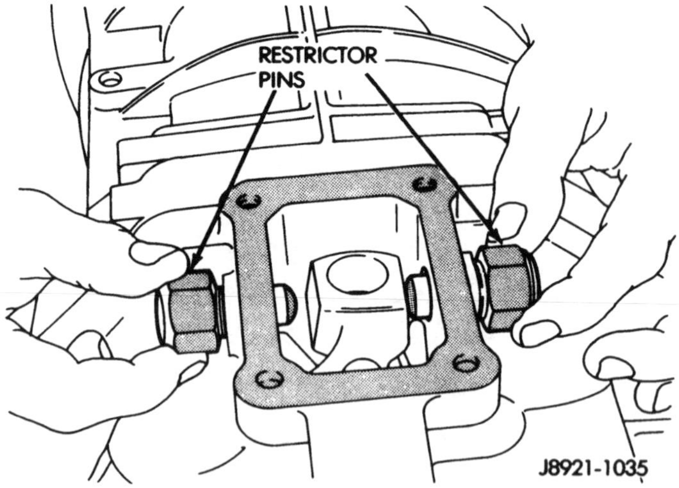

Fig. 12 Removing/Installing Restrictor Pins

DISASSEMBLY AND ASSEMBLY (Continued)

(7) Remove shift arm shaft plug (Fig. 13).

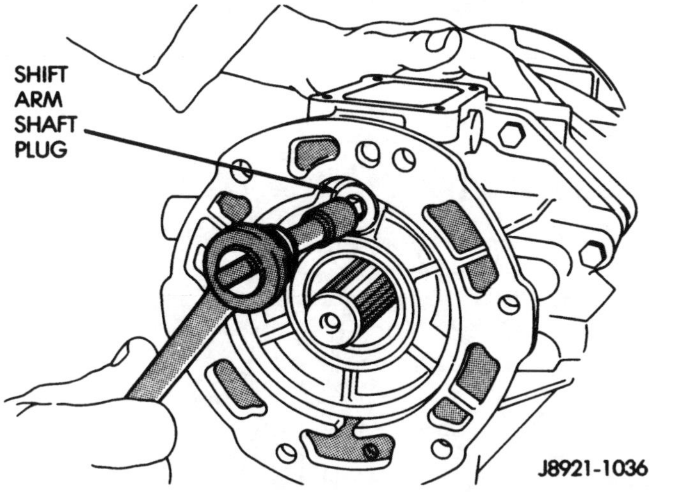

Fig. 13 Removing/Installing Shift Lever Shaft Plug

(8) Remove shift arm shaft with large magnet (Fig. 14).

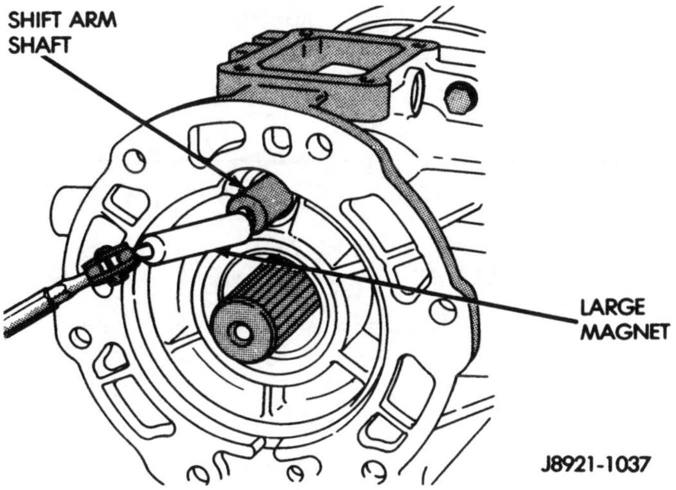

Fig. 14 Removing/Installing Shift Lever Shaft

(9) Remove shift arm (Fig. 15).

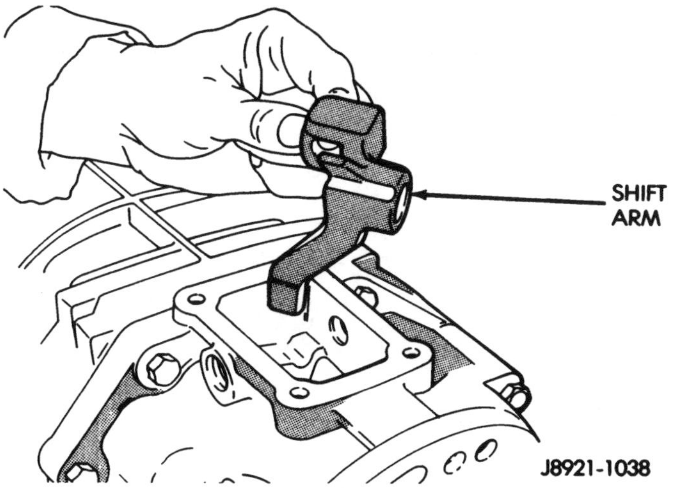

Fig. 15 Shift Arm Removal/Installation

(10) Remove plug for reverse shift head lock ball. Plug is at right side of adapter housing near backup light switch (Fig. 16).

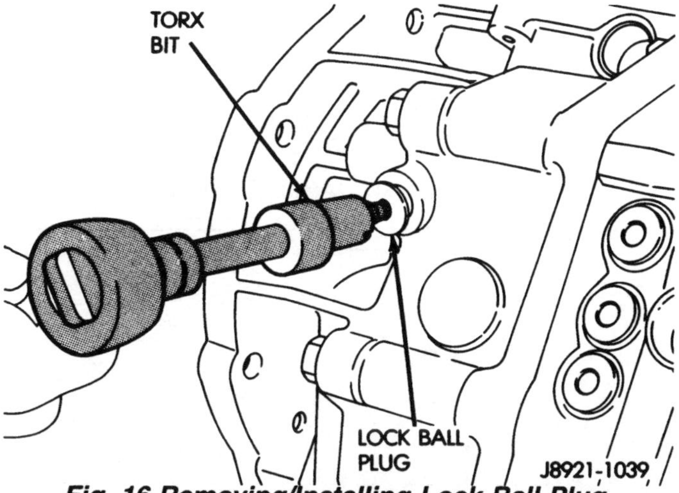

Fig. 16 Removing/Installing Lock Ball Plug

(11) Remove lock ball spring with pencil magnet (Fig. 17).

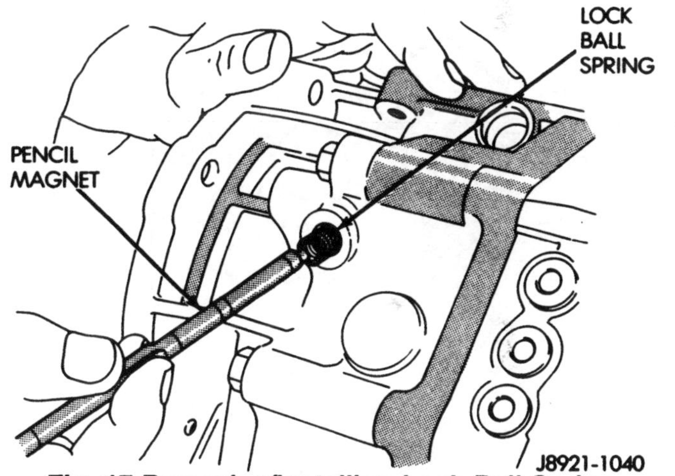

Fig. 17 Removing/Installing Lock Ball Spring

(12) Remove shift head lock ball with pencil magnet (Fig. 18).

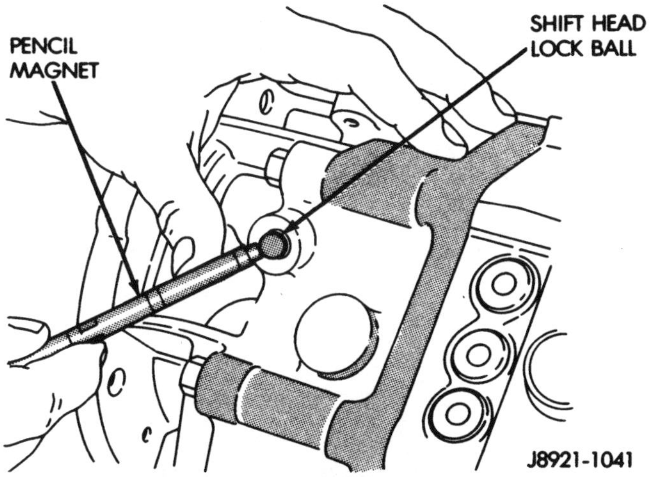

Fig. 18 Removing/Installing Shift Head Lock Ball

DISASSEMBLY AND ASSEMBLY (Continued)

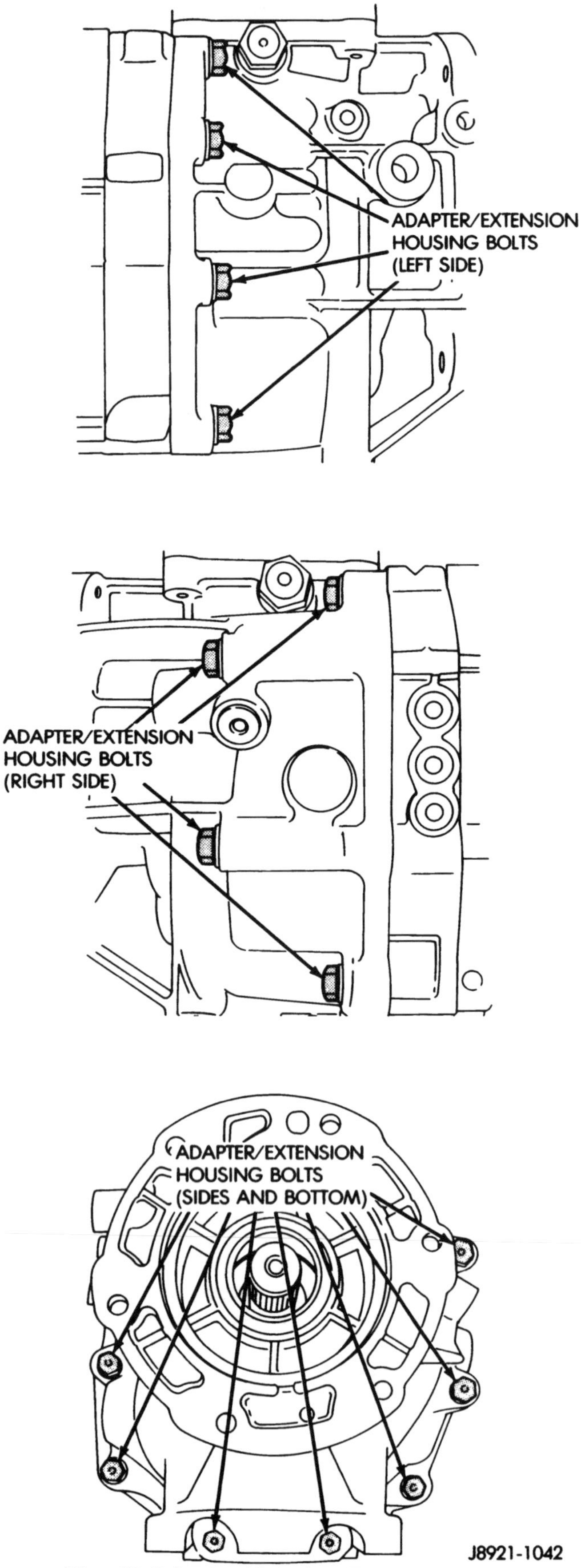

Fig. 19 Adapter Housing Bolt Locations

(13) Remove adapter housing bolts (Fig. 19).

(14) Loosen adapter housing with rubber mallet (Fig. 20).

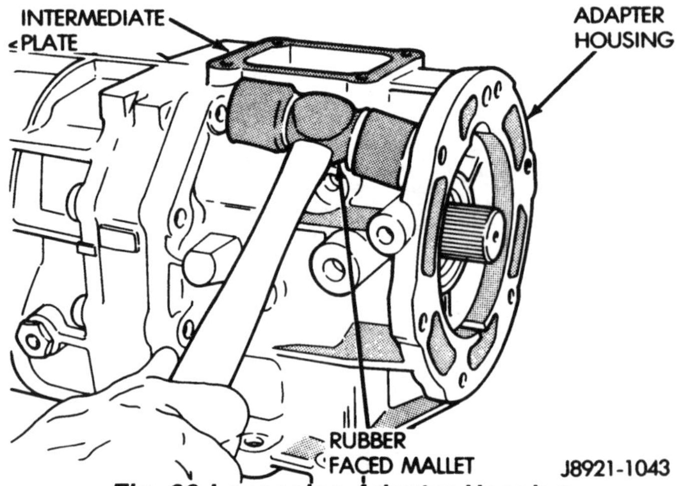

Fig. 20 Loosening Adapter Housing

(15) Remove housing after loosening it (Fig. 21)

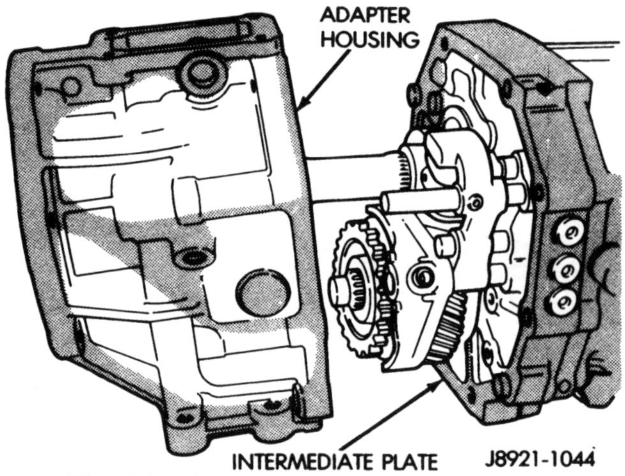

Fig. 21 Adapter Housing Removal

(16) Remove adapter housing oil seal with a pry tool (Fig. 22).

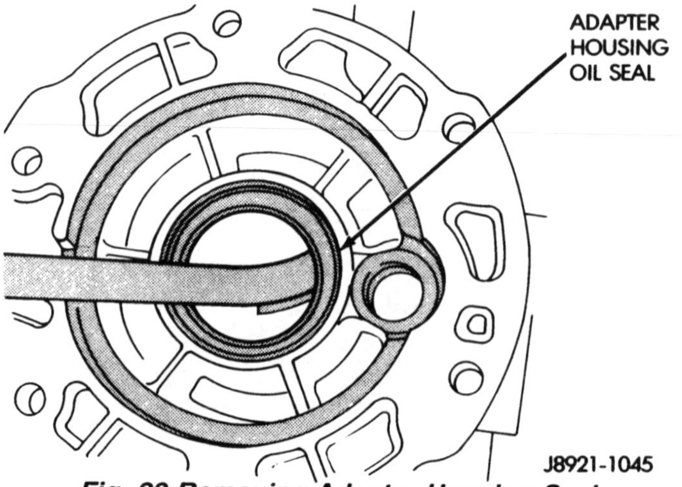

Fig. 22 Removing Adapter Housing Seal

DISASSEMBLY AND ASSEMBLY (Continued)

ADAPTER HOUSING INSTALLATION

(1) Inspect condition of reverse pin in adapter housing (Fig. 23). If pin is worn or damaged, replace it as described in following steps.

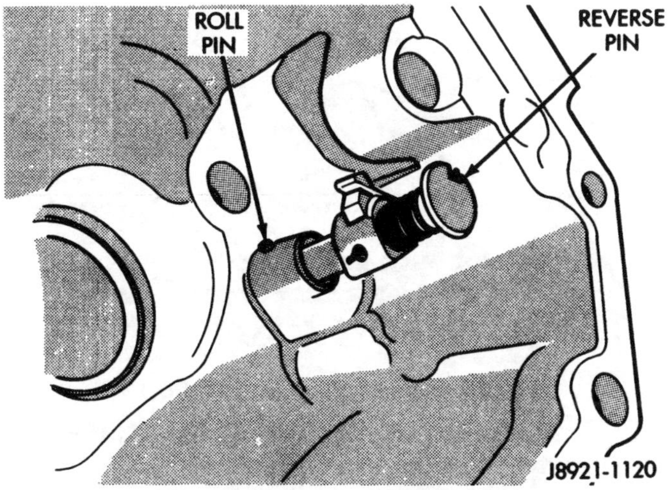

Fig. 23 Reverse Pin Position

(2) Remove roll pin access plug (Fig. 24).

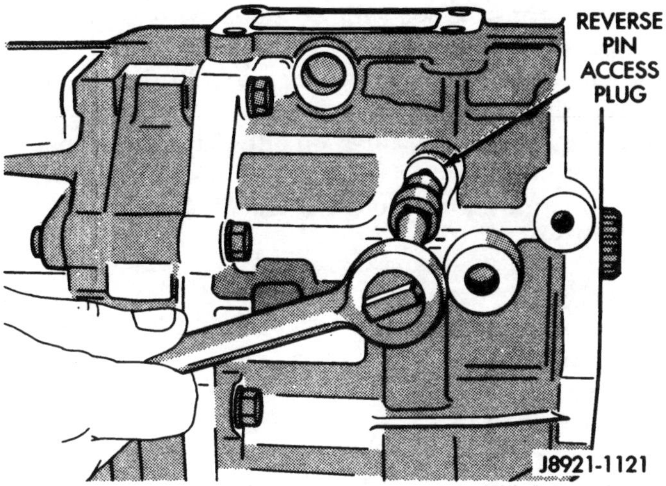

Fig. 24 Reverse Pin Access Plug Removal/Installation

(3) Tap roll pin out of housing with pin punch (Fig. 25). Then remove old reverse pin.

(4) Install new reverse pin and secure it with roll pin. Then install and tighten access plug to 19 N·m (14 ft. lbs.) torque.

(5) Clean sealing surfaces of adapter housing and intermediate plate with wax and grease remover. Then wipe dry with a clean cloth.

(6) Apply 3 mm (1/8 in.) wide bead of Mopar Gasket Maker, or Loctite 518 to sealing surface of adapter housing. Keep sealer bead inside bolt holes.

(7) Align and install adapter housing on intermediate plate. Be sure housing is seated on intermediate plate dowel pins.

(8) Coat threads of housing attaching bolts with Mopar silicone sealer. Then install and tighten bolts to 37 N·m (27 ft. lbs.) torque.

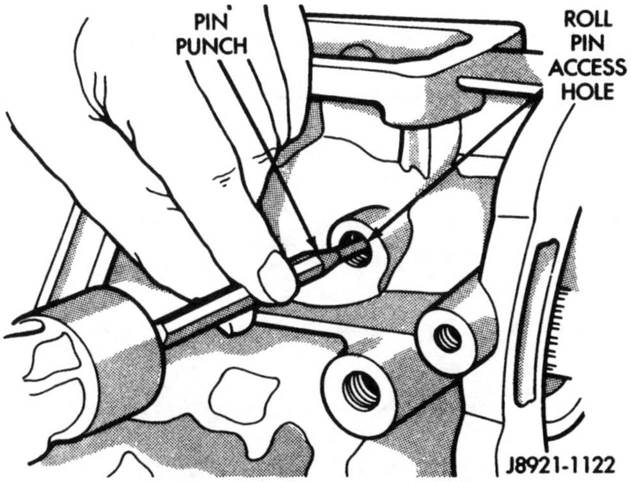

Fig. 25 Roll Pin Removal/Installation

(9) Install reverse shift head detent ball (Fig. 26). Then install detent spring and plug. Tighten plug to 19 N.m (14 ft. lbs.) torque.

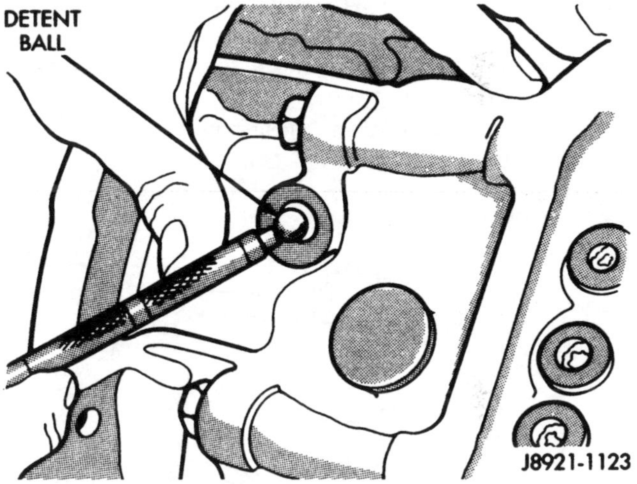

Fig. 26 Reverse Shift Head Detent Ball Installation

(10) Lubricate shift arm shaft and install it in adapter housing (Fig. 27).

Fig. 27 Shift Arm Shaft Installation

DISASSEMBLY AND ASSEMBLY (Continued)

(11) Position shift arm in adapter housing (Fig. 28). Be sure arm is engaged in shift rails.

Fig. 28 Shift Arm Installation

(12) Align shift arm with shaft and push shaft into arm.

(13) Rotate shift arm shaft until set screw holes in shaft and arm are aligned.

(14) Install and tighten shift arm set screw to 38 N·m (28 ft. lbs.) torque (Fig. 29).

(15) Install and tighten restrictor pins to 19 N·m (14 ft. lbs.) torque (Fig. 29).

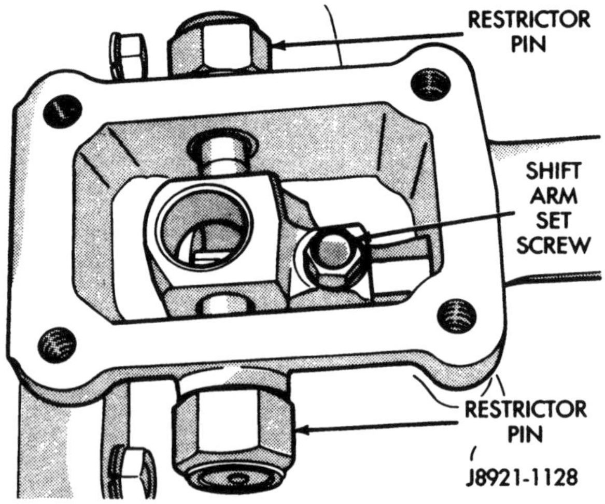

Fig. 29 Set Screw And Restrictor Pin Installation

(16) Install and tighten shift arm shaft access plug to 19 N·m (14 ft. lbs.) torque (Fig. 30).

(17) Position new shift tower gasket on adapter housing.

(18) Install shift tower. Tighten tower attaching bolts to 18 N·m (13 ft. lbs.) torque.

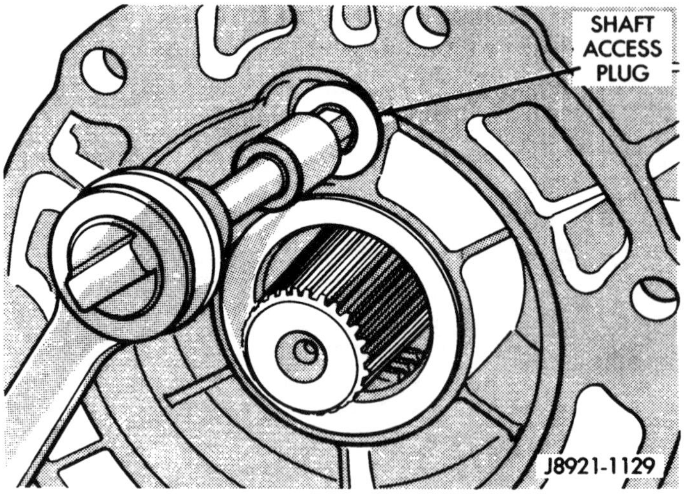

Fig. 30 Access Plug Installation

(19) Install new gasket on backup light switch and install switch. Tighten switch to 37 N·m (27 ft. lbs.) torque.

(20) Install new washer on drain plug. Then install and tighten plug to 37 N·m (27 ft. lbs.) torque.

(21) If transmission will be filled with gear lubricant before installation, place transmission in a level position. Then fill with Mopar 75W-90, grade GL-5 gear lubricant.

(22) Install new washer on fill plug. Then install and tighten plug to 37 N·m (27 ft. lbs.) torque.

(23) Install clutch housing and hydraulic concentric bearing.

GEAR CASE

DISASSEMBLE

(1) Remove bearing retainer bolts and remove retainer (Fig. 31).

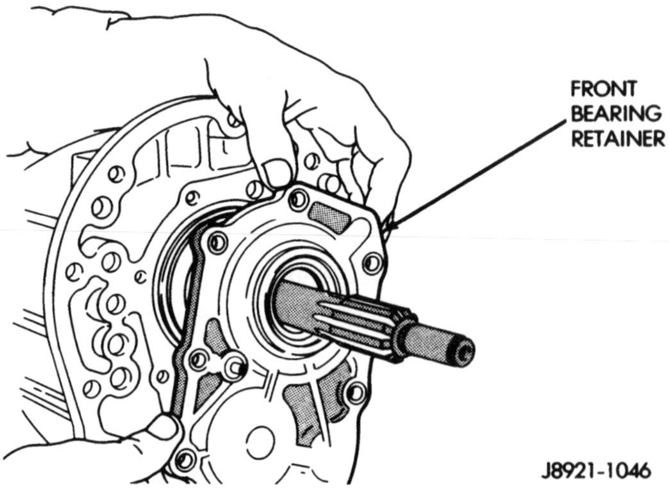

Fig. 31 Front Bearing Retainer Removal

DISASSEMBLY AND ASSEMBLY (Continued)

(2) Remove retainer oil seal with pry tool (Fig. 32).

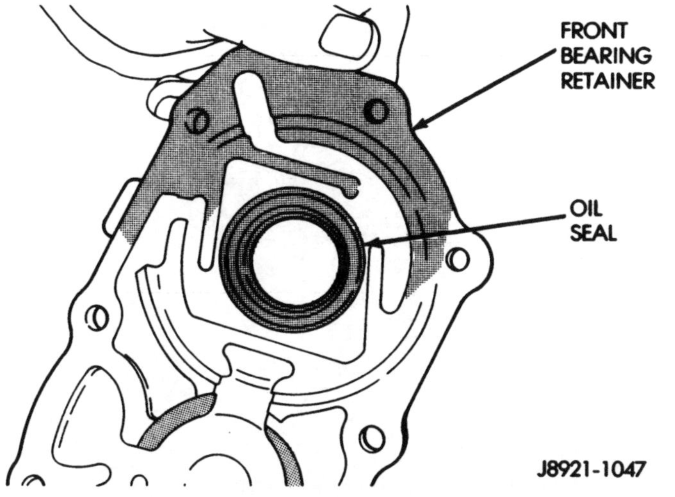

Fig. 32 Front Bearing Retainer Seal Location

(3) Remove input shaft bearing snap ring (Fig. 33).

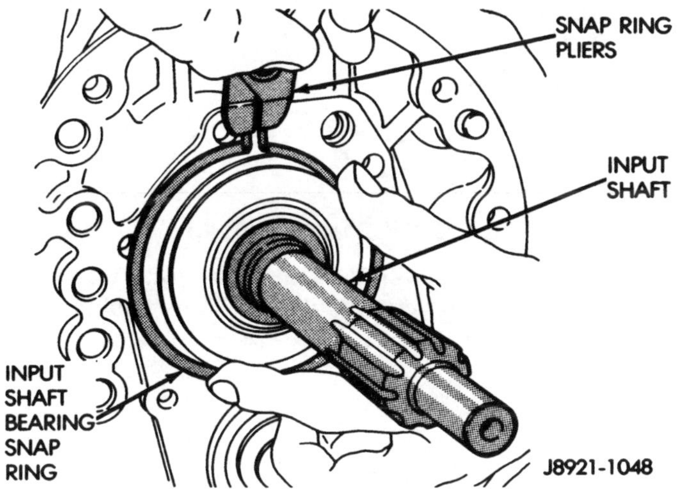

Fig. 33 Removing Input Shaft Bearing Snap Ring

(4) Remove cluster gear front bearing snap ring (Fig. 34).

(5) Loosen gear case by tapping it away from intermediate plate with rubber mallet (Fig. 35).

(6) Remove gear case from geartrain and intermediate plate (Fig. 36).

(7) Remove speedometer gear snap ring and remove speedometer gear and spacer from output shaft.

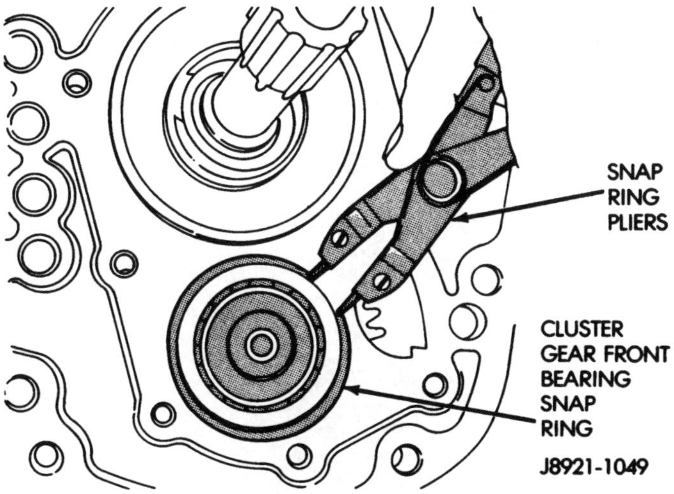

Fig. 34 Removing Cluster Gear Front Bearing Snap Ring

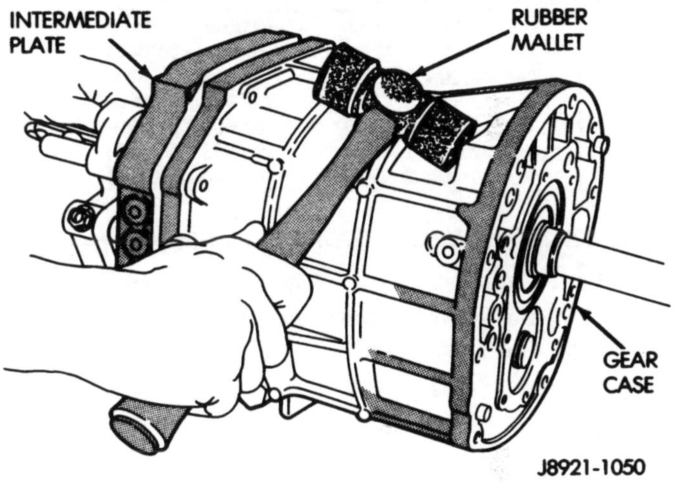

Fig. 35 Loosening Gear Case

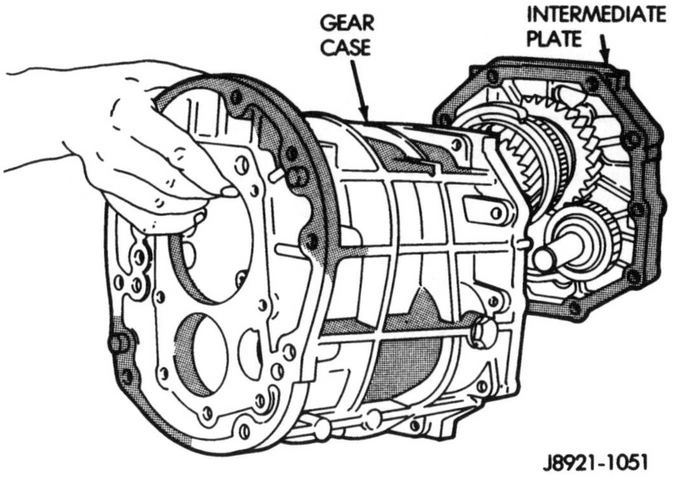

Fig. 36 Gear Case Removal

DISASSEMBLY AND ASSEMBLY (Continued)

GEAR CASE ASSEMBLE

(1) Press front bearing on input shaft. Then secure bearing with thickest snap ring that will fit in shaft groove (Fig. 37).

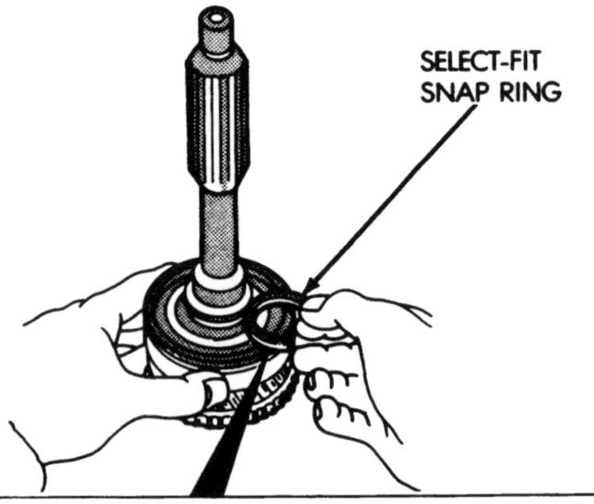

I.D. MARK	SNAP RING THICKNESS	MM (IN.)
A	2.10 - 2.15	(0.0827 - 0.0846)
B	2.15 - 2.20	(0.0846 - 0.0866)
C	2.20 - 2.25	(0.0866 - 0.0886)
D	2.25 - 2.30	(0.0886 - 0.0906)
E	2.30 - 2.35	(0.0906 - 0.0925)
F	2.35 - 2.40	(0.0925 - 0.0945)
G	2.40 - 2.45	(0.0945 - 0.0965)

J8921-1097

Fig. 37 Selecting Input Shaft Front Bearing Snap Ring

(2) Press front bearing on cluster gear. Then secure bearing with thickest snap ring that will fit in ring groove on gear (Fig. 38).

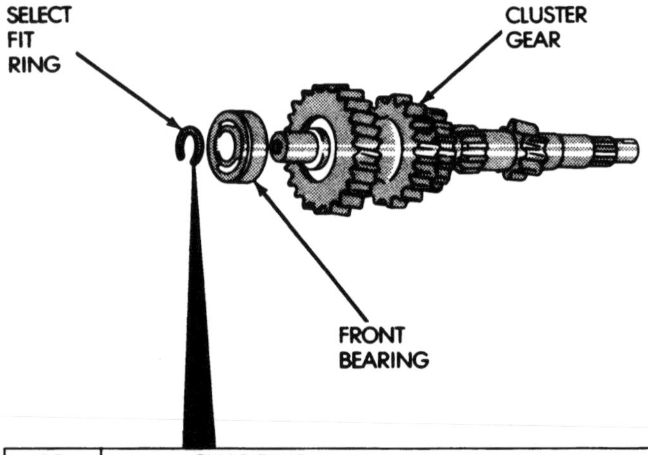

I.D. MARK	SNAP RING THICKNESS	MM (IN.)
A	2.00 - 2.05	(0.0787 - 0.0807)
B	2.05 - 2.10	(0.0807 - 0.0827)
C	2.10 - 2.15	(0.0827 - 0.0846)
D	2.15 - 2.20	(0.0846 - 0.0866)
E	2.20 - 2.25	(0.0866 - 0.0886)

J8921-1098

Fig. 38 Selecting Cluster Gear Front Bearing Snap Ring

(3) Install new oil seals in front bearing retainer and adapter housing (Fig. 39). Installation depth for bearing retainer seal is 10.5 to 11.5 mm (0.414 to 0.453 in.).

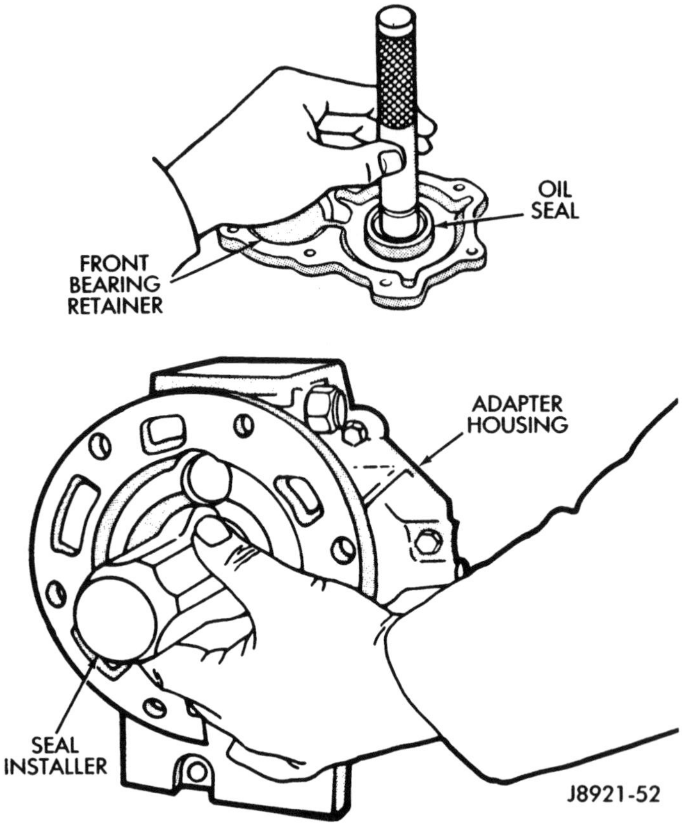

Fig. 39 Oil Seal Installation

(4) Install reverse shaft and shaft retaining pin in adapter housing. Then install access hole plug with torx bit (Fig. 40).

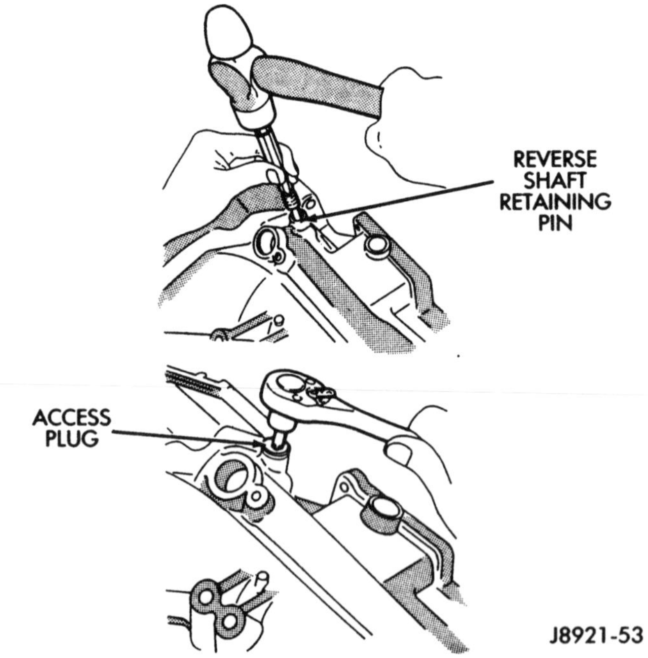

Fig. 40 Installing Reverse Shaft Pin

(5) Lubricate reverse shaft and gear components with Mopar 75W–90 gear lubricant.

DISASSEMBLY AND ASSEMBLY (Continued)

(6) Clean mating surfaces of intermediate plate and transmission gear case with wax and grease remover. Then wipe dry with a clean cloth.

(7) Apply 3 mm (1/8 in.) wide bead of Mopar Gasket Maker, or Loctite 518 to mating surface of gear-case. Keep sealer bead inside bolt holes as shown (Fig. 41).

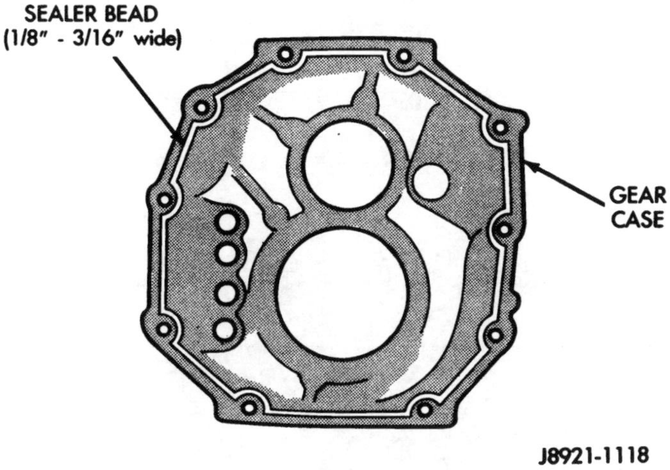

Fig. 41 Applying Sealer To Gear Case

(8) Install gear case (Fig. 42). Align shift rails and bearings in case and tap case into position.

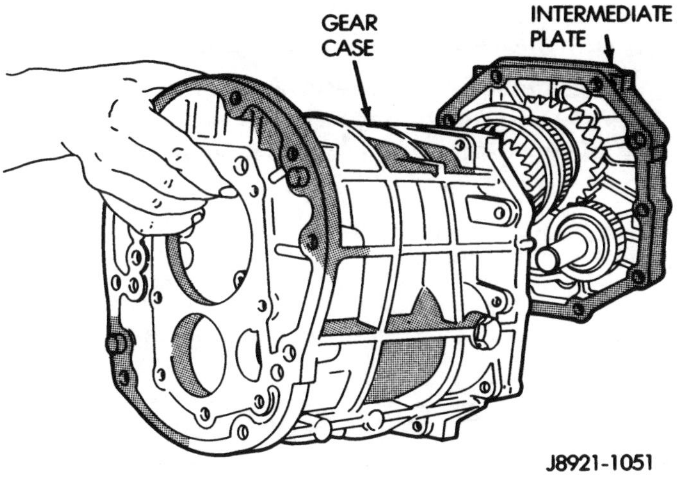

Fig. 42 Gear Case Installation

(9) Verify that gear case is seated on intermediate plate dowel pins.

(10) Install front bearing snap rings (Fig. 43).

(11) Clean gear case and front bearing retainer sealing surfaces with wax and grease remover. Then wipe dry with a clean cloth.

(12) Install new seal in front bearing retainer. Then lubricate seal lip with petroleum jelly. **Installation depth for seal is 10.5 to 11.5 mm (0.413 to 0.453 in.).**

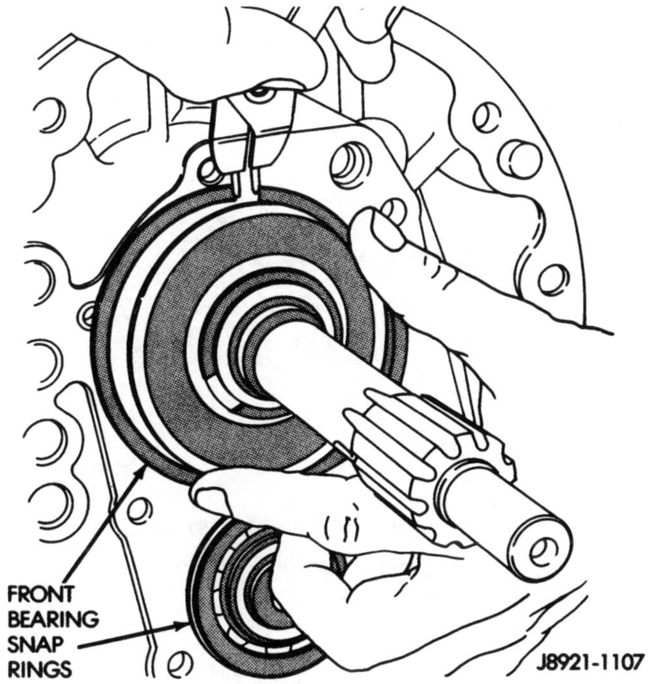

Fig. 43 Front Bearing Snap Ring Installation

(13) Apply a 3 mm (1/8 in.) wide bead of Mopar Gasket Maker, or Loctite 518 to front bearing retainer sealing surface.

(14) Align and install front bearing retainer (Fig. 44). Be sure retainer is properly seated on case and bearings.

(15) Install and tighten front bearing retainer bolts to 17 N·m (12 ft. lbs.) torque.

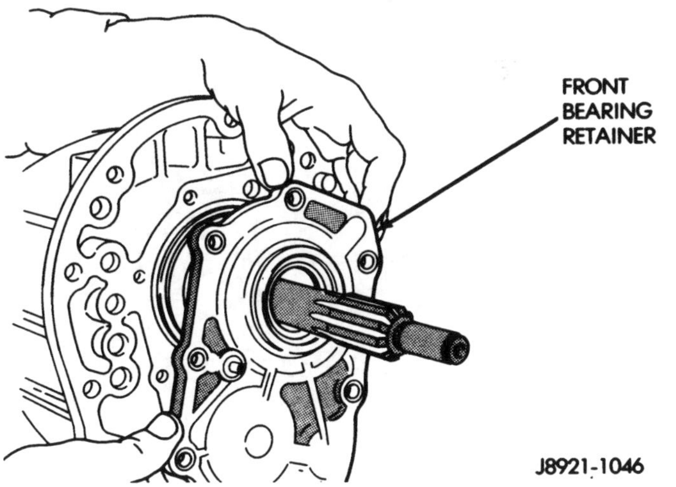

Fig. 44 Front Bearing Retainer Installation

DISASSEMBLY AND ASSEMBLY (Continued)

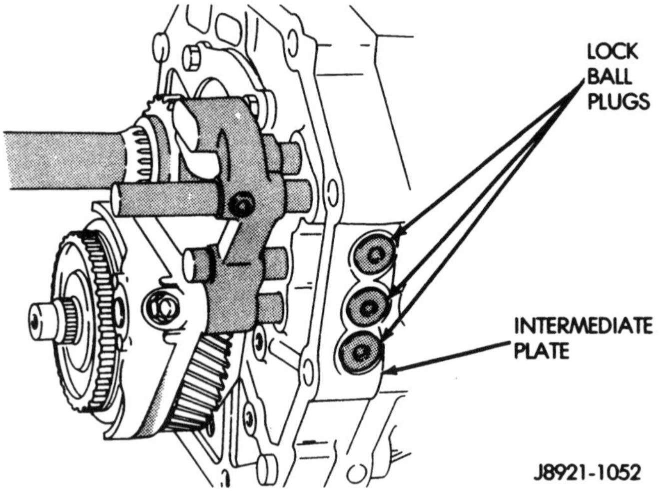

Fig. 45 Lock Ball Plug Locations

FIFTH GEAR AND SYNCHRO ASSEMBLY

DISASSEMBLE

(1) Remove three lock ball plugs from intermediate plate (Fig. 45).

(2) Remove three lock ball springs and lock balls from intermediate plate with pencil magnet (Fig. 46).

(3) Mount intermediate plate and geartrain assembly in vise as follows:

(a) Insert two spare bolts in one bottom bolt hole in intermediate plate. Insert bolts from opposite sides of plates (Fig. 47).

(b) Install enough flat washers under each bolt head to prevent bolts from touching (Fig. 47).

(c) Tape bolts and washers in place and mount intermediate plate in vise (Fig. 47).

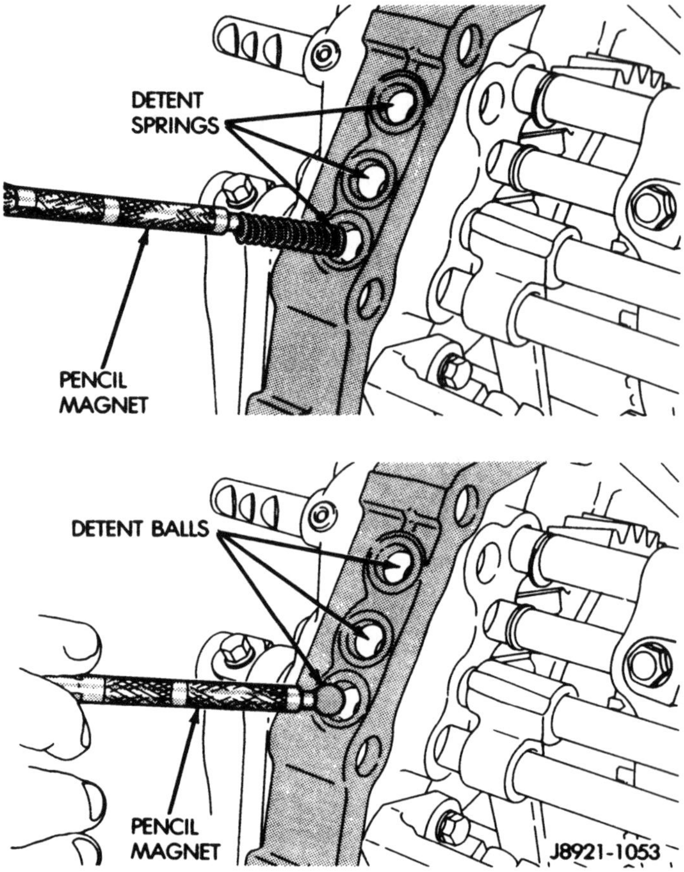

Fig. 46 Removing/Installing Lock Ball And Spring

(d) Clamp vise jaws securely against bolt heads (Fig. 47). **Do not clamp vise jaws on intermediate plate. Clamp only on bolt heads.**

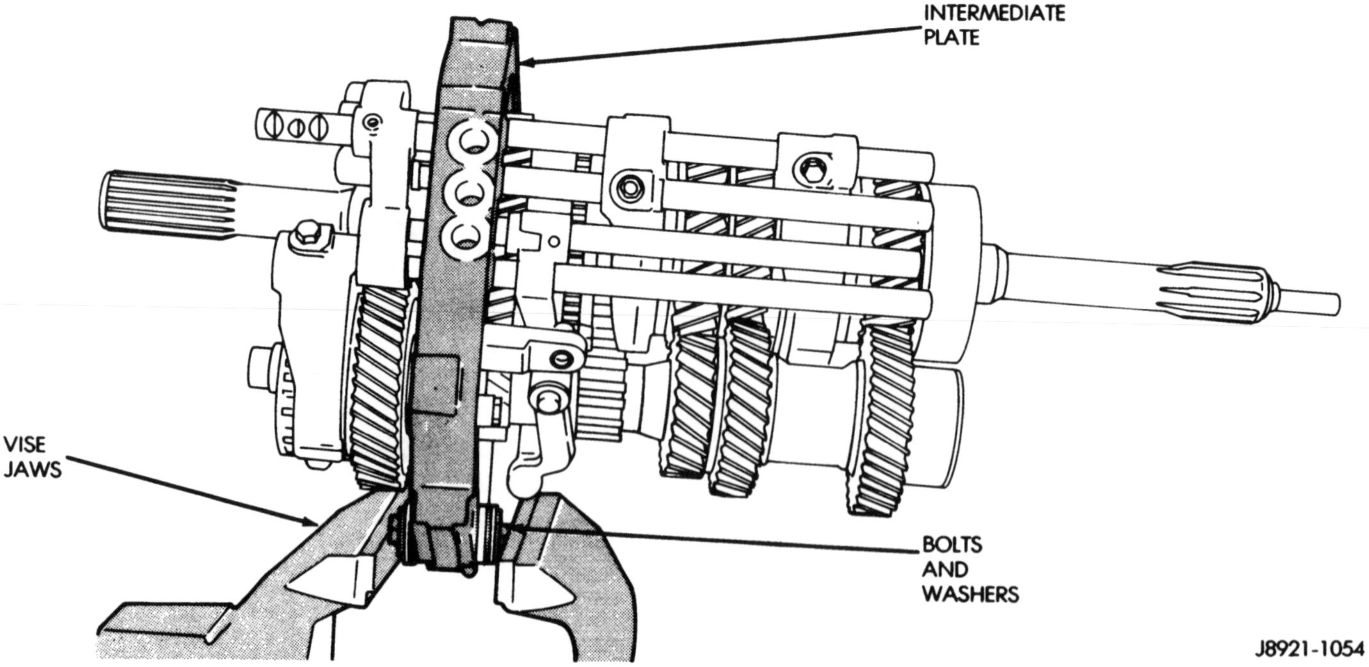

Fig. 47 Mounting Intermediate Plate And Geartrain In Vise

DISASSEMBLY AND ASSEMBLY (Continued)

(4) Remove fifth gear snap ring (Fig. 48). Retain snap ring for assembly reference. It is a select fit component.

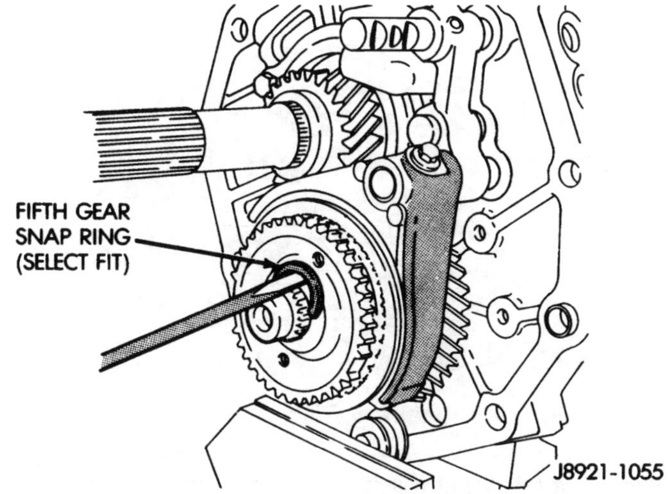

Fig. 48 Fifth Gear Snap Ring Removal

(5) Remove E–ring that secures reverse shift arm to fork (Fig. 49).

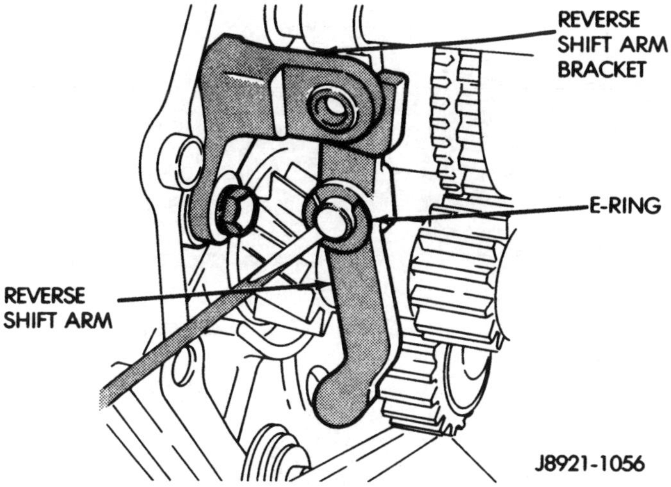

Fig. 49 Reverse Shift Arm E–Ring Removal

(6) Remove bolts attaching reverse shift arm bracket to intermediate plate. Then remove bracket (Fig. 50).

(7) Remove reverse shift arm and shoe (Fig. 51).

(8) Remove fifth gear shift fork set screw (Fig. 52).

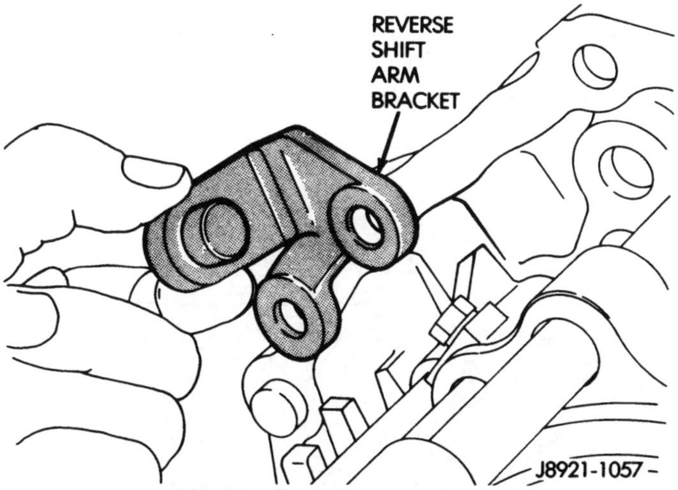

Fig. 50 Reverse Shift Arm Bracket Removal

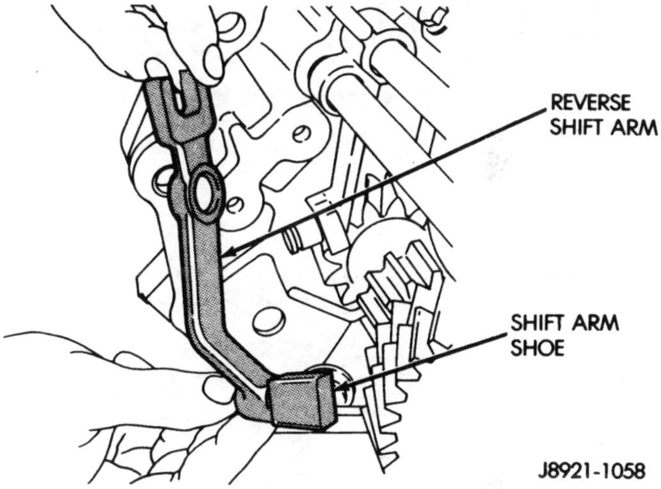

Fig. 51 Reverse Shift Arm And Shoe Removal

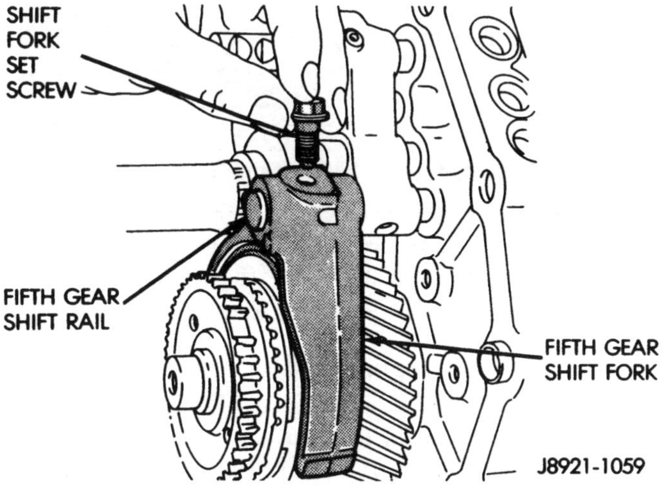

Fig. 52 Fifth Gear Fork Set Screw Removal

DISASSEMBLY AND ASSEMBLY (Continued)

(9) Move fifth gear shift rail forward until it clears shift fork.

(10) Remove fifth gear shift fork from synchro sleeve (Fig. 53).

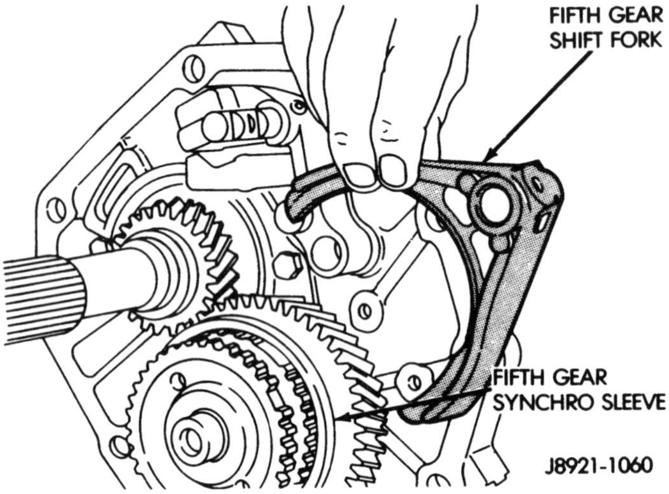

Fig. 53 Fifth Gear Shift Fork Removal

(11) Remove reverse shift rail and reverse shift head as assembly (Fig. 54).

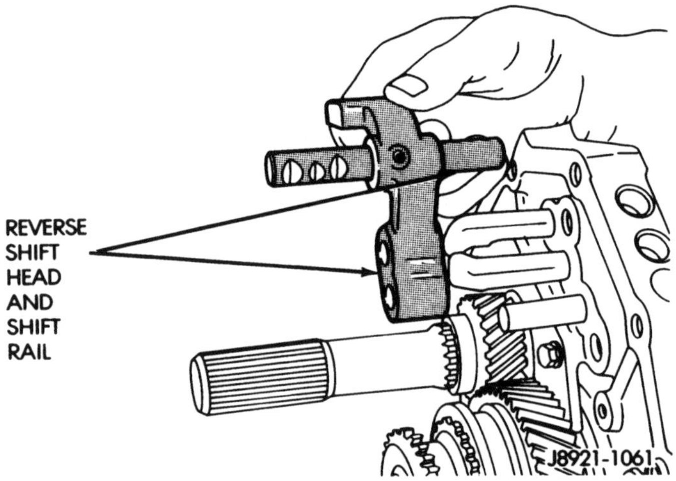

Fig. 54 Reverse Shift Head And Rail Removal

(12) Measure thrust clearance between counter fifth gear and thrust ring with feeler gauge. Clearance should be 0.10 to 0.40 mm (0.003 to 0.019 in.). If clearance exceeds limits, gear and/or ring will have to be replaced.

(13) Loosen fifth spline gear with standard two–jaw puller (Fig. 55). **Position puller jaws behind fifth counter gear as shown.**

(14) Remove fifth spline gear (Fig. 56).

(15) Remove fifth gear synchro ring (Fig. 57).

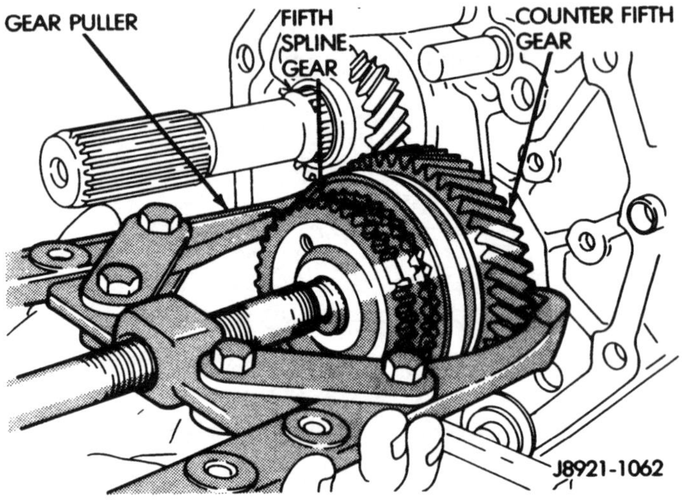

Fig. 55 Loosening Fifth Spline Gear

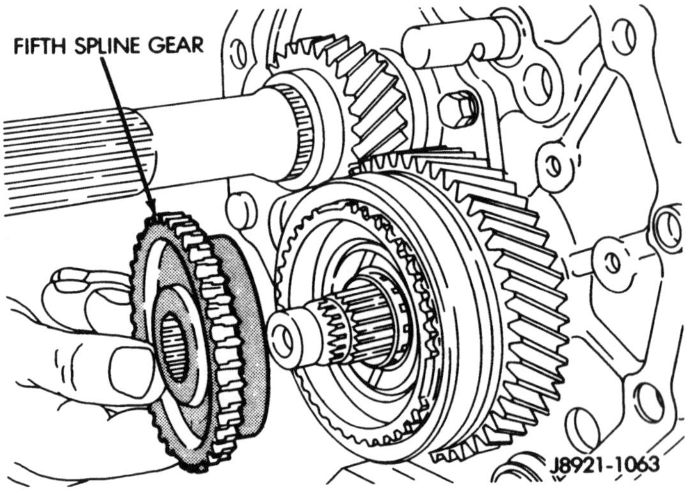

Fig. 56 Fifth Spline Gear Removal

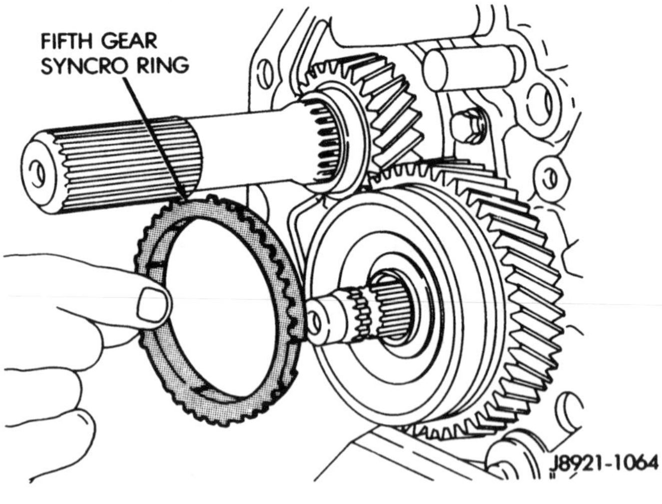

Fig. 57 Fifth Gear Synchro Ring Removal

DISASSEMBLY AND ASSEMBLY (Continued)

(16) Remove fifth gear synchro and sleeve assembly (Fig. 58).

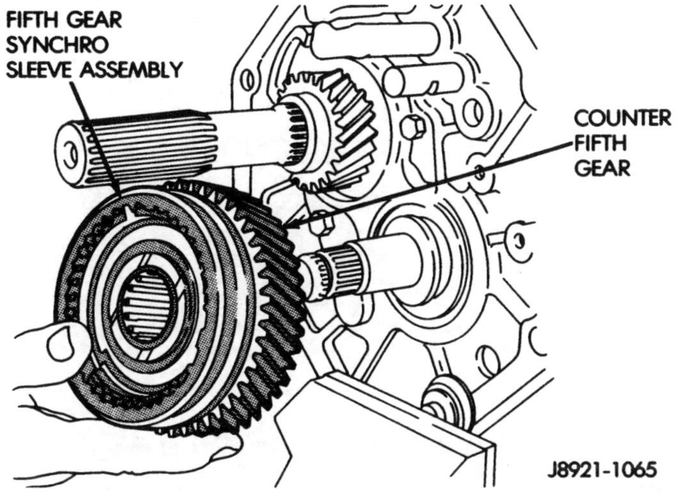

Fig. 58 Counter Fifth Gear And Synchro Assembly Removal

(17) Remove counter fifth gear thrust ring (Fig. 59).

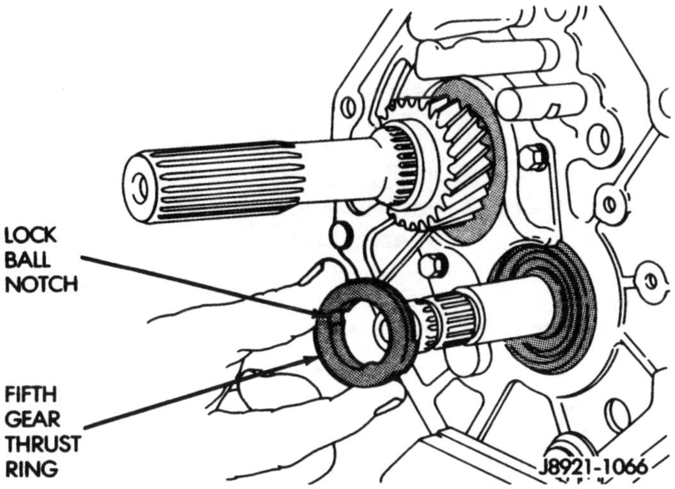

Fig. 59 Fifth Gear Thrust Ring Removal

(18) Remove thrust ring lock ball with pencil magnet (Fig. 60).

(19) Remove bolts attaching output shaft rear bearing retainer to intermediate plate (Fig. 61).

(20) Remove rear bearing retainer (Fig. 62).

(21) Remove reverse gear and shaft (Fig. 63).

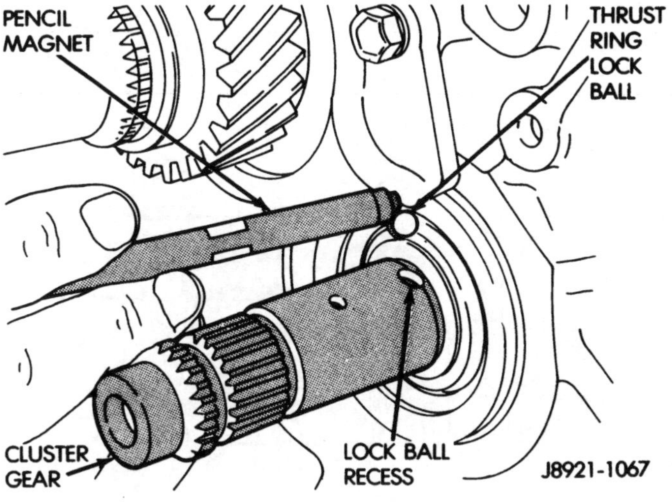

Fig. 60 Thrust Ring Lock Ball Removal

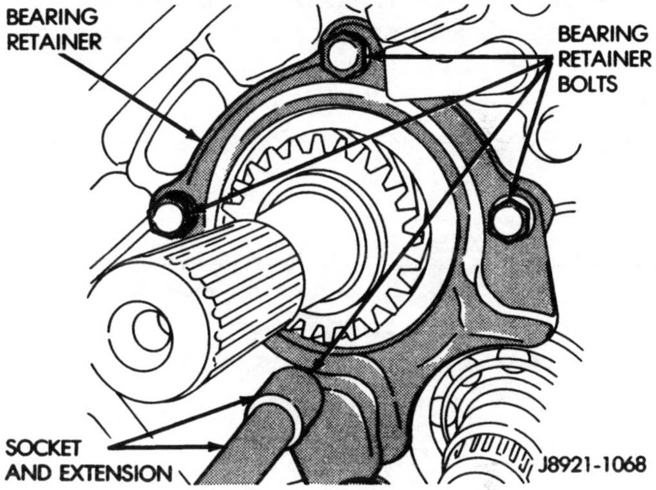

Fig. 61 Output Shaft Rear Bearing Retainer Bolt Removal

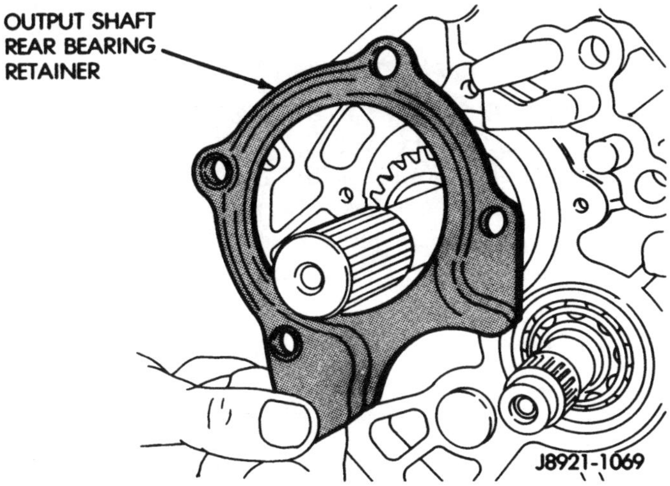

Fig. 62 Output Shaft Rear Bearing Retainer Removal

DISASSEMBLY AND ASSEMBLY (Continued)

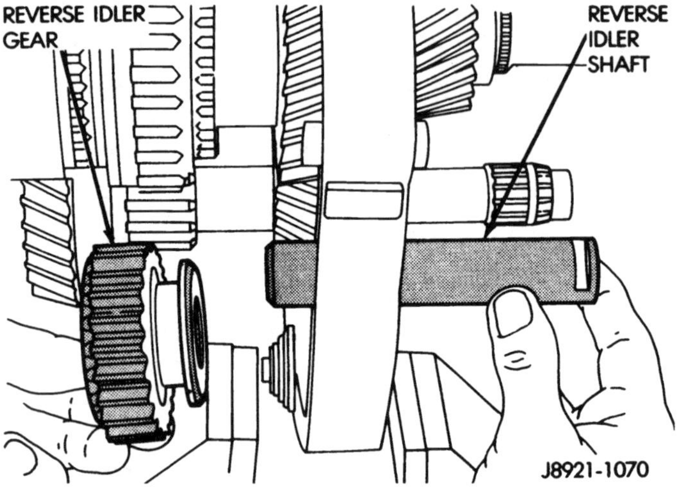

Fig. 63 Reverse Idler Gear And Shaft Removal

FIFTH GEAR AND SYNCHRO ASSEMBLE

(1) Install thrust ring lock ball in cluster gear journal (Fig. 64). Use petroleum jelly to hold ball in place.

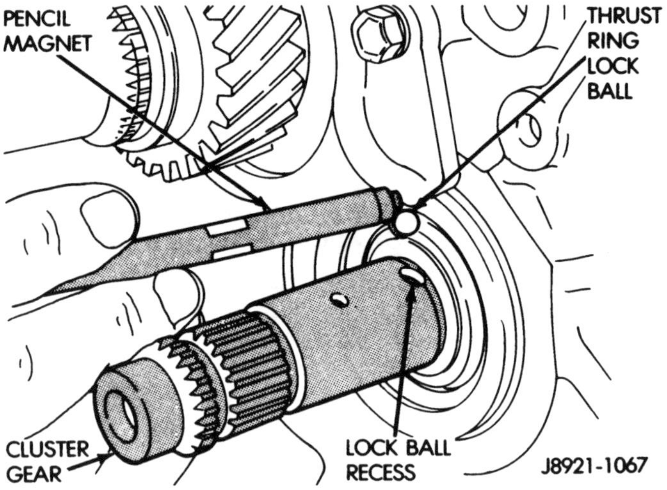

Fig. 64 Installing Thrust Ring Lock Ball

(2) Install fifth gear thrust ring (Fig. 65). Be sure thrust ring notch fits over lock ball.

(3) Assemble counter fifth gear, synchro sleeve, inserts and insert springs (Fig. 66).

(4) Lubricate two–piece bearing with petroleum jelly and install it in counter fifth gear (Fig. 67).

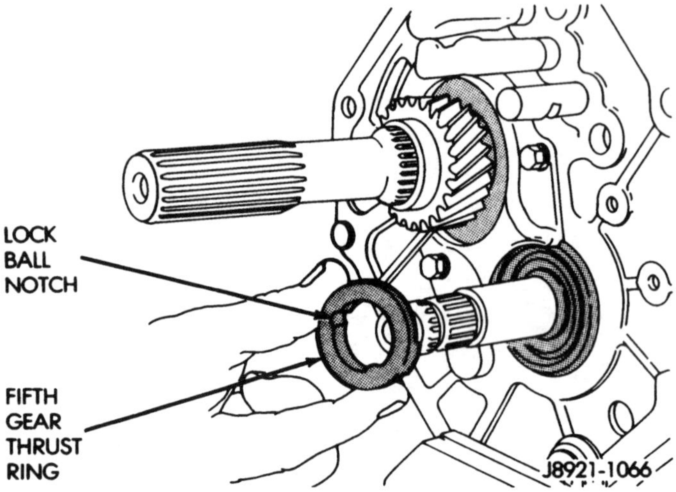

Fig. 65 Installing Fifth Gear Thrust Ring

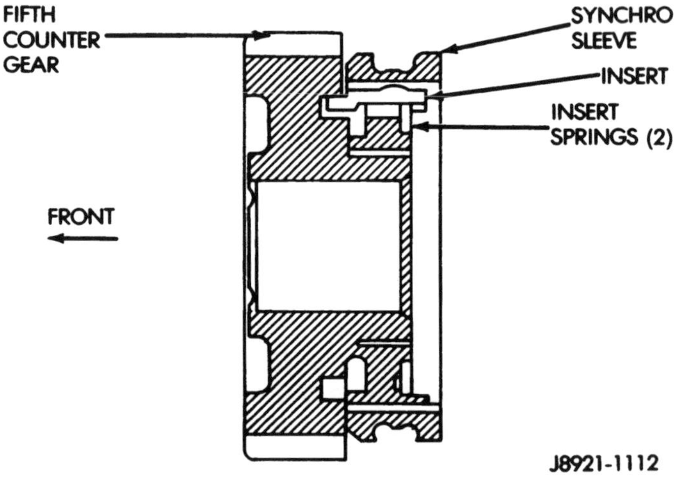

Fig. 66 Assembling Fifth Gear And Synchro Assembly

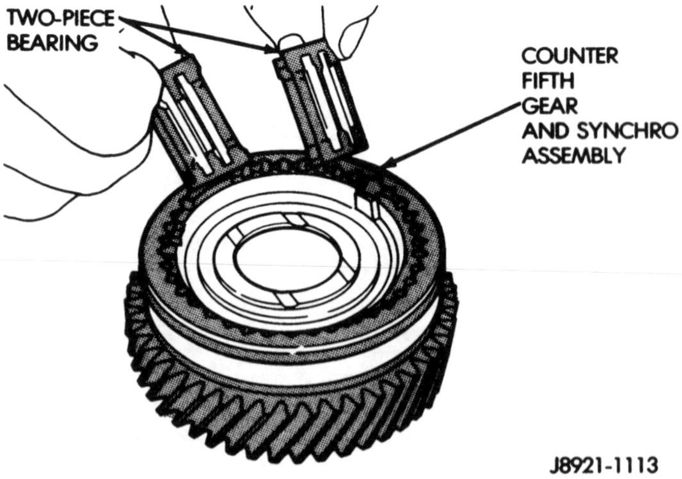

Fig. 67 Installing Counter Fifth Gear Bearing

DISASSEMBLY AND ASSEMBLY (Continued)

(5) Install counter fifth gear and synchro assembly on cluster gear journal (Fig. 68).

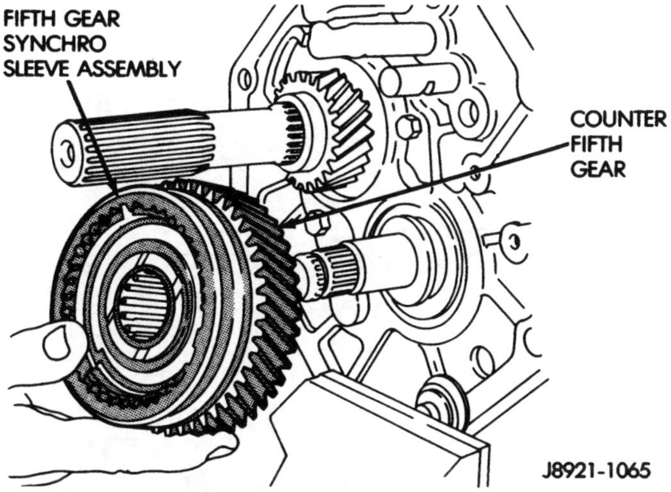

Fig. 68 Installing Counter Fifth Gear And Sleeve

(6) Install synchro ring in synchro sleeve (Fig. 69).

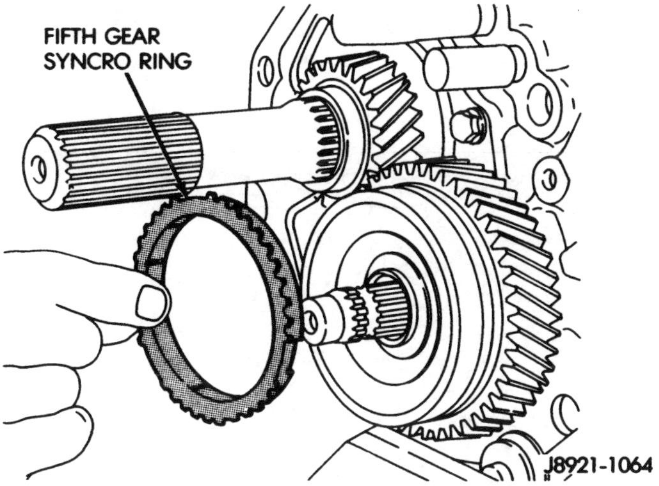

Fig. 69 Installing Fifth Gear Synchro Ring

(7) Install fifth spline gear on cluster journal (Fig. 70). Tap spline gear into place with plastic mallet if necessary.

(8) Install fifth gear selective snap ring (Fig. 71). Use thickest snap ring that will fit in shaft groove.

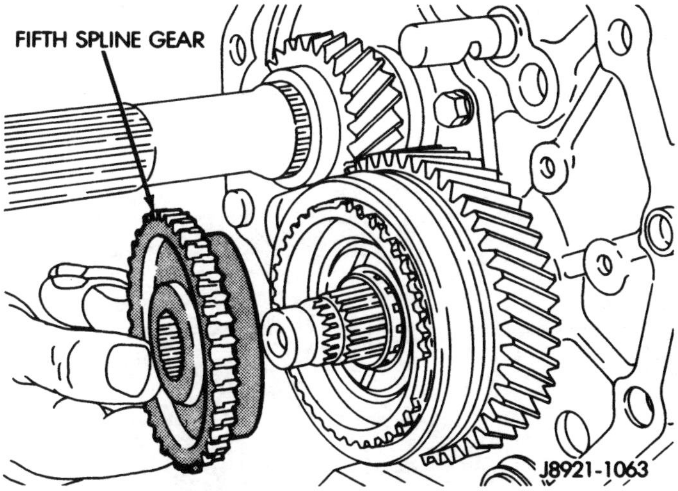

Fig. 70 Installing Fifth Spline Gear

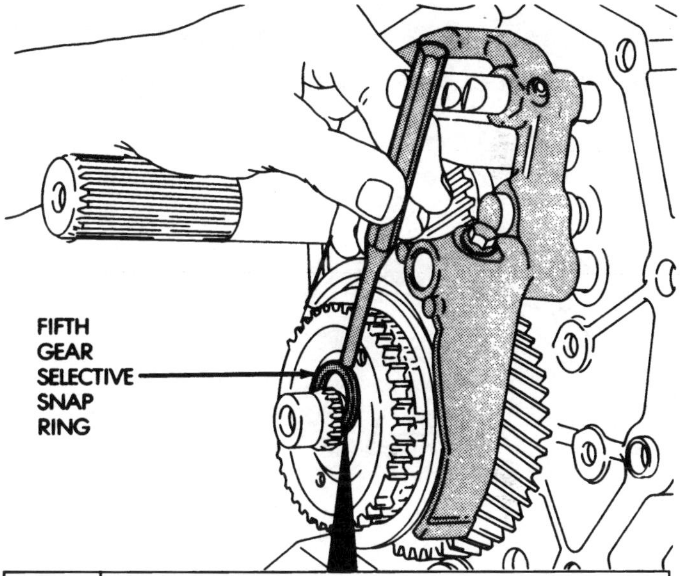

I.D. MARK	SNAP RING THICKNESS	MM (IN.)
A	2.85 - 2.90	(0.1122 - 0.1142)
B	2.90 - 2.95	(0.1142 - 0.1161)
C	2.95 - 3.00	(0.1161 - 0.1181)
D	3.00 - 3.05	(0.1181 - 0.1201)
E	3.05 - 3.10	(0.1201 - 0.1220)
F	3.10 - 3.15	(0.1220 - 0.1240)
G	3.15 - 3.20	(0.1240 - 0.1260)
H	3.20 - 3.25	(0.1260 - 0.1280)

J8921-1114

Fig. 71 Installing Fifth Gear Snap Ring

DISASSEMBLY AND ASSEMBLY (Continued)

(9) Install reverse shift head and rail (Fig. 72). Then install lock ball in shift head.

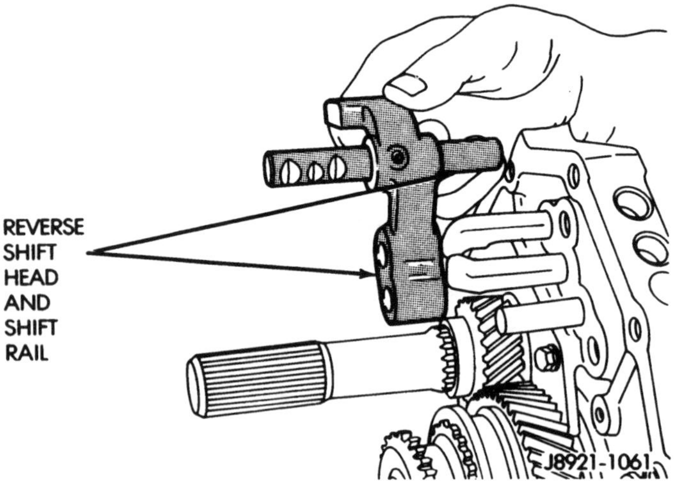

Fig. 72 Installing Reverse Shift Head And Rail

(10) Position fifth gear shift fork in synchro sleeve (Fig. 73).

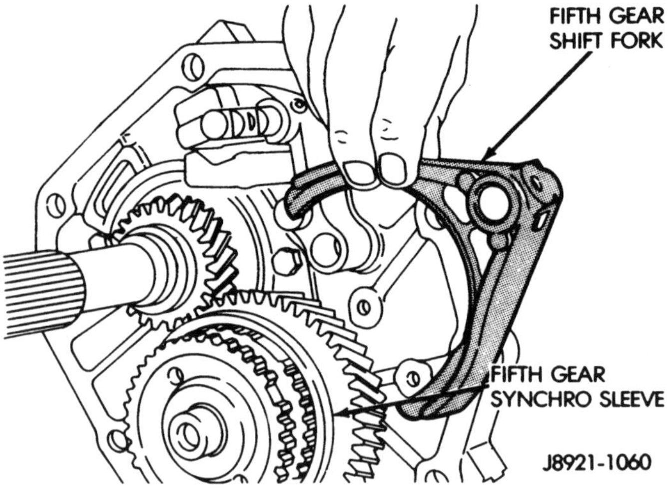

Fig. 73 Fifth Gear Shift Fork Installation

(11) Install fifth gear shift rail (Fig. 74). Slide rail through fork, shift head, intermediate plate and reverse shift fork. Be sure interlock ball is not displaced during installation.

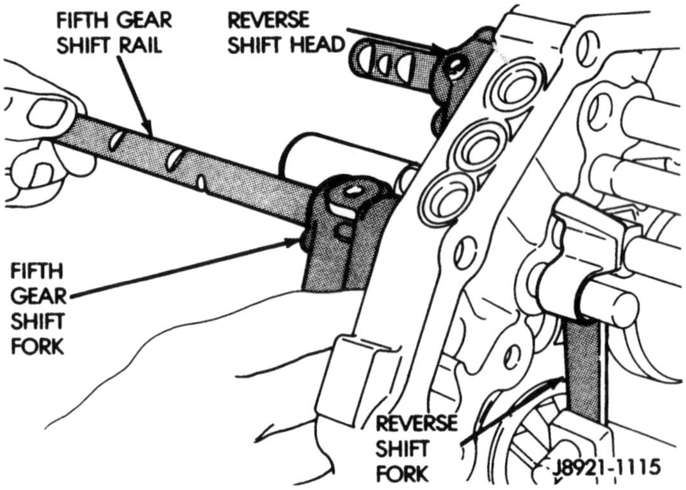

Fig. 74 Fifth Gear Shift Rail Installation

(12) Align screw holes in shift fork and rail and install set screw (Fig. 75). Tighten screw to 20 N·m (15 ft. lbs.) torque.

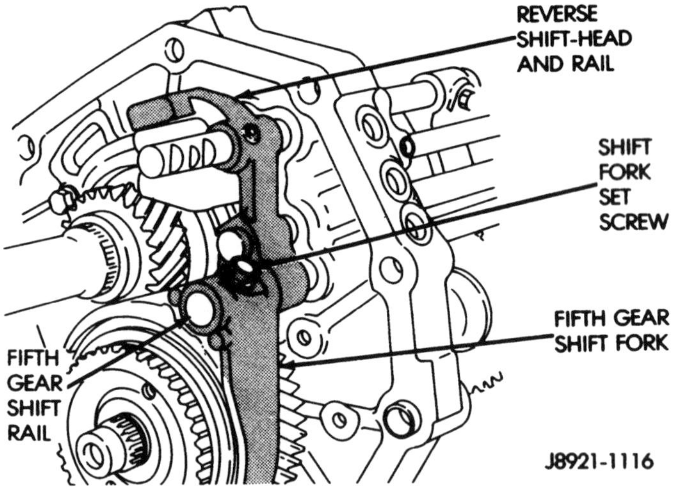

Fig. 75 Shift Fork Set Screw Installation

DISASSEMBLY AND ASSEMBLY (Continued)

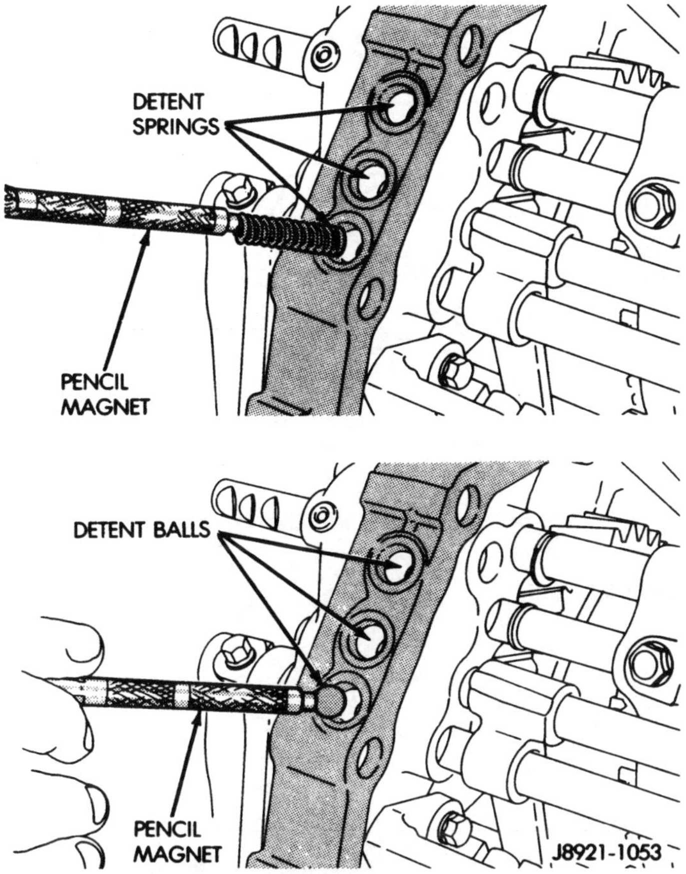

Fig. 76 Detent Ball And Spring Installation

(13) Install lock balls and springs in intermediate plate (Fig. 76). Then install and tighten lock ball plugs to 19 N·m (14 ft. lbs.) torque.

(14) Install reverse shift arm bracket (Fig. 77). Tighten bracket bolts to 18 N·m (13 ft. lbs.) torque.

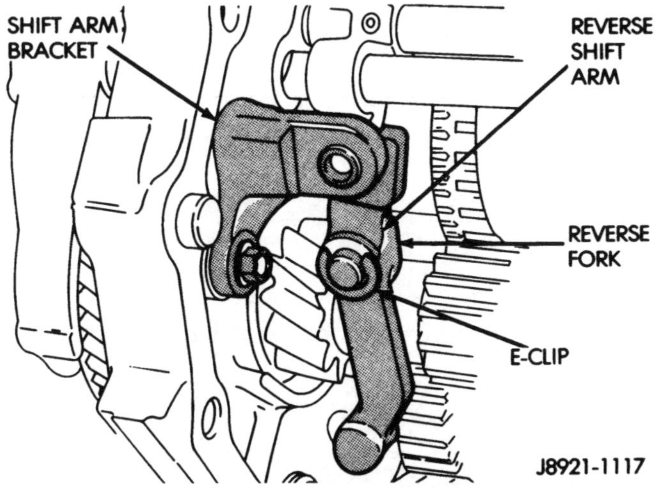

Fig. 77 Reverse Shift Arm And Bracket Installation

(15) Install reverse shift arm (Fig. 77). Position arm on reverse fork pin and engage it with pin on shift arm bracket.

(16) Verify that shift arm shoe is engaged in reverse idler gear. Then secure shift arm to pin on reverse fork with new E– clip.

SHIFT RAIL AND FORK

DISASSEMBLE

There are a total of five shift rails in the AX 15 transmission. The 1–2, 3–4, fifth gear and front reverse shift rails are shown in Figure 41.

Two shift rails are used for reverse gear range. The front reverse rail is at the forward side of the intermediate plate (Fig. 78). The short rear reverse rail

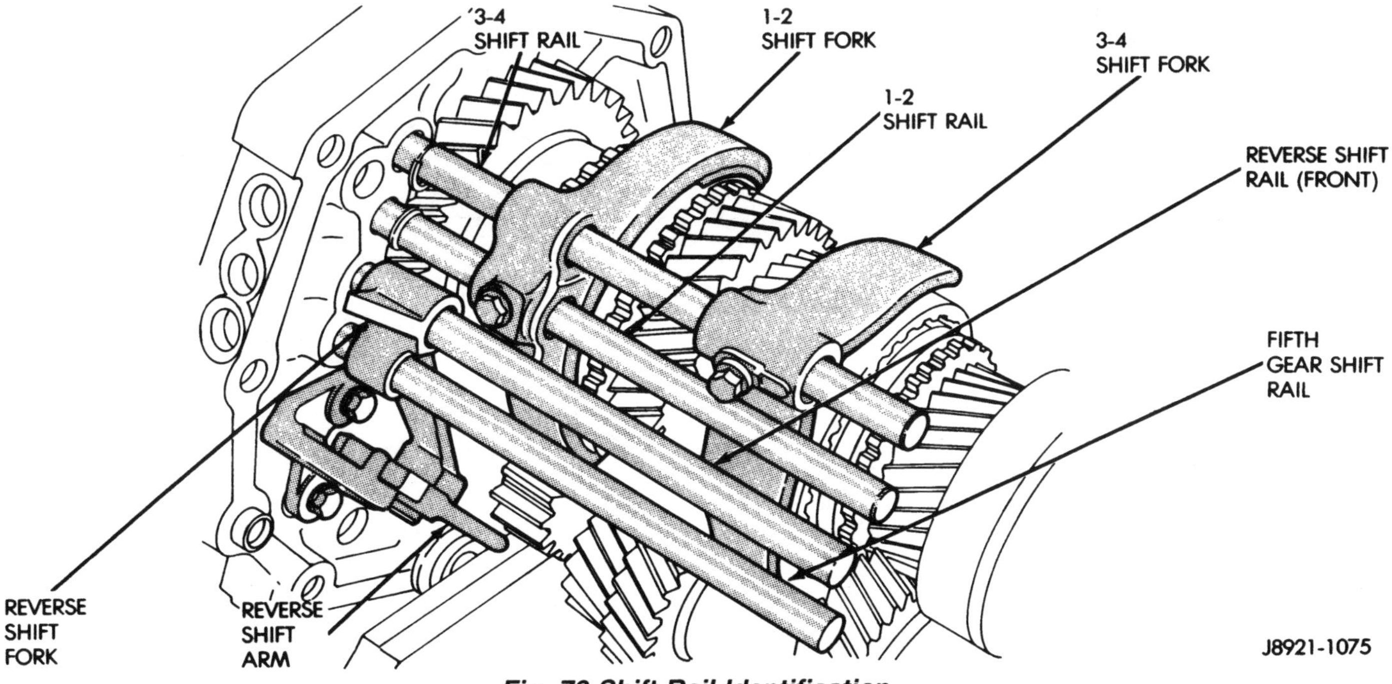

Fig. 78 Shift Rail Identification

DISASSEMBLY AND ASSEMBLY (Continued)

and reverse shift head are at the rear side of the intermediate plate.

It is not necessary to remove the shift rails if they are in good condition. Only the shift forks need be removed for access to the shafts and gears.

(1) Remove fifth gear shift rail (Fig. 78). Catch lock ball in your hand as rail comes out of intermediate plate.

(2) Remove 1–2 and 3–4 shift rail C–rings with two screwdrivers of equal size and length (Fig. 79).

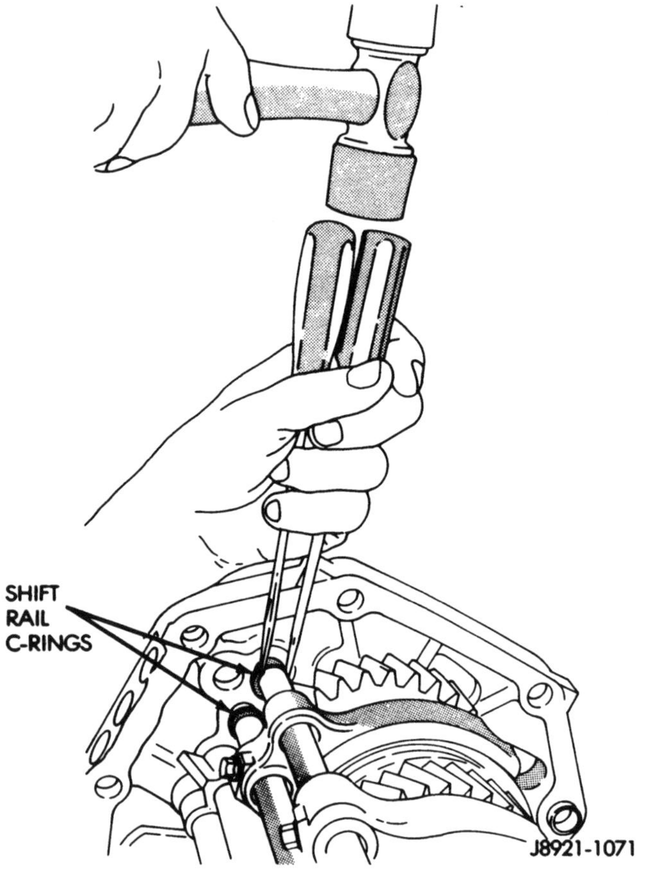

Fig. 79 Shift Rail C–Ring Removal

(3) Remove shift fork set screws (Fig. 80).

(4) Remove 3–4 shift rail from shift fork and intermediate plate (Fig. 81).

(5) Remove 3–4 shift rail interlock plug from intermediate plate with magnet (Fig. 82).

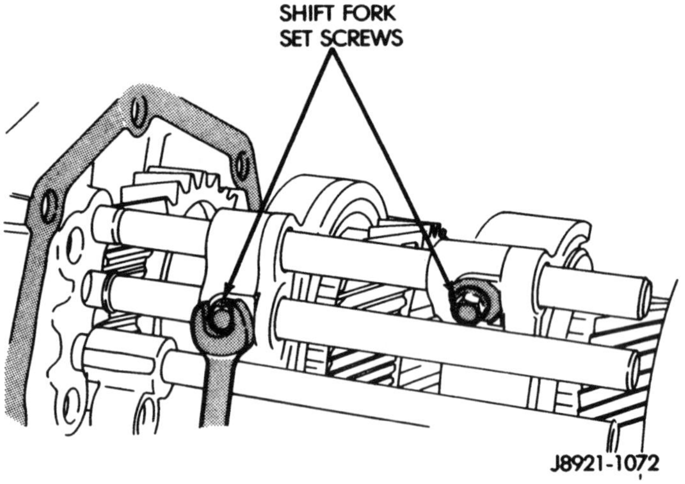

Fig. 80 Shift Fork Set Screw Removal

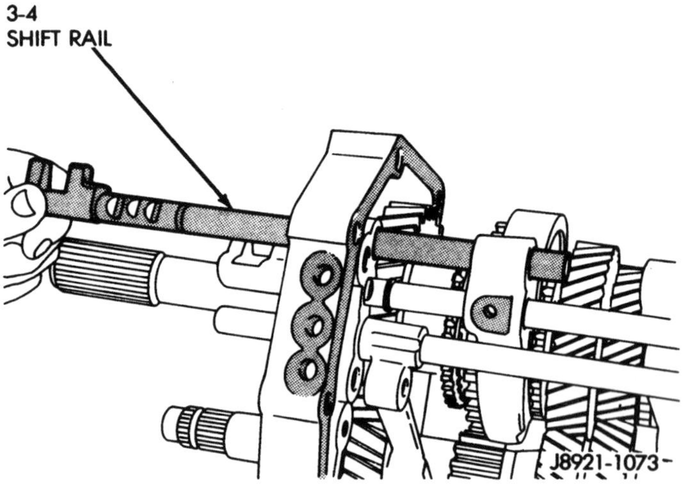

Fig. 81 Removing 3–4 Shift Rail

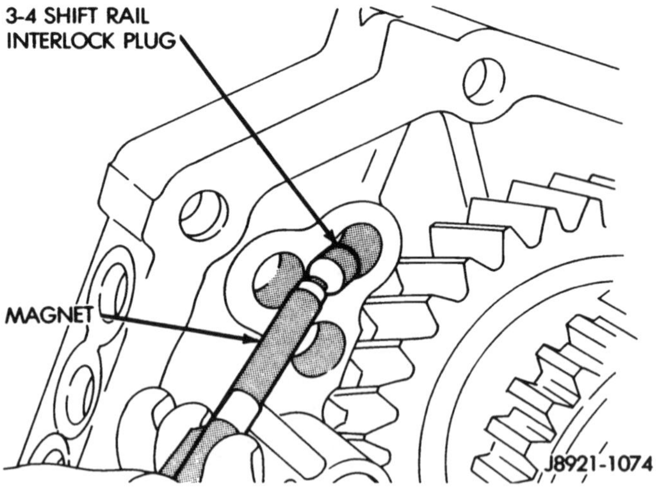

Fig. 82 Removing 3–4 Shift Rail Interlock Plug

DISASSEMBLY AND ASSEMBLY (Continued)

(6) Remove 1–2 shift rail from shift fork and intermediate plate (Fig. 83).

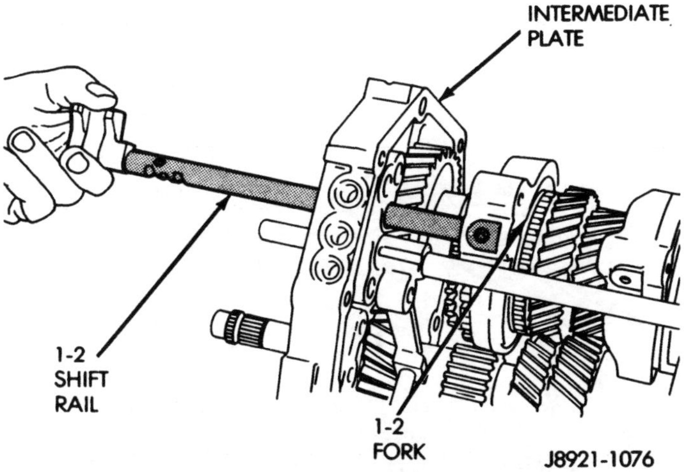

Fig. 83 Removing 1–2 Shift Rail

(7) Remove 1–2 shift rail interlock pin from shift rail (Fig. 84).

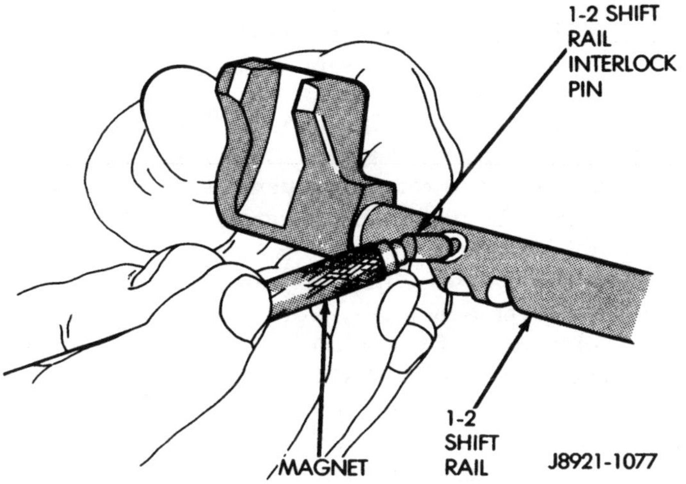

Fig. 84 Removing 1–2 Shift Rail Interlock Pin

(8) Remove 1–2 shift rail interlock plug from intermediate plate (Fig. 85).

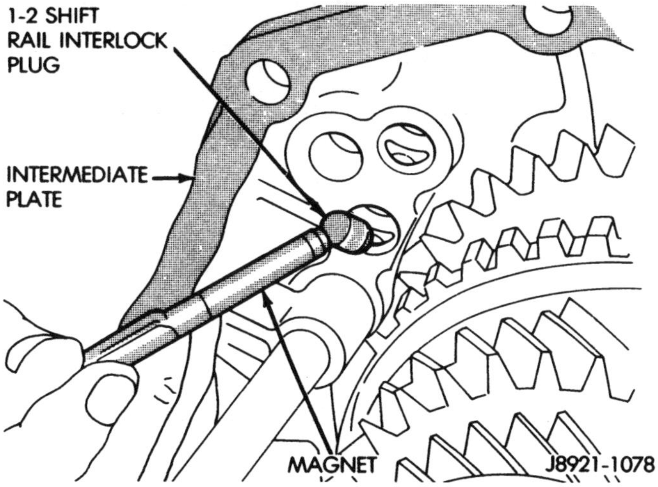

Fig. 85 Removing 1–2 Shift Rail Interlock Plug

(9) Lift reverse shift fork upward and remove fifth gear shift rail lock ball (Fig. 86).

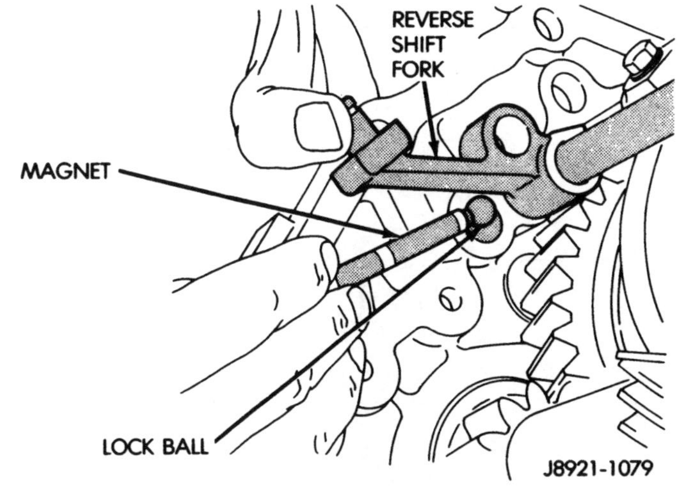

Fig. 86 Fifth Gear Shift Rail Lock Ball Removal

(10) Remove 3–4 shift fork (Fig. 87).

(11) Remove 1–2 shift fork (Fig. 87).

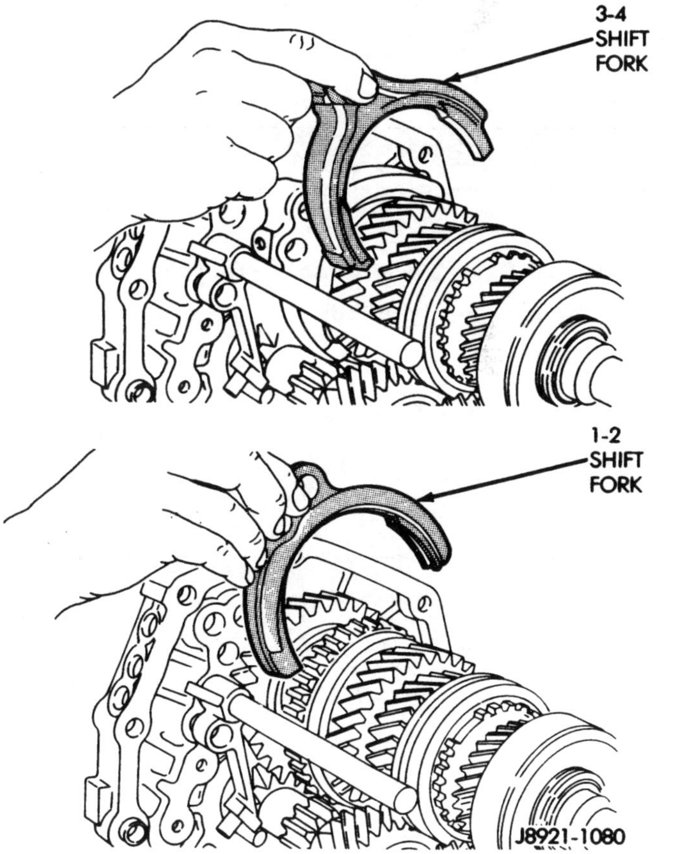

Fig. 87 Shift Fork Removal

DISASSEMBLY AND ASSEMBLY (Continued)

(12) Remove reverse shift rail C–ring with two equal length and size screwdrivers (Fig. 88).

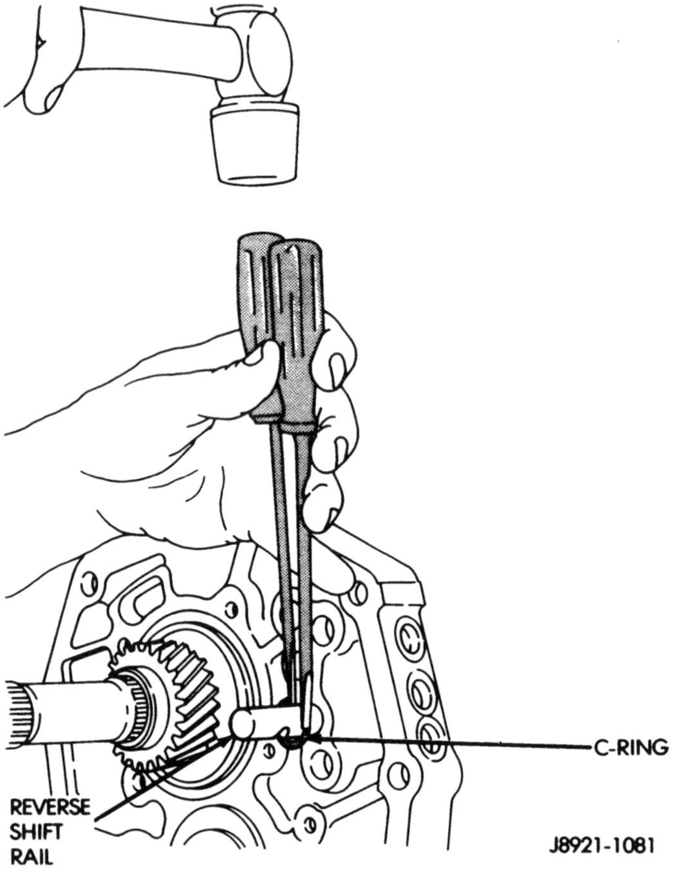

Fig. 88 Reverse Shift Rail C–Ring Removal

(13) Remove reverse shift rail and fork (Fig. 89).

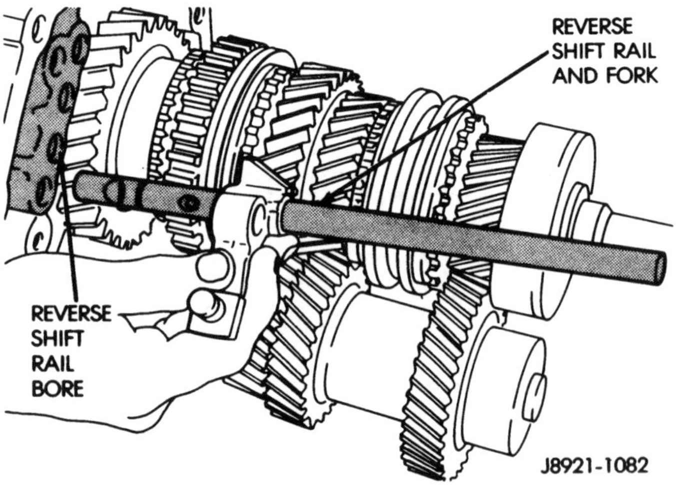

Fig. 89 Reverse Shift Rail And Fork Removal

(14) Remove interlock pin from reverse shift rail (Fig. 90).

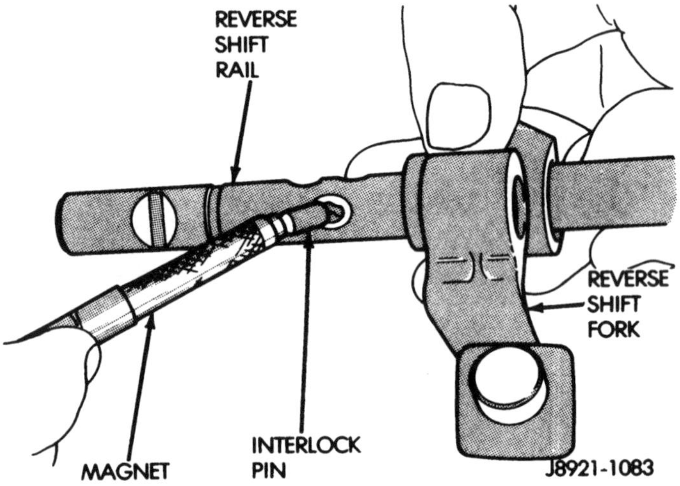

Fig. 90 Reverse Shift Rail Interlock Pin Removal

(15) Position shift rails, shift forks, lock balls, interlock plugs and interlock pins on the workbench in order of removal. This will help in identifying components during inspection and assembly.

SHIFT RAIL AND FORK ASSEMBLE

The shift rail interlock pins, balls and plugs must be installed in the correct sequence for proper shifting. Refer to the installation diagram (Fig. 91) during assembly.

Coat the intermediate plate shift rail bores and the interlock balls, pins and plugs with a thick covering of petroleum jelly before assembly. The jelly will hold the interlock components in place making installation easier. Use a pencil magnet to hold and insert the interlocks. Then use a small screwdriver to push the interlock components into place.

(1) Coat reverse rail interlock pin with petroleum jelly and install pin in rail (Fig. 92).

(2) Install reverse shift rail in intermediate plate (Fig. 93).

(3) Install reverse shift rail C–ring (Fig. 88).

DISASSEMBLY AND ASSEMBLY (Continued)

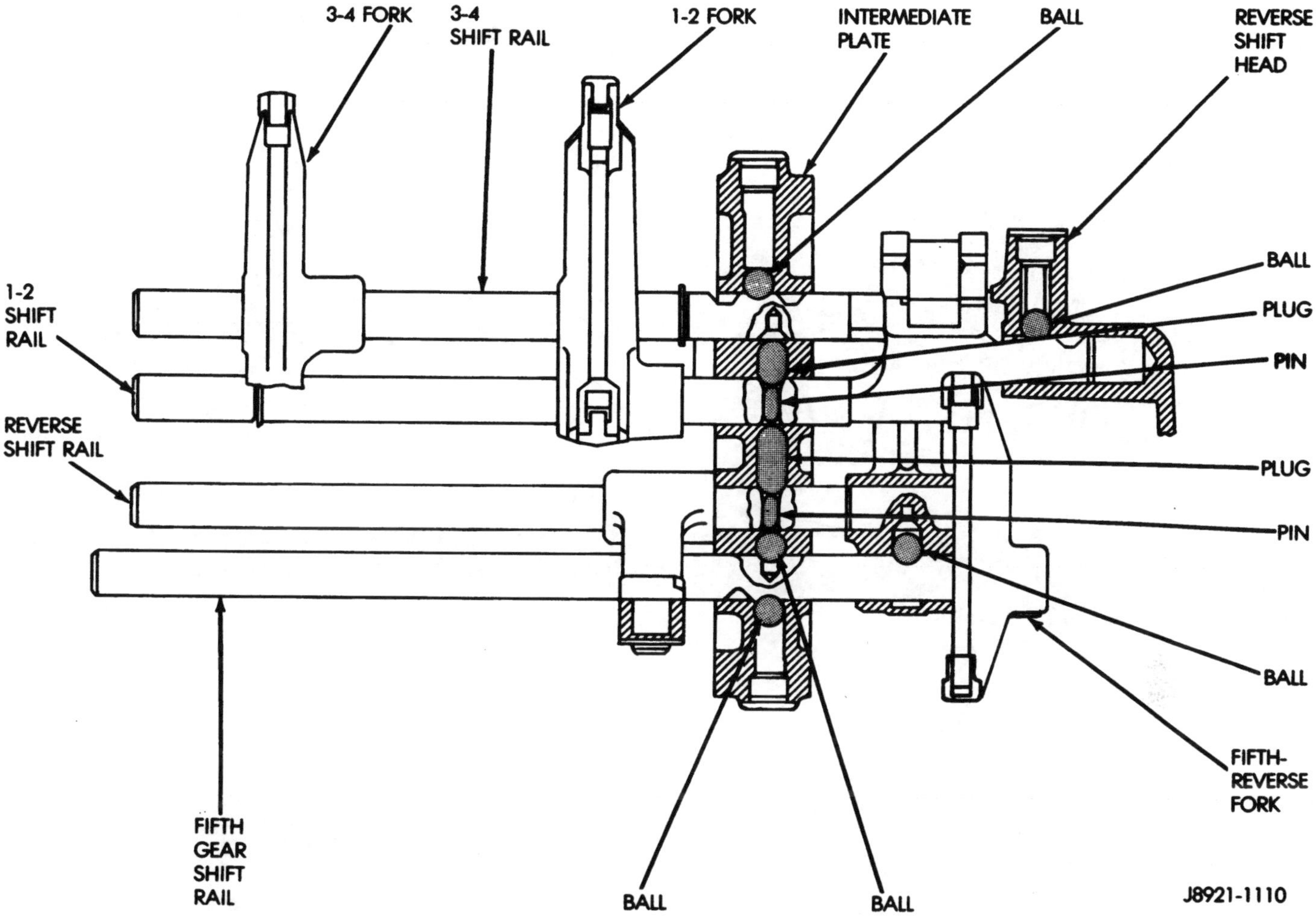

Fig. 91 Shift Rail Ball–Plug–Pin Position

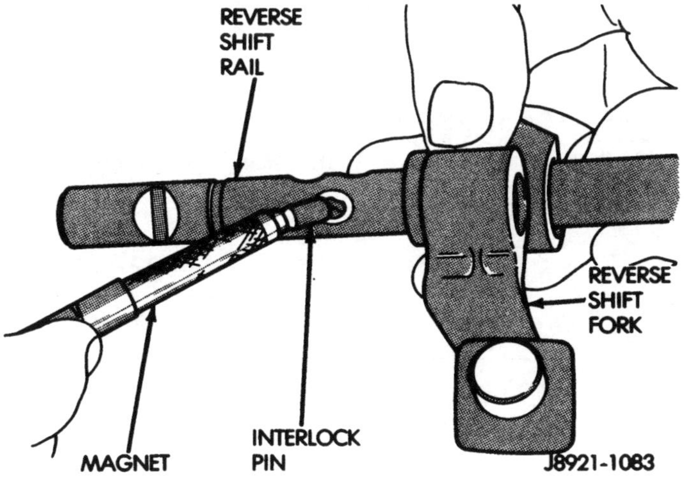

Fig. 92 Installing Reverse Shift Rail Interlock Pin

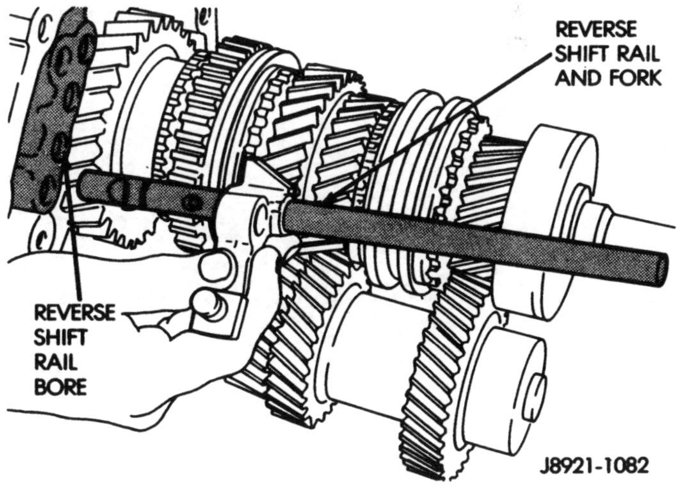

Fig. 93 Installing Reverse Shift Rail And Fork

DISASSEMBLY AND ASSEMBLY (Continued)

(4) Position 1–2 and 3–4 shift forks in synchro sleeves (Fig. 94).

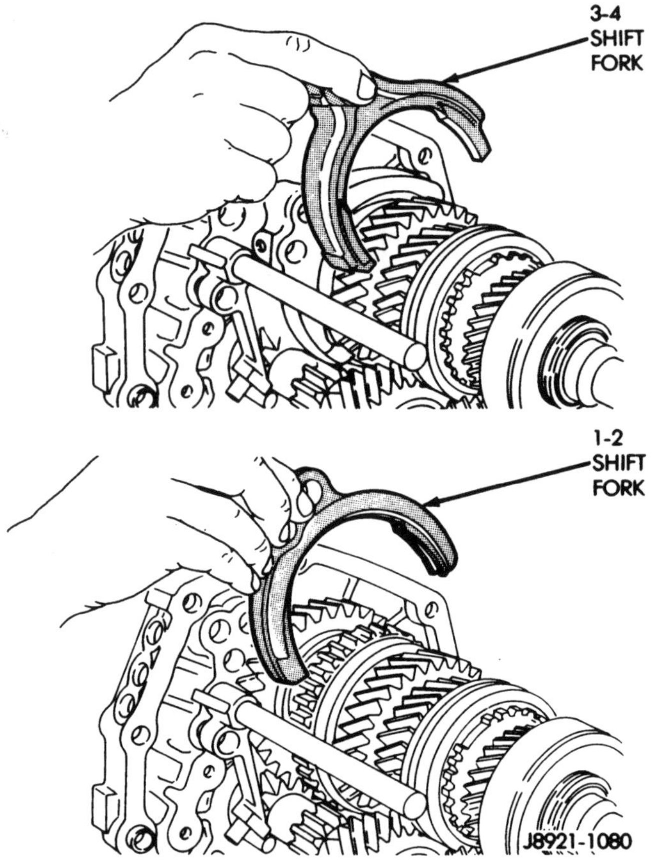

Fig. 94 Shift Fork Installation

(5) Coat reverse rail lock ball with petroleum jelly. Then tilt reverse shift fork upward and insert ball in intermediate plate (Fig. 95).

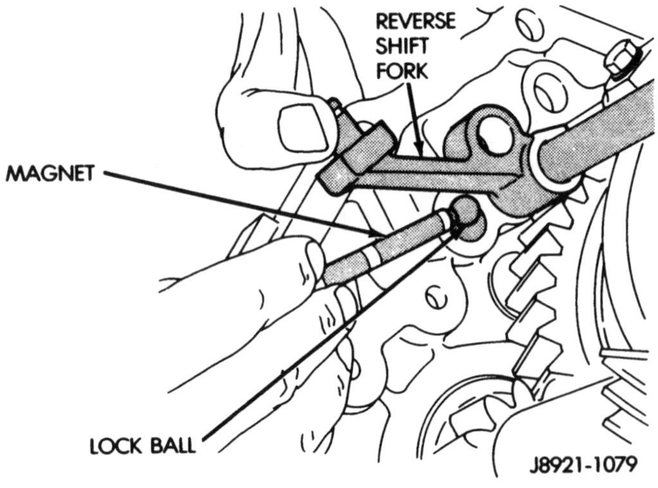

Fig. 95 Installing Reverse Shift Rail Lock Ball

(6) Coat 1–2 shift rail interlock plug with petroleum jelly and install it in intermediate plate bore (Fig. 96).

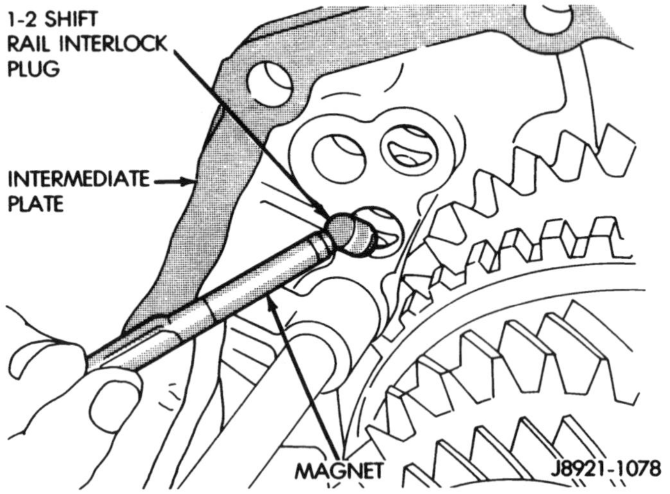

Fig. 96 Installing 1–2 Shift Rail Interlock Plug

(7) Coat 1–2 shift rail interlock pin with petroleum jelly and insert it in shift rail (Fig. 97).

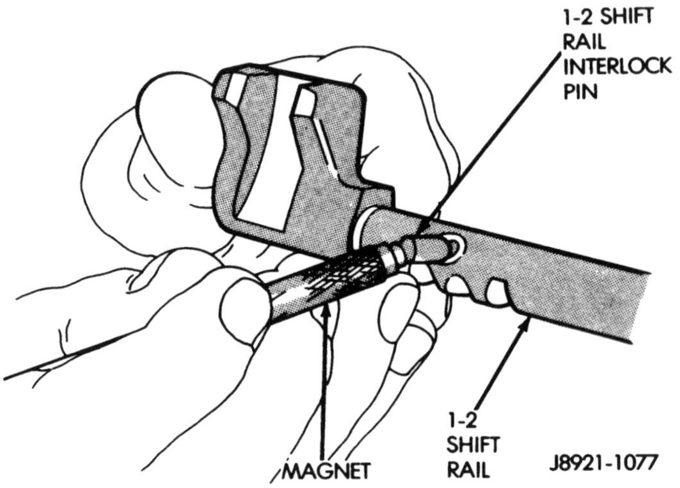

Fig. 97 Installing 1–2 Shift Rail Interlock Pin

(8) Install 1–2 shift rail in intermediate plate and 1–2 fork (Fig. 98).

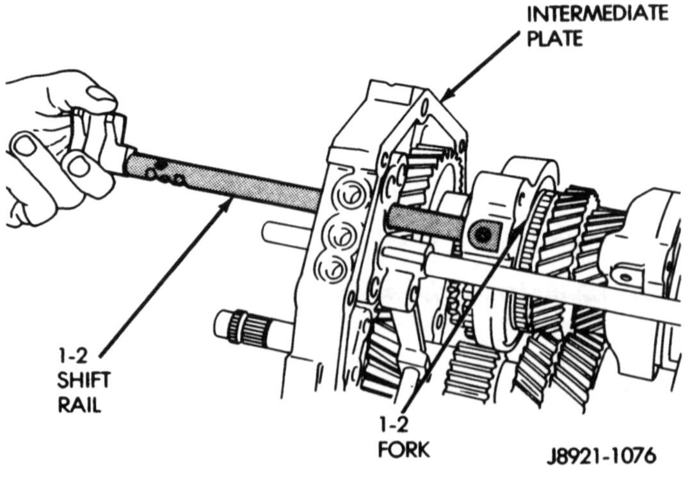

Fig. 98 Installing 1–2 Shift Rail

DISASSEMBLY AND ASSEMBLY (Continued)

(9) Coat 3–4 shift rail interlock plug with petroleum jelly and install plug in intermediate plate (Fig. 99).

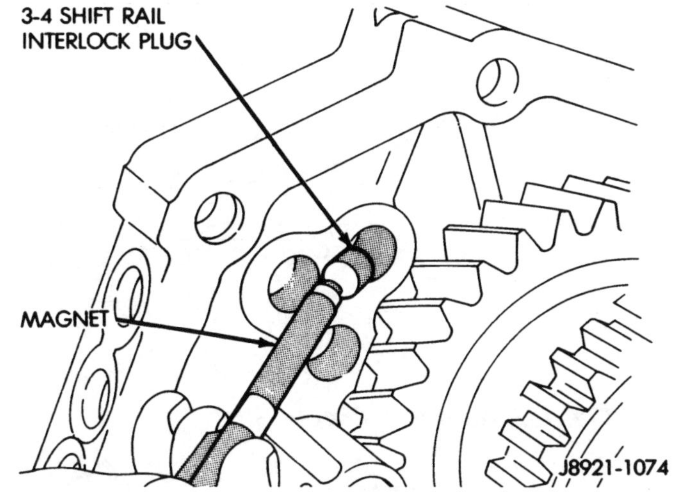

Fig. 99 Installing 3–4 Shift Rail Interlock Plug

(10) Install 3–4 shift rail in intermediate plate and in both shift forks (Fig. 100).

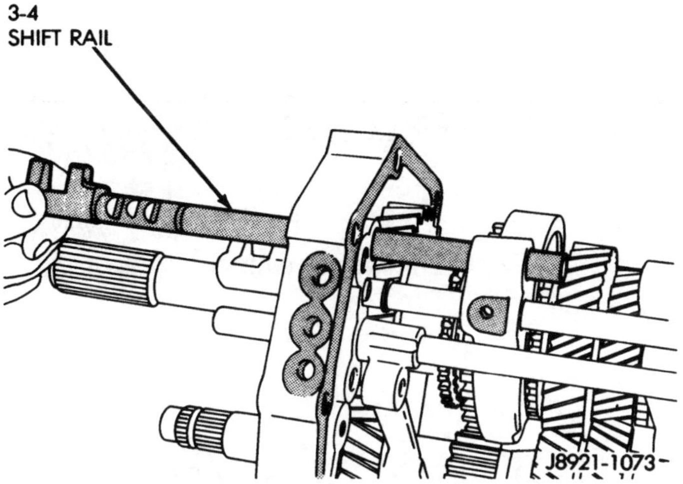

Fig. 100 Installing 3–4 Shift Rail

(11) Verify that none of the interlock balls, plugs, or pins were displaced during shift rail installation.

(12) Install and tighten shift fork setscrews to 20 N·m (14 ft. lbs.) torque (Fig. 101).

(13) Install 1–2 and 3–4 shift rail C–rings (Fig. 102).

(14) Insert fifth gear shift rail through reverse shift fork. **Then slide rail into intermediate plate just far enough to secure interlock ball. Do not fully install shift rail at this time.**

OUTPUT SHAFT AND CLUSTER GEAR

DISASSEMBLE

(1) Remove output shaft rear bearing snap ring (Fig. 103).

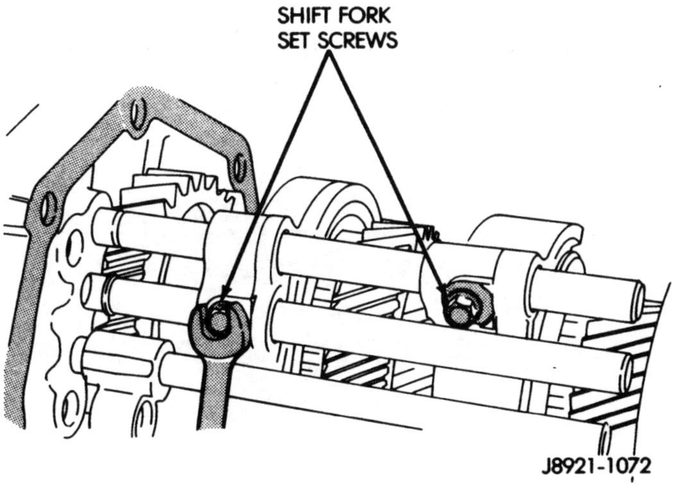

Fig. 101 Installing Shift Fork Set Screws

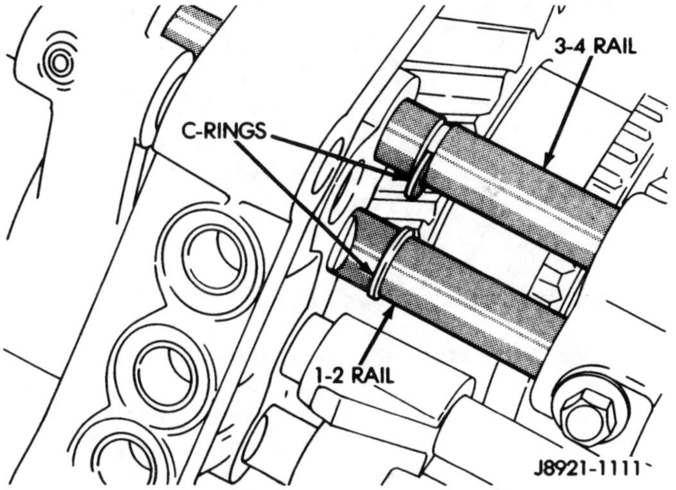

Fig. 102 Installing Shift Rail C–Rings

(2) Remove cluster gear rear bearing snap ring (Fig. 103).

(3) Tap end of output shaft with mallet to unseat and start rear bearing out of intermediate plate (Fig. 104).

(4) Remove output shaft by rocking it lightly until rear bearing comes out of intermediate plate (Fig. 105).

(5) Remove cluster gear by pulling it straight out of rear bearing (Fig. 106).

(6) Remove cluster gear rear bearing from intermediate plate (Fig. 107).

DISASSEMBLY AND ASSEMBLY (Continued)

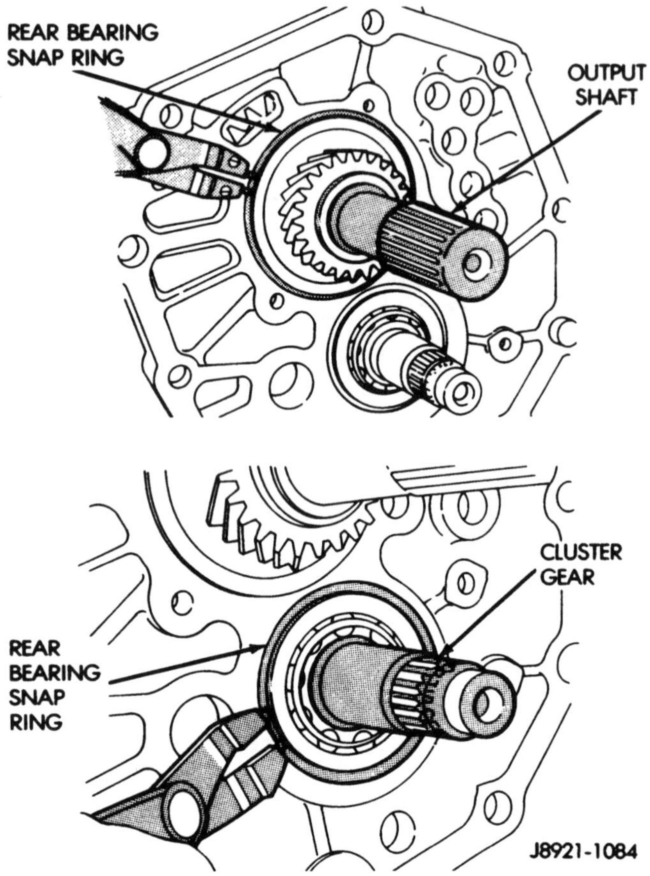

Fig. 103 Removing Bearing Snap Rings

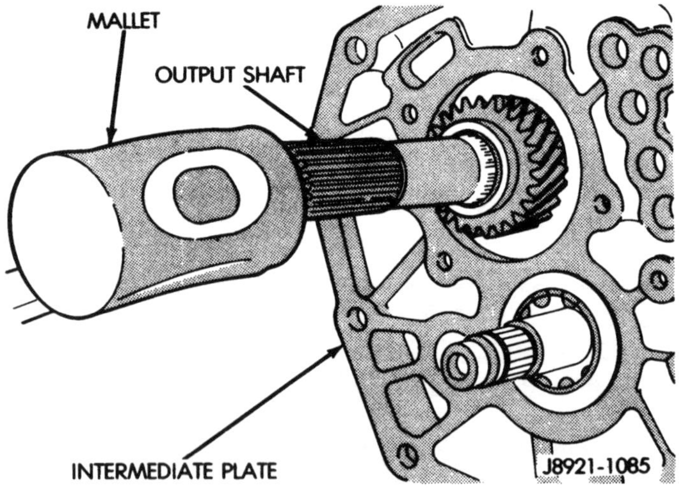

Fig. 104 Unseating Output Shaft Rear Bearing

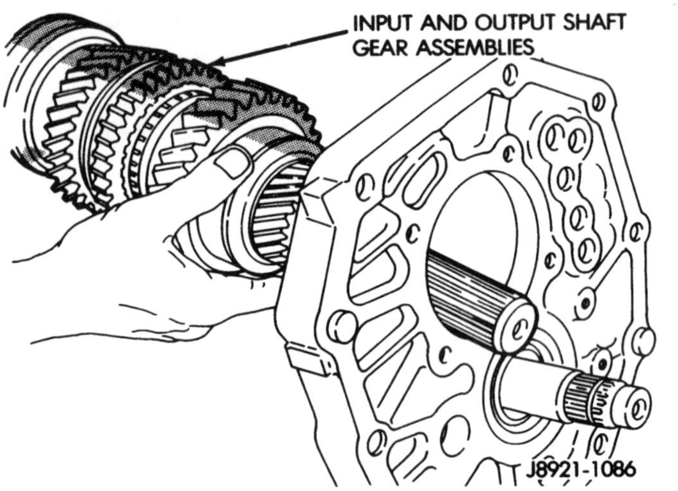

Fig. 105 Input And Output Shaft Removal

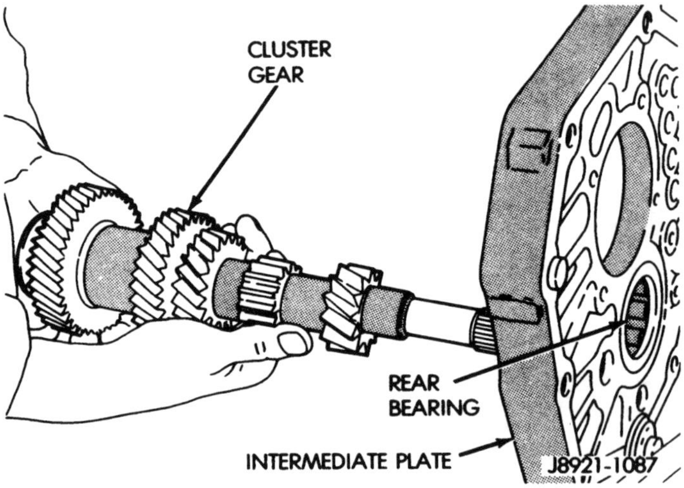

Fig. 106 Cluster Gear Removal

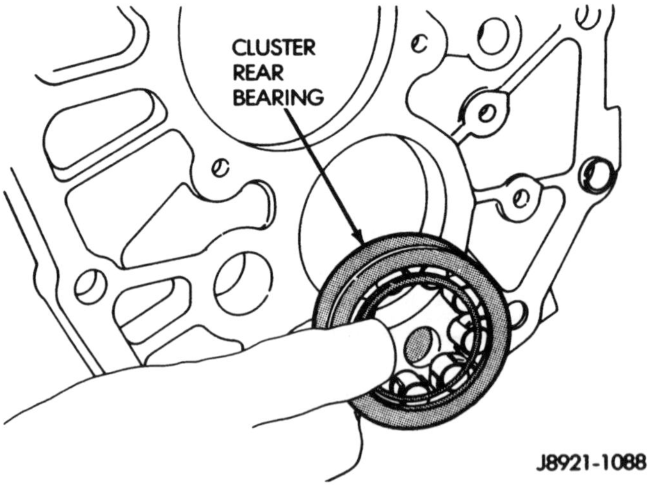

Fig. 107 Removing Cluster Gear Rear Bearing

DISASSEMBLY AND ASSEMBLY (Continued)

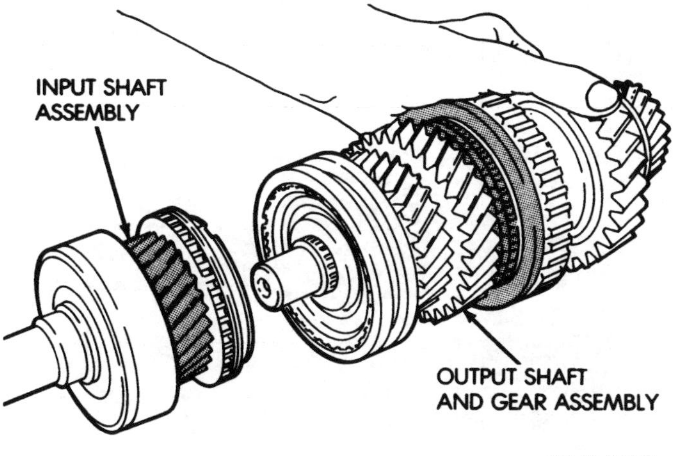

Fig. 108 Input Shaft Removal

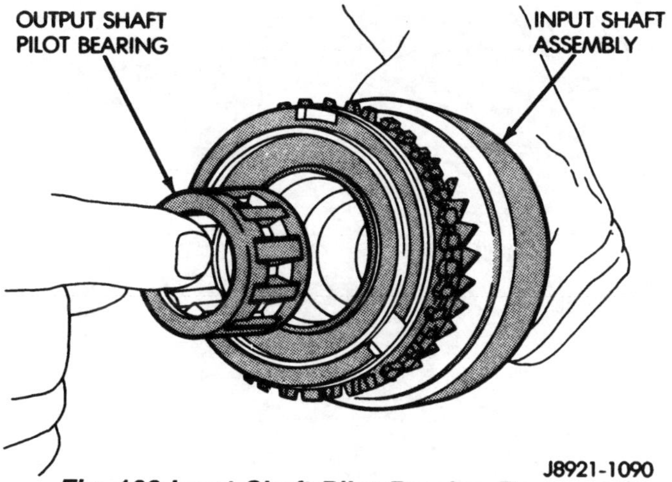

Fig. 109 Input Shaft Pilot Bearing Removal

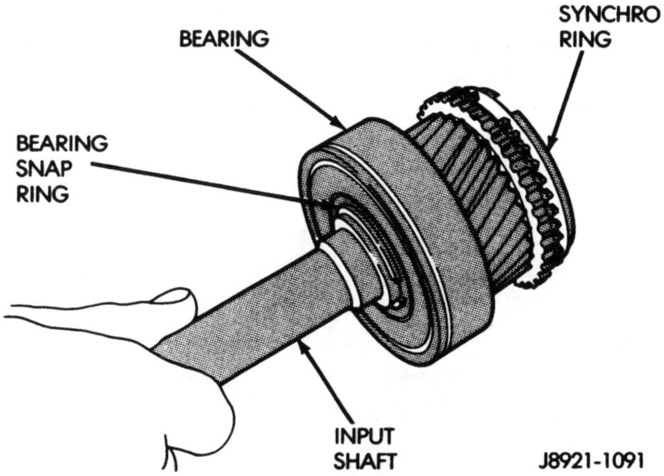

Fig. 110 Input Shaft Components

(7) Remove input shaft from output shaft (Fig. 108).

(8) Remove output shaft pilot bearing from input shaft (Fig. 109).

(9) Remove synchro ring from input shaft (Fig. 110).

(10) Remove bearing snap ring and press bearing off input shaft (Fig. 110).

OUTPUT SHAFT AND CLUSTER GEAR ASSEMBLE

(1) Mount intermediate plate in vise (Fig. 111).

(2) Lubricate cluster gear journal and rear bearing with petroleum jelly or gear lubricant.

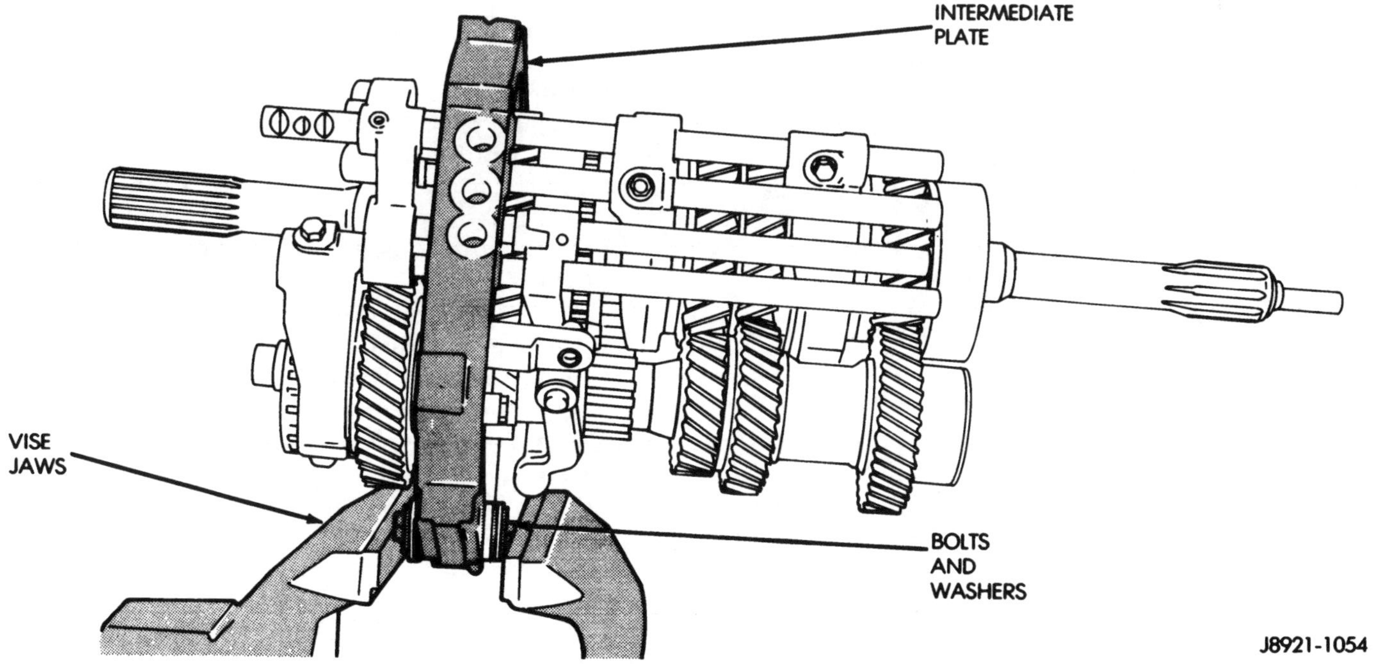

Fig. 111 Mounting Intermediate Plate And Geartrain In Vise

DISASSEMBLY AND ASSEMBLY (Continued)

(3) Install cluster gear rear bearing in intermediate plate (Fig. 112). Be sure snap ring groove in bearing is rearward as shown.

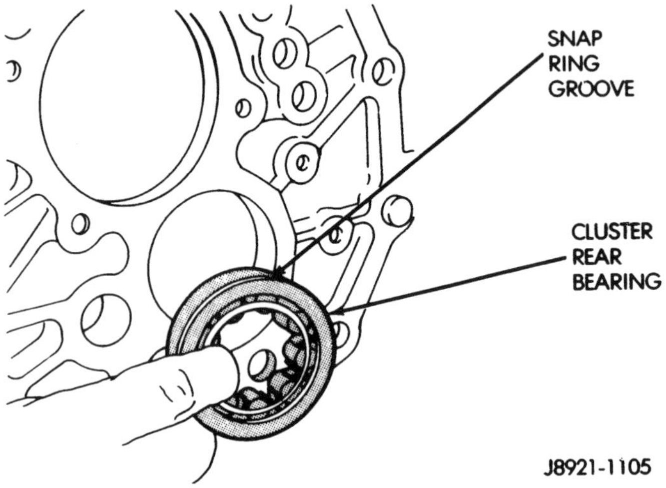

Fig. 112 Installing Cluster Gear Rear Bearing

(4) Start cluster gear into bearing (Fig. 106). Then hold bearing and push gear into place. Use plastic or rawhide mallet to seat bearing if necessary.

(5) Start output shaft rear bearing in intermediate plate. Push shaft rearward and tap intermediate plate with mallet to seat bearing.

(6) Install snap rings on cluster and output shaft **rear** bearings only (Fig. 113). Do not install front bearing snap rings at this time.

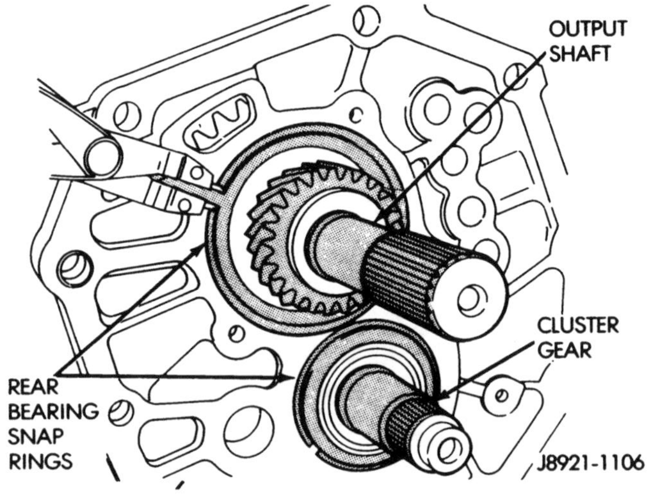

Fig. 113 Installing Rear Bearing Snap Rings

(7) Install reverse idler gear and shaft (Fig. 114).

(8) Position rear bearing retainer over output shaft and rear bearing. **Be sure bearing retainer tab is engaged in reverse idler shaft notch (Fig. 115).**

(9) Install and tighten rear bearing retainer bolts to 18 N·m (13 ft. lbs.).

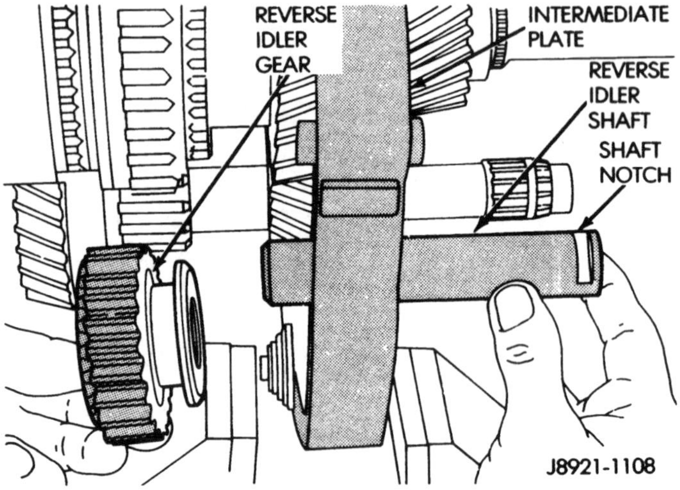

Fig. 114 Installing Reverse Idler Gear And Shaft

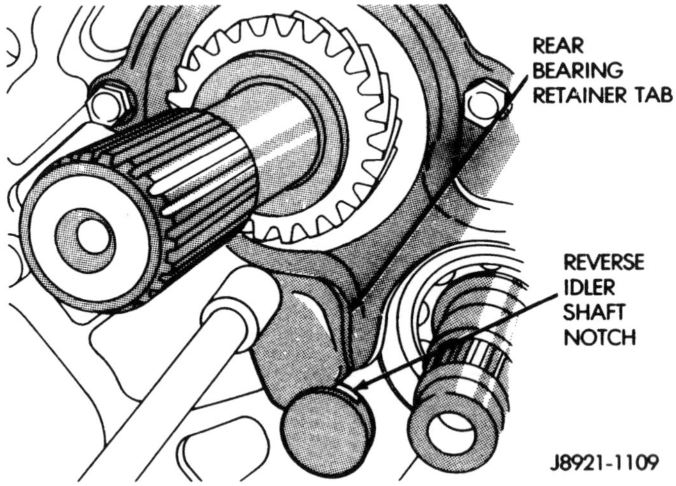

Fig. 115 Installing Rear Bearing Retainer

OUTPUT SHAFT

DISASSEMBLE

(1) Measure thrust clearance of output shaft first, second and third gears with feeler gauge (Fig. 116).

- First gear clearance should be 0.10—0.40 mm (0.003—0.0197 in).
- Second—third gear clearance should be 0.10—0.30 mm (0.003—0.0118 in.).

(2) If first gear thrust clearance is incorrect, replace gear and thrust washer. **If second or third gear clearance is incorrect, either gear and bearing, or output shaft flange is worn. Refer to output shaft inspection in Cleaning and Inspection section.**

(3) Press fifth gear and rear bearing off rear of output shaft.

(4) Remove thrust washer, pin, and first gear and bearing (Fig. 117).

(5) Remove first/reverse hub snap ring (Fig. 117).

(6) Remove synchro ring.

DISASSEMBLY AND ASSEMBLY (Continued)

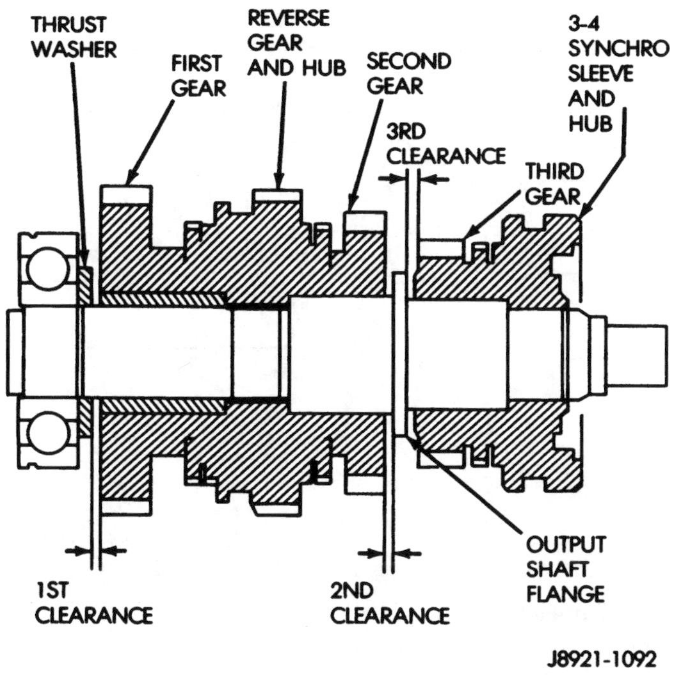

Fig. 116 Checking Output Shaft Gear Thrust Clearance

(7) Press reverse gear and first/reverse hub off shaft as assembly.

(8) Remove remaining synchro ring and second gear and bearing (Fig. 117).

(9) Remove snap ring at front of output shaft (Fig. 117).

(10) Press 3–4 hub and sleeve off output shaft as assembly (Fig. 117).

(11) Remove synchro ring.

(12) Remove third gear and needle bearing (Fig. 117).

OUTPUT SHAFT ASSEMBLY

(1) Lubricate output shaft journals, gears and needle bearings with recommended gear lubricant.

(2) Install third gear and needle bearing on shaft (Fig. 117)

(3) Install synchro ring on third gear (Fig. 117).

(4) Assemble 1–2 and 3–4 synchro hubs and sleeves (Fig. 118).

(5) Install inserts and springs in synchro sleeves. Position open ends of springs 180° apart as shown (Fig. 119).

(6) Install 3–4 synchro hub and sleeve on output shaft. Press hub onto shaft if necessary.

(7) Install 3–4 synchro hub snap ring (Fig. 120). Use thickest snap ring that will fit in shaft groove.

(8) Verify third gear thrust clearance with feeler gauge (Fig. 121). Clearance should be 0.10 to 0.25 mm (0.004 to 0.010 in.).

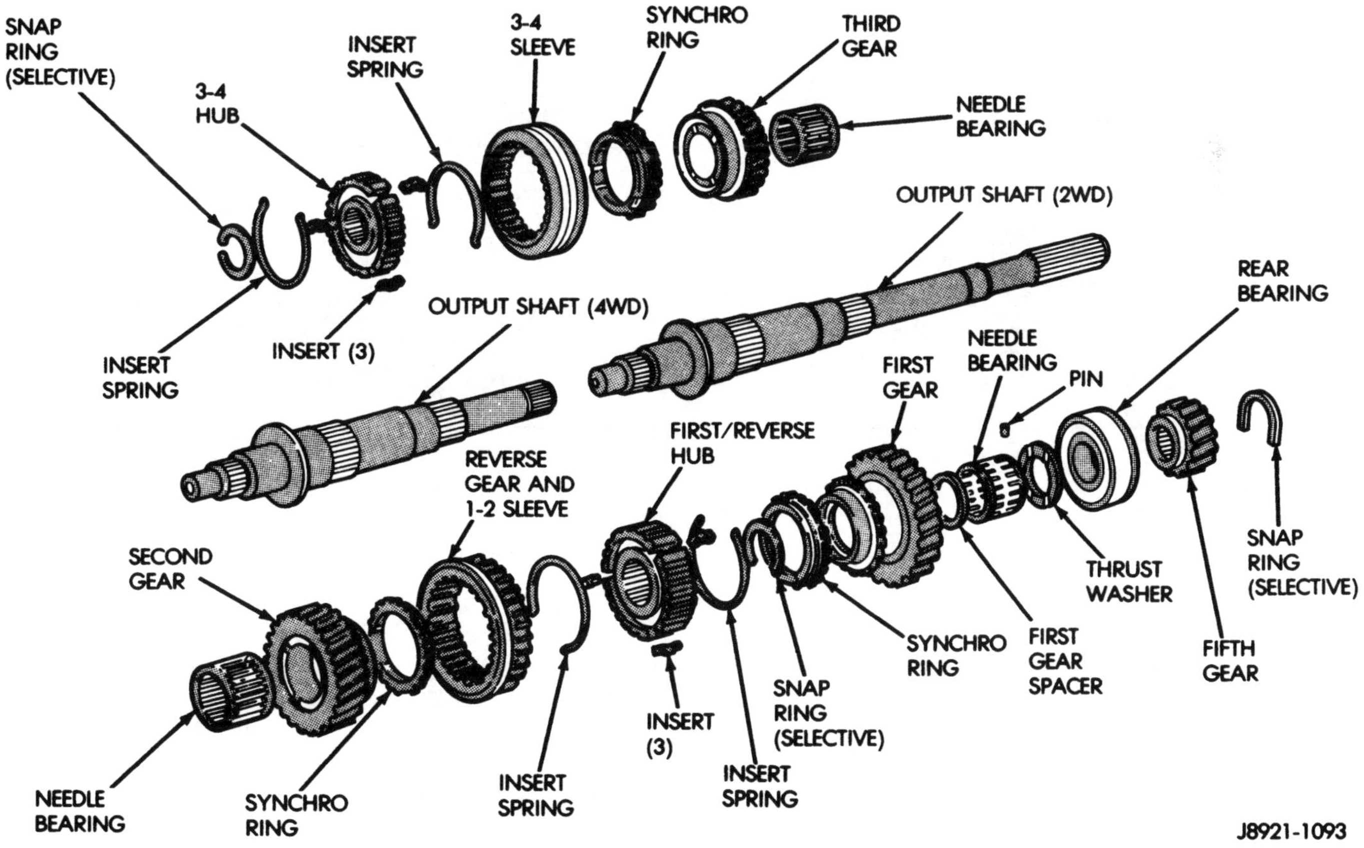

Fig. 117 Output Shaft And Gears

DISASSEMBLY AND ASSEMBLY (Continued)

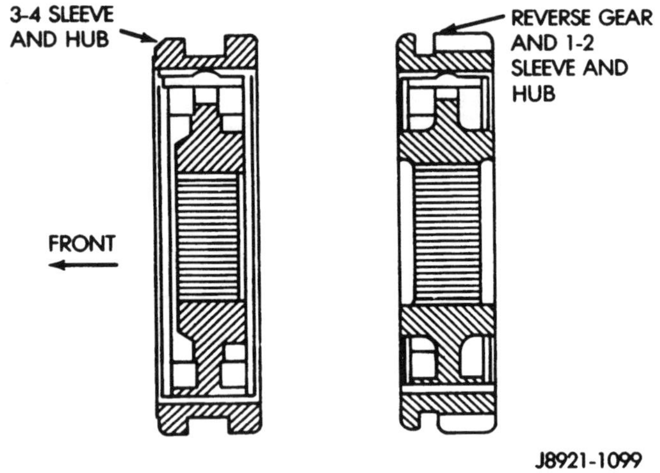

Fig. 118 Synchro Sleeve And Hub Identification

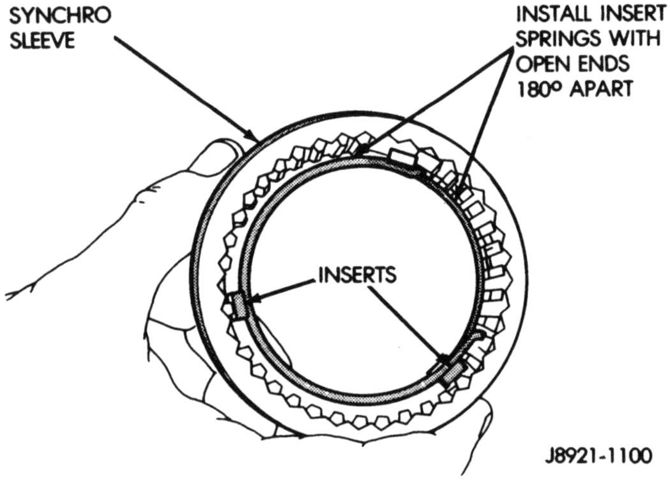

Fig. 119 Insert Spring Position

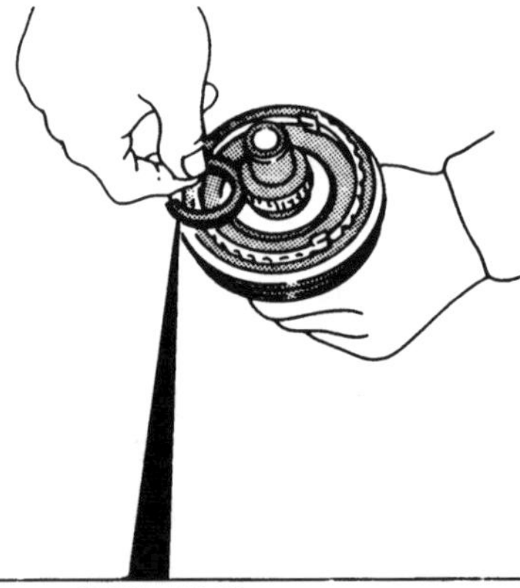

I.D. MARK	SNAP RING THICKNESS	MM (IN.)
A	1.80 - 1.85	(0.0709 - 0.0728)
B	1.85 - 1.90	(0.0728 - 0.0748)
C	1.90 - 1.95	(0.0748 - 0.0768)
D	1.95 - 2.00	(0.0768 - 0.0787)
E	2.00 - 2.05	(0.0787 - 0.0807)
F	2.05 - 2.10	(0.0807 - 0.0827)
G	2.10 - 2.15	(0.0827 - 0.0846)

J8921-1101

Fig. 120 Installing 3–4 Synchro Hub Snap Ring

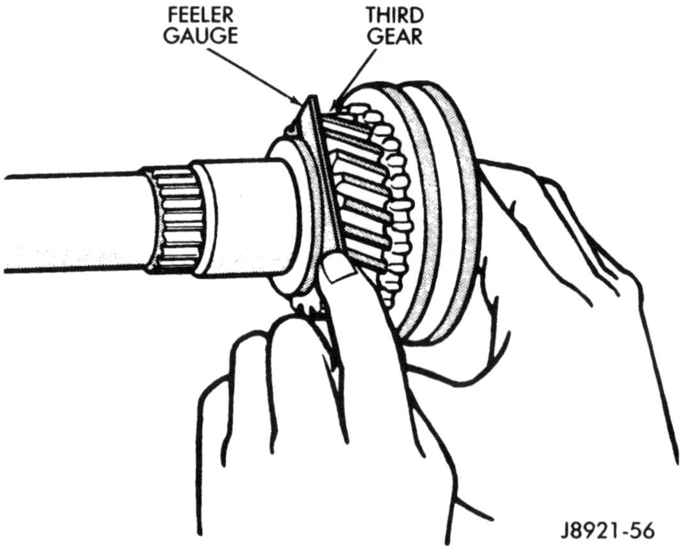

Fig. 121 Checking Third Gear Clearance

(9) Lubricate remaining output shaft gears and bearings with gear lubricant.

(10) Install second gear and needle bearing on shaft (Fig. 122).

(11) Install synchro ring on second gear (Fig. 122).

(12) Assemble first/reverse hub, insert springs, inserts, reverse gear and 1–2 sleeve (Fig. 122). **Be sure spring ends are 180° apart. Note that splines in hub bore are chamfered on one side. Install hub so chamfered side faces front of output shaft.**

(13) Press assembled hub and sleeve on output shaft.

(14) Install selective snap ring (Fig. 122). Use thickest snap ring that will fit in output shaft groove.

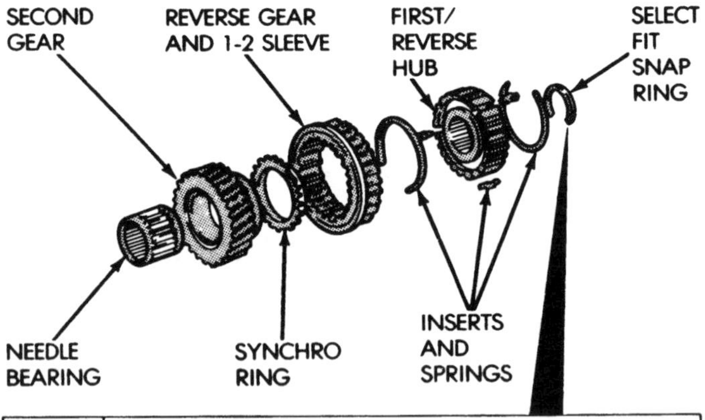

I.D. MARK	SNAP RING THICKNESS	MM (IN.)
B	2.35 - 2.40	(0.0925 - 0.0945)
C	2.40 - 2.45	(0.0945 - 0.0965)
D	2.45 - 2.50	(0.0965 - 0.0984)
E	2.50 - 2.55	(0.0984 - 0.1004)
F	2.55 - 2.60	(0.1004 - 0.1024)
G	2.60 - 2.65	(0.1024 - 0.1043)

J8921-1102

Fig. 122 Second Gear And Synchro Assembly

DISASSEMBLY AND ASSEMBLY (Continued)

(15) Install synchro ring on first gear (Fig. 123).

(16) Install first gear spacer on shaft and against selective fit snap ring (Fig. 123).

(17) Install first gear and needle bearing (Fig. 123) on output shaft.

(18) Install locating pin and thrust washer on shaft (Fig. 123).

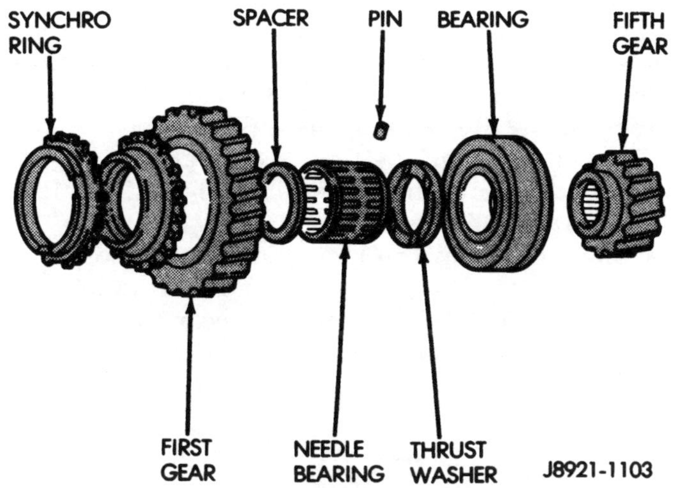

Fig. 123 First And Fifth Gear Components

(19) Press rear bearing on shaft. Position bearing snap ring groove so it is closest to end of output shaft.

(20) Check first and second gear thrust clearance with feeler gauge (Fig. 124).

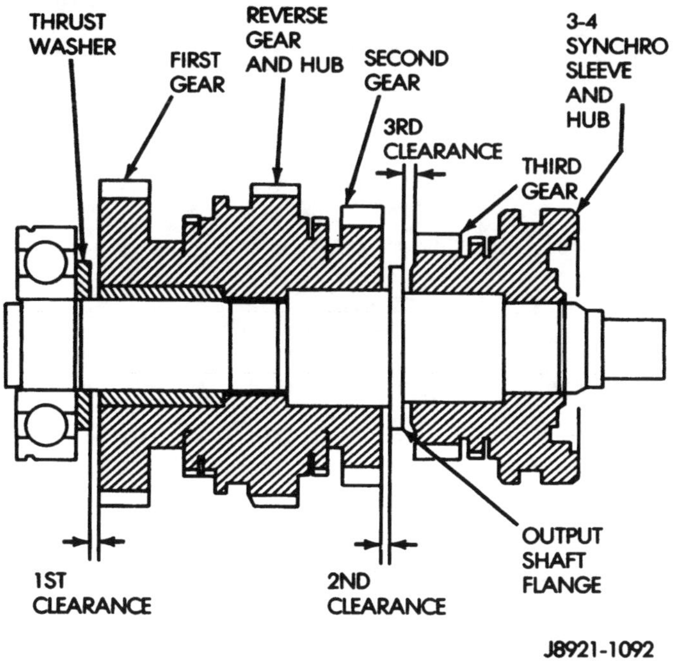

Fig. 124 Checking Output Shaft Gear Thrust Clearance

- First gear clearance should be 0.10 to 0.40 mm (0.003 to 0.0197 in.)
- Second gear clearance should be 0.10 to 0.30 mm (0.003 to 0.0118 in.)

(21) Press fifth gear onto output shaft. Then install select fit snap ring (Fig. 125). Use thickest snap ring that will fit in shaft groove.

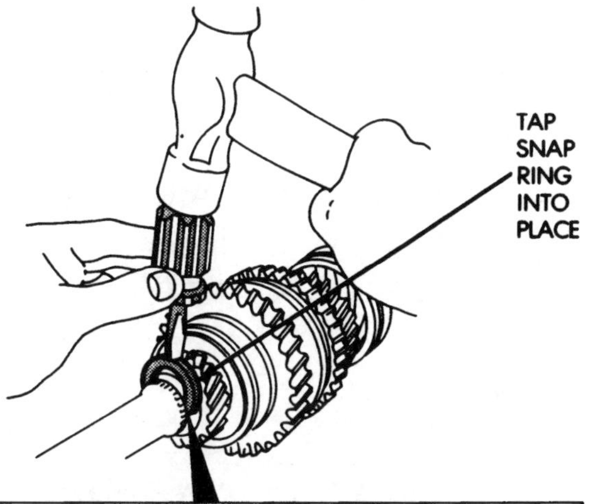

I.D. MARK	SNAP RING THICKNESS	MM (IN.)
A	2.75 - 2.80	(0.1083 - 0.1102)
B	2.80 - 2.85	(0.1002 - 0.1122)
C	2.85 - 2.90	(0.1122 - 0.1142)
D	2.90 - 2.95	(0.1142 - 0.1161)
E	2.95 - 3.00	(0.1161 - 0.1181)
F	3.00 - 3.05	(0.1181 - 0.1201)
G	3.05 - 3.10	(0.1201 - 0.1220)
H	3.10 - 3.15	(0.1220 - 0.1240)
J	3.15 - 3.20	(0.1240 - 0.1260)
K	3.20 - 3.25	(0.1260 - 0.1280)
L	3.25 - 3.30	(0.1280 - 0.1299)
M	3.30 - 3.35	(0.1299 - 0.1319)

J8921-1104

Fig. 125 Selecting Fifth Gear Snap Ring

(22) Lubricate input shaft pilot bearing with petroleum jelly and install bearing in shaft (Fig. 126).

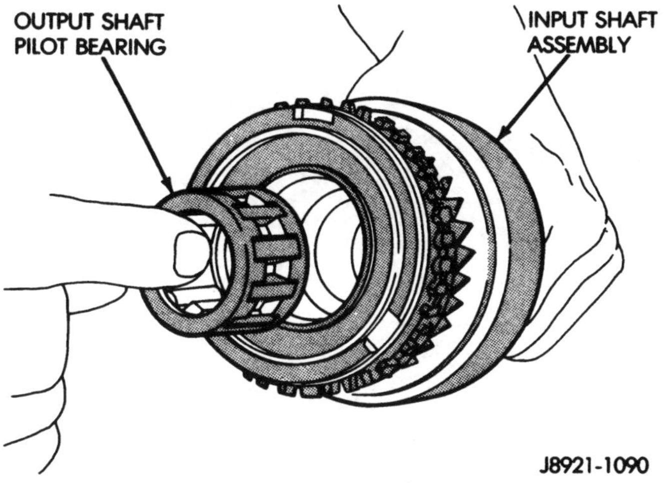

Fig. 126 Input Shaft Pilot Bearing Removal

DISASSEMBLY AND ASSEMBLY (Continued)

(23) Install input shaft on output shaft (Fig. 127). Be sure output shaft hub is fully seated in pilot bearing.

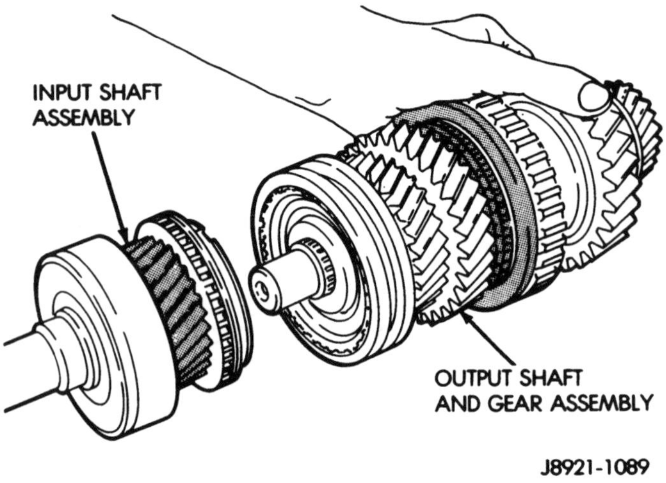

Fig. 127 Input Shaft Removal

CLEANING AND INSPECTION

AX15 TRANSMISSION

Clean the transmission components in solvent. Then dry the cases, gears, shift mechanism and shafts with compressed air. **Dry the bearings with clean, dry shop towels only. Never use compressed air on the bearings. This could damage the bearing rollers.**

Replace components that are obviously worn, cracked, chipped or damaged.

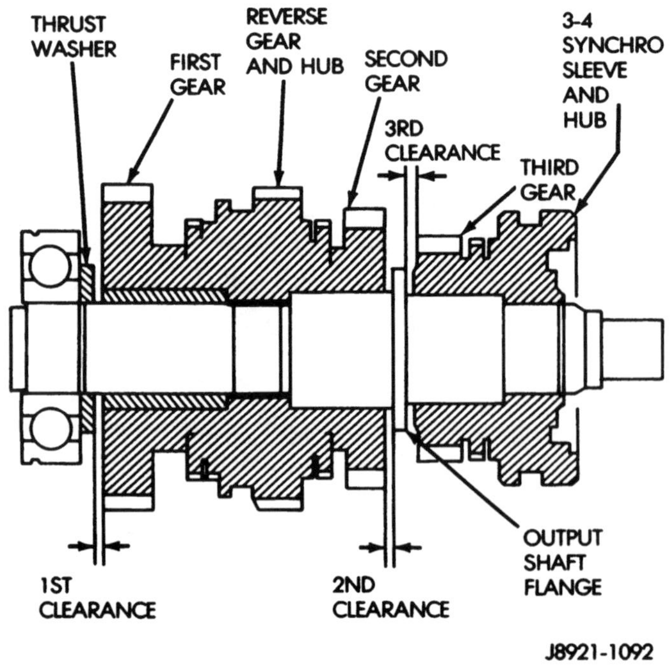

Fig. 128 Checking Output Shaft Gear Thrust Clearance

Inspect the transmission case. Replace the case if cracked or porous or if any of the bearing and gear bores are damaged.

OUTPUT SHAFT INSPECTION

Measure thickness of the output shaft flange with a micrometer (Fig. 129). Minimum allowable flange thickness is 4.70 mm (0.185 in).

If shaft flange thickness is OK but previously measured second/third gear thrust clearance was incorrect (Fig. 128), replace the necessary gear and needle bearing as an assembly.

Check diameter of the first, second and third gear bearing surfaces of the output shaft (Fig. 129). Minimum allowable diameters are:

- 38.86 mm (1.529 in.) for first gear surface
- 46.86 mm (1.844 in.) for second gear surface
- 37.86 mm (1.490 in.) for third gear surface

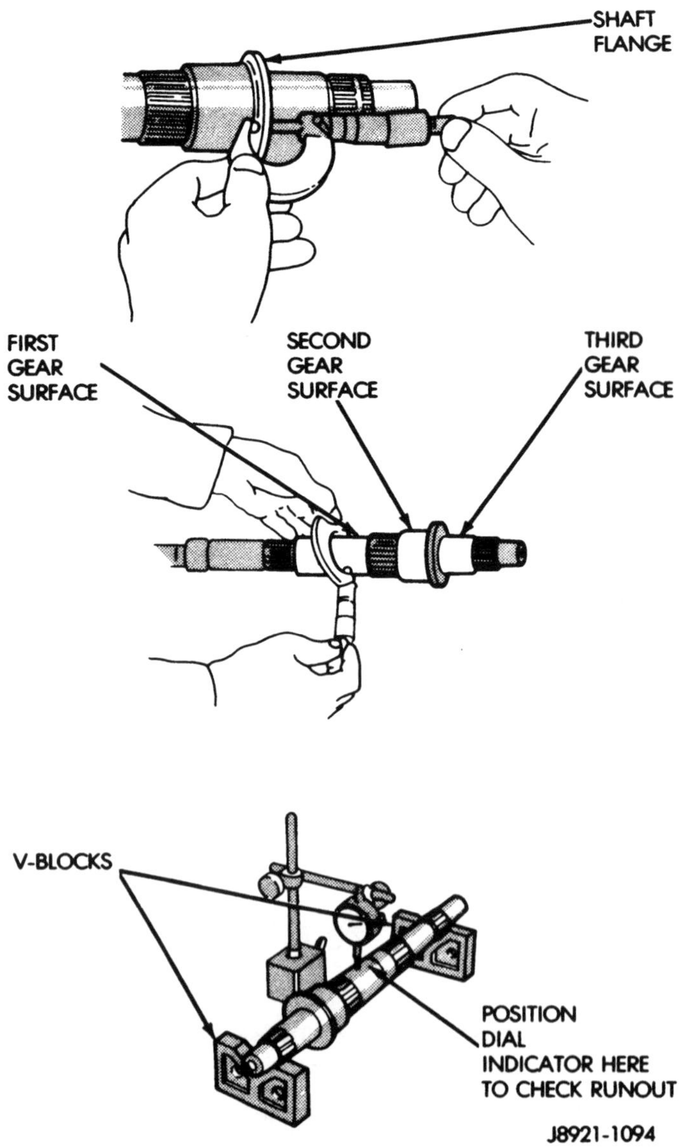

Fig. 129 Checking Output Shaft Tolerances

CLEANING AND INSPECTION (Continued)

Check output shaft runout with V–blocks and a dial indicator (Fig. 129). Maximum allowable runout is 0.06 mm (0.0024 in.).

Replace the output shaft if any surface measured fails to meet stated tolerance.

CLUSTER GEAR INSPECTION

Inspect the cluster gear teeth. Replace the gear if any teeth are worn or damaged or if the bearing surfaces are damaged.

Check diameter of the cluster gear journal with a micrometer (Fig. 130). Minimum allowable diameter is 27.860 mm (1.096 in.).

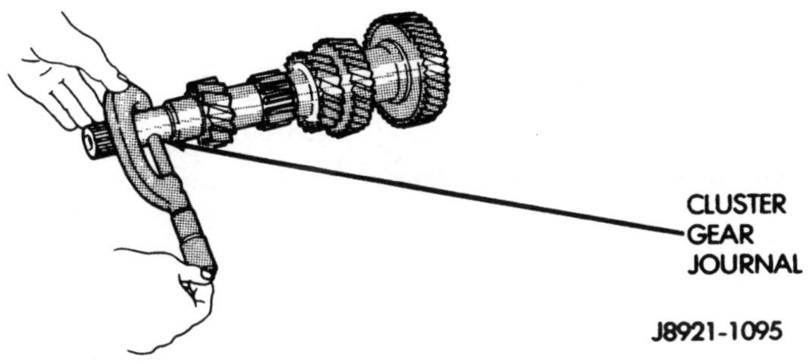

Fig. 130 Checking Cluster Gear Journal Diameter

Check condition of the cluster gear front bearing. Replace the bearing if worn, noisy, or damaged.

AX15 COMPONENTS

GEARTRAIN AND SYNCHRO

Install the synchro rings on their respective gears. Rotate each ring on the gear and note synchro action. Replace any synchro ring that exhibits a lack of braking action or binds on the gear. Also replace any ring that is worn or has chipped or broken teeth.

Measure end clearance between the synchro ring and the gear with a feeler gauge (Fig. 131). Clearance should be 0.06 mm to 1.6 mm (0.024 to 0.063 in.).

Install the needle bearings in the first, second and third gears. Then install the gears on the output shaft and check shaft–to–gear clearance with a dial indicator (Fig. 132).

Maximum allowable clearance is 0.16 mm (0.0063 in.). If any gear exhibits excessive clearance, replace the gear and needle bearing.

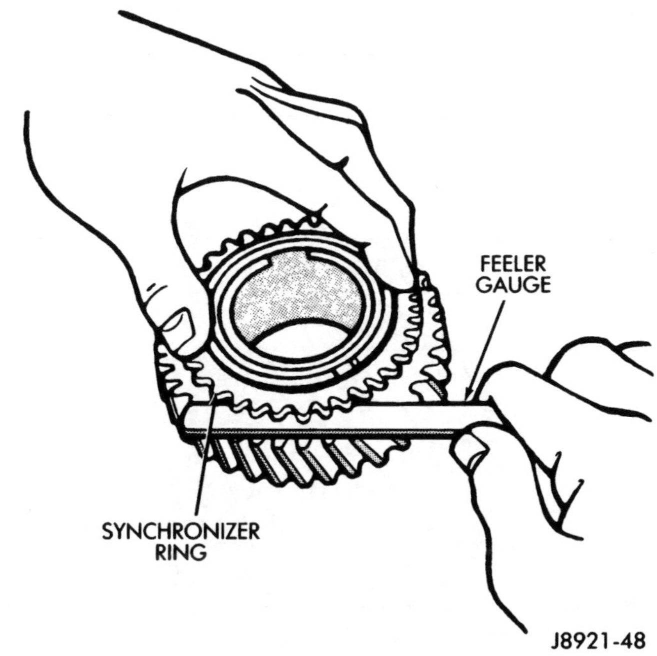

Fig. 131 Checking Synchro Ring End Clearance

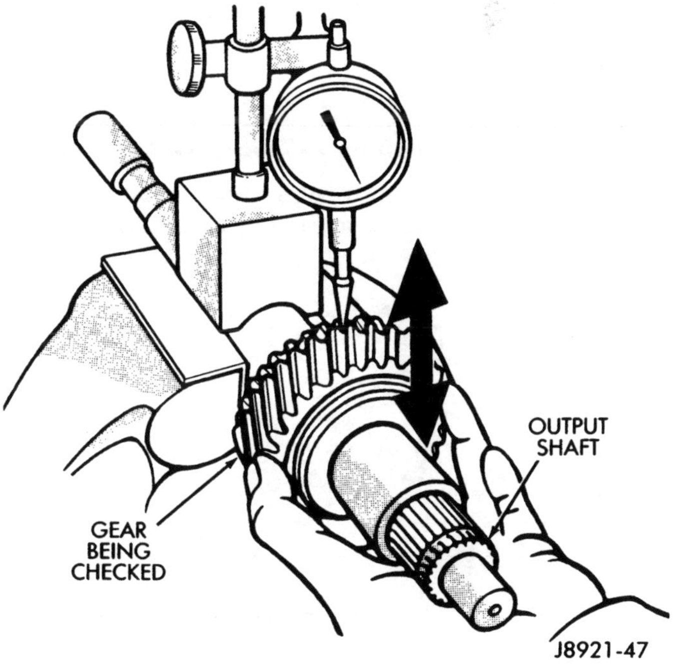

Fig. 132 Checking Gear–To–Shaft Clearance

CLEANING AND INSPECTION (Continued)

Check clearance between the shift forks and synchro sleeves with a feeler gauge (Fig. 133). Clearance should not exceed 1.0 mm (0.039 in.). Replace the synchro sleeve (and matching hub) if clearance exceeds the stated limit.

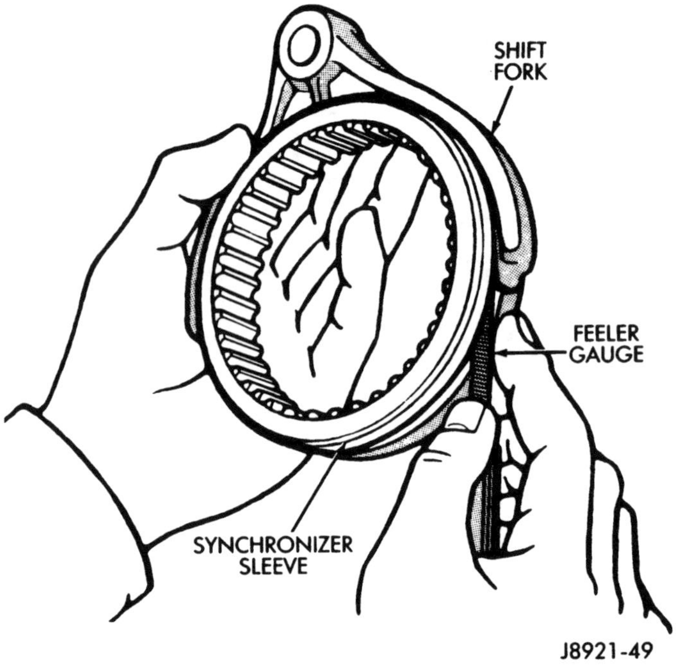

Fig. 133 Checking Shift Fork–To–Sleeve Clearance

Check condition of the reverse idler gear bushing (Fig. 134). Replace the gear if the bushing is scored or worn.

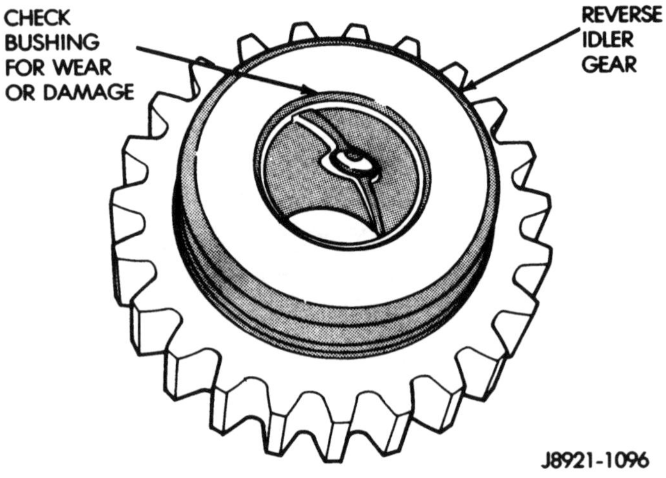

Fig. 134 Reverse Idler Gear Bushing

GEAR CASE, HOUSING AND INTERMEDIATE PLATE

Clean the case, housing and plate with solvent and dry with compressed air. Replace any component that is cracked, warped or damaged in any way.

Inspect the threads in the case, housing and plate. Minor thread damage can be repaired with steel thread inserts if necessary. However, do not attempt to repair if the cracks are evident around any threaded hole.

Inspect the reverse pin in the adapter/extension housing. Replace the pin if worn or damaged. Refer to the replacement procedure in the Transmission Assembly section.

SPECIFICATIONS

AX15 MANUAL TRANSMISSION

SPECIFICATIONS (Continued)

SELECTIVE SNAP RINGS

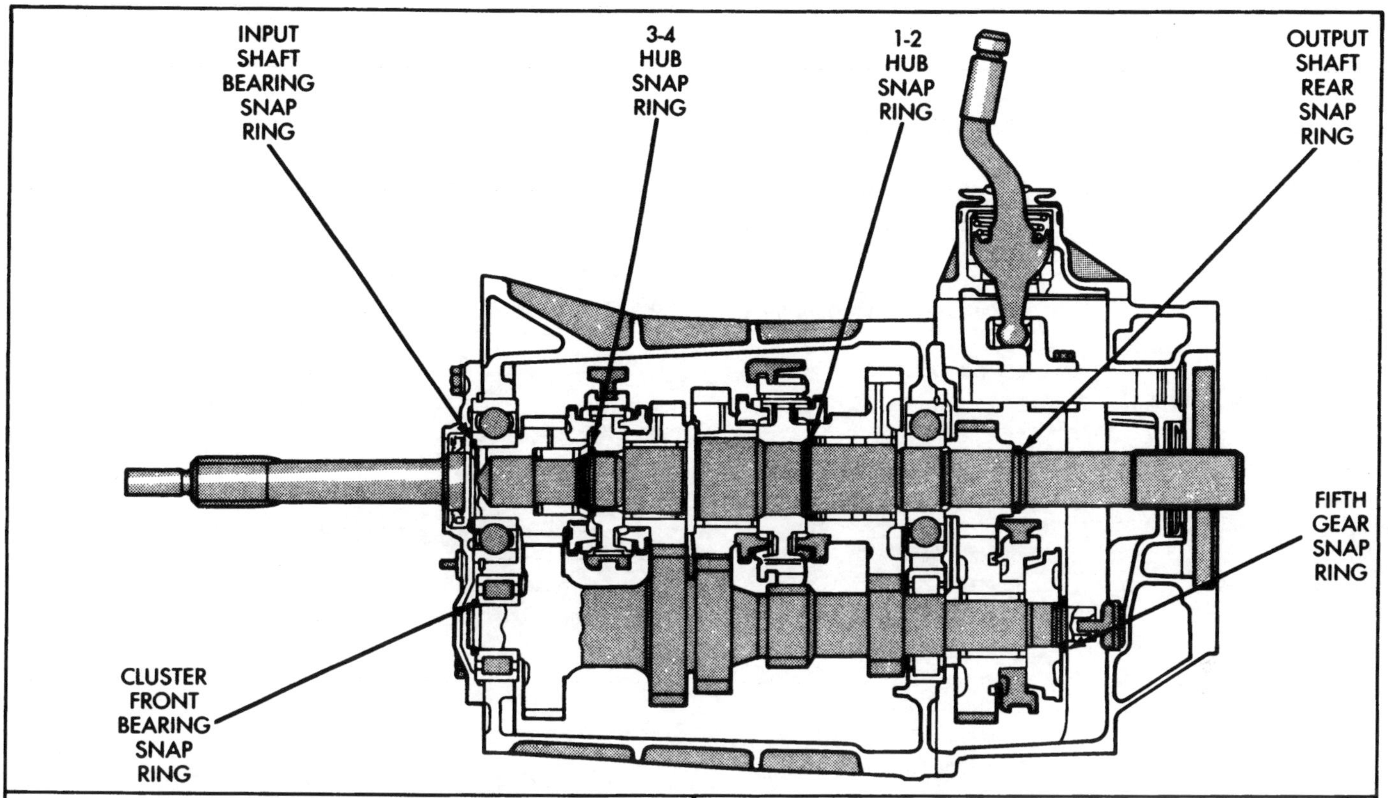

INPUT SHAFT BEARING SNAP RING

I.D. MARK	THICKNESS
A	2.10-2.15 mm
B	2.15-2.20 mm
C	2.20-2.25 mm
D	2.25-2.30 mm
E	2.30-2.35 mm
F	2.35-2.40 mm
G	2.40-2.45 mm

1-2 HUB SNAP RING

I.D. MARK	THICKNESS
B	2.35-2.40 mm
C	2.40-2.45 mm
D	2.45-2.50 mm
E	2.50-2.55 mm
F	2.55-2.60 mm
G	2.60-2.65 mm

CLUSTER FRONT BEARING SNAP RING

I.D. MARK	THICKNESS
A	2.00-2.05 mm
B	2.05-2.10 mm
C	2.10-2.15 mm
D	2.15-2.20 mm
E	2.20-2.25 mm

OUTPUT SHAFT REAR SNAP RING

I.D. MARK	THICKNESS
A	2.75-2.80 mm
B	2.80-2.85 mm
C	2.85-2.90 mm
D	2.90-2.95 mm
E	2.95-3.00 mm
F	3.00-3.05 mm
G	3.05-3.10 mm
H	3.10-3.15 mm
I	3.15-3.20 mm
J	3.20-3.25 mm
K	3.25-3.30 mm
L	3.30-3.35 mm

3-4 HUB SNAP RING

I.D. MARK	THICKNESS
A	1.80-1.85 mm
B	1.85-1.90 mm
C	1.90-1.95 mm
D	1.95-2.00 mm
E	2.00-2.05 mm
F	2.05-2.10 mm
G	2.10-2.15 mm

FIFTH GEAR SNAP RING

I.D. MARK	THICKNESS
A	2.80-2.85 mm
B	2.85-2.90 mm
C	2.90-2.95 mm
D	2.95-3.00 mm
E	3.00-3.05 mm
F	3.05-3.10 mm
G	3.10-3.15 mm
H	3.15-3.20 mm

J8921-1131

SPECIFICATIONS (Continued)

TORQUE

Description	Torque
Access Plugs	19 N•m (14 ft. lbs.)
Adapter Housing Bolts	37 N•m (27 ft. lbs.)
Backup Light Switch	37 N•m (27 ft. lbs.)
Drain and Fill Plugs	37 N•m (27 ft. lbs.)
Front Bearing Retainer Bolts	17 N•m (12 ft. lbs.)
Interlock and Detent Ball Plugs	19 N•m (14 ft. lbs.)
Propeller Shaft Clamp Screws	16-23 N•m (140-200 in. lbs.)
Rear Mount-To-Transmission Bolts	33-60 N•m (24-44 ft. lbs.)
Rear Mount Clevis Bolt/Nut	54-75 N•m (40-55 ft. lbs.)
Rear Mount-To-Crossmember Nuts	33-49 N•m (24-36 ft. lbs.)
Restrictor Pins	19 N•m (14 ft. lbs.)
Reverse Shift Arm Bracket Bolts	18 N•m (13 ft. lbs.)
Shift Arm Set Screw	38 N•m (28 ft. lbs.)
Shift Fork Set Screws	20 N•m (15 ft. lbs.)
Shift Knob Nut	20-34 N•m (15-25 ft. lbs.)
Shift Lever Floor Cover Screws	2-3 N•m (17-30 in. lbs.)
Shift Tower Bolts	18 N•m (13 ft. lbs.)
Transfer Case Mounting Nuts	30-41 N•m (22-30 ft. lbs.)

J9321-89

SPECIAL TOOLS

AX15

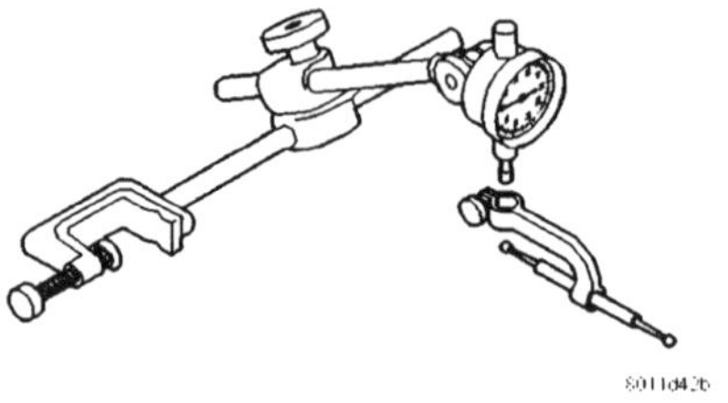

C-3339 Dial Indicator Set

C-4961 Michrometer, Two Inch

AUTOMATIC TRANSMISSION—30/32RH

INDEX

GENERAL INFORMATION

30/32RH AUTOMATIC TRANSMISSION

The 30RH automatic transmission is used with the 2.5L engine. The 32RH automatic transmission (Fig. 1) is used with the 4.0L engine. The 30/32RH are three speed transmissions with a lock-up clutch in the torque converter. The torque converter clutch is controlled by the Powertrain Control Module (PCM). The torque converter clutch is hydraulically applied and is released when fluid is vented from the hydraulic circuit by the torque converter control (TCC) solenoid on the valve body. The torque converter clutch engages in third gear when the vehicle is cruising on a level plane after the vehicle has warmed up. The torque converter clutch will disengage when the vehicle begins to go uphill or the accelerator is applied. The torque converter clutch feature increases fuel economy and reduces the transmission fluid temperature. The 30/32RH transmission is cooled by an integral fluid cooler inside the radiator.

GENERAL INFORMATION (Continued)

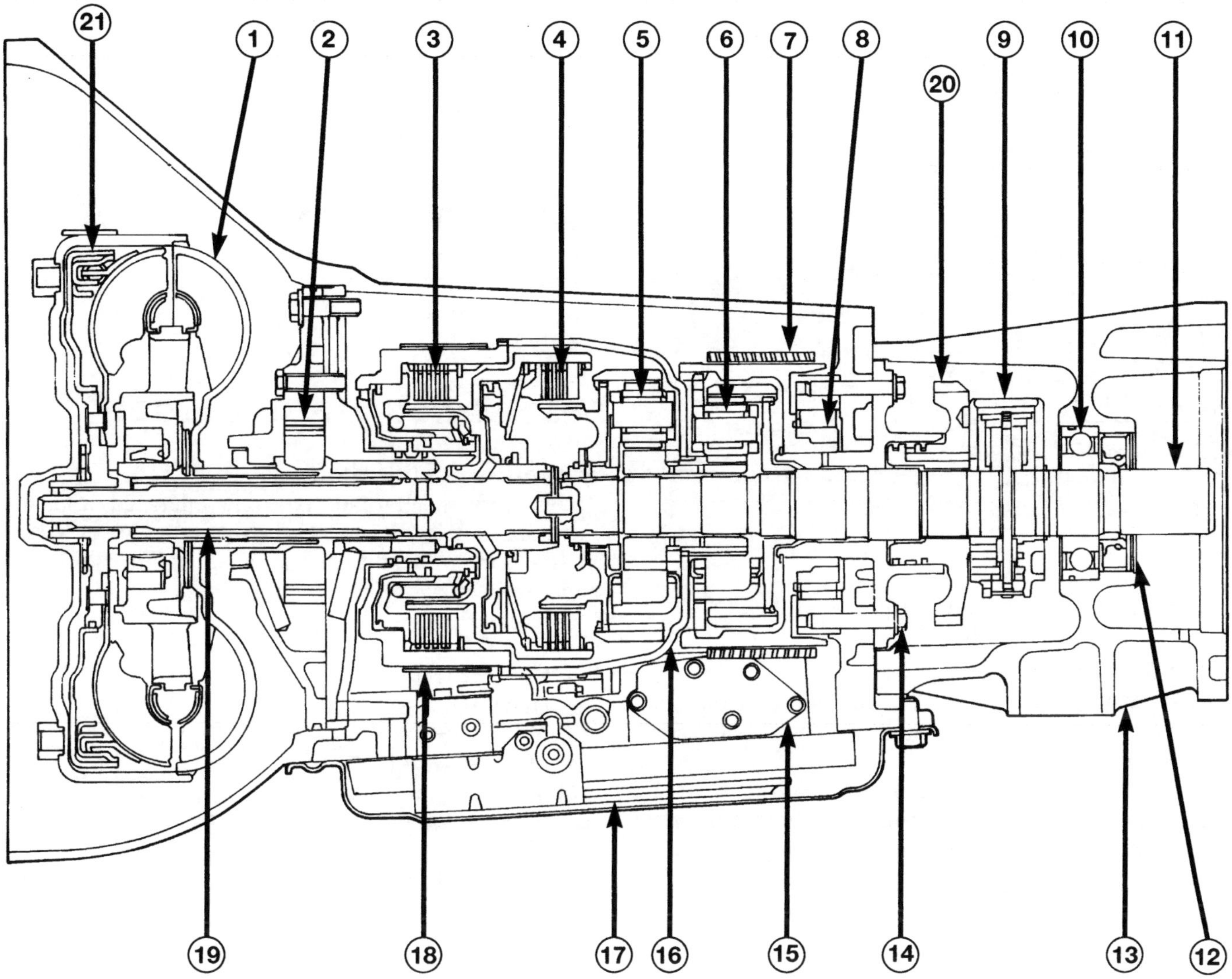

1	CONVERTER	11	OUTPUT SHAFT
2	OIL PUMP	12	SEAL
3	FRONT CLUTCH	13	ADAPTER HOUSING
4	REAR CLUTCH	14	PARK LOCK ROD
5	FRONT PLANETARY GEAR SET	15	VALVE BODY
6	REAR PLANETARY GEAR SET	16	SUN GEAR DRIVING SHELL
7	LOW AND REVERSE (REAR) BAND	17	OIL FILTER
8	OVERRUNNING CLUTCH	18	KICK DOWN (FRONT) BAND
9	GOVERNOR	19	INPUT SHAFT
10	BEARING	20	PARK GEAR
		21	CONVERTER CLUTCH

80a13873

Fig. 1 30/32 RH Automatic Transmission

GENERAL INFORMATION (Continued)

TRANSMISSION IDENTIFICATION

Transmission identification numbers are stamped on the left side of the case just above the oil pan gasket surface (Fig. 2). Refer to this information when ordering replacement parts.

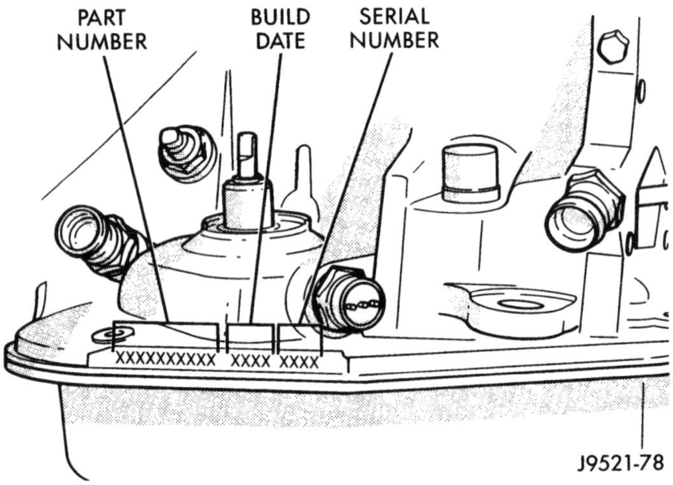

Fig. 2 Transmission Part And Serial Number Location

RECOMMENDED FLUID

Mopar ATF Plus, Type 7176 automatic transmission fluid is the recommended fluid for Chrysler automatic transmissions.

Dexron II fluid IS NOT recommended. Clutch chatter can result from the use of improper fluid. If Mopar ATF Plus is not available, Dexron II can be used as a supplement if the vehicle must be driven.

TORQUE CONVERTER—ELECTRONIC CLUTCH

The torque converter is a hydraulic device that couples the engine crankshaft to the transmission. The torque converter consists of an outer shell with an internal turbine, a stator, an overrunning clutch, an impeller and an electronically applied converter clutch. Torque multiplication is created when the stator directs the hydraulic flow from the turbine to rotate the impeller in the direction the engine crankshaft is turning. The turbine transfers power to the planetary gear sets in the transmission. The transfer of power into the impeller assists torque multiplication. At low vehicle speed, the overrunning clutch holds the stator (during torque multiplication) and allows the stator to free wheel at high vehicle speed. The converter clutch provides reduced engine speed and greater fuel economy when engaged. Clutch engagement also provides reduced transmission fluid temperatures. The converter clutch engages in third gear. The torque converter hub drives the transmission oil (fluid) pump.

The torque converter is a sealed, welded unit that is not repairable and is serviced as an assembly.

CAUTION: The torque converter must be replaced if a transmission failure resulted in large amounts of metal or fiber contamination in the fluid. If the fluid is contaminated, flush the fluid cooler and lines.

TRANSMISSION GEAR RATIOS

Forward gear ratios are:

- 2.74:1 (first gear)
- 1.54:1 (second gear)
- 1.00:1 (third gear)

DESCRIPTION AND OPERATION

GEARSHIFT MECHANISM

The shift mechanism is cable operated and provides six shift positions. The shift indicator is located on the console next to the gear shift. The shift positions are:

- Park (P)
- Reverse (R)
- Neutral (N)
- Drive (D)
- Manual Second (2)
- Manual Low (1)

Manual low (1) range provides first gear only. Over run braking is also provided in this range. Manual second (2) range provides first and second gear only. Drive range provides first, second, and third gear ranges.

HYDRAULIC CONTROL SYSTEM

The transmission hydraulic control system performs four basic functions.

- pressure supply
- pressure regulation
- flow control and lubrication
- clutch/band application

PRESSURE SUPPLY

The oil pump develops fluid pressure for clutch/band application and for lubrication. The pump is driven by the torque converter. The converter is driven by a driveplate attached to the engine crankshaft.

Pressure Regulation

The pressure regulator valve maintains line (operating) pressure. The amount of pressure developed is controlled by throttle pressure which is dependent on the degree of throttle opening. The regulator valve is located in the valve body.

DESCRIPTION AND OPERATION (Continued)

The throttle valve determines throttle pressure and shift speed. Governor pressure increases in proportion to vehicle speed. The throttle valve controls upshift and downshift speeds by regulating pressure according to throttle position.

Flow Control And Lubrication

The manual valve is operated by the gearshift linkage and provides the operating range selected by the driver.

The switch valve controls line pressure to the converter clutch. The valve also directs oil to the cooling and lubrication circuits. The switch valve regulates oil pressure to the torque converter by limiting maximum oil pressure to 130 psi.

The 1-2 shift valve provide 1-2 and 2-1 shifts and the 2-3 shift valve provide 2-3 and 3-2 shifts.

The 1-2 shift control valve transmits 1-2 shift pressure to the accumulator piston. This controls kickdown band capacity on 1-2 upshifts and 3-2 downshifts.

The 2-3 valve throttle pressure plug provides 3-2 downshifts at varying throttle openings depending on vehicle speed.

The kickdown valve provides forced downshifts depending on vehicle speed. Downshifts occur when the throttle is opened beyond downshift detent position. Detent is reached just before wide open throttle position.

The limit valve determines maximum speed at which a 3-2 part throttle kickdown can be made. Some transmissions do not have the limit valve and maximum speed for a 3-2 kickdown is at the detent position.

The shuttle valve has two functions. First is fast front band release and smooth engagement during "lift foot" 2-3 upshifts. Second is to regulate front clutch release and band application during 3-2 downshifts.

The fail safe valve restricts feed to the converter clutch if front clutch pressure drops. It permits clutch engagement only in direct (third) gear and provides fast clutch release during kickdown.

Clutch/Band Application

The front/rear clutch pistons and servo pistons are actuated by line pressure. When line pressure is removed, the pistons are released by spring tension.

On 2-3 upshifts, the front servo piston is released by spring tension and hydraulic pressure. The accumulator controls hydraulic pressure on the apply side of the front servo during 1-2 upshifts and at all throttle openings.

CONVERTER CLUTCH ENGAGEMENT

Converter clutch engagement in third gear is controlled by sensor inputs to the powertrain control module. Inputs that determine clutch engagement are: coolant temperature, vehicle speed and throttle position. The torque converter clutch is engaged by the clutch solenoid on the valve body. The clutch will engage at approximately 56 km/h (35 mph) with light throttle, after the shift to third gear.

CONVERTER DRAINBACK VALVE

The drainback valve is located in the transmission cooler outlet (pressure) line. The valve prevents fluid from draining from the converter into the cooler and lines when the vehicle is shut down for lengthy periods. Production valves have a hose nipple at one end, while the opposite end is threaded for a flare fitting. All valves have an arrow (or similar mark) to indicate direction of flow through the valve.

BRAKE TRANSMISSION SHIFT INTERLOCK MECHANISM

The Brake Transmission Shifter/Ignition Interlock (BTSI), is a cable and solenoid operated system. It interconnects the automatic transmission floor mounted shifter to the steering column ignition switch (Fig. 3). The system locks the shifter into the PARK position. The Interlock system is engaged whenever the ignition switch is in the LOCK or ACCESSORY position. An additional electrically activated feature will prevent shifting out of the PARK position unless the brake pedal is depressed at least one-half an inch. A magnetic holding device in line with the park/brake interlock cable is energized in PARK when the ignition is in the OFF-LOCK position. When the key is in the OFF or RUN position and the brake pedal is depressed, the shifter is unlocked and will move into any position. The interlock system also prevents the ignition switch from being turned to the LOCK or ACCESSORY position (Fig. 4). Unless the shifter is fully locked into the PARK position.

DIAGNOSIS AND TESTING

AUTOMATIC TRANSMISSION DIAGNOSIS

Automatic transmission problems can be a result of poor engine performance, incorrect fluid level, incorrect linkage or cable adjustment, band or hydraulic control pressure adjustments, hydraulic system malfunctions or electrical/mechanical component malfunctions. Begin diagnosis by checking the easily accessible items such as: fluid level, condition, and linkage adjustments. A road test will determine if further diagnosis is necessary.

On vehicles with 32RH transmission, check for a diagnostic trouble code (DTC). Access the DTC by cycling the ignition key ON-OFF-ON-OFF and ON. With the ignition ON, count the number of times the

DIAGNOSIS AND TESTING (Continued)

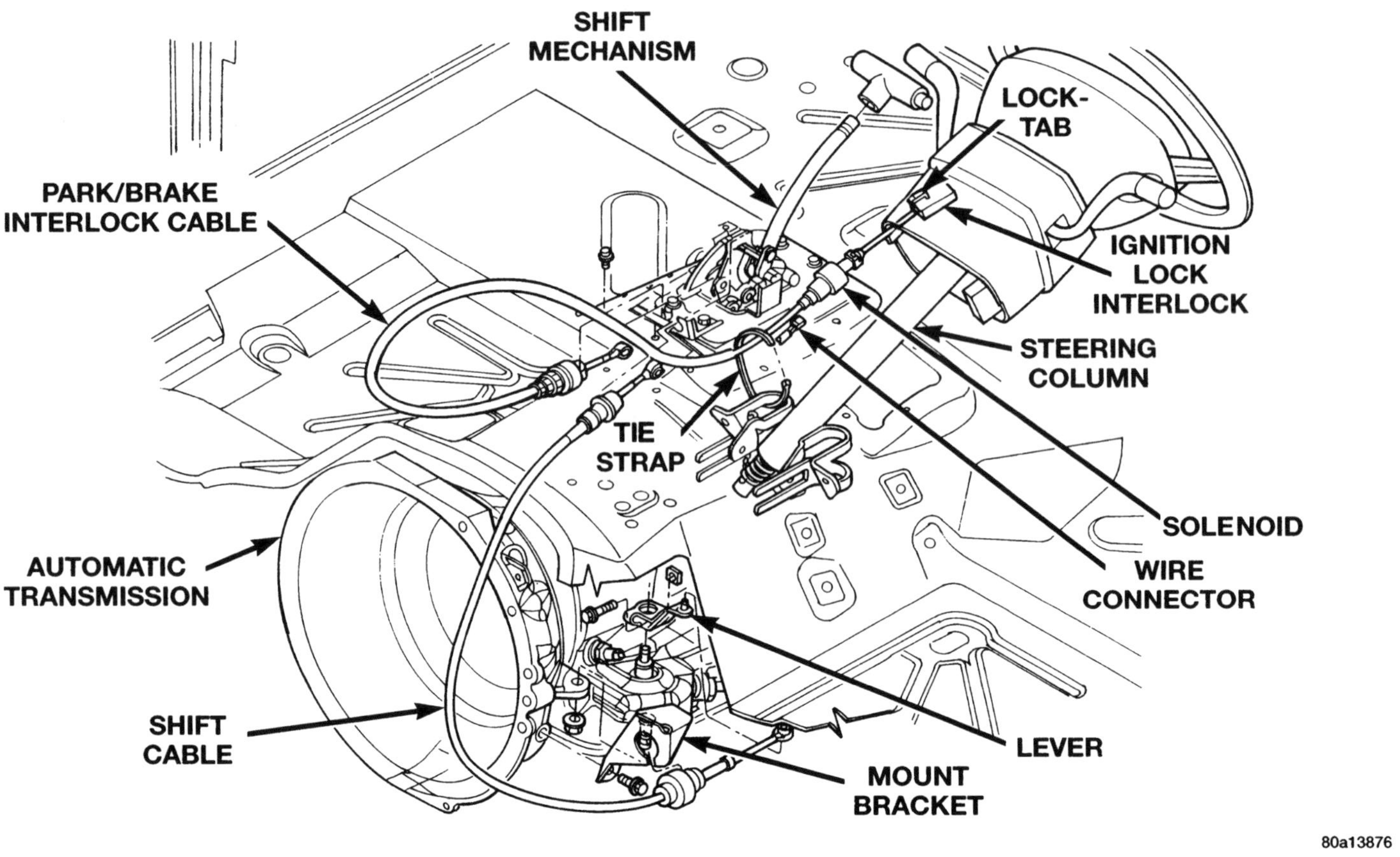

Fig. 3 Ignition Interlock Cable Routing

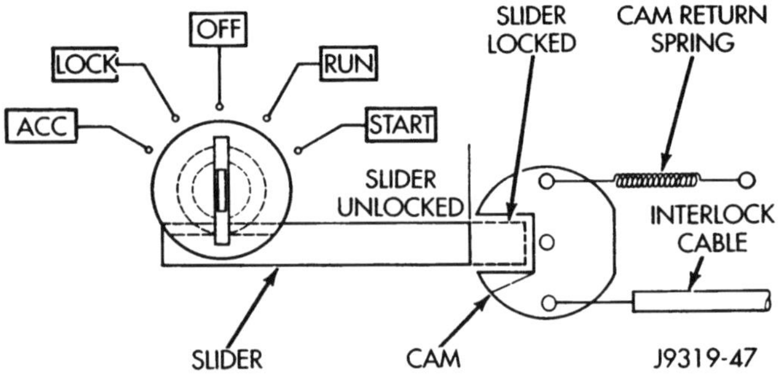

Fig. 4 Ignition Key Cylinder Actuation

malfunction indicator lamp (MIL) flashes. Three MIL flashes followed by seven indicate an open or shorted circuit in the torque converter clutch control system. Refer to the Group 8W, Wiring Diagrams for circuit information and component locations.

PRELIMINARY DIAGNOSIS

Two basic procedures are required. One procedure for vehicles that are drivable and an alternate procedure for disabled vehicles (will not back up or move forward).

VEHICLE IS DRIVABLE

(1) Check fluid level and condition.

(2) Adjust throttle and gearshift linkage if complaint was based on delayed, erratic, or harsh shifts.

(3) Road test and note how transmission upshifts, downshifts and engages.

(4) Perform stall test if complaint is based on sluggish acceleration. Or, if abnormal throttle opening is needed to maintain normal speeds with a properly tuned engine.

(5) Perform hydraulic pressure test if shift problems were noted during road test.

(6) Perform air pressure test to check clutch-band operation.

VEHICLE IS DISABLED

(1) Check fluid level and condition.

(2) Check for broken, disconnected gearshift and throttle linkage.

(3) Check for cracked, leaking cooler lines, or loose, missing pressure port plugs.

(4) Raise and support vehicle on safety stands, start engine, shift transmission into gear and note following:

(a) If propeller shaft turns but wheels do not, problem is with differential or axle shafts.

(b) If propeller shaft does not turn and transmission is noisy, stop engine. Remove oil pan, and check for debris. If pan is clear, remove transmis-

DIAGNOSIS AND TESTING (Continued)

sion and check for damaged drive plate, converter, oil pump or input shaft.

(c) If propeller shaft does not turn and transmission is not noisy, perform hydraulic pressure test to determine if problem is hydraulic or mechanical.

PARK/NEUTRAL POSITION SWITCH

The center terminal of the park/neutral position switch is the starter-circuit terminal. It provides the ground for the starter solenoid circuit through the selector lever in PARK and NEUTRAL positions only. The outer terminals on the switch are for the backup lamp circuit.

SWITCH TEST

To test the switch, remove the wiring connector. Then test for continuity between the center terminal and the transmission case. Continuity should exist only when the transmission is in PARK or NEUTRAL.

Shift the transmission into REVERSE and test continuity at the switch outer terminals (Fig. 5). Continuity should exist only when the transmission is in REVERSE. Continuity should not exist between the outer terminals and the case.

Check gearshift linkage adjustment before replacing a switch that tests bad.

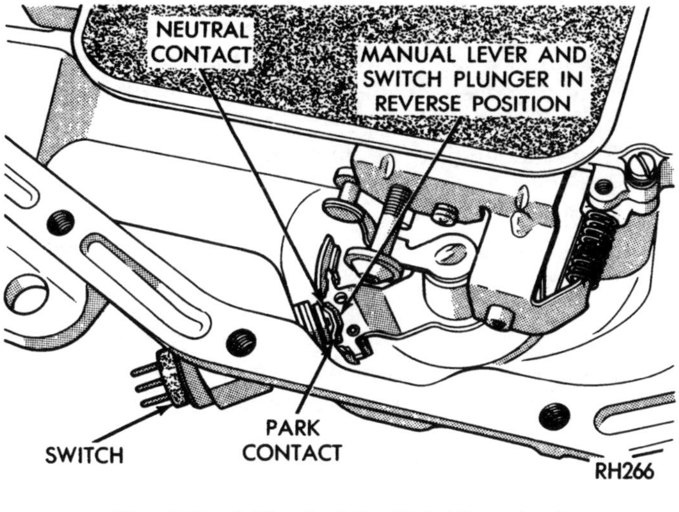

Fig. 5 Park/Neutral Switch Terminals

CHECKING FLUID LEVEL AND CONDITION

Transmission fluid level and condition should be checked a minimum of six times per year under normal operation. If the vehicle is used for commercial operation, trailer towing, or similar high load operation, fluid level and condition should be checked weekly.

Fluid level is checked with the engine running at curb idle speed, brakes applied, transmission in Neutral, and the transmission fluid at normal operating temperature (hot).

(1) Transmission fluid must be at normal operating temperature for accurate fluid level check. Drive vehicle if necessary to bring fluid temperature up to normal hot operating temperature of 82° C (180° F).

(2) Position vehicle on level surface. This is extremely important for accurate fluid level check.

(3) Start and run engine at curb idle speed.

(4) Apply parking brakes.

(5) Shift transmission momentarily into all gear ranges. Then shift transmission back to **Neutral.**

(6) Clean top of filler tube and dipstick to keep dirt from entering tube.

CAUTION: Do not overfill the transmission. Overfilling may cause leakage out the pump vent which can be mistaken for a pump seal leak. Overfilling will also cause fluid aeration and foaming as the excess fluid is picked up and churned by the gear train. This will significantly reduce fluid life.

(7) Remove dipstick and check **fluid level** as follows:

(a) Dipstick has three indicator levels (Fig. 6) which are a MIN dot, an OK crosshatch area, and a MAX fill arrow.

(b) Correct maximum level is to MAX arrow mark. Correct acceptable level is to OK mark in crosshatch area. Incorrect level is at or below MIN dot.

(c) If fluid is low, add only enough Mopar ATF Plus to restore correct level. Do not overfill.

(d) If transmission is overfilled, fluid can be removed with 1/8 to 3/16 in. diameter tubing and suction gun. Tubing will have to be adapted to nozzle of gun and be long enough to extend down fill tube and into transmission oil pan.

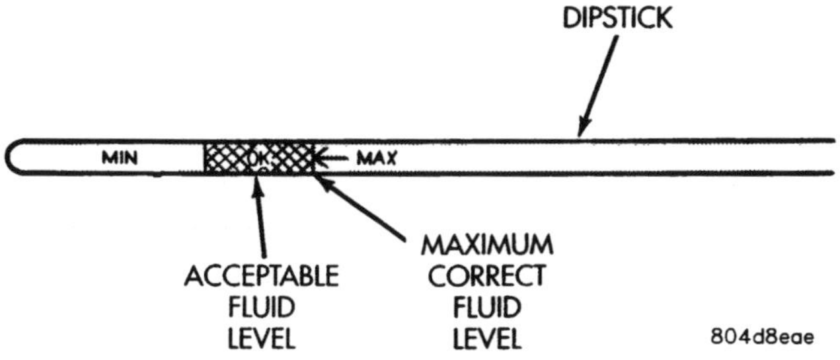

Fig. 6 Dipstick Fluid Level Marks

(8) Check **fluid condition** as follows:

(a) Fluid color should range from dark red to pink and be free of particles and sludge.

(b) If fluid is orange, brown, or smells burned but shifts were OK, flow test and reverse flush cooler and lines. Then change fluid and filter and road test again to confirm proper operation.

(c) If fluid is black, dark brown, turned to sludge, contains extensive amount of metal or fric-

DIAGNOSIS AND TESTING (Continued)

tion material particles, transmission will need overhaul. Main and auxiliary coolers will have to be flow tested and reverse flushed as well.

EFFECTS OF INCORRECT FLUID LEVEL

A low fluid level allows the pump to take in air along with the fluid. Air in the fluid will cause fluid pressures to be low and develop slower than normal. If the transmission is overfilled, the gears churn the fluid into foam. This aerates the fluid and causing the same conditions occurring with a low level. In either case, air bubbles cause fluid overheating, oxidation and varnish buildup which interferes with valve, clutch and servo operation. Foaming also causes fluid expansion which can result in fluid overflow from the transmission vent or fill tube. Fluid overflow can easily be mistaken for a leak if inspection is not careful.

CAUSES OF BURNT FLUID

Burnt, discolored fluid is a result of overheating which has two primary causes.

(1) A result of restricted fluid flow through the main and/or auxiliary cooler. This condition is usually the result of a faulty or improperly installed drainback valve, a damaged main cooler, or severe restrictions in the coolers and lines caused by debris or kinked lines.

(2) Heavy duty operation with a vehicle not properly equipped for this type of operation. Trailer towing or similar high load operation will overheat the transmission fluid if the vehicle is improperly equipped. Such vehicles should have an auxiliary transmission fluid cooler, a heavy duty cooling system, and the engine/axle ratio combination needed to handle heavy loads.

FLUID CONTAMINATION

Transmission fluid contamination is generally a result of:

- adding incorrect fluid
- failure to clean dipstick and fill tube when checking level
- engine coolant entering the fluid
- internal failure that generates debris
- overheat that generates sludge (fluid breakdown)
- failure to reverse flush cooler and lines after repair
- failure to replace contaminated converter after repair

The use of non recommended fluids can result in transmission failure. The usual results are erratic shifts, slippage, abnormal wear and eventual failure due to fluid breakdown and sludge formation. Avoid this condition by using recommended fluids only.

The dipstick cap and fill tube should be wiped clean before checking fluid level. Dirt, grease and other foreign material on the cap and tube could fall into the tube if not removed beforehand. Take the time to wipe the cap and tube clean before withdrawing the dipstick.

Engine coolant in the transmission fluid is generally caused by a cooler malfunction. The only remedy is to replace the radiator as the cooler in the radiator is not a serviceable part. If coolant has circulated through the transmission for some time, an overhaul may also be necessary; especially if shift problems had developed.

The transmission cooler and lines should be reverse flushed whenever a malfunction generates sludge and/or debris. The torque converter should also be replaced at the same time.

Failure to flush the cooler and lines will result in recontamination. Flushing applies to auxiliary coolers as well. The torque converter should also be replaced whenever a failure generates sludge and debris. This is necessary because normal converter flushing procedures will not remove all contaminants.

OIL COOLER FLOW CHECK

After the new or repaired transmission has been installed and filled, the oil cooler flow should be checked using the following procedure:

(1) Disconnect the **From cooler** line at the transmission and place a collecting container under the disconnected line.

(2) Run the engine at curb idle speed, with the shift selector in neutral.

(3) If the fluid flow is intermittent or takes more than 20 seconds to collect one quart, the cooler should be replaced.

CAUTION: With the fluid set at the proper level, fluid collection should not exceed (1) quart or internal damage to the transmission may occur.

(4) If flow is found to be within acceptable limits, reconnect the cooler line. Then fill transaxle to the proper level, using the approved type of automatic transmission fluid.

ROAD TESTING

Before road testing, be sure the fluid level and control cable adjustments have been checked and adjusted if necessary.

Observe engine performance during the road test. A poorly tuned engine will not allow accurate analysis of transmission operation.

Operate the transmission in all gear ranges. Check for shift variations and engine flare which indicates

DIAGNOSIS AND TESTING (Continued)

slippage. Note if shifts are harsh, spongy, delayed, early, or if part throttle downshifts are sensitive.

Slippage indicated by engine flare, usually means clutch, band or overrunning clutch problems. If the condition is advanced, an overhaul will be necessary to restore normal operation.

A slipping clutch or band can often be determined by comparing which internal units are applied in the various gear ranges. The Clutch and Band Application charts (Fig. 7) provide a basis for analyzing road test results.

DRIVE ELEMENTS	Gearshift Lever Position								
	P	R	N	D			2		1
				1	2	3	1	2	
FRONT CLUTCH		•				•			
FRONT BAND (KICKDOWN)					•			•	
REAR CLUTCH				•	•	•	•	•	•
REAR BAND (LOW-REV.)		•							•
OVER-RUNNING CLUTCH				•			•		•

J9021-33

Fig. 7 Clutch And Band Application

ANALYZING ROAD TEST

Refer to the Clutch and Band Application chart (Fig. 7) and note which elements are in use in the various gear ranges.

Verify that the rear clutch is applied in all forward ranges (D, 2, 1). The transmission overrunning clutch is applied in first gear (D, 2 and 1 ranges) only. The rear band is applied in 1 and R range only.

Verify that the overdrive clutch is applied only in fourth gear and the overdrive direct clutch and overrunning clutch are applied in all ranges except fourth gear. For example: If slippage occurs in first gear in D and 2 range but not in 1 range, the transmission overrunning clutch is faulty. Similarly, if slippage occurs in any two forward gears, the rear clutch is slipping.

Applying the same method of analysis, verify that the front and rear clutches are applied simultaneously only in D range third gear. If the transmission slips in third gear, either the front clutch or the rear clutch is slipping.

If slippage occurs during the third gear and the direct clutch were to fail, the transmission would lose both reverse gear and overrun braking in 2 position (manual second gear). If the transmission slips in any other forward gears, the transmission rear clutch is probably slipping.

This process of elimination can be used to identify a slipping unit and check operation. Proper use of the Clutch and Band Application Chart is the key.

Although road test analysis will help determine the slipping unit, the actual cause of a malfunction usually cannot be determined until hydraulic and air pressure tests are performed. Practically any condition can be caused by leaking hydraulic circuits or sticking valves.

Unless a malfunction is obvious, such as no drive in D range first gear, do not disassemble the transmission. Perform the hydraulic and air pressure tests to help the probable cause.

HYDRAULIC PRESSURE TEST

Hydraulic test pressures range from a low of one psi (6.895 kPa) governor pressure, to 300 psi (2068 kPa) at the rear servo pressure port in reverse. Use 100 psi Gauge C-3292 to check pressure at the accumulator, front servo and governor. Use 300 psi Gauge C-3293-SP to check pressure at the rear servo and overdrive port.

Pressure Test Port Locations

Pressure test ports locations are provided at the accumulator, front servo, and rear servo, governor passage, and overdrive clutch pressure passage (Fig. 8), (Fig. 9) and (Fig. 10).

An accurate tachometer and two test gauges are required for the pressure test. Test Gauge C-3292 has a 100 psi range and is used at the accumulator, governor, and front servo pressure ports. Test Gauge C-3293-SP has a 300 psi range and is used at the rear servo port and overdrive test ports where pressures are higher. In cases where two test gauges are required, the 300 psi gauge can be used at any of the other test ports.

Line pressure is checked at the accumulator port on the right side of the case. The front servo pressure port is at the right side of the case just behind the filler tube opening.

Connect a tachometer to the engine. Position the tachometer so it can be observed from under the vehicle. Raise the vehicle on a hoist that will allow the wheels to rotate freely.

PRESSURE TEST PROCEDURE

Test One - Transmission In 1 Range

This test checks pump output, pressure regulation, and condition of the rear clutch and servo circuit. Test Gauges C-3292 and C-3293-SP are required for

DIAGNOSIS AND TESTING (Continued)

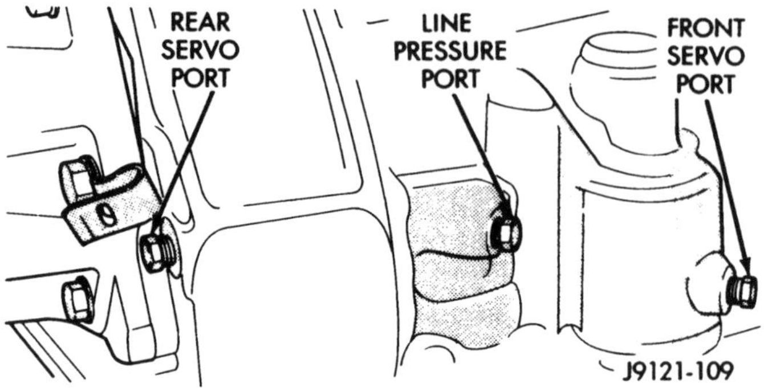

Fig. 8 Pressure Test Ports At Side Of Case

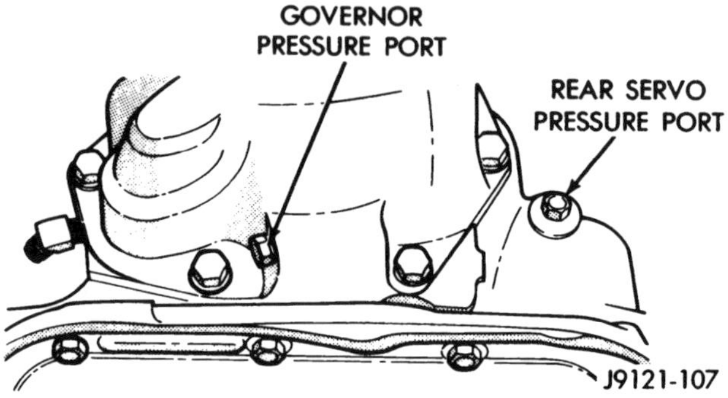

Fig. 9 Pressure Test Ports At Rear Of Case—2WD

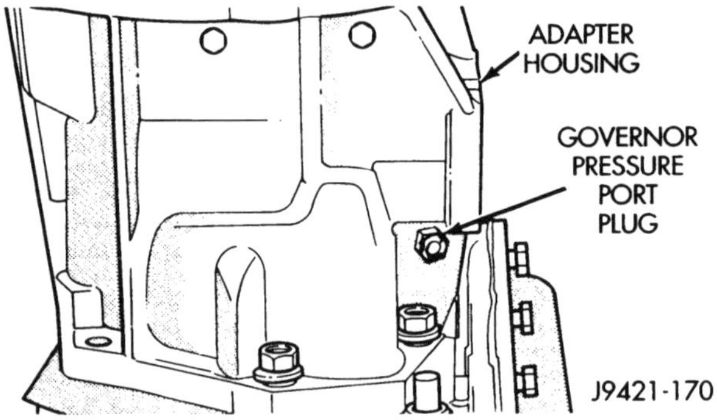

Fig. 10 Pressure Test Ports At Rear Of Case—4WD

this test. Gauge C-3292 has a 100 psi range. Gauge C-3293-SP has a 300 psi range.

(1) Connect 100 psi Gauge C-3292 to accumulator port.

(2) Connect 300 psi Gauge C-3293-SP to rear servo port (Fig. 8) and (Fig. 9).

(3) Disconnect throttle and gearshift rods from manual and throttle levers.

(4) Start and run engine at 1000 rpm.

(5) Move shift lever (on manual lever shaft) all the way forward into 1 range.

(6) Move transmission throttle lever from full forward to full rearward position and note pressures on both gauges.

(7) Line pressure at accumulator port should be 54-60 psi (372-414 kPa) with throttle lever forward and gradually increase to 90-96 psi (621-662 kPa) as lever is moved rearward.

(8) Rear servo pressure should be same as line pressure within 3 psi (20.68 kPa).

Test Two - Transmission In 2 Range

This test checks pump output and pressure regulation. Use 100 psi Test Gauge C-3292 for this test.

(1) Connect test gauge to accumulator pressure port (Fig. 8) and (Fig. 9).

(2) Start and run engine at 1000 rpm.

(3) Move shift lever on valve body manual lever shaft, one detent rearward from full forward position. This is 2 range.

(4) Move transmission throttle lever from full forward to full rearward position and read pressure at both gauges.

(5) Line pressure should be 54-60 psi (372-414 kPa) with throttle lever forward and gradually increase to 90-96 psi (621-662 kPa) as lever is moved rearward.

Test Three - Transmission In D Range

This test checks pressure regulation and condition of the clutch circuits. Use both pressure Test Gauges C-3292 and C-3293-SP for this test.

(1) Connect test gauges to accumulator and front servo ports (Fig. 8) and (Fig. 9). Use either test gauge at the two ports.

(2) Start and run engine at 1600 rpm for this test.

(3) Move selector lever to D range. This is two detents rearward from full forward position.

(4) Read pressures on both gauges as transmission throttle lever is moved from full forward to full rearward position.

(5) Line pressure should be 54-60 psi (372-414 kPa) with throttle lever forward and gradually increase as lever is moved rearward.

(6) Front servo is pressurized only in D range and should be same as line pressure within 3 psi (21 kPa) up to downshift point.

Test Four - Transmission In Reverse

This test checks pump output, pressure regulation and the front clutch and rear servo circuits. Use 300 psi Test Gauge C-3293-SP for this test.

(1) Connect 300 psi gauge to rear servo port (Fig. 8) and (Fig. 9).

(2) Start and run engine at 1600 rpm for test.

(3) Move valve body selector lever four detents rearward from the full forward position. This is Reverse range.

(4) Move throttle lever all way forward then all way rearward and note gauge readings.

(5) Pressure should be 145 - 175 psi (1000-1207 kPa) with lever forward and increase to 230 - 280 psi (1586-1931 kPa) as lever is moved rearward.

DIAGNOSIS AND TESTING (Continued)

Test Five - Governor Pressure

This test checks governor operation by measuring governor pressure response to changes in engine speed. It is usually not necessary to check governor operation unless shift speeds are incorrect or if the transmission will not downshift.

(1) Connect 100 psi Test Gauge C-3292 to governor pressure port (Fig. 8) and (Fig. 9).

(2) Move shift lever to D range.

(3) Start and run engine at curb idle speed and note pressure. At idle and with vehicle stopped, pressure should be zero to 1.5 psi maximum. If pressure exceeds this figure, governor valve or weights are sticking open.

(4) Slowly increase engine speed and observe speedometer and pressure test gauge. Governor pressure should increase in proportion to vehicle speed. Or approximately 1 psi for every 1 mph.

(5) Pressure rise should be smooth and drop back to 0 to 1.5 psi when wheels stop rotating.

(6) Compare results of pressure tests with analysis charts (Fig. 11).

TEST CONDITION	INDICATION
Line pressure OK during any one test	Pump and regulator valve OK
Line pressure OK in R but low in D, 2, 1	Leakage in rear clutch area (servo, clutch seals, governor support seal rings on park gear)
Pressure OK in 1, 2 but low in D3 and R	Leakage in front clutch area (servo, clutch seals, retainer bore, pump seal rings)
Pressure OK in 2 but low in R and 1	Leakage in rear servo
Front servo pressure in 2	Leakage in servo (broken servo ring or cracked servo piston)
Pressure low in all positions	Clogged filter, stuck pressure regulator valve, worn or defective pump
Governor pressure too high at idle speed	Governor valve sticking open
Governor pressure low at all mph figures	Governor valve sticking closed
Lubrication pressure low at all throttle positions	Clogged drainback valve, oil cooler or lines, seal rings leaking, output shaft plugged with debris, worn bushings in pump or clutch retainer

J9521-129

Fig. 11 Pressure Test Analysis

CONVERTER STALL TEST

Stall testing involves determining maximum engine speed obtainable at full throttle with the rear wheels locked and the transmission in D range. This test checks the holding ability of the converter overrunning and transmission clutches.

WARNING: NEVER ALLOW ANYONE TO STAND DIRECTLY IN LINE WITH THE VEHICLE FRONT OR REAR DURING A STALL TEST. ALWAYS BLOCK THE WHEELS AND FULLY APPLY THE SERVICE AND PARKING BRAKES DURING THE TEST.

STALL TEST PROCEDURE

(1) Connect tachometer to engine. Position tachometer so it can be viewed from driver's seat.

(2) Check transmission fluid level. Add fluid if necessary.

(3) Drive vehicle to bring transmission fluid up to normal operating temperature. Vehicle can be driven on road, or on chassis dynamometer, if available.

(4) Block front wheels.

(5) Fully apply service and parking brakes.

(6) Open throttle completely and record maximum engine speed registered on tachometer. It takes 4-10 seconds to reach max rpm. **Once max rpm has been achieved, do not hold wide open throttle for more than 4-5 seconds.**

CAUTION: Stalling the converter causes a rapid increase in fluid temperature. To avoid fluid overheating, hold the engine at maximum rpm for no more than 5 seconds. If engine exceeds 2500 rpm during the test, release the accelerator pedal immediately; transmission clutch slippage is occurring.

(7) If a second stall test is required, cool down fluid before proceeding. Shift into NEUTRAL and run engine at 1000 rpm for 20-30 seconds to cool fluid.

(8) Refer to Stall Test Analysis.

STALL TEST ANALYSIS

Stall Speed Too High

If the stall speed exceeds 1800-2300 rpm by more than 200 rpm, transmission clutch slippage is indicated.

Stall Speed Low

Low stall speed with a properly tuned engine indicate a torque converter overrunning clutch problem. The condition should be confirmed by road testing before to converter replacement. A stall speed 250-350 rpm below normal indicates the converter overrunning clutch is slipping. The vehicle also exhibits poor acceleration but operates normally once

DIAGNOSIS AND TESTING (Continued)

highway cruise speeds are reached. Torque converter replacement will be necessary.

Stall Speed Normal But Acceleration Poor

If stall speeds are normal (1800-2300 rpm) but abnormal throttle opening is required for acceleration, or to maintain cruise speed, the converter overrunning clutch is seized. The torque converter will have to be replaced.

Converter Noise During Test

A whining noise caused by fluid flow is normal during a stall test. However, loud metallic noises indicate a damaged converter. To confirm that noise is originating from the converter, operate the vehicle at light throttle in DRIVE and NEUTRAL on a hoist and listen for noise coming from the converter housing.

AIR TESTING TRANSMISSION CLUTCH AND BAND OPERATION

Air-pressure testing can be used to check transmission front/rear clutch and band operation. The test can be conducted with the transmission either in the vehicle or on the work bench, as a final check, after overhaul.

Air-pressure testing requires that the oil pan and valve body be removed from the transmission. The servo and clutch apply passages are shown (Fig. 12).

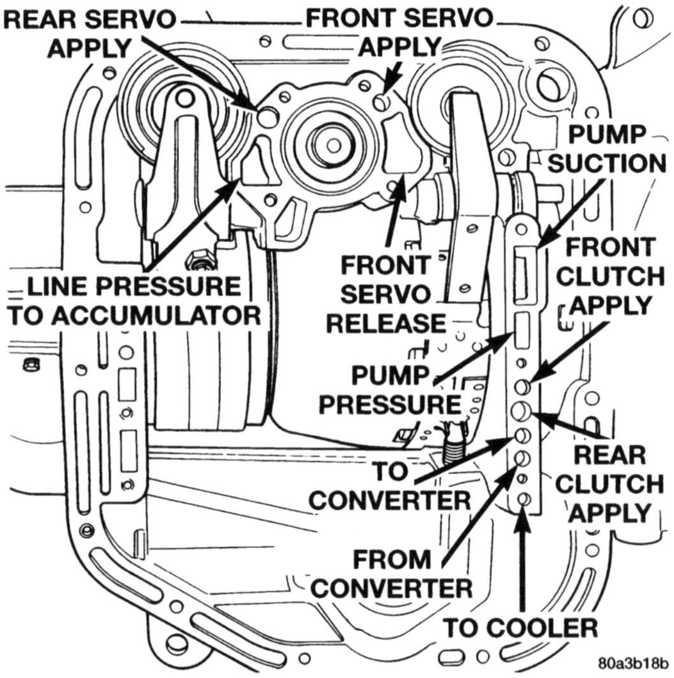

Fig. 12 Air Pressure Test Passages—Typical

Front Clutch Air Test

Place one or two fingers on the clutch housing and apply air pressure through front clutch apply passage. Piston movement can be felt and a soft thump heard as the clutch applies.

Rear Clutch Air Test

Place one or two fingers on the clutch housing and apply air pressure through rear clutch apply passage. Piston movement can be felt and a soft thump heard as the clutch applies.

Front Servo Air Test

Apply air pressure to the front servo apply passage. The servo rod should extend and cause the band to tighten around the drum. Spring pressure should release the servo when air pressure is removed.

Rear Servo Air Test

Apply air pressure to the rear servo apply passage. The servo rod should extend and cause the band to tighten around the drum. Spring pressure should release the servo when air pressure is removed.

CONVERTER HOUSING FLUID LEAK DIAGNOSIS

When diagnosing converter housing fluid leaks, two items must be established before repair.

(1) Verify that a leak condition actually exists.

(2) Determined the true source of the leak.

Some suspected converter housing fluid leaks may not be leaks at all. They may only be the result of residual fluid in the converter housing, or excess fluid spilled during factory fill or fill after repair. Converter housing leaks have several potential sources. Through careful observation, a leak source can be identified before removing the transmission for repair. Pump seal leaks tend to move along the drive hub and onto the rear of the converter. Pump O-ring or pump body leaks follow the same path as a seal leak (Fig. 13). Pump vent or pump attaching bolt leaks are generally deposited on the inside of the converter housing and not on the converter itself (Fig. 13). Pump seal or gasket leaks usually travel down the inside of the converter housing. Front band lever pin plug leaks are generally deposited on the housing and not on the converter.

LEAK DIAGNOSIS PROCEDURE

(1) Raise rear of vehicle and allow accumulated fluid to drain out of converter housing.

(2) Check and adjust transmission fluid level.

(3) Raise vehicle. Remove converter housing dust cover and wipe as much fluid as possible from converter housing.

(4) Fabricate test probe (Fig. 14). Attach probe to converter housing with a dust shield bolt.

(5) Have a helper run engine at 2500 rpm (with transmission in Neutral) for two minutes; then stop engine.

DIAGNOSIS AND TESTING (Continued)

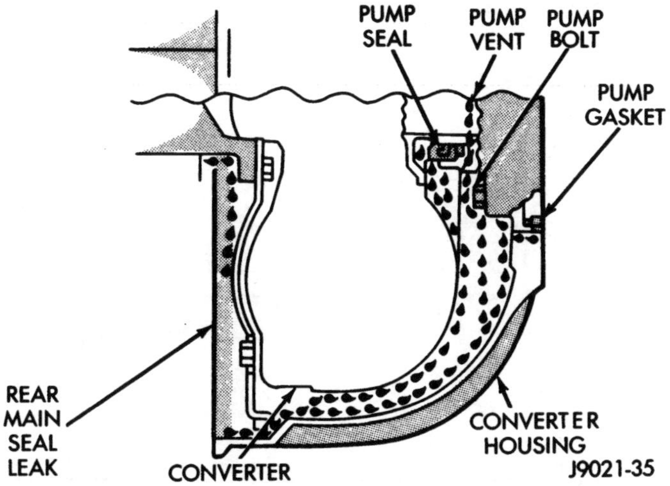

Fig. 13 Converter Housing Leak Paths

(6) Inspect test probe and converter housing. If a leak is evident, note color of fluid. Transmission fluid is red. Engine oil ranges in color from brown to green, or to black when oil is dirty.

(7) Check probe **upper surface**. If upper surface is dry, converter and seal are OK. If probe upper surface is wet, converter and/or seal is leaking.

(8) Fluid leaking **under** the probe is coming from pump housing area. Leak could be from: pump seal and/or bushing, pump vent, kickdown lever shaft access plug, pump bolts, or porous spots in pump body or transmission case (Fig. 15).

(9) If porous spots in the transmission case or pump body are the suspected leak source, pressurize transmission as described in Leak Testing With Air Pressure.

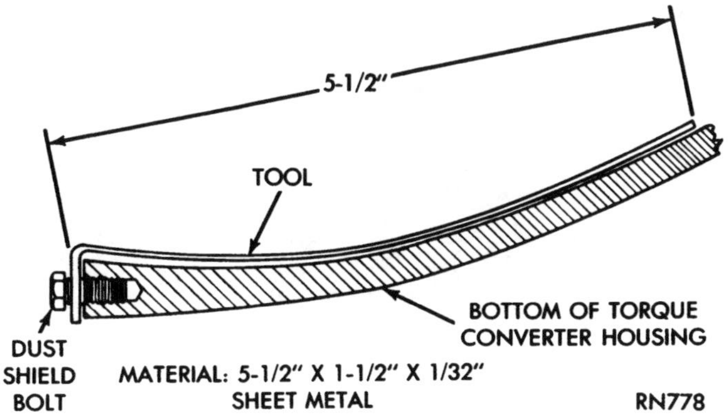

Fig. 14 Leak Test Probe

TORQUE CONVERTER LEAK POINTS

Possible sources of converter leaks are:

(1) Leaks at the weld joint around the outside diameter weld (Fig. 15).

(2) Leaks at the converter hub weld (Fig. 16).

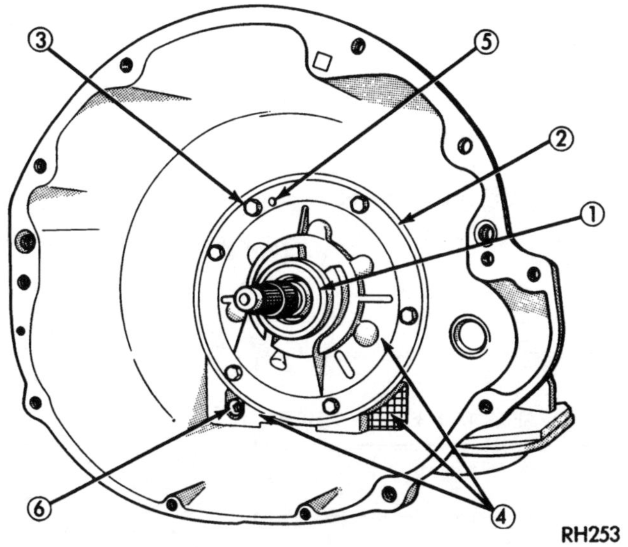

Fig. 15 Pump Area Inspection Points

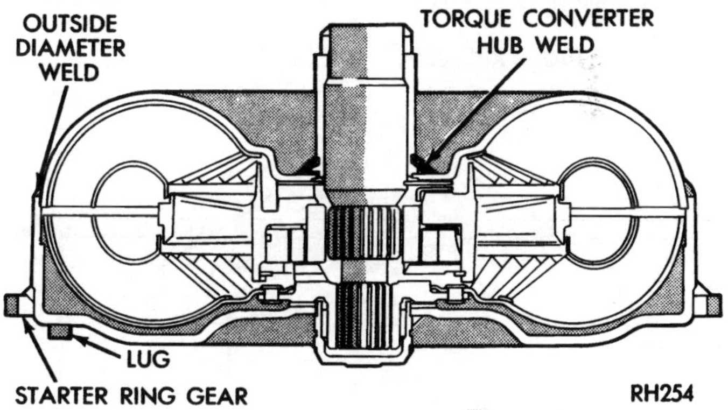

Fig. 16 Converter Leak Points—Typical

LEAK TESTING WITH AIR PRESSURE

This test involves closing off all openings and pressurizing the transmission to 8 psi with hand operated Air Pump Tool 7700.

A soapy water solution is applied to suspected leak points before and during the pressure test. Leaks will be indicated by the presence of air bubbles coming through the solution.

Some transmission openings such as the fill tube and front cooler line fitting can be closed off with a rubber plug or similar device. Plugs can secured with wire or duct tape.

The transmission rear output shaft opening is closed off simply by leaving the transfer case bolted in place. However, if the transfer case has been removed, a shipping plug can used to close off this opening.

The torque converter hub opening in the pump and the pump vent require special tools to close them off.

The converter hub seal cup is made from thin wall tube and a 3.17 mm (1/8 in.) thick disc (Fig. 17).

A retaining strap is needed to secure the seal cup for testing. The strap can be made from 31.75 mm

DIAGNOSIS AND TESTING (Continued)

(1-1/4 in.) wide stock (Fig. 18). The strap attaching hole positions are approximate only. Measure hole position on the converter housing before drilling.

The pump vent tool is made from 6.35 mm (1/4 in.) rod and 4.76 mm (3/16 in.) plate (Fig. 19).

The fabricated tools can all be made from mild steel or aluminum stock.

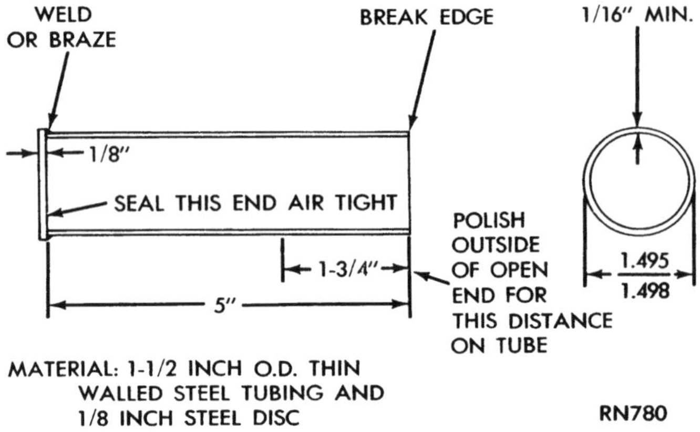

Fig. 17 Converter Hub Seal Cup

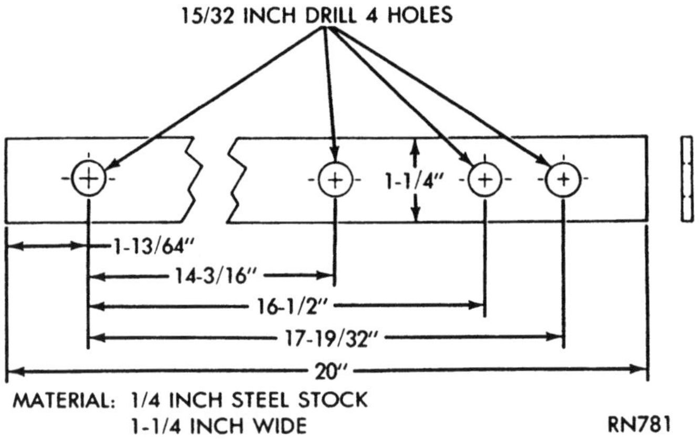

Fig. 18 Seal Cup Retaining Strap

AIR PRESSURE LEAK TEST PROCEDURE

(1) Install vent plug, converter hub seal cup and cup retaining strap (Fig. 20).

CAUTION: Be sure the surfaces of the hub seal cup are smooth and free of nicks, scratches, or burrs. Surface irregularities on the cup will damage the pump seal if not removed. Sand and/polish the cup with 400 grit sandpaper or crocus cloth to smooth the surface if necessary.

(2) Close off remaining transmission openings with rubber plugs, or stoppers or similar devices. **Do not close off rear cooler line fitting. Hand operated air pump will be attached to this fitting.**

(3) Attach Air Pump 7700 to rear cooler line fitting. Connect a length of copper tube to fitting. Then attach pump hose to tube with hose clamp (Fig. 21).

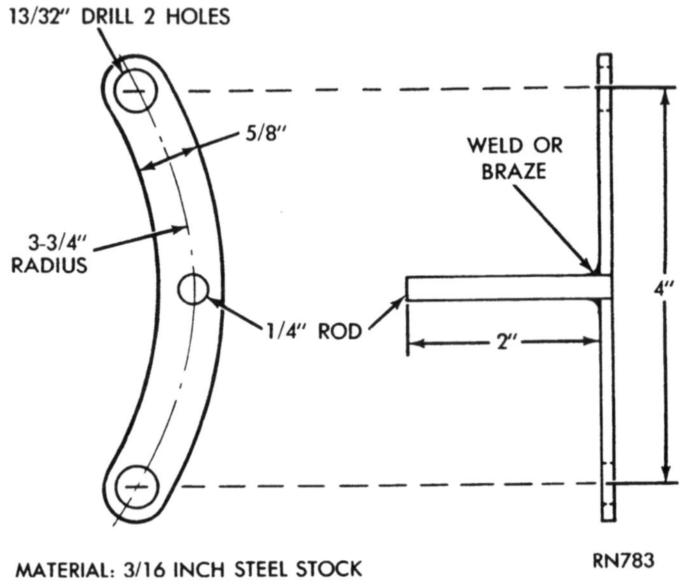

Fig. 19 Pump Vent Plug

(4) Apply a thick soapy water solution to suspected leak areas.

CAUTION: The recommended test pressure is 8 psi. The maximum allowable test pressure is 10 psi. Do not exceed specified pressure.

(5) Pressurize transmission to 8 psi. with air pump.

(6) Observe suspected leak areas. Air bubbles appearing in soapy water solution indicate leak points.

(7) Remove test tools and plugs after test completion and make necessary repairs as described in Leak Correction procedure.

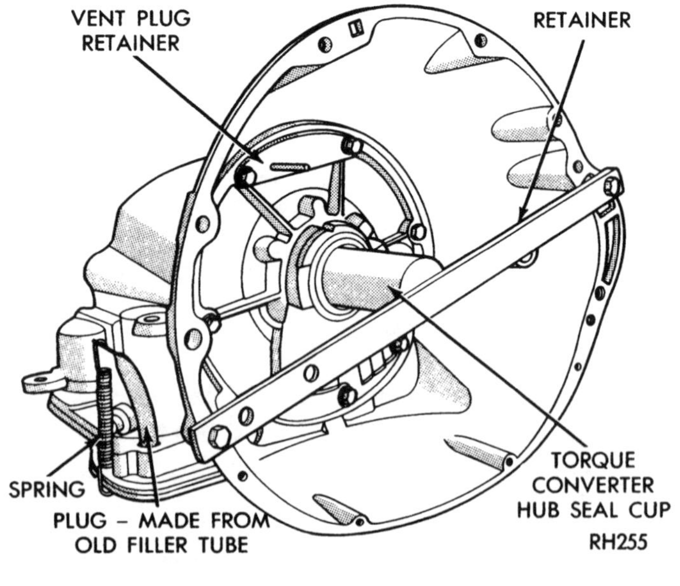

Fig. 20 Vent Plug And Hub Seal Cup Installation

DIAGNOSIS AND TESTING (Continued)

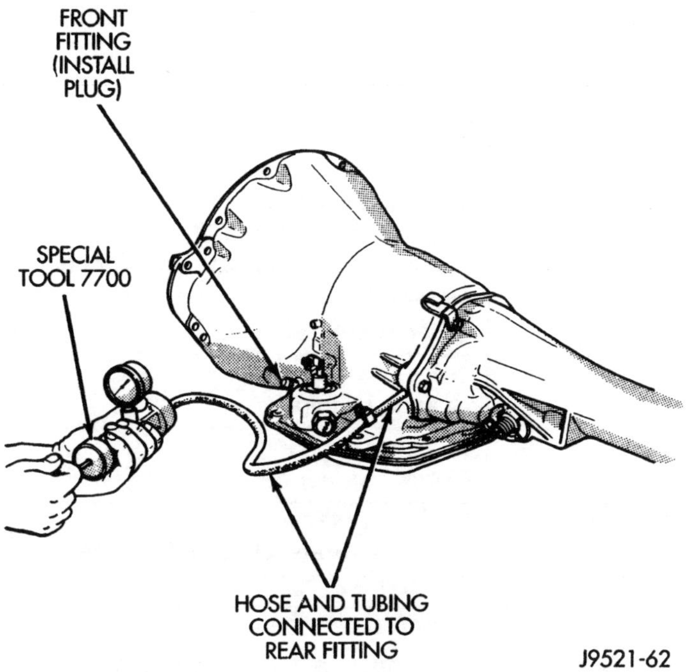

Fig. 21 Pressurizing Transmission With Tool 7700

CONVERTER HOUSING AREA LEAK CORRECTION

(1) Remove converter.

(2) Tighten front band adjusting screw until band is tight around front clutch retainer. This prevents front/rear clutches from coming out when oil pump is removed.

(3) Remove oil pump and remove pump seal. Inspect pump housing drainback and vent holes for obstructions. Clear holes with solvent and wire.

(4) Inspect pump bushing and converter hub. If bushing is scored, replace it. If converter hub is scored, either polish it with crocus cloth or replace converter if scoring is severe.

(5) Install new pump seal, O-ring, gasket, bushing. Replace oil pump if cracked, porous or damaged in any way.

(6) Loosen kickdown lever pin access plug three turns. Apply Loctite 592, or Permatex No. 2 to plug threads and tighten plug to 17 N·m (150 in. lbs.) torque.

(7) Adjust front band.

(8) Lubricate pump seal and converter hub with transmission fluid or petroleum jelly and install converter.

(9) Install transmission and converter housing dust shield.

(10) Lower vehicle.

DIAGNOSIS CHARTS

The diagnosis charts provide additional reference when diagnosing a transmission fault. The charts provide general information on a variety of transmission, overdrive unit and converter clutch fault conditions.

The hydraulic flow charts, in the Schematics and Diagrams section of this group, outline fluid flow and hydraulic circuitry. Circuit operation is provided for neutral, third, fourth and reverse gear ranges. Normal working pressures are also supplied for each of the gear ranges.

DIAGNOSIS AND TESTING (Continued)

CONDITION	POSSIBLE CAUSES	CORRECTION
HARSH ENGAGEMENT FROM NEUTRAL TO DRIVE OR REVERSE	1. Fluid Level Low	1. Add Fluid
	2. Throttle Linkage Misadjusted	2. Adjust linkage - setting may be too long.
	3. Mount and Driveline Bolts Loose	3. Check engine mount, transmission mount, propeller shaft, rear spring to body bolts, rear control arms, crossmember and axle bolt torque. Tighten loose bolts and replace missing bolts.
	4. U-Joint Worn/Broken	4. Remove propeller shaft and replace U-Joint.
	5. Axle Backlash Incorrect	5. Check per Service Manual. Correct as needed.
	6. Hydraulic Pressure Incorrect	6. Check pressure. Remove, overhaul or adjust valve body as needed.
	7. Band Misadjusted.	7. Adjust rear band.
	8. Valve Body Check Balls Missing.	8. Inspect valve body for proper check ball installation.
	9. Axle Pinion Flange Loose.	9. Replace nut and check pinion threads before installing new nut. Replace pinion gear if threads are damaged.
	10. Clutch, band or planetary component Damaged.	10. Remove, disassemble and repair transmission as necessary.
	11. Converter Clutch (if equipped) Faulty.	11. Replace converter and flush cooler and line before installing new converter.
DELAYED ENGAGEMENT FROM NEUTRAL TO DRIVE OR REVERSE	1. Fluid Level Low.	1. Correct level and check for leaks.
	2. Filter Clogged.	2. Change filter.
	3. Gearshift Linkage Misadjusted.	3. Adjust linkage and repair linkage if worn or damaged.
	5. Rear Band Misadjusted.	5. Adjust band.
	6. Valve Body Filter Plugged.	6. Replace fluid and filter. If oil pan and old fluid were full of clutch disc material and/or metal particles, overhaul will be necessary.
	7. Oil Pump Gears Worn/Damaged.	7. Remove transmission and replace oil pump.
	8. Hydraulic Pressure Incorrect.	8. Perform pressure test, remove transmission and repair as needed.
	9. Reaction Shaft Seal Rings Worn/Broken.	9. Remove transmission, remove oil pump and replace seal rings.
	10. Rear Clutch/Input Shaft, Rear Clutch Seal Rings Damaged.	10. Remove and disassemble transmission and repair as necessary.

DIAGNOSIS AND TESTING (Continued)

CONDITION	POSSIBLE CAUSES	CORRECTION
	11. Governor Valve Stuck.	11. Remove and inspect governor components. Replace worn or damaged parts.
	12. Regulator Valve Stuck.	12. Clean.
	13. Cooler Plugged.	13. Transfer case failure can plug cooler.
NO DRIVE RANGE (REVERSE OK)	1. Fluid Level Low.	1. Add fluid and check for leaks if drive is restored.
	2. Gearshift Linkage/Cable Loose/Misadjusted.	2. Repair or replace linkage components.
	3. Rear Clutch Burnt.	3. Remove and disassemble transmission and rear clutch and seals. Repair/replace worn or damaged parts as needed.
	4. Valve Body Malfunction.	4. Remove and disassemble valve body. Replace assembly if any valves or bores are damaged.
	5. Transmission Overrunning Clutch Broken.	5. Remove and disassemble transmission. Replace overrunning clutch.
	6. Input Shaft Seal Rings Worn/ Damaged.	6. Remove and disassemble transmission. Replace seal rings and any other worn or damaged parts.
	7. Front Planetary Failed Broken.	7. Remove and repair.
NO DRIVE OR REVERSE (VEHICLE WILL NOT MOVE)	1. Fluid Level Low.	1. Add fluid and check for leaks if drive is restored.
	2. Gearshift Linkage/Cable Loose/Misadjusted.	2. Inspect, adjust and reassemble linkage as needed. Replace worn/damaged parts.
	3. U-Joint/Axle/Transfer Case Broken.	3. Perform preliminary inspection procedure for vehicle that will not move. Refer to procedure in diagnosis section.
	4. Filter Plugged.	4. Remove and disassemble transmission. Repair or replace failed components as needed. Replace filter. If filter and fluid contained clutch material or metal particles, an overhaul may be necessary. Perform lube flow test. Flush oil. Replace cooler as necessary.
	5. Oil Pump Damaged.	5. Perform pressure test to confirm low pressure. Replace pump body assembly if necessary.

DIAGNOSIS AND TESTING (Continued)

CONDITION	POSSIBLE CAUSES	CORRECTION
	6. Valve Body Malfunctioned.	6. Check press and inspect valve body. Replace valve body (as assembly) if any valve or bore is damaged. Clean and reassemble correctly if all parts are in good condition.
	7. Transmission Internal Component Damaged.	7. Remove and disassemble transmission. Repair or replace failed components as needed. Remove and disassemble transmission. Repair or replace failed components as needed.
	8. Park Sprag not Releasing - Check Stall Speed, Worn/Damaged/ Stuck.	8. Remove, disassemble, repair.
	9. Torque Converter Damage.	9. Inspect and replace as required.
SHIFTS DELAYED OR ERRATIC (SHIFTS ALSO HARSH AT TIMES)	1. Fluid Level Low/High.	1. Correct fluid level and check for leaks if low.
	2. Fluid Filter Clogged.	2. Replace filter. If filter and fluid contained clutch material or metal particles, an overhaul may be necessary. Perform lube flow test.
	3. Throttle Linkage Misadjusted.	3. Adjust linkage as described in service section.
	4. Throttle Linkage Binding.	4. Check cable for binding. Check for return to closed throttle at transmission.
	5. Gearshift Linkage/Cable Misadjusted.	5. Adjust linkage/cable as described in service section.
	6. Governor Valve Sticking.	6. Inspect, clean or repair.
	7. Governor Seal Rings Worn/ Damaged.	7. Inspect/replace.
	8. Clutch or Servo Failure.	8. Remove valve body and air test clutch, and band servo operation. Disassemble and repair transmission as needed.
	9. Front Band Misadjusted.	9. Adjust band.
	10. Pump Suction Passage Leak.	10. Check for excessive foam on dipstick after normal driving. Check for loose pump bolts, defective gasket. Replace pump assembly if needed.
NO REVERSE (D RANGES OK)	1. Gearshift Linkage/Cable Misadjusted/Damaged.	1. Repair or replace linkage parts as needed.
	2. Park Sprag Sticking.	2. Replace overdrive annulus gear.
	3. Rear Band Misadjusted/Worn.	3. Adjust band; replace.
	4. Valve Body Malfunction.	4. Remove and service valve body. Replace valve body if any valves or valve bores are worn or damaged.

DIAGNOSIS AND TESTING (Continued)

CONDITION	POSSIBLE CAUSES	CORRECTION
	5. Rear Servo Malfunction.	5. Remove and disassemble transmission. Replace worn/ damaged servo parts as necessary.
	6. Direct Clutch in Overdrive Worn	6. Disassemble overdrive. Replace worn or damaged parts.
	7. Front Clutch Burnt.	7. Remove and disassemble transmission. Replace worn, damaged clutch parts as required.
HAS FIRST/REVERSE ONLY (NO 1-2 OR 2-3 UPSHIFT)	1. Governor Valve, Shaft, Weights or Body Damaged/Stuck.	1. Remove governor assembly and clean or repair as necessary.
	2. Valve Body Malfunction.	2. Stuck 1-2 shift valve or governor plug.
	3. Front Servo/Kickdown Band Damaged/Burned.	3. Repair/replace.
MOVES IN 2ND OR 3RD GEAR, ABRUPTLY DOWNSHIFTS TO LOW	1. Valve Body Malfunction.	1. Remove, clean and inspect. Look for stuck 1-2 valve or governor plug.
	2. Governor Valve Sticking.	2. Remove, clean and inspect. Replace faulty parts.
NO LOW GEAR (MOVES IN 2ND OR 3RD GEAR ONLY)	1. Governor Valve Sticking.	1. Remove governor, clean, inspect and repair as required.
	2. Valve Body Malfunction.	2. Remove, clean and inspect. Look for sticking 1-2 shift valve, 2-3 shift valve, governor plug or broken springs.
	3. Front Servo Piston Cocked in Bore.	3. Inspect servo and repair as required.
	4. Front Band Linkage Malfunction	4. Inspect linkage and look for bind in linkage.
NO KICKDOWN OR NORMAL DOWNSHIFT	1. Throttle Linkage Misadjusted.	1. Adjust linkage.
	2. Accelerator Pedal Travel Restricted.	2. Floor mat under pedal, accelerator cable worn or brackets bent.
	3. Governor/Valve Body Hydraulic Pressures Too High or Too Low Due to Sticking Governor, Valve Body Malfunction or Incorrect Hydraulic Control Pressure Adjustments.	3. Perform hydraulic pressure tests to determine cause and repair as required. Correct valve body pressure adjustments as required.
	4. Valve Body Malfunction.	4. Perform hydraulic pressure tests to determine cause and repair as required. Correct valve body pressure adjustments as required.
	5. TPS Malfunction.	5. Replace sensor, check with DRB scan tool.
	6. PCM Malfunction.	6. Check with DRB II and replace if required.
	7. Valve Body Malfunction.	7. Sticking 1-2, 2-3 shift valves, governor plugs, 3-4 solenoid, 3-4 shift valve, 3-4 timing valve.

DIAGNOSIS AND TESTING (Continued)

CONDITION	POSSIBLE CAUSES	CORRECTION
STUCK IN LOW GEAR (WILL NOT UPSHIFT)	1. Throttle Linkage Misadjusted/ Stuck.	1. Adjust linkage and repair linkage if worn or damaged. Check for binding cable or missing return spring.
	2. Gearshift Linkage Misadjusted.	2. Adjust linkage and repair linkage if worn or damaged.
	3. Governor/Valve Body, Governor Valve Stuck Closed; Loose Output Shaft Support or Governor Housing Bolts, Leaking Seal Rings or Valve Body Problem (i.e., Stuck 1- 2 Shift Valve/Gov. Plug).	3. Check line and governor pressures to determine cause. Correct as required.
	4. Governor Component (RE Only) Electrical Fault.	4. Check operating pressures and test with DRB scan tool, repair faulty component.
	5. Front Band Out of Adjustment.	5. Adjust Band.
	6. Clutch or Servo Malfunction.	6. Air pressure check operation of clutches and bands. Repair faulty component.
CREEPS IN NEUTRAL	1. Gearshift Linkage Misadjusted.	1. Adjust linkage.
	2. Rear Clutch Dragging/Warped Welded.	2. Disassemble and repair.
	3. Valve Body Malfunction.	3. Perform hydraulic pressure test to determine cause and repair as required.
BUZZING NOISE	1. Fluid Level Low	1. Add fluid and check for leaks.
	2. Shift Cable Misassembled.	2. Route cable away from engine and bell housing.
	3. Valve Body Misassembled.	3. Remove, disassemble, inspect valve body. Reassemble correctly if necessary. Replace assembly if valves or springs are damaged. Check for loose bolts or screws.
	4. Pump Passages Leaking	4. Check pump for porous casting, scores on mating surfaces and excess rotor clearance. Repair as required. Loose pump bolts.
	5. Cooling System Cooler Plugged.	5. Flow check cooler circuit. Repair as needed.
	6.Overrunning Clutch Damaged.	6. Replace clutch.
SLIPS IN REVERSE ONLY	1. Fluid Level Low.	1. Add fluid and check for leaks.
	2. Gearshift Linkage Misadjusted.	2. Adjust linkage.
	3. Rear Band Misadjusted.	3. Adjust band.
	4. Rear Band Worn.	4. Replace as required.
	5. Hydraulic Pressure Too Low.	5. Perform hydraulic pressure tests to determine cause.
	6. Rear Servo Leaking.	6. Air pressure check clutch-servo operation and repair as required.
	7. Band Linkage Binding.	7. Inspect and repair as required.

DIAGNOSIS AND TESTING (Continued)

CONDITION	POSSIBLE CAUSES	CORRECTION
SLIPS IN FORWARD DRIVE RANGES	1. Fluid Level Low.	1. Add fluid and check for leaks.
	2. Fluid Foaming.	2. Check for high oil level, bad pump gasket or seals, dirt between pump halves and loose pump bolts. Replace pump if necessary.
	3. Throttle Linkage Misadjusted.	3. Adjust linkage.
	4. Gearshift Linkage Misadjusted.	4. Adjust linkage.
	5. Rear Clutch Worn.	5. Inspect and replace as needed.
	6. Low Hydraulic Pressure Due to Worn Pump, Incorrect Control Pressure Adjustments, Valve Body Warpage or Malfunction, Sticking Governor, Leaking Seal Rings, Clutch Seals Leaking, Servo Leaks, Clogged Filter or Cooler Lines	6. Perform hydraulic and air pressure tests to determine cause.
	7. Rear Clutch Malfunction, Leaking Seals or Worn Plates.	7. Air pressure check clutch-servo operation and repair as required.
	8. Overrunning Clutch Worn, Not Holding (Slips in 1 Only).	8. Replace Clutch.
SLIPS IN LOW GEAR "D" ONLY, BUT NO IN 1 POSITION	Overrunning Clutch Faulty.	Replace overrunning clutch.
GROWLING, GRATING OR SCRAPING NOISES	1. Drive Plate Broken.	1. Replace.
	2. Torque Converter Bolts Hitting Dust Shield.	2. Dust shield bent. Replace or repair.
	3. Planetary Gear Set Broken/ Seized.	3. Check for debris in oil pan and repair as required.
	4. Overrunning Clutch Worn/Broken.	4. Inspect and check for debris in oil pan. Repair as required.
	5. Oil Pump Components Scored/ Binding.	5. Remove, inspect and repair as required.
	6. Output Shaft Bearing or Bushing Damaged.	6. Remove, inspect and repair as required.
	7. Clutch Operation Faulty.	7. Perform air pressure check and repair as required.
	8. Front and Rear Bands Misadjusted.	8. Adjust bands.
DRAGS OR LOCKS UP	1. Fluid Level Low.	1. Check and adjust level.
	2. Clutch Dragging/Failed	2. Air pressure check clutch operation and repair as required.
	3. Front or Rear Band Misadjusted.	3. Adjust bands.
	4. Case Leaks Internally.	4. Check for leakage between passages in case.
	5. Servo Band or Linkage Malfunction.	5. Air pressure check servo operation and repair as required.
	6. Overrunning Clutch Worn.	6. Remove and inspect clutch. Repair as required.
	7. Planetary Gears Broken.	7. Remove, inspect and repair as required (look for debris in oil pan).

DIAGNOSIS AND TESTING (Continued)

CONDITION	POSSIBLE CAUSES	CORRECTION
	8. Converter Clutch Dragging.	8. Check for plugged cooler. Perform flow check. Inspect pump for excessive side clearance. Replace pump as required.
WHINE/NOISE RELATED TO ENGINE SPEED	1. Fluid Level Low.	1. Add fluid and check for leaks.
	2. Shift Cable Incorrect Routing.	2. Check shift cable for correct routing. Should no touch engine or bell housing.
TORQUE CONVERTER LOCKS UP IN SECOND AND/OR THIRD GEAR	Lockup Solenoid, Relay or Wiring Shorted/Open.	Test solenoid, relay and wiring for continuity, shorts or grounds. Replace solenoid and relay if faulty. Repair wiring and connectors as necessary.
HARSH 1-2 OR 2-3 SHIFTS	Lockup Solenoid Malfunction.	Remove valve body and replace solenoid assembly.
NO START IN PARK OR NEUTRAL	1. Gearshift Linkage/Cable Misadjusted.	1. Adjust linkage/cable.
	2. Neutral Switch Wire Open/Cut.	2. Check continuity with test lamp. Repair as required.
	3. Neutral Switch Faulty.	3. Refer to service section for test and replacement procedure.
	4. Neutral Switch Connect Faulty.	4. Connectors spread open. Repair.
	5. Valve Body Manual Lever Assembly Bent/Worn/Broken.	5. Inspect lever assembly and replace if damaged.
NO REVERSE (OR SLIPS IN REVERSE)	1. Direct Clutch Pack (front clutch) Worn.	1. Disassemble unit and rebuild clutch pack.
	2. Rear Band Misadjusted.	2. Adjust band.
	3. Front Clutch Malfunctioned/Burnt.	3. Air pressure test clutch operation. Remove and rebuild if necessary.
OIL LEAKS (ITEMS LISTED REPRESENT POSSIBLE LEAK POINTS AND SHOULD ALL BE CHECKED.	1. Speedometer Adapter Leaks.	1. Replace both adapter seals.
	2. Fluid Lines and Fittings Loose/Leaks/Damaged.	2. Tighten fittings. If leaks persist, replace fittings and lines if necessary.
	3. Filler Tube (where tube enters case) Leaks/Damaged.	3. Replace O-ring seal. Inspect tube for cracks in tube.
	4. Pressure Port Plug Loose Loose/Damaged.	4. Tighten to correct torque. Replace plug or reseal if leak persists.
	5. Pan Gasket Leaks.	5. Tighten pan screws to 150 inch pounds. If leaks persist, replace gasket. Do no over tighten screws.
	6. Valve Body Manual Lever Shaft Seal Leaks/Worn.	6. Replace shaft seal.
	7. Rear Bearing Access Plate Leaks.	7. Replace gasket. Tighten screws.
	8. Gasket Damaged or Bolts are Loose.	8. Replace bolts or gasket or tighten both.

DIAGNOSIS AND TESTING (Continued)

CONDITION	POSSIBLE CAUSES	CORRECTION
	9. Adapter/Extension Gasket Damaged Leaks/Damaged.	9. Replace gasket.
	10. Neutral Switch Leaks/Damaged.	10. Replace switch and gasket.
	11. Converter Housing Area Leaks.	11. Check for leaks at seal caused by worn seal or burr on converter hub (cutting seal), worn bushing, missing oil return, oil in front pump housing or hole plugged. Check for leaks past O-ring seal on pump or past pump-to-case bolts; pump housing porous, oil coming out vent due to overfill or leak past front band shaft access plug.
	12. Pump Seal Leaks/Worn/ Damaged.	12. Replace seal.
	13. Torque Converter Weld Leak/Cracked Hub.	13. Replace converter.
	14. Case Porosity Leaks.	14. Replace case.

SERVICE PROCEDURES

FLUID LEVEL CHECK

Transmission fluid level should be checked monthly under normal operation. If the vehicle is used for trailer towing or similar heavy load hauling, check fluid level and condition weekly. Fluid level is checked with the engine running at curb idle speed, the transmission in NEUTRAL and the transmission fluid at normal operating temperature.

FLUID LEVEL CHECK PROCEDURE

(1) Transmission fluid must be at normal operating temperature for accurate fluid level check. Drive vehicle if necessary to bring fluid temperature up to normal hot operating temperature of 82°C (180°F).

(2) Position vehicle on level surface.

(3) Start and run engine at curb idle speed.

(4) Apply parking brakes.

(5) Shift transmission momentarily into all gear ranges. Then shift transmission back to Neutral.

(6) Clean top of filler tube and dipstick to keep dirt from entering tube.

(7) Remove dipstick (Fig. 22) and check fluid level as follows:

(a) Correct maximum level is to MAX arrow mark. Correct acceptable level is in crosshatch area.

(b) Incorrect level is at or below MIN line.

(c) If fluid is low, add only enough Mopar ATF Plus to restore correct level. Do not overfill.

CAUTION: Do not overfill the transmission. Overfilling may cause leakage out the pump vent which can be mistaken for a pump seal leak. Overfilling will also cause fluid aeration and foaming as the excess fluid is picked up and churned by the gear train. This will significantly reduce fluid life.

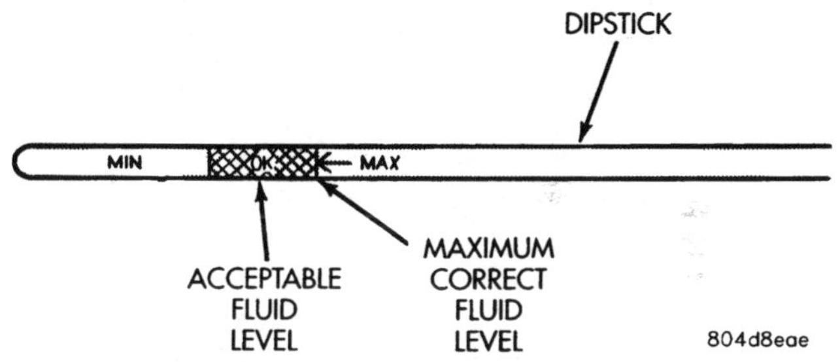

Fig. 22 Dipstick Fluid Level Marks—Typical

FLUID AND FILTER REPLACEMENT

Refer to the Maintenance Schedules in Group 0, Lubrication and Maintenance for proper service intervals. The service fluid fill after a filter change is approximately 3.8 liters (4.0 quarts).

PAN AND FILTER REMOVAL

(1) Hoist and support vehicle on safety stands.

(2) Place a large diameter shallow drain pan beneath the transmission pan.

(3) Remove bolts holding front and sides of pan to transmission (Fig. 23).

(4) Loosen bolts holding rear of pan to transmission.

(5) Slowly separate front of pan away from transmission allowing the fluid to drain into drain pan.

(6) Hold up pan and remove remaining bolt holding pan to transmission.

SERVICE PROCEDURES (Continued)

(7) While holding pan level, lower pan away from transmission.

(8) Pour remaining fluid in pan into drain pan.

(9) Remove screws holding filter to valve body (Fig. 24).

(10) Separate filter from valve body and pour fluid in filter into drain pan.

(11) Dispose used trans fluid and filter properly.

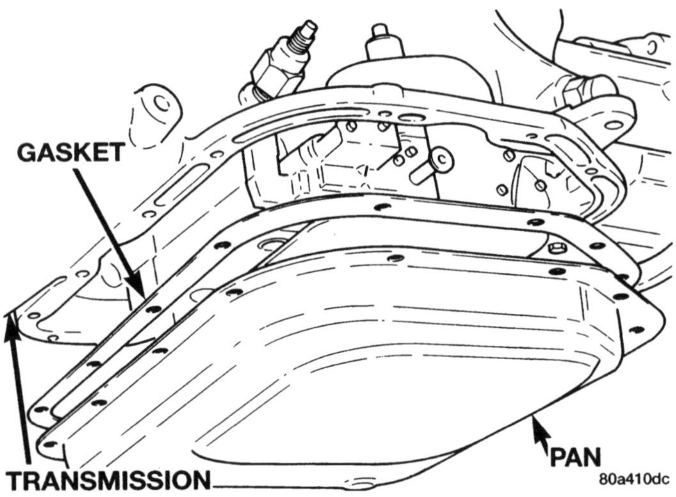

Fig. 23 Transmission Pan

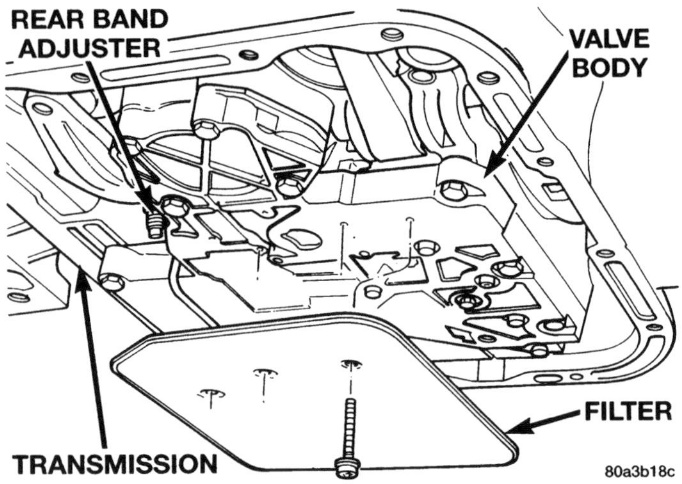

Fig. 24 Transmission Filter

INSPECTION AND CLEANING

INSPECTION

Inspect bottom of pan and magnet for excessive amounts of metal or fiber contamination. A light coating of clutch or band material on the bottom of the pan does not indicate a problem unless accompanied by slipping condition or shift lag. If fluid and pan are contaminated with excessive amounts or debris, refer to the diagnosis section of this group.

Check the adjustment of the front and rear bands, adjust if necessary. Refer to Adjustment section of this group for proper procedure.

CLEANING

(1) Using a suitable solvent, clean pan and magnet (Fig. 25).

(2) Using a suitable gasket scraper, clean gasket material from gasket surface of transmission case and the gasket flange around the pan.

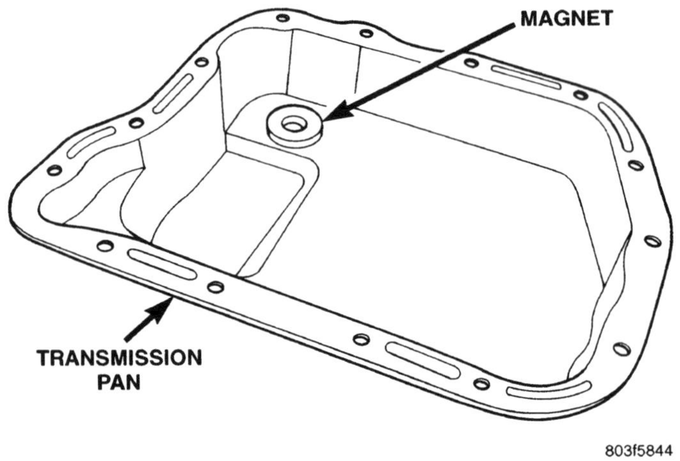

Fig. 25 Pan and Magnet

FILTER AND PAN INSTALLATION

(1) Place replacement filter in position on valve body.

(2) Install screws to hold filter to valve body (Fig. 24). Tighten screws to 4 N·m (35 in. lbs.) torque.

(3) Place new gasket in position on pan. and install pan on transmission.

(4) Place pan in position on transmission.

(5) Install screws to hold pan to transmission (Fig. 23). Tighten bolts to 17 N·m (150 in. lbs.) torque.

(6) Lower vehicle and fill transmission with Mopar ATF Plus, type 7176 fluid.

TRANSMISSION FILL PROCEDURE

To avoid overfilling transmission after a fluid change or overhaul, perform the following procedure:

(1) Remove dipstick and insert clean funnel in transmission fill tube.

(2) Add following initial quantity of Mopar ATF Plus to transmission:

(a) If only fluid and filter were changed, add **3 pints (1-1/2 quarts)** of ATF Plus to transmission.

(b) If transmission was completely overhauled, torque converter was replaced or drained, and cooler was flushed, add **12 pints (6 quarts)** of ATF Plus to transmission.

(3) Apply parking brakes.

(4) Start and run engine at normal curb idle speed.

(5) Apply service brakes, shift transmission through all gear ranges then back to NEUTRAL, set parking brake, and leave engine running at curb idle speed.

SERVICE PROCEDURES (Continued)

(6) Remove funnel, insert dipstick and check fluid level. If level is low, **add fluid to bring level to MIN mark on dipstick.**

(7) Drive vehicle until transmission fluid is at normal operating temperature.

(8) With the engine running at curb idle speed, the gear selector in NEUTRAL, and the parking brake applied, check the transmission fluid level.

CAUTION: Do not overfill transmission, fluid foaming and shifting problems can result.

(9) Add fluid to bring level up to MAX arrow mark.

When fluid level is correct, shut engine off, release park brake, remove funnel, and install dipstick in fill tube.

CONVERTER DRAINBACK CHECK VALVE SERVICE

The converter drainback check valve is located in the cooler outlet (pressure) line near the radiator lower tank. The valve prevents fluid drainback when the vehicle is parked for lengthy periods. The valve check ball is spring loaded and has an opening pressure of approximately 2 psi.

The valve is serviced as an assembly; it is not repairable. Do not clean the valve if restricted, or contaminated by sludge, or debris. If the valve fails, or if a transmission malfunction occurs that generates sludge and/or clutch particles and metal shavings, the valve must be replaced.

The valve must be removed whenever the cooler and lines are reverse flushed. The valve can be flow tested when necessary. The procedure is exactly the same as for flow testing a cooler.

If the valve is restricted, installed backwards, or in the wrong line, it will cause an overheating condition and possible transmission failure.

CAUTION: The drainback valve is a one-way flow device. It must be properly oriented in terms of flow direction for the cooler to function properly. The valve must be installed in the pressure line. Otherwise flow will be blocked and would cause an overheating condition and eventual transmission failure.

ALUMINUM THREAD REPAIR

Damaged or worn threads in the aluminum transaxle case and valve body can be repaired by the use of Heli-Coils, or equivalent. This repair consists of drilling out the worn-out damaged threads. Then tap the hole with a special Heli-Coil tap, or equivalent, and installing a Heli-Coil insert, or equivalent, into the hole. This brings the hole back to its original thread size.

Heli-Coil, or equivalent, tools and inserts are readily available from most automotive parts suppliers.

FLUSHING COOLERS AND TUBES

When a transmission failure has contaminated the fluid, the oil cooler(s) must be flushed. The cooler bypass valve in the transmission must be replaced also. The torque converter must also be replaced with an exchange unit. This will insure that metal particles or sludged oil are not later transferred back into the reconditioned (or replaced) transmission.

There are two different procedures for flushing coolers and lines. The recommended procedure is to use Tool 6906 Cooler Flusher. The other procedure is to use a hand suction gun and mineral spirits.

WARNING: WEAR PROTECTIVE EYEWEAR THAT MEETS THE REQUIREMENTS OF OSHA AND ANSI Z87.1–1968. WEAR STANDARD INDUSTRIAL RUBBER GLOVES.

KEEP LIGHTED CIGARETTES, SPARKS, FLAMES, AND OTHER IGNITION SOURCES AWAY FROM THE AREA TO PREVENT THE IGNITION OF COMBUSTIBLE LIQUIDS AND GASES. KEEP A CLASS (B) FIRE EXTINGUISHER IN THE AREA WHERE THE FLUSHER WILL BE USED.

KEEP THE AREA WELL VENTILATED.

DO NOT LET FLUSHING SOLVENT COME IN CONTACT WITH YOUR EYES OR SKIN: IF EYE CONTAMINATION OCCURS, FLUSH EYES WITH WATER FOR 15 TO 20 SECONDS. REMOVE CONTAMINATED CLOTHING AND WASH AFFECTED SKIN WITH SOAP AND WATER. SEEK MEDICAL ATTENTION.

COOLER FLUSH USING TOOL 6906

(1) Remove cover plate filler plug on Tool 6906. Fill reservoir 1/2 to 3/4 full of fresh flushing solution. Flushing solvents are petroleum based solutions generally used to clean automatic transmission components. **DO NOT** use solvents containing acids, water, gasoline, or any other corrosive liquids.

(2) Reinstall filler plug on Tool 6906.

(3) Verify pump power switch is turned OFF. Connect red alligator clip to positive (+) battery post. Connect black (-) alligator clip to a good ground.

(4) Disconnect the cooler lines at the transmission.

NOTE: When flushing transmission cooler and lines, ALWAYS reverse flush.

(5) Connect the BLUE pressure line to the OUTLET (From) cooler line.

(6) Connect the CLEAR return line to the INLET (To) cooler line

SERVICE PROCEDURES (Continued)

(7) Turn pump ON for two to three minutes to flush cooler(s) and lines. Monitor pressure readings and clear return lines. Pressure readings should stabilize below 20 psi. for vehicles equipped with a single cooler and 30 psi. for vehicles equipped with dual coolers. If flow is intermittent or exceeds these pressures, replace cooler.

(8) Turn pump OFF.

(9) Disconnect CLEAR suction line from reservoir at cover plate. Disconnect CLEAR return line at cover plate, and place it in a drain pan.

(10) Turn pump ON for 30 seconds to purge flushing solution from cooler and lines. Turn pump OFF.

(11) Place CLEAR suction line into a one quart container of Mopar® type 7176 automatic transmission fluid.

(12) Turn pump ON until all transmission fluid is removed from the one quart container and lines. This purges any residual cleaning solvent from the transmission cooler and lines. Turn pump OFF.

(13) Disconnect alligator clips from battery. Reconnect flusher lines to cover plate, and remove flushing adapters from cooler lines.

COOLER FLUSH USING SUCTION GUN AND MINERAL SPIRITS

(1) Disconnect the cooler lines at the transmission.

(2) Using a hand suction gun filled with mineral spirits, reverse flush the cooler. Force mineral spirits into the **From Cooler** line of the cooler and catch the exiting spirits from the **To Cooler** line. Observe for the presence of debris in the exiting fluid. Continue until fluid exiting is clear and free from debris.

(3) Using compressed air (under 40 psi.) in intermittent spurts, blow any remaining mineral spirits from the cooler, again in the reverse direction.

(4) Pump one (1) quart of automatic transmission fluid through the cooler before reconnecting.

(5) If at any stage of the cleaning process, the cooler does not freely pass fluid, the cooler must be replaced.

REMOVAL AND INSTALLATION

BRAKE TRANSMISSION SHIFT INTERLOCK

REMOVAL

(1) Remove lower steering column cover, refer to Group 8E, Instrument Panel and Gauges for proper procedure.

(2) Remove lower steering column shroud, refer to Group 19, Steering for proper procedure.

(3) With the ignition removed or in the unlocked position, disengage lock tab holding cable end to steering column (Fig. 26).

(4) Pull cable end from steering column.

(5) Remove the floor console and related trim. Refer to Group 23, Body for proper procedure.

(6) Disconnect the cable eyelet from the bellcrank (Fig. 27).

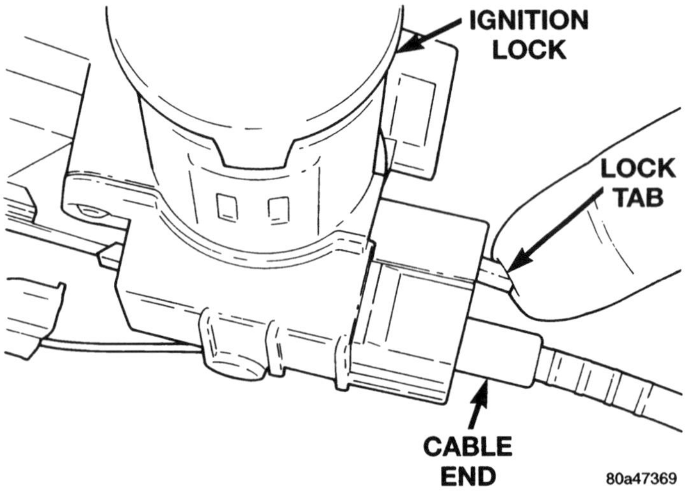

Fig. 26 Brake/Park Interlock Cable

(7) Disconnect and remove the cable from the shift bracket.

(8) Disengage wire connector from solenoid.

(9) Disengage cable from tie strap at base of steering column.

INSTALLATION

(1) Route replacement cable behind instrument panel and under floor console area to shift mechanism (Fig. 27)

(2) Insert cable end into opening in steering column hub under ignition lock. Push cable inward until lock tab engages.

(3) Connect the cable end eyelet onto shifter bellcrank pin.

(4) Place gear selector in PARK.

(5) Push the spring-loaded cable adjuster forward and snap cable into bracket.

(6) Push the cable adjuster lock clamp downward to lock it.

(7) Install the floor console and related trim.

(8) Test the park-lock cable operation.

(9) Install tie strap to hold cable to base of steering column.

(10) Install lower steering column shroud and ignition lock.

(11) Install lower steering column cover.

SPEEDOMETER SERVICE

Rear axle gear ratio and tire size determine speedometer pinion requirements. If the pinion must be replaced, refer to the parts catalogue information for the correct part.

REMOVAL AND INSTALLATION (Continued)

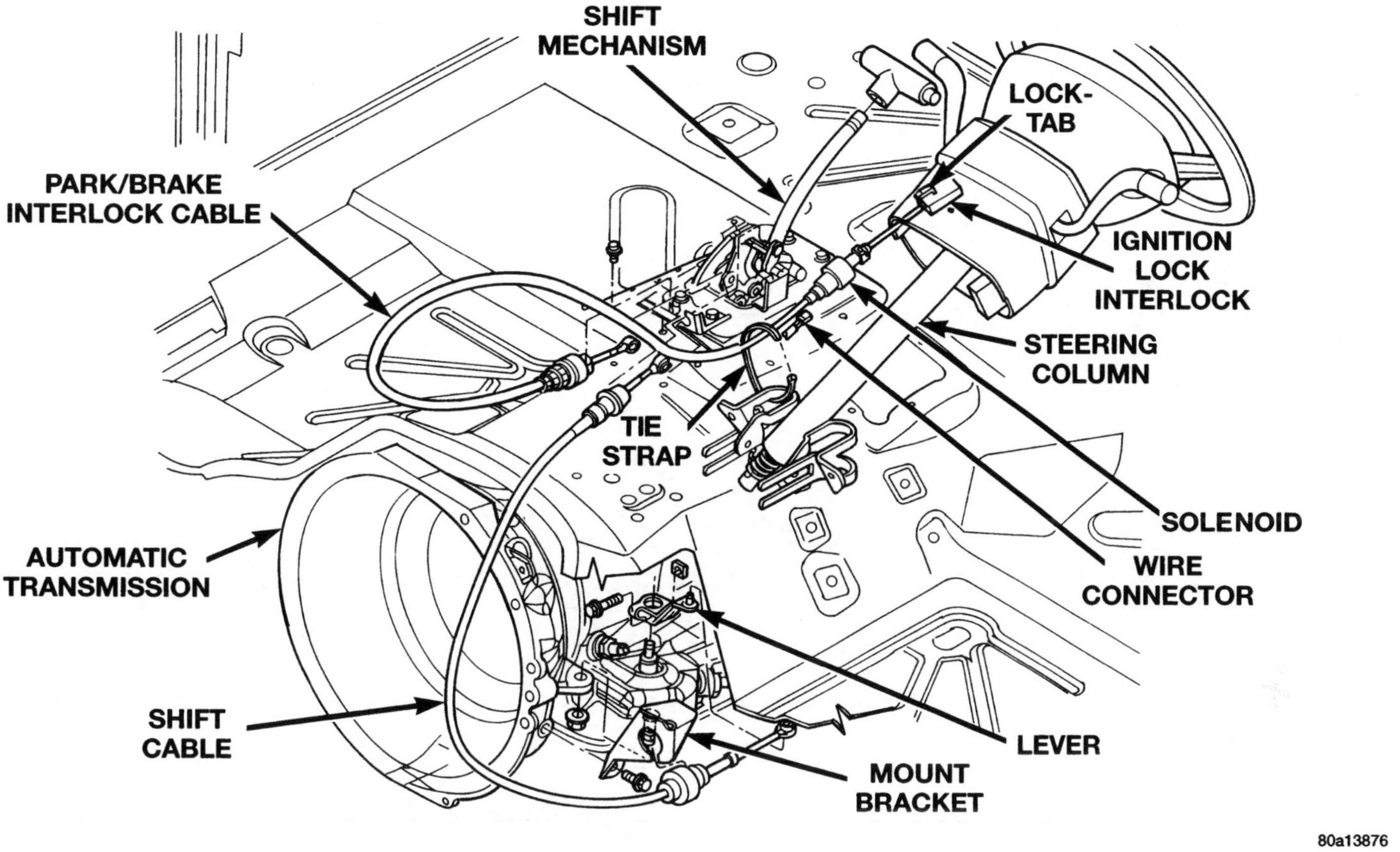

Fig. 27 Cable and Shifter

SPEEDOMETER ASSEMBLY REMOVAL

(1) Raise vehicle.

(2) Disconnect wires from vehicle speed sensor.

(3) Remove adapter clamp and screw (Fig. 28).

(4) Remove speed sensor and speedometer adapter as assembly.

(5) Remove speed sensor retaining screw and remove sensor from adapter.

(6) Remove speedometer pinion from adapter.

(7) Inspect sensor and adapter O-rings (Fig. 28). Remove and discard O-rings if worn or damaged.

(8) Inspect terminal pins in speed sensor. Clean pins with Mopar electrical spray cleaner if dirty or oxidized. Replace sensor if faulty, or pins are loose, severely corroded, or damaged.

SPEEDOMETER INSTALLATION AND INDEXING

(1) Thoroughly clean adapter flange and adapter mounting surface in housing. Surfaces must be clean for proper adapter alignment and speedometer operation.

(2) Install new O-rings on speed sensor and speedometer adapter if necessary (Fig. 28).

(3) Lubricate sensor and adapter O-rings with transmission fluid.

(4) Install vehicle speed sensor in speedometer adapter. Tighten sensor attaching screw to 2-3 N·m (15-27 in. lbs.) torque.

(5) Install speedometer pinion in adapter.

(6) Count number of teeth on speedometer pinion. Do this before installing assembly in housing. Then lubricate pinion teeth with transmission fluid.

(7) Note index numbers on adapter body (Fig. 29). These numbers will correspond to number of teeth on pinion.

(8) Install speedometer assembly in housing.

(9) Rotate adapter until required range numbers are at 6 o'clock position. Be sure range index numbers correspond to number of teeth on pinion gear.

(10) Install speedometer adapter clamp and retaining screw. Tighten clamp screw to 10-12 N·m (90-110 in. lbs.) torque.

(11) Connect wires to vehicle speed sensor.

(12) Lower vehicle and top off transmission fluid level if necessary.

PARK/NEUTRAL POSITION SWITCH

Switch Replacement

(1) Raise vehicle and position drain pan under switch.

(2) Disconnect switch wires.

REMOVAL AND INSTALLATION (Continued)

ITEM	TORQUE
A	2-3 N•m (15-27 in. lbs.)
B	10-12 N•m (90-110 in. lbs.)

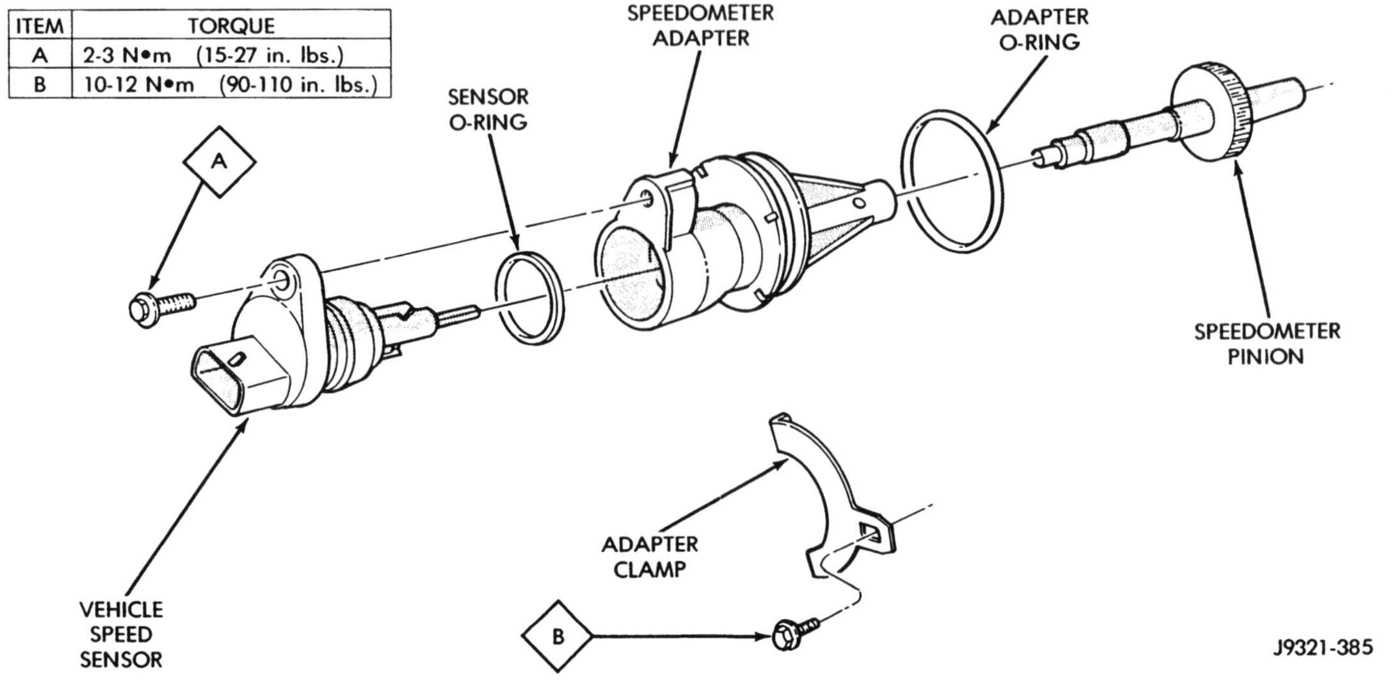

Fig. 28 Speedometer Pinion Adapter Components

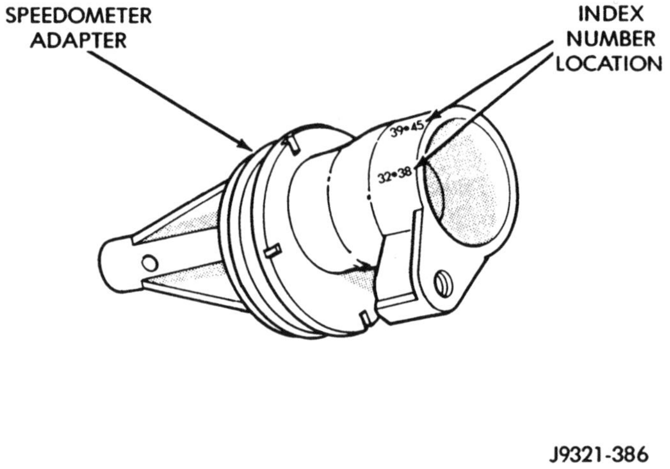

Fig. 29 Index Numbers On Speedometer Pinion Adapter

(3) Remove switch from case.

(4) Move shift lever to Park and Neutral positions. Verify that switch operating lever fingers are centered in switch opening in case (Fig. 30).

(5) Install new seal on switch and install switch in case. Tighten switch to 34 N·m (25 ft. lbs.) torque.

(6) Test continuity of new switch with 12V test lamp.

(7) Connect switch wires and lower vehicle.

(8) Top off transmission fluid level.

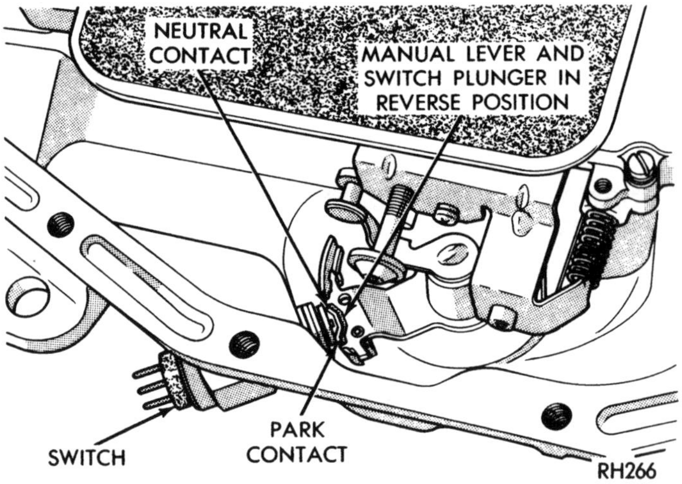

Fig. 30 Park/Neutral Position Switch

EXTENSION HOUSING

REMOVAL

(1) Hoist and support vehicle on safety stands.

(2) Support transmission with a suitable lifting device.

(3) Remove transmission skid plate, refer to Group 13 Bumpers and Frame for proper procedure.

(4) Remove propeller shafts, refer to Group 3, Differential and Driveline for proper procedure.

(5) Remove transfer case, refer to Transfer Case paragraph in this section.

(6) Remove bolts holding extension housing to transmission case (Fig. 31).

(7) Separate extension housing from transmission.

REMOVAL AND INSTALLATION (Continued)

(8) Slide extension housing rearward and off output shaft (Fig. 31).

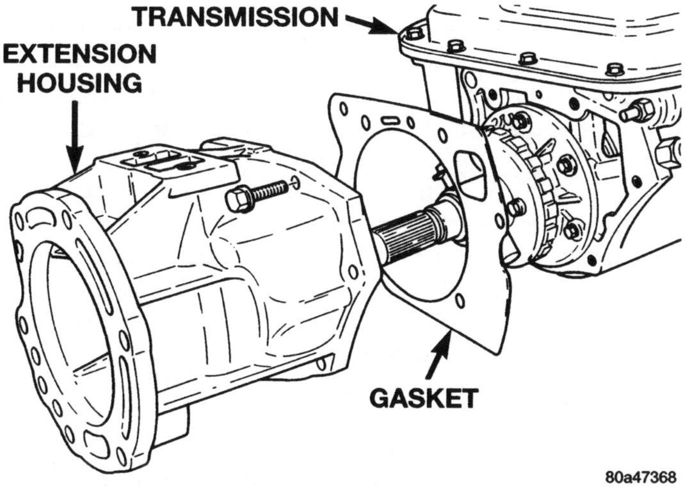

Fig. 31 Extension Housing

INSTALLATION

Clear gasket material from sealing surfaces on extension housing and rear of transmission. Replace output shaft bearing and seal if necessary.

(1) Place extension housing gasket in position on rear of transmission.

(2) Slide extension housing forward and over output shaft (Fig. 31).

(3) Guide park shaft into park sprag and push extension housing forward until rod passes through opening behind sprag. It may be necessary to use a wire to hold sprag to the side for rod to pass through.

(4) Install bolts to hold extension housing to rear of transmission.

(5) Install transfer case.

(6) Install propeller shafts.

(7) Install rear transmission mount and skid plate.

(8) Lower vehicle and verify transmission fluid level. Add fluid as necessary.

GOVERNOR AND PARK GEAR

REMOVAL

(1) Hoist and support vehicle on safety stands.

(2) Mark propeller shaft and axle yoke for assembly reference. Then disconnect and remove shaft.

(3) Disconnect parking brake cable at equalizer and disconnect exhaust components as necessary.

(4) Support transmission on a suitable lifting device.

(5) Remove skid plate and rear transmission mount.

(6) Remove extension housing.

(7) Loosen but do not remove bolts that hold governor body to park gear.

(8) Rotate transmission output shaft until governor weight assembly is accessible.

(9) Remove E-clip at end of governor valve shaft (Fig. 32).

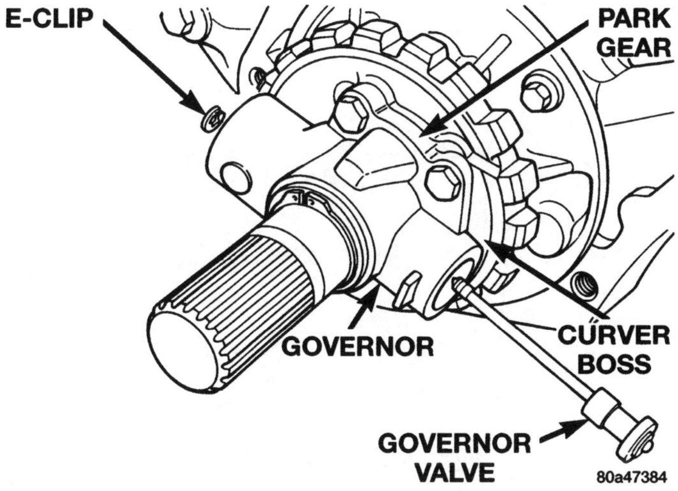

Fig. 32 Governor Valve

(10) Remove governor valve and shaft from governor body (Fig. 32).

(11) Remove snap rings and spacer that retain governor body and park gear assembly on output shaft (Fig. 33).

(12) Remove bolts holding governor body to park gear (Fig. 34).

(13) Separate governor from park gear.

(14) Pull park gear from rear support.

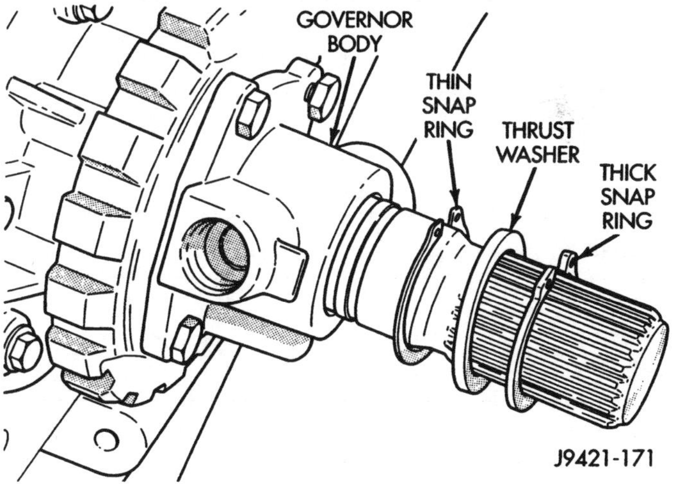

Fig. 33 Snap Rings And Spacer

INSTALLATION

(1) Install park gear into rear support so crown on curved boss is in line with hole through output shaft.

(2) Install governor filter in park gear.

(3) Slip governor body over output shaft and align port to filter.

(4) Install bolts to hold governor body to park gear. Tighten bolts to 11 N·m (95 in. lbs.) torque (Fig. 34).

(5) Install governor body-park gear snap rings and washer on output shaft as follows:

REMOVAL AND INSTALLATION (Continued)

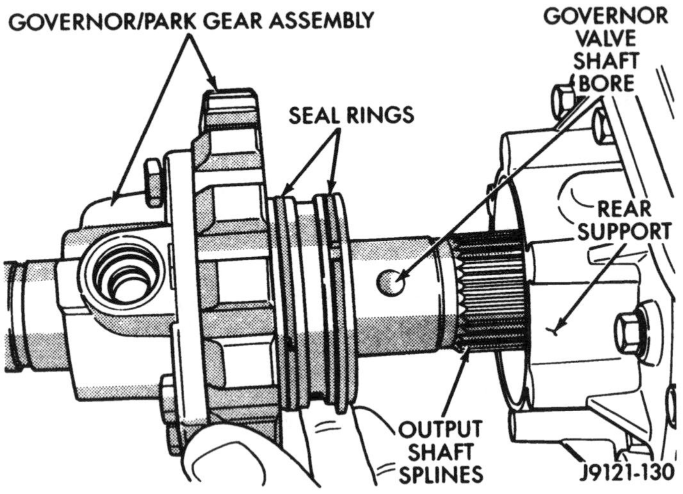

Fig. 34 Governor Body

(a) Install thin snap ring first. Then install thrust washer second, and thick snap ring last (Fig. 33).

(b) Verify correct position of snap rings. **Be sure flat side of each snap ring is toward governor body.**

(6) Insert governor valve and shaft through governor and install E-clip (Fig. 32).

(7) Install extension housing and gasket on transmission. Tighten housing bolts to 32 N·m (24 ft. lbs.).

(8) Install rear transmission mount and skid plate.

(9) Install speed sensor and speedometer components and connect speed sensor wires.

(10) Connect exhaust components and brake cable, if removed.

(11) Align and connect propeller shaft. Tighten shaft clamp bolts to 19 N·m (14 ft. lbs.) torque.

(12) Remove supports and lower vehicle.

(13) Check transmission fluid level, add fluid if necessary.

PARK LOCK

REMOVAL

(1) Raise vehicle and remove propeller shaft.

(2) Remove extension housing. Refer to procedure in this section.

(3) Slide sprag shaft out of extension housing and remove sprag and spring (Fig. 35).

(4) Remove snap ring and slide reaction plug and pin assembly out of housing.

(5) If park rod requires service, it will be necessary to remove valve body. Refer to Valve Body Service procedures in this section.

INSTALLATION

(1) Inspect sprag shaft for scores and free movement in housing and sprag. Inspect sprag and control rod springs for distortion and loss of tension. replace worn, damaged parts as necessary.

(2) Inspect square lug on sprag for broken edges. Check lugs on park gear for damage. Inspect knob on end of control rod for wear grooves, or being seized on rod. Replace rod if bent, if knob is worn/grooved, or it has seized on rod. Replace park gear if lugs are damaged.

(3) Install reaction plug and pin assembly in housing and secure with new snap ring (Fig. 35).

(4) Position sprag and spring in housing and insert sprag shaft. Be sure square lug on sprag is toward park gear. Also be sure spring is positioned so it moves sprag away from gear.

(5) Install extension housing as described in this section.

(6) Install propeller shaft and lower vehicle.

(7) Check transmission fluid level. Add fluid if necessary.

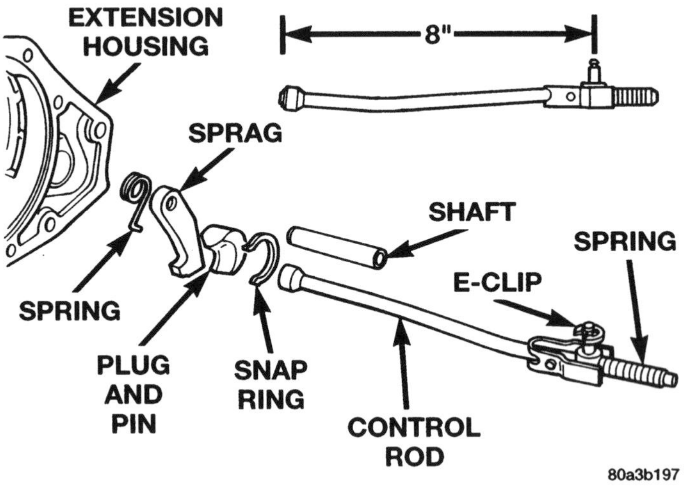

Fig. 35 Park Lock

VALVE BODY

The valve body can be removed for service without having to remove the entire transmission assembly.

The valve body can be disassembled for cleaning and inspection of the individual components. Refer to the procedures in the appropriate transmission overhaul section.

The only serviceable valve body components are the:

- manual lever
- manual lever washer/seal/E-clip and shaft seal
- lever detent ball and spring
- throttle lever
- fluid filter
- switch valve, spring and adjusting screw bracket
- park rod and E-clip
- converter clutch solenoid

The remaining valve body components are serviced only as part of a complete valve body assembly.

REMOVAL AND INSTALLATION (Continued)

REMOVAL

(1) Raise vehicle.

(2) Remove oil pan and drain fluid.

(3) Loosen clamp bolts and remove throttle and manual valve levers from manual lever shaft.

(4) Remove park/neutral position switch.

(5) Remove filter from valve body.

(6) Depress retaining clip and pull solenoid wire from case connector (Fig. 36).

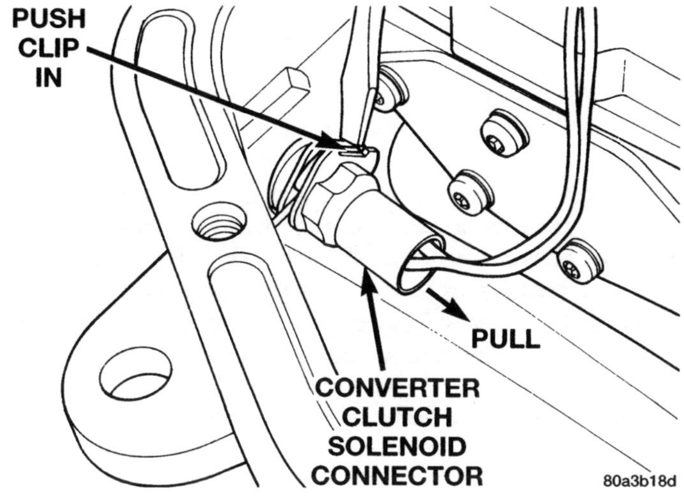

Fig. 36 Solenoid Wire Connector

(7) Remove valve body attaching screws.

(8) Lower valve body enough to remove accumulator piston and piston spring (Fig. 37).

(9) Pull valve body forward to disengage park rod.

(10) Push manual lever shaft and solenoid case connector out of transmission case.

(11) Lower valve body, rotate it away from case, pull park lock rod out of sprag, and remove valve body (Fig. 38).

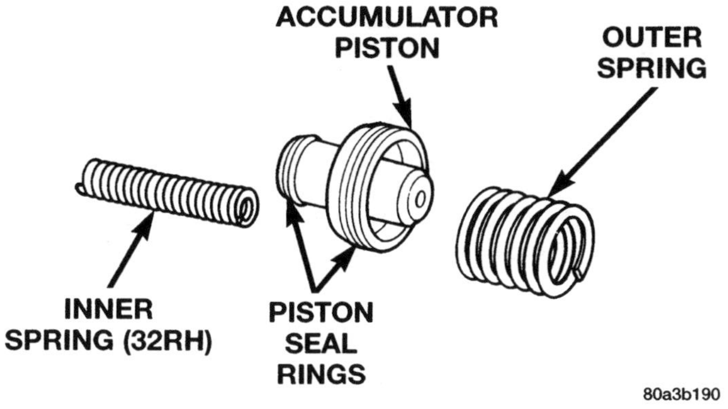

Fig. 37 Accumulator Piston And Springs

INSTALLATION

(1) Verify that park/neutral position switch is **NOT** installed. Valve body cannot be installed with switch in place. Remove switch if necessary.

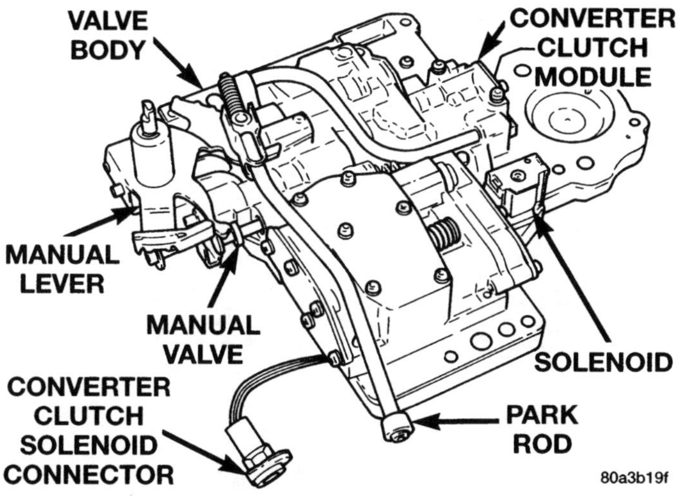

Fig. 38 Valve Body

(2) Install new seals on accumulator piston if necessary, and install piston in case. Use small amount of petroleum jelly to hold piston in place.

(3) Place valve body manual lever in low (1 position) to ease inserting park rod into sprag.

(4) Use screwdriver to push park sprag into engagement with park gear. This makes clearance for knob on lock rod to move past sprag when valve body is installed. Rotate output shaft to verify sprag engagement.

(5) Position accumulator spring between accumulator piston and valve body.

(6) Position valve body on transmission and work knob on park lock rod past sprag. Be sure accumulator piston and spring remain in position.

(7) Hold valve body in position and install valve body screws finger tight.

(8) Install park/neutral position switch.

(9) Tighten valve body screws alternately and evenly to 11 N·m (100 in. lbs.) torque.

(10) Install new fluid filter on valve body. Install and tighten filter screws to 4 N·m (35 in. lbs.) torque.

(11) Connect solenoid wire to case connector.

(12) Install manual and throttle levers on throttle lever shaft. Tighten lever clamp screws and check for free operation. Shaft and levers must operate freely without any bind.

(13) Install oil pan and new gasket. Tighten pan bolts to 17 N·m (150 in. lbs.) torque. Install gasket dry; do not use sealer.

(14) Connect park/neutral position switch and converter clutch solenoid wires.

(15) Install speedometer pinion gear, adapter and speed sensor.

(16) Lower vehicle.

(17) Fill transmission with Mopar ATF Plus, Type 7176 fluid.

(18) Adjust gearshift and throttle cable if necessary.

REMOVAL AND INSTALLATION (Continued)

TRANSMISSION COOLER LINE AND FITTINGS

The transmission cooler lines (Fig. 39) are attached to the transmission with quick connect fittings (Fig. 40).

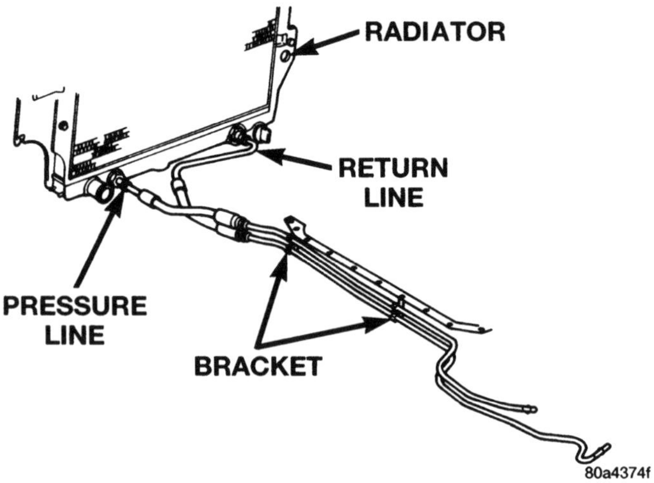

Fig. 39 Transmission Cooler Lines

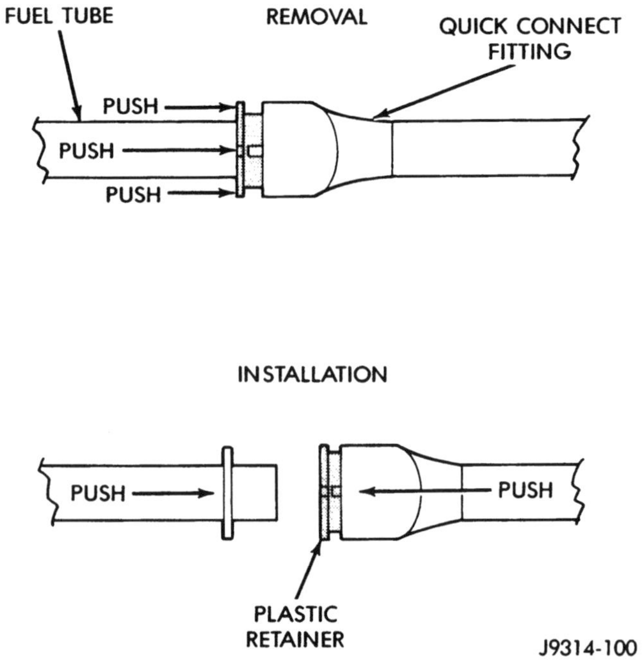

Fig. 40 Quick Connect Fitting

COOLER LINE AND FITTING SERVICE

The cooler lines and fittings are NOT serviceable. Damaged fittings or cooler lines are to be replaced as assemblies.

Fittings swedged into cooler line hoses are serviced only as part of the entire cooler line.

DISCONNECTING COOLER LINES

(1) If fitting and cooler line are covered with dirt, mud, or grease, clean fitting and cooler line with Mopar spray type carburetor or brake cleaner.

(2) Disengage retainer on fitting and pull cooler line out of fitting.

(3) Cover open ends of cooler lines and fittings to prevent dirt entry.

(4) Inspect condition of fitting. Replace transmission fitting as an assembly if fitting body or retainer clip is damaged. Replace cooler line as assembly, if fitting swedged into cooler line hose, is damaged.

CONNECTING COOLER LINES

(1) If transmission or radiator fittings require replacement, apply Mopar Lock N' Seal, or Loctite 242 to fitting threads before installation.

(2) Wipe off cooler line and fitting with clean, dry cloth.

(3) Insert cooler line into fitting. Then push line inward until retainer secures line. A snap or click will be heard and felt through the line when the retainer seats behind the cooler line flange.

(4) **Pull outward on cooler lines to verify that they are properly secured.**

TRANSMISSION COOLER—AUXILLARY

REMOVAL

(1) Release hood latch and open hood.

(2) Drain cooling system and remove radiator.

(3) Place a suitable pan under cooler line couplings.

(4) Disengage cooler lines from auxillary transmission cooler.

(5) Remove screws holding cooler to radiator closure panel.

(6) Separate auxillary transmission cooler from vehicle.

INSTALLATION

(1) Place auxillary transmission cooler in position on vehicle.

(2) Install screws to hold cooler to radiator closure panel.

(3) Engage cooler lines into auxillary transmission cooler.

(4) Install radiator and fill cooling system.

(5) If necessary, add transmission fluid.

(6) Close hood and road test vehicle to verify repair.

TRANSMISSION AND CONVERTER

REMOVAL

(1) Remove fan shroud attaching bolts.

(2) Disconnect transmission fill tube at upper bracket.

(3) Raise vehicle.

(4) Remove inspection cover from converter housing and remove skid plate for access, if necessary.

REMOVAL AND INSTALLATION (Continued)

(5) Remove transmission fill tube and fill tube O-ring.

(6) Remove starter motor.

(7) Mark propeller shafts and axle yokes for alignment reference.

(8) Disconnect propeller shafts at yokes. Secure shafts to frame rails with wire.

(9) Disconnect exhaust pipes at exhaust manifolds, if necessary.

(10) Drain transfer case lubricant, if transfer case will also be serviced.

(11) Disconnect vehicle speed sensor wires.

(12) Disconnect transfer case shift linkage.

(13) Disconnect gearshift cable/linkage and throttle valve cable at transmission levers.

(14) Disconnect transfer case vent hose. Then disconnect vacuum switch harness.

(15) Remove wire harness from clips on transfer case.

(16) Remove transfer case attaching nuts and remove transfer case. Use transmission jack or helper to support and remove transfer case.

(17) Disconnect park/neutral position switch wires.

(18) Disconnect and remove crankshaft position sensor (Fig. 41) or (Fig. 42). Retain sensor bolt (or bolts) for reinstallation.

CAUTION: The crankshaft position sensor can be damaged during transmission removal (or installation) if the sensor is still bolted to the engine block. To avoid damage, remove the sensor before removing the transmission.

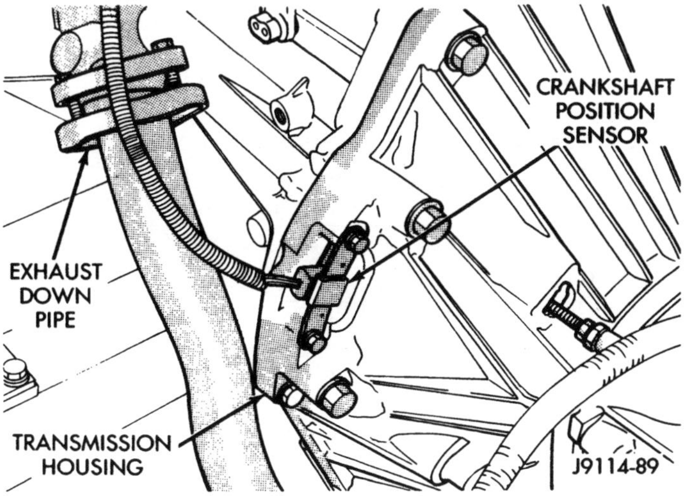

Fig. 41 Crankshaft Position Sensor—2.5L Engine

(19) Remove wire harnesses from clips/tie straps on transmission.

(20) Remove converter housing access cover and mark drive plate and converter for alignment reference.

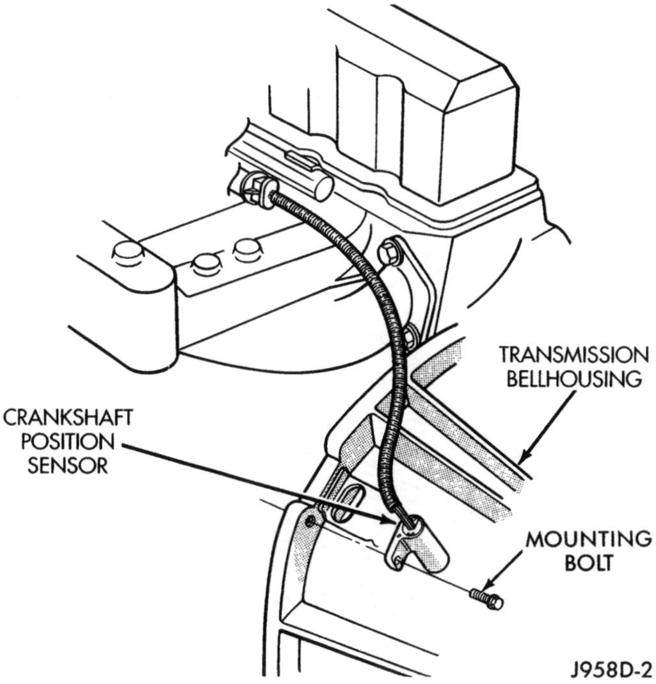

Fig. 42 Crankshaft Position Sensor—4.0L Engine

(21) Remove bolts attaching converter to drive plate.

(22) Support engine with support stand.

(23) Support transmission with transmission jack. Secure transmission to jack with safety chain.

(24) Remove bolts/nuts attaching cushion and torque arm bracket to skid plate (Fig. 43).

(25) Remove skid plate, or rear crossmember, if equipped.

(26) Lower transmission slightly and disconnect cooler lines at transmission.

(27) Remove bolts attaching transmission converter housing to engine block.

(28) Move transmission and converter rearward until clear of crankshaft.

(29) Hold converter in position and lower transmission until converter housing clears engine.

(30) Remove converter from transmission.

TRANSMISSION AND CONVERTER INSTALLATION

CAUTION: If the transmission was repaired to correct a problem that generated sludge and debris, the fluid cooler and lines must be reverse flushed and the torque converter and drainback valve replaced. Sludge and metal or friction particles must be removed from the cooler system before reinstalling the transmission. This avoids re-contaminating the repaired transmission. Failure to flush the system will result in repeat failure and a shop comeback.

REMOVAL AND INSTALLATION (Continued)

ITEM	TORQUE
A	41-68 N·m (30-50 ft. lbs.)

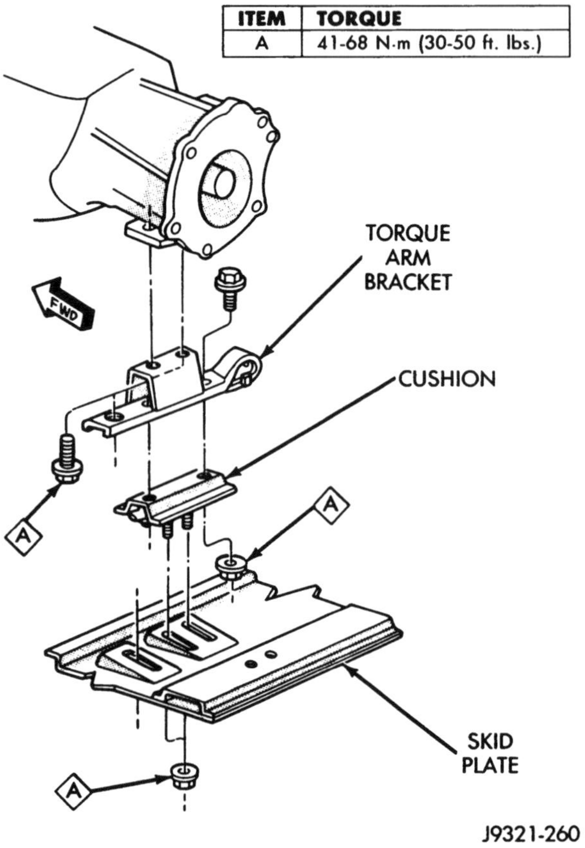

Fig. 43 Transmission Rear Mount

(1) Lubricate converter drive hub and pump seal with Mopar ATF Plus transmission fluid. Then install converter. Turn converter back and forth to align drive slots in converter hub with pump gear lugs. Be sure converter is fully seated in pump (Fig. 44).

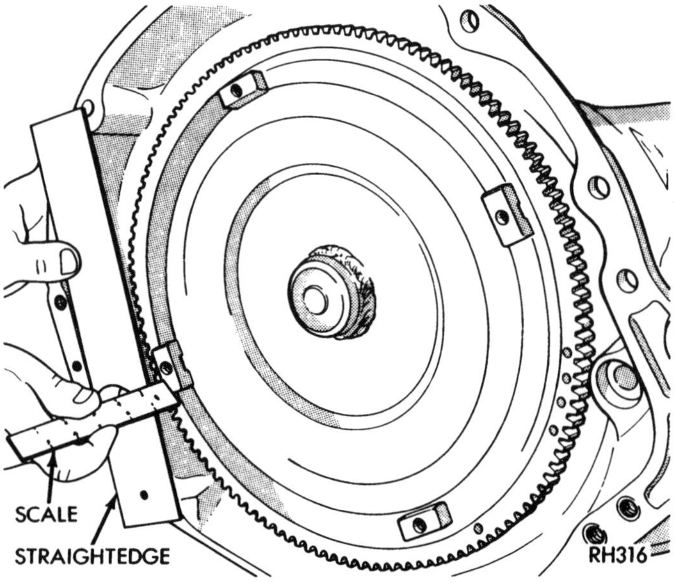

Fig. 44 Checking Torque Converter Seating

(2) Temporarily secure converter with C-clamp or metal strap attached across converter housing.

(3) Position transmission on jack and secure it with safety chains.

(4) Raise transmission and align converter with drive plate.

(5) Move transmission forward. Then raise, lower or tilt transmission to align converter housing with engine block dowels.

(6) Install two transmission attaching bolts. Tighten bolts just enough to hold transmission converter housing in place on block.

(7) Install torque converter attaching bolts. Tighten bolts to following torque.

- 54 N·m (40 ft. lbs.) with 9.5 in. 3-lug converter
- 74 N·m (55 ft. lbs.) with 9.5 in. 4-lug converter
- 74 N·m (55 ft. lbs.) with 10.0 in. 4-lug converter
- 31 N·m (270 in. lbs.) with 10.75 in. 4-lug converter

(8) Install and tighten remaining bolts that attach transmission converter housing to engine block (Fig. 45).

CAUTION: Be sure the converter housing is fully seated on the engine block dowels before tightening any bolts.

(9) Install crankshaft position sensor.

(10) Install transmission fill tube and O-ring.

(11) Connect transmission cooler lines to fittings (Fig. 46).

(12) Install transfer case on transmission. Tighten attaching nuts to 47 N·m (35 ft. lbs.) torque if case has 3/8 studs, or 35 N·m (26 ft. lbs.) if case has 5/16 studs.

(13) Install rear crossmember and attach transmission rear support to crossmember.

(14) Remove transmission jack.

(15) Connect vehicle speed sensor wires.

(16) Install inspection cover on converter housing.

(17) Install exhaust pipes and support brackets, if removed.

(18) Install starter motor.

(19) Connect wires to park/neutral position switch.

(20) Connect gearshift and linkage and throttle cable.

(21) Connect transfer case shift linkage.

(22) Connect propeller shafts to transfer case yokes.

(23) Connect front exhaust pipes and catalytic converter support bracket bolts (if removed).

(24) Install skid plate, rear cushion and bracket, if removed.

(25) Fill transfer case to bottom edge of fill plug hole with Mopar Dexron II.

(26) Lower vehicle and fill transmission to correct level with ATF Plus, type 7176 fluid.

REMOVAL AND INSTALLATION (Continued)

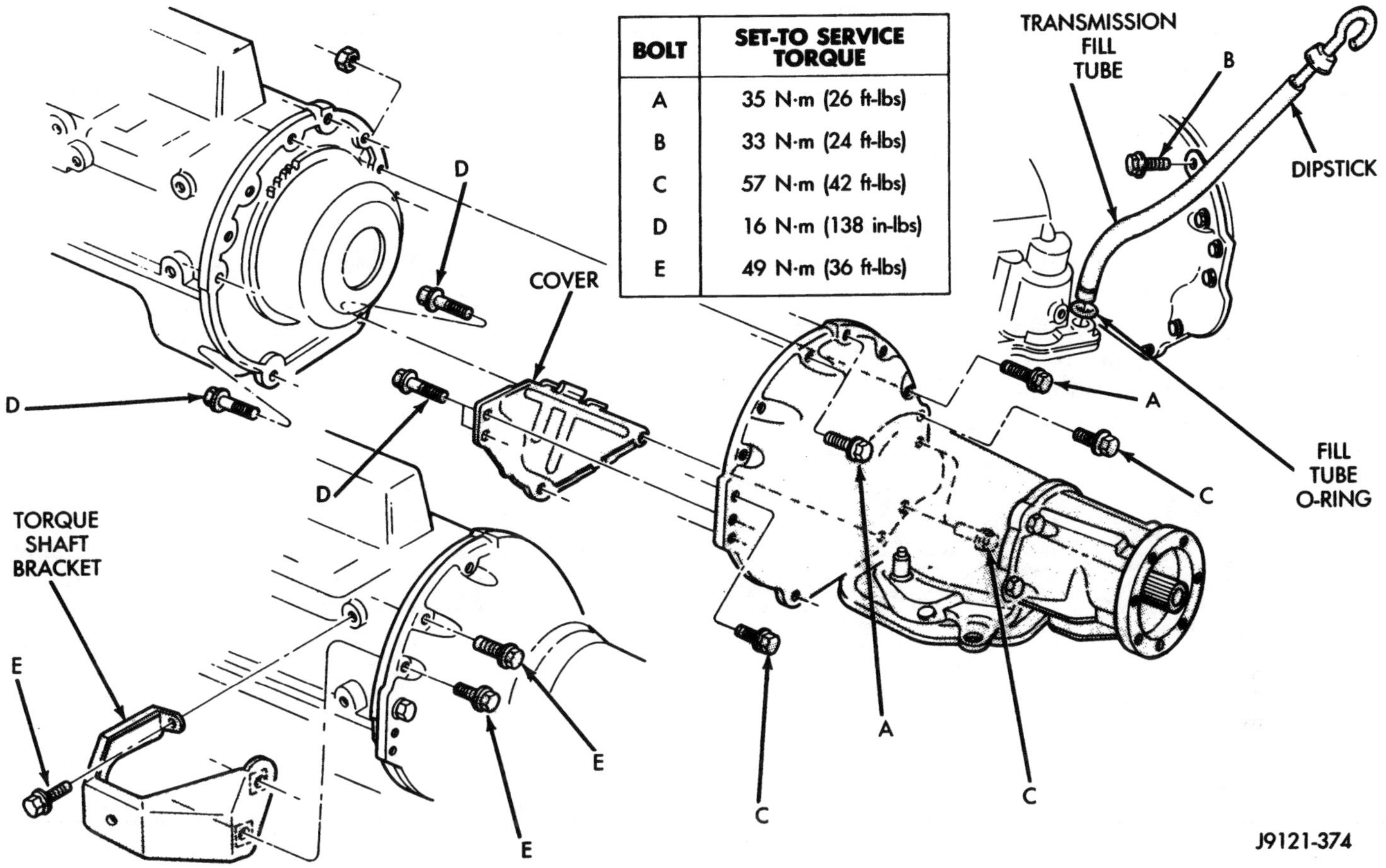

BOLT	SET-TO SERVICE TORQUE
A	35 N·m (26 ft-lbs)
B	33 N·m (24 ft-lbs)
C	57 N·m (42 ft-lbs)
D	16 N·m (138 in-lbs)
E	49 N·m (36 ft-lbs)

Fig. 45 Transmission Attachment

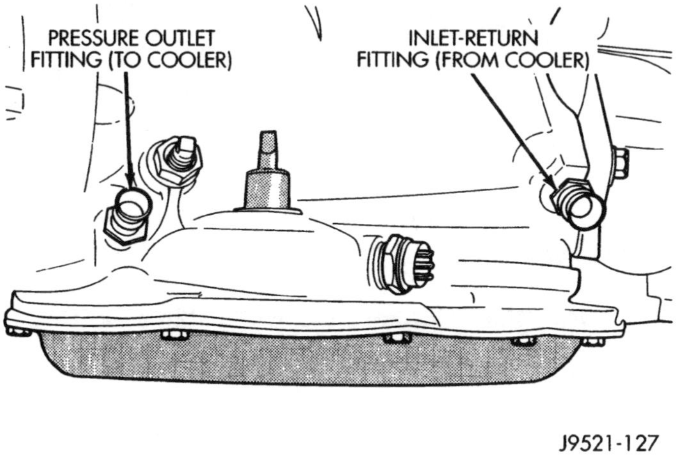

Fig. 46 Transmission Cooler Lines

(27) Install fan shroud and bolts (if removed).

TORQUE CONVERTER

REMOVAL

(1) Remove transmission and torque converter from vehicle.

(2) Place a suitable drain pan under the converter housing end of the transmission.

CAUTION: Verify that transmission is secure on the lifting device or work surface, the center of gravity of the transmission will shift when the torque converter is removed creating an unstable condition.

The torque converter is a heavy unit. Use caution when separating the torque converter from the transmission.

(3) Pull the torque converter forward until the center hub clears the oil pump seal.

(4) Separate the torque converter from the transmission.

INSTALLATION

Check converter hub and drive notches for sharp edges, burrs, scratches, or nicks. Polish the hub and notches with 320/400 grit paper or crocus cloth if necessary. The hub must be smooth to avoid damaging the pump seal at installation.

(1) Lubricate converter hub and oil pump seal lip with transmission fluid.

(2) Place torque converter in position on transmission.

CAUTION: Do not damage oil pump seal or bushing while inserting torque converter into the front of the transmission.

REMOVAL AND INSTALLATION (Continued)

(3) Align torque converter to oil pump seal opening.

(4) Insert torque converter hub into oil pump.

(5) While pushing torque converter inward, Rotate converter until converter is fully seated in the oil pump gears.

(6) Check converter seating with a scale and straightedge (Fig. 47). Surface of converter lugs should be 1/2 in. to rear of straightedge when converter is fully seated.

(7) If necessary, temporarily secure converter with C-clamp attached to the converter housing.

(8) Install the transmission in the vehicle.

(9) Fill the transmission with the recommended fluid.

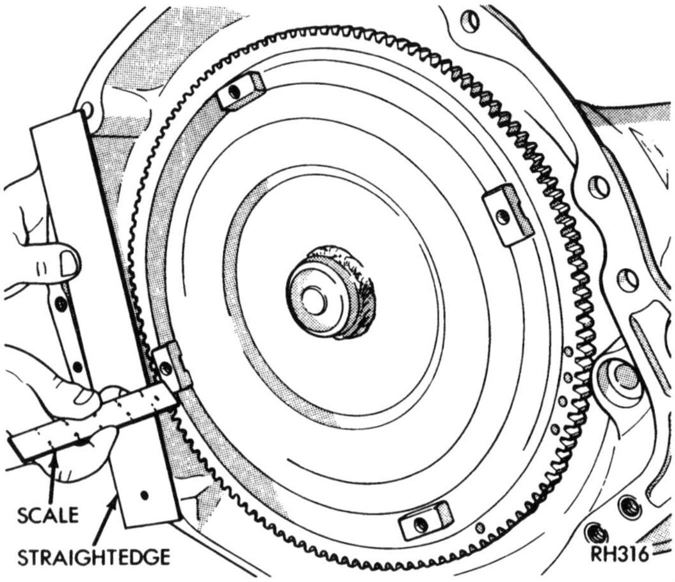

Fig. 47 Checking Torque Converter Seating

DISASSEMBLY AND ASSEMBLY

GOVERNOR AND PARK GEAR

DISASSEMBLY

(1) Remove governor body from transmission, refer to Governor and Park Gear removal and installation paragraph in this group.

(2) Clean and inspect governor filter (Fig. 48).

(3) Remove snap ring and washer that secure governor weight assembly in body (Fig. 49).

(4) Remove governor weight assembly from governor body bore.

(5) Slide intermediate and inner weight from outer weight.

(6) Position intermediate weight on suitable size socket (Fig. 50).

(7) Push inner weight downward with nut driver. Then remove inner weight snap ring with Miller Plier Tool 6823 (Fig. 50).

(8) Remove inner weight and spring from intermediate weight.

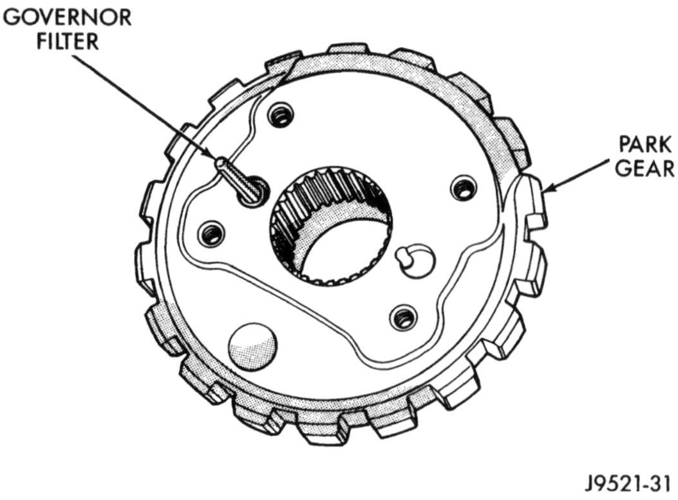

Fig. 48 Governor Filter

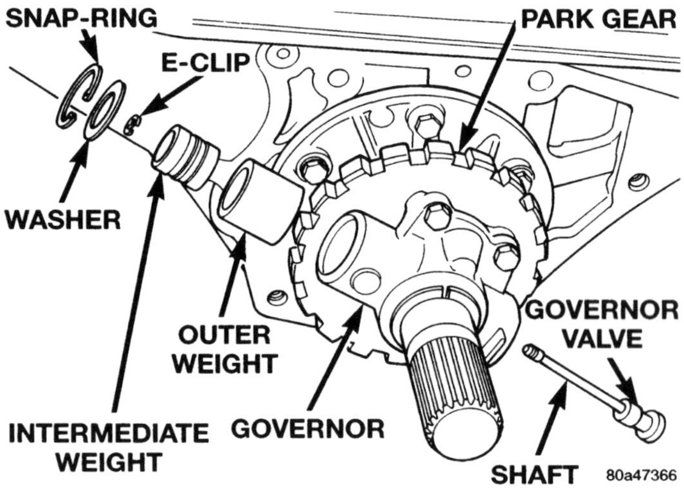

Fig. 49 Snap Ring, Washer, and Outer Weight

ASSEMBLY

CAUTION: Exercise care when installing the rings. They are easily broken if overspread or twisted during installation.

If it was necessary to remove the park gear, inspect the seal rings and bore in rear support. Install new seal rings on park gear hub only if original rings are damaged, or worn. Install ring with interlock ends first and ring with plain ends last. Slip each ring on hub and seat them in grooves. Verify that rear ring ends are securely interlocked before proceeding. If the bore in rear support is damaged, replace the rear support.

(1) Lubricate governor components with Mopar ATF Plus transmission fluid before assembly.

(2) Clean and inspect governor weights and bores for scoring or wear. Replace the governor body and

DISASSEMBLY AND ASSEMBLY (Continued)

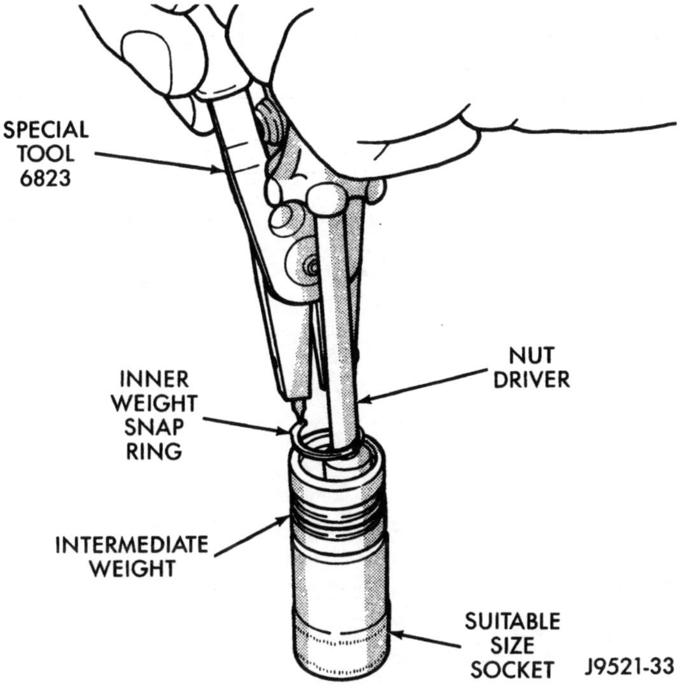

Fig. 50 Inner Weight Snap Ring

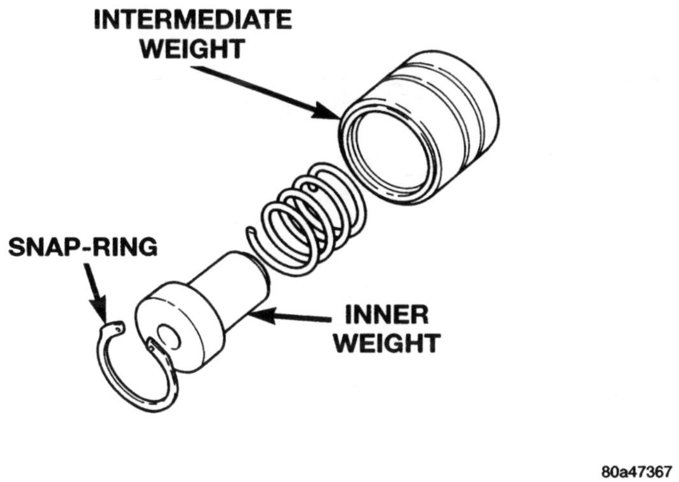

Fig. 51 Intermediate and Inner Governor Weights

weights if damaged. Refer to Cleaning and Inspection section of this group for proper procedure.

(3) Insert spring into intermediate weight.

(4) Insert inner weight into intermediate weight and install snap-ring (Fig. 51). Verify snap-ring is fully seated in groove in intermediate weight (Fig. 50).

(5) Assemble governor weights into governor body (Fig. 49).

(6) Install washer and snap ring to hold weights in governor body.

(7) Install governor body in transmission

VALVE BODY

Remove the valve body from the transmission, refer to the Removal and Installation procedures section of this group.

DISASSEMBLE

Remove valve body from the transmission following the procedures in the Removal and Installation section of this group. Position the valve body on a clean work surface to avoid contamination.

CAUTION: Do not clamp any part of the valve body assembly (Fig. 52) in a vise. This practice will distort the valve body and transfer plate resulting in valve bind. Slide valves and plugs out carefully. Do not use force at any time. The valves and valve body will be damaged if force is used. Also tag or mark the valve body springs for reference as they are removed. Do not allow them to become intermixed.

(1) Remove screws attaching adjusting screw bracket to valve body and transfer plate. Hold bracket firmly against spring force while removing last screw.

(2) Remove adjusting screw bracket, line pressure adjusting screw. (Fig. 53).

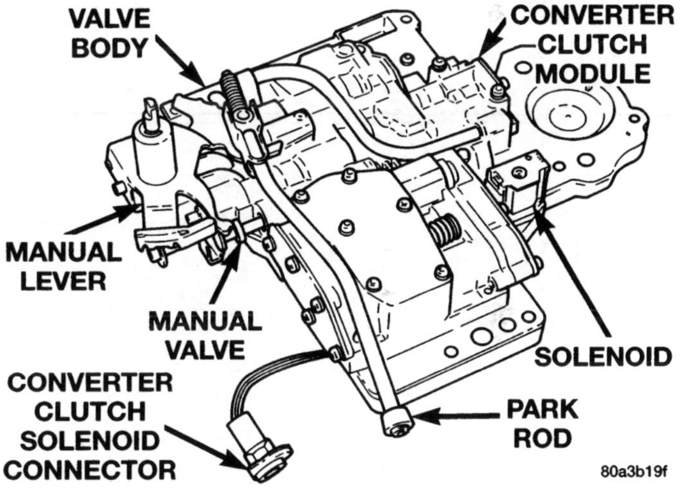

Fig. 52 Valve Body Assembly

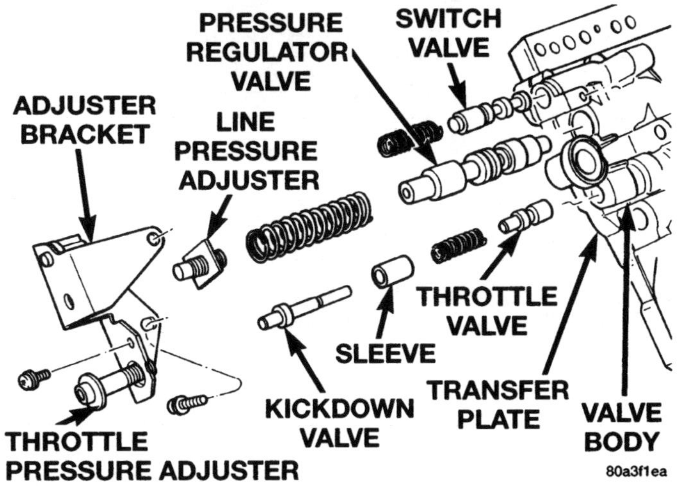

Fig. 53 Adjusting Screw Bracket, Springs, Valve Removal

DISASSEMBLY AND ASSEMBLY (Continued)

(3) Remove switch valve and spring, pressure regulator valve and spring, kickdown valve and spring, and throttle valve from valve body (Fig. 53).

(4) Secure detent ball and spring in housing with retainer tool 6583 (Fig. 54).

(5) Remove manual shaft E-clip, washer, and seal (Fig. 55).

(6) Pull manual shaft and park rod assembly upward out of valve body and off throttle lever (Fig. 55).

(7) Remove manual valve from valve body (Fig. 56)

(8) Remove Retainer Tool 6583. Then remove and retain detent ball and spring (Fig. 55).

(9) Remove throttle lever (Fig. 55).

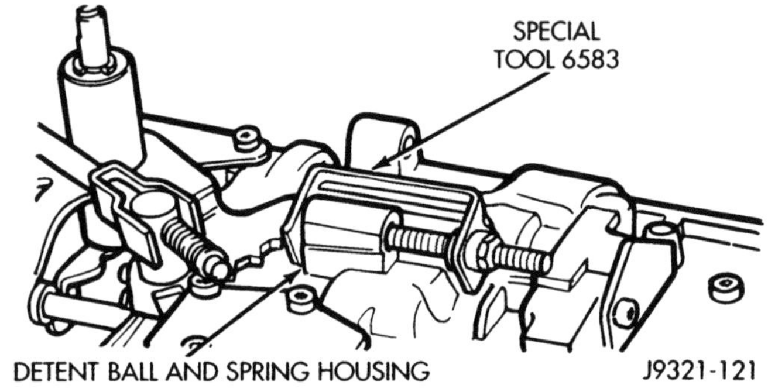

Fig. 54 Securing Detent Ball And Spring With Retainer Tool

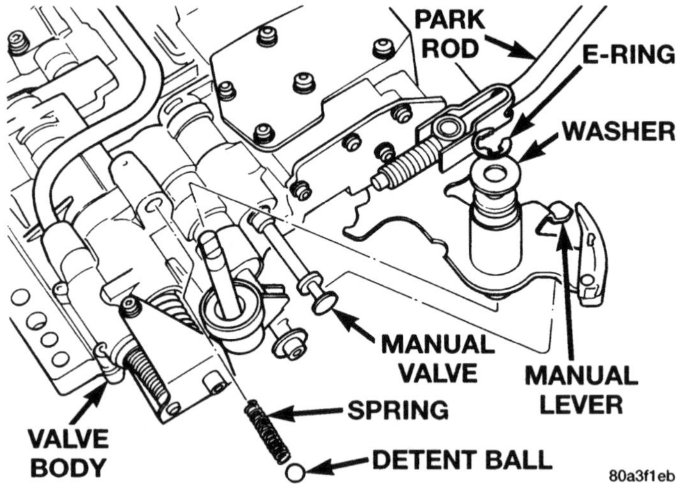

Fig. 55 Manual And Throttle Levers

(10) Remove park rod E-clip and separate rod from manual lever (Fig. 57).

(11) Remove converter clutch solenoid from separator plate (Fig. 58). A T25 torx bit is required to remove solenoid attaching screw.

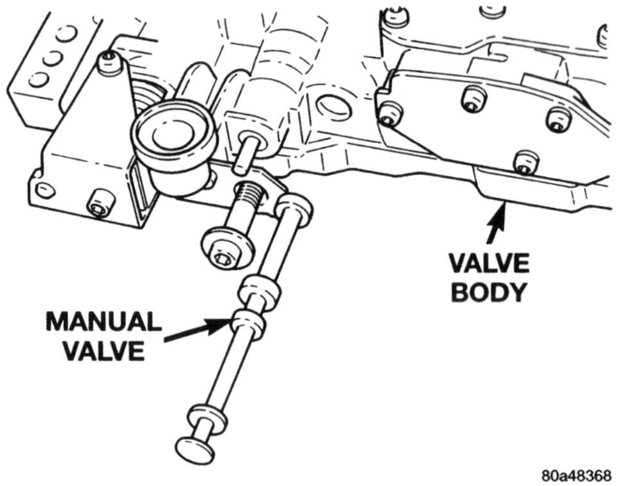

Fig. 56 Manual Valve

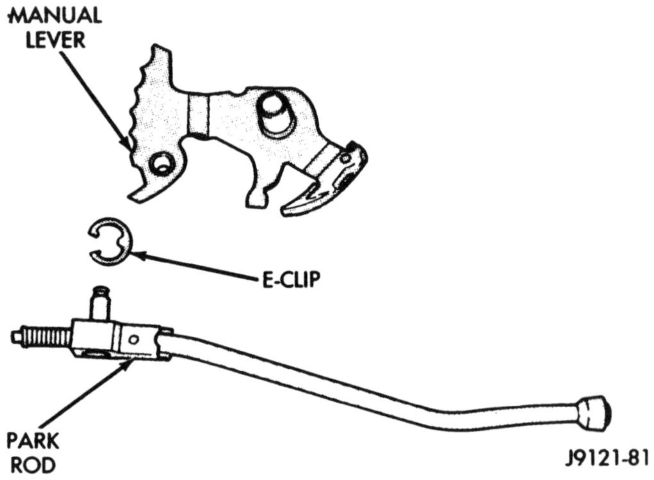

Fig. 57 Park Rod

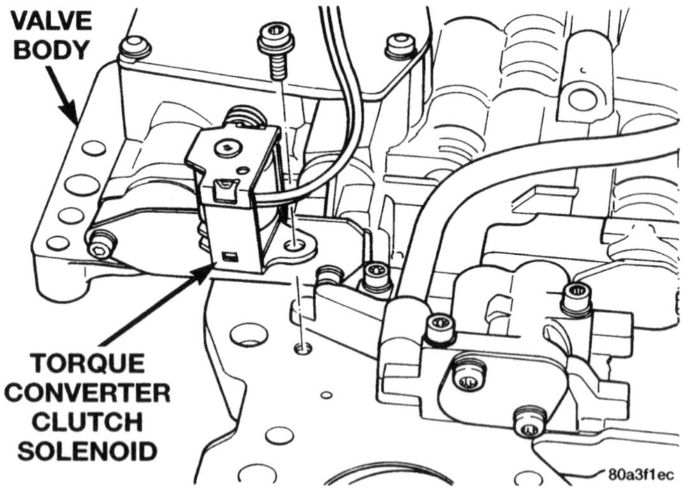

Fig. 58 Converter Clutch Solenoid

DISASSEMBLY AND ASSEMBLY (Continued)

(12) Remove screws attaching converter clutch module to valve body and remove module and connecting tube (Fig. 59).

(13) Remove screws attaching end cover plate to torque converter module (Fig. 60).

(14) Remove converter clutch valve, fail safe valve, and springs (Fig. 60)

(15) Turn valve body over so transfer plate is facing upward (Fig. 61). With valve body in this position, valve body check balls will remain in place and not fall out when transfer plate is removed.

(16) Remove screws attaching transfer plate to valve body (Fig. 61).

(17) Remove transfer plate and separator plate from valve body (Fig. 61). Note position of filter and clutch solenoid for reference. Remove valve body check balls. Note that check balls will be steel on very early production models, or plastic on later production models.

(18) Position transfer plate on bench so separator plate, and filter are facing up. This will avoid having rear clutch and rear servo check balls fall out when plates are separated.

(19) Remove screws attaching separator plate to transfer plate (Fig. 62).

(20) Note position of filter, rear clutch servo and rear servo check balls for assembly reference (Fig. 62) and (Fig. 63).

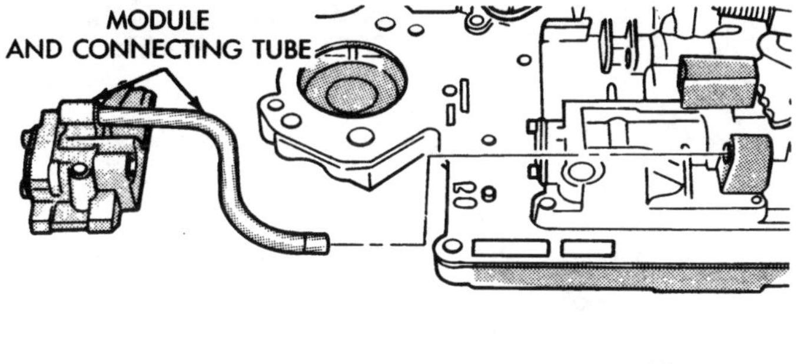

Fig. 59 Clutch Module And Connecting Tube

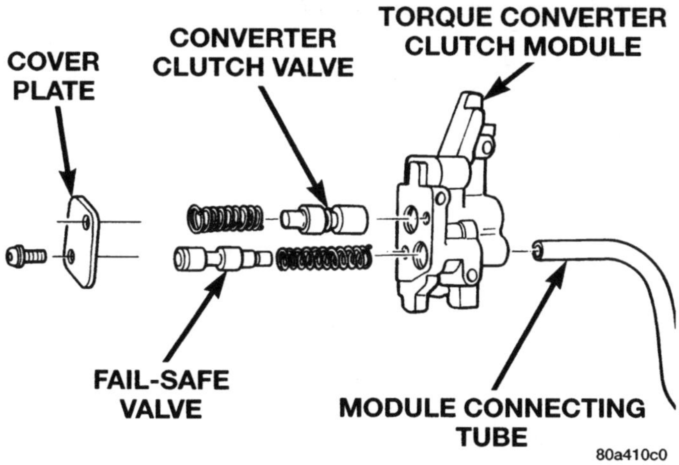

Fig. 60 Converter Clutch and Fail Safe Valves

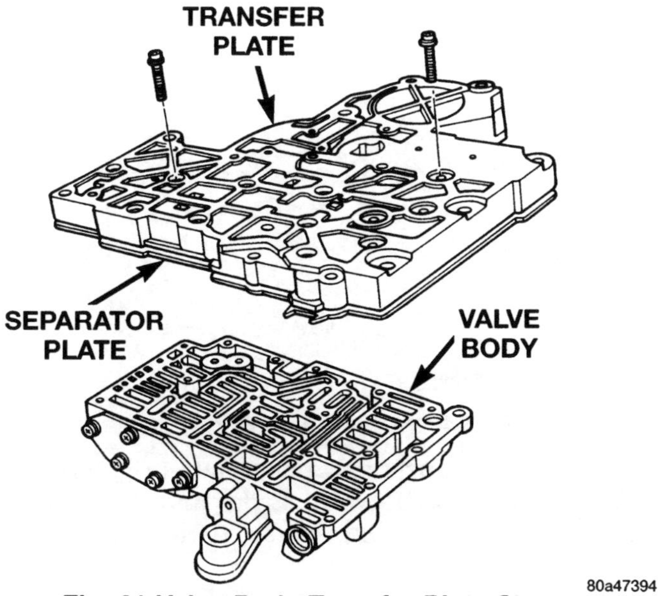

Fig. 61 Valve Body Transfer Plate Screws

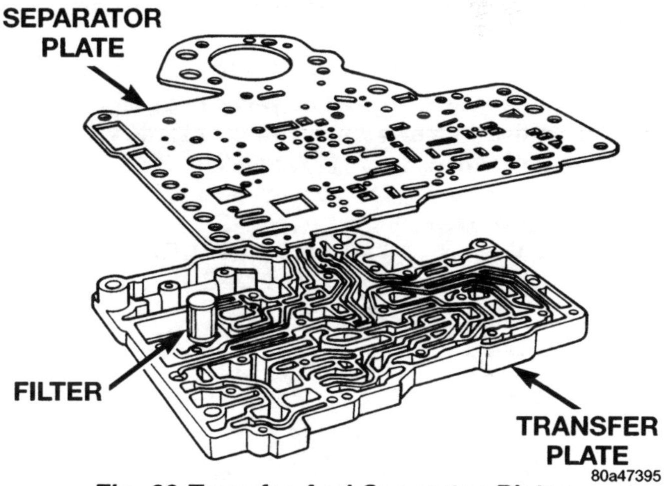

Fig. 62 Transfer And Separator Plates

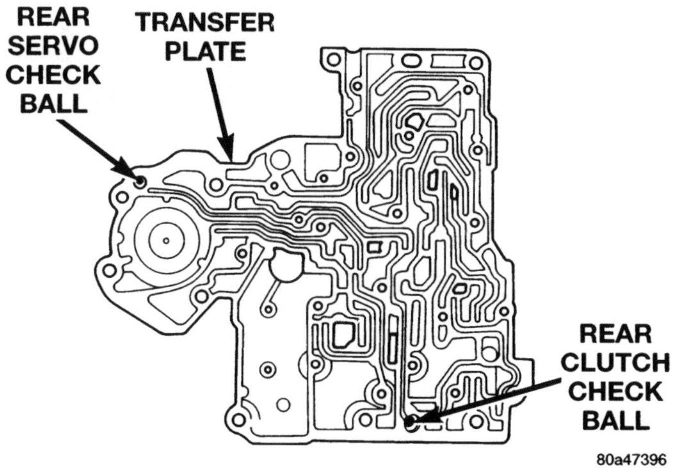

Fig. 63 Rear Servo and Rear Clutch Check Balls

DISASSEMBLY AND ASSEMBLY (Continued)

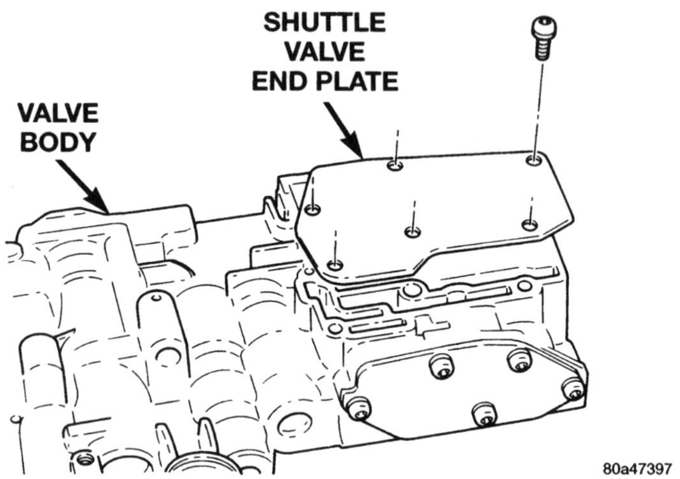

Fig. 64 Shuttle Valve End Plate

(21) Remove shuttle valve end plate (Fig. 64).

(22) Remove shuttle valve E-clip and remove secondary spring and spring guides from end of valve (Fig. 65).

(23) Remove governor plug end plate (Fig. 66).

(24) Remove 1-2 and 2-3 shift valve governor plugs from valve body (Fig. 66).

(25) Remove shuttle valve throttle plug, primary spring and shuttle valve from valve body (Fig. 66).

(26) Remove screws attaching kickdown limit valve body to valve body (Fig. 66).

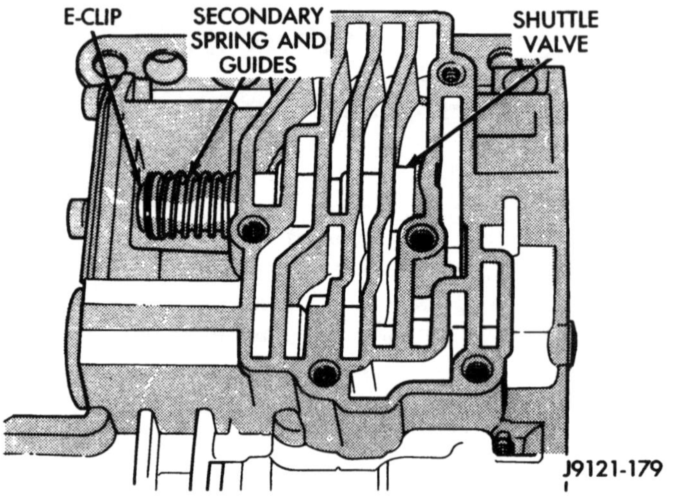

Fig. 65 Shuttle Valve E-Clip And Secondary Spring

(27) Remove 1-2 shift control valve and spring from valve body (Fig. 66).

(28) Remove 2-3 shift valve and spring from valve body (Fig. 66).

(29) Remove 1-2 shift valve and spring from valve body (Fig. 66).

(30) Remove throttle pressure plug from kickdown limit valve body (Fig. 66).

(31) Remove retainer from end of kickdown limit valve body (Fig. 66).

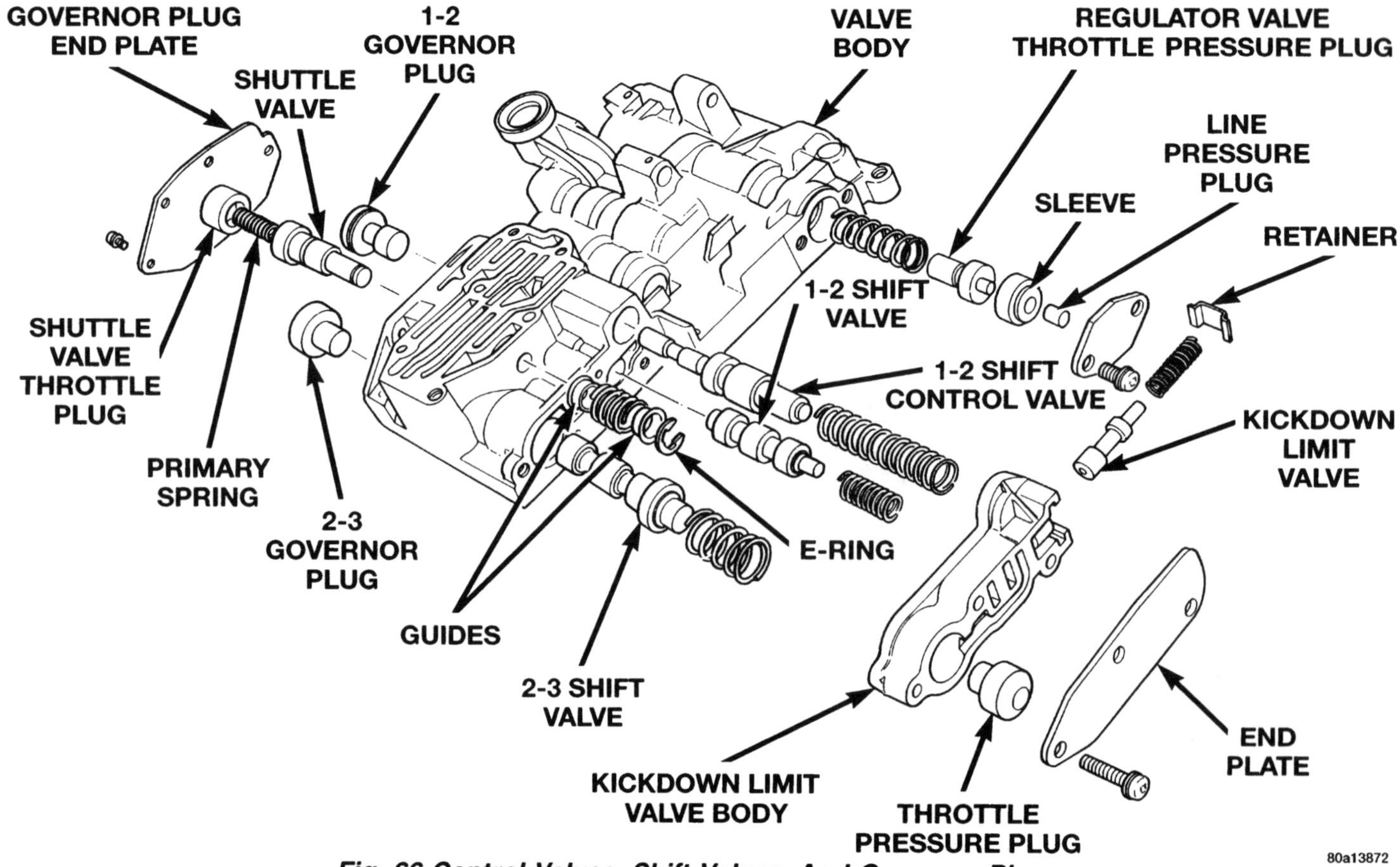

Fig. 66 Control Valves, Shift Valves, And Governor Plugs

DISASSEMBLY AND ASSEMBLY (Continued)

(32) Remove kickdown limit valve and spring from kickdown limit valve body (Fig. 66).

(33) Remove regulator valve end plate from valve body (Fig. 66).

(34) Remove regulator valve line pressure plug, pressure plug sleeve, regulator valve throttle pressure plug and spring (Fig. 66).

ASSEMBLE VALVE BODY

Clean and inspect all valve body components for damage or wear. Refer to the Cleaning and Inspection section of this group for proper procedure.

CAUTION: Do not force valves or plugs into place during reassembly. If the valve body bores, valves and plugs are free of distortion or burrs, the valve body components should all slide into place easily. In addition, do not overtighten the transfer plate and valve body screws during reassembly. Overtightening can distort the valve body resulting in valve sticking, cross leakage and unsatisfactory operation. Tighten valve body screws to recommended torque only.

(1) Lubricate valve body bores, valves and plugs with Mopar ATF Plus transmission fluid.

(2) Install regulator valve line pressure plug, pressure plug sleeve, regulator valve throttle pressure plug and spring into valve body (Fig. 66). Verify valve components slide freely.

(3) Install regulator valve end plate on valve body (Fig. 66).

(4) Install kickdown limit valve and spring in kickdown limit valve body (Fig. 66). Verify valve components slide freely.

(5) Compress spring into kickdown limit valve body.

(6) Install retainer in grooves at end of kickdown limit valve body (Fig. 66).

(7) Install throttle pressure plug in kickdown limit valve body (Fig. 66).

(8) Install 1-2 shift valve and spring into valve body (Fig. 66).

(9) Install 2-3 shift valve and spring into valve body (Fig. 66).

(10) Install 1-2 shift control valve and spring into valve body (Fig. 66).

(11) Verify valve components slide freely.

(12) Place kickdown limit valve body and end plate in position on valve body and compress springs (Fig. 66).

(13) Install screws to attach kickdown limit valve body to valve body (Fig. 66).

(14) Install shuttle valve throttle plug, primary spring and shuttle valve into valve body (Fig. 66). Verify valve components slide freely.

(15) Install 1-2 and 2-3 shift valve governor plugs into valve body (Fig. 66). Verify valve components slide freely.

(16) Place governor plug end plate in position on valve body and compress spring.

(17) Install screws to attach governor plug end plate to valve body (Fig. 66).

(18) Assemble shuttle valve spring and guides (Fig. 66). Place spring and guides in position on shuttle valve stem.

(19) Compress spring and install E-clip in groove on shuttle valve stem (Fig. 67).

(20) Place shuttle valve end plate in position on valve body (Fig. 68).

(21) Install screws to attach shuttle valve end plate to valve body (Fig. 68).

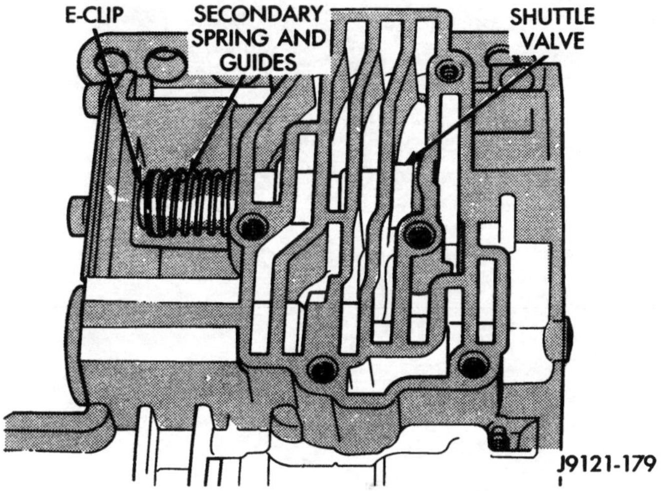

Fig. 67 Shuttle Valve E-Clip And Secondary Spring

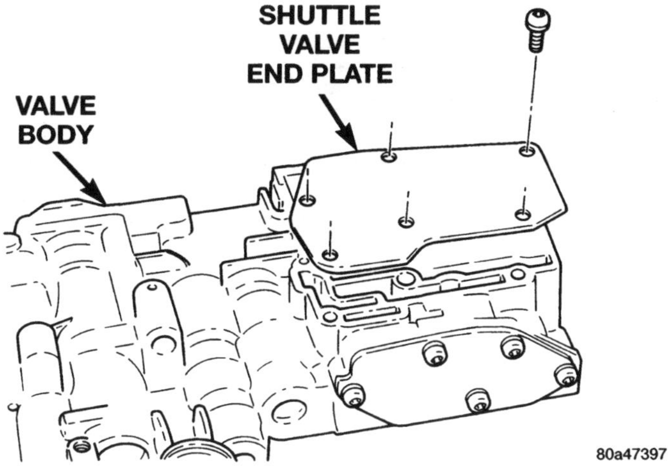

Fig. 68 Shuttle Valve End Plate

(22) Install rear clutch servo and rear servo check balls in proper cavities in transfer plate (Fig. 69).

DISASSEMBLY AND ASSEMBLY (Continued)

(23) Insert filter into opening in separator plate (Fig. 70).

(24) Place separator plate in position on transfer plate and install screws to attach separator plate to transfer plate (Fig. 70).

(25) Place one 11/32 in. check ball and six 1/4 in. check balls in the proper cavities in the valve body (Fig. 71)

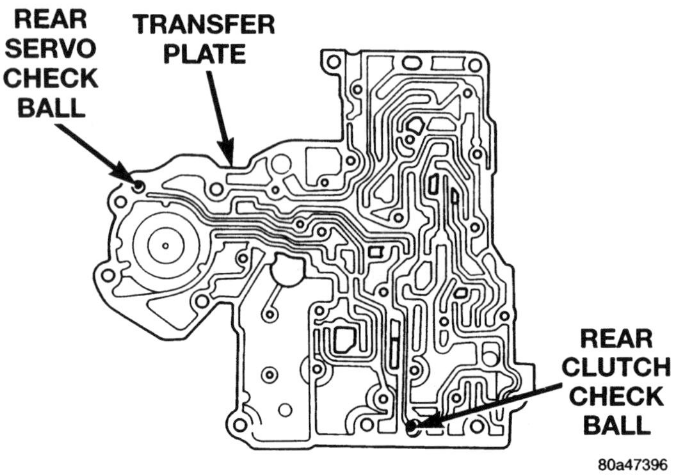

Fig. 69 Rear Servo and Rear Clutch Check Balls

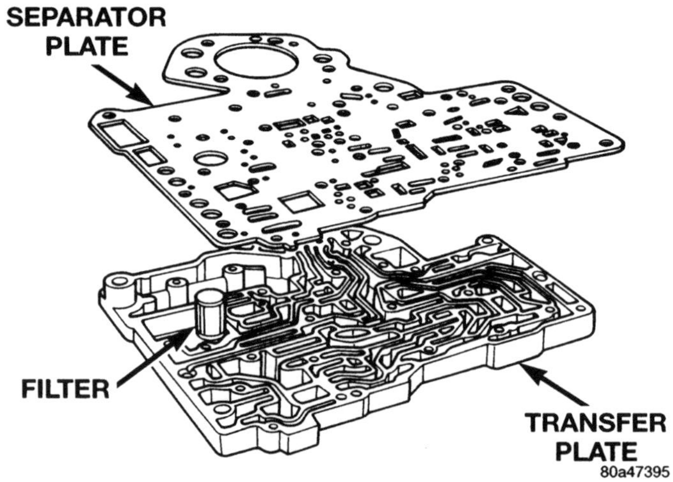

Fig. 70 Transfer And Separator Plates

(26) Place transfer plate in position on valve body (Fig. 72).

(27) Install screws to attach transfer plate to valve body (Fig. 72).

(28) Turn valve body over to expose the separator plate.

(29) Insert converter clutch valve and spring into converter clutch valve module (Fig. 73). Verify valve components slide freely.

(30) Insert spring and fail-safe valve into converter clutch valve module (Fig. 73). Verify valve components slide freely.

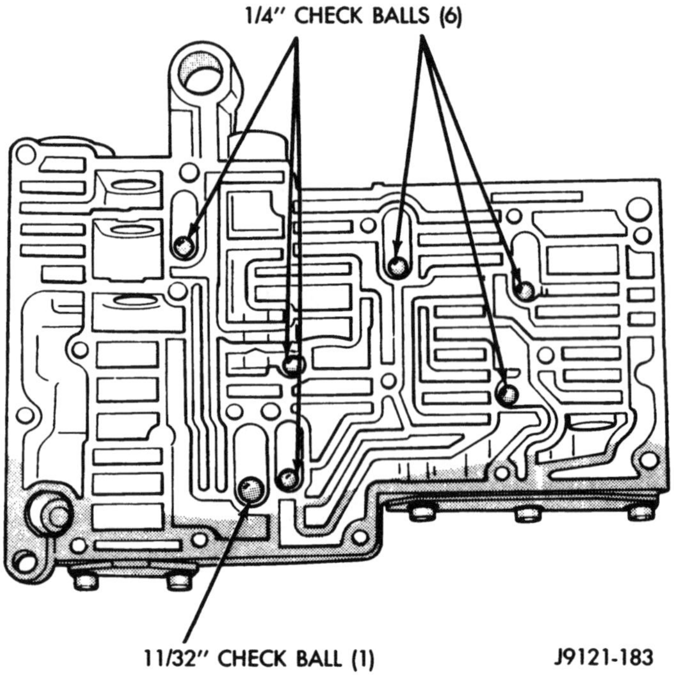

Fig. 71 Correct Position Of Valve Body Check Balls

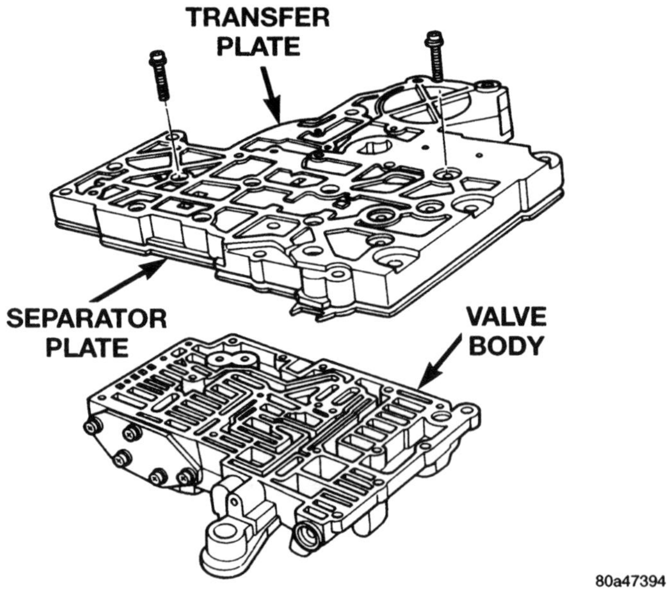

Fig. 72 Valve Body Transfer Plate Screws

(31) Place cover plate in position on converter clutch valve module (Fig. 73).

(32) Install screws to attach cover to converter clutch valve module (Fig. 73).

(33) Insert connecting tube into converter clutch valve module (Fig. 73).

(34) Insert connecting tube into valve body opening (Fig. 74).

DISASSEMBLY AND ASSEMBLY (Continued)

(35) Place converter clutch valve module in position on separator plate. Install screws to attach converter clutch module to valve body (Fig. 74).

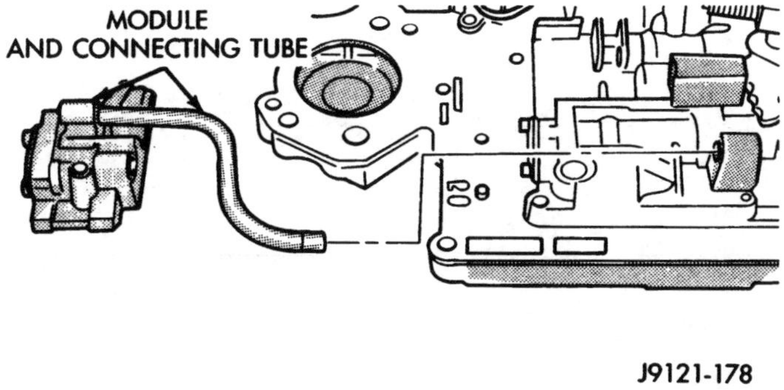

Fig. 74 Clutch Module And Connecting Tube

(36) If necessary, install a new O-ring on converter clutch solenoid (Fig. 75).

(37) Insert converter clutch solenoid into transfer plate (Fig. 75).

(38) Install screw to attach solenoid to transfer plate (Fig. 75).

(39) If necessary, adjust park rod to specified length (Fig. 76).

(40) If necessary, insert park rod end into manual lever and install E-clip (Fig. 77).

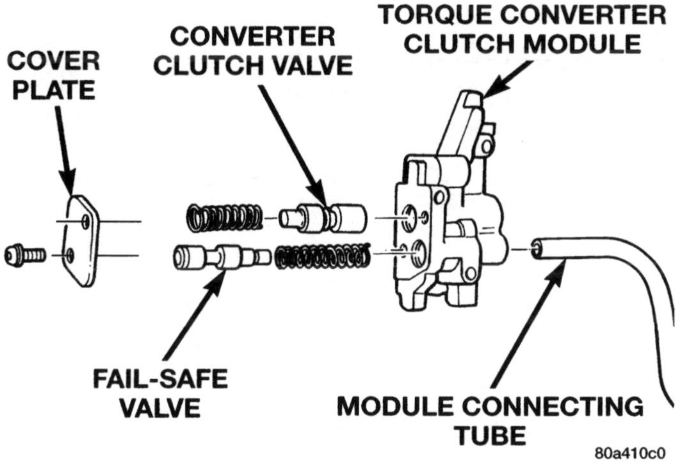

Fig. 73 Converter Clutch Valve Module

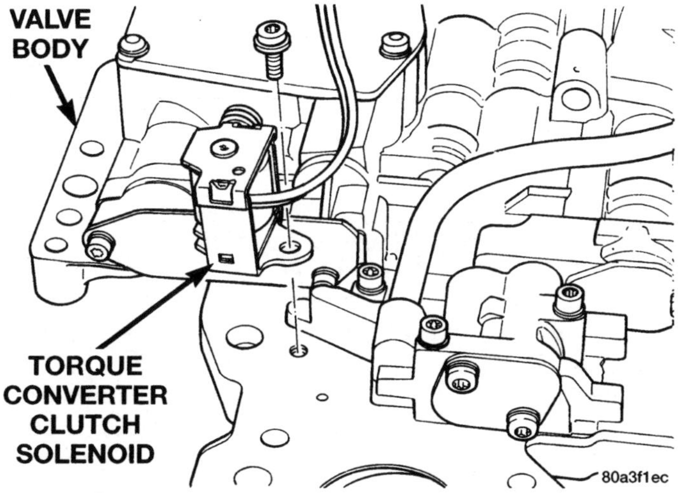

Fig. 75 Converter Clutch Solenoid

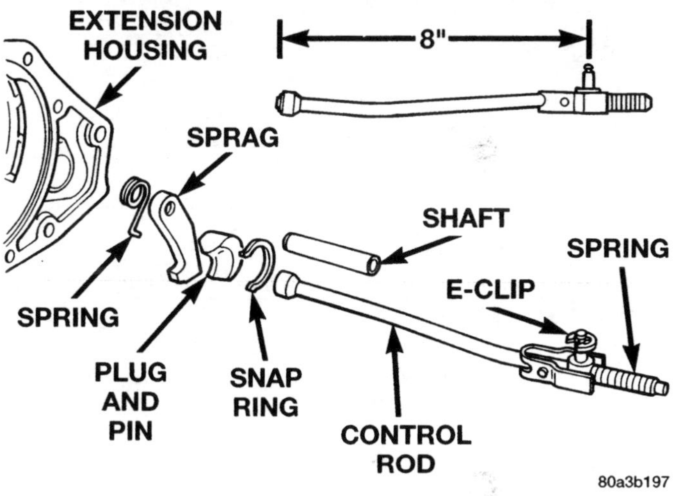

Fig. 76 Park Rod Measurement

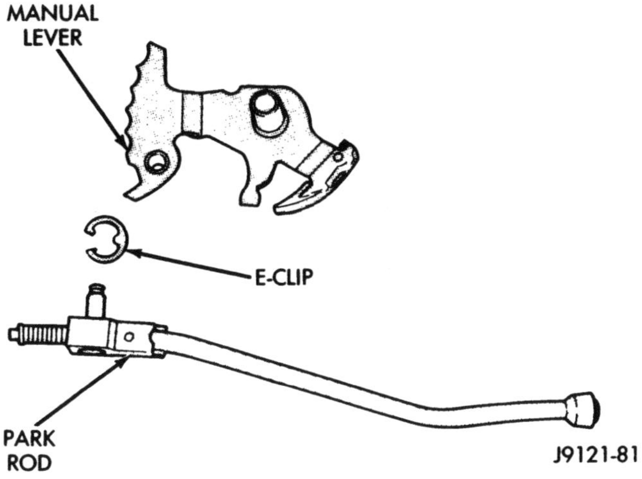

Fig. 77 Park Rod

DISASSEMBLY AND ASSEMBLY (Continued)

(41) Insert detent spring and ball into opening in valve body and install Retainer Tool 6583. (Fig. 78).

(42) Install manual valve into valve body (Fig. 79)

(43) Insert throttle lever through transfer plate side of valve body and upward (Fig. 80).

(44) Insert throttle lever into groove in manual valve (Fig. 81).

(45) Install seal, washer, and E-clip to retain manual shaft to valve body (Fig. 80).

(46) Install switch valve and spring, pressure regulator valve and spring, kickdown valve and spring, and throttle valve into valve body (Fig. 82).

(47) Place adjusting screw bracket and line pressure adjusting screw in position on valve body and compress springs. (Fig. 53).

(48) Install screws to attach adjuster bracket to valve body.

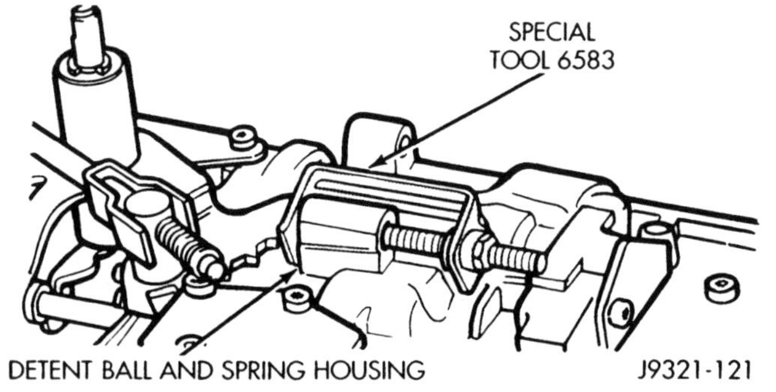

Fig. 78 Securing Detent Ball And Spring With Retainer Tool

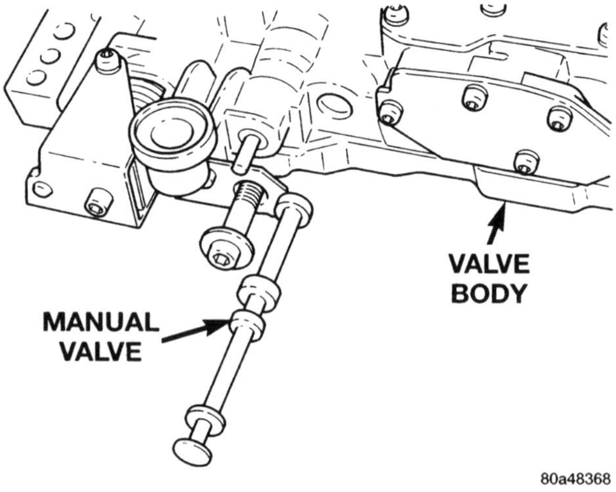

Fig. 79 Manual Valve

TRANSMISSION

DISASSEMBLE

(1) Drain fluid from transmission.

(2) Remove transmission from vehicle.

(3) Install a suitable tail shaft housing plug to avoid contaminating internal components with cleaning solvents.

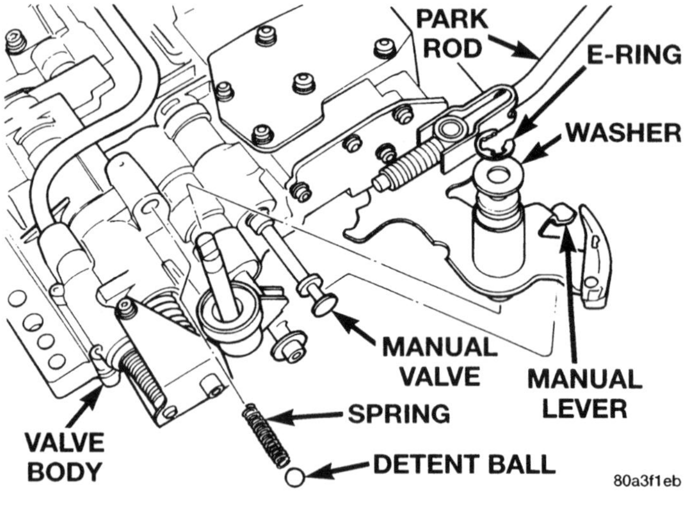

Fig. 80 Manual And Throttle Levers

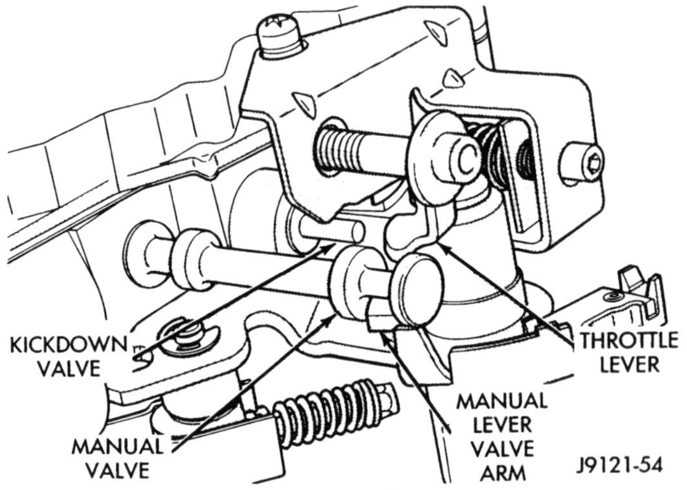

Fig. 81 Manual Valve And Throttle Lever Alignment

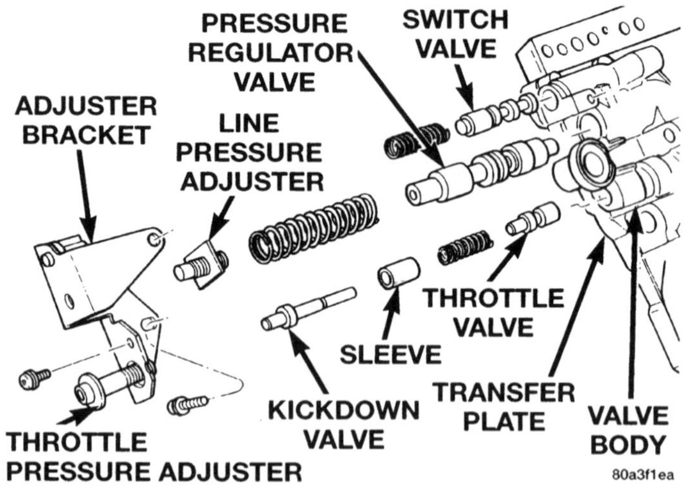

Fig. 82 Adjusting Screw Bracket, Springs, and Valves

(4) Clean exterior of transmission with suitable solvent or pressure washer.

(5) Remove torque converter from transmission.

DISASSEMBLY AND ASSEMBLY (Continued)

(6) Remove throttle and shift levers from valve body manual shaft and throttle lever shaft.

(7) Mount transmission in repair stand C-3750-B or similar type stand (Fig. 83).

(8) Remove extension housing.

(9) Remove fluid pan.

(10) Remove park/neutral position switch and seal (Fig. 84).

(11) Remove valve body.

(12) Remove accumulator spring and piston (Fig. 85). 32RH is equipped with a spring under the accumulator piston.

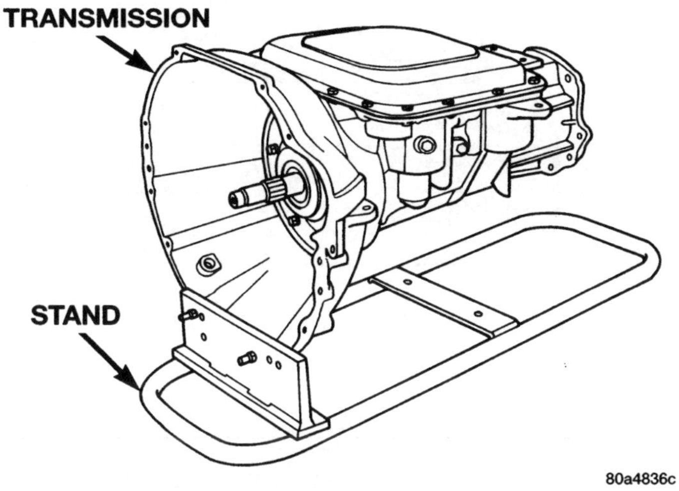

Fig. 83 Repair Stand

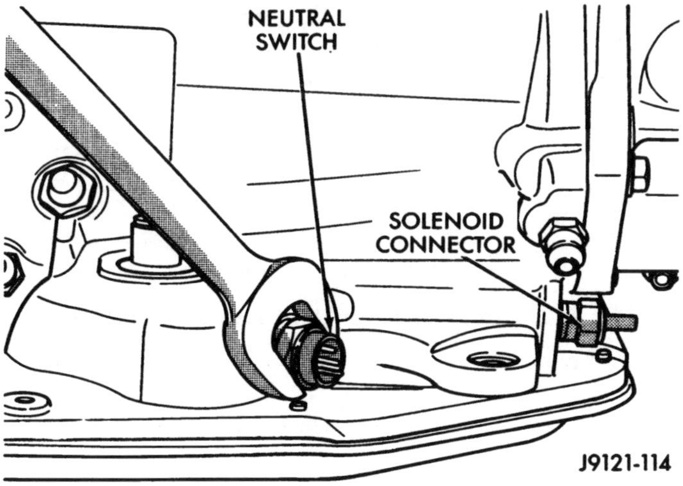

Fig. 84 Park/Neutral Position Switch

(13) Loosen front band adjusting screw lock nut (Fig. 86) 4-5 turns. Then tighten band adjusting screw until band is tight around front clutch. This prevents front/rear clutches from coming out with pump and possibly damaging clutch or pump components.

(14) Remove oil pump bolts.

(15) Thread bolts of Slide Hammer Tools C-3752 into threaded holes in pump body flange (Fig. 87).

Fig. 85 Accumulator Piston And Spring

(16) Bump slide hammer weights outward to remove pump and reaction shaft support assembly from case (Fig. 87).

(17) Loosen front band adjusting screw until band is completely loose (Fig. 86).

(18) Squeeze front band together and remove band strut (Fig. 88).

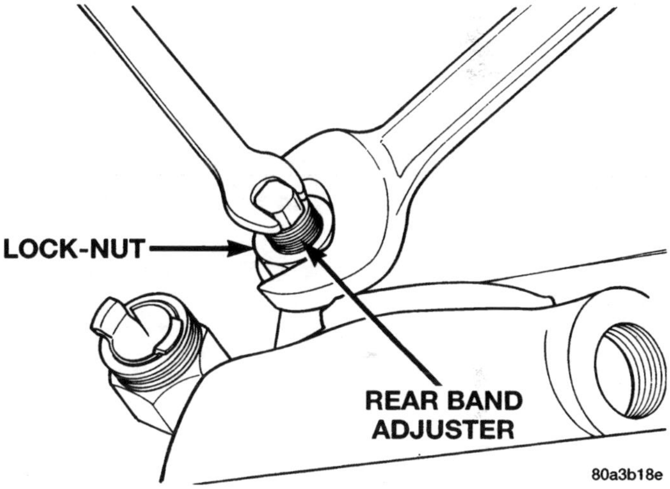

Fig. 86 Front Band Adjusting Screw Lock Nut

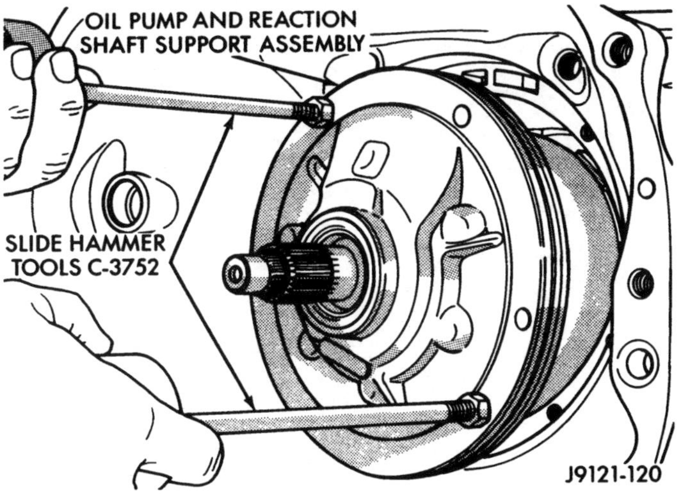

Fig. 87 Oil Pump/Reaction Shaft Support

DISASSEMBLY AND ASSEMBLY (Continued)

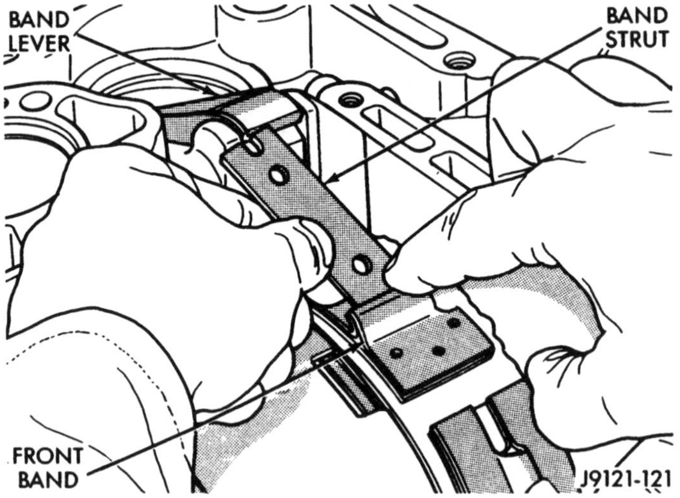

Fig. 88 Front Band Strut

(19) Remove front and rear clutch units as an assembly. Grasp input shaft, hold clutch units together and remove them from case (Fig. 89).

(20) Lift front clutch off rear clutch (Fig. 90). Set clutch units aside for overhaul.

(21) Remove output shaft thrust washer from output shaft (or from rear clutch hub) (Fig. 91).

(22) Remove output shaft thrust plate and washer from output shaft hub (Fig. 91).

(23) Remove front band from case (Fig. 92).

(24) Remove extension housing from transmission case. Refer to Removal and Installation section of this group.

(25) Remove governor body and park gear from output shaft. Refer to Removal and Installation procedures section of this group.

(26) Remove output shaft and planetary geartrain as assembly (Fig. 93). Support geartrain with both hands during removal. Do not allow machined surfaces on output shaft to become nicked or scratched.

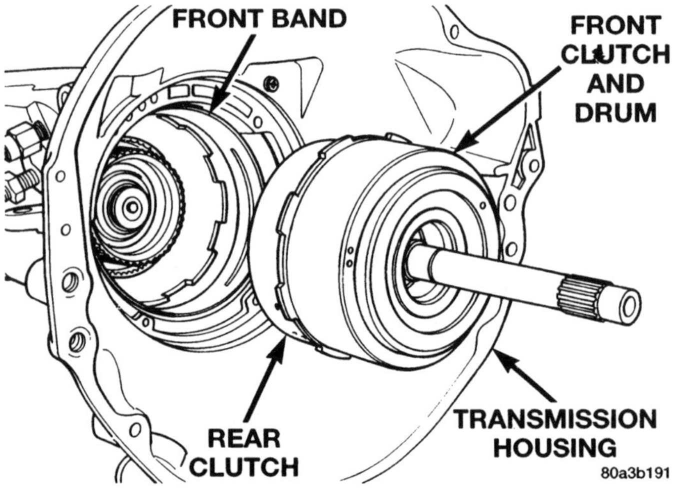

Fig. 89 Front/Rear Clutch Assemblies

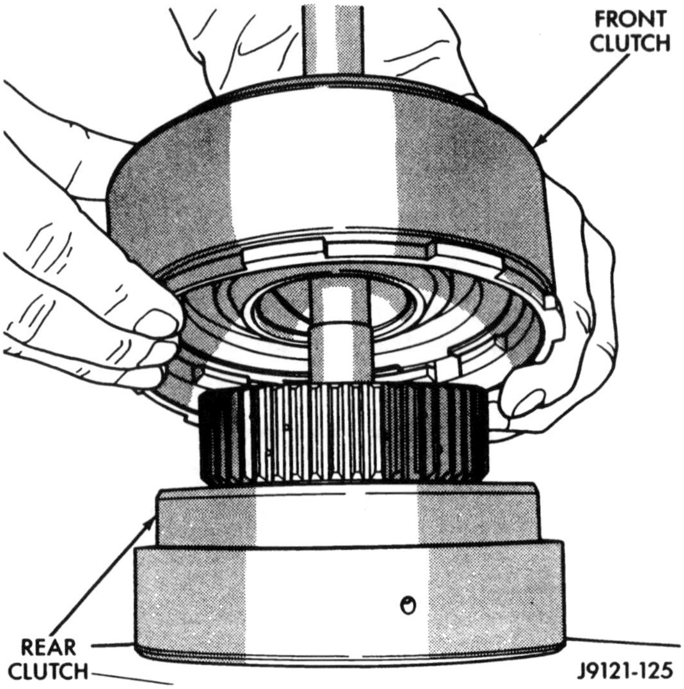

Fig. 90 Separating Front Clutch From Rear Clutch

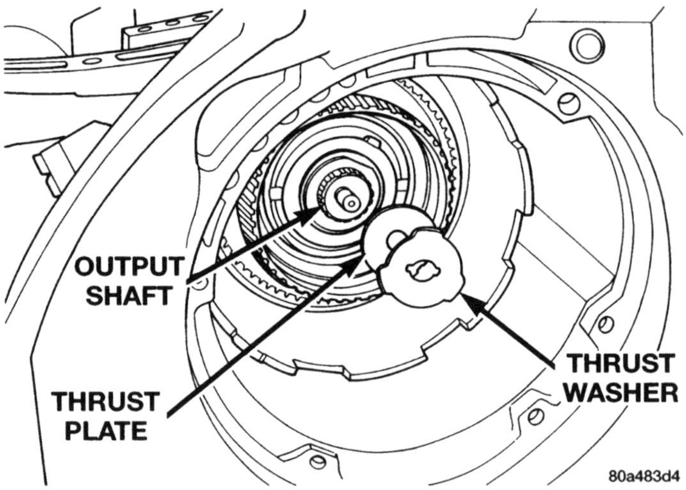

Fig. 91 Output Shaft Thrust Plate and Washer

(27) Loosen rear band adjusting screw 4-5 turns (Fig. 94).

(28) Remove snap ring that secures low-reverse drum to rear support hub, however do not remove drum at this time (Fig. 95).

(29) Remove bolts attaching rear support to transmission case and pull support from low-reverse drum (Fig. 96).

(30) Remove bolts attaching overrunning clutch cam and low-reverse drum to transmission case (Fig. 97).

REAR BAND—32RH.

(31) Remove rear band. The 32RH transmission is equipped with a double-wrap band that does not require a link bar.

DISASSEMBLY AND ASSEMBLY (Continued)

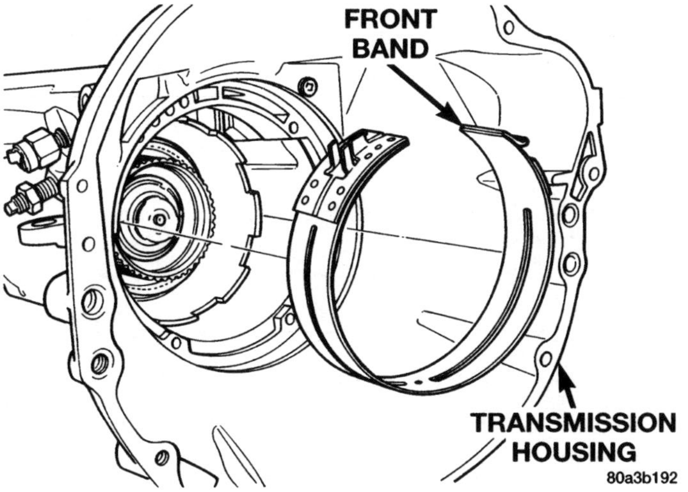

Fig. 92 Front Band

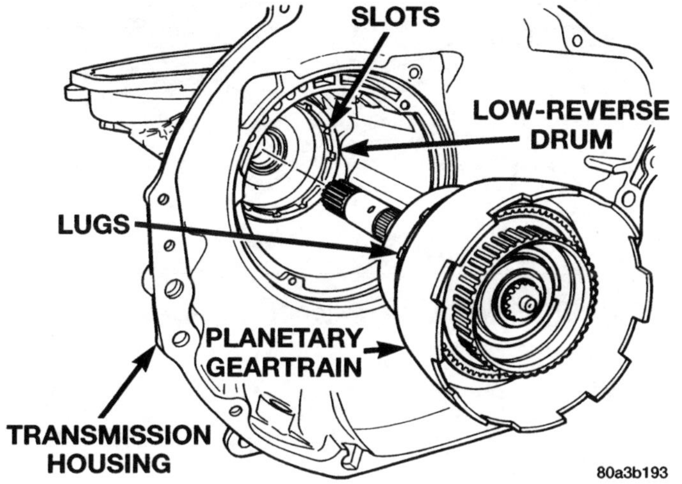

Fig. 93 Planetary Geartrain

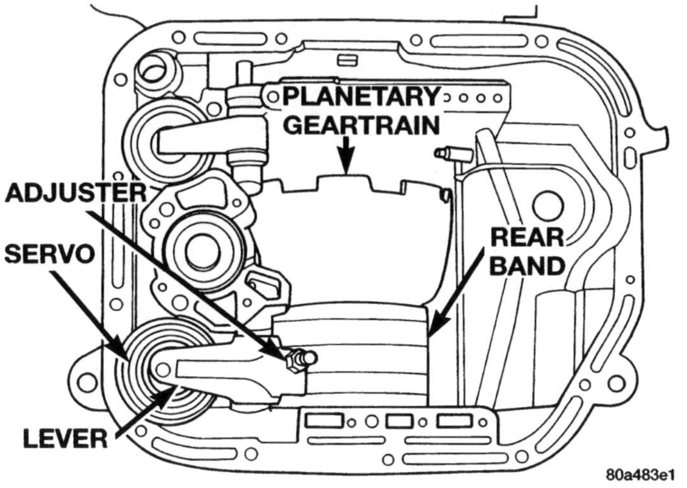

Fig. 94 Rear Band Adjuster Location

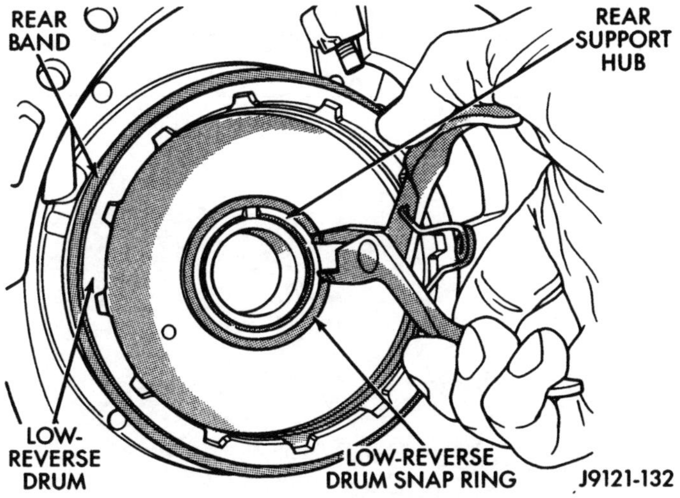

Fig. 95 Low-Reverse Drum Snap Ring

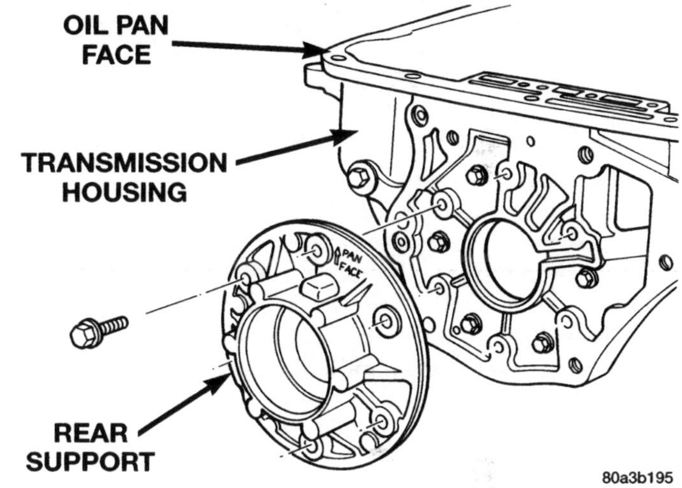

Fig. 96 Rear Support

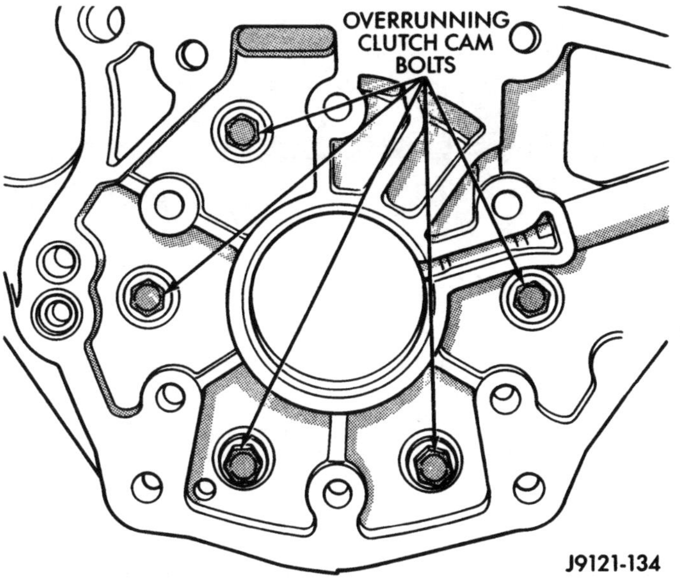

Fig. 97 Overrunning Clutch Cam Bolt Locations

DISASSEMBLY AND ASSEMBLY (Continued)

(a) Remove low-reverse drum and overrunning clutch as assembly. Slide drum and clutch through rear band and out of case (Fig. 98). Set drum and clutch assembly aside for cleaning and inspection.

(b) Remove rear band from case (Fig. 98).

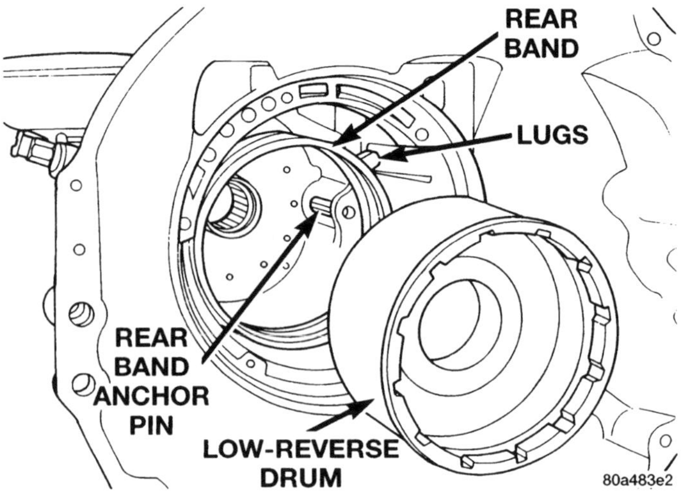

Fig. 98 Low- Reverse Band and Drum—32RH

REAR BAND—30RH

(32) Remove rear band. The 30RH transmission is equipped with a single-wrap band with a link bar.

(a) Using snap-ring plier, pull rear band anchor pin (located on the servo side of the rear support) from transmission case.

(b) Remove rear band and link from transmission (Fig. 99).

(c) Separate rear band from link (Fig. 100).

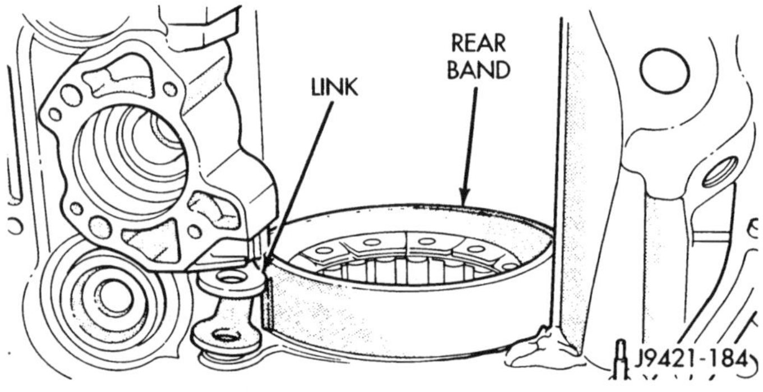

Fig. 99 Rear Band and Link—30RH

(33) If necessary remove front and rear band servo levers. All transmission components can be serviced without removing the levers.

(a) Using a 1/4 inch drive extension remove front band reaction pin access plug (Fig. 101).

(b) Remove front band reaction pin with pencil magnet. Pin is accessible from converter housing side of case (Fig. 102).

(c) Remove front band lever (Fig. 103).

(d) Using snap-ring plier, pull rear band lever pivot from transmission case (Fig. 104).

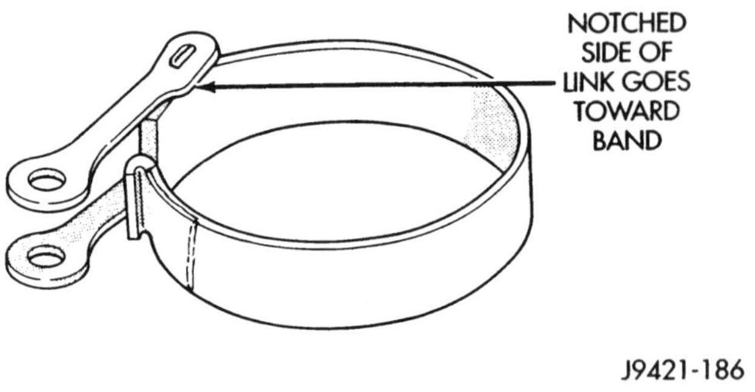

Fig. 100 Rear Band and Link—30RH

(e) Separate rear band servo lever from transmission.

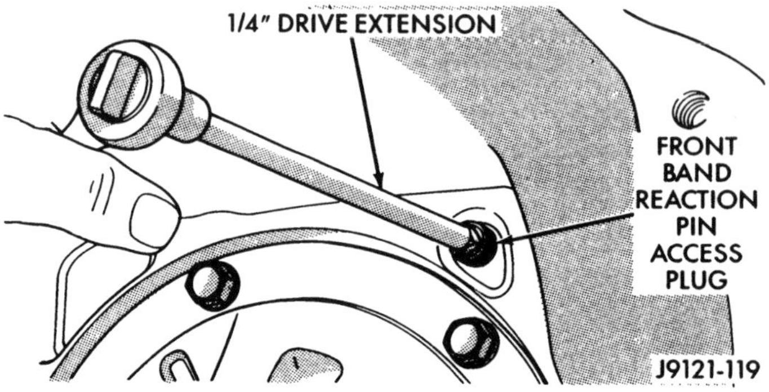

Fig. 101 Front Band Reaction Pin Access Plug

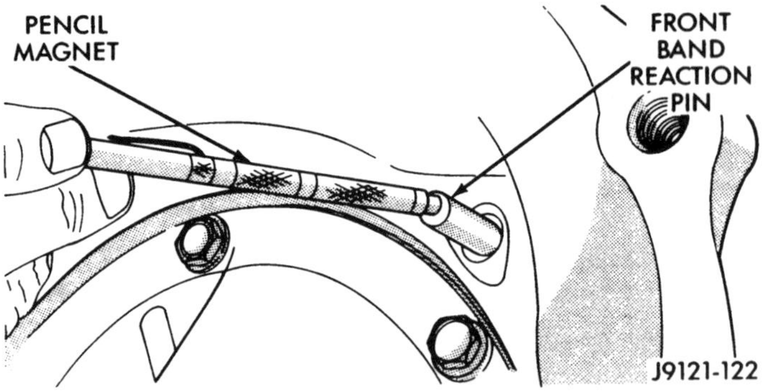

Fig. 102 Front Band Reaction Pin

(34) Compress front servo rod guide about 1/8 in. with large C-clamp and Tool C-4470, or Spring Compressor Tool C-3422-B (Fig. 105).

(35) Remove front servo rod guide snap ring (Fig. 105). **Exercise caution when removing snap ring. Servo bore can be scratched or nicked if care is not exercised.**

(36) Remove compressor tools and remove front servo rod guide, spring and servo piston.

(37) Compress rear servo spring retainer about 1/16 in. with C-clamp and Tool C-4470 or SP-5560 (Fig. 106). Valve Spring Compressor C-3422-B can also be used to compress spring retainer.

DISASSEMBLY AND ASSEMBLY (Continued)

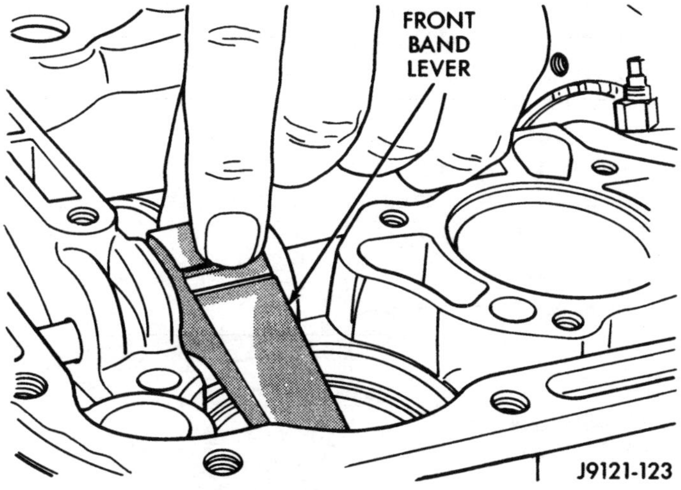

Fig. 103 Front Band Lever

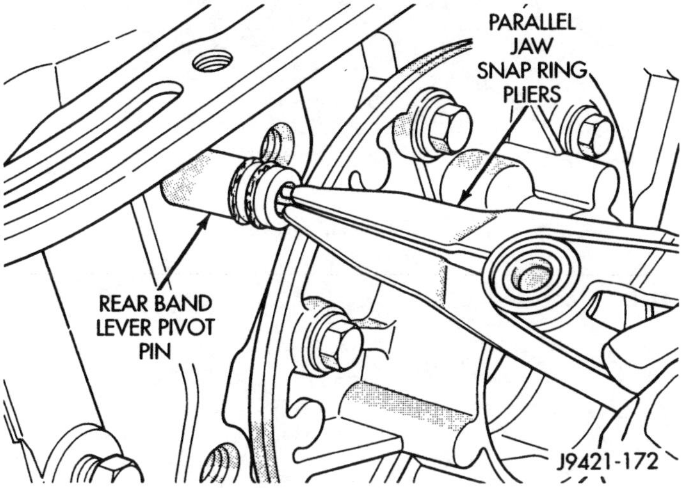

Fig. 104 Rear Band Servo Lever Pin

(38) Remove rear servo spring retainer snap ring. Then remove compressor tools and remove rear servo spring and piston.

TRANSMISSION ASSEMBLE

Disassemble, clean, inspect, assemble, and adjust internal components as necessary before assembling transmission.

(1) Install rear servo piston, spring and spring retainer. Compress rear servo spring and retainer with Compressor Tool C-3422-B (Fig. 106) or a large C-clamp.

(2) Install front servo piston, spring and rod guide. Compress front servo rod guide with Valve Spring Compressor C-3422-B and install servo snap ring (Fig. 105).

REAR BAND—32RH

(3) Install rear band

(a) Insert rear band through pan opening in transmission case. Single lug toward pan face.

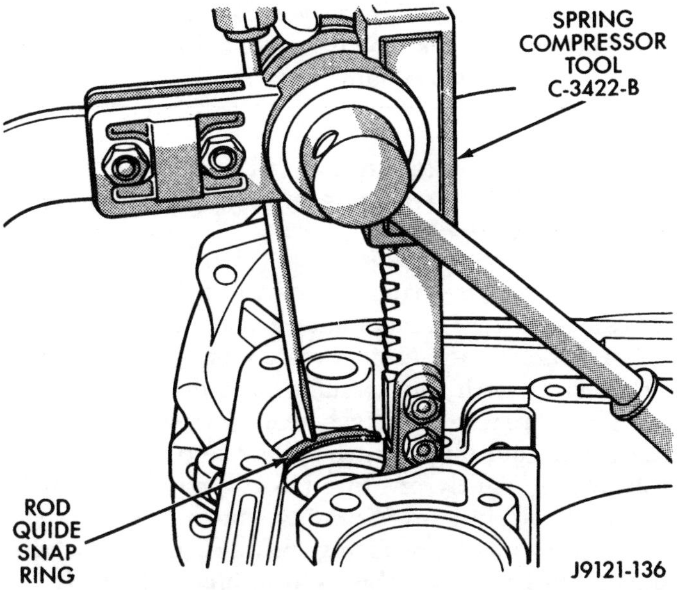

Fig. 105 Compressing Front Servo

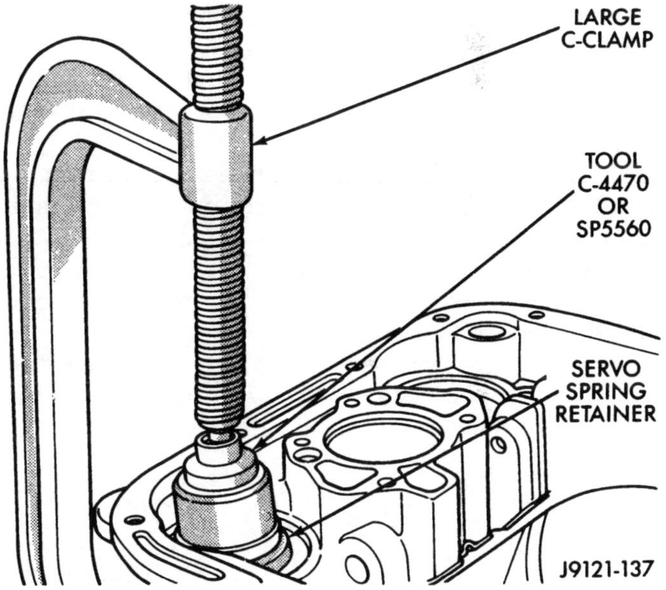

Fig. 106 Compressing Rear Servo Spring

(b) Place single lug under adjuster screw and two lugs over anchor pin in transmission case (Fig. 98).

REAR BAND—30RH

(4) Install rear band.

(a) Assemble link bar to band. Notched side of link toward band (Fig. 104).

(b) Insert rear band through pan opening in transmission case.

(c) Insert hook on band onto adjuster lever.

(d) Align holes in link bar with hole in transmission case outboard of rear support opening (Fig. 103).

(e) Insert anchor pin into case through link bar.

DISASSEMBLY AND ASSEMBLY (Continued)

(5) Examine bolt holes in overrunning clutch cam. Note that one hole is **not threaded** (Fig. 107). This hole must align with blank area in clutch cam bolt circle.

NOTE: The bolt holes in cam are slightly countersunk on one side. This side of cam faces rearward (toward rear support).

(6) Lubricate overrunning clutch rollers, springs and cam with ATF Plus transmission fluid.

(7) Position overrunning clutch on a clean, flat work surface with countersunk holes downward.

(8) Place rear of low-reverse drum over overrunning clutch and align clutch rollers to hub of drum.

(9) While slightly pivoting low-reverse drum, push hub of drum into overrunning clutch. Verify that countersunk holes are facing outward. **Cam should be able to rotate in the drum clockwise only.**

(10) Insert a suitable awl through the rear support mounting hole closest to the pan sealing face. The awl should be next to the wide space area at the back of transmission case.

(11) Insert low-reverse drum and overrunning clutch into front of transmission case and into rear band.

(12) Insert awl tip into the threaded hole next to the non-threaded hole in the overrunning clutch cam. Verify that non-threaded hole is aligned with wide space area on transmission case.

(13) Push low-reverse drum rearward to close gap between cam and case.

(14) Install overrunning clutch cam bolts. **Clutch cam bolts are shorter than rear support bolts.** Tighten cam bolts to 17 N·m (150 in. lbs. or 13 ft. lbs.) torque.

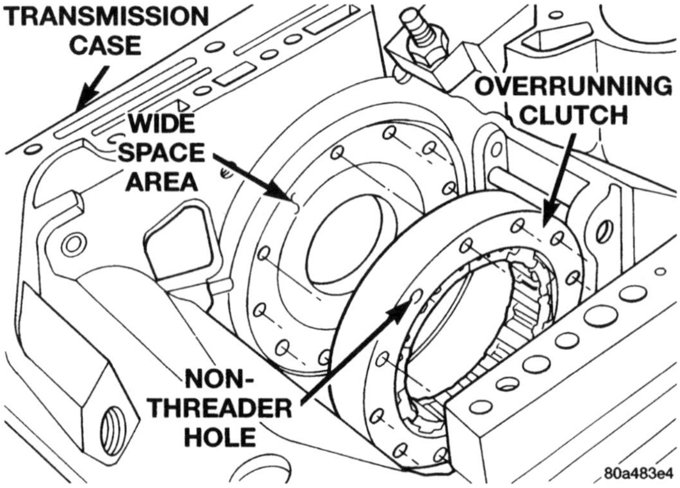

Fig. 107 Clutch Cam Alignment

(15) Hold low-reverse drum in position so rear support will not push it out of overrunning clutch.

(16) Insert rear support into opening at rear of transmission case (Fig. 108).

(17) Align support with the embossed arrow in the direction of the pan face.

(18) Install and tighten rear support bolts to 17 N·m (150 in. lbs.) torque.

(19) Install snap ring to retain low-reverse drum to hub of rear support (Fig. 109).

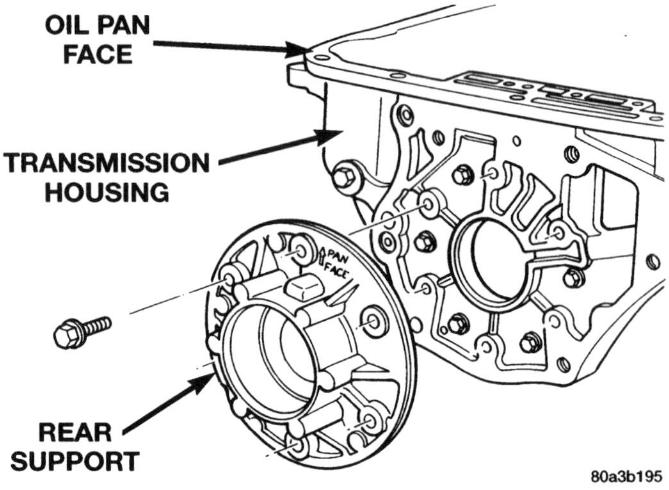

Fig. 108 Rear Support

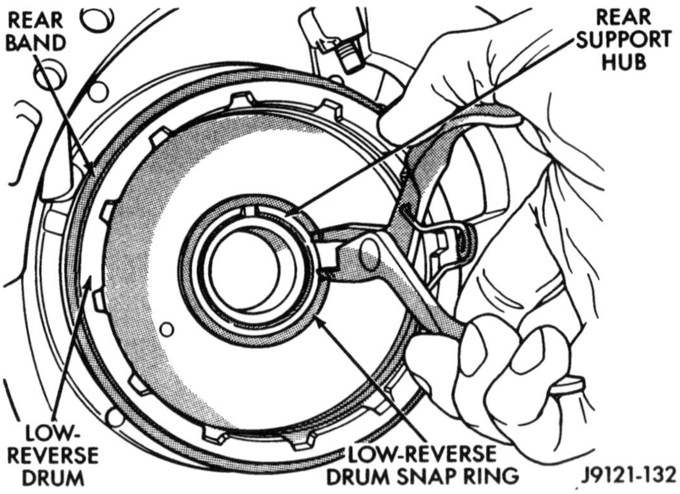

Fig. 109 Low-Reverse Drum Snap Ring

(20) Lubricate output shaft, rear support bore and low-reverse drum hub with transmission fluid.

(21) Install assembled output shaft and planetary geartrain in case (Fig. 110).

(22) Align drive lugs on rear planetary gear with slots in low-reverse drum (Fig. 110). Then seat planetary assembly in drum.

(23) Install governor on output shaft. Refer to Removal and Installation section of this group.

(24) Turn and secure transmission so that front opening is upward.

(25) Assemble front and rear clutches together.

DISASSEMBLY AND ASSEMBLY (Continued)

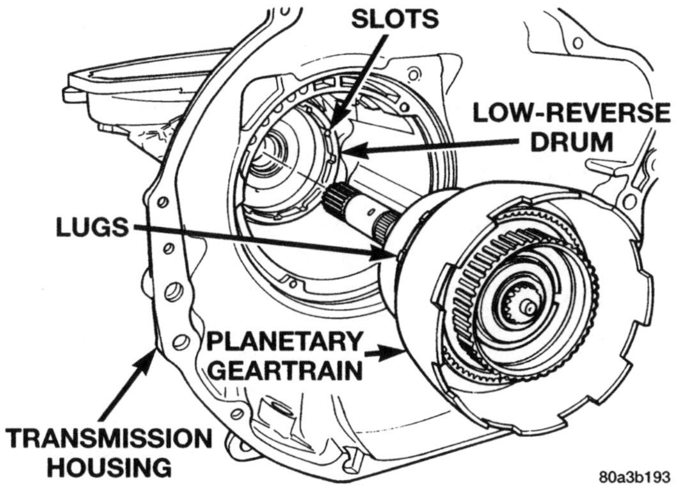

Fig. 110 Output Shaft And Planetary Geartrain

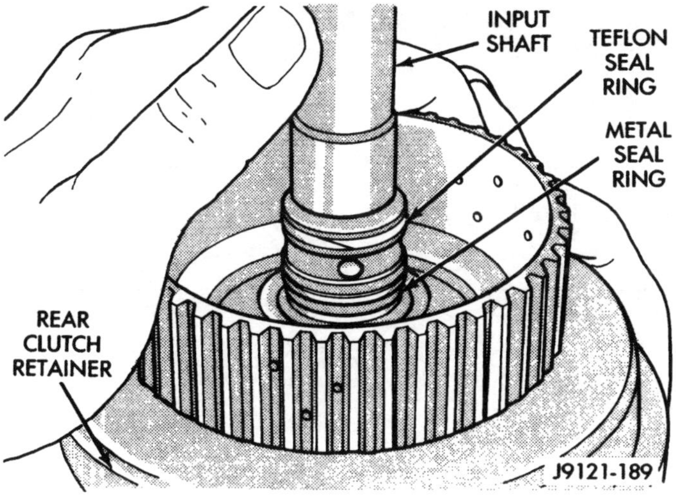

Fig. 111 Input Shaft Seal Ring Location

(a) Check input shaft seal rings (Fig. 111). Verify that diagonal-cut ends of Teflon™ seal ring are properly joined and ends of metal ring are correctly hooked together. Also be sure rings are installed in sequence shown.

(b) Align teeth on clutch discs in line.

(c) Insert input shaft on rear clutch into center of front clutch (Fig. 112).

(d) Engage teeth on rear clutch hub into teeth on clutch (Fig. 114). Rotate front clutch retainer back and forth until completely seated on rear clutch.

(26) Install output shaft thrust plate on shaft hub in planetary geartrain driving shell (Fig. 113). Use petroleum jelly to hold thrust plate in place.

(27) Check rear clutch thrust washer. Use additional petroleum jelly to hold washer in place if necessary.

(28) Coat output shaft thrust washer with petroleum jelly. Install washer in rear clutch hub (Fig. 115). Use enough petroleum jelly to hold washer in place. **Be sure grooved side of washer faces rearward (toward output shaft) as shown. Also note that washer only fits one way in clutch hub.**

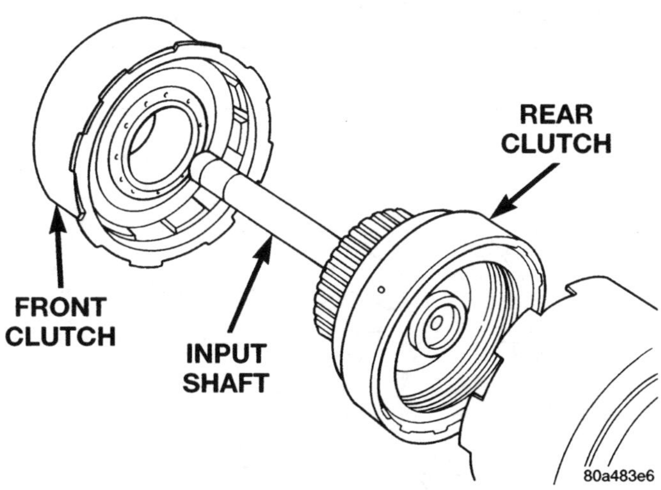

Fig. 112 Front and Rear Clutches

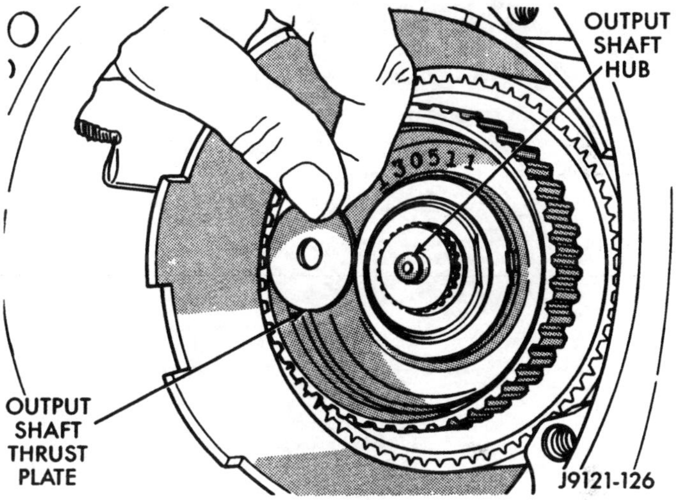

Fig. 113 Output Shaft Thrust Plate

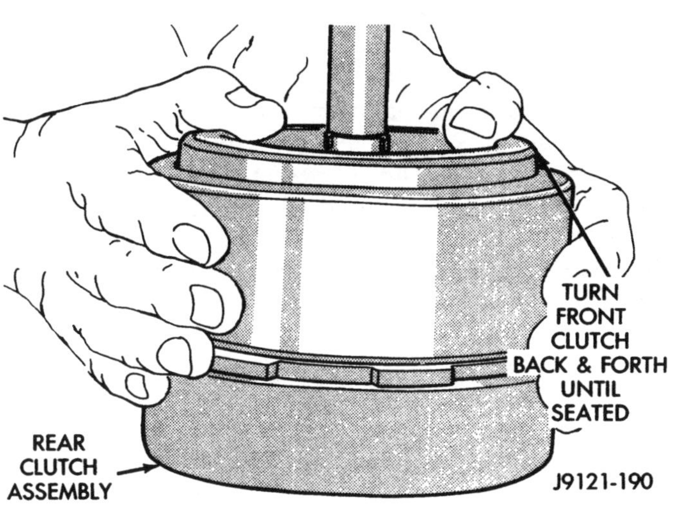

Fig. 114 Assembling Front And Rear Clutch Units

DISASSEMBLY AND ASSEMBLY (Continued)

(29) Align drive teeth on rear clutch discs with small screwdriver (Fig. 116). This will make installation into front of planetary geartrain easier.

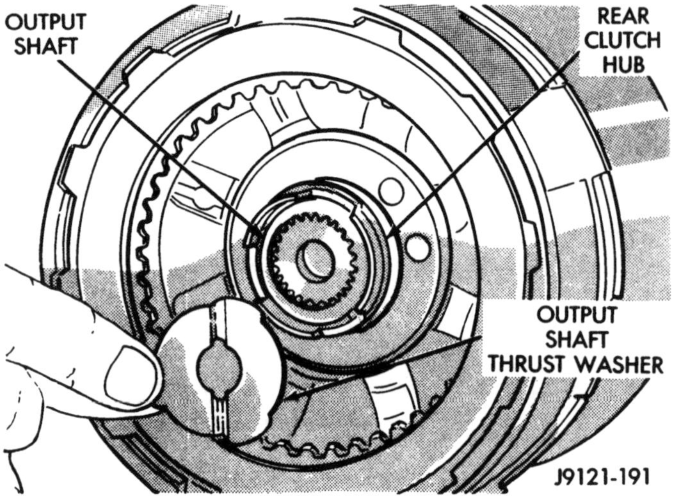

Fig. 115 Output Shaft Thrust Washer

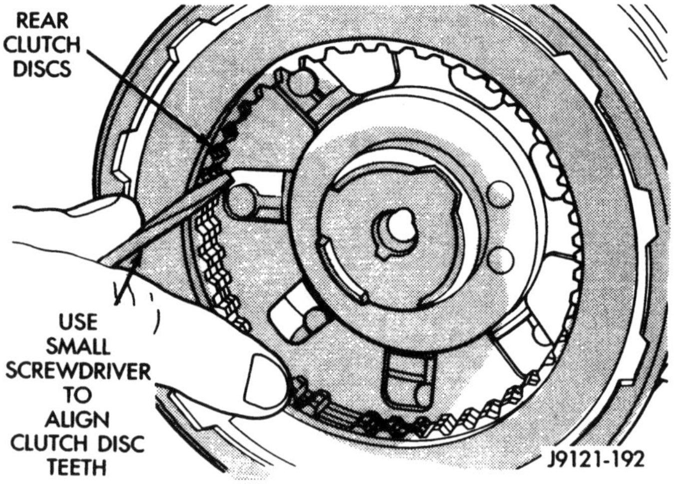

Fig. 116 Aligning Rear Clutch Disc Lugs

(30) Insert front band into opening at front of transmission case (Fig. 117).

(31) Install front and rear clutch units as assembly (Fig. 118). Align rear clutch with front annulus gear and install assembly in driving shell. **Be sure output shaft thrust washer and thrust plate are not displaced during installation.**

(32) Carefully work assembled clutches back and forth to engage and seat rear clutch discs on front annulus gear. Verify that front clutch drive lugs are fully engaged in slots of driving shell after installation.

(33) Engage front band on adjusting screw and hold band in place

(34) Install strut between band lever and front band (Fig. 119).

(35) Tighten front band adjusting screw until band just grips clutch retainer. Verify that front/rear clutches are still seated before continuing.

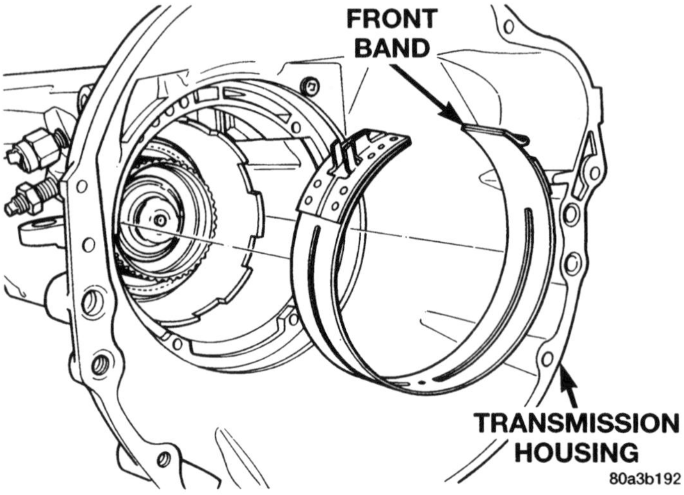

Fig. 117 Front Band

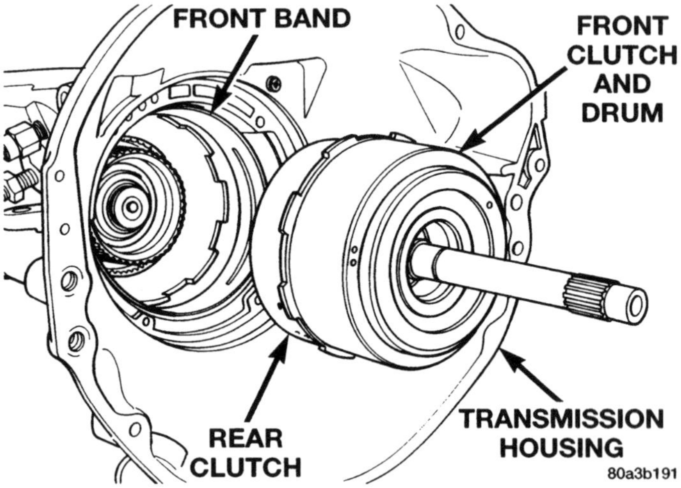

Fig. 118 Installing Front/Rear Clutch

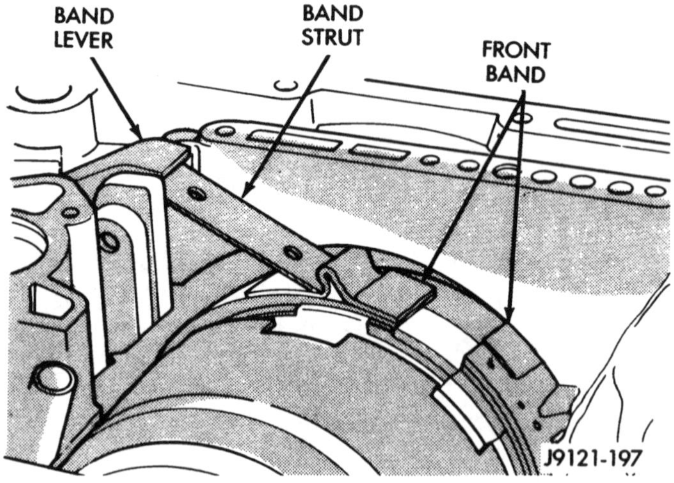

Fig. 119 Front Band Linkage Installation

DISASSEMBLY AND ASSEMBLY (Continued)

(36) Verify that reaction shaft support hub seal rings are hooked together (Fig. 120).

(37) Coat front clutch thrust washer with petroleum jelly to hold it in place. Then install washer over reaction shaft hub and seat it on pump (Fig. 121).

CAUTION: The thrust washer bore (I.D.), is chamfered on one side. Make sure the chamfered side is installed so it faces the pump.

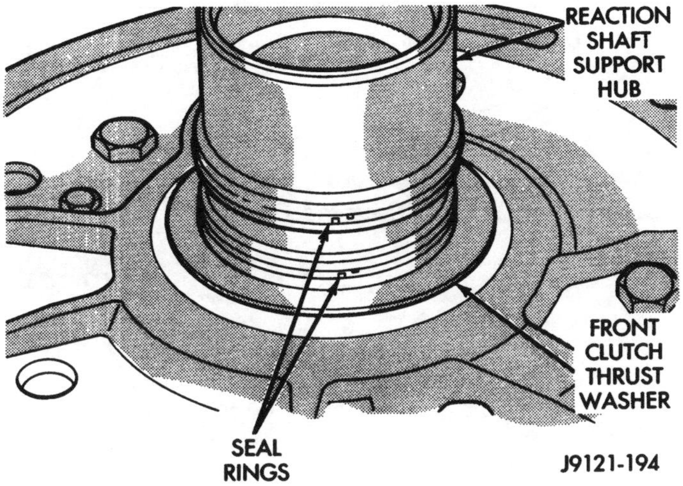

Fig. 120 Reaction Shaft Support Seal Rings

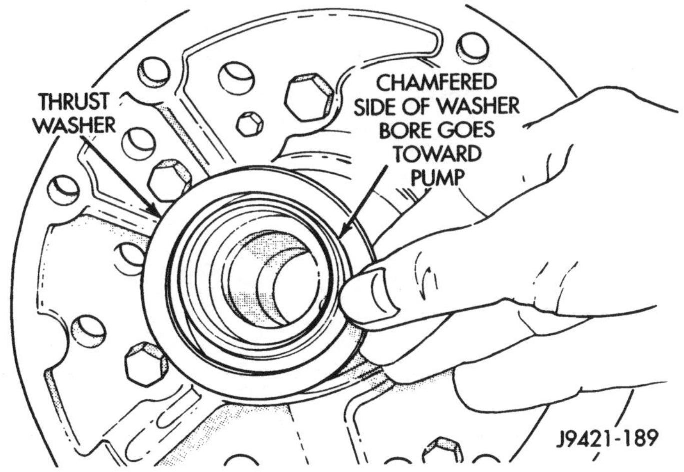

Fig. 121 Front Clutch Thrust Washer Installation

(38) Thread two Pilot Stud Tools C-3288-B into bolt holes in oil pump flange (Fig. 122).

(39) Align and install oil pump gasket (Fig. 122).

(40) Lubricate oil pump seals with Mopar Door-Ease, or Ru-Glyde, Door Eze, or ATF Plus.

(41) Install oil pump (Fig. 123). Align and position pump on pilot studs. Slide pump down studs and work it into front clutch hub and case by hand. Then install two or three pump bolts to hold pump in place.

(42) Remove pilot stud tools and install remaining oil pump bolts. Tighten bolts alternately in diagonal pattern to 20 N·m (15 ft. lbs.).

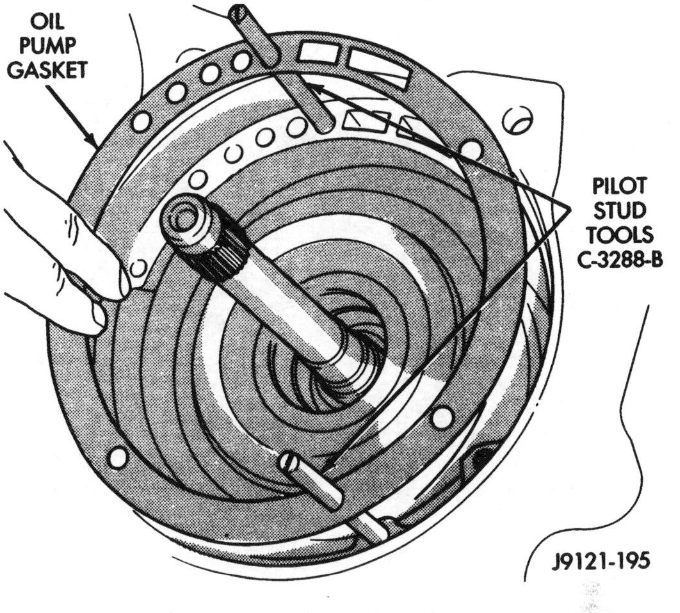

Fig. 122 Installing Pilot Studs And Oil Pump Gasket

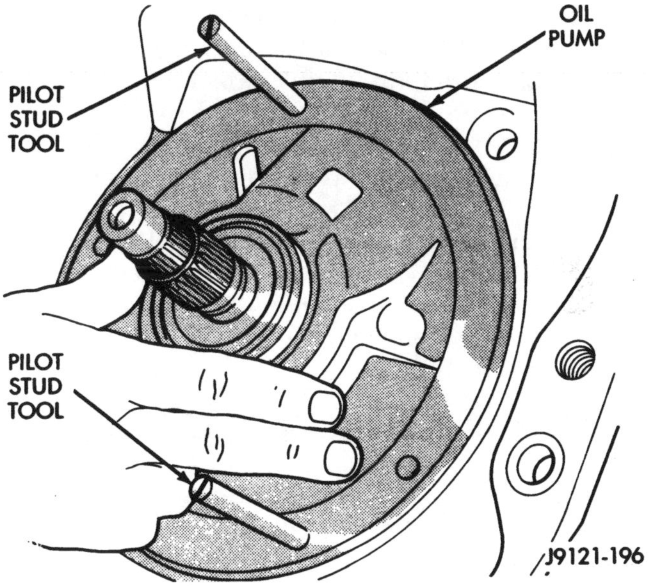

Fig. 123 Installing Oil Pump And Reaction Shaft Support

(43) Measure input shaft end play (Fig. 124).

NOTE: If end play is incorrect, transmission is incorrectly assembled, or output shaft thrust washer and/or thrust plate are worn and need to be changed.

(a) Attach dial indicator (C-3339) to converter housing. Position indicator plunger against input shaft and zero indicator.

DISASSEMBLY AND ASSEMBLY (Continued)

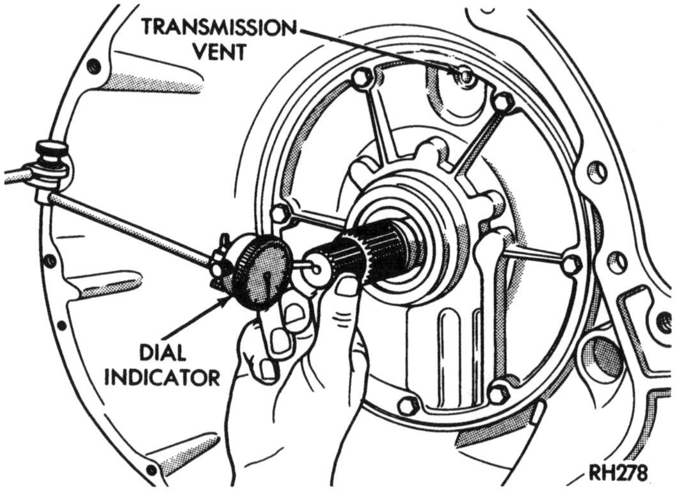

Fig. 124 Checking Input Shaft End Play

(b) Move input shaft in and out and record reading. End play should be 0.56 - 2.31 mm (0.022 - 0.091 in.).

(44) Position transmission on work surface with pan face upward.

(45) Install valve body, refer to Removal and Installation section of this group for procedure.

(46) Adjust front and rear bands, refer to Adjustments section of this group for procedure.

(47) Install fluid filter and pan, refer to Service Procedures section of this group for procedure.

(48) Install rear extension housing, refer to Removal and Installation section of this group for procedure.

(49) Install torque converter, refer to Removal and Installation section of this group for procedure.

(50) Install a small C-clamp at the bottom of torque converter housing to retain torque during transmission installation.

OVERRUNNING CLUTCH/LOW-REVERSE DRUM

DISASSEMBLE

If the clutch assembly came out with the low-reverse drum, thread two clutch cam bolts into the cam. Then lift the cam out of the drum with the bolts (Fig. 125). Rotate the cam back and forth to ease removal if necessary. Remove the clutch roller and spring assembly from the race afterward.

OVERRUNNING CLUTCH/LOW-REVERSE DRUM, ASSEMBLE

(1) Assemble clutch rollers and springs in retainer if necessary (Fig. 126).

(2) Install overrunning clutch roller, spring and retainer assembly in clutch cam (Fig. 127).

(3) Temporarily assemble and check overrunning clutch operation as follows:

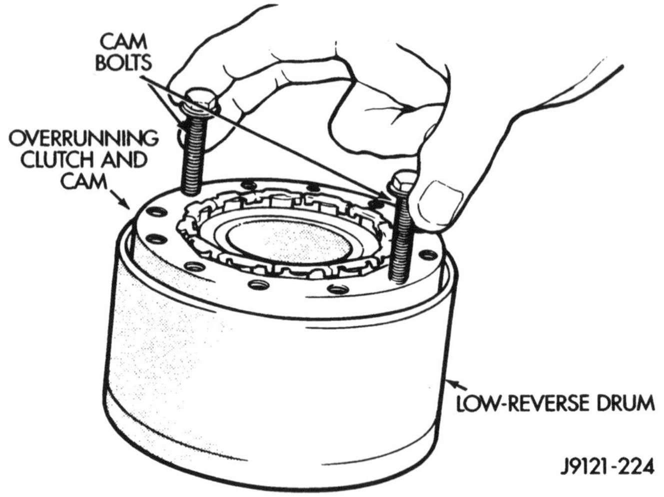

Fig. 125 Removing Overrunning Clutch From Low-Reverse Drum

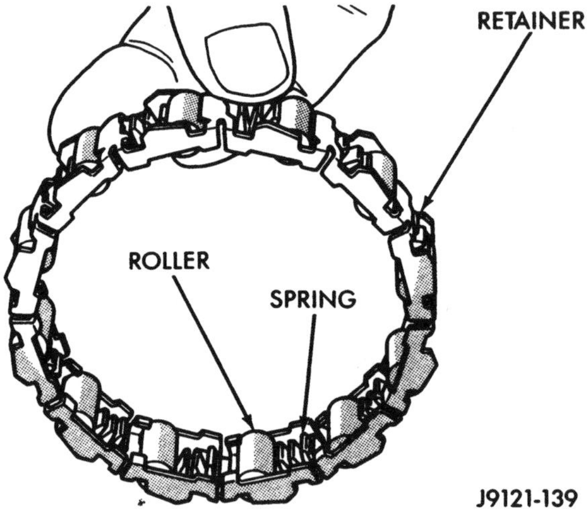

Fig. 126 Overrunning Clutch Rollers, Springs, Retainer

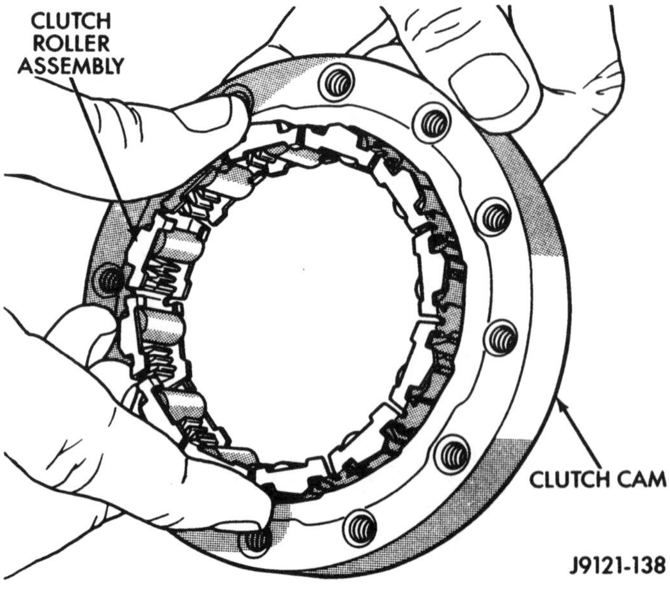

Fig. 127 Assembling Overrunning Clutch And Cam

DISASSEMBLY AND ASSEMBLY (Continued)

(a) Assemble cam and clutch.

(b) Install clutch assembly on low-reverse drum with twisting motion (Fig. 128).

(c) Install drum-clutch assembly in case and install clutch cam bolts.

(d) Install rear support and support attaching bolts.

(e) Check low-reverse drum rotation. **Drum should rotate freely in clockwise direction and lock when turned in counterclockwise direction (as viewed from front of case).**

(4) Note component position for assembly reference. Bolt holes in clutch cam are countersunk on one side, Be sure this side of cam will face rearward when installed (Fig. 129).

(5) Remove rear support, overrunning clutch and low-reverse drum. Set components aside for final assembly. **If overrunning clutch will be installed before final assembly, install cam only as described in Transmission Assembly And Adjustment section. Clutch cam must be properly indexed in case to fit and operate properly.**

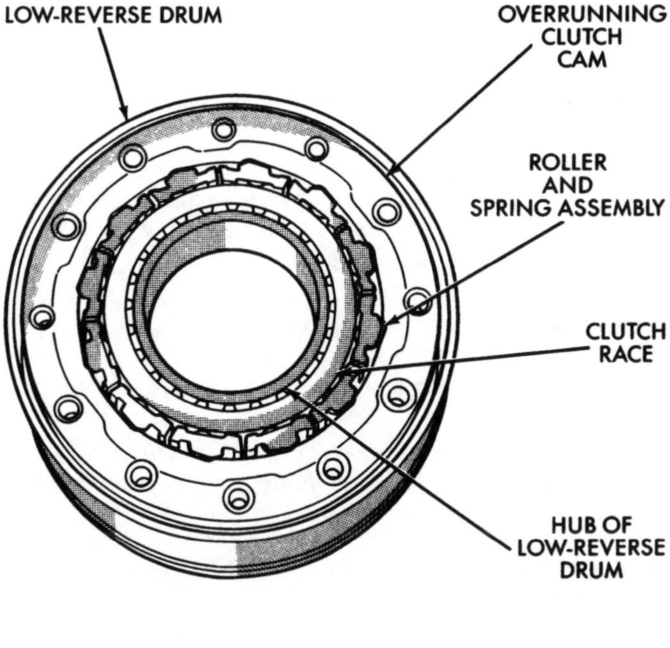

Fig. 129 Assembled Overrunning Clutch

FRONT SERVO PISTON

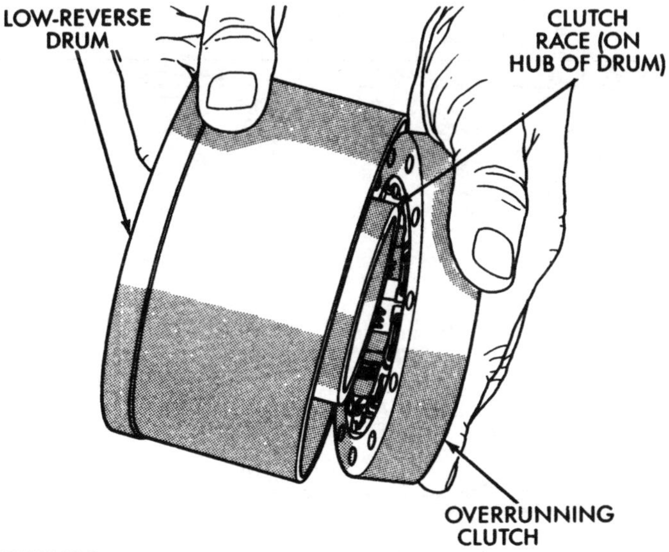

Fig. 128 Temporary Assembly Of Clutch And Drum To Check Operation

DISASSEMBLE

(1) Remove seal ring from rod guide (Fig. 130).

(2) Remove small snap ring from servo piston rod. Then remove piston rod, spring and washer from piston.

(3) Remove and discard servo component O-ring and seal rings.

ASSEMBLE

Clean and inspect front servo components.

(1) Lubricate new O-ring and seal rings with petroleum jelly and install them on piston, guide and rod.

(2) Install rod in piston. Install spring and washer on rod. Compress spring and install snap ring (Fig. 130).

(3) Set servo components aside for installation during transmission reassembly.

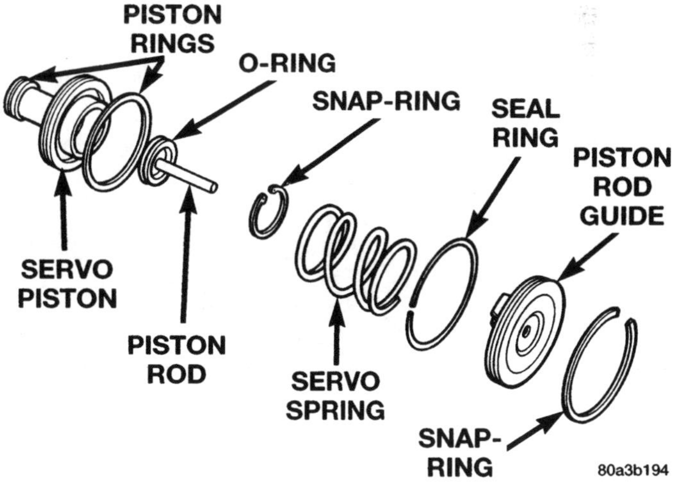

Fig. 130 Front Servo

DISASSEMBLY AND ASSEMBLY (Continued)

REAR SERVO PISTON

DISASSEMBLE

(1) Remove small snap ring and remove plug and spring from servo piston (Fig. 131).

(2) Remove and discard servo piston seal ring.

(3) Lubricate piston and guide seals with petroleum jelly. Lubricate other servo parts with Mopar ATF Plus transmission fluid.

ASSEMBLE

(1) Install new seal ring on servo piston.

(2) Assemble piston, plug, spring and new snap ring.

(3) Lubricate piston seal lip with petroleum jelly.

(4) Set servo components aside for assembly installation.

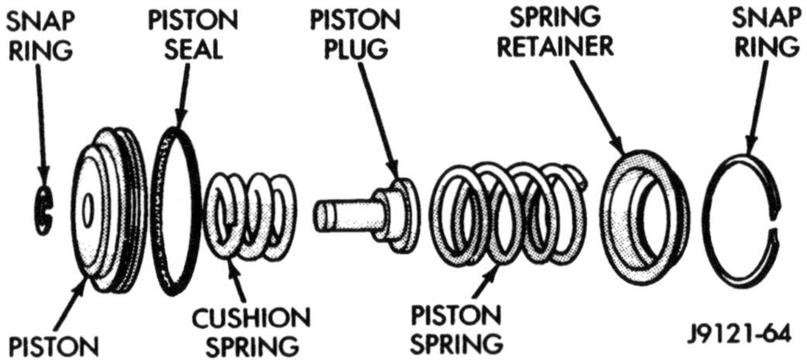

Fig. 131 Rear Servo Components

OIL PUMP AND REACTION SHAFT SUPPORT

DISASSEMBLE

(1) Remove seal ring from housing and reaction shaft support (Fig. 132).

(2) Mark pump housing and support assembly for alignment reference.

(3) Remove bolts attaching pump body to support (Fig. 133).

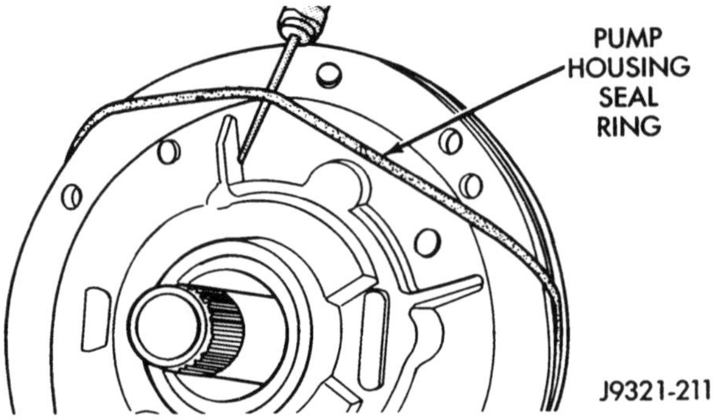

Fig. 132 Removing Pump Seal Ring

(4) Separate support from pump housing (Fig. 134).

(5) Remove inner and outer gears from reaction shaft support (Fig. 135).

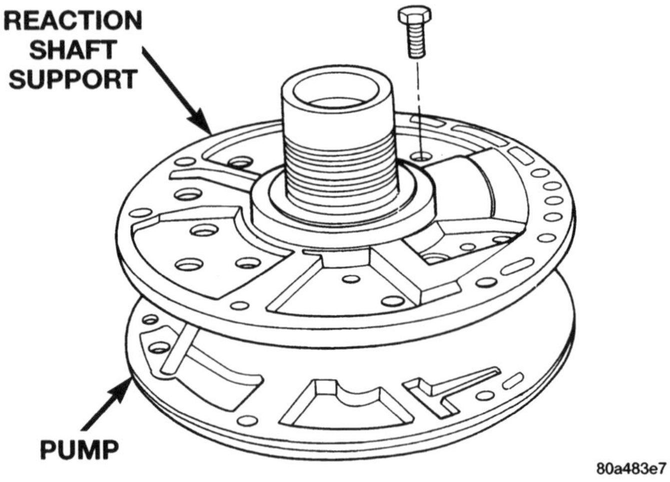

Fig. 133 Pump Support Bolts

(6) If pump seal was not removed during transmission disassembly, remove seal with punch and hammer.

(7) Remove front clutch thrust washer from support hub (Fig. 136).

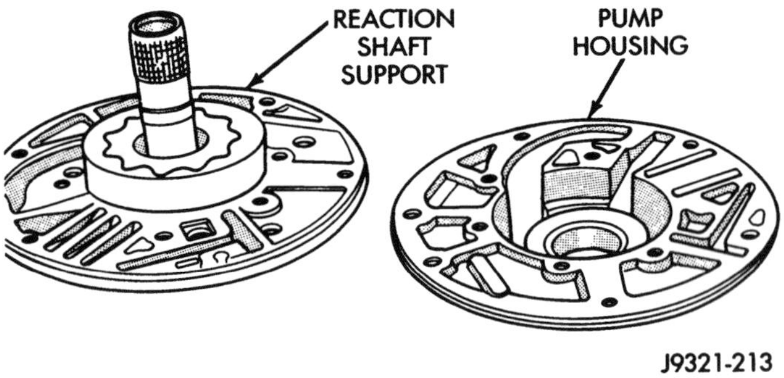

Fig. 134 Separating Pump Housing From Reaction Shaft Support

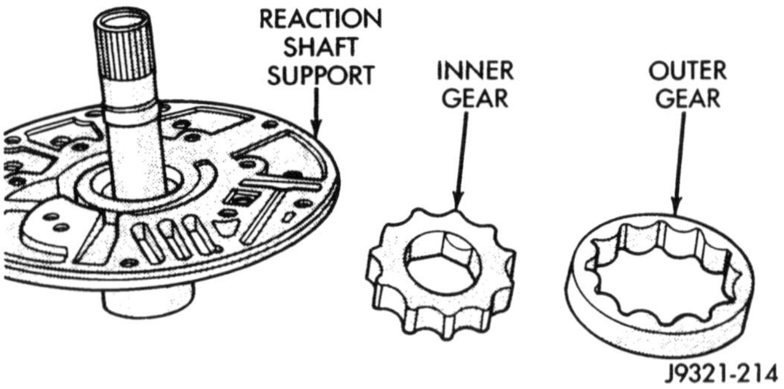

Fig. 135 Pump Gear Removal

DISASSEMBLY AND ASSEMBLY (Continued)

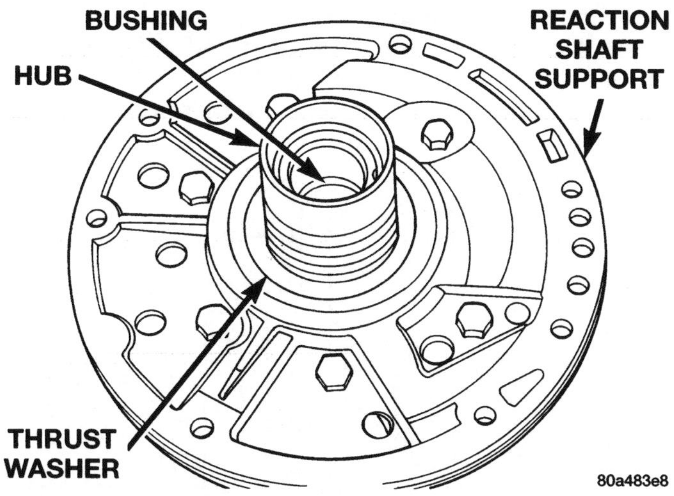

Fig. 136 Support Hub Thrust Washer

OIL PUMP BUSHING REPLACEMENT

(1) Remove pump bushing with Tool Handle C-4171 and Bushing Remover SP-3551 from Tool Set C-3887-J (Fig. 137).

(2) Install new pump bushing with Tool Handle C-4171 and Bushing Installer SP-5117 (Fig. 137). Bushing should be flush with pump housing bore.

(3) Stake new pump bushing in two places with blunt punch (Fig. 138). Remove burrs from stake points with knife blade afterward.

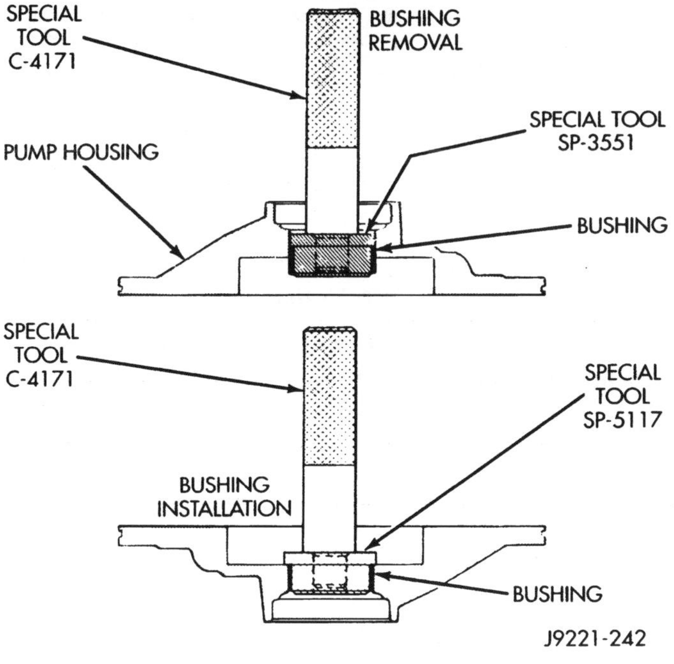

Fig. 137 Removing Oil Pump Bushing

REACTION SHAFT SUPPORT BUSHING REMOVAL

(1) Assemble Bushing Remover Tools SP-1191, 3633 and 5324 (Fig. 139). **Do not clamp any part of reaction shaft or support in vise.**

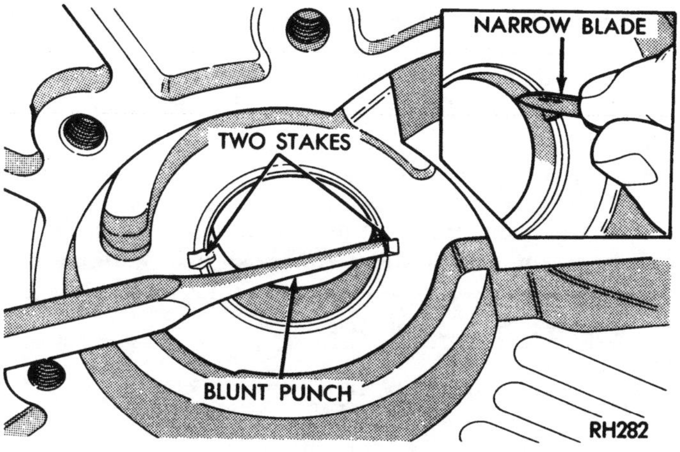

Fig. 138 Staking Oil Pump Bushing

(2) Hold Cup Tool SP-3633 firmly against reaction shaft and thread remover SP-5324 into bushing as far as possible by hand. Then thread remover tool 3-4 additional turns into bushing with a wrench.

(3) Turn remover tool hex nut down against remover cup to pull bushing from shaft. Clean all chips from shaft after bushing removal.

(4) Lightly grip old bushing in vise or with pliers and back remover tool out of bushing.

(5) Assemble Bushing Installer Tools C-4171 and SP-5325 (Fig. 139).

(6) Slide new bushing onto Installer Tool SP-5325.

(7) Position reaction shaft support upright on a clean smooth surface.

(8) Align bushing in bore. Then tap bushing into place until Bushing Installer SP-5325 bottoms.

(9) Clean reaction shaft support thoroughly after installing bushing.

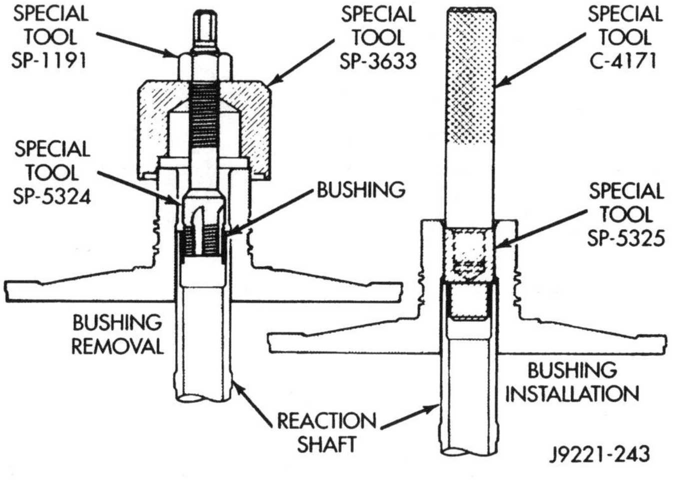

Fig. 139 Replacing Reaction Shaft Support Bushing

OIL PUMP AND REACTION SHAFT SUPPORT ASSEMBLE

(1) Lubricate gear bore in pump housing with transmission fluid.

(2) Lubricate pump gears with transmission fluid.

DISASSEMBLY AND ASSEMBLY (Continued)

(3) Support pump housing on wood blocks (Fig. 140).

(4) Install outer gear in pump housing (Fig. 140). Gear can be installed either way (it is not a one-way fit).

(5) Install pump inner gear (Fig. 141).

CAUTION: The pump inner gear is a one way fit. The bore on one side of the gear inside diameter (I.D.) is chamfered. Be sure the chamfered side faces forward (to front of pump).

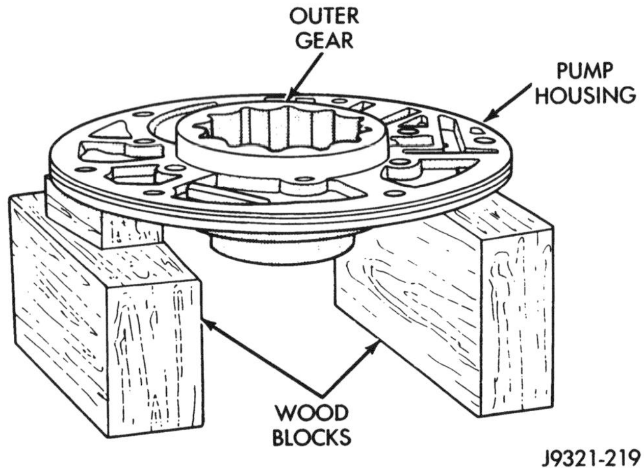

Fig. 140 Supporting Pump And Installing Outer Gear

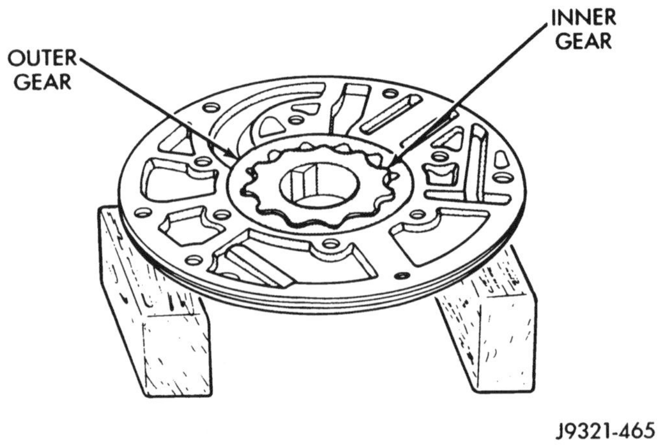

Fig. 141 Pump Inner Gear Installation

(6) Install new thrust washer on hub of reaction shaft support. Lubricate washer with transmission fluid or petroleum jelly.

(7) If reaction shaft seal rings are being replaced, install new seal rings on support hub (Fig. 142). Lubricate seal rings with transmission fluid or petroleum jelly after installation. Squeeze each ring until ring ends are securely hooked together.

CAUTION: The reaction shaft support seal rings will break if overspread, or twisted. If new rings are being installed, spread them only enough for installation. Also be very sure the ring ends are securely hooked together after installation. Otherwise, the rings will either prevent pump installation, or break during installation.

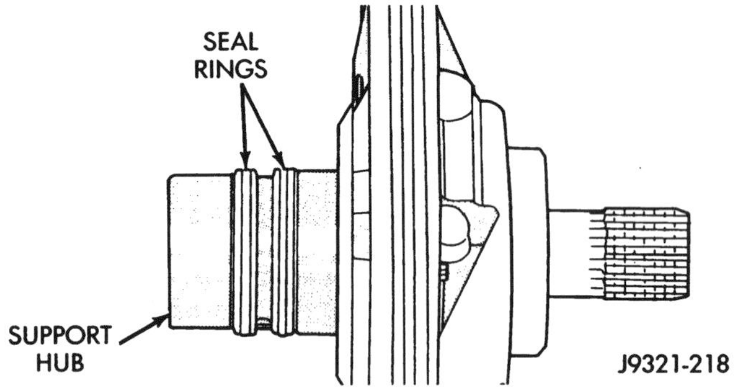

Fig. 142 Hub Seal Ring Position

(8) Install reaction shaft support on pump housing (Fig. 143).

(9) Align reaction support on pump housing. Use alignment marks made at disassembly. Or, rotate support until bolt holes in support and pump housing are all aligned (holes are offset for one-way fit).

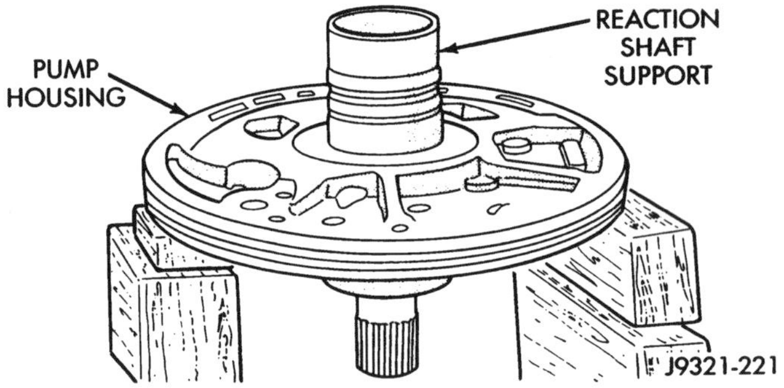

Fig. 143 Assembling Reaction Shaft Support And Pump Housing

(10) Install all bolts that attach support to pump housing. Then tighten bolts finger tight.

(11) Tighten support-to-pump bolts to required torque as follows:

(a) Reverse pump assembly and install it in transmission case. Position pump so bolts are facing out and are accessible.

(b) Secure pump assembly in case with 2 or 3 bolts, or with pilot studs.

(c) Tighten support-to-pump bolts to 20 N·m (15 ft. lbs.).

(d) Remove pump assembly from transmission case.

(12) Install new oil seal in pump with Special Tool C-4193 and Tool Handle C-4171 (Fig. 144). Be sure seal lip faces inward.

(13) Install new seal ring around pump housing. Be sure seal is properly seated in groove.

DISASSEMBLY AND ASSEMBLY (Continued)

(14) Lubricate lip of pump oil seal and O-ring seal with transmission fluid.

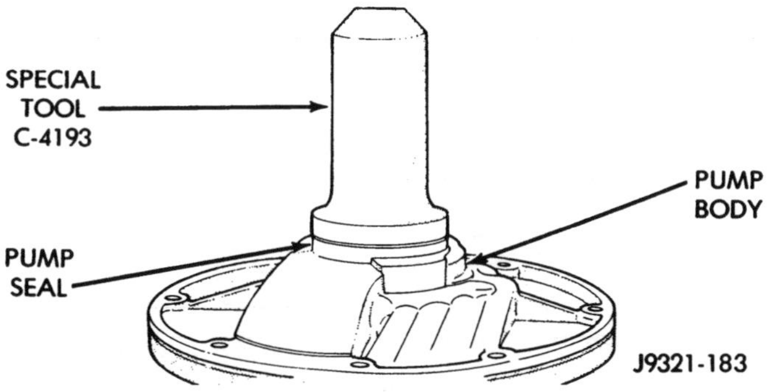

Fig. 144 Pump Oil Seal Installation

FRONT CLUTCH

DISASSEMBLE

(1) Remove waved snap ring and remove pressure plate, clutch plates and clutch discs (Fig. 145).

(2) Compress clutch piston spring with Compressor Tool C-3575-A (Fig. 146). Be sure legs of tool are seated squarely on spring retainer before compressing spring.

(3) Remove retainer snap ring and remove compressor tool.

(4) Remove spring retainer and clutch spring. Note position of retainer on spring for assembly reference.

(5) Remove clutch piston from clutch retainer. Remove piston by rotating it up and out of retainer.

(6) Remove seals from clutch piston and clutch retainer hub. Discard both seals as they are not reusable.

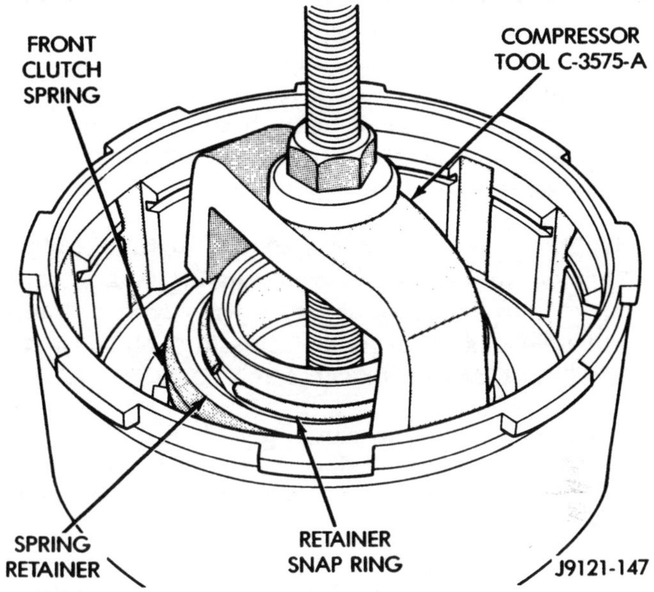

Fig. 146 Compressing Front Clutch Piston Spring

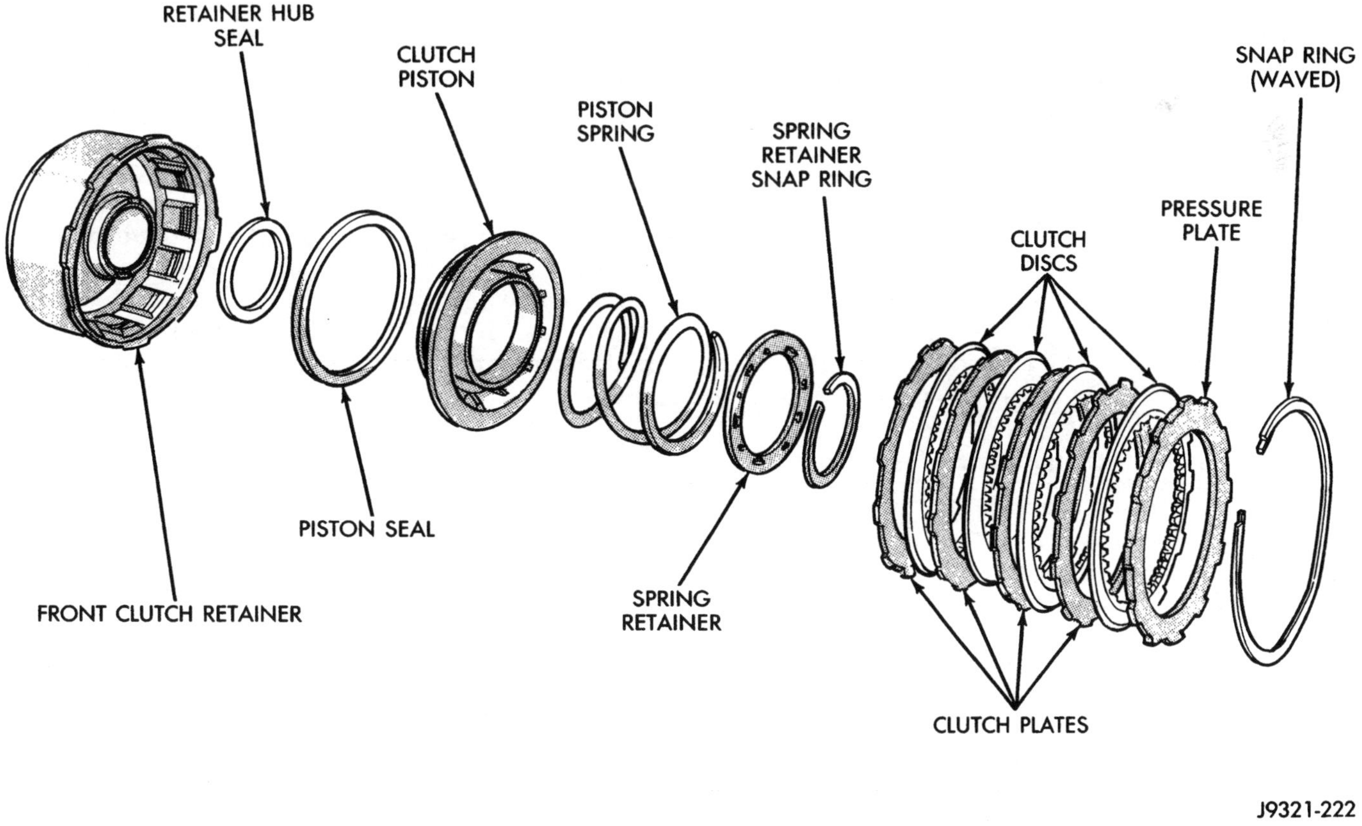

Fig. 145 Front Clutch Components

DISASSEMBLY AND ASSEMBLY (Continued)

ASSEMBLE

(1) Soak clutch discs in transmission fluid while assembling other clutch parts.

(2) Install new seals on piston and in hub of retainer. Be sure lip of each seal faces interior of clutch retainer.

(3) Lubricate lips of piston and retainer seals with liberal quantity of Mopar Door Ease, or Ru-Glyde. Then lubricate retainer hub, bore and piston with light coat of transmission fluid.

(4) Install clutch piston in retainer (Fig. 147). Use twisting motion to seat piston in bottom of retainer. A thin strip of plastic (about 0.020" thick), can be used to guide seals into place if necessary.

CAUTION: Never push the clutch piston straight in. This will fold the seals over causing leakage and clutch slip. In addition, never use any type of metal tool to help ease the piston seals into place. Metal tools will cut, shave, or score the seals.

(5) Position spring in clutch piston (Fig. 148).

(6) Position spring retainer on top of piston spring (Fig. 149). **Make sure retainer is properly installed. Small raised tabs should be facing upward. Semicircular lugs on underside of retainer are for positioning retainer in spring.**

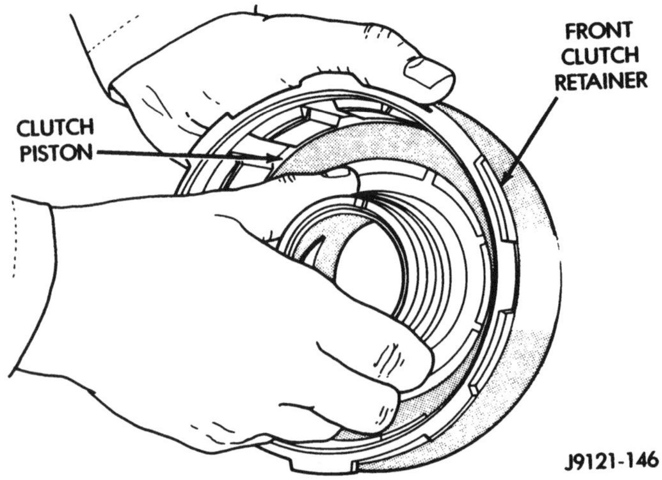

Fig. 147 Front Clutch Piston Installation

(7) Compress piston spring and retainer with Compressor Tool C-3575-A (Fig. 146). Then install new snap ring to secure spring retainer and spring.

(8) Install clutch plates and discs (Fig. 145). Install steel plate then disc until all plates and discs are installed. The front clutch uses 4 clutch discs.

(9) Install pressure plate and waved snap ring (Fig. 145).

(10) Using a suitable gauge bar and dial indicator, measure clutch plate clearance (Fig. 150).

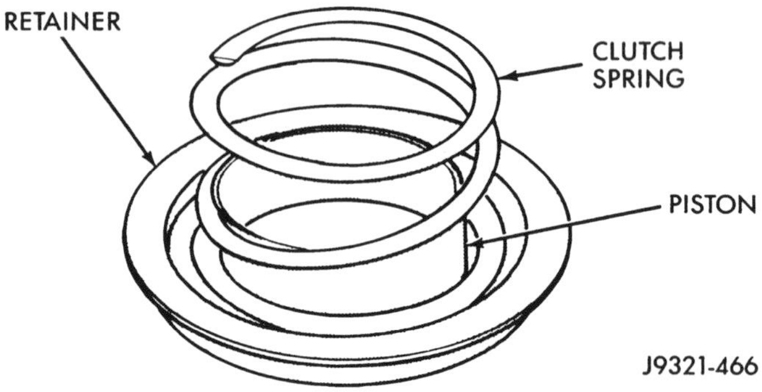

Fig. 148 Clutch Piston Spring Installation

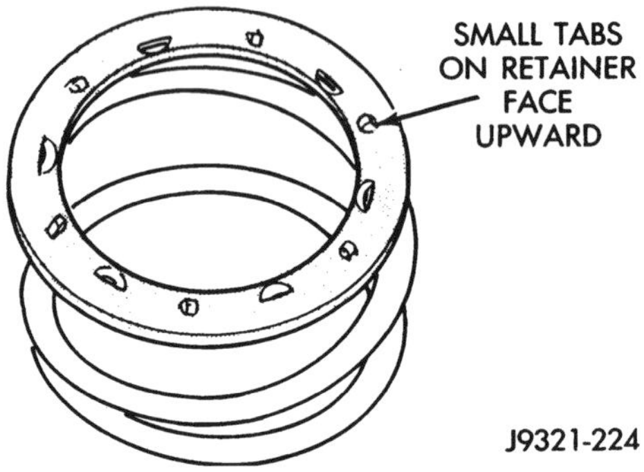

Fig. 149 Correct Spring Retainer Installed Position

(a) Position gauge bar across the clutch drum with the dial indicator pointer on the pressure plate (Fig. 150).

(b) Using two small screw drivers, lift the pressure plate and compress the waved snap-ring. This will assure that the snap-ring is at the top of the groove.

(c) Release the pressure plate and zero the dial indicator.

(d) Lift the pressure plate until it contacts the waved snap-ring and record the dial indicator reading.

Clearance should be 1.70 to 3.40 mm (0.067 to 0.134 in.). If clearance is incorrect, clutch discs, plates pressure plates and snap ring may have to be changed.

REAR CLUTCH

DISASSEMBLE

(1) Remove fiber thrust washer from forward side of clutch retainer.

(2) Remove selective clutch pack snap ring (Fig. 151).

(3) Remove top pressure plate, clutch discs, steel plates, bottom pressure plate and wave spring (Fig. 151).

(4) Remove clutch piston with rotating motion.

(5) Remove and discard piston seals.

(6) Remove input shaft snap ring (Fig. 152).

DISASSEMBLY AND ASSEMBLY (Continued)

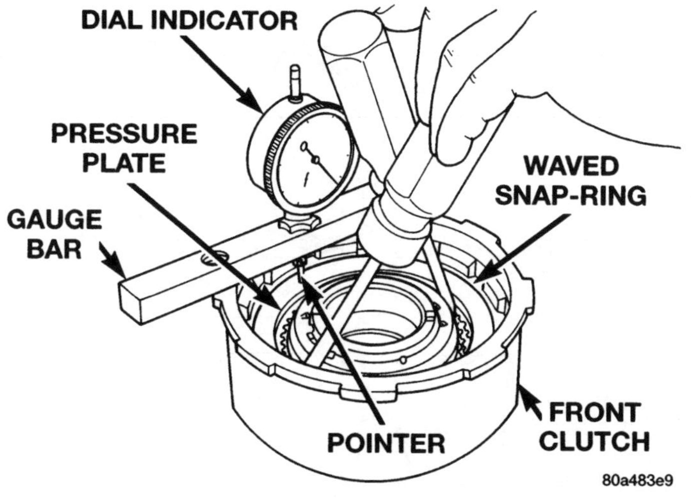

Fig. 150 Measuring Front Clutch Pack Clearance

(7) Press input shaft out of retainer with shop press and suitable size press tool (Fig. 153).

(8) Remove input shaft front/rear seal rings.

ASSEMBLE

(1) Soak clutch discs in transmission fluid while assembling other clutch parts.

(2) Install new seal rings on clutch retainer hub and input shaft if necessary (Fig. 154).

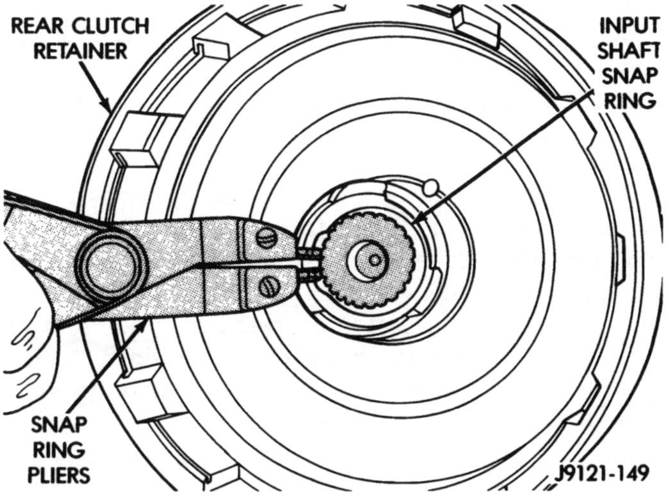

Fig. 152 Removing/Installing Input Shaft Snap Ring

(a) Be sure clutch hub seal ring is fully seated in groove and is not twisted.

(b) Note that input shaft front seal ring is teflon and rear seal ring is metal (Fig. 155). Be sure chamfered ends of teflon ring are properly joined and that ends of rear ring are securely hooked together. Lubricate both rings with transmission fluid after installation.

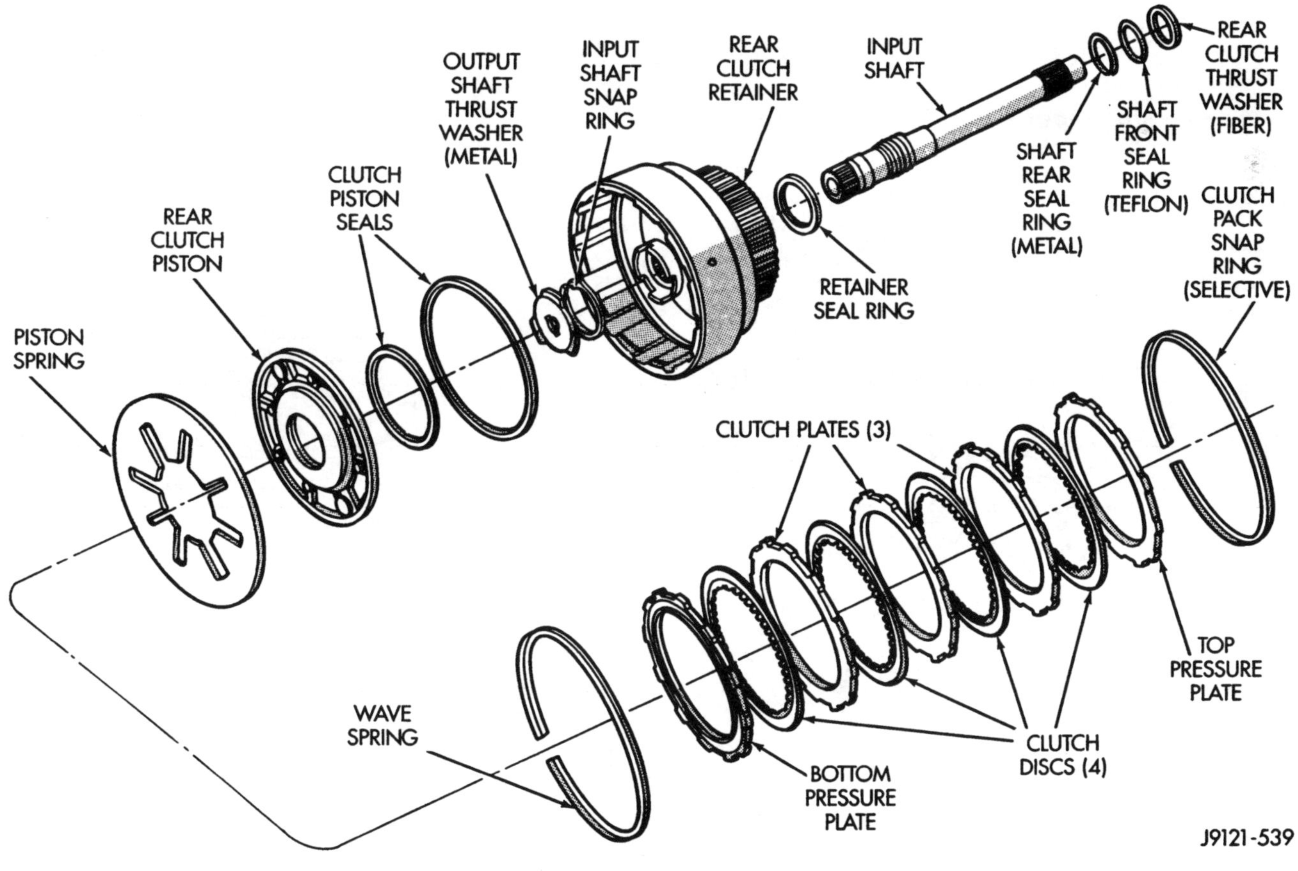

Fig. 151 Rear Clutch Components

DISASSEMBLY AND ASSEMBLY (Continued)

(3) Lubricate splined end of input shaft and clutch retainer with transmission fluid. Then press input shaft into retainer (Fig. 156).

(4) Install input shaft snap ring (Fig. 152).

(5) Install new seals on clutch piston. Be sure lip of each seal faces interior of clutch retainer.

(6) Lubricate lip of piston seals with generous quantity of Mopar Door Ease, or Ru-Glyde. Then lubricate retainer hub and bore with light coat of transmission fluid.

(7) Install clutch piston in retainer. Use twisting motion to seat piston in bottom of retainer. A thin strip of plastic (about 0.020″ thick), can be used to guide seals into place if necessary.

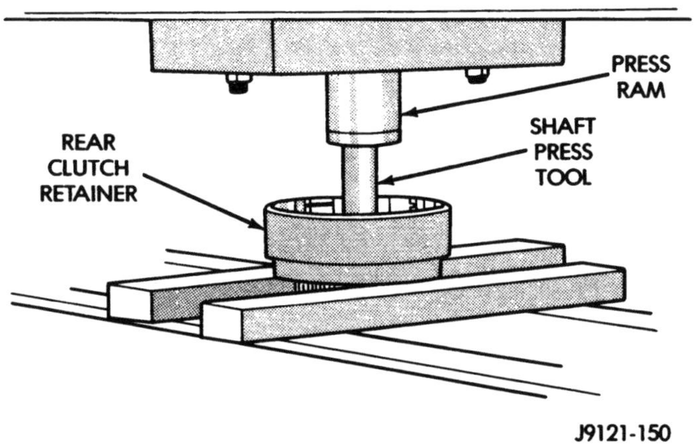

Fig. 153 Pressing Input Shaft Out Of Rear Clutch Retainer

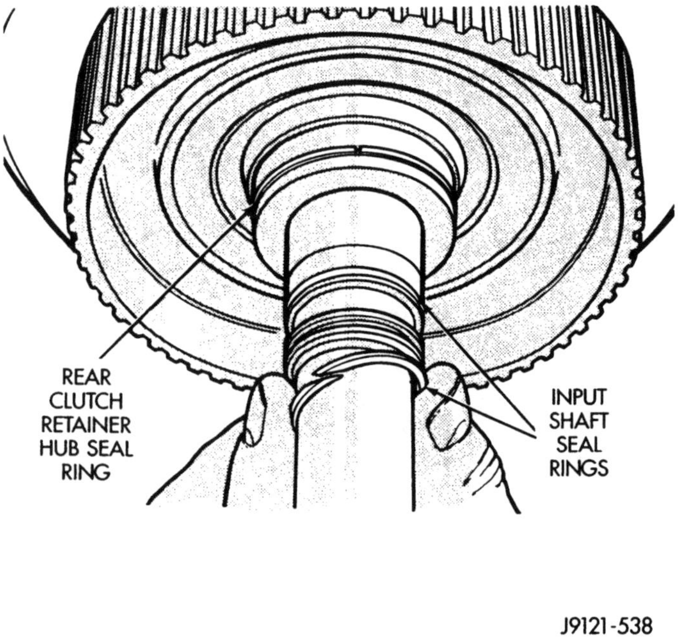

Fig. 154 Rear Clutch Retainer And Input Shaft Seal Ring Installation

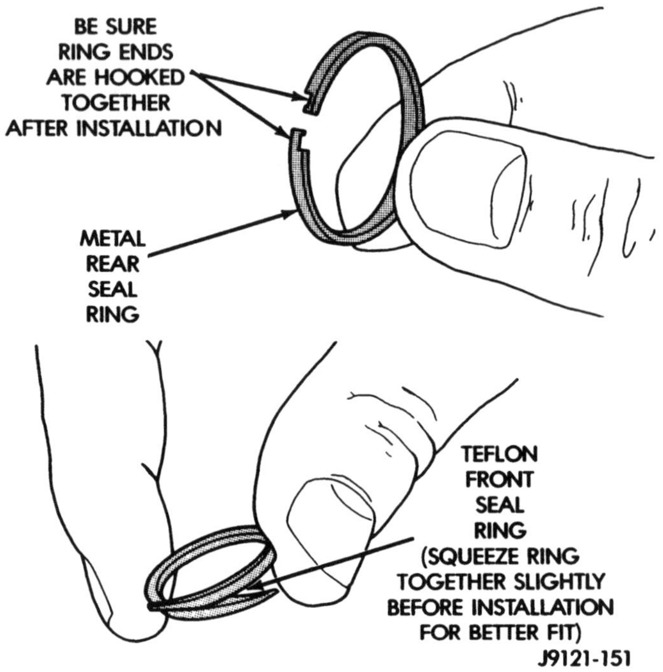

Fig. 155 Input Shaft Seal Ring Identification

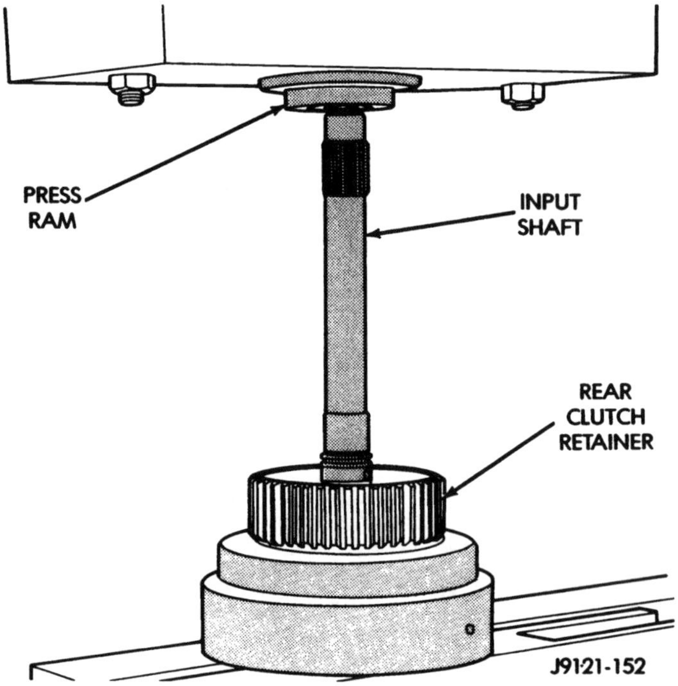

Fig. 156 Pressing Input Shaft Into Rear Clutch Retainer

CAUTION: Never push the clutch piston straight in. This will fold the seals over causing leakage and clutch slip. In addition, never use any type of metal tool to help ease the piston seals into place. Metal tools will cut, shave, or score the seals.

DISASSEMBLY AND ASSEMBLY (Continued)

(8) Install piston spring in retainer and on top of piston (Fig. 157). Concave side of spring faces downward (toward piston).

(9) Install wave spring in retainer (Fig. 157). Be sure spring is completely seated in retainer groove.

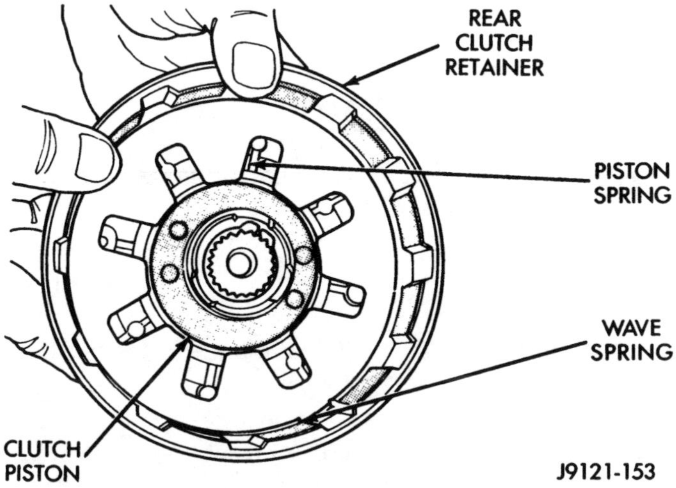

Fig. 157 Piston Spring/Wave Spring Position

(10) Install bottom pressure plate (Fig. 151). Ridged side of plate faces downward (toward piston) and flat side toward clutch pack.

(11) Install first clutch disc in retainer on top of bottom pressure plate. Then install a clutch plate followed by a clutch disc until entire clutch pack is installed (4 discs and 3 plates are required) (Fig. 151).

(12) Install top pressure plate.

(13) Install selective snap ring. Be sure snap ring is fully seated in retainer groove.

(14) Using a suitable gauge bar and dial indicator, measure clutch pack clearance (Fig. 158).

(a) Position gauge bar across the clutch drum with the dial indicator pointer on the pressure plate (Fig. 158).

(b) Using two small screw drivers, lift the pressure plate and release it.

(c) Zero the dial indicator.

(d) Lift the pressure plate until it contacts the snap-ring and record the dial indicator reading.

Clearance should be 0.64 - 1.14 mm (0.025 - 0.045 in.). If clearance is incorrect, steel plates, discs, selective snap ring and pressure plates may have to be changed.

(15) Coat rear clutch thrust washer with petroleum jelly and install washer over input shaft and into clutch retainer (Fig. 159). Use enough petroleum jelly to hold washer in place.

(16) Set rear clutch aside for installation during final assembly.

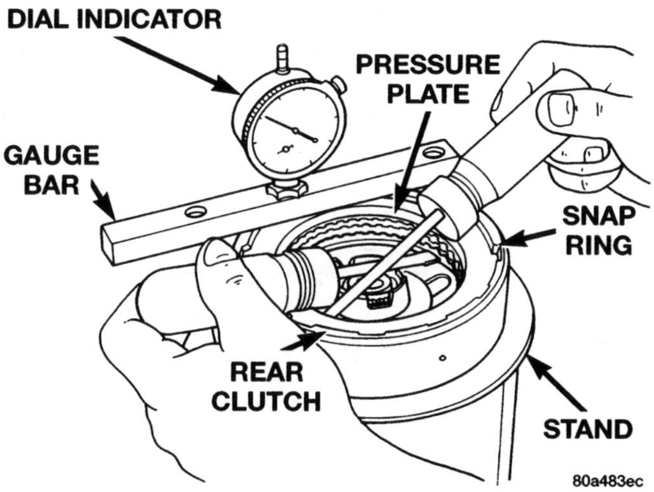

Fig. 158 Checking Rear Clutch Pack Clearance

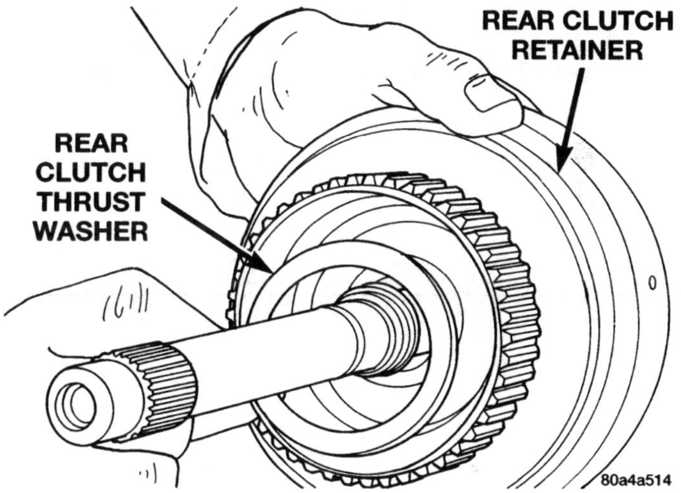

Fig. 159 Installing Rear Clutch Thrust Washer

PLANETARY GEARTRAIN/OUTPUT SHAFT

DISASSEMBLE

(1) Remove planetary snap ring (Fig. 160).

(2) Remove front annulus and planetary assembly from driving shell (Fig. 160).

(3) Remove snap ring that retains front planetary gear in annulus gear (Fig. 161).

(4) Remove tabbed thrust washer and tabbed thrust plate from hub of front annulus (Fig. 162).

(5) Separate front annulus and planetary gears (Fig. 162).

(6) Remove front planetary gear front thrust washer from annulus gear hub.

(7) Remove front planetary rear thrust washer from driving shell.

(8) Separate and remove driving shell, rear planetary and rear annulus from output shaft (Fig. 163).

(9) Remove tabbed thrust washers from rear planetary gear.

DISASSEMBLY AND ASSEMBLY (Continued)

(10) Remove snap ring that retains sun gear in driving shell. Then remove sun gear, spacer and thrust plates.

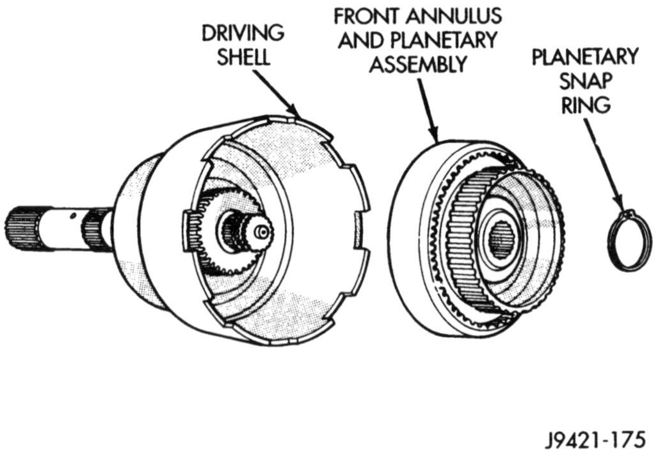

Fig. 160 Front Annulus And Planetary Assembly Removal

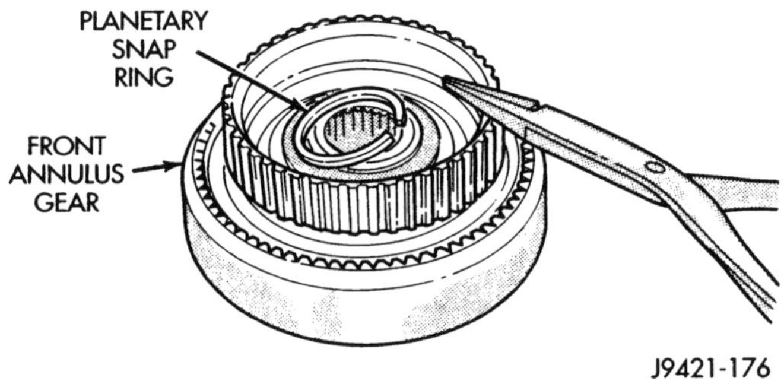

Fig. 161 Front Planetary Snap Ring Removal

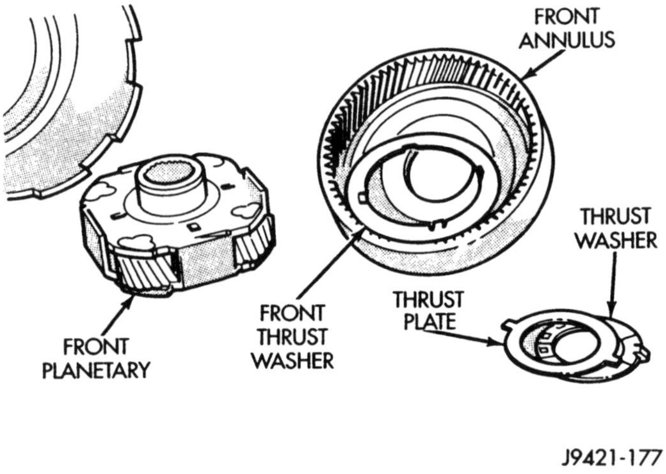

Fig. 162 Front Planetary And Annulus Gear Disassembly

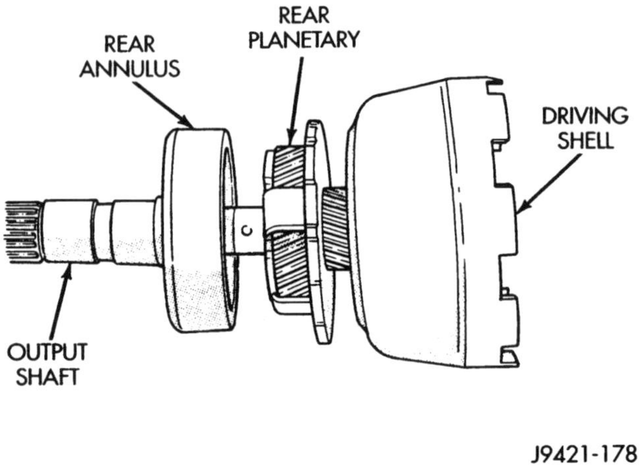

Fig. 163 Removing Driving Shell, Rear Planetary And Rear Annulus

ASSEMBLE

(1) Lubricate output shaft and planetary components with transmission fluid. Use petroleum jelly to lubricate and hold thrust washers and plates in position.

(2) Assemble rear annulus gear and support if disassembled. Be sure support snap ring is seated and that shoulder-side of support faces rearward (Fig. 165).

(3) Install rear thrust washer on rear planetary gear (Fig. 164). Use enough petroleum jelly to hold washer in place. Also be sure all four washer tabs are properly engaged in gear slots.

(4) Install rear annulus over and onto rear planetary gear (Fig. 165).

(5) Install assembled rear planetary and annulus gear on output shaft (Fig. 166). Verify that assembly is fully seated on shaft.

DISASSEMBLY AND ASSEMBLY (Continued)

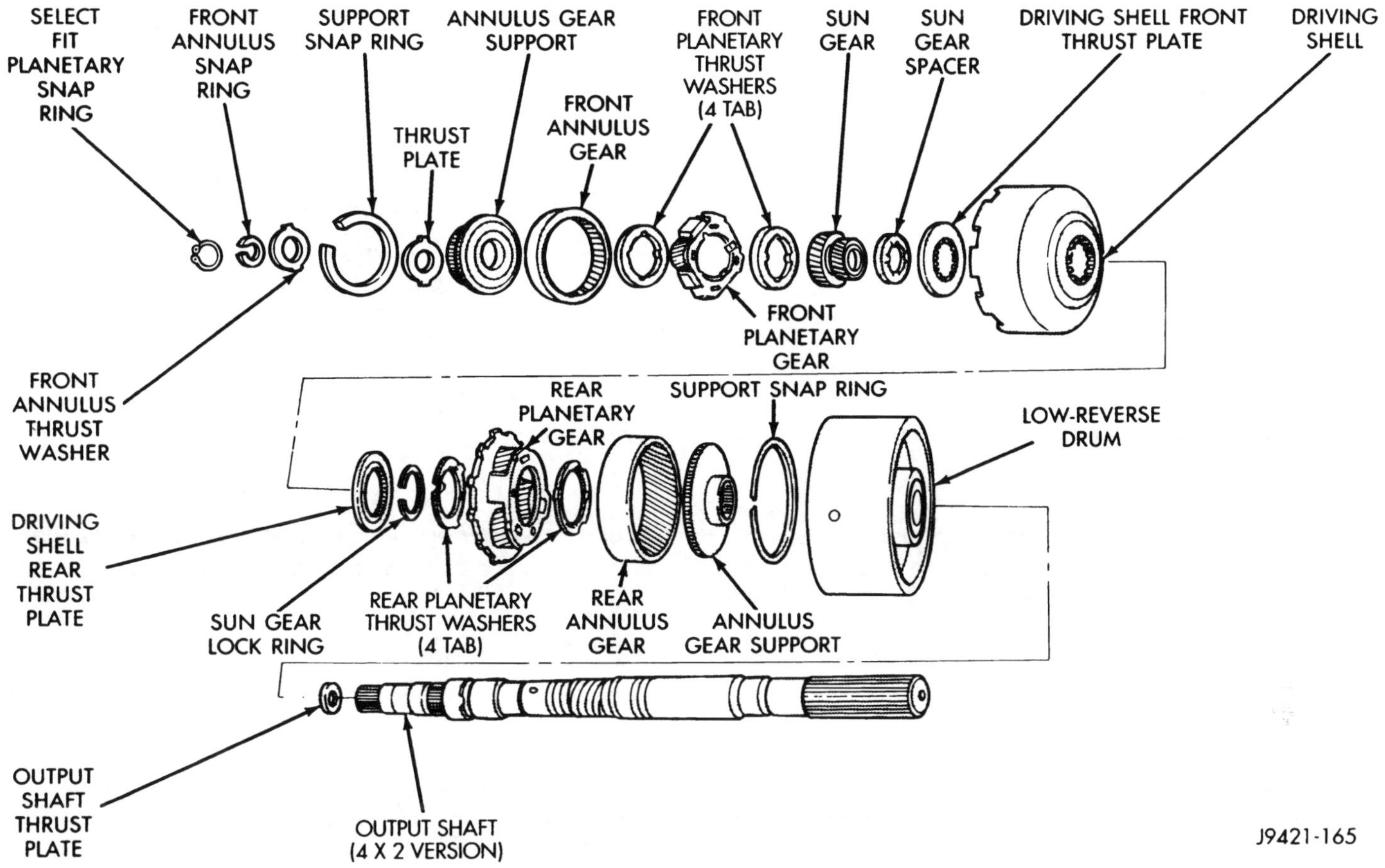

Fig. 164 Planetary Geartrain Components

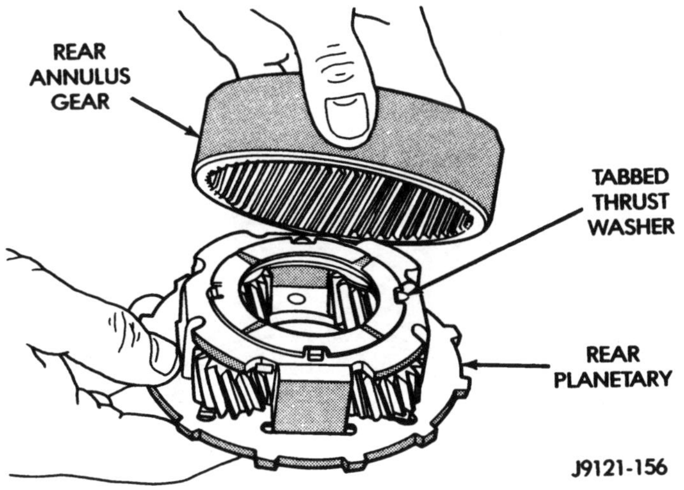

Fig. 165 Assembling Rear Annulus And Planetary Gear

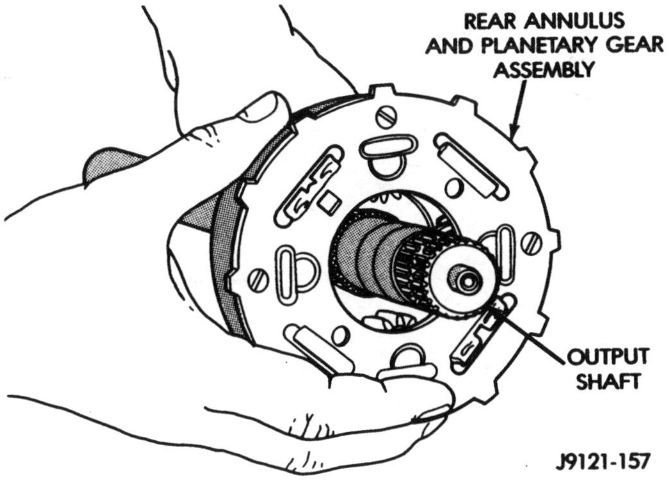

Fig. 166 Installing Rear Annulus And Planetary On Output Shaft

DISASSEMBLY AND ASSEMBLY (Continued)

(6) Install front thrust washer on rear planetary gear (Fig. 167). Use enough petroleum jelly to hold washer on gear. Be sure all four washer tabs are seated in slots.

(7) Install spacer on sun gear (Fig. 168).

(8) Install thrust plate on sun gear (Fig. 169). Note that driving shell thrust plates are interchangeable. Use either plate on sun gear and at front/rear of shell.

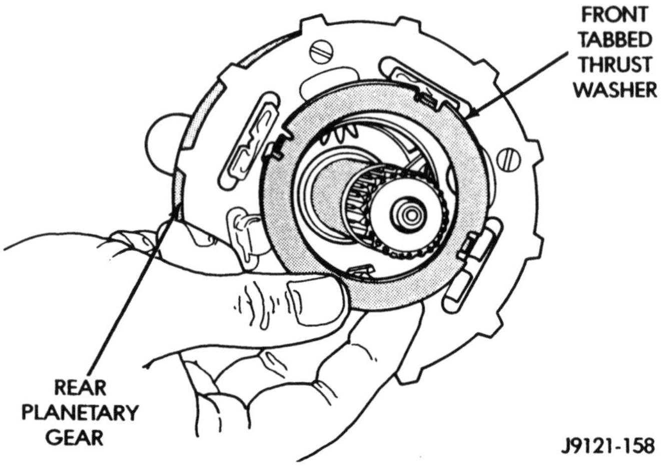

Fig. 167 Installing Rear Planetary Front Thrust Washer

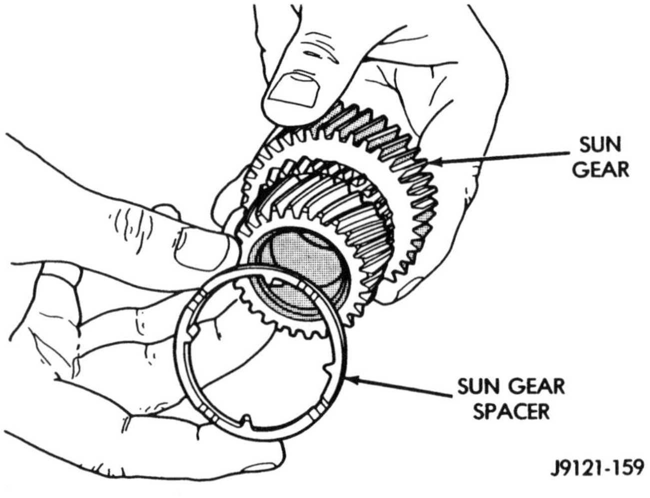

Fig. 168 Installing Spacer On Sun Gear

(9) Hold sun gear in place and install thrust plate over sun gear at rear of driving shell (Fig. 170).

(10) Position wood block on bench and support sun gear on block (Fig. 171). This makes it easier to align and install sun gear lock ring. Keep wood block handy as it will also be used for geartrain end play check.

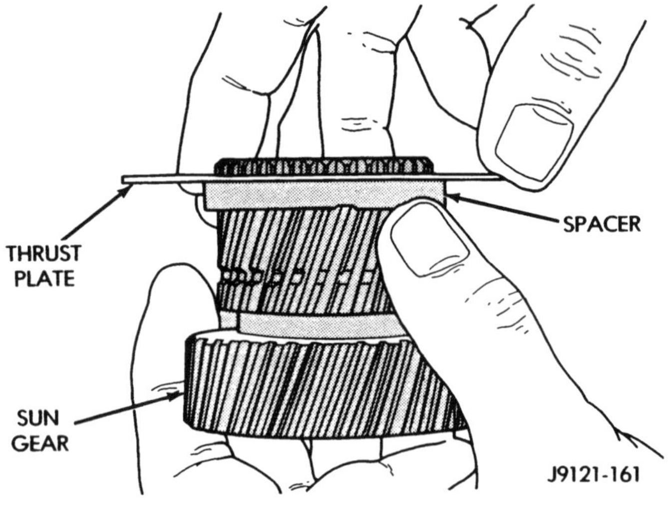

Fig. 169 Installing Driving Shell Front Thrust Plate On Sun Gear

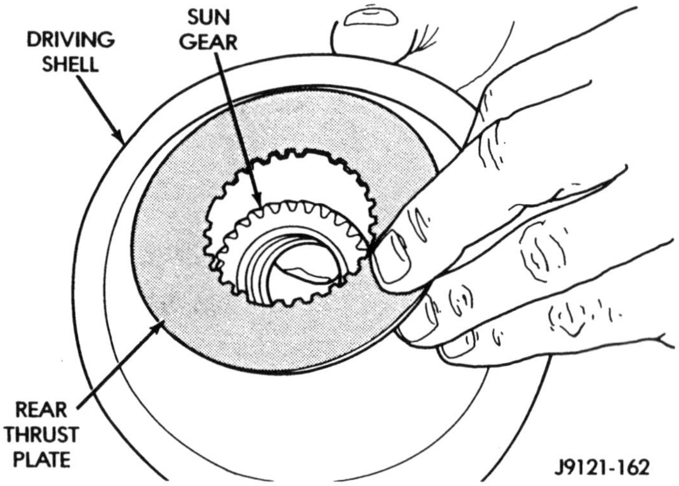

Fig. 170 Installing Driving Shell Rear Thrust Plate

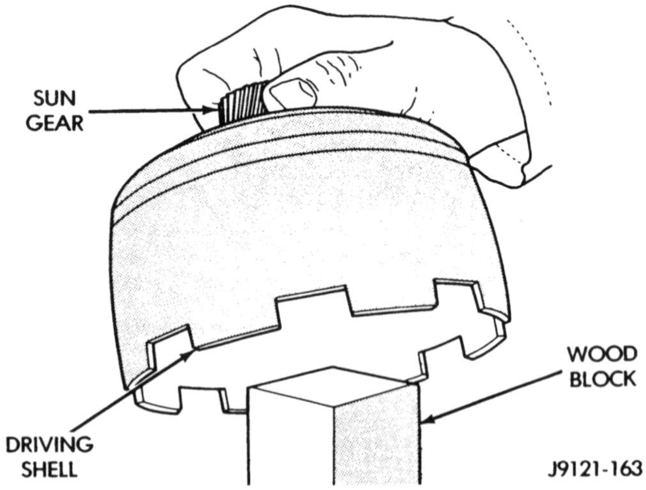

Fig. 171 Supporting Sun Gear On Wood Block

DISASSEMBLY AND ASSEMBLY (Continued)

(11) Align rear thrust plate on driving shell and install sun gear lock ring. Be sure ring is fully seated in sun gear ring groove (Fig. 172).

(12) Install assembled driving shell and sun gear on output shaft (Fig. 173).

(13) Install rear thrust washer on front planetary gear (Fig. 174). Use enough petroleum jelly to hold washer in place and be sure all four washer tabs are seated.

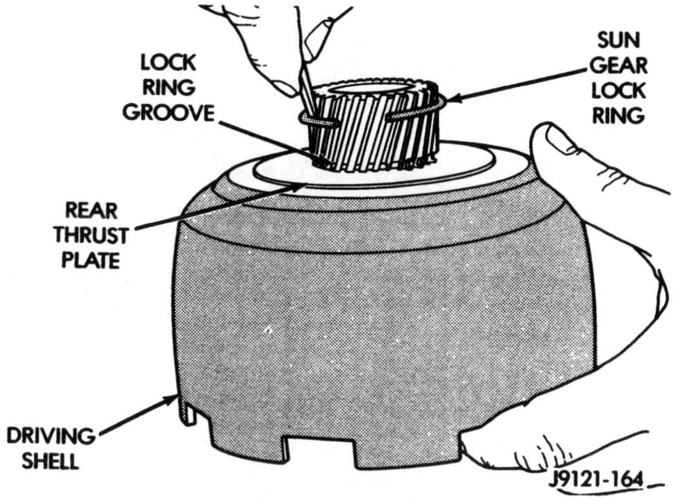

Fig. 172 Installing Sun Gear Lock Ring

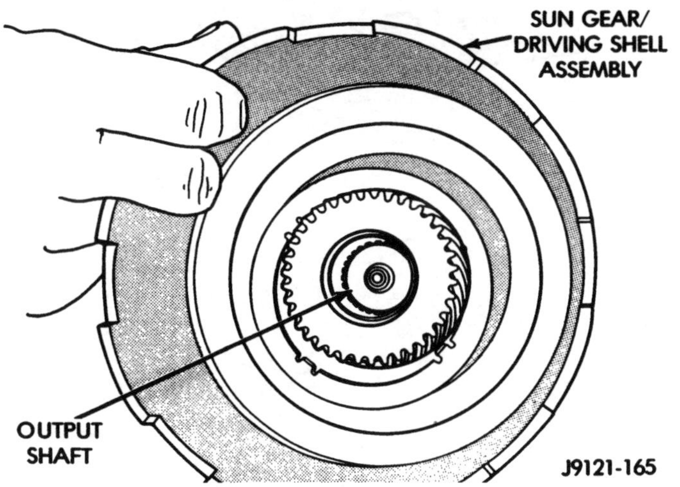

Fig. 173 Installing Assembled Sun Gear And Driving Shell On Output Shaft

(14) Install front planetary gear on output shaft and in driving shell (Fig. 175).

(15) Install front thrust washer on front planetary gear. Use enough petroleum jelly to hold washer in place and be sure all four washer tabs are seated.

(16) Assemble front annulus gear and support, if necessary. Be sure support snap ring is seated.

(17) Install front annulus on front planetary (Fig. 175).

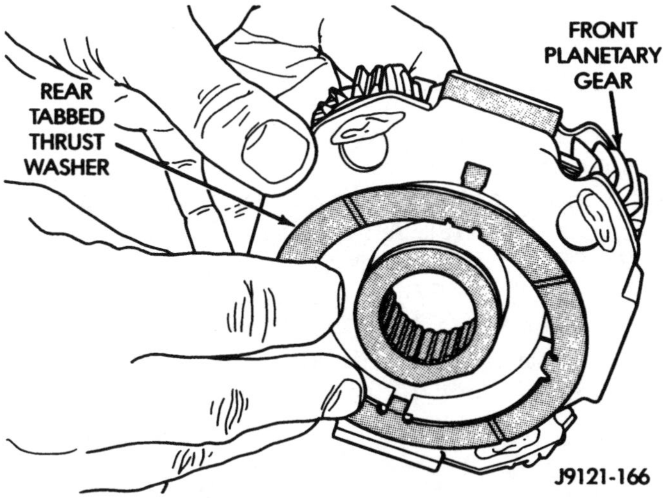

Fig. 174 Installing Rear Thrust Washer On Front Planetary Gear

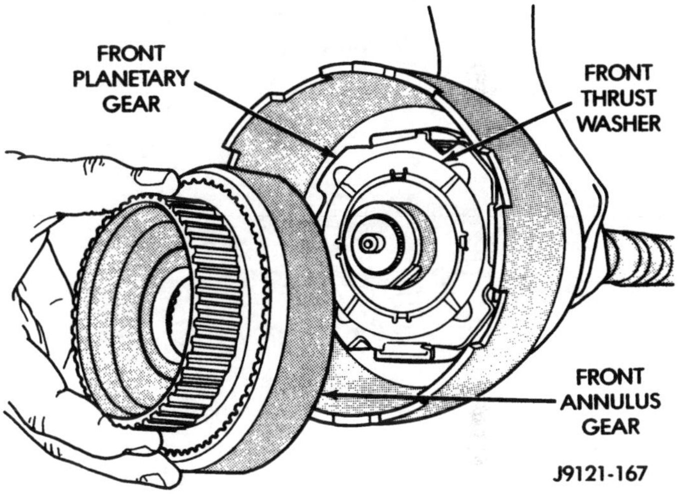

Fig. 175 Installing Front Planetary And Annulus Gears

(18) Position thrust plate on front annulus gear support (Fig. 176). **Note that plate has two tabs on it. These tabs fit in notches of annulus hub.**

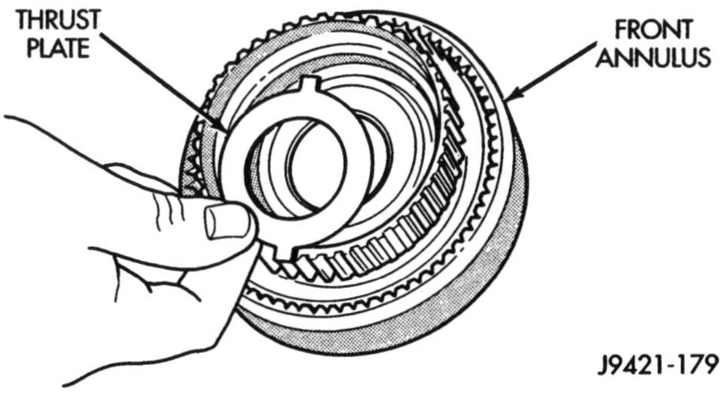

Fig. 176 Positioning Thrust Plate On Front Annulus Support

DISASSEMBLY AND ASSEMBLY (Continued)

(19) Install thrust washer in front annulus (Fig. 177). **Align flat on washer with flat on planetary hub. Also be sure washer tab is facing up.**

(20) Install front annulus snap ring (Fig. 178). Use snap ring pliers to avoid distorting ring during installation. Also be sure ring is fully seated.

(21) Install planetary selective snap ring with snap ring pliers (Fig. 179). Be sure ring is fully seated.

(22) Turn planetary geartrain assembly over so driving shell is facing workbench. Then support geartrain on wood block positioned under forward end of output shaft. This allows geartrain components to move forward for accurate end play check.

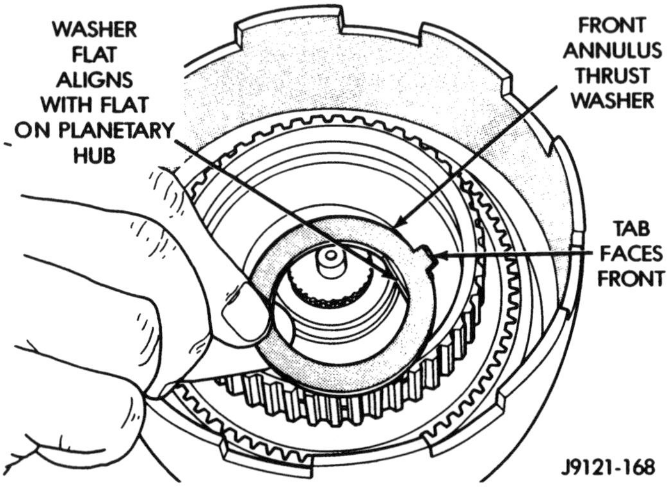

Fig. 177 Installing Front Annulus Thrust Washer

(23) Check planetary geartrain end play with feeler gauge (Fig. 180). Gauge goes between shoulder on output shaft and end of rear annulus support.

(24) Geartrain end play should be 0.12 to 1.22 mm (0.005 to 0.048 in.). If end play is incorrect, snap ring (or thrust washers) may have to be replaced. Snap ring is available in three different thicknesses for adjustment purposes.

CLEANING AND INSPECTION

GOVERNOR AND PARK GEAR

CLEANING AND INSPECTION

Thoroughly clean all the governor parts in a suitable cleaning solution but do not use any type of caustic cleaning agents.

The governor weight components (Fig. 181) and the governor valve (Fig. 182), must slide freely in their bores when clean and dry. Minor surface scratches and burrs can be smoothed with crocus cloth

The aluminum governor valve and outer weight have a hard coating on them. Check condition of this coating carefully. Do not reuse either part if the coating is damaged.

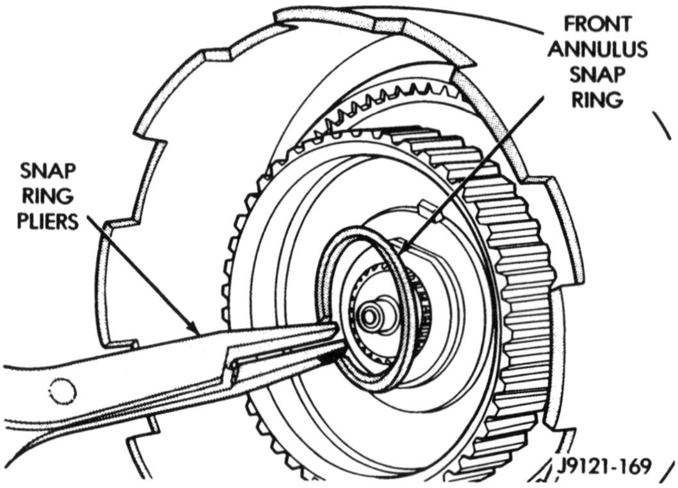

Fig. 178 Installing Front Annulus Snap Ring

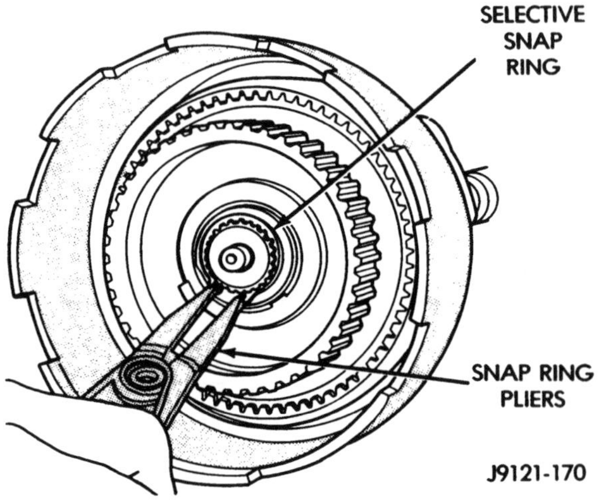

Fig. 179 Installing Planetary Selective Snap Ring

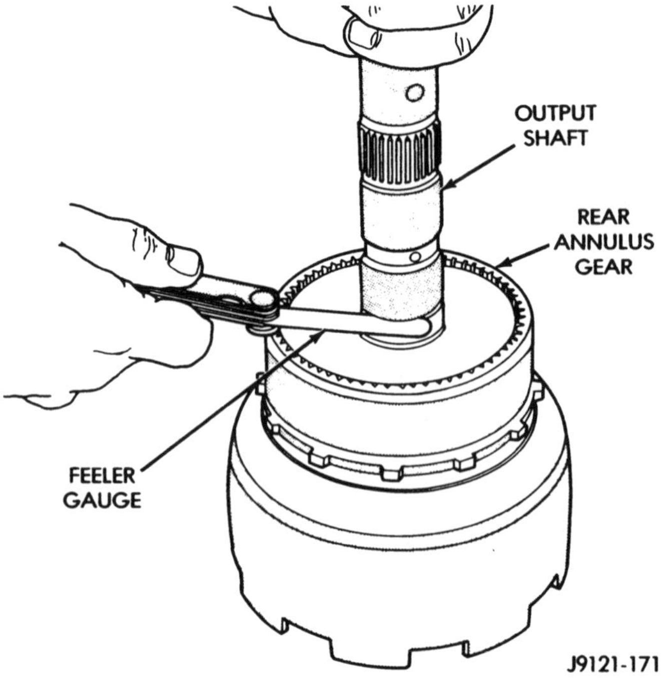

Fig. 180 Checking Planetary Geartrain End Play

CLEANING AND INSPECTION (Continued)

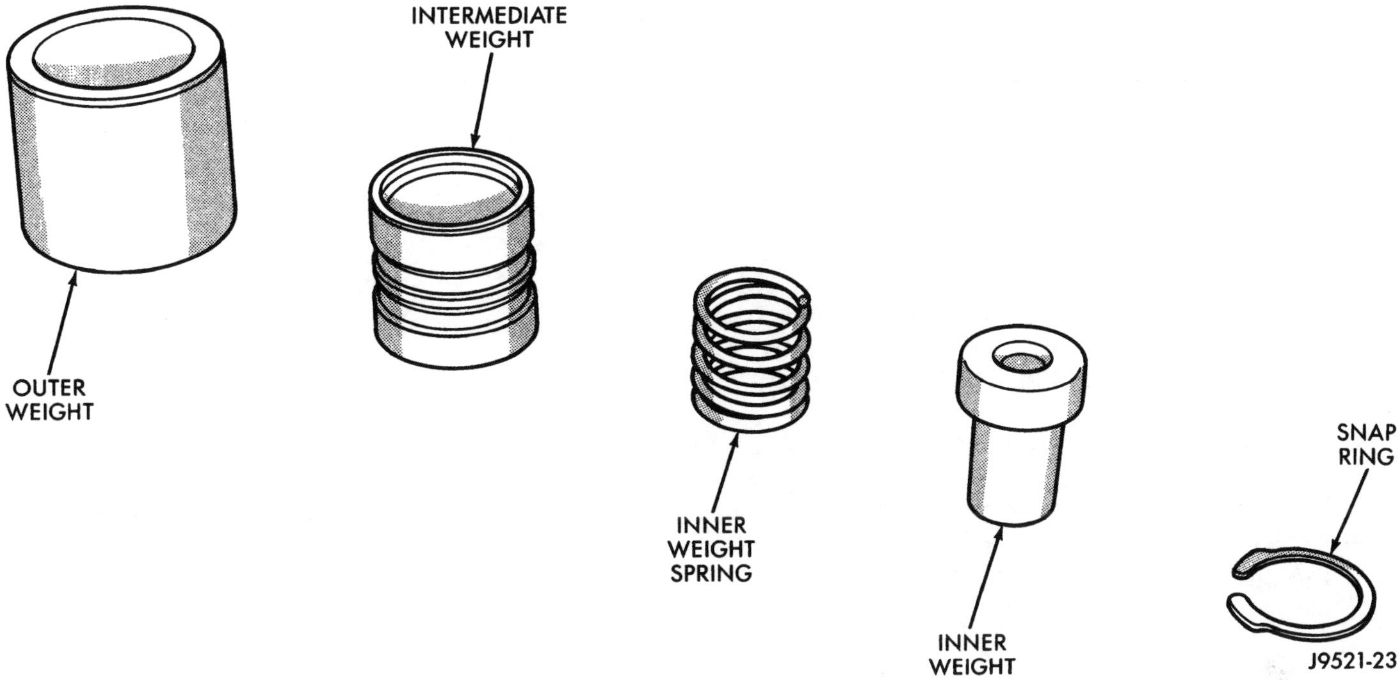

Fig. 181 Governor Weights

Inspect the governor weight spring for distortion. Replace the spring, if distorted, collapsed, or broken. Clean the filter in solvent and dry it with compressed air. Replace the filter, if damaged. Inspect the park gear for chipped or worn gear teeth or damaged ring grooves. Replace the gear, if damaged.

Check the teeth on the park gear for wear or damage. Replace the gear if necessary. Inspect the metal

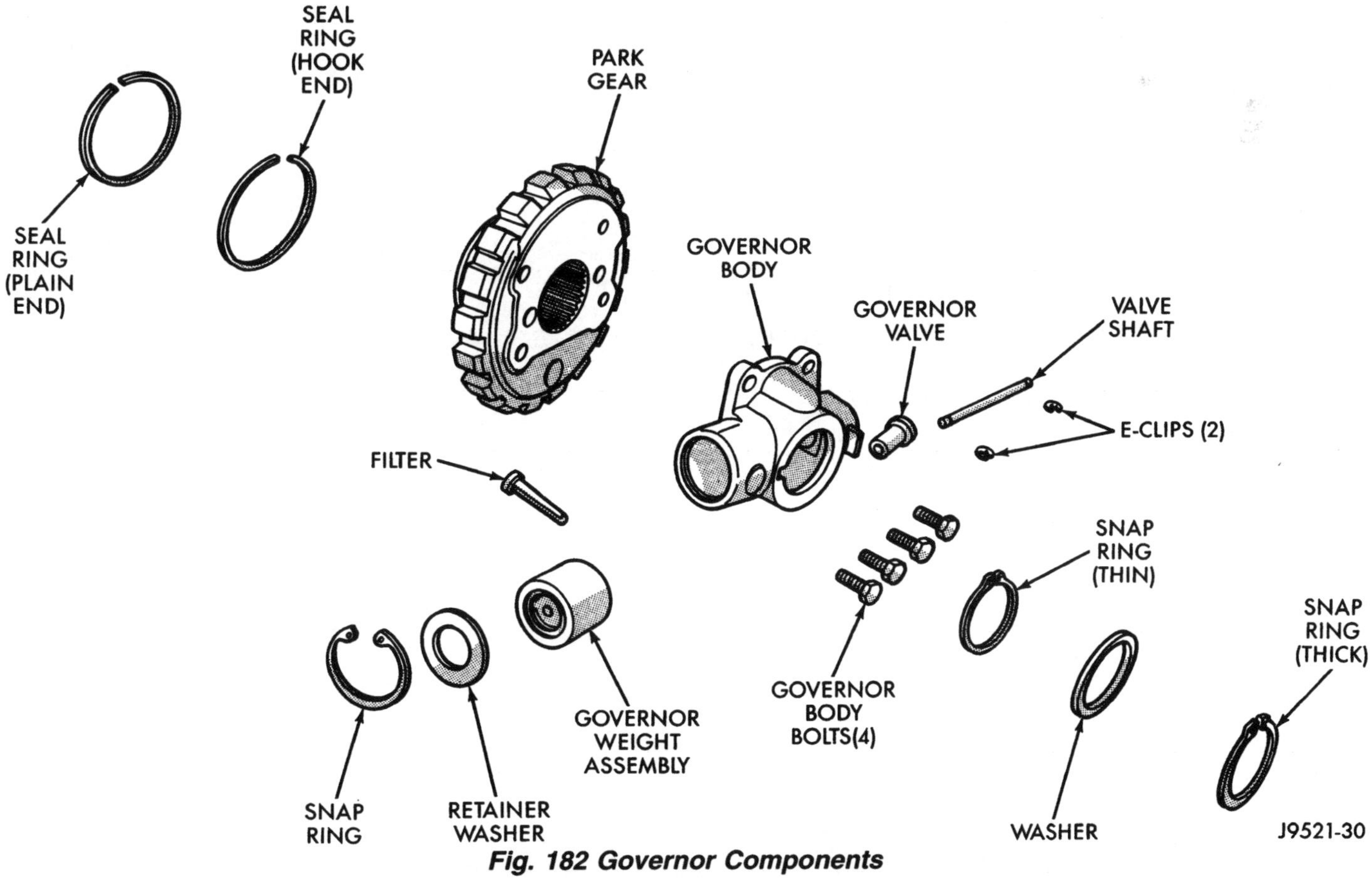

Fig. 182 Governor Components

CLEANING AND INSPECTION (Continued)

seal rings on the park gear hub. Replace the rings only if severely worn, or broken.

EXTENSION HOUSING AND PARK LOCK

Clean the housing and park lock components in solvent and dry them with compressed air.

Examine the park lock components in the housing. If replacement is necessary, remove the shaft with parallel jaw snap ring pliers (Fig. 183) and remove the sprag and spring. Then remove the spring clip and reaction plug (Fig. 184). **Compress the reaction plug spring clip only enough to remove and install it. Do not distort the clip during removal or installation.**

Be sure a replacement sprag is installed so the sprag locking lug will face the park gear (Fig. 185). Also be sure the spring is correctly positioned as shown (Fig. 185). The sprag may not retract if the spring is improperly installed.

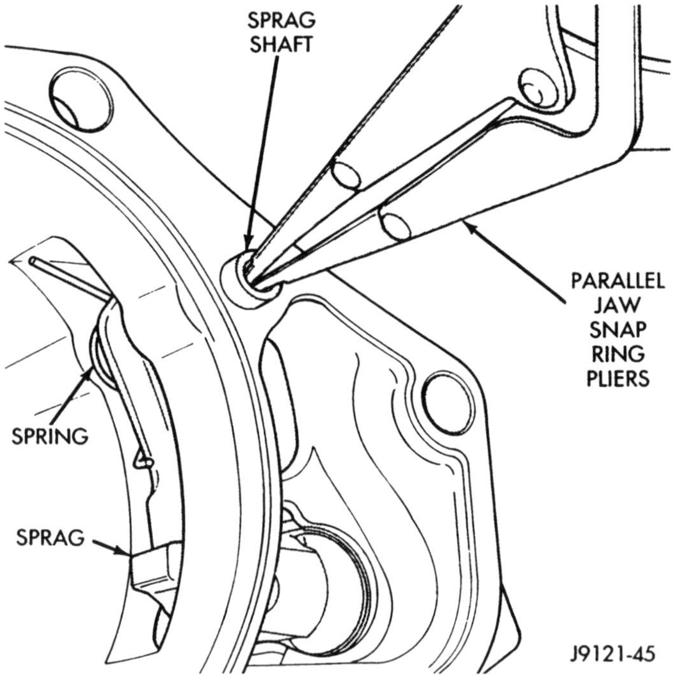

Fig. 183 Park Sprag, Shaft And Spring

VALVE BODY

Serviceable valve body components are:

- park lock rod and E-clip
- switch valve and spring
- pressure adjusting screw bracket
- throttle valve lever
- manual lever
- manual lever shaft seal, washer, E-clip and detent ball
- fluid filter
- converter clutch solenoid

The remaining valve body components are serviced only as part of a complete valve body assembly.

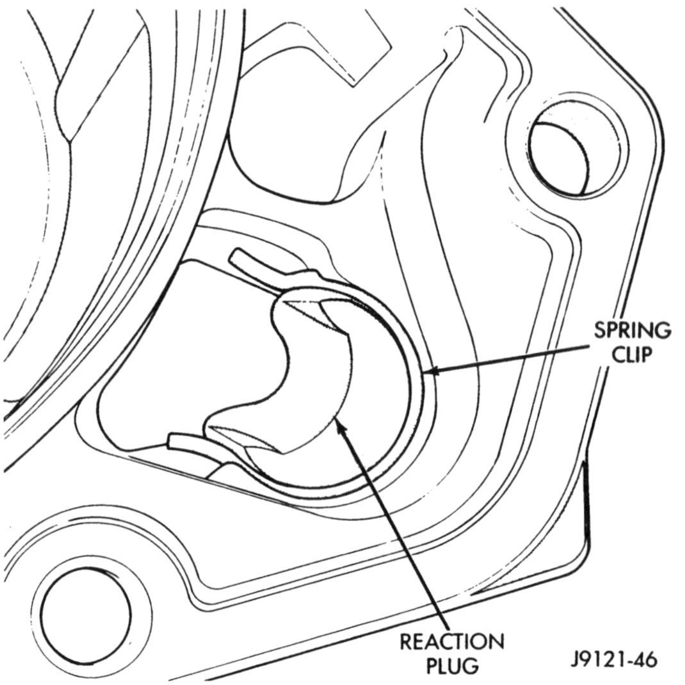

Fig. 184 Park Sprag Reaction Plug And Spring Location

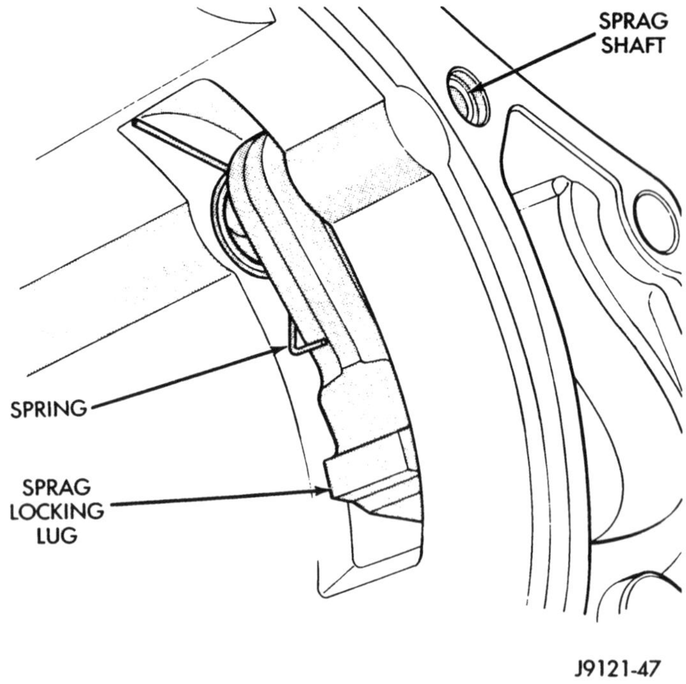

Fig. 185 Correct Position Of Sprag And Spring

Clean the valve body components in a parts cleaning solution only. Do not use gasoline, kerosene, or any type of caustic solution. Dry the parts with compressed air. Make sure all passages are clean and free from obstructions.

CLEANING AND INSPECTION (Continued)

NOTE: Do not use rags or shop towels to wipe off valve body components. Lint from these materials will adhere to the valve body components. Lint will interfere with valve operation and may clog filters and fluid passages.

Inspect the throttle and manual valve levers and shafts. Do not attempt to straighten a bent shaft or correct a loose lever. Replace these components if worn, bent, loose or damaged in any way.

Inspect all of the valve body mating surfaces for scratches, nicks, burrs, or distortion. Use a straightedge to check surface flatness. Minor scratches may be removed with crocus cloth using only very light pressure.

Minor distortion of a valve body mating surface may be corrected by smoothing the surface with crocus cloth. The cloth should be in sheet form and be positioned on a surface plate, sheet of plate glass, or equally flat surface. However, if distortion is severe or any surfaces are heavily scored, the valve body will have to be replaced.

CAUTION: Many of the valve body valves and plugs are made of coated aluminum. Aluminum components can be identified by the dark color of the special coating applied to the surface (or by testing with a magnet). DO NOT polish or sand aluminum valves or plugs with any type of material, or under any circumstances. This practice might damage the special coating and cause the valves and plugs to stick and bind.

Inspect the valves and plugs for scratches, burrs, nicks, or scores. Also inspect the coating on the aluminum valves and plugs (Fig. 186). If the coating is damaged or worn through, the valve (or valve body) should be replaced.

Aluminum valves and plugs should not be sanded or polished under any circumstances. However, minor burrs or scratches on steel valves and plugs can be removed with crocus cloth but do not round off the valve or plug edges. Squareness of these edges is vitally important. These edges prevent foreign matter from lodging between the valves, plugs and bore.

Inspect all the valve and plug bores in the valve body. Use a penlight to view the bore interiors. Replace the valve body if any bores are distorted or scored. Inspect all of the valve body springs. The springs must be free of distortion, warpage or broken coils.

Trial fit each valve and plug in its bore to check freedom of operation. When clean and dry, the valves and plugs should drop freely into the bores. Valve body bores do not change dimensionally with use. If the valve body functioned correctly when new, it will continue to operate properly after cleaning and inspection. It should not be necessary to replace a valve body assembly unless it is damaged in handling.

TRANSMISSION

INSPECTION AFTER DISASSEMBLY

Inspect all the transmission bushings during overhaul. Bushing condition is important as worn, scored bushings contribute to low pressures, clutch slip and accelerated wear of other components. Replace worn, or scored bushings, or if doubt exists about bushing condition.

Use recommended tools to replace bushings. The tools are sized and designed to remove, install and seat bushings correctly. The bushing replacement tools are included in Bushing Tool Sets C-3887-B, or C-3887-J.

Pre-sized service bushings are available for replacement purposes. Only the sun gear bushings are not serviced. Replace the gear as an assembly if the bushings are severely scored, or worn.

Heli-Coil inserts are recommended for repairing damaged, stripped or worn threads in aluminum parts. These inserts are available from most automotive jobbers. Stainless steel inserts are preferred.

The use of crocus cloth is permissible where necessary, providing it is used carefully. When used on valves, use extreme care to avoid rounding off sharp edges. Sharp edges are vital as they prevent foreign matter from getting between the valve and valve bore.

Do not reuse oil seals, gaskets, seal rings, or O-rings during overhaul. Replace these parts as a matter of course. Also do not reuse snap rings or E-clips that are bent or distorted. Replace these parts as well.

Lubricate transmission parts with Mopar ATF Plus, Type 7176 transmission fluid during assembly. Use Mopar Door Ease, or Ru-Glyde to lubricate piston seals and O-rings. Use petroleum jelly on thrust washers and to hold parts in place during reassembly.

TRANSMISSION CASE CLEANING AND INSPECTION

Clean the case in a solvent tank. Flush the case bores and fluid passages thoroughly with solvent. Dry the case and all fluid passages with compressed air. Be sure all solvent is removed from the case and that all fluid passages are clear.

CLEANING AND INSPECTION (Continued)

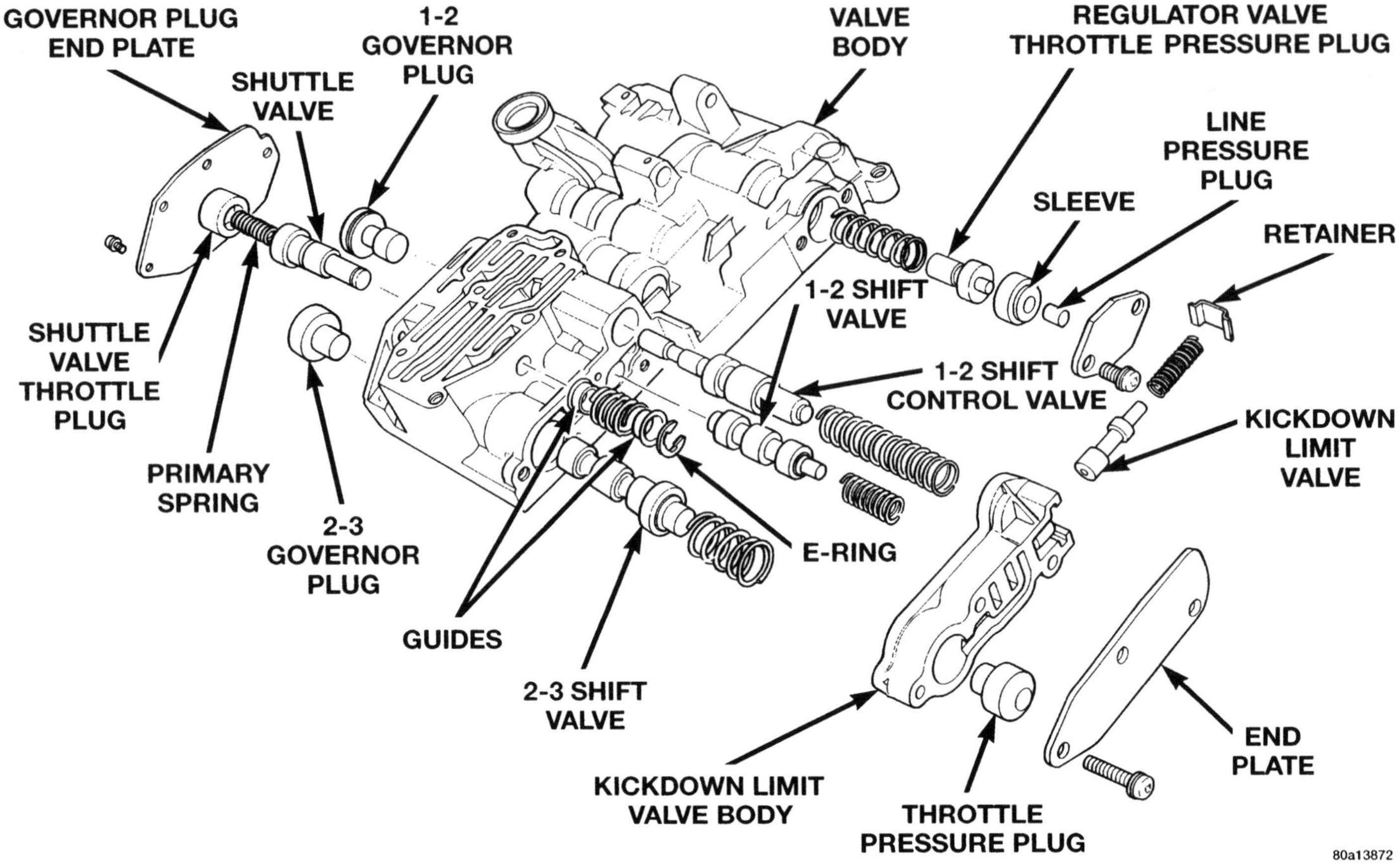

Fig. 186 Valve Body Components

NOTE: Do not use shop towels or rags to dry the case (or any other transmission component) unless they are made from lint-free materials. Lint will readily adhere to case surfaces and transmission components and will circulate throughout the transmission after assembly. A sufficient quantity of lint can block fluid passages and interfere with valve body operation.

Inspect the case for cracks, porous spots, worn servo bores, or damaged threads. Damaged threads can be repaired with Helicoil thread inserts. However, the case will have to be replaced if it exhibits damage or wear.

Lubricate the front band adjusting screw and locknut with petroleum jelly and thread it part way into the case. Be sure the screw turns freely and does not bind. Install the locknut on the screw after checking screw thread operation.

OVERRUNNING CLUTCH/LOW-REVERSE DRUM/REAR SUPPORT

Clean the overrunning clutch assembly, clutch cam, low-reverse drum and rear support in solvent. Dry them with compressed air after cleaning.

Inspect condition of each clutch part after cleaning. Replace the overrunning clutch roller and spring assembly if any rollers or springs are worn or damaged, or if the roller cage is distorted, or damaged. Replace the cam if worn, cracked or damaged.

Replace the low-reverse drum if the clutch race, roller surface or inside diameter is scored, worn or damaged. **Do not remove the clutch race from the low-reverse drum under any circumstances. Replace the drum and race as an assembly if either component is damaged.**

Examine the rear support carefully for wear, cracks, scoring or other damage. Be sure the support hub is a snug fit in the case and drum. Replace the support if worn or damaged.

FRONT SERVO

Clean the servo piston components with solvent and dry them with compressed air. Wipe the band clean with lint free shop towels.

Replace the front band if distorted, lining is burned, flaking off, or worn to the point where the grooves in the lining material are no longer visible.

Inspect the servo components (Fig. 187). Replace the springs if collapsed, distorted or broken. Replace the guide, rod and piston if cracked, bent, or worn. Discard the servo snap ring if distorted or warped.

CLEANING AND INSPECTION (Continued)

Check the servo piston bore for wear. If the bore is severely scored, or damaged, it will be necessary to replace the case.

Replace any servo component if doubt exists about condition. Do not reuse suspect parts.

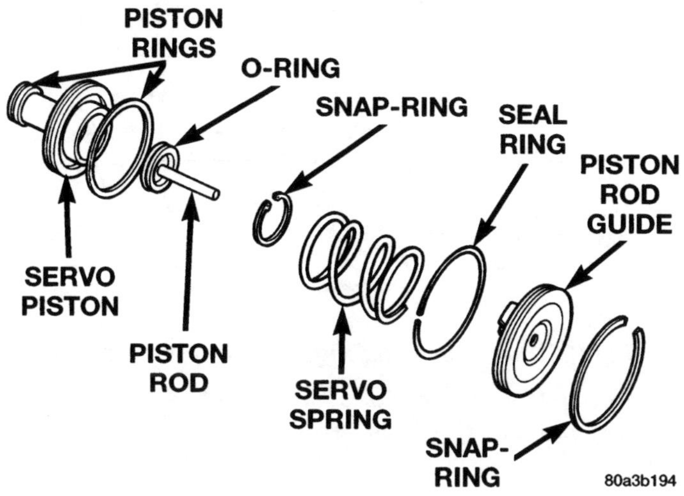

Fig. 187

REAR SERVO

Remove and discard the servo piston seal ring (Fig. 188). Then clean the servo components with solvent and dry with compressed air. Replace either spring if collapsed, distorted or broken. Replace the plug and piston if cracked, bent, or worn. Discard the servo snap rings and use a new ones at assembly.

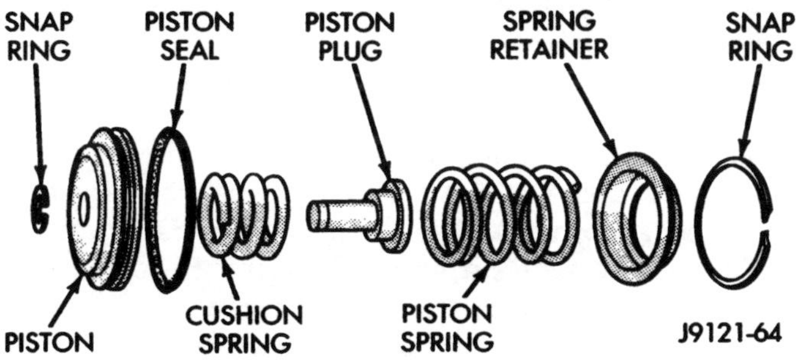

Fig. 188 Rear Servo Components

OIL PUMP AND REACTION SHAFT SUPPORT

Clean pump and reaction shaft support components with solvent and dry them with compressed air.

Inspect the pump housing and support components. Replace the housing or support if the seal ring grooves or machined surfaces are worn, scored, pitted, or damaged.

Replace the pump gears if pitted, worn chipped, or damaged. Inspect the thrust washer for wear or damage. Replace the washer if necessary.

Inspect the pump and reaction shaft support bushings. Minor bushing wear is acceptable. Replace the bushings only if scored, or severely worn.

Install the gears in the pump housing and measure end clearance with a feeler gauge and straightedge (Fig. 189). The pump inner gear is a one way fit. The bore on one side of the gear inside diameter is chamfered. Be sure the chamfered side faces forward (to front of pump). Clearance should be 0.010 - 0.06 mm (0.0004 - 0.0025 in.).

Fig. 189 Measuring Pump Gear End Clearance

Measure clearance between the outer gear and the pump body (Fig. 190). Clearance should be 0.08 - 0.19 mm (0.0035 - 0.0075 in.).

Measure gear tooth clearance with a feeler gauge. Align one tooth of the outer gear in inner gear and measure clearance (Fig. 191). Clearance should be 0.08 - 0.19 mm (0.0035 - 0.0075 in.).

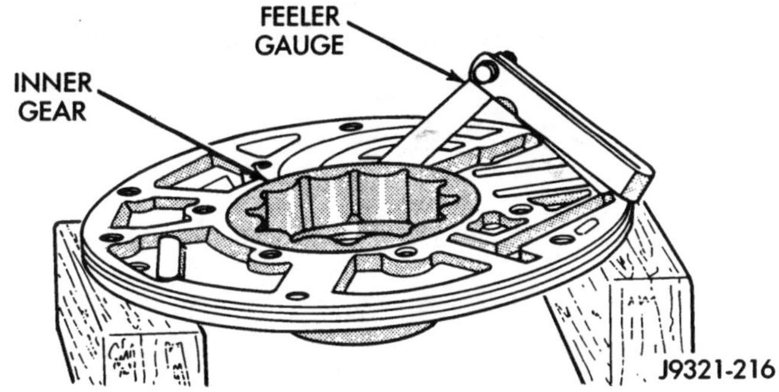

Fig. 190 Measuring Pump Housing-To-Inner Gear Clearance

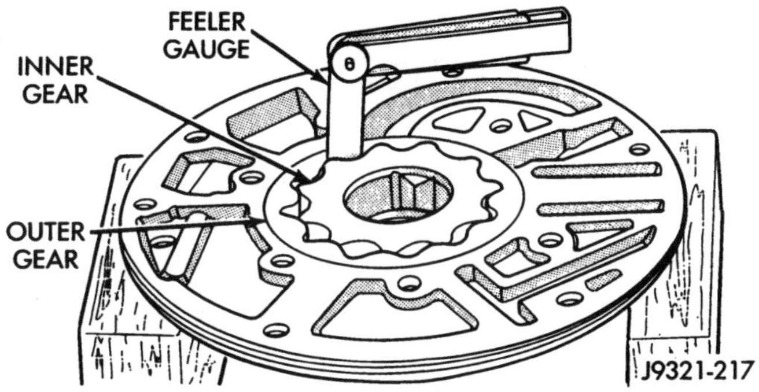

Fig. 191 Measuring Pump Gear Tooth Clearance

CLEANING AND INSPECTION (Continued)

FRONT CLUTCH

Clean the front clutch components in solvent and dry them with compressed air only. Do not use rags or shop towels to dry any of the clutch parts. Lint from such materials will adhere to the component surfaces and could restrict or block fluid passages after assembly.

Replace the clutch discs if warped, worn, scored, burned or charred, or if the facing is flaking off. Replace the steel plates if heavily scored, warped, or broken. Be sure the driving lugs on the plates are in good condition. The lugs must not be bent, cracked or damaged in any way.

Replace the clutch spring and spring retainer if either is distorted, warped or broken.

Check the lug grooves in the clutch retainer. The steel plates should slide freely in the slots. Replace the retainer if the grooves are worn or damaged.

Check action of the check ball in the retainer (Fig. 192). The ball must move freely and not stick.

NOTE: Inspect the clutch retainer bushings carefully (Fig. 193). The retainer bushings are NOT serviceable. It will be necessary to replace the retainer if either bushing is scored, or worn.

Inspect the piston and retainer seal surfaces for nicks or scratches. Minor scratches can be removed with crocus cloth. However, replace the piston and/or retainer if the seal surfaces are seriously scored.

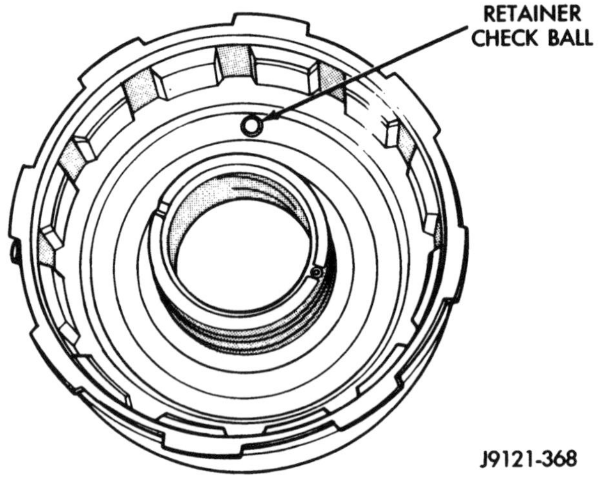

Fig. 192 Front Clutch Piston Retainer Check Ball Location

REAR CLUTCH

Clean the clutch components (Fig. 194) with solvent and dry them with compressed air. Do not use rags or shop towels to dry any of the clutch parts. Lint from such materials will adhere to component surfaces and could restrict or block fluid passages after assembly.

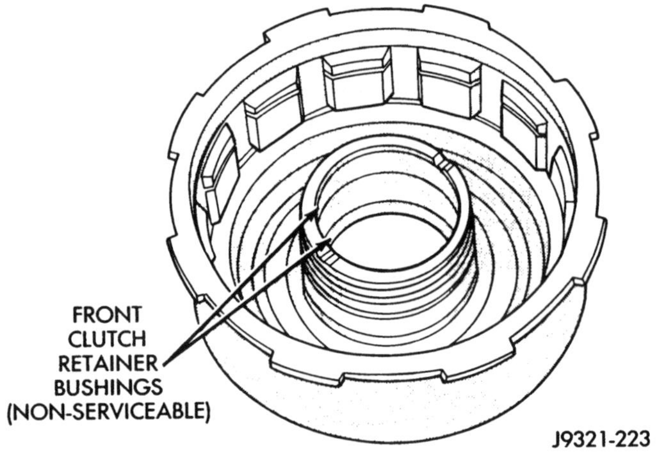

Fig. 193 Retainer Bushing Location/Inspection

Replace the clutch discs if warped, worn, scored, burned/charred, the lugs are damaged, or if the facing is flaking off. Replace the top and bottom pressure plates if scored, warped, or cracked. Be sure the driving lugs on the pressure and clutch plates are also in good condition. The lugs must not be bent, cracked or damaged in any way.

Replace the piston spring and wave spring if either part is distorted, warped or broken.

Check the lug grooves in the clutch retainer. The clutch and pressure plates should slide freely in the slots. Replace the retainer if the grooves are worn or damaged. Also check action of the check balls in the retainer and piston. Each check ball must move freely and not stick.

Replace the retainer bushing if worn, scored, or doubt exists about bushing condition.

Inspect the piston and retainer seal surfaces for nicks or scratches. Minor scratches can be removed with crocus cloth. However, replace the piston and/or retainer if the seal surfaces are seriously scored.

Check condition of the fiber thrust washer and metal output shaft thrust washer. Replace either washer if worn or damaged.

Check condition of the seal rings on the input shaft and clutch retainer hub. Replace the seal rings only if worn, distorted, or damaged. The input shaft front seal ring is teflon with chamfered ends. The rear ring is metal with interlocking ends.

Check the input shaft for wear, or damage. Replace the shaft if worn, scored or damaged in any way.

PLANETARY GEARTRAIN

Clean the planetary components in solvent and dry them with compressed air.

Check sun gear and driving shell condition (Fig. 195). Replace the gear if damaged or if the bushings are scored or worn. The bushings are not serviceable.

CLEANING AND INSPECTION (Continued)

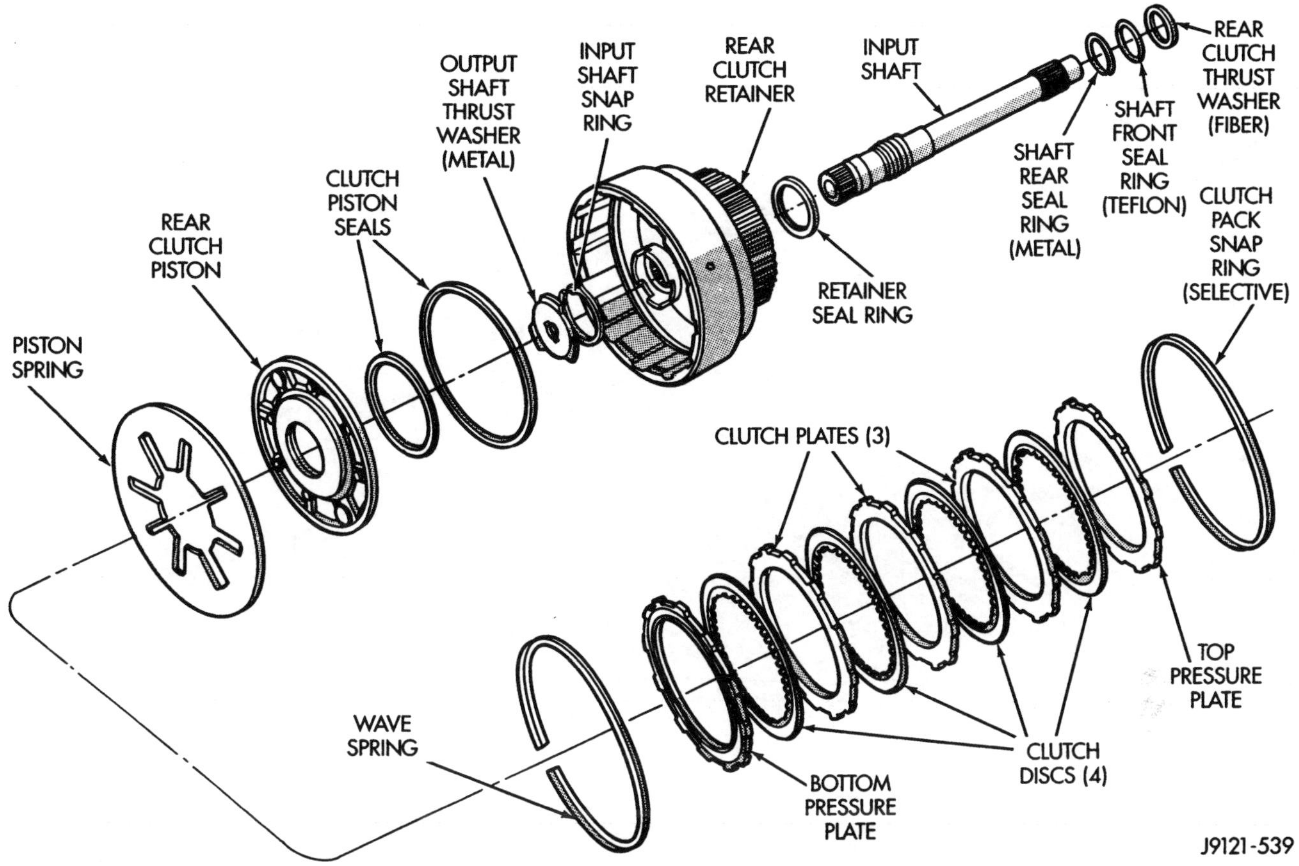

Fig. 194 Rear Clutch Components

Replace the driving shell if worn, cracked or damaged.

Replace planetary gear sets if gears, pinion pins, or carrier are damaged in any way. Replace the annulus gears and supports if either component is worn or damaged.

Inspect the geartrain spacers, thrust plates, snap rings, and thrust washers (Fig. 195). Replace any of these parts that are worn, distorted or damaged. Do not attempt to reuse these parts.

The planetary gear thrust washers are different sizes. The large diameter washers go on the front planetary and the smaller washers go on the rear planetary. All the washers have four locating tabs on them. These tabs fit in the holes or slots provided in each planetary gear.

Inspect the output shaft carefully. Pay particular attention to the machined bushing/bearing surfaces on the shaft and the governor valve shaft bore at the shaft rear.

Replace the output shaft if the machined surfaces are scored, pitted, or damaged in any way. Also replace the shaft if the splines are damaged, or exhibits cracks at any location (especially at the governor valve shaft bore).

The annulus gears can be removed from their supports if necessary. Just remove the snap rings and separate the two parts when replacement is necessary. In addition, the annulus gear bushings can be replaced if severely worn, or scored. However it is not necessary to replace the bushings if they only exhibit normal wear. Check bushing fit on the output shaft to be sure.

ADJUSTMENTS

SHIFT CABLE ADJUSTMENT

(1) Shift transmission into Park.

(2) Raise vehicle.

(3) Release cable adjuster clamp to unlock cable (Fig. 196) and (Fig. 197). Clamp is at transmission end of cable.

(4) Unsnap cable from transmission cable bracket.

(5) Move transmission shift lever fully rearward to Park detent. Lever is on manual valve shaft at driver side of case.

(6) Verify positive engagement of park lock by attempting to rotate propeller shaft. Shaft will not rotate when park lock is engaged.

(7) Snap cable into cable bracket.

(8) Lock shift cable by pressing cable adjuster clamp down until it snaps into place.

ADJUSTMENTS (Continued)

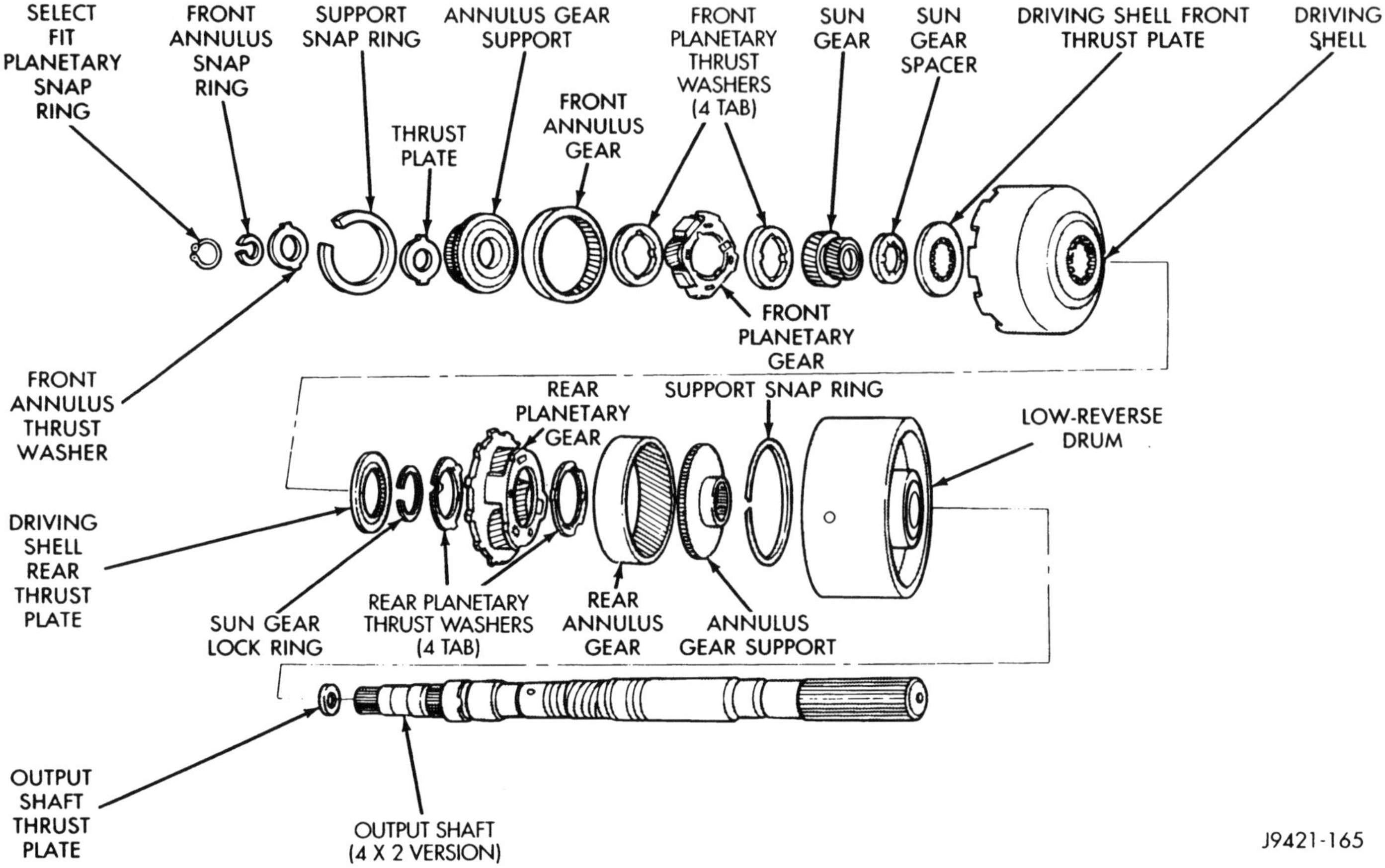

Fig. 195 Planetary Geartrain Components

(9) Check engine starting. Engine should start only in Park and Neutral.

(10) Lower vehicle.

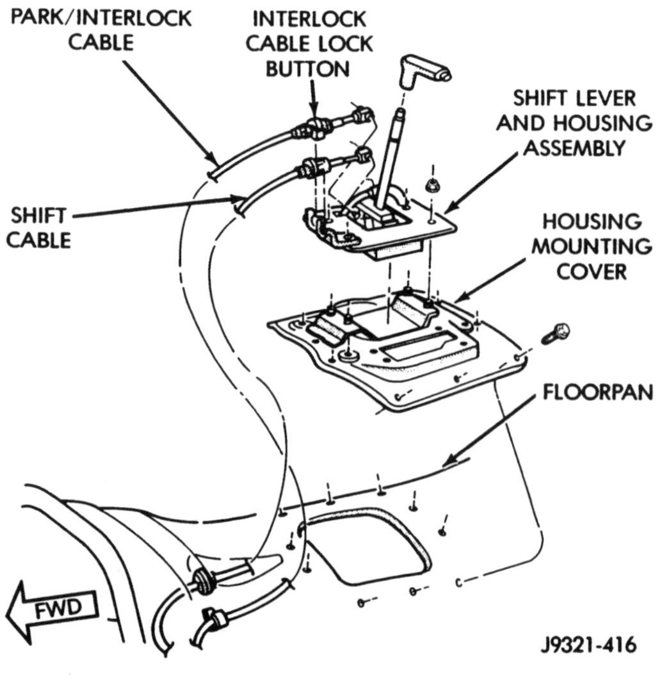

Fig. 196 Shift Cable

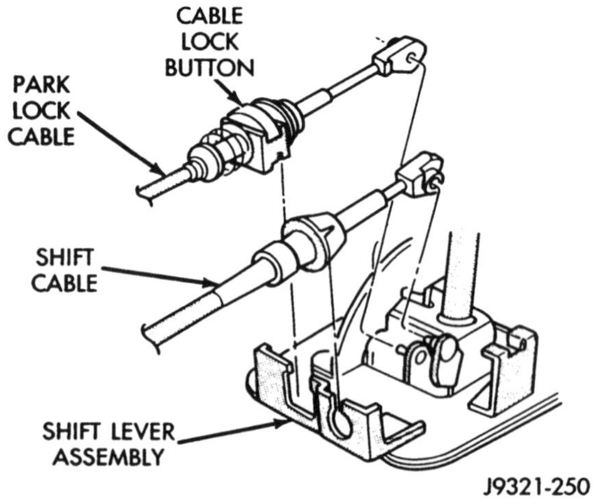

Fig. 197 Cable Attachment

THROTTLE VALVE CABLE ADJUSTMENT

The throttle valve cable controls throttle pressure and kickdown on 30RH transmissions (Fig. 198).

Correct cable adjustment is important to proper shifting. The cable positions the throttle valve which controls shift speed, shift quality and part throttle downshift sensitivity. If the setting is incorrect, shift quality and shift speeds will be unsatisfactory.

ADJUSTMENTS (Continued)

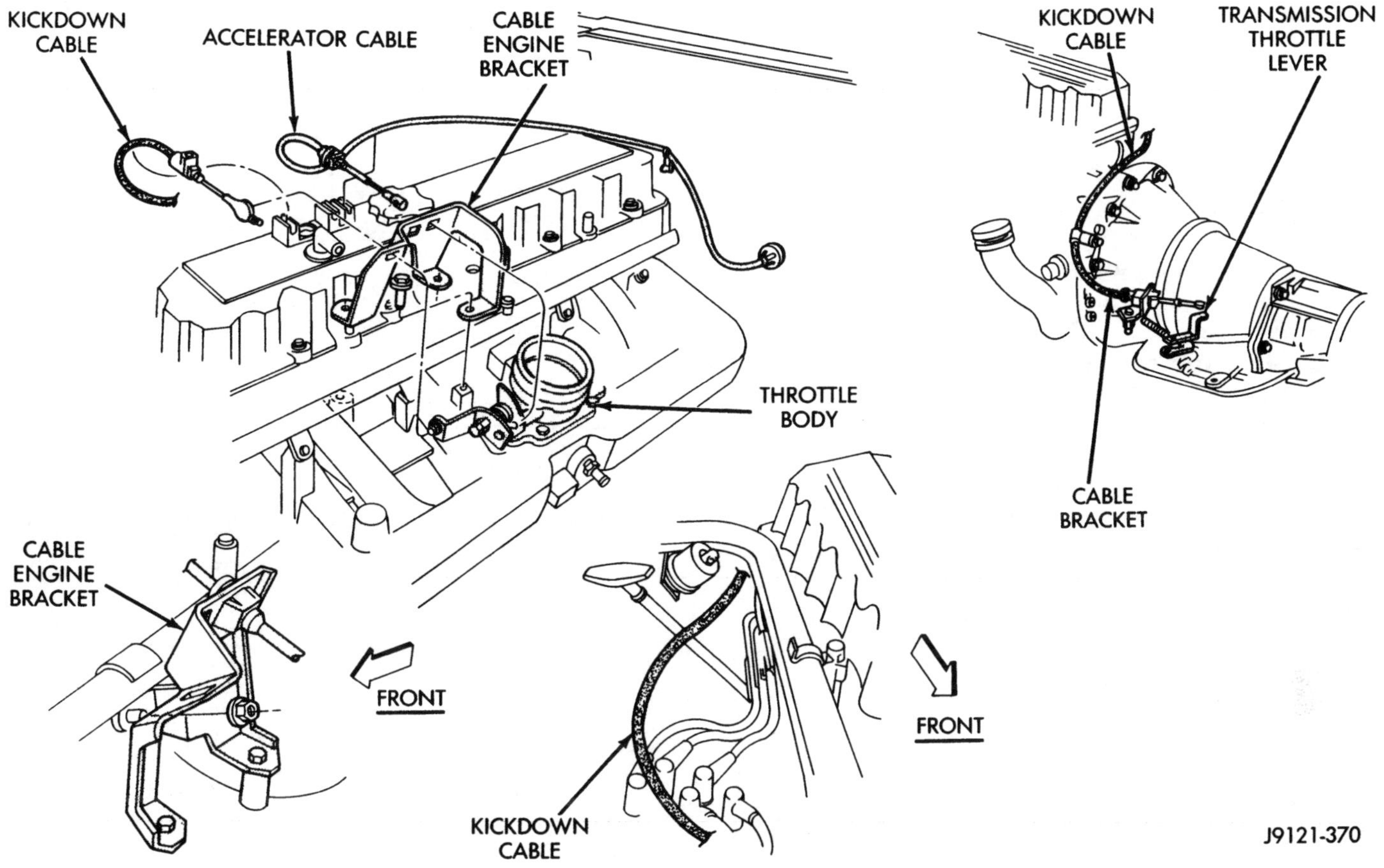

Fig. 198 Transmission Throttle Valve Cable

THROTTLE VALVE CABLE ADJUSTMENT PROCEDURE

Cable adjustment is performed in the engine compartment. It is not necessary to raise the vehicle for access.

(1) Shift transmission into Park and shut engine off.

(2) Disconnect cable end from throttle lever.

(3) Press cable release button (Fig. 199).

(4) Adjust cable end socket to center of ball on lever (Fig. 200).

(5) Connect cable to throttle lever (Fig. 200).

FRONT BAND ADJUSTMENT

The front band adjusting screw is located on the left side of the transmission case above the manual valve and throttle valve levers.

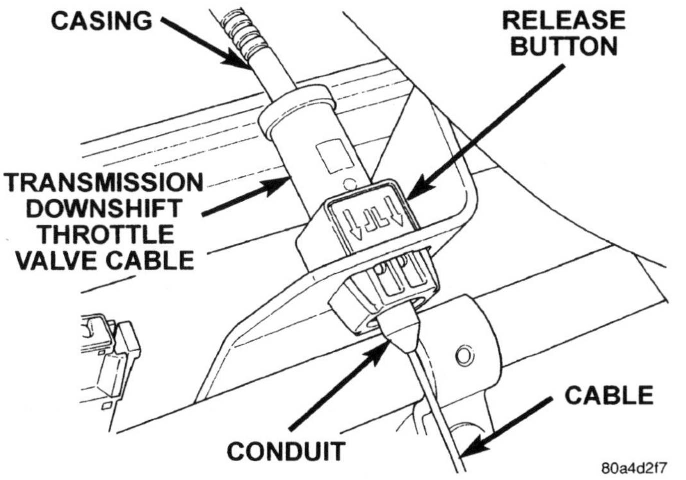

Fig. 199 Throttle Valve Cable Components

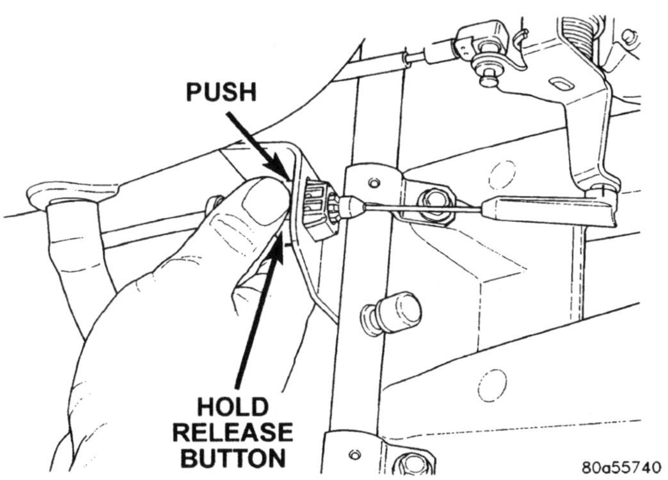

Fig. 200 Throttle Valve Cable Adjustment

ADJUSTMENTS (Continued)

(1) Raise vehicle.

(2) Loosen band adjusting screw locknut. Then back locknut off 4-5 turns.

(3) Clean adjusting screw threads with Mopar rust penetrant if necessary. Then lubricate threads with Mopar spray lube or petroleum jelly. Be sure screw turns freely in case. This is necessary for accurate adjustment.

(4) Tighten band adjusting screw to 8 N·m (72 in. lbs.) torque with inch-pound torque wrench. **If Adapter Extension C-3705 is needed in order to reach adjusting screw, tighten screw to only 5-6 N·m (47-50 in. lbs.) torque (Fig. 201).**

(5) Back off front band adjusting screw 2-1/2 turns.

(6) Hold adjuster screw in position and tighten locknut to 41 N·m (30 ft. lbs.) torque.

(7) Lower vehicle.

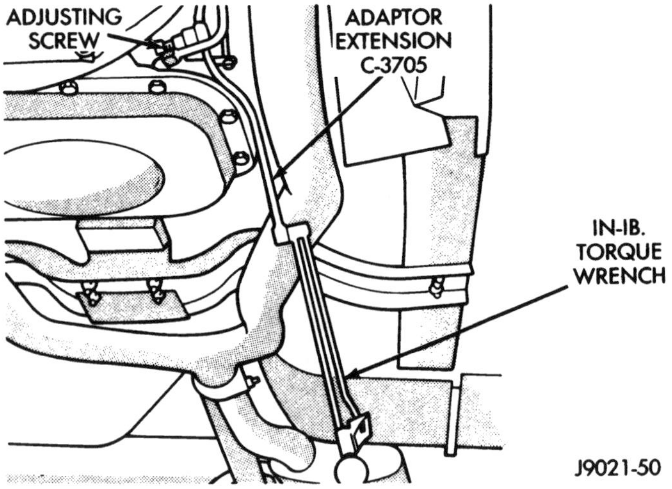

Fig. 201 Front Band Adjustment

REAR BAND ADJUSTMENT

The transmission oil pan must be removed for access to the rear (low-reverse) band adjusting screw.

(1) Raise vehicle.

(2) Remove transmission oil pan and drain fluid.

(3) Loosen band adjusting screw locknut 5-6 turns. Be sure adjusting screw turns freely in lever.

(4) Tighten adjusting screw to 5 N·m (41 in. lbs.) torque (Fig. 202).

(5) Back off rear band adjusting screw 7 turns.

(6) Hold adjusting screw in place and tighten locknut to 34 N·m (25 ft. lbs.) torque.

(7) Position new gasket on oil pan and install pan on transmission. Tighten pan bolts to 17 N·m (150 in. lbs.) torque.

(8) Lower vehicle and refill transmission with recommended fluid.

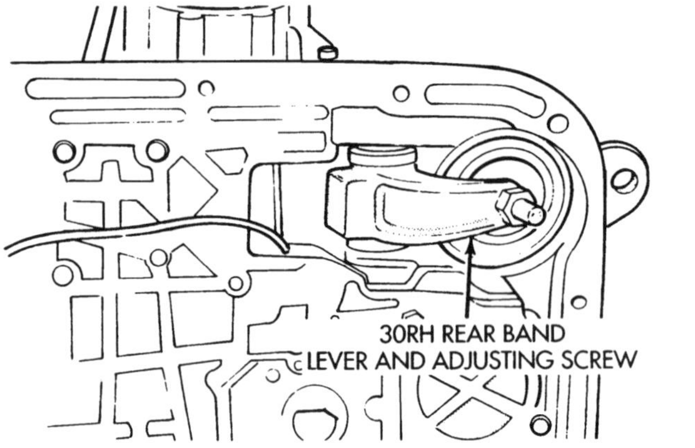

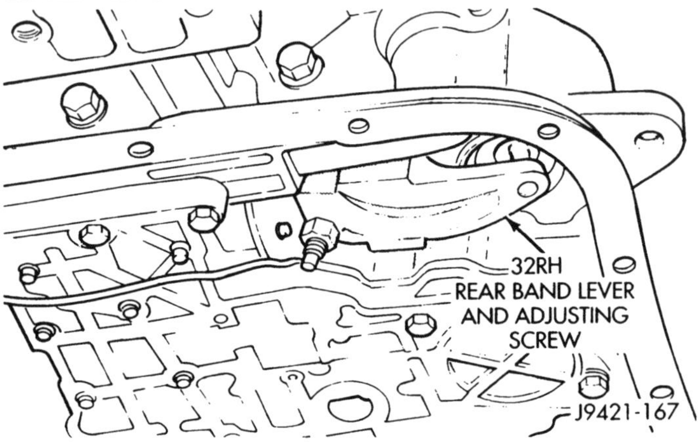

Fig. 202 Rear Band Lever And Adjusting Screw Location

VALVE BODY

CONTROL PRESSURE ADJUSTMENTS

There are two control pressure adjustments on the valve body;

- Line Pressure
- Throttle Pressure

Line and throttle pressures are interdependent because each affects shift quality and timing. As a result, both adjustments must be performed properly and in the correct sequence. Adjust line pressure first and throttle pressure last.

LINE PRESSURE ADJUSTMENT

Measure distance from the valve body to the inner edge of the adjusting screw with an accurate steel scale (Fig. 203).

Distance should be 33.4 mm (1-5/16 in.).

If adjustment is required, turn the adjusting screw in, or out, to obtain required distance setting.

NOTE: The 33.4 mm (1-5/16 in.) setting is an approximate setting. Manufacturing tolerances may make it necessary to vary from this dimension to obtain desired pressure.

ADJUSTMENTS (Continued)

One complete turn of the adjusting screw changes line pressure approximately 1-2/3 psi (9 kPa).

Turning the adjusting screw counterclockwise increases pressure while turning the screw clockwise decreases pressure.

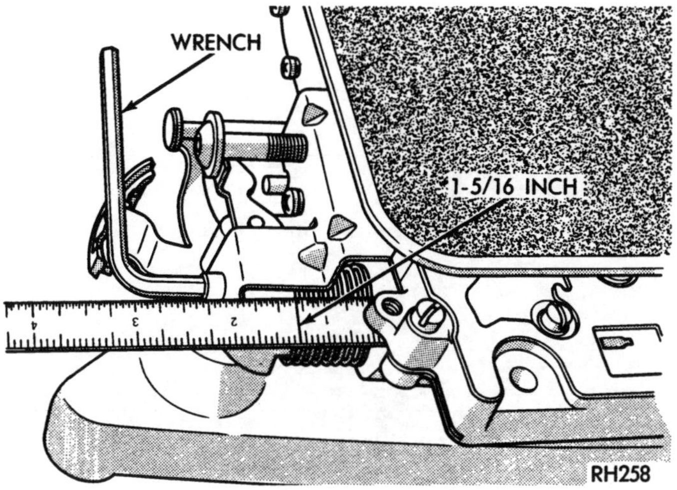

Fig. 203 Line Pressure Adjustment

THROTTLE PRESSURE ADJUSTMENT

Insert Gauge Tool C-3763 between the throttle lever cam and the kickdown valve stem (Fig. 204).

Push the gauge tool inward to compress the kickdown valve against the spring and bottom the throttle valve.

Maintain pressure against kickdown valve spring. Turn throttle lever stop screw until the screw head touches throttle lever tang and the throttle lever cam touches gauge tool.

NOTE: The kickdown valve spring must be fully compressed and the kickdown valve completely bottomed to obtain correct adjustment.

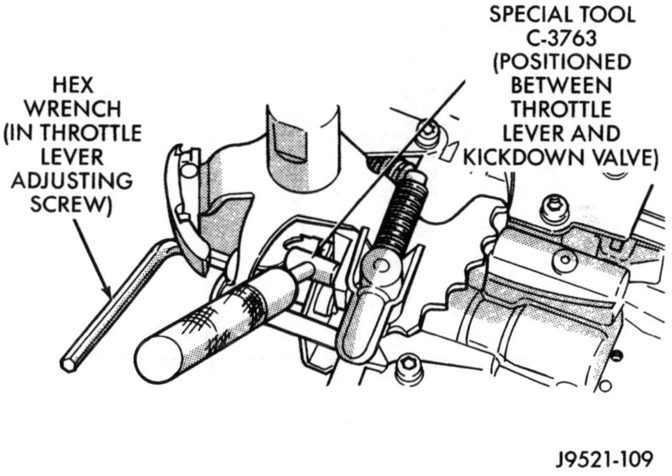

Fig. 204 Throttle Pressure Adjustment

SCHEMATICS AND DIAGRAMS

HYDRAULIC SCHEMATICS

SCHEMATICS AND DIAGRAMS (Continued)

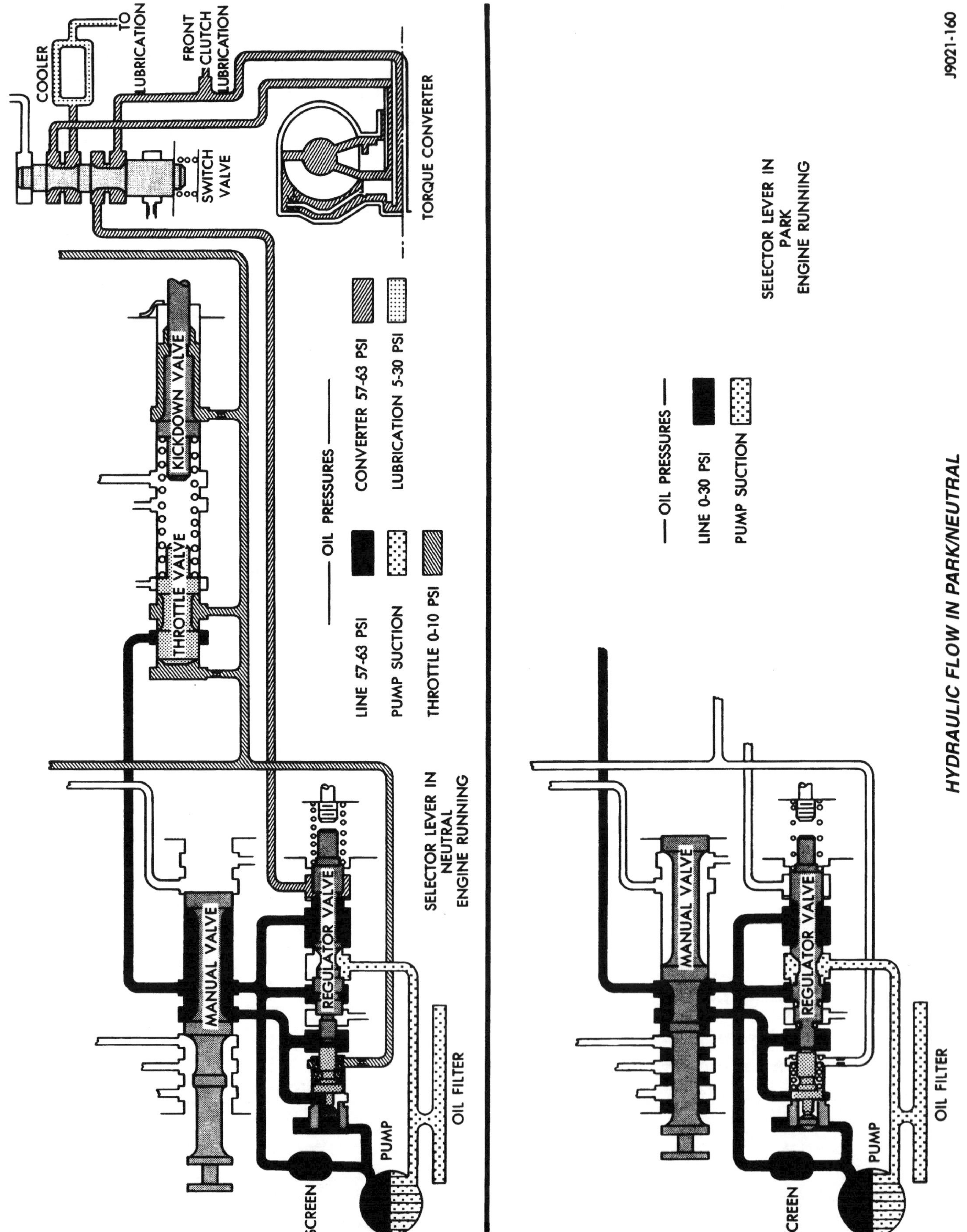

HYDRAULIC FLOW IN PARK/NEUTRAL

SCHEMATICS AND DIAGRAMS (Continued)

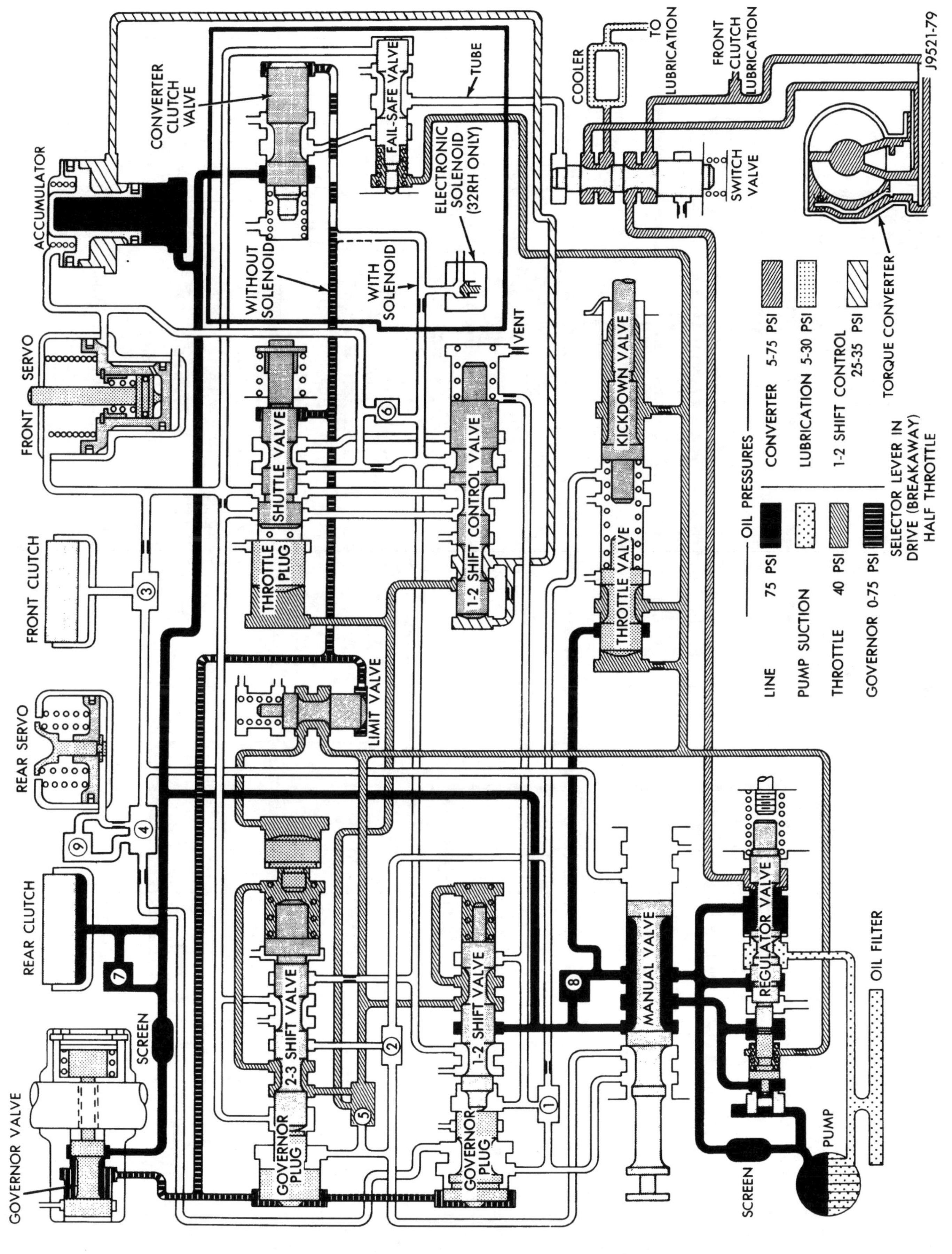

HYDRAULIC FLOW IN D-FIRST GEAR

SCHEMATICS AND DIAGRAMS (Continued)

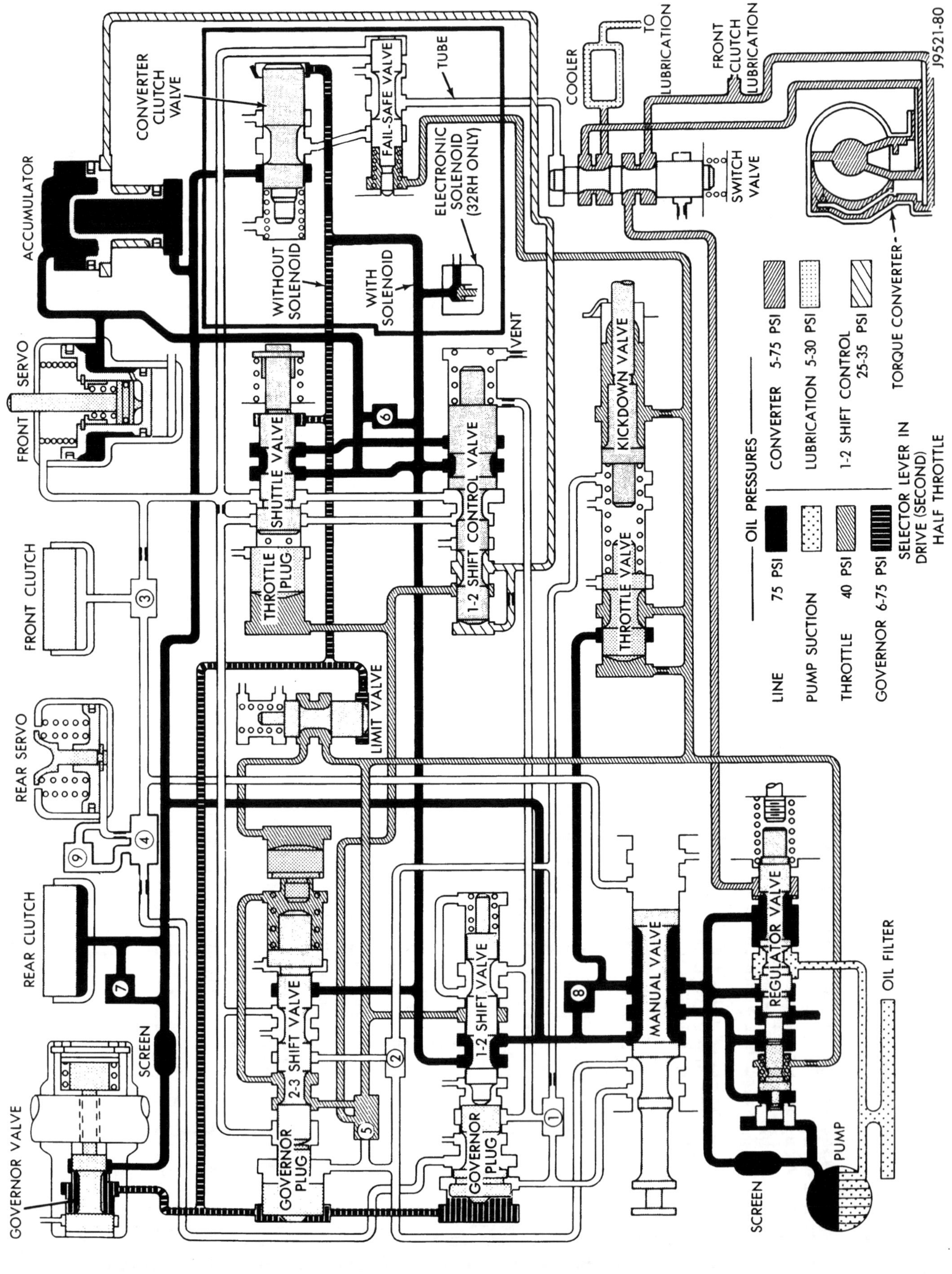

HYDRAULIC FLOW IN D-SECOND GEAR

SCHEMATICS AND DIAGRAMS (Continued)

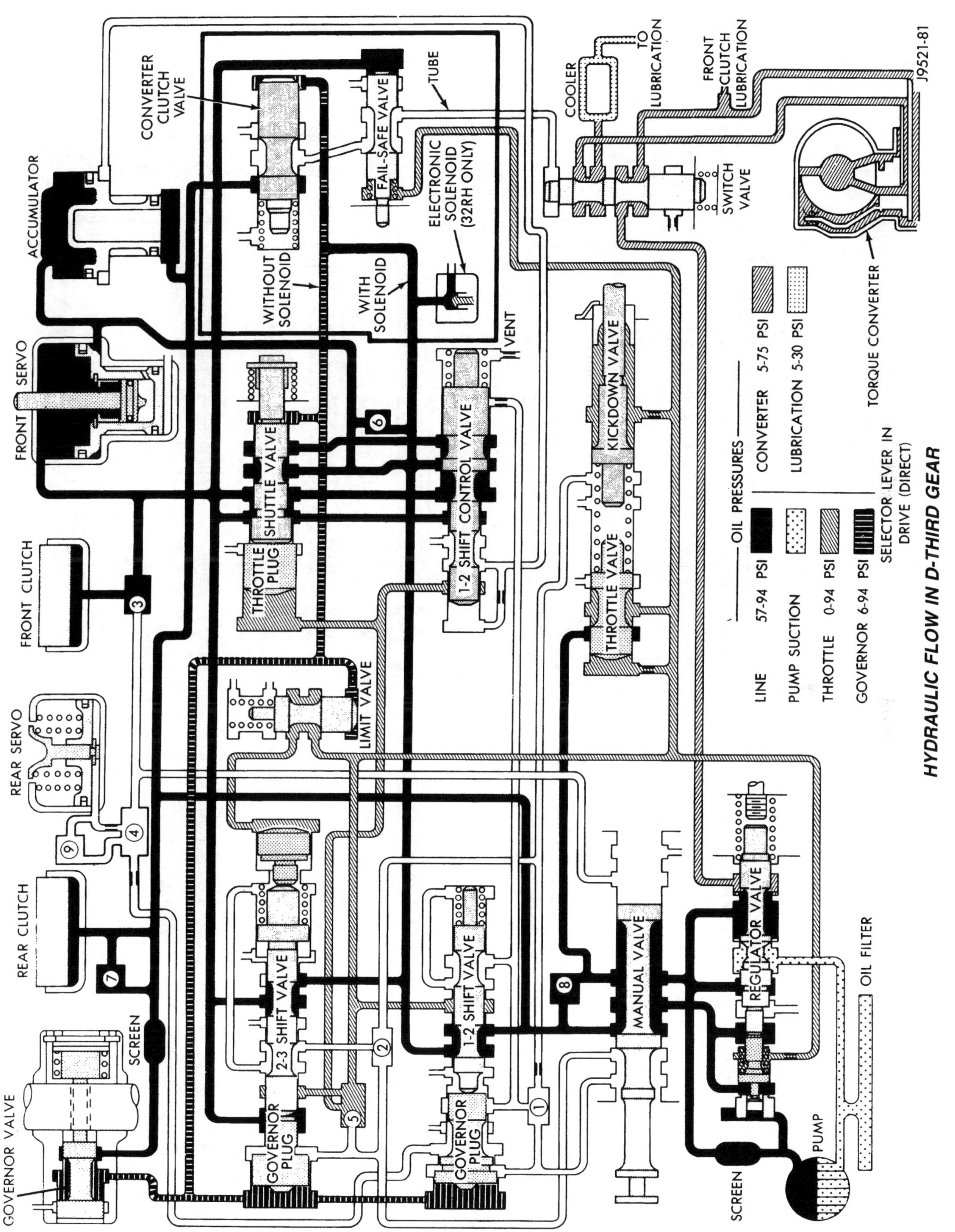

HYDRAULIC FLOW IN D-THIRD GEAR

SCHEMATICS AND DIAGRAMS (Continued)

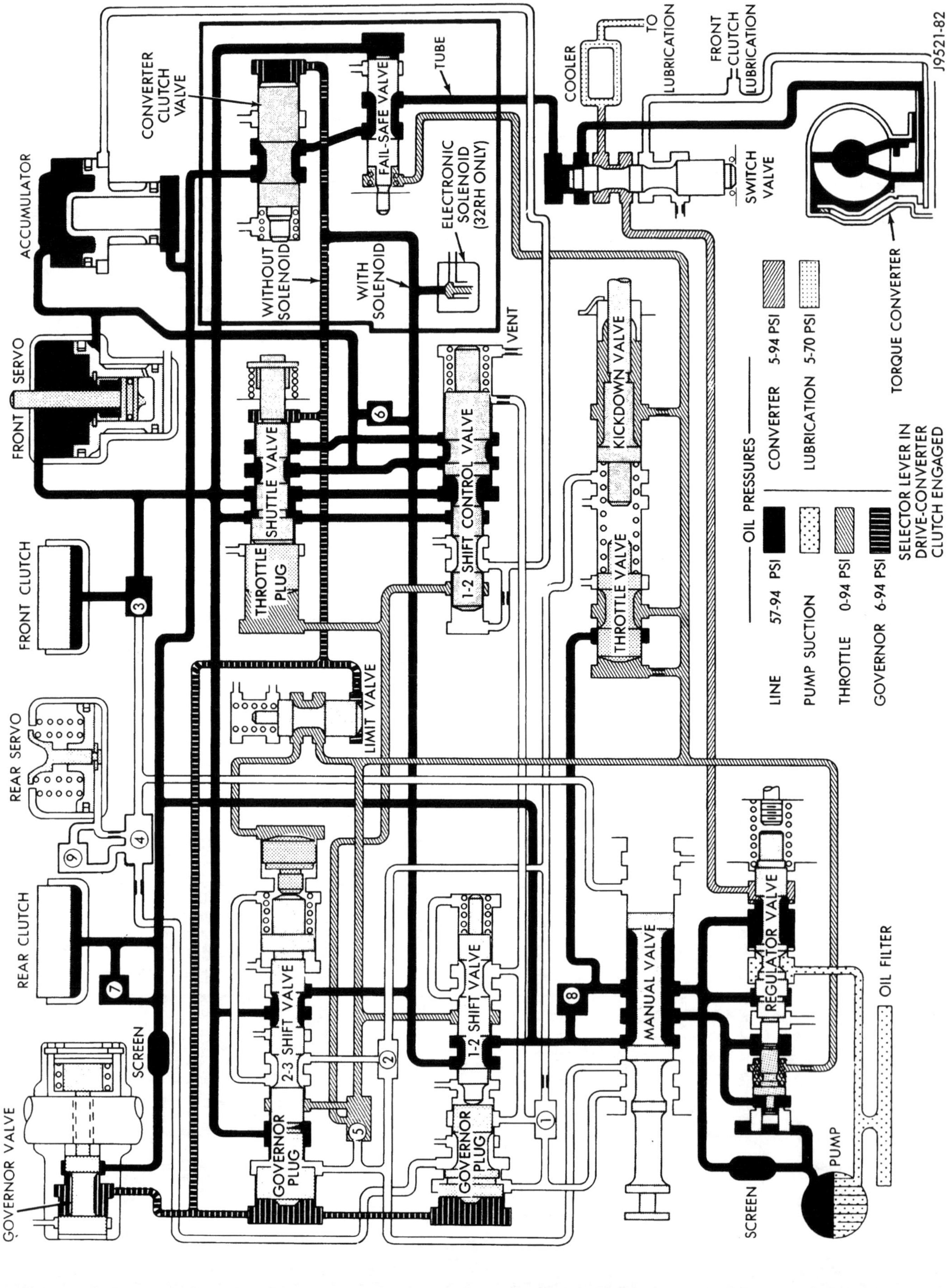

HYDRAULIC FLOW IN D-THIRD GEAR (CONVERTER CLUTCH APPLIED)

SCHEMATICS AND DIAGRAMS (Continued)

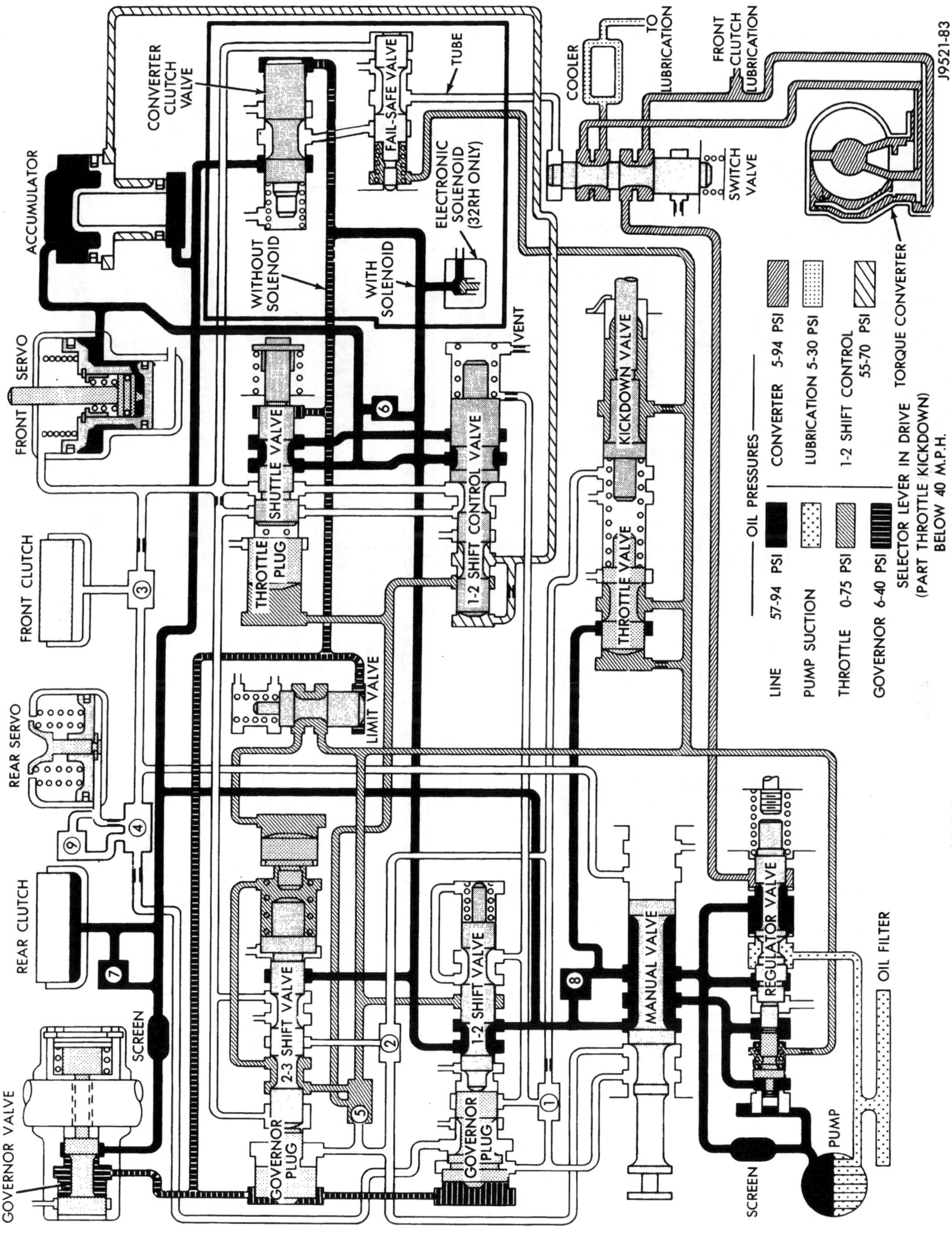

HYDRAULIC FLOW AT PART THROTTLE 3-2 KICKDOWN

SCHEMATICS AND DIAGRAMS (Continued)

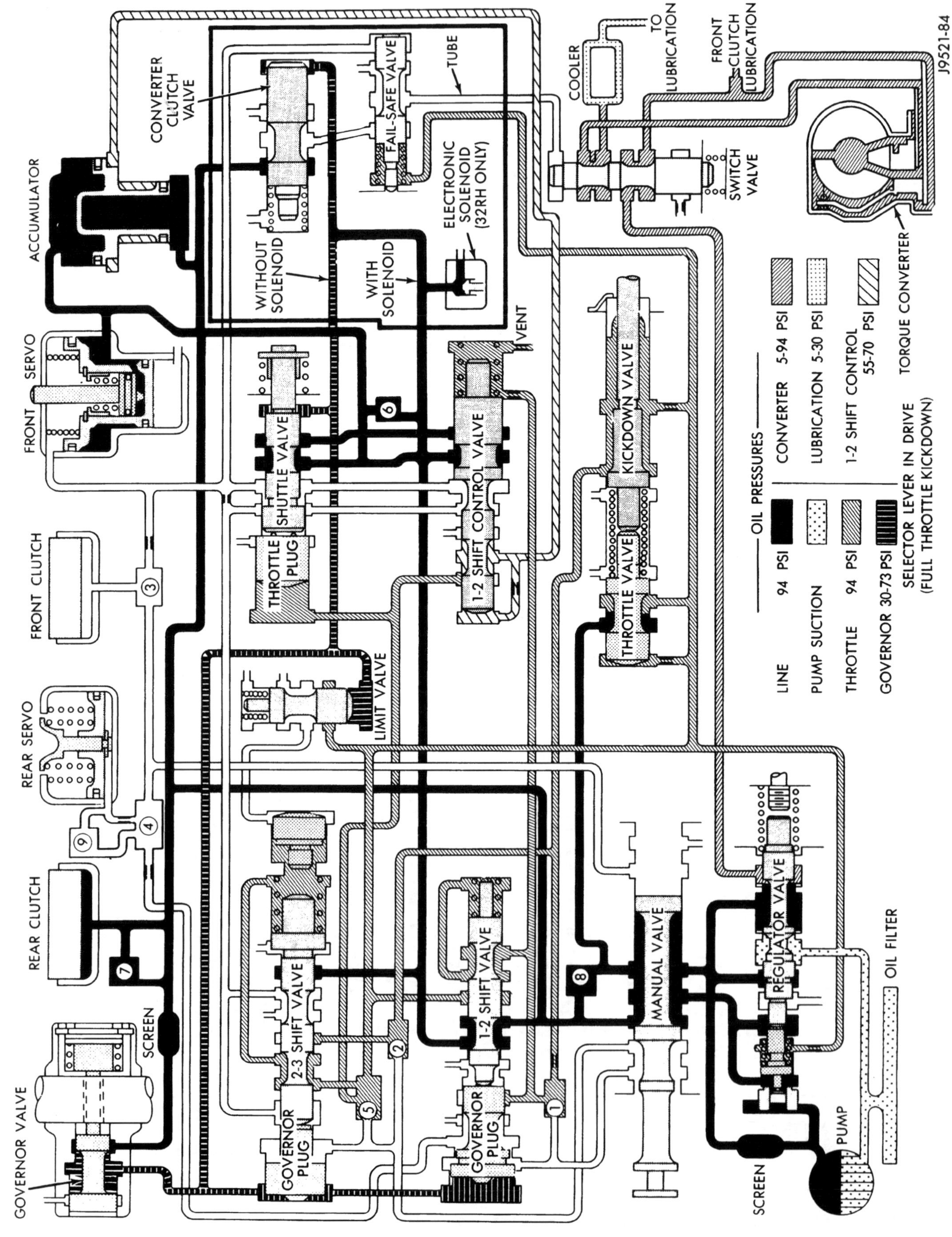

HYDRAULIC FLOW AT FULL THROTTLE 3-2 KICKDOWN

SCHEMATICS AND DIAGRAMS (Continued)

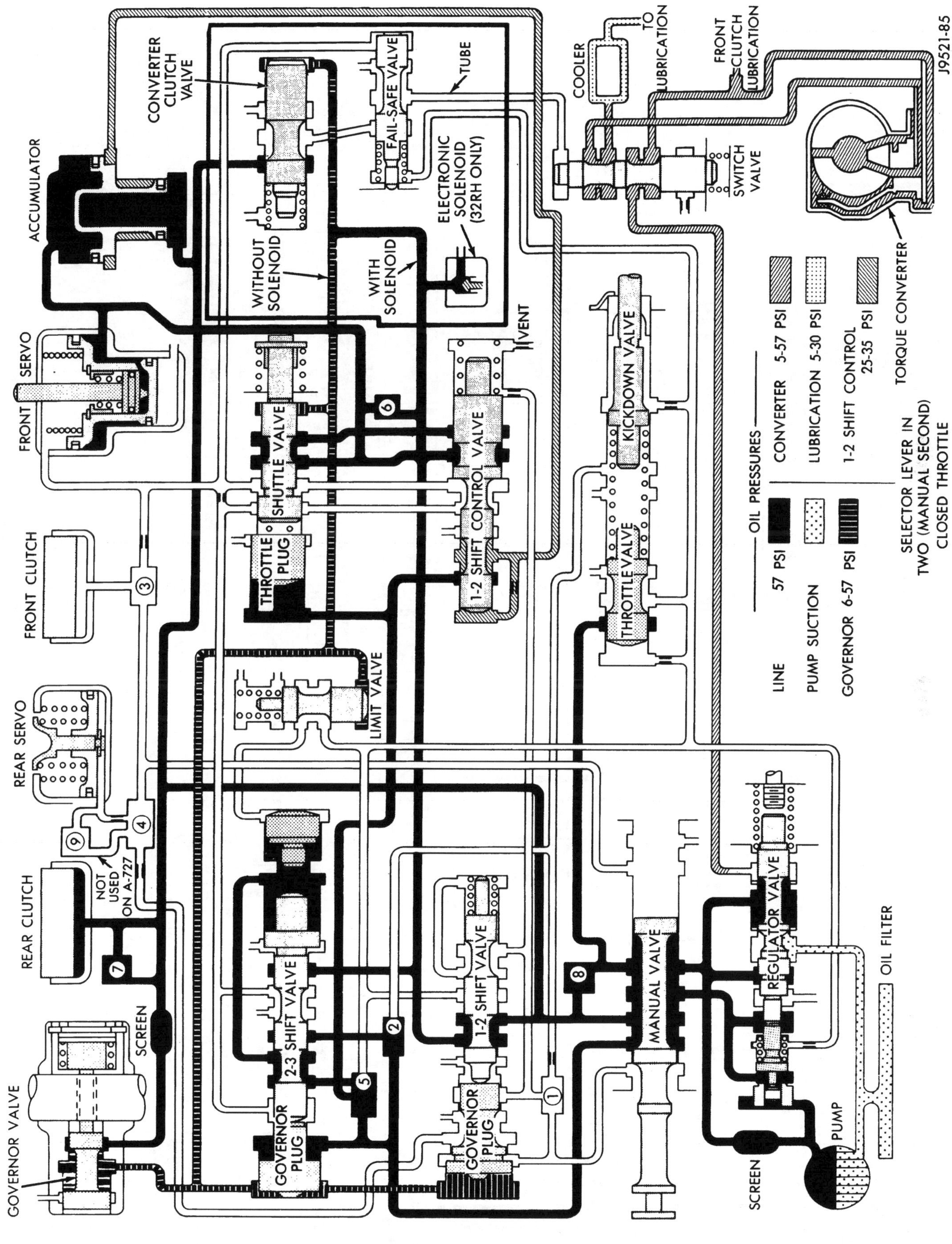

HYDRAULIC FLOW IN MANUAL SECOND

SCHEMATICS AND DIAGRAMS (Continued)

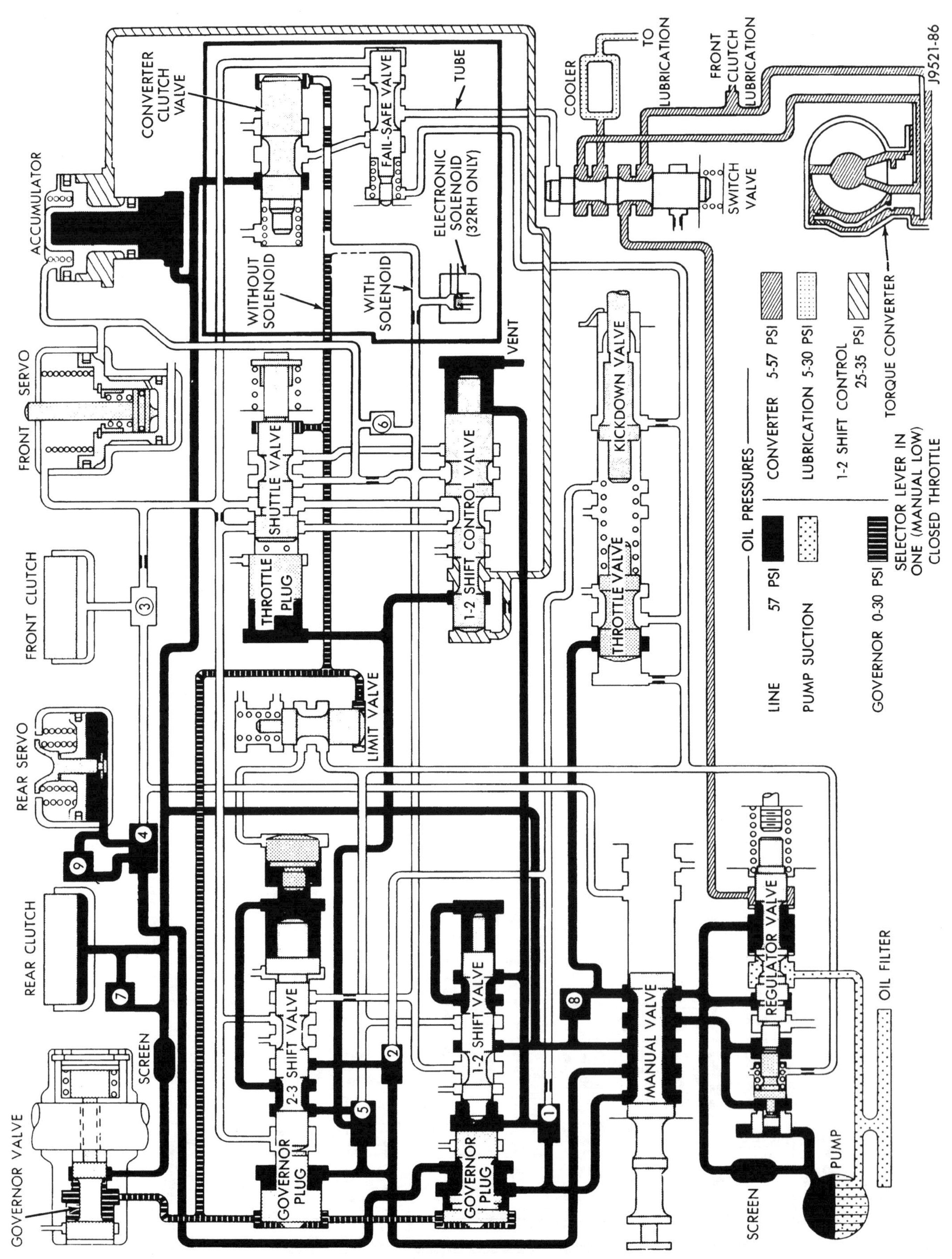

HYDRAULIC FLOW IN MANUAL LOW

SCHEMATICS AND DIAGRAMS (Continued)

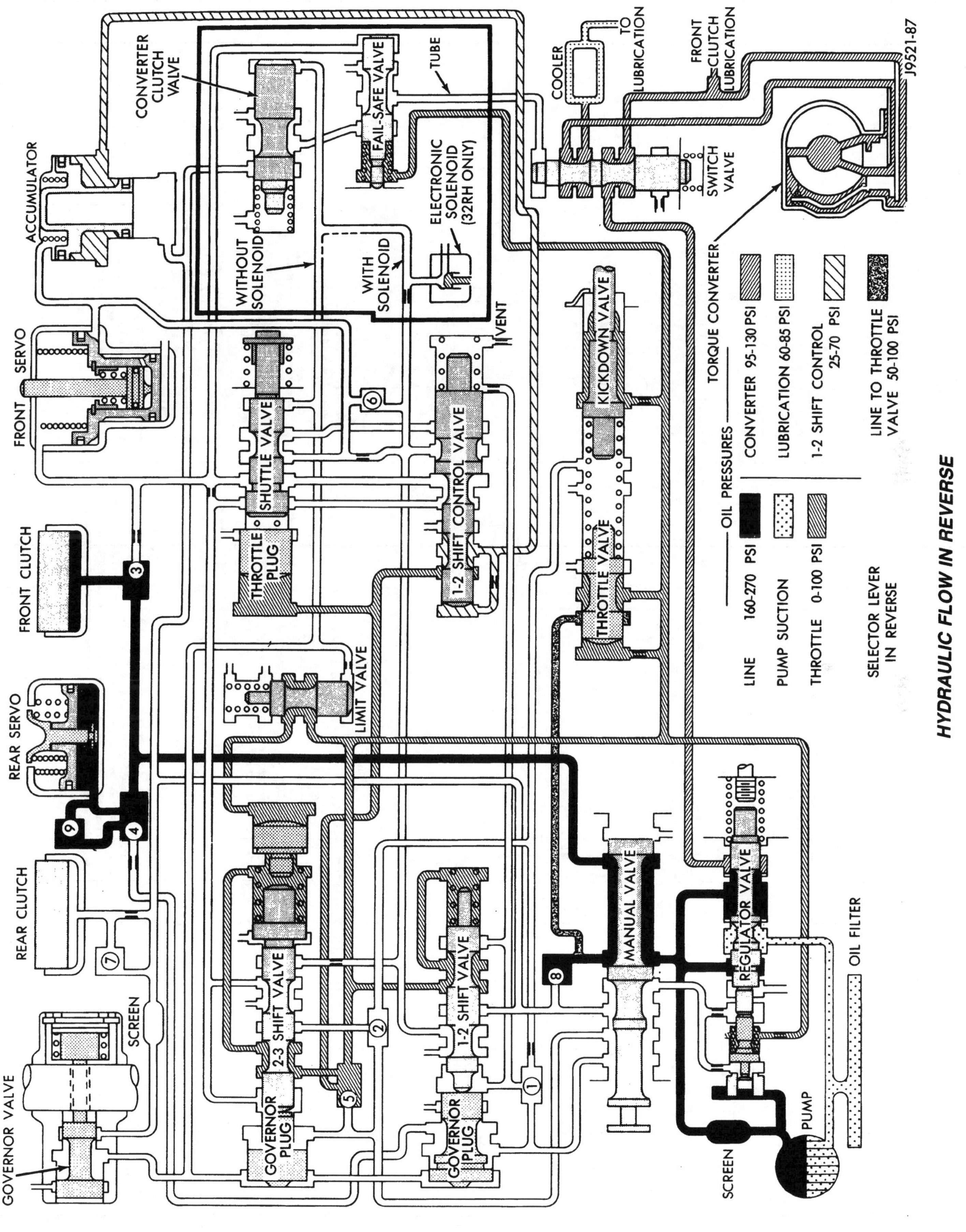

HYDRAULIC FLOW IN REVERSE

SCHEMATICS AND DIAGRAMS (Continued)

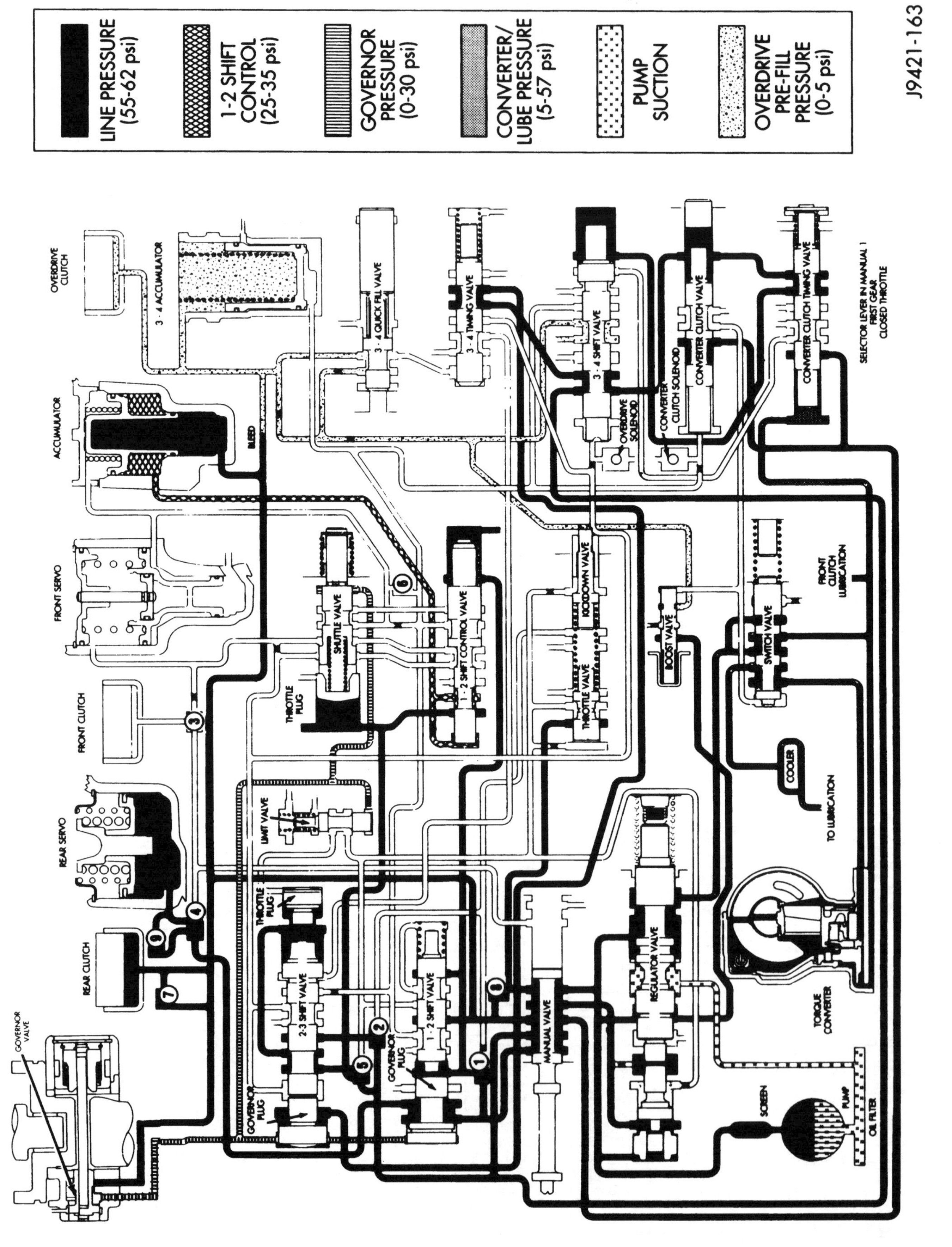

HYDRAULIC FLOW IN MANUAL FIRST GEAR (1)

SCHEMATICS AND DIAGRAMS (Continued)

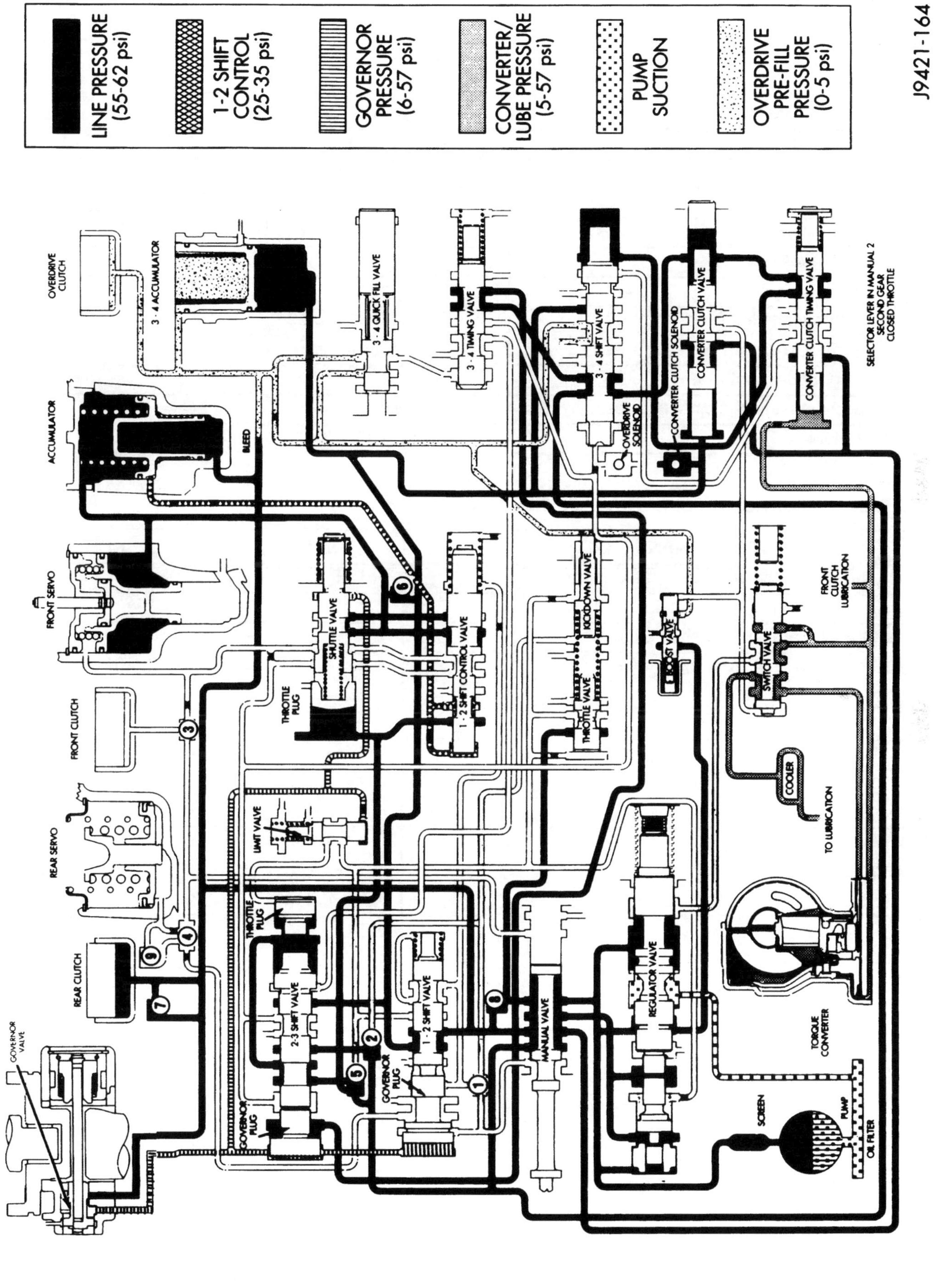

HYDRAULIC FLOW IN MANUAL SECOND GEAR (2)

SPECIFICATIONS

30RH AUTOMATIC TRANSMISSION

GENERAL

COMPONENT	METRIC	INCH
Oil pump gear tip clearance	0.089-0.190 mm	0.0035-0.0075 in.
Planetary end play	0.125-1.19 mm	0.001-0.047 in.
Input shaft end play	0.56-2.31 mm	0.022-0.091 in.
Clutch pack clearance/Front 4-disc.	1.70-3.40 mm	0.067-0.134 in.
Clutch pack clearance/Rear 4-disc.	0.635-1.14 mm	0.025-0.045 in.
Front clutch spring usage	1 spring	
32RH-Front Band adjustment from 72 in. lbs. 32RH-Rear Band adjustment from 72 in. lbs.	Back off 2.25 turns Back off 4 turns	
30RH-Front Band adjustment from 72 in. lbs.	Back off 2.5 turns	
30RH-Rear Band adjustment from 41 in. lbs.	Back off 7 turns	
Recommended fluid	Mopar, ATF Plus type 7176	

THRUST WASHER/SPACER/SNAP RING DIMENSIONS

COMPONENT	METRIC	INCH
Front clutch thrust washer (reaction shaft support hub)	1.55 mm	0.061 in.
Rear clutch thrust washer (clutch retainer)	1.55 mm	0.061 in.
Output shaft thrust plate (output shaft pilot hub)	1.5-1.6mm	0.060-0.063 in.
Output shaft thrust washer (rear clutch hub)	1.3-1.4 mm 1.7-1.8 mm 2.1-2.2 mm	0.052-0.054 in. 0.068-0.070 in. 0.083-0.086 in.
Rear clutch pack snap ring	1.5-1.6 mm 1.7-1.8 mm 1.9-2.0 mm	0.06-0.062 in. 0.068-0.070 in. 0.076-0.078 in.
Planetary geartrain snap ring (at front of output shaft)	1.0-1.1 mm 1.6-1.7 mm 2.1-2.2 mm	0.040-0.044 in. 0.062-0.066 in. 0.082-0.086 in.

SPECIFICATIONS (Continued)

PRESSURE TEST—ALL

ITEM	RANGE	PRESSURE
Overdrive clutch	Fourth gear only	Pressure should be 469-496 kPa (68-72 psi) with closed throttle and increase to 620-896 kPa (90-130 psi) at 1/2 to 3/4 throttle.
Line pressure (at accumulator)	Closed throttle	372-414 kPa (54-60 psi).
Front servo	Third gear only	No more than 21 kPa (3 psi) lower than line pressure.
Rear servo	1 range R range	No more than 21 kPa (3 psi) lower than line pressure. 1103 kPa (160 psi) at idle, builds to 1862 kPa (270 psi) at 1600 rpm.
Governor	D range closed throttle	Pressure should respond smoothly to changes in mph and return to 0-7 kPa (0-1.5 psi) when stopped with transmission in D, 1, 2. Pressure above 7 kPa (1.5 psi) at stand still will prevent transmission from downshifting.

TORQUE—ALL

DESCRIPTION	TORQUE
Bolt, torque convertor	31 N·m (23 ft. lbs.)
Bolt/nut, crossmember	68 N·m (50 ft. lbs.)
Bolt, driveplate to crankshaft	75 N·m (55 ft. lbs.)
Plug, front band reaction	17 N·m (13 ft. lbs.)
Locknut, front band adj.	34 N·m (25 ft. lbs.)
Switch, park/neutral	34 N·m (25 ft. lbs.)
Bolt, fluid pan	17 N·m (13 ft. lbs.)
Bolt, oil pump	20 N·m (15 ft. lbs.)
Bolt, overrunning clutch cam	17 N·m (13 ft. lbs.)
Bolt, O/D to trans.	34 N·m (25 ft. lbs.)
Bolt, O/D piston retainer	17 N·m (13 ft. lbs.)
Plug, pressure test port	14 N·m (10 ft. lbs.)
Bolt, reaction shaft support	20 N·m (15 ft. lbs.)
Locknut, rear band	41 N·m (30 ft. lbs.)
Bolt. speedometer adapter	11 N·m (8 ft. lbs.)
Screw, fluid filter	4 N·m (35 in. lbs.)
Bolt, valve body to case	12 N·m (100 in. lbs.)

SPECIAL TOOLS

30RH AUTOMATIC TRANSMISSION

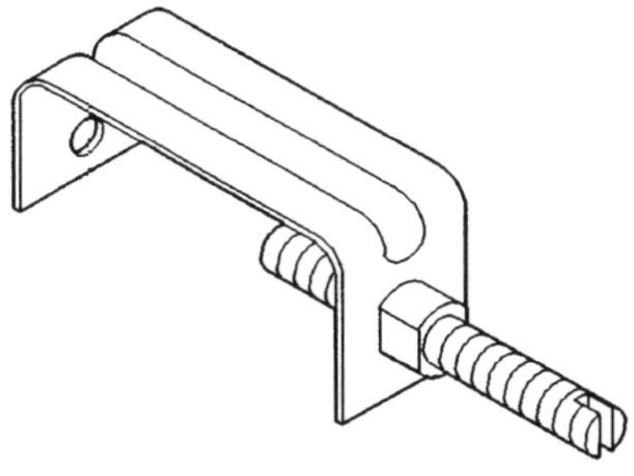

Retainer, Detent Ball and Spring—6583

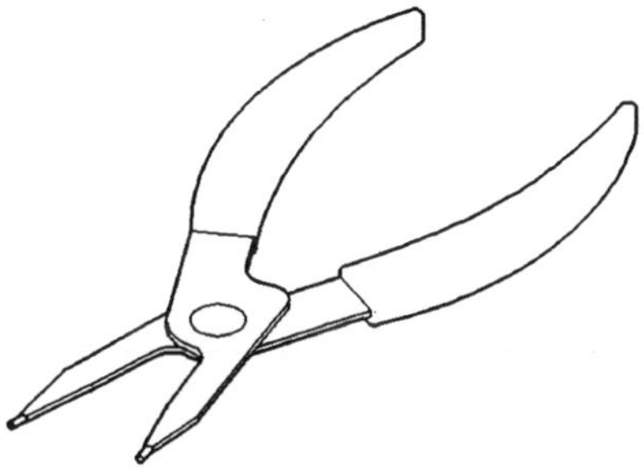

Snap-ring Plier—6823

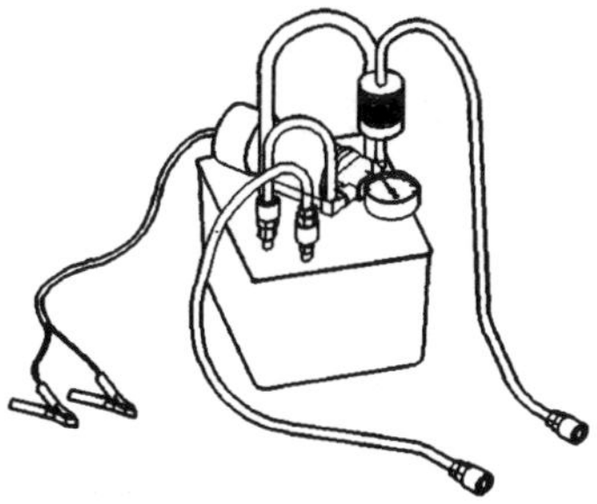

Flusher, Transmission Cooler—6906

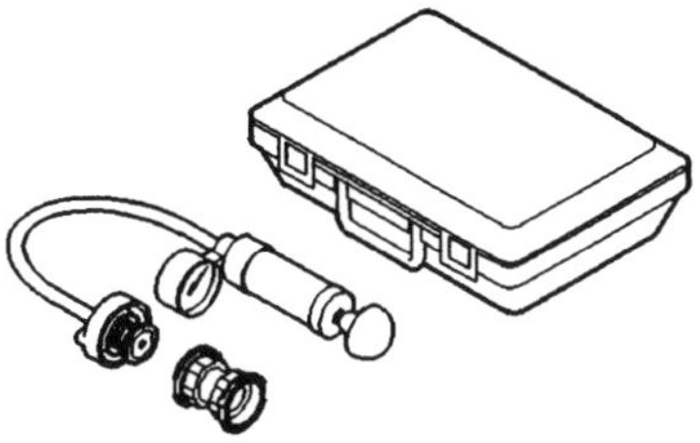

Pressure Tester—7700

SPECIAL TOOLS (Continued)

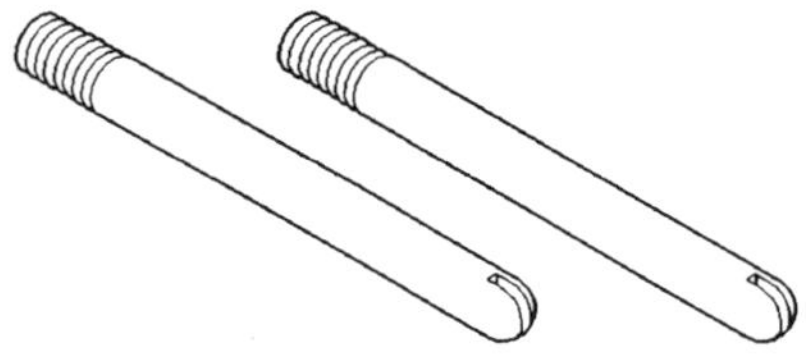

Extension Housing Pilot—C-3288-B

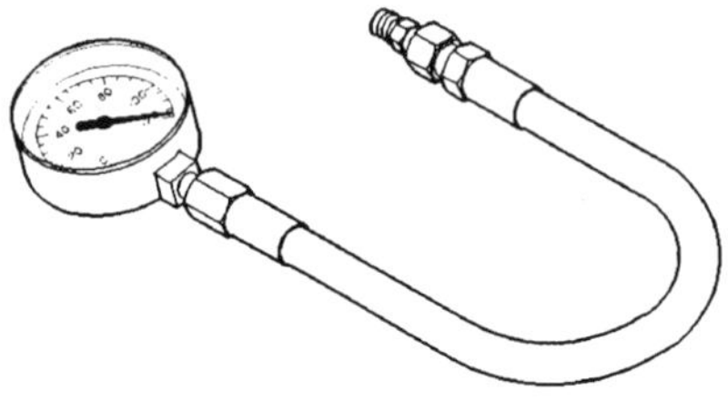

Pressure Gauge—C-3292

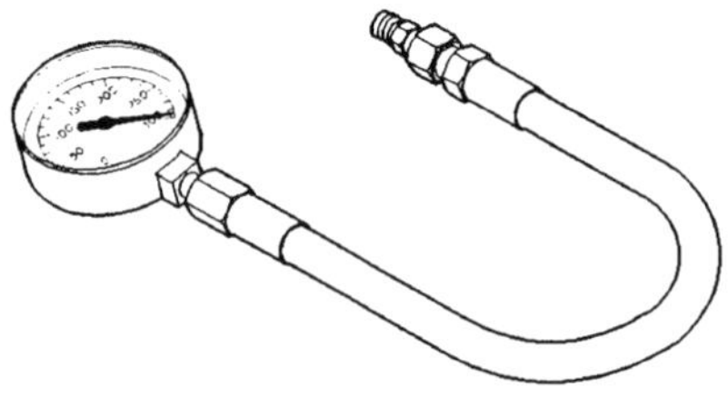

Pressure Gauge—C-3293SP

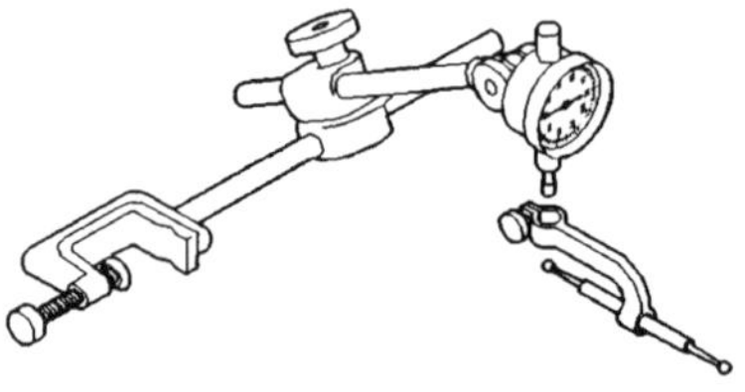

Dial Indicator—C-3339

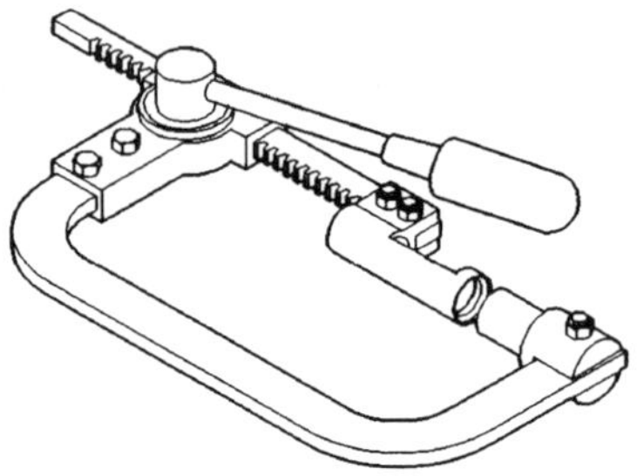

Spring Compressor—C-3422-B

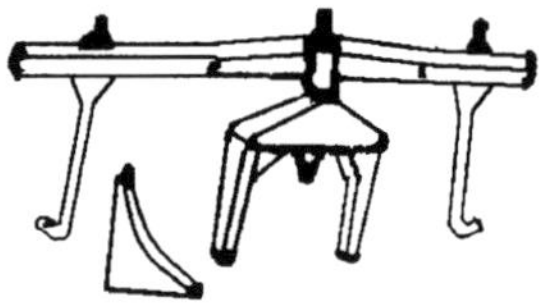

Fixture, Engine Support—C-3487-A

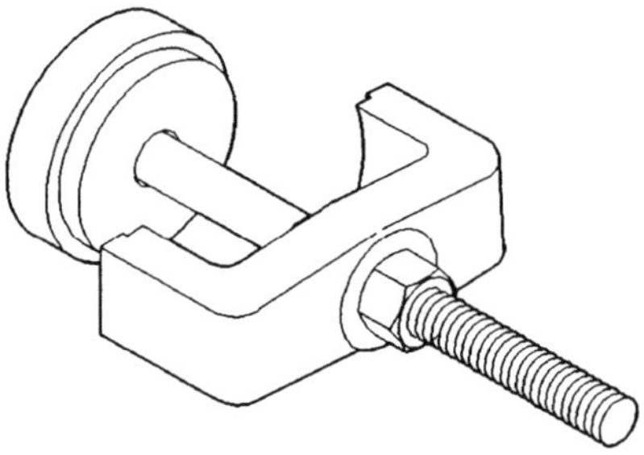

Spring Compressor—C-3575-A

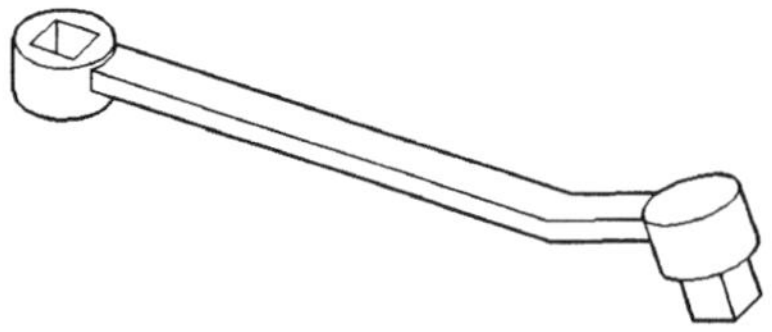

Adapter, Band Adjuster—C-3705

SPECIAL TOOLS (Continued)

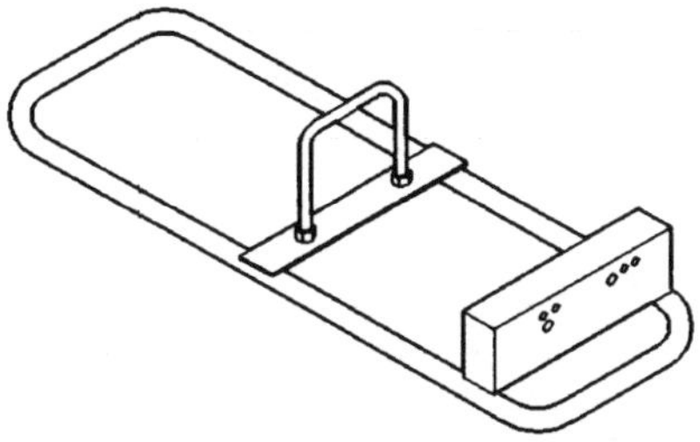

Transmission Repair Stand—C-3750-B

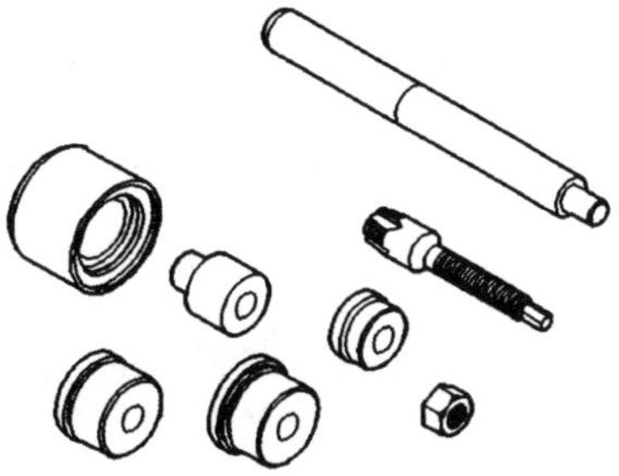

Bushing Remover/Intsaller Set—C-3887-J

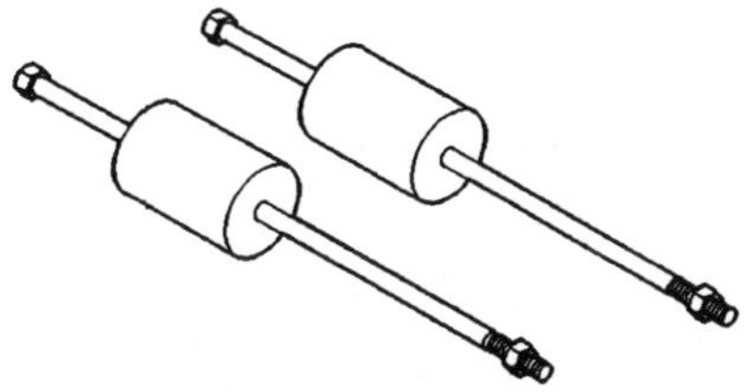

Puller, Slide Hammer—C-3752

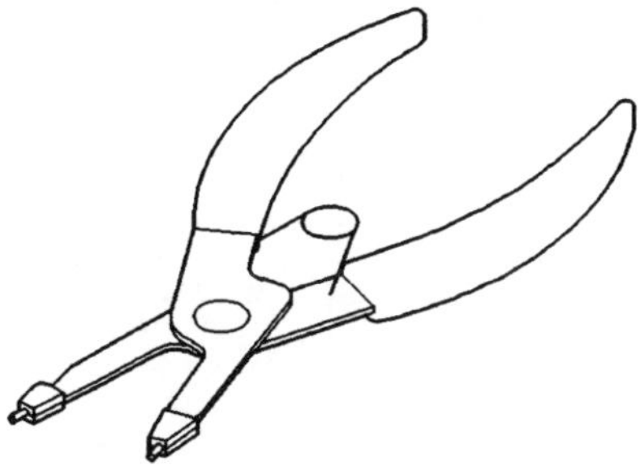

Snap-ring Plier—C-3915

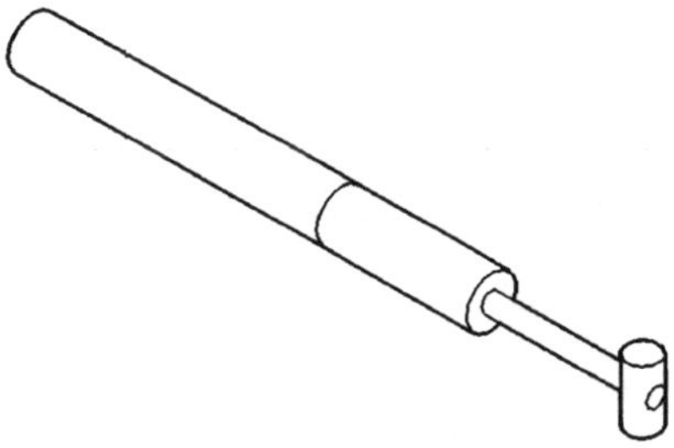

Gauge, Throttle Setting—C-3763

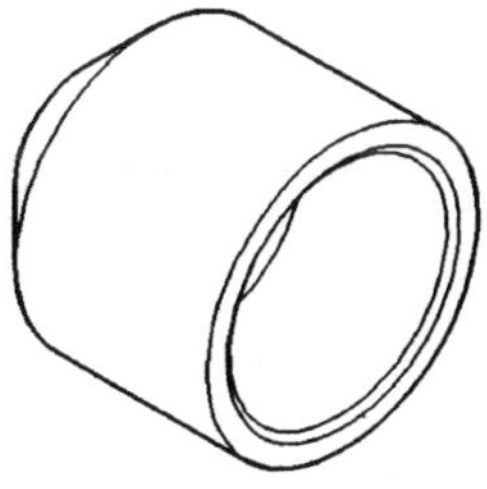

Seal Installer—C-3972-A

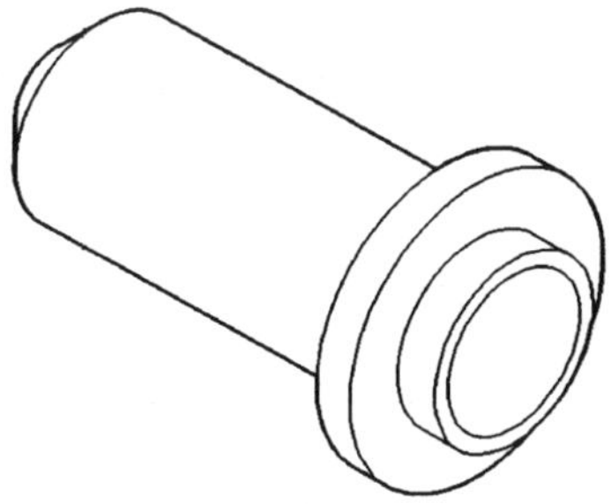

Seal Installer—C-3860-A

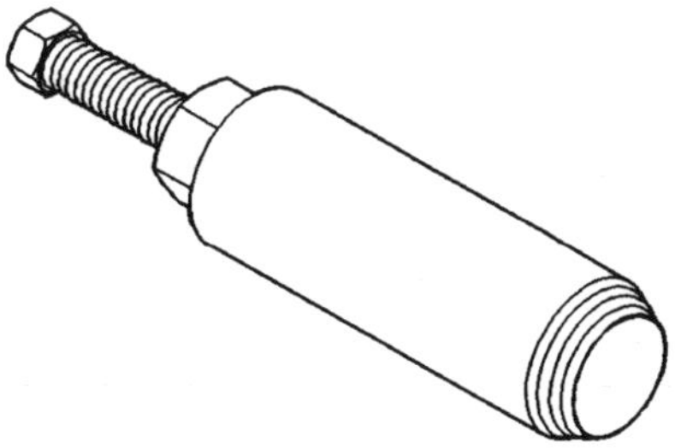

Seal Puller—C-3981-B

SPECIAL TOOLS (Continued)

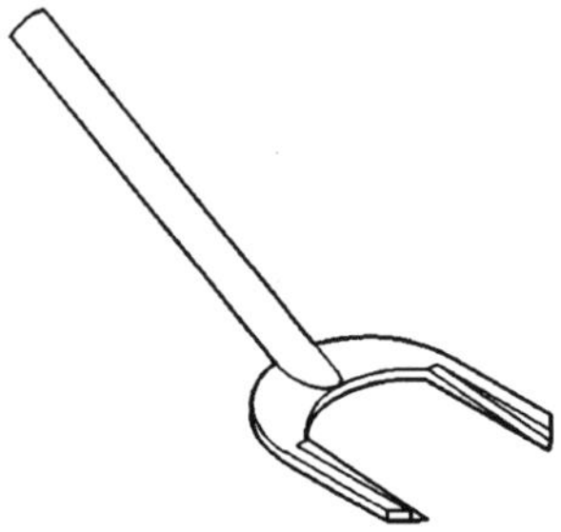

Seal Remover—C-3985-B

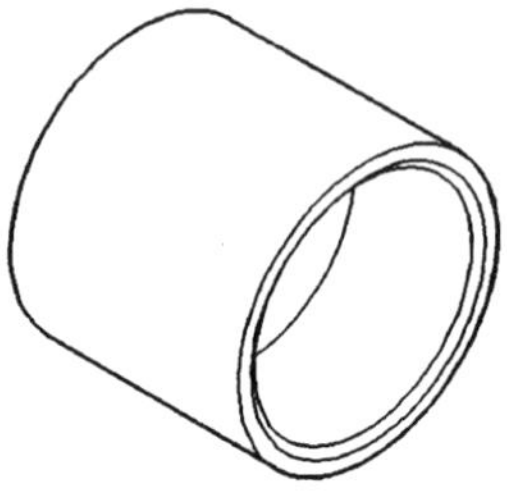

Installer—C-3995-A

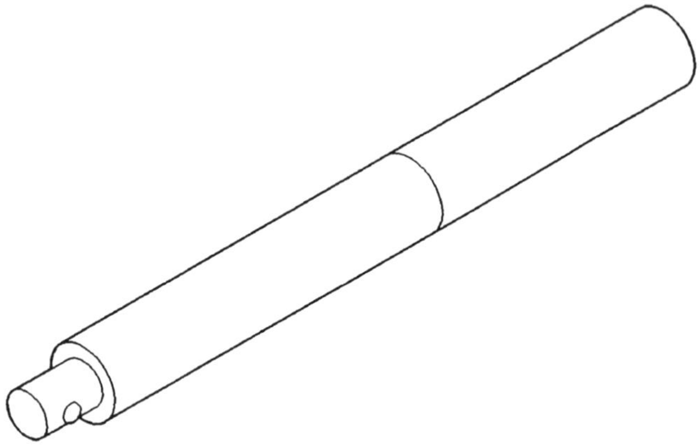

Universal Handle—C-4171

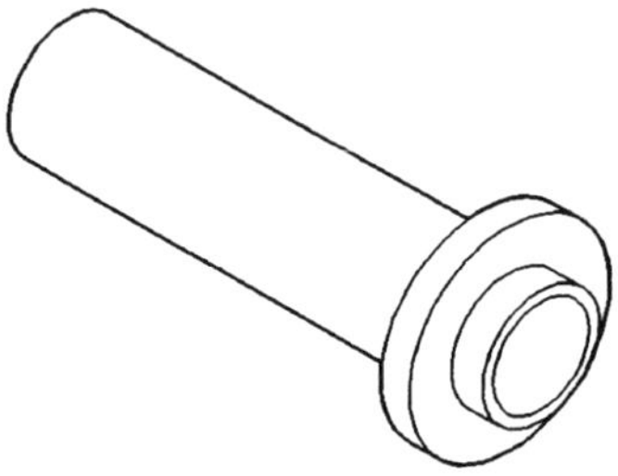

Seal Installer—C-4193-A

TRANSFER CASE—NV231

INDEX

GENERAL INFORMATION

GENERAL INFORMATION

The NV 231 is a part-time transfer case with a low range reduction gear mechanism.

The NV 231 has three operating ranges plus a Neutral position. The reduction gear mechanism consists of a planetary and annulus gear that provide a 2.7:1 reduction ratio when engaged. The annulus gear is fixed in the case; it does not rotate.

The input gear is splined to the transmission output shaft. It drives the mainshaft through the planetary gear and range hub. The front output shaft is operated by a drive chain that connects the shaft to a drive sprocket on the mainshaft. The drive sprocket is engaged/disengaged by the mode fork, which operates the mode sleeve and hub. The sleeve and hub are not equipped with a synchro mechanism for shifting.

The geartrain is mounted in two aluminum case halves attached with bolts. The mainshaft front and rear bearings are mounted in aluminum retainer housings bolted to the case halves.

OPERATING RANGES

NV 231 operating ranges are:

- 2-wheel drive high (2H)
- 4-wheel drive high (4H)
- 4-wheel drive low (4L)

Two-wheel drive range is for use on all road surfaces. The 4-wheel drive high and low ranges are not for use on paved roads. They are only recommended for off-road use on unpaved, low traction surfaces. The only time 4-wheel drive can be used on paved roads, is when the road surface is covered with snow or ice.

SHIFT MECHANISM

Operating ranges are selected with a floor mounted shift lever. The shift lever is connected to the transfer case range lever by an adjustable linkage rod. A straight line shift pattern is used. Range positions are marked on the shifter bezel cover plate, or on the shift knob.

TRANSFER CASE IDENTIFICATION

A circular ID tag is attached to the rear case of each transfer case (Fig. 1). The ID tag provides the transfer case model number, assembly number, serial number, and low range ratio.

The transfer case serial number also represents the date of build.

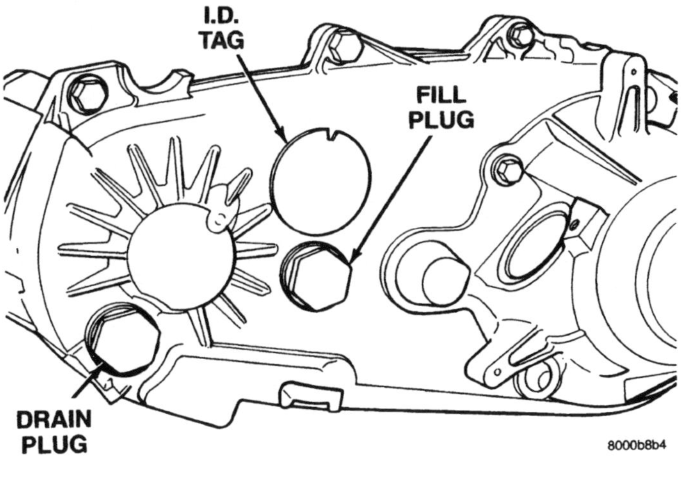

Fig. 1 Fill/Drain Plug And I.D. Tag Locations

RECOMMENDED LUBRICANT AND FILL LEVEL

Recommended lubricant for the NV 231 transfer case is Mopar Dexron II, or ATF Plus. Approximate lubricant fill capacity is 1.18 liters (2.2 pints).

The fill and drain plugs are both in the rear case (Fig. 1). Correct fill level is to the bottom edge of the fill plug hole. Be sure the vehicle is level to ensure an accurate fluid level check.

DIAGNOSIS AND TESTING

NV231 DIAGNOSIS

Condition	Possible Cause	Correction
TRANSFER CASE DIFFICULT TO SHIFT OR WILL NOT SHIFT INTO DESIRED RANGE	(1) Vehicle speed too great to permit shifting. (2) If vehicle was operated for extended period in 4H mode on dry paved surface, driveline torque load may cause difficulty. (3) Transfer case external shift linkage binding. (4) Insufficient or incorrect lubricant. (5) Internal components binding, worn or damaged.	(1) Stop vehicle and shift into desired range. Or reduce speed to 3-4 km/h (2-3 mph) before attempting to shift. (2) Stop vehicle, shift transmission to Neutral, shift transfer case to 2H mode and operate vehicle in 2H on dry paved surfaces. (3) Lubricate, repair or replace linkage bushings or tighten loose components as necessary. (4) Drain and refill to edge of fill hole with DEXRON II® or MOPAR-MERCON® Automatic Transmission Fluid. (5) Disassemble unit and replace worn or damaged components as necessary.
TRANSFER CASE NOISY IN ALL DRIVE MODES	(1) Insufficient or incorrect lubricant.	(1) Drain and refill to edge of fill hole with DEXRON II® or MOPAR-MERCON® Automatic Transmission Fluid. Check for leaks and repair if necessary. **Note: If unit is still noisy after drain and refill, disassembly and inspection may be required to locate source of noise.**
NOISY IN – OR JUMPS OUT OF – FOUR WHEEL DRIVE LOW RANGE	(1) Transfer case not completely engaged in 4L position. (2) Shift linkage out of adjustment. (3) Shift linkage loose or binding. (4) Range fork damaged, inserts worn, or fork is binding on shift rail. (5) Low range gear worn or damaged.	(1) Stop vehicle, shift transfer case to Neutral, then shift back into 4L position. (2) Adjust linkage. (3) Tighten, lubricate or repair linkage as necessary. (4) Disassemble unit and repair as necessary. (5) Disassemble and repair as necessary.
LUBRICANT LEAKING FROM OUTPUT SHAFT SEALS OR FROM VENT	(1) Transfer case overfilled. (2) Vent closed or restricted. (3) Output shaft seals damaged or installed incorrectly.	(1) Drain to correct level. (2) Clear or replace vent if necessary. (3) Replace seals. Be sure seal lip faces interior of case when installed. Also be sure yoke seal surfaces are not scored or nicked. Remove scores and nicks with fine sandpaper or replace yoke(s) if necessary.
ABNORMAL TIRE WEAR	(1) Extended operation on dry hard surface (paved) roads in 4H range.	(1) Operate in 2H on hard surface (paved) roads.

J9021-118

REMOVAL AND INSTALLATION

SHIFT LEVER

REMOVAL

(1) Shift transfer case into 4L.

(2) Raise vehicle.

(3) Loosen adjusting trunnion locknut and slide shift rod out of trunnion (Fig. 2). If rod lacks enough travel to come out of trunnion, push trunnion out of torque shaft.

(4) Lower vehicle.

(5) Remove console. Refer to park brake section in Group 5 for procedures.

(6) Remove screws attaching lever assembly to floorpan and remove assembly and shift rod (if left attached).

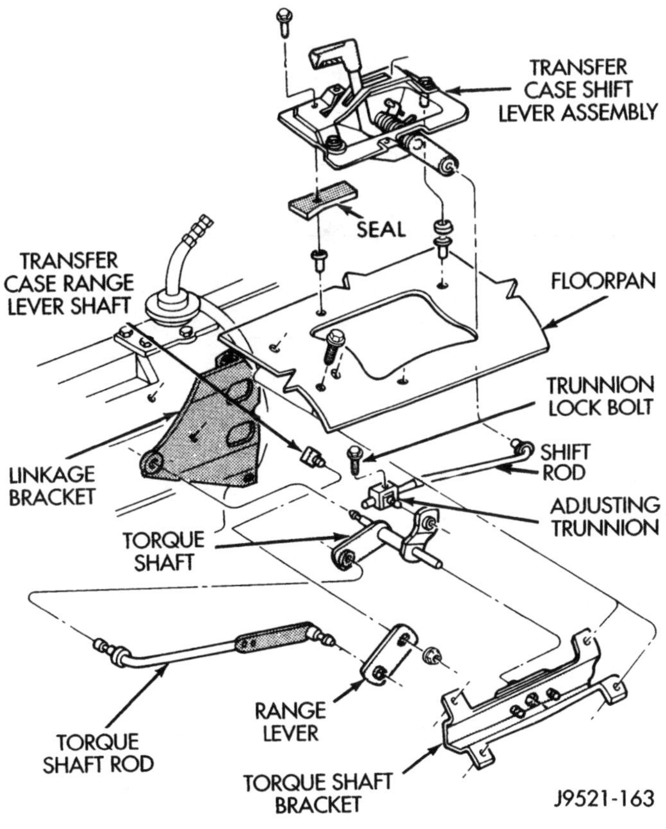

Fig. 2 Shift Linkage

INSTALLATION

(1) If shift rod was not removed from lever assembly, work rod down through floorpan opening. Then position lever assembly on floorpan and install assembly attaching screws.

(2) Install console.

(3) Raise vehicle.

(4) Connect trunnion to torque shaft arm. Or, slide shift rod into trunnion on range lever. Be sure shift rod slides freely in trunnion.

(5) Verify that range lever is in 4L position. Then tighten trunnion lock bolt.

(6) Lower vehicle and check transfer case shift operation.

TRANSFER CASE

REMOVAL

(1) Shift transfer case into Neutral.

(2) Raise vehicle.

(3) Drain transfer case lubricant.

(4) Mark front and rear propeller shaft yokes for alignment reference.

(5) Support transmission with jack stand.

(6) Remove rear crossmember, or skid plate.

(7) Disconnect front/rear propeller shafts at transfer case.

(8) Disconnect vehicle speed sensor wires.

(9) Disconnect transfer case linkage rod from range lever.

(10) Disconnect transfer case vent hose, and indicator or vacuum switch harness.

(11) Support transfer case with transmission jack.

(12) Remove nuts attaching transfer case to transmission.

(13) Secure transfer case to jack with chains.

(14) Pull transfer case and jack rearward to disengage transfer case.

(15) Remove transfer case from under vehicle.

(16) If transfer case was removed for overhaul, remove damper from rear retainer.

TRANSFER CASE INSTALLATION

(1) Mount transfer case on a transmission jack. Secure transfer case to jack with chains.

(2) Position transfer case under vehicle.

(3) Align transfer case and transmission shafts and install transfer case on transmission.

(4) Install and tighten transfer case attaching nuts to 35 N·m (26 ft. lbs.) torque.

(5) Install damper on rear retainer (Fig. 3). Tighten damper attaching nuts to 54 N·m (40 ft. lbs.) torque.

(6) Connect vehicle speed sensor wires, and vent hose.

(7) Connect indicator or vacuum switch harness to transfer case switch. Secure wire harnesses to clips on transfer case.

(8) Align and connect propeller shafts. Tighten shaft attaching bolts to 19 N·m (170 in. lbs.) torque.

(9) Fill transfer case with Mopar Dexron II fluid.

(10) Install rear crossmember, or skid plate. Tighten crossmember bolts to 41 N·m (30 ft. lbs.) torque.

(11) Remove transmission jack and support stand.

(12) Connect shift rod to transfer case range lever.

(13) Adjust transfer case shift linkage.

REMOVAL AND INSTALLATION (Continued)

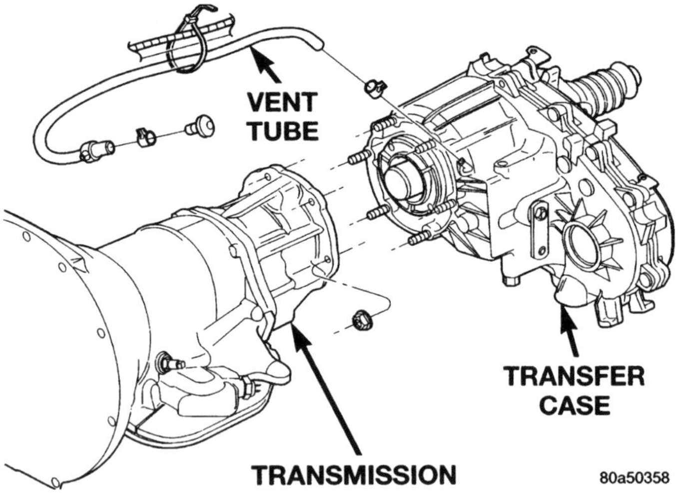

Fig. 3 Transfer Case Mounting

(14) Lower vehicle and verify transfer case shift operation.

DISASSEMBLY AND ASSEMBLY

NV231 TRANSFER CASE

DISASSEMBLE

SPEEDOMETER/YOKE/RANGE LEVER REMOVAL

(1) Remove speedometer adapter.

(2) Remove front yoke nut:

(a) Move range lever to 4L position.

(b) Then remove nut with 1–1/8 socket and impact wrench (Fig. 4).

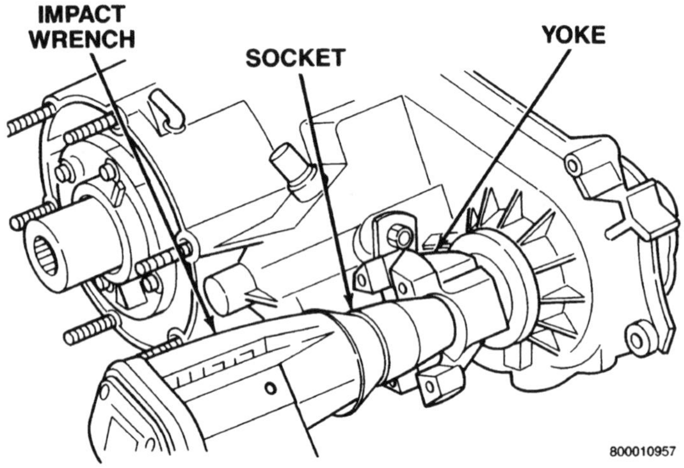

Fig. 4 Yoke Nut Removal

(3) Remove yoke. If yoke is difficult to remove by hand, remove it with bearing splitter, or with standard two jaw puller (Fig. 5). Be sure puller tool is positioned on yoke and not on slinger as slinger will be damaged.

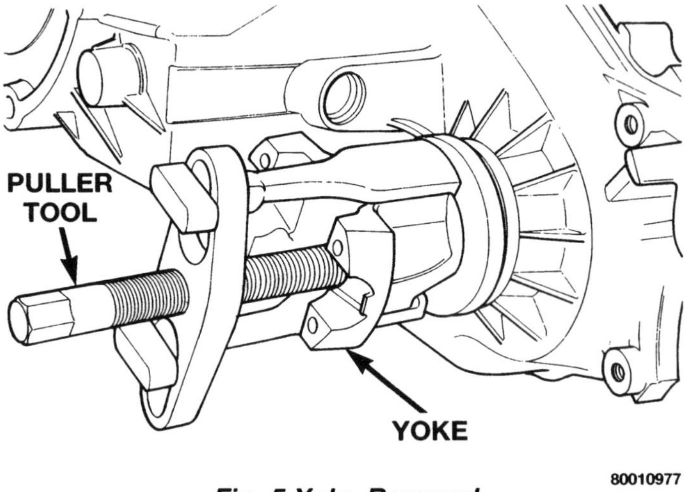

Fig. 5 Yoke Removal

(4) Remove seal washer from front output shaft. Discard washer as it should not be reused.

(5) Remove nut and washer that attach range lever to sector shaft. Then move sector to neutral position and remove range lever from shaft. (Fig. 6)

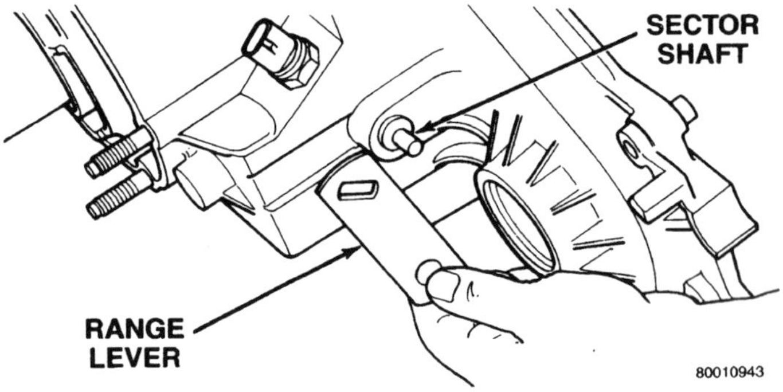

Fig. 6 Range Lever Removal

REAR RETAINER REMOVAL AND DISASSEMBLY

(1) Remove output shaft boot. Spread band clamp that secures boot on slinger with a suitable awl. Then slide boot off shaft (Fig. 7).

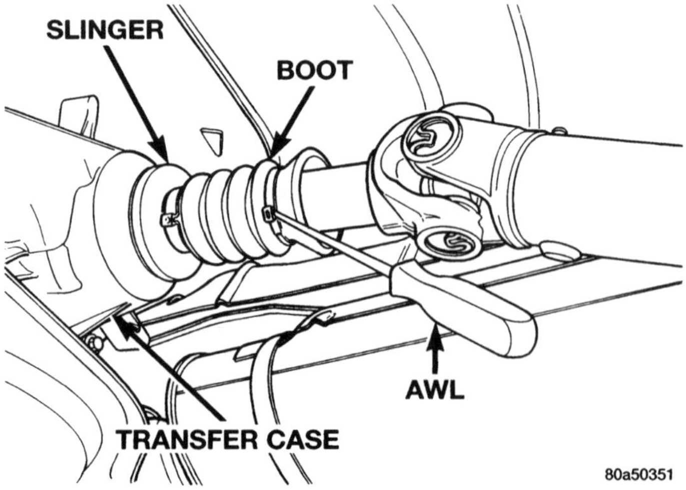

Fig. 7 Output Boot—Typical

DISASSEMBLY AND ASSEMBLY (Continued)

(2) Using puller MD-998056-A, remove rear slinger (Fig. 8).

(3) Remove slinger stop spacer and snap-ring from output shaft (Fig. 9).

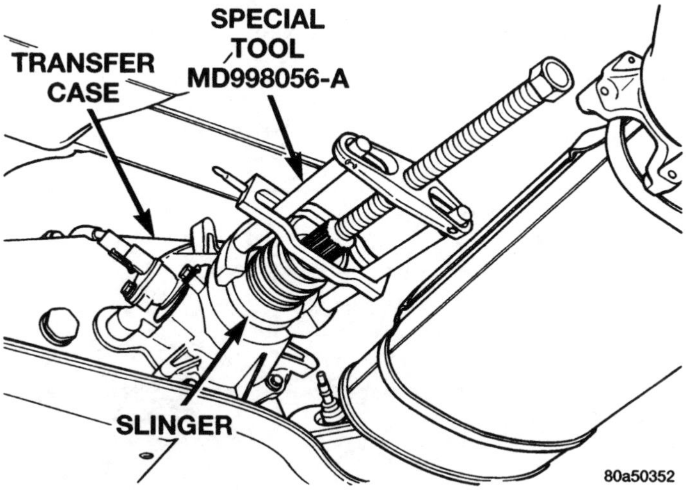

Fig. 8 Rear Slinger Removal

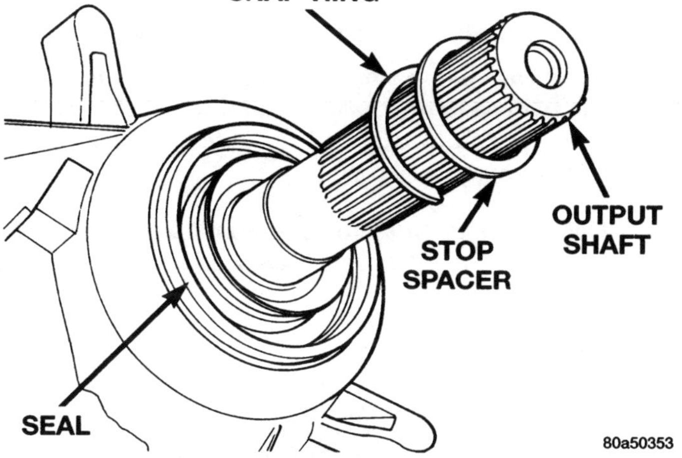

Fig. 9 Slinger Stop Spacer and Snap-ring

(4) Remove rear seal from retainer (Fig. 10). Use pry tool, or collapse seal with punch to remove it.

(5) Remove rear output bearing I.D. retaining ring (Fig. 11).

(6) Remove rear retainer bolts with 10mm socket and air ratchet.

(7) Remove rear retainer. Tap retainer with mallet and pry upward to break sealer bead. Then slide retainer off case and output shaft (Fig. 12).

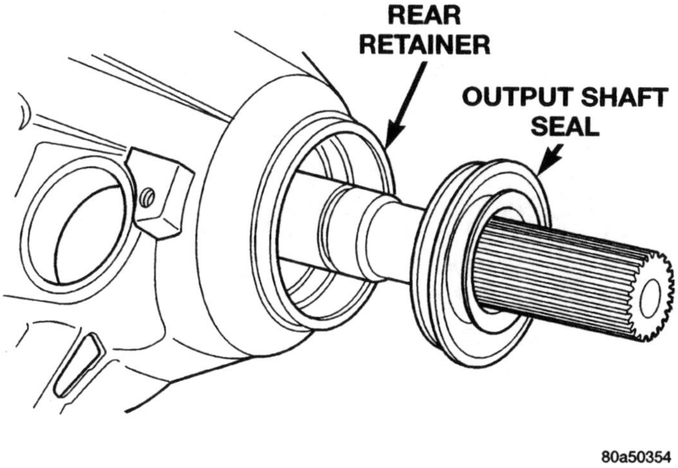

Fig. 10 Rear Seal Removal

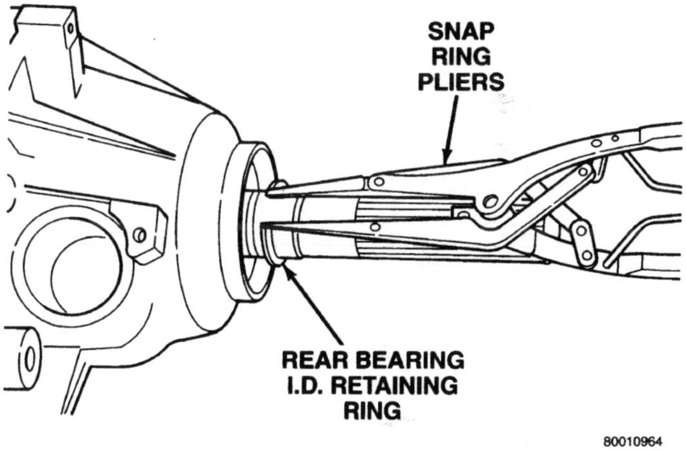

Fig. 11 Rear Bearing I.D. Retaining Ring Removal

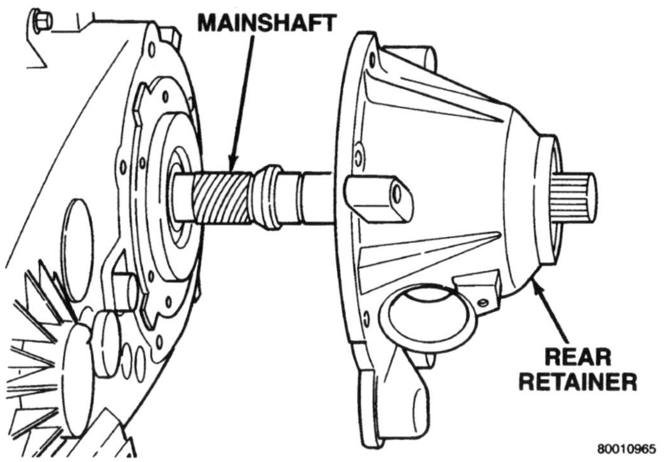

Fig. 12 Rear Retainer Removal

DISASSEMBLY AND ASSEMBLY (Continued)

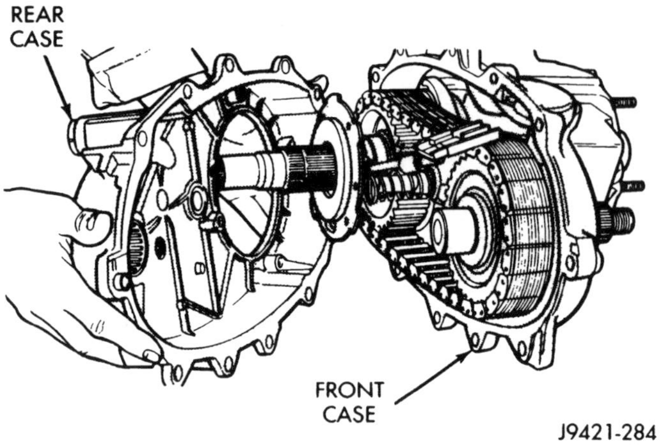

Fig. 13 Oil Pump/Rear Case Removal

(8) Remove rear bearing O.D. retaining ring with snap ring pliers. Then tilt pump and slide it off output shaft (Fig. 14)

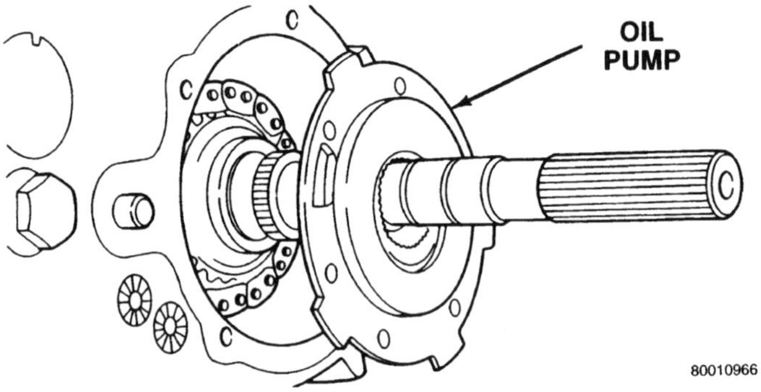

Fig. 14 Oil Pump Removal

(9) Remove pickup tube O-ring from pump (Fig. 15) but do not disassemble pump; it is not a repairable part.

(10) Remove seal from oil pump with pry tool.

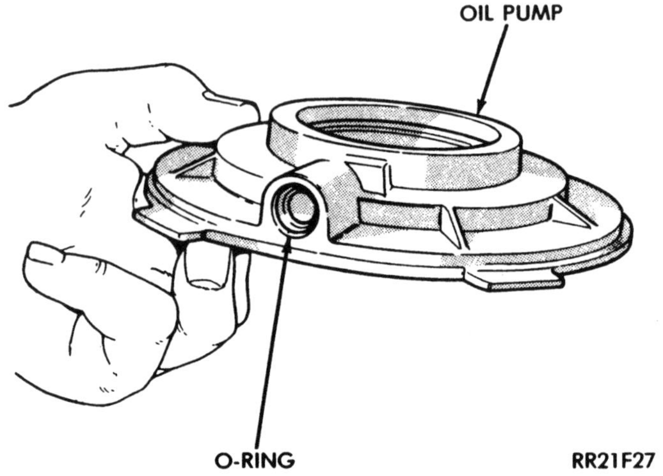

Fig. 15 Pickup Tube O-Ring Location

(11) Remove bolts attaching rear case to front case. A 10 mm, 12 point socket is needed for the spline head bolt (Fig. 13). A 15 mm socket is needed for the remaining bolts. Note position of the two black finish bolts at each end of the case. These bolts go through the case dowels and require a washer under the bolt head (Fig. 16)

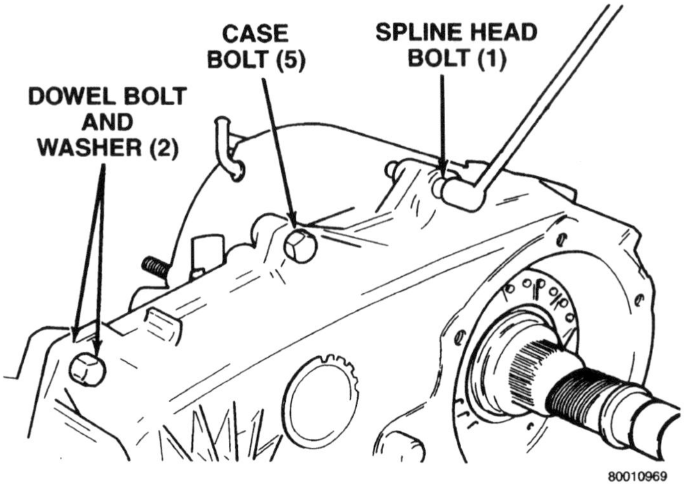

Fig. 16 Spline And Dowel Bolt Locations

(12) Remove rear case from front case (Fig. 17). Insert screwdrivers into slots cast into each end of case. Then pry upward to break sealer bead and remove rear case.

CAUTION: Do not pry on the sealing surface of either case half as the surfaces will become damaged.

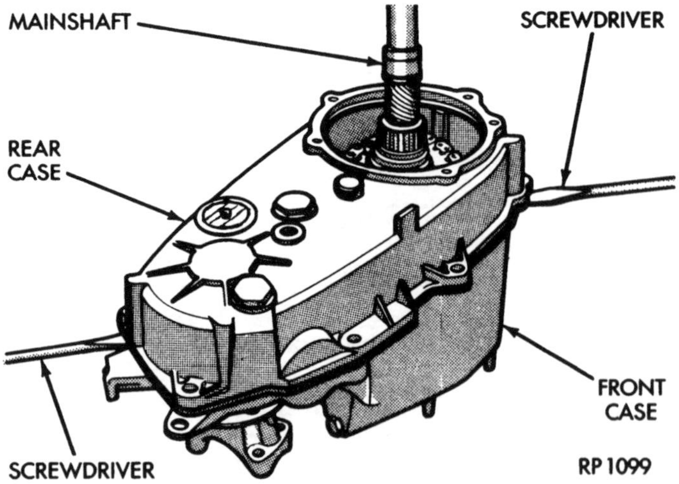

Fig. 17 Loosening/Removing Rear case

DISASSEMBLY AND ASSEMBLY (Continued)

(13) Remove oil pickup tube and screen from rear case (Fig. 18).

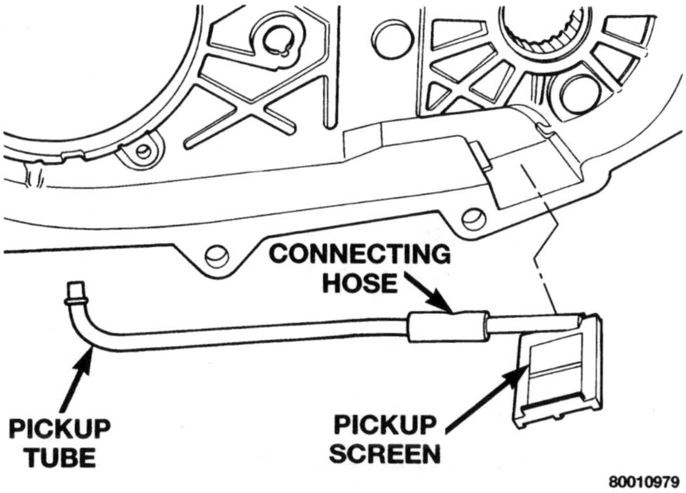

Fig. 18 Oil Pickup Screen, Hose And Tube Removal

FRONT SHAFT/DRIVE CHAIN/POPPET REMOVAL

(1) Remove poppet plug, spring and plunger (Fig. 19).

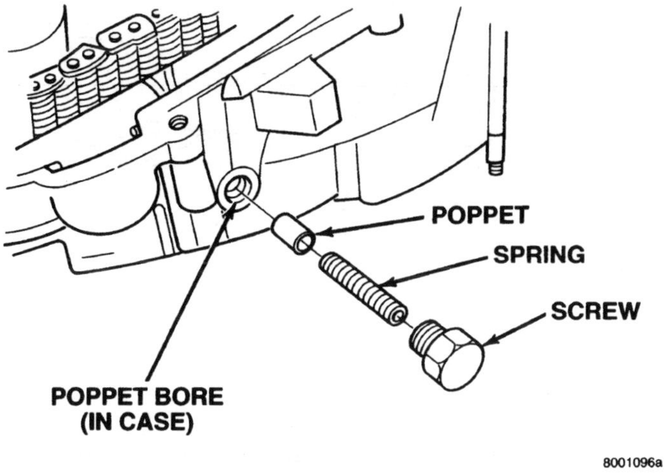

Fig. 19 Poppet Components

(2) Pull front output shaft upward and out of front bearing (Fig. 20).

(3) Slide drive chain off output shaft sprocket and remove front output shaft and chain as assembly (Fig. 21).

OUTPUT SHAFT REMOVAL AND DISASSEMBLY

(1) Grasp end of output shaft and remove shaft, drive sprocket and mode hub as assembly (Fig. 22).

(2) Remove mode hub retaining ring with heavy duty snap ring pliers (Fig. 23).

(3) Slide mode hub off output shaft (Fig. 24).

(4) Slide drive sprocket off output shaft (Fig. 25).

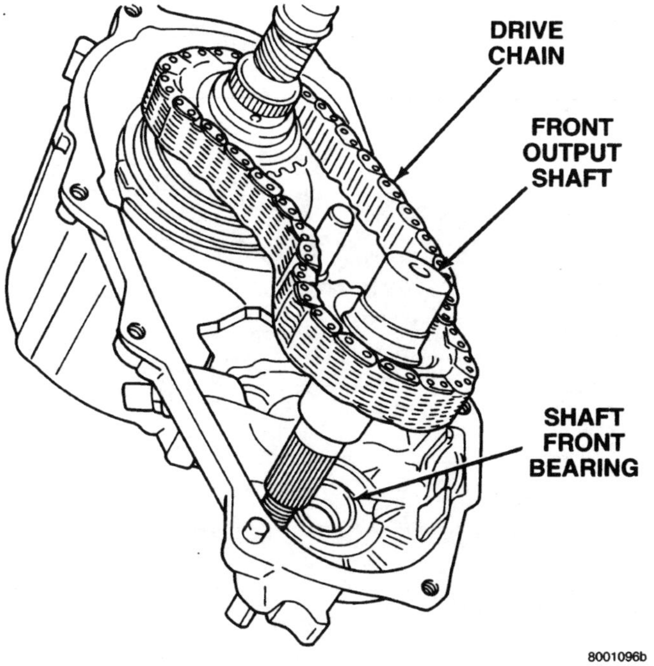

Fig. 20 Disengaging Front Output Shaft From Front Bearing

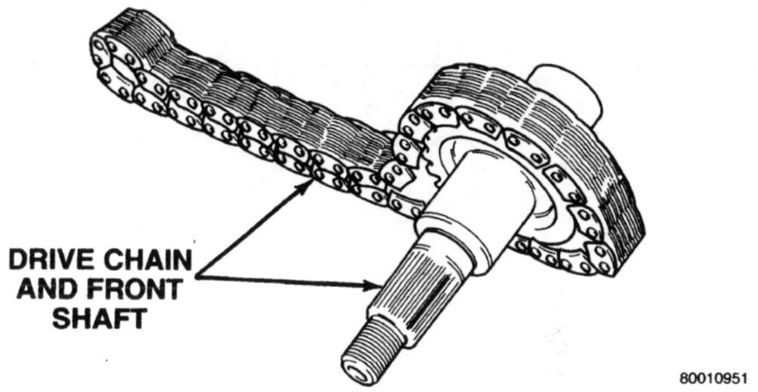

Fig. 21 Front Output Shaft And Drive Chain Removal

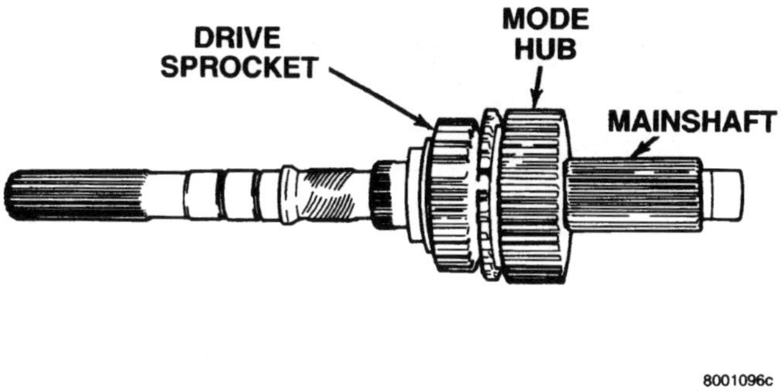

Fig. 22 Output Shaft Assembly Removal

SHIFT FORK/SLEEVE/HUB REMOVAL

(1) Remove mode spring from end of mode fork rail.

DISASSEMBLY AND ASSEMBLY (Continued)

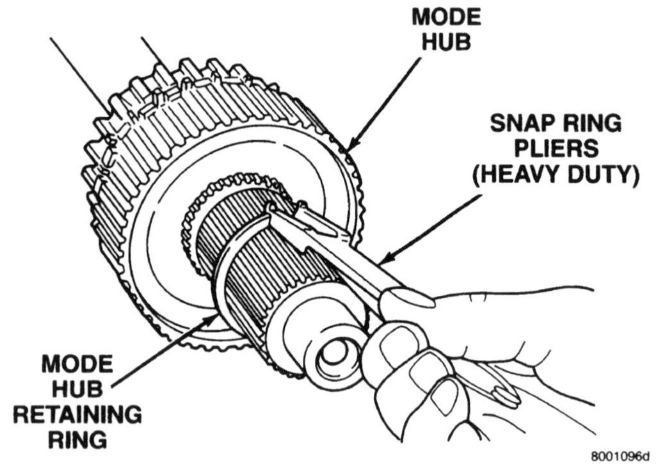

Fig. 23 Mode Hub retaining Ring Removal

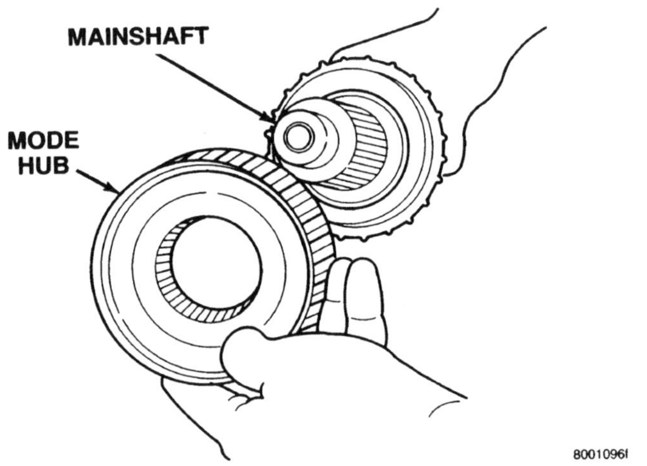

Fig. 24 Mode Hub Removal

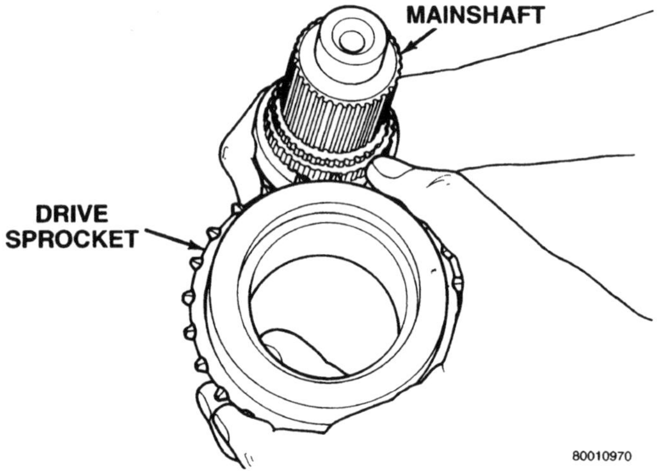

Fig. 25 Drive Sprocket Removal

(2) Remove mode fork and sleeve as assembly (Fig. 26). Note position of sleeve for assembly installation (short side of sleeve faces up).

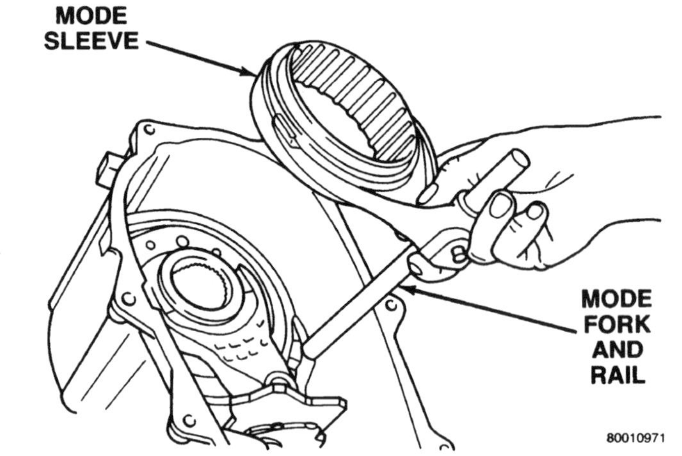

Fig. 26 Mode Fork And Sleeve Removal

(3) Remove range fork and hub as assembly. Note fork position for installation reference (Fig. 27).

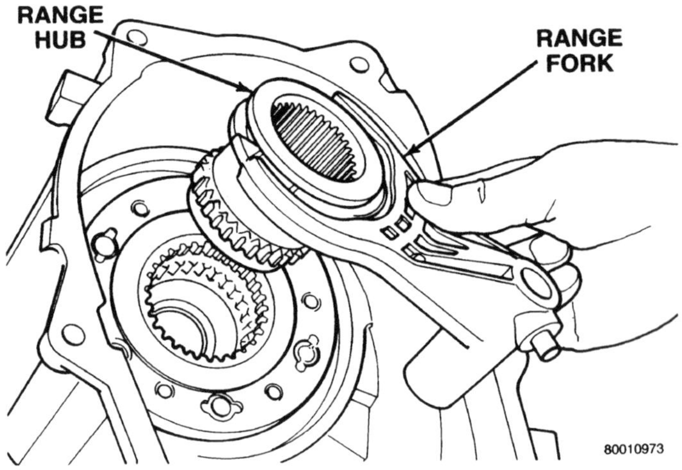

Fig. 27 Range Fork And Hub Removal

(4) Remove shift sector from front case (Fig. 28).

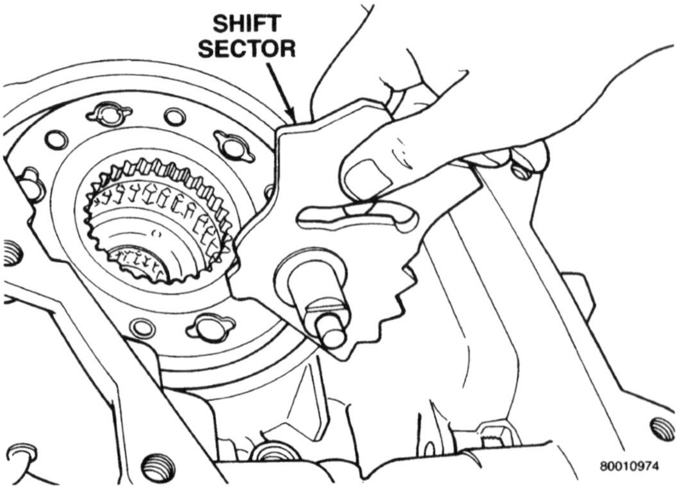

Fig. 28 Shift Sector Removal

DISASSEMBLY AND ASSEMBLY (Continued)

(5) Remove sector shaft O-ring seal and nylon retainer (Fig. 29)

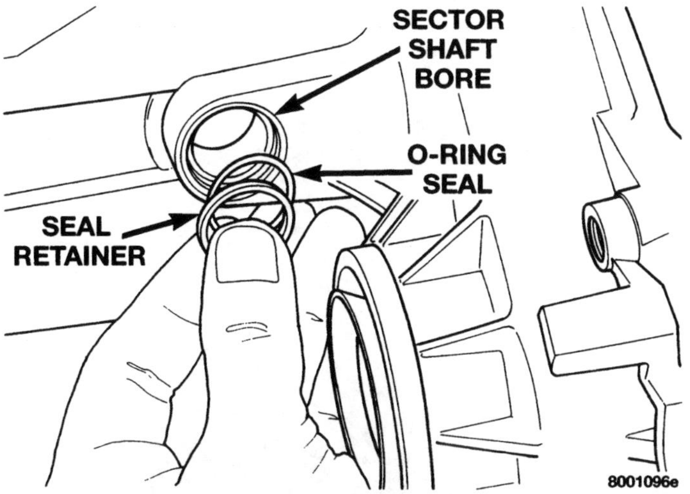

Fig. 29 Sector Shaft Seal And Retainer Removal

INPUT GEAR/PLANETARY CARRIER REMOVAL AND DISASSEMBLY

(1) Remove input retainer attaching bolts with 10mm socket and air ratchet.

(2) Remove input retainer. Pry retainer loose with screwdriver positioned in slots at each end of retainer (Fig. 30)

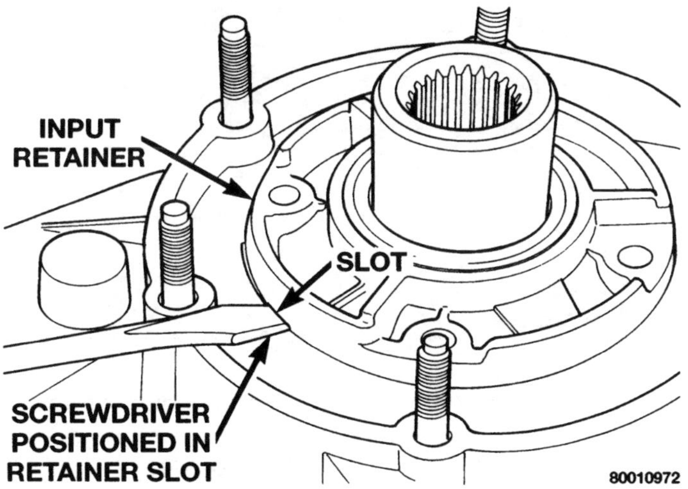

Fig. 30 Input Retainer Removal

(3) Remove input retainer seal. Position retainer upside down over front case bearing. Then tap seal out with drift and hammer.

(4) Remove input gear bearing retaining ring with heavy duty snap ring pliers (Fig. 31)

(5) Place front case in horizontal position. Then remove input gear and planetary carrier as assembly (Fig. 32). Tap gear out of bearing with plastic mallet if necessary.

(6) Remove carrier lock retaining ring (Fig. 33).

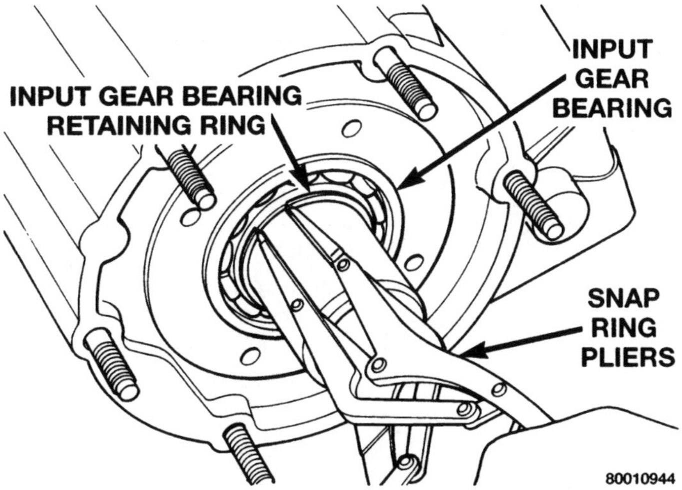

Fig. 31 Removing Input Bearing retaining ring

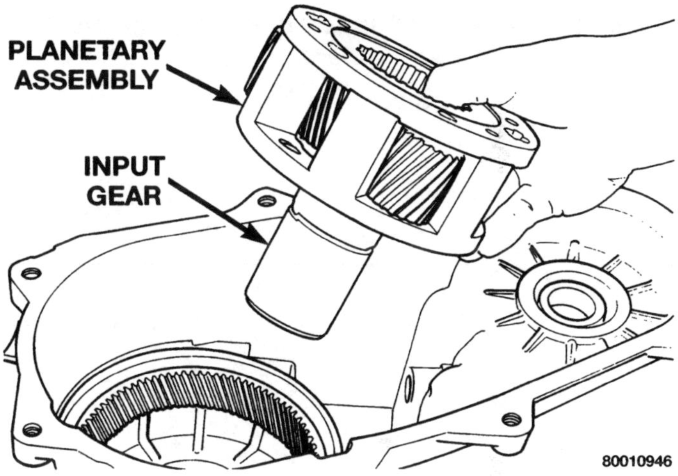

Fig. 32 Input Gear And Planetary Carrier Removal

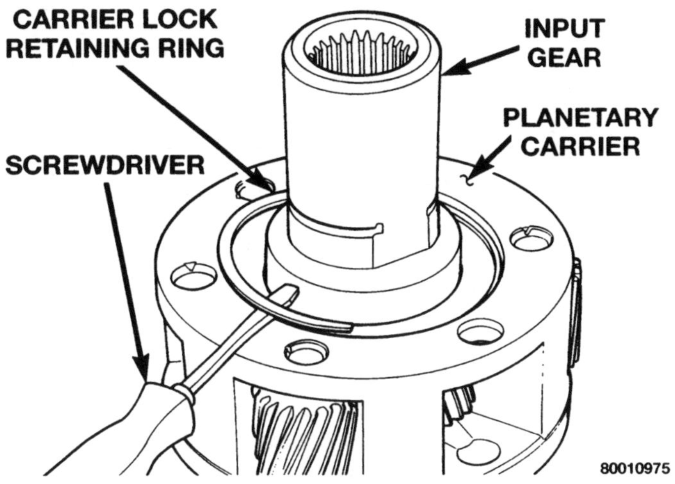

Fig. 33 Carrier Lock Retaining Ring Removal

DISASSEMBLY AND ASSEMBLY (Continued)

(7) Remove input gear, lock ring, and front thrust washer from planetary carrier (Fig. 34).

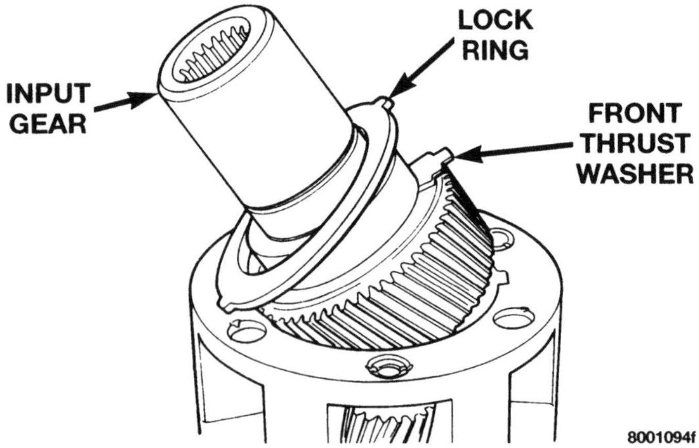

Fig. 34 Input Gear, Carrier Lock Ring, And Rear thrust Washer Removal

(8) Remove rear thrust washer from carrier (Fig. 35).

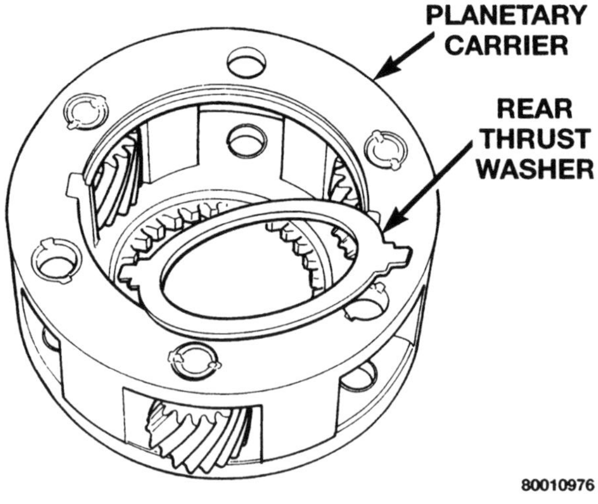

Fig. 35 Rear Thrust washer Removal

(9) Remove pilot bearing from input gear with Tool MD-998346 as follows:

(a) Turn puller tool bolt until jaws retract enough to fit into bearing (Fig. 36)

(b) .

(c) Insert puller bolt and jaws into bearing. Then turn puller bolt clockwise so ramp on bolt spreads jaws forcing them under bearing (Fig. 37).

(d) Install puller bridge over puller bolt (Fig. 38). Then install flat washer and nut on bolt.

(e) Hold puller bridge from turning with locking pliers. Then tighten nut on puller bolt in clockwise direction to draw bearing out of input gear (Fig. 39).

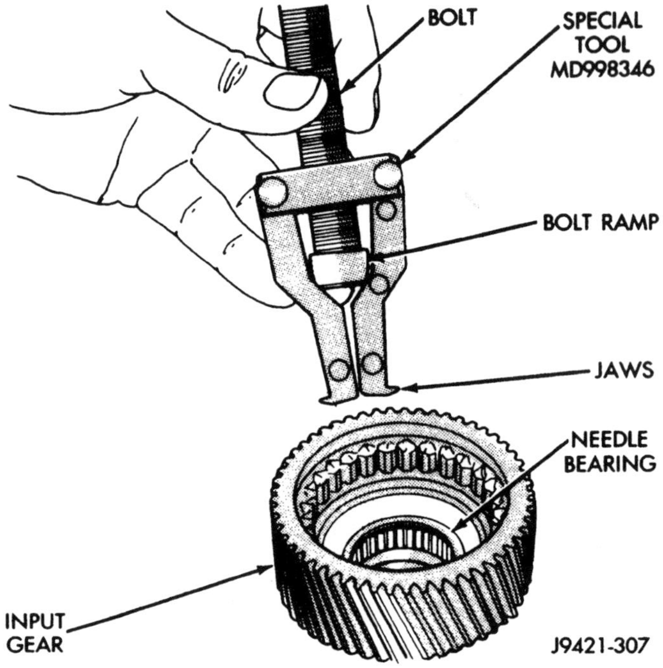

Fig. 36 Puller Jaws In Retracted Position

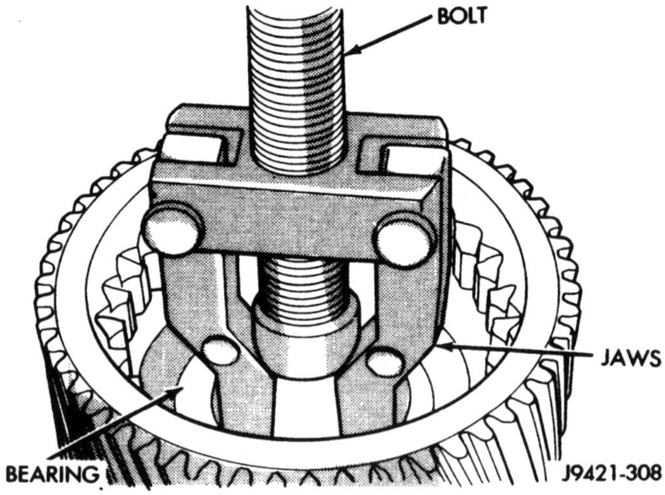

Fig. 37 Puller Bolt And Jaws Seated Under Pilot Bearing

FRONT/REAR CASE BEARING AND SEAL REMOVAL

(1) Remove front output shaft front bearing and seal as follows:

(a) Remove seal from case with pry tool (Fig. 40).

(b) Remove bearing retaining ring with screwdriver (Fig. 41).

(c) Remove bearing with Tool Handle C-4171 and Tool 5065 (Fig. 42).

(2) Remove front output shaft rear bearing from rear case with Tool MD-998346 (Fig. 43). Be sure tool jaws are seated under bearing before tightening puller nut.

DISASSEMBLY AND ASSEMBLY (Continued)

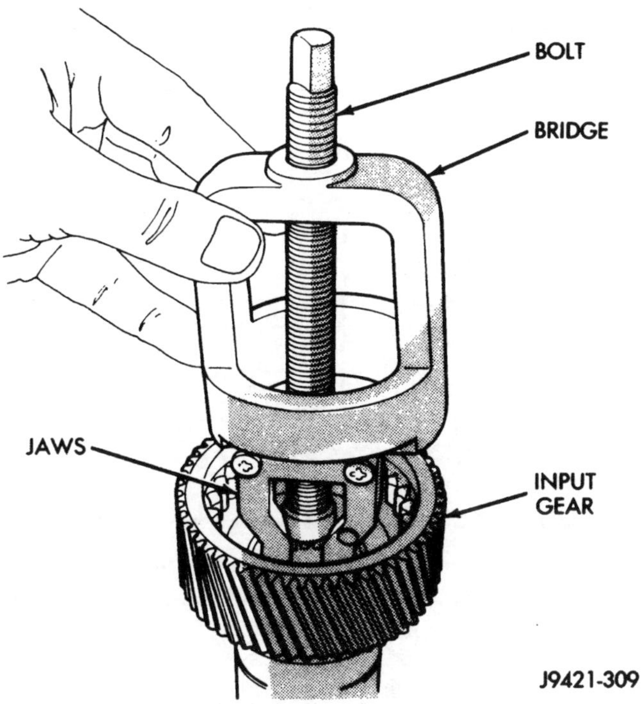

Fig. 38 Installing Puller Bridge

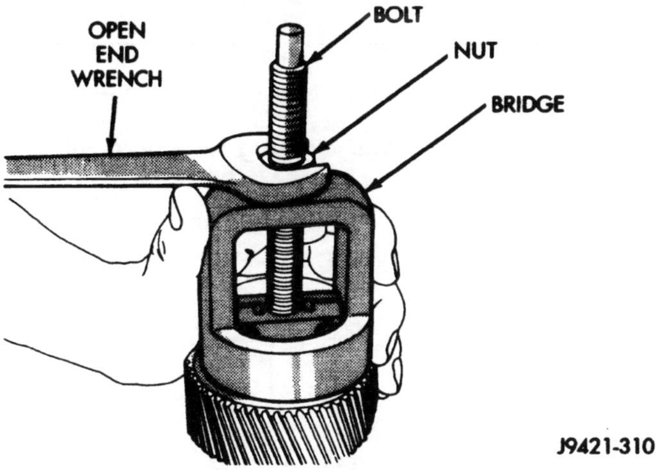

Fig. 39 Pilot Bearing Removal

(3) Remove input bearing from front case. Tap bearing out from inside of case with brass drift and hammer.

NV231 TRANSFER CASE ASSEMBLE

CAUTION: The bearing bores in various transfer case components contain oil feed holes. Make sure replacement bearings do not block the holes.

INPUT GEAR, PLANETARY CARRIER, AND INPUT RETAINER INSTALLATION

(1) Lubricate bearings, input gear, and planetary carrier with transmission fluid during installation.

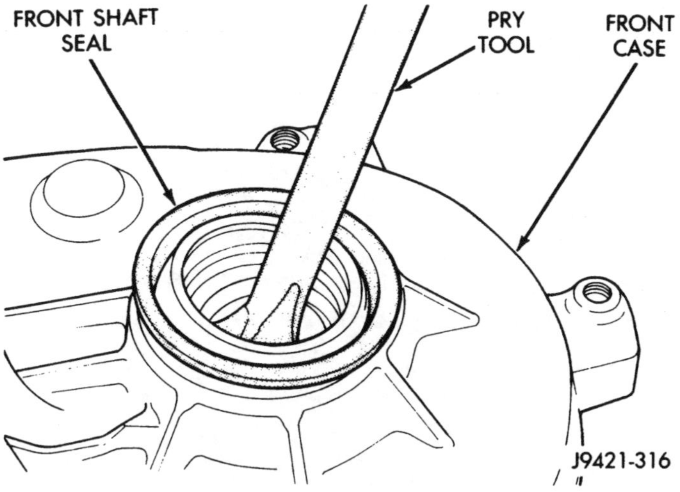

Fig. 40 Front Output Seal Removal

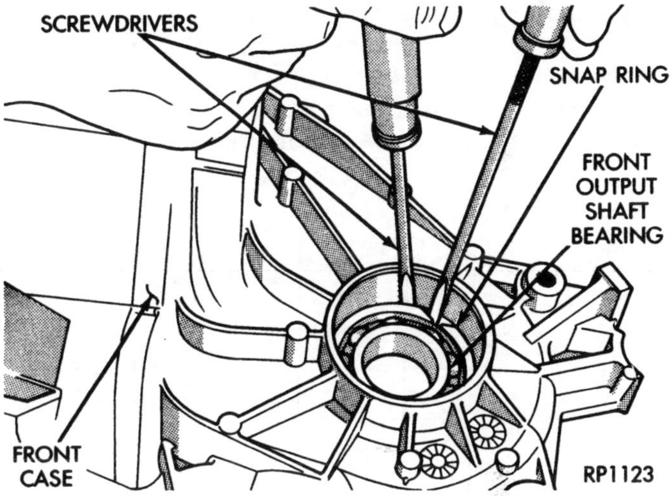

Fig. 41 Front Shaft Front Bearing Retaining Ring Removal

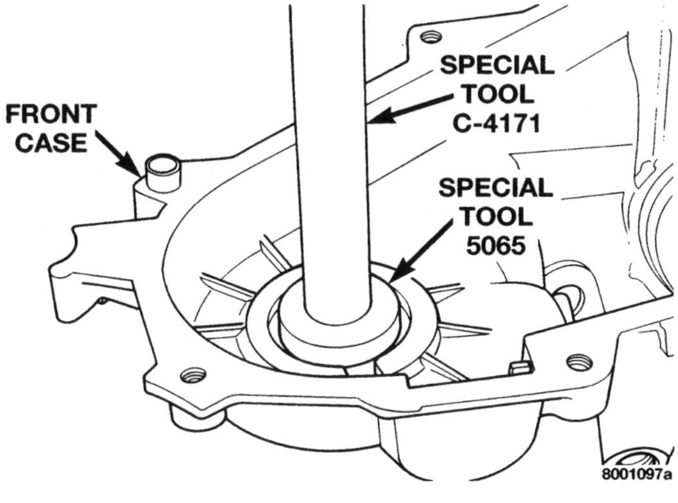

Fig. 42 Front Shaft Front Bearing Removal

Seals can be lubricated with transmission fluid, petrolatum, or Ru-Glyde if desired.

DISASSEMBLY AND ASSEMBLY (Continued)

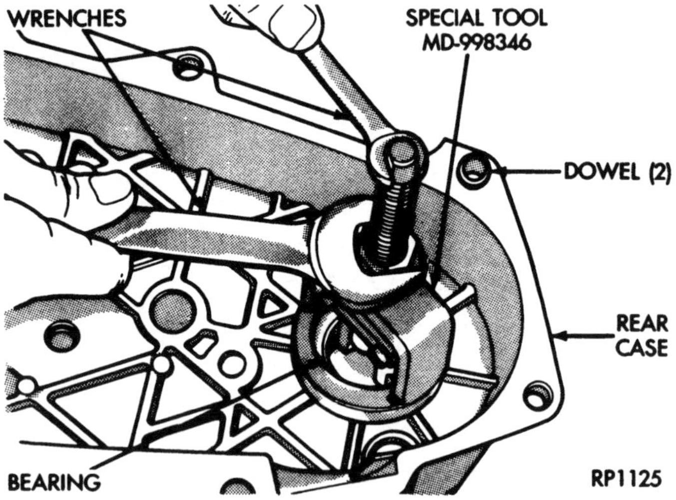

Fig. 43 Front Shaft Rear Bearing Removal

(2) Install new input bearing in front case. Start bearing in bore with copper mallet. Tap bearing at 6–8 points around outer race to start it evenly. Mount case in shop press and seat bearing in case using hard wood block as press tool. Press bearing inward until bearing locating ring stops against case surface (Fig. 44).

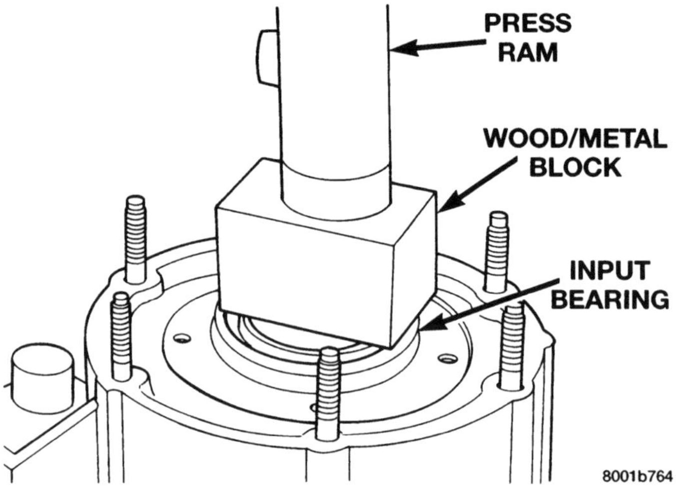

Fig. 44 Input Bearing Installation

(3) Install front output shaft front bearing in case with Tool Handle C-4171 and Installer 5064 (Fig. 45).

(4) Install shaft front bearing retaining ring (Fig. 46). Start ring into place by hand. Then use small screwdriver to work ring into case groove. Be sure ring is fully seated before proceeding.

(5) Install new front output seal in case bore with Tools C-4171 and 7934 (Fig. 47).

(6) Install pilot bearing in input gear with Tools C-4171 and 5065 (Fig. 48).

(7) Assemble input gear and planetary carrier as follows:

(a) Install rear thrust washer in carrier. Be sure washer tabs are aligned and seated in carrier slots

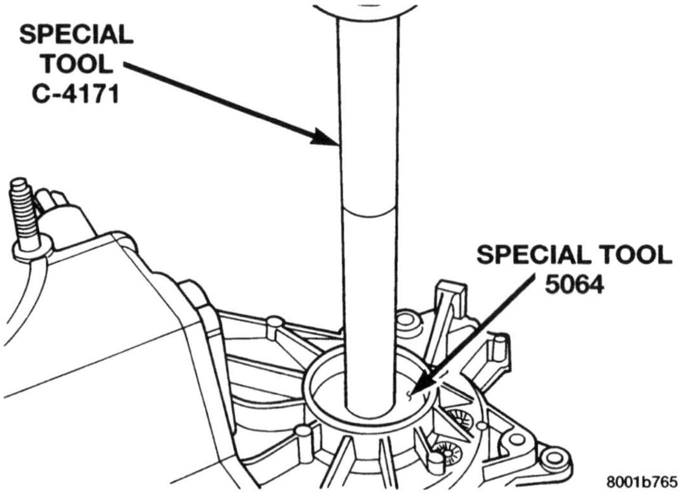

Fig. 45 Front Shaft Front Bearing Installation

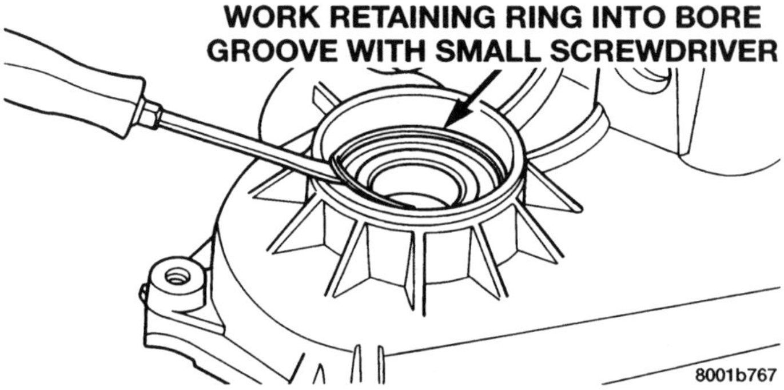

Fig. 46 Installing Front Bearing Retaining Ring

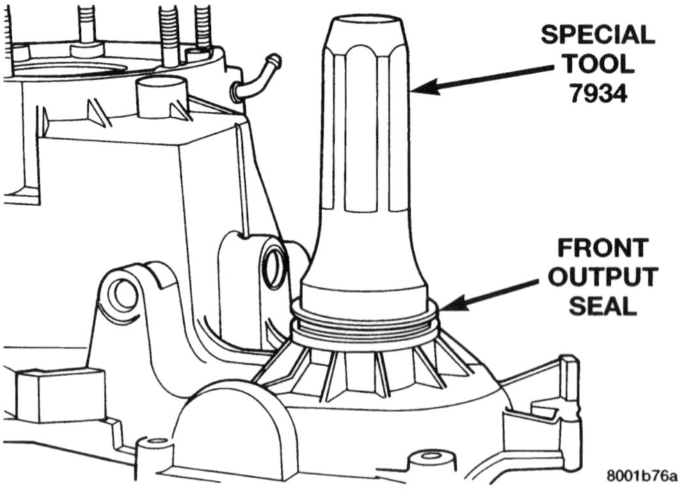

Fig. 47 Front output Seal Installation

(Fig. 49). Also note that washers are the same and therefore interchangeable.

(b) Position front thrust washer and lock ring on input gear. Then install assembled parts in carrier (Fig. 50)

(c) Install carrier lock retaining ring. Use small screwdriver to work ring into place. Be sure ring is fully seated before proceeding (Fig. 51).

DISASSEMBLY AND ASSEMBLY (Continued)

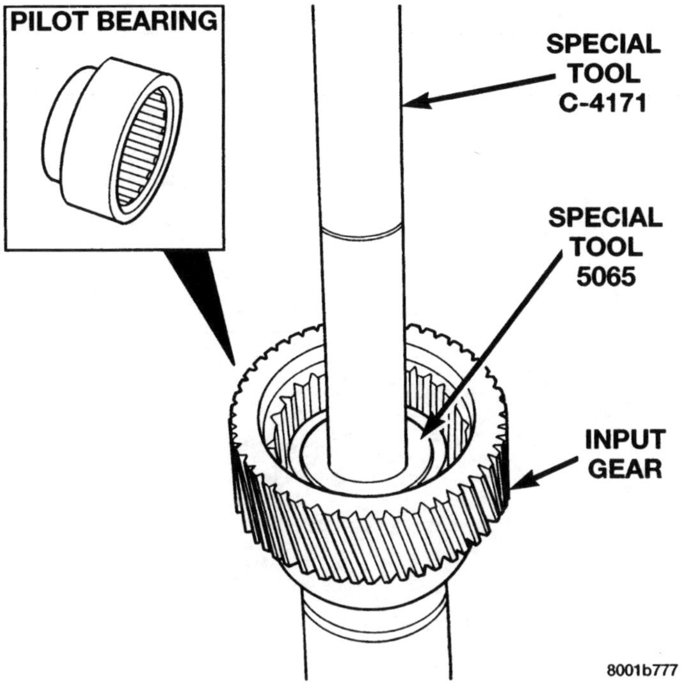

Fig. 48 Pilot Bearing Installation

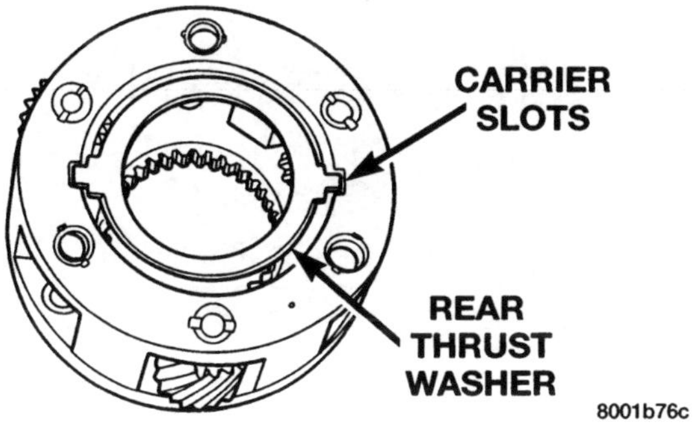

Fig. 49 Input Gear Rear Thrust Washer Installation

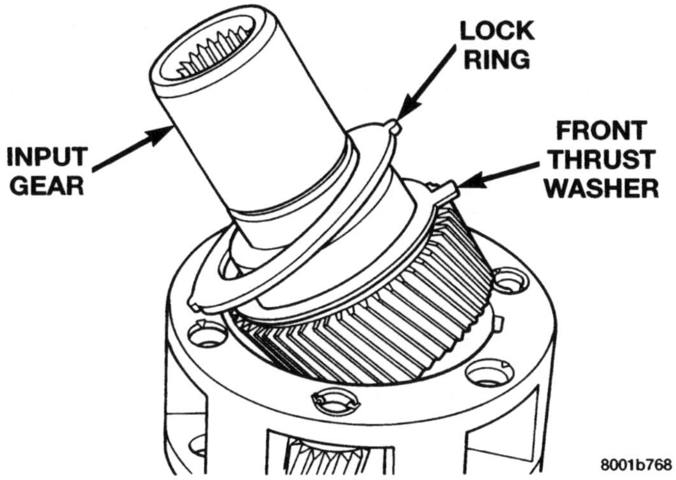

Fig. 50 Input Gear, Front Thrust Washer, And Carrier Lock Ring Installation

(8) Install assembled input gear/planetary carrier in front case (Fig. 52). Be sure to align carrier pinions in annulus gear. Use wood hammer handle or rawhide mallet to seat assembly if necessary.

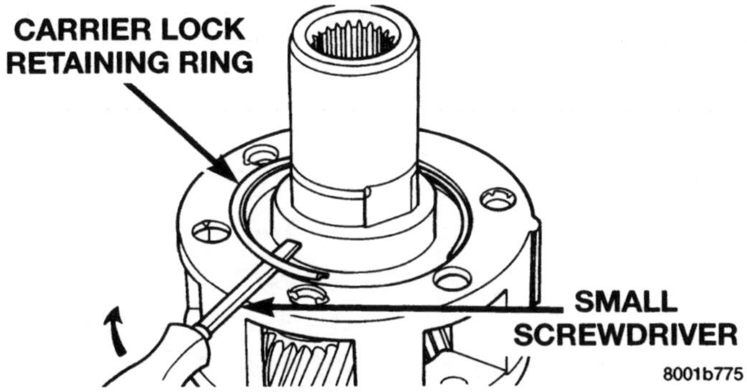

Fig. 51 Carrier Lock Retaining Ring Installation

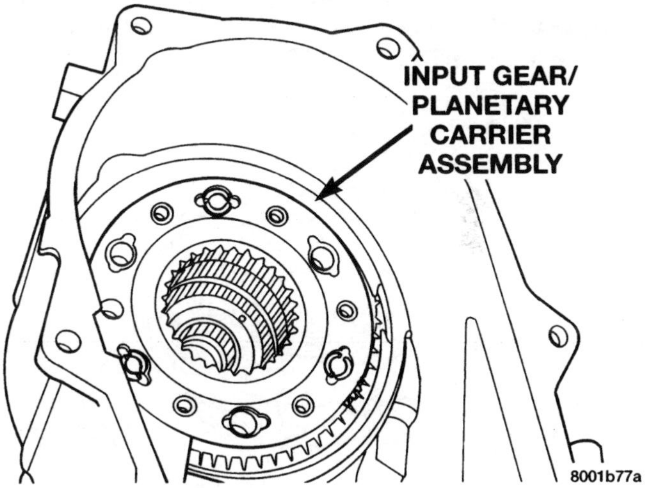

Fig. 52 Input Gear And Carrier Installation

(9) Install input gear retaining ring (Fig. 53). Be sure to install the correct retaining ring as the input gear and mode hub retaining rings are almost the same diameter. The difference is in ring thickness with the input gear retaining ring being substantially thicker.

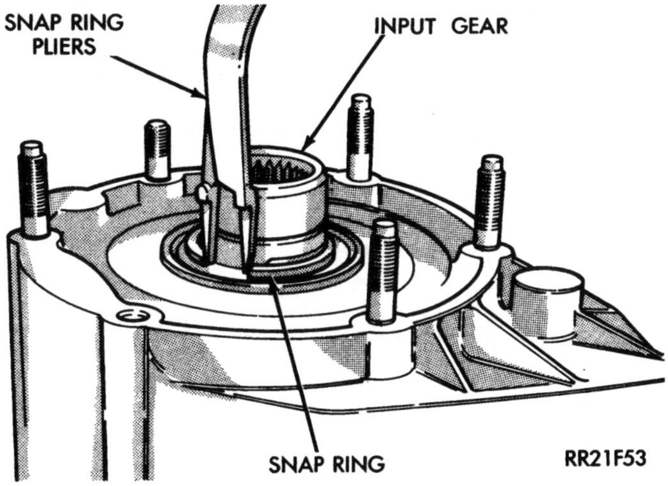

Fig. 53 Input Gear Retaining Ring Installation

DISASSEMBLY AND ASSEMBLY (Continued)

(10) Install new seal in input retainer with Tools C-4171 and 7884 (Fig. 54).

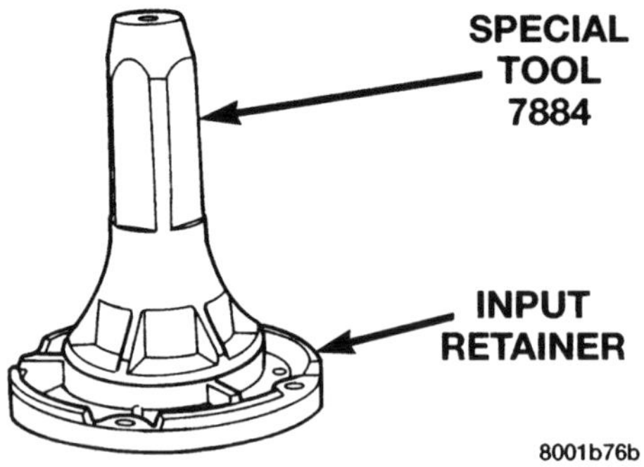

Fig. 54 Input Retainer Seal Installation

(11) Apply 3 mm bead of Mopar Sealer P/N 82300234, or Loctite Ultra Gray to front bearing retainer seal surface (Fig. 55).

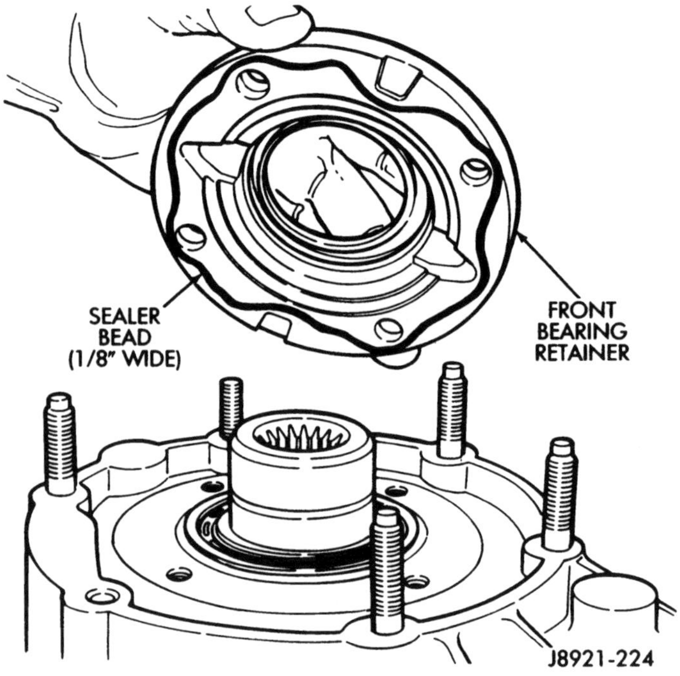

Fig. 55 Applying Sealer Bead To Input Bearing Retainer

(12) Align oil channel in retainer with oil feed hole in front case (Fig. 56).

(13) Align and install input retainer on front case (Fig. 57).

(14) Install and tighten input retainer bolts to 16–24 N.m (12–18 ft. lbs.) torque.

SHIFT SECTOR/POPPET/RANGE FORK/RANGE HUB INSTALLATION

(1) Install shift sector O-ring and nylon retainer in case bore. Note that one side of retainer is slightly rounded and that the opposite side has a shallow groove. Groove side goes toward seal and rounded side faces out.

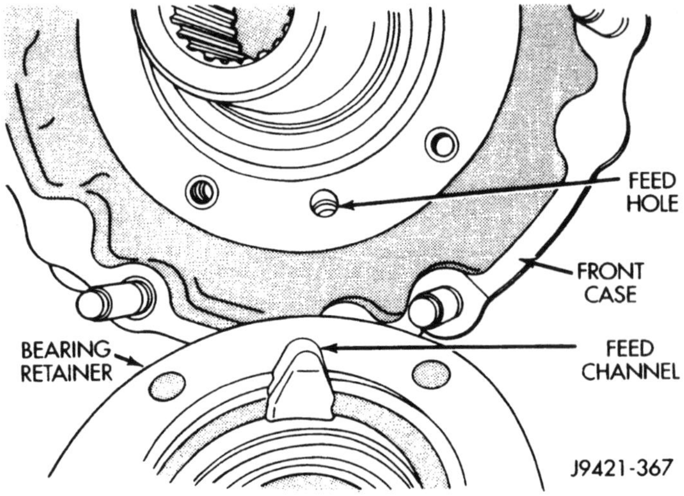

Fig. 56 Aligning Retainer Oil Channel With Feed Hole In Front Case

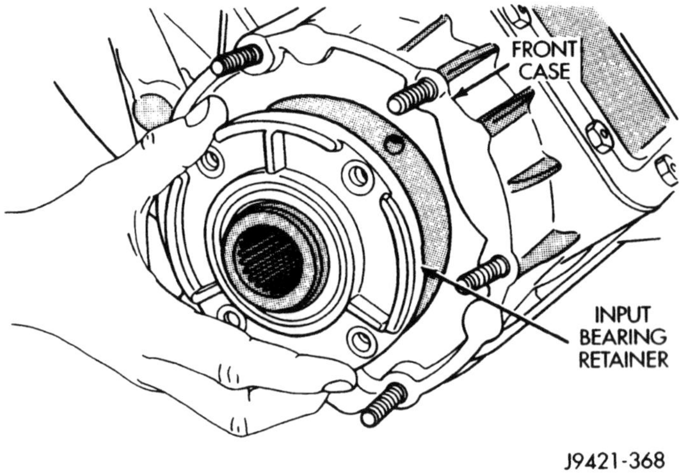

Fig. 57 Input Retainer Installation

(2) Install shift sector in case (Fig. 58). Lubricate sector shaft with transmission fluid before installation.

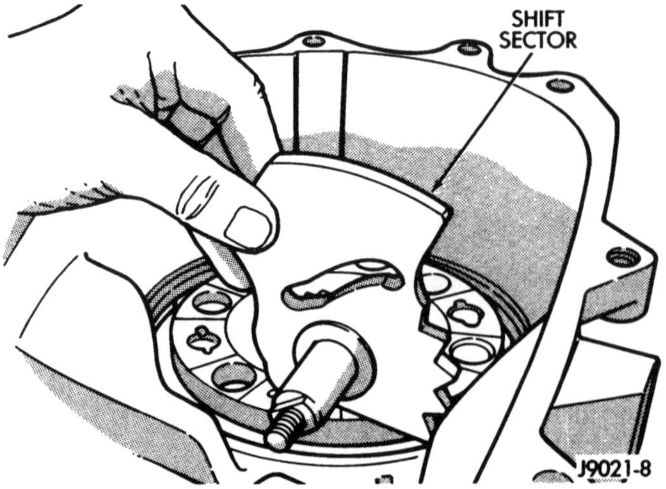

Fig. 58 Shift Sector Installation

DISASSEMBLY AND ASSEMBLY (Continued)

(3) Install range lever, washer, and nut on sector shaft (Fig. 59). Tighten range lever nut to 27–34 N.m (20–25 ft. lbs.) torque.

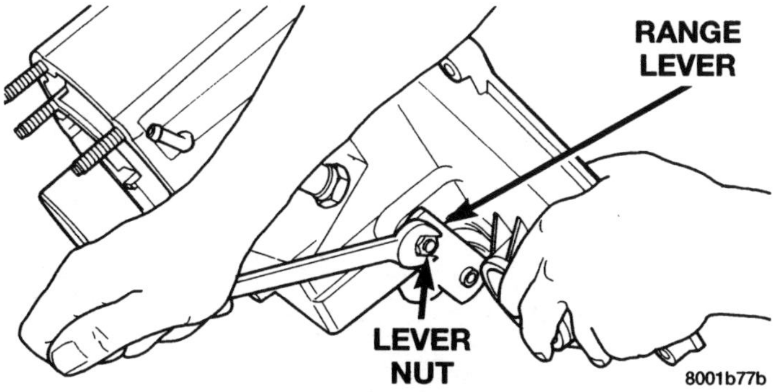

Fig. 59 Range Lever Installation

(4) Assemble and install range fork and hub (Fig. 60). Be sure hub is properly seated in planetary carrier and engaged with input gear.

(5) Align and insert range fork pin in shift sector slot.

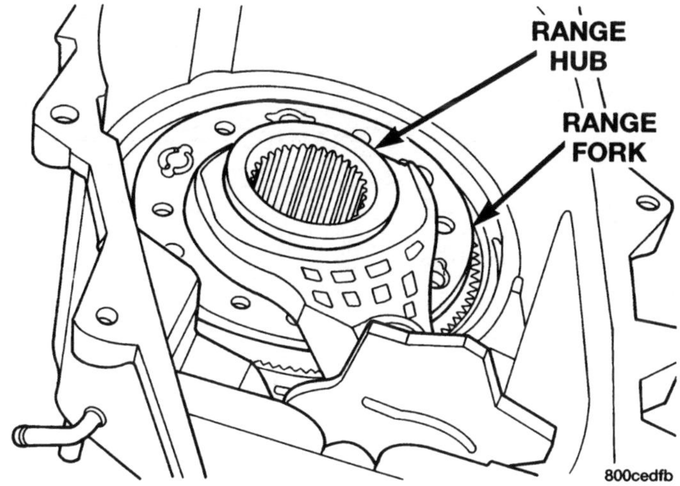

Fig. 60 Range Fork And Hub Assembly/Installation

(6) Install poppet plunger, spring, and screw plug (Fig. 19). Install new O-ring on screw plug if necessary. Tighten plug to 16–24 N.m (12–18 ft. lbs.) torque.

OUTPUT SHAFT AND MODE FORK INSTALLATION

(1) Lubricate output shaft and hub and sprocket bores with transmission fluid.

(2) Install drive sprocket on output shaft.

(3) Install mode hub on output shaft.

(4) Install mode hub retaining ring. Be sure ring is fully seated in shaft groove before proceeding.

(5) Install assembled output shaft, sprocket and hub (Fig. 61). Be sure shaft is seated in pilot bearing, planetary, and range sleeve.

(6) Install new pads on mode fork if necessary.

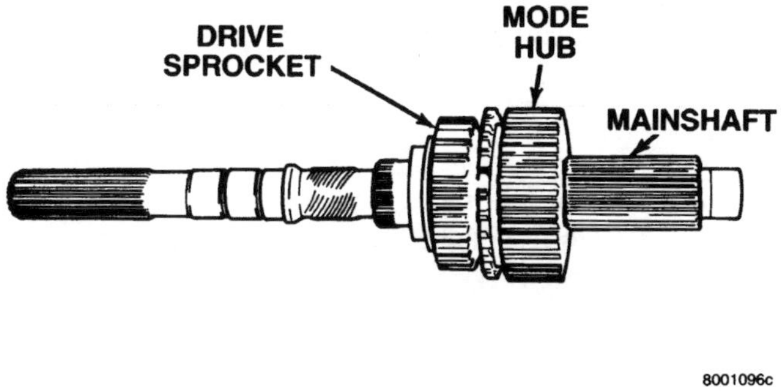

Fig. 61 Output Shaft Assembly Installation

(7) Insert mode sleeve in mode fork mode fork. Be sure long side of sleeve is toward long end of shift rail (Fig. 62).

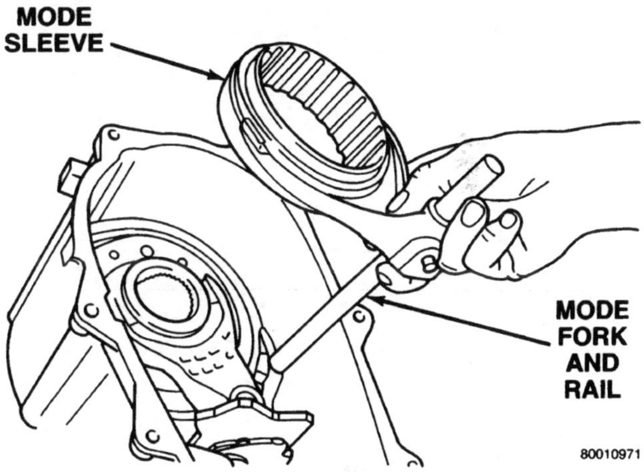

Fig. 62 Assembling Mode Fork And Sleeve

(8) Install assembled mode fork and sleeve (Fig. 63). Be sure fork rail goes through range fork and into case bore. Also be sure sleeve is aligned and seated on output shaft hub.

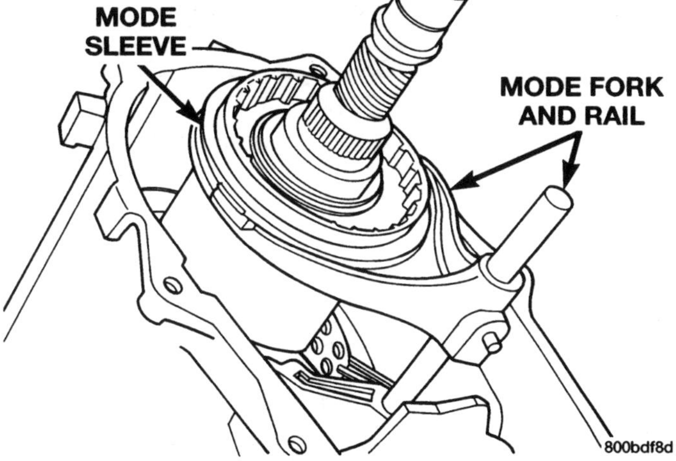

Fig. 63 Mode Fork And Sleeve Installation

DISASSEMBLY AND ASSEMBLY (Continued)

DRIVE CHAIN AND FRONT OUTPUT SHAFT INSTALLATION

(1) Lubricate chain and front shaft with automatic transmission fluid.

(2) Install drive chain on front output shaft.

(3) Lift chain and shaft upward and start chain around output shaft drive sprocket.

(4) Install front output shaft. Tilt shaft and insert it into front bearing. Then work shaft and drive chain into place (Fig. 64).

(5) Install mode spring on upper end of mode fork shift rail (Fig. 64).

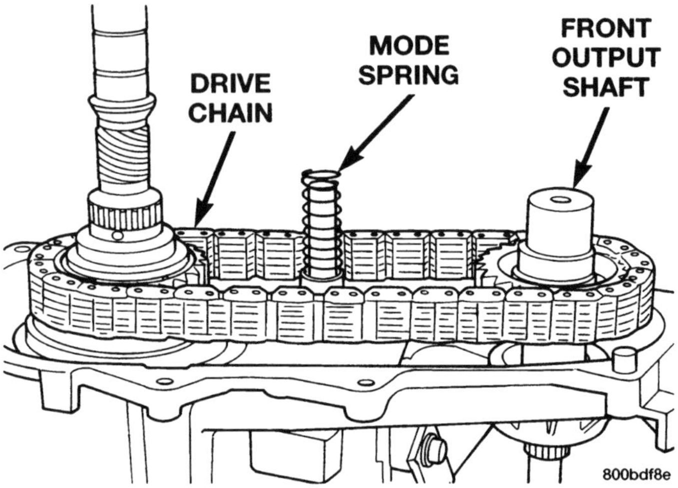

Fig. 64 Front Output Shaft And Drive Chain Installation

OIL PUMP AND REAR CASE ASSEMBLY/INSTALLATION

(1) Assemble oil pickup screen, connecting hose, and tube.

(2) Install new pickup tube O-ring in oil pump (Fig. 65).

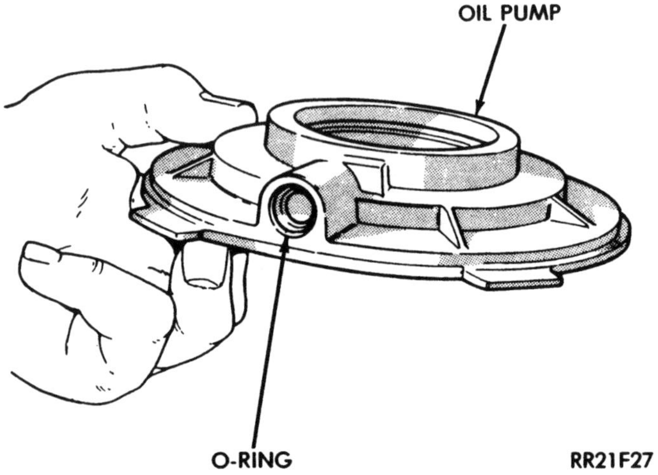

Fig. 65 Pickup Tube O-Ring Position

(3) Install new seal in oil pump with Installer Tool 7588 (Fig. 66).

(4) Insert oil pickup tube in oil pump inlet.

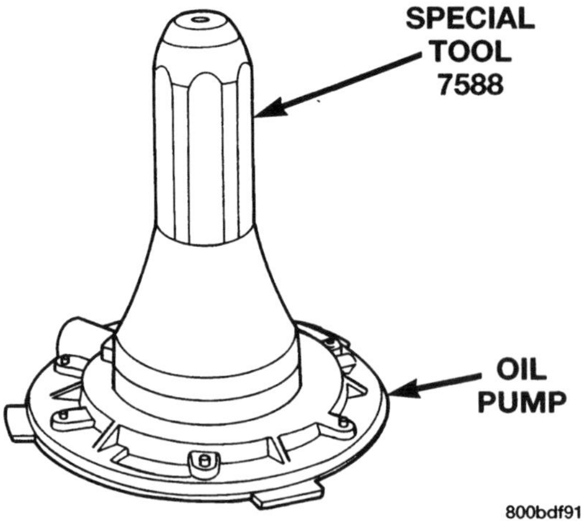

Fig. 66 Oil Pump Seal Installation

(5) Position assembled oil pump and pickup tube in rear case. Be sure pickup screen is securely seated in case slot. Also be sure oil pump locating tabs are outside rear case (Fig. 67).

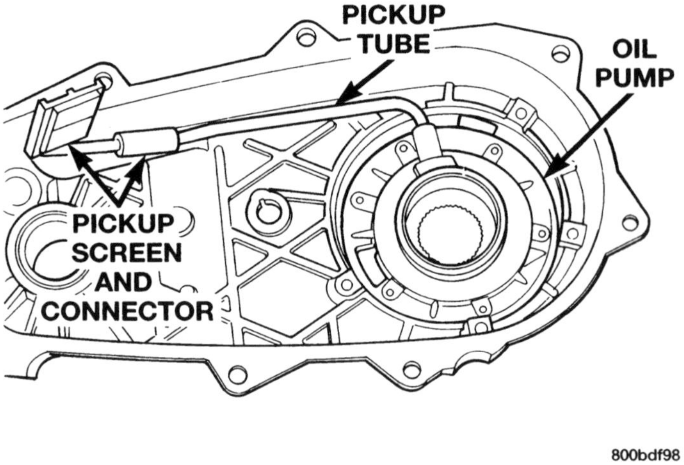

Fig. 67 Oil Pump And Pickup Tube Installation

(6) Apply bead of sealer to mating surface of front case. Use Mopar Sealer P/N 82300234, or Loctite Ultra Gray. Sealer bead should not exceed 3/16 in. in diameter.

(7) Lift rear case and oil pump and carefully position assembly on front case. Be sure case dowels are aligned and that mode fork rail extends through rear case before seating rear case on front case.

(8) Install bolts that attach rear case to front case. Be sure to use a washer with each of the two dowel bolts (Fig. 16). Tighten all bolts (including spline head bolt), to 27– 34 N.m (20–25 ft. lbs.) torque.

REAR RETAINER ASSEMBLY AND INSTALLATION

(1) Install rear bearing in retainer with Tools C-4171 and 5064 (Fig. 68).

DISASSEMBLY AND ASSEMBLY (Continued)

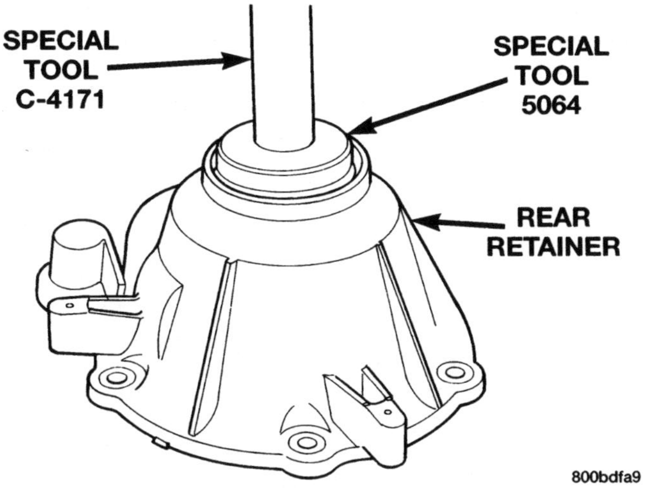

Fig. 68 Installing Rear Bearing In Retainer

(2) Install rear bearing O.D. retaining ring with snap ring pliers (Fig. 69). Be sure retaining ring is fully seated in retainer groove.

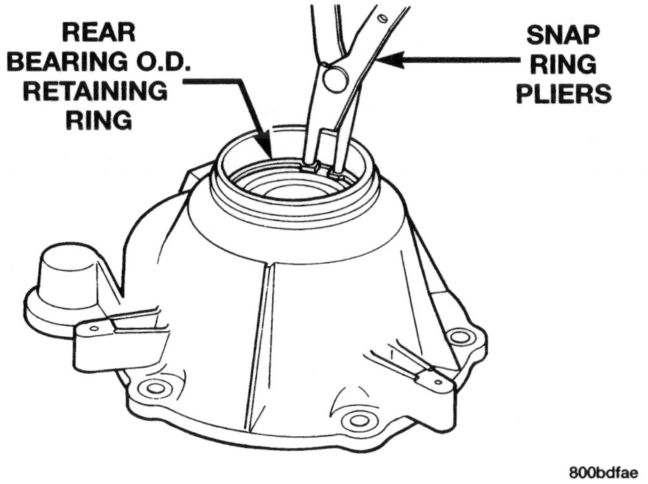

Fig. 69 Rear Bearing Retaining Ring Installation

(3) Apply bead of Mopar Sealer P/N 82300234, or Loctite Ultra Gray to mating surface of rear retainer. Sealer bead should be a maximum of 3/16 in.

(4) Install rear retainer on rear case. Tighten retainer bolts to 20–27 N.m (15–20 ft. lbs.) torque.

(5) Install rear bearing I.D. retaining ring and spacer on output shaft.

(6) Apply liberal quantity of petroleum jelly to new rear seal and to output shaft. Petroleum jelly is needed to protect seal lips during installation.

(7) Slide seal onto seal protector 6992 (Fig. 70). Slide seal protector and seal onto output shaft.

(8) Drive seal into rear bearing retainer with installer C-4076-A and handle MD-998323 (Fig. 71).

(9) Install rear slinger with installer C-4076-A and handle MD-998323 (Fig. 71).

(10) Install boot on output shaft slinger and crimp retaining clamp with tool C-4975-A (Fig. 72).

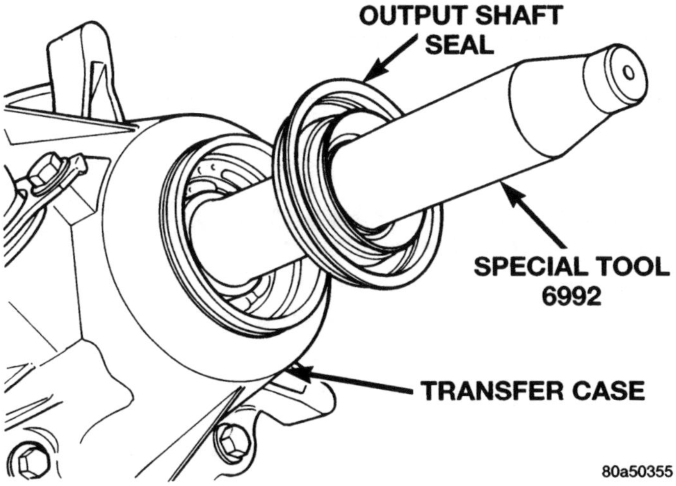

Fig. 70 Output Shaft Seal and Protector

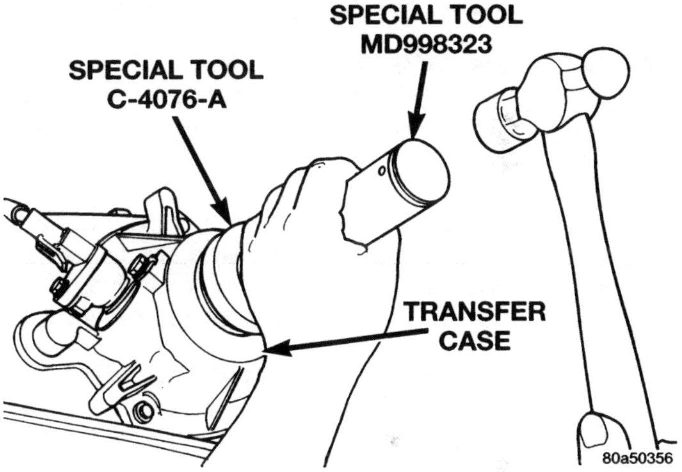

Fig. 71 Rear Seal Installation

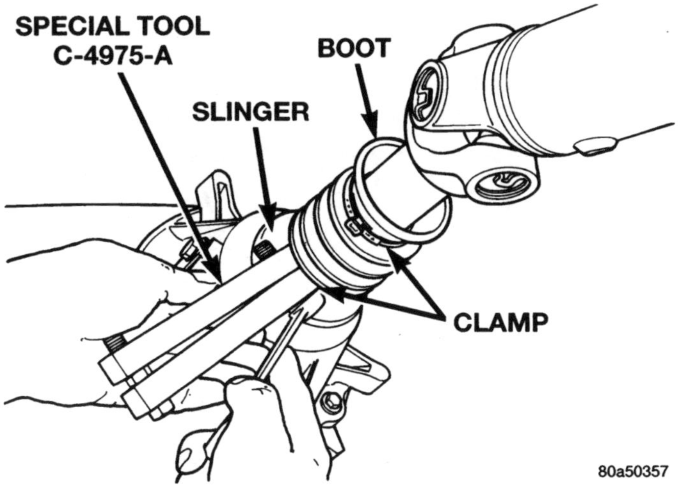

Fig. 72 Slinger Boot Installation

FRONT YOKE AND SWITCH INSTALLATION

(1) Install vacuum or indicator switch in front case. Tighten switch to 20–34 N.m (15–25 ft. lbs.) torque.

DISASSEMBLY AND ASSEMBLY (Continued)

(2) Lubricate yoke hub with transmission fluid and install yoke on front shaft.

(3) Install new seal washer on front shaft.

(4) Install yoke on front shaft. Secure yoke with new nut.

CLEANING AND INSPECTION

NV231 TRANSFER CASE

Clean the transfer case parts with a standard parts cleaning solvent. Remove all traces of sealer from the cases and retainers with a scraper and 3M all purpose cleaner. Use compressed air to remove solvent residue from oil feed passages in the case halves, retainers, gears, and shafts.

The oil pickup screen can be cleaned with solvent. Shake excess solvent from the screen after cleaning and allow it to air dry. Do not use compressed air.

MAINSHAFT/SPROCKET/HUB INSPECTION

Inspect the splines on the hub and shaft and the teeth on the sprocket (Fig. 73). Minor nicks and scratches can be smoothed with an oilstone, however, replace any part is damaged.

Check the contact surfaces in the sprocket bore and on the mainshaft. Minor nicks and scratches can be smoothed with 320–400 grit emery cloth but do not try to salvage the shaft if nicks or wear is severe.

INPUT GEAR AND PLANETARY CARRIER

Check the teeth on the gear (Fig. 74). Minor nicks can be dressed off with an oilstone but replace the gear if any teeth are broken, cracked, or chipped. The bearing surface on the gear can be smoothed with 300–400 grit emery cloth if necessary.

Examine the carrier body and pinion gears for wear or damage. The carrier will have to be replaced as an assembly if the body, pinion pins, or pinion gears are damaged.

Check the lock ring and both thrust washers for wear or cracks. Replace them if necessary. Also replace the lock retaining ring if bent, distorted, or broken.

SHIFT FORKS/HUBS/SLEEVES

Check condition of the shift forks and mode fork shift rail (Fig. 75). Minor nicks on the shift rail can be smoothed with 320–400 grit emery cloth.

Inspect the shift fork wear pads (Fig. 76). The mode fork pads are serviceable and can be replaced if necessary. The range fork pads are not serviceable. The fork must be replaced as an assembly if the pads are worn or damaged.

Check both of the sleeves for wear or damage, especially on the interior teeth. Replace the sleeves if wear or damage is evident.

REAR RETAINER/BEARING/ SEAL/SLINGER/ BOOT

Inspect the retainer components (Fig. 77). Replace the bearing if rough or noisy. Check the retainer for cracks or wear in the bearing bore. Clean the retainer sealing surfaces with a scraper and 3M all purpose cleaner. This will ensure proper adhesion of the sealer during reassembly.

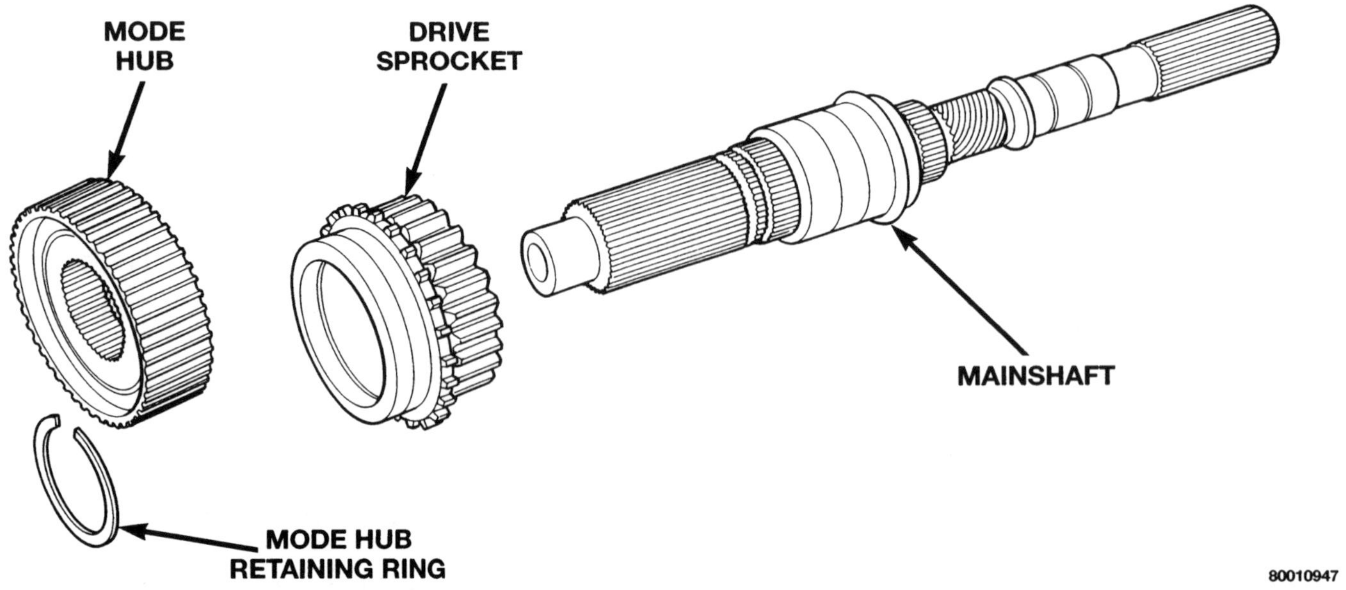

Fig. 73 Mainshaft, Mode Hub, And Drive Sprocket

CLEANING AND INSPECTION (Continued)

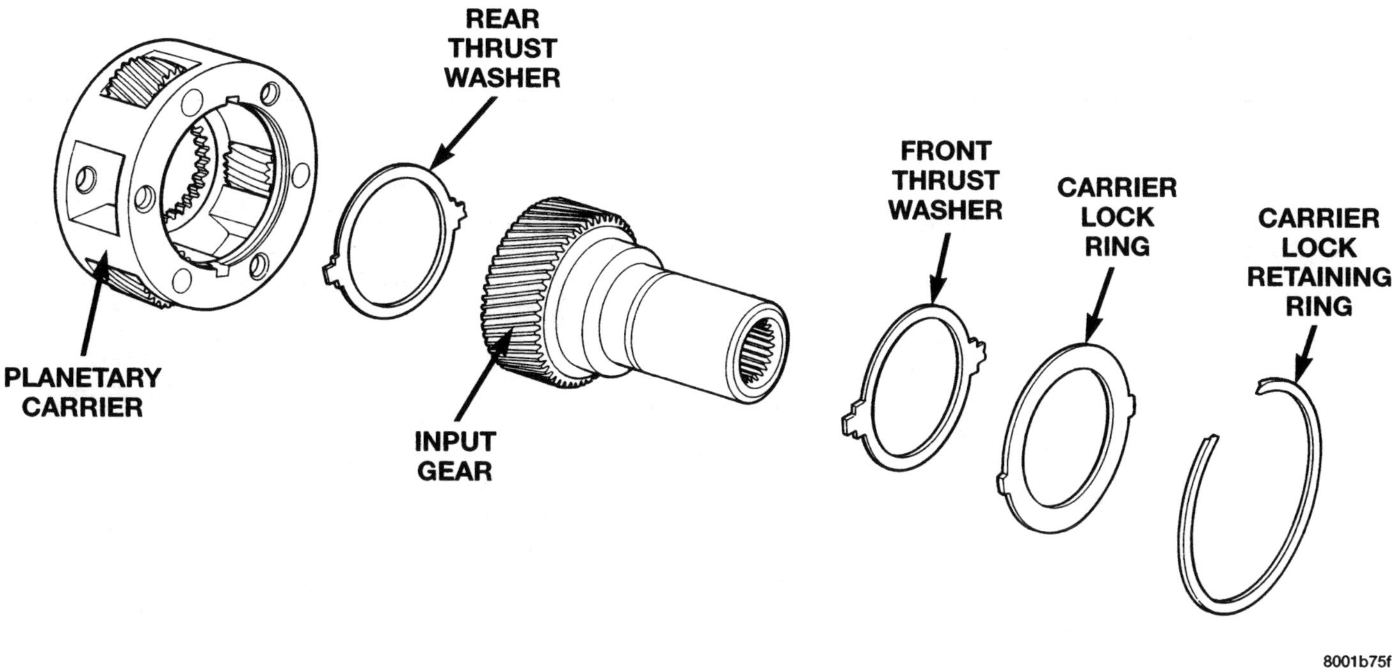

Fig. 74 Input Gear And Carrier Components

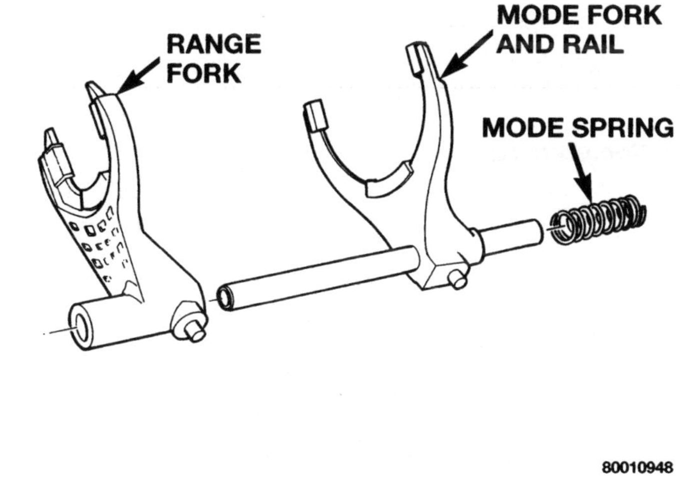

Fig. 75 Shift forks

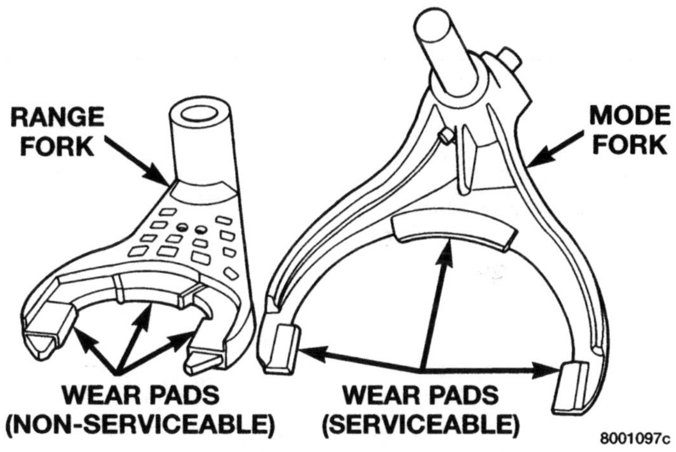

Fig. 76 Shift Fork And Wear Pad Locations

Replace the slinger and seal outright; do not reuse either part.

Inspect the retaining rings and washers. Replace any part if distorted, bent, or broken. Reuse is not recommended. Also replace the boot if cut or torn. Replace the boot band clamps, do not reuse them.

REAR OUTPUT SHAFT/YOKE/DRIVE CHAIN

Check condition of the seal contact surfaces of the yoke slinger (Fig. 78). This surface must be clean and smooth to ensure proper seal life. Replace the yoke nut and seal washer as neither part should be reused.

Inspect the shaft threads, sprocket teeth, and bearing surfaces. Minor nicks on the teeth can be smoothed with an oilstone. Use 320–400 grit emery to smooth minor scratches on the shaft bearing surfaces. Rough threads on the shaft can be chased if necessary. Replace the shaft if the threads are damaged, bearing surfaces are scored, or if any sprocket teeth are cracked or broken.

Examine the drive chain and shaft bearings. replace the chain if stretched, distorted, or if any of the links bind. Replace the bearings if rough, or noisy.

LOW RANGE ANNULUS GEAR

Inspect annulus gear condition carefully. The gear is only serviced as part of the front case. If the gear is damaged, it will be necessary to replace the gear and front case as an assembly. Do not attempt to remove the gear (Fig. 79)

CLEANING AND INSPECTION (Continued)

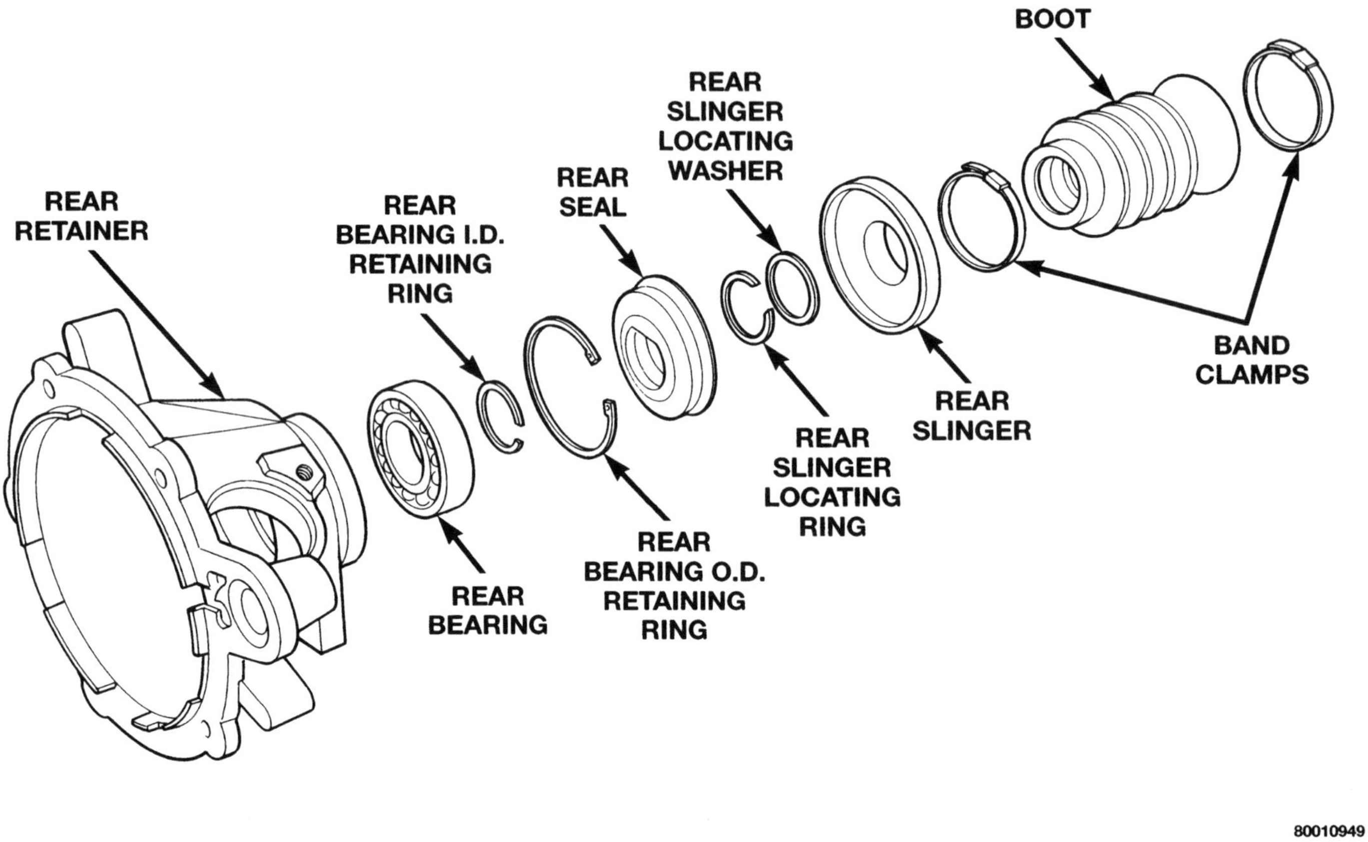

Fig. 77 Rear Retainer Components

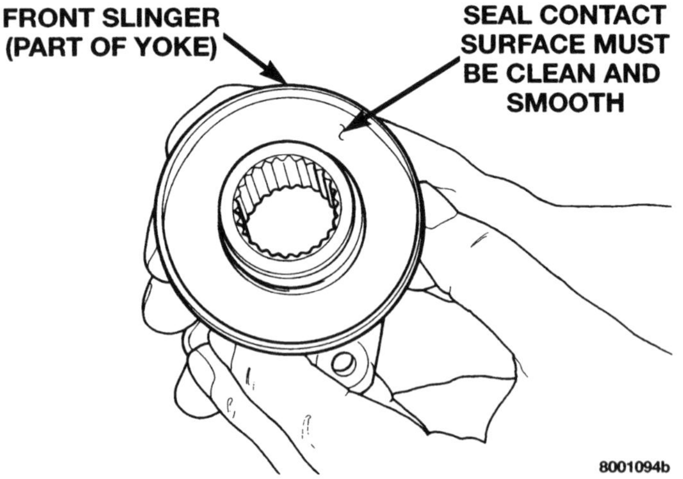

Fig. 78 Seal Contact Surface Of Yoke Slinger

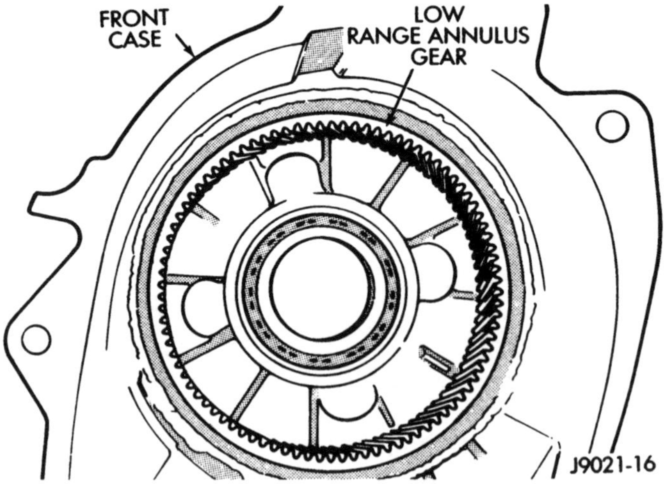

Fig. 79 Low Range Annulus Gear

FRONT-REAR CASES AND FRONT RETAINER

Inspect the cases and retainer for wear and damage. Clean the sealing surfaces with a scraper and 3M all purpose cleaner. This will ensure proper sealer adhesion at assembly. Replace the input retainer seal; do not reuse it.

Check case condition. If leaks were a problem, look for gouges and severe scoring of case sealing surfaces. Also make sure the front case mounting studs are in good condition.

Check the front case mounting studs and vent tube. The tube can be secured with Loctite 271 or 680 if loose. The stud threads can be cleaned up with a die if necessary. Also check condition of the fill/drain plug threads in the rear case. The threads can be repaired with a thread chaser or tap if necessary. Or the threads can be repaired with Helicoil stainless steel inserts if required.

CLEANING AND INSPECTION (Continued)

OIL PUMP/OIL PICKUP

Examine the oil pump pickup parts. Replace the pump if any part appears to be worn or damaged. Do not disassemble the pump as individual parts are not available. The pump is only available as a complete assembly. The pickup screen, hose, and tube are the only serviceable parts and are available separately.

ADJUSTMENTS

SHIFT LINKAGE ADJUSTMENT

(1) Shift transfer case into 4L position.

(2) Raise vehicle.

(3) Loosen lock bolt on adjusting trunnion (Fig. 80).

(4) Be sure linkage rod slides freely in trunnion. Clean rod and apply spray lube if necessary.

(5) Verify that transfer case range lever is fully engaged in 4L position.

(6) Tighten adjusting trunnion lock bolt.

(7) Lower vehicle.

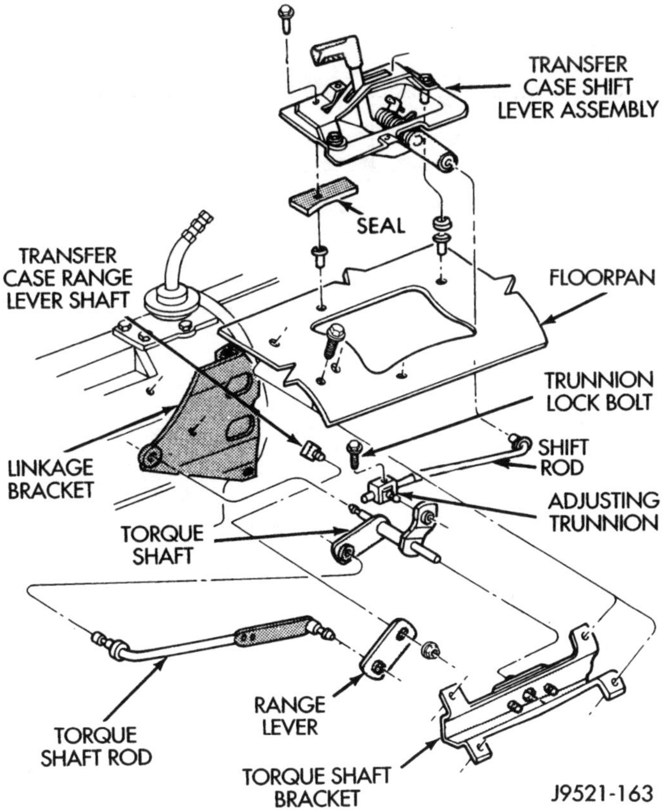

Fig. 80 Shift Linkage

SPECIFICATIONS

TORQUE

DESCRIPTION	TORQUE
Plug, Detent	16–24 N·m (12–18 ft. lbs.)
Bolt, Diff. Case	17–27 N·m (15–24 ft. lbs.)
Plug, Drain/Fill	40–45 N·m (30–40 ft. lbs.)
Bolt, Extension Housing	35–46 N·m (26–34 ft. lbs.)
Bolt, Front Brg. Retainer	16–27 N·m (12–20 ft. lbs.)
Bolt, Case Half	35–46 N·m (26–34 ft. lbs.)
Nut, Front Yoke	122–176 N·m (90–130 ft. lbs.)
Screw, Oil Pump	1.2–1.8 N·m (12–15 in. lbs.)
Nut, Range Lever	27–34 N·m (20–25 ft. lbs.)
Bolt, Rear Retainer	35–46 N·m (26–34 ft. lbs.)
Nuts, Mounting	35–47 N·m (26–35 ft. lbs.)
Bolts, U-Joint	19 N·m (17 ft. lbs.)
Vacuum Switch	20–34 N·m (15–25 ft. lbs.)

SPECIAL TOOLS

NV231

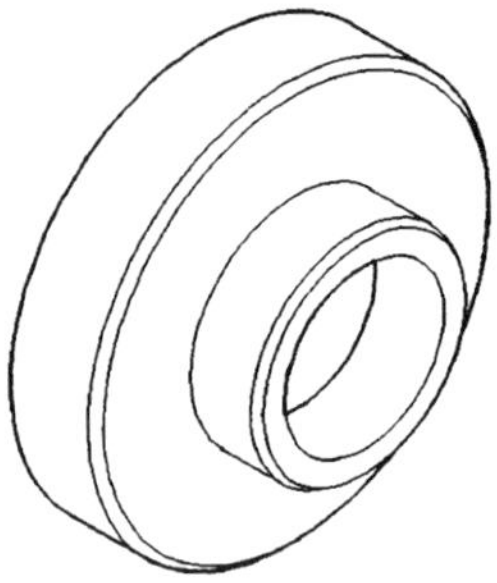

Installer—C-4076-A

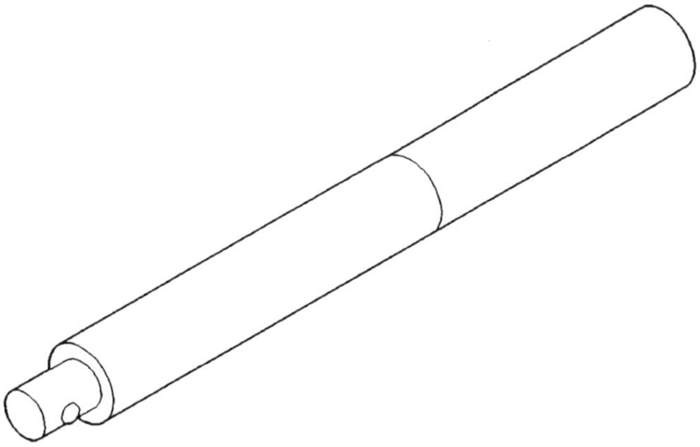

Handle, Universal—C-4171

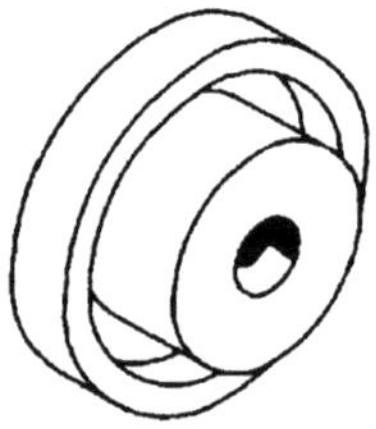

Installer, Seal—C-4210

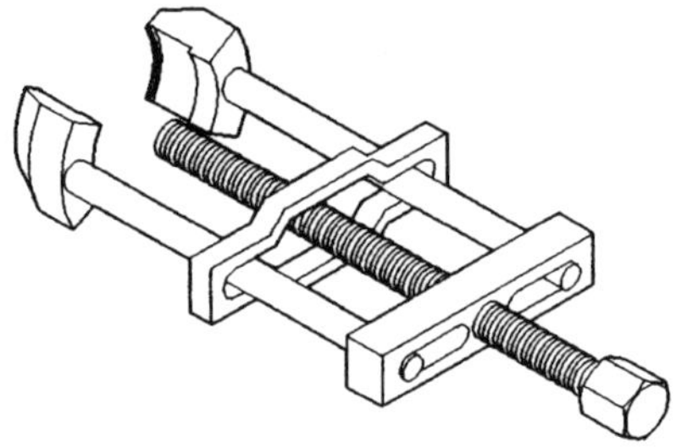

Puller, Slinger—MD-998056–A

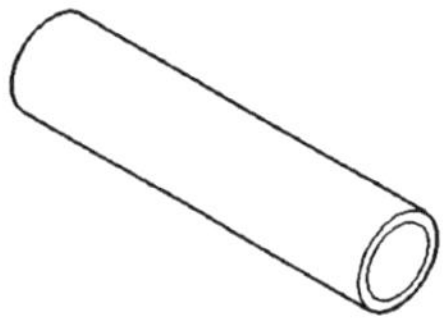

Installer—MD-998323

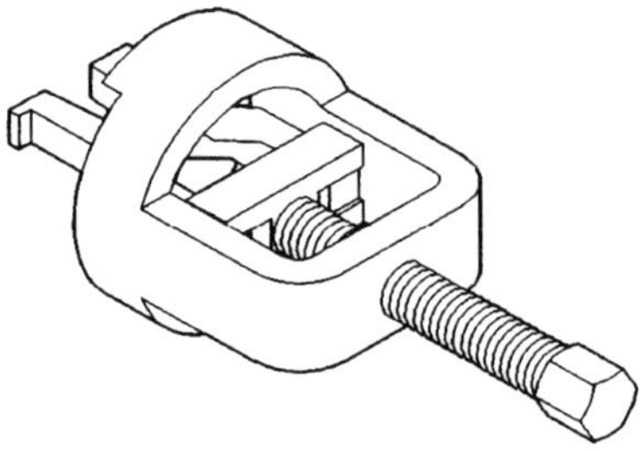

Puller, Bearing—MD-998346

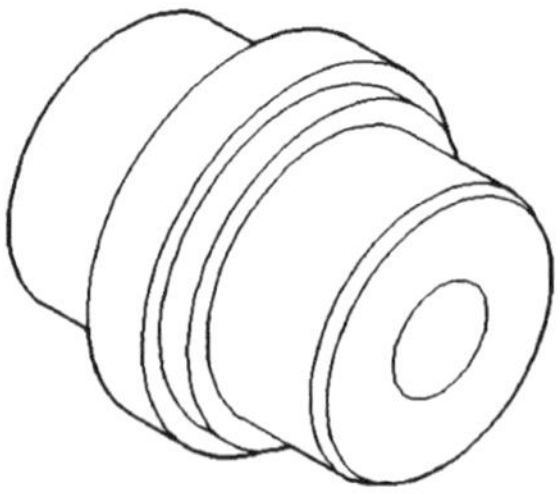

Installer, Bearing—5061

SPECIAL TOOLS (Continued)

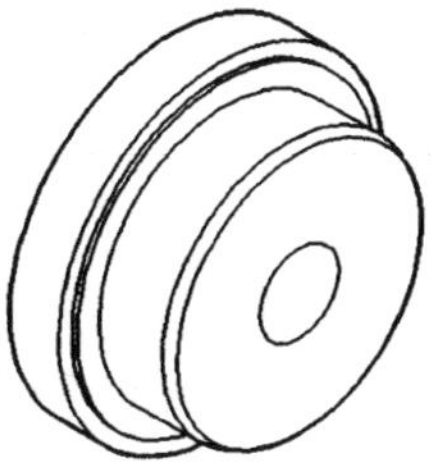

Installer, Bearing—5062

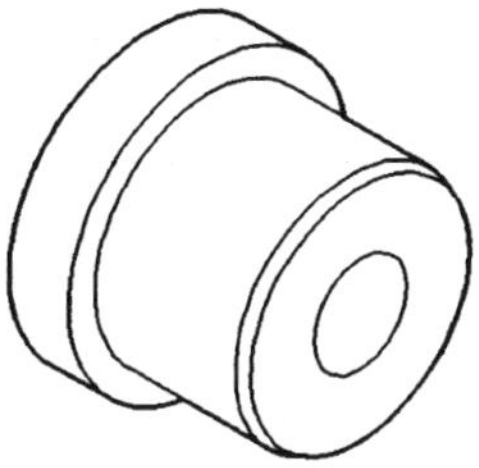

Installer, Bushing—5066

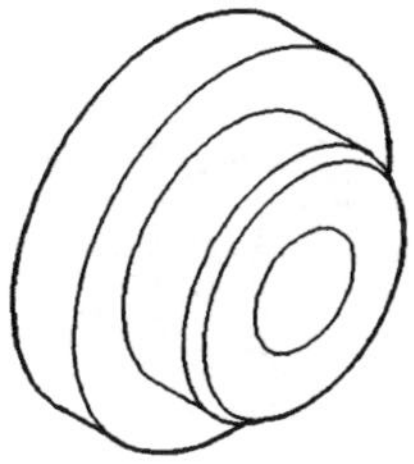

Installer, Bearing—5063

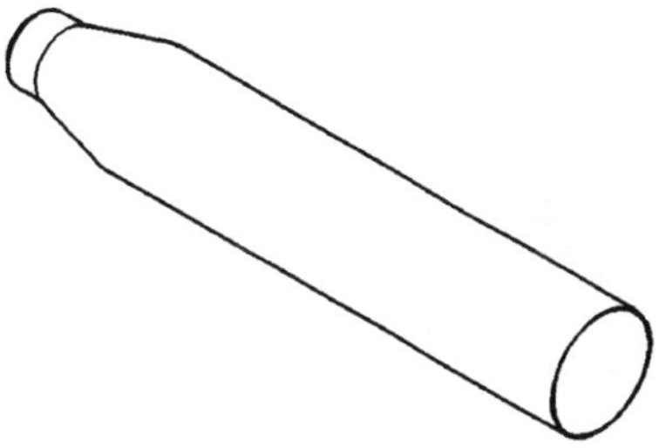

Seal Protector—6692

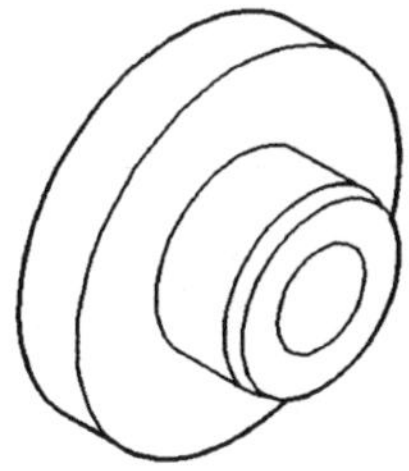

Installer, Bearing—5064

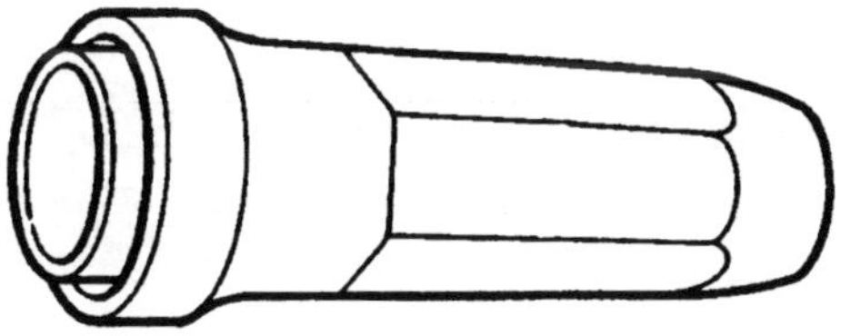

Installer, Seal—7588

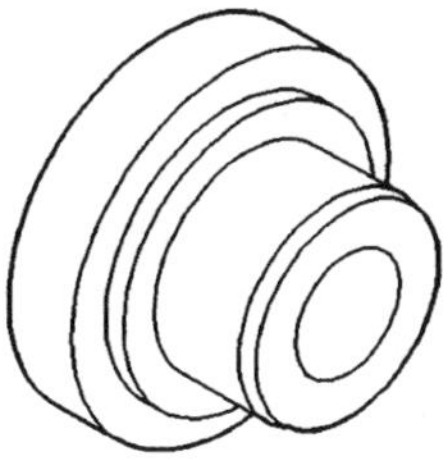

Installer, Bearing—5065

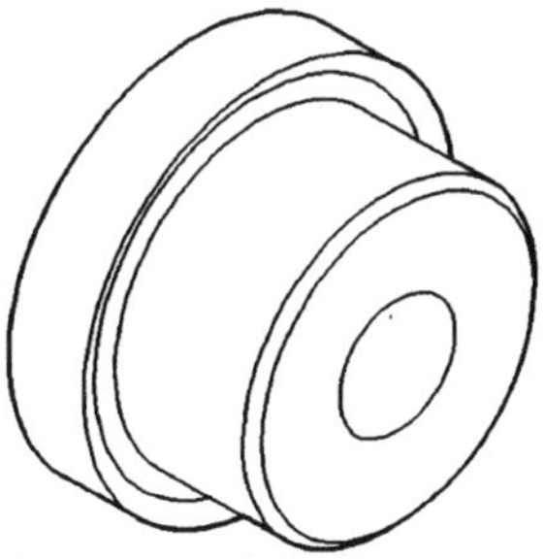

Installer, Input Gear Bearing—7828-A

SPECIAL TOOLS (Continued)

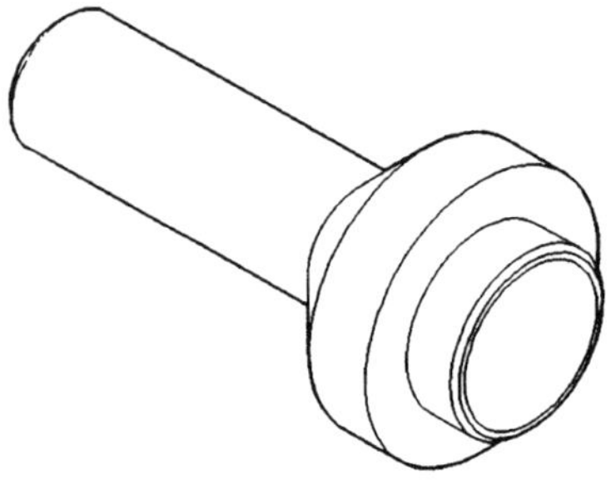

Installer, Seal—7884

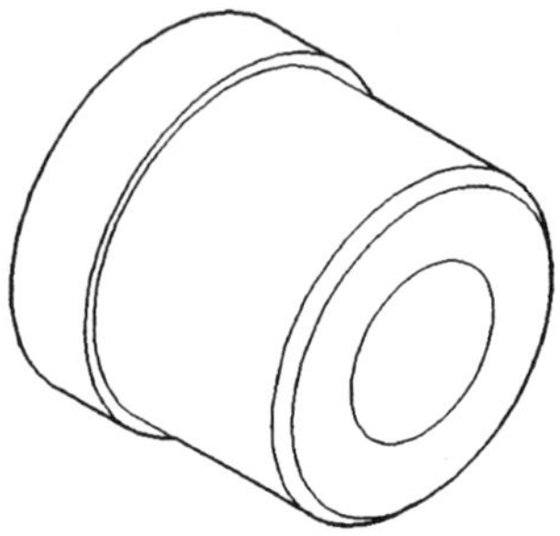

Remover, Rear Output Shaft Bushing—7889-A

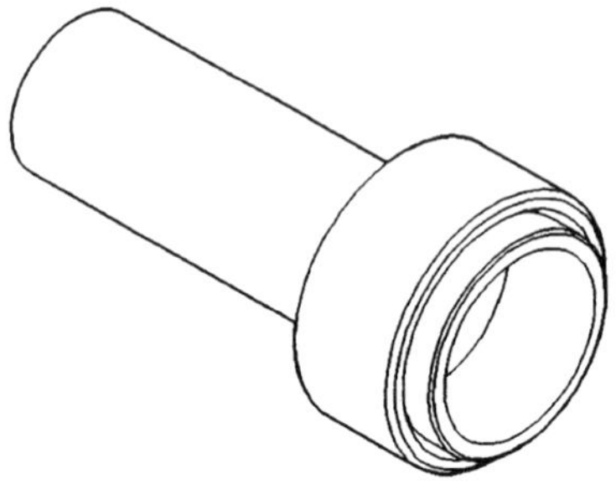

Installer, Pump Housing Seal—7888

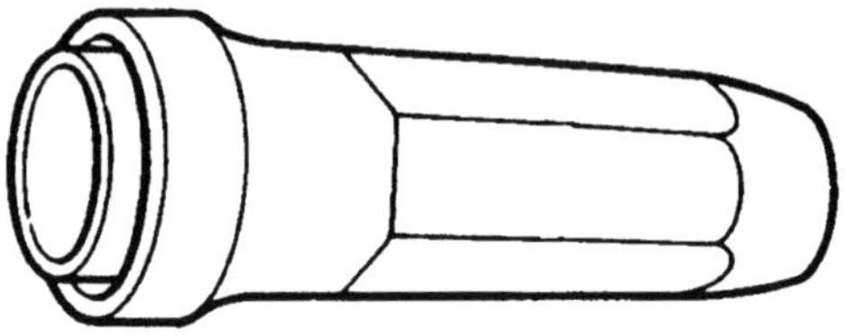

Installer, Seal—7934

TIRES AND WHEELS

CONTENTS

TIRES

INDEX

DESCRIPTION AND OPERATION

TIRE INFORMATION

Tires are designed and engineered for each specific vehicle. They provide the best overall performance for normal operation. The ride and handling characteristics match the vehicle's requirements. With proper care they will give excellent reliability, traction, skid resistance, and tread life.

Driving habits have more effect on tire life than any other factor. Careful drivers will obtain, in most cases, much greater mileage than severe use or careless drivers. A few of the driving habits which will shorten the life of any tire are:

- Rapid acceleration
- Severe application of brakes
- High-speed driving
- Taking turns at excessive speeds
- Striking curbs and other obstacles

Radial ply tires are more prone to irregular tread wear. It is important to follow the tire rotation interval shown in the section on Tire Rotation. This will help to achieve a greater tread-life potential.

TIRE IDENTIFICATION

Tire type, size, aspect ratio and speed rating are encoded in the letters and numbers imprinted on the side wall of the tire. Refer to the chart to decipher the tire identification code (Fig. 1).

Performance tires will have a speed rating letter after the aspect ratio number. The speed rating is not always printed on the tire sidewall. The letter **S** indicates that the tire is speed rated up to 112 mph.

- **Q** up to 100 mph
- **T** up to 118 mph
- **U** up to 124 mph
- **H** up to 130 mph
- **V** up to 149 mph
- **Z** more than 149 mph (consult the tire manufacturer for the specific speed rating)

An All Season type tire will have either **M + S, M & S or M—S** (indicating mud and snow traction) imprinted on the side wall.

TIRE CHAINS

Tire snow chains may be used on **certain** models. Refer to Owner's Manual for more information.

DESCRIPTION AND OPERATION (Continued)

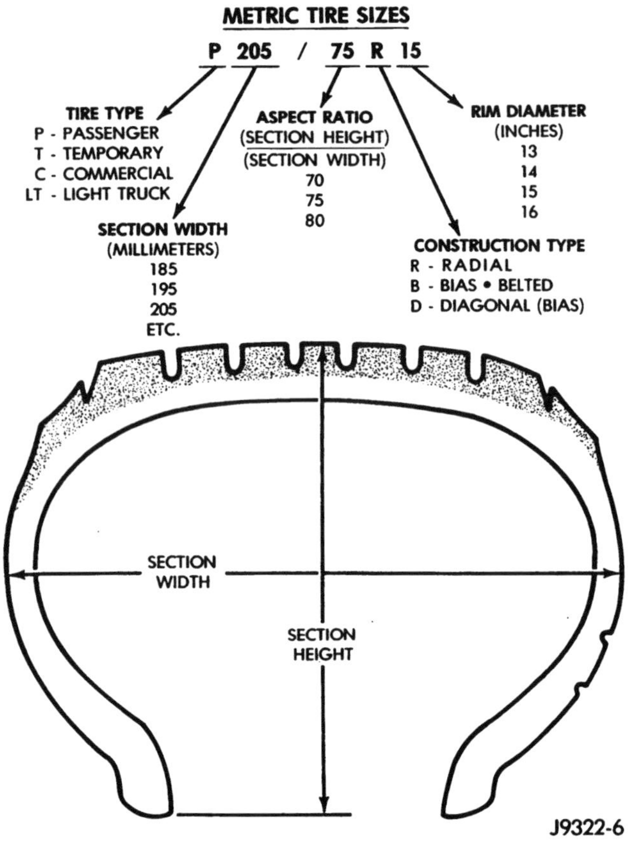

Fig. 1 Tire Identification

RADIAL-PLY TIRES

Radial-ply tires improve handling, tread life, ride quality and decrease rolling resistance.

Radial-ply tires must always be used in sets of four and under no circumstances should they be used on the front only. They may be mixed with temporary spare tires when necessary. A maximum speed of 50 MPH is recommended while a temporary spare is in use.

Radial-ply tires have the same load-carrying capacity as other types of tires of the same size. They also use the same recommended inflation pressures.

The use of oversized tires, either in the front or rear of the vehicle, can cause vehicle drive train failure. This could also cause inaccurate wheel speed signals when the vehicle is equipped with Anti-Lock Brakes.

It is recommended that tires from different manufactures NOT be mixed. The proper tire pressure should be maintained on all four tires. For proper tire pressure refer to the Tire Inflation Pressure Chart provided with the vehicle.

SPARE TIRE (TEMPORARY)

The temporary spare tire is designed for emergency use only. The original tire should be repaired and reinstalled at the first opportunity, or a new tire purchased. Do not exceed speeds of 50 MPH. Refer to Owner's Manual for complete details.

TIRE INFLATION PRESSURES

Under inflation causes rapid shoulder wear, tire flexing, and can result in tire failure (Fig. 2).

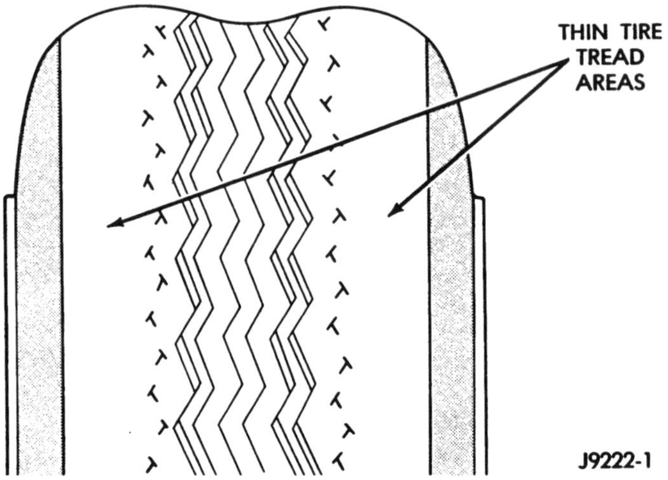

Fig. 2 Under Inflation Wear

Over inflation causes rapid center wear and loss of the tire's ability to cushion shocks (Fig. 3).

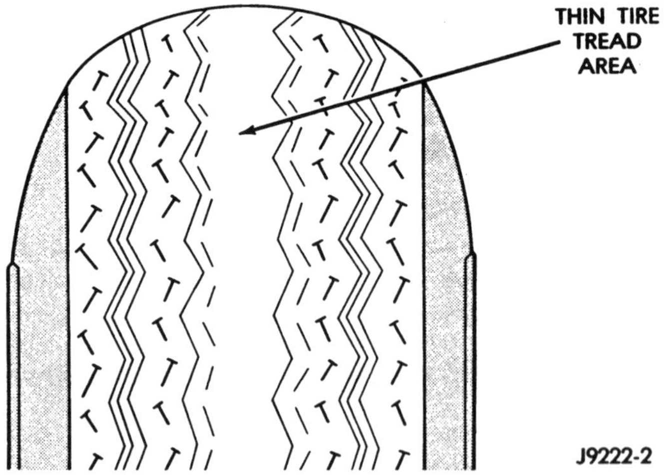

Fig. 3 Over Inflation Wear

Improper inflation can cause:

- Uneven wear patterns
- Reduced tread life
- Reduced fuel economy
- Unsatisfactory ride
- The vehicle to drift.

For proper tire pressure specification refer to the Tire Inflation Pressure Chart provided with the vehicle.

Tire pressures have been chosen to provide safe operation, vehicle stability, and a smooth ride. Tire pressure should be checked cold once per month. Check tire pressure more frequently when the

DESCRIPTION AND OPERATION (Continued)

weather temperature varies widely. Tire pressure will decreases when the outdoor temperature drops.

Inflation pressures specified on the placards are always cold inflation pressure. Cold inflation pressure is obtained after the vehicle has not been operated for at least 3 hours. Or the vehicle is driven less than one mile after being inoperative for 3 hours. Tire inflation pressures may increase from 2 to 6 pounds per square inch (psi) during operation. Do not reduce this normal pressure build-up.

WARNING: OVER OR UNDER INFLATED TIRES CAN AFFECT VEHICLE HANDLING. THE TIRE CAN FAIL SUDDENLY, RESULTING IN LOSS OF VEHICLE CONTROL.

TIRE PRESSURE FOR HIGH—SPEED OPERATION

WARNING: OVER OR UNDER INFLATED TIRES CAN AFFECT VEHICLE HANDLING. THE TIRE CAN FAIL SUDDENLY, RESULTING IN LOSS OF VEHICLE CONTROL.

Chrysler Corporation advocates driving at safe speeds within posted speed limits. Where speed limits allow the vehicle to be driven at high speeds, correct tire inflation pressure is very important. For speeds up to and including 75 mph (120 km/h), tires must be inflated to the pressures shown on the tire placard. For continuous speeds in excess of 75 mph (120 km/h), tires must be inflated to the maximum pressure specified on the tire sidewall.

Vehicles loaded to the maximum capacity should not be driven at continuous speeds above 75 mph (120 km/h).

For emergency vehicles that are driven at speeds over 90 mph (144 km/h), special high-speed tires must be used. Consult tire manufacturer for correct inflation pressure recommendations.

REPLACEMENT TIRES

The original equipment tires provide a proper balance of many characteristics such as:

- Ride
- Noise
- Handling
- Durability
- Tread life
- Traction
- Rolling resistance
- Speed capability

It is recommend that tires equivalent to the original equipment tires be used when replacement is needed.

Failure to use equivalent replacement tires may adversely affect the safety and handling of the vehicle.

The use of oversize tires not listed in the specification charts may cause interference with vehicle components. Under extremes of suspension and steering travel, interference with vehicle components may cause tire damage.

WARNING: FAILURE TO EQUIP THE VEHICLE WITH TIRES HAVING ADEQUATE SPEED CAPABILITY CAN RESULT IN SUDDEN TIRE FAILURE.

DIAGNOSIS AND TESTING

PRESSURE GAUGES

A high-quality air-pressure gauge is recommended to check tire pressure. After checking with the gauge, replace valve caps and finger tighten.

TREAD WEAR INDICATORS

Tread wear indicators are molded into the bottom of the tread grooves. When tread depth is 1.6 mm (1/16 in.), the tread wear indicators will appear as a 13 mm (1/2 in.) band.

Tire replacement is necessary when indicators appear in two or more grooves or if localized balding occurs (Fig. 4).

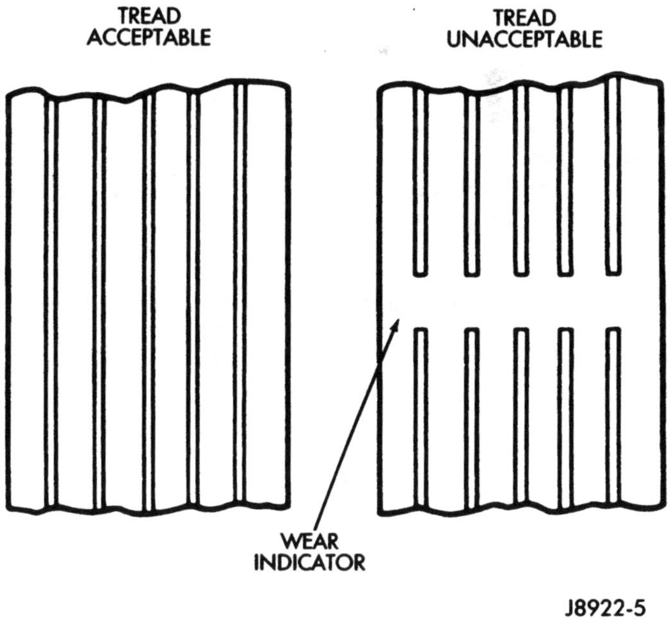

Fig. 4 Tread Wear Indicators

TIRE WEAR PATTERNS

Under inflation results in faster wear on shoulders of tire. Over inflation causes faster wear at center of tread.

DIAGNOSIS AND TESTING (Continued)

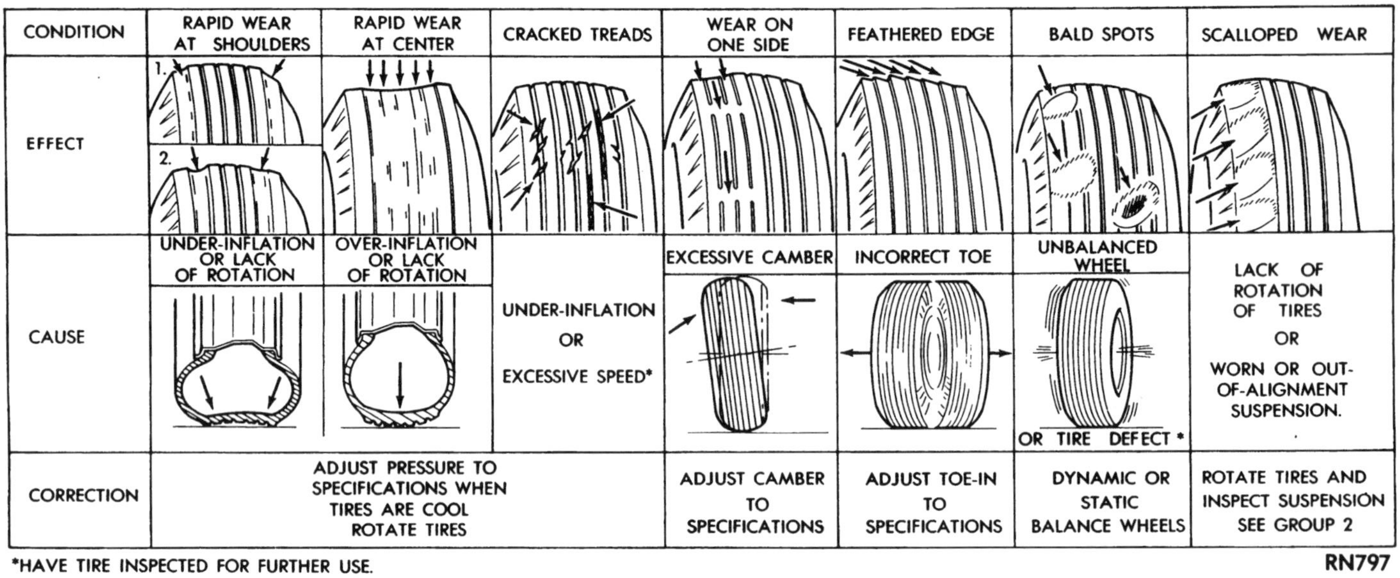

Fig. 5 Tire Wear Patterns

Excessive camber causes the tire to run at an angle to the road. One side of tread is worn more than the other.

Excessive toe-in or toe-out causes wear on the tread edges of the tire, from dragging of tire. There is a feathered effect across the tread (Fig. 5).

TIRE NOISE OR VIBRATION

Radial-ply tires are sensitive to force impulses caused by improper mounting, vibration, wheel defects, or possibly tire imbalance.

To find out if tires are causing the noise or vibration, drive the vehicle over a smooth road at varying speeds. Note the effect of acceleration and deceleration on noise level. Differential and exhaust noises will change in intensity as speed varies, while tire noise will usually remain constant.

SERVICE PROCEDURES

ROTATION

Tires on the front and rear axles operate at different loads and perform different steering, driving, and braking functions. For these reasons;

- They wear at unequal rates
- Tend to develop irregular wear patterns

These effects can be reduced by timely rotation of tires. The benefits of rotation are especially worthwhile. Rotation will:

- Increase tread life
- Help to maintain mud, snow, and wet traction levels
- Contribute to a smooth, quiet ride

The suggested method of tire rotation is (Fig. 6). Other rotation methods can be used, but they will not provide all the tire longevity benefits.

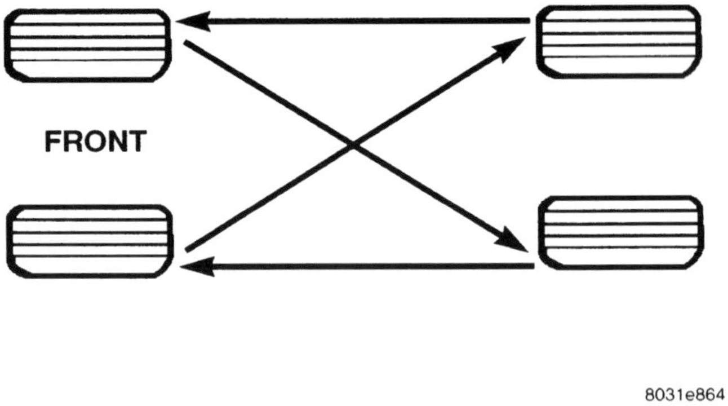

Fig. 6 Tire Rotation Pattern

MATCH MOUNTING

NOTE: Tires and wheels are currently match mounted at the factory.

Match mounting is a technique used to reduce runout in the wheel/tire assembly. This means that the high spot of the tire is aligned with the low spot on the wheel rim. The high spot on the tire is marked with a paint mark or a bright colored adhesive label on the outboard sidewall. The low spot on the rim is identified with a label on the outside of the rim and a dot on the inside of the rim. If the outside label has been removed the tire will have to be removed to locate the dot on the inside of the rim.

SERVICE PROCEDURES (Continued)

Before dismounting a tire from its wheel, a reference mark should be placed on the tire at the valve stem location. This reference will ensure that it is remounted in the original position on the wheel.

(1) Measure the total indicator runout on the center of the tire tread rib. Record the indicator reading. Mark the tire to indicate the high spot. Place a mark on the tire at the valve stem location (Fig. 7).

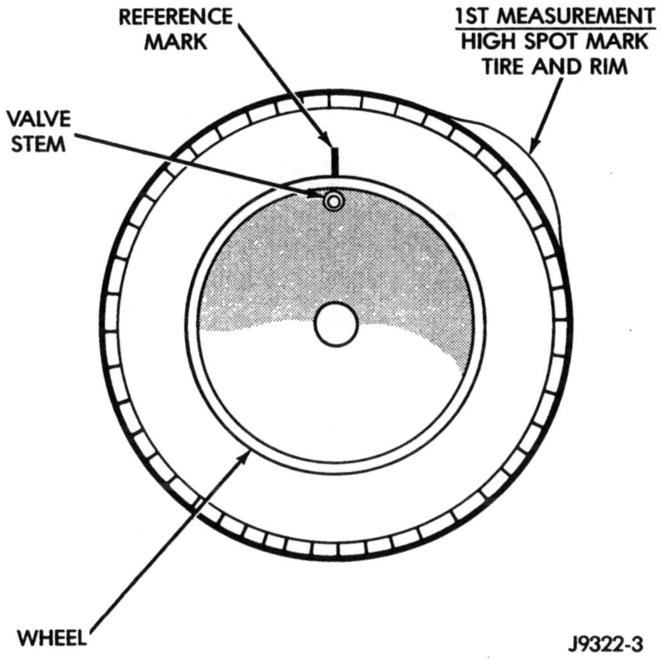

Fig. 7 First Measurement On Tire

(2) Break down the tire and remount it 180 degrees on the rim (Fig. 8).

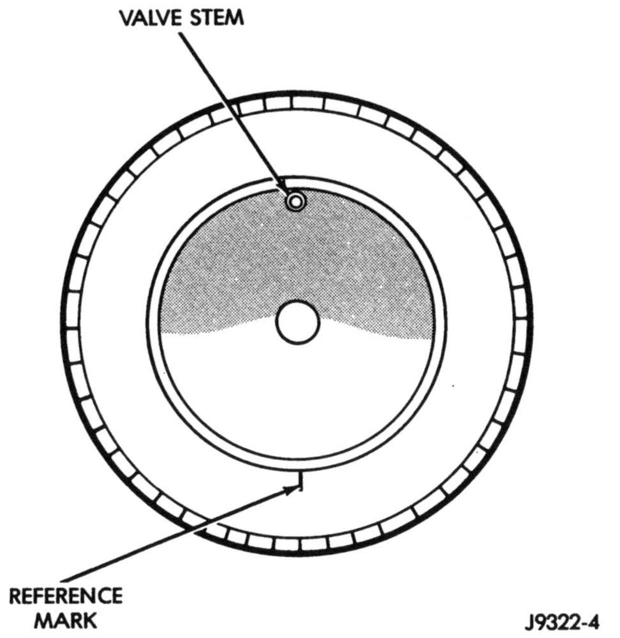

Fig. 8 Remount Tire 180 Degrees

(3) Measure the total indicator runout again. Mark the tire to indicate the high spot.

(4) If runout is still excessive, the following procedures must be done.

- If the high spot is within 101.6 mm (4.0 in.) of the first spot and is still excessive, replace the tire.
- If the high spot is within 101.6 mm (4.0 in.) of the first spot on the wheel, the wheel may be out of specifications. Refer to Wheel and Tire Runout.
- If the high spot is NOT within 101.6 mm (4.0 in.) of either high spot, draw an arrow on the tread from second high spot to first. Break down the tire and remount it 90 degrees on rim in that direction (Fig. 9). This procedure will normally reduce the runout to an acceptable amount.

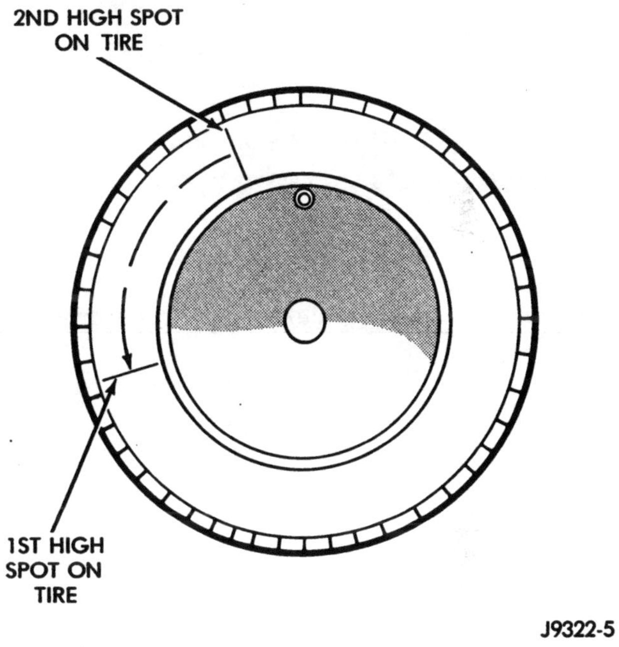

Fig. 9 Remount Tire 90 Degrees In Direction of Arrow

REPAIRING LEAKS

For proper repairing, a radial tire must be removed from the wheel. Repairs should only be made if the defect, or puncture, is in the tread area (Fig. 10). The tire should be replaced if the puncture is located in the sidewall.

Deflate tire completely before dismounting tire from the wheel. Use lubrication such as a mild soap solution when dismounting or mounting tire. Use tools free of burrs or sharp edges which could damage the tire or wheel rim.

Before mounting tire on wheel, make sure all rust is removed from the rim bead and repaint if necessary.

Install wheel on vehicle, and tighten to proper torque specification.

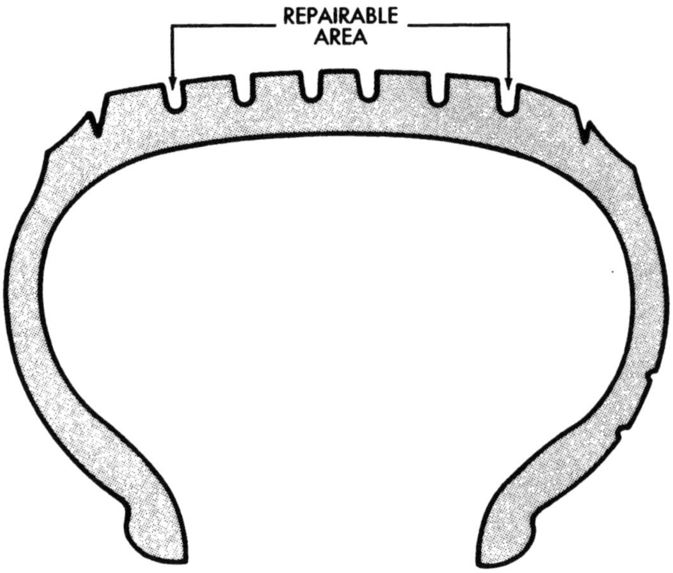

Fig. 10 Tire Repair Area

CLEANING AND INSPECTION

CLEANING OF TIRES

Remove protective coating on tires before delivery of vehicle. The coating could cause deterioration of tires.

Remove protective coating by:

- Applying warm water
- Letting it soak one minute
- Scrubbing the coating away with a soft bristle brush.
- Steam cleaning may also be used for cleaning.
- DO NOT use gasoline or wire brush for cleaning.
- DO NOT use mineral oil or an oil-based solvent.

WHEELS

INDEX

DESCRIPTION AND OPERATION

WHEEL

Available rim sizes are on the safety certification label located on the drivers door shut face.

Rim size is determined by the drivetrain package.

Original equipment wheels are designed for operation up to the specified maximum vehicle capacity.

All models use steel or cast aluminum wheels. Every wheel has raised sections between the rim flanges and rim drop well called safety humps (Fig. 1).

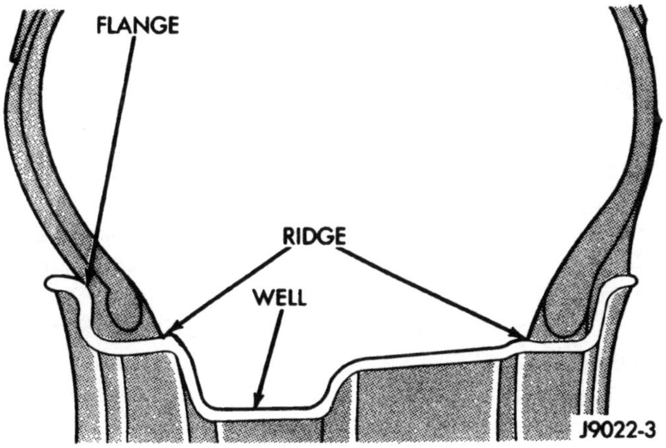

Fig. 1 Safety Rim

Initial inflation of the tire forces the bead over these raised sections. In case of rapid loss of air pressure, the raised sections help hold the tire on the wheel.

Cast aluminum wheels require coated balance weights and special alignment equipment.

The wheel studs and nuts are designed for specific applications and must be replaced with equivalent parts. Do not use replacement parts of lesser quality or a substitute design. All aluminum and some steel wheels have wheel stud nuts with an enlarged nose. This enlarged nose is necessary to ensure proper retention of the wheels.

Before installing the wheel, remove any build up of corrosion on the wheel mounting surfaces.

WARNING: INSTALLING WHEELS WITHOUT GOOD METAL-TO-METAL CONTACT COULD CAUSE LOOSENING OF WHEEL NUTS. THIS COULD ADVERSELY AFFECT THE SAFETY AND HANDLING OF YOUR VEHICLE.

DIAGNOSIS AND TESTING

WHEEL INSPECTION

Wheels must be replaced if they:

- Have excessive run out
- Are bent or dented
- Leak air
- Have damaged bolt holes

Wheel repairs employing hammering, heating, welding or repairing leaks are not allowed.

Original equipment replacement wheels should be used. When obtaining replacement wheels, they should be equivalent in load carrying capacity. The physical dimensions (diameter, width, offset, and bolt circle) of the wheel should be the same as the original wheel.

WARNING: FAILURE TO USE EQUIVALENT REPLACEMENT WHEELS MAY ADVERSELY AFFECT THE SAFETY AND HANDLING OF THE VEHICLE. REPLACEMENT WITH USED WHEELS IS NOT RECOMMENDED. THE SERVICE HISTORY OF THE RIM MAY HAVE INCLUDED SEVERE TREATMENT OR VERY HIGH MILEAGE. THE RIM COULD FAIL WITHOUT WARNING.

TIRE AND WHEEL RUNOUT

Radial runout is the difference between the high and low points on the tire or wheel (Fig. 2).

Lateral runout is the **wobble** of the tire or wheel.

DIAGNOSIS AND TESTING (Continued)

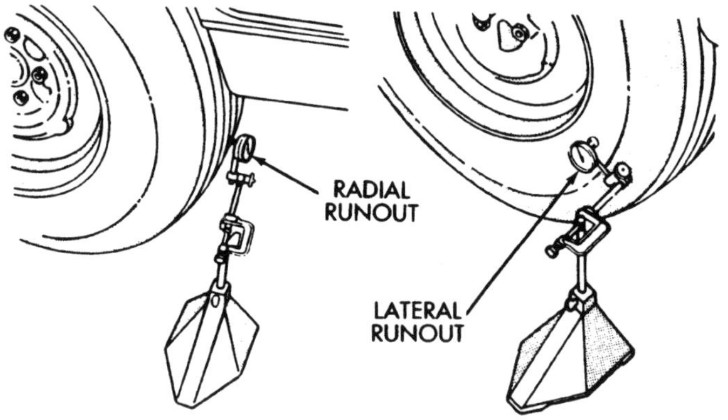

Fig. 2 Checking Tire Runout

Radial runout of more than 1.5 mm (.060 inch) measured at the center line of the tread may cause the vehicle to shake.

Lateral runout of more than 2.0 mm (.080 inch) measured near the shoulder of the tire may cause the vehicle to shake.

Sometimes radial runout can be reduced. Relocate the wheel and tire assembly on the mounting studs (See Method 1). If this does not reduce runout to an acceptable level, the tire can be rotated on the wheel. (See Method 2).

METHOD 1 (RELOCATE WHEEL ON HUB)

Check accuracy of the wheel mounting surface; adjust wheel bearings.

Drive vehicle a short distance to eliminate tire flat spotting from a parked position.

Make sure all wheel nuts are properly torqued.

Relocate wheel on the mounting, two studs over from the original position.

Re-tighten wheel nuts until all are properly torqued, to eliminate brake distortion.

Check radial runout. If still excessive, mark tire sidewall, wheel, and stud at point of maximum runout and proceed to Method 2.

METHOD 2 (RELOCATE TIRE ON WHEEL)

Rotating tire on wheel is particularly effective when there is runout in both tire and wheel.

Remove tire from wheel and re-mount wheel on hub in former position.

Check wheel radial runout (Fig. 3).

NOTE: If the vehicle is equipped with aluminum or full faced wheels the tire must be removed to check radial runout.

- STEEL WHEELS: Radial runout 0.040 in., Lateral runout 0.045 in.
- ALUMINUM WHEELS: Radial runout 0.030 in., Lateral runout 0.035 in.

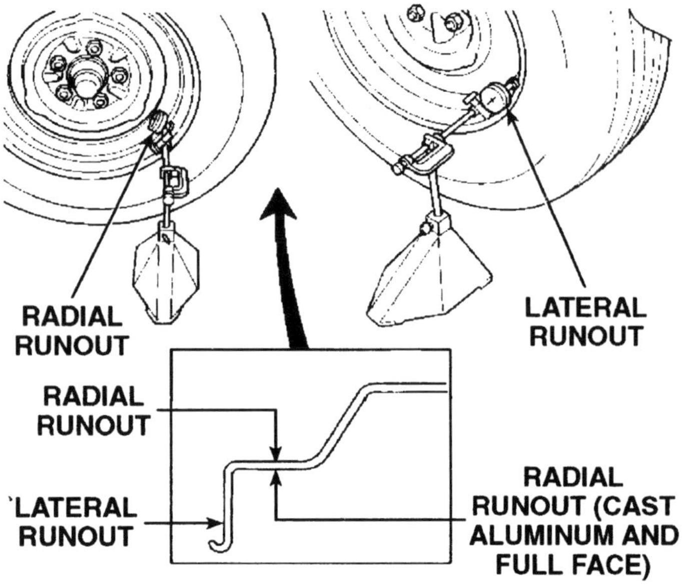

Fig. 3 Checking Wheel Runout

If point of greatest runout is near original chalk mark, remount tire 180 degrees. Recheck runout.

SERVICE PROCEDURES

WHEEL INSTALLATION

The wheel studs and nuts are designed for specific applications. They must be replaced with equivalent parts. Do not use replacement parts of lesser quality or a substitute design. All aluminum and some steel wheels have wheel stud nuts which feature an enlarged nose. This enlarged nose is necessary to ensure proper retention of the aluminum wheels.

NOTE: Do not use chrome plated lug nuts with chrome plated wheels.

Before installing the wheel, be sure to remove any build up of corrosion on the wheel mounting surfaces. Ensure wheels are installed with good metal-to-metal contact. Improper installation could cause loosening of wheel nuts. This could affect the safety and handling of your vehicle.

To install the wheel, first position it properly on the mounting surface. All wheel nuts should then be tightened just snug. Gradually tighten them in sequence to the proper torque specification (Fig. 4). **Never use oil or grease on studs or nuts.**

SERVICE PROCEDURES (Continued)

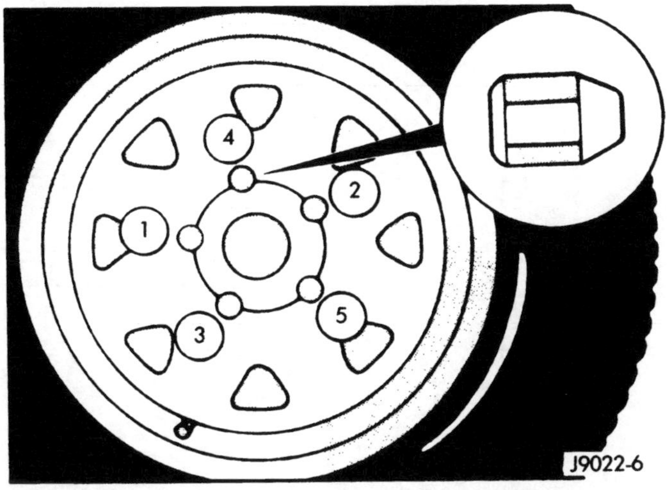

Fig. 4 Lug Nut Tightening Pattern

WHEEL REPLACEMENT

Wheels must be replaced if they have:

- Excessive runout
- Bent or dented
- Leak air through welds
- Have damaged bolt holes

Wheel repairs employing hammering, heating, or welding are not allowed.

Original equipment wheels are available through your dealer. Replacement wheels from any other source should be equivalent in:

- Load carrying capacity
- Diameter
- Width
- Offset
- Mounting configuration

Failure to use equivalent replacement wheels may affect the safety and handling of your vehicle. Replacement with **used** wheels is not recommended. Their service history may have included severe treatment.

TIRE AND WHEEL BALANCE

It is recommended that a two plane dynamic balancer be used when a wheel and tire assembly require balancing. Static should be used only when a two plane balancer is not available.

For static imbalance, find location of heavy spot causing imbalance. Counter balance wheel directly opposite the heavy spot. Determine weight required to counterbalance the area of imbalance. Place half of this weight on the **inner** rim flange and the other half on the **outer** rim flange (Fig. 5) and (Fig. 6). Off-vehicle balancing is necessary.

Wheel balancing can be accomplished with either on or off vehicle equipment. When using on-vehicle balancing equipment, remove the opposite wheel/tire.

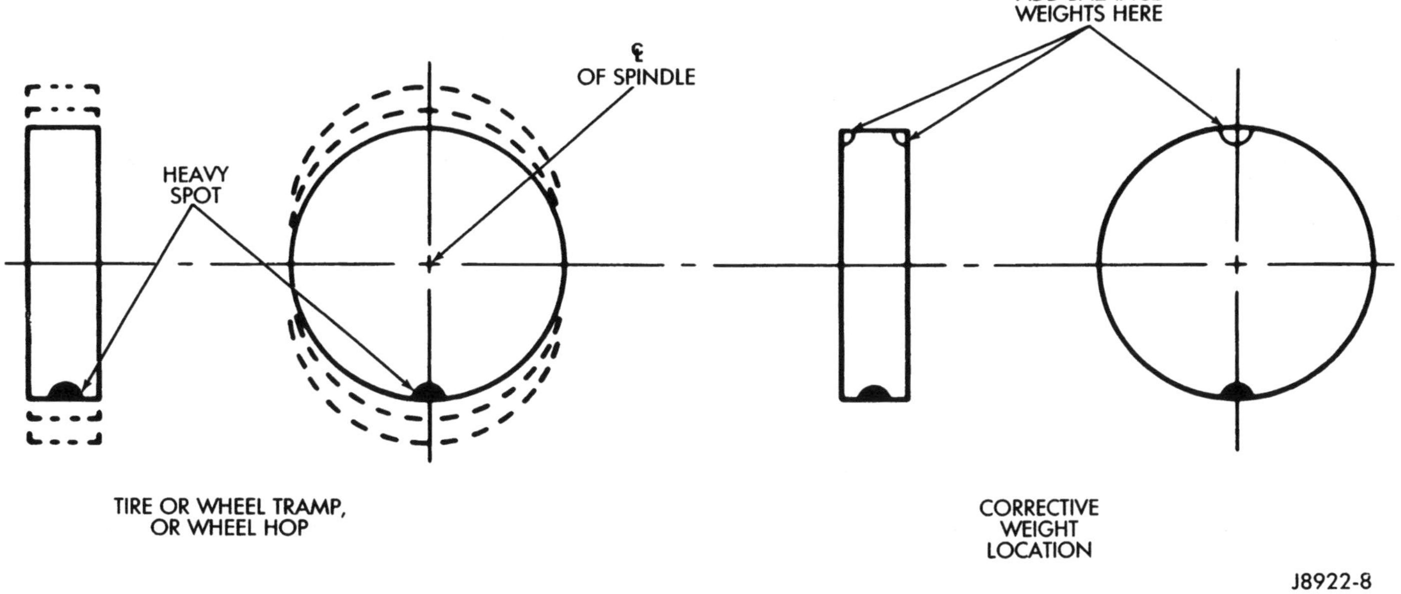

Fig. 5 Static Unbalance & Balance

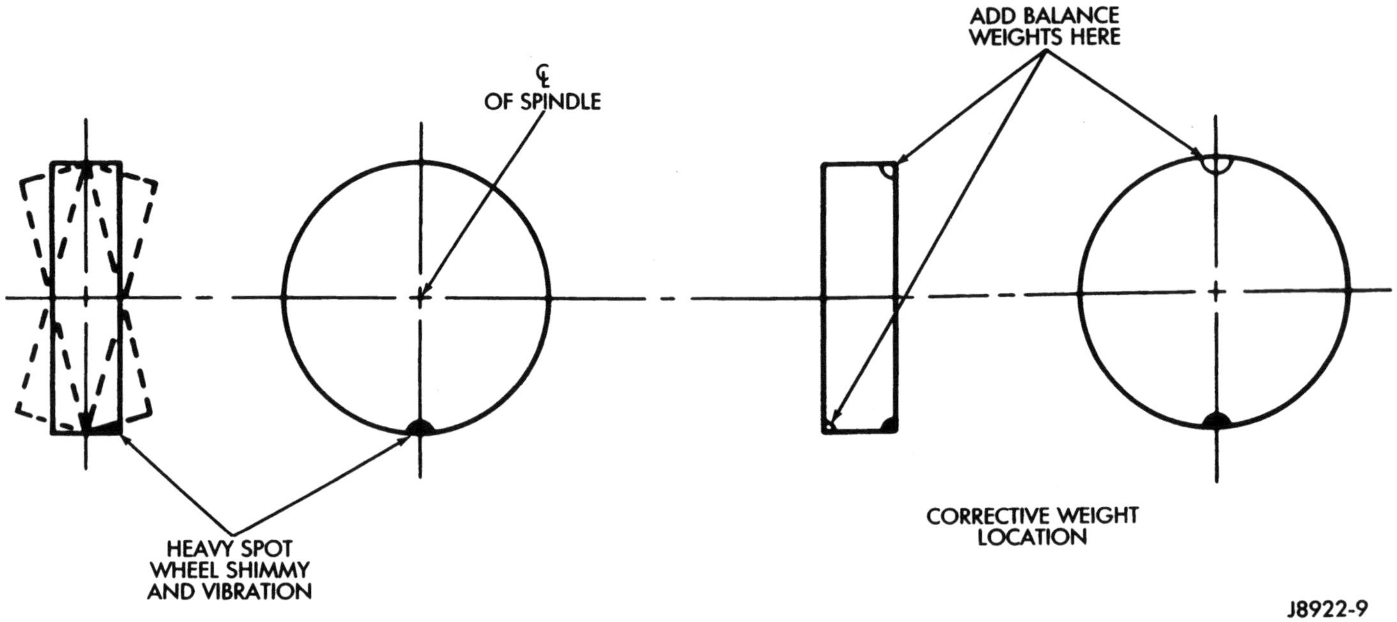

Fig. 6 Dynamic Unbalance & Balance

SPECIFICATIONS

TORQUE CHART

DESCRIPTION	TORQUE
Lug Nut	
1/2 X 20 with 60° Cone	109 to 150 N·m (80 to 110 ft. lbs.)

BODY

CONTENTS

GENERAL SERVICE INFORMATION

INDEX

GENERAL INFORMATION

SAFETY PRECAUTIONS AND WARNINGS

WARNING: EYE PROTECTION SHOULD BE USED WHEN SERVICING GLASS COMPONENTS. PERSONAL INJURY CAN RESULT.

USE A OSHA APPROVED BREATHING FILTER WHEN SPRAYING PAINT OR SOLVENTS IN A CONFINED AREA. PERSONAL INJURY CAN RESULT.

AVOID PROLONGED SKIN CONTACT WITH PETROLEUM OR ALCOHOL– BASED CLEANING SOLVENTS. PERSONAL INJURY CAN RESULT.

DO NOT STAND UNDER A HOISTED VEHICLE THAT IS NOT PROPERLY SUPPORTED ON SAFETY STANDS. PERSONAL INJURY CAN RESULT.

CAUTION: When holes must be drilled or punched in an inner body panel, verify depth of space to the outer body panel, electrical wiring, or other components. Damage to vehicle can result.

Do not weld exterior panels unless combustible material on the interior of vehicle is removed from the repair area. Fire or hazardous conditions, can result.

Always have a fire extinguisher ready for use when welding.

Disconnect the negative (-) cable clamp from the battery when servicing electrical components that are live when the ignition is OFF. Damage to electrical system can result.

Do not use abrasive chemicals or compounds on painted surfaces. Damage to finish can result.

Do not use harsh alkaline based cleaning solvents on painted or upholstered surfaces. Damage to finish or color can result.

Do not hammer or pound on plastic trim panel when servicing interior trim. Plastic panels can break.

Chrysler Corporation uses many different types of push-in fasteners to secure the interior and exterior trim to the body. Most of these fasteners can be reused to assemble the trim during various repair procedures. At times, a push-in fastener cannot be removed without damaging the fastener or the component it is holding. If it is not possible to remove a fastener without damaging a component or body, cut or break the fastener and use a new one when installing the component. Never pry or pound on a plastic or pressed-board trim component. Using a suitable fork-type prying device, pry the fastener from the retaining hole behind the component being removed. When installing, verify fastener alignment with the retaining hole by hand. Push directly on or over the fastener until it seats. Apply a low-force pull to the panel to verify that it is secure.

When it is necessary to remove components to service another, it should not be necessary to apply excessive force or bend a component to remove it. Before damaging a trim component, verify hidden fasteners or captured edges holding the component in place.

PAINT

INDEX

GENERAL INFORMATION

PAINT CODE

Exterior vehicle body colors are identified on the Body Code plate. The plate is located on the floor pan under the driver's seat. Refer to the Introduction section at the front of this manual for, body code plate description. The paint code is also identified on the Vehicle Safety Certification Label, which is located on the driver's door shut face The color names, provided in the Paint and Trim Code Description chart, are the color names used on most repair product containers.

BASE COAT/CLEAR COAT FINISH

On most vehicles a two-stage paint application (base coat/clear coat) is used. Color that is applied to primer is called base coat. The clear coat protects the base coat from ultraviolet light and provides a durable high-gloss finish.

FINESSE SANDING, BUFFING, AND POLISHING

Minor acid etching, orange peel, or surface scratches in clear coat or single-stage finishes can be reduced with light finesse sanding, buffing, and polishing. **If the finish has been wet sanded in the past, it cannot be repeated. Wet sanding operation should be performed by a trained automotive paint technician.**

CAUTION: Do not remove clear coat finish more than .5 mils, if equipped (Use a paint thickness gauge to verify paint thickness). Base coat paint must retain clear coat for durability.

PAINTED SURFACE TOUCHUP

When a painted metal surface has been scratched or chipped, it should be touched-up as soon as possible to avoid corrosion. For best results, use Mopar® Scratch Filler/Primer, Touch-Up Paints and Clear Top Coat. Refer to Introduction group of this manual for Body Code Plate information.

TOUCHUP PROCEDURE

(1) Scrape loose paint and corrosion from inside scratch or chip.

(2) Clean affected area with Mopar® Tar/Road Oil Remover, and allow to dry.

(3) Fill the inside of the scratch or chip with a coat of filler/primer. Do not overlap primer onto good surface finish. The applicator brush should be wet enough to puddle-fill the defect without running. Do not stroke brush applicator on body surface. Allow the filler/primer to dry hard.

(4) Cover the filler/primer with color touch-up paint. Do not overlap touchup color onto the original color coat around the scratch or chip. Butt the new color to the original color, if possible. Do not stroke applicator brush on body surface. Allow touchup paint to dry hard.

(5) On vehicles without clear coat, the touchup color can be lightly wet sanded (600 grit) and polished with rubbing compound.

(6) On vehicles with clear coat, apply clear top coat to touchup paint with the same technique as described in Step 4. Allow clear top coat to dry hard. If desired, Step 5 can be performed on clear top coat.

GENERAL INFORMATION (Continued)

AFTERMARKET PAINT REPAIR PRODUCTS

1997 EXTERIOR COLOR

EXTERIOR COLOR	CHRY CODE *	PPG	BASF	DuPONT	S-W ACME M-S	AKZO/NOBEL SIKKENS
Flame Red Clear Coat	PR4	4679	23043	B9326	46916	CHA93:PR4
Magenta Clear Coat	SH1	74171	26079	B9615	51522	CHA96:SH1
Citron Pearl Coat	SJV	47694	26081	B9672	51524	CHA96:SJV
Light Pearlstone Pearl Coat	HV1	4189	22125	B8952	41824	CHA89:HV1
Moss Green Pearl Coat	RJN	47383	25036	B9533	50277	CHA95:RJN
Emerald Green Pearl Coat	PGF	4785	24075	B9460	48539	CHA94:PGF
Bright Jade Satin Glow	SQP	47586	26088	B9636	51533	CHA96:SQP
Lapis Blue Clear Coat	RC4	4935	24098	B9531	50218	CHA95:RC4
Dark Blue Pearl Coat	PCJ	4783	24072	B9453	48543	CHA94:PCJ
Black Clear Coat	DX8	9700	15214	99	34858 90-5950	CHA85:DX8
Stone White Clear Coat	SW1	83542	26089	B9622	51539	CHA96:SW1

NOTE: * Herberts Standox and Spies Hecker use the Chrysler paint code as listed on the Body Code Plate.

1996 INTERIOR COLOR

INTERIOR COLOR	CHRY CODE	PPG	BASF	DuPONT	S-W ACME M-S
Mist Gray	C3	35799 / 2-1576	25065	C9507	50508
Saddle	T6	27917 / 2-1594	26121	C9604	51542
Saddle / Moss Green	TJ	N/A	26121 25069	C9604 C9513	51542 50512

SERVICE PROCEDURES

HARD TOP REPAIR

The hard top fiberglass material can be repaired. The required repair materials include:

- Fiberglass mat or cloth.
- Fiberglass resin and hardener.
- structural adhesive (3M brand or an equivalent product).
- Glazing putty.
- Plastic spreader.

HARD TOP HOLE REPAIR

(1) Use a grinder to remove the paint and outline the damaged area. Use a grade 24 grit disc for paint removal.

(2) Grind the outlined surface area again with a 50 grit disc to prevent coarse scratches from appearing in the final finish.

(3) If cracks extend from the hole, it will be necessary to stop-drill the crack(s) with a 3-mm (1/8-in) diameter drill bit.

(4) Position a fiberglass mat or cloth on the repair surface area. Cut the mat to allow a 2.5-cm (1-in) overlap of the repair surface area.

(5) Clean the repair surface area.

(6) Place the fiberglass cloth on aluminum foil.

(7) Pour the fiberglass resin into a clean container.

(8) Mix the appropriate amount of hardener and resin. Follow the manufacturers instructions.

(9) Apply the hardener/resin mixture to both sides of the fiberglass cloth.

(10) Place the fiberglass cloth over the repair surface area. Next, place the aluminum foil over the cloth. Use a plastic spreader to smooth-out the cloth and resin. Use firm pressure to remove air bubbles and to smooth-out the cloth.

(11) Allow the resin to cure.

SERVICE PROCEDURES (Continued)

(12) Smooth-out the surface area to the contour of the hard top with a 50-grit disc.
(13) Apply plastic filler to complete the repair. Finish smoothing the surface area with 80-grit paper.
(14) Repeat the previous step on the inside surface area of the hard top.
(15) Featheredge the repaired surface area.
(16) Prime the repaired surface area with PPG Epoxy Primer, or an equivalent product.
(17) Apply surface primer to the surface area.
(18) Prime the surface area for the color coat.
(19) Apply color coat to the repaired surface area.

FRACTURE REPAIR

(1) Use a grinder to remove the paint (from both, the inner and outer surface areas of the hard top) and to outline the damaged area.
(2) Stop-drill the crack(s) with a 3-mm (1/8-in) diameter drill bit.
(3) Bevel the edges of the crack(s) on both sides with a rotary file.

NOTE: The edges should be beveled on the inside and outside of the top to ensure sufficient surface area for good bonding.

(4) Complete the repairs with fiberglass cloth and resin as described above in the hard top hole repair procedure.

STATIONARY GLASS

INDEX

GENERAL INFORMATION

SAFETY PRECAUTIONS

WARNING: DO NOT OPERATE THE VEHICLE WITHIN 24 HOURS OF WINDSHIELD INSTALLATION. IT TAKES AT LEAST 24 HOURS FOR URETHANE ADHESIVE TO CURE. IF IT IS NOT CURED, THE WINDSHIELD MAY NOT PERFORM PROPERLY IN AN ACCIDENT.

URETHANE ADHESIVES ARE APPLIED AS A SYSTEM. USE GLASS CLEANER, GLASS PREP SOLVENT, GLASS PRIMER, PVC (VINYL) PRIMER AND PINCHWELD (FENCE) PRIMER PROVIDED BY THE ADHESIVE MANUFACTURER. IF NOT, STRUCTURAL INTEGRITY COULD BE COMPROMISED.

BE SURE TO REFER TO THE URETHANE MANUFACTURER'S DIRECTIONS FOR CURING TIME SPECIFICATIONS, AND DO NOT USE ADHESIVE AFTER ITS EXPIRATION DATE.

VAPORS THAT ARE EMITTED FROM THE URETHANE ADHESIVE OR PRIMER COULD CAUSE PERSONAL INJURY. USE THEM IN A WELL-VENTILATED AREA.

SKIN CONTACT WITH URETHANE ADHESIVE SHOULD BE AVOIDED. PERSONAL INJURY MAY RESULT.

ALWAYS WEAR EYE AND HAND PROTECTION WHEN WORKING WITH GLASS.

CAUTION: Protect all painted and trimmed surfaces from coming in contact with urethane or primers.

Be careful not to damage painted surfaces when removing moldings or cutting urethane around windshield.

It is difficult to salvage a windshield during the removal operation. The urethane bonding used to secure the windshield to the fence is difficult to cut or clean from any surface. If the moldings are set in urethane, it would also be unlikely they could be salvaged. Before removing the windshield, check the availability of the windshield and moldings from the parts supplier.

REMOVAL AND INSTALLATION

WINDSHIELD

The windshield is positioned in the reveal molding and is bonded to the windshield frame with urethane adhesive. The windshield interior trim molding is positioned onto the inner windshield frame pinchweld.

REMOVAL

(1) Cover body surface areas with protective covering to avoid paint damage and extra clean-up time.

(2) Remove the windshield wiper arms and the rearview mirror.

(3) Using a razor knife, slide the blade between the windshield glass and the inboard edge of the reveal molding.

(4) Cut around the interior perimeter of the reveal molding and sever the cap of the reveal molding.

(5) Using a cold knife, cut the urethane around the perimeter of the windshield (Fig. 1).

(6) Remove the windshield glass from the frame (Fig. 2).

INSTALLATION

(1) Trim the urethane from the pinchweld flanges. Leave a 3 mm (0.1 in.) level base of urethane on the pinchweld flanges.

(2) Place replacement windshield into windshield opening and position glass in the center of the opening against pinchweld flange.

(3) Verify the glass lays evenly against the pinch weld fence at the sides, top and bottom of the replacement windshield. If not, the pinchweld flange must be formed to the shape of the new glass. Next, make alignment marks on glass and body with a grease pencil.

(4) Remove replacement windshield from windshield opening.

REMOVAL AND INSTALLATION (Continued)

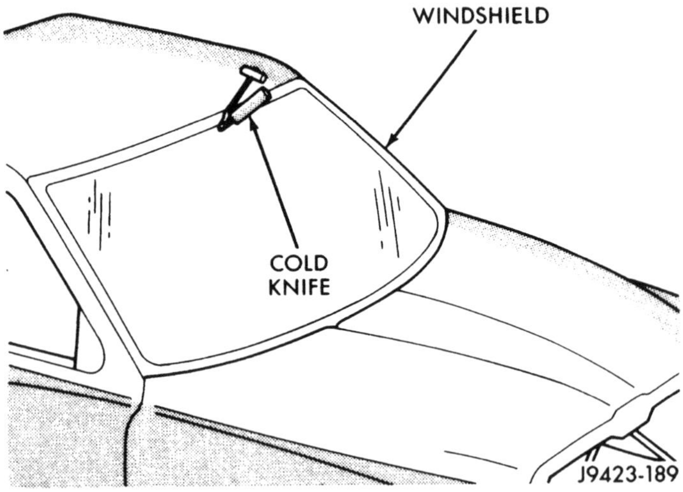

Fig. 1 Cutting Urethane Around Windshield—Typical

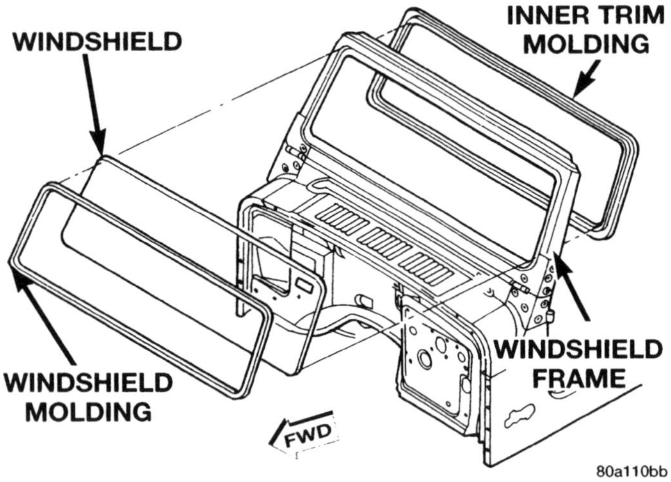

Fig. 2 Windshield

(5) Position the windshield inside up on a suitable work surface with two padded, wood 10 cm by 10 cm by 50 cm (4 in. by 4 in. by 20 in.) blocks, placed parallel 75 cm (2.5 ft.) apart (Fig. 3).

WARNING: DO NOT USE SOLVENT BASED GLASS CLEANER TO CLEAN WINDSHIELD BEFORE APPLYING GLASS PREP AND PRIMER. POOR ADHESION CAN RESULT.

(6) Clean inside of windshield with ammonia based glass cleaner and lint-free cloth.

(7) Apply molding to perimeter of windshield. The butt weld of the molding should be centered at the bottom edge of the windshield.

(8) Apply Glass Prep adhesion promoter 25 mm (1 in.) wide around perimeter of windshield and wipe with clean/dry lint-free cloth until no streaks are visible.

(9) Apply Glass Primer 25 mm (1 in.) wide around perimeter of windshield. Allow at least three minutes drying time.

(10) Apply Pinchweld primer 15 mm (.75 in.) wide around the windshield fence. Allow at least three minutes drying time.

(11) Apply a 10 mm (0.4 in.) diameter bead of urethane on the pinchweld flange surface area 6 mm (.25 in.) from the outboard edge.

CAUTION: Be prepared to install the windshield glass immediately after applying the adhesive. The adhesive begins to cure within 10-15 minutes.

(12) Align the windshield with the grease pencil marks and position windshield on pinchweld flanges.

(13) Push the windshield glass inward until the reveal molding is seated on the windshield frame. Use care to avoid excessive squeeze-out of adhesive.

(14) Open windows and liftgate to prevent pressure build-up while the urethane is curing.

(15) Apply 150 mm (6 in.) lengths of 50 mm (2 in.) masking tape spaced 250 mm (10 in.) apart to hold windshield in place until urethane cures.

(16) Install the rearview mirror on the mirror button.

(17) Install the wiper arms.

(18) After urethane has cured, remove tape strips and water test windshield to verify repair.

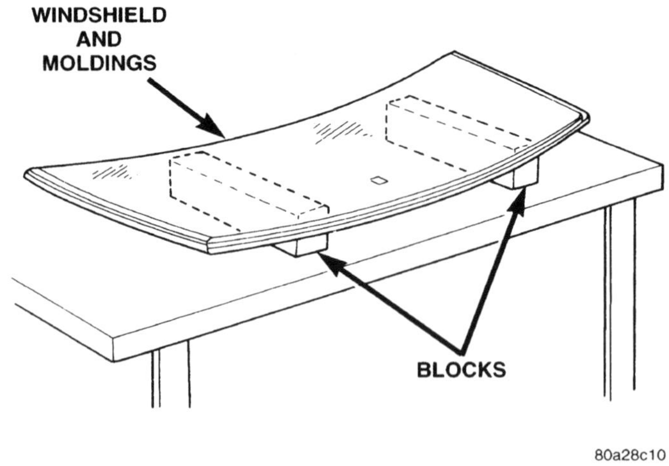

Fig. 3 Work Surface Set up and Molding Installation

QUARTER GLASS

REMOVAL

(1) Cover surface areas with protective covering to avoid paint damage and extra clean-up time.

(2) Using a razor knife, slide the blade between the quarter glass and the inboard edge of the reveal molding.

(3) Cut around the interior perimeter of the reveal molding and sever the cap of the reveal molding.

REMOVAL AND INSTALLATION (Continued)

(4) Using a cold knife, cut the urethane around the perimeter of the quarter glass.

(5) Remove the quarter glass from the opening (Fig. 4).

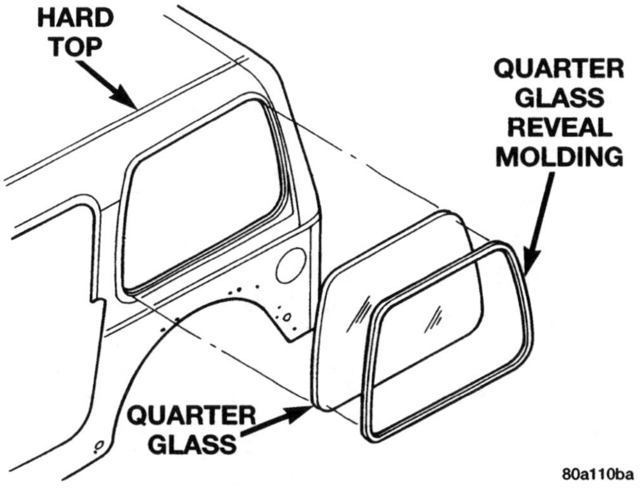

Fig. 4 Hard Top Quarter Glass

INSTALLATION

(1) Trim the urethane from the quarter glass opening fence. Leave a 3 mm (0.1 in.) level base of urethane on the quarter glass opening fence.

(2) Place replacement quarter glass into quarter glass opening and position glass in the center of the opening against fence.

(3) Verify the glass lays evenly against the fence at the sides, top and bottom of the replacement quarter glass. Next, make alignment marks on glass and top with a grease pencil.

(4) Remove replacement quarter glass from opening.

(5) Position the quarter glass inside up on a suitable work surface.

WARNING: DO NOT USE SOLVENT BASED GLASS CLEANER TO CLEAN QUARTER GLASS BEFORE APPLYING GLASS PREP AND PRIMER. POOR ADHESION CAN RESULT.

(6) Clean inside of quarter glass with ammonia based glass cleaner and lint-free cloth.

(7) Clean the outer edge of the window glass with naphtha or a similar product.

(8) Apply molding to perimeter of quarter glass. The butt weld of the molding should be centered at the bottom edge of the quarter glass.

(9) Apply Glass Prep adhesion promoter 25 mm (1 in.) wide around perimeter of the quarter glass and wipe with clean/dry lint-free cloth until no streaks are visible.

(10) Apply Glass Primer 25 mm (1 in.) wide around perimeter of quarter glass. Allow at least three minutes drying time.

(11) Apply Pinchweld primer 15 mm (.75 in.) wide around the quarter glass fence. Allow at least three minutes drying time.

(12) Apply a 10 mm (0.4 in.) diameter bead of urethane to the center of the quarter glass fence surface area.

CAUTION: Be prepared to install the quarter glass immediately after applying the adhesive. The adhesive begins to cure within 10-15 minutes.

(13) Align the quarter glass with the grease pencil marks and position quarter glass on fence.

(14) Push the quarter glass inward until the reveal molding is seated on the hardtop. Use care to avoid excessive squeeze-out of adhesive.

(15) Open windows and liftgate to prevent pressure build-up while the urethane is curing.

(16) Apply 150 mm (6 in.) lengths of 50 mm (2 in.) masking tape spaced 250 mm (10 in.) apart to hold quarter glass in place until urethane cures.

(17) After urethane has cured, remove tape strips and water test quarter glass to verify repair.

SEATS

INDEX

REMOVAL AND INSTALLATION

BUCKET SEATBACK

REMOVAL

(1) Remove seat.

(2) Remove the inboard seatback pivot bolt.

(3) Disengage the retainers attaching the cushion cover to the outboard seat cushion frame (Fig. 1).

(4) Disengage the seat cushion corner cover zipper.

(5) Remove the bolts attaching the recliner to the seat cushion frame (Fig. 2).

(6) Passenger seat only:

(a) From the underside of the seat cushion, disengage the seat track release cable (Fig. 3).

(b) Disengage recliner release cable (Fig. 4) from the seat back pivot bracket.

(7) Route the recliner handle through the seat cushion cover and separate the seatback from the seat cushion.

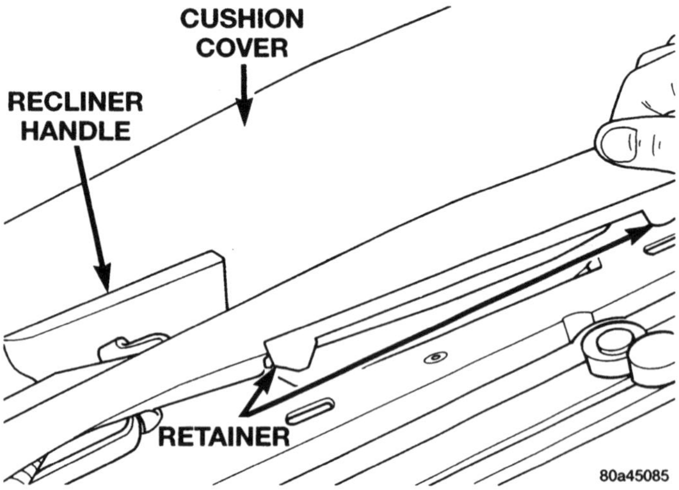

Fig. 1 Cushion Cover Retainers

INSTALLATION

(1) Position the seatback on the seat cushion while routing the recliner handle through the cushion cover opening.

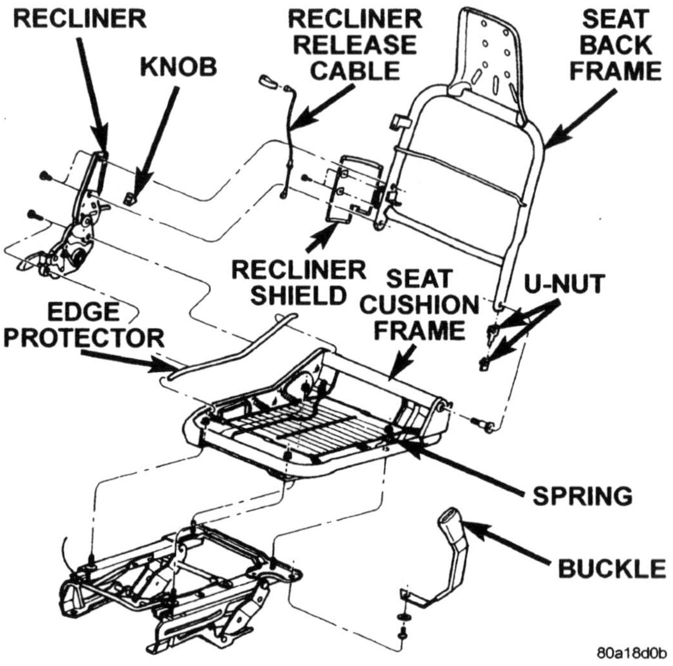

Fig. 2 Passenger Seat

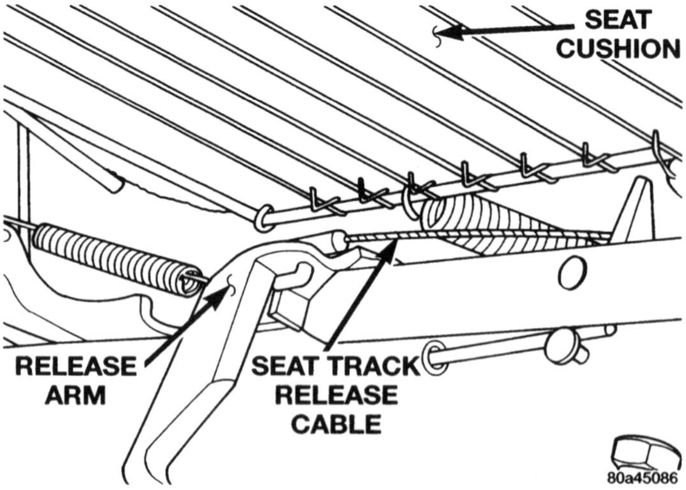

Fig. 3 Seat Track Release Cable

(2) Passenger seat only:

(a) Engage recliner release cable to the seat back pivot bracket.

REMOVAL AND INSTALLATION (Continued)

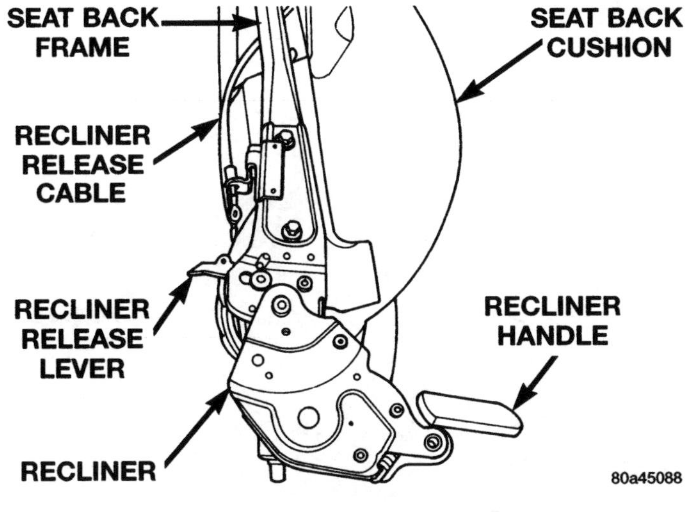

Fig. 4 Recliner Release Cable

(b) From the underside of the seat cushion, engage the seat track release cable.

(3) Install the bolts attaching the recliner to the seat cushion frame.

(4) Engage the seat cushion corner cover zipper.

(5) Engage the retainers attaching the cushion cover to the outboard seat cushion frame.

(6) Install the inboard seatback pivot bolt.

(7) Install seat.

BUCKET SEATBACK COVER

REMOVAL

(1) Remove seat.

(2) Remove seatback.

(3) Disengage zipper at seatback base.

(4) Using a trim stick, carefully pry off tilt release knob.

(5) Roll cover upward and over tilt release lever.

(6) Continue to roll cover upward and disengage hook and loop fastener (Fig. 5).

(7) Passenger seat only:

(a) Route recliner release cable/strap through cover.

(8) Separate cover from seatback.

INSTALLATION

(1) Position cover on seatback.

(2) Passenger seat only:

(a) Route recliner release cable/strap through cover.

(3) Roll cover downward and engage hook and loop fastener.

(4) Roll cover over tilt release lever.

(5) Install tilt release knob.

(6) Engage zipper at seatback base.

(7) Install seatback.

(8) Install seat.

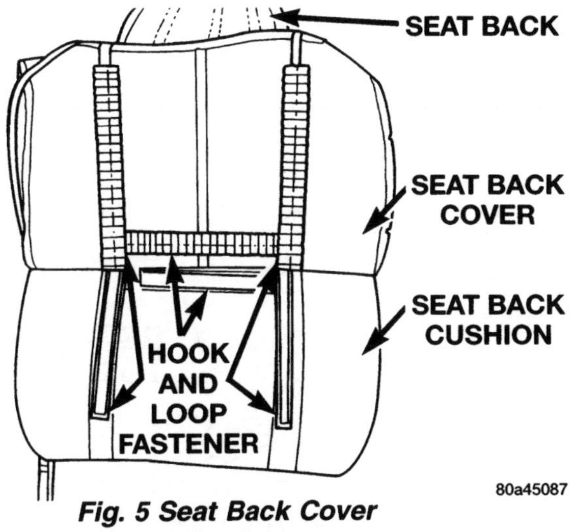

Fig. 5 Seat Back Cover

BUCKET SEAT CUSHION COVER

REMOVAL

(1) Remove seat.

(2) Remove seatback.

(3) Disengage inboard J-strap.

(4) Disengage front J-strap.

(5) Roll cover up to access hog rings.

(6) Disengage inboard, outboard and front hog rings.

(7) From the underside of the cushion, disengage the rear hog rings (Fig. 6).

(8) Separate cover from cushion.

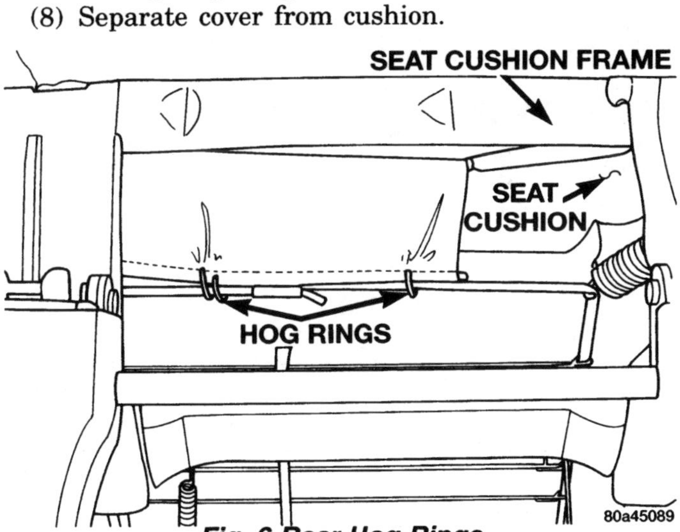

Fig. 6 Rear Hog Rings

INSTALLATION

(1) Position cover on cushion and align seams.

(2) From the underside of the cushion, engage the rear hog rings.

(3) Engage inboard, outboard and front hog rings.

(4) Roll cover over cushion edges and engage front J-strap.

(5) Engage inboard J-strap.

(6) Engage front J-strap.

(7) Install seatback.

(8) Install seat.

REMOVAL AND INSTALLATION (Continued)

REAR SEATBACK

REMOVAL

(1) Remove rear seat from vehicle.
(2) Remove torx bolts attaching seatback to seat cushion (Fig. 7).
(3) Separate the seat back from the seat cushion.

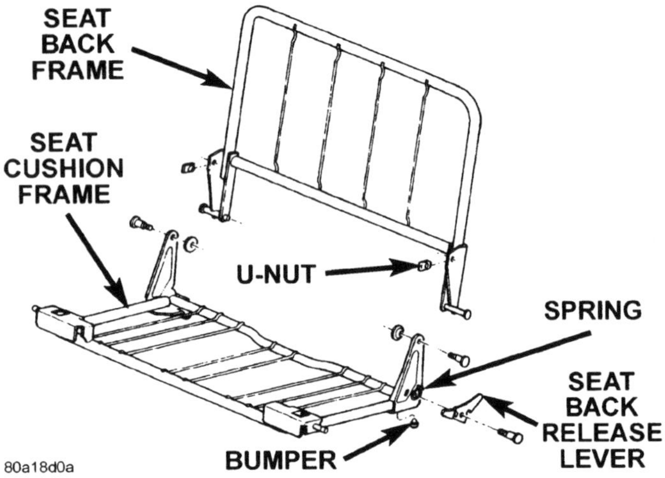

Fig. 7 Rear Seat Components

INSTALLATION

(1) Position the seat back on the seat cushion.
(2) Install the torx bolts attaching seatback to seat cushion.
(3) Install rear seat.

REAR SEATBACK COVER

REMOVAL

(1) Remove rear seat.
(2) Remove the seatback.
(3) Disengage the hook and loop fasteners at the seatback lower corners (Fig. 8).
(4) Disengage the seatback cover zipper.
(5) Carefully, remove the seatback frame from the cushion/cover.
(6) Roll the seatback cover upward and disengage the hook and loop fasteners.

INSTALLATION

(1) Position the cover on the seatback cushion.
(2) Roll the seatback cover downward over the cushion.
(3) Install the seatback frame into the cushion/cover.
(4) Engage the seatback cover zipper.
(5) Engage the hook and loop fasteners at the seat-back lower corners.
(6) Install the seatback.
(7) Install rear seat.

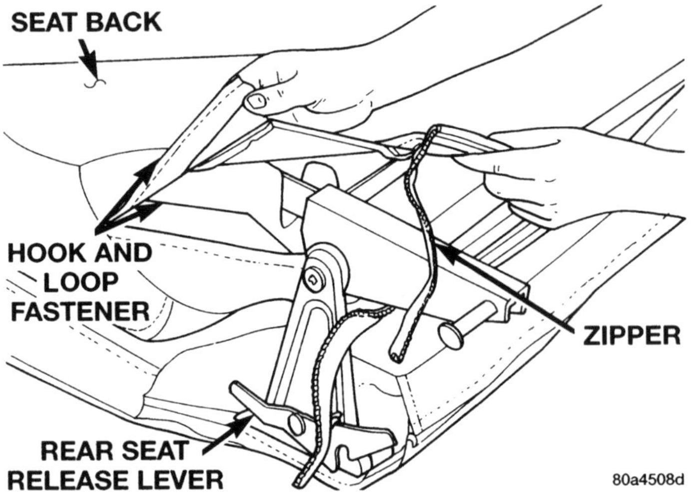

Fig. 8 Seat Back Cover

REAR SEAT CUSHION COVER

REMOVAL

(1) Remove rear seat.
(2) Remove the seatback.
(3) Disengage the J-straps at the rear cushion corners.
(4) Disengage the seat cushion cover zipper.
(5) Carefully, remove the seat cushion frame from the cushion/cover.
(6) Roll the cover from seat cushion and disengage the hook and loop fasteners (Fig. 9).

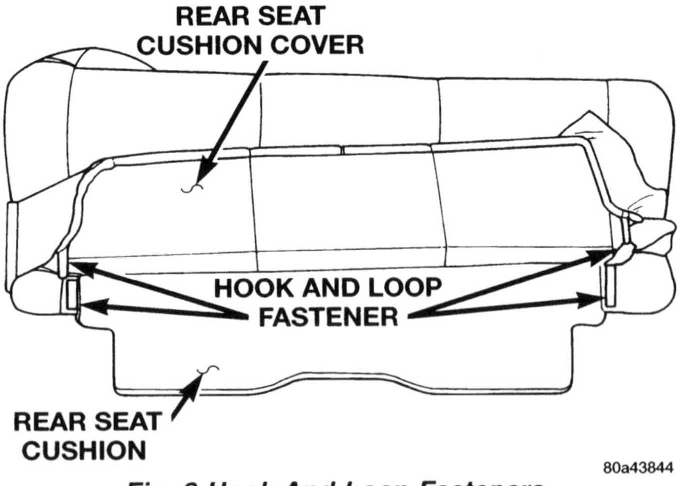

Fig. 9 Hook And Loop Fasteners

INSTALLATION

(1) Position the cover on the cushion and roll cover downward over the corners.
(2) Install the seat cushion frame into the cushion/cover.
(3) Engage the seat cushion cover zipper.
(4) Engage the J-straps at the rear cushion corners.
(5) Install the seatback.
(6) Install rear seat.

BODY COMPONENT SERVICE

INDEX

SERVICE PROCEDURES

BODY LUBRICATION

All mechanisms and linkages should be lubricated when necessary. This will maintain ease of operation and provide protection against rust and excessive wear. The weatherstrip seals should be lubricated to prolong their life as well as to improve door sealing.

All applicable exterior and interior vehicle operating mechanisms should be inspected and cleaned. Pivot/sliding contact areas on the mechanisms should then be lubricated.

(1) When necessary, lubricate the operating mechanisms with the specified lubricants.

(2) Apply silicone lubricant to a cloth and wipe it on door seals to avoid over-spray that can soil passenger's clothing.

(3) Before applying lubricant, the component should be wiped clean. After lubrication, any excess lubricant should be removed.

(4) The hood latch, latch release mechanism, latch striker, and safety latch should be lubricated periodically.

(5) The door lock cylinders should be lubricated twice each year (preferably autumn and spring):

- Spray a small amount of lock cylinder lubricant directly into the lock cylinder.
- Apply a small amount to the key and insert it into the lock cylinder.
- Rotate it to the locked position and then back to the unlocked position several times.
- Remove the key. Wipe the lubricant from it with a clean cloth to avoid soiling of clothing.

REMOVAL AND INSTALLATION

RADIATOR GRILLE PANEL

REMOVAL

(1) Remove the front crossmember cover.

(2) Remove the crossmember valence cover.

(3) Remove the radiator overflow bottle.

(4) Remove the bolts that attach the radiator and shroud from the grille panel.

(5) If A/C equipped:

(a) Evacuate the system.

(b) Disconnect the high and low pressure lines at the quick disconnect couplings.

(c) Cover (cap) the lines to prevent contamination.

(6) Remove the bolts attaching the radiator support rods to the grille panel.

(7) Disconnect the head lamp, turn signal, marker lamp and horn wire harness connectors.

(8) Remove the bolts attaching the fenders to the grille panel.

(9) Remove the bolt attaching the grille to the frame mount.

(10) Separate the grille from the vehicle.

INSTALLATION

Transfer all related components.

(1) Position the grille panel on the vehicle. Ensure the rubber support bumpers are aligned (Fig. 1).

(2) Install the bolt attaching the grille to the frame mount.

(3) Install the bolts attaching the fenders to the grille panel.

(4) Connect the head lamp, turn signal, marker lamp and horn wire harness connectors.

(5) Install the bolts attaching the radiator support rods to the grille panel.

(6) If A/C equipped:

(a) Connect the high and low pressure lines at the quick disconnect couplings.

(b) Evacuate and charge the system.

(7) Install the radiator and shroud to the grille panel.

(8) Install the radiator overflow bottle.

(9) Install the crossmember valence cover.

(10) Install the front crossmember cover.

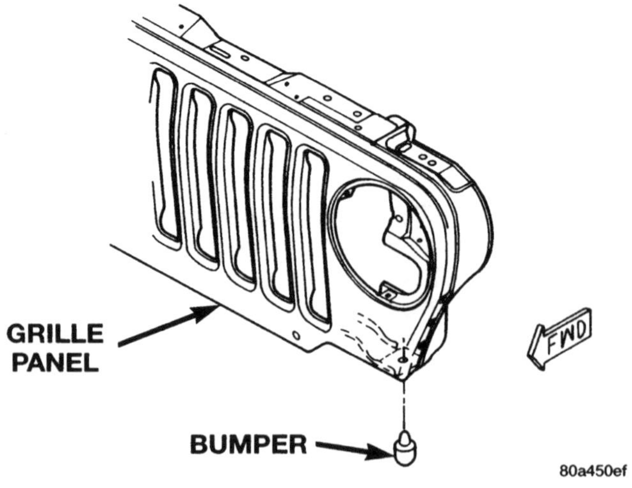

Fig. 1 Grille Bumpers

REMOVAL AND INSTALLATION (Continued)

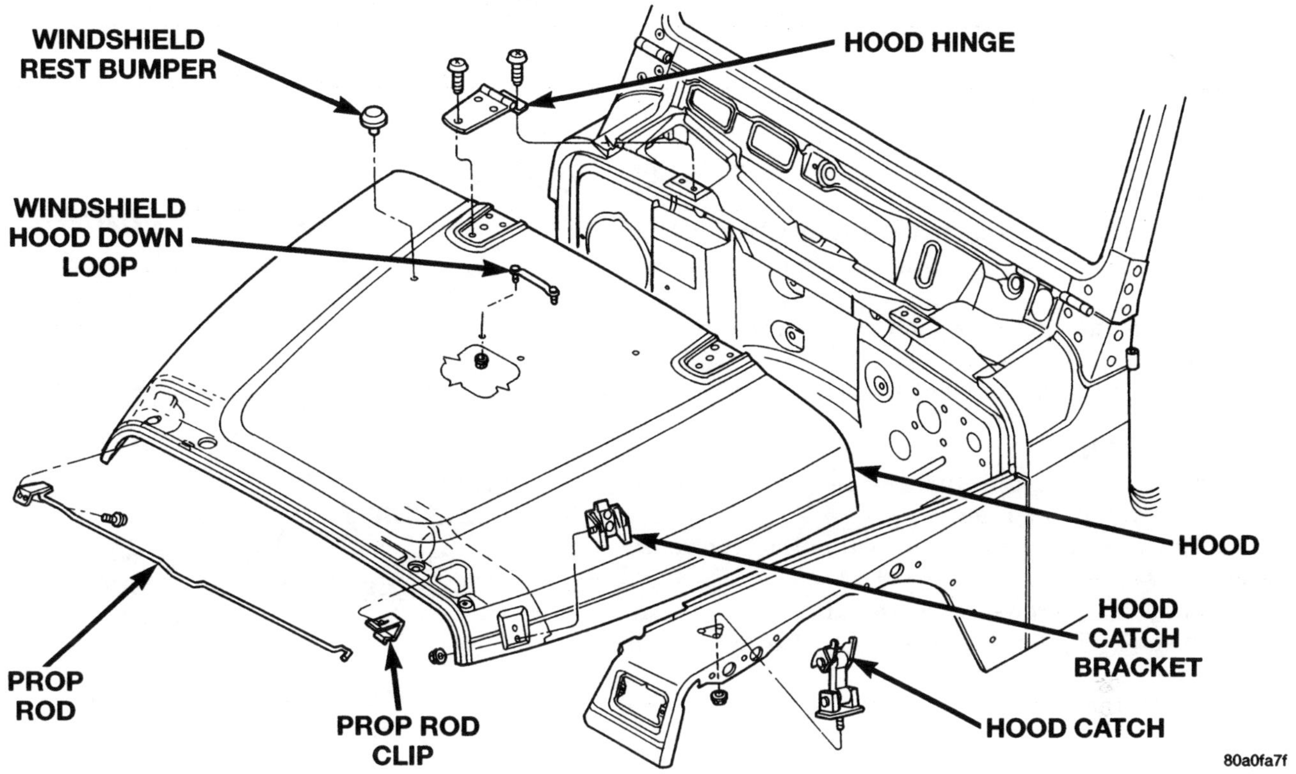

Fig. 2 Hood Components

HOOD

REMOVAL

(1) Raise and support the hood.
(2) Disconnect the underhood lamp wire harness connector.
(3) Disconnect the windshield washer nozzles.
(4) Disconnect the ground strap.
(5) Mark the position of the hinges on the hood for installation alignment reference.
(6) Remove the screws attaching the hood to the hinge and remove the hood (Fig. 2).
(7) If the hood must be replaced, remove and transfer the insulator panel, hinges, latches, bumpers, brackets, footman loop, hood lamp, support rod, and safety latch to the replacement hood (Fig. 2).

INSTALLATION

(1) Position the hood on the vehicle and install the screws attaching the hinge to the hood.
(2) Align the hinges with the installation reference marks on the hood and tighten the hinge screws securely.
(3) Connect the underhood lamp wire harness connector.
(4) Connect the windshield washer nozzles.
(5) Connect the ground strap.
(6) Close the hood.

HOOD INSULATION PANEL

REMOVAL

(1) Raise and support the hood.
(2) Remove the insulation panel fasteners (Fig. 3).
(3) Remove the insulation panel from the hood.

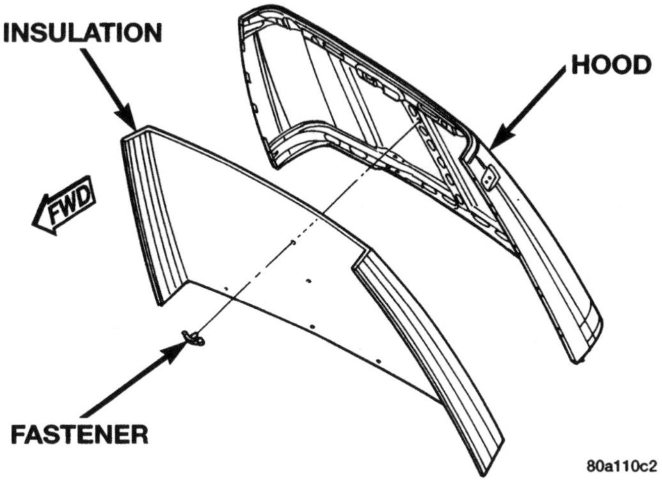

Fig. 3 Hood Insulation Panel

INSTALLATION

(1) Position the insulation panel on the hood.
(2) Install the insulation panel fasteners.
(3) Remove the support rod and close the hood.

REMOVAL AND INSTALLATION (Continued)

HOOD HINGE

REMOVAL

(1) Remove the wiper arms.
(2) Remove the cowl panel and screen.
(3) Remove the bolts attaching the hinge to the cowl.
(4) Using a wax pencil, mark the position of the hinge on the hood for installation alignment reference.
(5) Remove the screws attaching the hinge to the hood (Fig. 2).
(6) Separate the hinge from the hood.

INSTALLATION

(1) Prepare and paint the replacement hinge to match the body paint color.
(2) Align the hinge with the installation reference marks on the hood
(3) Install the screws attaching the hinge to the hood and cowl. Tighten the screws to 17 N·m (155 in. lbs.) torque.
(4) Install the bolts attaching the hinge to the cowl.
(5) Install the cowl panel and screen.
(6) Install the wiper arms.

HOOD SAFETY LATCH

REMOVAL

(1) Raise and support the hood.
(2) Remove the screws attaching the safety latch to the grille panel (Fig. 4).
(3) Remove the latch from the grille panel.

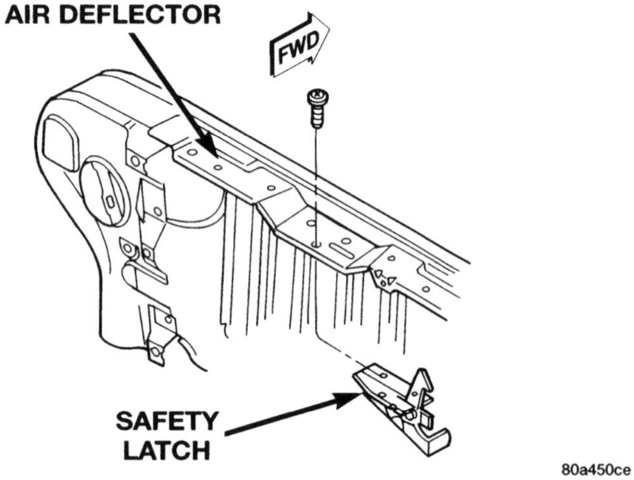

Fig. 4 Hood Safety Latch

INSTALLATION

(1) Position the latch on the grille panel.
(2) Install the screws attaching the safety latch to the grille panel.
(3) Remove the support rod and close the hood.

COWL WEATHERSTRIP

REMOVAL

(1) Carefully separate the weatherstrip from the cowl flange (Fig. 5).

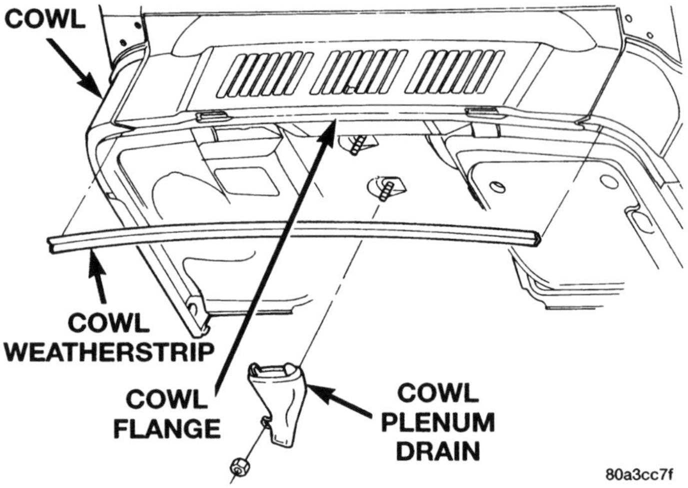

Fig. 5 Cowl Weatherstrip

INSTALLATION

(1) Position the weatherstrip on the cowl flange and press it into place.

COWL GRILLE AND SCREEN

REMOVAL

(1) Open the hood and remove the screws that attach the cowl grille and screen to the cowl (Fig. 6).
(2) Remove the grille and screen from the cowl.

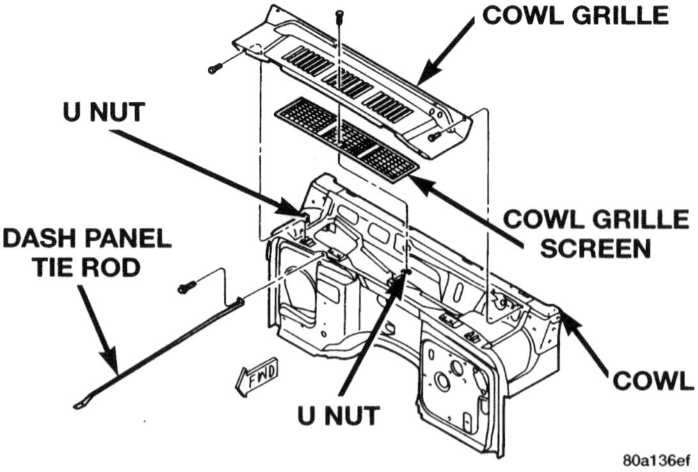

Fig. 6 Cowl Grille And Screen

INSTALLATION

(1) Position the cowl screen and grille on the cowl.
(2) Install the screws that attach the grille and screen to the cowl.

REMOVAL AND INSTALLATION (Continued)

WINDSHIELD FRAME

REMOVAL

(1) Unlatch top.

(2) Remove the bolts attaching the sport bar to the windshield frame.

(3) Remove the windshield wiper arms.

(4) Remove the torx screw closest to the hinge pivot point and tilt the windshield forward.

(5) Remove the torx screws attaching the windshield hinge to the windshield frame (Fig. 7).

(6) Separate the windshield frame from the vehicle.

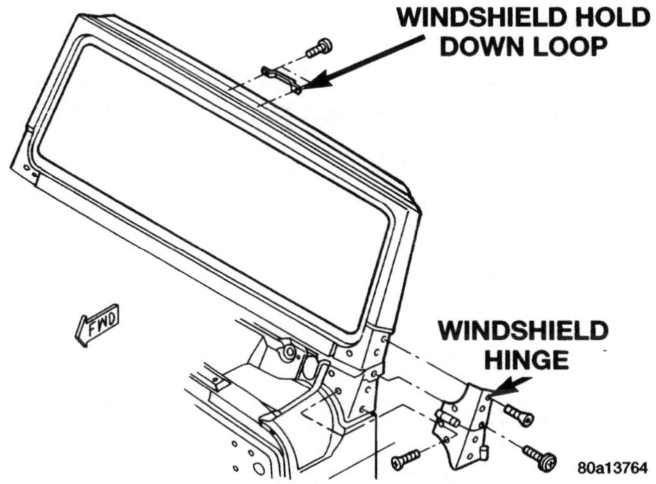

Fig. 7 Windshield Frame

INSTALLATION

(1) Position the windshield frame on the vehicle.

(2) Install the torx screws attaching the windshield hinge to the windshield frame.

(3) Tilt the windshield rearward.

(4) Install the torx screw closest to the hinge pivot point and lock the windshield in the upright position.

(5) Install the windshield wiper arms.

(6) Install the bolts attaching the sport bar to the windshield frame.

(7) Latch top.

WINDSHIELD FRAME WEATHERSTRIP

UPPER FRAME WEATHERSTRIP REMOVAL

(1) Disconnect the top from the windshield frame.

(2) Peel the weatherstrip from the frame.

UPPER FRAME WEATHERSTRIP INSTALLATION

(1) Clean the seal contact surface on the windshield frame with isopropyl alcohol or equivalent.

(2) Remove adhesive backing from the weatherstrip.

(3) Position the weatherstrip on the windshield frame and press it into place (Fig. 8).

(4) Connect the top to the windshield frame.

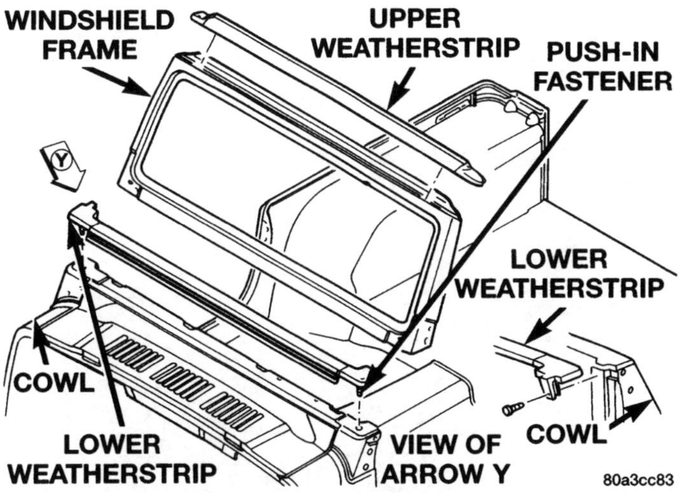

Fig. 8 Windshield Frame Weatherstrip

LOWER FRAME WEATHERSTRIP REMOVAL

The lower windshield frame weatherstrip can be removed with the frame tilted forward to the full horizontal position.

(1) Mark the position of the wiper arms and remove the arms.

(2) Disconnect the top from the windshield frame.

(3) Remove the cowl grille.

(4) Remove the torx screws on each side of the windshield frame allowing the windshield frame to tilt to the full horizontal position.

(5) Disengage the outboard push-in fasteners at the top of cowl and unscrew the fasteners that hold the weatherstrip on each hinge pillar (Fig. 8).

(6) Remove the weatherstrip from the cowl.

LOWER FRAME WEATHERSTRIP INSTALLATION

(1) Clean the seal contact surface on the cowl with isopropyl alcohol or equivalent.

(2) Position the weatherstrip on the cowl, align the push-in fasteners and press it into place.

(3) Install the screws attaching the lower weatherstrip to the hinge pillars.

(4) Tilt the windshield frame rearward to the full vertical position.

(5) Connect the top to the windshield frame.

(6) Install cowl grille and wiper arms.

WINDSHIELD HINGE

REMOVAL

If both hinges are to be replaced, the windshield must be tilted to the full forward position. Refer to the Windshield Frame Removal/Installation procedure in this group for windshield frame lowering information.

(1) Remove door.

REMOVAL AND INSTALLATION (Continued)

(2) Remove the bolts attaching the hinge to the cowl (Fig. 9).

(3) Remove the bolts attaching the hinge to the windshield frame.

(4) Separate the hinge from the vehicle.

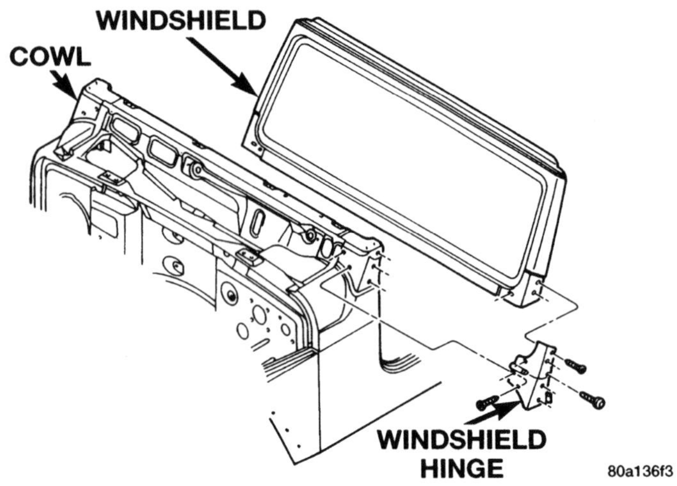

Fig. 9 Windshield Hinge

INSTALLATION

(1) Paint as required.

(2) Clean the contact surface of the hinge and cowl with isopropyl alcohol or equivalent.

(3) Apply a 4 mm bead of Mopar Vinyl Acrylic Sealant or equivalent around the perimeter of the hinge contact surface. The bead should be 10 mm inboard of the edge.

(4) Position the hinge on the vehicle.

(5) Install the bolts attaching the hinge to the windshield frame.

(6) Install the bolts attaching the hinge to the cowl.

(7) Ensure that the sealant provides complete coverage. Wipe away excess sealant.

(8) Install door.

BODY DECALS

TJ decals (Fig. 10) are durable tape decals with a adhesive backing.

To eliminate blisters and air bubbles in a decal, pierce them with a needle or pin. Force the trapped air out of the hole.

A heat gun can also be used to remove small wrinkles and irregularities in a decal.

REMOVAL

NOTE: The key to successful decal removal is to apply heat to area and slowly peel the decal from panel.

(1) Clean the surface as necessary.

(2) Place a piece of masking tape above or below the decal as a reference mark.

(3) Start at one end of the decal and apply heat with a heat gun. Slowly peel the decal from the panel by pulling it back. **Do not pull the decal outward from the panel.**

INSTALLATION

(1) The area that will be covered by the decal must be cleaned with an cleaning solution to remove any residue paint. Freshly painted surfaces must be thoroughly dry.

(2) Clean painted surface with a commercial wax and silicone removal solution. Wipe surface with a clean cloth and allow to dry.

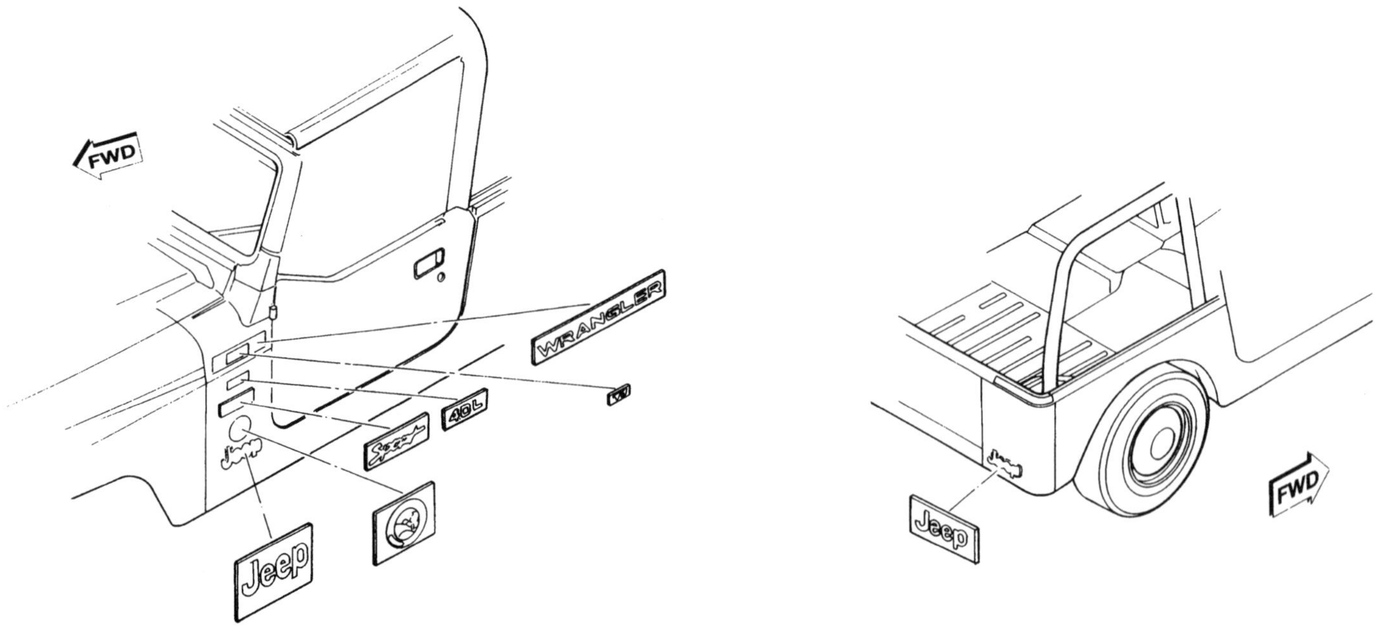

Fig. 10 TJ—Decals

REMOVAL AND INSTALLATION (Continued)

(3) Position decal and carrier on panel and hold it in-place with pieces masking tape.

(4) Lift the bottom edge of the decal and carrier, use the tape sections as hinges, and reverse the position of the decal and carrier.

CAUTION: Always remove the carrier from the tape stripe/decal, never remove the tape stripe/decal from the carrier.

(5) Bend a corner of the carrier outward, separate the corner of the carrier from the decal.

(6) Using the masking tape on the body panel, align the decal.

(7) Separate the carrier from one end of the decal.

(8) Hold tape decal firmly against the panel surface while separating the carrier from the decal.

(9) Inspect tape decal with reflected light to check for defects that could have developed during the installation process. Remove all air and/or moisture bubbles.

SIDE VIEW MIRROR

REMOVAL

(1) Remove the screws attaching the mirror to the door hinge (Fig. 11).

(2) Remove the mirror from the door hinge.

INSTALLATION

(1) Clean the door hinge-mirror base contact surface.

(2) Position the mirror base at the door hinge.

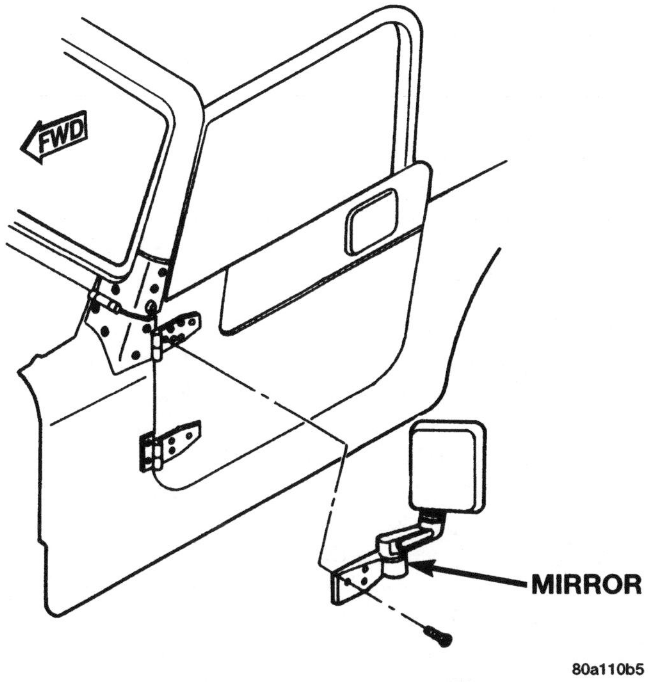

Fig. 11 Side View Mirror

(3) Install the screws attaching the mirror base to the door hinge.

FENDER FLARE

REMOVAL

(1) Remove the side marker lamp.

(2) Remove the screws that attach the flare to the front fender or rear wheelhouse (Fig. 12).

(3) Separate the flare from the body.

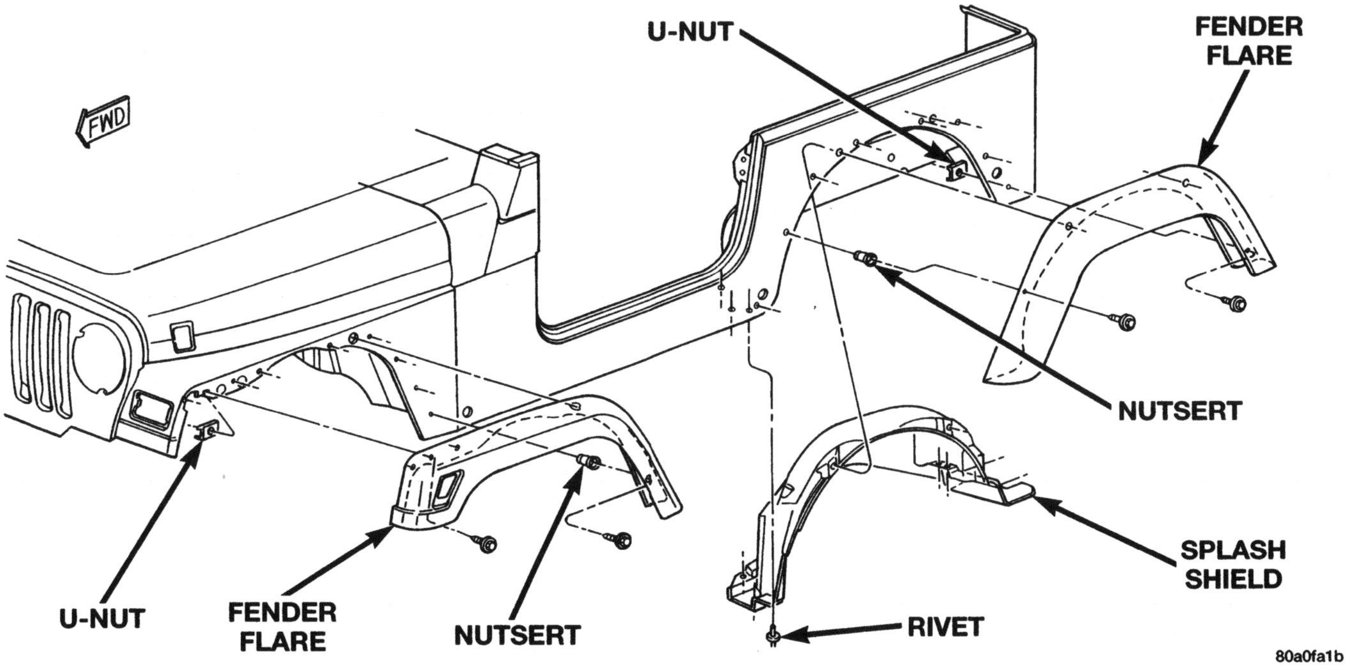

Fig. 12 Fender Flares

REMOVAL AND INSTALLATION (Continued)

INSTALLATION

(1) Clean the contact surface on the body.

(2) Clean the contact surface on the flare and position it on the front fender or wheelhouse.

(3) Install the screws attaching the flares to the front fender or wheelhouse.

(4) If removed, install the side marker lamp.

FRONT FENDER

RIGHT FENDER REMOVAL

(1) Disconnect and remove the battery.

(2) Remove the air cleaner housing.

(3) Remove the bolts attaching the Power Distribution Center (PDC) to the fender.

(4) Disengage the PDC wire harness retainers on the battery tray and fender.

(5) Move and secure the PDC.

(6) Disengage the high pressure air conditioning line retainer on the fender.

(7) Disengage the front end lighting wire harness retainers on the fender.

(8) Remove the battery tray.

(9) Disengage the battery temperature sensor connector.

(10) Disengage the vacuum line at the reservoir under the battery tray reinforcement bracket.

(11) Disengage the headlamp wire connector.

(12) Route the fog lamp (if equipped), park lamp and side marker wire harness through the access hole in the fender well.

(13) If equipped, remove the fender flare extension and body side molding (Fig. 13).

(14) Remove the bolts attaching the fender to the cowl (Fig. 14).

(15) Remove the bolts attaching the fender to the battery tray reinforcement bracket.

(16) Remove the bolts attaching the fender to the grille.

(17) Separate the fender from the vehicle.

RIGHT FENDER INSTALLATION

Transfer all related components. Replace harness retainers if damaged.

(1) Position the fender on the vehicle.

(2) Install the bolts attaching the fender to the grille.

(3) Install the bolts attaching the fender to the battery tray reinforcement bracket.

(4) Install the bolts attaching the fender to the cowl.

(5) If equipped, install the fender flare extension and body side molding.

(6) Route the fog lamp (if equipped), park lamp and side marker wire harness through the access hole in the fender well. Seat the grommet

(7) Engage the headlamp wire connector.

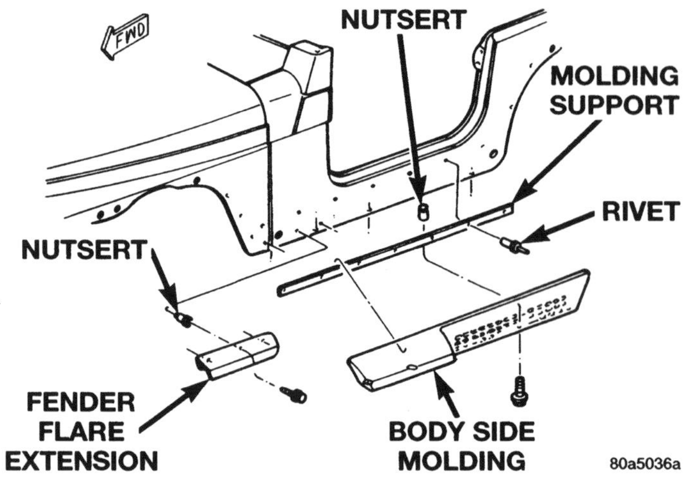

Fig. 13 Body Side Molding

(8) Engage the battery temperature sensor connector.

(9) Engage the vacuum line at the reservoir under the battery tray reinforcement bracket.

(10) Install the battery tray.

(11) Position the front end lighting wire harness into the retainers on the fender. Engage the retainers to secure.

(12) Position the high pressure air conditioning line into the retainer on the fender. Engage the retainer to secure.

(13) Position the PDC on the fender and install the bolts.

(14) Position the PDC wire harness into the retainers on the fender and battery tray. Engage the retainers to secure.

(15) Install the air cleaner housing.

(16) Install and connect the battery.

LEFT FENDER REMOVAL

(1) Disconnect the negative terminal on the battery.

(2) Remove the windshield washer reservoir.

(3) Disengage horn wire connectors.

(4) Remove horns.

(5) Remove EVAP canister.

(6) Remove the bolts attaching the ABS Hydraulic Control Unit (HCU) to the support tray.

(7) Secure the HCU.

(8) Remove the HCU tray.

(9) Disengage the front end lighting wire harness retainers on the fender.

(10) Disengage the headlamp wire connector.

(11) Route the fog lamp (if equipped), park lamp and side marker wire harness through the access hole in the fender well.

(12) If equipped, remove the body side molding (Fig. 13).

REMOVAL AND INSTALLATION (Continued)

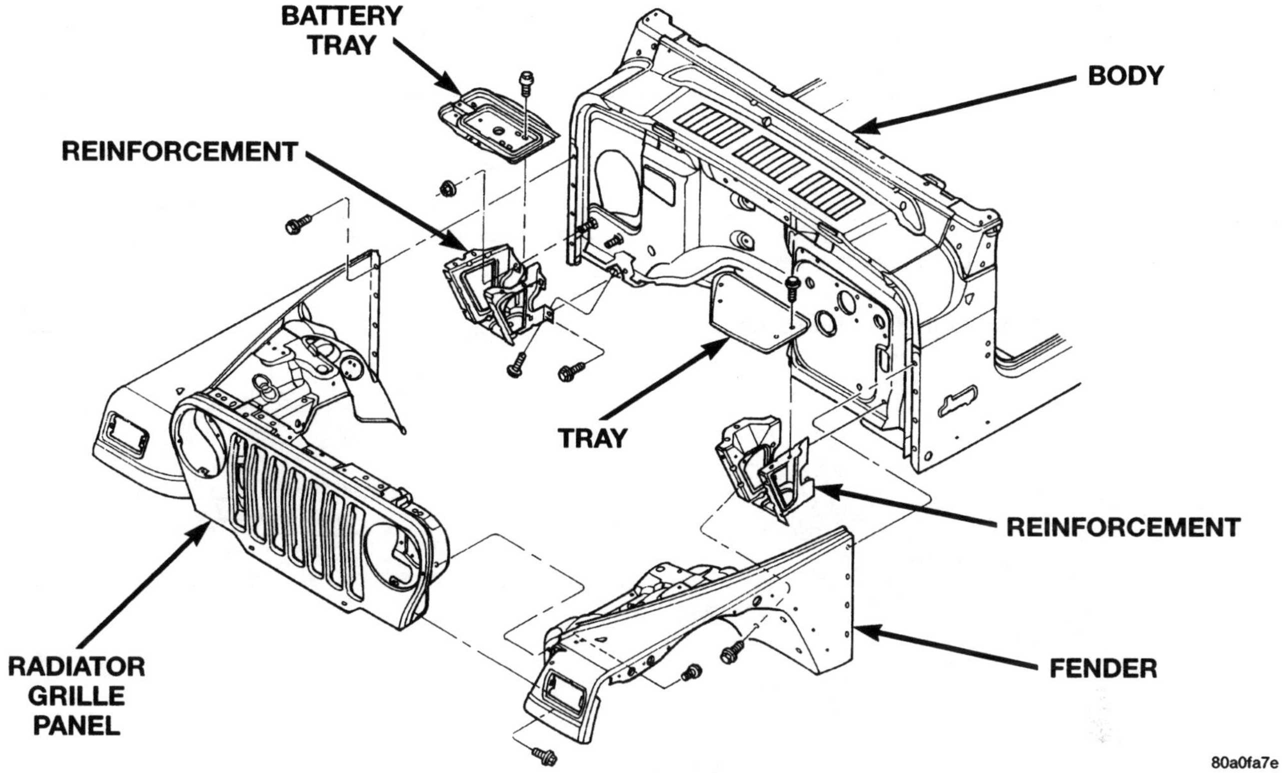

Fig. 14 Front Fender

(13) Remove the bolts attaching the fender to the cowl (Fig. 14).

(14) Remove the bolts attaching the fender to the HCU tray reinforcement bracket.

(15) Remove the bolts attaching the fender to the grille.

(16) Separate the fender from the vehicle.

LEFT FENDER INSTALLATION

Transfer all related components. Replace harness retainers if damaged.

(1) Position the fender on the vehicle.

(2) Install the bolts attaching the fender to the grille.

(3) Position the front end lighting wire harness into the retainers on the fender. Engage the retainers to secure.

(4) Install the bolts attaching the fender to the HCU tray reinforcement bracket.

(5) Install the bolts attaching the fender to the cowl.

(6) If equipped, install the body side molding.

(7) Route the fog lamp (if equipped), park lamp and side marker wire harness through the access hole in the fender well. Seat the grommet

(8) Engage the headlamp wire connector.

(9) Install the HCU tray.

(10) Position the HCU on the support tray and install the bolts.

(11) Install EVAP canister.

(12) Install horns.

(13) Engage horn wire connectors.

(14) Install the windshield washer reservoir.

(15) Connect the negative terminal on the battery.

BODY SIDE MOLDING

REMOVAL

(1) Remove the bolts from underside of the body side molding (Fig. 15).

(2) Lift the molding upward to release it from the molding support.

(3) Remove the molding support by drilling out the rivets.

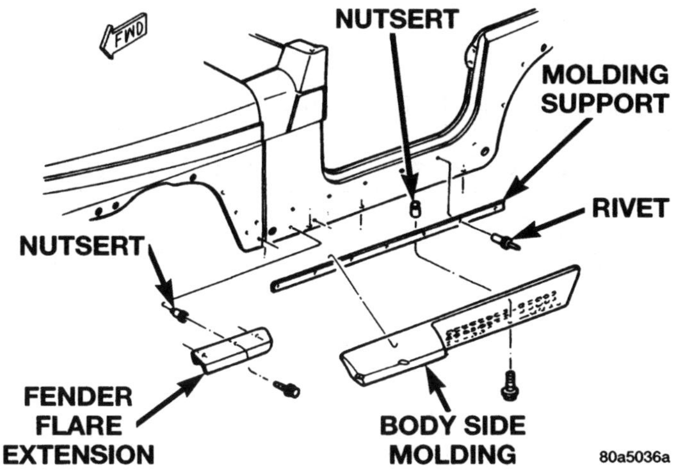

Fig. 15 Body Side Molding

INSTALLATION

(1) If removed, position the molding support on the body and install the rivets.

REMOVAL AND INSTALLATION (Continued)

(2) Place the upper edge of the molding over the top of the molding support and slide it downward.

(3) Install the bolts into the underside of the body side molding.

SIDE STEP

REMOVAL

(1) Remove the bolts that attach the side step to the frame (Fig. 16).

(2) Separate the side step from the frame.

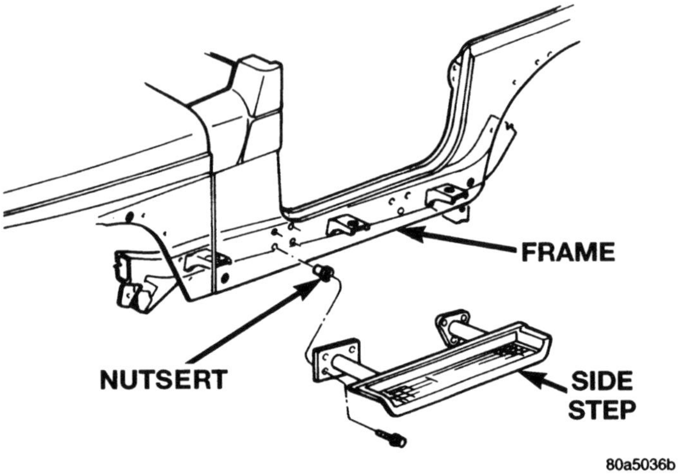

Fig. 16 Side Step

INSTALLATION

(1) Postion the side step on the frame.

(2) Install the bolts that attach the side step to the frame.

FULL DOOR TRIM PANEL

REMOVAL

(1) Lower the window.

(2) Remove the clip attaching the window glass regulator handle to the regulator. Remove the handle.

(3) Remove the screws attaching trim panel to door.

(4) Remove push-in fasteners attaching trim panel to door with special tool C-4829.

(5) Lift the trim panel upward and separate the trim panel from the door.

INSTALLATION

(1) Position the trim panel on the door.

(2) Press the push-in fasteners attaching trim panel to door into place.

(3) Install the screws attaching trim panel to door.

(4) Position the clip on regulator handle and install the handle on the regulator.

FULL DOOR

REMOVAL

(1) Open the door.

(2) Disconnect the door restraint strap from the pin (Fig. 17).

(3) Remove the nuts at the door hinge pivots and lift the door from the body.

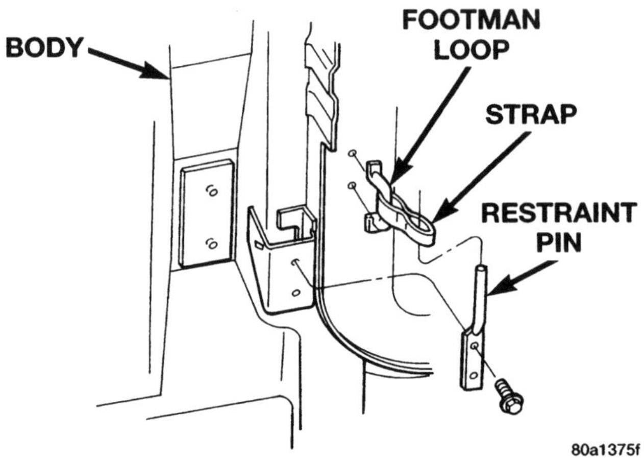

Fig. 17 Restraint Strap

INSTALLATION

(1) Position the door in the hinge and install the nuts.

(2) Connect the door restraint strap at the pin.

FULL DOOR HINGE

REMOVAL

(1) Remove the door.

(2) Mark the outline of the existing hinge on the body and the door with a wax pencil for installation alignment reference.

(3) Remove the nut from the upper hinge pin (Fig. 18).

NOTE: When removing the door or hinge DO NOT discard the plastic shims or the hinge pin.

(4) Remove the hinge-to-body screws and the hinge-to-door screws. Remove the hinge from the door and body. Support the door as necessary.

The upper hinge is integrated with the windshield hinge. When removing it, support the windshield frame with an appropriate device prior to removal.

INSTALLATION

(1) Clean the replacement hinge with an appropriate solvent and dry it with compressed air.

(2) Paint the hinge to match the vehicle body.

(3) Lubricate the hinge with spray lubricant.

REMOVAL AND INSTALLATION (Continued)

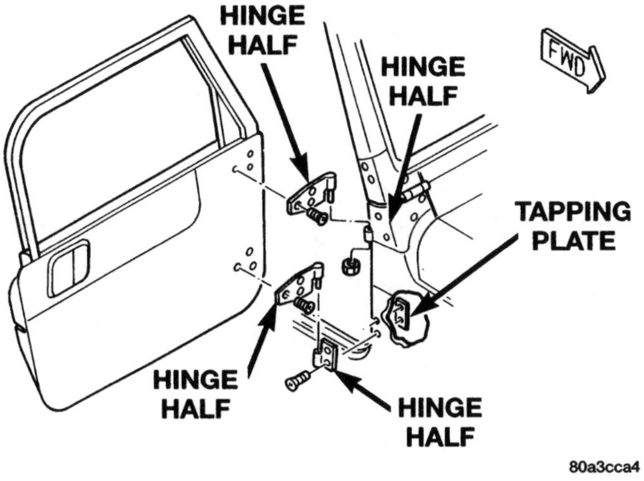

Fig. 18 Full Door Hinge

(4) Position the hinge on the door, align carefully with the wax pencil installation alignment reference marks, and install the screws.

(5) Position the hinge on the vehicle body. Align the wax pencil marks installation alignment reference marks. Install the screws.

(6) Install the door,

(7) Inspect the windshield alignment after hinge installation.

(8) Inspect the door alignment. Adjust, if necessary.

FULL DOOR OUTSIDE RELEASE HANDLE

REMOVAL

(1) Remove the door trim panel.

(2) Position the window in the full upward position.

(3) Remove the grab handle support bracket (Fig. 19).

(4) Peel back the waterdam from the door inner panel to access the door latch.

(5) Disconnect from the latch, the inside lock knob to latch rod and, the outside release handle to latch rod (Fig. 20).

(6) Using a long flat blade, tap the handle keepers upward and remove from the door handle (Fig. 21).

(7) Remove the latch release rod from the door handle.

(8) Separate the handle and gasket from the door.

INSTALLATION

(1) Engage the latch release rod to the door handle.

(2) Position the gasket and handle in the door.

(3) Slide the keepers into the door handle from the top.

(4) Lower the window.

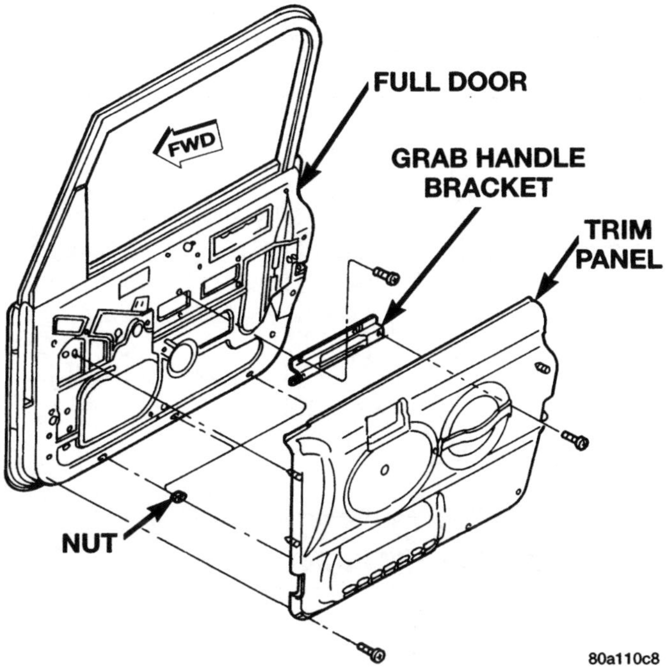

Fig. 19 Grab Handle Support Bracket

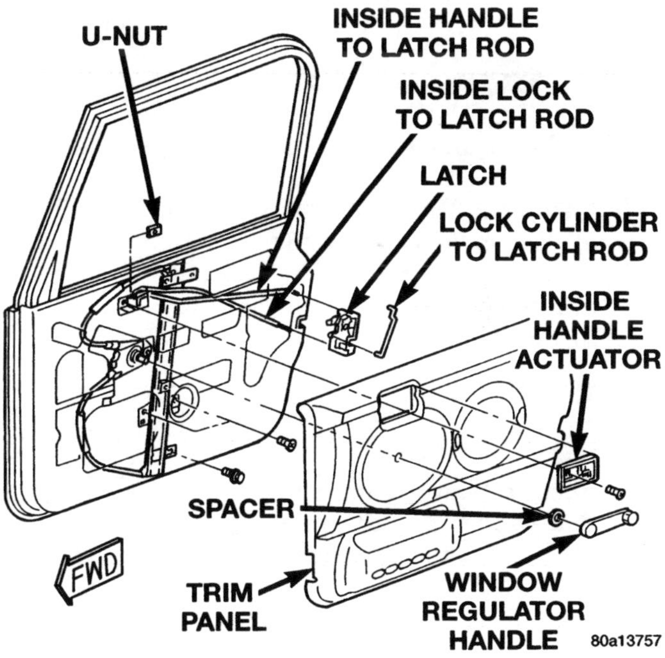

Fig. 20 Latch Rods

(5) Using a long flat blade, lightly tap the handle keepers downward to secure the handle.

(6) Raise the window.

(7) Connect to the latch, the inside lock knob to latch rod and, the outside release handle to latch rod.

(8) Install the waterdam

(9) Install the grab handle support bracket.

(10) Install the door trim panel.

REMOVAL AND INSTALLATION (Continued)

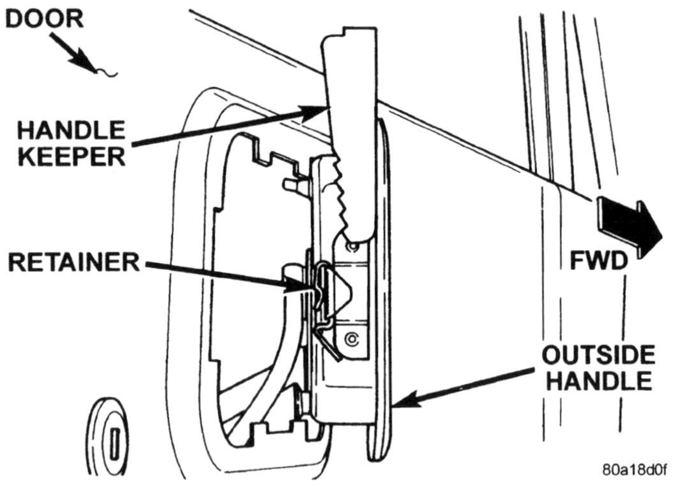

Fig. 21 Outside Door Handle Removal

FULL DOOR LOCK CYLINDER

REMOVAL

(1) Remove trim panel.
(2) Peel back waterdam.
(3) Disconnect lock cylinder to latch rod.
(4) Remove lock cylinder retaining clip.
(5) Remove the lock cylinder from the door.

INSTALLATION

(1) Install the lock cylinder in the door. Install lock cylinder retaining clip.
(2) Connect lock cylinder to latch rod.
(3) Install the lock cylinder in the door. Install lock cylinder retaining clip.
(4) Connect lock cylinder to latch rod.
(5) Secure the waterdam to the door.
(6) Install trim panel.

FULL DOOR LATCH

REMOVAL

(1) Remove trim panel.
(2) Roll window to full upward position.
(3) Disconnect the lock cylinder to latch rod (Fig. 22).
(4) Disconnect the lock knob to latch rod.
(5) Disconnect the outside handle to latch rod.
(6) Remove the screws attaching the latch to the door (Fig. 23).
(7) Lower the latch in the door and disconnect the inside handle to latch rod.
(8) Remove the latch from the door.

INSTALLATION

(1) Position the latch in the door.
(2) Connect the inside handle to latch rod.
(3) Install the screws attaching the latch to the door.

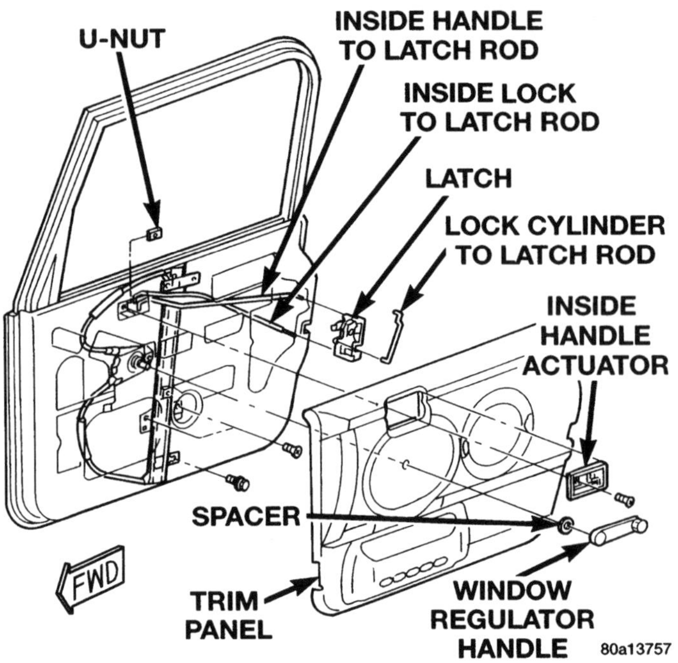

Fig. 22 Latch Rods

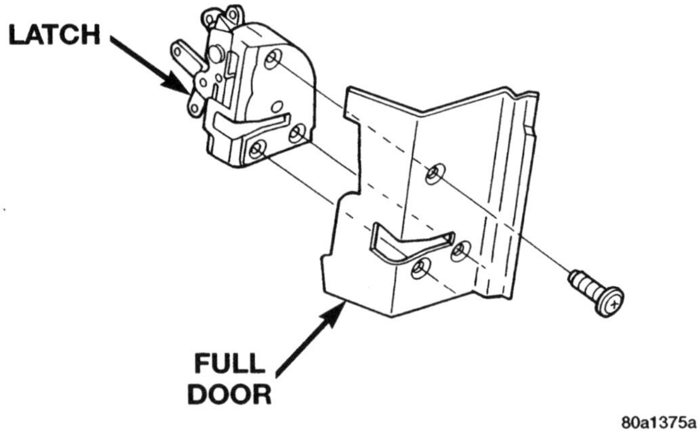

Fig. 23 Full Door Latch

(4) Position the door weatherstrip in place, apply adhesive as necessary.
(5) Connect the outside handle to latch rod.
(6) Connect the lock knob to latch rod.
(7) Connect the lock cylinder to latch rod.
(8) Install trim panel.

FULL DOOR LATCH STRIKER

REMOVAL

(1) Remove the screws attaching the striker to the body.
(2) Separate the striker and the spacer from the body (Fig. 24).

REMOVAL AND INSTALLATION (Continued)

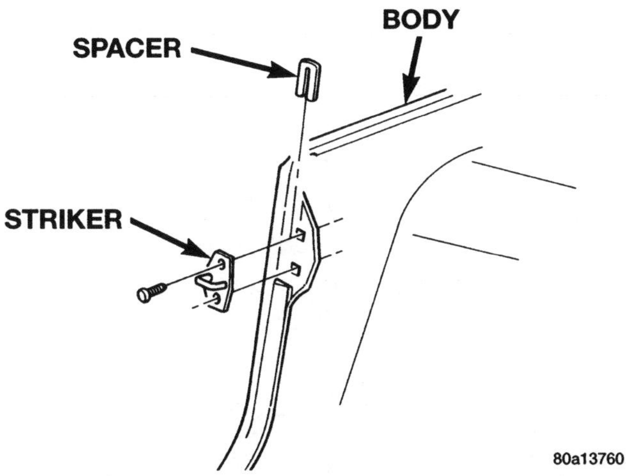

Fig. 24 Latch Striker

INSTALLATION

(1) Position the striker and the spacer on the body.

(2) Install the screws attaching the striker and spacer to the body.

FULL DOOR INSIDE HANDLE ACTUATOR

REMOVAL

(1) Remove the torx screw attaching the inside handle to the door.

(2) Carefully pull the handle from the door.

(3) Disconnect the latch rods from the handle (Fig. 25).

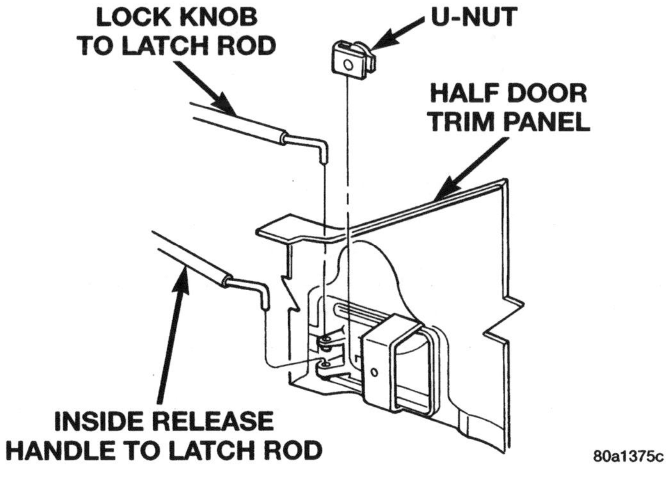

Fig. 25 Inside Handle Actuator

INSTALLATION

INSTALLATION

(1) Connect the latch rods to the handle.

(2) Position handle and seal in door.

(3) Install the torx screw attaching the inside handle the to door.

FULL DOOR GLASS

REMOVAL

(1) Remove the door trim panel and the waterdam.

(2) Pull the door glass run channel from the door sail.

(3) Roll glass fully downward.

(4) Remove the door sail panel (Fig. 26) and (Fig. 27).

(5) Roll glass 1/4 upward to access regulator arm guide.

(6) Remove the screws that attach the regulator arm guide to the glass.

(7) Lift the glass upward while tilting inward and remove from the door.

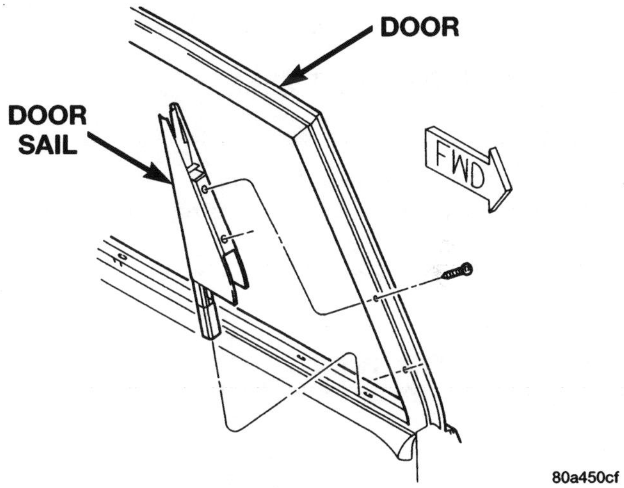

Fig. 26 Door Sail Screws

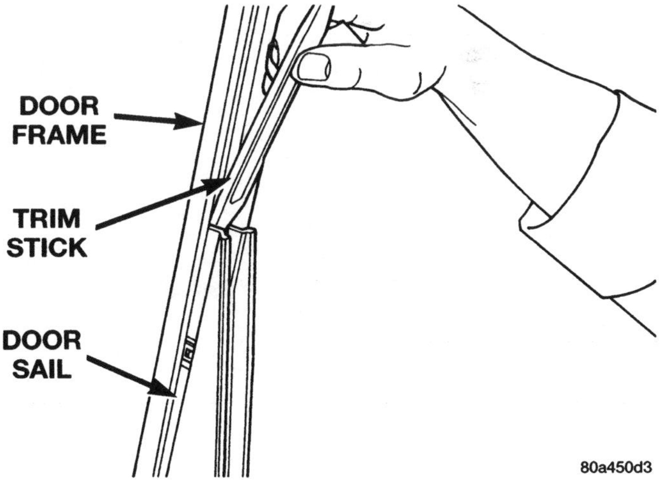

Fig. 27 Door Sail Removal

INSTALLATION

(1) Position the glass in the door ensuring the glass is aligned in the glass run channel.

(2) Install the screws that attach the regulator arm guide to the glass.

(3) Install the door sail panel.

(4) Install the run channel in the door sail.

(5) Install the waterdam and the door trim panel.

REMOVAL AND INSTALLATION (Continued)

FULL DOOR INNER BELT WEATHERSTRIP

REMOVAL

The inner belt weatherstrip is attached to the door trim panel.

(1) Remove the door trim panel.

(2) Remove the staples attaching the inner belt weatherstrip to the trim panel.

INSTALLATION

(1) Align the inner belt weatherstrip to the door trim panel.

(2) Install staples to hold weatherstrip to trim panel at original locations using a heavy duty stapler.

(3) Install the door trim panel.

FULL DOOR OUTER BELT SEAL

REMOVAL

(1) Remove the door sail panel.

(2) Disengage the clips attaching the outer belt seal to the door (Fig. 28).

(3) Separate the seal from the door.

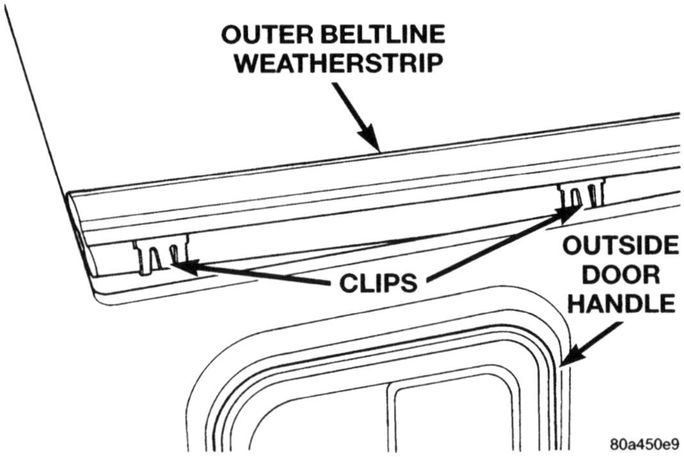

Fig. 28 Full Door Outer Belt Seal

INSTALLATION

(1) Position the seal on the door.

(2) Engage the clips attaching the outer belt seal to the door.

(3) Install the door sail panel.

FULL DOOR GLASS RUN CHANNEL WEATHERSTRIP

REMOVAL

(1) Lower the window.

(2) Using a trim stick, carefully pry the glass run channel weatherstrip from the window opening frame.

(3) Remove the door glass.

(4) Grasp the glass run channel weatherstrip in the door (Fig. 29) and pull from the channel.

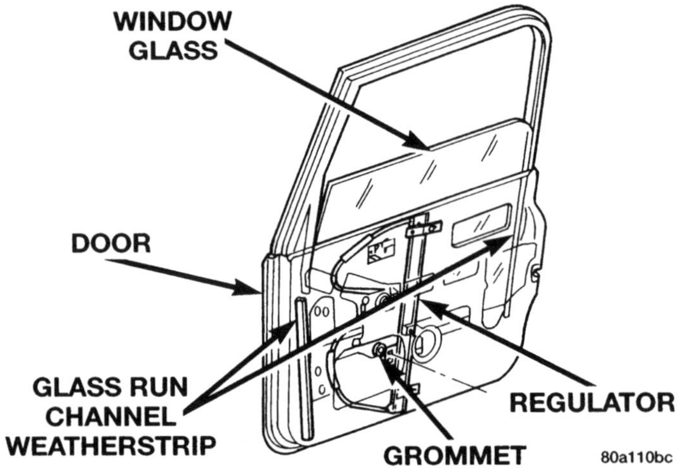

Fig. 29 Full Door Glass Run Channel Weatherstrip

INSTALLATION

Applying a small amount of lubricant to the weatherstrip may ease the installation.

(1) Position the weatherstrip in the door channels and press into place.

(2) Install the door glass.

(3) Position the weatherstrip in the window opening frame and press into place.

FULL DOOR WEATHERSTRIP

The upper portion of the weatherstrip is seated into a channel around the window opening frame. The channel that seats the lower portion of the weatherstrip is attached to the door with push-in fasteners and double sided tape.

REMOVAL

(1) Peel the weatherstrip from the channel.

(2) Separate the weatherstrip from the door.

(3) If necessary, remove the push-in fasteners attaching the weatherstrip channel to the door and peel the channel from the door (Fig. 30).

INSTALLATION

(1) If the weatherstrip channel has been removed, clean the contact surfaces with isopropyl alcohol or equivalent.

(2) Remove paper backing from the weatherstrip channel, position the channel on the door and install the push-in fasteners.

(3) Install the weatherstrip in the upper and lower weatherstrip channels ensuring that the weatherstrip is completely engaged to the weatherstrip channels.

REMOVAL AND INSTALLATION (Continued)

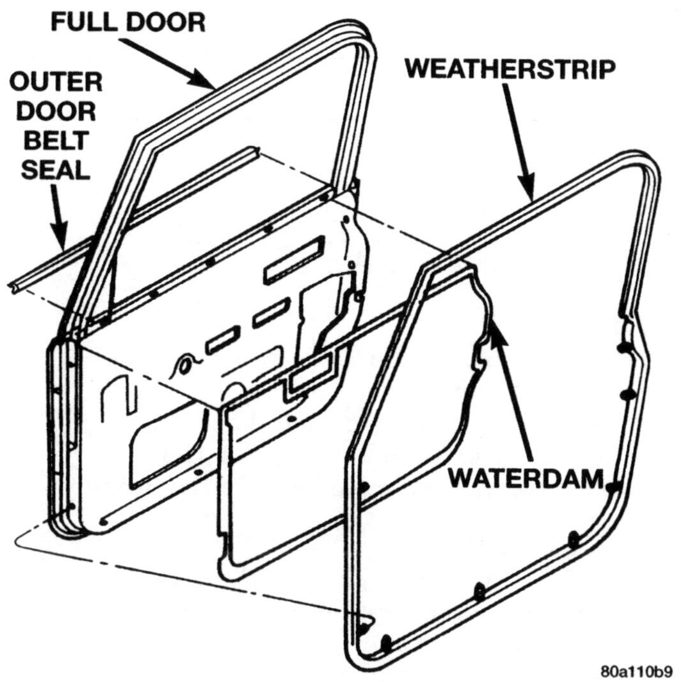

Fig. 30 Full Door Weatherstrip

FULL DOOR WINDOW REGULATOR

REMOVAL

(1) Remove door trim panel.
(2) Remove door glass.
(3) Loosen the bolts in the slotted holes (Fig. 31).
(4) Remove the bolts attaching the regulator to the door inner panel.
(5) Lift the regulator upward to free it from the slotted holes in the door inner panel.
(6) Lower the regulator and remove it through the access hole in the door inner panel (Fig. 32).

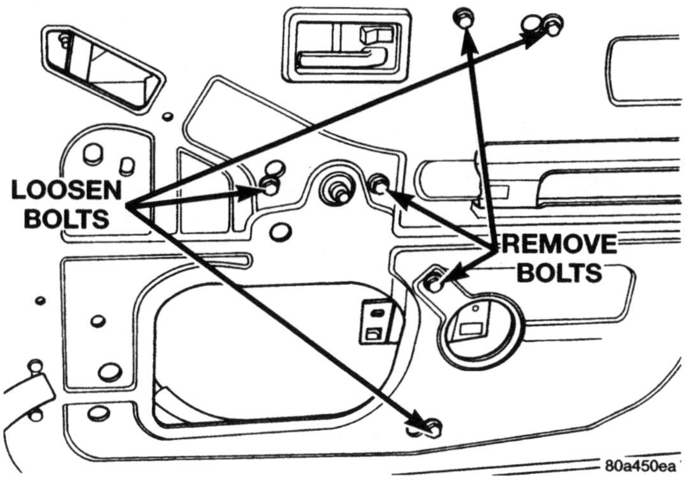

Fig. 31 Window Regulator Bolts

INSTALLATION

(1) Position the regulator in the door.
(2) Align regulator bolts into slotted holes.

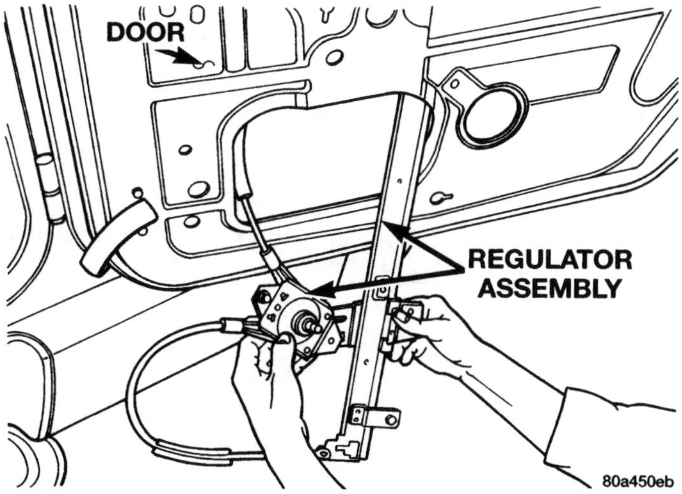

Fig. 32 Regulator Removal

(3) Install bolts attaching regulator to the inner door panel.
(4) Tighten the bolts in the slotted holes.
(5) Install door glass.
(6) Install door trim panel.

HALF DOOR TRIM PANEL

REMOVAL

(1) Remove half door window.
(2) Rotate window retainer sleeves 90°. Using a trim stick, pry sleeve retainers from door.
(3) Remove the screws attaching trim panel to door.
(4) Remove push-in fasteners attaching trim panel to door with special tool C-4829.
(5) Separate the trim panel from the door.

INSTALLATION

(1) Position the trim panel on the door.
(2) Press the push-in fasteners attaching trim panel to door into place.
(3) Install the screws attaching trim panel to door.
(4) Position retainer sleeves into door. Rotate retainer sleeves 90° to secure into place.
(5) Install half door window.

HALF DOOR

REMOVAL

(1) Open the door.
(2) Disconnect the door restraint strap from the pin (Fig. 33).
(3) Remove the nuts at the door hinge pivots and lift the door from the body.

INSTALLATION

(1) Position the door in the hinge and install the nuts.
(2) Connect the door restraint strap at the pin.

REMOVAL AND INSTALLATION (Continued)

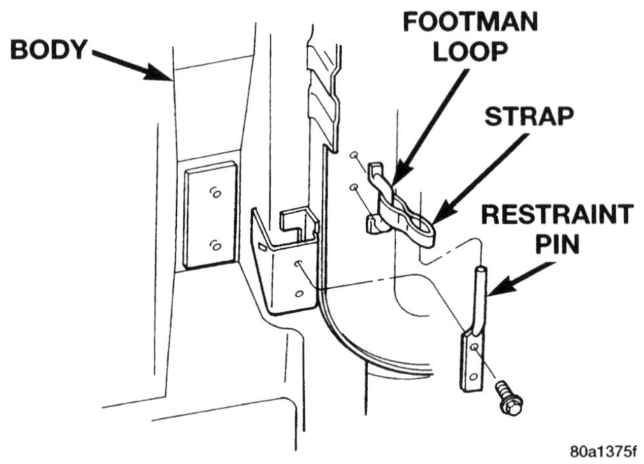

Fig. 33 Restraint Strap

HALF DOOR HINGE

The service procedures for the half door hinge are the same as the full door hinge. Refer to, Full Door Hinge Removal/Installation procedures in this group.

HALF DOOR OUTSIDE HANDLE

REMOVAL

(1) Remove trim panel.

(2) Disconnect the outside handle to latch rod (Fig. 34).

(3) Remove screws attaching the outside handle to the door.

(4) Separate the outside handle and seal from the door.

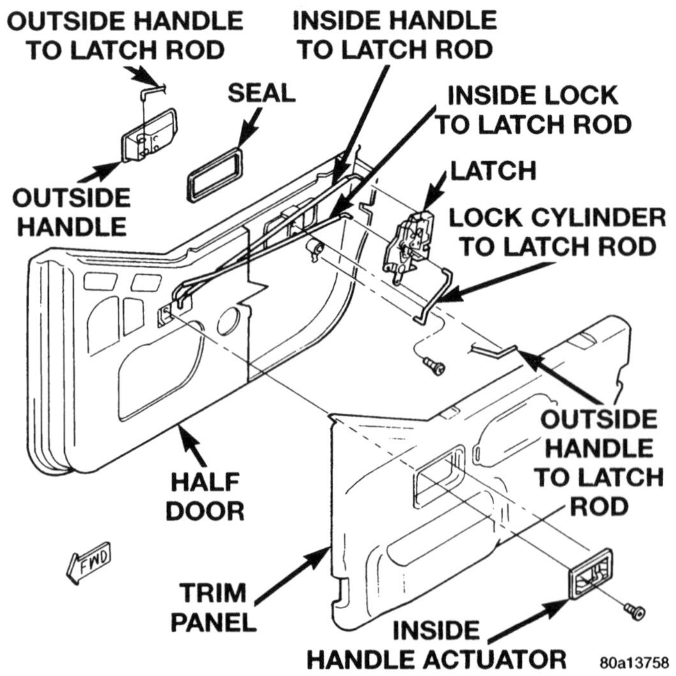

Fig. 34 Outside Handle

INSTALLATION

(1) Position the outside handle and seal in the door.

(2) Install screws attaching the outside handle to the door.

(3) Connect the outside handle to latch rod.

(4) Install trim panel.

HALF DOOR LOCK CYLINDER

REMOVAL

(1) Remove trim panel.

(2) Peel back the waterdam.

(3) Disconnect lock cylinder to latch rod (Fig. 35).

(4) Remove lock cylinder retaining clip.

(5) Remove the lock cylinder from the door.

INSTALLATION

(1) Install the lock cylinder in the door.
Install lock cylinder retaining clip.

(2) Connect lock cylinder to latch rod.

(3) Secure the waterdam.

(4) Install trim panel.

HALF DOOR LATCH

REMOVAL

(1) Remove trim panel.

(2) Disconnect the lock cylinder to latch rod (Fig. 35).

(3) Disconnect the lock knob to latch rod.

(4) Disconnect the outside handle to latch rod.

(5) Using a trim stick or equivalent, pry back the door weatherstip at the latch to access the screw attaching the latch to the door.

(6) Remove the screws attaching the latch to the door (Fig. 36).

(7) Lower the latch in the door and disconnect the inside handle to latch rod.

(8) Remove the latch from the door.

INSTALLATION

(1) Position the latch in the door.

(2) Connect the inside handle to latch rod.

(3) Install the screws attaching the latch to the door.

(4) Position the door weatherstrip in place, apply adhesive as necessary.

(5) Connect the outside handle to latch rod.

(6) Connect the lock knob to latch rod.

(7) Connect the lock cylinder to latch rod (Fig. 35).

(8) Install trim panel.

REMOVAL AND INSTALLATION (Continued)

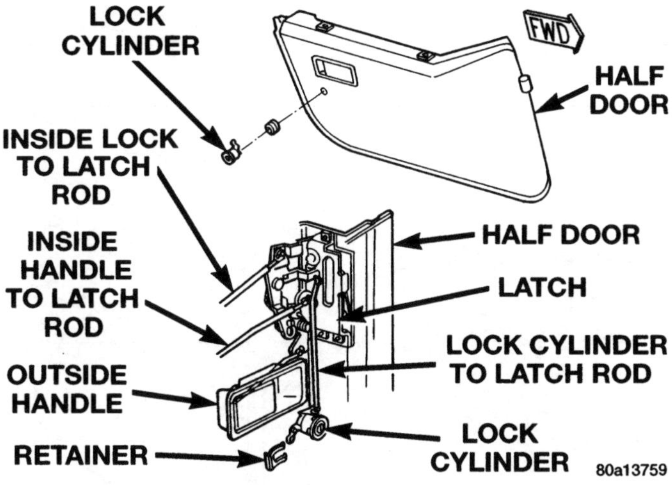

Fig. 35 Half Door Latch Rods

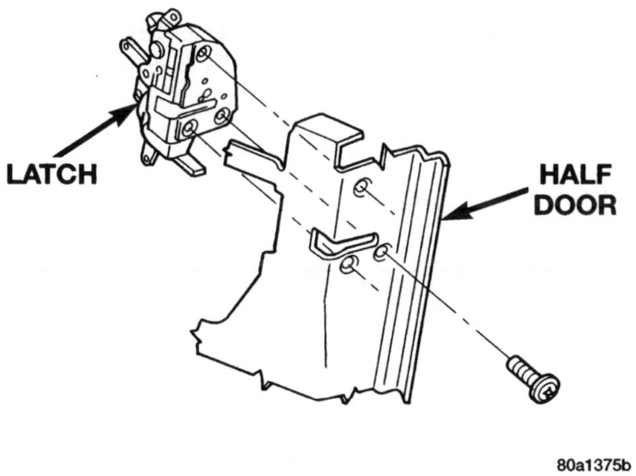

Fig. 36 Door Latch

HALF DOOR LATCH STRIKER

REMOVAL

(1) Remove the screws attaching the striker to the body.

(2) Separate the striker and the spacer from the body (Fig. 37).

INSTALLATION

(1) Position the striker and the spacer on the body.

(2) Install the screws attaching the striker and spacer to the body.

HALF DOOR INSIDE HANDLE ACTUATOR

REMOVAL

(1) Remove the torx screw attaching the inside handle to the door.

(2) Carefully pull handle from door.

(3) Disconnect the latch rods from the handle (Fig. 38).

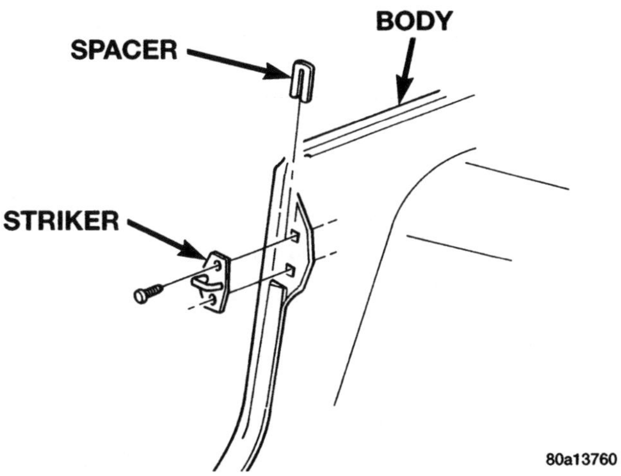

Fig. 37 Latch Striker

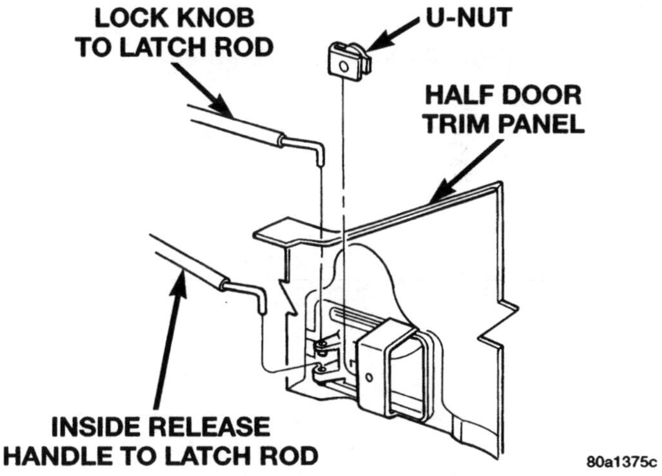

Fig. 38 Inside Handle Actuator

INSTALLATION

(1) Connect the latch rods to the handle.

(2) Position handle and seal in door.

(3) Install the torx screw attaching the inside handle the to door.

HALF DOOR WEATHERSTRIP

The weatherstrip is seated into a channel around the door. The channel that seats the weatherstrip is attached to the door with push-in fasteners and double sided tape.

REMOVAL

(1) Remove trim panel.

(2) Remove window retaining sleeve.

(3) Remove the push-in fasteners attaching the weatherstrip to the top of the door.

(4) Peel the weatherstrip from the channel.

REMOVAL AND INSTALLATION (Continued)

(5) If necessary, remove the push-in fasteners attaching the weatherstrip channel to the door and peel the channel from the door (Fig. 39).

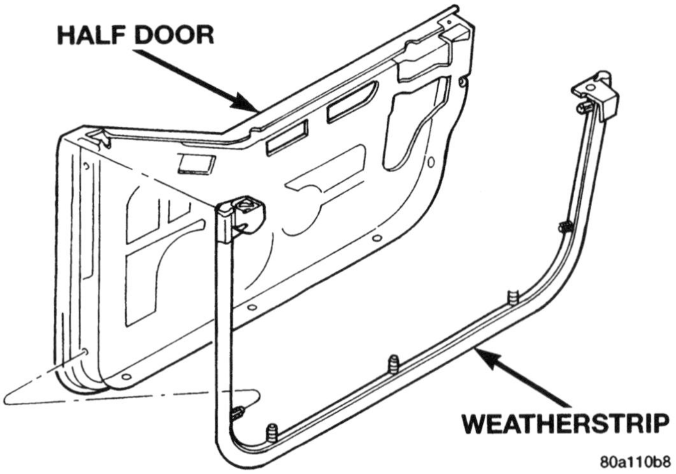

Fig. 39 Half Door Weatherstrip

INSTALLATION

(1) If the weatherstrip channel has been removed, clean the contact surfaces with isopropyl alcohol or equivalent.

(2) Remove the paper backing from the weatherstrip channel, position the channel on the door and install the push-in fasteners.

(3) Position the seal on the door and press it into place.

(4) Install the weatherstrip in the weatherstrip channel ensuring that the weatherstrip is fully engaged in the weatherstrip channel.

(5) Install window retaining sleeve.

(6) Install trim panel.

HALF DOOR WINDOW

REMOVAL

(1) Open the door.

(2) Grasp the window at both front and rear edges and firmly lift upward (Fig. 40).

INSTALLATION

(1) Position the window alignment pins into the restraint sleeves and push downward until seated.

HARD TOP

REMOVAL

(1) Disengage latches at windshield frame (Fig. 41).

(2) Remove the bolts that attach the hard top to the body (Fig. 42).

(3) Using a flat blade or equivalent, disconnect the rear wiper wire harness connector (Fig. 43).

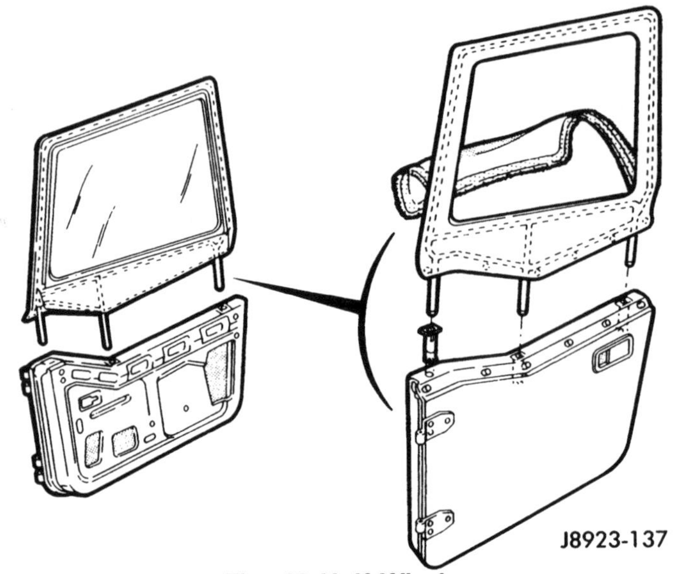

Fig. 40 Half Window

(4) Disconnect the rear washer fluid hose. Cap the hose to prevent washer fluid leakage (Fig. 44).

(5) Remove the hard top from the vehicle.

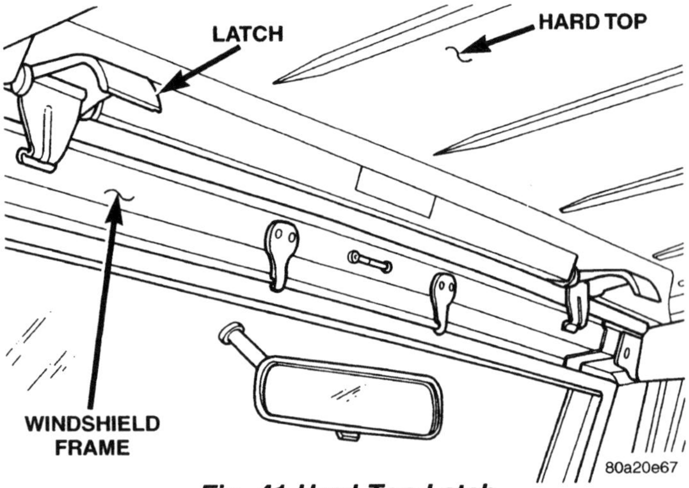

Fig. 41 Hard Top Latch

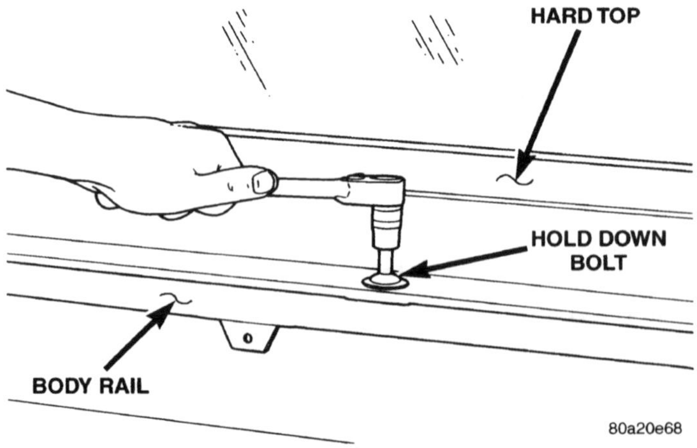

Fig. 42 Hard Top Removal

REMOVAL AND INSTALLATION (Continued)

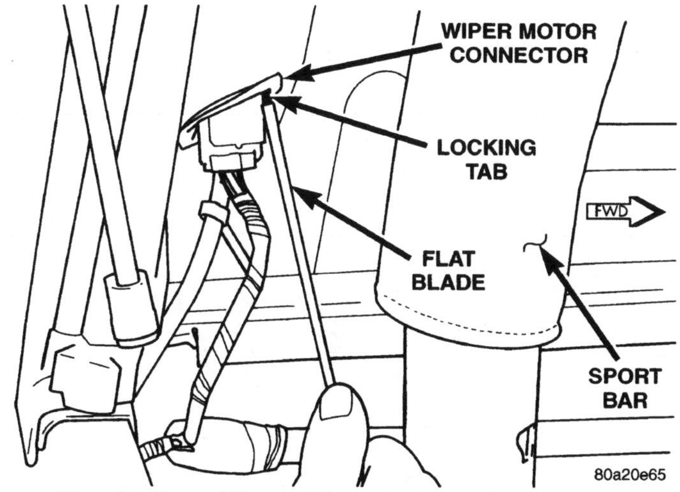

Fig. 43 Rear Wiper Wire Harness Connector

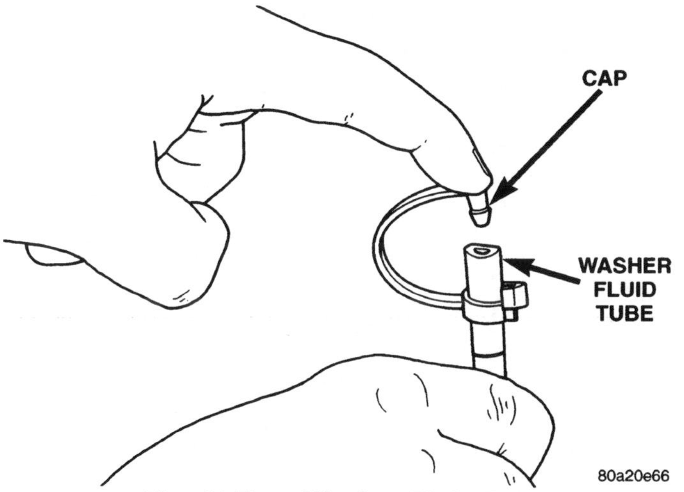

Fig. 44 Rear Washer Fluid Tube

INSTALLATION

(1) Inspect the hard top seals for damage and replace, if necessary.

(2) Carefully position the hard top on the vehicle. Ensure that the latches are not pinched between the top and windshield frame.

(3) Loosely install the bolts. Ensure that the top is centered on the vehicle. Tighten the bolts securely.

(4) Connect the wire harness connector.

(5) Connect the rear washer fluid hose.

(6) Engage the latches at windshield frame.

HARD TOP AIR EXHAUSTER

The hard top air exhauster fits very tightly into the hard top and generally cannot be removed wihout being damaged. It is recommended that availibility of a replacement air exhauster is determined prior to attempting to remove it.

REMOVAL

(1) Using a trim stick, C-4755, between air exhaster and hard top, disengage one edge of exhauster from hard top.

(2) Separate the air exhauster from the hard top.

INSTALLATION

(1) Position the air exhauster on the hard top.

(2) Press air exhauster into opening in hard top until fully seated.

SOFT TOP

REMOVAL

(1) Unlatch top at windshield frame.

(2) Disengage J-straps at upper door opening frame.

(3) Remove quarter windows.

(4) Disengage J-straps at soft top rear corners (Fig. 45).

(5) Disengage the retainers attaching the rear window to the body.

(6) Remove rear window.

(7) Lower the top to the rearward position.

(8) Remove the screws attaching the roof bows to the pivot bracket (Fig. 46).

(9) Remove the top (Fig. 47).

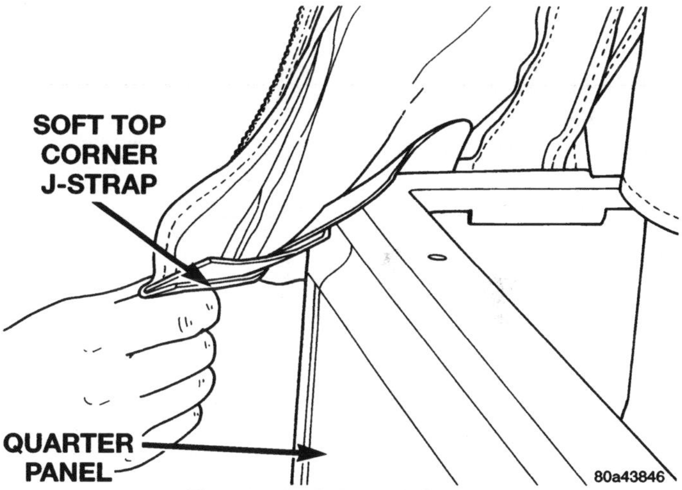

Fig. 45 Soft Top J-Straps

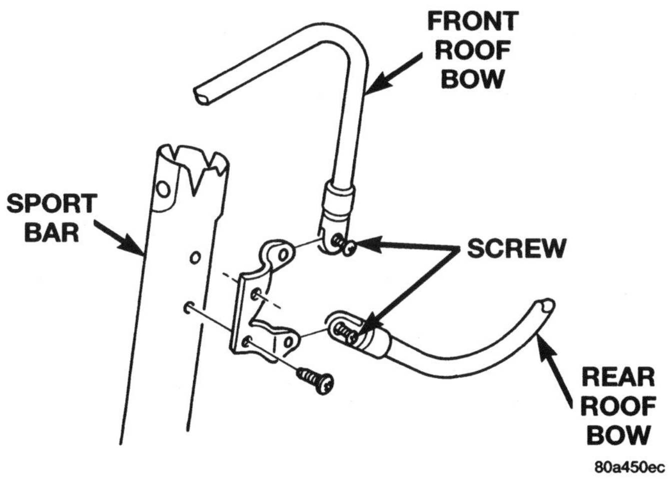

Fig. 46 Roof Bow Removal

REMOVAL AND INSTALLATION (Continued)

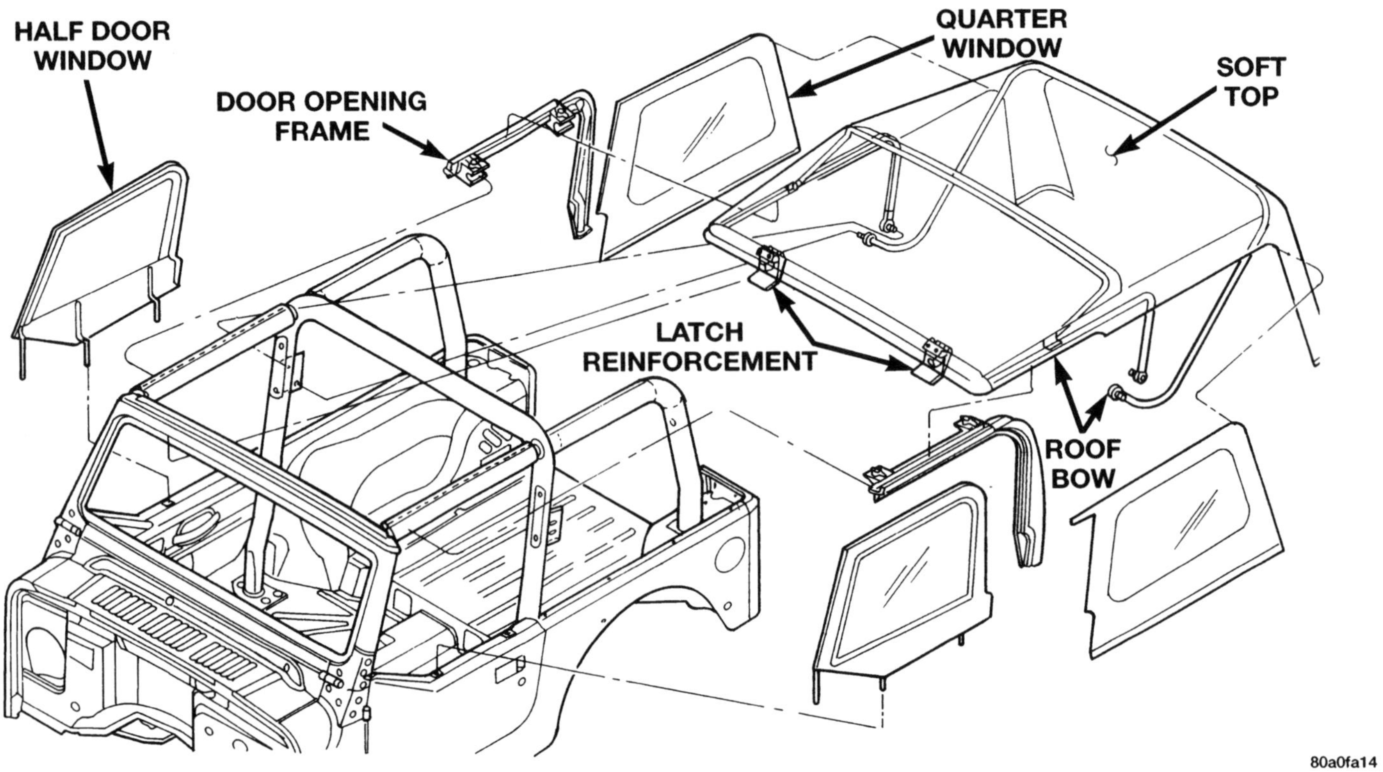

Fig. 47 Soft Top

INSTALLATION

(1) Position the top on the vehicle.

(2) Install the screws attaching the roof bows to the pivot bracket.

(3) Raise the top.

(4) Install rear window.

(5) Latch top at windshield frame.

(6) Engage J-straps at door opening frame.

(7) Install the quarter windows.

(8) Engage J-straps at soft top rear corners.

(9) Engage the retainers attaching the rear window to the body.

SOFT TOP FABRIC

REMOVAL

(1) Unlatch top at windshield frame.

(2) Disengage J-straps at door opening frame.

(3) Disengage the J-straps attaching the quarter windows to the body.

(4) Disengage the retainers attaching the rear window to the body.

(5) Remove the screws attaching the soft top fabric to the front roof bow.

(6) Disengage the hook and loop fastener attaching soft top fabric to the center roof bow.

(7) Disengage the snaps attaching the soft top fabric to the rear roof bow.

(8) Separate the soft top fabric from the frame.

INSTALLATION

(1) Position the soft top fabric on the frame.

(2) Install the screws attaching the soft top fabric to the front roof bow.

(3) Engage the hook and loop fastener attaching soft top fabric to the center roof bow.

(4) Engage the snaps attaching the soft top fabric to the rear roof bow.

(5) Latch the top at windshield frame.

(6) Engage J-straps at door opening frame.

(7) Engage the J-straps attaching the quarter windows to the body.

(8) Engage the retainers attaching the rear window to the body.

REMOVAL AND INSTALLATION (Continued)

HARD/SOFT TOP LATCH

REMOVAL

(1) Unlatch the top (Fig. 48).

(2) Using a wax pencil, mark the position of the latch on the top.

(3) Remove the screws attaching the latch to the top.

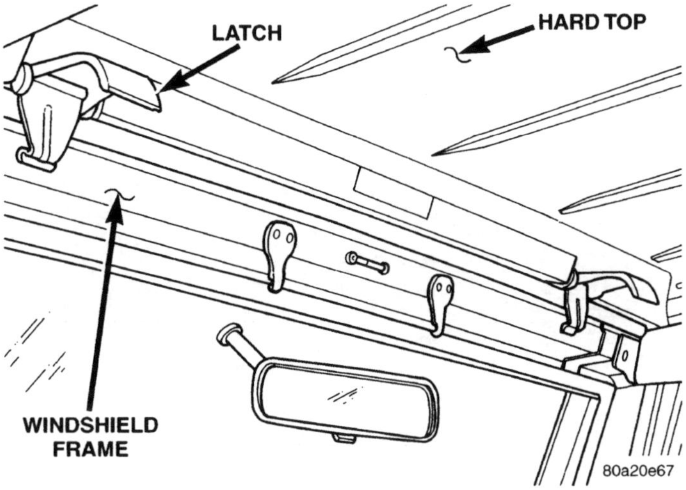

Fig. 48 Hard/Soft Top Latch

INSTALLATION

(1) Position the latch on the top and install the screws.

DOOR OPENING FRAME

Vehicles equipped with a soft top require a door opening frame to complete the seal for the soft top door assembly.

REMOVAL

(1) Open door.

(2) Unlatch top at windshield frame.

(3) Disengage J-straps at upper door opening frame.

(4) Remove quarter windows.

(5) Disengage J-straps at soft top rear corners (Fig. 45).

(6) Disengage the retainers attaching the rear window to the body.

(7) Remove rear window.

(8) Lower the top to the rearward position.

(9) Turn the knobs located on top of the door opening frame counter clockwise and remove completely (Fig. 49).

(10) Pull door opening frame outward and up. Separate from vehicle.

INSTALLATION

(1) Install the alignment pin at the base of the door opening frame into the hole at the top of the quarter panel.

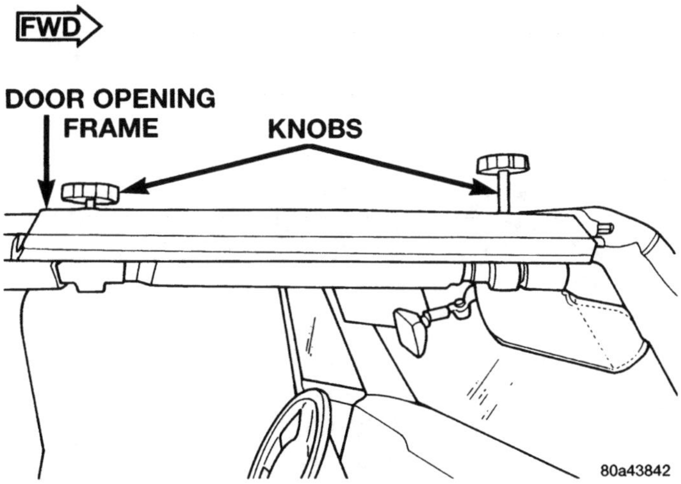

Fig. 49 Door Opening Frame

(2) Position the door opening frame on the side support bar and install the knobs.

(3) Raise the top.

(4) Install rear window.

(5) Latch top at windshield frame.

(6) Engage J-straps at door opening frame.

(7) Install the quarter windows.

(8) Engage J-straps at soft top rear corners.

(9) Engage the retainers attaching the rear window to the body.

FRONT SHOULDER/LAP BELT AND BUCKLE

FRONT SHOULDER/LAP BELT AND RETRACTOR REMOVAL

(1) Move front seat to the full forward position.

(2) Remove the bolt attaching the retractor to the sport bar (Fig. 50).

(3) Using a small flat blade, pry the cover from the turning loop.

(4) Remove the bolt attaching the turning loop to the height adjuster (Fig. 51).

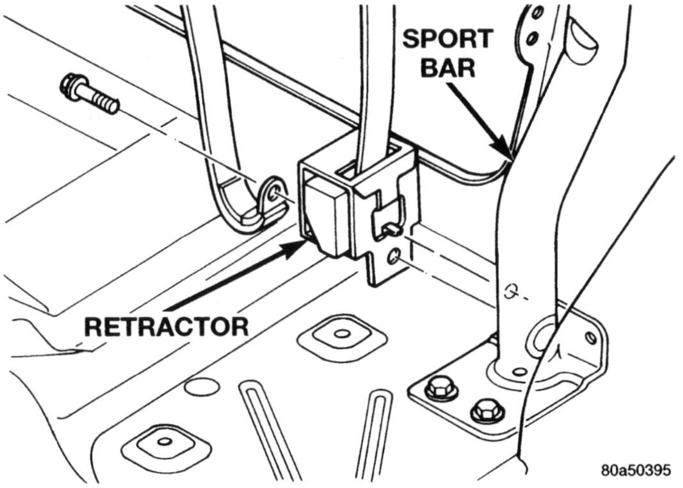

Fig. 50 Front Retractor

REMOVAL AND INSTALLATION (Continued)

(5) Separate the belt assembly from the vehicle.

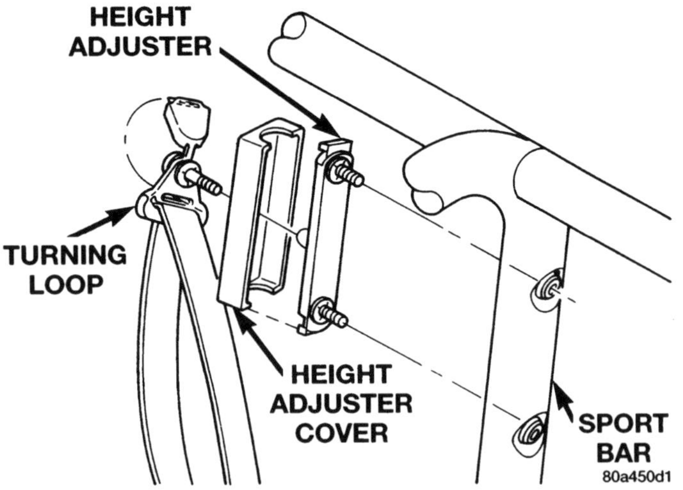

Fig. 51 Front Turning Loop

FRONT SHOULDER/LAP BELT AND RETRACTOR INSTALLATION

(1) Position the turning loop on the height adjuster and install the bolt. Tighten the bolt to 47 N·m (35 ft. lbs.) torque.

(2) Close the cover on the turning loop.

(3) Install the bolt attaching the retractor to the sport bar. Tighten the bolt to 47 N·m (35 ft. lbs.) torque.

FRONT SEAT BELT BUCKLE REMOVAL

(1) Remove the bolt attaching the seat belt buckle to the seat track/seat riser (Fig. 52).

(2) Disengage seat belt harness connector (driver's seat only).

(3) Remove buckle from vehicle.

FRONT SEAT BELT BUCKLE INSTALLATION

(1) Position the buckle on the seat track/seat riser and install the bolt.

(2) Engage seat belt harness connector (driver's seat only).

REAR SHOULDER/LAP BELT AND BUCKLE

SEAT/LAP BELT AND RETRACTOR REMOVAL

(1) Move the rear seat to the forward tumble position.

(2) Remove the anchor bolt attaching the belt to the wheelhouse (Fig. 55).

(3) Using a flat blade, pry the cover off the turning loop (Fig. 53).

(4) Remove the bolt attaching the turning loop to the sport bar (Fig. 54).

(5) Remove the bolt attaching the retractor to the sport bar.

(6) Separate the belt assembly from the vehicle.

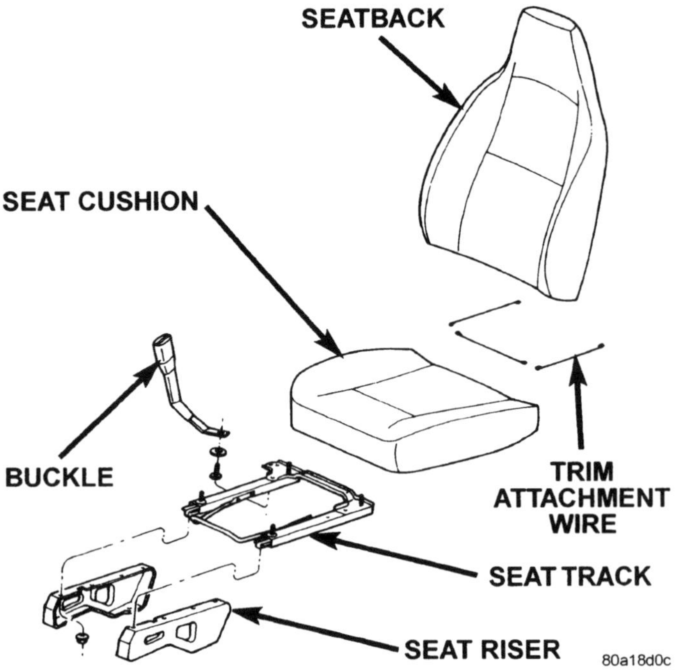

Fig. 52 Seat Belt Buckle

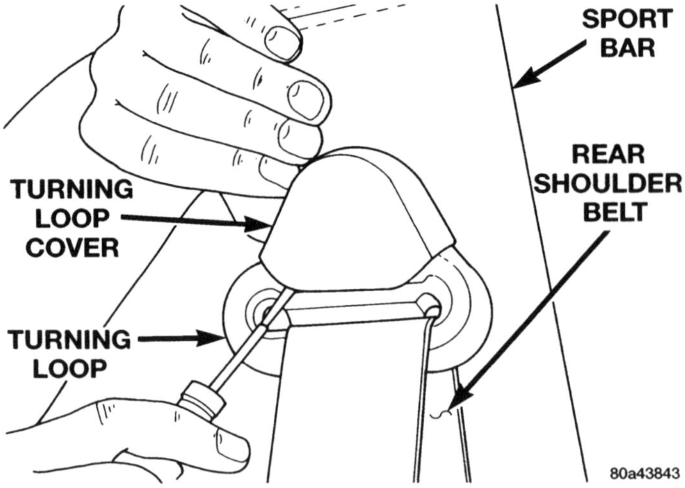

Fig. 53 Turning Loop Cover

SEAT/LAP BELT AND RETRACTOR INSTALLATION

(1) Position the retractor on the sport bar and install the bolt. Tighten the bolt to 47 N·m (35 ft. lbs.) torque.

(2) Position the turning loop on the sport bar and install the bolt. Tighten the bolt to 47 N·m (35 ft. lbs.) torque.

(3) Close cover on turning loop.

(4) Position the belt anchor on the wheelhouse and install the bolt. Tighten the bolt to 47 N·m (35 ft. lbs.) torque.

(5) Move the rear seat back to the latch position.

REMOVAL AND INSTALLATION (Continued)

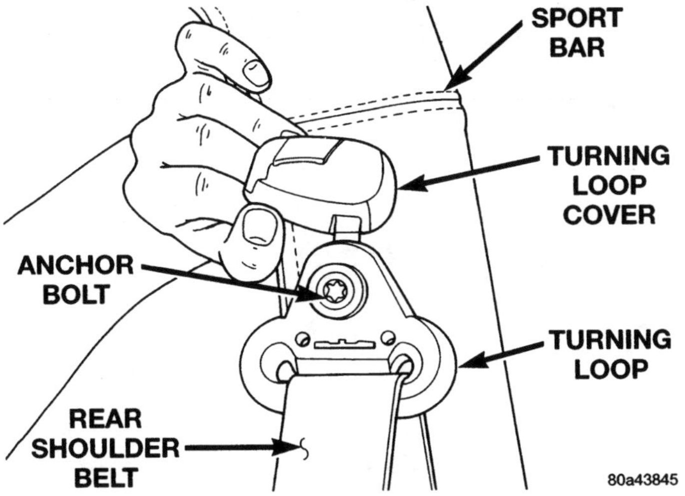

Fig. 54 Turning Loop

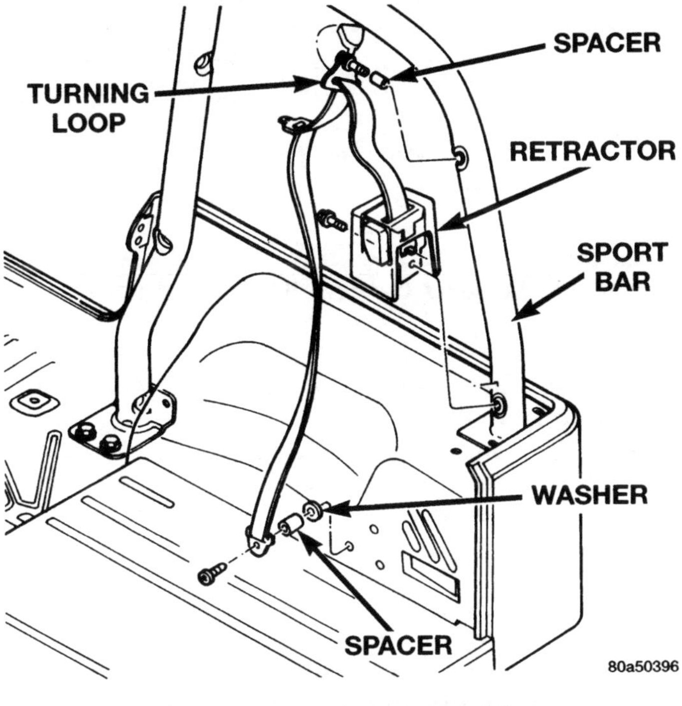

Fig. 55 Rear Belt Assembly

REAR BUCKLE REMOVAL

(1) Move the rear seat to the forward tumble position.

(2) Grasp the carpet between the buckles and lift to access the anchor bolt.

(3) Remove the anchor bolt and separate the buckle from the vehicle (Fig. 56).

REAR BUCKLE INSTALLATION

(1) Route the buckle through the carpet and align the holes.

(2) Install the anchor bolt. Tighten the bolt to 43 N·m (32 ft. lbs.) torque.

(3) Move the rear seat back to the latch position.

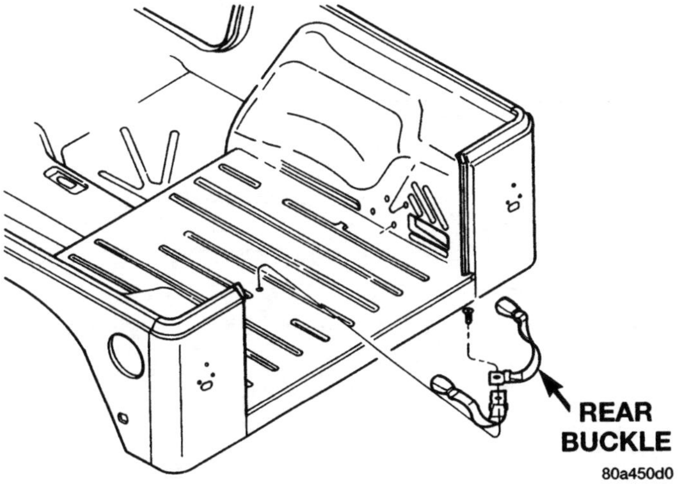

Fig. 56 Rear Buckle

BUCKET SEAT

REMOVAL

(1) Disengage seat belt electrical connector (Fig. 57).

(2) Remove the bolts attaching the rear of the seat frame to the floor panel.

(3) Remove the nuts attaching the front of the seat frame to floor panel (Fig. 58).

(4) Remove the seat from the vehicle.

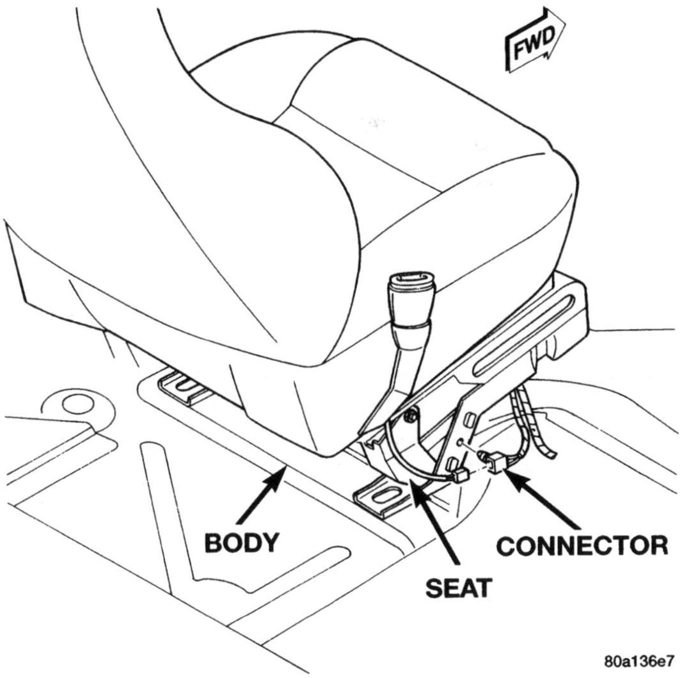

Fig. 57 Bucket Seat

INSTALLATION

(1) Position the seat in the vehicle.

(2) Install the bolts attaching the rear of seat frame to the floor panel. Tighten outboard bolts to 33

REMOVAL AND INSTALLATION (Continued)

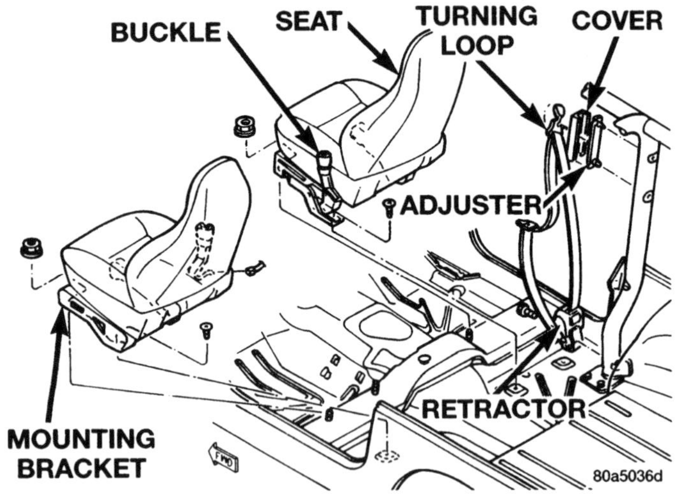

Fig. 58 Bucket Seat Removal

N·m (25 ft. lbs.) torque. Tighten inboard bolts to 47 N·m (35 ft. lbs.) torque.

(3) Install the nuts attaching the front of seat frame to the floor panel. Tighten nuts to 33 N·m (25 ft. lbs.) torque.

(4) Engage seat belt electrical connector.

MINI FLOOR CONSOLE

REMOVAL

(1) Move the seats to the full rearward position.

(2) Grasp shift handle (auto trans only) and firmly pull upward to remove.

(3) Using a small flat blade, pry up shift indicator bezel, disengage bezel lamp connector and remove bezel (auto trans only).

(4) Using a trim stick, pry up shift boot and remove (manual trans only).

(5) Remove the trim disc from the bottom of the cup holder.

(6) Remove the bolts attaching the console to the floor pan (Fig. 59).

(7) Shift transfer case to four low position.

(8) Lift the console upward and shift transmission to L (2nd gear for man. trans.).

(9) Remove console through the passenger door.

INSTALLATION

(1) Position and align the console in the vehicle.

(2) Install the bolts attaching the console to the floor pan.

(3) Install the trim disc

(4) Install shift boot/indicator bezel.

(5) Return seats to normal position.

(6) Install the shift handle.

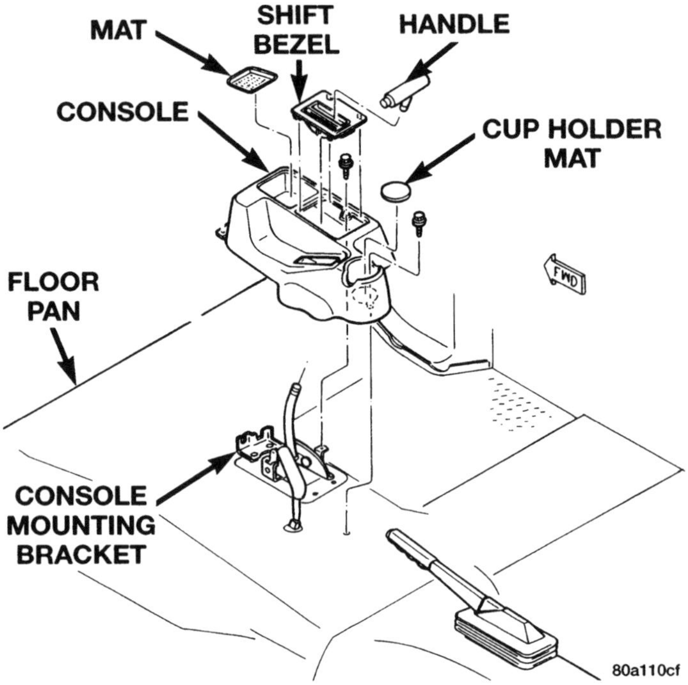

Fig. 59 Mini Floor Console

FULL FLOOR CONSOLE

REMOVAL

(1) Move the seats to the full rearward position.

(2) Move the passenger seat in the full recline position.

(3) Grasp shift handle (auto trans only) and firmly pull upward to remove.

(4) Using a small flat blade, pry up shift indicator bezel, disengage bezel lamp connector and remove bezel (auto trans only).

(5) Using a trim stick, pry up shift boot and remove (manual trans only).

(6) Remove the bolts attaching the console to the floor pan (Fig. 60).

(7) Shift transfer case to four low position.

(8) Engage parking brake.

(9) Lift the console upward and rotate to remove through the passenger door.

INSTALLATION

(1) Position and align the console in the vehicle.

(2) Install the bolts attaching the console to the floor pan.

(3) Install shift boot/indicator bezel.

(4) Return seats to normal position.

(5) Install the shift handle.

CONSOLE LOCK CYLINDER

REMOVAL

(1) Open the console cover.

REMOVAL AND INSTALLATION (Continued)

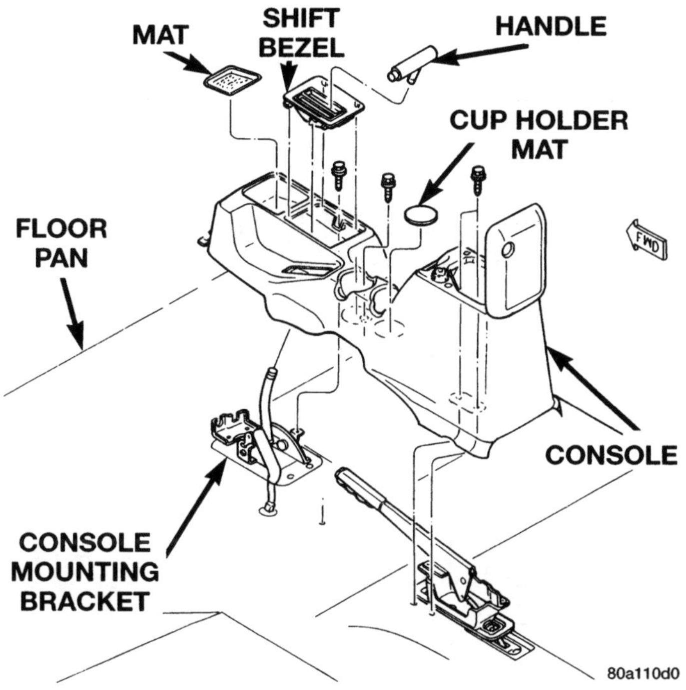

Fig. 60 Full Floor Console

(2) Remove the screw that attaches the retainer to the lock and then remove the retainer from the lock (Fig. 61).

(3) Remove the lock cylinder from the console cover.

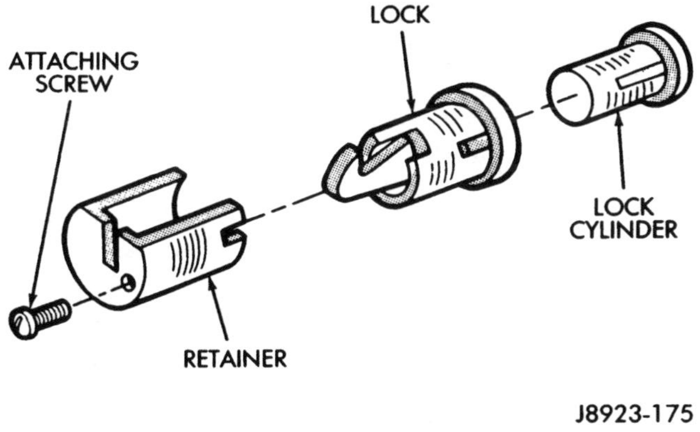

Fig. 61 Console Lock Cylinder

INSTALLATION

(1) Insert the assembled lock in the console cover hole and position the retainer on the lock and install the screw.

SHIFT BOOT

REMOVAL

(1) Using a trim stick, pry the shift boot from the bezel.

(2) Using a small flat blade, pry the shift pattern insert from the shift knob.

(3) Remove the nut attaching the shift knob to the shift lever (Fig. 62).

(4) Remove the knob and slide the shift boot from the shift lever.

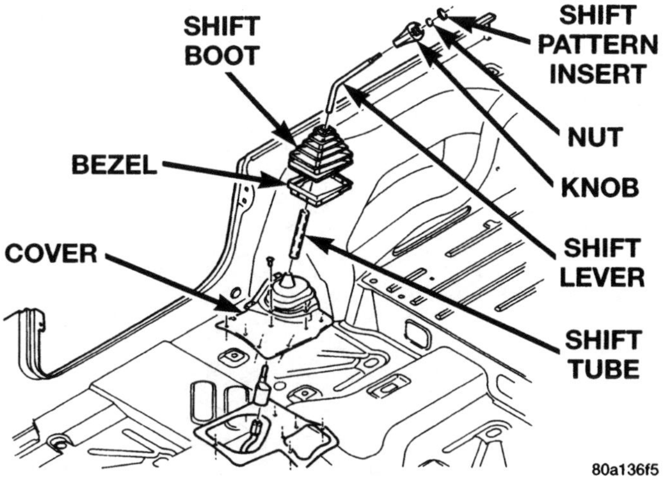

Fig. 62 Shift Boot

INSTALLATION

(1) Slide the shift boot over the shift lever.

(2) Position the shift knob on the lever and install the nut.

(3) Position the shift pattern insert on the knob and press into place.

REAR SEAT

REMOVAL

(1) Move the front seats to the full forward position.

(2) Pull on the rear seat latch to disengage the rear seat from the striker.

(3) Lift the rear seat to the forward tumble position.

(4) Remove the hitch pins from the seat frame pivot pins.

(5) Slide the seat to the left to disengage the pivot pin from the pivot bracket.

(6) Slide the seat to the right to disengage the opposite pivot pin from the pivot bracket (Fig. 63).

(7) Remove the seat through the passenger door opening.

INSTALLATION

(1) Position the seat on the rear floor panel and engage the seat frame pivot pins with the pivot brackets.

(2) Install the hitch pins on the seat frame pivot pins.

(3) Move the seat back to the latch position and engage the strikers with the latch brackets.

REMOVAL AND INSTALLATION (Continued)

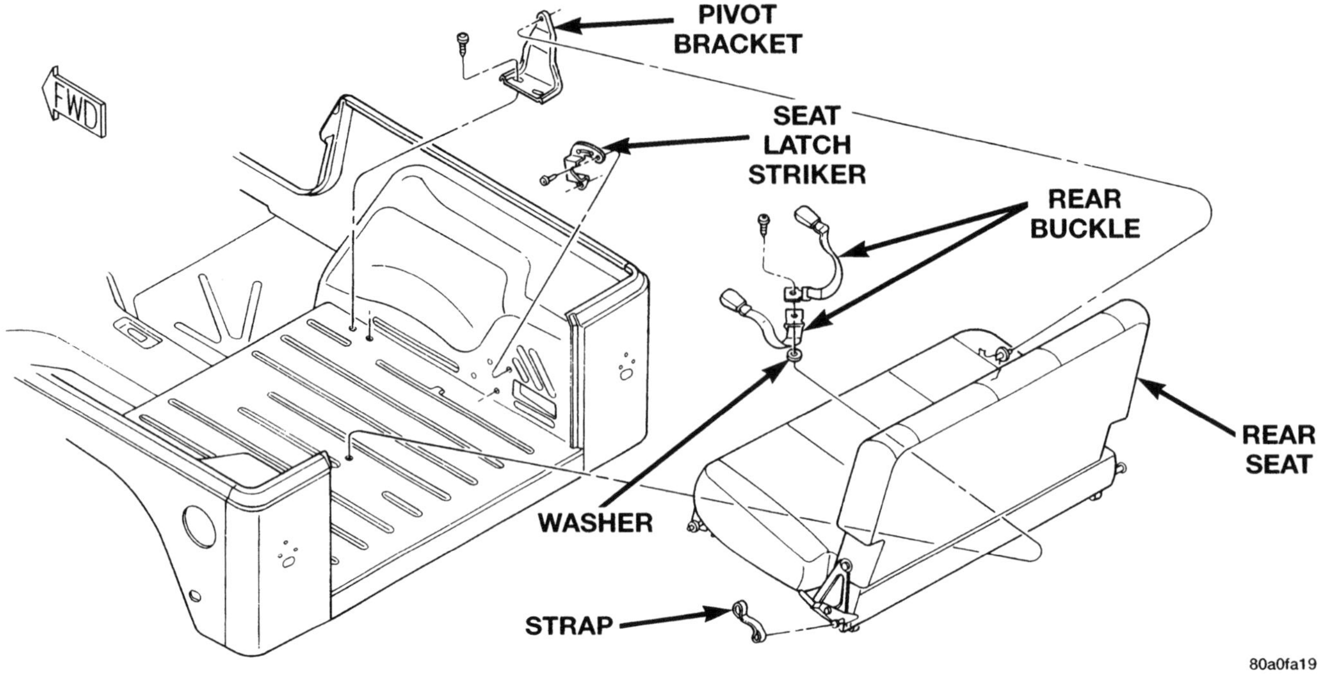

Fig. 63 Rear Seat

ADD-A-TRUNK

REMOVAL

(1) Release latches under trunk panel and lift panel up.

(2) Remove bolts attaching trunk to inner body panel (Fig. 64).

(3) Separate trunk from vehicle.

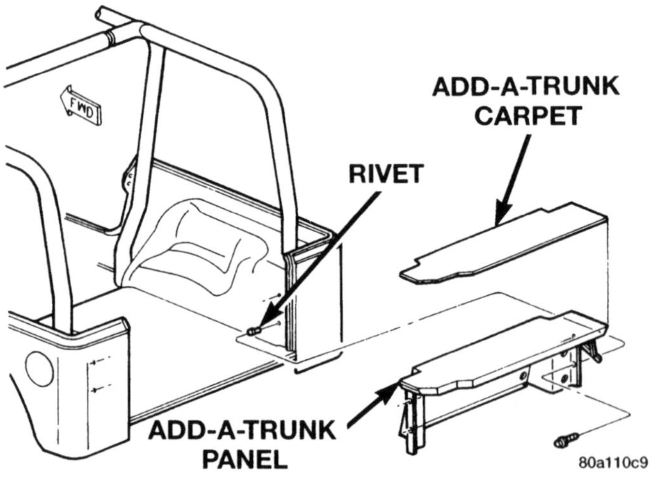

Fig. 64 Add-A-Trunk

INSTALLATION

(1) Position the trunk in the cargo space.

(2) Install the bolts.

FRONT CARPET/MAT

REMOVAL

(1) Remove the screws attaching the console to the floor pan.

(2) If equipped, remove the retainers attaching the carpet/mat to the dash panel (Fig. 65).

(3) Disengage the snaps around the perimeter of the seats.

(4) Remove carpet/mat from the vehicle

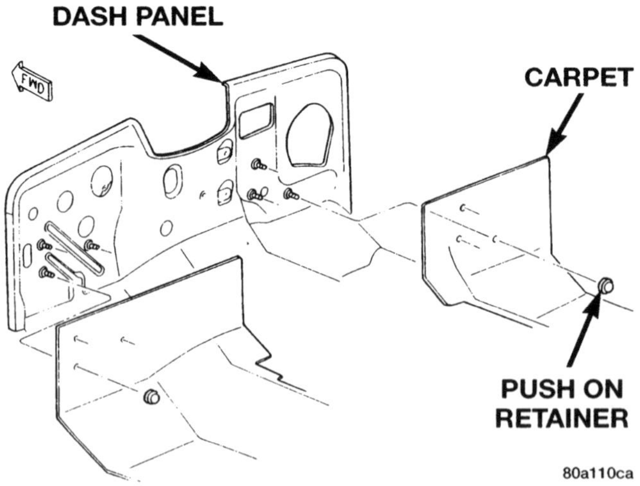

Fig. 65 Front Carpet/Mat

INSTALLATION

(1) Position the carpet/mat in the vehicle

(2) Engage the snaps around the perimeter of the seats.

REMOVAL AND INSTALLATION (Continued)

(3) If equipped, Install the retainers attaching the carpet/mat to the dash panel.

(4) Install the screws attaching the console to the floor pan.

CENTER CARPET

REMOVAL

(1) Disengage the snaps around the perimeter of the bucket seats.

(2) Remove the carpet.

INSTALLATION

(1) Position the carpet in the vehicle.

(2) Engage the snaps around the perimeter of the bucket seats.

CARGO AREA CARPET/MAT

REMOVAL

(1) Position the rear seat in the full forward position.

(2) Pull the from under the rear seat.

(3) If equipped, remove the Add-A-Trunk.

(4) Route the rear seat belt buckles through the cargo area carpet/mat

(5) Separate the carpet/mat from the vehicle (Fig. 66).

INSTALLATION

(1) Position the carpet/mat in the vehicle.

(2) If necessary, cut access slits into carpet for cargo holddown loops and rear seat belt buckle anchors.

(3) Route the rear seat belt buckles through the cargo area carpet/mat

(4) If equipped, install the Add-A-Trunk.

(5) Position the rear seat in the full rearward position.

WHEELHOUSE CARPET

REMOVAL

(1) Position the rear seat in the full forward position.

(2) If equipped, remove the Add-A-trunk.

(3) Grasp wheelhouse carpet and remove from vehicle (Fig. 66).

INSTALLATION

(1) Position wheelhouse carpet in vehicle and adjust as necessary.

(2) If equipped, install the Add-A-trunk.

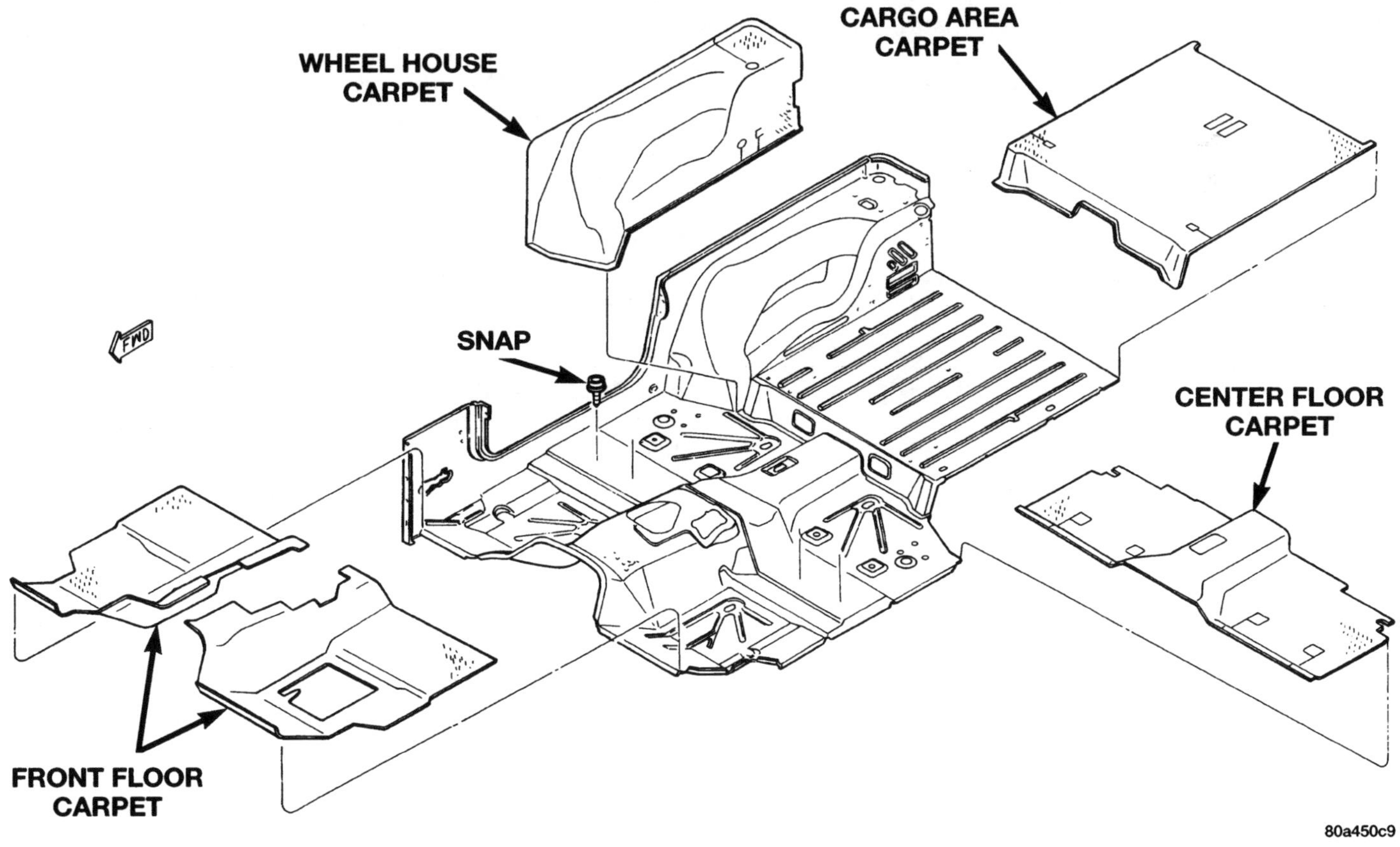

Fig. 66 Vehicle Carpet

REMOVAL AND INSTALLATION (Continued)

(3) Position the rear seat in the full rearward position.

SPORT BAR

REMOVAL

(1) Remove hard top and/or soft top.
(2) Remove the door opening frames.
(3) Remove the sunvisors.
(4) Remove the A-pillar weatherstrips strips (Fig. 67).
(5) Disengage center support bar cover zipper.
(6) Remove the bolts attaching the side support bars to the center support bar (Fig. 68).
(7) Remove the bolts attaching the side support bars to the windshield frame.
(8) Separate the side support bars from the vehicle.
(9) Pull back the center section of the car/mat and remove the bolts attaching the sport bar to the cargo floor panel.
(10) Lower the rear seat and lift rear seat to the full forward position.
(11) Pull back wheelhouse carpet and remove bolts attaching the directional cross bars to the wheelhouse.
(12) Remove the bolts attaching the seatbelt anchors to the wheelhouse.
(13) Disconnect sound bar. Refer to Group 8F, Audio Systems for removal and installation procedures.
(14) Carefully lift the sport bar upward and remove it from the vehicle.
(15) If necessary, remove the pads and covers from the sport bar.

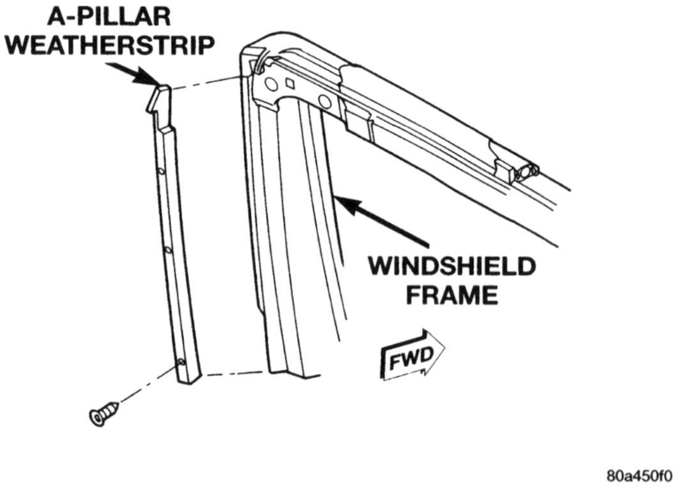

Fig. 67 A-Pillar Weatherstrip

INSTALLATION

(1) If necessary, transfer all attached components.
(2) Clean the base plate contact surface areas on the floor and wheelhouse panels.
(3) Apply epoxy chromate primer to the attaching hole edges for protection against corrosion.
(4) Position the sport bar base plates on the floor and wheelhouse panels with the holes aligned.

NOTE: To prevent water seepage, apply 3M Drip-Chek Sealant (or an equivalent product) to the underside of the sport bar base flanges and all the bolt heads before installation.

(5) Connect sound bar. Refer to Group 8F, Audio Systems for removal and installation procedures.
(6) Install the bolts attaching the seatbelt anchors to the wheelhouse.
(7) Install the bolts attaching the directional cross bars to the wheelhouse and install the wheelhouse carpet. Tighten the bolts to 40 N·m (30 ft. lbs.) torque.
(8) Return seat back to upright position.
(9) Install the bolts attaching the sport bar to the cargo floor panel and install the center carpet. Tighten the bolts to 40 N·m (30 ft. lbs.) torque.
(10) Position side supports at the windshield and install the bolts attaching the side support bars to the windshield frame. Tighten the bolts to 32 N·m (24 ft. lbs.) torque.
(11) Install the bolts attaching the side support bars to the center support bar. Tighten the bolts to 71 N·m (53 ft. lbs.) torque.
(12) Engage center support bar cover zipper.
(13) Install the A-pillar windshield strips.
(14) Install the door opening frames.
(15) Install hard top and/or soft top.

REAR VIEW MIRROR

REMOVAL

(1) Loosen the mirror set screw.
(2) Slide the mirror up and off the support button (bracket) (Fig. 69).

INSTALLATION

(1) Slide the mirror onto the support button (bracket).

CAUTION: Do not over-tighten the setscrew because glass chipping and/or breakage could result.

(2) Tighten the mirror setscrew to 1 N·m (9 in. lbs.) torque.

REARVIEW MIRROR SUPPORT BRACKET

INSTALLATION

(1) Mark the position for the mirror bracket on the outside of the windshield glass with a wax pencil.

REMOVAL AND INSTALLATION (Continued)

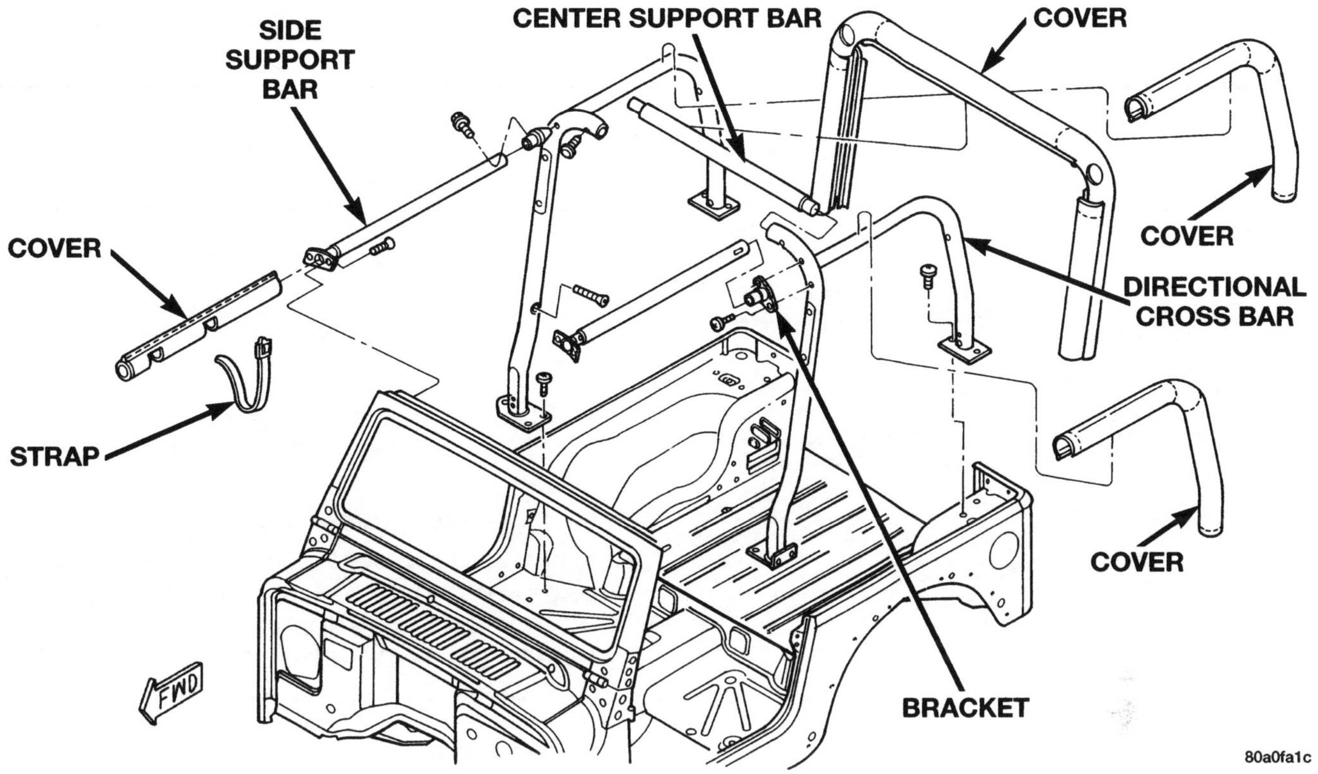

Fig. 68 Sport Bar

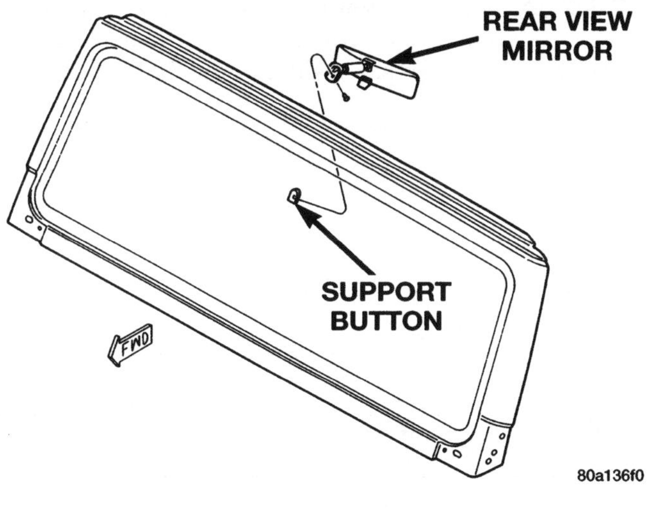

Fig. 69 Rear View Mirror

(2) Clean the bracket contact area on the glass. Use a mild powdered cleanser on a cloth saturated with isopropyl (rubbing) alcohol. Finally, clean the glass with a paper towel dampened with alcohol.

(3) Sand the surface on the support bracket with fine grit-sandpaper. Wipe the bracket surface clean with a paper towel.

(4) Apply accelerator to the surface on the bracket according to the following instructions:

- Crush the vial to saturate the felt applicator.
- Remove the paper sleeve.
- Apply accelerator to the contact surface on the bracket.
- Allow the accelerator to dry for five minutes.
- Do not touch the bracket contact surface after the accelerator has been applied.

(5) Apply adhesive accelerator to the bracket contact surface on the windshield glass. Allow the accelerator to dry for one minute. Do not touch the glass contact surface after the accelerator has been applied.

(6) Install the bracket according to the following instructions:

- Apply one drop of adhesive at the center of the bracket contact-surface on the windshield glass.
- Apply an even coat of adhesive to the contact surface on the bracket.
- Align the bracket with the marked position on the windshield glass.
- Press and hold the bracket in place for at least one minute.

NOTE: Verify that the mirror support bracket is correctly aligned, because the adhesive will cure rapidly.

(7) Allow the adhesive to cure for 8-10 minutes. Remove any excess adhesive with an alcohol-dampened cloth.

(8) Allow the adhesive to cure for an additional 8-10 minutes before installing the mirror.

REMOVAL AND INSTALLATION (Continued)

SUNVISOR

REMOVAL

(1) Remove the screws that attach the sunvisor arm support brackets to the windshield frame (Fig. 70).

(2) Remove the sunvisor from the windshield frame

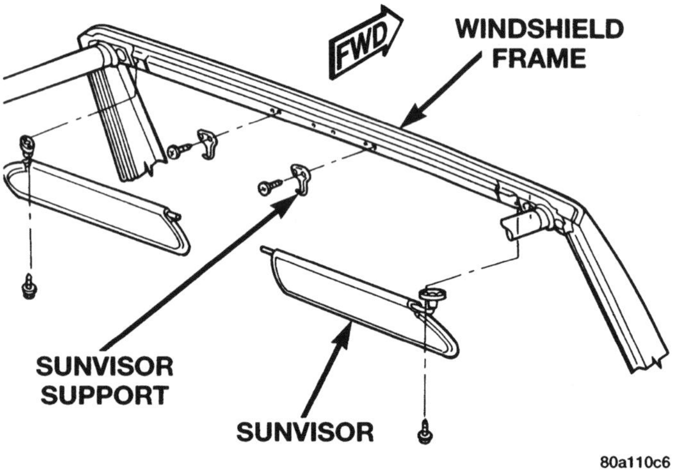

Fig. 70 Sunvisor

INSTALLATION

(1) Position the sunvisor on the windshield frame and align the arm support bracket holes with the frame.

(2) Install the screws that attach the sunvisor arm support brackets to the frame. Tighten the screws securely.

WHEELHOUSE SPLASH SHIELD

REMOVAL

(1) Remove the plastic rivets that attach the splash shield to the wheelhouse (Fig. 71).

(2) Remove the push-in fasteners attaching the splash shield to the wheelhouse. (The push-in fasteners are molded into the splash shield.)

(3) Remove the splash shield from the wheelhouse.

INSTALLATION

(1) Position the splash shield in the wheelhouse.

(2) Press the splash shield push-in fasteners into place.

(3) Attach the splash shield to the wheelhouse with rivets.

LIFTGATE GLASS SUPPORT CYLINDER

REMOVAL

WARNING: DO NOT REMOVE THE LIFTGATE SUPPORT RODS WITH THE LIFTGATE CLOSED. THE

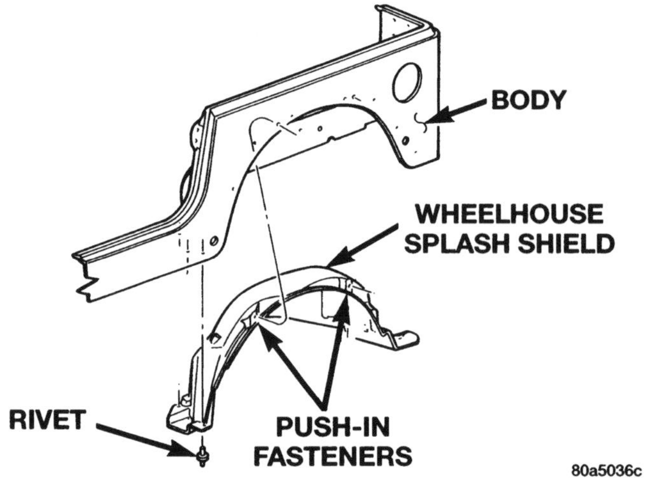

Fig. 71 Wheelhouse Splash Shield

SUPPORT ROD PISTONS ARE OPERATED BY HIGH PRESSURE GAS AND COULD CAUSE PERSONAL INJURY AND/OR VEHICLE DAMAGE IF THEY ARE REMOVED WITH THE PISTONS COMPRESSED (LIFTGATE CLOSED). ONCE REMOVED, DO NOT ATTEMPT TO DISASSEMBLE OR REPAIR THE SUPPORT RODS.

(1) Open and support the liftgate glass.

(2) Remove the support rod cylinder retaining clips at both ends of each support rod cylinder (Fig. 72).

(3) Pull the support rods off the ball studs (Fig. 73).

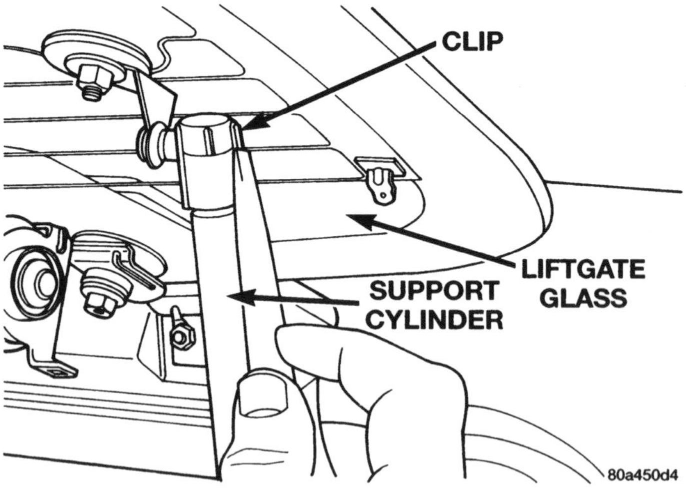

Fig. 72 Support Rod Cylinder

INSTALLATION

(1) Position the support rod cylinders on the ball studs.

(2) Install the support rod cylinder retainer clips.

REMOVAL AND INSTALLATION (Continued)

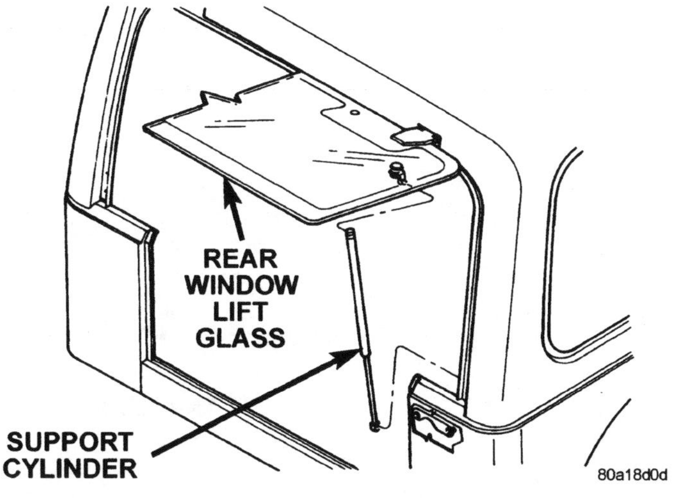

Fig. 73 Support Rod Cylinder Removal

LIFTGATE GLASS

REMOVAL

(1) If equipped, disconnect the rear defroster harness connectors (Fig. 74).

(2) If equipped, disconnect the wiper motor harness connectors.

WARNING: DO NOT REMOVE THE LIFTGATE SUPPORT RODS WITH THE LIFTGATE CLOSED. THE SUPPORT ROD PISTONS ARE OPERATED BY HIGH PRESSURE GAS AND COULD CAUSE PERSONAL INJURY AND/OR VEHICLE DAMAGE IF THEY ARE REMOVED WITH THE PISTONS COMPRESSED (LIFTGATE CLOSED). ONCE REMOVED, DO NOT ATTEMPT TO DISASSEMBLE OR REPAIR THE SUPPORT RODS.

(3) Open the tailgate and liftgate.

(4) Remove support rod cylinders.

(5) Remove the bolts attaching the liftgate hinge to the hardtop (Fig. 75).

(6) Separate the liftgate glass from the hard top.

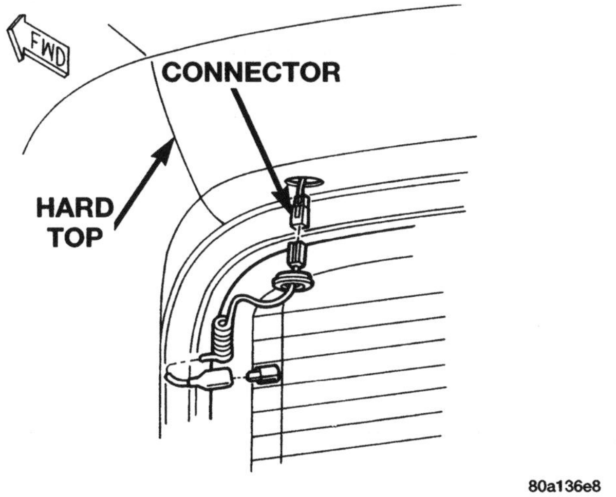

Fig. 74 Rear Defroster Connectors

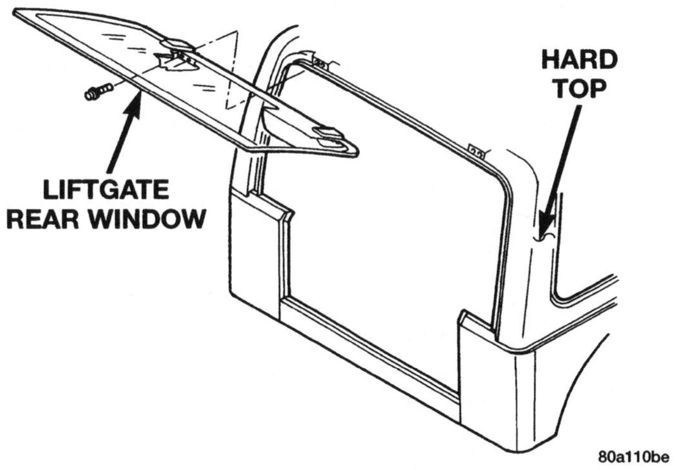

Fig. 75 Liftgate Glass

INSTALLATION

Transfer all related components

(1) If removed, install support rod ball studs. Tighten the nut to 12 N·m (112 in. lbs.) torque.

(2) Position the liftgate glass at the hard top.

(3) Install the bolts attaching the liftgate hinge to the hardtop. Tighten the bolts to 10 N·m (95 in. lbs.) torque.

(4) Position the support rod cylinders on the ball studs and install the clips.

LIFTGATE GLASS HINGE

REMOVAL

(1) Open tailgate.

(2) Open and support liftgate glass.

(3) Remove wiper motor cover (right hinge only).

(4) Remove the nut attaching the liftgate hinge to the liftgate glass.

(5) Mark the position of the hinge in the top and remove the bolts attaching the hinge to the top (Fig. 76).

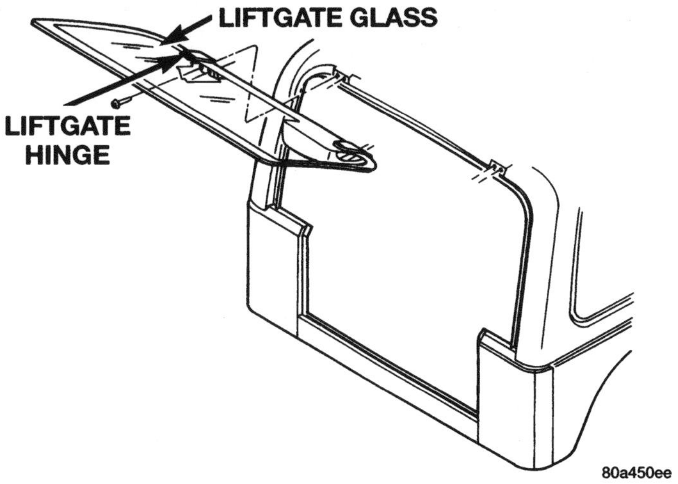

Fig. 76 Liftgate Hinge

REMOVAL AND INSTALLATION (Continued)

INSTALLATION

(1) Align and position the hinge on the top and install the bolts.

(2) Install the nut attaching the liftgate hinge to the liftgate glass. Tighten the nut to 6 N·m (53 in. lbs.) torque.

(3) If removed, install wiper motor cover.

LIFTGATE GLASS WEATHERSTRIP

REMOVAL

(1) Open the liftgate.

(2) Peel back corner of weatherstrip and slide weatherstrip out of liftgate glass channel.

INSTALLATION

(1) Position the weatherstrip in the liftgate glass weatherstrip channel.

(2) Slide weatherstrip through channel until seated.

SPARE TIRE CARRIER

REMOVAL

(1) Remove the spare tire from the wheel bracket (Fig. 77).

(2) Remove the bolts that attach the tire bracket to the tailgate (Fig. 78).

(3) Disconnect CHMSL.

(4) Remove the bracket and the gaskets from the tailgate.

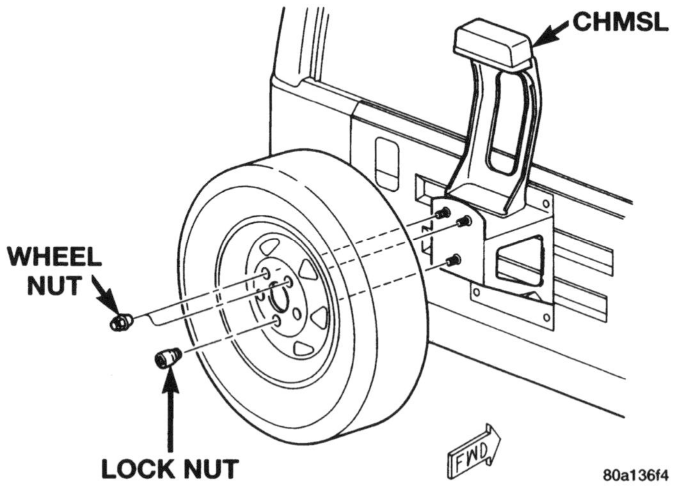

Fig. 77 Spare Tire

INSTALLATION

(1) Position the gaskets and the tire bracket on the tailgate and install the bolts. Tighten the bolts to 24 N·m (17 ft. lbs.) torque.

(2) Connect CHMSL connector.

(3) Install the spare tire on the tire bracket.

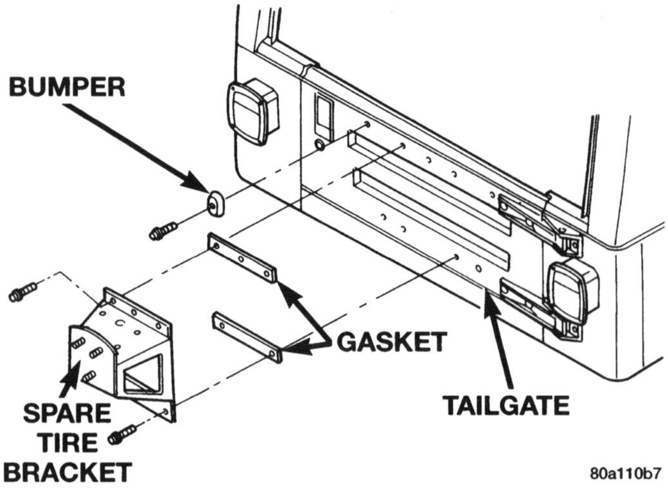

Fig. 78 Spare Tire Bracket

LICENSE PLATE BEZEL

REMOVAL

(1) If installed, remove the license plate.

(2) Remove the screws attaching the license plate bezel to the body (Fig. 79).

(3) Separate the bezel from the body.

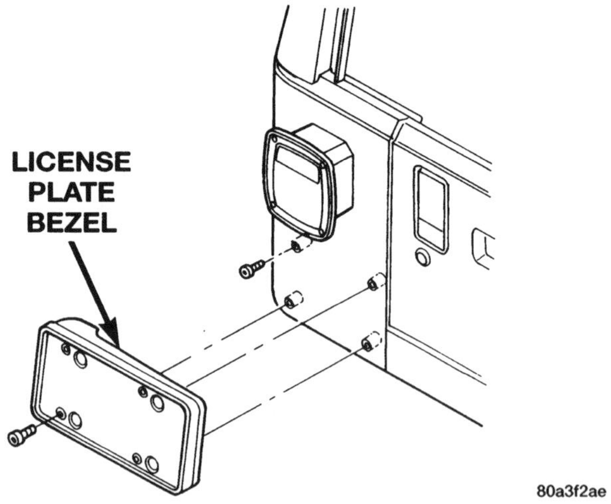

Fig. 79 License Plate Bezel

INSTALLATION

(1) Position the bezel on the body.

(2) Install the screws attaching the license plate bezel to the body.

(3) If removed, install the license plate.

TAILGATE

REMOVAL

(1) Remove the spare tire.

(2) Open the tailgate and remove the CHMSL contact cover (Fig. 80).

(3) Disengage the CHMSL electrical connectors.

REMOVAL AND INSTALLATION (Continued)

(4) Remove the screws that attach the tailgate hinge to the tailgate.

(5) Separate the tailgate from the vehicle.

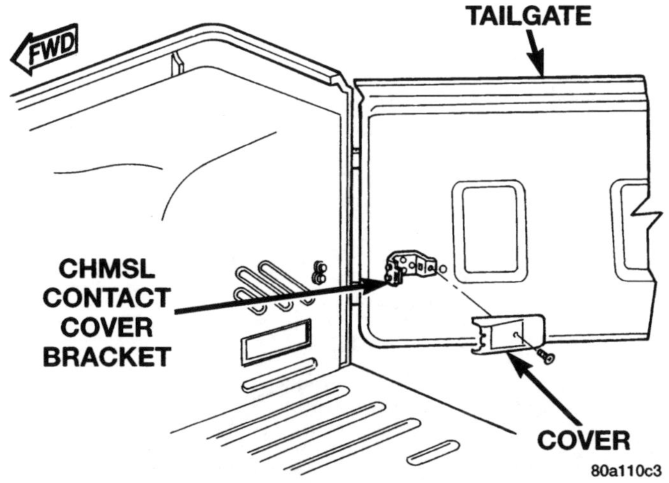

Fig. 80 CHMSL Contact Cover

INSTALLATION

If necessary, transfer tailgate related components.

(1) Install the screws that attach the tailgate hinge to the tailgate.

(2) Engage the CHMSL electrical connectors.

(3) Install the CHMSL contact cover.

(4) Close the tailgate and install the spare tire.

TAILGATE HINGE

Hinges may be serviced individually. If both are to be serviced, remove/install hinges one at a time.

REMOVAL

(1) Using a wax pencil, mark the position of the hinge on the body.

(2) Remove the screws attaching the hinge to the body and tailgate (Fig. 81).

(3) Separate the hinge from the tailgate.

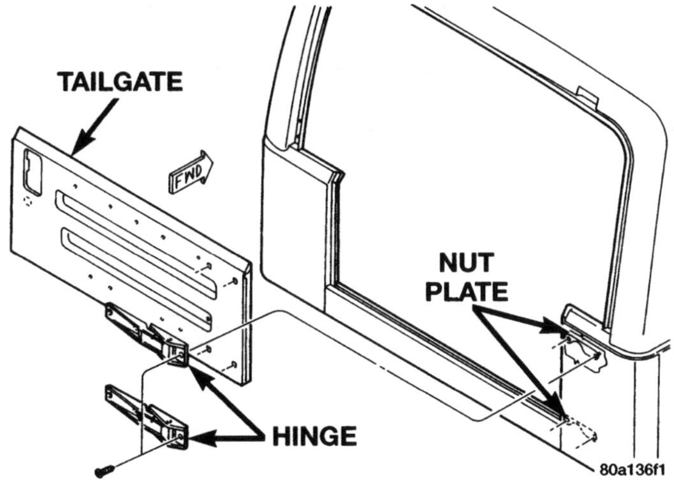

Fig. 81 Tailgate Hinge

INSTALLATION

(1) Prepare and paint the replacement hinge to match the body paint color.

(2) Lubricate the hinge with spray lubricant.

(3) Align and position the hinge on the body and tailgate.

(4) Install the screws. Tighten the screws to 23 N·m (200 in. lbs.) torque

TAILGATE OUTSIDE HANDLE

REMOVAL

(1) Remove the latch from the tailgate.

(2) Remove the screws attaching the outside handle to the tailgate (Fig. 82).

(3) Separate the outside handle and seal from the tailgate.

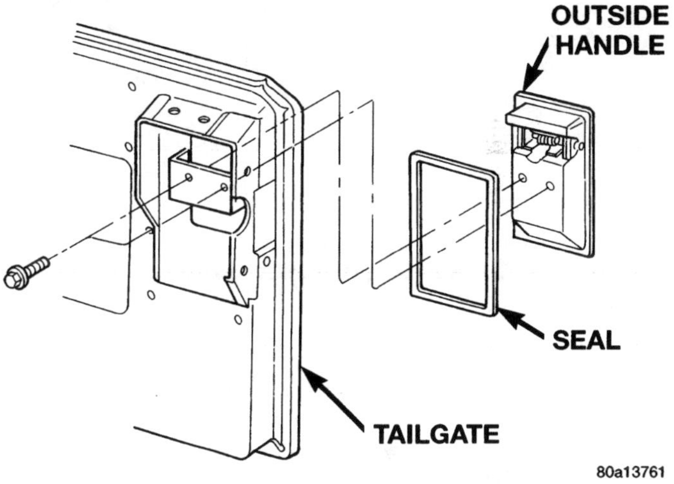

Fig. 82 Tailgate Outside Handle

INSTALLATION

(1) Position the seal and outside release handle on the tailgate. and install screws.

(2) Install the screws attaching the outside handle to the tailgate.

(3) Install the latch.

TAILGATE LOCK CYLINDER

REMOVAL

(1) Open the tailgate.

(2) Remove the latch cover.

(3) Remove the lock cylinder retainer clip.

Remove the lock cylinder from the tailgate opening.

INSTALLATION

(1) Position the lock cylinder in the tailgate opening.

(2) Connect the lock cylinder to latch rod.

(3) Install the lock cylinder retainer clip.

(4) Install the latch cover.

REMOVAL AND INSTALLATION (Continued)

TAILGATE LATCH

REMOVAL

(1) Open the tailgate and remove the latch trim cover (Fig. 83).
(2) Disconnect the outside handle to latch rod.
(3) Disconnect the lock cylinder to latch rod.
(4) Remove the screw attaching latch to tailgate.
(5) Separate the latch from the tailgate.

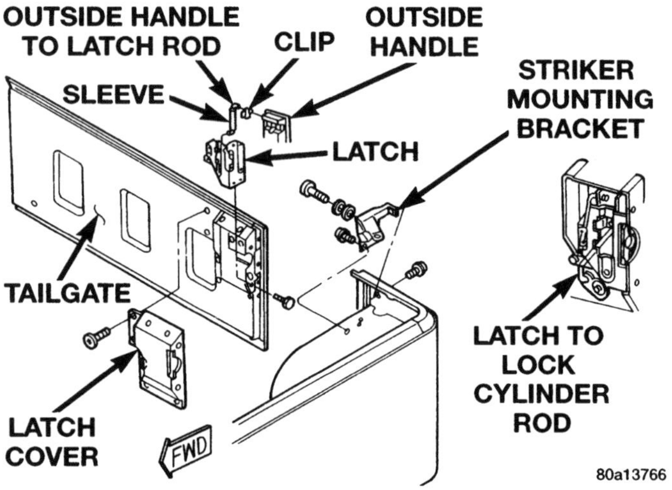

Fig. 83 Tailgate Latch Cover

INSTALLATION

(1) Position the latch in the tailgate.
(2) Install the screw attaching latch to tailgate. Do not tighten screw.
(3) Connect the lock cylinder to latch rod.
(4) Connect the outside handle to latch rod.
(5) Install the latch trim cover. Tighten all screws.

TAILGATE LATCH STRIKER

REMOVAL

(1) Remove the striker from the bracket with a Torx bit.
(2) Remove the shim washers from the bracket.
(3) Remove the screws attaching the striker bracket to the body.

INSTALLATION

(1) Position the striker bracket on the body and install the screws.
(2) Position the striker and shim washers on the striker bracket.
(3) Install the striker in the bracket with a Torx bit. Tighten the striker to 71 N·m (52 ft. lbs.) torque.

TAILGATE WEATHERSTRIP AND CHANNEL

REMOVAL

(1) Open the tailgate.
(2) Remove the push-in fasteners attaching the weatherstrip to the top corners of the tailgate (Fig. 84).
(3) Peel the weatherstrip from the upper tailgate corners.
(4) Slide the weatherstrip out of the tailgate.
(5) If the weatherstrip channel requires replacement, peel the weatherstrip channel from the tailgate.

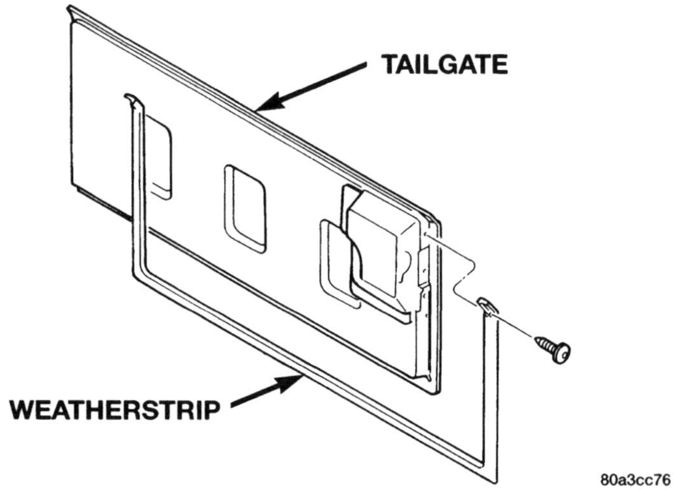

Fig. 84 Tailgate Weatherstrip

INSTALLATION

(1) If the weatherstrip channel is being replaced;
(a) Clean the channel contact surface on the tailgate with isopropyl alcohol, or equivalent.
(b) Peel the paper backing from the weatherstrip channel.
(c) Position weatherstrip channel to the tailgate and press into place.
(d) Use hand pressure or a roller to wet out the tape adhesive holding the weatherstrip channel to the tailgate.
(2) Slide the weatherstrip into the weatherstrip channel.
(3) Clean the weatherstrip contact surface on the tailgate with isopropyl alcohol, or equivalent.
(4) Remove paper backing from upper ends of weatherstrip.
(5) Position the weatherstrip to the tailgate and press it into place.
(6) Install the push-in fasteners attaching the weatherstrip to the tailgate.
(7) Use hand pressure or a roller to wet out the tape adhesive holding the weatherstrip to the tailgate.

ADJUSTMENTS

HOOD ADJUSTMENT

The hood hinge screw holes are oversized to facilitate hood adjustment movement.

(1) Loosen the screws.

(2) Move the hood in the direction(s) required for correct alignment.

(3) Tighten the screws.

DOOR ADJUSTMENT

The doors are adjusted at the hinge attaching locations on either the body or the door. Enlarged holes are located in the body (lower hinge only) for fore, aft and tilt adjustments. Enlarged holes are also located in the door (upper and lower hinges) for up, down, fore, aft and tilt adjustments.

Prior to door adjustment or alignment, the door latch must be removed to allow the door to close freely and be properly aligned.

The door latch striker should be adjusted in or out to allow the door latch to be fully engaged. The door should be flush with the adjacent body panels.

TAILGATE ADJUSTMENT

(1) Loosen the tailgate hinge-to-body screws.

(2) Align the tailgate in the body opening and tighten the hinge screws.

SPECIFICATIONS

BODY LUBRICANTS

COMPONENT	SERVICE INTERVAL	LUBRICANT
Door Latches	As Required	Multi-Purpose Grease NLGI GC-LB (Water Resistant) (1)
Hood Latch, Release Mechanism & Safety Latch	As Required (When Performing Other Underhood Service)	Multi-Purpose Grease NLGI GC-LB 2 EP (2)
Hood Hinges	As Required	Engine Oil
Seat Track & Release Mechanism	As Required	Multi-Purpose Grease NLGI GC-LB 2 EP (2)
Tailgate Hinge	As Required	Multi-Purpose Grease NLGI GC-LB 2 EP (2)
Liftgate Support Arms	As Required	Engine Oil
Tailgate Latches	As Required	White Spray Lubricant (3)
Tailgate Release Handle	As Required	Multi-Purpose Grease NLGI GC-LB 2 EP (2)
Window System Components	As Required	White Spray Lubricant (3)
Lock Cylinders	Twice A Year	Lock Cylinder Lubricant (4)
Parking Brake Mechanism	As Required	Multi-Purpose Grease NLGI GC-LB 2 EP (1)
1 = Mopar Wheel Bering Grease (High Temp) 2 = Mopar Multi-Mileage Lubricant 3 = Mopar Spray White Lube 4 = Mopar Lock Cylinder Lubricant		

SPECIFICATIONS (Continued)

TORQUE SPECIFICATIONS

DESCRIPTION	TORQUE
Hood hinge screws	17 N·m (155 in. lbs.)
Bucket seat front anchor nut	47 N·m (35 ft. lbs.)
Bucket seat rear inboard anchor bolt	47 N·m (35 ft. lbs.)
Bucket seat rear outboard anchor bolt	33 N·m (25 ft. lbs.)
Liftgate glass ball stud nut	12 N·m (112 in. lbs.)
Liftgate glass hinge nut	6 N·m (53 in. lbs.)
Liftgate hinge to hardtop bolt	10 N·m (95 in. lbs.)
Front turning loop bolt	47 N·m (35 ft. lbs.)
Front retractor bolt	47 N·m (35 ft. lbs.)
Rear retractor bolt	47 N·m (35 ft. lbs.)
Rear turning loop bolt	47 N·m (35 ft. lbs.)
Rear belt anchor bolt	47 N·m (35 ft. lbs.)
Rearview mirror setscrew	1 N·m (9 in. lbs.)
Rear buckle anchor bolt	43 N·m (32 ft. lbs.)
Side support bar to sport bar bolts	71 N·m (53 ft. lbs.)
Sport bar to wheelhouse bolts	40 N·m (30 ft. lbs.)
Sport bar to cargo floor bolts	40 N·m (30 ft. lbs.)
Sport bar to windshield frame bolts	32 N·m (24 ft. lbs.)
Tailgate hinge screws	23 N·m (200 in. lbs.)
Tailgate striker	71 N·m (52 ft. lbs.)

SPECIAL TOOLS

BODY

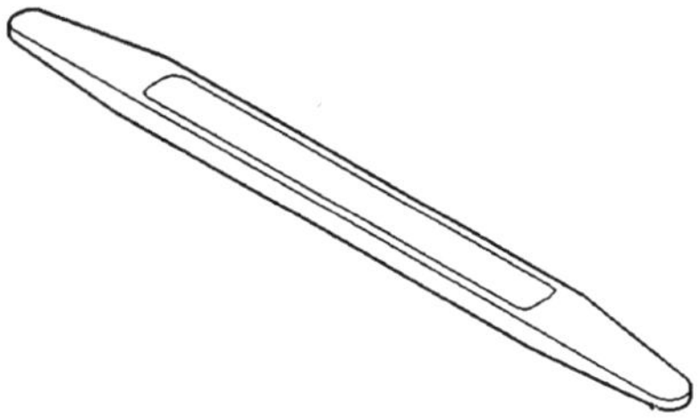

Trim Stick C-4755

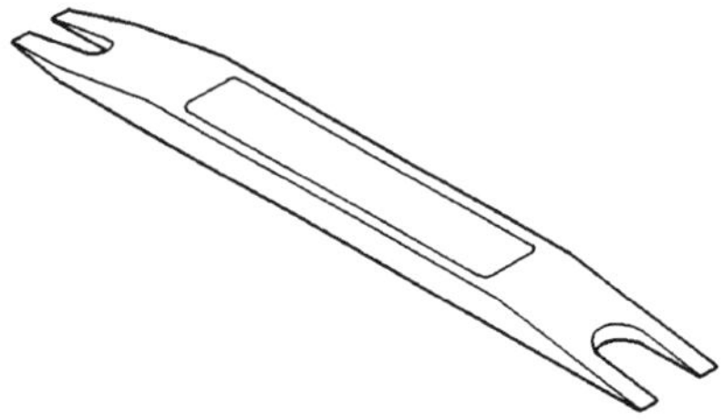

Remover, Moldings C-4829

HEATING AND AIR CONDITIONING

CONTENTS

GENERAL INFORMATION

HEATER AND AIR CONDITIONER

All vehicles are equipped with a common heater-A/C housing assembly (Fig. 1). The system combines air conditioning, heating, and ventilating capabilities in a single unit housing mounted under the instrument panel. On heater-only systems, the evaporator coil and recirculating air door are omitted from the housing.

Outside fresh air enters the vehicle through the cowl top opening at the base of the windshield, and

GENERAL INFORMATION (Continued)

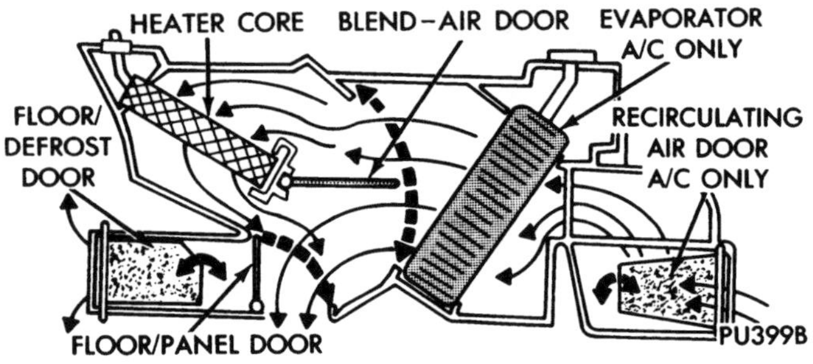

Fig. 1 Common Blend-Air Heater-Air Conditioner System - Typical

passes through a plenum chamber to the heater-A/C system blower housing. Air flow velocity can then be adjusted with the blower motor speed selector switch on the heater-A/C control panel. The air intake openings must be kept free of snow, ice, leaves, and other obstructions for the heater-A/C system to receive a sufficient volume of outside air.

The heater and optional air conditioner are blend-air type systems. In a blend-air system, a blend-air door controls the amount of unconditioned air (or cooled air from the evaporator on models with air conditioning) is allowed to flow through, or around, the heater core. A temperature control lever on the heater-A/C control panel determines the discharge air temperature by moving a cable, which operates the blend-air door. This allows an almost immediate manual control of the system's output air temperature.

The mode control lever on the heater-A/C control panel is used to direct the conditioned air to the selected system outlets. Both mode control switches use engine vacuum to control the mode doors, which are operated by vacuum actuator motors.

On air conditioned vehicles, the outside air intake can be shut off by selecting the Recirculation Mode with the mode control lever. This will open a vacuum actuated recirculating air door and recirculate the air that is already inside the vehicle.

The optional air conditioner for all models is designed for the use of non-CFC, R-134a refrigerant. The air conditioning system has an evaporator to cool and dehumidify the incoming air prior to blending it with the heated air. This system uses a fixed orifice tube in the liquid line near the condenser outlet tube to meter refrigerant flow to the evaporator coil. To maintain minimum evaporator temperature, a fixed pressure setting switch on the accumulator cycles the compressor clutch.

HEATER AND AIR CONDITIONER CONTROLS

Both the heater and heater-A/C systems use a combination of mechanical, electrical, and vacuum controls. These controls provide the vehicle operator with a number of setting options to help control the climate and comfort within the vehicle. Refer to the Owner's Manual for more information on the suggested operation and use of these controls.

The heater-only or heater-A/C control panel is located in the instrument panel center bezel below the radio and above the accessory switch bezel and ash receiver. The control panel contains a sliding-type temperature control knob, a sliding-type mode control switch knob, and a rotary-type blower motor speed switch knob.

SERVICE WARNINGS AND PRECAUTIONS

WARNING:

- **THE AIR CONDITIONING SYSTEM CONTAINS REFRIGERANT UNDER HIGH PRESSURE. SEVERE PERSONAL INJURY MAY RESULT FROM IMPROPER SERVICE PROCEDURES. REPAIRS SHOULD ONLY BE PERFORMED BY QUALIFIED SERVICE PERSONNEL.**
- **AVOID BREATHING THE REFRIGERANT AND REFRIGERANT OIL VAPOR OR MIST. EXPOSURE MAY IRRITATE EYES, NOSE, AND/OR THROAT. WEAR EYE PROTECTION WHEN SERVICING THE AIR CONDITIONING REFRIGERANT SYSTEM. SERIOUS EYE INJURY CAN RESULT FROM DIRECT CONTACT WITH THE REFRIGERANT. IF EYE CONTACT OCCURS, SEEK MEDICAL ATTENTION IMMEDIATELY.**
- **DO NOT EXPOSE THE REFRIGERANT TO OPEN FLAME. POISONOUS GAS IS CREATED WHEN REFRIGERANT IS BURNED. AN ELECTRONIC LEAK DETECTOR IS RECOMMENDED.**
- **IF ACCIDENTAL SYSTEM DISCHARGE OCCURS, VENTILATE THE WORK AREA BEFORE RESUMING SERVICE. LARGE AMOUNTS OF REFRIGERANT RELEASED IN A CLOSED WORK AREA WILL DISPLACE THE OXYGEN AND CAUSE SUFFOCATION.**
- **THE EVAPORATION RATE OF R-134a REFRIGERANT AT AVERAGE TEMPERATURE AND ALTITUDE IS EXTREMELY HIGH. AS A RESULT, ANYTHING THAT COMES IN CONTACT WITH THE REFRIGERANT WILL FREEZE. ALWAYS PROTECT THE SKIN OR DELICATE OBJECTS FROM DIRECT CONTACT WITH THE REFRIGERANT.**
- **THE R-134a SERVICE EQUIPMENT OR THE VEHICLE REFRIGERANT SYSTEM SHOULD NOT BE PRESSURE TESTED OR LEAK TESTED WITH COMPRESSED AIR. SOME MIXTURES OF AIR AND R-134a HAVE BEEN SHOWN TO BE COMBUSTIBLE AT ELEVATED PRESSURES. THESE MIXTURES ARE POTENTIALLY DANGEROUS, AND MAY RESULT IN FIRE OR EXPLOSION CAUSING INJURY OR PROPERTY DAMAGE.**

GENERAL INFORMATION (Continued)

CAUTION:

• Liquid refrigerant is corrosive to metal surfaces. Follow the operating instructions supplied with the service equipment being used.

• Never add R-12 to a refrigerant system designed to use R-134a. Damage to the system will result.

• R-12 refrigerant oil must not be mixed with R-134a refrigerant oil. They are not compatible.

• Do not use R-12 equipment or parts on the R-134a system. Damage to the system will result.

• Do not overcharge the refrigerant system. This will cause excessive compressor head pressure and can cause noise and system failure.

In addition to the warnings and cautions listed above, the following precautions must also be observed whenever servicing the air conditioning system:

• Recover the refrigerant before opening any fitting or connection. Open the fittings with caution, even after the system has been discharged. Never open or loosen a connection before recovering the refrigerant.

• The refrigerant system must always be evacuated before charging.

• Do not open the refrigerant system or uncap a replacement component until you are ready to service the system. This will prevent contamination in the system.

• Before disconnecting a component, clean the outside of the fittings thoroughly to prevent contamination from entering the refrigerant system.

• Immediately after disconnecting a component from the refrigerant system, seal the open fittings with a cap or plug.

• Before connecting an open refrigerant fitting, always install a new seal or gasket. Coat the fitting and seal with clean refrigerant oil before connecting.

• Do not remove the sealing caps from a replacement component until it is installed.

• When installing a refrigerant line, avoid sharp bends that may restrict refrigerant flow. Position the refrigerant lines away from exhaust system components or any sharp edges, which may damage the line.

• Tighten refrigerant fittings only to the specified torque. The aluminum fittings used in the refrigerant system will not tolerate overtightening.

• When disconnecting a refrigerant fitting, use a wrench on both halves of the fitting. This will prevent twisting of the refrigerant lines or tubes.

• Refrigerant oil will absorb moisture from the atmosphere if left uncapped. Do not open a container of refrigerant oil until you are ready to use it. Replace the cap on the oil container immediately after using. Store refrigerant oil only in a clean, airtight, and moisture-free container.

• Keep service tools and the work area clean. Contamination of the refrigerant system through careless work habits must be avoided.

COOLING SYSTEM REQUIREMENTS

To maintain the performance level of the heating-air conditioning system, the engine cooling system must be properly maintained.

The use of a bug screen is not recommended. Any obstructions in front of the radiator or condenser will reduce the performance of the air conditioning and engine cooling systems.

COOLANT PRECAUTIONS

WARNING:

• ANTIFREEZE IS AN ETHYLENE GLYCOL BASED COOLANT AND IS HARMFUL IF SWALLOWED OR INHALED. IF SWALLOWED, DRINK TWO GLASSES OF WATER AND INDUCE VOMITING. IF INHALED, MOVE TO A FRESH AIR AREA. SEEK MEDICAL ATTENTION IMMEDIATELY.

• WASH THE SKIN AND CLOTHING THOROUGHLY AFTER COMING IN CONTACT WITH ETHYLENE GLYCOL.

• KEEP OUT OF THE REACH OF CHILDREN AND PETS.

• DO NOT OPEN A COOLING SYSTEM WHEN THE ENGINE IS AT OPERATING TEMPERATURE. PERSONAL INJURY MAY RESULT.

• DO NOT STORE ENGINE COOLANT IN OPEN OR UNMARKED CONTAINERS.

• HOT ENGINE COOLANT CAN CAUSE SEVERE BURNS. DO NOT OPEN THE RADIATOR DRAIN COCK WHEN THE COOLING SYSTEM IS HOT AND PRESSURIZED. ALLOW THE COOLANT TO DECREASE TO ROOM TEMPERATURE BEFORE STARTING REPAIR OPERATIONS.

The engine cooling system is designed to develop internal pressures of 97 to 124 kPa (14 to 18 psi). Allow the vehicle 15 minutes to cool down, or wait until a safe temperature and pressure are attained, before opening the cooling system. Refer to Group 7 - Cooling System for more information.

REFRIGERANT HOSES/LINES/TUBES PRECAUTIONS

Kinks or sharp bends in the refrigerant plumbing will reduce the capacity of the entire system. High pressures are produced in the system when it is operating. Extreme care must be exercised to make sure that all refrigerant system connections are pressure tight.

GENERAL INFORMATION (Continued)

A good rule for the flexible hose refrigerant lines is to keep the radius of all bends at least ten times the diameter of the hose. Sharp bends will reduce the flow of refrigerant. The flexible hose lines should be routed so they are at least 80 mm (3 inches) from the exhaust manifold. It is a good practice to inspect all flexible refrigerant system hose lines at least once a year to make sure they are in good condition and properly routed.

There are two types of refrigerant fittings:

- All fittings with O-rings need to be coated with refrigerant oil before installation. Use only O-rings approved for use with R-134a refrigerant. Failure to do so may result in a leak.
- Unified plumbing connections with aluminum gaskets cannot be serviced with O-rings. The gaskets are not reusable and new gaskets do not require lubrication before installing.

Using the proper tools when making a refrigerant plumbing connection is very important. Improper tools or improper use of the tools can damage the refrigerant fittings. Always use two wrenches when loosening or tightening tube fittings. Use one wrench to hold one side of the connection stationary, while loosening or tightening the other side of the connection with a second wrench.

The refrigerant must be recovered completely from the system before opening any fitting or connection. Open the fittings with caution, even after the refrigerant has been recovered. If any pressure is noticed as a fitting is loosened, tighten the fitting and recover the refrigerant from the system again.

Do not discharge refrigerant into the atmosphere. Use an R-134a refrigerant recovery/recycling device that meets SAE Standard J2210.

The refrigerant system will remain chemically stable as long as pure, moisture-free R-134a refrigerant oil is used. Dirt, moisture, or air can upset this chemical stability. Operational troubles or serious damage can occur if foreign material is present in the refrigerant system.

When it is necessary to open the refrigerant system, have everything needed to service the system ready. The refrigerant system should not be left open to the atmosphere any longer than necessary. Cap or plug all lines and fittings as soon as they are opened to prevent the entrance of dirt and moisture. All lines and components in parts stock should be capped or sealed until they are installed.

All tools, including the refrigerant recycling equipment, the manifold gauge set, and test hoses should be kept clean and dry. All tools and equipment must be designed for R-134a refrigerant.

DESCRIPTION AND OPERATION

ACCUMULATOR

The accumulator is mounted in the engine compartment between the evaporator coil outlet tube and the compressor inlet. Refrigerant enters the accumulator canister as a low pressure vapor through the inlet tube. Any liquid, oil-laden refrigerant falls to the bottom of the canister, which acts as a separator. A desiccant bag is mounted inside the accumulator canister to absorb any moisture which may have entered and become trapped in the refrigerant system (Fig. 2).

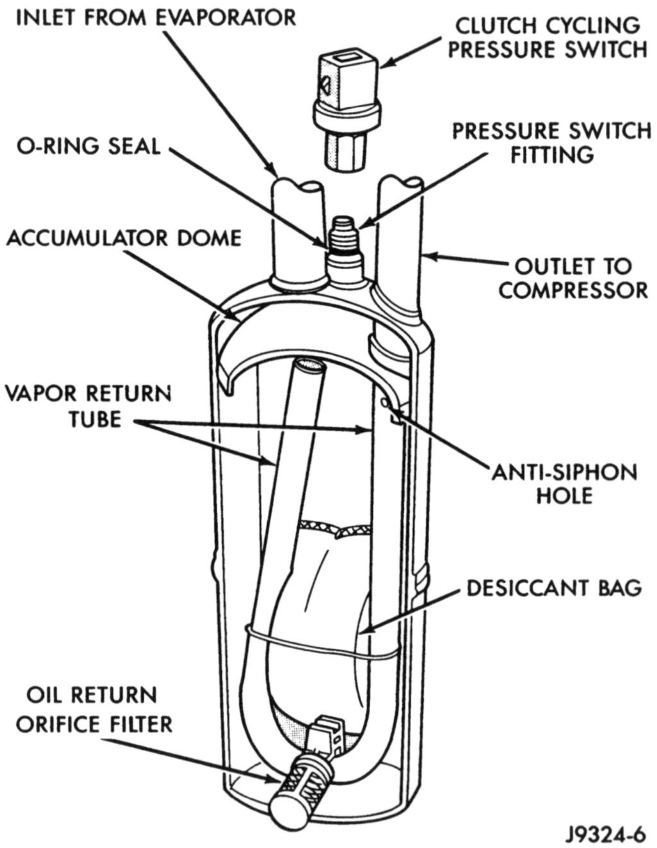

Fig. 2 Accumulator - Typical

BLOWER MOTOR

The blower motor and blower wheel are located in the passenger side end of the heater-A/C housing, below the glove box. The blower motor controls the velocity of air flowing through the heater-A/C housing by spinning a squirrel cage-type blower wheel within the housing at the selected speed. The blower motor and wheel can be removed from the engine compartment side of the housing without heater-A/C housing removal.

The blower motor will only operate when the ignition switch is in the On position, and the heater-A/C mode control switch knob is in any position, except Off. The blower motor receives a ground feed at all

DESCRIPTION AND OPERATION (Continued)

times. The blower motor battery feed circuit is protected by a fuse in the fuseblock module. Blower motor speed is controlled by regulating the battery feed through the blower motor switch, blower motor resistor, and high speed blower motor relay.

The blower motor and blower motor wheel cannot be repaired and, if faulty, they must be replaced. The blower motor and blower wheel are serviced only as a unit.

BLOWER MOTOR RESISTOR

The blower motor resistor is mounted to the bottom of the heater-A/C housing on the passenger side of the vehicle under the instrument panel. On models with the optional air conditioning, it can be accessed by removing the recirculation air door actuator kick cover.

The resistor has multiple resistor wires, each of which reduce the current flow to the blower motor, to change the blower motor speed. The blower motor switch directs the current through the correct resistor wire to obtain the selected speed.

The blower motor resistor cannot be repaired and, if faulty, it must be replaced.

BLOWER MOTOR SWITCH

The heater or heater-A/C blower motor is controlled by a four position rotary-type blower motor switch, mounted in the heater-A/C control panel. The switch allows the selection of one of four blower motor speeds, but can only be turned off by selecting the Off position with the heater-A/C mode control switch knob.

The blower motor switch receives ignition-switched battery feed through the mode control switch from a fuse in the fuseblock module. The switch directs the current to the blower motor resistor, or to the high speed blower motor relay, as required to achieve the selected blower motor speed.

The blower motor switch cannot be repaired and, if faulty, it must be replaced.

COMPRESSOR

The air conditioning system uses a Sanden SD7H15 fixed displacement compressor on all models. A label identifying the use of R-134a refrigerant is located on the compressor. The purpose of the compressor is to compress the low-pressure refrigerant vapor from the evaporator into a high-pressure, high-temperature vapor. The compressor is serviced only as an assembly.

COMPRESSOR CLUTCH

The compressor clutch assembly consists of a stationary electromagnetic coil, a hub bearing and pulley assembly, and a clutch plate (Fig. 3). The electromagnetic coil and pulley are retained on the compressor with snap rings. The clutch plate is mounted on the compressor shaft and secured with a nut.

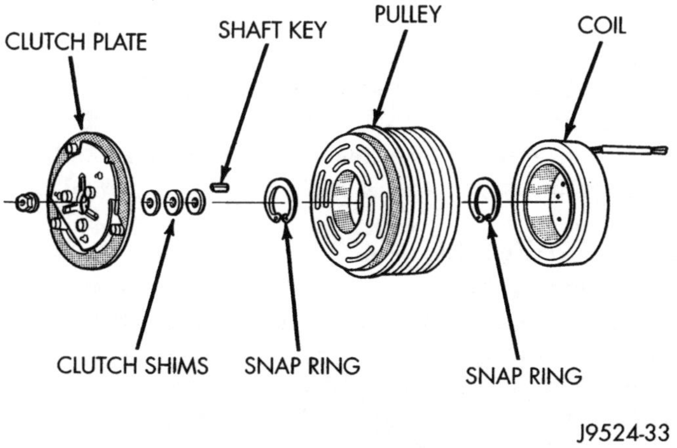

Fig. 3 Compressor Clutch

These components provide the means to engage and disengage the compressor from the engine serpentine accessory drive belt. When the clutch coil is energized, it magnetically draws the clutch into contact with the pulley and drives the compressor shaft. When the coil is not energized, the pulley freewheels on the clutch hub bearing, which is part of the pulley. The compressor clutch and coil are the only serviced parts on the compressor.

The compressor clutch is controlled by several components: the heater-A/C mode control switch, the low pressure cycling clutch switch, the high pressure cut-off switch, the compressor clutch relay, and the Powertrain Control Module (PCM). The PCM may delay compressor clutch engagement for up to 30 seconds. Refer to Group 14 - Fuel System for more information on the PCM controls.

COMPRESSOR CLUTCH RELAY

The compressor clutch relay is a International Standards Organization (ISO) micro-relay. The terminal designations and functions are the same as a conventional ISO relay. However, the micro-relay terminal orientation (footprint) is different, current capacity is lower, and the relay case dimensions are smaller than on the conventional ISO relay.

The compressor clutch relay is a electro-mechanical device that switches current to the compressor clutch coil when the Powertrain Control Module (PCM) grounds the coil side of the relay. The PCM responds to inputs from the heater-A/C mode control switch, the low pressure cycling clutch switch, and the high pressure cut-off switch.

The compressor clutch relay is located in the Power Distribution Center (PDC) in the engine compart-

DESCRIPTION AND OPERATION (Continued)

ment. Refer to the PDC label for relay identification and location.

CONDENSER

The condenser is located in front of the engine cooling radiator. It is a heat exchanger that allows the high-pressure refrigerant gas to give up its heat to the air passing over the condenser fins. This causes the refrigerant gas to condense into a high-pressure liquid refrigerant. The condenser is serviced only as an assembly.

EVAPORATOR COIL

The evaporator coil is located in the heater-A/C housing, under the instrument panel. Refrigerant enters the evaporator as a low-temperature, low-pressure liquid. As air passes over the fins of the evaporator, the humidity in the air condenses on the fins, and the heat from the air is absorbed by the refrigerant. Heat absorption causes the refrigerant to become a low-pressure gas before it leaves the evaporator.

The evaporator coil cannot be repaired and, if faulty, it must be replaced.

FIXED ORIFICE TUBE

The fixed orifice tube is installed in the liquid line between the outlet tube of the condenser and the inlet tube of the evaporator. The fixed orifice tube is located in the end of the liquid line that connects to the condenser outlet tube.

The inlet and outlet ends of the tube have a screen to filter the refrigerant. O-rings on the tube body prevent the refrigerant from bypassing the fixed orifice. The fixed orifice tube is used to meter the flow of liquid refrigerant into the evaporator coil.

The fixed orifice tube cannot be repaired and, if faulty or plugged, it must be replaced.

HEATER CORE

The heater core is located in the heater-A/C housing, under the instrument panel. It is a heat exchanger made of rows of tubes and fins. Engine coolant is circulated through heater hoses to the heater core at all times. As the coolant flows through the heater core, heat removed from the engine is transferred to the heater core fins and tubes.

Air directed through the heater core picks up the heat from the heater core fins. The blend air door allows control of the heater output air temperature by controlling how much of the air flowing through the heater-A/C housing is directed through the heater core. The blower motor speed controls the amount of air flowing through the heater-A/C housing.

The heater core cannot be repaired and, if faulty, it must be replaced.

HIGH PRESSURE CUT-OFF SWITCH

The high pressure cut-off switch is located on the discharge line near the compressor. This switch is connected in series with the low pressure cycling clutch switch between ground and the Powertrain Control Module (PCM). The switch contacts open and close causing the PCM to turn the compressor clutch on and off. This prevents compressor operation when the discharge line pressure approaches high levels.

The high pressure cut-off switch contacts are open when the discharge line pressure rises above 3100-3375 kPa (450-490 psi). The switch contacts will close when the discharge line pressure drops to 1860-2275 kPa (270-330 psi).

The high pressure cut-off switch is a factory-calibrated unit. The switch cannot be adjusted or repaired and, if faulty, it must be replaced.

HIGH PRESSURE RELIEF VALVE

The high pressure relief valve is located on the compressor. The valve is used to prevent excessive refrigerant system pressure. The valve vents the system when a pressure of 3445 to 4135 kPa (500 to 600 psi), and above, is reached. This prevents damage to the compressor and other system components due to condenser air flow being restricted or an overcharge of refrigerant. The valve closes with a minimum pressure of 2756 kPa (400 psi).

The high pressure relief valve vents only enough refrigerant to reduce system pressure, and then re-seats itself. The majority of the refrigerant is conserved in the system. If the valve vents refrigerant, it does not mean the valve is faulty. The valve is part of the compressor assembly and must not be removed or otherwise disturbed.

HIGH SPEED BLOWER MOTOR RELAY

The high speed blower motor relay is a International Standards Organization (ISO)-type relay. The relay is a electro-mechanical device that switches battery current from a fuse in the Power Distribution Center (PDC) to the blower motor, bypassing the remainder of the blower motor feed circuit. The relay is energized when the relay coil is provided a voltage signal by the blower motor switch. See the Diagnosis and Testing section of this group for more information on the relay's operation.

The high speed blower motor relay is located near the passenger side end of the heater-A/C housing, next to the heater-A/C wire harness connector. The relay cannot be repaired and, if faulty, it must be replaced.

DESCRIPTION AND OPERATION (Continued)

LOW PRESSURE CYCLING CLUTCH SWITCH

The low pressure cycling clutch switch is mounted on top of the accumulator. The switch is connected in series with the high pressure cut-off switch, between ground and the Powertrain Control Module (PCM). The switch contacts open and close causing the PCM to turn the compressor clutch on and off. This regulates the system pressure and controls evaporator temperature. Controlling evaporator temperature prevents condensate water on the evaporator fins from freezing and obstructing air conditioning system air flow.

The low pressure cycling clutch switch contacts are open when the suction pressure is approximately 141 kPa (20.5 psi) or lower. The switch contacts will close when the suction pressure rises to approximately 234-262 kPa (34-38 psi) or above. Lower ambient temperatures, below approximately -1°C (30°F) during cold weather will also open the switch contacts. This is due to the pressure/temperature relationship of the refrigerant in the system.

The low pressure cycling clutch switch is a factory-calibrated unit. It cannot be adjusted or repaired and, if faulty, it must be replaced.

REFRIGERANT

The R-134a refrigerant used in this air conditioning system is a non-toxic, non-flammable, clear, and colorless liquefied gas. R-134a refrigerant is not compatible with R-12 refrigerant in an air conditioning system. Even a small amount of R-12 added to a R-134a refrigerant system, will cause compressor failure, refrigerant oil sludge, or poor air conditioning system performance.

The refrigerant system service ports have been designed to ensure that the system is not accidentally filled with the wrong refrigerant (R-12).

REFRIGERANT LINES

The refrigerant lines are used to carry the refrigerant between the various air conditioning system components. A barrier hose design is used for the air conditioning system on this vehicle. The ends of the refrigerant hoses are made from lightweight aluminum, and use braze-less fittings. The refrigerant lines and hoses cannot be repaired and, if faulty, they must be replaced.

REFRIGERANT LINE COUPLERS

Spring-locking refrigerant line couplers are used to connect refrigerant lines and other components to the refrigerant system. The coupling is held together by a garter spring inside a circular cage.

When the coupling halves are connected, the flared end of the female fitting slips behind the garter spring inside the cage of the male fitting. The garter spring and cage prevent the flared end of the female fitting from pulling out of the cage. Secondary clips are installed over the coupling at the factory for added blowoff protection.

O-rings are used to seal the coupling. These O-rings are compatible with R-134a refrigerant and must be replaced with O-rings made of the same material.

REFRIGERANT OIL

The oil used in the SD7H15 compressor is a polyalkylene glycol, synthetic (SP-20 PAG), wax-free refrigerant oil. Use only refrigerant oil of the same type to service the system.

Refrigerant oil will absorb any moisture it comes in contact with, even moisture in the air. The oil container should be kept tightly capped until it is ready to be used. Then, cap the oil immediately after using, to prevent contamination.

REFRIGERANT SYSTEM SERVICE EQUIPMENT

WARNING: EYE PROTECTION MUST BE WORN WHEN SERVICING AN AIR CONDITIONING REFRIGERANT SYSTEM. TURN OFF (ROTATE CLOCKWISE) ALL VALVES ON THE EQUIPMENT BEING USED, BEFORE CONNECTING TO OR DISCONNECTING FROM THE REFRIGERANT SYSTEM. FAILURE TO OBSERVE THESE WARNINGS MAY RESULT IN PERSONAL INJURY.

When servicing the air conditioning system, a refrigerant charging station and a recovery/recycling device for R-134a must be used. This device must meet SAE Standard J2210. Contact an automotive service equipment supplier for refrigerant charging and recycling/recovering equipment. Refer to the operating instructions provided with the equipment for proper operation.

A manifold gauge set may be needed with some charging and/or recovery/recycling devices (Fig. 4). The service hoses on the gauge set being used should have manual (turn wheel), or automatic back-flow valves at the service port connector ends. This will prevent refrigerant from being released into the atmosphere.

MANIFOLD GAUGE SET CONNECTIONS

CAUTION: Do not use an R-12 manifold gauge set on an R-134a system. The refrigerants are not compatible and system damage will result.

LOW PRESSURE GAUGE HOSE

The low pressure hose (Blue with Black stripe) attaches to the suction service port. This port is

DESCRIPTION AND OPERATION (Continued)

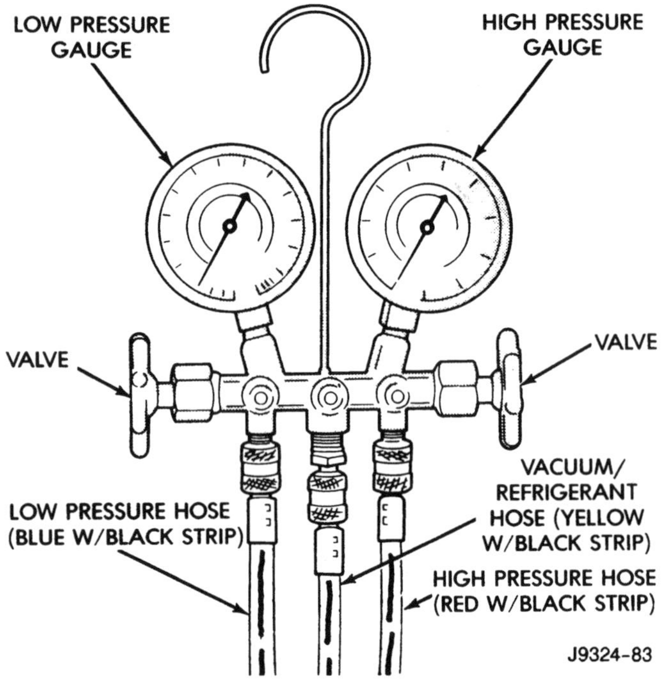

Fig. 4 Manifold Gauge Set

located on the liquid line near the evaporator inlet tube at the rear of the engine compartment.

HIGH PRESSURE GAUGE HOSE

The high pressure hose (Red with Black stripe) attaches to the discharge service port. This port is located on the discharge line between the compressor and the condenser.

RECOVERY/RECYCLING/EVACUATION/CHARGING HOSE

The center manifold hose (Yellow, or White, with Black stripe) is used to recover, evacuate, and charge the refrigerant system. When the low or high pressure valves on the manifold gauge set are opened, the refrigerant in the system will escape through this hose.

REFRIGERANT SYSTEM SERVICE PORTS

The refrigerant system service ports are used to charge, recover/recycle, evacuate, and test the air conditioning refrigerant system. Unique service port coupler sizes are used on the R-134a system, to ensure that the refrigerant system is not accidentally contaminated by the use of the wrong refrigerant (R-12), or refrigerant system service equipment.

The high pressure service port is located on the compressor manifold or plumbing. The low pressure service port is located on the liquid line. After servicing the refrigerant system, always reinstall the service port caps.

VACUUM CHECK VALVE

A one-way vacuum check valve is installed in the accessory vacuum supply line near the vacuum tap on the engine intake manifold. This check valve helps to maintain the system vacuum needed to retain the selected heater-A/C mode settings by preventing the engine from bleeding down system vacuum through the intake manifold during extended heavy engine load (low engine vacuum) operation.

The vacuum check valve cannot be repaired and, if faulty, it must be replaced.

VACUUM RESERVOIR

The vacuum reservoir is mounted in the engine compartment on the rear of the front wheelhouse inner panel and under the battery tray. Vacuum stored in the reservoir is used to operate the vacuum-controlled vehicle accessories during periods of low engine vacuum, such as when the vehicle is climbing a steep grade or under other high engine load operating conditions.

The vacuum reservoir cannot be repaired and, if faulty, it must be replaced.

DIAGNOSIS AND TESTING

A/C PERFORMANCE

The air conditioning system is designed to provide the passenger compartment with low temperature and low humidity air. The evaporator, located in the heater-A/C housing on the dash panel below the instrument panel, is cooled to temperatures near the freezing point. As warm damp air passes over the fins in the evaporator, the air is cooled and the moisture is removed as it condenses on the fins. During periods of high heat and humidity, an air conditioning system will be more effective in the Recirculation Mode. With the system in the Recirculation Mode, only air from the passenger compartment passes through the evaporator. As the passenger compartment air dehumidifies, the air conditioning system performance levels improve.

Humidity has an important bearing on the temperature of the air delivered to the interior of the vehicle. It is important to understand the effect that humidity has on the performance of the air conditioning system. When humidity is high, the evaporator has to perform a double duty. It must lower the air temperature, and it must lower the temperature of the moisture in the air that condenses on the evaporator fins. Condensing the moisture in the air transfers heat energy into the evaporator fins and tubing. This reduces the amount of heat the evaporator can absorb from the air. High humidity greatly reduces the ability of the evaporator to lower the temperature of the air.

DIAGNOSIS AND TESTING (Continued)

However, evaporator capacity used to reduce the amount of moisture in the air is not wasted. Wringing some of the moisture out of the air entering the vehicle adds to the comfort of the passengers. Although, an owner may expect too much from their air conditioning system on humid days. A performance test is the best way to determine whether the system is performing up to standard. This test also provides valuable clues as to the possible cause of trouble with the air conditioning system.

Review the Service Warnings and Precautions in the front of this group before performing this procedure. The air temperature in the test room and in the vehicle must be a minimum of 21°C (70°F) for this test.

(1) Connect a tachometer and a manifold gauge set.

(2) Set the heater-A/C mode control switch knob in the Recirculation Mode position, the temperature control knob in the full cool position, and the blower motor switch knob in the highest speed position.

(3) Start the engine and hold the idle at 1,000 rpm with the compressor clutch engaged.

(4) The engine should be at operating temperature. The doors and windows must be open.

(5) Insert a thermometer in the driver's side center A/C (panel) outlet. Operate the engine for five minutes.

(6) The compressor clutch may cycle, depending upon the ambient temperature and humidity. If the clutch cycles, remove the low pressure cycling clutch switch connector from the switch located on the accumulator (Fig. 5). Place a jumper wire across the terminals of the low pressure cycling clutch switch connector.

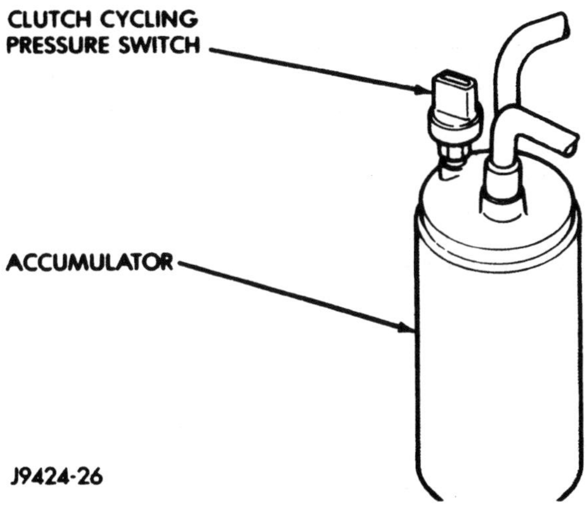

Fig. 5 Low Pressure Cycling Clutch Switch

(7) With the compressor clutch engaged, record the discharge air temperature and the compressor discharge pressure.

(8) Compare the discharge air temperature to the Performance Temperature and Pressure chart. If the discharge air temperature is high, see Refrigerant System Leaks and Refrigerant System Charge in this group.

(9) Compare the compressor discharge pressure to the Performance Temperature and Pressure chart. If the compressor discharge pressure is high, see the Pressure Diagnosis chart.

Ambient Temperature	21°C (70°F)	27°C (80°F)	32°C (90°F)	38°C (100°F)	43°C (110°F)
Air Temperature at Center Panel Outlet	-3 to 3°C (27-38°F)	1 to 7°C (33-44°F)	3 to 9°C (37-48°F)	6 to 13°C (43-55°F)	10 to 18°C (50-64°F)
Evaporator Inlet Pressure at Charge Port	179-241 kPa (26-35 psi)	221-283 kPa (32-41 psi)	262-324 kPa (38-47 psi)	303-365 kPa (44-53 psi)	345-414 kPa (50-60 psi)
Compressor Discharge Pressure	1240-1655 kPa (180-240 psi)	1380-1790 kPa (200-260 psi)	1720-2070 kPa (250-300 psi)	1860-2345 kPa (270-340 psi)	2070-2690 kPa (300-390 psi)

J9324-74

Performance Temperature and Pressure Chart

DIAGNOSIS AND TESTING (Continued)

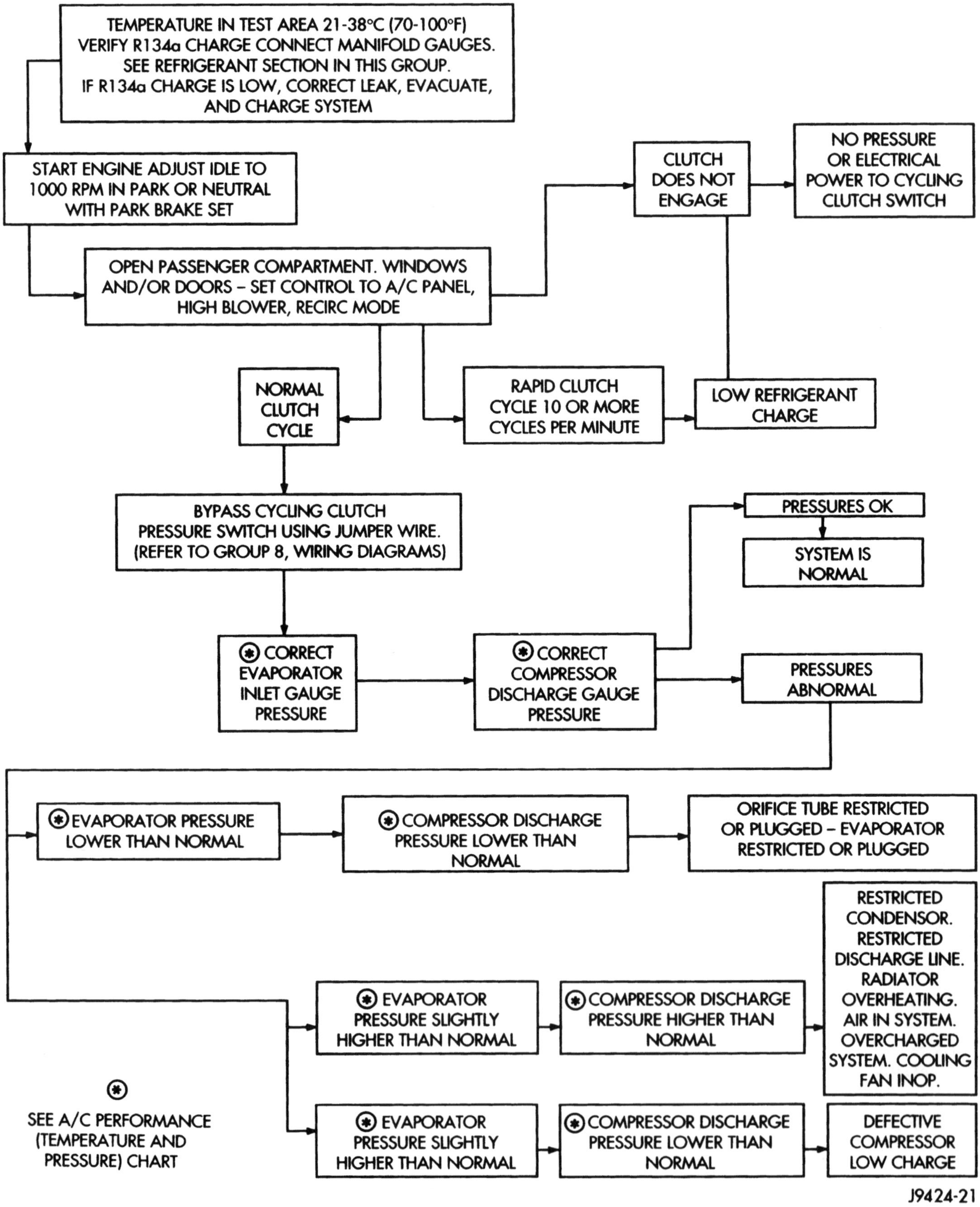

Pressure Diagnosis

DIAGNOSIS AND TESTING (Continued)

HEATER PERFORMANCE

PREPARATIONS

Review the Service Warnings and Precautions in the front of this group before performing the following procedures.

Check the radiator coolant level, serpentine drive belt tension, and engine vacuum line connections. Also check the radiator air flow and the radiator fan operation. Start the engine and allow it to warm up to normal operating temperature.

WARNING: DO NOT REMOVE THE RADIATOR PRESSURE CAP WHEN THE ENGINE IS AT OPERATING TEMPERATURE, PERSONAL INJURY MAY RESULT.

If the vehicle has been operated recently, wait 15 minutes or longer before removing the radiator pressure cap. Place a rag over the cap and turn it to the first safety stop. Allow any pressure to escape through the overflow tube. When the system stabilizes, remove the cap completely.

MAXIMUM HEATER OUTPUT

Engine coolant is delivered to the heater core through two heater hoses. With the engine idling at normal operating temperature, set the temperature control knob in the full hot position, the mode control switch knob in the Floor position, and the blower motor switch knob in the highest speed position. Using a test thermometer, check the air temperature coming from the floor outlets, refer to the Temperature Reference Chart.

Ambient Temperature		Minimum Heater System Floor Outlet Temperature	
Celsius	Fahrenheit	Celsius	Fahrenheit
15.5°	60°	62.2°	144°
21.1°	70°	63.8°	147°
26.6°	80°	65.5°	150°
32.2°	90°	67.2°	153°

9124-4

Temperature Reference Chart

If the floor outlet air temperature is low, refer to Group 7 - Cooling System for the coolant temperature specifications. Both of the heater hoses should be hot to the touch. The coolant return hose should be slightly cooler than the supply hose. If the coolant return hose is much cooler than the supply hose, locate and repair the engine coolant flow obstruction in the heater system.

OBSTRUCTED COOLANT FLOW

Possible locations or causes of obstructed coolant flow:

- Pinched or kinked heater hoses.
- Improper heater hose routing.
- Plugged heater hoses or supply and return ports at the cooling system connections (refer to Group 7 - Cooling System).
- A plugged heater core.

If proper coolant flow through the heater system is verified, and outlet air temperature is still low, a mechanical problem may exist.

MECHANICAL PROBLEMS

Possible locations or causes of insufficient heat:

- An obstructed cowl air intake.
- Obstructed heater system outlets.
- A blend-air door not functioning properly.

TEMPERATURE CONTROL

If the heater discharge air temperature cannot be adjusted with the temperature control knob on the heater-A/C control panel, the following could require service:

- The heater-A/C control.
- The temperature control cable.
- The blend-air door.
- Improper engine coolant temperature.

VACUUM SYSTEM

Vacuum control is used to operate the mode doors in the heater-A/C housing. Testing of the heater-A/C mode control switch operation will determine if the vacuum, and mechanical controls are functioning. However, it is possible that a vacuum control system that operates perfectly at engine idle (high engine vacuum) may not function properly at high engine speeds or loads (low engine vacuum). This can be caused by leaks in the vacuum system, or a faulty vacuum check valve.

A vacuum system test will help to identify the source of poor vacuum system performance, or vacuum system leaks. Before starting this test, stop the engine and make certain that the problem isn't a disconnected vacuum supply tube at the engine intake manifold vacuum tap or the vacuum reservoir.

Use an adjustable vacuum test set (Special Tool C-3707) and a suitable vacuum pump to test the heater-A/C vacuum control system. With a finger placed over the end of the vacuum test hose probe (Fig. 6), adjust the bleed valve on the test set gauge to obtain a vacuum of exactly 27 kPa (8 in. Hg.). Release and block the end of the probe several times to verify that the vacuum reading returns to the exact 27 kPa (8 in. Hg.) setting. Otherwise, a false reading will be obtained during testing.

DIAGNOSIS AND TESTING (Continued)

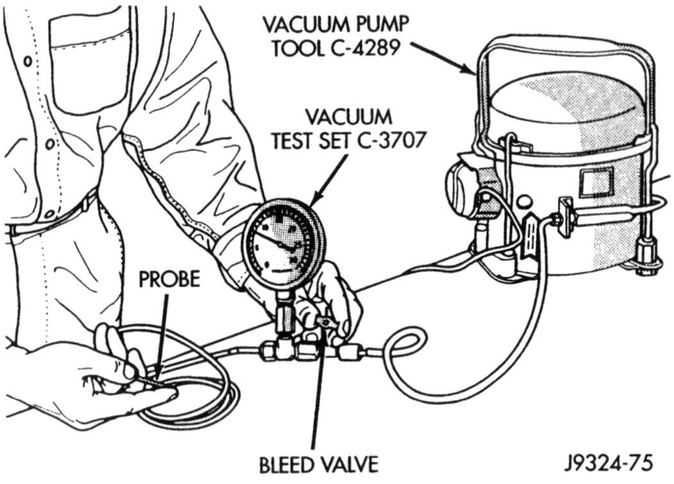

Fig. 6 Adjust Vacuum Test Bleed Valve

VACUUM CHECK VALVE

(1) Remove the vacuum check valve. The valve is located in the (black) vacuum supply tube at the intake manifold vacuum tap.

(2) Connect the test set vacuum supply hose to the heater (natural color) side of the valve. When connected to this side of the check valve, no vacuum should pass and the test set gauge should return to the 27 kPa (8 in. Hg.) setting. If OK, go to Step 3. If not OK, replace the faulty valve.

(3) Connect the test set vacuum supply hose to the engine vacuum (black color) side of the valve. When connected to this side of the check valve, vacuum should flow through the valve without restriction. If not OK, replace the faulty valve.

HEATER-A/C CONTROLS

(1) Connect the test set vacuum probe to the heater-A/C vacuum supply (black) tube in the engine compartment. Position the test set gauge so that it can be viewed from the passenger compartment.

(2) Place the heater-A/C mode control switch knob in each mode position, one at a time, and pause after each selection. The test set gauge should return to the 27 kPa (8 in. Hg.) setting shortly after each selection is made. If not OK, a component or vacuum line in the selected mode's vacuum circuit has a leak. See the procedure in Locating Vacuum Leaks.

CAUTION: Do not use lubricant on the switch ports or in the holes in the plug, as lubricant will ruin the vacuum valve in the switch. A drop of clean water in the connector plug holes will help the connector slide onto the switch ports.

LOCATING VACUUM LEAKS

WARNING: ON VEHICLES EQUIPPED WITH AIRBAGS, REFER TO GROUP 8M - PASSIVE RESTRAINT SYSTEMS BEFORE ATTEMPTING STEERING WHEEL, STEERING COLUMN, OR INSTRUMENT PANEL COMPONENT DIAGNOSIS OR SERVICE. FAILURE TO TAKE THE PROPER PRECAUTIONS COULD RESULT IN ACCIDENTAL AIRBAG DEPLOYMENT AND POSSIBLE PERSONAL INJURY.

(1) Disconnect the vacuum connector from the back of the heater-A/C mode control switch on the control panel.

(2) Connect the test set vacuum hose probe to each port in the vacuum harness connector, one at a time, and pause after each connection (Fig. 7). The test set gauge should return to the 27 kPa (8 in. Hg.) setting shortly after each connection is made. If OK, replace the faulty mode control switch. If not OK, go to Step 3.

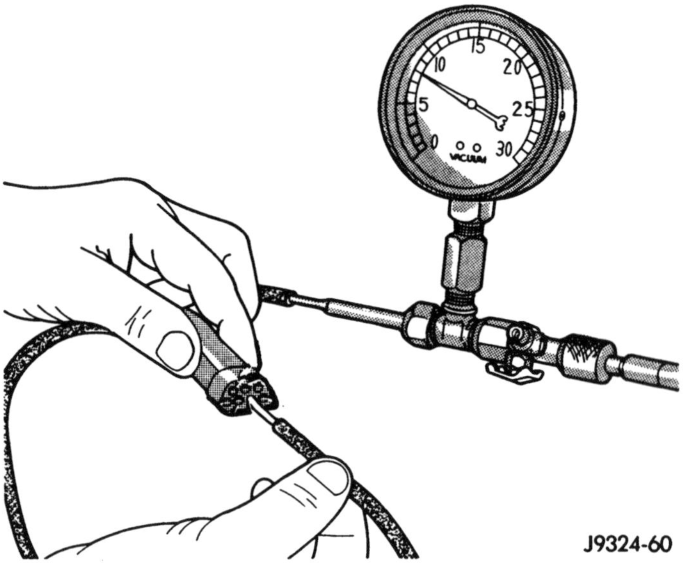

Fig. 7 Vacuum Circuit Test

(3) Determine the vacuum line color of the vacuum circuit that is leaking. To determine the vacuum line colors, refer to the Vacuum Circuits chart (Fig. 8) or (Fig. 9).

(4) Disconnect and plug the vacuum line from the component (fitting, actuator, valve, switch, or reservoir) on the other end of the leaking circuit. Instrument panel disassembly or removal may be necessary to gain access to some components.

(5) Connect the test set hose or probe to the open end of the leaking circuit. The test set gauge should return to the 27 kPa (8 in. Hg.) setting shortly after each connection is made. If OK, replace the faulty disconnected component. If not OK, go to Step 6.

(6) To locate a leak in a vacuum line, leave one end of the line plugged and connect the test set hose or probe to the other end. Run your fingers slowly along the line while watching the test set gauge. The

**** DIAGNOSIS AND TESTING (Continued) ****

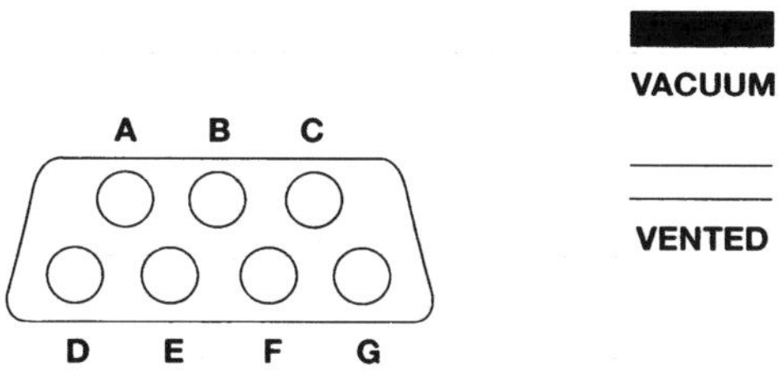

VACUUM CIRCUIT LEGEND		
I.D.	Function	Color
A	Not Used	N/A
B	Defrost Actuator (Full Position)	Yellow
C	Floor Actuator	Brown
D	Defrost Actuator (Mid-Position)	Blue
E	Vacuum Supply (Reservoir)	Black
F	Panel Actuator	Red
G	Not Used	N/A

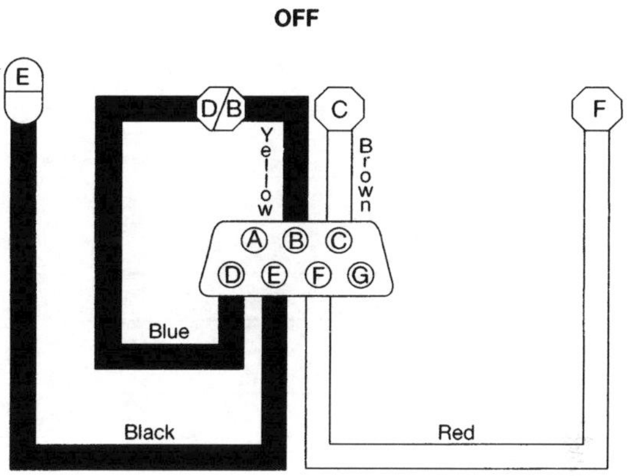

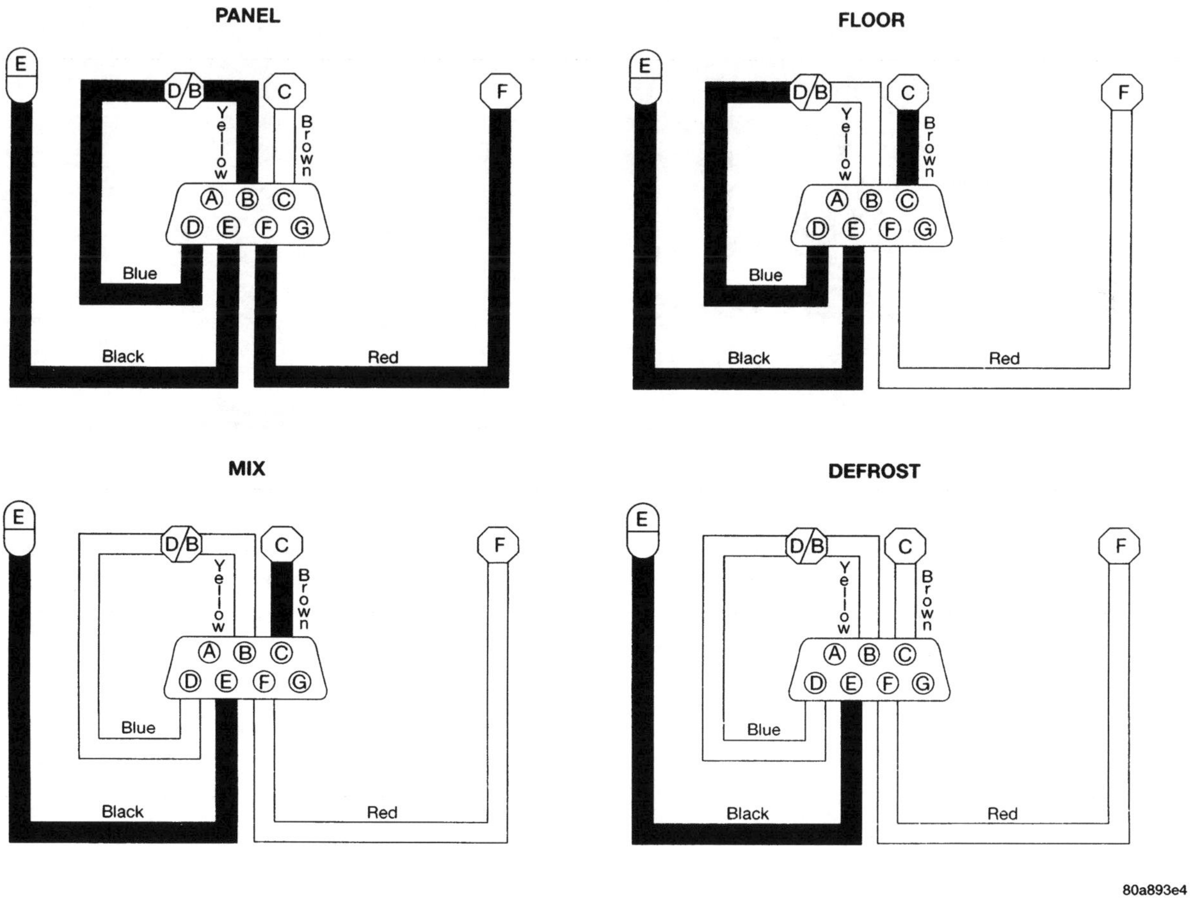

Fig. 8 Vacuum Circuits - Heater Only

1997 Wrangler
Publication No. 81-370-7148
TSB 26-06-96 June, 1996

** DIAGNOSIS AND TESTING (Continued) **

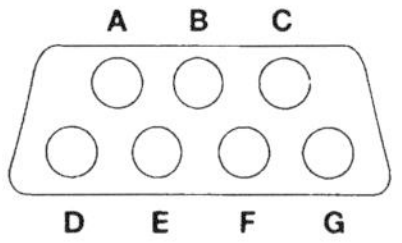

VACUUM CIRCUIT LEGEND		
I.D.	Function	Color
A	Not Used	N/A
B	Defrost Actuator (Full Position)	Yellow
C	Floor Actuator	Brown
D	Defrost Actuator (Mid-Position)	Blue
E	Vacuum Supply (Reservoir)	Black
F	Panel Actuator	Red
G	Recirculation Actuator	Green

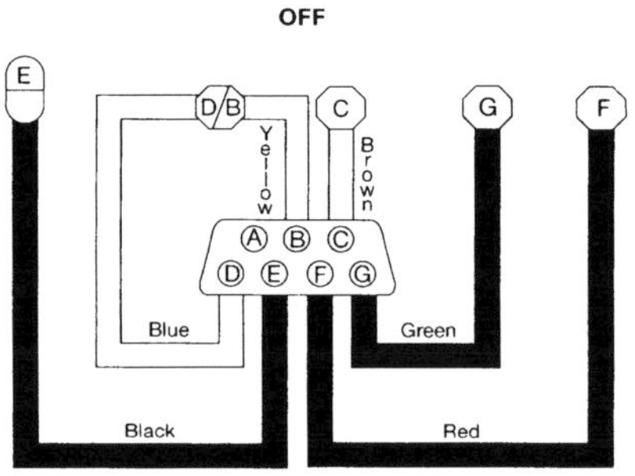

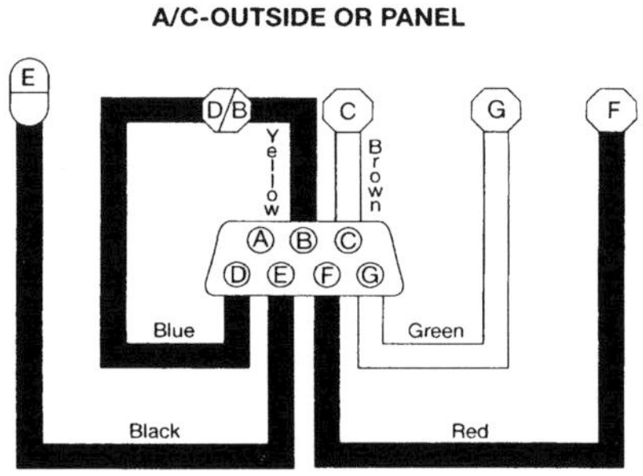

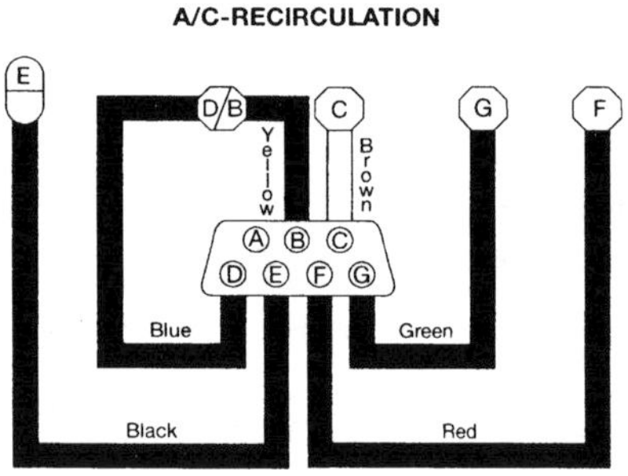

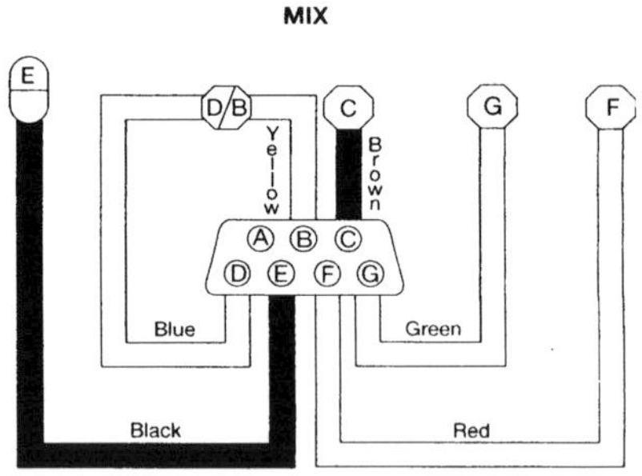

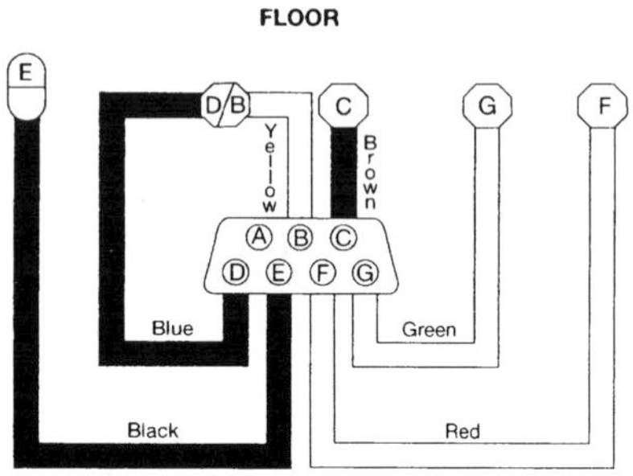

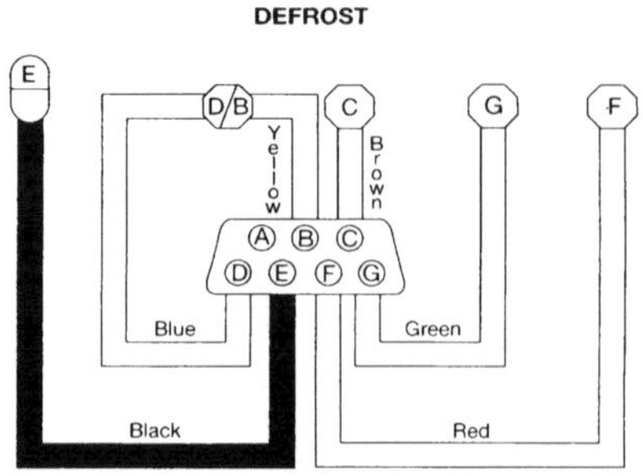

80a893e5

Fig. 9 Vacuum Circuits - Heater-A/C

1997 Wrangler
Publication No. 81-370-7148
TSB 26-06-96 June, 1996

DIAGNOSIS AND TESTING (Continued)

vacuum reading will fluctuate when your fingers contact the source of the leak. To repair the vacuum line, cut out the leaking section of the line. Then, insert the loose ends of the line into a suitable length of 3 mm (1/8-inch) inside diameter rubber hose.

BLOWER MOTOR

WARNING: ON VEHICLES EQUIPPED WITH AIRBAGS, REFER TO GROUP 8M - PASSIVE RESTRAINT SYSTEMS BEFORE ATTEMPTING STEERING WHEEL, STEERING COLUMN, OR INSTRUMENT PANEL COMPONENT DIAGNOSIS OR SERVICE. FAILURE TO TAKE THE PROPER PRECAUTIONS COULD RESULT IN ACCIDENTAL AIRBAG DEPLOYMENT AND POSSIBLE PERSONAL INJURY.

For circuit descriptions and diagrams, refer to 8W-42 - Air Conditioning/Heater in Group 8W - Wiring Diagrams. Possible causes of an inoperative blower motor include:

- Faulty fuse
- Faulty blower motor ground circuit wiring or connectors
- Faulty blower motor resistor
- Faulty high speed blower motor relay
- Faulty blower motor switch
- Faulty heater-A/C mode control switch
- Faulty blower motor feed circuit wiring or connectors
- Faulty blower motor.

Possible causes of the blower motor not operating in all speeds include:

- Faulty fuse
- Faulty blower motor switch
- Faulty blower motor resistor
- Faulty high speed blower motor relay
- Faulty blower motor circuit wiring or connectors.

VIBRATION

Possible causes of blower motor vibration include:

- Improper blower motor mounting
- Improper blower wheel mounting
- Blower wheel out of balance or bent
- Blower motor faulty.

NOISE

To verify that the blower is the source of the noise, disconnect the blower motor connector and operate the heater-A/C system. If the noise goes away, possible causes include:

- Foreign material in the heater-A/C housing
- Improper blower motor mounting
- Improper blower wheel mounting
- Blower motor faulty.

BLOWER MOTOR RESISTOR

For circuit descriptions and diagrams, refer to 8W-42 - Air Conditioning/Heater in Group 8W - Wiring Diagrams.

WARNING: ON VEHICLES EQUIPPED WITH AIRBAGS, REFER TO GROUP 8M - PASSIVE RESTRAINT SYSTEMS BEFORE ATTEMPTING STEERING WHEEL, STEERING COLUMN, OR INSTRUMENT PANEL COMPONENT DIAGNOSIS OR SERVICE. FAILURE TO TAKE THE PROPER PRECAUTIONS COULD RESULT IN ACCIDENTAL AIRBAG DEPLOYMENT AND POSSIBLE PERSONAL INJURY.

To test the blower motor resistor, unplug the resistor connector. Each blower motor switch input terminal on the resistor must have continuity to the resistor output terminal, which is connected to the circuit going to the blower motor. If the blower motor resistor continuity does not check OK, replace the faulty resistor.

BLOWER MOTOR SWITCH

For circuit descriptions and diagrams, refer to 8W-42 - Air Conditioning/Heater in Group 8W - Wiring Diagrams.

WARNING: ON VEHICLES EQUIPPED WITH AIRBAGS, REFER TO GROUP 8M - PASSIVE RESTRAINT SYSTEMS BEFORE ATTEMPTING STEERING WHEEL, STEERING COLUMN, OR INSTRUMENT PANEL COMPONENT DIAGNOSIS OR SERVICE. FAILURE TO TAKE THE PROPER PRECAUTIONS COULD RESULT IN ACCIDENTAL AIRBAG DEPLOYMENT AND POSSIBLE PERSONAL INJURY.

(1) Turn the ignition switch to the On position and check for battery voltage at the fuse in the fuseblock module. If OK, go to Step 2. If not OK, replace the faulty fuse.

(2) Turn the ignition switch to the Off position. Remove the heater-A/C control from the instrument panel, but do not unplug the wiring connectors. Turn the ignition switch to the On position. Check for battery voltage at the **fused ignition switch output (run)** circuit cavity of the heater-A/C mode control switch connector. If OK, go to Step 3. If not OK, repair the open circuit to the fuseblock module as required.

(3) Select any one of the heater-A/C mode control positions except Off to turn the system on. Check for battery voltage at the **low blower motor driver** circuit cavity of the heater-A/C mode control switch connector. If OK, go to Step 4. If not OK, replace the faulty heater-A/C mode control switch.

DIAGNOSIS AND TESTING (Continued)

(4) Check for battery voltage at the **low blower motor driver** circuit cavity of the blower motor switch connector. If OK, go to Step 5. If not OK, repair the open circuit to the heater-A/C mode control switch connector as required.

(5) Check for battery voltage at each of the remaining blower motor switch connector cavities as you move the switch to each blower motor speed position. Voltage should be present in each cavity at only one switch position. If OK, see the diagnosis for the blower motor resistor and/or the high speed blower motor relay. If not OK, replace the faulty blower motor switch.

COMPRESSOR

When investigating an air conditioning related noise, you must first know the conditions under which the noise occurs. These conditions include: weather, vehicle speed, transmission in gear or neutral, engine temperature, and any other special conditions.

Noises that develop during air conditioning operation can often be misleading. For example: What sounds like a failed front bearing or connecting rod, may be caused by loose bolts, nuts, mounting brackets, or a loose clutch assembly. Verify serpentine drive belt tension. Improper belt tension can cause a misleading noise when the compressor is engaged. The noise may not occur when the compressor is disengaged.

Drive belts are speed sensitive. At different engine speeds and depending upon belt tension, belts can develop noises that are mistaken for a compressor noise.

(1) Select a quiet area for testing. Duplicate the complaint conditions as much as possible. Switch the compressor on and off several times to clearly identify the compressor noise. Listen to the compressor clutch while engaged and disengaged.

(2) To duplicate a high-ambient temperature condition (high head pressure), restrict the air flow through the condenser. Install a manifold gauge set to make sure that the discharge pressure does not exceed 2070 kPa (300 psi).

(3) Tighten all compressor mounting bolts, the clutch mounting nut, the clutch coil mounting screw or nut, and the serpentine drive belt to the correct specifications.

(4) Check the refrigerant system plumbing for rubbing or interference, which can cause unusual noises.

(5) Check the refrigerant system charge. See Charging Refrigerant System in this group.

(6) Check the compressor noise as in Step 1.

(7) If the noise still exists, loosen the compressor mounting bolts and tighten again. Repeat Step 1.

(8) If the noise continues, replace the compressor and repeat Step 1.

COMPRESSOR CLUTCH COIL

For circuit descriptions and diagrams, refer to 8W-42 - Air Conditioning/Heater in Group 8W - Wiring Diagrams. The battery must be fully-charged before performing the following tests. Refer to Group 8A - Battery for more information.

WARNING: ON VEHICLES EQUIPPED WITH AIRBAGS, REFER TO GROUP 8M - PASSIVE RESTRAINT SYSTEMS BEFORE ATTEMPTING STEERING WHEEL, STEERING COLUMN, OR INSTRUMENT PANEL COMPONENT DIAGNOSIS OR SERVICE. FAILURE TO TAKE THE PROPER PRECAUTIONS COULD RESULT IN ACCIDENTAL AIRBAG DEPLOYMENT AND POSSIBLE PERSONAL INJURY.

(1) Connect an ammeter (0-10 ampere scale) in series with the clutch coil terminal. Use a voltmeter (0-20 volt scale) with clip-type leads for measuring the voltage across the battery and the compressor clutch coil.

(2) With the heater-A/C mode control switch in any A/C mode, and the blower motor switch in the lowest speed position, start the engine and run it at normal idle.

(3) The compressor clutch coil voltage should read within two volts of the battery voltage. If there is voltage at the clutch coil, but the reading is not within two volts of the battery voltage, test the clutch coil feed circuit for excessive voltage drop and repair as required. If there is no voltage reading at the clutch coil, refer to the proper Powertrain Diagnostic Procedures manual for testing of the compressor clutch circuit. The following components must be checked and repaired as required before you can complete testing of the clutch coil:

- Fuses in the fuseblock module and the Power Distribution Center
- Heater-A/C mode control switch
- Compressor clutch relay
- High pressure cut-off switch
- Low pressure cycling clutch switch
- Powertrain Control Module.

(4) The compressor clutch coil is acceptable if the current draw measured at the clutch coil is 2.0 to 3.9 amperes with the electrical system voltage at 11.5 to 12.5 volts. This should only be checked with the work area temperature at 21°C (70°F). If system voltage is more than 12.5 volts, add electrical loads by turning on electrical accessories until the system voltage drops below 12.5 volts.

DIAGNOSIS AND TESTING (Continued)

(a) If the clutch coil current reading is four amperes or more, the coil is shorted and should be replaced.

(b) If the clutch coil current reading is zero, the coil is open and should be replaced.

COMPRESSOR CLUTCH RELAY

For circuit descriptions and diagrams, refer to 8W-42 - Air Conditioning/Heater in Group 8W - Wiring Diagrams.

WARNING: ON VEHICLES EQUIPPED WITH AIRBAGS, REFER TO GROUP 8M - PASSIVE RESTRAINT SYSTEMS BEFORE ATTEMPTING STEERING WHEEL, STEERING COLUMN, OR INSTRUMENT PANEL COMPONENT DIAGNOSIS OR SERVICE. FAILURE TO TAKE THE PROPER PRECAUTIONS COULD RESULT IN ACCIDENTAL AIRBAG DEPLOYMENT AND POSSIBLE PERSONAL INJURY.

The compressor clutch relay is located in the Power Distribution Center (PDC). Refer to the PDC label for relay identification and location. Remove the relay from the PDC to perform the following tests:

(1) A relay in the de-energized position should have continuity between terminals 87A and 30, and no continuity between terminals 87 and 30. If OK, go to Step 2. If not OK, replace the faulty relay.

(2) Resistance between terminals 85 and 86 (electromagnet) should be 75±5 ohms. If OK, go to Step 3. If not OK, replace the faulty relay.

(3) Connect a battery to terminals 85 and 86. There should now be continuity between terminals 30 and 87, and no continuity between terminals 87A and 30. If OK, see the Circuit Test in this group. If not OK, replace the faulty relay.

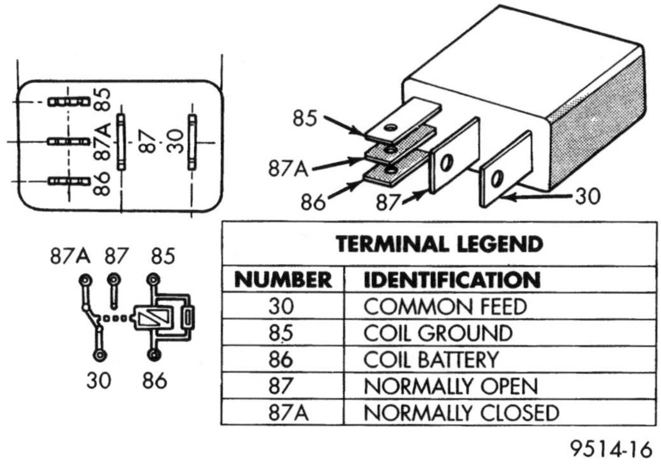

TERMINAL LEGEND	
NUMBER	IDENTIFICATION
30	COMMON FEED
85	COIL GROUND
86	COIL BATTERY
87	NORMALLY OPEN
87A	NORMALLY CLOSED

Compressor Clutch Relay

CIRCUIT TEST

For circuit descriptions and diagrams, refer to 8W-42 - Air Conditioning/Heater in Group 8W - Wiring Diagrams.

(1) The relay common feed terminal cavity (30) is connected to fused battery feed. There should be battery voltage at the cavity for relay terminal 30 at all times. If OK, go to Step 2. If not OK, repair the open circuit to the PDC fuse as required.

(2) The relay normally closed terminal (87A) is not used in this application. Go to Step 3.

(3) The relay normally open terminal cavity (87) is connected to the compressor clutch coil. There should be continuity between this cavity and the **A/C compressor clutch relay output** circuit cavity of the compressor clutch coil connector. If OK, go to Step 4. If not OK, repair the open circuit as required.

(4) The relay coil battery terminal (86) is connected to the **fused ignition switch output (run/start)** circuit. There should be battery voltage at the cavity for relay terminal 86 with the ignition switch in the On position. If OK, go to Step 5. If not OK, repair the open circuit to the fuseblock module as required.

(5) The coil ground terminal cavity (85) is switched to ground through the Powertrain Control Module (PCM). There should be continuity between this cavity and the **A/C compressor clutch relay control** circuit cavity of the PCM connector at all times. If not OK, repair the open circuit as required.

HIGH PRESSURE CUT-OFF SWITCH

For circuit descriptions and diagrams, refer to 8W-42 - Air Conditioning/Heater in Group 8W - Wiring Diagrams.

(1) Verify that the refrigerant system is properly charged.

(2) Unplug the high pressure switch connector and test for continuity between the switch terminals. There should be continuity. If OK, refer to the wiring diagrams and repair the circuits as required. If not OK, replace the faulty switch.

HIGH SPEED BLOWER MOTOR RELAY

WARNING: ON VEHICLES EQUIPPED WITH AIRBAGS, REFER TO GROUP 8M - PASSIVE RESTRAINT SYSTEMS BEFORE ATTEMPTING STEERING WHEEL, STEERING COLUMN, OR INSTRUMENT PANEL COMPONENT DIAGNOSIS OR SERVICE. FAILURE TO TAKE THE PROPER PRECAUTIONS COULD RESULT IN ACCIDENTAL AIRBAG DEPLOYMENT AND POSSIBLE PERSONAL INJURY.

DIAGNOSIS AND TESTING (Continued)

RELAY TEST

The high speed blower motor relay is located near the passenger side end of the heater-A/C housing next to the heater-A/C wire harness connector under the instrument panel. Remove the relay from its connector to perform the following tests:

(1) A relay in the de-energized position should have continuity between terminals 87A and 30, and no continuity between terminals 87 and 30. If OK, go to Step 2. If not OK, replace the faulty relay.

(2) Resistance between terminals 85 and 86 (electromagnet) should be 75±5 ohms. If OK, go to Step 3. If not OK, replace the faulty relay.

(3) Connect a battery to terminals 85 and 86. There should now be continuity between terminals 30 and 87, and no continuity between terminals 87A and 30. If OK, see the Relay Circuit Test in this group. If not OK, replace the faulty relay.

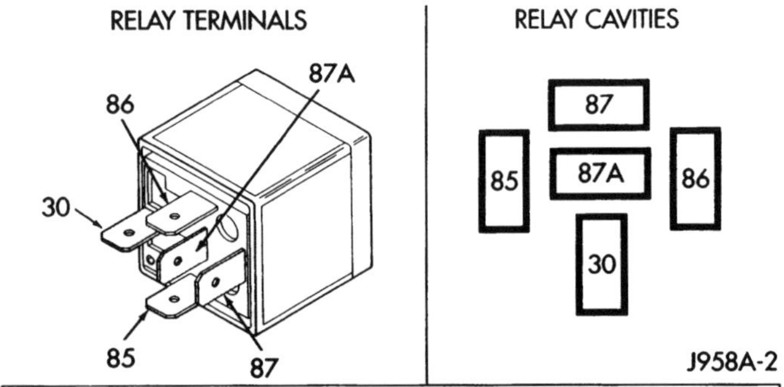

TERMINAL LEGEND	
NUMBER	IDENTIFICATION
30	COMMON FEED
85	COIL GROUND
86	COIL BATTERY
87	NORMALLY OPEN
87A	NORMALLY CLOSED

High Speed Blower Motor Relay

RELAY CIRCUIT TEST

(1) The relay common feed terminal cavity (30) is connected to the blower motor. This terminal supplies fused battery feed directly from a fuse in the Power Distribution Center (PDC) when the relay is energized, and ignition switched battery feed from a fuse in the fuseblock module through the blower motor resistor when the relay is de-energized. There should be continuity between this cavity and the **blower motor feed** circuit cavity of the blower motor connector at all times. If OK, go to Step 2. If not OK, repair the open circuit as required.

(2) The relay normally closed terminal cavity (87A) is connected to the blower motor resistor output. When the relay is de-energized, terminal 87A is connected to terminal 30 and provides the blower motor resistor output to the **blower motor feed** circuit. There should be continuity between this cavity and the **blower resistor outputs** circuit cavity of the blower motor resistor connector at all times. If OK, go to Step 3. If not OK, repair the open circuit as required.

(3) The relay normally open terminal cavity (87) is connected to a fused battery feed from the PDC. When the relay is energized, terminal 87 is connected to terminal 30 and provides full battery current to the **blower motor feed** circuit. There should be battery voltage at this cavity at all times. If OK, go to Step 4. If not OK, repair the open circuit to the PDC as required.

(4) The coil battery terminal cavity (86) is connected to the high speed output contacts of the blower motor switch. When the blower motor switch is placed in the high speed position, fused ignition switch output is directed to the relay electromagnetic coil to energize the relay. There should be continuity between the cavity for relay terminal 86 and the **high blower motor relay control** circuit cavity of the blower motor switch connector at all times. If OK, go to Step 5. If not OK, repair the open circuit as required.

(5) The coil ground terminal cavity (85) is connected to ground. This terminal supplies the ground for the relay electromagnet coil. There should be continuity between the cavity for relay terminal 85 and a good ground at all times. If not OK, repair the open circuit as required.

LOW PRESSURE CYCLING CLUTCH SWITCH

Verify that the refrigerant system has the correct refrigerant charge. For circuit descriptions and diagrams, refer to 8W-42 - Air Conditioning/Heater in Group 8W - Wiring Diagrams.

(1) Unplug the low pressure cycling clutch switch connector from the switch on the accumulator, and install a jumper wire between the two connector cavities.

(2) Connect a manifold gauge set to the refrigerant system service ports.

(3) Place the heater-A/C mode control switch knob in any A/C position and start the engine.

(4) Check the continuity between the two terminals of the low pressure switch. There should be continuity with a suction pressure reading of 262 kPa (38 psi) or above, and no continuity with a suction pressure reading of 141 kPa (20.5 psi) or below. If OK, test and repair the **A/C switch sense** circuit as required. If not OK, replace the faulty switch.

REFRIGERANT SYSTEM LEAKS

WARNING: REVIEW THE WARNINGS AND CAUTIONS IN THE FRONT OF THIS GROUP BEFORE LEAK TESTING THE SYSTEM.

If the air conditioning system is not cooling properly, determine if the refrigerant system is fully-charged. See A/C Performance in this group. If the refrigerant system is low or empty, a leak at a line, fitting, or component seal is likely. Fittings, lines, or

DIAGNOSIS AND TESTING (Continued)

components that appear to be oily indicate a possible refrigerant leak. To detect a leak in the refrigerant system, perform one of the following procedures:

SYSTEM EMPTY

(1) Evacuate the refrigerant system. See Refrigerant System Evacuate in this group.

(2) Connect and dispense 0.283 kPa (0.6 lbs. or 10 oz.) of R-134a refrigerant into the evacuated refrigerant system. See Refrigerant System Charge in this group.

(3) Position the vehicle in a wind-free work area. This will aid in detecting small leaks.

(4) With the engine not running, use a electronic R-134a leak detector and search for leaks. Move the leak detector probe slowly along the bottom side of all lines and fittings, because R-134a is heavier than air.

(5) To inspect the evaporator coil for leaks, insert the leak detector probe into the center panel outlet. Set the blower motor switch to the lowest speed position, and the mode control switch in the Recirculation Mode.

SYSTEM LOW

(1) Position the vehicle in a wind-free work area. This will aid in detecting small leaks.

(2) Bring the refrigerant system up to operating temperature and pressure. This is done by allowing the engine to run with the air conditioning system on for five minutes.

(3) With the engine not running, use a electronic R-134a leak detector and search for leaks. Move the leak detector probe slowly along the bottom side of all lines and fittings, because R-134a is heavier than air.

(4) To inspect the evaporator coil for leaks, insert the leak detector probe into the center panel outlet. Set the blower motor switch to the lowest speed position, and the mode control switch in the Recirculation Mode.

SERVICE PROCEDURES

REFRIGERANT RECOVERY

WARNING: REVIEW THE WARNINGS AND CAUTIONS IN THE FRONT OF THIS GROUP BEFORE RECOVERING REFRIGERANT.

R-134a refrigerant is a hydrofluorocarbon (HFC) that does not contain chlorine. A R-134a refrigerant recovery/recycling station that meets SAE Standard J2210 must be used to recover the refrigerant. Refer to the operating instructions provided with the equipment for proper operation.

REFRIGERANT SYSTEM EVACUATE

WARNING: REVIEW THE WARNINGS AND CAUTIONS IN THE FRONT OF THIS GROUP BEFORE EVACUATING THE SYSTEM.

If the refrigerant system has been open to the atmosphere, it must be evacuated before the system can be charged. Moisture and air mixed with the refrigerant will raise the compressor head pressure above acceptable operating levels. This will reduce the performance of the air conditioner and damage the compressor. Evacuating will boil the moisture out of the refrigerant system at near room temperature. To evacuate the refrigerant system, use the following procedure:

(1) Connect a suitable charging station and manifold gauge set to the vehicle.

(2) Open the low and high side valves and start the vacuum pump. When the suction gauge reads 88 kPa (26 in. Hg.) vacuum or greater, close all of the valves and turn off the vacuum pump. If the system fails to reach the specified vacuum, the system has a leak that must be corrected. If the system maintains the specified vacuum for five minutes, restart the vacuum pump. Then open the suction and discharge valves and evacuate an additional ten minutes.

(3) Close all of the valves. Turn off and disconnect the vacuum pump.

(4) The refrigerant system is now ready to be charged with refrigerant.

REFRIGERANT SYSTEM CHARGE

WARNING: REVIEW THE WARNINGS AND CAUTIONS IN THE FRONT OF THIS GROUP BEFORE CHARGING THE REFRIGERANT SYSTEM.

After the system has been tested for leaks and evacuated, a refrigerant charge can be injected into the system. See Refrigerant Charge Capacity for the proper amount of the refrigerant charge. Charge the system using a recovery/recycling/charging station approved for R-134a refrigerant. This device must meet SAE Standard J2210. Refer to the instructions provided with the equipment for proper operation.

REFRIGERANT CHARGE CAPACITY

The R-134a system charge capacity is 0.567 kg (1.25 lbs.).

REFRIGERANT OIL LEVEL

When an air conditioning system is assembled at the factory, all components (except the compressor) are refrigerant oil free. After the system has been charged and operated, the oil in the compressor is dispersed through the refrigerant system. The accu-

SERVICE PROCEDURES (Continued)

mulator, evaporator, condenser, and compressor will retain a significant amount of oil.

It is important to have the correct amount of oil in the refrigerant system. This will ensure proper lubrication of the compressor. Too little oil will result in damage to the compressor. Too much oil will reduce the cooling capacity of the system.

It will not be necessary to check oil level in the compressor or to add oil, unless there has been an oil loss. This may be due to a rupture or leak from a refrigerant line, a compressor shaft seal, an evaporator, or a condenser. If a rupture occurs, add 1 ounce of oil to the system after the repair has been made. Oil loss at a leak point will be evident by the presence of a wet, shiny surface around the leak.

Refrigerant oil must be added when a accumulator, evaporator, or condenser are replaced. Refer to the Refrigerant Oil Capacities chart. When a compressor is replaced, the oil must be drained from the old compressor and measured. Drain all the oil from the new compressor, then fill the new compressor with the same amount of oil that was drained out of the old compressor.

Refrigerant Oil Capacities		
Component	**ml**	**oz**
A/C System	240	8.1
Accumulator	120	4
Condenser	30	1
Evaporator	60	2
Compressor	drain and measure the oil from the old compressor - see text.	

REMOVAL AND INSTALLATION

REFRIGERANT LINE COUPLERS

WARNING: REVIEW THE WARNINGS AND CAUTIONS IN THE FRONT OF THIS GROUP BEFORE PERFORMING THE FOLLOWING OPERATION.

REMOVAL

(1) Recover the refrigerant from the refrigerant system as described in this group.

(2) Remove the secondary clip from the coupling. Fit the appropriate spring lock coupling tool from the A/C Tool Kit (Special Tool 6125) (Fig. 10).

(3) Close the tool and push it into the open side of the cage to expand the garter spring and release the female fitting.

NOTE: The garter spring may not release if the tool is cocked while pushing it into the cage opening.

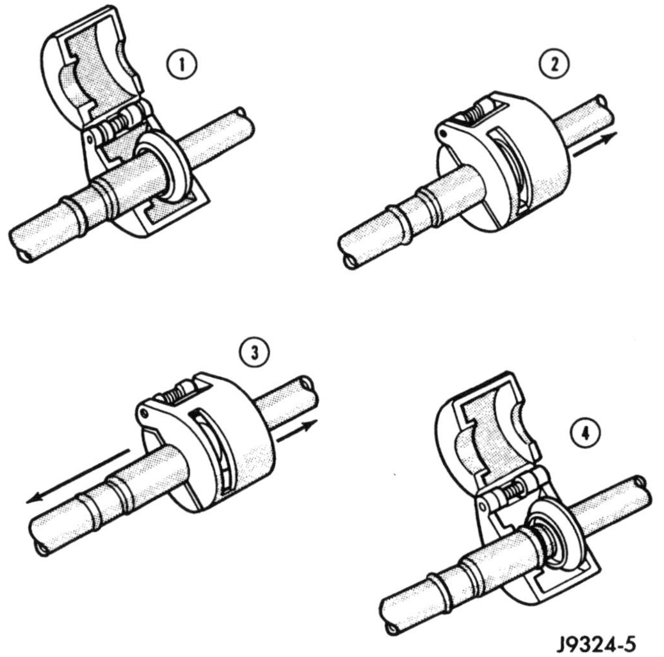

Fig. 10 Spring Lock Coupling Disconnect

(4) After the garter spring is expanded, pull the fittings apart within the tool.

(5) Remove the tool from the disconnected coupling.

(6) Separate the two ends of the coupling.

INSTALLATION

(1) Check to ensure that the garter spring is in the cage of the male fitting. If the garter spring is missing, install a new spring by pushing it into the cage opening. If the garter spring is damaged, remove it from the cage with a small wire hook (DO NOT use a screwdriver) and install a new garter spring.

(2) Clean any dirt or foreign material from both halves of the coupling.

(3) Install new O-rings on the male fitting.

CAUTION: Use only the specified O-rings as they are made of a special material for the R-134a system. The use of any other O-ring may allow the connection to leak intermittently during vehicle operation.

(4) Lubricate the male fitting and O-ring, and the inside of the female fitting with clean R-134a (SP20 PAG) refrigerant oil.

(5) Fit the female fitting to the male fitting and push together until the garter spring snaps over the flared end of the female fitting.

(6) Ensure the coupling is fully engaged by pulling back on the lines on either side of the coupling.

REMOVAL AND INSTALLATION (Continued)

(7) Install the secondary clip on the coupling.

COMPRESSOR

The compressor may be removed and repositioned without disconnecting the refrigerant lines or discharging the refrigerant system. Discharging is not necessary if servicing the compressor clutch or clutch coil, the engine, the cylinder head, or the generator.

WARNING: REVIEW THE WARNINGS AND CAUTIONS IN THE FRONT OF THIS GROUP BEFORE PERFORMING THE FOLLOWING OPERATION.

REMOVAL

(1) Disconnect and isolate the battery negative cable.

(2) Loosen and remove the serpentine drive belt. Refer to Group 7 - Cooling System for the procedures.

(3) Unplug the compressor clutch coil and high pressure cut-off switch wiring connectors.

(4) Recover the refrigerant from the refrigerant system as described in this group.

(5) Remove the manifold and refrigerant lines from the compressor. Install plugs in, or tape over, all of the open refrigerant fittings (Fig. 11).

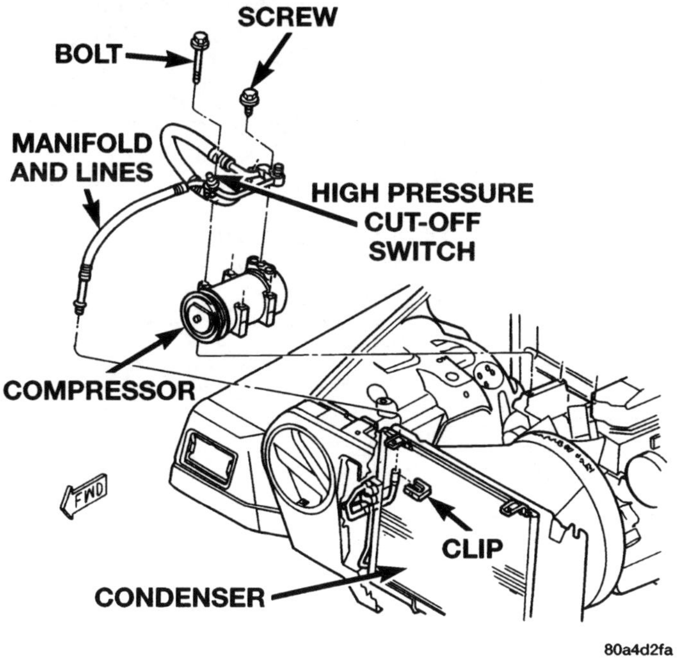

Fig. 11 Compressor Remove/Install

(6) Remove the compressor mounting bolts, and lift the compressor from the mounting bracket.

INSTALLATION

NOTE: If a replacement compressor is being installed, be certain to check the oil level. See Refrigerant Oil Level in this group.

(1) If the compressor mounting bracket was removed, install the bracket to the engine. Tighten the mounting bolts to 27 N·m (20 ft. lbs.).

(2) Install the compressor on the mounting bracket. Tighten the bolts to 28 N·m (21 ft. lbs.).

(3) Remove the tape or plugs from all of the refrigerant fittings, and install the manifold and refrigerant lines on the compressor.

(4) Install the serpentine drive belt. Refer to Group 7 - Cooling System for the procedures.

(5) Connect the compressor clutch coil and high pressure cut-off switch wiring.

(6) Connect the battery negative cable.

(7) Evacuate and charge the refrigerant system as described in this group.

COMPRESSOR CLUTCH

The refrigerant system can remain fully-charged during compressor clutch, pulley, or coil replacement. The compressor clutch can be serviced in the vehicle.

REMOVAL

(1) Disconnect and isolate the battery negative cable.

(2) Remove the serpentine drive belt. Refer to Group 7 - Cooling System for the procedures.

(3) Remove the compressor mounting bolts and lift the compressor from the mounting bracket. Support the compressor to work on the clutch.

(4) Insert the two pins of the spanner wrench (Special Tool C-4489) into the holes of the clutch plate. Hold the clutch plate stationary and remove the hex nut (Fig. 12).

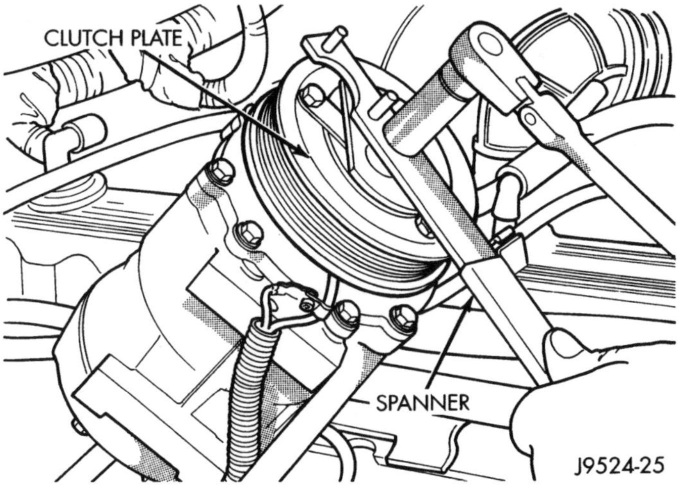

Fig. 12 Clutch Nut Remove

REMOVAL AND INSTALLATION (Continued)

(5) Remove the clutch plate with a puller (Special Tool C-6461) (Fig. 13).

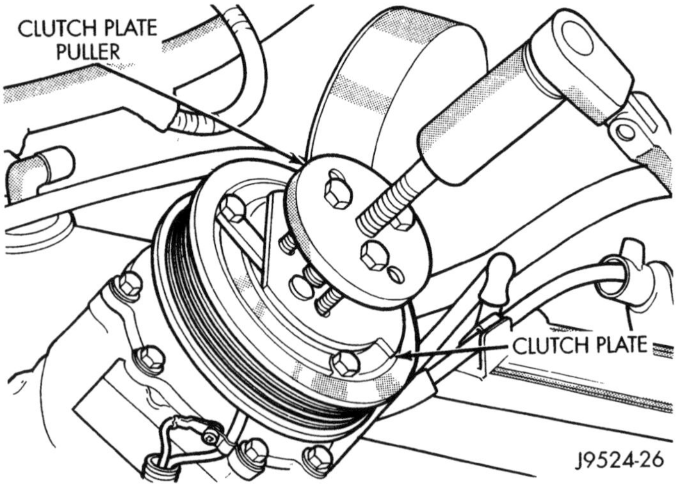

Fig. 13 Clutch Plate Remove

(6) Remove the compressor shaft key and the clutch shims.

(7) Remove the external front housing snap ring with snap ring pliers (Fig. 14).

Fig. 14 External Snap Ring Remove

(8) Install the lip of the rotor puller (Special Tool C-6141-1) into the snap ring groove exposed in the previous step, and install the shaft protector (Special Tool C-6141-2) (Fig. 15).

(9) Install the puller through-bolts (Special Tool C-6461) through the puller flange and into the jaws of the rotor puller and tighten (Fig. 16). Turn the puller center bolt clockwise until the rotor pulley is free.

(10) Remove the screw and retainer from the clutch coil lead wire on the compressor front housing (Fig. 17).

(11) Remove the snap ring from the compressor hub and remove the clutch field coil (Fig. 18). Slide the clutch field coil off of the compressor hub.

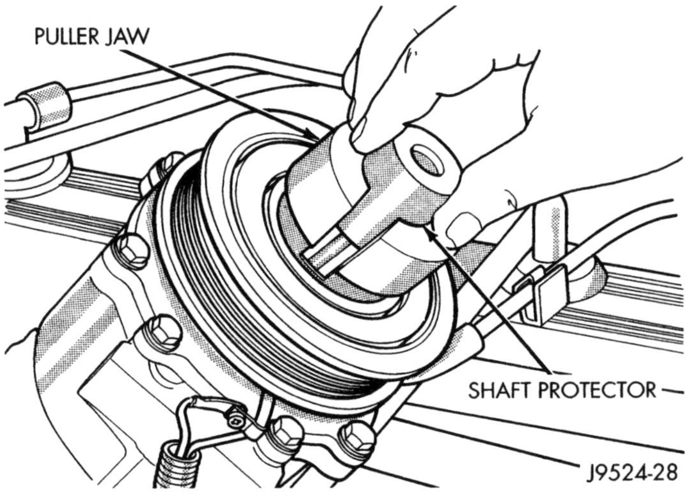

Fig. 15 Shaft Protector and Puller

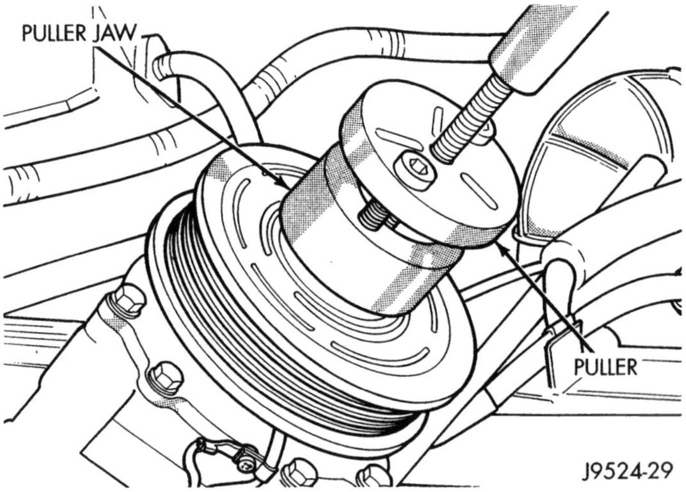

Fig. 16 Install Puller Plate

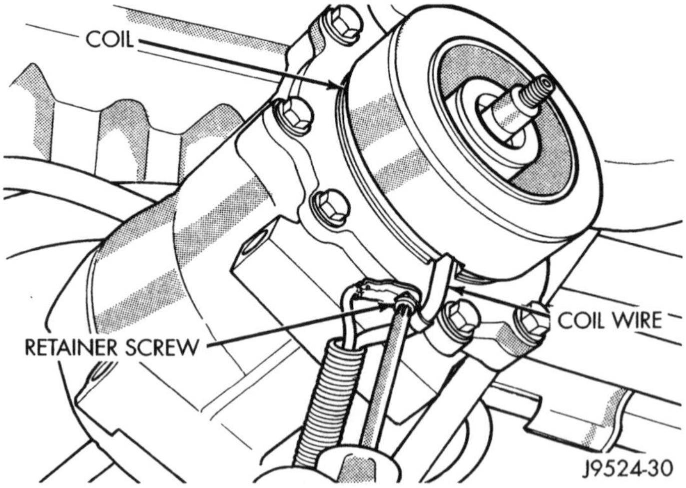

Fig. 17 Clutch Coil Lead Wire

INSPECTION

Examine the friction surfaces of the clutch pulley and the front plate for wear. The pulley and front

REMOVAL AND INSTALLATION (Continued)

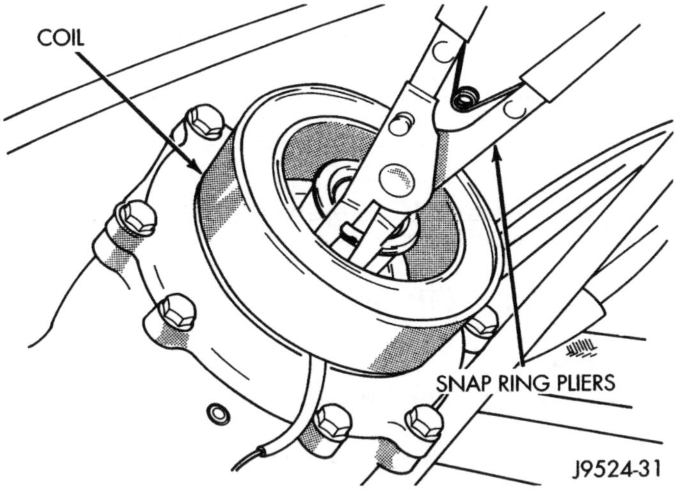

Fig. 18 Clutch Field Coil Snap Ring Remove

plate should be replaced if there is excessive wear or scoring.

If the friction surfaces are oily, inspect the shaft and nose area of the compressor for oil. Remove the felt from the front cover. If the felt is saturated with oil, the shaft seal is leaking and the compressor must be replaced.

Check the clutch pulley bearing for roughness or excessive leakage of grease. Replace the bearing, if required.

INSTALLATION

(1) Install the clutch field coil and snap ring.

(2) Install the clutch coil wire lead retaining clip on the compressor front housing and tighten the retaining screw.

(3) Align the rotor assembly squarely on the front compressor housing hub.

(4) Install the pulley bearing assembly with the installer (Special Tool C-6871) (Fig. 19). Thread the installer on the shaft, then turn the nut until the pulley assembly is seated.

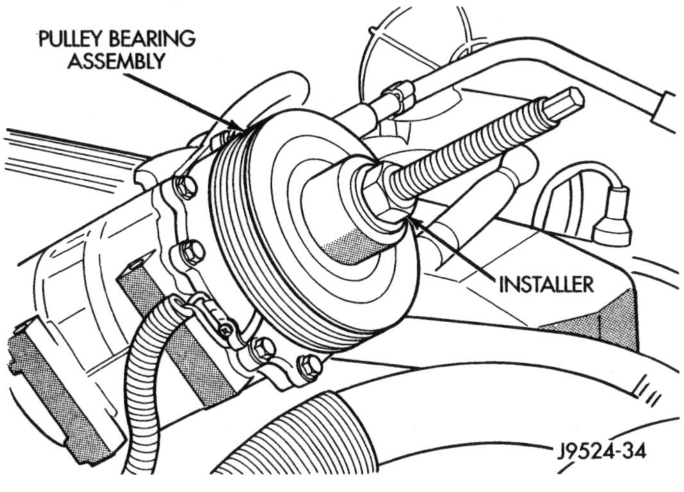

Fig. 19 Clutch Pulley Install

(5) Install the external front snap ring with snap ring pliers. The bevel side of the snap ring must be facing outward. Press the snap ring to make sure it is properly seated in the groove.

CAUTION: If the snap ring is not fully seated in the groove it will vibrate out, resulting in a clutch failure and severe damage to the front housing of the compressor.

(6) Install the compressor shaft key and the original clutch shims on the compressor shaft.

(7) Install the clutch plate with the driver (Special Tool C-6463) (Fig. 20). Install the shaft hex nut and tighten to 14.4 N·m (10.5 ft. lbs.).

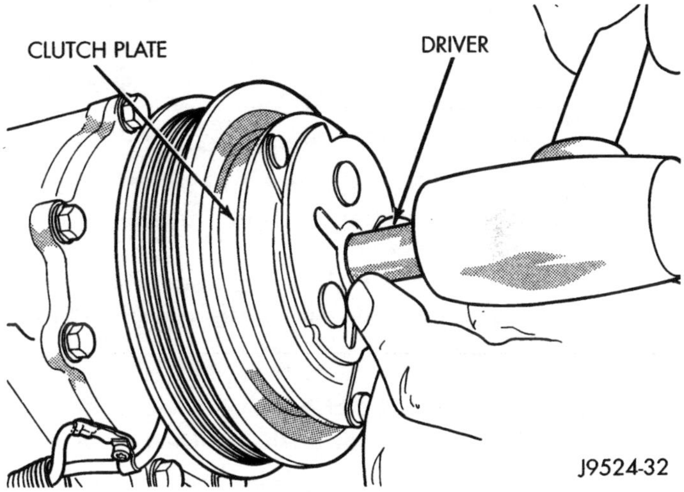

Fig. 20 Clutch Plate Driver

(8) Check the clutch air gap with a feeler gauge (Fig. 21). If the air gap does not meet the specification, add or subtract shims as required. The air gap specification is 0.41-0.79 mm (0.016-0.031 inch). If the air gap is not consistent around the circumference of the clutch, lightly pry up at the minimum variations. Lightly tap down at the points of maximum variation.

NOTE: The air gap is determined by the spacer shims. When installing an original, or a new clutch assembly, try the original shims first. When installing a new clutch onto a compressor that previously did not have a clutch, use 0.040, 0.020, and 0.005 shims from the clutch hardware package that is provided with the new clutch.

(9) Reverse the remaining removal procedures to complete the installation.

CLUTCH BREAK-IN

After a new compressor clutch has been installed, cycle the compressor clutch approximately twenty times (5 seconds on, then 5 seconds off). During this

REMOVAL AND INSTALLATION (Continued)

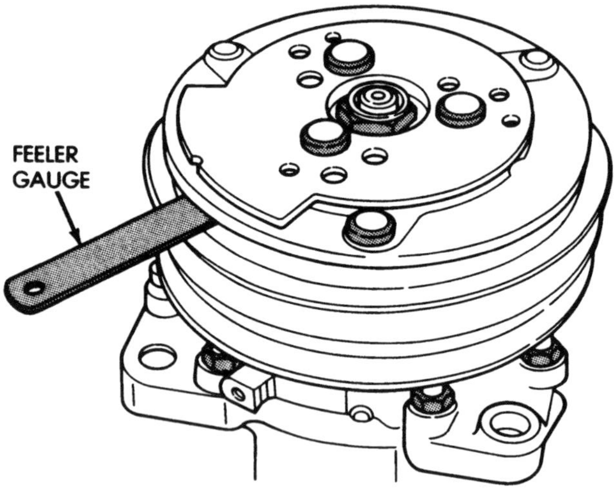

Fig. 21 Check Clutch Air Gap

procedure, set the heater-A/C control to the Recirculation Mode, the blower motor switch in the highest speed position, and the engine speed at 1500 - 2000 rpm. This procedure (burnishing) will seat the opposing friction surfaces and provide a higher compressor clutch torque capability.

COMPRESSOR CLUTCH RELAY

(1) Disconnect and isolate the battery negative cable.

(2) Remove the cover from the Power Distribution Center (PDC) (Fig. 22).

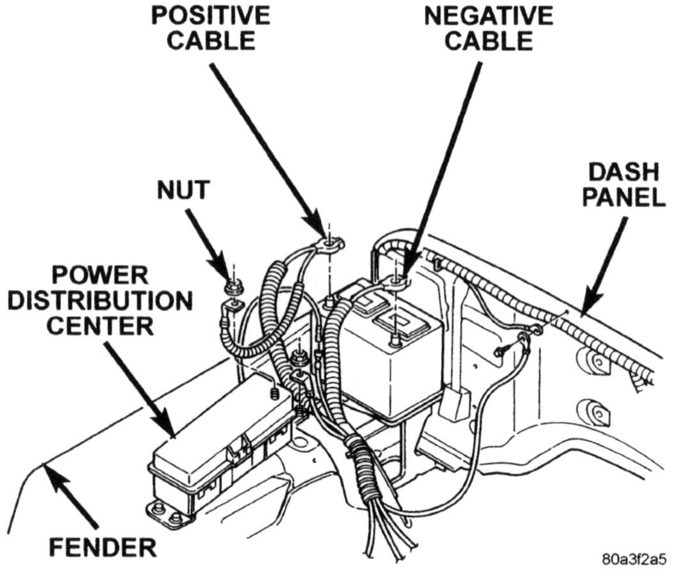

Fig. 22 Power Distribution Center

(3) Refer to the label on the PDC for compressor clutch relay identification and location.

(4) Remove the compressor clutch relay by unplugging it from the PDC.

(5) Install the compressor clutch relay by aligning the relay terminals with the cavities in the PDC and pushing the relay firmly into place.

(6) Install the PDC cover.

(7) Connect the battery negative cable.

(8) Test the relay operation.

HIGH PRESSURE CUT-OFF SWITCH

REMOVAL

(1) Disconnect and isolate the battery negative cable.

(2) Unplug the wiring connector from the switch (Fig. 23).

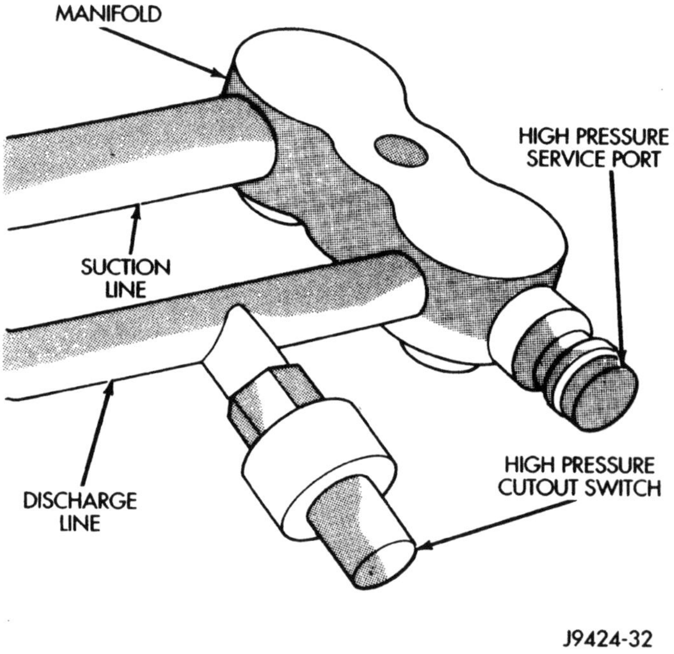

Fig. 23 High Pressure Cut-Off Switch - Typical

(3) Unscrew the switch from the discharge line fitting.

INSTALLATION

(1) Install and tighten the switch.

(2) Plug the wiring connector into the switch.

(3) Connect the battery negative cable.

CONDENSER

WARNING: REVIEW THE WARNINGS AND CAUTIONS IN THE FRONT OF THIS GROUP BEFORE PERFORMING THE FOLLOWING OPERATION.

REMOVAL AND INSTALLATION (Continued)

CAUTION: When removing the condenser note the locations of all of the radiator and condenser air seals. These seals are used to direct air through the condenser and radiator. They must be installed in their original locations to prevent engine overheating.

REMOVAL

(1) Disconnect and isolate the battery negative cable.

(2) Recover the refrigerant from the refrigerant system as described in this group.

(3) Remove the two retainers securing the upper condenser air seal to the grille panel and remove the air seal (Fig. 24).

(4) Remove the two screws securing the upper condenser mounting brackets to the grille panel.

(5) Reach through the grille panel opening from the front of the vehicle to remove the two screws securing the condenser refrigerant tube and flange unit to the condenser. Install plugs in, or tape over, all of the open refrigerant fittings.

(6) Remove the four retainers securing the lower condenser air seal to the frame rails and the grille panel and remove the air seal.

(7) Remove the two screws securing the lower condenser mounting bracket to the grille panel.

(8) Remove the three screws on each side of the radiator securing the radiator mounting brackets to the grille panel.

(9) Tilt the radiator and shroud unit back towards the engine using care to prevent the cooling fan blades from damaging the radiator.

(10) Carefully lift the condenser out of the vehicle.

INSTALLATION

(1) Carefully position the condenser in the vehicle.

(2) Install and tighten the two screws securing the upper condenser mounting brackets to the grille panel.

(3) Align the holes of the radiator mounting brackets to the grille panel. Install and tighten the six screws securing the radiator and shroud unit to the grille panel.

(4) Install the upper condenser air seal to the grille panel with two retainers.

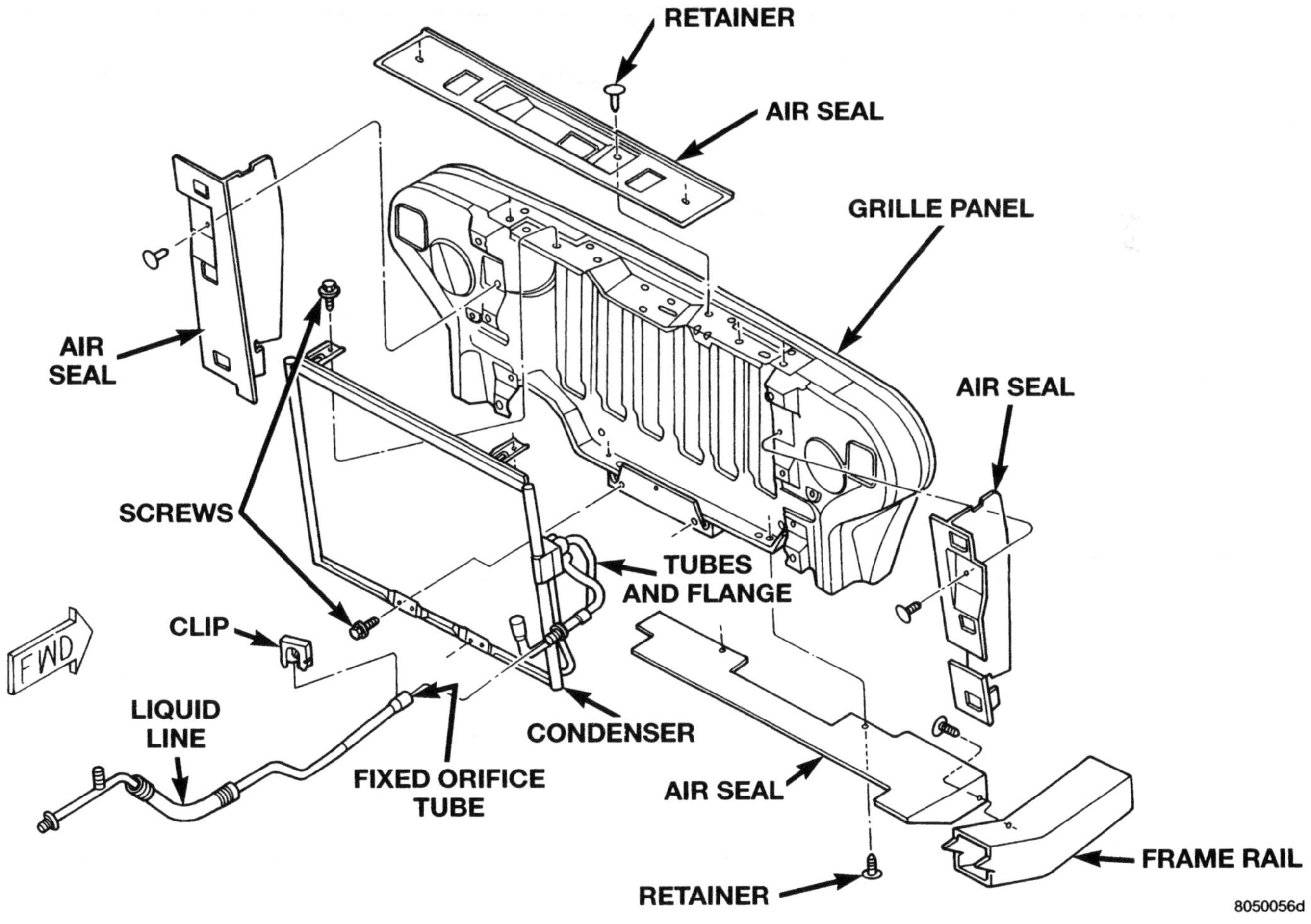

Fig. 24 Condenser Remove/Install

REMOVAL AND INSTALLATION (Continued)

(5) Remove the tape or plugs from the refrigerant fittings. Reach through the grille opening to install the condenser tubes and flange to the condenser with two screws.

(6) Install and tighten the two screws securing the lower condenser bracket to the grille panel.

(7) Install the lower condenser air seal to the grille panel and the frame rails with four retainers.

(8) Evacuate the refrigerant system as described in this group.

(9) Charge the refrigerant system as described in this group.

(10) Connect the battery negative cable.

NOTE: If the condenser is replaced, add 30 ml (1 oz.) of refrigerant oil to the refrigerant system.

FIXED ORIFICE TUBE

WARNING: REVIEW THE WARNINGS AND CAUTIONS IN THE FRONT OF THIS GROUP BEFORE PERFORMING THE FOLLOWING OPERATION.

REMOVAL

(1) Disconnect and isolate the battery negative cable.

(2) Recover the refrigerant from the refrigerant system as described in this group.

(3) Disconnect the liquid line refrigerant line coupler at the condenser outlet tube.

(4) Remove the fixed orifice tube using a needle nose pliers. Note the orientation of the fixed orifice tube for correct reinstallation.

INSTALLATION

(1) Install the fixed orifice tube in the liquid line.

(2) Connect the liquid line to the condenser outlet tube.

(3) Evacuate and charge the refrigerant system as described in this group.

(4) Connect the battery negative cable.

ACCUMULATOR

WARNING: REVIEW THE WARNINGS AND CAUTIONS IN THE FRONT OF THIS GROUP BEFORE PERFORMING THE FOLLOWING OPERATION.

REMOVAL

(1) Disconnect and isolate the battery negative cable.

(2) Recover the refrigerant from the refrigerant system as described in this group.

(3) Disconnect the two refrigerant line couplers from the accumulator tubes. Install plugs in, or tape over, all of the open refrigerant fittings (Fig. 25).

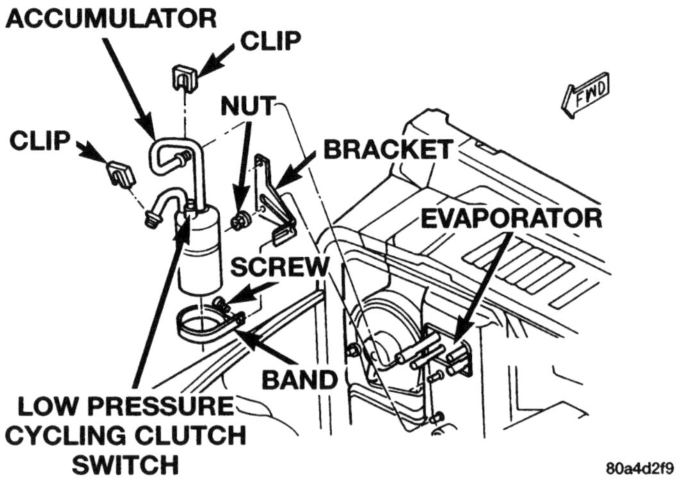

Fig. 25 Accumulator Remove/Install

(4) Unplug the wire harness connector from the low pressure cycling clutch switch.

(5) Loosen the screw securing the accumulator and band to the mounting bracket.

(6) Slide the accumulator and band unit screw out of the slotted hole in the mounting bracket.

INSTALLATION

(1) Install the accumulator and band unit screw into the slotted mounting bracket hole.

(2) Tighten the screw.

(3) Plug the wire harness connector into the low pressure cycling clutch switch.

(4) Remove the plugs or tape from the refrigerant line fittings. Connect the refrigerant lines to the accumulator tubes.

(5) Evacuate and charge the refrigerant system as described in this group.

(6) Connect the battery negative cable.

NOTE: If the accumulator is replaced, add 120 ml (4 oz.) of refrigerant oil to the refrigerant system.

LOW PRESSURE CYCLING CLUTCH SWITCH

(1) Disconnect and isolate the battery negative cable.

(2) Unplug the wire harness connector from the switch on the top of the accumulator.

(3) Unscrew the switch from the fitting on the accumulator.

(4) Reverse the removal procedures to install.

REMOVAL AND INSTALLATION (Continued)

BLOWER MOTOR

REMOVAL

(1) Remove the battery from the battery tray. Refer to Group 8A - Battery for the procedures.

(2) Remove the three screws securing the Powertrain Control Module (PCM) to the mounting bracket on the engine compartment side of the dash panel. Move the PCM away from the blower motor opening in the dash panel (Fig. 26).

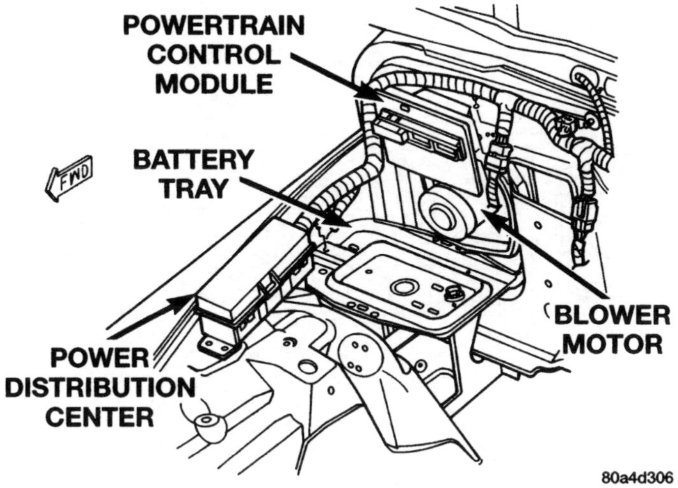

Fig. 26 Blower Motor Remove/Install

(3) Unplug the blower motor wiring connector.

(4) Remove the three blower motor and wheel assembly mounting screws.

(5) Remove the blower motor and wheel from the heater-A/C housing.

(6) Remove the blower motor wheel retainer clip and remove the wheel from the blower motor shaft

INSTALLATION

(1) Install the blower motor and wheel into the heater-A/C housing.

(2) Install and tighten the three blower motor mounting screws.

(3) Connect the blower motor wiring connector.

(4) Install the PCM to the mounting bracket with three screws.

(5) Install the battery in the battery tray. Refer to Group 8A - Battery for the procedures.

VACUUM CHECK VALVE

(1) Unplug the vacuum supply line at the intake manifold.

(2) Note the orientation of the check valve in the vacuum line for correct installation. The black colored end of the valve should be oriented towards the intake manifold, and the natural colored end towards the vacuum reservoir.

(3) Unplug the valve from the vacuum supply line fittings.

(4) Reverse the removal procedures to install.

VACUUM RESERVOIR

(1) Remove the battery and battery tray as described in Group 8A - Battery.

(2) Disconnect the vacuum supply line from the vacuum reservoir (Fig. 27).

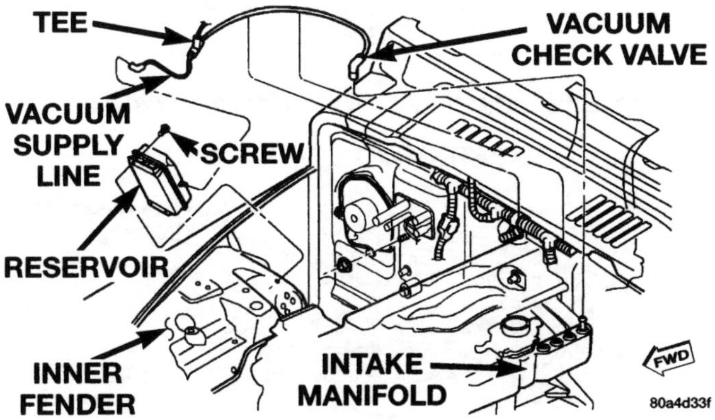

Fig. 27 Vacuum Reservoir Remove/Install

(3) Remove the one screw securing the reservoir to the inner fender panel beneath the battery tray.

(4) Remove the vacuum reservoir.

(5) Reverse the removal procedures to install.

HEATER-A/C CONTROL

WARNING: ON VEHICLES EQUIPPED WITH AIRBAGS, REFER TO GROUP 8M - PASSIVE RESTRAINT SYSTEMS BEFORE ATTEMPTING STEERING WHEEL, STEERING COLUMN, OR INSTRUMENT PANEL COMPONENT DIAGNOSIS OR SERVICE. FAILURE TO TAKE THE PROPER PRECAUTIONS COULD RESULT IN ACCIDENTAL AIRBAG DEPLOYMENT AND POSSIBLE PERSONAL INJURY.

REMOVAL

(1) Disconnect and isolate the battery negative cable.

(2) Remove the instrument panel center bezel and the glove box. Refer to Group 8E - Instrument Panel Systems for the procedures.

(3) Reach through the glove box opening and unplug the two halves of the vacuum harness connector.

(4) Remove the four screws securing the heater-A/C control to the instrument panel (Fig. 28).

(5) Pull the heater-A/C control out from the instrument panel far enough to access the connectors on the back of the control.

(6) Unplug the three electrical connectors from the back of the heater-A/C control (Fig. 29).

REMOVAL AND INSTALLATION (Continued)

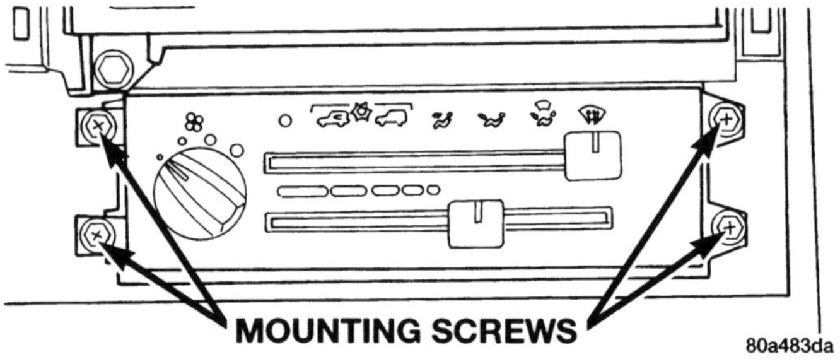

Fig. 28 Heater-A/C Control Remove/Install

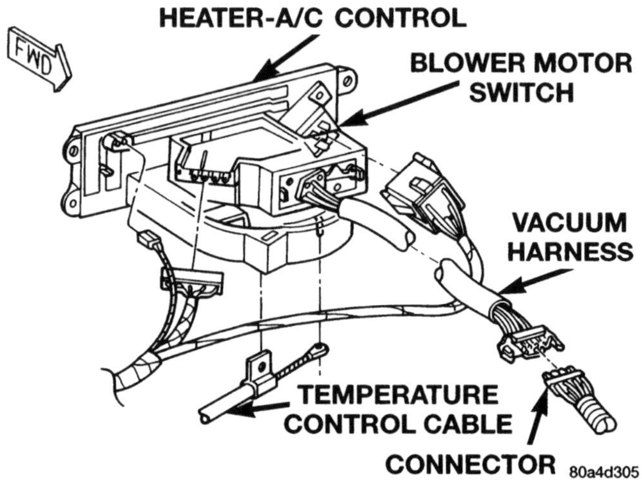

Fig. 29 Heater-A/C Control Connectors

(7) Disconnect the temperature control cable and cable housing from the heater-A/C control.

(8) Remove the heater-A/C control from the instrument panel.

INSTALLATION

(1) Connect the temperature control cable and cable housing to the heater-A/C control.

(2) Plug the three electrical connectors into the heater-A/C control.

(3) Install the heater-A/C control to the instrument panel with four screws.

(4) Reach through the glove box opening and plug the two halves of the vacuum harness together.

(5) Install the glove box and the instrument panel center bezel. Refer to Group 8E - Instrument Panel Systems for the procedures.

(6) Connect the battery negative cable.

BLOWER MOTOR SWITCH

WARNING: ON VEHICLES EQUIPPED WITH AIRBAGS, REFER TO GROUP 8M - PASSIVE RESTRAINT SYSTEMS BEFORE ATTEMPTING STEERING WHEEL, STEERING COLUMN, OR INSTRUMENT PANEL COMPONENT DIAGNOSIS OR SERVICE. FAILURE TO TAKE THE PROPER PRECAUTIONS COULD RESULT IN ACCIDENTAL AIRBAG DEPLOYMENT AND POSSIBLE PERSONAL INJURY.

(1) Disconnect and isolate the battery negative cable.

(2) Pull the blower motor switch knob on the front of the heater-A/C control off of the blower motor switch stem.

(3) Remove the heater-A/C control as described in this group.

(4) Remove the two screws securing the blower motor switch to the rear of the heater-A/C control and remove the switch (Fig. 30).

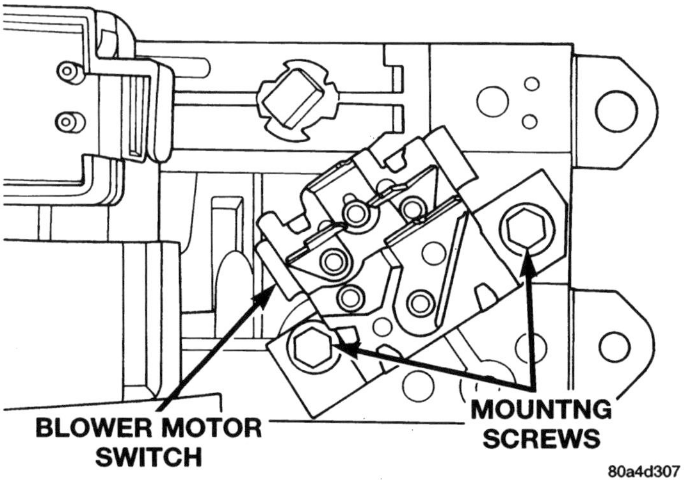

Fig. 30 Blower Motor Switch Remove/Install

(5) Reverse the removal procedures to install.

TEMPERATURE CONTROL CABLE

WARNING: ON VEHICLES EQUIPPED WITH AIRBAGS, REFER TO GROUP 8M - PASSIVE RESTRAINT SYSTEMS BEFORE ATTEMPTING STEERING WHEEL, STEERING COLUMN, OR INSTRUMENT PANEL COMPONENT DIAGNOSIS OR SERVICE. FAILURE TO TAKE THE PROPER PRECAUTIONS COULD RESULT IN ACCIDENTAL AIRBAG DEPLOYMENT AND POSSIBLE PERSONAL INJURY.

(1) Disconnect and isolate the battery negative cable.

(2) Remove the heater-A/C control as described in this group.

(3) Disconnect the cable retainer from the heater-A/C housing (Fig. 31).

(4) Remove the push nut attaching the cable to the blend air door crank arm and remove the cable.

(5) Reach through the glove box opening to route the cable through the strap retaining it to the heater-A/C housing support bracket on the dash panel, and

REMOVAL AND INSTALLATION (Continued)

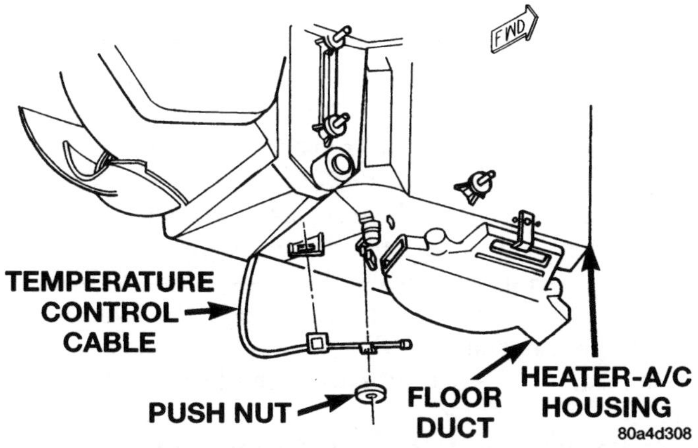

Fig. 31 Temperature Control Cable Remove/Install

to remove the cable from the retainer clips on the heater-A/C housing.

(6) Reverse the removal procedures to install. Be certain that the push nut is reinstalled.

HIGH SPEED BLOWER MOTOR RELAY

WARNING: ON VEHICLES EQUIPPED WITH AIRBAGS, REFER TO GROUP 8M - PASSIVE RESTRAINT SYSTEMS BEFORE ATTEMPTING STEERING WHEEL, STEERING COLUMN, OR INSTRUMENT PANEL COMPONENT DIAGNOSIS OR SERVICE. FAILURE TO TAKE THE PROPER PRECAUTIONS COULD RESULT IN ACCIDENTAL AIRBAG DEPLOYMENT AND POSSIBLE PERSONAL INJURY.

(1) Disconnect and isolate the battery negative cable.

(2) Remove the glove box as described in Group 8E - Instrument Panel Systems.

(3) Locate the relay near the right end of the heater-A/C housing under the instrument panel (Fig. 32).

(4) Unplug the relay from the connector.

(5) To install the relay, align the terminals with the cavities in the relay center and push the relay firmly into place.

(6) Install the glove box.

(7) Connect the battery negative cable.

(8) Test the relay operation.

BLOWER MOTOR RESISTOR

WARNING: ON VEHICLES EQUIPPED WITH AIRBAGS, REFER TO GROUP 8M - PASSIVE RESTRAINT SYSTEMS BEFORE ATTEMPTING STEERING WHEEL, STEERING COLUMN, OR INSTRUMENT PANEL COMPONENT DIAGNOSIS OR SERVICE. FAILURE TO TAKE THE PROPER PRECAUTIONS COULD RESULT IN ACCIDENTAL AIRBAG DEPLOYMENT AND POSSIBLE PERSONAL INJURY.

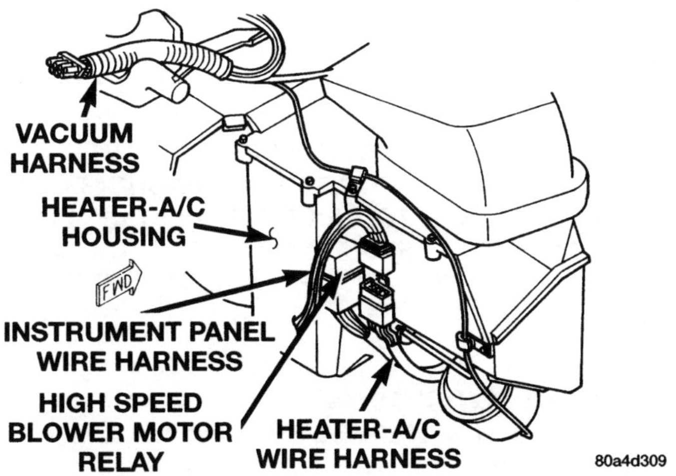

Fig. 32 High Speed Blower Motor Relay

(1) Disconnect and isolate the battery negative cable.

(2) Remove the kick cover from the passenger side outboard end of the heater-A/C housing under the instrument panel. There are two screws securing the outboard end of the cover to the housing, and one screw secures the inboard end of the cover to the housing.

(3) Pull out on the blower motor resistor wiring connector latch and unplug the connector from the resistor (Fig. 33).

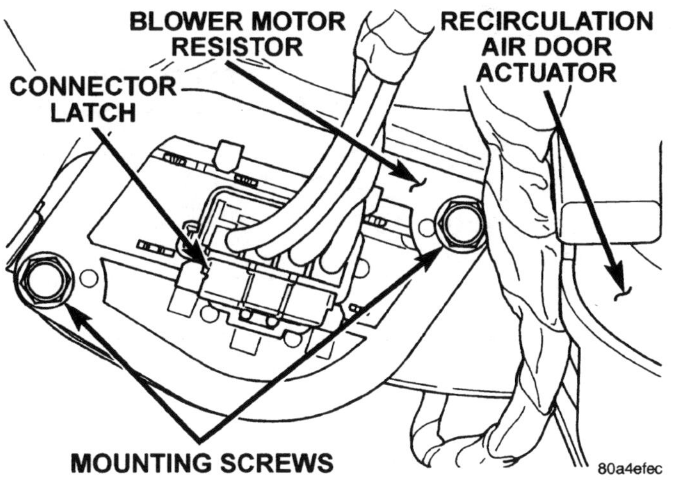

Fig. 33 Blower Motor Resistor Remove/Install

(4) Remove the two screws securing the resistor to the heater-A/C housing.

(5) Remove the resistor from the housing.

(6) Reverse the removal procedures to install.

REMOVAL AND INSTALLATION (Continued)

MODE DOOR VACUUM ACTUATORS

WARNING: ON VEHICLES EQUIPPED WITH AIRBAGS, REFER TO GROUP 8M - PASSIVE RESTRAINT SYSTEMS BEFORE ATTEMPTING STEERING WHEEL, STEERING COLUMN, OR INSTRUMENT PANEL COMPONENT DIAGNOSIS OR SERVICE. FAILURE TO TAKE THE PROPER PRECAUTIONS COULD RESULT IN ACCIDENTAL AIRBAG DEPLOYMENT AND POSSIBLE PERSONAL INJURY.

DEFROST/DEMIST DOOR

(1) Disconnect and isolate the battery negative cable.

(2) Remove the steering column cover and knee blocker as described in Group 8E - Instrument Panel Systems.

(3) Unplug the two actuator vacuum lines from the actuator (Fig. 34).

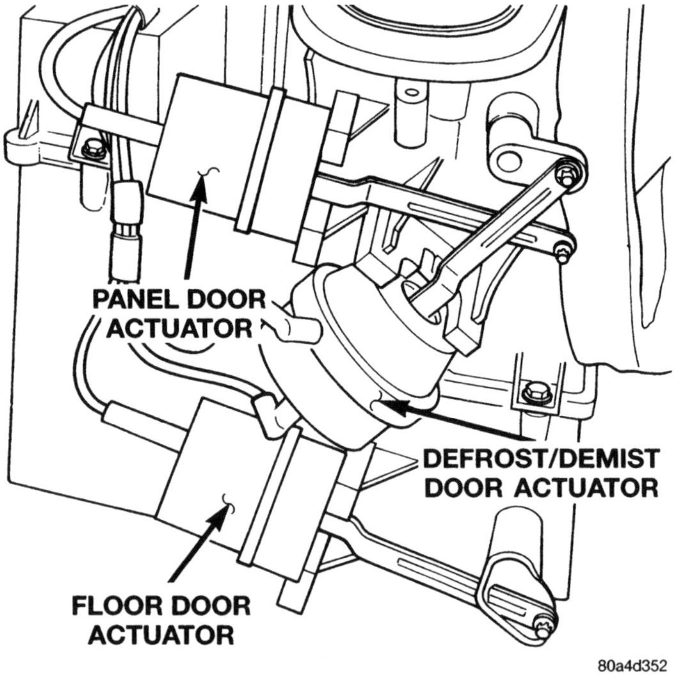

Fig. 34 Defrost/Demist, Floor, and Panel Door Vacuum Actuators

(4) Remove the push nut securing the actuator arm to the stud on the defrost/demist door lever.

(5) Pull firmly outwards on the actuator to release the snap-fit actuator mounts from the mounting stanchions molded into the heater-A/C housing.

(6) Remove the actuator from the heater-A/C housing.

(7) Reverse the removal procedures to install. Be certain that the push nut is reinstalled.

FLOOR DOOR

(1) Disconnect and isolate the battery negative cable.

(2) Remove the steering column cover and knee blocker as described in Group 8E - Instrument Panel Systems.

(3) Unplug the actuator vacuum line from the actuator (Fig. 34).

(4) Remove the push nut securing the actuator arm to the stud on the floor door lever.

(5) Pull firmly outwards on the actuator to release the snap-fit actuator mounts from the mounting stanchions molded into the heater-A/C housing.

(6) Remove the actuator from the heater-A/C housing.

(7) Reverse the removal procedures to install. Be certain that the push nut is reinstalled.

PANEL DOOR

(1) Disconnect and isolate the battery negative cable.

(2) Remove the steering column cover and knee blocker as described in Group 8E - Instrument Panel Systems.

(3) Remove the defrost/demist door actuator as described in this group.

(4) Unplug the actuator vacuum line from the actuator (Fig. 34).

(5) Remove the push nut securing the actuator arm to the stud on the panel door lever.

(6) Pull firmly outwards on the actuator to release the snap-fit actuator mounts from the mounting stanchions molded into the heater-A/C housing.

(7) Remove the actuator from the heater-A/C housing.

(8) Reverse the removal procedures to install. Be certain that the push nut is reinstalled.

RECIRCULATION AIR DOOR

A recirculation air door and actuator are used only on models with the optional air conditioning system.

(1) Disconnect and isolate the battery negative cable.

(2) Remove the kick cover from the passenger side outboard end of the heater-A/C housing under the instrument panel. There are two screws securing the outboard end of the cover to the housing, and one screw secures the inboard end of the cover to the housing.

(3) Unplug the actuator vacuum line from the actuator (Fig. 35).

(4) Remove the push nut securing the actuator arm to the stud on the recirculation air door lever.

(5) Pull firmly downwards on the actuator to release the snap-fit actuator mounts from the mounting stanchions molded into the heater-A/C housing.

REMOVAL AND INSTALLATION (Continued)

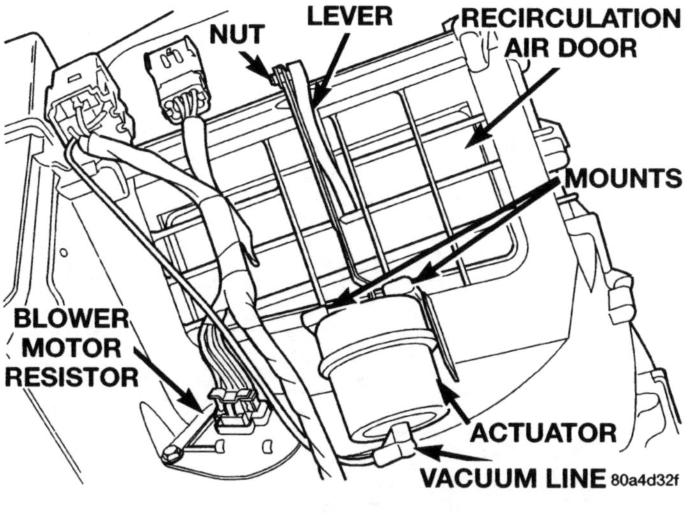

Fig. 35 Recirculation Air Door Vacuum Actuator Remove/Install

(6) Remove the actuator from the heater-A/C housing.

(7) Reverse the removal procedures to install. Be certain that the push nut is reinstalled.

HEATER-A/C HOUSING

The heater-A/C housing assembly must be removed from the vehicle and the two halves of the housing separated for service access of the heater core, evaporator coil, blend-air door, and each of the various mode control doors.

WARNING: ON VEHICLES EQUIPPED WITH AIRBAGS, REFER TO GROUP 8M - PASSIVE RESTRAINT SYSTEMS BEFORE ATTEMPTING STEERING WHEEL, STEERING COLUMN, OR INSTRUMENT PANEL COMPONENT DIAGNOSIS OR SERVICE. FAILURE TO TAKE THE PROPER PRECAUTIONS COULD RESULT IN ACCIDENTAL AIRBAG DEPLOYMENT AND POSSIBLE PERSONAL INJURY.

REMOVAL

(1) Disconnect and isolate the battery negative cable.

(2) Remove the instrument panel assembly as described in Group 8E - Instrument Panel Systems.

(3) If the vehicle is not equipped with air conditioning, go to Step 5. If the vehicle is equipped with air conditioning, recover the refrigerant from the refrigerant system as described in this group.

(4) Disconnect the refrigerant lines from the evaporator tubes. Install plugs in, or tape over all of the open refrigerant fittings.

(5) Drain the cooling system. Refer to Group 7 - Cooling System for the procedures.

(6) Disconnect the heater hoses from the heater core tubes.

(7) Disconnect the heater-A/C system vacuum supply line from the tee fitting near the heater core tubes.

(8) Remove the five heater-A/C housing mounting nuts from the studs on the engine compartment side of the dash panel (Fig. 36). Loosen the battery hold-downs and reposition the battery for access, if required.

(9) Remove the cowl plenum drain tube from the stud directly behind the engine.

(10) Remove one screw securing the heater-A/C housing to the bracket on the dash panel.

(11) Pull the heater-A/C housing rearward and down far enough for the mounting studs to clear the dash panel holes and the housing to clear the defrost/demist and fresh air ducts.

(12) Remove the heater-A/C housing from the vehicle.

DISASSEMBLY

(1) Disengage the heater-A/C wiring and high speed blower motor relay connector retainers from their mounting holes in the heater-A/C housing.

(2) Unplug the vacuum harness connectors at the recirculation air door and floor door actuators.

(3) Remove the three screws securing the blower motor and wheel unit to the heater-A/C housing.

(4) Unplug the blower motor wire connector and remove the blower motor and wheel from the heater-A/C housing.

(5) Remove the screws and snap clips holding the upper and lower heater-A/C housing halves together.

(6) Separate the upper heater-A/C housing half from the lower half.

ASSEMBLY

(1) Assemble the upper heater-A/C housing half to the lower half. Be certain that the upper blend-air door pivot is engaged in its hole in the upper housing half.

(2) Install the screws and snap clips holding the upper and lower heater-A/C housing halves together.

(3) Plug the blower motor wire connector into the heater-A/C wire harness and install the blower motor and wheel into the heater-A/C housing.

(4) Install the three screws securing the blower motor and wheel unit to the heater-A/C housing.

(5) Plug in the vacuum harness connectors at the recirculation air door and floor door actuators.

(6) Engage the heater-A/C wiring and high speed blower motor relay connector retainers with their mounting holes in the heater-A/C housing.

INSTALLATION

(1) Position the heater-A/C housing to the dash panel. Be sure the drain tube is installed through the dash panel drain hole and that the defrost/demist and fresh air ducts are in their proper positions.

REMOVAL AND INSTALLATION (Continued)

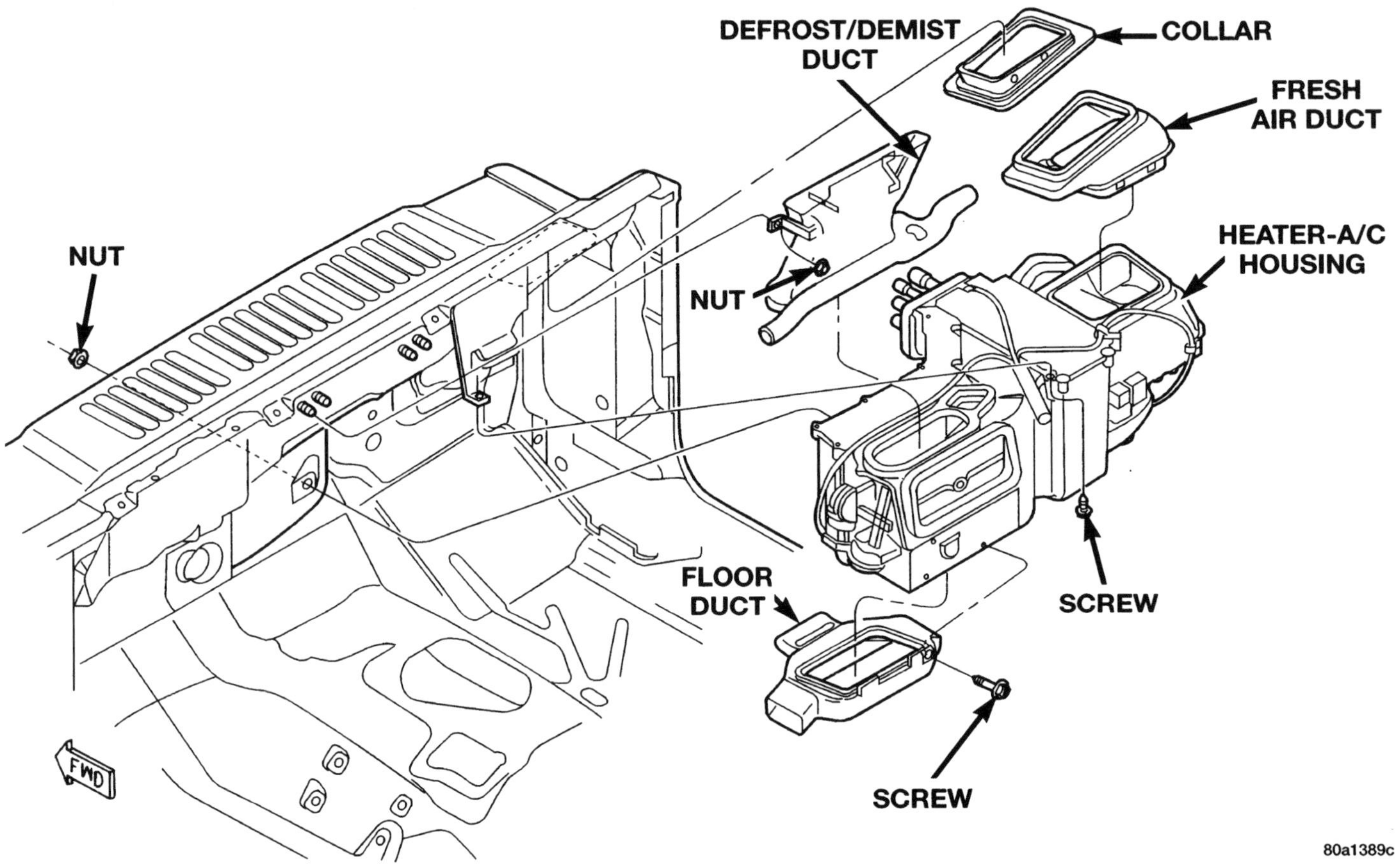

Fig. 36 Heater-A/C Housing Remove/Install

(2) Install the one mounting screw to secure the heater-A/C housing to the dash panel bracket.

(3) Install the cowl drain tube onto the stud located directly behind the engine.

(4) Install the five nuts to the mounting studs on the engine compartment side of the dash panel. If the battery was repositioned during the removal procedure, position the battery and tighten the hold-downs.

(5) Connect the heater-A/C system vacuum supply tube to the tee fitting near the heater core tubes.

(6) Connect the heater hoses to the heater core tubes.

(7) Unplug or remove the tape from the refrigerant fittings, and connect the refrigerant lines to the evaporator tubes.

(8) Install the instrument panel assembly as described in Group 8E - Instrument Panel Systems.

(9) Connect the battery negative cable.

(10) Fill the cooling system. Refer to Group 7 - Cooling System for the procedures.

(11) Evacuate and charge the refrigerant system as described in this group.

(12) Start the vehicle and check for proper operation of the heating and air conditioning systems.

HEATER-A/C HOUSING DOORS

WARNING: ON VEHICLES EQUIPPED WITH AIRBAGS, REFER TO GROUP 8M - PASSIVE RESTRAINT SYSTEMS BEFORE ATTEMPTING STEERING WHEEL, STEERING COLUMN, OR INSTRUMENT PANEL COMPONENT DIAGNOSIS OR SERVICE. FAILURE TO TAKE THE PROPER PRECAUTIONS COULD RESULT IN ACCIDENTAL AIRBAG DEPLOYMENT AND POSSIBLE PERSONAL INJURY.

BLEND-AIR DOOR

(1) Remove and disassemble the heater-A/C housing as described in this group.

(2) Pry the blend-air door lever out of the door pivot from the outside of the lower housing half.

(3) Lift the door pivot out of the pivot hole from the inside of the lower housing half.

(4) Reverse the removal procedures to install.

DEFROST/DEMIST DOOR

(1) Remove and disassemble the heater-A/C housing as described in this group.

(2) Remove the defrost/demist door vacuum actuator as described in this group.

REMOVAL AND INSTALLATION (Continued)

(3) Pry the defrost/demist door lever out of the door pivot from the outside of the inboard end of the upper housing half.

(4) Reach inside the upper housing half and gently flex the doors enough so that the door pivot clears the pivot hole in the housing.

(5) Remove the defrost/demist doors from the housing as a unit.

(6) Reverse the removal procedures to install.

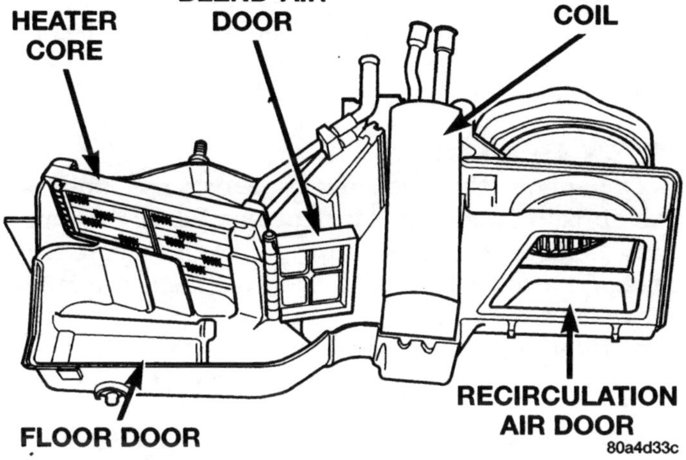

Lower Heater-A/C Housing

FLOOR DOOR

(1) Remove and disassemble the heater-A/C housing as described in this group.

(2) Remove the floor door vacuum actuator as described in this group.

(3) Pry the floor door lever out of the door pivot from the outside of the inboard end of the lower housing half.

(4) Reach inside the lower housing half and gently flex the door enough so that the door pivot clears the pivot hole in the housing.

(5) Remove the floor door from the housing.

(6) Reverse the removal procedures to install.

PANEL DOOR

(1) Remove and disassemble the heater-A/C housing as described in this group.

(2) Remove the panel door vacuum actuator as described in this group.

(3) Pry the panel door lever out of the door pivot from the outside of the inboard end of the upper housing half.

(4) Reach inside the upper housing half and gently flex the door enough so that the door pivot clears the pivot hole in the housing.

(5) Remove the panel door from the housing.

(6) Reverse the removal procedures to install.

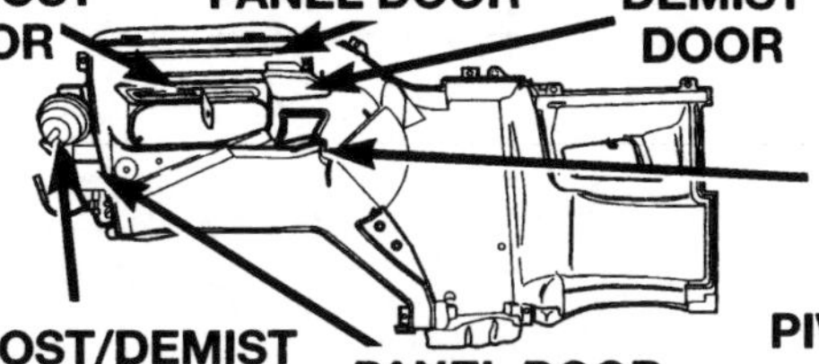

Upper Heater-A/C Housing

RECIRCULATION AIR DOOR

(1) Remove and disassemble the heater-A/C housing as described in this group.

(2) Remove the recirculation air door vacuum actuator as described in this group.

(3) Reach inside the lower housing half and gently flex the door enough so that the door pivot clears the pivot hole in the housing.

(4) Remove the recirculation air door from the housing.

(5) Reverse the removal procedures to install.

EVAPORATOR COIL

WARNING: ON VEHICLES EQUIPPED WITH AIRBAGS, REFER TO GROUP 8M - PASSIVE RESTRAINT SYSTEMS BEFORE ATTEMPTING STEERING WHEEL, STEERING COLUMN, OR INSTRUMENT PANEL COMPONENT DIAGNOSIS OR SERVICE. FAILURE TO TAKE THE PROPER PRECAUTIONS COULD RESULT IN ACCIDENTAL AIRBAG DEPLOYMENT AND POSSIBLE PERSONAL INJURY.

(1) Remove and disassemble the heater-A/C housing as described in this group.

(2) Lift the evaporator coil out of the lower half of the heater-A/C housing.

(3) Reverse the removal procedures to install. Be certain that the evaporator foam insulator is reinstalled.

NOTE: If the evaporator is replaced, add 60 ml (2 oz.) of refrigerant oil to the refrigerant system.

HEATER CORE

WARNING: ON VEHICLES EQUIPPED WITH AIRBAGS, REFER TO GROUP 8M - PASSIVE RESTRAINT SYSTEMS BEFORE ATTEMPTING STEERING WHEEL, STEERING COLUMN, OR INSTRUMENT PANEL COMPONENT DIAGNOSIS OR SERVICE. FAILURE TO TAKE THE PROPER PRECAUTIONS COULD RESULT IN ACCIDENTAL AIRBAG DEPLOYMENT AND POSSIBLE PERSONAL INJURY.

REMOVAL AND INSTALLATION (Continued)

(1) Remove and disassemble the heater-A/C housing as described in this group.

(2) Lift the heater core out of the lower half of the heater-A/C housing.

(3) Reverse the removal procedures to install. Be certain that the heater core foam insulator is reinstalled.

DUCTS AND OUTLETS

Only the demister hoses and the panel outlet barrels can be removed without instrument panel assembly removal. Removal of the fresh air duct and collar require that the heater-A/C housing also be partially removed. The panel outlet housings and demister outlets are serviced only as a part of the instrument panel or instrument panel center bezel.

WARNING: ON VEHICLES EQUIPPED WITH AIRBAGS, REFER TO GROUP 8M - PASSIVE RESTRAINT SYSTEMS BEFORE ATTEMPTING STEERING WHEEL, STEERING COLUMN, OR INSTRUMENT PANEL COMPONENT DIAGNOSIS OR SERVICE. FAILURE TO TAKE THE PROPER PRECAUTIONS COULD RESULT IN ACCIDENTAL AIRBAG DEPLOYMENT AND POSSIBLE PERSONAL INJURY.

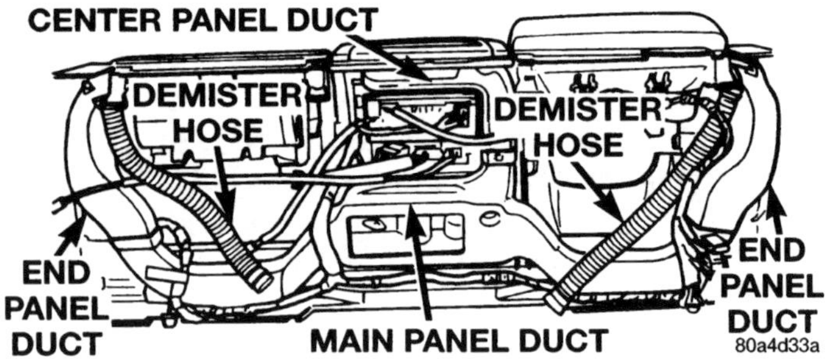

Heater-A/C Ducts and Outlets Remove/Install

DEFROST/DEMIST DUCT

(1) Remove the instrument panel assembly as described in Group 8E - Instrument Panel Systems.

(2) Remove the two screws securing the defrost/demist duct to the studs on the dash panel.

(3) Remove the defrost/demist duct.

(4) Reverse the removal procedures to install.

DEMISTER HOSES

(1) Disconnect and isolate the battery negative cable.

(2) Remove the glove box to service the passenger side demister hose. Remove the steering column cover and knee blocker to service the driver side demister hose. Refer to Group 8E - Instrument Panel Systems for the procedures.

(3) Disconnect the ends of the demister hose from the demister outlet and the defrost/demist duct.

(4) Reverse the removal procedures to install.

FLOOR DUCT

(1) Remove the instrument panel as described in Group 8E - Instrument Panel Systems.

(2) Remove the two screws securing the rear of the duct to the heater-A/C housing.

(3) Release the front of the duct from the snap clip securing it to the heater-A/C housing.

(4) Slide the floor duct out from under the heater-A/C housing.

(5) Reverse the removal procedures to install.

FRESH AIR DUCT

(1) Remove the instrument panel assembly as described in Group 8E - Instrument Panel Systems.

(2) Remove the five nuts from the heater-A/C housing studs on the engine compartment side of the dash panel.

(3) Remove the one screw securing the heater-A/C housing to the bracket on the passenger compartment side of the dash panel.

(4) Push gently down on the top of the heater-A/C housing until sufficient clearance is obtained to remove the fresh air duct from the housing.

(5) Remove the fresh air duct collar from the cowl plenum panel by reaching up above the heater-A/C housing fresh air duct opening and pulling the collar downward. The collar is retained by a light snap fit.

(6) Reverse the removal procedures to install.

PANEL DUCTS

(1) Remove the instrument panel assembly as described in Group 8E - Instrument Panel Systems.

(2) Remove the demister hoses as described in this group.

(3) Remove the two screws from the rearward facing side of the instrument panel securing the main panel duct to the instrument panel base.

(4) Remove the one screw securing each end panel duct and/or the center panel duct to the instrument panel base.

(5) Remove the panel ducts from the instrument panel.

(6) Reverse the removal procedures to install.

PANEL OUTLET BARRELS

(1) Use a trim stick or other suitable flat wide-blade tool to pry the panel outlet barrel out of the panel outlet housing. The barrel is retained by a light snap fit.

(2) To install, position the barrel in the panel outlet housing and press firmly until the barrel snaps into place.

EMISSION CONTROL SYSTEMS

CONTENTS

ON-BOARD DIAGNOSTICS

INDEX

GENERAL INFORMATION

SYSTEM DESCRIPTION

The Powertrain Control Module (PCM) monitors many different circuits in the fuel injection, ignition, emission and engine systems. If the PCM senses a problem with a monitored circuit often enough to indicate an actual problem, it stores a Diagnostic Trouble Code (DTC) in the PCM's memory. If the problem is repaired or ceases to exist, the PCM cancels the code after 40 warm-up cycles. Diagnostic trouble codes that affect vehicle emissions will cause the Malfunction Indicator (check engine) Lamp to illuminate continuously if the engine is running. Refer to Malfunction Indicator Lamp in this section.

Certain criteria must be met before the PCM stores a DTC in memory. The criteria may be a specific range of engine RPM, engine temperature, and/or input voltage to the PCM.

The PCM might not store a DTC for a monitored circuit even though a malfunction has occurred. This may happen because one of the DTC criteria for the circuit has not been met. **For example**, assume the diagnostic trouble code criteria requires the PCM to monitor the circuit only when the engine operates between 750 and 2000 RPM. Suppose the sensor's output circuit shorts to ground when engine operates above 2400 RPM (resulting in 0 volt input to the PCM). Because the condition happens at an engine speed above the maximum threshold (2000 rpm), the PCM will not store a DTC.

There are several operating conditions for which the PCM monitors and sets DTC's. Refer to Monitored Systems, Components, and Non-Monitored Circuits in this section.

NOTE: Various diagnostic procedures may actually cause a diagnostic monitor to set a DTC. For instance, pulling a spark plug wire to perform a spark test may set the misfire code. When a repair is completed and verified, connect the DRB scan tool to the 16–way data link connector (Fig. 1) to erase all DTC's and extinguish the MIL.

Technicians can display stored DTC's by two different methods. Refer to Diagnostic Trouble Codes in this section. For DTC information, refer to charts in this section.

DESCRIPTION AND OPERATION

MALFUNCTION INDICATOR LAMP (MIL)

As a functional test, the MIL (check engine) illuminates at key-on before engine cranking. Whenever the Powertrain Control Module (PCM) sets a Diagnostic Trouble Code (DTC) that affects vehicle emissions, it illuminates the MIL. If a problem is detected, the PCM sends a message to the instru-

DESCRIPTION AND OPERATION (Continued)

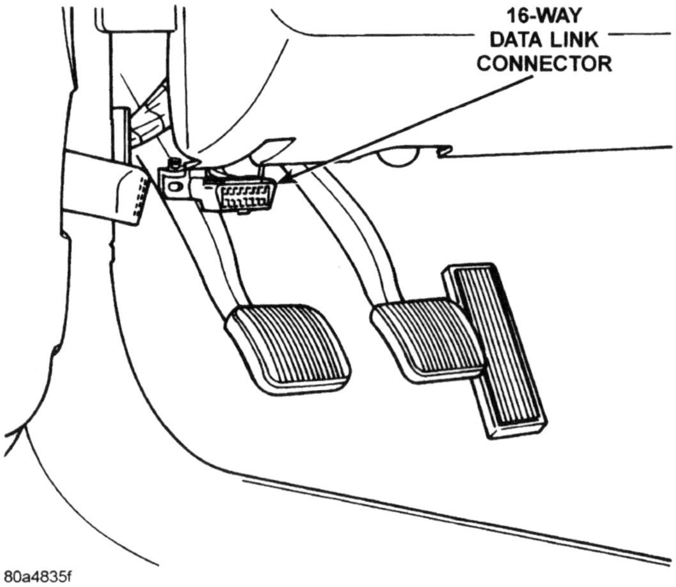

Fig. 1 Data Link (Diagnostic) Connector Location

ment cluster to illuminate the lamp. The PCM illuminates the MIL only for DTC's that affect vehicle emissions. There are some monitors that may take two consecutive trips, with a detected fault, before the MIL is illuminated. The MIL stays on continuously when the PCM has entered a Limp-In mode or identified a failed emission component. Refer to the Diagnostic Trouble Code charts in this group for emission related codes.

Also, the MIL either flashes or illuminates continuously when the PCM detects active engine misfire. Refer to Misfire Monitoring in this section.

Additionally, the PCM may reset (turn off) the MIL when one of the following occur:

- PCM does not detect the malfunction for 3 consecutive trips (except misfire and Fuel system Monitors).
- PCM does not detect a malfunction while performing three successive engine misfire or fuel system tests. The PCM performs these tests while the engine is operating within ± 375 RPM of and within 10 % of the load of the operating condition at which the malfunction was first detected.

STATE DISPLAY TEST MODE

The switch inputs to the Powertrain Control Module (PCM) have two recognized states; HIGH and LOW. For this reason, the PCM cannot recognize the difference between a selected switch position versus an open circuit, a short circuit, or a defective switch. If the State Display screen shows the change from HIGH to LOW or LOW to HIGH, assume the entire switch circuit to the PCM functions properly. Connect the DRB scan tool to the data link connector and access the state display screen. Then access either State Display Inputs and Outputs or State Display Sensors.

CIRCUIT ACTUATION TEST MODE

The Circuit Actuation Test Mode checks for proper operation of output circuits or devices the Powertrain Control Module (PCM) may not internally recognize. The PCM attempts to activate these outputs and allow an observer to verify proper operation. Most of the tests provide an audible or visual indication of device operation (click of relay contacts, fuel spray, etc.). Except for intermittent conditions, if a device functions properly during testing, assume the device, its associated wiring, and driver circuit work correctly. Connect the DRB scan tool to the data link connector and access the Actuators screen.

DIAGNOSTIC TROUBLE CODES

A Diagnostic Trouble Code (DTC) indicates the PCM has recognized an abnormal condition in the system.

The technician can display a DTC in three different ways:

- a two-digit number flashed on the Malfunction Indicator (Check Engine) Lamp
- a two-digit number displayed on the vehicle odometer
- a description of the DTC can be read using the DRB scan tool

Diagnostic trouble codes are the results of a system or circuit failure, but do not directly identify the failed component or components.

NOTE: For a list of DTC's, refer to the charts in this section.

OBTAINING DIAGNOSTIC TROUBLE CODES

USING DRB SCAN TOOL

WARNING: APPLY PARKING BRAKE AND/OR BLOCK WHEELS BEFORE PERFORMING ANY TEST ON AN OPERATING ENGINE.

(1) Connect the DRB scan tool to data link (diagnostic) connector located in passengers compartment, below instrument cluster near bottom of steering column (Fig. 1).

(2) Turn the ignition switch on, access Read Fault Screen. Record all the DTC's shown on the DRB scan tool. Observe the malfunction indicator (check engine) lamp on the instrument panel. The lamp should light for 2 seconds then go out (bulb check).

(3) To erase DTC's, use the Erase Trouble Code data screen on the DRB scan tool.

DESCRIPTION AND OPERATION (Continued)

USING THE MALFUNCTION INDICATOR LAMP (MIL)

(1) Cycle the ignition key On - Off - On - Off - On within 5 seconds.

(2) Count the number of times the MIL (check engine lamp) on the instrument panel flashes on and off. The number of flashes represents the trouble code. There is a slight pause between the flashes representing the first and second digits of the code. Longer pauses separate individual two digit trouble codes.

An example of a flashed DTC is as follows:

(3) Lamp flashes 1 time, pauses, and then flashes 5 more times. This indicates a DTC code number 15.

(4) Lamp flashes 5 times, pauses, and flashes 5 more times. This indicates a DTC code number 55. A DTC code number 55 will always be the last code to be displayed. This will indicate the end of all stored codes.

(5) To erase DTC's, use the Erase Trouble Code data screen on the DRB scan tool.

USING THE VEHICLE ODOMETER

(1) Cycle the ignition key On - Off - On - Off - On within 5 seconds.

(2) Read the actual DTC number displayed on the vehicle odometer. Each number will be displayed with a slight delay between numbers. A DTC code number 55 will always be the last code to be displayed. This will indicate the end of all stored codes.

(3) To erase DTC's, use the Erase Trouble Code data screen on the DRB scan tool.

DIAGNOSTIC TROUBLE CODE DESCRIPTIONS

HEX CODE	MIL CODE	GENERIC SCAN TOOL CODE	DRB SCAN TOOL DISPLAY	DESCRIPTION OF DIAGNOSTIC TROUBLE CODE
	12*		Battery Disconnect	Direct battery input to PCM was disconnected within the last 50 Key-on cycles.
	55*			Completion of fault code display on Check Engine lamp.
01	54**	P0340	No Cam Signal at PCM	No camshaft signal detected during engine cranking.
02	53**	P0601	Internal Controller Failure	PCM Internal fault condition detected.
05	47***		Charging System Voltage Too Low	Battery voltage sense input below target charging during engine operation. Also, no significant change detected in battery voltage during active test of generator output circuit.
06	46***		Charging System Voltage Too High	Battery voltage sense input above target charging voltage during engine operation.
0A	42*		Auto Shutdown Relay Control Circuit	An open or shorted condition detected in the auto shutdown relay circuit.
0B	41***		Generator Field Not Switching Properly	An open or shorted condition detected in the generator field control circuit.
0C	37**	P0743	Torque Converter Clutch Soleniod CKT	An open or shorted condition detected in the torque converter part throttle unlock solenoid control circuit (3 speed auto RH trans. only).
0F	34*		Speed Control Solenoid Circuits	An open or shorted condition detected in the Speed Control vacuum or vent solenoid circuits.
10	33*		A/C Clutch Relay Circuit	An open or shorted condition detected in the A/C clutch relay circuit.
12	31**	P0443	EVAP Purge Solenoid Circuit	An open or shorted condition detected in the duty cycle purge solenoid circuit.
13	27**	P0203	Injector #3 Control Circuit	Injector #3 output driver does not respond properly to the control signal.

DESCRIPTION AND OPERATION (Continued)

HEX CODE	MIL CODE	GENERIC SCAN TOOL CODE	DRB SCAN TOOL DISPLAY	DESCRIPTION OF DIAGNOSTIC TROUBLE CODE
		or		
14		P0202	Injector #2 Control Circuit	Injector #2 output driver does not respond properly to the control signal.
		or		
15		P0201	Injector #1 Control Circuit	Injector #1 output driver does not respond properly to the control signal.
19	25**	P0505	Idle Air Control Motor Circuits	A shorted or open condition detected in one or more of the idle air control motor circuits.
1A	24**	P0122	Throttle Position Sensor Voltage Low	Throttle position sensor input below the minimum acceptable voltage
		or		
1B		P0123	Throttle Position Sensor Voltage High	Throttle position sensor input above the maximum acceptable voltage.
1E	22**	P0117	ECT Sensor Voltage Too Low	Engine coolant temperature sensor input below minimum acceptable voltage.
		or		
1F		P0118	ECT Sensor Voltage Too High	Engine coolant temperature sensor input above maximum acceptable voltage.
21	17*		Engine Is Cold Too Long	Engine did not reach operating temperature within acceptable limits.
23	15**	P0500	No Vehicle Speed Sensor Signal	No vehicle speed sensor signal detected during road load conditions.
24	14**	P0107	MAP Sensor Voltage Too Low	MAP sensor input below minimum acceptable voltage.
		or		
25		P0108	MAP Sensor Voltage Too High	MAP sensor input above maximum acceptable voltage.
27	13**	P1297	No Change in MAP From Start to Run	No difference recognized between the engine MAP reading and the barometric (atmospheric) pressure reading from start-up.
28	11*		No Crank Reference Signal at PCM	No crank reference signal detected during engine cranking.
2B	43*	P0351	Ignition Coil #1 Primary Circuit	Peak primary circuit current not achieved with maximum dwell time.
2C	42*		No ASD Relay Output Voltage at PCM	An Open condition Detected In The ASD Relay Output Circuit.
31	63*	P1698	PCM Failure EEPROM Write Denied	Unsuccessful attempt to write to an EEPROM location by the PCM.
39	23**	P0112	Intake Air Temp Sensor Voltage Low	Intake air temperature sensor input below the maximum acceptable voltage.
		or		
3A		P0113	Intake Air Temp Sensor Voltage High	Intake air temperature sensor input above the minimum acceptable voltage.

DESCRIPTION AND OPERATION (Continued)

HEX CODE	MIL CODE	GENERIC SCAN TOOL CODE	DRB SCAN TOOL DISPLAY	DESCRIPTION OF DIAGNOSTIC TROUBLE CODE
3D	27**	P0204	Injector #4 Control Circuit	Injector #4 output driver does not respond properly to the control signal.
3E	21**	P0132	Left O2 Sensor Shorted to Voltage	Left oxygen sensor input voltage maintained above the normal operating range.
44	53*	P0600	PCM Failure SPI Communications	PCM Internal fault condition detected.
45 46	27**	P0205 or P0206	Injector #5 Control Circuit Injector #6 Control Circuit	Injector #5 output driver does not respond properly to the control signal. Injector #6 output driver does not respond properly to the control signal.
52	77*		S/C Power Relay Circuit	Malfunction detected with power feed to speed control servo solenoids.
57	34*		Speed Control Switch Always Low	Speed control switch input below the minimum acceptable voltage.
65	42*		Fuel Pump Relay Control Circuit	An open or shorted condition detected in the fuel pump relay control circuit.
66 67 69	21**	P0133 or P0135 or P0141	Upstream O2 Sensor Slow Response Upstream O2 Sensor Heater Failure Downstream O2 Sensor Heater Failure	Upstream oxygen sensor response slower than minimum required switching frequency. Upstream oxygen sensor heating element circuit malfunction Downstream oxygen sensor heating element circuit malfunction
6A 6B 6C 6D 6E	43**	P0300 or P0301 or P0302 or P0303 or P0304	Multiple Cylinder Misfire Cylinder #1 Misfire Cylinder #2 Misfire Cylinder #3 Misfire Cylinder #4 Misfire	Misfire detected in multiple cylinders. Misfire detected in cylinder #1. Misfire detected in cylinder #2. Misfire detected in cylinder #3. Misfire detected in cylinder #4.
70	72**	P0420	Catalytic Converter Efficency Failure	Catalyst efficiency below required level.
70	64**	P0420	Catalytic Converter Efficiency Failure	Catalyst efficiency below required level.
71	31*	P0441	Evap Purge Flow Monitor Failure	Insufficient or excessive vapor flow detected during evaporative emission system operation.
72	37**	P1899	Park/Neutral Switch Failure	Incorrect input state detected for the Park/Neutral switch, auto. trans. only.

DESCRIPTION AND OPERATION (Continued)

HEX CODE	MIL CODE	GENERIC SCAN TOOL CODE	DRB SCAN TOOL DISPLAY	DESCRIPTION OF DIAGNOSTIC TROUBLE CODE
73	65*	P0551	Power Steering Switch Failure	Power steering high pressure seen at high speed (2.5L only).
76	52**	P0172	Fuel System Rich	A rich air/fuel mixture has been indicated by an abnormally lean correction factor.
77	51**	P0171	Fuel System Lean	A lean air/fuel mixture has been indicated by an abnormally rich correction factor.
7E	21**	P0138	Downstream O2 Sensor Shorted to Voltage	Downstream oxygen sensor input voltage maintained above the normal operating range.
80	17**	P0125	Closed Loop Temp Not Reached	Engine does not reach 20°F within 5 minutes with a vehicle speed signal.
84	24**	P0121	TPS Voltage Does Not Agree With MAP	TPS signal does not correlate to MAP sensor
87	14**	P1296	No 5 Volts To MAP Sensor	5 Volt output to MAP sensor open
8A	25**	P1294	Target Idle Not Reached	Actual idle speed does not equal target idle speed.
94	37*	P0740	Torq Conv Clu, No RPM Drop At Lockup	Relationship between engine speed and vehicle speed indicates no torque converter clutch engagement (auto. trans. only).
95	42*		Fuel Level Sending Unit Volts Too Low	Open circuit between PCM and fuel gauge sending unit.
		or		
96			Fuel Level Sending Unit Volts Too High	Circuit shorted to voltage between PCM and fuel gauge sending unit.
		or		
97			Fuel Level Unit No Change Over Miles	No movement of fuel level sender detected.
99	44**	P1493	Battery Temp Sensor Voltage Too Low	Battery temperature sensor input voltage below an acceptable range.
		or		
9A		P1492	Battery Temp Sensor Voltage Too High	Battery temperature sensor input voltage above an acceptable range.
9B	21**	P0131	Upstream O2s Voltage Shorted to Ground	O2 sensor voltage too low, tested after cold start.
		or		
9C		P0137	Downstream O2s Voltage Shorted to Ground	O2 sensor voltage too low, tested after cold start.
9D	11**	P1391	Intermittent Loss of CMP or CKP	Intermittent loss of either camshaft or crankshaft position sensor
AE	43**	P0305	Cylinder #5 Misfire	Misfire detected in cylinder #5.
		or		
AF		P0306	Cylinder #6 Misfire	Misfire detected in cylinder #6.

DESCRIPTION AND OPERATION (Continued)

HEX CODE	MIL CODE	GENERIC SCAN TOOL CODE	DRB SCAN TOOL DISPLAY	DESCRIPTION OF DIAGNOSTIC TROUBLE CODE
BA	11**	P1398	Misfire Adaptive Numerator at Limit	CKP sensor target windows have too much variation

* Check Engine Lamp (MIL) will not illuminate if this Diagnostic Trouble Code was recorded. Cycle Ignition key as described in manual and observe code flashed by Check Engine lamp.

** Check Engine Lamp (MIL) will illuminate during engine operation if this Diagnostic Trouble Code was recorded.

*** Generator Lamp illuminated

MONITORED SYSTEMS

There are new electronic circuit monitors that check fuel, emission, engine and ignition performance. These monitors use information from various sensor circuits to indicate the overall operation of the fuel, engine, ignition and emission systems and thus the emissions performance of the vehicle.

The fuel, engine, ignition and emission systems monitors do not indicate a specific component problem. They do indicate that there is an implied problem within one of the systems and that a specific problem must be diagnosed.

If any of these monitors detect a problem affecting vehicle emissions, the Malfunction Indicator (Check Engine) Lamp will be illuminated. These monitors generate Diagnostic Trouble Codes that can be displayed with the check engine lamp or a scan tool.

The following is a list of the system monitors:

- Misfire Monitor
- Fuel System Monitor
- Oxygen Sensor Monitor
- Oxygen Sensor Heater Monitor
- Catalyst Monitor

All these system monitors require two consecutive trips with the malfunction present to set a fault.

Following is a description of each system monitor, and its DTC.

Refer to the appropriate Powertrain Diagnostics Procedures manual for diagnostic procedures.

DTC 21—OXYGEN SENSOR (O2S) MONITOR

Effective control of exhaust emissions is achieved by an oxygen feedback system. The most important element of the feedback system is the O2S. The O2S is located in the exhaust path. Once it reaches operating temperature 300° to 350°C (572° to 662°F), the sensor generates a voltage that is inversely proportional to the amount of oxygen in the exhaust. The information obtained by the sensor is used to calculate the fuel injector pulse width. This maintains a 14.7 to 1 Air Fuel (A/F) ratio. At this mixture ratio, the catalyst works best to remove hydrocarbons (HC), carbon monoxide (CO) and nitrogen oxide (NOx) from the exhaust.

The O2S is also the main sensing element for the Catalyst and Fuel Monitors.

The O2S can fail in any or all of the following manners:

- slow response rate
- reduced output voltage
- dynamic shift
- shorted or open circuits

Response rate is the time required for the sensor to switch from lean to rich once it is exposed to a richer than optimum A/F mixture or vice versa. As the sensor starts malfunctioning, it could take longer to detect the changes in the oxygen content of the exhaust gas.

The output voltage of the O2S ranges from 0 to 1 volt. A good sensor can easily generate any output voltage in this range as it is exposed to different concentrations of oxygen. To detect a shift in the A/F mixture (lean or rich), the output voltage has to change beyond a threshold value. A malfunctioning sensor could have difficulty changing beyond the threshold value.

DTC 21—OXYGEN SENSOR HEATER MONITOR

If there is an oxygen sensor (O2S) shorted to voltage DTC, as well as a O2S heater DTC, the O2S fault MUST be repaired first. Before checking the O2S fault, verify that the heater circuit is operating correctly.

Effective control of exhaust emissions is achieved by an oxygen feedback system. The most important element of the feedback system is the O2S. The O2S is located in the exhaust path. Once it reaches operating temperature 300° to 350°C (572 ° to 662°F), the sensor generates a voltage that is inversely proportional to the amount of oxygen in the exhaust. The information obtained by the sensor is used to calculate the fuel injector pulse width. This maintains a 14.7 to 1 Air Fuel (A/F) ratio. At this mixture ratio, the catalyst works best to remove hydrocarbons (HC),

DESCRIPTION AND OPERATION (Continued)

carbon monoxide (CO) and nitrogen oxide (NOx) from the exhaust.

The voltage readings taken from the O2S sensor are very temperature sensitive. The readings are not accurate below 300°C. Heating of the O2S sensor is done to allow the engine controller to shift to closed loop control as soon as possible. The heating element used to heat the O2S sensor must be tested to ensure that it is heating the sensor properly.

The O2S sensor circuit is monitored for a drop in voltage. The sensor output is used to test the heater by isolating the effect of the heater element on the O2S sensor output voltage from the other effects.

DTC 43—MISFIRE MONITOR

Excessive engine misfire results in increased catalyst temperature and causes an increase in HC emissions. Severe misfires could cause catalyst damage. To prevent catalytic convertor damage, the PCM monitors engine misfire.

The Powertrain Control Module (PCM) monitors for misfire during most engine operating conditions (positive torque) by looking at changes in the crankshaft speed. If a misfire occurs the speed of the crankshaft will vary more than normal.

DTC 51/52—FUEL SYSTEM MONITOR

To comply with clean air regulations, vehicles are equipped with catalytic converters. These converters reduce the emission of hydrocarbons, oxides of nitrogen and carbon monoxide. The catalyst works best when the Air Fuel (A/F) ratio is at or near the optimum of 14.7 to 1.

The PCM is programmed to maintain the optimum air/fuel ratio of 14.7 to 1. This is done by making short term corrections in the fuel injector pulse width based on the O2S sensor output. The programmed memory acts as a self calibration tool that the engine controller uses to compensate for variations in engine specifications, sensor tolerances and engine fatigue over the life span of the engine. By monitoring the actual fuel-air ratio with the O2S sensor (short term) and multiplying that with the program long-term (adaptive) memory and comparing that to the limit, it can be determined whether it will pass an emissions test. If a malfunction occurs such that the PCM cannot maintain the optimum A/F ratio, then the MIL will be illuminated.

DTC 64—CATALYST MONITOR

To comply with clean air regulations, vehicles are equipped with catalytic converters. These converters reduce the emission of hydrocarbons, oxides of nitrogen and carbon monoxide.

Normal vehicle miles or engine misfire can cause a catalyst to decay. A meltdown of the ceramic core can cause a reduction of the exhaust passage. This can increase vehicle emissions and deteriorate engine performance, driveability and fuel economy.

The catalyst monitor uses dual oxygen sensors (O2S's) to monitor the efficiency of the converter. The dual O2S's sensor strategy is based on the fact that as a catalyst deteriorates, its oxygen storage capacity and its efficiency are both reduced. By monitoring the oxygen storage capacity of a catalyst, its efficiency can be indirectly calculated. The upstream O2S is used to detect the amount of oxygen in the exhaust gas before the gas enters the catalytic converter. The PCM calculates the A/F mixture from the output of the O2S. A low voltage indicates high oxygen content (lean mixture). A high voltage indicates a low content of oxygen (rich mixture).

When the upstream O2S detects a lean condition, there is an abundance of oxygen in the exhaust gas. A functioning converter would store this oxygen so it can use it for the oxidation of HC and CO. As the converter absorbs the oxygen, there will be a lack of oxygen downstream of the converter. The output of the downstream O2S will indicate limited activity in this condition.

As the converter loses the ability to store oxygen, the condition can be detected from the behavior of the downstream O2S. When the efficiency drops, no chemical reaction takes place. This means the concentration of oxygen will be the same downstream as upstream. The output voltage of the downstream O2S copies the voltage of the upstream sensor. The only difference is a time lag (seen by the PCM) between the switching of the O2S's.

To monitor the system, the number of lean-to-rich switches of upstream and downstream O2S's is counted. The ratio of downstream switches to upstream switches is used to determine whether the catalyst is operating properly. An effective catalyst will have fewer downstream switches than it has upstream switches i.e., a ratio closer to zero. For a totally ineffective catalyst, this ratio will be one-to-one, indicating that no oxidation occurs in the device.

The system must be monitored so that when catalyst efficiency deteriorates and exhaust emissions increase to over the legal limit, the MIL (check engine lamp) will be illuminated.

TRIP DEFINITION

For a component monitor to erase or turn off a MIL illumination for open/short diagnostics, the PCM must first recognize that the engine has operated for 2 minutes, 3 consecutive times, with no failures.

All system monitors, component rationality and functionality monitors have their own trip counters. Once the appropriate conditions have been met, the monitor will be run. If the monitor fails its test, the MIL will be illuminated after completion of the first

DESCRIPTION AND OPERATION (Continued)

or second failed test (1 trip or 2 trips). If conditions can be repeated for 3 consecutive trips with no malfunctions, the MIL will be turned off.

Anytime the MIL is illuminated, a DTC is stored. It takes three good trips without the condition present to extinguish the MIL. The DTC remains in PCM memory even though the MIL has been extinguished. Once the MIL is extinguished, the PCM must pass the diagnostic test for the most recent DTC for 40 warm-up cycles for the DTC to be erased from memory.

A warm-up cycle can best be described by the following:

- The engine must be running
- A rise of 40°F in engine temperature must occur from the time when the engine was started
- Engine coolant temperature must reach at least 160°F

Once the above conditions occur, the PCM is considered to have passed a warm-up cycle. Due to the conditions required to extinguish the MIL and erase the DTC, it is most important that after a repair has been made, all DTC's be erased and the repair verified.

COMPONENT MONITORS

There are several components that will affect vehicle emissions if they malfunction. If one of these components malfunctions the Malfunction Indicator Lamp (Check Engine) will illuminate.

Some of the component monitors are checking for proper operation of the part. Electrically operated components now have input (rationality) and output (functionality) checks. Previously, a component like the Throttle Position sensor (TPS) was checked by the PCM for an open or shorted circuit. If one of these conditions occurred, a DTC was set. Now there is a check to ensure that the component is working. This is done by watching for a TPS indication of a greater or lesser throttle opening than MAP and engine rpm indicate. In the case of the TPS, if engine vacuum is high and engine rpm is 1600 or greater and the TPS indicates a large throttle opening, a DTC will be set. The same applies to low vacuum if the TPS indicates a small throttle opening.

All open/short circuit checks or any component that has an associated limp in will set a fault after 1 trip with the malfunction present. Components without an associated limp in will take two trips to illuminate the MIL.

Refer to the Diagnostic Trouble Codes Description Charts in this section and the appropriate Powertrain Diagnostic Procedure Manual for diagnostic procedures.

NON-MONITORED CIRCUITS

The PCM does not monitor the following circuits, systems and conditions that could have malfunctions causing driveability problems. The PCM might not store diagnostic trouble codes for these conditions. However, problems with these systems may cause the PCM to store diagnostic trouble codes for other systems or components. For example, a fuel pressure problem will not register a fault directly, but could cause a rich/lean condition or misfire. This could cause the PCM to store an oxygen sensor or misfire diagnostic trouble code

FUEL PRESSURE

The fuel pressure regulator controls fuel system pressure. The PCM cannot detect a clogged fuel pump inlet filter, clogged in-line fuel filter, or a pinched fuel supply or return line. However, these could result in a rich or lean condition causing the PCM to store an oxygen sensor or fuel system diagnostic trouble code.

SECONDARY IGNITION CIRCUIT

The PCM cannot detect an inoperative ignition coil, fouled or worn spark plugs, ignition cross firing, or open spark plug cables.

CYLINDER COMPRESSION

The PCM cannot detect uneven, low, or high engine cylinder compression.

EXHAUST SYSTEM

The PCM cannot detect a plugged, restricted or leaking exhaust system, although it may set a fuel system fault.

FUEL INJECTOR MECHANICAL MALFUNCTIONS

The PCM cannot determine if a fuel injector is clogged, the needle is sticking or if the wrong injector is installed. However, these could result in a rich or lean condition causing the PCM to store a diagnostic trouble code for either misfire, an oxygen sensor, or the fuel system.

EXCESSIVE OIL CONSUMPTION

Although the PCM monitors engine exhaust oxygen content when the system is in closed loop, it cannot determine excessive oil consumption.

THROTTLE BODY AIR FLOW

The PCM cannot detect a clogged or restricted air cleaner inlet or filter element.

VACUUM ASSIST

The PCM cannot detect leaks or restrictions in the vacuum circuits of vacuum assisted engine control system devices. However, these could cause the PCM

DESCRIPTION AND OPERATION (Continued)

to store a MAP sensor diagnostic trouble code and cause a high idle condition.

PCM SYSTEM GROUND

The PCM cannot determine a poor system ground. However, one or more diagnostic trouble codes may be generated as a result of this condition. The module should be mounted to the body at all times, also during diagnostic.

PCM CONNECTOR ENGAGEMENT

The PCM may not be able to determine spread or damaged connector pins. However, it might store diagnostic trouble codes as a result of spread connector pins.

HIGH AND LOW LIMITS

The PCM compares input signal voltages from each input device with established high and low limits for the device. If the input voltage is not within limits and other criteria are met, the PCM stores a diagnostic trouble code in memory. Other diagnostic trouble code criteria might include engine RPM limits or input voltages from other sensors or switches that must be present before verifying a diagnostic trouble code condition.

LOAD VALUE

ENGINE	IDLE/NEUTRAL	2500 RPM/NEUTRAL
All Engines	2% to 8% of Maximum Load	9% to 17% of Maximum Load

EVAPORATIVE EMISSION CONTROLS

INDEX

DESCRIPTION AND OPERATION

EVAPORATION (EVAP) CONTROL SYSTEM

The function of the EVAP control system is to prevent the emissions of gasoline vapors from the fuel tank into the atmosphere. When fuel evaporates in the fuel tank, the vapors pass through vent hoses or tubes to a carbon filled EVAP canister. They are temporarily held in the canister until they can be drawn into the intake manifold when the engine is running.

All engines use a duty cycle purge system. The PCM controls vapor flow by operating the duty cycle EVAP purge solenoid. Refer to Duty Cycle Solenoid for additional information.

The EVAP canister is a feature on all models for the storage of fuel vapors from the fuel tank.

NOTE: The hoses used in this system are specially manufactured. If replacement becomes necessary, it is important to use only fuel resistant hose.

ROLLOVER VALVE

The fuel tank is equipped with 2 interconnected rollover valves. The valves are located on the top of the fuel tank (Fig. 1). These valves will prevent fuel flow through the fuel tank vent (EVAP) hoses in the event of an accidental vehicle rollover. The EVAP canister draws fuel vapors from the fuel tank through these valves.

The valves are not serviced separately. If replacement is necessary, the fuel tank must be replaced. Refer to the Fuel Tank section of Group 14, Fuel Systems for removal and installation procedures.

EVAP CANISTER

A maintenance free, EVAP canister is used on all vehicles. The EVAP canister is located in the engine compartment on the left inner fender (Fig. 2). The EVAP canister is filled with granules of an activated carbon mixture. Fuel vapors entering the EVAP canister are absorbed by the charcoal granules.

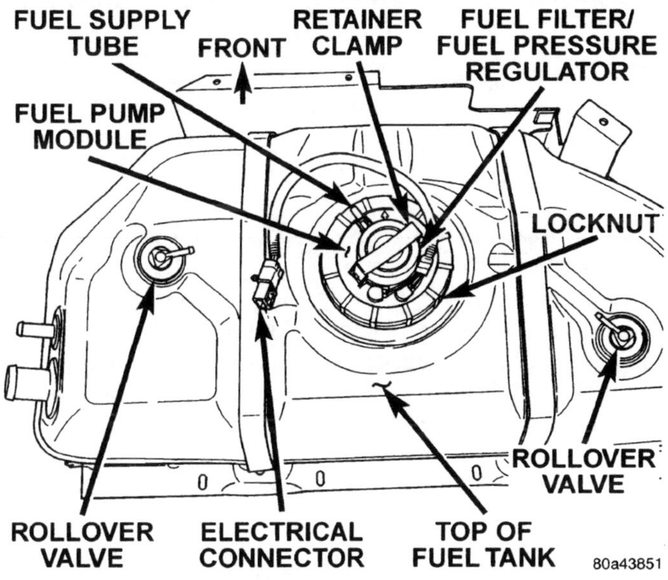

Fig. 1 Rollover Valve Location

Fuel tank pressure vents into the EVAP canister. Fuel vapors are temporarily held in the canister until they can be drawn into the intake manifold. The duty cycle EVAP canister purge solenoid allows the EVAP canister to be purged at predetermined times and at certain engine operating conditions.

DUTY CYCLE EVAP CANISTER PURGE SOLENOID

All models are equipped with a duty cycle EVAP canister purge solenoid. The solenoid regulates the rate of vapor flow from the EVAP canister to the intake manifold. The PCM operates the solenoid.

DESCRIPTION AND OPERATION (Continued)

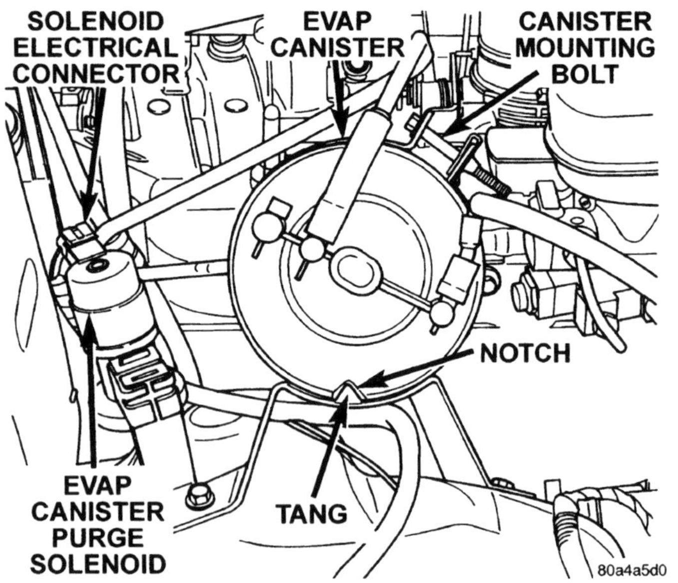

Fig. 2 EVAP Canister and Canister Purge Solenoid Location

During the cold start warm-up period and the hot start time delay, the PCM does not energize the solenoid. When de-energized, no vapors are purged. The PCM de-energizes the solenoid during open loop operation.

The engine enters closed loop operation after it reaches a specified temperature and the time delay ends. During closed loop operation, the PCM cycles (energizes and de-energizes) the solenoid 5 or 10 times per second, depending upon operating conditions. The PCM varies the vapor flow rate by changing solenoid pulse width. Pulse width is the amount of time that the solenoid is energized. The PCM adjusts solenoid pulse width based on engine operating condition.

The solenoid attaches to a bracket located in the engine compartment near the EVAP canister (Fig. 2). The top of the solenoid has the word UP or TOP on it. The solenoid will not operate properly unless it is installed correctly.

FUEL TANK FILLER TUBE CAP

The fuel tank is sealed with a pressure-vacuum relief fuel tank filler tube cap (Fig. 3). The relief valves in the cap are a safety feature. They operate only to prevent excessive pressure or vacuum in tank caused by a malfunction in system or damage to vent lines.

The cap has a threaded configuration. This allows the seal to be broken and pressure to be relieved without separation of cap from filler tube. Approximately two and a half turns are required to remove the cap.

If replacement of filler tube cap is necessary, it must be replaced with an identical cap to be sure of correct system operation.

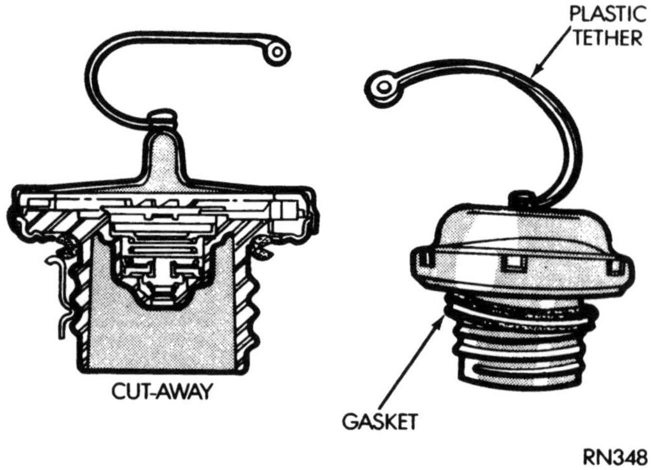

Fig. 3 Fuel Tank Filler Tube Cap—Typical

CAUTION: Remove the fuel tank filler tube cap (fuel tank cap) to relieve any fuel tank pressure. The cap must be removed prior to disconnecting any fuel system component or before draining the fuel tank.

CRANKCASE VENTILATION SYSTEM

All 2.5L 4–cylinder and 4.0L 6–cylinder engines are equipped with a Crankcase Ventilation (CCV) system (Fig. 4) or (Fig. 5). The CCV system performs the same function as a conventional PCV system, but does not use a vacuum controlled valve.

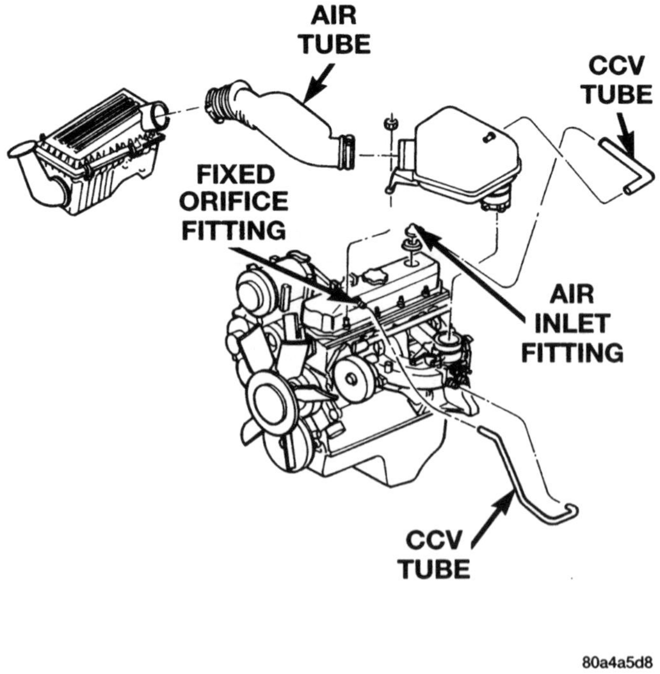

Fig. 4 CCV System—2.5L Engine

On 4.0L 6–cylinder engines, a molded vacuum tube connects manifold vacuum to top of cylinder head (valve) cover at dash panel end. The vacuum fitting

DESCRIPTION AND OPERATION (Continued)

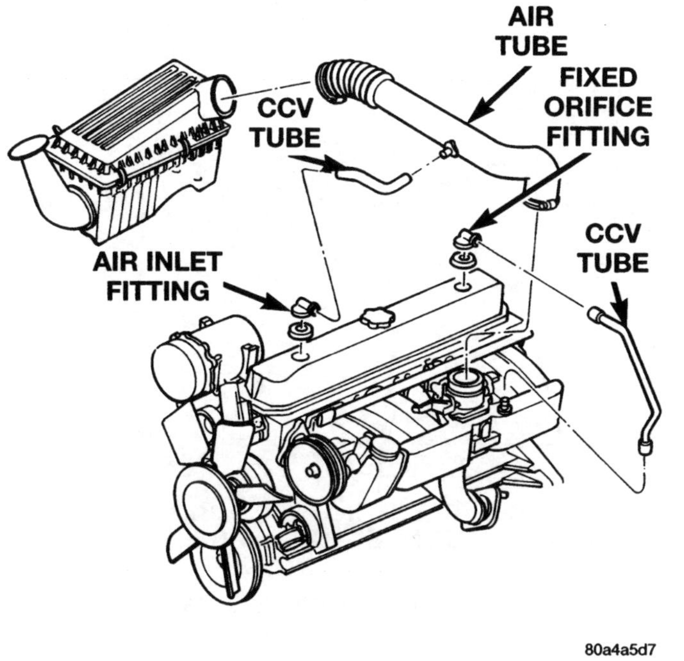

Fig. 5 CCV System—4.0L Engine

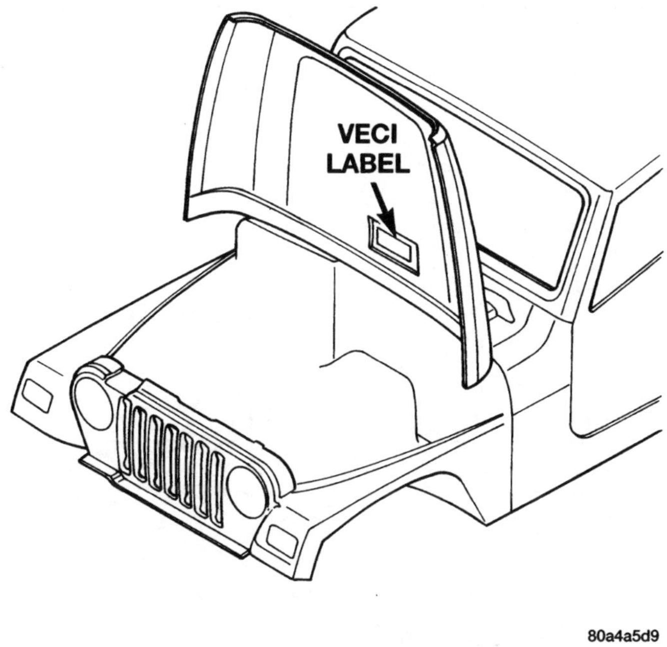

Fig. 6 VECI Label Location

contains a fixed orifice of a calibrated size. It meters the amount of crankcase vapors drawn out of the engine.

On 2.5L 4–cylinder engines, a fitting on drivers side of cylinder head (valve) cover contains the metered orifice. It is connected to manifold vacuum.

A fresh air supply CCV tube (hose) from the air cleaner is connected to front of cylinder head cover on 4.0L engines. It is connected to rear of cover on 2.5L engines.

When the engine is operating, fresh air enters the engine and mixes with crankcase vapors. Manifold vacuum draws the vapor/air mixture through the fixed orifice and into the intake manifold. The vapors are then consumed during combustion.

VEHICLE EMISSION CONTROL INFORMATION (VECI) LABEL

All vehicles are equipped with a combined VECI label. This label is located in the engine compartment (Fig. 6) and contains the following:

- Engine family and displacement
- Evaporative family
- Emission control system schematic
- Certification application
- Engine timing specifications (if adjustable)
- Idle speeds (if adjustable)
- Spark plug and gap

The label also contains an engine vacuum schematic. There are unique labels for vehicles built for sale in the state of California and the country of Canada. Canadian labels are written in both the English and French languages. These labels are permanently attached and cannot be removed without defacing information and destroying label.

DIAGNOSIS AND TESTING

VACUUM SCHEMATICS

A vacuum schematic for emission related items can be found on the Vehicle Emission Control Information (VECI) Label. Refer to VECI Label in this group for label location.

REMOVAL AND INSTALLATION

EVAP CANISTER

The EVAP canister is located in the engine compartment on the left front inner fender (Fig. 7).

REMOVAL/INSTALLATION

(1) Disconnect vacuum lines at EVAP canister. Note location of lines before removal.

(2) Remove canister retaining strap bolt.

(3) Remove canister from vehicle.

(4) Reverse the removal procedure for installation. Align notch (Fig. 7) on EVAP canister to locating tang on canister mounting bracket.

(5) Tighten canister strap bolt to 5 N·m (45 in. lbs.) torque.

REMOVAL AND INSTALLATION (Continued)

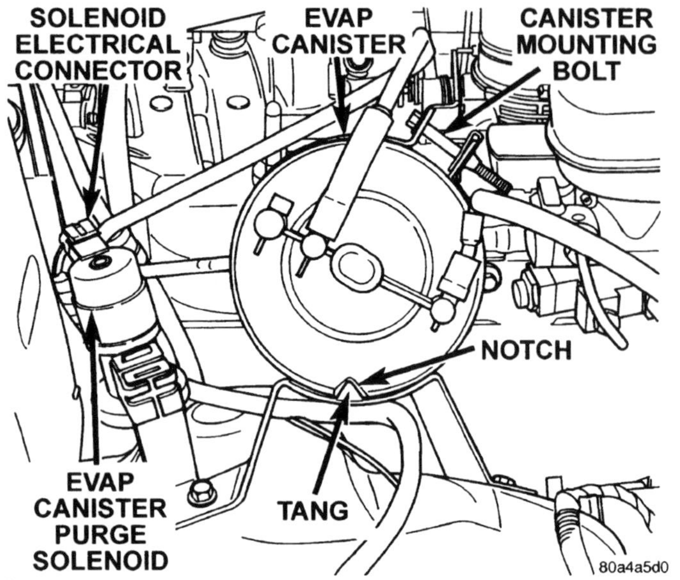

Fig. 7 EVAP Canister and Purge Solenoid Location

EVAP CANISTER PURGE SOLENOID

REMOVAL

The duty cycle EVAP canister purge solenoid is located in the engine compartment near the EVAP canister (Fig. 7).

(1) Disconnect electrical wiring connector at solenoid.

(2) Disconnect vacuum harness at solenoid.

(3) Lift solenoid and rubber solenoid support from mounting bracket.

INSTALLATION

(1) Install purge solenoid and rubber support to its mounting bracket.

(2) Connect vacuum harness and wiring connector.

ROLLOVER VALVE

The fuel tank is equipped with 2 interconnected rollover valves. The valves are located on the top of the fuel tank (Fig. 8).

The valves are not serviced separately. If replacement is necessary, the fuel tank must be replaced. Refer to the Fuel Tank section of Group 14, Fuel Systems for removal and installation procedures.

FUEL TANK FILLER TUBE CAP

If replacement of the fuel tank filler tube cap (Fig. 9) is necessary, it must be replaced with an identical cap to be sure of correct system operation.

CAUTION: Remove the fuel tank filler tube cap to relieve fuel tank pressure. The cap must be removed prior to disconnecting any fuel system component or before draining the fuel tank.

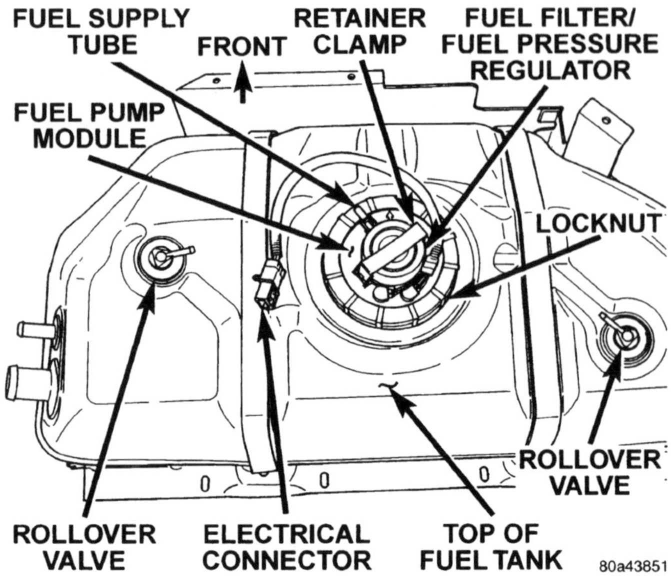

Fig. 8 Rollover Valve Location

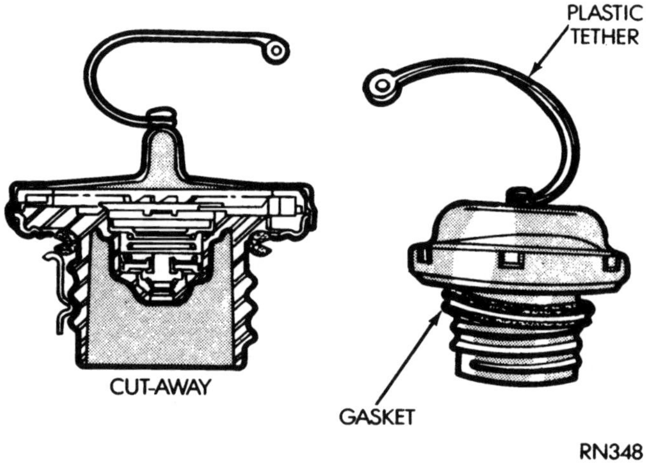

Fig. 9 Fuel Tank Filler Tube Cap—Typical

SPECIFICATIONS

TORQUE CHART

Description	Torque
EVAP Canister Mounting Bolt	5 N·m (45 in. lbs.)